UNIVERSITY CASEBOOK SERIES®

DOMESTIC RELATIONS

CASES AND MATERIALS

EIGHTH EDITION

WALTER WADLINGTON
James Madison Professor of Law Emeritus
University of Virginia School of Law

RAYMOND C. O'BRIEN
Professor of Law
The Catholic University of America

ROBIN FRETWELL WILSON
Roger and Stephany Joslin Professor of Law
University of Illinois College of Law

FOUNDATION
PRESS

444 Cedar Street, Suite 700
St. Paul, MN 55101
1-877-888-1330

Printed in the United States of America

ISBN: 978-1-63460-885-5

WW

For our grandchildren
~ their presence is a continuing blessing.

ROB

For James D. Waller & John W. Holsinger
~ family arises from commitment and a bit of fun.

RFW

To Lynn, Sandie, Connie, And Trudy
~ with fondest hopes for a summer of evenings at the Tiki bar and a season without hurricanes.

PREFACE TO EIGHTH EDITION

The eighth edition of this casebook is the continuation of a series of domestic relations casebooks originating with Professors Albert C. Jacobs and Julius Goebel, Jr. more than three-quarters of a century ago. Many of the topics in the eighth edition were discussed in the earliest edition, but today's emphasis on national and international application, assisted reproductive technology, nonmarital arrangements, and no-fault divorce would have been absent from both the earliest editions and the imaginations of these originating authors. What has been a consistent feature throughout the decades is the careful attention to court decisions that highlight the law. Any casebook attempts to build upon past understandings and indicate where the future lies; we seek to do this by providing engaging and informative teaching cases, concise statutory formulations, and references to legal periodicals, state surveys and Internet sites. Our constant link with past editions is our retention of the words "Domestic Relations" rather than family law. We believe that the former offers a comprehensive title in which the developments in interpersonal relationships will continue to find reconstruction building upon the twentieth century and continuing through the twenty-first.

Like the seventh edition, the eighth edition is shorter than the previous edition. Professors familiar with the book will notice that we have edited some of the longer cases and deleted some cases and materials that no longer seem as relevant in today's society. Annulment, long-term alimony and lengthy exploration of fault grounds for divorce seem to be among these less-discussed topics. To supplement the casebook we rely upon two additional books by the same coauthors as the casebook that may be purchased separately: Family Law in Perspective (4th ed. 2017); and Family Law Statutes: Selected Uniform Laws, Model Legislation, Federal Statutes, State Statutes, and International Treaties (5th ed. 2017). Among the evolving features of the eighth edition are references to the rights of same-sex couples to marry and adopt, accommodation and the First Amendment, pre and postmarital agreements and the 2012 Uniform Premarital and Marital Agreements Act, assisted reproductive technology cases, school vouchers, relocation of custodial parents, Safe Haven statutes, and state and third-party intervention in the parent-child relationship.

Several themes recognizable in previous editions appear again. First, this casebook is meant to provide professors at law schools and universities with cases pertinent to the practice of law in the United States. The legal casebook method of teaching requires factual scenarios that combine constitutional, common law, federal and state statutes, and human personalities in such a way as to allow the professor the opportunity to springboard to other relevant rules and principles; we hope that current events and legal developments may be included too. We have tried to retain and to choose cases that condense decades of decisions and refinements into a few pages of instructive history. We think the cases themselves offer problems to be solved by students and teachers and we like the fact that the highest court or the legislative process offers solutions, even though these may not be permanent.

A second theme recognizes the continuing interaction between federal and state law. Increasingly we have seen federal involvement in the enforcement of support obligations, welfare benefits, interstate and international custody disputes, Native American child placement, individual liberties, marriage, and termination of parental rights. There are specific references to federal involvement in these issues in the material covered. For instance, federal welfare legislation mandates that states enact statutes and policies or suffer the loss of federal benefits; federal law defines reasonable services to be offered to parents prior to termination of parental rights; and federal efforts to prohibit child trafficking proliferate at the national and international level. Nonetheless, states remain what they have traditionally been, laboratories for changes in the area of domestic relations. We witness this in areas such as domestic violence, infant safe haven laws, emerging forms of assisted reproductive rights and responsibilities, and equitable remedies available to nonmarital couples.

Finally, the authors wish to extend our sincere appreciation to those persons providing research and editorial assistance in the production of this book. They are: Rachel Bernal, Breanna Taylor, and Samuel Mott.

NOTE ON EDITING

Some citations, footnotes, and text have been omitted in order to keep the materials at manageable size for a several hour credit course, or to eliminate portions of a decision focusing on an unrelated issue. When some footnotes have been omitted, those that have been retained bear the original numbering from the reporter or other source from which the passage was excerpted. Some citations to cases and secondary material (including some "string" citations with brief explanatory notes about cases in the string) have been omitted without notes or symbols indicating their omission. Ellipses, or brackets summarizing omitted text, indicate whether other text has been deleted in the editing process.

SPECIAL ACKNOWLEDGMENT

We thank the National Conference of Commissioners on Uniform State Laws for their permission to reprint excerpts from copyrighted text of their various UNIFORM LAWS.

TABLE OF WEB SITES

Subject

ADOPTION

http://www.adopting.org [General site on adoption for people considering adoption.]

http://www.adopt.org [Website of the National Adoption Center; significant amount of adoption advice found under the link for "How to Adopt."]

http://www.acf.hhs.gov/programs/cb/stats_research/index.htm [Statistics on adoption, provided by the Administration for Children & Families, within HHS.]

http://pediatrics.aappublications.org/content/131/4/827 [American Academy of Pediatrics endorsing adoptions by same sex partners.]

AIDS/HIV

https://www.cdc.gov/hiv/library/reports/hiv-surveillance.html [Recent statistics]

http://www.unaids.org/en/resources/publications [Provides link to United Nations "Report on the Global Aids Epidemic."]

ANTENUPTIAL CONTRACTING

http://family.findlaw.com/marriage/prenuptial-agreements.html [Contains basic information on prenuptial agreements.]

ASSISTED REPRODUCTIVE TECHNOLOGIES

http://www.health.ny.gov/regulations/task_force/reports_publications/execsum.htm

CHILD ABUSE REPORTING

https://www.childwelfare.gov/topics/systemwide/laws-policies/statutes/manda/ [Provides overview on the child abuse reporting obligations for various persons.]

CHILD CUSTODY

http://www.divorcesupport.com/childcustody/custody.shtml [Information on child custody issues.]

CHILD SUPPORT GUIDELINES/CHILD SUPPORT INFORMATION

http://www.acf.hhs.gov/programs/cse/ [This is the website for the U.S. Office of Child Support Enforcement, within HHS.]

http://www.uniformlaws.org/Act.aspx?title=Interstate%20Family%20Support%20Act%20Amendments%20(2008) [UIFSA Home Page.]

http://www.ncsl.org/issues-research/human-services/termination-of-child-support-age-of-majority.aspx

http://www.ncsl.org/issues-research/human-services/termination-of-child-support-exception-for-adult.aspx

http://www.ncsl.org/research/human-services/termination-of-support-college-support.aspx

COHABITATION AGREEMENT

http://www.AAML.org

COUNSELING RESOURCES

http://www.divorcenet.com

http://www.divorcesource.com/archives/counseling.shtml

DOMESTIC PARTNERSHIPS

http://www.thetaskforce.org/ [This is the website of the National Gay and Lesbian Task Force.]

DOMESTIC VIOLENCE

http://www.usdoj.gov/ovw/ [U.S. Department of Justice's Office on Violence Against Women.]

http://www.hrc.org/ [Human Rights Campaign.]

DRUGS AND CHILD PROTECTION

https://www.childwelfare.gov/topics/systemwide/laws-policies/statutes/drugexposed/ [Contains information on state statutes regarding parental drug use as child abuse.]

http://www.d.umn.edu/~jgarriso/specialtopics/alcoholism/aod brochure%5B1%5D.pdf [Website from the Child Welfare League of America. In addition to a broad range of other information, it contains some statistics on children and substance abuse.]

HEALTH CARE DIRECTIVES

http://www.helpguide.org/elder/advance_directive_end_of_life_care.htm [Information on the use of health care directives and living wills.]

http://www.agingwithdignity.org. [General information of planning for incapacity.]

http://www.nhpco.org. [National Hospice and Palliative Care Organization, providing information on end of life decisionmaking.]

http://www.mayoclinic.com. [Mayo Clinic's Advance Directive Resources.]

IN VITRO FERTILIZATION

http://www.americanpregnancy.org/infertility/ivf.html [This site is run by the American Pregnancy Association, and contains general information on in vitro fertilization, the variations on IVF, and information on pregnancy in general.]

MEDICAID

https://www.medicaid.gov/medicaid/eligibility/spousal-impoverishment/index.html [Medicaid Spousal Impoverishment Standards.]

PARENTAL ALIENATION

http://www.parentalalienation.com/ [General site on parental alienation.]

SCHOOL VOUCHERS

http://www.topix.com/education/school-vouchers [This is a news site on the issue of school vouchers.]

http://www.ncsl.org/research/education/school-choice-vouchers.aspx [This is link for the National Conference of State Legislatures; provides an overview of the issue.]

SPOUSAL SUPPORT

http://www.divorceinfo.com/alimony.htm

http://www.divorcehq.com/alimony.html

UNMARRIED COHABITANTS

https://www.census.gov/hhes/families/data/cps.html [Provides statistics.]

VIOLENCE AGAINST WOMEN ACT

https://www.justice.gov/ovw [Department of Justice Office on Violence Agaisnt Women.]

WOMAN'S SUPPORT RESOURCES

http://www.divorcesupport.com/search/women.shtml [Resources specific to women.]

SUMMARY OF CONTENTS

TABLE OF CONTENTS

TABLE OF CASES

The principal cases are in bold type.

UNIVERSITY CASEBOOK SERIES®

DOMESTIC RELATIONS

CASES AND MATERIALS

EIGHTH EDITION

CHAPTER I

CHANGING CONCEPTS OF MARRIAGE AND FAMILY

A. FORM AND FUNCTION RELATIONSHIPS

City of Ladue v. Horn

Missouri Court of Appeals, Eastern District, Division Three, 1986
720 S.W.2d 745

■ CRANDALL, JUDGE.

Defendants, Joan Horn and E. Terrence Jones, appeal from the judgment of the trial court in favor of plaintiff, City of Ladue (Ladue), which enjoined defendants from occupying their home in violation of Ladue's zoning ordinance and which dismissed defendants' counterclaim. We affirm.

The case was submitted to the trial court on stipulated facts. Ladue's Zoning Ordinance No. 1175 was in effect at all times pertinent to the present action. Certain zones were designated as one-family residential. The zoning ordinance defined family as: "One or more persons related by blood, marriage or adoption, occupying a dwelling unit as an individual housekeeping organization." The only authorized accessory use in residential districts was for "[a]ccommodations for domestic persons employed and living on the premises and home occupations." The purpose of Ladue's zoning ordinance was broadly stated as to promote "the health, safety, morals and general welfare" of Ladue.

In July, 1981, defendants purchased a seven-bedroom, four-bathroom house which was located in a single-family residential zone in Ladue. Residing in defendants' home were Horn's two children (aged 16 and 19) and Jones's one child (age 18). The two older children attended out-of-state universities and lived in the house only on a part-time basis. Although defendants were not married, they shared a common bedroom, maintained a joint checking account for the household expenses, ate their meals together, entertained together, and disciplined each other's children. Ladue made demands upon defendants to vacate their home because their household did not comprise a family, as defined by Ladue's zoning ordinance, and therefore they could not live in an area zoned for single-family dwellings. When defendants refused to vacate, Ladue sought to enjoin defendants' continued violation of the zoning ordinance. Defendants counterclaimed, seeking a declaration that the zoning ordinance was constitutionally void. They also sought attorneys' fees and costs. The trial court entered a permanent injunction in favor of Ladue and dismissed defendants' counterclaim. Enforcement of the injunction was stayed pending this appeal.

Preliminarily, we note that the ordinance in question clearly restricts the use of the property rather than the character of the structure. It is therefore a legal impossibility to uphold the validity of the ordinance and, at the same time, permit defendants to occupy their residence.

In Missouri, the scope of appellate review in zoning matters is limited; and the reviewing court may not substitute its judgment for that of the zoning authority. A zoning ordinance is presumed valid. The legislative body is vested with broad discretion and the appellate court cannot interfere unless it is shown that the legislative body has acted arbitrarily. . . .

Capsulated, defendants' attack on Ladue's ordinance is three-pronged. First, the zoning limitations foreclose them from exercising their right to associate freely with whomever they wish. *Roberts v. United States Jaycees*, 468 U.S. 609, 104 S.Ct. 3244, 82 L.Ed.2d 462 (1984). Second, their right to privacy is violated by the zoning restrictions. *Stanley v. Georgia*, 394 U.S. 557, 89 S.Ct. 1243, 22 L.Ed.2d 542 (1969). Third, the zoning classification distinguishes between related persons and unrelated persons. *United States Dept. of Agriculture v. Moreno*, 413 U.S. 528, 93 S.Ct. 2821, 37 L.Ed.2d 782 (1973). Defendants allege that the United States and Missouri Constitutions grant each of them the right to share his or her residence with whomever he or she chooses. They assert that Ladue has not demonstrated a compelling, much less rational, justification for the overly proscriptive blood or legal relationship requirement in its zoning ordinance.

Defendants posit that the term "family" is susceptible to several meanings. They contend that, since their household is the "functional and factual equivalent of a natural family," the ordinance may not preclude them from living in a single-family residential Ladue neighborhood. *See, e.g., McMinn v. Town of Oyster Bay*, 66 N.Y.2d 544, 498 N.Y.S.2d 128, 488 N.E.2d 1240 (Ct.App.1985). Defendants argue in their brief as follows:

> The record amply demonstrates that the private, intimate interests of Horn and Jones are substantial. Horn, Jones, and their respective children have historically lived together as a single family unit. They use and occupy their home for the identical purposes and in the identical manners as families which are biologically or maritally related.

To bolster this contention, defendants elaborate on their shared duties, as set forth earlier in this opinion. Defendants acknowledge the importance of viewing themselves as a family unit, albeit a "conceptual family" as opposed to a "true non-family," in order to prevent the application of the ordinance.[3]

The fallacy in defendants' syllogism is that the stipulated facts do not compel the conclusion that defendants are living as a family. A man and woman living together, sharing pleasures and certain responsibilities, does not *per se* constitute a family in even the conceptual sense. To approximate a family relationship, there must exist a commitment to a permanent relationship and a perceived reciprocal obligation to support and to care for each other. *See, e.g., State ex rel. Ellis v. Liddle*, 520 S.W.2d 644, 650 (Mo.App.1975). Only when these characteristics are present can the conceptual family, perhaps, equate with the traditional family. In a traditional family, certain of its inherent attributes arise from the legal relationship of the family members. In a non-traditional family, those same qualities arise in fact, either by explicit agreement or by tacit understanding among the parties.

While the stipulated facts could arguably support an inference by the trial court that defendants and their children comprised a non-traditional family, they do not compel that inference. Absent findings of fact and conclusions of law, we cannot assume that the trial court's perception of defendants' familial status comported with defendants' characterization of themselves as a conceptual family. In fact, if a finding by the trial court that defendants' living arrangement constituted a conceptual family is critical to a determination in defendants' favor, we can assume that the court's finding was adverse to defendants' position. Ordinarily, given our deference to the decision of the trial court, that would dispose of this appeal. We decline, however, to restrict our ruling to such a narrow basis. We therefore consider the broader issues presented by the parties. We assume, *arguendo,* that the sole basis for the judgment entered by the trial court was that defendants were not related by blood, marriage or adoption, as required by Ladue's ordinance.

We first consider whether the ordinance violates any federally protected rights of the defendants. Generally, federal court decisions hold that a zoning classification based upon a biological or a legal relationship among household members is justifiable under constitutional police powers to protect the public health, safety, morals or welfare of the community.

More specifically, the United States Supreme Court has developed a two-tiered approach by which to examine legislation challenged as violative of the equal protection clause. If the personal interest affected by the ordinance is fundamental, "strict scrutiny" is applied and the ordinance is sustained only upon a showing that the burden imposed is

---

[3] The distinction between "conceptual" or "non-traditional" families and true non-families may well be a distinction without a difference, the distinction resting in speculation and stereotypical presumptions. Further, recognition of the conceptual family suffers from the defect of commanding inquiry into who are the users rather than focusing on the use itself. See generally Note, *City of Santa Barbara v. Adamson*: An Associational Right of Privacy and the End of Family Zones, 69 Calif.L.Rev. 1052, 1068–70 (1981).

necessary to protect a compelling governmental interest. If the ordinance does not contain a suspect class or impinge upon a fundamental interest, the more relaxed "rational basis" test is applied and the classification imposed by the ordinance is upheld if any facts can reasonably justify it. *McGowan v. Maryland*, 366 U.S. 420, 426, 81 S.Ct. 1101, 1105, 6 L.Ed.2d 393 (1961). Defendants urge this court to recognize that their interest in choosing their own living arrangement inexorably involves their fundamental rights of freedom of association and of privacy.

In *Village of Euclid v. Ambler Realty Co.*, 272 U.S. 365, 47 S.Ct. 114, 71 L.Ed. 303 (1926) and in *Nectow v. City of Cambridge*, 277 U.S. 183, 48 S.Ct. 447, 72 L.Ed. 842 (1928), the United States Supreme Court also established the due process parameters of permissible legislation. The ordinance in question must have a "foundation in reason" and bear a "substantial relation to the public health, the public morals, the public safety or the public welfare in its proper sense."

In the *Village of Belle Terre v. Boraas*, 416 U.S. 1, 94 S.Ct. 1536, 39 L.Ed.2d 797 (1974), the court addressed a zoning regulation of the type at issue in this case. The court held that the Village of Belle Terre ordinance involved no fundamental right, but was typical of economic and social legislation which is upheld if it is reasonably related to a permissible governmental objective. The challenged zoning ordinance of the Village of Belle Terre defined family as:

> One or more persons related by blood, adoption or marriage, living and cooking together as a single housekeeping unit [or] a number of persons but not exceeding two (2) living and cooking together as a single housekeeping unit though not related by blood, adoption, or marriage. . . .

The court upheld the ordinance, reasoning that the ordinance constituted valid land use legislation reasonably designed to maintain traditional family values and patterns.

The importance of the family was reaffirmed *in Moore v. City of East Cleveland*, 431 U.S. 494, 97 S.Ct. 1932, 52 L.Ed.2d 531 (1977), wherein the United States Supreme Court was confronted with a housing ordinance which defined a "family" as only certain closely related individuals. Consequently, a grandmother who lived with her son and two grandsons was convicted of violating the ordinance because her two grandsons were first cousins rather than brothers. The United States Supreme Court struck down the East Cleveland ordinance for violating the freedom of personal choice in matters of marriage and family life. The court distinguished *Belle Terre* by stating that the ordinance in that case allowed all individuals related by blood, marriage or adoption to live together; whereas East Cleveland, by restricting the number of related persons who could live together, sought "to regulate the occupancy of its housing by slicing deeply into the family itself." The court pointed out that the institution of the family is protected by the Constitution precisely because it is so deeply rooted in the American tradition and that "[o]urs is by no means a tradition limited to respect for the bonds uniting the members of the nuclear family."

Here, because we are dealing with economic and social legislation and not with a fundamental interest or a suspect classification, the test of constitutionality is whether the ordinance is reasonable and not arbitrary and bears a rational relationship to a permissible state objective. . . .

Ladue has a legitimate concern with laying out guidelines for land use addressed to family needs . . . The question of whether Ladue could have chosen more precise means to effectuate its legislative goals is immaterial. Ladue's zoning ordinance is rationally related to its expressed purposes and violates no provisions of the Constitution of the United States. Further, defendants' assertion that they have a constitutional right to share their residence with whomever they please amounts to the same argument that was made and found unpersuasive by the court in *Belle Terre.*

We next consider whether the Ladue ordinance violates any rights of defendants protected by the Missouri Constitution. Defendants rely on several Missouri cases which they allege have "expanded the definition of 'family.' " We disagree with defendants' conclusion.

In *State ex rel. Ellis v. Liddle*, 520 S.W.2d 644 (Mo.App.1975), the zoning ordinance divided the term "family" into two distinct categories, as follows:

> First, "one or more persons related by blood, marriage, or adoption living together in one dwelling unit" in a "common household" including servants, guests, boarders, roomers or lodgers. The ordinance places no limitation on the number of such persons occupying the dwelling unit. Second, persons "not related by blood, marriage, or adoption". Such occupancy may not exceed 10 persons in any one dwelling unit.

Id. at 650. Given this definition, the court permitted the operation of a group home for six to eight juvenile boys and two "teaching parents" in a single-family residential neighborhood in Maryville, Missouri. The court stated that it was clear that, "*both under the specific terms of the ordinance* and under common law" (emphasis added), the operation of the group home did no violence to the single-family residence requirement.

In *City of Vinita Park v. Girls Sheltercare*, Inc., 664 S.W.2d 256 (Mo.App.1984), this court allowed the use of a single-family residence as a girls' group home operated by the Juvenile Court of St. Louis County in the City of Vinita Park. The Vinita Park Zoning Ordinance defined family as "[o]ne or more persons related by blood or marriage occupying a premises and living as a single housekeeping unit." Id. at 258. The housing ordinance contained a more expansive definition of family:

> [A]n individual or married couple and the children thereof and no more than two other persons related directly to the individual

> or married couple by blood or marriage and not more than three persons not related by blood or marriage living together as a single housekeeping unit in a dwelling unit.

Id. at 259 n. 1.

The court stated that, although the group did not "conform to the letter of either of the *ordinances* which defines family," it did conform to "the spirit of the *ordinances*." Id. at 259. (emphasis added). After addressing the "family" issue, the court addressed what it referred to as the "pivotal issue" of the case concerning what limitations there are on the power of a municipality to zone public uses. The court held that "the leasing of the premises pursuant to the statutory authority for the county and juvenile court to establish a group home is a governmental function (use) and thereby immune from the City of Vinita Park's zoning ordinance."

In both of these cases, the reviewing court looked to the definition of family as set forth in the ordinance. Defendants' argument that these cases "expand" the definition of family is unpersuasive. The clear implication of these cases is that the appellate court will give deference to a zoning ordinance, particularly when there is no overriding governmental interest or statutory authority to negate the legislative prerogative to define family based upon biological or legal relationships.

For purposes of its zoning code, Ladue has in precise language defined the term family. It chose the definition which comports with the historical and traditional notions of family; namely, those people related by blood, marriage or adoption. That definition of family has been upheld in numerous Missouri decisions. *See, e.g., London v. Handicapped Facilities Board of St. Charles County*, 637 S.W.2d 212 (Mo.App.1982) (group home not a "family" as used in restrictive covenant); *Feely v. Birenbaum*, 554 S.W.2d 432 (Mo.App.1977) (two unrelated males not a "family" as used in restrictive covenant); *Cash v. Catholic Diocese*, 414 S.W.2d 346 (Mo.App.1967) (nuns not a "family" as used in a restrictive covenant).

Decisions from other state jurisdictions have addressed identical constitutional challenges to zoning ordinances similar to the ordinance in the instant case. The reviewing courts have upheld their respective ordinances on the ground that maintenance of a traditional family environment constitutes a reasonable basis for excluding uses that may impair the stability of that environment and erode the values associated with traditional family life.

The essence of zoning is selection; and, if it is not invidious or discriminatory against those not selected, it is proper. There is no doubt that there is a governmental interest in marriage and in preserving the integrity of the biological or legal family. There is no concomitant governmental interest in keeping together a group of unrelated persons, no matter how closely they simulate a family. Further, there is no state policy which commands that groups of people may live under the same roof in any section of a municipality they choose. . . .

NOTES

The *Ladue* decision offers an illustration of how the law may "use marriage as an administratively convenient mechanism for identifying couples who are likely to have made a long-term commitment to each other, and/or likely to have intertwined finances." Deborah A. Widiss, *Non-Marital Families and (Or After) Marriage Equality*, 42 FLA. ST. U. L. REV. 547, 563 (2015). Marriage provides a rational basis, and a rational basis for the law is sufficient to rebut any claimants other than those basing claims on fundamental rights or suspect classification. But fewer adult are entering into marriage, thereby lessening the opportunity to utilize this mechanism. "Barely half of all adults are currently married, as compared to seventy-two percent of adults in 1960." *Id.* Indeed, during the last forty years the number of married couples with their own children decreased from 40.3% to 20.9% of all families, and there was a corresponding 41% increase in unmarried partner households. U.S. Census Bureau, Current Population Survey, Statistical Abstract of the United States, Table 59 (2012) at http://www2.census.gov/library/publications/2011/compendia/statab/131ed/tables/pop.pdf *See also* U.S. Census Bureau, Unmarried and Single Americans Week Sept. 20–26, at http://www.census.gov/newsroom/facts-for-features/2015/cb15-ff19.html (reporting that there were 7 million unmarried partner households in 2013 and that of this number 573,530 were same-sex households). For additional commentary on cohabitation and marriage, *see* Serena Mayeri, *Marital Supremacy and the Constitution of the Nonmarital Family*, 103 CAL. L. REV. 1277 (2015); Lawrence W. Waggoner, *With Marriage on the Decline and Cohabitation on the Rise, What About Marital Rights for Unmarried Partners?*, 41 ACTEC L.J. 49 (2015) (advocating a new status, de facto marriage). Increasing numbers of cohabitating adults prompts disputes over property rights, support obligations, parentage, and custody determinations. Each of these will be discussed *infra*, but the *Marvin* trilogy, which follows, provides the underpinnings of the discussion.

B. THE ELEMENTS OF NONMARITAL CONTRACTING

Marvin v. Marvin (I)

Supreme Court of California, In Bank, 1976
557 P.2d 106

■ TOBRINER, JUSTICE.

During the past 15 years, there has been a substantial increase in the number of couples living together without marrying. Such nonmarital relationships lead to legal controversy when one partner dies or the couple separates. Courts of Appeal, faced with the task of determining property rights in such cases, have arrived at conflicting positions: two cases (In re Marriage of Cary (1973) 34 Cal.App.3d 345,

109 Cal.Rptr. 862; Estate of Atherley (1975) 44 Cal.App.3d 758, 119 Cal.Rptr. 41) have held that the Family Law Act (Civ.Code, § 4000 et seq.) requires division of the property according to community property principles, and one decision (*Beckman v. Mayhew* (1975) 49 Cal.App.3d 529, 122 Cal.Rptr. 604) has rejected that holding. . . .

We conclude: (1) The provisions of the Family Law Act do not govern the distribution of property acquired during a non-marital relationship; such a relationship remains subject solely to judicial decision. (2) The courts should enforce express contracts between non-marital partners except to the extent that the contract is explicitly founded on the consideration of meretricious sexual services. (3) In the absence of an express contract, the court should inquire into the conduct of the parties to determine whether that conduct demonstrates an implied contract, agreement of partnership or joint venture, or some other tacit understanding between the parties. The courts may also employ the doctrine of quantum meruit, or equitable remedies such as constructive or resulting trusts, when warranted by the facts of the case.

In the instant case plaintiff and defendant lived together for seven years without marrying; all property acquired during this period was taken in defendant's name. When plaintiff sued to enforce a contract under which she was entitled to half the property and to support payments, the trial court granted judgment on the pleadings for defendant, thus leaving him with all property accumulated by the couple during their relationship. Since the trial court denied plaintiff a trial on the merits of her claim, its decision conflicts with the principle stated above, and must be reversed.

1. *The factual setting of this appeal. . . .*

Plaintiff avers that in October of 1964 she and defendant "entered into an oral agreement" that while "the parties lived together they would combine their efforts and earnings and would share equally any and all property accumulated as a result of their efforts whether individual or combined." Furthermore, they agreed to "hold themselves out to the general public as husband and wife" and that "plaintiff would further render her services as a companion, homemaker, housekeeper and cook to . . . defendant."

Shortly thereafter plaintiff agreed to "give up her lucrative career as an entertainer [and] singer" in order to "devote her full time to defendant . . . as a companion, homemaker, housekeeper and cook;" in return defendant agreed to "provide for all of plaintiff's financial support and needs for the rest of her life."

Plaintiff alleges that she lived with defendant from October of 1964 through May of 1970 and fulfilled her obligations under the agreement. During this period the parties as a result of their efforts and earnings acquired in defendant's name substantial real and personal property, including motion picture rights worth over $1 million. In May of 1970, however, defendant compelled plaintiff to leave his household. He continued to support plaintiff until November of 1971, but thereafter refused to provide further support.

On the basis of these allegations plaintiff asserts two causes of action. The first, for declaratory relief, asks the court to determine her contract and property rights; the second seeks to impose a constructive trust upon one half of the property acquired during the course of the relationship.

Defendant demurred unsuccessfully, and then answered the complaint. Following extensive discovery and pretrial proceedings, the case came to trial. Defendant renewed his attack on the complaint by a motion to dismiss. Since the parties had stipulated that defendant's marriage to Betty Marvin did not terminate until the filing of a final decree of divorce in January 1967, the trial court treated defendant's motion as one for judgment on the pleadings augmented by the stipulation.

After hearing argument the court granted defendant's motion and entered judgment for defendant. Plaintiff moved to set aside the judgment and asked leave to amend her complaint to allege that she and defendant reaffirmed their agreement after defendant's divorce was final. The trial court denied plaintiff's motion, and she appealed from the judgment.

2. *Plaintiff's complaint states a cause of action for breach of an express contract. . . .*

Defendant first and principally relies on the contention that the alleged contract is so closely related to the supposed "immoral" character of the relationship between plaintiff and himself that the enforcement of the contract would violate public policy. He points to cases asserting that a contract between non-marital partners is unenforceable if it is "involved in" an illicit relationship or made in "contemplation" of such a relationship. A review of the numerous California decisions concerning contracts between non-marital partners, however, reveals that the courts have not employed such broad and uncertain standards to strike down contracts. The decisions instead disclose a narrower and more precise standard: a contract between non-marital partners is unenforceable only *to the extent* that it *explicitly* rests upon the immoral and illicit consideration of meretricious sexual services. . . .

[W]e base our opinion on the principle that adults who voluntarily live together and engage in sexual relations are nonetheless as competent as any other persons to contract respecting their earnings and property rights. Of course, they cannot lawfully contract to pay for the performance of sexual services, for such a contract is, in essence, an agreement for prostitution and unlawful for that reason. But they may agree to pool their earnings and to hold all property acquired during the relationship in accord with the law governing community property;

conversely they may agree that each partner's earnings and the property acquired from those earnings remains the separate property of the earning partner. So long as the agreement does not rest upon illicit meretricious consideration, the parties may order their economic affairs as they choose, and no policy precludes the courts from enforcing such agreements.

In the present instance, plaintiff alleges that the parties agreed to pool their earnings, that they contracted to share equally in all property acquired, and that defendant agreed to support plaintiff. The terms of the contract as alleged do not rest upon any unlawful consideration. We therefore conclude that the complaint furnishes a suitable basis upon which the trial court can render declaratory relief. The trial court consequently erred in granting defendant's motion for judgment on the pleadings.

3. *Plaintiff's complaint can be amended to state a cause of action founded upon theories of implied contract or equitable relief.*

As we have noted, both causes of action in plaintiff's complaint allege an express contract; neither assert any basis for relief independent from the contract. In In re Marriage of Cary, 34 Cal.App.3d 345, 109 Cal.Rptr. 862, however, the Court of Appeal held that, in view of the policy of the Family Law Act, property accumulated by non-marital partners in an actual family relationship should be divided equally. Upon examining the Cary opinion, the parties to the present case realized that plaintiff's alleged relationship with defendant might arguably support a cause of action independent of any express contract between the parties. The parties have therefore briefed and discussed the issue of the property rights of a non-marital partner in the absence of an express contract. Although our conclusion that plaintiff's complaint states a cause of action based on an express contract alone compels us to reverse the judgment for defendant, resolution of the Cary issue will serve both to guide the parties upon retrial and to resolve a conflict presently manifest in published Court of Appeal decisions.

Both plaintiff and defendant stand in broad agreement that the law should be fashioned to carry out the reasonable expectations of the parties. Plaintiff, however, presents the following contentions: that the decisions prior to *Cary* rest upon implicit and erroneous notions of punishing a party for his or her guilt in entering into a non-marital relationship, that such decisions result in an inequitable distribution of property accumulated during the relationship, and that *Cary* correctly held that the enactment of the Family Law Act in 1970 overturned those prior decisions. Defendant in response maintains that the prior decisions merely applied common law principles of contract and property to persons who have deliberately elected to remain outside the bounds of the community property system.[11] *Cary,* defendant contends, erred in

[11] We note that a deliberate decision to avoid the strictures of the community property system is not the only reason that couples live together without marriage. Some couples may

holding that the Family Law Act vitiated the force of the prior precedents. . . .

In summary, we believe that the prevalence of non-marital relationships in modern society and the social acceptance of them, marks this as a time when our courts should by no means apply the doctrine of the unlawfulness of the so-called meretricious relationship to the instant case. As we have explained, the nonenforceability of agreements expressly providing for meretricious conduct rested upon the fact that such conduct, as the word suggests, pertained to and encompassed prostitution. To equate the non-marital relationship of today to such a subject matter is to do violence to an accepted and wholly different practice.

We are aware that many young couples live together without the solemnization of marriage, in order to make sure that they can successfully later undertake marriage. This trial period, preliminary to marriage, serves as some assurance that the marriage will not subsequently end in dissolution to the harm of both parties. We are aware, as we have stated, of the pervasiveness of non-marital relationships in other situations.

The mores of the society have indeed changed so radically in regard to cohabitation that we cannot impose a standard based on alleged moral considerations that have apparently been so widely abandoned by so many. Lest we be misunderstood, however, we take this occasion to point out that the structure of society itself largely depends upon the institution of marriage, and nothing we have said in this opinion should be taken to derogate from that institution. The joining of the man and woman in marriage is at once the most socially productive and individually fulfilling relationship that one can enjoy in the course of a lifetime.

We conclude that the judicial barriers that may stand in the way of a policy based upon the fulfillment of the reasonable expectations of the parties to a non-marital relationship should be removed. As we have explained, the courts now hold that express agreements will be enforced unless they rest on an unlawful meretricious consideration. We add that

---

wish to avoid the permanent commitment that marriage implies, yet be willing to share equally any property acquired during the relationship; others may fear the loss of pension, welfare, or tax benefits resulting from marriage (see Beckman v. Mayhew, 49 Cal.App.3d 529, 122 Cal.Rptr. 604). Others may engage in the relationship as a possible prelude to marriage. In lower socio-economic groups the difficulty and expense of dissolving a former marriage often leads couples to choose a non-marital relationship; many unmarried couples may also incorrectly believe that the doctrine of common law marriage prevails in California, and thus that they are in fact married. Consequently we conclude that the mere fact that a couple have not participated in a valid marriage ceremony cannot serve as a basis for a court's inference that the couple intend to keep their earnings and property separate and independent; the parties' intention can only be as ascertained by a more searching inquiry into the nature of their relationship.

in the absence of an express agreement, the courts may look to a variety of other remedies in order to protect the parties' lawful expectations.[24]

The courts may inquire into the conduct of the parties to determine whether that conduct demonstrates an implied contract or implied agreement of partnership or joint venture, or some other tacit understanding between the parties. The courts may, when appropriate, employ principles of constructive trust or resulting trust. Finally, a non-marital partner may recover in quantum meruit for the reasonable value of household services rendered less the reasonable value of support received if he can show that he rendered services with the expectation of monetary reward.[25]

Since we have determined that plaintiff's complaint states a cause of action for breach of an express contract, and, as we have explained, can be amended to state a cause of action independent of allegations of express contract,[26] we must conclude that the trial court erred in granting defendant a judgment on the pleadings.

The judgment is reversed and the cause remanded for further proceedings consistent with the views expressed herein.

■ CLARK, JUSTICE (concurring and dissenting).

The majority opinion properly permits recovery on the basis of either express or implied in fact agreement between the parties. These being the issues presented, their resolution requires reversal of the judgment. Here, the opinion should stop.

This court should not attempt to determine all anticipated rights, duties and remedies within every meretricious relationship—particularly in vague terms. Rather, these complex issues should be determined as each arises in a concrete case.

The majority broadly indicates that a party to a meretricious relationship may recover on the basis of equitable principles and in quantum meruit. However, the majority fails to advise us of the circumstances permitting recovery, limitations on recovery, or whether their numerous remedies are cumulative or exclusive. Conceivably, under the majority opinion a party may recover half of the property acquired during the relationship on the basis of general equitable

---

[24] We do not seek to resurrect the doctrine of common law marriage, which was abolished in California by statute in 1895. Thus we do not hold that plaintiff and defendant were "married," nor do we extend to plaintiff the rights which the Family Law Act grants valid or putative spouses; we hold only that she has the same rights to enforce contracts and to assert her equitable interest in property acquired through her effort as does any other unmarried person.

[25] Our opinion does not preclude the evolution of additional equitable remedies to protect the expectations of the parties to a non-marital relationship in cases in which existing remedies prove inadequate; the suitability of such remedies may be determined in later cases in light of the factual setting in which they arise.

[26] We do not pass upon the question whether, in the absence of an express or implied contractual obligation, a party to a non-marital relationship is entitled to support payments from the other party after the relationship terminates.

principles, recover a bonus based on specific equitable considerations, and recover a second bonus in quantum meruit.

The general sweep of the majority opinion raises but fails to answer several questions. First, because the Legislature specifically excluded some parties to a meretricious relationship from the equal division rule of Civil Code section 4452, is this court now free to create an equal division rule? Second, upon termination of the relationship, is it equitable to impose the economic obligations of lawful spouses on meretricious parties when the latter may have rejected matrimony to avoid such obligations? Third, does not application of equitable principles—necessitating examination of the conduct of the parties—violate the spirit of the Family Law Act of 1969, designed to eliminate the bitterness and acrimony resulting from the former fault system in divorce? Fourth, will not application of equitable principles reimpose upon trial courts the unmanageable burden of arbitrating domestic disputes? Fifth, will not a quantum meruit system of compensation for services—discounted by benefits received—place meretricious spouses in a better position than lawful spouses? Sixth, if a quantum meruit system is to be allowed, does fairness not require inclusion of all services and all benefits regardless of how difficult the evaluation?

When the parties to a meretricious relationship show by express or implied in fact agreement they intend to create mutual obligations, the court should enforce the agreement. However, in the absence of agreement, we should stop and consider the ramifications before creating economic obligations which may violate legislative intent, contravene the intention of the parties, and surely generate undue burdens on our trial courts.

By judicial overreach, the majority perform a nunc pro tunc marriage, dissolve it, and distribute its property on terms never contemplated by the parties, case law or the Legislature.

NOTES

Upon remand, the Los Angeles Superior Court ordered Lee Marvin to pay Michelle $104,000 to assist with her economic rehabilitation. Marvin v. Marvin, 5 FAM. L. REPORTER 3077 (April 24, 1979). This opinion may properly be called *Marvin II.*

Marvin v. Marvin (III)

Court of Appeal, Second District, Division 3, 1981
122 Cal.App.3d 871

■ COBEY, ASSOCIATE JUSTICE.

Defendant, Lee Marvin, appeals from that portion of a judgment ordering him to pay to plaintiff, Michelle Marvin, the sum of $104,000, to be used by her primarily for her economic rehabilitation. . . .

This statement of facts is taken wholly from the findings of the trial court, which tried the case without a jury. The parties met in June 1964 and started living together occasionally in October of that year. They lived together almost continuously (except for business absences of his) from the spring of 1965 to May or June of 1970, when their cohabitation was ended at his insistence. This cohabitation was the result of an initial agreement between them to live together as unmarried persons so long as they both enjoyed their mutual companionship and affection.

More specifically, the parties to this lawsuit never agreed during their cohabitation that they would combine their efforts and earnings or would share equally in any property accumulated as a result of their efforts, whether individual or combined. They also never agreed during this period that plaintiff would relinquish her professional career as an entertainer and singer in order to devote her efforts full time to defendant as his companion and homemaker generally. Defendant did not agree during this period of cohabitation that he would provide all of plaintiff's financial needs and support for the rest of her life.

Furthermore, the trial court specifically found that: (1) defendant has never had any obligation to pay plaintiff a reasonable sum as and for her maintenance; (2) plaintiff suffered no damage resulting from her relationship with defendant, including its termination and thus defendant did not become monetarily liable to plaintiff at all; (3) plaintiff actually benefited economically and socially from the cohabitation of the parties, including payment by defendant for goods and services for plaintiff's sole benefit in the approximate amount of $72,900.00, payment by defendant of the living expenses of the two of them of approximately $221,400.00, and other substantial specified gifts;[3] (4) a confidential and fiduciary relationship never existed between the parties with respect to property; (5) defendant was never unjustly enriched as a result of the relationship of the parties or of the services performed by plaintiff for him or for them; (6) defendant never acquired any property or money from plaintiff by any wrongful act.

The trial court specifically found in support of its challenged rehabilitation award that the market value of defendant's property at the time the parties separated exceeded $1 million, that plaintiff at the time of the trial of this case had been recently receiving unemployment insurance benefits, that it was doubtful that plaintiff could return to the career that she had enjoyed before the relationship of the parties commenced, namely, that of singer, that plaintiff was in need of rehabilitation—i.e., to learn new employable skills, that she should be able to accomplish such rehabilitation in two years and that the sum of $104,000 was not only necessary primarily for such rehabilitation, but also for her living expenses (including her debts) during this period of

[3] The trial court also found that "Defendant made a substantial financial effort to launch Plaintiff's career as a recording singer and to continue her career as a nightclub singer."

rehabilitation, and that defendant had the ability to pay this sum forthwith.

Moreover, the trial court concluded as a matter of law that inasmuch as defendant had terminated the relationship of the parties and plaintiff had no visible means of support, "in equity", she had a right to assistance by defendant until she could become self-supporting. The trial court explained that it fixed the award at the highest salary that the plaintiff had ever earned, namely, $1,000 a week for two years, although plaintiff's salary had been at that level for only two weeks and she ordinarily had earned less than one-half that amount weekly. . . .

The trial court apparently based its rehabilitative award upon two footnotes in the opinion of our Supreme Court in this case. (*Marvin v. Marvin* (1976) 18 Cal.3d 660, 134 Cal.Rptr. 815, 557 P.2d 106.) These are footnotes 25 and 26, which respectively read as follows:

> "Our opinion does not preclude the evolution of additional equitable remedies to protect the expectations of the parties to a non-marital relationship in cases in which existing remedies prove inadequate; the suitability of such remedies may be determined in later cases in light of the factual setting in which they arise." (Id., at p. 684, 134 Cal.Rptr. 815, 557 P.2d 106.)
>
> "We do not pass upon the question whether, in the absence of an express or implied contractual obligation, a party to a non-marital relationship is entitled to support payments from the other party after the relationship terminates." (Id. at p. 685, 134 Cal.Rptr. 815, 557 P.2d 106.)

There is no doubt that footnote 26 opens the door to a support award in appropriate circumstances. Likewise, under footnote 25, equitable remedies should be devised "to protect the expectations of the parties to a non-marital relationship." The difficulty in applying either of these footnotes in the manner in which the trial court has done in this case is that, as already pointed out, the challenged limited rehabilitative award of the trial court is not within the issues of the case as framed by the pleadings and there is nothing in the trial court's findings to suggest that such an award is warranted to protect the expectations of *both* parties.

Quite to the contrary, as already noted, the trial court expressly found that plaintiff benefited economically and socially from her relationship with defendant and suffered no damage therefrom, even with respect to its termination. Furthermore, the trial court also expressly found that defendant never had any obligation to pay plaintiff a reasonable sum as and for her maintenance and that defendant had not been unjustly enriched by reason of the relationship or its termination and that defendant had never acquired anything of value from plaintiff by any wrongful act.

Furthermore, the special findings in support of the challenged rehabilitative award merely established plaintiff's need therefore and defendant's ability to respond to that need. This is not enough. The award, being nonconsensual in nature, must be supported by some recognized underlying obligation in law or in equity. A court of equity admittedly has broad powers, but it may not create totally new substantive rights under the guise of doing equity.

The trial court in its special conclusions of law addressed to this point attempted to state an underlying obligation by saying that plaintiff had a right to assistance from defendant until she became self-supporting. But this special conclusion obviously conflicts with the earlier, more general, finding of the court that defendant has never had and did not then have any obligation to provide plaintiff with a reasonable sum for her support and maintenance and, in view of the already-mentioned findings of no damage (but benefit instead), no unjust enrichment and no wrongful act on the part of defendant with respect to either the relationship or its termination, it is clear that no basis whatsoever, either in equity or in law, exists for the challenged rehabilitative award. . . .

The judgment under appeal is modified by deleting therefrom the portion thereof under appeal, namely, the rehabilitative award of $104,000 to plaintiff, Michelle Marvin. As modified it is affirmed. . . .

NOTES

Nonmarital cohabitation is not synonymous with either statutory or common law marriage, or with another equitable device called putative spouse. Each of these will be discussed, *infra*, but it is important to note that economic remedies available at divorce will not be available at the cessation of a nonmarital cohabitation. Without an express contract, how should a court divide property or issue support? The *Marvin* court adopts an equitable remedy approach so as to accommodate the clearly and convincingly proven expectations of both parties. The lack of clear and convincing expectations forms the basis for the court's holding in *Marvin III*. It is not surprising that the majority of courts hold that without statutory authority any remedies available at divorce are unavailable to nonmarital cohabitants. *See, e.g.*, Gunderson v. Golden, 360 P.3d 353, 356 (Id.App. 2015) (holding that when couple ended their twenty-five years of nonmarital cohabitation the property accumulated could not be divided in accordance with the state's divorce law). Increasingly there is one exception, occurring when a couple cohabits prior to marriage, sharing the economic benefits and responsibilities, and then eventually marry one another, courts are willing to consider the period of premarital cohabitation when dividing the couple's property upon divorce. *See, e.g.*, Collins v. Wassell, 323 P.3d 1216 (Haw. 2014) (holding that premarital contributions are a relevant consideration when dividing property upon divorce where the parties cohabited and formed a premarital economic partnership at that time). For commentary on nonmarital contracting, *see, e.g.*, Emily E. Diederich, Student Work, *'Cause Breaking Up is Hard to Do': The Need for Uniform Enforcement of Cohabitation Agreements in West Virginia*, 113 W. VA. L. REV. 1073 (2011). But a few courts have been willing to apply provisions pertinent to divorce to nonmarital cohabitation dissolution. As the following decision illustrates, courts have struggled to make a just and equitable distribution of property acquired by the parties during their nonmarital cohabitation.

Connell v. Francisco

Supreme Court of Washington, 1995
898 P.2d 831

■ GUY, JUSTICE.

Petitioner Richard Francisco and Respondent Shannon Connell met in Toronto, Canada, in June 1983. Connell was a dancer in a stage show produced by Francisco. She resided in New York, New York. She owned clothing and a leasehold interest in a New York apartment. Francisco resided in Las Vegas, Nevada. He owned personal property, real property, and several companies, including Prince Productions, Inc. and Las Vegas Talent, Ltd., which produced stage shows for hotels. Francisco's net worth was approximately $1,300,000 in February 1984.

Connell, at Francisco's invitation, moved to Las Vegas in November 1983. They cohabited in Francisco's Las Vegas home from November 1983 to June 1986. While living in Las Vegas, Connell worked as a paid dancer in several stage shows. She also assisted Francisco as needed with his various business enterprises. Francisco managed his companies and produced several profitable stage shows. In November 1985, Prince Productions, Inc. purchased a bed and breakfast, the Whidbey Inn, on Whidbey Island, Washington. Connell moved to Whidbey Island in June 1986 to manage the Inn. Shortly thereafter Francisco moved to Whidbey Island to join her. Connell and Francisco resided and cohabited on Whidbey Island until the relationship ended in March 1990. While living on Whidbey Island, Connell and Francisco were viewed by many in the community as being married. Francisco acquiesced in Connell's use of his surname for business purposes. A last will and testament, dated December 11, 1987, left the corpus of Francisco's estate to Connell. Both Connell and Francisco had surgery to enhance their fertility. In the summer of 1986, Francisco gave Connell an engagement ring.

From June 1986 to September 1990 Connell continuously managed and worked at the Inn. She prepared breakfast, cleaned rooms, took reservations, laundered linens, paid bills, and maintained and repaired the Inn. Connell received no compensation for her services at the Inn from 1986 to 1988. From January 1989 to September 1990 she received $400 per week in salary. Francisco produced another profitable stage show and acquired several pieces of real property during the period from June 1986 to September 1990. Property acquired by Francisco included: a condominium in Langley, Washington, for $65,000; a waterfront lot next to the Inn for $35,000; property identified as the Alan May property for $225,000; real property identified as the restaurant property for

$320,000; a house in Langley, Washington, for $105,000; and a condominium in Las Vegas, Nevada, for $110,000. In addition to the real property acquired by Francisco, Prince Productions, Inc. acquired two pieces of real property next to the Inn. Connell did not contribute financially toward the purchase of any of the properties, and title to the properties was held in Francisco's name individually or in the name of Prince Productions, Inc. Connell and Francisco separated in March 1990. When the relationship ended Connell had $10,000 in savings, $10,000 in jewelry, her clothes, an automobile, and her leasehold interest in the New York apartment. She continued to receive her $400 per week salary from the Inn until September 1990. In contrast, Francisco's net worth was over $2,700,000, a net increase since February 1984 of almost $1,400,000. In March 1990, he was receiving $5,000 per week in salary from Prince Productions, Inc.[2]

Connell filed a lawsuit against Francisco in December 1990 seeking a just and equitable distribution of the property acquired during the relationship. The Island County Superior Court determined Connell and Francisco's relationship was sufficiently long term and stable to require a just and equitable distribution. The Superior Court limited the property subject to distribution to the property that would have been community in character had they been married. The trial court held property owned by each party prior to the relationship could not be distributed. In addition, the Superior Court required Connell to prove by a preponderance of the evidence that the property acquired during their relationship would have been community property had they been married. The only property characterized by the Superior Court as being property that would have been community in character had Connell and Francisco been married was the increased value of Francisco's pension plan. The increased value of the pension plan, $169,000, was divided equally, with $84,500 distributed to Connell. The Superior Court, concluding Connell did not satisfy her burden of proof with respect to the remaining property, distributed to Francisco the remainder of the pension plan and all real property.

The Court of Appeals reversed, holding both property owned by each prior to the relationship and property that would have been community in character had the parties been married may be distributed following a meretricious relationship. *Connell v. Francisco,* 74 Wash.App. 306, 317, 872 P.2d 1150 (1994). The Court of Appeals also ruled the analogous application of RCW 26.09.080 by the Superior Court to meretricious relationships would be meaningless without a community-property-like presumption attaching to all property acquired during the relationship. *Connell,* 74 Wash.App. at 320, 872 P.2d 1150. The Court of Appeals remanded the case to the Superior Court. Francisco petitioned this court

[2] During the relationship Francisco was paid $490,548 in salary from Prince Productions, Inc. The Superior Court concluded Prince Productions, Inc. paid Francisco a reasonable salary for his services.

for discretionary review. He argues property owned by each party prior to the relationship may not be distributed following a meretricious relationship, and a community-property-like presumption is inapplicable when a trial court distributes property following a meretricious relationship. We granted discretionary review.

A meretricious relationship is a stable, marital-like relationship where both parties cohabit with knowledge that a lawful marriage between them does not exist. *In re Marriage of Lindsey,* 101 Wash.2d 299, 304, 678 P.2d 328 (1984); Harry M. Cross, *Community Property Law in Washington (Revised 1985),* 61 Wash.L.Rev. 13, 23 (1986). Relevant factors establishing a meretricious relationship include, but are not limited to: continuous cohabitation, duration of the relationship, purpose of the relationship, pooling of resources and services for joint projects, and the intent of the parties. *Lindsey,* 101 Wash.2d at 304–05, 678 P.2d 328; *Latham v. Hennessey,* 87 Wash.2d 550, 554, 554 P.2d 1057 (1976); *In re Marriage of DeHollander,* 53 Wash.App. 695, 699, 770 P.2d 638 (1989). In *Lindsey,* this court ruled a relationship need not be "long term" to be characterized as a meretricious relationship. *Lindsey,* 101 Wash.2d at 305, 678 P.2d 328. While a "long term" relationship is not a threshold requirement, duration is a significant factor. A "short term" relationship may be characterized as meretricious, but a number of significant and substantial factors must be present. *See Lindsey,* 101 Wash.2d at 304–05, 678 P.2d 328 (a less than 2-year meretricious relationship preceded marriage). The Superior Court found Connell and Francisco were parties to a meretricious relationship. This finding is not contested.

Historically, property acquired during a meretricious relationship was presumed to belong to the person in whose name title to the property was placed. "[I]n the absence of any evidence to the contrary, it should be presumed *as a matter of law* that the parties intended to dispose of the property exactly as they did dispose of it." *Creasman v. Boyle,* 31 Wash.2d 345, 356, 196 P.2d 835 (1948). This presumption is commonly referred to as "the *Creasman* presumption". To avoid inequitable results under "the *Creasman* presumption", Washington courts developed a number of exceptions. *In re Estate of Thornton,* 81 Wash.2d 72, 79–81, 499 P.2d 864 (1972) (implied partnership); *Hennessey,* 87 Wash.2d 550, 554 P.2d 1057 (implied partnership); *Humphries v. Riveland,* 67 Wash.2d 376, 407 P.2d 967 (1965) (constructive trust); *West v. Knowles,* 50 Wash.2d 311, 311 P.2d 689 (1957) (tracing source of funds); *Dahlgren v. Blomeen,* 49 Wash.2d 47, 298 P.2d 479 (1956) (contract theory); *Omer v. Omer,* 11 Wash.App. 386, 523 P.2d 957, *review denied,* 84 Wash.2d 1009 (1974) (constructive trust); *see generally* Washington State Bar Ass'n, *Community Property Deskbook* §§ 2.70–2.76 (1989).

In 1984, this court overruled *Creasman. Lindsey,* 101 Wash.2d at 304, 678 P.2d 328. In its place, the court adopted a general rule requiring a just and equitable distribution of property following a meretricious relationship.

> [W]e adopt the rule that courts must "examine the [meretricious] relationship and the property accumulations and make a just and equitable disposition of the property." *Latham v. Hennessey, supra* at 554 [554 P.2d 1057]. *Cf.* RCW 26.09.080. *See West v. Knowles, supra* at 320 [311 P.2d 689]; *Poole v. Schrichte,* 39 Wn.2d 558, 569, 236 P.2d 1044 (1951). *Cf. Buckley v. Buckley,* 50 Wash. 213, 96 P. 1079 (1908).

Lindsey, 101 Wash.2d at 304, 678 P.2d 328.

In *Lindsey,* the parties cohabited for less than 2 years prior to marriage. When they subsequently divorced, the wife argued the increase in value of property acquired during the meretricious portion of their relationship was also subject to an equitable distribution as if the property were community in character. We agreed, citing former RCW 26.09.080.[3] *Lindsey,* 101 Wash.2d at 304, 678 P.2d 328. The citation to former RCW 26.09.080, however, was preceded by the "*Cf.*" signal. The "*Cf.*" signal means: "Cited authority *supports a proposition different from the main proposition but sufficiently analogous to lend support.*" Harvard Law Review Ass'n, *A Uniform System of Citation* 23 (15th ed. 1991). The dispute in the present case arises from this court's reference in *Lindsey* to former RCW 26.09.080 by use of the "*Cf.*" signal. At issue is to what extent the principles contained in RCW 26.09.080 govern the disposition of property following a meretricious relationship.

Francisco contends the Court of Appeals misinterpreted *Lindsey* when it applied all the principles contained in RCW 26.09.080 to meretricious relationships. We agree. A meretricious relationship is not the same as a marriage. *Davis v. Department of Employment Sec.,* 108 Wash.2d 272, 278–79, 737 P.2d 1262 (1987) (an unmarried cohabitant is ineligible for benefits triggered by a "marital status" provision under Washington's unemployment compensation statute); *see also Western Comm'ty Bank v. Helmer,* 48 Wash.App. 694, 740 P.2d 359 (1987) (RCW 26.09.140, which permits an award of attorney fees in a marriage dissolution action, is inapplicable to an action to distribute property following a meretricious relationship); *Continental Cas. Co. v. Weaver,* 48 Wash.App. 607, 612, 739 P.2d 1192 (1987) (a person cohabiting in a non-marital relationship with an insured is not a member of the insured's

---

[3] Former RCW 26.09.080 provides: "In a proceeding for dissolution of the marriage, legal separation, declaration of invalidity, or in a proceeding for disposition of property following dissolution of the marriage by a court which lacked personal jurisdiction over the absent spouse or lacked jurisdiction over the absent spouse or lacked jurisdiction to dispose of the property, the court shall, without regard to marital misconduct, make such disposition of the property and the liabilities of the parties, either community or separate, as shall appear just and equitable after considering all relevant factors including, but not limited to: (1) The nature and extent of the community property; (2) The nature and extent of the separate property; (3) The duration of the marriage; and (4) The economic circumstances of each spouse at the time the division of property is to become effective, including the desirability of awarding the family home or the right to live therein for reasonable periods to a spouse having custody of any children." In 1989 the Legislature amended RCW 26.09.080, replacing "spouse having custody of any children" with "with whom the children reside the majority of the time." Laws of 1989, ch. 375, § 5, amending Laws of 1978, 1st Ex.Sess., ch. 157, § 8.

"immediate family"); *Roe v. Ludtke Trucking, Inc.*, 46 Wash.App. 816, 732 P.2d 1021 (1987) (under the wrongful death statute an unmarried cohabitant is not included within the statutory category of "wife"). *But see Warden v. Warden,* 36 Wash.App. 693, 698, 676 P.2d 1037, *review denied,* 101 Wash.2d 1016 (1984); *Foster v. Thilges,* 61 Wash.App. 880, 886, 812 P.2d 523 (1991). As such, the laws involving the distribution of marital property do not directly apply to the division of property following a meretricious relationship. Washington courts may look toward those laws for guidance. Once a trial court determines the existence of a meretricious relationship, the trial court then: (1) evaluates the interest each party has in the property acquired during the relationship, and (2) makes a just and equitable distribution of the property. *Lindsey,* 101 Wash.2d at 307, 678 P.2d 328; *Community Property Deskbook* § 2.64. The critical focus is on property that would have been characterized as community property had the parties been married. This property is properly before a trial court and is subject to a just and equitable distribution.

While portions of RCW 26.09.080 may apply by analogy to meretricious relationships, not all provisions of the statute should be applied. The parties to such a relationship have chosen not to get married and therefore the property owned by each party prior to the relationship should not be before the court for distribution at the end of the relationship. However, the property acquired during the relationship should be before the trial court so that one party is not unjustly enriched at the end of such a relationship. *Peffley-Warner,* 113 Wash.2d 243, 252, 778 P.2d 1022 (1989). We conclude a trial court may not distribute property acquired by each party prior to the relationship at the termination of a meretricious relationship. Until the Legislature, as a matter of public policy, concludes meretricious relationships are the legal equivalent to marriages, we limit the distribution of property following a meretricious relationship to property that would have been characterized as community property had the parties been married. This will allow the trial court to justly divide property the couple has earned during the relationship through their efforts without creating a common law marriage or making a decision for a couple which they have declined to make for themselves. Any other interpretation equates cohabitation with marriage; ignores the conscious decision by many couples not to marry; confers benefits when few, if any, economic risks or legal obligations are assumed; and disregards the explicit intent of the Legislature that RCW 26.09.080 apply to property distributions following a marriage.

Francisco argues the Court of Appeals erred in requiring the application of a community-property-like presumption to property acquired during a meretricious relationship. We disagree. In a marital context, property acquired during marriage is presumptively community property. *In re Marriage of Short,* 125 Wash.2d 865, 870, 890 P.2d 12 (1995). When no marriage exists there is, by definition, no community property. However, only by treating the property acquired in a meretricious relationship similarly can this court's reversal of "the *Creasman* presumption" be given effect. Failure to apply a community-property-like presumption to the *property acquired during a meretricious relationship* places the burden of proof on the non-acquiring partner. This would overrule *In re Marriage of Lindsey,* 101 Wash.2d 299, 678 P.2d 328 (1984) and reinstate the presumption expressed in *Creasman v. Boyle,* 31 Wash.2d 345, 196 P.2d 835 (1948). The Court of Appeals properly rejected the resurrection of "the *Creasman* presumption". We hold income and property acquired during a meretricious relationship should be characterized in a similar manner as income and property acquired during marriage. Therefore, all property acquired during a meretricious relationship is presumed to be owned by both parties. This presumption can be rebutted. *See Estate of Madsen v. Commissioner of Internal Rev.,* 97 Wash.2d 792, 796, 650 P.2d 196 (1982). All property considered to be owned by both parties is before the court and is subject to a just and equitable distribution. *Lindsey,* 101 Wash.2d at 307, 678 P.2d 328. The fact title has been taken in the name of one of the parties does not, in itself, rebut the presumption of common ownership. *See Lindsey,* 101 Wash.2d at 306–07, 678 P.2d 328; *Merritt v. Newkirk,* 155 Wash. 517, 520, 285 P. 442 (1930).

For the purpose of dividing property at the end of a meretricious relationship, the definitions of "separate" and "community" property found in RCW 26.16.010–.030 are useful and we apply them by analogy. Therefore, property owned by one of the parties prior to the meretricious relationship and property acquired during the meretricious relationship by gift, bequest, devise, or descent with the rents, issues and profits thereof, is not before the court for division. All other property acquired during the relationship would be presumed to be owned by both of the parties. *See In re Marriage of Elam,* 97 Wash.2d 811, 816, 650 P.2d 213 (1982); *In re Marriage of Pearson-Maines,* 70 Wash.App. 860, 869, 855 P.2d 1210 (1993). Furthermore, when the funds or services owned by both parties are used to increase the equity or to maintain or increase the value of property that would have been separate property had the couple been married, there may arise a right of reimbursement in the "community". *See, e.g., Pearson-Maines,* 70 Wash.App. at 869–70, 855 P.2d 1210; Harry M. Cross, *Community Property Law in Washington (Revised 1985),* 61 Wash.L.Rev. 13, 61, 67 (1986). A court may offset the "community's" right of reimbursement against any reciprocal benefit received by the "community" for its use and enjoyment of the individually owned property. *See In re Marriage of Miracle,* 101 Wash.2d 137, 139, 675 P.2d 1229 (1984); Cross, at 70.

In the case before us, the majority of real property was purchased during Connell and Francisco's meretricious relationship. This real property is presumed to be owned by both parties, notwithstanding the fact the real property is not held in both parties' names. Francisco may overcome this presumption with evidence showing the real property was acquired with funds that would have been characterized as his separate property had the parties been married. With respect to any real property found by the trial court to be owned by Francisco, Connell may establish that any increase in value of Francisco's property occurred during their meretricious relationship and is attributable to "community" funds or efforts. If Connell can establish Francisco's property increased in value due to unreimbursed community funds or efforts, then there arises in the "community" a right of reimbursement for those contributions. Any such increase in value would be before the trial court for a just and equitable distribution. To the extent one, or both, of the parties received a fair wage for their efforts, the "community" may have already been reimbursed. Since these inquiries are factual, we leave their resolution to the trial court.

In summary, we hold that property which would have been characterized as separate property had the couple been married is not before the trial court for division at the end of the relationship. The property that would have been characterized as community property had the couple been married is before the trial court for a just and equitable distribution. There is a rebuttable presumption that property acquired during the relationship is owned by both of the parties and is therefore before the court for a fair division.

We reverse the Court of Appeals in part, affirm in part, and remand the case to the Superior Court for a just and equitable distribution of property.

■ DURHAM, C.J., and SMITH, JOHNSON, MADSEN, ALEXANDER and TALMADGE, JJ., concur.

■ JUSTICE UTTER, dissenting.

I disagree with the majority's conclusion that the Court of Appeals misinterpreted our decision in *In re Marriage of Lindsey,* 101 Wash.2d 299, 678 P.2d 328 (1984) when it applied the principles found in RCW 26.09.080 to meretricious relationships. By limiting the distribution of property following a meretricious relationship to property that would have been characterized as community property had the parties been married, the majority establishes a new rule that will be uncertain in application and will likely interfere with the ability of the courts to "make a just and equitable distribution of the property" as is required by *Lindsey.* Given the increasing number of these cases in our trial courts, what is needed in this context is a simple rule that is easy to apply. Our holding in *Lindsey,* as understood by the Court of Appeals, does just that.

The majority is correct in pointing out that a meretricious relationship is not the same as a marriage. In citing a number of cases in which this court has refused to treat them the same, however, the majority fails to realize that the question of how closely these two types of relationships are treated depends upon the context. We discussed

Lindsey in *Davis v. Department of Empl. Sec.,* 108 Wash.2d 272, 737 P.2d 1262 (1987), a case in which we held that an unmarried cohabitant is not eligible for benefits triggered by a "marital status" provision under our state's unemployment compensation statutes. There we noted that while *Lindsey* treated meretricious relationships like marriages in the context of property distribution, "the extension of property distribution rights of spouses to partners in meretricious relationships does not elevate meretricious relationships themselves to the level of marriages for any and all purposes." *Davis,* 108 Wash.2d at 279, 737 P.2d 1262. Thus, the Court of Appeals was correct in concluding that in *Lindsey* we did not interpret RCW 26.09.080 to include meretricious relationships. *Connell v. Francisco,* 74 Wash.App. 306, 315, 872 P.2d 1150 (1994). Such an interpretation, as the majority notes, would have ignored the explicit language of the statute. Instead, we adopted a common law rule applicable to meretricious relationships which mirrored the provisions of RCW 26.09.080 applicable to marriages.

Both the majority and the Court of Appeals note that in support of our holding in *Lindsey,* we cited RCW 26.09.080, preceded by the "*cf.*" signal. The Court of Appeals' understanding of our *Lindsey* holding is consistent with our use of that signal in that case. RCW 26.09.080 does support a somewhat different proposition than what we held in *Lindsey,* but it is "sufficiently analogous to lend support". *The Bluebook: A Uniform System of Citation* 23 (15th ed. 1991) (defining the "*cf.*" signal). The statute applies certain principles to property distribution following the dissolution of a marriage; *Lindsey* applies those same principles to property distribution following the dissolution of a meretricious relationship. The type of relationship is different, but the governing principles are the same. If, on the other hand, neither the type of relationship nor the applicable principles were the same, RCW 26.09.080 would not be "sufficiently analogous to lend support" to our *Lindsey* holding.

Finally, the rule articulated by the majority is likely to be difficult and uncertain in application. In many cases, it will be impossible to carry out the requirement of *Lindsey* that there be "a just and equitable distribution of the property" while limiting distribution to only that property that would be characterized as community property had the parties been married. The requirement that there be a court finding of a meretricious relationship prior to the distribution of property is enough of a safeguard in these cases without the need to limit the type of property subject to distribution as the majority does. Additionally, the majority's rule, which will make the outcome of the property distribution depend upon how the court may characterize each individual piece of property, creates a great deal of uncertainty and makes the distribution unnecessarily complicated.

I, therefore, would affirm the opinion of the Court of Appeals in its entirety.

■ DOLLIVER, J., concurs with UTTER, J Pro Tem.

NOTES

The Supreme Court of Washington offers a definition of what constitutes a "meretricious relationship." Connell v. Francisco, 898 P.2d 831, 834 (Wash. 1995). And the decision then holds that trial courts may justly divide property the couple has earned during the relationship in a manner similar to marriage, applying a presumption that all property acquired by the parties during the relationship is owned by both parties. *Id.* at 836. As the dissent points out, the broad scope of this holding may cause confusion because it appears that the majority is elevating meretricious relationships to the status of marriage. *Id.* at 838. For commentary on the decision, *see* Gavin M. Parr, *What is a "Meretricious Relationship"?: An Analysis of Cohabitant Property Rights Under* Connell v. Francisco, 74 WASH. L. REV. 1243 (1999). In 2007 the Washington Supreme Court revisited the issue of meretricious relationships, affirming the holding in *Connell* that a trial court may equitably divide property acquired by the nonmarital cohabitants during the period of cohabitation so as to prevent unjust enrichment. *See* Olver v. Fowler, 168 P.3d 348, 355–356 (2007) (couple had lived in a nonmarital cohabitation for fourteen years until both were killed in an automobile accident and the estate of each decedent petitioned for an award of assets).

Not all commentators agree with the approach of the Washington courts, but all commentators recommend caution when courts are tasked with approximating the expectations of nonmarital couples in any situation. *See, e.g.*, Marsha Garrison, *Nonmarital Cohabitation: Social Revolution and Legal Regulation*, 42 FAM. L.Q. 309, 331 (2008) ("Given the public and private advantages associated with formal marriage, the variety of cohabiting relationships and attendant difficulty of drafting standards that separate relationships involving expectations of sharing from the majority that do not give rise to such expectations, and the risk of creating bandwagon effects that might reduce public support for formal marriage and marital childbearing, there is every reason for courts and legislatures to remain cautious."); Marsha Garrison, *Is Consent Necessary? An Evaluation of the Emerging Law of Cohabitant Obligation*, 52 UCLA L. REV. 815 (2005) ("It would be unfair to impose marital obligations on cohabitants simply because a relationship has survived for a legislatively determined time period. Individualized inquiry into the nature of a couple's relationship is also undesirable as it is likely to produce uncertain and inconsistent results."). The following decision illustrates another approach to establishing property rights during a nonmarital relationship.

Hofstad v. Christie

Supreme Court of Wyoming, 2010
240 P.3d 816

■ HILL, JUSTICE.

Appellant Jerald Korwin Hofstad challenges the district court's judgment equally partitioning a home owned by him and Appellee Cathryn Anne Christie as tenants in common. We affirm. . . .

From February of 1996 to July of 2007, Mr. Hofstad and Ms. Christie were involved in a relationship and lived together for extended periods of time, but never married. However, their relationship produced twin boys born in 1996. The couple and their children, including five children from Mr. Hofstad's prior relationship, lived together in Casper from 1998 to 2005. Their home, located on Monument Road, was owned alone by Mr. Hofstad.

In 2005, Hofstad decided to purchase a new home in Casper located at 1120 Donegal Street. At the time he entered into the contract on the Donegal home, he and Ms. Christie were separated. However, in April of 2005, the parties reconciled, and the warranty deed of the Donegal home conveyed the property to "Jerald K. Hofstad and Cathryn Anne Christie, grantee(s)." Mr. Hofstad paid the down payment, the closing costs, and entered into the loan obligation for the Donegal home. He used $124,053.15 from the sale of the Monument Road home, which was sold in May of 2005, to pay down the mortgage on the Donegal home.

From May of 2005 until July of 2007, the parties and their children lived in the Donegal home. Mr. Hofstad paid all mortgage payments and utilities. Christie contributed to various improvements and was the homemaker of the home. In July of 2007, Christie moved out of the Donegal home.

In December of 2007, Christie filed suit seeking partition of the Donegal home. After a bench trial, the court ruled that the home should be partitioned equally. The court reasoned that although Mr. Hofstad and Christie contributed unequal monetary amounts to the Donegal home, with Mr. Hofstad contributing substantially more money than Ms. Christie, Mr. Hofstad nevertheless failed to prove that there was not a family relationship or donative intent. Ms. Christie was awarded $70,767.40, one-half of the home's equity. Mr. Hofstad appealed that decision. . . .

It is widely accepted that, "if the instrument does not specify the shares of each co-tenant, it will be presumed that they take equal, undivided interests." *Bixler v. Oro Management*, 2004 WY 29, ¶ 19, 86 P.3d 843, 850 (Wyo.2004); see also 20 Am.Jur.2d *Cotenancy and Joint Ownership* § 121 (1995). However, this presumption may be rebutted by parol evidence, such as proof that the co-tenants contributed unequal amounts toward the purchase price of the property, and there is neither a family relationship among the co-tenants nor any evidence of donative intent on the part of those who contributed more than their pro rata amounts toward the purchase price. *Bixler*, ¶ 19, 86 P.3d at 850 (citations omitted); see also *D.M. v. D.A.*, 885 P.2d 94, 96 (Alaska 1994). See *Lawrence v. Harvey*, 186 Mont. 314, 607 P.2d 551, 556–57 (1980).

In the instant case, both parties agree that the Donegal property is held by them as tenants in common, inasmuch as the warranty deed did not specify a joint tenancy. Also, both parties agree with the district court's assessment that Mr. Hofstad contributed a substantially greater financial amount. Having established that the parties are tenants in common, but that Mr. Hofstad contributed substantially more money than Ms. Christie towards the property, we are faced with considering whether there is either evidence of a family relationship or evidence of donative intent on the part of Mr. Hofstad, or lack thereof.

First, we consider the more difficult of the two questions: whether there is evidence of the existence of a family relationship. Mr. Hofstad argues that the district court improperly applied a family presumption to himself and Ms. Christie as an "unmarried couple." Mr. Hofstad insists that there is absolutely no family relationship between himself and Ms. Christie because they are not related and they are unmarried.[1] This is a matter of first impression in Wyoming, so we therefore look to other jurisdictions for guidance. A Missouri court stated as follows:

> The record is clear that for several years prior to his death Phillips and Margaret conducted their joint household in the same manner as if they were married. Such a relationship, even in the absence of sexual relations, gave rise to a "family relation" between Margaret and Phillips. *Wells v. Goff*, [361 Mo. 1188] 239 S.W.2d 301 (Mo.1951); *Manning v. Driscoll's Estate*, 174 S.W.2d 921 (Mo.App.1943). In each of those cases a woman filed a claim against the estate of a male decedent for general housework performed for him during his lifetime. In each case, a "family relation" was found to exist.

Johnston v. Estate of Phillips, 706 S.W.2d 554, 556 (Mo.Ct.App.1986). Similarly, an Oregon court stated:

> [T]he legislature expressly defined "members of the same family" to mean "persons who are members of a family as parents, stepparents, grandparents, spouses, sons-in-law, daughters-in-law, brothers, sisters, children, stepchildren, adopted children or grandchildren." The definition expressly requires a family relationship between "persons." In particular, those persons must be members of a family "as" parents, stepparents, and so on. As the department correctly observes, a person cannot be a parent to himself, a spouse to himself, his own child, his own in-law, or have any of the other relationships specified in the statute. In keeping with that understanding of

1 Wyoming does not recognize common law marriage.

> the legislature's intended meaning, the statute consistently uses plural rather than singular references (*e.g.*, corporate "officers," corporate "directors," and family "members"). See *Schuette v. Dept. of Revenue*, 326 Or. 213, 217–18, 951 P.2d 690 (1997) (the repeated use of a singular or plural noun form provides some indication of the legislature's intent). [Emphasis in original.]
>
> Finally, as the department correctly argues, even apart from the definition provided by the legislature, the term "family" is a "quintessential example" of a collective noun—*i.e.*, a noun that most naturally refers to a collection of things or persons as a unit. See *Webster's Third New Int'l Dictionary* 444 (unabridged ed. 2002) (defining "collective": "1 a *of a word or term*: indicating a number of persons or things considered as constituting one group or aggregate *family* and *flock* are *collective* words> b *of a noun or pronoun*: singular in form but sometimes or always plural in construction *family* in 'the family were proud' is a *collective* word>"). Various dictionary definitions of the word "family" similarly denote a group of individuals with a common affiliation or ancestry.

Empl. Dep't v. Stock Secrets, Inc., 210 Or.App. 426, 150 P.3d 1090, 1092 (2007).

Our own statute defines "family members" as follows:

> (x) "Member of the minor's family" means the minor's parent, stepparent, spouse, grandparent, brother, sister, uncle or aunt, whether of whole or half blood or by adoption[.]

Wyo. Stat. Ann. § 34–13–114(a)(x) (LexisNexis 2009).

Even the United States Supreme Court recognizes that "family is a much broader term" than just parents and their children. *Moore v. City of East Cleveland*, 431 U.S. 494, 543, 97 S.Ct. 1932, 52 L.Ed.2d 531 (1977). The district court in this case echoed that sentiment when it stated in its conclusions of law that:

> Mr. Hofstad and Ms. Christie cohabited and shared an intimate relationship which resulted in the birth of two children of that relationship, and they resided together with their children at the 1120 Donegal residence, and accordingly, there was a family relationship[.]

Although the term "family relationship" is by no means absolute, we agree with the district court and Ms. Christie that in this case, the parties do share a family relationship, largely by way of their sharing two children. Even if Mr. Hofstad and Ms. Christie are not married, nor related by blood, that they lived together on and off for approximately ten years, all the while sharing an intimate relationship which resulted in the birth of their twins is evidence that a family relationship exists. Mr. Hofstad and Ms. Christie may never consider themselves "family," having never been married; however, their twin sons bind the four of them inextricably and forever, resulting in a family relationship. We disagree with Mr. Hofstad's argument that he does not share a family relationship with Ms. Christie.

Next we turn to whether or not there was any evidence of donative intent on the part of Mr. Hofstad, who argues that not only did he not gift Ms. Christie one-half of the value of the Donegal home, but also that she should have been required to actually prove that a gift of one-half of the value of the home was given to her.

Again, because this is an issue of first impression in Wyoming, we look to other states for direction. Other states have applied the "equal share presumption rule" to tenancies in common. In *D.M.*, the plaintiffs rebutted the general presumption of equal shares between tenants in common by demonstrating unequal contribution to equity in real property. There, the court found that this evidence created a presumption that they intended to share property in proportion to their respective contributions, and that was enough to rebut the general presumption of equal shares. *D.M.*, 885 P.2d at 97–98. The court held that if the parties intend to hold a tenancy in common in a particular proportion or if intent to determine proportion by a particular method can be discovered, this intent controls over the equal share presumption rule of cotenancy. *Id.*, at 97. Nonetheless, the court recognized that the common law presumptions concerning the respective interests of tenants in common where one contributes unequally to the purchase price are not applicable where the relationship between the parties indicates that one might have intended to make a gift to the other. *Id.*, at 97, n. 7 (citing *People v. Varel*, 351 Ill. 96, 184 N.E. 209, 211 (1932); *Wood v. Collins*, 812 P.2d 951, 956 (Alaska 1991)). In *Wood*, the court held that where the parties cohabitate and share an intimate relationship, it is more likely than otherwise that one party may contribute more of the acquisition or upkeep costs and still expect an equal share of the property. *Id.*, 812 P.2d at 956. The court in *Wood* went on to explain that the court must still find, however, that it was in fact the intent of the party making the excess contribution to confer it on the other party as a gift. *Id.*, at 957.

Using the rules of cotenancy, when the conveyance is taken in both names, the parties would be presumed to share equally or to share based upon the amount contributed, if the contributions were traceable (rebuttable by donative intent or a family relationship). *West v. Knowles*, 50 Wash.2d 311, 311 P.2d 689 (1957); A.C. Freeman on Cotenancy and Partition, 172 § 105 *Presumption of Relative Interests* (2nd ed. 1886). *See, e.g., Mayo v. Jones*, 8 Wash.App. 140, 505 P.2d 157 (Wash.App.1972); *Huls v. Huls*, 98 Ohio App. 509, 130 N.E.2d 412 (1954); *Williams v. Monzingo*, 235 Iowa 434, 16 N.W.2d 619 (Iowa 1944). Such rules of cotenancy could also result in requiring a showing of who paid various items, such as taxes, mortgage payments, or repairs. 2 Tiffany, Law of Real Property 282, § 461 (1939 and 2001 Cum.Supp.). The difficulty with the application of the rules of cotenancy is that their mechanical operation does not consider the nature of the relationship of the parties. While this may be appropriate for commercial investments, a mechanistic application of these rules will not often accurately reflect the expectations of the parties.

In *Beal v. Beal*, 282 Or. 115, 577 P.2d 507 (1978), the Supreme Court of Oregon found that property accumulated during cohabitation should be divided by determining the express or implied intent of the parties. *Id.*, at 510. There, Barbara and Raymond Beal, recently divorced, purchased property together, listing themselves as husband and wife. Both contributed to the down payment, Barbara paying $500.00 more than Raymond. Barbara made the first monthly payment; Raymond made all subsequent payments. The parties lived together in the house and both contributed to the household. After two years, Barbara moved out. Raymond remained and made all monthly payments on the house. The court decided the property dispute should be resolved by looking at the parties' intent. Before Barbara moved out, the trial court found that the parties intended to pool their resources for their common benefit. Therefore, both parties were held to have an undivided interest in the property. *Id.* The court rejected the regular rules of cotenancy, which would have required the parties to share expenses based upon their ownership share, because these rules failed to account for the relationship between the parties. Instead, the court stated,

> We believe a division of property accumulated during a period of cohabitation must be begun by inquiring into the intent of the parties, and if an intent can be found, it should control that property distribution. While this is obviously true when the parties have executed a written agreement, it is just as true if there is no written agreement. The difference is often only the sophistication of the parties. Thus, absent an express agreement, courts should closely examine the facts in evidence to determine what the parties implicitly agreed upon. . . .
>
> [W]e hold that courts, when dealing with the property disputes of a man and a woman who have been living together in a nonmarital domestic relationship, should distribute the property based upon the express or implied intent of those parties.

Beal, 577 P.2d at 510. We agree with Beal that property accumulated before separation should be divided by determining the express or implied intent of the parties. Here, the district court stated that

> Mr. Hofstad's representation and promise that Ms. Christie would be a "co-owner" or "equal owner" of the 1120 Donegal residence, and that if they would get back together again he would put title to the property in both names, is evidence of donative intent on his part with respect to the equal undivided one-half interest in the property vested in Ms. Christie.

After reviewing the record, we agree with the district court. Among the evidence that leads us to this conclusion is that in 2005, after the parties were briefly separated, they became engaged, and Mr. Hofstad represented to Ms. Christie that he would "change," they would be married within three months, that he would undergo counseling, and that Ms. Christie would be a co-owner or equal owner in the Donegal home. Furthermore, as conclusive evidence of Mr. Hofstad's intent, he put Ms. Christie's name on the Donegal deed after they rekindled their relationship. He initiated the purchase of the Donegal property of his own volition, but switched course after rekindling his relationship with Ms. Christie. We find this to be persuasive evidence of Mr. Hofstad's donative intent.

The district court's judgment partitioning equally a home the parties owned as tenants in common is affirmed. Given the parties' children and living situation over the course of the past ten years, a family relationship existed. Furthermore, given the circumstances surrounding the purchase of 1120 Donegal and the parties' reconciliation, evidence of donative intent existed. We affirm the district court.

NOTES

In deciding that unmarried cohabitants and their children constituted a "family relationship," the Wyoming Supreme Court went beyond equity and found that the family relationship adopted by the participants rebutted the presumption of unequal division of assets when cotenants contribute disproportionate amounts to the purchase of property. Other courts have provided additional benefits usually reserved to marriage and made them available to nonmarital cohabitants. *See, e.g.,* Owens v. Auto. Machinists Pension Trust, 551 F.3d 1138 (9th Cir. 2009) (holding nonmarital cohabitant was entitled to a portion of her former partner's pension, enforceable under a qualified domestic relations order (QDRO)); Byrne v. Laura, 60 Cal. Rptr.2d 908 (Cal. App. 1997) (holding that after either party's death, property may be distributed in a manner that best enforces an express or implied agreement). For commentary on nonmarital cohabitations, *see* PRINCIPLES OF THE LAW OF FAMILY DISSOLUTION: ANALYSES AND RECOMMENDATIONS § 6.03 (AM. LAW INST. 2002) (defining those persons qualifying for nonmarital cohabitation.); *see also* Candace Kovacic-Fleischer, *Cohabitation and the Restatement (Third) of Restitution & Unjust Enrichment*, 68 WASH. & LEE L. REV. 1407 (2011); Marsha B. Freeman, *Their Love is Here to Stay: Why The Supreme Court Cannot Turn Back the Hands of Time*, 17 CARDOZO J.L. & GENDER 1 (2010); Grace Ganz Blumberg, *The Regularization of Nonmarital Cohabitation: Rights and Responsibilities in the American Welfare State*, 76 NOTRE DAME L. REV. 1265 (2001).

PROBLEM ONE

Miguel Braschi and Leslie Blanchard, two men, met and began an intimate same-sex relationship in New York City. Throughout their relationship of nearly eleven years, they lived in Blanchard's rent-controlled apartment, sharing expenses, back accounts, and their common household, but they never married. Their relationship ended when Blanchard died and because the apartment was listed in his name, the landlord sought to evict Braschi or at least raise his rent to what it would be without rent control. But Braschi resisted, arguing that he was family to Blanchard and since the city code permitted family to remain in the apartment protected by rent control, he should be able to stay. The city code provision on rent control did not explicitly define family, but the landlord argued that it should be interpreted as incorporating only persons related by blood, marriage, or adoption and that Braschi was none of these. How would you argue on behalf of Miguel Braschi?

C. JURISDICTIONAL BASIS

Anastasi v. Anastasi

United States District Court, District of New Jersey, 1982
544 F. Supp. 866

■ DEBEVOISE, DISTRICT JUDGE.

Plaintiff instituted this action in the Chancery Division of the Superior Court of New Jersey, charging that defendant had breached his agreement "to provide plaintiff with all of her financial support and needs for the rest of her life". Defendant removed the case to the federal court . . . on the basis of diversity of citizenship. I raised the question whether the case should be remanded to the state court on the ground that it is within the domestic relations exception to federal jurisdiction notwithstanding that there is diversity of citizenship. After briefing and oral argument I concluded that under applicable New Jersey law the action was akin to a contract action rather than a domestic relations action and therefore the domestic relations exception to jurisdiction did not require remand. Anastasi v. Anastasi, 532 F. Supp. 720 (D.N.J.1982).

In reaching my conclusion I relied heavily upon two New Jersey cases which dealt with agreements for life support entered into by two cohabiting but unmarried persons. Kozlowski v. Kozlowski, 80 N.J. 378, 403 A.2d 902 (1979); Crowe v. DeGioia, 179 N.J.Super. 36, 430 A.2d 251 (App.Div.1981). Each held that such agreements were to be treated under the rules established by the law of contracts. In Crowe v. DeGioia the Court (with one judge dissenting) reversed an order of the trial court awarding plaintiff weekly support payments *pendente lite,* requiring defendant to pay plaintiff's outstanding medical, dental, drug and other bills, permitting plaintiff the exclusive use of defendant's dwelling, and requiring defendant to continue to pay all costs, enjoining defendant from disposing of his assets and awarding plaintiff a counsel fee *pendente lite.*

In ruling as I did I stated:

> I conclude that the exception will apply only if two conditions are met: first, the state exhibits a significant interest

> in this kind of relationship akin to the state's interest in the marriage and the parent-child relationships; and, second, in order to protect this interest a court must make the same kinds of inquiries that have traditionally brought into play the domestic relations exception. . . .
>
> Had the views of the trial court and of the dissenting opinion on appeal prevailed in *DeGioia,* I would have concluded that the domestic relations exception to jurisdiction should be applied were such an action instituted in the federal court. The state would have evidenced a sufficient interest in the relationship of unmarried couples to have devised legal mechanisms to protect the parties upon dissolution of the relationship. It would be necessary for a court to inquire into the details of the relationship and into the financial circumstances of the parties. It would be necessary to do this on a continuing basis at least during the course of the litigation. This is precisely what the domestic relations exception is designed to avoid.

Anastasi v. Anastasi, supra, at 724, 725.

On July 8, 1982 the New Jersey Supreme Court reversed the judgment of the Appellate Division of the Superior Court in Crowe v. DeGioia, 90 N.J. 126, 447 A.2d 173 (1982). The Supreme Court ruled that Crowe should be permitted to remain in the home, that support payments to meet "her minimal needs" should be continued *pendente lite,* and that "necessary" medical, dental and pharmaceutical bills should continue to be paid by DeGioia. The Supreme Court held that DeGioia should not be restrained from transferring his assets and that costs and counsel fees should not be awarded in the application for temporary relief. Observing that the Chancery Division rather than the Law Division was the more appropriate forum for the case, the Court stated:

> Moreover, a similarity exists between many of the issues and proofs in this type of case and those in a matrimonial action, the exclusive province of the Chancery Division under R. 4:75. Consequently, in this case, as we anticipate will be true in the majority of such cases, the Chancery Division is the appropriate forum. Selection of the Law or Chancery Division in future cases should reflect the responsible exercise of judgment by counsel, subject to the control of the court, to best achieve a just result in this evolving cause of action.

At 138, 447 A.2d 173.

After the New Jersey Supreme Court's opinion was issued I directed the parties to show cause why the instant action should or should not be remanded to the state courts. A hearing was held and I conclude that in the present posture of New Jersey law this kind of case is within the domestic relations exception to jurisdiction and must be remanded. New Jersey's Supreme Court emphasized that it was not awarding alimony because "alimony may be awarded only in a matrimonial action for divorce or nullity". It was, it stated, "applying traditional equitable principles" in an attempt to "achieve substantial justice" by adjusting "the rights and duties of parties in light of the realities of their relationship". At 135, 447 A.2d 173. For federal jurisdictional purposes, it is immaterial what label is ascribed to the actions New Jersey courts are now required to take in "palimony" cases. What matters is not the label but rather the function the courts are called upon to perform. As delineated by the New Jersey Supreme Court, a palimony case applying New Jersey law is a domestic relations case within the exception to federal jurisdiction.

In Crowe v. DeGioia the Supreme Court defined a significant state interest in living relationships established by agreement rather than by formal marriage. It noted the frequency of such relationships and the need to protect the interests of the parties to them, stating:

> Increasing numbers of unmarried couples live together. The number of households comprised of unmarried partners rose from approximately 12,000 in 1960 to more than 1.5 million in 1980. U.S. Bureau of Census, Dept. of Commerce, 1960 Census of Population, "Persons by Family Characteristics," Table 15 (1960) and Current Population Report, Series P–20, No. 365, "Marital Status in Living Arrangements," Table 7 (1980). Although plaintiff need not be rewarded for cohabiting with defendant, she should not be penalized simply because she lived with him in consideration of a promise for support. Our endeavor is to shape a remedy that will protect the legally cognizable interests of the parties and serve the needs of justice.

At 135, 447 A.2d 173.

The Court evidently contemplates that palimony actions will be commenced with increasing frequency and in its opinion provided guidance as to the Division of the Superior Court in which such actions should be filed—normally the Chancery Division. At 137, 447 A.2d 173. Not only does Crowe v. DeGioia announce a significant state interest in the consensual live-in relationship, it requires that in order to protect this interest a trial court must make the same kinds of inquiries that have traditionally brought into play the domestic relations exception to federal jurisdiction. In Crowe v. DeGioia the Court's rationale requires a finding of a reasonable basis for one of the parties to remain in the non-marital home. It requires a finding of the minimal needs of the moving party in order to form a basis for an award of interim support payments. It requires a finding as to the necessity of medical, dental and pharmaceutical bills. Final resolution of the controversy will inevitably require extensive probing into many other issues similar to those in a matrimonial action in order "to best achieve a just result in this evolving cause of action"....

[T]hese are the kinds of inquiries and judgments which the state courts are best equipped to handle. They are the kinds of inquiries and judgments which, under the domestic relations exception to jurisdiction, may not be made by federal courts.

For these reasons the case will be remanded to the Superior Court of New Jersey, Chancery Division. . . .

NOTES

Nonmarital Partnerships and the Domestic Relations Exception to Federal Jurisdiction. In Barber v. Barber, 62 U.S. 582, (21 How.) 582, 584, 16 L.Ed. 226 (1858), the Supreme Court of the United States said in dictum:

> We disclaim altogether any jurisdiction in the courts of the United States upon the subject of divorce, or for the allowance of alimony, either as an original proceeding in chancery or as an incident to divorce *a vinculo,* or to one from bed and board.

That statement led to what became known as a "domestic relations exception" to subject matter jurisdiction in federal courts. Under this doctrine, even though with diversity of citizenship and the requisite jurisdictional amount in controversy, federal courts will not hear divorce cases. In the past, the exception was far wider; some believe that longstanding inaccessibility to federal courts even to challenge arbitrary state regulation of marriage and divorce contributed significantly to the slow pace of reform until only two or three decades ago. Considerable question has been voiced about the appropriate scope and even the desirability of an exception, and there are signs that it is now beginning to erode. Even so, there continue to be strong views that federal courts should abstain from hearing family law matters. Such a position was articulated by Justice Rehnquist as recently as 1982 in his dissenting opinion in *Santosky v. Kramer*:

> If ever there were an area in which federal courts should heed the admonition of Justice Holmes that "a page of history is worth a volume of logic," it is in the area of domestic relations. This area has been left to the states from time immemorial, and not without good reason.

455 U.S. 745, 769, 102 S.Ct. 1388, 71 L.Ed.2d 599 (1982).

In Ankenbrandt v. Richards, 504 U.S. 689, 112 S.Ct. 2206, 119 L.Ed.2d 468 (1992), the Supreme Court of the United States was asked to decide whether the exception should apply to tort suits brought in federal court solely pursuant to diversity jurisdiction. Justice White, seeking a firmer foundation for the federal domestic relations exception than the century and one-half old *Barber*, wrote that the exception cannot be found explicitly within the Constitution but rather in the power of Congress to grant jurisdiction under Article III. He explained that

> Article I, § 8, cl. 9, for example, authorizes Congress "[t]o constitute Tribunals inferior to the supreme Court" and Article III, § 1, states

> that "[t]he judicial Power of the United States shall be vested in one supreme Court, and in such inferior courts as the Congress may from time to time ordain and establish." The court cases state the rule that "if inferior courts were created, [Congress was not] required to invest them with all the jurisdiction it was authorized to bestow under Article III. Palmore v. United States, 411 U.S. 389, 401."

Id. at 697. . . .

> We thus are content to rest our conclusion that a domestic relations exception exists as a matter of statutory construction not on the accuracy of the historical justifications on which it was based, but rather on Congress' apparent acceptance of this construction of the diversity jurisdiction. . . .

Id. at 700. . . .

> We conclude, therefore, that the domestic relations exception, as articulated by this Court since *Barber*, divests the federal courts of power to issue divorce, alimony, and child custody decrees. Given the long passage of time without any expression of congressional dissatisfaction, we have no trouble today reaffirming the validity of the exception as it pertains to divorce and alimony decrees and child custody orders.

Id. at 706–7.

Fisher v. Fisher

Court of Appeals of New York, 1929
165 N.E. 460

■ KELLOGG, J.

In this action for a separation the complaint alleges "that the parties hereto were duly married on the 24th day of October, 1925." The answer denies the allegation. Concededly, on the day named the parties to the action were on board the steamship Leviathan, then on the high seas, bound from the port of New York to Southampton, England. When the ship was 40 miles out from the port of New York, its captain performed a marriage ceremony, wherein these parties were the principals. In the course of the ceremony the captain asked the plaintiff if she took the defendant for her husband, asked the defendant if he took the plaintiff for his wife, received an affirmative answer from each, and thereupon pronounced them man and wife. Cohabitation of the principals followed the ceremony. The only question which survives for discussion here is this: Were the parties upon the occasion in question lawfully united in marriage?

It is elementary that marriage is a civil contract; that the law deals with it as it does with all other contracts; that it pronounces a marriage to be valid wherever a man and woman, able and willing to contract, do, per verba de praesenti, promise to become husband and wife. A formal ceremony of marriage, whether in due form or not, must be assumed to be by consent, and, therefore, prima facie a contract of marriage per verba de praesenti. According to the common law of all Christendom, consensual marriages—i.e., marriages resting simply on consent per verba de praesenti—between competent parties, are valid marriages. . . . The sanction which the law of civilized nations bestows upon marriages by mere consent is of course not inclusive of marriages which civilization commonly condemns. . . . Otherwise, regulations restrictive of the common right of marriage by mere consent, or imposing conditions upon it, are exceptional; they depend upon local statutes, and, as in other cases of exceptions, if one claims that a case falls within them, the burden is upon him to show the fact . . . [A]lthough no law of any state, territory or district of the United States, *sanctioning* the marriage of the parties to this action, may have followed the ship Leviathan upon the high seas, in the absence of any such law which *condemned* the marriage, we think that they were lawfully married. It becomes necessary now to inquire whether a controlling law of any state did condemn the marriage.

The defendant, prior to the performance of the marriage ceremony in question, was already a married man. His former wife had procured, in this jurisdiction, a decree of divorce against him, dissolving the marriage on the ground of adultery. According to the terms of the decree and the laws of this state the defendant was forbidden to remarry during the life of his then wife. The wife, who procured the decree, is still living. It is well settled that the provisions of our statute forbidding the remarriage of a party who has been divorced for adultery have no extraterritorial effect; that a subsequent marriage of the guilty party, during the life of the innocent party, in a sister state, if valid in that state, will be recognized here as a lawful marriage. The question then arises, Did the laws of the State of New York follow the steamship Leviathan in its journey upon the high seas?

"The Steamship Leviathan of New York, N.Y." was registered in the port of New York. The certificate of registry specifies that the "United States of America represented by the United States Shipping Board is the only owner of the vessel called the Leviathan of New York, N.Y." On the high seas it flew the flag of the United States. A ship in the open sea is regarded by the law of nations as a part of the territory whose flag such ship carries. Wharton, Conflict of Laws, § 356. Wharton says: "As between the several states in the American Union, a ship at sea is presumed to belong to the state in which it is registered." For this statement the sole authority is Crapo v. Kelly, 16 Wall. 610, 21 L.Ed. 430. We think that the learned author misconceived the decision in that case. The ship there considered was a vessel owned by residents of the state of Massachusetts. It was, likewise, registered at a port within the state of Massachusetts. As we read the case, the court decided that the vessel was a Massachusetts ship, not because it had a Massachusetts registry, but because its owners were citizens of Massachusetts. The court said:

"Again, the owners of this vessel and the assignees in insolvency were citizens of Massachusetts, and subject to her laws. It is not doubted that a sale of property between them of property on board of this vessel, or of the vessel itself, would be regulated by the laws of Massachusetts." In The Havana (C.C.A.) 64 F. 496, it was held that a vessel owned by a New Jersey corporation, although registered in New York, was a New Jersey vessel. In International Nav. Co. v. Lindstrom (C.C.A.) 123 F. 475, it was said: "It is plain that the New York statute did not reach the case, because, inasmuch as the steamship belonged to a citizen of New Jersey, it was a vessel of that state, notwithstanding its registry in New York." . . . We think it clear, under the authorities, that the laws which follow a ship upon the high seas are the laws of the state where the owner resides, not the laws of the state within which the ship is registered. Therefore, if we assume that the United States was the owner of the steamship Leviathan, the laws of the state of New York did not follow the ship as a part of its territory, since the United States certainly is not domiciled in that state. The presumption of the validity of the marriage, therefore, was not destroyed by proof that one of the parties thereto, within the state of New York, was incompetent to marry.

We have hitherto assumed that the marriage in question had not the positive sanction of any Federal statute, or of the common law of any state, territory or district of the United States, carried upon the high seas by the steamship Leviathan. We think the fact is otherwise.

Congress had provided that: "Every vessel making voyages from a port in the United States to any foreign port" should have an official log book; that every master of such a vessel should make entry therein of "Every marriage taking place on board, with the names and ages of the parties." Mason's U.S. Code, vol. 3, title 46, § 201 (46 U.S.C.A. § 201), "Every marriage taking place on board" is certainly inclusive of marriages other than those sanctioned by the municipal laws of the state of the ship's ownership. We take it that Congress had thus recognized that on board a ship at sea, notwithstanding the absence of municipal laws so carried, there is nevertheless a law of marriage. That law can be none other than the law, common to all nations, which pronounces valid all consensual marriages between a man and woman who are, in the view of all civilized people, competent to marry. In this view, the marriage between the parties to this action, by force of a federal statute, which Congress was fully empowered to enact, was a valid marriage.

If the federal statute cannot thus be interpreted, then we think that the common law of the District of Columbia prevailed to give sanction to the marriage. We have thus far assumed that the title to the steamship Leviathan was in the United States. The certificate of registry so states, and the referee has so found. Moreover, the respondent does not appear to have disputed the point. However, we think that such was not the fact. An act of Congress of June 5, 1920, provided in part as follows: "All vessels . . . acquired by the President . . . in pursuance of the joint resolution entitled 'Joint Resolution authorizing the President to take over for the United States the possession and title of any vessel within its jurisdiction, which at the time of coming therein was owned in whole or in part by any corporation, citizen, or subject of any nation with which the United States may be at war, or was under register of any such nation, and for other purposes,' approved May 12, 1917, . . . are hereby transferred to the board. . . ." (46 U.S.C.A. § 863). The "board" is the United States Shipping Board. The steamship Leviathan was a vessel of the class referred to by the joint resolution. . . . It seems to be clear, therefore, that the title to the steamship Leviathan was in the United States Shipping Board. That board had its domicile in the District of Columbia. Therefore, if the law of Congress referred to did not occupy the field, the law of the District of Columbia in relation to marriage followed the steamship on its journey upon the high seas, and was controlling. . . .

In the absence of proof of the statutes of the District, we must assume that the common law, which would give sanction to the marriage in question, prevails in the District of Columbia; that this law obtained on board the steamship Leviathan when upon the high seas; that the marriage between the parties was, therefore, legal. . . .

NOTES

Marriage is not a public act, record, or judicial proceeding of a state entitled to Full Faith and Credit under the United States Constitution. Therefore, a marriage may be valid in one state but not in another because the marriage celebrated in another jurisdiction offends the strong state public policy of the second state in which recognition is sought. *See, e.g.*, N. H. REV. STAT. § 457:13. Recognition of Out-of-State Marriages (2014). State public policies may differ on issues such as incest, capacity, permitted age to marry, and prior to the decision of the United States Supreme Court in 2015, same-sex marriage. *See* Obergefell v. Hodges, 135 S.Ct. 2584 (2015). Lacking mandatory Constitutional recognition, the validity of a marriage can be subject to the vagaries of individual states. Likewise, in addition to marriage, any modifiable support award or custody determination made by a court in one state *may not* be entitled to Full Faith and Credit in another state. In order to promote and enforce uniformity among the states the states have adopted, at federal insistence, the Uniform Child-Custody Jurisdiction and Enforcement Act (1997), 9 U.L.A. Pt. IA 649 *et seq.* (1999) (custody and visitation awards), and the Uniform Interstate Family Support Act (2008). 9 U.L.A. Pt. IB 133 *et seq.* (2015) (spousal and child support awards). Both of these statutes may be found in the Statutory Supplement to this casebook. *See* WALTER WADLINGTON, RAYMOND C. O'BRIEN, & ROBIN FRETWELL WILSON, FAMILY LAW STATUTES: SELECTED UNIFORM LAWS, MODEL LEGISLATION, FEDERAL STATUTES, STATE STATUTES, AND INTERNATIONAL TREATIES (5th ed. 2017).

D. CONSTITUTIONAL PARAMETERS OF FAMILY LAW

1. FREEDOM OF RELIGION

Reynolds v. United States

Supreme Court of the United States, 1878
98 U.S. 145

Error to the Supreme Court of the Territory of Utah. This is an indictment found in the District Court for the third judicial district of the Territory of Utah, charging George Reynolds with bigamy, in violation of section 5352 of the Revised Statutes, which omitting its exceptions, is as follows:—

"Every person having a husband or wife living, who marries another, whether married or single, in a Territory, or other place over which the United States have exclusive jurisdiction, is guilty of bigamy, and shall be punished by a fine of not more than $500, and by imprisonment for a term of not more than five years." . . .

Evidence was admitted that showed that the prisoner had married Mary Ann Tuddenham, and subsequently had married Amelia Jane Schofield, during the lifetime of said Mary. . . . The jury found him guilty . . . and the judgment that he be imprisoned at hard labor for a term of two years, and pay a fine of $500, rendered by the District Court, having been affirmed by the Supreme Court of the Territory, he sued out this writ of error.

■ WAITE, C.J.

. . .

On the trial, the plaintiff in error, the accused proved that at the time of his alleged second marriage he was, and for many years before had been a member of the Church of Jesus Christ of Latter-Day Saints, commonly called the Mormon Church, and a believer in its doctrines; that it was an accepted doctrine of that church "that it was the duty of the male members of said church, circumstances permitting, to practice polygamy; . . . that this duty was enjoined by different books which the members of said church believed to be of divine origin, and among others the Holy Bible, and also, that the members of the church believed that the practice of polygamy was directly enjoined upon the male members thereof by the Almighty God, in a revelation to Joseph Smith, the founder and prophet of said church; and that failing or refusing to practice polygamy by such male members of said church, when circumstances would admit, would be punished, and that the penalty for such failure and refusal would be damnation of the life to come." He also proved "that he had received permission from the recognized authorities in said church to enter into polygamous marriage; . . . and that such marriage ceremony was performed under and pursuant to the doctrines of said church."

Upon this proof he asked the court to instruct the jury that if they found from the evidence that he "was married as charged—if he was married—in pursuance of and in conformity with what he believed at the time to be a religious duty, that the verdict must be 'not guilty.'" This request was refused, and the court did charge "that there must have been a criminal intent, but that if the defendant under the influence of a religious belief that it was right,—under an inspiration, if you please, that it was right,—deliberately married a second time, having a first wife living, the want of consciousness of evil intent—the want of understanding on his part that he was committing a crime—did not excuse him; but the law inexorably in such case implied the criminal intent."

Upon this charge and refusal to charge the question is raised whether religious belief can be accepted as a justification of an overt act made criminal by the law of the land. . . .

Congress cannot pass a law for the government of the Territories which shall prohibit the free exercise of religion. The first amendment to the Constitution expressly forbids such legislation. Religious freedom is guaranteed everywhere throughout the United States, so far as congressional interference is concerned. The question to be determined is, whether the law now under consideration comes within this prohibition.

The word "religion" is not defined in the Constitution. We must go elsewhere, therefore, to ascertain its meaning, and nowhere more appropriately, we think, than to the history of the times in the midst of which the provision was adopted. The precise point of the inquiry, is what is the religious freedom which has been guaranteed. . . .

Polygamy has always been odious among the northern and western nations of Europe, and, until the establishment of the Mormon Church, was almost exclusively a feature of the life of Asiatic and of African people. At common law, the second marriage was always void (2 Kent Com. 79), and from the earliest history of England polygamy has been treated as an offence against society. After the establishment of the ecclesiastical courts, and until the time of James I., it was punished through the instrumentality of those tribunals, not merely because ecclesiastical rights had been violated, but because upon the separation of the ecclesiastical courts from the civil the ecclesiastical were supposed to be the most appropriate for the trial of matrimonial causes and offences against the rights of marriage, just as they were for testamentary causes and the settlement of the estates of deceased persons.

By the statute of 1 James I. (c. 11), the offence, if committed in England or Wales, was made punishable in the civil courts, and the penalty was death. As this statute was limited in its operation to England and Wales, it was at a very early period re-enacted, generally with some modifications, in all the colonies. In connection with the case we are now considering, it is a significant fact that on the 8th day of December, 1788, after the passage of the act establishing religious freedom, and after the convention of Virginia had recommended as an amendment to the Constitution of the United States the declaration in a bill of rights that "all men have an equal, natural, and unalienable right to the free exercise of religion, according to the dictates of conscience," the legislature of that State substantially enacted the statute of James I., death penalty included, because, as recited in the preamble, "it hath been doubted whether bigamy or polygamy be punishable by the laws of this Commonwealth." 12 Hening's Stat. 691. From that day to this we think it may safely be said there never has been a time in any State of the Union when polygamy has not been an offence against society, cognizable by the civil courts and punishable with more or less severity. In the face of all this evidence, it is impossible to believe that the constitutional guaranty of religious freedom was intended to prohibit legislation in respect to this most important feature of social life. Marriage, while from its very nature, a sacred obligation, is nevertheless, in most civilized nations, a civil contract, and usually regulated by law. Upon it society may be said to be built, and out of its fruits spring social relations and social obligations and duties, with which government is necessarily required to deal. In fact, according as monogamous or polygamous marriages are allowed, do we find the principles on which the government of the people, to a greater or less extent rests. . . .

In our opinion, the statute immediately under consideration is within the legislative power of Congress . . . This being so, the only question which remains is, whether those who make polygamy a part of their religion are excepted from the operation of the statute. If they are, then those who do not make polygamy a part of their religious belief may be found guilty and punished, while those who do, must be acquitted and go free. This would be introducing a new element into criminal law. Laws are made for government of actions, and while they cannot interfere with mere religious belief and opinions, they may with practices. Suppose one believed that human sacrifices were a necessary part of religious worship, would it be seriously contended that the civil government under which he lived could not interfere to prevent a sacrifice? Or if a wife religiously believed it was her duty to burn herself upon the funeral pile of her dead husband would it be beyond the power of the civil government to prevent her carrying her belief into practice?

So here, as a law of the organization of society under the exclusive dominion of the United States, it provided that plural marriage shall not be allowed. Can a man excuse his practices to the contrary because of his religious belief? To permit this would be to make the professed doctrines of religious belief superior to the law of the land, and in effect to permit every citizen to become a law unto himself. Government could exist only in name under such circumstances. . . .

Every act necessary to constitute the crime was knowingly done. . . The only defence of the accused in this case is his belief that the law ought not to have been enacted. It matters not that his belief was a part of his professed religion: it was still belief, and belief only. . . .

Judgment affirmed.

NOTES

Reynolds initiated free exercise jurisprudence, discussing whether a neutral and generally applicable law could be bypassed by an individual's right to religious freedom. The Court's distinction between religious beliefs and religious practices dictates resolution of religious freedom cases today. When the Court issued its decision in Sherbert v. Verner, 374 U.S. 398 (1963), religious organizations and individuals gained a modicum of protection from legislative acts because the Court subsequently required laws that infringed on religious liberty to be subjected to a strict scrutiny standard. Under this standard, the legislation would have to be the least restrictive means of achieving a compelling state interest. In 1990, however, the Court returned to the belief-practice distinction adopted in *Reynolds*. *See* Emp't Div. v. Smith, 494 U.S. 872 (1990). The state does not need to demonstrate a compelling state interest. If the legal prohibition is "merely the incidental effect of a generally applicable and otherwise valid provision, the First Amendment has not been offended." *Id.* at 878.

Unable to find refuge in judicial requirements of strict scrutiny, free exercise claimants must find recourse in the political process, specifically in accommodation statutes exempting religious persons and organizations from complying with legislation. The following decision is illustrative.

On polygamy generally, *see* John Witte, Jr., *Why No Polygamy*, in THE CONTESTED PLACE OF RELIGION IN FAMILY LAW (Robin Fretwell Wilson, ed. 2017).

PROBLEM TWO

Within a week of the Supreme Court's *Obergefell* decision, Nathan Collier, a Montana man, applied for a marriage license to "legally wed his second wife." He had broken away from the Church of the Latter-Day Saints or Mormon church and "now belongs to no religious organization. He said he and his wives hid their relationship for years but decided to go public by appearing on the reality cable television show 'Sister Wives.' " If you were representing Collier, what would you argue after *Obergefell* that might overcome the hurdle of the *Reynolds* decision, which has not been overruled?

Catholic Charities of Sacramento Inc. v. Superior Court

Supreme Court of California, 2004
85 P.3d 67

■ WERDEGAR, J.

In this case, we address a church-affiliated employer's constitutional challenges to the Women's Contraception Equity Act (WCEA), under which certain health and disability insurance contracts must cover prescription contraceptives. The plaintiff employer, which opposes contraceptives on religious grounds, claims the statute violates the establishment and free exercise clauses of the United States and California Constitutions. (U.S. Const., 1st Amend.; Cal. Const., art. I, § 4.) The lower courts rejected the employer's claims. We affirm.

The Legislature enacted the WCEA in 1999 to eliminate gender discrimination in health care benefits and to improve access to prescription contraceptives. Evidence before the Legislature showed that women during their reproductive years spent as much as 68 percent more than men in out-of-pocket health care costs, due in large part to the cost of prescription contraceptives and the various costs of unintended pregnancies, including health risks, premature deliveries and increased neonatal care. Evidence also showed that, while most health maintenance organizations (HMO's) covered prescription contraceptives, not all preferred provider organization (PPO) and indemnity plans did. As a result, approximately 10 percent of commercially insured Californians did not have coverage for prescription contraceptives.

The Legislature chose to address these problems by regulating the terms of insurance contracts. The WCEA does not require any employer to offer coverage for prescription drugs. Under the WCEA, however, certain health and disability insurance plans that cover prescription drugs must cover prescription contraceptives. As an exception, the law permits a "religious employer" to request a policy that includes drug coverage but excludes coverage for "contraceptive methods that are contrary to the religious employer's religious tenets." Health and Safety Code section 1367.25 governs group health care service plan contracts; Insurance Code section 10123.196 governs individual and group disability insurance policies.

Plaintiff Catholic Charities of Sacramento, Inc. (hereafter Catholic Charities) is a California nonprofit public benefit corporation. (See Corp.Code, § 5110 et seq.) Although independently incorporated, Catholic Charities describes itself as "operated in connection with the Roman Catholic Bishop of Sacramento" and as "an organ of the Roman Catholic Church." The nonprofit corporation "offer[s] a multitude of social services and private welfare programs to the general public, as part of the social justice ministry of the Roman Catholic Church." These services and programs include "providing immigrant resettlement programs, elder care, counseling, food, clothing and affordable housing for the poor and needy, housing and vocational training of the developmentally disabled and the like."

Catholic Charities offers health insurance, including prescription drug coverage, to its 183 full-time employees through group health care plans underwritten by Blue Shield of California and Kaiser Permanente. Catholic Charities does not, however, offer insurance for prescription contraceptives because it considers itself obliged to follow the Roman Catholic Church's religious teachings, because the Church considers contraception a sin, and because Catholic Charities believes it cannot offer insurance for prescription contraceptives without improperly facilitating that sin.

As mentioned, the WCEA permits a "religious employer" to offer prescription drug insurance without coverage for contraceptives that violate the employer's religious tenets. (Health & Saf. Code, § 1367.25, subd. (b).) The act defines a "religious employer" as "an entity for which each of the following is true: (A) The inculcation of religious values is the purpose of the entity. (B) The entity primarily employs persons who share the religious tenets of the entity. (C) The entity serves primarily persons who share the religious tenets of the entity. (D) The entity is a nonprofit organization as described in Section 6033(a)(2)(A)I or iii, of the Internal Revenue Code of 1986, as amended." (*Ibid.*) The cited provisions of the Internal Revenue Code exempt, from the obligation to file an annual return, "churches, their integrated auxiliaries, and conventions or associations of churches" (26 U.S.C. § 6033(a)(2)(A)(I)) and "the exclusively religious activities of any religious order" (*id.*, § 6033(a)(2)(A)(I) and (iii)).

Catholic Charities does not qualify as a "religious employer" under the WCEA because it does not meet any of the definition's four criteria. (See Health & Saf. Code, § 1367.25, subd. (b)(1)(A)–(D).) The organization candidly acknowledges this in its complaint, offering the following explanation: "The corporate purpose of Catholic Charities is not the direct inculcation of religious values. Rather, [its] purpose . . . is to offer social services to the general public that promote a just, compassionate society that supports the dignity of individuals and families, to reduce the causes and results of poverty, and to build healthy communities through social service programs such as counseling, mental health and immigration services, low-income housing, and supportive social services to the poor and vulnerable. Further, Catholic Charities does not primarily employ persons who share its Roman Catholic religious beliefs, but, rather, employs a diverse group of persons of many religious backgrounds, all of whom share [its] Gospel-based commitment to promote a just, compassionate society that supports the dignity of individuals and families. Moreover, Catholic Charities serves people of all faith backgrounds, a significant majority of [whom] do not share [its] Roman Catholic faith. Finally . . . Catholic Charities, although an exempt organization under 26 U.S.C. § 501(c)(3), is not a nonprofit organization pursuant to [s]ection 6033(a)(2)(A)(I) or (iii) of the Internal Revenue Code of 1986. Consequently . . . Catholic Charities is not entitled . . . to an exemption from the mandate imposed by [the WCEA]."

As mentioned, the WCEA implicitly permits any employer to avoid covering contraceptives by not offering coverage for prescription drugs. But this option, according to Catholic Charities, does not eliminate all conflict between the law and its religious beliefs. Catholic Charities feels obliged to offer prescription drug insurance to its employees under what it describes as the "Roman Catholic religious teaching" that "an employer has a moral obligation at all times to consider the well-being of its employees and to offer just wages and benefits in order to provide a dignified livelihood for the employee and his or her family."

Perceiving no option consistent with both its beliefs and the law, Catholic Charities filed this action seeking a declaratory judgment that the WCEA is unconstitutional and an injunction barring the law's enforcement. Defendants are the State of California, the Department of Managed Health Care and the Department of Insurance . . . Catholic Charities' challenges to the WCEA arise under the establishment and free exercise clauses of the United States and California Constitutions. (U.S. Const., 1st Amend.; Cal. Const., art. I, § 4.) The superior court, finding no reasonable likelihood that Catholic Charities would prevail on the merits, denied its motion for a preliminary injunction. Catholic Charities sought review of this ruling by petition for writ of mandate, which the Court of Appeal denied. We granted review of the Court of Appeal's decision.

Catholic Charities, in its brief to this court, asserts eight constitutional challenges to the WCEA. All refer to the religion clauses of the federal and state Constitutions. (U.S. Const., 1st Amend.; Cal. Const., art. I, § 4.) Catholic Charities begins with a set of three arguments to the effect that the WCEA impermissibly interferes with the autonomy of religious organizations. (See 10 Cal.Rptr.3d p. 294, 85 P.3d p. 76 et seq., *post.*) Next, Catholic Charities claims the WCEA impermissibly burdens its right of free exercise. As part of this claim, Catholic Charities offers four arguments for subjecting the WCEA to strict scrutiny, despite the United States Supreme Court's holding that the right of free exercise does not excuse compliance with neutral, generally applicable laws. (*Employment Div., Ore. Dept. of Human Res. v. Smith* (1990) 494 U.S. 872, 876–890, 110 S.Ct. 1595, 108 L.Ed.2d 876; see 10 Cal.Rptr.3d p. 299, 85 P.3d p. 81 et seq., *post.*) Finally, Catholic Charities contends the WCEA fails even the rational basis test. (See p. 315, 85 P.3d p. 94 et seq., *post.*)

A. RELIGIOUS AUTONOMY

1. INTERFERENCE WITH MATTERS OF RELIGIOUS DOCTRINE AND INTERNAL CHURCH GOVERNANCE

. . .

Catholic Charities asserts that the Legislature, in enacting the WCEA, violated the rule of church property cases by interfering with matters of internal church governance and by rejecting the Catholic Church's decision that prescription contraceptives are sinful. These assertions are incorrect. This case does not implicate internal church governance; it implicates the relationship between a nonprofit public benefit corporation and its employees, most of whom do not belong to the Catholic Church. Only those who join a church impliedly consent to its religious governance on matters of faith and discipline. (*Watson, supra,* 13 Wall. 679, 80 U.S. 679, 729.) Certainly the WCEA conflicts with Catholic Charities' religious beliefs, but this does not mean the Legislature has decided a religious question. Congress has created, and the high court has resolved, similar conflicts between employment law and religious beliefs without deciding religious questions and without reference to the church property cases. (E.g., *Tony and Susan Alamo Foundation v. Sec'y of Labor* (1985) 471 U.S. 290, 303–306, 105 S.Ct. 1953, 85 L.Ed.2d 278 [religious organization must comply with federal minimum wage laws]; *United States v. Lee* (1982) 455 U.S. 252, 256–261, 102 S.Ct. 1051, 71 L.Ed.2d 127 [Amish employer must pay Social Security and unemployment taxes].) Neither does this case require us to decide any religious questions. Instead, we need only apply the usual rules for assessing whether state-imposed burdens on religious exercise are constitutional. (See *Church of Lukumi Babalu Aye, Inc. v. Hialeah* (1993) 508 U.S. 520, 531–533, 113 S.Ct. 2217, 124 L.Ed.2d 472; *Employment Div., Ore. Dept. of Human Res. v. Smith, supra,* 494 U.S. 872, 876–882, 110 S.Ct. 1595.) This we do below, in the context of Catholic Charities' separate claims under the free exercise clause. (See 10 Cal.Rptr.3d p. 299, 85 P.3d p. 81 et seq., *post.*) . . .

2. DISTINCTION BETWEEN RELIGIOUS AND SECULAR ACTIVITIES

Catholic Charities next argues that the First Amendment forbids the government to "premis[e] a religious institution's eligibility for an exemption from government regulation upon whether the activities of the institution are deemed by the government to be 'religious' or 'secular'. . . ." The argument is directed against the four statutory criteria an employer must satisfy to claim exemption from the WCEA as a "religious employer." (Health & Saf. Code, § 1367.25, subd. (b)(1)(A)–(D); see 10 Cal.Rptr.3d p. 292, 85 P.3d p. 75, *ante.*) The argument lacks merit.

The exception to the WCEA accommodates religious exercise by relieving statutorily defined "religious employers" (Health & Saf. Code, § 1367.25, subd. (b)) of the burden of paying for contraceptive methods that violate their religious beliefs. The United States Supreme Court has long recognized that the alleviation of significant governmentally created burdens on religious exercise is a permissible legislative purpose that does not offend the establishment clause. (*Corporation of Presiding Bishop v. Amos* (1978) 483 U.S. 327, 334–335, 107 S.Ct. 2862, 97 L.Ed.2d 273; *Hobbie v. Unemployment Appeals Comm'n of Fla.* (1987) 480 U.S. 136, 144–145, 107 S.Ct. 1046, 94 L.Ed.2d 190; cf. *Employment Div., Ore. Dept. of Human Res. v. Smith, supra,* 494 U.S. 872, 890, 110 S.Ct. 1595.) Such legislative accommodations would be impossible as a practical matter if the government were, as Catholic Charities argues, forbidden to distinguish between the religious entities and activities that are entitled to accommodation and the secular entities and activities that are not. In fact, Congress and the state legislatures have drawn such distinctions for this purpose, and laws embodying such distinctions have passed constitutional muster. (E.g., *Corporation of Presiding Bishop v. Amos, supra,* 483 U.S. 327, 334–340, 107 S.Ct. 2862 [upholding statutory exemption of "religious" employers from liability for religious discrimination; 42 U.S.C. § 2000e–1(a)]; *East Bay Asian Local Development Corp. v. State of California* (2000) 24 Cal.4th 693, 704–718, 102 Cal.Rptr.2d 280, 13 P.3d 1122 [upholding state laws exempting "religiously affiliated" organizations from landmark preservation laws, Gov.Code, §§ 25373, subds. (c) & (d), 37361, subd. (c)].). . . .

Our conclusion that the government may properly distinguish between secular and religious entities and activities for the purpose of accommodating religious exercise does not mean that any given statute purporting to draw such distinctions necessarily passes muster under the free exercise clause. "[A] law targeting religious beliefs as such is never permissible," and a court " 'must survey meticulously the circumstances of governmental categories to eliminate, as it were, religious gerrymanders.' " (*Church of Lukumi Babalu Aye, Inc. v. Hialeah, supra,* 508 U.S. 520, 533–534, 113 S.Ct. 2217, quoting *Walz v. Tax Commission* (1970) 397 U.S. 664, 696, 90 S.Ct. 1409, 25 L.Ed.2d 697 (conc. opn. of Harlan, J.).) We address below Catholic Charities' separate argument that the WCEA's definition of "religious employer" in fact embodies a legislative effort to target Catholic organizations for unfavorable treatment. (See 10 Cal.Rptr.3d p. 303, 85 P.3d p. 84 et seq., *post.*)

3. EXCESSIVE ENTANGLEMENT

Catholic Charities contends that the WCEA's exemption for "religious employer[s]" (Health & Saf. Code, § 1367.25, subd. (b)) violates the establishment clause by mandating an entangling inquiry into the employer's religious purpose and into its employees' and clients' religious beliefs. The argument refers to the first three of the four statutory criteria for identifying a "religious employer," namely, whether "[t]he inculcation of religious values is the purpose of the entity" (*id.,* subd. (b)(1)(A)), whether "[t]he entity primarily employs persons who share the religious tenets of the entity" (*id.,* subd. (b)(1)(B)), and whether "[t]he entity serves primarily persons who share the religious tenets of the entity" (*id.,* subd. (b)(1)(C)). A law that fosters an excessive governmental entanglement with religion can for that reason violate the establishment clause. (*Lemon v. Kurtzman* (1971) 403 U.S. 602, 612–613, 91 S.Ct. 2105, 29 L.Ed.2d 745.)[6] Moreover, recent judicial opinions have criticized rules and laws that invite official "trolling through a person's or institution's religious beliefs." (*Mitchell v. Helms* (2000) 530 U.S. 793, 828, 120 S.Ct. 2530, 147 L.Ed.2d 660 (plur. opn. of Thomas, J.); *University of Great Falls v. N.L.R.B.* (D.C.Cir.2002) 278 F.3d 1335, 1342–1348.)

The argument might have merit as applied to a hypothetical employer that sought to qualify under the WCEA's exemption for religious employers (Health & Saf. Code, § 1367.25, subd. (b)) but objected on establishment clause grounds to an entangling official effort to verify that its purpose was the inculcation of religious values, and that it primarily employed and served persons who shared its religious tenets. But Catholic Charities candidly alleges in its complaint that it does not qualify under the exemption because it does not satisfy any of the four criteria. More specifically, Catholic Charities concedes that its purpose is not the inculcation of religious values, that it does not primarily hire and serve Catholics, and that it does not fall within either of the relevant provisions of the Internal Revenue Code (26 U.S.C. § 6033(a)(2)(A)(I) and (iii), cited in Health & Saf. Code, § 1367.25, subd. (b)(1)(D)). Consequently, no entangling inquiry into Catholic Charities' purpose or beliefs, or the beliefs of its employees and clients, has occurred or is likely to occur. Therefore, even if in some other case the statute might require an entangling inquiry, in this case, as applied to Catholic Charities, the establishment clause offers no basis for holding the statute unconstitutional.

B. FREE EXERCISE OF RELIGION

Catholic Charities argues the WCEA violates the free exercise clauses of the federal and state Constitutions (U.S. Const., 1st Amend.; Cal. Const., art. I, § 4) by coercing the organization to violate its religious beliefs, in that the WCEA, by regulating the content of insurance policies, in effect requires employers who offer their workers insurance for prescription drugs to offer coverage for prescription contraceptives. Catholic Charities wishes to offer insurance, but may not facilitate the use of contraceptives without violating its religious beliefs. . . .

The general rule affirmed in *Smith, supra,* 494 U.S. 872, 110 S.Ct. 1595, would at first glance appear to dispose of Catholic Charities' free exercise claim. The WCEA's requirements apply neutrally and generally to all employers, regardless of religious affiliation, except to those few

[6] The court in *Lemon v. Kurtzman, supra,* 403 U.S. 602, 91 S.Ct. 2105, 29 L.Ed.2d 745, "gleaned from [its prior] cases" three tests for determining whether a statute violates the establishment clause: "First, the statute must have a secular legislative purpose; second its principal or primary effect must be one that neither advances nor inhibits religion . . . finally, the statute must not foster 'an excessive governmental entanglement with religion.' " (*Id.,* at pp. 612–613, 91 S.Ct. 2105, quoting *Walz v. Tax Commission, supra,* 397 U.S. 664, 674, 90 S.Ct. 1409.)

who satisfy the statute's strict requirements for exemption on religious grounds. (Health & Saf. Code, § 1367.25, subd. (b).) The act also addresses a matter the state is free to regulate; it regulates the content of insurance policies for the purpose of eliminating a form of gender discrimination in health benefits. The act conflicts with Catholic Charities' religious beliefs only incidentally, because those beliefs happen to make prescription contraceptives sinful. Accordingly, it appears Catholic Charities may successfully challenge the WCEA only by demonstrating an exception to the general rule. . . .

2. RELIGIOUS GERRYMANDER

Our analysis does not end with the conclusion that the WCEA is facially neutral towards religion. The First Amendment requires more than facial neutrality. It protects against " 'subtle departures from neutrality' " and "governmental hostility which is masked as well as overt." (*Lukumi, supra,* 508 U.S. 520, 534, 113 S.Ct. 2217, quoting *Gillette v. United States, supra,* 401 U.S. 437, 452, 91 S.Ct. 828.) Thus, a court " 'must survey meticulously the circumstances of governmental categories to eliminate, as it were, religious gerrymanders.' " (*Ibid.,* quoting *Walz v. Tax Commission, supra,* 397 U.S. 664, 696, 90 S.Ct. 1409 (conc. opn. of Harlan, J.).) Catholic Charities argues the Legislature gerrymandered the WCEA to deny the benefit of the exemption to Catholic organizations. The law discriminates, Catholic Charities contends, both against the Catholic Church and against religious organizations of any denomination that engage in charitable work, as opposed to work that is purely spiritual or evangelical.

We find no merit in the argument that the WCEA discriminates against the Catholic Church. It was at the request of Catholic organizations that the Legislature added an exception permitting religious employers to deny coverage for "contraceptive methods that are contrary to the religious employer's religious tenets." (Health & Saf. Code, § 1367.25, subd. (b).) Because most religions do not object to prescription contraceptives, most religious employers are subject to the WCEA. The Legislature's decision to grant preferential treatment to religious employers who do object is justifiable as an accommodation of religious exercise under the principles discussed above. (*Amos, supra,* 483 U.S. 327, 334–335, 107 S.Ct. 2862.) That the exemption is not sufficiently broad to cover all organizations affiliated with the Catholic Church does not mean the exemption discriminates against the Catholic Church.[9]. . .

[9] Indeed, rather than discriminating against the Catholic Church, the WCEA can more plausibly be viewed as benefiting the Catholic Church in practical effect, since no other religious group opposed to prescription contraceptives has been identified. But the WCEA does not for this reason violate the establishment clause. A law intended not to discriminate among religions but to alleviate a governmentally created burden on religious exercise does not necessarily violate the establishment clause, even though only a single religion in need of accommodation has been identified, if the law is phrased neutrally, to allow for the possibility that other as-yet-unidentified religions in need of the same accommodation will be able to claim it. (See, e.g., *Kong*

Catholic Charities' intent may be to argue that the WCEA discriminates against charitable social work *as a religious practice*. Such an argument would implicate "[t]he principle that government, in pursuit of legitimate interests, cannot in a selective manner impose burdens only on conduct motivated by religious belief. . . ." (*Lukumi, supra,* 508 U.S. 520, 543, 113 S.Ct. 2217.) Applying this principle, the high court in *Lukumi* held unconstitutional an ordinance that permitted the killing of animals for food or sport, but not in religious rituals. The ordinance had " 'every appearance of a prohibition that society is prepared to impose upon [Santeria worshippers] but not upon itself.' " (*Id.,* at p. 545, 113 S.Ct. 2217, quoting *The Florida Star v. B.J.F.* (1989) 491 U.S. 524, 542, 109 S.Ct. 2603, 105 L.Ed.2d 443.) The WCEA is not similar. If a religiously affiliated organization fails to qualify for exemption because its purpose is something other than the "inculcation of religious values" (Health & Saf. Code, § 1367. 25, subd. (b)(1)(A)), then the result is simply that the organization becomes subject to the same obligations that apply to all other employers. Because the WCEA applies to all nonreligious employers engaged in charitable social work, no argument can logically be made that the WCEA imposes a burden on charitable social work only when performed for religious reasons.

As additional support for its claim that the WCEA's purpose is to discriminate against the Catholic Church, Catholic Charities contends the Legislature drafted the "religious employer" exception (Health & Saf. Code, § 1367.25, subd. (b)) with the specific intention of excluding Catholic hospitals and social service agencies like Catholic Charities. Catholic Charities draws an analogy to *Lukumi, supra,* 508 U.S. 520, 540–542, 113 S.Ct. 2217, in which the high court considered specific statements by members of the Hialeah City Council as evidence that the ordinance prohibiting animal sacrifice was intended to suppress the Santeria religion. Catholic Charities' assertions about the legislative history of the WCEA do not justify a similar conclusion in this case.

According to Catholic Charities, the history of the WCEA suggests the Legislature intended the law to close a "Catholic gap" in insurance coverage for prescription contraceptives. The evidence does not support the contention. The phrase "Catholic gap" appears only in Catholic Charities' brief, not in the legislative history. Catholic Charities refers to the Senate testimony of a representative of Planned Parenthood, which opposed any exception for religious employers. Explaining that organization's position, the witness stated: "Primarily our intent was to close the gap in insurance coverage for contraception and prescription benefit plans. Our concern with granting an exemption is that that defeats the original purpose of the bill." The "gap" to which the witness apparently referred was the gap identified by a national consulting firm's 1999 study of health insurance for prescription contraceptives. This

---

v. Scully (9th Cir.2003) 341 F.3d 1132; *Children's Health Is a Legal Duty v. Min De Parle* (8th Cir.2000) 212 F.3d 1084; *Droz v. Commissioner of I.R.S.* (9th Cir.1995) 48 F.3d 1120.)

study, which received much attention in the Legislature, concluded that approximately 10 percent of commercially insured Californians did not already have insurance coverage for prescription contraceptives. The study identified this minority not as the employees of Catholic organizations, but as persons covered by PPO and indemnity plans. While most HMO's covered prescription contraceptives, not all PPO and indemnity plans did. Catholic Charities' assertion that the purpose of the WCEA was to close a "Catholic gap" rather than a statewide statistical gap in coverage has no apparent evidentiary support.[11]

Next, Catholic Charities argues the Legislature deliberately narrowed the statutory exception for "religious employer[s]" (Health & Saf. Code, § 1367.25, subd. (b)) to include as few Catholic organizations as possible and specifically to exclude Catholic hospitals and social service organizations. The legislative history does show that the bill's sponsors argued against a broader exception. The bill's Senate sponsor, for example, stated in a committee hearing that "the intention of the authors as it relates to creating a religious exemption may not be the same intentions of the religions themselves in wanting to be exempted. The intention of the religious exemption in both these bills is an intention to provide for exemption for what is religious activity. The more secular the activity gets, the less religiously based it is, and the more we believe that they should be required to cover prescription drug benefits for contraception." Catholic Charities describes this and similar statements as evidence that the Legislature targeted specific Catholic organizations for disadvantageous treatment. But we have already examined and rejected that argument. The law treats some Catholic organizations more favorably than all other employers by exempting them; nonexempt Catholic organizations are treated the same as all other employers. . . .

C. RATIONAL BASIS

Catholic Charities' final challenge to the WCEA is that it violates the rational basis test. More specifically, Catholic Charities argues the State has defined the exempt category of "religious employer" (Health & Saf. Code, § 1367.25, subd. (b)) with arbitrary criteria. "In effect," according to Catholic Charities, "the Legislature decided that any religious institution that employs individuals of other faiths or that ministers to persons of all faiths (or no faith)—in effect any 'missionary' church or church with social outreach—is not sufficiently 'religious' to

---

[11] Catholic Charities also argues that the Legislature acted out of antipathy and spite towards the Catholic Church. Through this argument, Catholic Charities seeks to compare the Legislature's consideration of the WCEA with the Hialeah City Council's decision (see *Lukumi*, *supra*, 508 U.S. 520, 113 S.Ct. 2217) to ban animal sacrifice as a way of suppressing the Santeria religion. In discussing the council's decision, the high court noted that Hialeah city officials had castigated Santeria as an "abomination to the Lord" and "the worship of demons," and that a public crowd attending the city council's meeting had interrupted with jeers and taunts the President of the Santeria Church. (*Id.*, at p. 541, 113 S.Ct. 2217.) The legislative history of the WCEA discloses no comparable antipathy to the Catholic Church.

qualify for exemption," and that these classifications are "wholly unrelated to any legitimate state interest."

The argument lacks merit. The WCEA's exemption for religious organizations, even if not applicable to Catholic Charities, rationally serves the legitimate interest of complying with the rule barring interference with the relationship between a church and its ministers. (See *ante,* 10 Cal.Rptr.3d at p. 296, 85 P.3d at p. 78 et seq.) Although the high court has not spoken on the subject, the lower federal courts have held that the constitutionally based ministerial exemption survives the decision in *Smith, supra,* 494 U.S. 872, 110 S.Ct. 1595. . . . Most organizations entitled to invoke the ministerial exemption will be involved in the "inculcation of religious values," which the first criterion requires. (Health & Saf. Code, § 1367.25, subd. (b)(1)(A).) many will also satisfy the WCEA's fourth exemption criterion, which requires that a religious employer qualify for federal tax exemption as a church, an integrated auxiliary of a church, a convention or association of churches, or a religious order. (See 26 U.S.C. § 6033(a)(2)(A)(I) and (iii), cited in Health & Saf. Code, § 1367.25, subd. (b)(1)(D).) If in any case the constitutionally required ministerial exception were broader than the statutory exemption, the former would of course take precedence.

The second criterion, to which Catholic Charities specifically objects as lacking a rational basis, requires that an employer "primarily employ [ ] persons who share the religious tenets of the entity." (Health & Saf. Code, § 1367.25, subd. (b)(1)(B).) This provision, in effect, accommodates religious employers more broadly than the ministerial exemption requires by extending the WCEA's exemption to employees who could not fall within the ministerial exemption. The provision has the legitimate, rational purpose of accommodating a state-imposed burden on religious exercise. (*Amos, supra,* 483 U.S. 327, 334–335, 107 S.Ct. 2862.)

The third criterion, to which Catholic Charities also objects, is problematic. To qualify under it, an employer must "serve[ ] primarily persons who share the religious tenets of the entity." (Health & Saf. Code, § 1367.25, subd. (b)(1)(C).) To imagine a legitimate purpose for such a requirement is difficult. Reading the provision literally, a hypothetical soup kitchen run entirely by the ministers of a church, which inculcates religious values to those who come to eat (thus satisfying the first, second, and fourth criteria), would lose its claim to an exemption from the WCEA if it chose to serve the hungry without discrimination instead of serving co-religionists only. The Legislature may wish to address this problem. Catholic Charities, however, cannot successfully challenge the WCEA on this ground because the organization concedes it does not qualify under any of the criteria for exemption, including the relatively objective terms of the federal tax statute cited in the fourth criterion. (Health & Saf. Code, § 1367.25, subd. (b)(1)(D).) Catholic Charities thus cannot qualify for exemption in any event.

The decision of the Court of Appeal is affirmed.

■ WE CONCUR: GEORGE, C.J., BAXTER, CHIN, and MORENO, JJ.

[The separate concurring opinion by KENNARD, J. and the dissenting opinion by BROWN, J. have been omitted.]

NOTES

The 2004 decision from the California Supreme Court illustrates the more current and ongoing litigation involving the passage of the Federal Patient Protection and Affordable Care Act of 2010. *See* Code Sec. 9815(a)(1), and ERISA 715(a)(1). The Affordable Care Act contains statutory mandates, implemented by regulations promulgated by the Department of Health and Human Services, which require large employers to provide group health insurance coverage that offers contraceptive drugs, devices, and related counseling at no charge to the employer's employees. Some of these contraceptive drugs would promote the destruction of embryos. Many employers viewed this "contraceptive mandate" as morally objectionable and challenged the mandate as a substantial violation of the Constitution's Free Exercise Clause. Specifically, they argue that the mandates compels them to violate sincerely held religious beliefs. Religious nonprofit organizations, such as churches, are exempt from the mandate, but other employers, to include for-profit organizations, argue that they are entitled to engage in "free exercise" and should be exempt as well. In 2014, the Supreme Court held that the Religious Freedom Restoration Act of 1993, 42 U.S.C. §§ 2000bb–1(a), (b), as amended by the Religious Land Use and Institutionalized Persons Act of 2000, applies to any exercise of religion, whether or not compelled by, or central to, a system of religious belief (*see* § 2000cc–5(7)(A)). Therefore free exercise protection applies to for-profit organizations as well as nonprofit ones. *See* Burwell v. Hobby Lobby Stores, Inc., 134 S.Ct. 2751 (2014). Penalties for not complying with the contraceptive mandate are significant: "If [the employers] refuse to provide contraceptive coverage, they face severe economic consequences: about $475 million per year for [one for-profit], $33 million per year [for another], and $15 million per year for [a third]. And if they drop coverage altogether, they could face penalties of roughly $26 million . . . $1.8 million . . . and $800,000 . . . " *Id.* at 2757.

Seeking to arrive at a compromise with nonprofit and for-profit employers asserting sincere Free Exercise objections to the contraceptive mandate, Federal government officials offered to exempt employers from the terms of the mandate if they submit a form stating that they object on religious grounds to providing contraceptive coverage. But some of the employers affected refused to sub the form and "allege that submitting this notice substantially burdens the exercise of their religion, in violation of the Religious Freedom Restoration Act of 1993, 107 Stat. 1488, 42 U.S.C. § 2000bb *et seq.*" Zubik v. Burwell, 136 S.Ct. 1557 (2016). Confronting this judicial First Amendment stalemate, the Supreme Court in 2016 vacated lower court decisions and remanded the issue "to the respective United States Courts of Appeal for the Third, Fifth, Tenth, and D.C. Circuits." *Id.* at 1560. "Given the gravity of the dispute and the substantial clarification and refinement in the positions of the parties, the parties on remand should be afforded an opportunity to arrive at an approach going forward that accommodates petitioners' religious exercise while at the same time ensuring that women covered by petitioners' health plans 'receive full and equal health coverage, including contraceptive coverage.' " *Id.* at 1560. Pending a resolution, the government "may not impose taxes or penalties on petitioners for failure to provide the relevant notice." *Id.* at 1560. And "the Court does not decide whether petitioners' religious exercise has been substantially burdened, whether the Government has a compelling interest, or whether the current regulations are the least restrictive means of serving that interest." *Id.* at 1560.

Free Exercise of Religion claims will continue to arise in other contexts too. Repeated instances have occurred associated with same-sex marriage, participation in assisted reproductive technologies, participation in assisted suicide, and abortion regulations. For further commentary, *see* Courtney Miller, Note, *"Spiritual But Not Religious": Rethinking the Legal Definition of Religion,* 102 VA. L. REV. 833 (2016); Trey O'Callaghan, *Going to Hell in a HHS Notice: The Contraceptive Mandate's Next Impermissible Burden on Religious Freedom*, 11 DUKE J. CONST. L. & PUB. POL'Y SIDEBAR 269 (2016); Robert Post, *RFRA and First Amendment Freedom of Expression*, 125 YALE L. J. FORUM 387 (2016); Mark Strasser, *Hobby Lobby, RFRA, and Family Burden*, 25 B.U. PUB. INT. L. J. 239 (2016); Raymond C. O'Brien, *Family Law's Challenge to Religious Liberty*, 35 UNIV. ARK. (LR) L. REV. 3 (2012); Laura Underkuffler-Freund, *The Separation of the Religious and the Secular: A Foundational Challenge to First Amendment Theory*, 36 WM. & MARY L. REV. 837 (1995); Michael W. McConnell, *The Origins and Historical Understanding of Free Exercise of Religion*, 103 HARV. L. REV. 1409 (1990).

PROBLEM THREE

Denise is a board-certified physician serving patients at the North Coast Women's Care Medical Group. In addition to being a medical professional she considers herself a person with deeply held religious beliefs and, as a result of those beliefs, she has refused to perform an intrauterine insemination (IUI) procedure on a lesbian woman living with her long-term female partner. The procedure would result in the birth of a child that the two women plan to raise together, but the physician has refused to participate because she is of the opinion that a child should not be raised by two persons of the same-sex living together in an intimate relationship. Although Denise refused to perform the medical procedure, the physician did suggest other physicians on staff who would be willing to perform the procedure. Nonetheless, there were no other physicians available and eventually the lesbian woman sued the physician under the state's Civil Rights Act, asserting that the physician discriminated against her based on her sexual orientation, a protected status under the Act. The physician argues that she cannot be compelled to violate her religious beliefs. How would you decide on the merits of the plaintiff's petition if you were a judge and this case were presented to you in court?

2. THE RIGHT TO PRIVACY

Griswold v. Connecticut

Supreme Court of the United States, 1965
381 U.S. 479

■ MR. JUSTICE DOUGLAS delivered the opinion of the Court.

Appellant Griswold is Executive Director of the Planned Parenthood League of Connecticut. Appellant Buxton is a licensed physician and a professor at the Yale Medical School who served as Medical Director for the League at its Center in New Haven—a center open and operating from November 1 to November 10, 1961, when appellants were arrested. They gave information, instruction, and medical advice to *married persons* as to the means of preventing conception. They examined the wife and prescribed the best contraceptive device or material for her use. Fees were usually charged, although some couples were serviced free.

The statutes whose constitutionality is involved in this appeal are §§ 53–32 and 54–196 of the General Statutes of Connecticut (1958 rev.). The former provides:

> "Any person who uses any drug, medicinal article or instrument for the purpose of preventing conception shall be fined not less than fifty dollars or imprisoned not less than sixty days nor more than one year or be both fined and imprisoned."

Section 54–196 provides:

> "Any person who assists, abets, counsels, causes, hires or commands another to commit any offense may be prosecuted and punished as if he were the principal offender."

The appellants were found guilty as accessories and fined $100 each, against the claim that the accessory statute as so applied violated the Fourteenth Amendment. . . .

Coming to the merits, we are met with a wide range of questions that implicate the Due Process Clause of the Fourteenth Amendment . . . We do not sit as a super-legislature to determine the wisdom, need, and propriety of laws that touch economic problems, business affairs, or social conditions. This law, however, operates directly on an intimate relation of husband and wife and their physician's role in one aspect of that relation.

The association of people is not mentioned in the Constitution nor in the Bill of Rights. The right to educate a child in a school of the parents' choice—whether public or private or parochial—is also not mentioned. Nor is the right to study any particular subject or any foreign language. Yet the First Amendment has been construed to include certain of those rights. By Pierce v. Society of Sisters [268 U.S. 510, 45 S.Ct. 571], the right to educate one's children as one chooses is made applicable to the States by the force of the First and Fourteenth Amendments. By Meyer

v. State of Nebraska [262 U.S. 390, 43 S.Ct. 625], the same dignity is given the right to study the German language in a private school. In other words, the State may not, consistently with the spirit of the First Amendment, contract the spectrum of available knowledge. The right of freedom of speech and press includes not only the right to utter or to print, but the right to distribute, the right to receive, the right to read and freedom of inquiry, freedom of thought, and freedom to teach—indeed the freedom of the entire university community . . . Without those peripheral rights the specific rights would be less secure. And so we reaffirm the principle of the Pierce and the Meyer cases.

In NAACP v. State of Alabama, 357 U.S. 449, 462, 78 S.Ct. 1163, 1172, we protected the "freedom to associate and privacy in one's associations," noting that freedom of association was a peripheral First Amendment right. Disclosure of membership lists of a constitutionally valid association, we held, was invalid "as entailing the likelihood of a substantial restraint upon the exercise by petitioner's members of their right to freedom of association." Ibid. In other words, the First Amendment has a penumbra where privacy is protected from governmental intrusion. In like context, we have protected forms of "association" that are not political in the customary sense but pertain to the social, legal, and economic benefit of the members. NAACP v. Button, 371 U.S. 415, 430–431, 83 S.Ct. 328, 336–337, 9 L.Ed.2d 405. . . .

Those cases involved more than the "right of assembly"—a right that extends to all irrespective of their race or ideology. De Jonge v. State of Oregon, 299 U.S. 353, 57 S.Ct. 255, 81 L.Ed. 278. The right of "association," like the right of belief (West Virginia State Board of Education v. Barnette, 319 U.S. 624, 63 S.Ct. 1178), is more than the right to attend a meeting; it includes the right to express one's attitudes or philosophies by membership in a group or by affiliation with it or by other lawful means. Association in that context is a form of expression of opinion; and while it is not expressly included in the First Amendment its existence is necessary in making the express guarantees fully meaningful.

The foregoing cases suggest that specific guarantees in the Bill of Rights have penumbras, formed by emanations from those guarantees that help give them life and substance. . . . Various guarantees create zones of privacy. The right of association contained in the penumbra of the First Amendment is one, as we have seen. The Third Amendment in its prohibition against the quartering of soldiers "in any house" in time of peace without the consent of the owner is another facet of that privacy. The Fourth Amendment explicitly affirms the "right of the people to be secure in their persons, houses, papers, and effects, against unreasonable searches and seizures." The Fifth Amendment in its Self-Incrimination Clause enables the citizen to create a zone of privacy which government may not force him to surrender to his detriment. The Ninth Amendment provides: "The enumeration in the Constitution, of certain rights, shall not be construed to deny or disparage others retained by the people." . . .

The present case, then, concerns a relationship lying within the zone of privacy created by several fundamental constitutional guarantees. And it concerns a law which, in forbidding the *use* of contraceptives rather than regulating their manufacture or sale, seeks to achieve its goals by means having a maximum destructive impact upon that relationship. Such a law cannot stand in light of the familiar principle, so often applied by this Court, that a "governmental purpose to control or prevent activities constitutionally subject to state regulation may not be achieved by means which sweep unnecessarily broadly and thereby invade the area of protected freedoms." NAACP v. Alabama, 377 U.S. 288, 307, 84 S.Ct. 1302, 1314, 12 L.Ed.2d 325. Would we allow the police to search the sacred precincts of marital bedrooms for telltale signs of the use of contraceptives? The very idea is repulsive to the notions of privacy surrounding the marriage relationship.

We deal with a right of privacy older than the Bill of Rights—older than our political parties, older than our school system. Marriage is a coming together for better or for worse, hopefully enduring, and intimate to the degree of being sacred. It is an association that promotes a way of life, not causes; a harmony in living, not political faiths; a bilateral loyalty, not commercial or social projects. Yet it is an association for as noble a purpose as any involved in our prior decisions.

Reversed.

■ MR. JUSTICE GOLDBERG who THE CHIEF JUSTICE and MR. JUSTICE BRENNAN join, concurring.

. . . .

The language and history of the Ninth Amendment reveal that the Framers of the Constitution believed that there are additional fundamental rights, protected from governmental infringement, which exist alongside those fundamental rights specifically mentioned in the first eight constitutional amendments.

The Ninth Amendment reads, "The enumeration in the Constitution, of certain rights, shall not be construed to deny or disparage others retained by the people." The Amendment is almost entirely the work of James Madison. It was introduced in Congress by him and passed the House and Senate with little or no debate and virtually no change in language. It was proffered to quiet expressed fears that a bill of specifically enumerated rights could not be sufficiently broad to cover all essential rights and that the specific mention of certain rights would be interpreted as a denial that others were protected. . . .

The Connecticut statutes here involved deal with a particularly important and sensitive area of privacy—that of the marital relation and the marital home. This Court recognized in Meyer v. Nebraska, supra, that the right "to marry, establish a home and bring up children" was an essential part of the liberty guaranteed by the Fourteenth Amendment. In Pierce v. Society of Sisters, the Court held unconstitutional an Oregon Act which forbade parents from sending their children to private schools because such an act "unreasonably interferes with the liberty of parents and guardians to direct the upbringing and education of children under their control." As this Court said in Prince v. Massachusetts, 321 U.S. 158, at 166, 64 S.Ct. 438, at 442, 88 L.Ed. 645, the Meyer and Pierce decisions "have respected the private realm of family life which the state cannot enter."

I agree with Mr. Justice Harlan's statement in his dissenting opinion in Poe v. Ullman, 367 U.S. 497, 551–552, 81 S.Ct. 1752, 1781:

> "Certainly the safeguarding of the home does not follow merely from the sanctity of property rights. The home derives its preeminence as the seat of family life. And the integrity of that life is something so fundamental that it has been found to draw to its protection the principles of more than one explicitly granted Constitutional right . . . Of this whole 'private realm of family life' it is difficult to imagine what is more private or more intimate than a husband and wife's marital relations."

The entire fabric of the Constitution and the purposes that clearly underlie its specific guarantees demonstrate that the rights to marital privacy and to marry and raise a family are of similar order and magnitude as the fundamental rights specifically protected. Although the Constitution does not speak in so many words of the right of privacy in marriage, I cannot believe that it offers these fundamental rights no protection. . . .

Finally, it should be said of the Court's holding today that it in no way interferes with a State's proper regulation of sexual promiscuity or misconduct. As my Brother Harlan so well stated in his dissenting opinion in Poe v. Ullman, supra, 367 U.S. at 553, 81 S.Ct. at 1782.

> "Adultery, homosexuality and the like are sexual intimacies which the State forbids . . . but the intimacy of husband and wife is necessarily an essential and accepted feature of the institution of marriage, an institution which the State not only must allow, but which always and in every age it has fostered and protected. It is one thing when the State exerts its power either to forbid extra-marital sexuality . . . or to say who may marry, but it is quite another when, having acknowledged a marriage and the intimacies inherent in it, it undertakes to regulate by means of the criminal law the details of that intimacy."

In sum, I believe that the right of privacy in the marital relation is fundamental and basic—a personal right "retained by the people" within the meaning of the Ninth Amendment. Connecticut cannot constitutionally abridge this fundamental right, which is protected by the

Fourteenth Amendment from infringement by the States. I agree with the Court that petitioners' convictions must therefore be reversed.

[The concurring opinions of JUSTICES HARLAN and WHITE, and the dissenting opinions of JUSTICES BLACK and STEWART are omitted.]

NOTES

The preceding excerpts from *Griswold* were chosen because they relate to marital privacy. The right to privacy announced in the plurality decision has been expanded to encompass many other aspects of family law. Throughout the following decisions of this section, the impact of *Griswold* will be manifest in issues ranging from artificial reproductive technology to sodomy.

Eisenstadt v. Baird

Supreme Court of the United States, 1972
405 U.S. 438

■ MR. JUSTICE BRENNAN delivered the opinion of the Court.

Appellee William Baird was convicted at a bench trial in the Massachusetts Superior Court under Massachusetts General Laws c. 272, § 21, first, for exhibiting contraceptive articles in the course of delivering a lecture on contraception to a group of students at Boston University and, second, for giving a young woman a package of Emko vaginal foam at the close of his address.[1] The Massachusetts Supreme Judicial Court unanimously set aside the conviction for exhibiting contraceptives on the ground that it violated Baird's First Amendment rights, but by a four-to-three vote sustained the conviction for giving away the foam. Commonwealth v. Baird, 355 Mass. 746, 247 N.E.2d 574 (1969). Baird subsequently filed a petition for a Federal writ of habeas corpus, which the District Court dismissed. 310 F. Supp. 951 (1970). On appeal, however, the Court of Appeals for the First Circuit vacated the dismissal and remanded the action with directions to grant the writ discharging Baird. 429 F.2d 1398 (1970). This appeal by the Sheriff of Suffolk County, Massachusetts, followed. . . .

Massachusetts General Laws c. 272, § 21, under which Baird was convicted, provides a maximum five-year term of imprisonment for "whoever . . . gives away . . . any drug, medicine, instrument or article whatever for the prevention of conception," except as authorized in § 21A. Under § 21A, "[a] registered physician may administer to or prescribe for any married person drugs or articles intended for the prevention of pregnancy or conception. [And a] registered pharmacist actually engaged in the business of pharmacy may furnish such drugs or articles to any married person presenting a prescription from a registered physician."

[1] The Court of Appeals below described the recipient of the foam as "an unmarried adult woman." 429 F.2d 1398, 1399 (1970). However, there is no evidence in the record about her marital status.

As interpreted by the State Supreme Judicial Court, these provisions make it a felony for anyone, other than a registered physician or pharmacist acting in accordance with the terms of § 21A, to dispense any article with the intention that it be used for the prevention of conception. The statutory scheme distinguishes among three distinct classes of distributees—*first,* married persons may obtain contraceptives to prevent pregnancy, but only from doctors or druggists on prescription; *second,* single persons may not obtain contraceptives from anyone to prevent pregnancy; and, *third,* married or single persons may obtain contraceptives from anyone to prevent not pregnancy, but the spread of disease. . . .

The legislative purposes that the statute is meant to serve are not altogether clear. In Commonwealth v. Baird, supra, the Supreme Judicial Court noted only the State's interest in protecting the health of its citizens: "[T]he prohibition in § 21," the court declared, "is directly related to" the State's goal of "preventing the distribution of articles designed to prevent conception which may have undesirable, if not dangerous, physical consequences." 355 Mass., at 753, 247 N.E.2d, at 578. In a subsequent decision, Sturgis v. Attorney General, Mass., 260 N.E.2d 687, 690 (1970), the court, however, found "a second and more compelling ground for upholding the statute"—namely, to protect morals through "regulating the private sexual lives of single persons."[3] The Court of Appeals, for reasons that will appear, did not consider the promotion of health or the protection—of morals through the deterrence of fornication to be the legislative aim. Instead, the court concluded that the statutory goal was to limit contraception in and of itself—a purpose that the court held conflicted "with fundamental human rights" under Griswold v. Connecticut, 381 U.S. 479, 85 S.Ct. 1678 (1965), where this Court struck down Connecticut's prohibition against the use of contraceptives as an unconstitutional infringement of the right of marital privacy. 429 F.2d, at 1401–1402.

We agree that the goals of deterring premarital sex and regulating the distribution of potentially harmful articles cannot reasonably be regarded as legislative aims of §§ 21 and 21A. And we hold that the statute, viewed as a prohibition on contraception *per se,* violates the rights of single persons under the Equal Protection Clause of the Fourteenth Amendment. . . .

The question for our determination in this case is whether there is some ground of difference that rationally explains the different treatment accorded married and unmarried persons under

[3] Appellant suggests that the purpose of the Massachusetts statute is to promote marital fidelity as well as to discourage premarital sex. Under § 21A, however, contraceptives may be made available to married persons without regard to whether they are living with their spouses or the uses to which the contraceptives are to be put. Plainly the legislation has no deterrent effect on extramarital sexual relations.

Massachusetts General Laws c. 272, §§ 21 and 21A.[7] For the reasons that follow, we conclude that no such ground exists.

First. Section 21 stems from Stat.1879, c. 159, § 1, which prohibited, without exception, distribution of articles intended to be used as contraceptives. In Commonwealth v. Allison, 227 Mass. 57, 62, 116 N.E. 265, 266 (1917), the Massachusetts Supreme Judicial Court explained that the law's "plain purpose is to protect purity, to preserve chastity, to encourage continence and self restraint, to defend the sanctity of the home, and thus to engender in the State and nation a virile and virtuous race of men and women." Although the State clearly abandoned that purpose with the enactment of § 21A at least insofar as the illicit sexual activities of married persons are concerned, see n. 3 supra, the court reiterated in Sturgis v. Attorney General, supra, that the object of the legislation is to discourage premarital sexual intercourse. Conceding that the State could, consistently with the Equal Protection Clause, regard the problems of extramarital and premarital sexual relations as "[e]vils . . . of different dimensions and proportions, requiring different remedies," Williamson v. Lee Optical Co., 348 U.S. 483, 489, 75 S.Ct. 461, 465, 99 L.Ed. 563 (1955), we cannot agree that the deterrence of premarital sex may reasonably be regarded as the purpose of the Massachusetts law.

It would be plainly unreasonable to assume that Massachusetts has prescribed pregnancy and the birth of an unwanted child as punishment for fornication, which is a misdemeanor under Massachusetts General Laws c. 272, § 18. Aside from the scheme of values that assumption would attribute to the State, it is abundantly clear that the effect of the ban on distribution of contraceptives to unmarried persons has at best a marginal relation to the proffered objective. What Mr. Justice Goldberg said in Griswold v. Connecticut, supra, 381 U.S. at 498, 85 S.Ct. at 1689, 14 L.Ed.2d 510 (concurring opinion), concerning the effect of Connecticut's prohibition on the use of contraceptives in discouraging extra-marital sexual relations, is equally applicable here. "The rationality of this justification is dubious, particularly in light of the admitted widespread availability to all persons in the State of Connecticut, unmarried as well as married, of birth-control devices for the prevention of disease, as distinguished from the prevention of conception." Like Connecticut's laws, §§ 21 and 21A do not at all regulate the distribution of contraceptives when they are to be used to prevent not pregnancy, but the spread of disease. Commonwealth v. Corbett, 307 Mass. 7, 29 N.E.2d 151 (1940), cited with approval in Commonwealth v.

---

[7] Of course, if we were to conclude that the Massachusetts statute impinges upon fundamental freedoms under *Griswold,* the statutory classification would have to be not merely *rationally related* to a valid public purpose but *necessary* to the achievement of a *compelling* state interest. E.g., Shapiro v. Thompson, 394 U.S. 618, 89 S.Ct. 1322, 22 L.Ed.2d 600 (1969); Loving v. Virginia, 388 U.S. 1, 87 S.Ct. 1817, 18 L.Ed.2d 1010 (1967). But just as in Reed v. Reed, supra, we do not have to address the statute's validity under that test because the law fails to satisfy even the more lenient equal protection standard.

Baird, 355 Mass., at 754, 247 N.E.2d, at 579. Nor, in making contraceptives available to married persons without regard to their intended use, does Massachusetts attempt to deter married persons from engaging in illicit sexual relations with unmarried persons. Even on the assumption that the fear of pregnancy operates as a deterrent to fornication, the Massachusetts statute is thus so riddled with exceptions that deterrence of premarital sex cannot reasonably be regarded as its aim.

Moreover, §§ 21 and 21A on their face have a dubious relation to the State's criminal prohibition on fornication. As the Court of Appeals explained, "Fornication is a misdemeanor [in Massachusetts], entailing a thirty dollar fine, or three months in jail. Violation of the present statute is a felony, punishable by five years in prison. We find it hard to believe that the legislature adopted a statute carrying a five-year penalty for its possible, obviously by no means fully effective, deterrence of the commission of a ninety-day misdemeanor." 429 F.2d, at 1401. Even conceding the legislature a full measure of discretion in fashioning remedies for fornication, and recognizing that the State may seek to deter prohibited conduct by punishing more severely those who facilitate than those who actually engage in its commission, we, like the Court of Appeals, cannot believe that in this instance Massachusetts has chosen to expose the aider and abetter who simply *gives away* a contraceptive to *20* times the *90-day* sentence of the offender himself. The very terms of the State's criminal statutes, coupled with the *de minimis* effect of §§ 21 and 21A in deterring fornication, thus compel the conclusion that such deterrence cannot reasonably be taken as the purpose of the ban on distribution of contraceptives to unmarried persons.

Second. Section 21A was added to the Massachusetts General Laws by Stat.1966, c. 265, § 1. The Supreme Judicial Court in Commonwealth v. Baird, supra, held that the purpose of the amendment was to serve the health needs of the community by regulating the distribution of potentially harmful articles. It is plain that Massachusetts had no such purpose in mind before the enactment of § 21A. As the Court of Appeals remarked, "Consistent with the fact that the statute was contained in a chapter dealing with 'Crimes Against Chastity, Morality, Decency and Good Order,' it was cast only in terms of morals. A physician was forbidden to prescribe contraceptives even when needed for the protection of health." Commonwealth v. Gardner, 1938, 300 Mass. 372, 15 N.E.2d 222, 429 F.2d, at 1401. Nor did the Court of Appeals "believe that the legislature [in enacting § 21A] suddenly reversed its field and developed an interest in health. Rather, it merely made what it thought to be the precise accommodation necessary to escape the *Griswold* ruling." Ibid.

Again, we must agree with the Court of Appeals. If health were the rationale of § 21A, the statute would be both discriminatory and overbroad. Dissenting in Commonwealth v. Baird, 355 Mass., at 758, 247

N.E.2d, at 581, Justices Whittemore and Cutter stated that they saw "in § 21 and § 21A, read together, no public health purpose. If there is need to have a physician prescribe (and a pharmacist dispense) contraceptives, that need is as great for unmarried persons as for married persons." The Court of Appeals added: "If the prohibition [on distribution to unmarried persons] is to be taken to mean that the same physician who can prescribe for married patients does not have sufficient skill to protect the health of patients who lack a marriage certificate, or who may be currently divorced, it is illogical to the point of irrationality." 429 F.2d, at 1401.[8] Furthermore, we must join the Court of Appeals in noting that not all contraceptives are potentially dangerous.[9] As a result, if the Massachusetts statute were a health measure, it would not only invidiously discriminate against the unmarried, but also be overbroad with respect to the married, a fact that the Supreme Judicial Court itself seems to have conceded in Sturgis v. Attorney General, Mass., 260 N.E.2d, at 690, where it noted that "it may well be that certain contraceptive medication and devices constitute no hazard to health, in which event it could be argued that the statute swept too broadly in its prohibition." "In this posture," as the Court of Appeals concluded, "it is impossible to think of the statute as intended as a health measure for the unmarried, and it is almost as difficult to think of it as so intended even as to the married." 429 F.2d, at 1401.

But if further proof that the Massachusetts statute is not a health measure is necessary, the argument of Justice Spiegel, who also dissented in Commonwealth v. Baird, 355 Mass., at 759, 247 N.E.2d, at 582, is conclusive: "It is at best a strained conception to say that the Legislature intended to prevent the distribution of articles 'which may have undesirable, if not dangerous, physical consequences.' If that was the Legislature's goal, § 21 is not required" in view of the federal and State laws *already* regulating the distribution of harmful drugs. We conclude, accordingly, that, despite the statute's superficial earmarks as a health measure, health, on the face of the statute, may no more reasonably be regarded as its purpose than the deterrence of premarital sexual relations.

---

8 Appellant insists that the unmarried have no right to engage in sexual intercourse and hence no health interest in contraception that needs to be served. The short answer to this contention is that the same devices the distribution of which the State purports to regulate when their asserted purpose is to forestall pregnancy are available without any controls whatsoever so long as their asserted purpose is to prevent the spread of disease. It is inconceivable that the need for health controls varies with the purpose for which the contraceptive is to be used when the physical act in all cases is one and the same.

9 The Court of Appeals stated, 429 F.2d at 1401:

> "[W]e must take notice that not all contraceptive devices risk 'undesirable . . . [or] dangerous physical consequences.' It is 200 years since Casanova recorded the ubiquitous article which, perhaps because of the birthplace of its inventor, he termed a 'redingote anglais.' The reputed nationality of the condom has now changed, but we have never heard criticism of it on the side of health. We cannot think that the legislature was unaware of it, or could have thought that it needed a medical prescription. We believe the same could be said of certain other products."

Third. If the Massachusetts statute cannot be upheld as a deterrent to fornication or as a health measure, may it, nevertheless, be sustained simply as a prohibition on contraception? The Court of Appeals analysis "led inevitably to the conclusion that, so far as morals are concerned, it is contraceptives per se that are considered immoral—to the extent that *Griswold* will permit such a declaration." 429 F.2d, at 1401–1402. The Court of Appeals went on to hold, id., at 1402:

> "To say that contraceptives are immoral as such, and are to be forbidden to unmarried persons who will nevertheless persist in having intercourse, means that such persons must risk for themselves an unwanted pregnancy, for the child, illegitimacy, and for society, a possible obligation of support. Such a view of morality is not only the very mirror image of sensible legislation; we consider that it conflicts with fundamental human rights. In the absence of demonstrated harm, we hold it is beyond the competency of the state."

We need not and do not, however, decide that important question in this case because, whatever the rights of the individual to access to contraceptives may be, the rights must be the same for the unmarried and the married alike.

If under *Griswold* the distribution of contraceptives to married persons cannot be prohibited, a ban on distribution to unmarried persons would be equally impermissible. It is true that in *Griswold* the right of privacy in question inhered in the marital relationship. Yet the marital couple is not an independent entity with a mind and heart of its own, but an association of two individuals each with a separate intellectual and emotional make-up. If the right of privacy means anything, it is the right of the *individual*, married or single, to be free from unwarranted governmental intrusion into matters so fundamentally affecting a person as the decision whether to bear or beget a child. See Stanley v. Georgia, 394 U.S. 557, 89 S.Ct. 1243.[10] See also Skinner v. Oklahoma ex rel. Williamson, 316 U.S. 535, 62 S.Ct. 1110 (1942); Jacobson v. Massachusetts, 197 U.S. 11, 29, 25 S.Ct. 358, 362 (1905).

On the other hand, if *Griswold* is no bar to a prohibition on the distribution of contraceptives, the State could not, consistently with the Equal Protection Clause, outlaw distribution to unmarried but not to

---

[10] In Stanley, 394 U.S., at 564, 89 S.Ct., at 1247, the Court stated:

"[A]lso fundamental is the right to be free, except in very limited circumstances, from unwanted governmental intrusions into one's privacy.

" 'The makers of our Constitution undertook to secure conditions favorable to the pursuit of happiness. They recognized the significance of man's spiritual nature, of his feelings and of his intellect. They knew that only a part of the pain, pleasure and satisfactions of life are to be found in material things. They sought to protect Americans in their beliefs, their thoughts, their emotions, and their sensations. They conferred, as against the Government, the right to be let aloneCthe most comprehensive of rights and the right most valued by civilized man.' Olmstead v. United States, 277 U.S. 438, 478, 48 S.Ct. 564, 572 (1928) (Brandeis, J., dissenting). . . ."

married persons. In each case the evil, as perceived by the State, would be identical, and the underinclusion would be invidious. . . .

We hold that by providing dissimilar treatment for married and unmarried persons who are similarly situated, Massachusetts General Laws c. 272, §§ 21 and 21A, violate the Equal Protection Clause. The judgment of the Court of Appeals is affirmed.

NOTES

Justice Douglas joined the opinion of the Court but filed a separate concurring opinion expressing his view that it was "a simple First Amendment case" which could have been affirmed on that narrower ground. He added that "The teachings of Baird and those of Galileo might be of a different order; but the suppression of either is equally repugnant." 405 U.S. 438, 457 (1972).

Justice White concurred in the result reached by the Court, filing a separate opinion in which Mr. Justice Blackmun joined. He stated that "Had Baird distributed a supply of the so-called 'pill', I would sustain his conviction" under the Massachusetts law, and added:

> That Baird could not be convicted for distributing Emko to a married person disposes of this case. Assuming *arguendo* that the result would be otherwise had the recipient been unmarried, nothing has been placed in the record to indicate her marital status. The State has maintained that marital status is irrelevant because an unlicensed person cannot legally dispense vaginal foam either to married or unmarried persons. This approach is plainly erroneous and requires the reversal of Baird's conviction; for on the facts of this case, it deprives us of knowing whether Baird was in fact convicted for making a constitutionally protected distribution of Emko to a married person. Id. at 462–64.

Chief Justice Burger dissented and also disagreed with the concurring opinion of Justice White, stating that: "The need for dissemination of information on birth control is not impinged in the slightest by limiting the distribution of medicinal substances to medical and pharmaceutical channels as Massachusetts has done by statute." Id. at 470.

Does *Baird* guarantee a right to procreate, within or without marriage? Does it suggest any clear limitation on distinctions that can be made between permissible conduct of parties in other contexts based upon being married rather than single?

Roe v. Wade

Supreme Court of the United States, 1973
410 U.S. 113

■ MR. JUSTICE BLACKMUN delivered the opinion of the Court.

. . .

The Texas statutes that concern us here are Arts. 1191–1194 and 1196 of the State's Penal Code, Vernon's Ann.P.C. These make it a crime to "procure an abortion," as therein defined, or to attempt one, except with respect to "an abortion procured or attempted by medical advice for the purpose of saving the life of the mother." Similar statutes are in existence in a majority of the States. . . .

Jane Roe,[4] a single woman who was residing in Dallas County, Texas, instituted this federal action in March 1970. . . . She sought a declaratory judgment that the Texas criminal abortion statutes were unconstitutional on their face, and an injunction restraining the defendant from enforcing the statutes.

Roe alleged that she was unmarried and pregnant; that she wished to terminate her pregnancy by an abortion "performed by a competent, licensed physician, under safe, clinical conditions"; that she was unable to get a "legal" abortion in Texas because her life did not appear to be threatened by the continuation of her pregnancy; and that she could not afford to travel to another jurisdiction in order to secure a legal abortion under safe conditions. She claimed that the Texas statutes were unconstitutionally vague and that they abridged her right of personal privacy, protected by the First, Fourth, Fifth, Ninth, and Fourteenth Amendments. By an amendment to her complaint Roe purported to sue "on behalf of herself and all other women" similarly situated. . . .

It perhaps is not generally appreciated that the restrictive criminal abortion laws in effect in a majority of States today are of relatively recent vintage. Those laws, generally proscribing abortion or its attempt at any time during pregnancy except when necessary to preserve the pregnant woman's life, are not of ancient or even of common-law origin. Instead, they derive from statutory changes effected, for the most part, in the latter half of the 19th century. . . .

In this country, the law in effect in all but a few States until mid-19th century was the pre-existing English common law. Connecticut, the first State to enact abortion legislation, adopted in 1821 that part of Lord Ellenborough's Act that related to a woman "quick with child." The death penalty was not imposed. Abortion before quickening was made a crime in that State only in 1860. In 1828, New York enacted legislation that, in two respects, was to serve as a model for early anti-abortion statutes. First, while barring destruction of an unquickend fetus as well as a quick fetus, it made the former only a misdemeanor, but the latter second-

[4] The name is a pseudonym.

degree manslaughter. Second, it incorporated a concept of therapeutic abortion by providing that an abortion was excused if it "shall have been necessary to preserve the life of such mother, or shall have been advised by two physicians to be necessary for such purpose." By 1840, when Texas had received the common law, only eight American States had statutes dealing with abortion. It was not until after the War Between the States that legislation began generally to replace the common law. Most of these initial statutes dealt severely with abortion after quickening but were lenient with it before quickening. Most punished attempts equally with completed abortions. While many statutes included the exception for an abortion thought by one or more physicians to be necessary to save the mother's life, that provision soon disappeared and the typical law required that the procedure actually be necessary for that purpose.

Gradually, in the middle and late 19th century the quickening distinction disappeared from the statutory law of most States and the degree of the offense and the penalties were increased. By the end of the 1950's a large majority of the jurisdictions banned abortion, however and whenever performed, unless done to save or preserve the life of the mother. The exceptions, Alabama and the District of Columbia, permitted abortion to preserve the mother's health. Three States permitted abortions that were not "unlawfully" performed or that were not "without lawful justification," leaving interpretation of those standards to the courts. In the past several years, however, a trend toward liberalization of abortion statutes has resulted in adoption, by about one-third of the States, of less stringent laws, most of them patterned after the American Law Institute's Model Penal Code, § 230.3. . . .

It is thus apparent that at common law, at the time of the adoption of our Constitution, and throughout the major portion of the 19th century, abortion was viewed with less disfavor than under most American statutes currently in effect. Phrasing it another way, a woman enjoyed a substantially broader right to terminate a pregnancy than she does in most States today. At least with respect to the early stage of pregnancy, and very possibly without such a limitation, the opportunity to make this choice was present in this country well into the 19th century. Even later, the law continued for some time to treat less punitively an abortion procured in early pregnancy.

6. The position of the American Medical Association. . . .

In 1970, after the introduction of a variety of proposed resolutions, and of a report from its Board of Trustees, a reference committee noted "polarization of the medical profession on this controversial issue"; division among those who had testified; a difference of opinion among AMA councils and committees; "the remarkable shift in testimony" in six months, felt to be influenced "by the rapid changes in state laws and by the judicial decisions which tend to make abortion more freely available;" and a feeling "that this trend will continue." On June 25, 1970, the House of Delegates adopted preambles and most of the resolutions proposed by the reference committee. The preambles emphasized "the best interests of the patient," "sound clinical judgment," and "informed patient consent," in contrast to "mere acquiescence to the patient's demand." The resolutions asserted that abortion is a medical procedure that should be performed by a licensed physician in an accredited hospital only after consultation with two other physicians and in conformity with state law, and that no party to the procedure should be required to violate personally held moral principles. Proceedings of the AMA House of Delegates 220 (June 1970). The AMA Judicial Council rendered a complementary opinion. . . .

8. The position of the American Bar Association.

At its meeting in February 1972 the ABA House of Delegates approved, with 17 opposing votes, the Uniform Abortion Act that had been drafted and approved the preceding August by the Conference of Commissioners on Uniform State Laws.[40] 58 A.B.A.J. 380 (1972).

VII

Three reasons have been advanced to explain historically the enactment of criminal abortion laws in the 19th century and to justify their continued existence.

It has been argued occasionally that these laws were the product of a Victorian social concern to discourage illicit sexual conduct. Texas, however, does not advance this justification in the present case, and it appears that no court or commentator has taken the argument seriously. . . .

A second reason is concerned with abortion as a medical procedure. . . [I]t has been argued that a State's real concern in enacting a criminal abortion law was to protect the pregnant woman, that is, to

---

[40] "Section 1. (*Abortion Defined; When Authorized.*)

"(a) 'Abortion' means the termination of human pregnancy with an intention other than to produce a live birth or to remove a dead fetus.

"(b) An abortion may be performed in this state only if it is performed:

"(1) by a physician licensed to practice medicine (or osteopathy) in this state or by a physician practicing medicine (or osteopathy) in the employ of the government of the United States or of this state, (and the abortion is performed (in the physician's office or in a medical clinic, or) in a hospital approved by the (Department of Health) or operated by the United States, this state, or any department, agency, or political subdivision of either;) or by a female upon herself upon the advice of the physician; and

"(2) within (20) weeks after the commencement of the pregnancy (or after (20) weeks only if the physician has reasonable cause to believe (i) there is a substantial risk that continuance of the pregnancy would endanger the life of the mother or would gravely impair the physical or mental health of the mother, (ii) that the child would be born with grave physical or mental defect, or (iii) that the pregnancy resulted from rape or incest, or illicit intercourse with a girl under the age of 16 years).

"Section 2. (Penalty.) Any person who performs or procures an abortion other than authorized by this Act is guilty of a (felony) and, upon conviction thereof, may be sentenced to pay a fine not exceeding ($1,000) or to imprisonment (in the state penitentiary) not exceeding (5 years), or both."

restrain her from submitting to a procedure that placed her life in serious jeopardy.

Modern medical techniques have altered this situation. Appellants and various amici refer to medical data indicating that abortion in early pregnancy, that is, prior to the end of the first trimester, although not without its risk, is now relatively safe. Mortality rates for women undergoing early abortions, where the procedure is legal, appear to be as low as or lower than the rates for normal childbirth. Consequently, any interest of the State in protecting the woman from an inherently hazardous procedure, except when it would be equally dangerous for her to forgo it, has largely disappeared. . . .

The third reason is the State's interest—some phrase it in terms of duty—in protecting prenatal life. Some of the argument for this justification rests on the theory that a new human life is present from the moment of conception. The State's interest and general obligation to protect life then extends, it is argued, to prenatal life. Only when the life of the pregnant mother herself is at stake, balanced against the life she carries within her, should the interest of the embryo or fetus not prevail. Logically, of course, a legitimate state interest in this area need not stand or fall on acceptance of the belief that life begins at conception or at some other point prior to life birth. In assessing the State's interest, recognition may be given to the less rigid claim that as long as at least potential life is involved, the State may assert interests beyond the protection of the pregnant woman alone.

Parties challenging state abortion laws have sharply disputed in some courts the contention that a purpose of these laws, when enacted, was to protect prenatal life. Pointing to the absence of legislative history to support the contention, they claim that most state laws were designed solely to protect the woman. Because medical advances have lessened this concern, at least with respect to abortion in early pregnancy, they argue that with respect to such abortions the laws can no longer be justified by any state interest . . .

VIII

The Constitution does not explicitly mention any right of privacy. In a line of decisions, however, going back perhaps as far as Union Pacific R. Co. v. Botsford, 141 U.S. 250, 251, 11 S.Ct. 1000, 1001, 35 L.Ed. 734 (1891), the Court has recognized that a right of personal privacy, or a guarantee of certain areas or zones of privacy, does exist under the Constitution. In varying contexts, the Court or individual Justices have, indeed, found at least the roots of that right in the First Amendment. . . .

This right of privacy, whether it be founded in the Fourteenth Amendment's concept of personal liberty and restrictions upon state action, as we feel it is, or, as the District Court determined, in the Ninth Amendment's reservation of rights to the people, is broad enough to encompass a woman's decision whether or not to terminate her pregnancy. The detriment that the State would impose upon the pregnant woman by denying this choice altogether is apparent. Specific and direct harm medically diagnosable even in early pregnancy may be involved. Maternity, or additional offspring, may force upon the woman a distressful life and future. Psychological harm may be imminent. Mental and physical health may be taxed by child care. There is also the distress, for all concerned, associated with the unwanted child, and there is the problem of bringing a child into a family already unable, psychologically and otherwise, to care for it. In other cases, as in this one, the additional difficulties and continuing stigma of unwed motherhood may be involved. All these are factors the woman and her responsible physician necessarily will consider in consultation.

On the basis of elements such as these, appellant and some amici argue that the woman's right is absolute and that she is entitled to terminate her pregnancy at whatever time, in whatever way, and for whatever reason she alone chooses. With this we do not agree. Appellant's arguments that Texas either has no valid interest at all in regulating the abortion decision, or no interest strong enough to support any limitation upon the woman's sole determination, are unpersuasive. The Court's decisions recognizing a right of privacy also acknowledge that some state regulation in areas protected by that right is appropriate. As noted above, a State may properly assert important interests in safeguarding health, in maintaining medical standards, and in protecting potential life. At some point in pregnancy, these respective interests become sufficiently compelling to sustain regulation of the factors that govern the abortion decision. The privacy right involved, therefore, cannot be said to be absolute. In fact, it is not clear to us that the claim asserted by some amici that one has an unlimited right to do with one's body as one pleases bears a close relationship to the right of privacy previously articulated in the Court's decisions. The Court has refused to recognize an unlimited right of this kind in the past. Jacobson v. Massachusetts, 197 U.S. 11, 25 S.Ct. 358, 49 L.Ed. 643 (1905) (vaccination); Buck v. Bell, 274 U.S. 200, 47 S.Ct. 584, 71 L.Ed. 1000 (1927) (sterilization).

We, therefore, conclude that the right of personal privacy includes the abortion decision, but that this right is not unqualified and must be considered against important state interests in regulation. . . .

IX

. . .

A. The appellee and certain amici argue that the fetus is a "person" within the language and meaning of the Fourteenth Amendment. In support of this, they outline at length and in detail the well-known facts of fetal development. If this suggestion of personhood is established, the appellant's case, of course, collapses, for the fetus' right to life would then be guaranteed specifically by the Amendment. The appellant conceded as much on reargument. On the other hand, the appellee conceded on reargument that no case could be cited that holds that a fetus is a person within the meaning of the Fourteenth Amendment.

The Constitution does not define "person" in so many words. [The opinion reviews the use of the term in various parts of the Constitution, concluding that in nearly all the instances cited, "the use of the word is such that it has application only postnatally"]. All this, together with our observation, supra, that throughout the major portion of the 19th century prevailing legal abortion practices were far freer than they are today, persuades us that the word "person," as used in the Fourteenth Amendment, does not include the unborn "moment of conception." This conclusion, however, does not of itself fully answer the contentions raised by Texas, and we pass on to other considerations.

B. The pregnant woman cannot be isolated in her privacy. She carries an embryo and, later, a fetus, if one accepts the medical definitions of the developing young in the human uterus. See Dorland's Illustrated Medical Dictionary 478–479, 547 (24th ed. 1965). The situation therefore is inherently different from marital intimacy, or bedroom possession of obscene material, or marriage, or procreation, or education, with which Eisenstadt and Griswold, Stanley, Loving, Skinner and Pierce and Meyer were respectively concerned. As we have intimated above, it is reasonable and appropriate for a State to decide that at some point in time another interest, that of health of the mother or that of potential human life, becomes significantly involved. The woman's privacy is no longer sole and any right of privacy she possesses must be measured accordingly.

Texas urges that, apart from the Fourteenth Amendment, life begins at conception and is present throughout pregnancy, and that, therefore, the State has a compelling interest in protecting that life from and after conception. We need not resolve the difficult question of when life begins. When those trained in the respective disciplines of medicine, philosophy, and theology are unable to arrive at any consensus, the judiciary, at this point in the development of man's knowledge, is not in a position to speculate as to the answer.

It should be sufficient to note briefly the wide divergence of thinking on this most sensitive and difficult question. There has always been strong support for the view that life does not begin until live birth. . . . As we have noted, the common law found greater significance in quickening. Physicians and their scientific colleagues have regarded that event with less interest and have tended to focus either upon conception, upon live birth, or upon the interim point at which the fetus becomes "viable," that is, potentially able to live outside the mother's womb, albeit with artificial aid. Viability is usually placed at about seven months (28 weeks) but may occur earlier, even at 24 weeks. The Aristotelian theory of "mediate animation," that held sway throughout the Middle Ages and the Renaissance in Europe, continued to be official Roman Catholic dogma until the 19th century, despite opposition to this "ensoulment" theory from those in the Church who would recognize the existence of life from the moment of conception. The latter is now, of course, the official belief of the Catholic Church. As one brief amicus discloses, this is a view strongly held by many non-Catholics as well, and by many physicians. Substantial problems for precise definition of this view are posed, however, by new embryological data that purport to indicate that conception is a "process" over time, rather than an event, and by new medical techniques such as menstrual extraction, the "morning-after" pill, implantation of embryos, artificial insemination, and even artificial wombs.

In areas other than criminal abortion, the law has been reluctant to endorse any theory that life, as we recognize it, begins before live birth or to accord legal rights to the unborn except in narrowly defined situations and except when the rights are contingent upon life birth. For example, the traditional rule of tort law denied recovery for prenatal injuries even though the child was born alive. That rule has been changed in almost every jurisdiction. In most States, recovery is said to be permitted only if the fetus was viable, or at least quick, when the injuries were sustained, though few courts have squarely so held. In a recent development, generally opposed by the commentators, some States permit the parents of a stillborn child to maintain an action for wrongful death because of prenatal injuries. Such an action, however, would appear to be one to vindicate the parents' interest and is thus consistent with the view that the fetus, at most, represents only the potentiality of life. Similarly, unborn children have been recognized as acquiring rights or interests by way of inheritance or other devolution of property, and have been represented by guardians ad litem. Perfection of the interests involved, again, has generally been contingent upon live birth. In short, the unborn have never been recognized in the law as persons in the whole sense.

X

In view of all this, we do not agree that, by adopting one theory of life, Texas may override the rights of the pregnant woman that are at stake. We repeat, however, that the State does have an important and legitimate interest in preserving and protecting the health of the pregnant woman, whether she be a resident of the State or a non-resident who seeks medical consultation and treatment there, and that it has still another important and legitimate interest in protecting the potentiality of human life. These interests are separate and distinct. Each grows in substantiality as the woman approaches term and, at a point during pregnancy, each becomes "compelling."

With respect to the State's important and legitimate interest in the health of the mother, the "compelling" point, in the light of present medical knowledge, is at approximately the end of the first trimester. This is so because of the now-established medical fact, referred to above at 725, that until the end of the first trimester mortality in abortion may be less than mortality in normal childbirth. It follows that, from and after this point, a State may regulate the abortion procedure to the extent that the regulation reasonably relates to the preservation and protection of maternal health. Examples of permissible state regulation in this area are requirements as to the qualifications of the person who is to perform the abortion; as to the licensure of that person; as to the facility in which the procedure is to be performed, that is, whether it must be a hospital or may be a clinic or some other place of less-than-hospital status; as to the licensing of the facility; and the like.

This means, on the other hand, that, for the period of pregnancy prior to this "compelling" point, the attending physician, in consultation with his patient, is free to determine, without regulation by the State, that, in his medical judgment, the patient's pregnancy should be terminated. If that decision is reached, the judgment may be effectuated by an abortion free of interference by the State.

With respect to the State's important and legitimate interest in potential life, the "compelling" point is at viability. This is so because the fetus then presumably has the capability of meaningful life outside the mother's womb. State regulation protective of fetal life after viability thus has both logical and biological justifications. If the State is interested in protecting fetal life after viability, it may go so far as to proscribe abortion during that period, except when it is necessary to preserve the life or health of the mother.

Measured against these standards, Art. 1196 of the Texas Penal Code, in restricting legal abortions to those "procured or attempted by medical advice for the purpose of saving the life of the mother," sweeps too broadly. The statute makes no distinction between abortions performed early in pregnancy and those performed later, and it limits to a single reason, "saving" the mother's life, the legal justification for the procedure. The statute, therefore, cannot survive the constitutional attack made upon it here. . . .

To summarize and to repeat:

1. A state criminal abortion statute of the current Texas type, that excepts from criminality only a *life-saving* procedure on behalf of the mother, without regard to pregnancy stage and without recognition of the other interests involved, is violative of the Due Process Clause of the Fourteenth Amendment.

(a) For the stage prior to approximately the end of the first trimester, the abortion decision and its effectuation must be left to the medical judgment of the pregnant woman's attending physician.

(b) For the stage subsequent to approximately the end of the first trimester, the State, in promoting its interest in the health of the mother, may, if it chooses, regulate the abortion procedure in ways that are reasonably related to maternal health.

(c) For the stage subsequent to viability, the State in promoting its interest in the potentiality of human life may, if it chooses, regulate, and even proscribe, abortion except where it is necessary, in appropriate medical judgment, for the preservation of the life or health of the mother.

2. The State may define the term "physician," as it has been employed in the preceding paragraphs of this Part XI of this opinion, to mean only a physician currently licensed by the State, and may proscribe any abortion by a person who is not a physician as so defined. . . .

This holding, we feel, is consistent with the relative weights of the respective interests involved, with the lessons and examples of medical and legal history, with the lenity of the common law, and with the demands of the profound problems of the present day. The decision leaves the State free to place increasing restrictions on abortion as the period of pregnancy lengthens, so long as those restrictions are tailored to the recognized state interests. The decision vindicates the right of the physician to administer medical treatment according to his professional judgment up to the points where important state interests provide compelling justifications for intervention. Up to those points, the abortion decision in all its aspects is inherently, and primarily, a medical decision, and basic responsibility for it must rest with the physician. If an individual practitioner abuses the privilege of exercising proper medical judgment, the usual remedies, judicial and intra-professional, are available. . . .

■ [The concurring opinion of JUSTICE STEWART and the dissent of JUSTICE REHNQUIST have been omitted.]

Gonzales v. Carhart

Supreme Court of the United States, 2007
550 U.S. 124

■ JUSTICE KENNEDY delivered the opinion of the Court.

These cases require us to consider the validity of the Partial-Birth Abortion Ban Act of 2003 (Act), 18 U.S.C. § 1531 (2000 ed., Supp. IV), a federal statute regulating abortion procedures. In recitations preceding its operative provisions the Act refers to the Court's opinion in *Stenberg v. Carhart*, 530 U.S. 914 (2000), which also addressed the subject of abortion procedures used in the later stages of pregnancy. Compared to the state statute at issue in *Stenberg*, the Act is more specific concerning the instances to which it applies and in this respect more precise in its coverage. We conclude the Act should be sustained against the objections lodged by the broad, facial attack brought against it. . . .

The Act proscribes a particular manner of ending fetal life, so it is necessary here, as it was in *Stenberg*, to discuss abortion procedures in some detail. Three United States District Courts heard extensive evidence describing the procedures. In addition to the two courts involved in the instant cases the District Court for the Southern District of New

York also considered the constitutionality of the Act. *Nat. Abortion Federation v. Ashcroft*, 330 F. Supp. 2d 436 (2004). It found the Act unconstitutional, *id.*, at 493, and the Court of Appeals for the Second Circuit affirmed, *Nat. Abortion Federation v. Gonzales*, 437 F. 3d 278 (2006). The three District Courts relied on similar medical evidence; indeed, much of the evidence submitted to the *Carhart* court previously had been submitted to the other two courts. 331 F. Supp. 2d, at 809–810. We refer to the District Courts' exhaustive opinions in our own discussion of abortion procedures.

Abortion methods vary depending to some extent on the preferences of the physician and, of course, on the term of the pregnancy and the resulting stage of the unborn child's development. Between 85 and 90 percent of the approximately 1.3 million abortions performed each year in the United States take place in the first three months of pregnancy, which is to say in the first trimester. *Planned Parenthood*, 320 F. Supp. 2d, at 960, and n. 4; App. in No. 05–1382, pp. 45–48. The most common first-trimester abortion method is vacuum aspiration (otherwise known as suction curettage) in which the physician vacuums out the embryonic tissue. Early in this trimester an alternative is to use medication, such as mifepristone (commonly known as RU–486), to terminate the pregnancy. *Nat. Abortion Federation, supra,* at 464, n. 20. The Act does not regulate these procedures.

Of the remaining abortions that take place each year, most occur in the second trimester. The surgical procedure referred to as "dilation and evacuation" or "D&E" is the usual abortion method in this trimester. *Planned Parenthood*, 320 F. Supp. 2d, at 960–961. Although individual techniques for performing D&E differ, the general steps are the same.

A doctor must first dilate the cervix at least to the extent needed to insert surgical instruments into the uterus and to maneuver them to evacuate the fetus. *Nat. Abortion Federation, supra*, at 465; App. in No. 05–1382, at 61. The steps taken to cause dilation differ by physician and gestational age of the fetus. *See, e.g., Carhart*, 331 F. Supp. 2d, at 852, 856, 859, 862–865, 868, 870, 873–874, 876–877, 880, 883, 886. A doctor often begins the dilation process by inserting osmotic dilators, such as laminaria (sticks of seaweed), into the cervix. The dilators can be used in combination with drugs, such as misoprostol, that increase dilation. The resulting amount of dilation is not uniform, and a doctor does not know in advance how an individual patient will respond. In general the longer dilators remain in the cervix, the more it will dilate. Yet the length of time doctors employ osmotic dilators varies. Some may keep dilators in the cervix for two days, while others use dilators for a day or less. *Nat. Abortion Federation, supra*, at 464–465; *Planned Parenthood, supra*, at 961.

After sufficient dilation the surgical operation can commence. The woman is placed under general anesthesia or conscious sedation. The doctor, often guided by ultrasound, inserts grasping forceps through the woman's cervix and into the uterus to grab the fetus. The doctor grips a fetal part with the forceps and pulls it back through the cervix and vagina, continuing to pull even after meeting resistance from the cervix. The friction causes the fetus to tear apart. For example, a leg might be ripped off the fetus as it is pulled through the cervix and out of the woman. The process of evacuating the fetus piece by piece continues until it has been completely removed. A doctor may make 10 to 15 passes with the forceps to evacuate the fetus in its entirety, though sometimes removal is completed with fewer passes. Once the fetus has been evacuated, the placenta and any remaining fetal material are suctioned or scraped out of the uterus. The doctor examines the different parts to ensure the entire fetal body has been removed. *See, e.g., Nat. Abortion Federation, supra*, at 465; *Planned Parenthood, supra*, at 962.

Some doctors, especially later in the second trimester, may kill the fetus a day or two before performing the surgical evacuation. They inject digoxin or potassium chloride into the fetus, the umbilical cord, or the amniotic fluid. Fetal demise may cause contractions and make greater dilation possible. Once dead, moreover, the fetus' body will soften, and its removal will be easier. Other doctors refrain from injecting chemical agents, believing it adds risk with little or no medical benefit. *Carhart, supra*, at 907–912; *Nat. Abortion Federation, supra*, at 474–475.

The abortion procedure that was the impetus for the numerous bans on "partial-birth abortion," including the Act, is a variation of this standard D&E. See M. Haskell, Dilation and Extraction for Late Second Trimester Abortion (1992), 1 Appellant's App. in No. 04–3379 (CA8), p. 109 (hereinafter Dilation and Extraction). The medical community has not reached unanimity on the appropriate name for this D&E variation. It has been referred to as "intact D&E," "dilation and extraction" (D&X), and "intact D&X." *Nat. Abortion Federation, supra*, at 440, n. 2; see also F. Cunningham et al., Williams Obstetrics 243 (22d ed. 2005) (identifying the procedure as D&X); Danforth's Obstetrics and Gynecology 567 (J. Scott, R. Gibbs, B. Karlan, & A. Haney eds. 9th ed. 2003) (identifying the procedure as intact D&X); M. Paul, E. Lichtenberg, L. Borgatta, D. Grimes, & P. Stubblefield, A Clinician's Guide to Medical and Surgical Abortion 136 (1999) (identifying the procedure as intact D&E). For discussion purposes this D&E variation will be referred to as intact D&E. The main difference between the two procedures is that in intact D&E a doctor extracts the fetus intact or largely intact with only a few passes. There are no comprehensive statistics indicating what percentage of all D&Es are performed in this manner.

Intact D&E, like regular D&E, begins with dilation of the cervix. Sufficient dilation is essential for the procedure. To achieve intact extraction some doctors thus may attempt to dilate the cervix to a greater degree. This approach has been called "serial" dilation. *Carhart, supra*, at 856, 870, 873; *Planned Parenthood, supra*, at 965. Doctors who attempt at the outset to perform intact D&E may dilate for two full days or use up to 25 osmotic dilators. *See, e.g.,* Dilation and Extraction 110; *Carhart, supra*, at 865, 868, 876, 886.

In an intact D&E procedure the doctor extracts the fetus in a way conducive to pulling out its entire body, instead of ripping it apart. One doctor, for example, testified:

> "If I know I have good dilation and I reach in and the fetus starts to come out and I think I can accomplish it, the abortion with an intact delivery, then I use my forceps a little bit differently. I don't close them quite so much, and I just gently draw the tissue out attempting to have an intact delivery, if possible." App. in No. 05–1382, at 74.

Rotating the fetus as it is being pulled decreases the odds of dismemberment. *Carhart, supra*, at 868–869; App. in No. 05–380, pp. 40–41; 5 Appellant's App. in No. 04–3379 (CA8), p. 1469. A doctor also "may use forceps to grasp a fetal part, pull it down, and re-grasp the fetus at a higher level—sometimes using both his hand and a forceps—to exert traction to retrieve the fetus intact until the head is lodged in the [cervix]." *Carhart*, 331 F. Supp. 2d, at 886–887. . . .

D&E and intact D&E are not the only second-trimester abortion methods. Doctors also may abort a fetus through medical induction. The doctor medicates the woman to induce labor, and contractions occur to deliver the fetus. Induction, which unlike D&E should occur in a hospital, can last as little as 6 hours but can take longer than 48. It accounts for about five percent of second-trimester abortions before 20 weeks of gestation and 15 percent of those after 20 weeks. Doctors turn to two other methods of second-trimester abortion, hysterotomy and hysterectomy, only in emergency situations because they carry increased risk of complications. In a hysterotomy, as in a cesarean section, the doctor removes the fetus by making an incision through the abdomen and uterine wall to gain access to the uterine cavity. A hysterectomy requires the removal of the entire uterus. These two procedures represent about .07% of second-trimester abortions. *Nat. Abortion Federation*, 330 F. Supp. 2d, at 467; *Planned Parenthood, supra*, at 962–963. . . .

The Act responded to *Stenberg* in two ways. First, Congress made factual findings. Congress determined that this Court in *Stenberg* "was required to accept the very questionable findings issued by the district court judge," § 2(7), 117 Stat. 1202, notes following 18 U.S.C. § 1531 (2000 ed., Supp. IV), p. 768, ¶ (7) (Congressional Findings), but that Congress was "not bound to accept the same factual findings," *ibid.*, ¶ (8). Congress found, among other things, that "[a] moral, medical, and ethical consensus exists that the practice of performing a partial-birth abortion . . . is a gruesome and inhumane procedure that is never medically necessary and should be prohibited." *Id.*, at 767, ¶ (1).

Second, and more relevant here, the Act's language differs from that of the Nebraska statute struck down in *Stenberg*. See 530 U.S., at 921–

922 (quoting Neb. Rev. Stat. Ann. §§ 28–328(1), 28–326(9) (Supp. 1999)). The operative provisions of the Act provide in relevant part:

"(a) Any physician who, in or affecting interstate or foreign commerce, knowingly performs a partial-birth abortion and thereby kills a human fetus shall be fined under this title or imprisoned not more than 2 years, or both. This subsection does not apply to a partial-birth abortion that is necessary to save the life of a mother whose life is endangered by a physical disorder, physical illness, or physical injury, including a life-endangering physical condition caused by or arising from the pregnancy itself. This subsection takes effect 1 day after the enactment.

"(b) As used in this section—

"(1) the term 'partial-birth abortion' means an abortion in which the person performing the abortion—

"(A) deliberately and intentionally vaginally delivers a living fetus until, in the case of a head-first presentation, the entire fetal head is outside the body of the mother, or, in the case of breech presentation, any part of the fetal trunk past the navel is outside the body of the mother, for the purpose of performing an overt act that the person knows will kill the partially delivered living fetus; and

"(B) performs the overt act, other than completion of delivery, that kills the partially delivered living fetus; and

"(2) the term 'physician' means a doctor of medicine or osteopathy legally authorized to practice medicine and surgery by the State in which the doctor performs such activity, or any other individual legally authorized by the State to perform abortions: *Provided, however,* That any individual who is not a physician or not otherwise legally authorized by the State to perform abortions, but who nevertheless directly performs a partial-birth abortion, shall be subject to the provisions of this section. . . .

"(d)(1) A defendant accused of an offense under this section may seek a hearing before the State Medical Board on whether the physician's conduct was necessary to save the life of the mother whose life was endangered by a physical disorder, physical illness, or physical injury, including a life-endangering physical condition caused by or arising from the pregnancy itself.

"(2) The findings on that issue are admissible on that issue at the trial of the defendant. Upon a motion of the defendant, the court shall delay the beginning of the trial for not more than 30 days to permit such a hearing to take place.

> "(e) A woman upon whom a partial-birth abortion is performed may not be prosecuted under this section, for a conspiracy to violate this section, or for an offense under section 2, 3, or 4 of this title based on a violation of this section." 18 U.S.C. § 1531 (2000 ed., Supp. IV).

The Act also includes a provision authorizing civil actions that is not of relevance here. § 1531(c). . . .

Whatever one's views concerning the *Casey* joint opinion, it is evident a premise central to its conclusion—that the government has a legitimate and substantial interest in preserving and promoting fetal life—would be repudiated were the Court now to affirm the judgments of the Courts of Appeals. . . .

We assume the following principles for the purposes of this opinion. Before viability, a State "may not prohibit any woman from making the ultimate decision to terminate her pregnancy." 505 U.S., at 879 (plurality opinion). It also may not impose upon this right an undue burden, which exists if a regulation's "purpose or effect is to place a substantial obstacle in the path of a woman seeking an abortion before the fetus attains viability." *Id.*, at 878. On the other hand, "[r]egulations which do no more than create a structural mechanism by which the State, or the parent or guardian of a minor, may express profound respect for the life of the unborn are permitted, if they are not a substantial obstacle to the woman's exercise of the right to choose." *Id.*, at 877. *Casey*, in short, struck a balance. The balance was central to its holding. We now apply its standard to the cases at bar. . . .

We conclude that the Act is not void for vagueness, does not impose an undue burden from any overbreadth, and is not invalid on its face. The Act punishes "knowingly perform[ing]" a "partial-birth abortion." § 1531(a) (2000 ed., Supp. IV). It defines the unlawful abortion in explicit terms. § 1531(b)(1).

First, the person performing the abortion must "vaginally delive[r] a living fetus." § 1531(b)(1)(A). The Act does not restrict an abortion procedure involving the delivery of an expired fetus. The Act, furthermore, is inapplicable to abortions that do not involve vaginal delivery (for instance, hysterotomy or hysterectomy). The Act does apply both previability and postviability because, by common understanding and scientific terminology, a fetus is a living organism while within the womb, whether or not it is viable outside the womb. *See, e.g., Planned Parenthood*, 320 F. Supp. 2d, at 971–972. We do not understand this point to be contested by the parties.

Second, the Act's definition of partial-birth abortion requires the fetus to be delivered "until, in the case of a head-first presentation, the entire fetal head is outside the body of the mother, or, in the case of breech presentation, any part of the fetal trunk past the navel is outside the body of the mother." § 1531(b)(1)(A) (2000 ed., Supp. IV). The

Attorney General concedes, and we agree, that if an abortion procedure does not involve the delivery of a living fetus to one of these "anatomical 'landmarks' "—where, depending on the presentation, either the fetal head or the fetal trunk past the navel is outside the body of the mother—the prohibitions of the Act do not apply. Brief for Petitioner in No. 05–380, p. 46.

Third, to fall within the Act, a doctor must perform an "overt act, other than completion of delivery, that kills the partially delivered living fetus." § 1531(b)(1)(B) (2000 ed., Supp. IV). For purposes of criminal liability, the overt act causing the fetus' death must be separate from delivery. And the overt act must occur after the delivery to an anatomical landmark. This is because the Act proscribes killing "the partially delivered" fetus, which, when read in context, refers to a fetus that has been delivered to an anatomical landmark. *Ibid.*

Fourth, the Act contains scienter requirements concerning all the actions involved in the prohibited abortion. To begin with, the physician must have "deliberately and intentionally" delivered the fetus to one of the Act's anatomical landmarks. § 1531(b)(1)(A). If a living fetus is delivered past the critical point by accident or inadvertence, the Act is inapplicable. In addition, the fetus must have been delivered "for the purpose of performing an overt act that the [doctor] knows will kill [it]." *Ibid.* If either intent is absent, no crime has occurred. This follows from the general principle that where scienter is required no crime is committed absent the requisite state of mind. . . .

Under the principles accepted as controlling here, the Act, as we have interpreted it, would be unconstitutional "if its purpose or effect is to place a substantial obstacle in the path of a woman seeking an abortion before the fetus attains viability." *Casey*, 505 U.S., at 878 (plurality opinion). The abortions affected by the Act's regulations take place both previability and postviability; so the quoted language and the undue burden analysis it relies upon are applicable. The question is whether the Act, measured by its text in this facial attack, imposes a substantial obstacle to late-term, but previability, abortions. The Act does not on its face impose a substantial obstacle, and we reject this further facial challenge to its validity. . . .

The Act's ban on abortions that involve partial delivery of a living fetus furthers the Government's objectives. No one would dispute that, for many, D&E is a procedure itself laden with the power to devalue human life. Congress could nonetheless conclude that the type of abortion proscribed by the Act requires specific regulation because it implicates additional ethical and moral concerns that justify a special prohibition. Congress determined that the abortion methods it proscribed had a "disturbing similarity to the killing of a newborn infant," Congressional Findings (14)(L), in notes following 18 U.S.C. § 1531 (2000 ed., Supp. IV), p. 769, and thus it was concerned with "draw[ing] a bright line that clearly distinguishes abortion and infanticide." Congressional

Findings (14)(G), *ibid.* The Court has in the past confirmed the validity of drawing boundaries to prevent certain practices that extinguish life and are close to actions that are condemned. *Glucksberg* found reasonable the State's "fear that permitting assisted suicide will start it down the path to voluntary and perhaps even involuntary euthanasia." 521 U.S., at 732–735, and n. 23.

Respect for human life finds an ultimate expression in the bond of love the mother has for her child. The Act recognizes this reality as well. Whether to have an abortion requires a difficult and painful moral decision. *Casey, supra,* at 852–853 (opinion of the Court). While we find no reliable data to measure the phenomenon, it seems unexceptionable to conclude some women come to regret their choice to abort the infant life they once created and sustained. See Brief for Sandra Cano et al. as *Amici Curiae* in No. 05–380, pp. 22–24. Severe depression and loss of esteem can follow. See *ibid.*

In a decision so fraught with emotional consequence some doctors may prefer not to disclose precise details of the means that will be used, confining themselves to the required statement of risks the procedure entails. From one standpoint this ought not to be surprising. Any number of patients facing imminent surgical procedures would prefer not to hear all details, lest the usual anxiety preceding invasive medical procedures become the more intense. This is likely the case with the abortion procedures here in issue. *See, e.g., Nat. Abortion Federation,* 330 F. Supp. 2d, at 466, n. 22 ("Most of [the plaintiffs'] experts acknowledged that they do not describe to their patients what [the D&E and intact D&E] procedures entail in clear and precise terms"); see also *id.,* at 479.

It is, however, precisely this lack of information concerning the way in which the fetus will be killed that is of legitimate concern to the State. *Casey, supra,* at 873 (plurality opinion) ("States are free to enact laws to provide a reasonable framework for a woman to make a decision that has such profound and lasting meaning"). The State has an interest in ensuring so grave a choice is well informed. It is self-evident that a mother who comes to regret her choice to abort must struggle with grief more anguished and sorrow more profound when she learns, only after the event, what she once did not know: that she allowed a doctor to pierce the skull and vacuum the fast-developing brain of her unborn child, a child assuming the human form.

It is a reasonable inference that a necessary effect of the regulation and the knowledge it conveys will be to encourage some women to carry the infant to full term, thus reducing the absolute number of late-term abortions. The medical profession, furthermore, may find different and less shocking methods to abort the fetus in the second trimester, thereby accommodating legislative demand. The State's interest in respect for life is advanced by the dialogue that better informs the political and legal systems, the medical profession, expectant mothers, and society as a whole of the consequences that follow from a decision to elect a late-term abortion. . . .

The conclusion that the Act does not impose an undue burden is supported by other considerations. Alternatives are available to the prohibited procedure. As we have noted, the Act does not proscribe D&E. One District Court found D&E to have extremely low rates of medical complications. *Planned Parenthood, supra*, at 1000. Another indicated D&E was "generally the safest method of abortion during the second trimester." *Carhart*, 331 F. Supp. 2d, at 1031; see also *Nat. Abortion Federation, supra*, at 467–468 (explaining that "[e]xperts testifying for both sides" agreed D&E was safe). In addition the Act's prohibition only applies to the delivery of "a living fetus." 18 U.S.C. § 1531(b)(1)(A) (2000 ed., Supp. IV). If the intact D&E procedure is truly necessary in some circumstances, it appears likely an injection that kills the fetus is an alternative under the Act that allows the doctor to perform the procedure. . . .

A zero tolerance policy would strike down legitimate abortion regulations, like the present one, if some part of the medical community were disinclined to follow the proscription. This is too exacting a standard to impose on the legislative power, exercised in this instance under the Commerce Clause, to regulate the medical profession. Considerations of marginal safety, including the balance of risks, are within the legislative competence when the regulation is rational and in pursuit of legitimate ends. When standard medical options are available, mere convenience does not suffice to displace them; and if some procedures have different risks than others, it does not follow that the State is altogether barred from imposing reasonable regulations. The Act is not invalid on its face where there is uncertainty over whether the barred procedure is ever necessary to preserve a woman's health, given the availability of other abortion procedures that are considered to be safe alternatives. . . .

Respondents have not demonstrated that the Act, as a facial matter, is void for vagueness, or that it imposes an undue burden on a woman's right to abortion based on its overbreadth or lack of a health exception. For these reasons the judgments of the Courts of Appeals for the Eighth and Ninth Circuits are reversed.

It is so ordered.

■ JUSTICE THOMAS, with whom JUSTICE SCALIA joins, concurring.

I join the Court's opinion because it accurately applies current jurisprudence, including *Planned Parenthood of Southeastern Pa. v. Casey*, 505 U.S. 833 (1992). I write separately to reiterate my view that the Court's abortion jurisprudence, including *Casey* and *Roe v. Wade*, 410 U.S. 113 (1973), has no basis in the Constitution. See *Casey, supra*, at 979 (SCALIA, J., concurring in judgment in part and dissenting in part); *Stenberg v. Carhart*, 530 U.S. 914, 980–983 (2000) (THOMAS, J., dissenting). . . .

■ JUSTICE GINSBURG, with whom JUSTICE STEVENS, JUSTICE SOUTER, and JUSTICE BREYER join, dissenting.

. . .

Today's decision is alarming. It refuses to take *Casey* and *Stenberg* seriously. It tolerates, indeed applauds, federal intervention to ban nationwide a procedure found necessary and proper in certain cases by the American College of Obstetricians and Gynecologists (ACOG). It blurs the line, firmly drawn in *Casey*, between previability and postviability abortions. And, for the first time since *Roe*, the Court blesses a prohibition with no exception safeguarding a woman's health. . . .

The Court offers flimsy and transparent justifications for upholding a nationwide ban on intact D&E *sans* any exception to safeguard a women's health. Today's ruling, the Court declares, advances "a premise central to [*Casey*'s] conclusion"—*i.e.*, the Government's "legitimate and substantial interest in preserving and promoting fetal life." *Ante*, at 14. See also *ante*, at 15 ("[W]e must determine whether the Act furthers the legitimate interest of the Government in protecting the life of the fetus that may become a child."). But the Act scarcely furthers that interest: The law saves not a single fetus from destruction, for it targets only a *method* of performing abortion. . . .

Delivery of an intact, albeit nonviable, fetus warrants special condemnation, the Court maintains, because a fetus that is not dismembered resembles an infant. *Ante,* at 28. But so, too, does a fetus delivered intact after it is terminated by injection a day or two before the surgical evacuation, *ante,* at 5, 34–35, or a fetus delivered through medical induction or cesarean, *ante,* at 9. Yet, the availability of those procedures—along with D&E by dismemberment—the Court says, saves the ban on intact D&E from a declaration of unconstitutionality. *Ante,* at 34–35. Never mind that the procedures deemed acceptable might put a woman's health at greater risk. . . .

Ultimately, the Court admits that "moral concerns" are at work, concerns that could yield prohibitions on any abortion. See *ante*, at 28 ("Congress could . . . conclude that the type of abortion proscribed by the Act requires specific regulation because it implicates additional ethical and moral concerns that justify a special prohibition."). Notably, the concerns expressed are untethered to any ground genuinely serving the Government's interest in preserving life. By allowing such concerns to carry the day and case, overriding fundamental rights, the Court dishonors our precedent. *See, e.g., Casey*, 505 U.S., at 850 ("Some of us as individuals find abortion offensive to our most basic principles of morality, but that cannot control our decision. Our obligation is to define the liberty of all, not to mandate our own moral code."); *Lawrence v. Texas*, 539 U.S. 558, 571 (2003) (Though "[f]or many persons [objections to homosexual conduct] are not trivial concerns but profound and deep convictions accepted as ethical and moral principles," the power of the State may not be used "to enforce these views on the whole society through operation of the criminal law." (citing *Casey*, 505 U.S., at 850)). . . .

As the Court wrote in *Casey*, "overruling *Roe*'s central holding would not only reach an unjustifiable result under principles of *stare decisis*, but would seriously weaken the Court's capacity to exercise the judicial power and to function as the Supreme Court of a Nation dedicated to the rule of law." 505 U.S., at 865. "[T]he very concept of the rule of law underlying our own Constitution requires such continuity over time that a respect for precedent is, by definition, indispensable." *Id.*, at 854. See also *id.*, at 867 ("[T]o overrule under fire in the absence of the most compelling reason to reexamine a watershed decision would subvert the Court's legitimacy beyond any serious question.").

Though today's opinion does not go so far as to discard *Roe* or *Casey*, the Court, differently composed than it was when we last considered a restrictive abortion regulation, is hardly faithful to our earlier invocations of "the rule of law" and the "principles of *stare decisis*." Congress imposed a ban despite our clear prior holdings that the State cannot proscribe an abortion procedure when its use is necessary to protect a woman's health. See *supra*, at 7, n. 4. Although Congress' findings could not withstand the crucible of trial, the Court defers to the legislative override of our Constitution-based rulings. See *supra*, at 7–9. A decision so at odds with our jurisprudence should not have staying power.

In sum, the notion that the Partial-Birth Abortion Ban Act furthers any legitimate governmental interest is, quite simply, irrational. The Court's defense of the statute provides no saving explanation. In candor, the Act, and the Court's defense of it, cannot be understood as anything other than an effort to chip away at a right declared again and again by this Court—and with increasing comprehension of its centrality to women's lives. See *supra*, at 3, n. 2; *supra*, at 7, n. 4. When "a statute burdens constitutional rights and all that can be said on its behalf is that it is the vehicle that legislators have chosen for expressing their hostility to those rights, the burden is undue." *Stenberg*, 530 U.S., at 952 (GINSBURG, J., concurring) (quoting *Hope Clinic v. Ryan*, 195 F. 3d 857, 881 (CA7 1999) (POSNER, C. J., dissenting)). . . .

For the reasons stated, I dissent from the Court's disposition and would affirm the judgments before us for review.

NOTES

Many articles have been written on the parameters of privacy since the Supreme Court upheld the validity of the Partial-Birth Abortion Ban Act of 2003. *See, e.g.,* Susan F. Appleton, *Reproduction and Regret*, 23 YALE J.L. & FEMINISM, 255 (2011); Erika Bachiochi, *Embodied Equality: Debunking Equal Protection Arguments for Abortion Rights*, 34 HARV. J.L. & PUB. POL'Y 889 (2011); I. Glenn Cohen, *Regulating Reproduction: The Problem with Best Interests*, 96 MINN. L. REV. 423 (2011); Linda Greenhouse and Reva B. Siegel,

Before (and after) Roe v. Wade*: New Questions About Backlash*, 120 YALE L.J. 2028 (2011); John A. Robertson, *Abortion and Technology: Sonograms, Fetal Pain, Viability, and Early Prenatal Diagnosis*, 14 U. PA. J. CONST. L. 327 (2011); Jeffrey C. Tuomala, *Nuremberg and the Crime of Abortion*, 42 U. TOL. L. REV. 283 (2011); Beth A. Burkstrand, *The More Things Change . . . : Abortion Politics & Regulation of Assisted Reproductive Technology*, 79 UMKC L. REV. 361 (2010); Fred H. Cate, *Protecting Privacy in Health Research: The Limits of Individual Choice*, 98 CAL. L. REV. 1765 (2010); Jessie B. Hill, *A Radically Immodest Judicial Modesty: The End of Facial Challenges to Abortion Regulations and the Future of the Health Exception in the Roberts Era*, 59 CASE W. RES. L. REV. 997 (2009). For text of the Act, *see* WALTER WADLINGTON, RAYMOND C. O'BRIEN, & ROBIN FRETWELL WILSON, FAMILY LAW STATUTES: SELECTED UNIFORM LAWS, MODEL LEGISLATION, FEDERAL STATUTES, STATE STATUTES, AND INTERNATIONAL TREATIES (5th ed. 2017).

3. DUE PROCESS LIBERTY INTEREST

Lawrence v. Texas

Supreme Court of the United States, 2003
539 U.S. 558

■ JUSTICE KENNEDY delivered the opinion of the Court.

Liberty protects the person from unwarranted government intrusions into a dwelling or other private places. In our tradition the State is not omnipresent in the home. And there are other spheres of our lives and existence, outside the home, where the State should not be a dominant presence. Freedom extends beyond spatial bounds. Liberty presumes an autonomy of self that includes freedom of thought, belief, expression, and certain intimate conduct. The instant case involves liberty of the person both in its spatial and more transcendent dimensions.

The question before the Court is the validity of a Texas statute making it a crime for two persons of the same sex to engage in certain intimate sexual conduct.

In Houston, Texas, officers of the Harris County Police Department were dispatched to a private residence in response to a reported weapons disturbance. They entered an apartment where one of the petitioners, John Geddes Lawrence, resided. The right of the police to enter does not seem to have been questioned. The officers observed Lawrence and another man, Tyron Garner, engaging in a sexual act. The two petitioners were arrested, held in custody overnight, and charged and convicted before a Justice of the Peace.

The complaints described their crime as "deviate sexual intercourse, namely anal sex, with a member of the same sex (man)." App. to Pet. for Cert. 127a, 139a. The applicable state law is Tex. Penal Code Ann. § 21.06(a) (2003). It provides: "A person commits an offense if he engages in deviate sexual intercourse with another individual of the same sex." The statute defines "[d]eviate sexual intercourse" as follows:

> "(A) any contact between any part of the genitals of one person and the mouth or anus of another person; or
>
> "(B) the penetration of the genitals or the anus of another person with an object." § 21.01(1). . . .

We conclude the case should be resolved by determining whether the petitioners were free as adults to engage in the private conduct in the exercise of their liberty under the Due Process Clause of the Fourteenth Amendment to the Constitution. For this inquiry we deem it necessary to reconsider the Court's holding in *Bowers.*

There are broad statements of the substantive reach of liberty under the Due Process Clause in earlier cases, including *Pierce v. Society of Sisters,* 268 U.S. 510, 45 S.Ct. 571, 69 L.Ed. 1070 (1925), and *Meyer v. Nebraska,* 262 U.S. 390, 43 S.Ct. 625, 67 L.Ed. 1042 (1923); but the most pertinent beginning point is our decision in *Griswold v. Connecticut,* 381 U.S. 479, 85 S.Ct. 1678, 14 L.Ed.2d 510 (1965).

In *Griswold* the Court invalidated a state law prohibiting the use of drugs or devices of contraception and counseling or aiding and abetting the use of contraceptives. The Court described the protected interest as a right to privacy and placed emphasis on the marriage relation and the protected space of the marital bedroom. *Id.,* at 485, 85 S.Ct. 1678.

After *Griswold* it was established that the right to make certain decisions regarding sexual conduct extends beyond the marital relationship. In *Eisenstadt v. Baird,* 405 U.S. 438, 92 S.Ct. 1029, 31 L.Ed.2d 349 (1972), the Court invalidated a law prohibiting the distribution of contraceptives to unmarried persons. The case was decided under the Equal Protection Clause, *id.,* at 454, 92 S.Ct. 1029; but with respect to unmarried persons, the Court went on to state the fundamental proposition that the law impaired the exercise of their personal rights, *ibid.* It quoted from the statement of the Court of Appeals finding the law to be in conflict with fundamental human rights, and it followed with this statement of its own:

> "It is true that in *Griswold* the right of privacy in question inhered in the marital relationship. . . . If the right of privacy means anything, it is the right of the *individual,* married or single, to be free from unwarranted governmental intrusion into matters so fundamentally affecting a person as the decision whether to bear or beget a child." *Id.,* at 453, 92 S.Ct. 1029.

The opinions in *Griswold* and *Eisenstadt* were part of the background for the decision in *Roe v. Wade,* 410 U.S. 113, 93 S.Ct. 705, 35 L.Ed.2d 147 (1973). As is well known, the case involved a challenge to the Texas law prohibiting abortions, but the laws of other States were affected as well. Although the Court held the woman's rights were not absolute, her right to elect an abortion did have real and substantial protection as an exercise of her liberty under the Due Process Clause. The Court cited cases that protect spatial freedom and cases that go well beyond it. *Roe* recognized the right of a woman to make certain fundamental decisions affecting her destiny and confirmed once more that the protection of liberty under the Due Process Clause has a substantive dimension of fundamental significance in defining the rights of the person.

In *Carey v. Population Services Int'l,* 431 U.S. 678, 97 S.Ct. 2010, 52 L.Ed.2d 675 (1977), the Court confronted a New York law forbidding sale or distribution of contraceptive devices to persons under 16 years of age. Although there was no single opinion for the Court, the law was invalidated. Both *Eisenstadt* and *Carey,* as well as the holding and rationale in *Roe,* confirmed that the reasoning of *Griswold* could not be confined to the protection of rights of married adults. This was the state of the law with respect to some of the most relevant cases when the Court considered *Bowers v. Hardwick.*

The facts in *Bowers* had some similarities to the instant case. A police officer, whose right to enter seems not to have been in question, observed Hardwick, in his own bedroom, engaging in intimate sexual conduct with another adult male. The conduct was in violation of a Georgia statute making it a criminal offense to engage in sodomy. One difference between the two cases is that the Georgia statute prohibited the conduct whether or not the participants were of the same sex, while the Texas statute, as we have seen, applies only to participants of the same sex. Hardwick was not prosecuted, but he brought an action in federal court to declare the state statute invalid. He alleged he was a practicing homosexual and that the criminal prohibition violated rights guaranteed to him by the Constitution. The Court, in an opinion by Justice White, sustained the Georgia law. Chief Justice Burger and Justice Powell joined the opinion of the Court and filed separate, concurring opinions. Four Justices dissented. 478 U.S., at 199, 106 S.Ct. 2841 (opinion of Blackmun, J., joined by Brennan, Marshall, and STEVENS, JJ.); *id.,* at 214, 106 S.Ct. 2841 (opinion of STEVENS, J., joined by Brennan and Marshall, JJ.).

The Court began its substantive discussion in *Bowers* as follows: "The issue presented is whether the Federal Constitution confers a fundamental right upon homosexuals to engage in sodomy and hence invalidates the laws of the many States that still make such conduct illegal and have done so for a very long time." *Id.,* at 190, 106 S.Ct. 2841. That statement, we now conclude, discloses the Court's own failure to appreciate the extent of the liberty at stake. To say that the issue in *Bowers* was simply the right to engage in certain sexual conduct demeans the claim the individual put forward, just as it would demean a married couple were it to be said marriage is simply about the right to have sexual intercourse. The laws involved in *Bowers* and here are, to be sure, statutes that purport to do no more than prohibit a particular sexual act.

Their penalties and purposes, though, have more far-reaching consequences, touching upon the most private human conduct, sexual behavior, and in the most private of places, the home. The statutes do seek to control a personal relationship that, whether or not entitled to formal recognition in the law, is within the liberty of persons to choose without being punished as criminals.

This, as a general rule, should counsel against attempts by the State, or a court, to define the meaning of the relationship or to set its boundaries absent injury to a person or abuse of an institution the law protects. It suffices for us to acknowledge that adults may choose to enter upon this relationship in the confines of their homes and their own private lives and still retain their dignity as free persons. When sexuality finds overt expression in intimate conduct with another person, the conduct can be but one element in a personal bond that is more enduring. The liberty protected by the Constitution allows homosexual persons the right to make this choice.

Having misapprehended the claim of liberty there presented to it, and thus stating the claim to be whether there is a fundamental right to engage in consensual sodomy, the *Bowers* Court said: "Proscriptions against that conduct have ancient roots." *Id.,* at 192, 106 S.Ct. 2841. In academic writings, and in many of the scholarly *amicus* briefs filed to assist the Court in this case, there are fundamental criticisms of the historical premises relied upon by the majority and concurring opinions in *Bowers.* Brief for Cato Institute as *Amicus Curiae* 16–17; Brief for American Civil Liberties Union et al. as *Amici Curiae* 15–21; Brief for Professors of History et al. as *Amici Curiae* 3–10. We need not enter this debate in the attempt to reach a definitive historical judgment, but the following considerations counsel against adopting the definitive conclusions upon which *Bowers* placed such reliance.

At the outset it should be noted that there is no longstanding history in this country of laws directed at homosexual conduct as a distinct matter. Beginning in colonial times there were prohibitions of sodomy derived from the English criminal laws passed in the first instance by the Reformation Parliament of 1533. The English prohibition was understood to include relations between men and women as well as relations between men and men. *See, e.g., King v. Wiseman,* 92 Eng. Rep. 774, 775 (K.B.1718) (interpreting "mankind" in Act of 1533 as including women and girls). Nineteenth-century commentators similarly read American sodomy, buggery, and crime-against-nature statutes as criminalizing certain relations between men and women and between men and men. *See, e.g.,* 2 J. Bishop, Criminal Law § 1028 (1858); . . . J. May, The Law of Crimes § 203 (2d ed. 1893). The absence of legal prohibitions focusing on homosexual conduct may be explained in part by noting that according to some scholars the concept of the homosexual as a distinct category of person did not emerge until the late 19th century. *See, e.g.,* J. Katz, The Invention of Heterosexuality 10 (1995); J. D'Emilio and E. Freedman, Intimate Matters: A History of Sexuality in America 121 (2d ed. 1997) ("The modern terms *homosexuality* and *heterosexuality* do not apply to an era that had not yet articulated these distinctions"). Thus early American sodomy laws were not directed at homosexuals as such but instead sought to prohibit nonprocreative sexual activity more generally. This does not suggest approval of homosexual conduct. It does tend to show that this particular form of conduct was not thought of as a separate category from like conduct between heterosexual persons.

Laws prohibiting sodomy do not seem to have been enforced against consenting adults acting in private. A substantial number of sodomy prosecutions and convictions for which there are surviving records were for predatory acts against those who could not or did not consent, as in the case of a minor or the victim of an assault. As to these, one purpose for the prohibitions was to ensure there would be no lack of coverage if a predator committed a sexual assault that did not constitute rape as defined by the criminal law. Thus the model sodomy indictments presented in a 19th-century treatise, see 2 Chitty, *supra,* at 49, addressed the predatory acts of an adult man against a minor girl or minor boy. Instead of targeting relations between consenting adults in private, 19th-century sodomy prosecutions typically involved relations between men and minor girls or minor boys, relations between adults involving force, relations between adults implicating disparity in status, or relations between men and animals.

To the extent that there were any prosecutions for the acts in question, 19th-century evidence rules imposed a burden that would make a conviction more difficult to obtain even taking into account the problems always inherent in prosecuting consensual acts committed in private. Under then-prevailing standards, a man could not be convicted of sodomy based upon testimony of a consenting partner, because the partner was considered an accomplice. A partner's testimony, however, was admissible if he or she had not consented to the act or was a minor, and therefore incapable of consent. *See, e.g.,* F. Wharton, Criminal Law 443 (2d ed. 1852); 1 F. Wharton, Criminal Law 512 (8th ed. 1880). The rule may explain in part the infrequency of these prosecutions. In all events that infrequency makes it difficult to say that society approved of a rigorous and systematic punishment of the consensual acts committed in private and by adults. The longstanding criminal prohibition of homosexual sodomy upon which the *Bowers* decision placed such reliance is as consistent with a general condemnation of nonprocreative sex as it is with an established tradition of prosecuting acts because of their homosexual character.

The policy of punishing consenting adults for private acts was not much discussed in the early legal literature. We can infer that one reason for this was the very private nature of the conduct. Despite the absence of prosecutions, there may have been periods in which there was public criticism of homosexuals as such and an insistence that the criminal laws be enforced to discourage their practices. But far from possessing "ancient roots," *Bowers,* 478 U.S., at 192, 106 S.Ct. 2841, American laws targeting same sex couples did not develop until the last third of the 20th century. The reported decisions concerning the prosecution of consensual, homosexual sodomy between adults for the years 1880–1995 are not always clear in the details, but a significant number involved conduct in a public place. See Brief for American Civil Liberties Union et al. as *Amici Curiae* 14–15, and n. 18. It was not until the 1970's that any State singled out same sex relations for criminal prosecution, and only nine States have done so. [Cases and statutes omitted.]

In summary, the historical grounds relied upon in *Bowers* are more complex than the majority opinion and the concurring opinion by Chief Justice Burger indicate. Their historical premises are not without doubt and, at the very least, are overstated.

It must be acknowledged, of course, that the Court in *Bowers* was making the broader point that for centuries there have been powerful voices to condemn homosexual conduct as immoral. The condemnation has been shaped by religious beliefs, conceptions of right and acceptable behavior, and respect for the traditional family. For many persons these are not trivial concerns but profound and deep convictions accepted as ethical and moral principles to which they aspire and which thus determine the course of their lives. These considerations do not answer the question before us, however. The issue is whether the majority may use the power of the State to enforce these views on the whole society through operation of the criminal law. "Our obligation is to define the liberty of all, not to mandate our own moral code." *Planned Parenthood of Southeastern Pa. v. Casey,* 505 U.S. 833, 850, 112 S.Ct. 2791, 120 L.Ed.2d 674 (1992). . . .

Equality of treatment and the due process right to demand respect for conduct protected by the substantive guarantee of liberty are linked in important respects, and a decision on the latter point advances both interests. If protected conduct is made criminal and the law which does so remains unexamined for its substantive validity, its stigma might remain even if it were not enforceable as drawn for equal protection reasons. When homosexual conduct is made criminal by the law of the State, that declaration in and of itself is an invitation to subject homosexual persons to discrimination both in the public and in the private spheres. The central holding of *Bowers* has been brought in question by this case, and it should be addressed. Its continuance as precedent demeans the lives of homosexual persons. . . .

To the extent *Bowers* relied on values we share with a wider civilization, it should be noted that the reasoning and holding in *Bowers* have been rejected elsewhere. The European Court of Human Rights has followed not *Bowers* but its own decision in *Dudgeon v. United Kingdom.* See *P.G. & J.H. v. United Kingdom,* App. No. 00044787/98, & ¶ 56 (Eur.Ct.H. R., Sept. 25, 2001); *Modinos v. Cyprus,* 259 Eur. Ct. H.R.

(1993); *Norris v. Ireland,* 142 Eur. Ct. H.R. (1988). Other nations, too, have taken action consistent with an affirmation of the protected right of homosexual adults to engage in intimate, consensual conduct. See Brief for Mary Robinson et al. as *Amici Curiae* 11–12. The right the petitioners seek in this case has been accepted as an integral part of human freedom in many other countries. There has been no showing that in this country the governmental interest in circumscribing personal choice is somehow more legitimate or urgent. . . .

The rationale of *Bowers* does not withstand careful analysis. In his dissenting opinion in Bowers Justice STEVENS came to these conclusions:

> "Our prior cases make two propositions abundantly clear. First, the fact that the governing majority in a State has traditionally viewed a particular practice as immoral is not a sufficient reason for upholding a law prohibiting the practice; neither history nor tradition could save a law prohibiting miscegenation from constitutional attack. Second, individual decisions by married persons, concerning the intimacies of their physical relationship, even when not intended to produce offspring, are a form of 'liberty' protected by the Due Process Clause of the Fourteenth Amendment. Moreover, this protection extends to intimate choices by unmarried as well as married persons." 478 U.S., at 216, 106 S.Ct. 2841 (footnotes and citations omitted).

Justice STEVENS' analysis, in our view, should have been controlling in *Bowers* and should control here. Bowers was not correct when it was decided, and it is not correct today. It ought not to remain binding precedent. *Bowers v. Hardwick* should be and now is overruled.

The present case does not involve minors. It does not involve persons who might be injured or coerced or who are situated in relationships where consent might not easily be refused. It does not involve public conduct or prostitution. It does not involve whether the government must give formal recognition to any relationship that homosexual persons seek to enter. The case does involve two adults who, with full and mutual consent from each other, engaged in sexual practices common to a homosexual lifestyle. The petitioners are entitled to respect for their private lives. The State cannot demean their existence or control their destiny by making their private sexual conduct a crime. Their right to liberty under the Due Process Clause gives them the full right to engage in their conduct without intervention of the government. "It is a promise of the Constitution that there is a realm of personal liberty which the government may not enter." *Casey, supra,* at 847, 112 S.Ct. 2791. The Texas statute furthers no legitimate state interest which can justify its intrusion into the personal and private life of the individual.

Had those who drew and ratified the Due Process Clauses of the Fifth Amendment or the Fourteenth Amendment known the components of liberty in its manifold possibilities, they might have been more specific.

They did not presume to have this insight. They knew times can blind us to certain truths and later generations can see that laws once thought necessary and proper in fact serve only to oppress. As the Constitution endures, persons in every generation can invoke its principles in their own search for greater freedom.

The judgment of the Court of Appeals for the Texas Fourteenth District is reversed, and the case is remanded for further proceedings not inconsistent with this opinion.

■ JUSTICE O'CONNOR, concurring in the judgment.

The Court today overrules *Bowers v. Hardwick,* 478 U.S. 186, 106 S.Ct. 2841, 92 L.Ed.2d 140 (1986). I joined *Bowers,* and do not join the Court in overruling it. Nevertheless, I agree with the Court that Texas' statute banning same sex sodomy is unconstitutional. See Tex. Penal Code Ann. § 21.06 (2003). Rather than relying on the substantive component of the Fourteenth Amendment's Due Process Clause, as the Court does, I base my conclusion on the Fourteenth Amendment's Equal Protection Clause. . . .

The statute at issue here makes sodomy a crime only if a person "engages in deviate sexual intercourse with another individual of the same sex." Tex. Penal Code Ann. § 21.06(a) (2003). Sodomy between opposite-sex partners, however, is not a crime in Texas. That is, Texas treats the same conduct differently based solely on the participants. Those harmed by this law are people who have a same sex sexual orientation and thus are more likely to engage in behavior prohibited by § 21.06. . . .

A law branding one class of persons as criminal based solely on the State's moral disapproval of that class and the conduct associated with that class runs contrary to the values of the Constitution and the Equal Protection Clause, under any standard of review. I therefore concur in the Court's judgment that Texas' sodomy law banning "deviate sexual intercourse" between consenting adults of the same sex, but not between consenting adults of different sexes, is unconstitutional.

■ JUSTICE SCALIA, with whom THE CHIEF JUSTICE and JUSTICE THOMAS join, dissenting.

"Liberty finds no refuge in a jurisprudence of doubt." *Planned Parenthood of Southeastern Pa. v. Casey,* 505 U.S. 833, 844, 112 S.Ct. 2791, 120 L.Ed.2d 674 (1992). That was the Court's sententious response, barely more than a decade ago, to those seeking to overrule *Roe v. Wade,* 410 U.S. 113, 93 S.Ct. 705, 35 L.Ed.2d 147 (1973). The Court's response today, to those who have engaged in a 17-year crusade to overrule *Bowers v. Hardwick,* 478 U.S. 186, 106 S.Ct. 2841, 92 L.Ed.2d 140 (1986), is very different. The need for stability and certainty presents no barrier.

Most of the rest of today's opinion has no relevance to its actual holding—that the Texas statute "furthers no legitimate state interest which can justify" its application to petitioners under rational-basis review. *Ante,* at 2484 (overruling *Bowers* to the extent it sustained Georgia's anti-sodomy statute under the rational-basis test). Though there is discussion of "fundamental proposition[s]," *ante,* at 2477, and "fundamental decisions," *ibid.* nowhere does the Court's opinion declare that homosexual sodomy is a "fundamental right" under the Due Process Clause; nor does it subject the Texas law to the standard of review that would be appropriate (strict scrutiny) if homosexual sodomy *were* a "fundamental right." Thus, while overruling the *outcome* of *Bowers,* the Court leaves strangely untouched its central legal conclusion: "[R]espondent would have us announce . . . a fundamental right to engage in homosexual sodomy. This we are quite unwilling to do." 478 U.S., at 191, 106 S.Ct. 2841. Instead the Court simply describes petitioners' conduct as "an exercise of their liberty"—which it undoubtedly is—and proceeds to apply an unheard-of form of rational-basis review that will have far-reaching implications beyond this case. *Ante,* at 2476. . . .

I turn now to the ground on which the Court squarely rests its holding: the contention that there is no rational basis for the law here under attack. This proposition is so out of accord with our jurisprudence—indeed, with the jurisprudence of *any* society we know—that it requires little discussion.

The Texas statute undeniably seeks to further the belief of its citizens that certain forms of sexual behavior are "immoral and unacceptable," *Bowers, supra,* at 196, 106 S.Ct. 2841—the same interest furthered by criminal laws against fornication, bigamy, adultery, adult incest, bestiality, and obscenity. *Bowers* held that this *was* a legitimate state interest. The Court today reaches the opposite conclusion. The Texas statute, it says, "furthers *no legitimate state interest* which can justify its intrusion into the personal and private life of the individual," *ante,* at 2484 (emphasis added). The Court embraces instead Justice STEVENS' declaration in his *Bowers* dissent, that "the fact that the governing majority in a State has traditionally viewed a particular practice as immoral is not a sufficient reason for upholding a law prohibiting the practice," *ante,* at 2483. This effectively decrees the end of all morals legislation. If, as the Court asserts, the promotion of majoritarian sexual morality is not even a *legitimate* state interest, none of the above-mentioned laws can survive rational-basis review. . . .

Today's opinion is the product of a Court, which is the product of a law-profession culture, that has largely signed on to the so-called homosexual agenda, by which I mean the agenda promoted by some homosexual activists directed at eliminating the moral opprobrium that has traditionally attached to homosexual conduct. I noted in an earlier opinion the fact that the American Association of Law Schools (to which any reputable law school *must* seek to belong) excludes from membership any school that refuses to ban from its job-interview facilities a law firm (no matter how small) that does not wish to hire as a prospective partner a person who openly engages in homosexual conduct. See *Romer, supra,* at 653, 116 S.Ct. 1620.

One of the most revealing statements in today's opinion is the Court's grim warning that the criminalization of homosexual conduct is "an invitation to subject homosexual persons to discrimination both in the public and in the private spheres." *Ante,* at 2482. It is clear from this that the Court has taken sides in the culture war, departing from its role of assuring, as neutral observer, that the democratic rules of engagement are observed. Many Americans do not want persons who openly engage in homosexual conduct as partners in their business, as scoutmasters for their children, as teachers in their children's schools, or as boarders in their home. They view this as protecting themselves and their families from a lifestyle that they believe to be immoral and destructive. The Court views it as "discrimination" which it is the function of our judgments to deter. So imbued is the Court with the law profession's anti-anti-homosexual culture, that it is seemingly unaware that the attitudes of that culture are not obviously "mainstream"; that in most States what the Court calls "discrimination" against those who engage in homosexual acts is perfectly legal; that proposals to ban such "discrimination" under Title VII have repeatedly been rejected by Congress, see Employment Non-Discrimination Act of 1994, S. 2238, 103d Cong., 2d Sess. (1994); Civil Rights Amendments, H.R. 5452, 94th Cong., 1st Sess. (1975); that in some cases such "discrimination" is *mandated* by federal statute, see 10 U.S.C. § 654(b)(1) (mandating discharge from the armed forces of any service member who engages in or intends to engage in homosexual acts); and that in some cases such "discrimination" is a constitutional right, see *Boy Scouts of America v. Dale,* 530 U.S. 640, 120 S.Ct. 2446, 147 L.Ed.2d 554 (2000).

Let me be clear that I have nothing against homosexuals, or any other group, promoting their agenda through normal democratic means. Social perceptions of sexual and other morality change over time, and every group has the right to persuade its fellow citizens that its view of such matters is the best. That homosexuals have achieved some success in that enterprise is attested to by the fact that Texas is one of the few remaining States that criminalize private, consensual homosexual acts. But persuading one's fellow citizens is one thing, and imposing one's views in absence of democratic majority will is something else. I would no more *require* a State to criminalize homosexual acts—or, for that matter, display *any* moral disapprobation of them—than I would *forbid* it to do so. What Texas has chosen to do is well within the range of traditional democratic action, and its hand should not be stayed through the invention of a brand-new "constitutional right" by a Court that is impatient of democratic change. It is indeed true that "later generations can see that laws once thought necessary and proper in fact serve only to oppress," *ante,* at 2484; and when that happens, later generations can repeal those laws. But it is the premise of our system that those judgments are to be made by the people, and not imposed by a governing caste that knows best.

One of the benefits of leaving regulation of this matter to the people rather than to the courts is that the people, unlike judges, need not carry things to their logical conclusion. The people may feel that their disapprobation of homosexual conduct is strong enough to disallow homosexual marriage, but not strong enough to criminalize private homosexual acts—and may legislate accordingly. The Court today pretends that it possesses a similar freedom of action, so that that we need not fear judicial imposition of homosexual marriage, as has recently occurred in Canada (in a decision that the Canadian Government has chosen not to appeal). See *Halpern v. Toronto,* 2003 WL 34950 (Ontario Ct.App.); Cohen, Dozens in Canada Follow Gay Couple's Lead, Washington Post, June 12, 2003, p. A25. At the end of its opinion—after having laid waste the foundations of our rational-basis jurisprudence—the Court says that the present case "does not involve whether the government must give formal recognition to any relationship that homosexual persons seek to enter." *Ante,* at 2484. Do not believe it. More illuminating than this bald, unreasoned disclaimer is the progression of thought displayed by an earlier passage in the Court's opinion, which notes the constitutional protections afforded to "personal decisions relating to *marriage,* procreation, contraception, family relationships, child rearing, and education," and then declares that "[p]ersons in a homosexual relationship may seek autonomy for these purposes, just as heterosexual persons do." *Ante,* at 2482 (emphasis added). Today's opinion dismantles the structure of constitutional law that has permitted a distinction to be made between heterosexual and homosexual unions, insofar as formal recognition in marriage is concerned. If moral disapprobation of homosexual conduct is "no legitimate state interest" for purposes of proscribing that conduct, *ante,* at 2484; and if, as the Court coos (casting aside all pretense of neutrality), "[w]hen sexuality finds overt expression in intimate conduct with another person, the conduct can be but one element in a personal bond that is more enduring," *ante,* at 2478; what justification could there possibly be for denying the benefits of marriage to homosexual couples exercising "[t]he liberty protected by the Constitution," *ibid.*? Surely not the encouragement of procreation, since the sterile and the elderly are allowed to marry. This case "does not involve" the issue of homosexual marriage only if one entertains the belief that principle and logic have nothing to do with the decisions of this Court. Many will hope that, as the Court comfortingly assures us, this is so.

The matters appropriate for this Court's resolution are only three: Texas's prohibition of sodomy neither infringes a "fundamental right" (which the Court does not dispute), nor is unsupported by a rational relation to what the Constitution considers a legitimate state interest, nor denies the equal protection of the laws. I dissent.

■ JUSTICE THOMAS, dissenting.

I join Justice SCALIA's dissenting opinion. I write separately to note that the law before the Court today "is . . . uncommonly silly." *Griswold v. Connecticut,* 381 U.S. 479, 527, 85 S.Ct. 1678, 14 L.Ed.2d 510 (1965) (Stewart, J., dissenting). If I were a member of the Texas Legislature, I would vote to repeal it. Punishing someone for expressing his sexual preference through noncommercial consensual conduct with another adult does not appear to be a worthy way to expend valuable law enforcement resources.

Notwithstanding this, I recognize that as a member of this Court I am not empowered to help petitioners and others similarly situated. My duty, rather, is to "decide cases 'agreeably to the Constitution and laws of the United States.' " *Id.,* at 530, 85 S.Ct. 1678. And, just like Justice Stewart, I "can find [neither in the Bill of Rights nor any other part of the Constitution a] general right of privacy," *ibid.,* or as the Court terms it today, the "liberty of the person both in its spatial and more transcendent dimensions," *ante,* at 2475.

NOTES

Justice Kennedy's opinion in *Lawrence* effectively overruled any state criminal sanctions, such as for sodomy, which could be brought against same-sex adults engaging in sexual activity. *Lawrence* effectively overruled the 1984 decision of *Bowers*, but because the decision utilizes an expansive definition of liberty, it provides the basis for the eventual recognition of same-sex marriage in 2015. *See* Obergefell v. Hodges, 135 S.Ct. 2584 (2015): "[T]he right to marry is a fundamental right inherent in the liberty of the person, and under the Due Process and Equal Protection Clauses of the Fourteenth Amendment couples of the same-sex may not be deprived of that right and that liberty." *Id.* at 22. It is arguable that Justice Kennedy's majority decision in *Lawrence* is the basis for his majority decision in *Obergefell.* For commentary on what is meant by liberty as utilized by *Lawrence* and *Obergefell, see* Melissa Murray, Essay, *Rights and Regulation: The Evolution of Sexual Regulation*, 116 COLUM. L. REV. 573 (2016); Ronald Turner, *Marriage Equality and Obergefell's Generational (Not Glucksberg's Traditional) Due Process Clause*, 23 DUKE J. GENDER L. & POL'Y 145 (2016); Kenji Yoshino, *A New Birth of Freedom?:* Obergefell v. Hodges, 129 HARV. L. REV. 147 (2015).

4. EQUAL PROTECTION

Loving v. Virginia

Supreme Court of the United States, 1967
388 U.S. 1

■ MR. CHIEF JUSTICE WARREN delivered the opinion of the Court.

This case presents a constitutional question never addressed by this Court: whether a statutory scheme adopted by the State of Virginia to prevent marriages between persons solely on the basis of racial classifications violates the Equal Protection and Due Process Clauses of the Fourteenth Amendment. For reasons which seem to us to reflect the central meaning of those constitutional commands, we conclude that these statutes cannot stand consistently with the Fourteenth Amendment.

In June 1958, two residents of Virginia, Mildred Jeter, a Negro woman, and Richard Loving, a white man, were married in the District of Columbia pursuant to its laws. Shortly after their marriage, the Lovings returned to Virginia and established their marital abode in Caroline County. At the October Term, 1958, of the Circuit Court of Caroline County, a grand jury issued an indictment charging the Lovings with violating Virginia's ban on interracial marriages. On January 6, 1959, the Lovings pleaded guilty to the charge and were sentenced to one year in jail; however, the trial judge suspended the sentence for a period of 25 years on the condition that the Lovings leave the State and not return to Virginia together for 25 years. . . .

After their convictions, the Lovings took up residence in the District of Columbia. On November 6, 1963, they filed a motion in the state trial court to vacate the judgment and set aside the sentence on the ground that the statutes which they had violated were repugnant to the Fourteenth Amendment. The motion not having been decided by October 28, 1964, the Lovings instituted a class action in the United States District Court for the Eastern District of Virginia requesting that a three-judge court be convened to declare the Virginia antimiscegenation statutes unconstitutional and to enjoin state officials from enforcing their convictions. On January 22, 1965, the state trial judge denied the motion to vacate the sentences, and the Lovings perfected an appeal to the Supreme Court of Appeals of Virginia. On February 11, 1965, the three-judge District Court continued the case to allow the Lovings to present their constitutional claims to the highest state court.

The Supreme Court of Appeals upheld the constitutionality of the antimiscegenation statutes and, after modifying the sentence, affirmed the convictions.[2] The Lovings appealed this decision. . . .

---

[2] 206 Va. 924, 147 S.E.2d 78 (1966).

The two statutes under which appellants were convicted and sentenced are part of a comprehensive statutory scheme aimed at prohibiting and punishing interracial marriages. The Lovings were convicted of violating § 20–58 of the Virginia Code:

> "*Leaving State to evade law.*—If any white person and colored person shall go out of this State, for the purpose of being married, and with the intention of returning, and be married out of it, and afterwards return to and reside in it, cohabiting as man and wife, they shall be punished as provided in § 20–59, and the marriage shall be governed by the same law as if it had been solemnized in this State. The fact of their cohabitation here as man and wife shall be evidence of their marriage."

Section 20–59, which defines the penalty for miscegenation, provides:

> "*Punishment for marriage.*—If any white person intermarry with a colored person, or any colored person intermarry with a white person, he shall be guilty of a felony and shall be punished by confinement in the penitentiary for not less than one nor more than five years."

Other central provisions in the Virginia statutory scheme are § 20–57, which automatically voids all marriages between "a white person and a colored person" without any judicial proceeding, and §§ 20–54 and 1–14 which, respectively, define "white persons" and "colored persons and Indians" for purposes of the statutory prohibitions.[4] The Lovings have never disputed in the course of this litigation that Mrs. Loving is a "colored person" or that Mr. Loving is a "white person" within the meanings given those terms by the Virginia statutes.

---

[4] Section 20–54 of the Virginia Code provides:

> "Intermarriage prohibited; meaning of term 'white persons.'—It shall hereafter be unlawful for any white person in this State to marry any save a white person, or a person with no other admixture of blood than white and American Indian. For the purpose of this chapter, the term 'white person' shall apply only to such person as has no trace whatever of any blood other than Caucasian; but persons who have one-sixteenth or less of the blood of the American Indian and have no other non-Caucasic blood shall be deemed to be white persons. All laws heretofore passed and now in effect regarding the intermarriage of white and colored persons shall apply to marriages prohibited by this chapter." Va.Code Ann. § 20–54 (1960 Repl.Vol.).

The exception for persons with less than one-sixteenth "of the blood of the American Indian" is apparently accounted for, in the words of a tract issued by the Registrar of the State Bureau of Vital Statistics, by "the desire of all to recognize as an integral and honored part of the white race the descendants of John Rolfe and Pocahontas. . . ." Plecker, The New Family and Race Improvement, 17 Va.Health Bull., Extra No. 12, at 25–26 (New Family Series No. 5, 1925), cited in Wadlington, The Loving Case; Virginia's AntiBMiscegenation Statute in Historical Perspective, 52 Va.L.Rev. 1189, 1202, n. 93 (1966).

Section 1–14 of the Virginia Code provides:

> "Colored persons and Indians defined. Every person in whom there is ascertainable any Negro blood shall be deemed and taken to be a colored person, and every person not a colored person having one fourth or more of American Indian blood shall be deemed an American Indian; except that members of Indian tribes existing in this Commonwealth having one fourth or more of Indian blood and less than one sixteenth of Negro blood shall be deemed tribal Indians." Va.Code Ann. § 1–14 (1960 Repl.Vol.).

Virginia is now one of 16 States which prohibit and punish marriages on the basis of racial classifications. Penalties for miscegenation arose as an incident to slavery and have been common in Virginia since the colonial period. The present statutory scheme dates from the adoption of the Racial Integrity Act of 1924, passed during the period of extreme nativism which followed the end of the First World War. The central features of this Act, and current Virginia law, are the absolute prohibition of a "white person" marrying other than another "white person," a prohibition against issuing marriage licenses until the issuing official is satisfied that the applicants' statements as to their race are correct, certificates of "racial composition" to be kept by both local and state registrars, and the carrying forward of earlier prohibitions against racial intermarriage.

In upholding the constitutionality of these provisions in the decision below, the Supreme Court of Appeals of Virginia referred to its 1955 decision in Naim v. Naim, 197 Va. 80, 87 S.E.2d 749, as stating the reasons supporting the validity of these laws. In *Naim*, the state court concluded that the State's legitimate purposes were "to preserve the racial integrity of its citizens," and to prevent "the corruption of blood," "a mongrel breed of citizens," and "the obliteration of racial pride," obviously an endorsement of the doctrine of White Supremacy. Id., at 90, 87 S.E.2d at 756. The court also reasoned that marriage has traditionally been subject to state regulation without federal intervention, and, consequently, the regulation of marriage should be left to exclusive state control by the Tenth Amendment.

While the state court is no doubt correct in asserting that marriage is a social relation subject to the State's police power, Maynard v. Hill, 125 U.S. 190, 8 S.Ct. 723, 31 L.Ed. 654 (1888), the State does not contend in its argument before this Court that its powers to regulate marriage are unlimited notwithstanding the commands of the Fourteenth Amendment. Nor could it do so in light of Meyer v. State of Nebraska, 262 U.S. 390, 43 S.Ct. 625, 67 L.Ed. 1042 (1923), and Skinner v. State of Oklahoma, 316 U.S. 535, 62 S.Ct. 1110, 86 L.Ed. 1655 (1942). Instead, the State argues that the meaning of the Equal Protection Clause, as illuminated by the statements of the Framers, is only that state penal laws containing an interracial element as part of the definition of the offense must apply equally to whites and Negroes in the sense that members of each race are punished to the same degree. Thus, the State contends that, because its miscegenation statutes punish equally both the white and the Negro participants in an interracial marriage, these statutes, despite their reliance on racial classifications do not constitute an invidious discrimination based upon race. The second argument advanced by the State assumes the validity of its equal application theory. The argument is that, if the Equal Protection Clause does not outlaw miscegenation statutes because of their reliance on racial classifications, the question of constitutionality would thus become whether there was any rational basis for a State to treat interracial marriages differently from other marriages. On this question, the State argues, the scientific evidence is substantially in doubt and, consequently, this Court should defer to the wisdom of the state legislature in adopting its policy of discouraging interracial marriages.

Because we reject the notion that the mere "equal application" of a statute containing racial classifications is enough to remove the classifications from the Fourteenth Amendment's proscription of all invidious racial discriminations, we do not accept the State's contention that these statutes should be upheld if there is any possible basis for concluding that they serve a rational purpose. . . .

There can be no question but that Virginia's miscegenation statutes rest solely upon distinctions drawn according to race. The statutes proscribe generally accepted conduct if engaged in by members of different races. Over the years, this Court has consistently repudiated "[d]istinctions between citizens solely because of their ancestry" as being "odious to a free people whose institutions are founded upon the doctrine of equality." Hirabayashi v. United States, 320 U.S. 81, 100, 63 S.Ct. 1375, 1385, 87 L.Ed. 1774 (1943). At the very least, the Equal Protection Clause demands that racial classifications, especially suspect in criminal statutes, be subjected to the "most rigid scrutiny," Korematsu v. United States, 323 U.S. 214, 216, 65 S.Ct. 193, 194, 89 L.Ed. 194 (1944), and, if they are ever to be upheld, they must be shown to be necessary to the accomplishment of some permissible state objective, independent of the racial discrimination which it was the object of the Fourteenth Amendment to eliminate. . . .

There is patently no legitimate overriding purpose independent of invidious racial discrimination which justifies this classification. The fact that Virginia prohibits only interracial marriages involving white persons demonstrates that the racial classifications must stand on their own justification, as measures designed to maintain White Supremacy.[11] We have consistently denied the constitutionality of measures which restrict the rights of citizens on account of race. There can be no doubt that restricting the freedom to marry solely because of racial classifications violates the central meaning of the Equal Protection Clause.

These statutes also deprive the Lovings of liberty without due process of law in violation of the Due Process Clause of the Fourteenth

11 Appellants point out that the State's concern in these statutes, as expressed in the words of the 1924 Act's title, "An Act to Preserve Racial Integrity," extends only to the integrity of the white race. While Virginia prohibits whites from marrying any nonwhite (subject to the exception for the descendants of Pocahontas), Negroes, Orientals, and any other racial class may intermarry without statutory interference. Appellants contend that this distinction renders Virginia's miscegenation statutes arbitrary and unreasonable even assuming the constitutional validity of an official purpose to preserve "racial integrity." We need not reach this contention because we find the racial classifications in these statutes repugnant to the Fourteenth Amendment, even assuming an even-handed state purpose to protect the "integrity" of all races.

Amendment. The freedom to marry has long been recognized as one of the vital personal rights essential to the orderly pursuit of happiness by free men.

Marriage is one of the "basic civil rights of man," fundamental to our very existence and survival. Skinner v. State of Oklahoma, 316 U.S. 535, 541, 62 S.Ct. 1110, 1113, 86 L.Ed. 1655 (1942). To deny this fundamental freedom on so unsupportable a basis as the racial classifications embodied in these statutes, classifications so directly subversive of the principle of equality at the heart of the Fourteenth Amendment, is surely to deprive all the State's citizens of liberty without due process of law. The Fourteenth Amendment requires that the freedom of choice to marry not be restricted by invidious racial discriminations. Under our Constitution, the freedom to marry or not marry, a person of another race resides with the individual and cannot be infringed by the State. . . .

5. DUE PROCESS OF LAW

Zablocki v. Redhail

Supreme Court of the United States, 1978
434 U.S. 374

■ MARSHALL, JUSTICE delivered the opinion of the Court.

At issue in this case is the constitutionality of a Wisconsin statute, Wis.Stat. §§ 245.10(1), (4), (5) (1973), which provides that members of a certain class of Wisconsin residents may not marry, within the State or elsewhere, without first obtaining a court order granting permission to marry. The class is defined by the statute to include any "Wisconsin resident having minor issue not in his custody and which he is under an obligation to support by any court order or judgment." The statute specifies that court permission cannot be granted unless the marriage applicant submits proof of compliance with the support obligation and, in addition, demonstrates that the children covered by the support order "are not then and are not likely thereafter to become public charges." No marriage license may lawfully be issued in Wisconsin to a person covered by the statute, except upon court order; any marriage entered into without compliance with § 245.10 is declared void; and persons acquiring marriage licenses in violation of the section are subject to criminal penalties. . . .

Appellee Redhail is a Wisconsin resident who, under the terms of § 245.10, is unable to enter into a lawful marriage in Wisconsin or elsewhere so long as he maintains his Wisconsin residency. The facts, according to the stipulation filed by the parties in the District Court, are as follows. In January 1972, when appellee was a minor and a high school student, a paternity action was instituted against him in Milwaukee County Court, alleging that he was the father of a baby girl born out of wedlock on July 5, 1971. After he appeared and admitted that he was the child's father, the court entered an order on May 12, 1972, adjudging appellee the father and ordering him to pay $109 per month as support for the child until she reached 18 years of age. From May 1972 until August 1974, appellee was unemployed and indigent, and consequently was unable to make any support payments.

On September 27, 1974, appellee filed an application for a marriage license with appellant Zablocki, the County Clerk of Milwaukee County, and a few days later the application was denied on the sole ground that appellee had not obtained a court order granting him permission to marry, as required by § 245.10. Although appellee did not petition a state court thereafter, it is stipulated that he would not have been able to satisfy either of the statutory prerequisites for an order granting permission to marry. First, he had not satisfied his support obligations to his illegitimate child, and as of December 1974 there was an arrearage in excess of $3,700. Second, the child had been a public charge since her birth, receiving benefits under the Aid to Families with Dependent Children program. It is stipulated that the child's benefit payments were such that she would have been a public charge even if appellee had been current in his support payments. . . .

The leading decision of this Court on the right to marry is Loving v. Virginia, 388 U.S. 1 (1967). In that case, an interracial couple who had been convicted of violating Virginia's miscegenation laws challenged the statutory scheme on both equal protection and due process grounds. The Court's opinion could have rested solely on the ground that the statutes discriminated on the basis of race in violation of the Equal Protection Clause. But the Court went on to hold that the laws arbitrarily deprived the couple of a fundamental liberty protected by the Due Process Clause, the freedom to marry. . . .

[R]ecent decisions have established that the right to marry is part of the fundamental "right of privacy" implicit in the Fourteenth Amendment's Due Process Clause. . . .*

It is not surprising that the decision to marry has been placed on the same level of importance as decisions relating to procreation, childbirth, child-rearing, and family relationships. As the facts of this case illustrate, it would make little sense to recognize a right of privacy with respect to other matters of family life and not with respect to the decision to enter the relationship that is the foundation of the family in our society. The woman whom appellee desired to marry had a fundamental right to seek an abortion of their expected child, see Roe v. Wade, supra, or to bring the child into life to suffer the myriad social, if not economic, disabilities that the status of illegitimacy brings, see Trimble v. Gordon, 430 U.S. 762, 768–770, and n. 13 (1977); Weber v. Aetna Casualty & Surety Co., 406 U.S. 164, 175–176 (1972). Surely, a decision to marry and raise the child in a traditional family setting must receive equivalent

* [The opinion quotes from Griswold v. Connecticut, 381 U.S. 479, 486 (1965).—*EDS.*]

protection. And, if appellee's right to procreate means anything at all, it must imply some right to enter the only relationship in which the State of Wisconsin allows sexual relations legally to take place.[11]

By reaffirming the fundamental character of the right to marry, we do not mean to suggest that every state regulation which relates in any way to the incidents of or prerequisites for marriage must be subjected to rigorous scrutiny. To the contrary, reasonable regulations that do not significantly interfere with decisions to enter into the marital relationship may legitimately be imposed. The statutory classification at issue here, however, clearly does interfere directly and substantially with the right to marry.

Under the challenged statute, no Wisconsin resident in the affected class may marry in Wisconsin or elsewhere without a court order, and marriages contracted in violation of the statute are both void and punishable as criminal offenses. Some of those in the affected class, like appellee, will never be able to obtain the necessary court order, because they either lack the financial means to meet their support obligations or cannot prove that their children will not become public charges. These persons are absolutely prevented from getting married. Many others, able in theory to satisfy the statute's requirements, will be sufficiently burdened by having to do so that they will in effect be coerced into foregoing their right to marry. And even those who can be persuaded to meet the statute's requirements suffer a serious intrusion into their freedom of choice in an area in which we have held such freedom to be fundamental.

When a statutory classification significantly interferes with the exercise of a fundamental right, it cannot be upheld unless it is supported by sufficiently important state interests and is closely tailored to effectuate only those interests. . . . Appellant asserts that two interests are served by the challenged statute: the permission-to-marry proceeding furnishes an opportunity to counsel the applicant as to the necessity of fulfilling his prior support obligations; and the welfare of the out-of-custody children is protected. We may accept for present purposes that these are legitimate and substantial interests, but, since the means selected by the State for achieving these interests unnecessarily impinge on the right to marry, the statute cannot be sustained.

There is evidence that the challenged statute, as originally introduced in the Wisconsin Legislature, was intended merely to establish a mechanism whereby persons with support obligations to children from prior marriages could be counselled before they entered into new marital relationships and incurred further support obligations. Court permission to marry was to be required, but apparently permission was automatically to be granted after counselling was completed. The

---

[11] Wisconsin punishes fornication as a criminal offense:

"Whoever has sexual intercourse with a person not his spouse may be fined not more than $200 or imprisoned not more than 6 months or both." Wis.Stat. § 944.15 (1973).

statute actually enacted, however, does not expressly require or provide for any counselling whatsoever, nor for any automatic granting of permission to marry by the court, and thus it can hardly be justified as a means for ensuring counselling of the persons within its coverage. Even assuming that counselling does take place—a fact as to which there is no evidence in the record—this interest obviously cannot support the withholding of court permission to marry once counselling is completed.

With regard to safeguarding the welfare of the out-of-custody children, appellant's brief does not make clear the connection between the State's interest and the statute's requirements. At argument, appellant's counsel suggested that, since permission to marry cannot be granted unless the applicant shows that he has satisfied his court-determined support obligations to the prior children and that those children will not become public charges, the statute provides incentive for the applicant to make support payments to his children. This "collection device" rationale cannot justify the statute's broad infringement on the right to marry.

First, with respect to individuals who are unable to meet the statutory requirements, the statute merely prevents the applicant from getting married, without delivering any money at all into the hands of the applicant's prior children. More importantly, regardless of the applicant's ability or willingness to meet the statutory requirements, the State already has numerous other means for exacting compliance with support obligations, means that are at least as effective as the instant statute's and yet do not impinge upon the right to marry. Under Wisconsin law, whether the children are from a prior marriage or were born out of wedlock, court-determined support obligations may be enforced directly via wage assignments, civil contempt proceedings, and criminal penalties. And, if the State believes that parents of children out of their custody should be responsible for ensuring that those children do not become public charges, this interest can be achieved by adjusting the criteria used for determining the amounts to be paid under their support orders.

There is also some suggestion that § 245.10 protects the ability of marriage applicants to meet support obligations to prior children by preventing the applicants from incurring new support obligations. But the challenged provisions of § 245.10 are grossly underinclusive with respect to this purpose, since they do not limit in any way new financial commitments by the applicant other than those arising out of the contemplated marriage. The statutory classification is substantially overinclusive as well: given the possibility that the new spouse will actually better the applicant's financial situation, by contributing income from a job or otherwise, the statute in many cases may prevent affected individuals from improving their ability to satisfy their prior support obligations. And, although it is true that the applicant will incur support obligations to any children born during the contemplated marriage, preventing the marriage may only result in the children being born out of wedlock, as in fact occurred in appellee's case. Since the support obligation is the same whether the child is born in or out of wedlock, the net result of preventing the marriage is simply more illegitimate children.

The statutory classification created by § 245.101(1), (4), (5) thus cannot be justified by the interests advanced in support of it. The judgment of the District Court is, accordingly,

Affirmed.

■ POWELL, JUSTICE concurring in the judgment.

I concur in the judgment of the Court that Wisconsin's restrictions . . . cannot meet applicable constitutional standards. I write separately because the majority's rationale sweeps too broadly in an area which traditionally has been subject to pervasive state regulation. The Court apparently would subject all state regulation which "directly and substantially" interferes with the decision to marry in a traditional family setting to "critical examination" or "compelling state interest" analysis. Presumably, "reasonable regulations that do not significantly interfere with the decision to enter into the marital relationship may legitimately be imposed." The Court does not present, however, any principled means for distinguishing between the two types of regulations. Since state regulation in this area typically takes the form of a prerequisite or barrier to marriage or divorce, the degree of "direct" interference with the decision to marry or to divorce is unlikely to provide either guidance for state legislatures or a basis for judicial oversight. . . .

[I]t is fair to say that there is a right of marital and familial privacy which places some substantive limits on the regulatory power of government. But the Court has yet to hold that all regulation touching upon marriage implicates a "fundamental right" triggering the most exacting judicial scrutiny. . . .

[Noting that Loving v. Virginia is the principal authority cited by the majority, the opinion explains that because of the issue of racial discrimination] *Loving* involved a denial of a "fundamental freedom" on a wholly unsupportable basis—the use of classifications "directly subversive of the principle of equality at the heart of the Fourteenth Amendment. . . ." It does not speak to the level of judicial scrutiny of, or governmental justification for, "supportable" restrictions on the "fundamental freedom" of individuals to marry or divorce.

In my view, analysis must start from the recognition of domestic relations as "an area that has long been regarded as a virtually exclusive province of the States." Sosna v. Iowa, 419 U.S. 393, 404 (1975). The marriage relation traditionally has been subject to regulation, initially by the ecclesiastical authorities, and later by the secular state. As early as Pennoyer v. Neff, 95 U.S. 714, 734–735 (1877), this Court noted that a State "has absolute right to prescribe the conditions upon which the marriage relation between its own citizens shall be created, and the causes for which it may be dissolved." The State, representing the collective expression of moral aspirations, has an undeniable interest in ensuring that its rules of domestic relations reflect the widely held values of its people. . . .

State regulation has included bans on incest, bigamy, and homosexuality, as well as various preconditions to marriage, such as blood tests. Likewise, a showing of fault on the part of one of the partners traditionally has been a prerequisite to the dissolution of an unsuccessful union. A "compelling state purpose" inquiry would cast doubt on the network of restrictions that the States have fashioned to govern marriage and divorce.

State power over domestic relations is not without constitutional limits. The Due Process Clause requires a showing of justification "when the government intrudes on choices concerning family living arrangements" in a manner which is contrary to deeply rooted traditions. Moore v. City of East Cleveland, Ohio, 431 U.S. 494, 499, 503–504 (1977) (plurality opinion). Due process constraints also limit the extent to which the State may monopolize the process of ordering certain human relationships while excluding the truly indigent from that process. Boddie v. Connecticut, 401 U.S. 371 (1971). Furthermore, under the Equal Protection Clause the means chosen by the State in this case must bear "a fair and substantial relation" to the object of the legislation.

The Wisconsin measure in this case does not pass muster under either due process or equal protection standards. Appellant identifies three objectives which are supposedly furthered by the statute in question: (i) a counseling function; (ii) an incentive to satisfy outstanding support obligations; and (iii) a deterrent against incurring further obligations. The opinion of the Court amply demonstrates that the asserted counseling objective bears no relation to this statute. . . .

The so-called "collection device" rationale presents a somewhat more difficult question. I do not agree with the suggestion in the Court's opinion that a State may never condition the right to marry on satisfaction of existing support obligations simply because the State has alternative methods of compelling such payments. To the extent this restriction applies to persons who are able to make the required support payments but simply wish to shirk their moral and legal obligation, the Constitution interposes no bar to this additional collection mechanism. The vice inheres not in the collection concept, but in the failure to make provision for those without the means to comply with child support obligations. I draw support from Justice Harlan's opinion in Boddie v. Connecticut. In that case, the Court struck down filing fees for divorce actions as applied to those wholly unable to pay, holding "that a State may not, consistent with the obligations imposed on it by the Due Process Clause of the Fourteenth Amendment, preempt the right to dissolve this legal relationship without affording all citizens access to the means it has prescribed for doing so." 401 U.S. at 383. The monopolization present in this case is total, for Wisconsin will not recognize foreign marriages that fail to conform to the requirements of § 245.10.

The third justification, only obliquely advanced by appellant, is that the statute preserves the ability of marriage applicants to support their prior issue by preventing them from incurring new obligations. The challenged provisions of § 245.10 are so grossly underinclusive with respect to this objective, given the many ways that additional financial obligations may be incurred by the applicant quite apart from a contemplated marriage, that the classification "does not bear a fair and substantial relation to the object of the legislation." Craig v. Boren, 429 U.S., at 211 (Powell, J., concurring). . . .

■ [The concurring opinions of CHIEF JUSTICE BURGER, JUSTICES STEWART, and STEVENS, and the dissent of JUSTICE REHNQUIST, have been omitted.]

NOTES

Is there really a fundamental right to marry? Is it "implicit in the concept of ordered liberty"? *See* Palko v. State of Connecticut, 302 U.S. 319, 325, 58 S.Ct. 149, 82 L.Ed. 288 (1937). Note the cautionary language in the concurring opinion of Justice Powell in *Zablocki* that "A 'compelling state purpose' inquiry would cast doubt on the network of restrictions that the States have fashioned to govern marriage and divorce." But the Court has said that "marriage involves interests of basic importance in our society", Boddie v. Connecticut, 401 U.S. 371, 376, 91 S.Ct. 780, 28 L.Ed.2d 113 (1971); has pointed to "the favored treatment of marriages", Califano v. Jobst, 434 U.S. 47, 58, 98 S.Ct. 95, 54 L.Ed.2d 228 (1977); and has given "categorical preference" to marriage (Michael H. v. Gerald D., 491 U.S. 110, 129, 109 S.Ct. 2333, 105 L.Ed.2d 91 (1989)). Of course the Court in Loving v. Virginia, 388 U.S. 1, 12, 87 S.Ct. 1817, 18 L.Ed.2d 1010 (1967), stated that "marriage is one of the 'basic civil rights of man', fundamental to our very existence and survival. . . ." If marriage is a fundamental right, is it so because marriage has as its traditional purpose the procreation and raising of children? And the Court also stated that "Marriage responds to the universal fear that a lonely person might call out only to find no one there. It offers the hope of companionship and understanding and assurance that while both still live there be someone to care for the other." Obergefell v. Hodges, 135 S.Ct. 2584 (2015).

In *The Right to Marry and Divorce: A New Look At Some Unanswered Questions*, 63 WASH. U. L.Q. 577 (1985), Professor Cathy Jones examined prevalent restrictions on marriage and concluded that most or all would fail a true "fundamental rights/strict scrutiny" approach. However, she suggests several ways in which courts might interpret or apply *Zablocki* to avoid upsetting "economic or moral reality."

CHAPTER II

GETTING MARRIED

A. INTRODUCTION

Entry into the status of marriage, dissolution of marriage through divorce, and recognition of foreign marriages remains subject to the laws and public policies of individual states. This state sovereignty is illustrated by state laws pertaining to the age of consent to marry, incest prohibitions, the necessity and qualifications pertaining to solemnization requirements, blood and premarital counseling requirements, and whether invalid or void marriages may be ratified. Entering into a valid marriage prompts significant state and federal benefits. Among these are inheritance rights, taxation benefits, social security benefits, obligations for support and division of property, and priority when making decisions for the other spouse. Federal involvement in state marriage laws has been restrained, unlike more aggressive federal initiatives pertaining to child custody and support, domestic violence, and efforts to promote parent-child reunification when there has been sufficient grounds to prompt removing of a child from the custody of a parent.

Some state marriage laws have prompted challenges based on the Constitution of the United States. For example, when a few states prohibited interracial marriages, the Supreme Court of the United States held that the prohibition violated Equal Protection. *See* Loving v. Virginia, 388 U.S. 1 (1967). Also, when a state prohibited a marriage license being issued to an applicant with a history of child support arrears, the Court held that the prohibition violated Due Process. *See* Zablocki v. Redhail, 434 U.S. 374 (1978). And finally, when states prohibited persons of the same sex to marry, or refused to recognize same-sex marriages celebrated in other states, the Court held that the prohibition violated fundamental liberties protected by the Fourteenth Amendment's Due Process Clause. *See* Obergefell v. Hodges, 135 S.Ct. 2584 (2015).

There has been a steady decline in the percentage of the population of the United States entering into marriage. Between 1867 and 1967, the annual marriage rate changed very little: 0.96% of the population married in 1867 and 0.97% in 1967. Lawrence W. Waggoner, *With Marriage on the Decline and Cohabitation on the Rise, What About Marital Rights for Unmarried Partners?*, 41 ACTEC L. J. 49 (2015). But by the year 2000 the marriage rate had declined to 0.82%, and the rate continued to decline, reaching an historic low of slightly less than 0.68% in 2009. *Id.* From 2009 to 2012, the marriage rate stabilized at that historically low rate of slightly less than 0.68%. *Id.* As the marriage rate has declined, the rate of cohabitation has risen. The number of unmarried cohabiting partners grew 41% between 2000 and 2010. *Id.* at 53.

The status of marriage will continue. But in a society characterized by mobility, individuality, and greater prosperity, there are alternatives to marriage that may offer an increasing array of benefits.

B. COURTSHIP AND THE MARRIAGE PROMISE

Legal regulation of the parties' conduct during "courtship" once took a number of forms: (1) attempts at enforcing a promise to marry through a mélange of tort, contract, or penal sanctions; (2) tort actions for seduction between unmarried adults who engage in sexual intercourse; and (3) rules and principles for deciding ownership of property transferred in contemplation of marriages that did not take place.

Today, "heartbalm" actions for breach of the promise to marry and seduction have been largely abolished, although actions to recover gifts in contemplation of marriage have not.

1. ENFORCING A PROMISE TO MARRY

As the United States Court of Appeals for the Seventh Circuit noted in Wildey v. Springs, 47 F.3d 1475 (7th Cir. 1995):

> The action for the breach of a promise to marry is of antique vintage. First conceived as a creature of the English ecclesiastical courts, the action was originally used to pressure a reluctant lover into fulfilling a marital promise. W.J. Brockelbank, *The Nature of the Promise to Marry—A Study in Comparative Law*, 41 ILL. L. REV. 1, 3 (1946); Michael Grossberg, Governing the Hearth: Law and the Family in Nineteenth-Century America 34 (1985). The common law eventually adopted the action, however, and permitted the recovery of monetary damages. Although developed by English courts, the action found its way into the American colonies and was later used by post-revolutionary American lawyers.
>
> The action served dual ideals in colonial America. On the one hand, a breach of promise action continued to appeal to vestiges of the older notion that marriage was a property transaction completed after complex family negotiations. Grossberg, *supra*, at 35. But on the other hand, the action began to pay tribute to the emerging ideal that marriage was a sacred contract premised upon affection and emotional commitment. Id. The suits soon became utilized almost universally by women, and were justified by lawmakers largely on these grounds. Id. at 37. Marriage was considered necessary to secure both a woman's social and financial security. Margaret F. Brinig, *Rings and Promises*, 6 J. LAW, ECONOMICS, AND ORGANIZATION 203, 204–05 (1990). But more importantly, the actions, and the judges

> who were willing to enforce them, recognized that promises to marry sometimes occasioned a loss of virginity. Id. at 205. Because of the importance the society of that day placed on premarital chastity, the economic and social harm suffered by a jilted woman were often reflected in large damage awards. Id.
>
> The actions were characterized by a lack of legal formality peculiar for the law of that time. Foreign observers noted that, unlike wills or commercial contracts, little was needed to support an allegation that the parties had become engaged. Grossberg, *supra*, at 51. Consequently, appellate courts deferred widely to jury determinations in credibility contests. Id. at 49. Traditional rules relating to damages, too, were relaxed. Despite the originally contractual nature of the action, judges refused to confine the damage measure to immediate loss. Instead, they permitted recovery for elements such as mental anguish and a loss of social position. *Id.* at 43.
>
> Largely because of the perceived vagaries of the suits, the actions had fallen into disrepute by the early twentieth century. Three principal reasons are given for their decline in popularity. The first is the unfounded use of the suit, given the lax standards of proof, to extort out-of-court settlements. Brockelbank, *supra*, at 13; Note, *Heartbalm Statutes and Deceit Actions*, 83 MICH. L. REV. 1770, 1776 (1985). Second, the excessive damages awarded prompted disdain for the actions. Id. at 1774. Finally, the ideals that the action served came to be viewed as anachronistic. The greater social and economic freedom incident to women's entry into the workforce meant that the loss of an initial suitor posed a lower threat to future prospects than it might have in the nineteenth century. Grossberg, *supra*, at [55].

The court pointed out that "[a]s concerns grew, legislatures began to act." Today, most jurisdictions have abolished the action either by statute or jurisprudence, typically eliminating other "heart balm" actions as well. *See* Laura Belleau, *Farewell to Heart Balm Doctrines and the Tender Years Presumption, Hello to the Genderless Family*, 24 J. AM. ACAD. OF MATRIM. LAW 365, 375 (2012). New York Civil Rights Law §§ 80–84 (McKinney 2016) is one example of a broad abolition statute.

The cause of action continues in some states, but is sharply circumscribed. *See* T. Foster, Annotation, *Liability of One Putative Spouse to Other for Wrongfully Inducing Entry into Cohabitation Under Illegal, Void or Nonexistent Marriage* 72 A.L.R. 2d 956 (1960). Like many states, the Illinois legislature repealed its Breach of Promise Act, which allowed recovery only for actual damages and required notice to be given within three months from the date that the breach of promise occurred. 740 ILL. COMP. ST. § 15/0.01 et seq. (West 2014), repealed by P.A. 99–90, § 1–25, eff. Jan. 1, 2016. It was under that statute that the breach of promise action reached the courts in *Wildey, supra*. Although the lower court initially returned a verdict in favor of the plaintiff, this was reversed on appeal because her notice had not provided the defendant with the date on which the parties became engaged, as required in the Breach of Promise Act. *Id.* at § 15/4.

Possible defenses to an action for breach of promise to marry included: fraudulent misrepresentation or concealment, insanity at time of the engagement, development of certain serious illnesses or physical conditions, or that the plaintiff was married at the time of the engagement. For more on enforcement of promises to marry, *see* Kelsey M. May, Comment, *Bachelors Beware: The Current Validity and Future Feasibility of a Cause of Action for Breach of Promise to Marry*, 45 TULSA L. REV. 331 (2009).

Some lawyers faced with statutes and cases abolishing anti-heart balm actions attempted to pursue recovery for breaches of a promise to marry using other legal theories, with little success. The Supreme Judicial Court of Maine dismissed an action by parents of a minor to recover compensatory and punitive damages for defendant's breach of a promise to marry their minor daughter and for malicious and intentional infliction of mental suffering by plaintiffs resulting from the defendant's failure to seasonably inform them that he intended not to show for the wedding. The court concluded that the policy considerations barring actions for damages for breach of promise to marry in a suit based on fraud or deceit apply equally to an action for intentional infliction of mental distress resulting from the facts. Waddell v. Briggs, 381 A.2d 1132 (Me. 1978).

2. SEDUCTION

The common law tort of seduction has been abolished in nearly every jurisdiction. *See* Laura Belleau, *Farewell to Heart Balm Doctrines and the Tender Years Presumption, Hello to the Genderless Family*, 24 J. AM. ACAD. OF MATRIM. LAW 365, 373–74 (2012). Historically, the action centered on the element of fraud and was "actionable by a parent against an individual for violating their daughter's virginity. It was intended to recompense an aggrieved parent for the 'consequent degradation, mortification, and wounded feelings visited upon [the daughter] as well as upon her parents, stemming from the child's 'loss of chastity.' " C.M. v. J.M., 726 A.2d 998, 1001 (N.J.Sup. 1999). In Franklin v. Hill, 444 S.E.2d 778 (Ga. 1994), the Supreme Court of Georgia struck down as unconstitutional Georgia's statute giving parents a cause of action for seduction of their unmarried daughter. The statute violated the equal protection clause of the Georgia Constitution because only men could be civilly liable under the statute. Other courts have struck state laws as unconstitutional, albeit on slightly different grounds. In Edwards v. Moore, 699 So. 2d 220, 222–23 (Ala.App. 1997), the Court of Civil Appeals of Alabama held that:

> [e]ven assuming that the seduction statute was designed to redress "wrongful conduct inducing [the] loss of chastity by the female," including the "consequent degradation, mortification and wounded feelings visited upon her, as well as her parents," the statute is not substantially related to that governmental interest. The gender-based limitations of the statute ignore the same "degradation, mortification and wounded feelings" visited upon a daughter seduced by a woman—the emotional and physical consequences of such a seduction should arguably also be guarded against. [The statute] does not afford such protection and thereby discriminates, allowing only the prosecution of men. Based on the language, history, and judicial interpretation of the seduction statute's gender-based classification, we conclude that this classification does not bear a substantial relationship to any important governmental objective. . . . We decline to amend it to extend liability to women.

Some courts and legislatures allowed women to bring seduction actions in their own right for damages based on reputation loss, embarrassment, or other such harm. In a few jurisdictions today, only minor women or their parents are permitted to bring an action for seduction. *See* IND. CODE § 34–12–2–1(a)(4) (2016); L.N.K. ex rel. Kavanaugh v. St. Mary's Med. Ctr., 785 N.E.2d 303 (Ind. Ct. App. 2003).

3. GIFTS IN CONTEMPLATION OF MARRIAGE

Because anti-heart balm statutes limited claims for recovery for breach of the promise to marry, it was sometimes unclear whether one could recover property that was given in anticipation of marriage, like an engagement ring. Some legislatures eventually amended their anti-heartbalm statutes to explicitly permit recovery. New York Law provides:

NEW YORK CIVIL RIGHTS LAW (McKinney 2016)

§ 80–b. Gifts made in contemplation of marriage

> Nothing in this article contained shall be construed to bar a right of action for the recovery of a chattel, the return of money or securities, or the rescission of a deed to real property when the sole consideration for the transfer of the chattel, money or securities or real property was a contemplated marriage which has not occurred. . . .

In other jurisdictions, the question of recovery was resolved in the courts.

Vigil v. Haber

Supreme Court of New Mexico, 1994
888 P.2d 455

■ FRANCHINI, JUSTICE.

Glenn Haber appeals from an order adjudging that Haber's former fiancée, Jannel M. Vigil, should be given permanent possession of an engagement ring she received from Haber. We hold that the ring was a conditional gift dependent upon the parties' marriage, that the question of whose fault it was that the engagement was broken is irrelevant, and that therefore the ring should be returned to Haber. . . .

Haber and Vigil exchanged engagement rings in February 1992. Unfortunately, their relationship deteriorated and each accused the other of threats and assaults. In May 1992 the couple separated and Vigil filed for a temporary order of protection. A special hearing commissioner resolved all protection issues and determined that the parties should return the rings they had given to each other. Haber immediately returned the ring he had, along with some of Vigil's other possessions. At a later hearing, however, Vigil objected to returning the engagement ring Haber had given to her. The commissioner instructed the Santa Fe Police to hold the ring until the dispute was resolved and referred the matter to the district court. Haber filed a motion in district court for an order to release the ring to him. After a hearing, the court determined that Vigil canceled the wedding plans but that she justifiably did so because of Haber's misconduct. The court then ordered that Vigil should keep the ring because Haber caused the failure of the condition (marriage) upon which the gift was based. . . .

Determination of the ownership of an engagement gift does not require a finding of who caused breakup of the engagement. The issue raised in this case is one of first impression in New Mexico. In determining who should be granted possession of an engagement ring in cases in which the marriage has not occurred, courts in other states have used a rationale "based upon a contract theory, i.e., the ring is a symbol of an agreement to marry. If that agreement is not performed, then the parties should be restored to the status quo." Spinnell v. Quigley, 785 P.2d 1149, 1150 (Wash. App. 1990). Using a kind of equitable estoppel, some courts at common law have created a policy exception to the rule that engagement gifts should be returned. Under this exception, if the marriage is not finalized because the donor breached the marriage agreement, the donor may not benefit from his breach by regaining the ring given as an engagement gift. The rationale for the exception is that " '[n]o man should take advantage of his own wrong.' " Id. (quoting Mate v. Abrahams, 62 A.2d 754, 755 (N.J.1948)). The practice of determining possession based upon fault is the majority rule. Aronow v. Silver, 538 A.2d 851, 852 (N.J. Super. Ct. Ch. Div.1987). However, application of this rationale makes changing one's mind about the choice of a marriage partner legally wrong unless the court determines that the donor was justified in changing his or her mind.

Following a modern trend, legislatures and courts have moved toward a policy that removes fault-finding from the personal-relationship dynamics of marriage and divorce. New Mexico was the first state to legislatively recognize "no-fault" divorce. . . . When determining whether a divorce should be granted on grounds of incompatibility, fault is not relevant to the determination. . . . We agree with the court in Brown v. Thomas, 379 N.W.2d 868, 873 (Wisc. Ct. App. 1985), that the policy statements that govern "our approach to broken marriages [are] equally relevant to broken engagements." . . .

In *Gaden*, the court stated that the result of basing entitlement to keep engagement gifts on the fault of another would "encourage every disappointed donee to resist the return of engagement gifts by blaming the donor for the breakup of the contemplated marriage, thereby promoting dramatic courtroom accusations and counter-accusations of fault." Gaden v. Gaden, 272 N.E.2d 471, 476 (N.Y. 1971). That is exactly what happened in this case. In attempting to prove that her cancellation of the marriage was justified, Vigil introduced testimony that Haber had physically abused her. Haber testified that Vigil made her own contributions to the domestic conflict. The trial court stated that it would not find that one side was lying and one side was telling the truth, but ultimately determined that it was Haber's fault that the engagement was broken. The court applied the exception to the common-law principle that the parties should be returned to the status quo, but the court also ordered Vigil to pay to Haber the value of the ring Haber had returned to her, which was approximately $500.00.

We agree that "fault, in an engagement setting, cannot be ascertained," Aronow, 538 A.2d at 853, and follow the lead of Iowa, New Jersey, New York, and Wisconsin in holding that when the condition precedent of marriage fails, an engagement gift must be returned. . . .

It is uncontroverted that the engagement ring was given to Vigil on condition and in contemplation of marriage. The condition having failed, Haber is entitled to return of the ring and Vigil is not required to pay to Haber the value of the ring that he returned to her. The order of the trial court is vacated and we remand for entry of an order releasing the ring to Haber.

NOTES

In Heiman v. Parrish, 942 P.2d 631, 637 (Kan. 1997), the Supreme Court of Kansas emphasized how difficult it would be for courts to assess fault in determining whether engagement rings or other property should be returned:

> What is fault or the unjustifiable calling off of an engagement? By way of illustration, should courts be asked to determine which of

the following grounds for breaking an engagement is fault or justified? (1) The parties have nothing in common; (2) one party cannot stand prospective in-laws; (3) a minor child of one of the parties is hostile to and will not accept the other party; (4) an adult child of one of the parties will not accept the other party; (5) the parties' pets do not get along; (6) a party was too hasty in proposing or accepting the proposal; (7) the engagement was a rebound situation which is now regretted; (8) one party has untidy habits that irritate the other; or (9) the parties[ ] have religious differences. The list could be endless.

C. MARRIAGE PROCEDURES, FORMAL AND INFORMAL

The law in every state provides a formal route into marriage. Approximately a dozen states recognize informal, or "common law" marriage between parties who agree to be bound and hold themselves out as married without having complied with the formal statutory requirements for marriage. Some states permit proxy marriage, in which one party designates someone to stand-in for the absent party at the formal ceremony. Each of these routes to marriage results in equally valid marriages that would have to be dissolved or annulled in order to exit them.

1. INFORMAL OR "COMMON-LAW" MARRIAGE

Although most states have abolished common-law marriage by statute, ten states and the District of Columbia retain the status. The ten states are Alabama, Colorado, Iowa, Kansas, Montana, Oklahoma, Rhode Island, South Carolina, Texas, and Utah. In order to enter into a valid common-law marriage a couple, otherwise able to enter into marriage, must objectively hold themselves out as spouses for a period of time sufficient to allow for community recognition in a state that permits common-law marriage. Obviously, there is no license and there is no solemnization by a third person designated by the state. Once there is a common-law marriage it is entitled to all of the benefits of marriage, including recognition in another state unless contrary to that state's strong public policy. In addition, a common-law marriage may only be dissolved by a court-ordered divorce. There is no common law divorce.

The *Crosson* decision illustrates the vagaries of common-law marriage.

Crosson v. Crosson

Court of Civil Appeals of Alabama, 1995
668 So. 2d 868

■ CRAWLEY, JUDGE.

Bruce Crosson and Barbara Crosson were married in February 1982 in a ceremonial marriage. The Crossons were divorced in June 1993. It is undisputed that after the divorce Mr. Crosson asked his former wife to come back and be his wife. Mrs. Crosson (the "wife") accepted the invitation to move back in with Mr. Crosson (the "husband").[1] They began living together in August 1993. Unknown to the wife, the husband married another woman in October 1994. Upon discovering that fact, the wife immediately sued for a divorce from the husband, contending that she was his common-law wife, and that he had committed adultery and bigamy, and that there was an irretrievable breakdown of the marriage.

The trial court found that the wife had failed to prove a common-law marriage and dismissed her complaint for divorce. At the conclusion of the testimony, the trial court stated:

> "When these [elements of common-law marriage] are met there is a presumption that a man and woman are married, however, that presumption does not exist where the parties are separated and one of the parties marries under a legal marriage. That is subject to rebuttal but it takes a very strong rebuttal to reach to the level of common law marriage to basically void a legal marriage or a ceremonial marriage. . . . [B]ased upon the testimony that has been presented the court has no recourse but to find that there did not exist a common law marriage at this time in this case and dismiss the petition for divorce."

The trial court's final judgment simply stated, "The Plaintiff's Complaint for Divorce is hereby DISMISSED, the Plaintiff having failed to prove the existence of a common law marriage." The trial court, in reaching its decision, applied this principle of law stated in White v. White, 142 So. 524, 526 (Ala. 1932): "[T]he presumption of an actual marriage from the fact of cohabitation, etc., is rebutted by the fact of a subsequent permanent separation, without apparent cause, and the actual marriage soon after of one of the parties." (Citations omitted.)

We must determine if the trial court erred in finding that a common-law marriage did not exist between the parties, on the basis that the husband's marriage to another vitiated the presumption of the common-law marriage between the parties.

The first issue is whether the parties entered into a common-law marriage.

> "This Court has recently reaffirmed the requirements for a common-law marriage in Alabama in Etheridge v. Yeager, 465 So.2d 378 (Ala. 1985). In that opinion, citing various cases as precedent, we held that while no ceremony or particular words are necessary, there are common elements which must be present, either explicitly expressed or implicitly inferred from the circumstances, in order for a common-law marriage to exist. Those elements are: 1) capacity; 2) present, mutual agreement

[1] Although the determination of whether the parties are, in fact, husband and wife is before this court, for convenience, they will be referred to as such.

to permanently enter the marriage relationship to the exclusion of all other relationships; and 3) public recognition of the relationship as a marriage and public assumption of marital duties and cohabitation."

Boswell v. Boswell, 497 So.2d 479, 480 (Ala. 1986) (citations omitted). "No specific words of assent are required; present intention is inferred from cohabitation and public recognition." Waller v. Waller, 567 So.2d 869, 869 (Ala. Civ. App. 1990) (citation omitted). In Copeland v. Richardson, 551 So.2d 353, 355 (Ala. 1989), our Supreme Court stated, "This Court has recognized valid common law marriages between parties who were once formally married to each other, when the proof has been sufficient to establish common law relationships." (Citations omitted.)

Both parties testified that immediately after their divorce, neither party married anyone else and that there was no other impediment to their remarriage. Therefore, both parties had the capacity to enter into the marital relationship.

The wife testified that she and the husband intended to enter into a marital relationship when "Bruce told me that he loved me and that he knew that he had made some mistakes, that I had taught him a very valuable lesson and that he loved me and *he wanted me to come back and be his wife and I did.*" (Emphasis added.) The husband did not deny making this statement. The wife returned to the husband's home that day. Both stated that while living together they had sexual relations. The wife testified that this second relationship "was a lot better" than the previous marital relationship because during their prior marriage, the husband never "accepted" her children by a previous marriage. She further testified that before living together again, they talked about this problem, and that the husband said he loved her children and that he was sorry that he had treated them as he had. During their alleged common-law relationship, the parties signed an agreement allowing the wife's daughter and her family to place a mortgaged mobile home on these parties' real property. Under the terms of the divorce, the wife still had an interest in the land. The wife testified that, except for the husband's relationship with her children, there was no difference between the relationship she and he had had before the divorce and the relationship they had after they began living together in August 1993. The wife never dropped him as a beneficiary of her health insurance. The husband maintained insurance on the wife's automobile. The husband obtained a pistol license for the wife in December 1993 by signing her name to the license, which showed her address at the home where they were living together.

This case is similar to *Copeland*, wherein our Supreme Court affirmed a judgment based on a finding of a common-law marriage and held that the finding of the parties' present intent to become married upon their reunification was based upon the husband's asking the wife to " 'come and be my wife.' " 551 So.2d at 355. In *Copeland*, the wife promised at that time that she would try harder to get along with the husband's daughters.

The husband's only contradictory testimony as to their mutual assent to be married is his testimony that he dated others and that he and the others were seen together at restaurants. He did not tell the wife, and he contends that he did not intend to enter into an agreement to get married when the wife replied "maybe" to his proposal of marriage; however, the wife moved in and began living with him on the same day. The husband's subjective intent, *i.e.*, any unexpressed intent he may have had not to be married, must yield to the reasonable conclusion to be drawn from his objective acts such as his failure to dispute what appeared to be a marital relationship. These acts speak for themselves. McGiffert v. State ex rel. Stowe, 366 So.2d 680 (Ala. 1978). Because the husband's subjective intent is insufficient to rebut the objective acts of the parties, we must take it as undisputed that when these parties began to live together they had a mutual agreement to permanently enter the marriage relationship, to the exclusion of all other relationships.

The husband admitted that after she moved back to his home she kept her clothes, personal belongings, furnishings, etc., at the house, and that they shared household duties. The wife did not remove her wedding band when she was divorced. In April 1994, the parties filed a federal tax return for the year 1993, stating that their status was "married filing joint return." This return included a Schedule C, "Profit or Loss From Business," for the husband's installation business, which stated a net income of approximately one half of the parties' adjusted gross income. This return was signed following this statement: "Under penalties of perjury, I declare that I have examined this return and accompanying schedules and statements, and to the best of my knowledge and belief, they are true, correct, and complete."

The parties lived together until the wife's job required her to move to Mississippi in March 1994. The wife took an apartment in Mississippi, listing the husband as her "husband" on an application for utilities. Upon the husband's first visit to the wife's apartment, he went to the office where she worked to obtain a key to the apartment, and the office manager asked him if he was "Barbara's husband," to which he replied, "Yes." On that occasion, the husband was driving the wife's vehicle, and her grandson was with him. The husband picked up a U-Haul truck and assisted her in moving to Tupelo. The husband and the wife saw each other on weekends, with each party driving every other weekend to the home of the other.

On several social occasions the wife introduced him as her husband, and he made no comment regarding that introduction, but now contends that he made no comment because he did not want to embarrass his wife by correcting her. The same office manager testified that at a company picnic and at the office manager's home several months after that, the husband was introduced as the wife's husband, and that he did not on either occasion deny being her husband. Another office manager testified that she attended a company Christmas party in 1993 where the husband was introduced as the wife's husband, by a company manager and by the wife, and the husband made no denial. This office manager also testified that after the divorce the husband talked with her about the separation and stated that he wanted to be back together with his wife again. This court has held that a man's knowingly allowing himself to be referred to as someone's husband, on several occasions, presented an objective manifestation of a mutual assent to be husband and wife. O'Dell v. O'Dell, 326 So.2d 747 (Ala. App. 1976).

These facts meet the required elements, stated in *Boswell*, *supra*, of capacity, present mutual agreement, and public recognition of the relationship as a marriage and public assumption of marital duties and cohabitation, thereby, inferring consent to enter a matrimonial relationship to the exclusion of all other relationships. *Waller*, *supra*.

The husband contends that the relationship did not amount to a common-law marriage because they discussed having a ceremonial marriage, which never occurred. We disagree. The husband admitted that on several occasions after the divorce he asked her to marry him, and she said "maybe." The wife stated that she agreed to remarry, but that they just never got around to having a ceremonial marriage. In Huffmaster v. Huffmaster, 188 So.2d 552 (Ala. 1966), the court held that the evidence supported a finding of a common-law marriage between parties who had lived together continuously from 1933 until 1961, except for a few months in 1945 after a divorce, where the parties filed joint income tax returns as husband and wife subsequent to their divorce. As in this case, the wife in *Huffmaster* testified that the parties "just never did have time to get around to getting married." Id. at 553.

"[T]he intent to participate in a marriage ceremony in the future does not prove a couple's nonmarriage." Mattison v. Kirk, 497 So.2d 120, 123 (Ala. 1986) (citation omitted) (overruled on other grounds, Carbon Hill Mfg., Inc. v. Moore, 602 So.2d 354 (Ala. 1992)). The rule was enunciated in King v. King, 114 So.2d 145, 147 (Ala. 1959), where the court said: "The mere fact that the parties could not get together on the time when and the place where they were to have another ceremonial marriage is not sufficient to overcome the presumption of the common-law marriage." In Mattison, 497 So.2d at 123, the court noted, "It is not uncommon even for ceremonially married couples to have a second marriage ceremony—a sort of celebration and renewal of marriage vows." The fact that two people are planning a wedding ceremony does not mean that they are not presently married.

The husband contends that he could not be found to have intended to be in a marital relationship, permanent and exclusive of all others, because he had dated other women and had been seen with them in public places, although the wife had no knowledge of these actions. We disagree. Although the husband testified that he was dating "others," he identified only one woman, Cheryl Gaddy Rollings, and he stated that he begin dating her in August 1994, one year after the wife had accepted his invitation to move in with him and become his wife. When asked why he did not tell the wife he was dating others, the husband stated, "Why should I? I don't have no ties with her. She is not—I'm not married to her."

> "Once there is a marriage, common law or ceremonial, it is *not* 'transitory, ephemeral, or conditional.' Once married, by common law or by ceremony, the spouses are married. There is no such thing as being a 'little bit' married; and once married, one spouse's *liaison amoureuse* does not end the marital status, whether that status was created by common law or by ceremony, though it may afford the other spouse a ground for judicially terminating the legal relationship."

Adams v. Boan, 559 So.2d 1084, 1087 (Ala. 1990) (citations omitted) (emphasis in original).

The husband contends that his ceremonial marriage on October 1, 1994, to Cheryl Gaddy Rollings was evidence that could be considered by the trial court to rebut the presumption of an actual marriage between the husband and wife, based upon their cohabitation, etc. We disagree. This principle, stated in White v. White, 142 So. 524 (Ala. 1932), does not apply in this case, because, as discussed above, we must take it as undisputed that when the parties resumed living together in August 1993 they fully intended a marital relationship. This occurred when the wife accepted the husband's invitation to come back and be his wife; she agreed and moved in with him that same day.

> "A subsequent asserting 'we knew we were not married' by a party to such an agreement [to enter into a marital relationship] will hardly vitiate a valid marriage where the *original* understanding was to presently enter into the marriage relationship, followed by a public recognition of the relationship."

Huffmaster, 188 So.2d at 554 (emphasis added).

> "[T]he *operative time* is when the agreement is initially entered into, and once other conditions of public recognition and cohabitation are met the only ways to terminate a common-law marriage are by death or divorce. A party cannot legally terminate the marriage by simply changing his or her mind . . . or by telling selected individuals, 'We're not really married.'"

Skipworth v. Skipworth, 360 So.2d 975, 977 (Ala. 1978) (emphasis added). The operative time, in the instant case, was when the *husband* asked the wife to come back and be his wife *and she did* return for that purpose.

Because we must take it as undisputed that the parties intended to become husband and wife in August 1993, and because they immediately began public assumption of marital duties and cohabitation, we must conclude that a common-law marriage was formed and that the husband's marriage to another, a year later, could not "untie the knot." Therefore, the principle stated in *White*, and relied upon by the trial judge, is not applicable. The trial court misapplied the law to the facts, and no presumption of correctness exists as to the court's judgment. Griggs v. Driftwood Landing, Inc., 620 So.2d 582 (Ala. 1993).

The arguments raised to rebut the contention that these parties had a common-law marriage—(1) their discussion of a ceremonial marriage, (2) the husband's dating others, and (3) the husband's subsequent marriage to another—are, as discussed before, insufficient to rebut the facts suggesting a common-law marriage. . . .

The trial court's judgment is reversed, and this case is remanded for further proceedings consistent with this opinion.

NOTES

As *Crosson* illustrates, in some states a common-law marriage may be formed only when there is no impediment to the marriage, such as another extant marriage. UMDA § 207(b) includes a curative mechanism for recognizing common-law marriages after the prior impediment is lifted:

UNIFORM MARRIAGE AND DIVORCE ACT (2015)

§ 207(b). Prohibited Marriages

> Parties to a marriage prohibited under this section who cohabit after removal of the impediment are lawfully married as of the date of removal of the impediment.

One question that arises is whether a common-law marriage will be assumed to have automatically formed between parties who continue to cohabit after removal of an impediment. In Callen v. Callen, 620 S.E.2d 59 (S.C. 2005), Page Callen filed for divorce from her putative husband, Sean Callen, alleging they had entered into a common-law marriage while living in Florida some fifteen years earlier. During their relationship Sean moved a number of times between different states and countries that did not recognize common-law marriage, with the exception of South Carolina. Sean claimed to have lived alone, receiving only occasional visits from Page, though Page alleged she lived with him throughout this time and that the two ultimately relocated to South Carolina. At the time of the divorce action, Sean claimed to reside in Georgia. The trial court determined there was a common-law marriage under South Carolina law, based upon a rebuttable presumption arising from the parties' cohabitation and reputation in the community as married. The Supreme Court of South Carolina reversed, holding that the trial court erred in part by applying a presumption of common-law marriage as a result of the cohabitation:

> When [no common-law marriage can be formed under the laws of another jurisdiction, and the couple relocates to South Carolina,] . . . the relationship is not automatically transformed into a

> common-law marriage. Instead, it is presumed that relationship remains nonmarital. For the relationship to become marital, "there must be a new mutual agreement either by way of civil ceremony or by way of recognition of the illicit relation and a new agreement to enter into a common law marriage. . . ."
>
> Even assuming, as Page urges, that the parties lived together in Florida, New York, Massachusetts, and Ireland, and further assuming that they moved together from Florida to South Carolina in August 2000, no common-law marriage could have been formed, if at all, until after the move. Since none of those other jurisdictions sanctions common-law marriages, there was an impediment to marriage until the parties took residency here. It must be presumed that Sean and Page's relationship remained nonmarital after the move, after the impediment disappeared. Consequently, Page has the burden of proving that the parties entered into a marital agreement after moving to South Carolina. . . . Instead, the family court considered Page and Sean's relationship in its entirety, relying heavily on the parties' conduct prior to coming to South Carolina. This constitutes reversible error.

Id. at 62–3.

States disagree about the effect of temporary cohabitation in a jurisdiction other than the parties' domicile or residence. Because a marriage that is valid at the place of celebration generally will be valid elsewhere, the extraterritorial impact of common-law marriage can be significant. In Grant v. Superior Court In and For County of Pima, 555 P.2d 895 (Ariz. Ct. App. 1976), it was alleged that the parties had gone to a motel in Texas for a few hours, consummated their marriage after agreeing to be husband and wife, and then told another couple accompanying them that they were married. The rest of the day was spent in Mexico. The parties then returned to Arizona where they lived together and held themselves out as husband and wife. In refusing to recognize that a common-law marriage was created under these circumstances, the Arizona court first pointed out that:

> The elements of such a relationship in Texas are (1) an agreement presently to be husband and wife; (2) living together and cohabiting as husband and wife; (3) holding each other out to the public as such.

Id. at 897. In refusing to find that a marriage had been effected, the court stated:

> It is not the requirement of domicile . . . that makes the difference, but rather the connection by the couple with the state that recognizes common law marriages. The only connection these parties had with the State of Texas was as mere transients.

Id. at 898.

Whether a court finds a common-law marriage between two parties can have significant repercussions beyond a simple divorce proceeding. At stake are questions as varied as: the availability of the husband-wife privilege in criminal cases, whether the appropriate action for dissolution should be divorce or annulment, and what the relationship will mean in terms of alimony, determination of an insurance beneficiary, or the ordering of heirs under intestacy laws.

The use of state law to establish a common-law marriage for federal criminal law purposes also has raised questions. In U.S. v. Seay, 718 F.2d 1279 (4th Cir. 1983), the United States Court of Appeals for the Fourth Circuit affirmed the conviction of a widow for making false statements to the Department of Labor and accepting benefits under the Federal Employee Compensation Act (FECA) when she was not entitled to them. After the death of her husband on active military duty, defendant was eligible for FECA benefits until she remarried. Her subsequent prosecution turned on whether she had entered into a later common-law marriage in South Carolina. In a dissenting opinion, Butzner, J. stated:

> In 32 states which do not recognize common law marriages, a soldier's widow can live with a man without forfeiting her pension or suffering prosecution for fraud because she signed the identical form the defendant signed. When the government through criminal prosecution draws a distinction between the marital status of soldiers' widows living in 18 states and those living in the other 32, the government should be required to give fair notice that signing a form, which it provides, is a criminal act in some states although innocent in others.

Id. at 1286–87.

For a sensitive discussion of the impact on women of abolishing common-law marriage and whether it should be revived, *see* Jean Hoefer Toal, *A Response to the Principals' Domestic Partnership Scheme*, in RECONCEIVING THE FAMILY: CRITIQUE OF THE AMERICAN LAW INSTITUTE'S PRINCIPLES OF THE LAW OF FAMILY DISSOLUTION 425–31 (Robin Fretwell Wilson, ed. 2006); Cynthia Grant Bowman, *A Feminist Proposal to Bring Back Common Law Marriage*, 75 OREGON L. REV. 709 (1997). For more on common-law marriage in the United States, *see* JOHN WITTE, FROM SACRAMENT TO CONTRACT: MARRIAGE, RELIGION, AND LAW IN THE WESTERN TRADITION (2d. ed. 2012); GORAN LIND, COMMON LAW MARRIAGE: A LEGAL INSTITUTION FOR COHABITATION (2008).

PROBLEM ONE

In 2005, famed women's tennis star Marianne Christoper and her now-partner, Jennifer Jones, meet in Los Angeles and quickly fall in love. Over the years they fall into comfortable couple-hood. In 2010, they hit a rough patch, partly because Jennifer is stir crazy since they now travel less. Jennifer catches Marianne flirting with another woman, and storms out, refusing to return home for weeks. To make amends, Marianne buys Jennifer a "rock for her finger." Jennifer moves back in and feeling more secure, starts to call herself Jennifer.Christopher Marianne laughs the first time she hears the name because it rhymes, "baby, call yourself whatever you like, so long as you stay mine." At the end of 2014, Marianne is asked to be on the President's Council on Sports, Fitness, and Nutrition. The pair move to

Washington D.C. for Marianne's new job on January 1, 2015. Yet Jennifer is still not satisfied with their status as a couple, and tells Marianne that she wants more. Marianne then offers to get herself a matching "rock," and starts introducing Jennifer as her "wife," knowing that D.C. recognizes common-law marriage. This makes Jennifer ecstatic, believing that she and Marianne are now closer than ever. Marianne wants Jennifer to be content but also wants to keep Jennifer from leaving her. On June 30, 2015, months after their move to D.C., the couple gathers on the steps of the U.S. Supreme Court to hear *Obergefell* (included infra) as it is handed down. Like others gathered, both break out in tears when they hear the Court granted same-sex couples a right to marry. Jennifer gushes to Marianne, "now we can get married at the courthouse!" Marianne is noticeably silent, and brushes off Jennifer's attempts to broach the subject over the next six months, saying "we don't need such silliness." They continue their relationship as before. When they meet new friends, they refer to each other as "wives," always wearing their rings. But Jennifer constant pestering about "a big ceremony" wears on Marianne. On New Year's Eve 2016, Marianne and Jennifer have a hateful, unpleasant breakup. Jennifer had expected Marianne to "pop the big question," and Marianne refused. What is the legal status of the couple's relationship? Was there proper intent on Marianne's side to form a common law marriage? Did the couple's plan for "a big ceremony" prove that Marianne and Jennifer never intended their actions to form a valid marriage?

2. PROXY MARRIAGE

Proxy or "picture" marriages usually involve the situation in which a ceremony takes place between parties who are in different jurisdictions. One method for this is to designate a "stand-in" who appears for the absent party at the ceremony, with the idea that the law where celebrated should govern. Such marriages could not be effected in some states because of requirements that both parties be present at the ceremony, and federal law limits their recognition for immigration purposes regardless of local validity. According to the United States Code:

8 UNITED STATES CODE (2016)

§ 1101(a)(35). Definitions

> The term *[sic]* "spouse", "wife", or "husband" do not include a spouse, wife or husband by reason of any marriage ceremony where the contracting parties thereto are not physically present in the presence of each other, unless the marriage shall have been consummated.

The Uniform Marriage and Divorce Act contains the following provision specifically authorizing proxy marriages:

UNIFORM MARRIAGE AND DIVORCE ACT (2015)

§ 206(b). Solemnization and Registration

> If a party to a marriage is unable to be present at the solemnization, he may authorize in writing a third person to act as his proxy. If the person solemnizing the marriage is satisfied that the absent party is unable to be present and has consented to the marriage, he may solemnize the marriage by proxy. If he is not satisfied, the parties may petition the [____] court for an order permitting the marriage to be solemnized by proxy.

For general issues concerning the impact of immigration laws on marriage, *see* Kerry Abrams, *Immigration Law and the Regulation of Marriage*, 91 MINN. L. REV. 1625 (2007); Maria Pabon Lopez, *A Tale of Two Systems: Analyzing the Treatment of Non-Citizen Families in State Family Law Systems and Under the Immigration Law System*, 11 HARV. LATINO L. REV. 229 (2008).

3. STATUTORILY REQUIRED FORMALITIES

All states have laws today permitting marriage after a couple receives a license from the state. Such laws will often specify who may legally join parties in a marriage recognized by the state and whether the parties must comply with a specified waiting period after receiving the license and before a ceremony, among other requirements. Questions then arise when a couple fails to comply with statutorily required formalities. In some states a valid marriage may be effected without obtaining a license, as *Carabetta* illustrates. This usually results from interpretation of the statutes as directory rather than mandatory. It also is consonant with the strong public policy favoring the validity of marriages.

Carabetta v. Carabetta

Supreme Court of Connecticut, 1980
438 A.2d 109

■ PETERS, ASSOCIATE JUSTICE.

This is an appeal from the dismissal of an action for the dissolution of the marriage. . . . The trial court . . . determined that the parties had never been legally married and thereupon granted the defendant's motion to dismiss. . . .

The plaintiff and the defendant exchanged marital vows before a priest in the rectory of Our Lady of Mt. Carmel Church of Meriden, on August 25, 1955, according to the rite of the Roman Catholic Church, although they had failed to obtain a marriage license. Thereafter they lived together as husband and wife, raising a family of four children, all of whose birth certificates listed the defendant as their father. Until the present action, the defendant had no memory or recollection of ever having denied that the plaintiff and the defendant were married.

The issue before us is whether, under Connecticut law, despite solemnization according to an appropriate religious ceremony, a marriage is void where there has been noncompliance with the statutory requirement of a marriage license. This is a question of first impression in this state. The trial court held that failure to obtain a marriage license was a flaw fatal to the creation of a legally valid marriage and that the court therefore lacked subject matter jurisdiction over an action for dissolution. . . .

The governing statutes at the time of the purported marriage between these parties contained two kinds of regulations concerning the requirements for a legally valid marriage. One kind of regulation concerned substantive requirements determining those eligible to be married. . . . The other kind of regulation concerns the formalities prescribed by the state for the effectuation of a legally valid marriage. These required formalities, in turn, are of two sorts: a marriage license and a solemnization. In Hames v. Hames, 316 A.2d 379 [(Conn. 1972)], we interpreted our statutes not to make void a marriage consummated after the issuance of a license but deficient for want of due solemnization. Today we examine the statutes in the reverse case, a marriage duly solemnized but deficient for want of a marriage license.

As to licensing, the governing statute in 1955 was a section entitled "Marriage licenses." It provided, in subsection (a): "No persons shall be joined in marriage until both have joined in an application . . . for a license for such marriage." Its only provision for the consequence of noncompliance with the license requirement was contained in subsection (e): ". . . any person who shall join any persons in marriage without having received such [license] shall be fined not more than one hundred dollars." General Statutes (Rev.1949) § 7302, as amended by § 1280b (1951 Sup.) and by § 2250c (1953 Sup.).[2] Neither this section, nor any other, described as void a marriage celebrated without license.

As to solemnization, the governing section, entitled "Who may join persons in marriage," provided in 1955: "All judges and justices of the peace may join persons in marriage . . . and all ordained or licensed clergymen belonging to this state or any other state so long as they continue in the work of the ministry may join persons in marriage and all marriages attempted to be celebrated by any other persons shall be void; but all marriages which shall be solemnized according to the forms and usages of any religious denomination in this state shall be valid." General Statutes (Rev.1949) § 7306, as amended by § 1281b (1951 Sup.) and by § 2251c (1953 Sup.).[3] Although solemnization is not at issue in the case before us, this language is illuminating since it demonstrates that

---

[2] Now General Statutes § 46b–24.

[3] Now General Statutes § 46b–22.

the legislature has on occasion exercised its power to declare expressly that failure to observe some kinds of formalities, e.g., the celebration of a marriage by a person not authorized by this section to do so, renders a marriage void. . . .

In the absence of express language in the governing statute declaring a marriage void for failure to observe a statutory requirement, this court has held in an unbroken line of cases since Gould v. Gould, 61 A. 604 (Conn. 1905), that such a marriage, though imperfect, is dissoluble rather than void. We see no reason to import into the language "[n]o persons shall be joined in marriage until [they have applied for] a license," a meaning more drastic than that assigned in *Gould v. Gould*, *supra*, to the statute that then provided that "[n]o man and woman, either of whom is epileptic . . . shall intermarry." Although the state may well have a legitimate interest in the health of those who are about to marry, *Gould v. Gould* held that the legislature would not be deemed to have entirely invalidated a marriage contract in violation of such health requirements unless the statute itself expressly declared the marriage to be void. Then as now, the legislature had chosen to use the language of voidness selectively, applying it to some but not to all of the statutory requirements for the creation of a legal marriage. Now as then, the legislature has the competence to choose to sanction those who solemnize a marriage without a marriage license rather than those who marry without a marriage license. In sum, we conclude that the legislature's failure expressly to characterize as void a marriage properly celebrated without a license means that such a marriage is not invalid.

Since the marriage that the trial court was asked to dissolve was not void, the trial court erred in granting the motion to dismiss for lack of jurisdiction over the subject matter. . . .

NOTES

Licensure. Marriage licensing goes back to colonial times, but such regulations developed slowly among the states. A Marriage Licensing Act making licensure essential to a valid marriage was recommended by the Commissioners on Uniform State Laws in 1911, but only two states adopted its substance while five others accepted some of its provisions.

Attempts to enforce requirements for licensure by imposing penalties against applicants for false statements, or against clerks for issuing licenses to unqualified persons, have largely been ineffective. Few states have evidenced interest in prosecuting persons who procure marriage licenses through false statements.

Some states require a specific waiting period before a marriage can be solemnized within its borders. *See, e.g.*, S.C. CODE ANN. § 20–1–220 (2016) ("No marriage license may be issued unless a written application has been filed with the probate judge . . . at least twenty-four hours before the issuance of the license."); WISC. STAT. ANN. § 765.08(1) (2016) (stating that, except at the discretion of the clerk, "no marriage license may be issued within 5 days of application for the marriage license"). Because neither domicile nor residence is required before a license can be obtained or a marriage performed in some jurisdictions, persons who wish to marry immediately may simply go to a jurisdiction without such a waiting period.

Ceremony. Today each state generally specifies who may perform marriages and the conditions that are placed on authorized celebrants. Ordinarily no specific form of ceremony is required though some statutes still require specifically that the parties take each other as husband and wife. West Virginia provides a scripted "Ritual for ceremony of marriage by a judge or justice." W. VA. CODE § 48–2–404 (2016).

Despite specific designations of authorized celebrants in state statutes, problems still arise regarding who has authority to solemnize marriages. For example, in Cramer v. Commonwealth, 202 S.E.2d 911 (Va. 1974), the Supreme Court of Virginia held that "ordained" ministers of the Universal Life Church, Inc. did not qualify as "ministers" within the meaning of the Virginia statute describing who could celebrate the rites of marriage. The court noted that the organization's only dogma was "that each person believe that which is right and that each person shall judge for himself what is right." It explained that:

> The interest of the state is not only in marriage as an institution, but in the contract between the parties who marry, and in the proper memorializing of the entry into, and execution of, such a contract. In the proper exercise of its legislative authority it can require that the person who performs a marriage ceremony be certified or licensed. . . .
>
> It is apparent that we have here an organization of ministers—over one million in number says Universal. . . . It appears that Universal encourages all who subscribe to its one tenet to become ministers. A church which consists of all ministers, and in which all new converts can become instant ministers, in fact has no "minister" within the contemplation of [the statute].

Id. at 915.

Statutes in some jurisdictions provide that if the parties believed in good faith that the person who solemnized their marriage was legally authorized to do so, then annulment will not be available on that ground. In such cases, however, there may be criminal sanctions that can be imposed against the unauthorized celebrant. *See, e.g.,* VA. CODE ANN. §§ 20–28, 20–31 (2016).

4. SAME-SEX MARRIAGE

Obergefell v. Hodges

Supreme Court of the United States, 2015
135 S.Ct. 2584

■ KENNEDY, JUSTICE.

. . .

From their beginning to their most recent page, the annals of human history reveal the transcendent importance of marriage. The lifelong union of a man and a woman always has promised nobility and dignity to all persons, without regard to their station in life. Marriage is sacred to those who live by their religions and offers unique fulfillment to those who find meaning in the secular realm. Its dynamic allows two people to find a life that could not be found alone, for a marriage becomes greater than just the two persons. Rising from the most basic human needs, marriage is essential to our most profound hopes and aspirations.

The centrality of marriage to the human condition makes it unsurprising that the institution has existed for millennia and across civilizations. Since the dawn of history, marriage has transformed strangers into relatives, binding families and societies together. Confucius taught that marriage lies at the foundation of government. 2 Li Chi: Book of Rites 266 (C. Chai & W. Chai eds., J. Legge transl. 1967). This wisdom was echoed centuries later and half a world away by Cicero, who wrote, "The first bond of society is marriage; next, children; and then the family." *See* De Officiis 57 (W. Miller transl. 1913). There are untold references to the beauty of marriage in religious and philosophical texts spanning time, cultures, and faiths, as well as in art and literature in all their forms. It is fair and necessary to say these references were based on the understanding that marriage is a union between two persons of the opposite sex.

That history is the beginning of these cases. The respondents say it should be the end as well. To them, it would demean a timeless institution if the concept and lawful status of marriage were extended to two persons of the same sex. Marriage, in their view, is by its nature a gender-differentiated union of man and woman. This view long has been held—and continues to be held—in good faith by reasonable and sincere people here and throughout the world. The petitioners acknowledge this history but contend that these cases cannot end there. Were their intent to demean the revered idea and reality of marriage, the petitioners' claims would be of a different order. But that is neither their purpose nor their submission. To the contrary, it is the enduring importance of marriage that underlies the petitioners' contentions. This, they say, is their whole point. Far from seeking to devalue marriage, the petitioners seek it for themselves because of their respect—and need—for its privileges and responsibilities. And their immutable nature dictates that same-sex marriage is their only real path to this profound commitment.

Recounting the circumstances of three of these cases illustrates the urgency of the petitioners' cause from their perspective. Petitioner James Obergefell, a plaintiff in the Ohio case, met John Arthur over two decades ago. They fell in love and started a life together, establishing a lasting, committed relation. In 2011, however, Arthur was diagnosed with amyotrophic lateral sclerosis, or ALS. This debilitating disease is progressive, with no known cure. Two years ago, Obergefell and Arthur decided to commit to one another, resolving to marry before Arthur died. To fulfill their mutual promise, they traveled from Ohio to Maryland, where same-sex marriage was legal. It was difficult for Arthur to move, and so the couple were wed inside a medical transport plane as it remained on the tarmac in Baltimore. Three months later, Arthur died. Ohio law does not permit Obergefell to be listed as the surviving spouse on Arthur's death certificate. By statute, they must remain strangers even in death, a state-imposed separation Obergefell deems "hurtful for the rest of time." . . . He brought suit to be shown as the surviving spouse on Arthur's death certificate.

April DeBoer and Jayne Rowse are co-plaintiffs in the case from Michigan. They celebrated a commitment ceremony to honor their permanent relation in 2007. They both work as nurses, DeBoer in a neonatal unit and Rowse in an emergency unit. In 2009, DeBoer and Rowse fostered and then adopted a baby boy. Later that same year, they welcomed another son into their family. The new baby, born prematurely and abandoned by his biological mother, required around-the-clock care. The next year, a baby girl with special needs joined their family. Michigan, however, permits only opposite-sex married couples or single individuals to adopt, so each child can have only one woman as his or her legal parent. If an emergency were to arise, schools and hospitals may treat the three children as if they had only one parent. And, were tragedy to befall either DeBoer or Rowse, the other would have no legal rights over the children she had not been permitted to adopt. This couple seeks relief from the continuing uncertainty their unmarried status creates in their lives.

Army Reserve Sergeant First Class Ijpe DeKoe and his partner Thomas Kostura, co-plaintiffs in the Tennessee case, fell in love. In 2011, DeKoe received orders to deploy to Afghanistan. Before leaving, he and Kostura married in New York. A week later, DeKoe began his deployment, which lasted for almost a year. When he returned, the two settled in Tennessee, where DeKoe works full-time for the Army Reserve. Their lawful marriage is stripped from them whenever they reside in Tennessee, returning and disappearing as they travel across state lines. DeKoe, who served this Nation to preserve the freedom the Constitution protects, must endure a substantial burden. The cases now before the Court involve other petitioners as well, each with their own experiences.

Their stories reveal that they seek not to denigrate marriage but rather to live their lives, or honor their spouses' memory, joined by its bond.

. . .

In the late 20th century, following substantial cultural and political developments, same-sex couples began to lead more open and public lives and to establish families. This development was followed by a quite extensive discussion of the issue in both governmental and private sectors and by a shift in public attitudes toward greater tolerance. As a result, questions about the rights of gays and lesbians soon reached the courts, where the issue could be discussed in the formal discourse of the law. This Court first gave detailed consideration to the legal status of homosexuals in *Bowers v. Hardwick,* 478 U.S. 186, 106 S.Ct. 2841, 92 L.Ed.2d 140 (1986). There it upheld the constitutionality of a Georgia law deemed to criminalize certain homosexual acts. Ten years later, in *Romer v. Evans,* 517 U.S. 620, 116 S.Ct. 1620, 134 L.Ed.2d 855 (1996), the Court invalidated an amendment to Colorado's Constitution that sought to foreclose any branch or political subdivision of the State from protecting persons against discrimination based on sexual orientation. Then, in 2003, the Court overruled *Bowers,* holding that laws making same-sex intimacy a crime "demea [n] the lives of homosexual persons." *Lawrence v. Texas,* 539 U.S. 558, 575, 123 S.Ct. 2472, 156 L.Ed.2d 508.

Against this background, the legal question of same-sex marriage arose. In 1993, the Hawaii Supreme Court held Hawaii's law restricting marriage to opposite-sex couples constituted a classification on the basis of sex and was therefore subject to strict scrutiny under the Hawaii Constitution. *Baehr v. Lewin,* 74 Haw. 530, 852 P.2d 44. Although this decision did not mandate that same-sex marriage be allowed, some States were concerned by its implications and reaffirmed in their laws that marriage is defined as a union between opposite-sex partners. So too in 1996, Congress passed the Defense of Marriage Act (DOMA), 110 Stat. 2419, defining marriage for all federal-law purposes as "only a legal union between one man and one woman as husband and wife." 1 U.S.C. § 7. The new and widespread discussion of the subject led other States to a different conclusion. In 2003, the Supreme Judicial Court of Massachusetts held the State's Constitution guaranteed same-sex couples the right to marry. See *Goodridge v. Department of Public Health,* 440 Mass. 309, 798 N.E.2d 941 (2003). After that ruling, some additional States granted marriage rights to same-sex couples, either through judicial or legislative processes. These decisions and statutes are cited in Appendix B, *infra.* Two Terms ago, in *United States v. Windsor,* 570 U.S. ___, 133 S.Ct. 2675, 186 L.Ed.2d 808 (2013), this Court invalidated DOMA to the extent it barred the Federal Government from treating same-sex marriages as valid even when they were lawful in the State where they were licensed. DOMA, the Court held, impermissibly disparaged those same-sex couples "who wanted to affirm their commitment to one another before their children, their family, their friends, and their community." *Id.*, at ___, 133 S.Ct., at 2689.

Numerous cases about same-sex marriage have reached the United States Courts of Appeals in recent years. In accordance with the judicial duty to base their decisions on principled reasons and neutral discussions, without scornful or disparaging commentary, courts have written a substantial body of law considering all sides of these issues. That case law helps to explain and formulate the underlying principles this Court now must consider. With the exception of the opinion here under review and one other, see *Citizens for Equal Protection v. Bruning,* 455 F.3d 859, 864–868 (C.A.8 2006), the Courts of Appeals have held that excluding same-sex couples from marriage violates the Constitution. There also have been many thoughtful District Court decisions addressing same-sex marriage—and most of them, too, have concluded same-sex couples must be allowed to marry. In addition the highest courts of many States have contributed to this ongoing dialogue in decisions interpreting their own State Constitutions. . . . After years of litigation, legislation, referenda, and the discussions that attended these public acts, the States are now divided on the issue of same-sex marriage. . . .

Under the Due Process Clause of the Fourteenth Amendment, no State shall "deprive any person of life, liberty, or property, without due process of law." The fundamental liberties protected by this Clause include most of the rights enumerated in the Bill of Rights. See *Duncan v. Louisiana,* 391 U.S. 145, 147–149, 88 S.Ct. 1444, 20 L.Ed.2d 491 (1968). In addition these liberties extend to certain personal choices central to individual dignity and autonomy, including intimate choices that define personal identity and beliefs. See, *e.g., Eisenstadt v. Baird,* 405 U.S. 438, 453, 92 S.Ct. 1029, 31 L.Ed.2d 349 (1972); *Griswold v. Connecticut,* 381 U.S. 479, 484–486, 85 S.Ct. 1678, 14 L.Ed.2d 510 (1965). The identification and protection of fundamental rights is an enduring part of the judicial duty to interpret the Constitution. That responsibility, however, "has not been reduced to any formula." *Poe v. Ullman,* 367 U.S. 497, 542, 81 S.Ct. 1752, 6 L.Ed.2d 989 (1961) (Harlan, J., dissenting). Rather, it requires courts to exercise reasoned judgment in identifying interests of the person so fundamental that the State must accord them its respect. See *ibid.* That process is guided by many of the same considerations relevant to analysis of other constitutional provisions that set forth broad principles rather than specific requirements. History and tradition guide and discipline this inquiry but do not set its outer boundaries. See *Lawrence, supra,* at 572, 123 S.Ct. 2472. That method respects our history and learns from it without allowing the past alone to rule the present. The nature of injustice is that we may not always see it in our own times. The generations that wrote and ratified the Bill of Rights and the Fourteenth Amendment did not presume to know the extent of freedom in all of its dimensions, and so they entrusted to future generations a charter protecting the right of all persons to enjoy liberty as we learn its meaning. When new insight reveals discord between the Constitution's central protections and a received legal stricture, a claim to liberty must be addressed.

Applying these established tenets, the Court has long held the right to marry is protected by the Constitution. In *Loving v. Virginia,* 388 U.S. 1, 12, 87 S.Ct. 1817, 18 L.Ed.2d 1010 (1967), which invalidated bans on interracial unions, a unanimous Court held marriage is "one of the vital personal rights essential to the orderly pursuit of happiness by free men." The Court reaffirmed that holding in *Zablocki v. Redhail,* 434 U.S. 374, 384, 98 S.Ct. 673, 54 L.Ed.2d 618 (1978), which held the right to marry was burdened by a law prohibiting fathers who were behind on child support from marrying. The Court again applied this principle in *Turner v. Safley,* 482 U.S. 78, 95, 107 S.Ct. 2254, 96 L.Ed.2d 64 (1987), which held the right to marry was abridged by regulations limiting the privilege of prison inmates to marry. Over time and in other contexts, the Court has reiterated that the right to marry is fundamental under the Due Process Clause. See, *e.g., M.L.B. v. S.L.J.,* 519 U.S. 102, 116, 117 S.Ct. 555, 136 L.Ed.2d 473 (1996); *Cleveland Bd. of Ed. v. LaFleur,* 414 U.S. 632, 639–640, 94 S.Ct. 791, 39 L.Ed.2d 52 (1974); *Griswold, supra,* at 486, 85 S.Ct. 1678; *Skinner v. Oklahoma ex rel. Williamson,* 316 U.S. 535, 541, 62 S.Ct. 1110, 86 L.Ed. 1655 (1942); *Meyer v. Nebraska,* 262 U.S. 390, 399, 43 S.Ct. 625, 67 L.Ed. 1042 (1923).

It cannot be denied that this Court's cases describing the right to marry presumed a relationship involving opposite-sex partners. The Court, like many institutions, has made assumptions defined by the world and time of which it is a part. This was evident in *Baker v. Nelson,* 409 U.S. 810, 93 S.Ct. 37, 34 L.Ed.2d 65, a one-line summary decision issued in 1972, holding the exclusion of same-sex couples from marriage did not present a substantial federal question. Still, there are other, more instructive precedents. This Court's cases have expressed constitutional principles of broader reach. In defining the right to marry these cases have identified essential attributes of that right based in history, tradition, and other constitutional liberties inherent in this intimate bond. See, *e.g., Lawrence,* 539 U.S., at 574, 123 S.Ct. 2472; *Turner, supra,* at 95, 107 S.Ct. 2254; *Zablocki, supra,* at 384, 98 S.Ct. 673; *Loving, supra,* at 12, 87 S.Ct. 1817; *Griswold, supra,* at 486, 85 S.Ct. 1678. And in assessing whether the force and rationale of its cases apply to same-sex couples, the Court must respect the basic reasons why the right to marry has been long protected. See, *e.g., Eisenstadt, supra,* at 453–454, 92 S.Ct. 1029; *Poe, supra,* at 542–553, 81 S.Ct. 1752 (Harlan, J., dissenting).

This analysis compels the conclusion that same-sex couples may exercise the right to marry. The four principles and traditions to be discussed demonstrate that the reasons marriage is fundamental under the Constitution apply with equal force to same-sex couples. A first premise of the Court's relevant precedents is that the right to personal choice regarding marriage is inherent in the concept of individual autonomy. This abiding connection between marriage and liberty is why *Loving* invalidated interracial marriage bans under the Due Process Clause. See 388 U.S., at 12, 87 S.Ct. 1817; see also *Zablocki, supra,* at 384, 98 S.Ct. 673 (observing *Loving* held "the right to marry is of fundamental importance for all individuals"). Like choices concerning contraception, family relationships, procreation, and childrearing, all of which are protected by the Constitution, decisions concerning marriage are among the most intimate that an individual can make. See *Lawrence, supra,* at 574, 123 S.Ct. 2472. Indeed, the Court has noted it would be contradictory "to recognize a right of privacy with respect to other matters of family life and not with respect to the decision to enter the relationship that is the foundation of the family in our society." *Zablocki, supra,* at 386, 98 S.Ct. 673.

Choices about marriage shape an individual's destiny. As the Supreme Judicial Court of Massachusetts has explained, because "it fulfils yearnings for security, safe haven, and connection that express our common humanity, civil marriage is an esteemed institution, and the decision whether and whom to marry is among life's momentous acts of self-definition." *Goodridge,* 440 Mass., at 322, 798 N.E.2d, at 955. The nature of marriage is that, through its enduring bond, two persons together can find other freedoms, such as expression, intimacy, and spirituality. This is true for all persons, whatever their sexual orientation. See *Windsor,* 570 U.S., at ___, 133 S.Ct., at 2693–2695. There is dignity in the bond between two men or two women who seek to marry and in their autonomy to make such profound choices. Cf. *Loving, supra,* at 12, 87 S.Ct. 1817 ("[T]he freedom to marry, or not marry, a person of another race resides with the individual and cannot be infringed by the State").

A second principle in this Court's jurisprudence is that the right to marry is fundamental because it supports a two-person union unlike any other in its importance to the committed individuals. This point was central to *Griswold v. Connecticut,* which held the Constitution protects the right of married couples to use contraception. 381 U.S., at 485, 85 S.Ct. 1678. Suggesting that marriage is a right "older than the Bill of Rights," *Griswold* described marriage this way: "Marriage is a coming together for better or for worse, hopefully enduring, and intimate to the degree of being sacred. It is an association that promotes a way of life, not causes; a harmony in living, not political faiths; a bilateral loyalty, not commercial or social projects. Yet it is an association for as noble a purpose as any involved in our prior decisions." *Id.,* at 486, 85 S.Ct. 1678. And in *Turner,* the Court again acknowledged the intimate association protected by this right, holding prisoners could not be denied the right to marry because their committed relationships satisfied the basic reasons why marriage is a fundamental right. See 482 U.S., at 95–96, 107 S.Ct. 2254. The right to marry thus dignifies couples who "wish to define themselves by their commitment to each other." *Windsor, supra,* at ___, 133 S.Ct., at 2689. Marriage responds to the universal fear that a lonely person might call out only to find no one there. It offers the hope of companionship and understanding and assurance that while both still live there will be someone to care for the other.

As this Court held in *Lawrence,* same-sex couples have the same right as opposite-sex couples to enjoy intimate association. *Lawrence* invalidated laws that made same-sex intimacy a criminal act. And it acknowledged that "[w]hen sexuality finds overt expression in intimate conduct with another person, the conduct can be but one element in a personal bond that is more enduring." 539 U.S., at 567, 123 S.Ct. 2472. But while *Lawrence* confirmed a dimension of freedom that allows individuals to engage in intimate association without criminal liability, it does not follow that freedom stops there. Outlaw to outcast may be a step forward, but it does not achieve the full promise of liberty.

A third basis for protecting the right to marry is that it safeguards children and families and thus draws meaning from related rights of childrearing, procreation, and education. See *Pierce v. Society of Sisters,* 268 U.S. 510, 45 S.Ct. 571, 69 L.Ed. 1070 (1925); *Meyer,* 262 U.S., at 399, 43 S.Ct. 625. The Court has recognized these connections by describing the varied rights as a unified whole: "[T]he right to 'marry, establish a home and bring up children' is a central part of the liberty protected by the Due Process Clause." *Zablocki,* 434 U.S., at 384, 98 S.Ct. 673 (quoting *Meyer, supra,* at 399, 43 S.Ct. 625). Under the laws of the several States, some of marriage's protections for children and families are material. But marriage also confers more profound benefits. By giving recognition and legal structure to their parents' relationship, marriage allows children "to understand the integrity and closeness of their own family and its concord with other families in their community and in their daily lives." *Windsor, supra,* at ___, 133 S.Ct., at 2694–2695. Marriage also affords the permanency and stability important to children's best interests. . . . As all parties agree, many same-sex couples provide loving and nurturing homes to their children, whether biological or adopted. And hundreds of thousands of children are presently being raised by such couples. See Brief for Gary J. Gates as *Amicus Curiae* 4. Most States have allowed gays and lesbians to adopt, either as individuals or as couples, and many adopted and foster children have same-sex parents, see *id.,* at 5. This provides powerful confirmation from the law itself that gays and lesbians can create loving, supportive families. Excluding same-sex couples from marriage thus conflicts with a central premise of the right to marry. Without the recognition, stability, and predictability marriage offers, their children suffer the stigma of knowing their families are somehow lesser. They also suffer the significant material costs of being raised by unmarried parents, relegated through no fault of their own to a more difficult and uncertain family life. The marriage laws at issue here thus harm and humiliate the children of same-sex couples. See *Windsor, supra,* at ___, 133 S.Ct., at 2694–2695. That is not to say the right to marry is less meaningful for those who do not or cannot have children. An ability, desire, or promise to procreate is not and has not been a prerequisite for a valid marriage in any State. In light of precedent protecting the right of a married couple not to procreate, it cannot be said the Court or the States have conditioned the right to marry on the capacity or commitment to procreate. The constitutional marriage right has many aspects, of which childbearing is only one.

Fourth and finally, this Court's cases and the Nation's traditions make clear that marriage is a keystone of our social order. Alexis de Tocqueville recognized this truth on his travels through the United States almost two centuries ago:

> "There is certainly no country in the world where the tie of marriage is so much respected as in America . . . [W]hen the American retires from the turmoil of public life to the bosom of his family, he finds in it the image of order and of peace. . . . [H]e afterwards carries [that image] with him into public affairs." 1 Democracy in America 309 (H. Reeve transl., rev. ed. 1990).

In *Maynard v. Hill,* 125 U.S. 190, 211, 8 S.Ct. 723, 31 L.Ed. 654 (1888), the Court echoed de Tocqueville, explaining that marriage is "the foundation of the family and of society, without which there would be neither civilization nor progress." Marriage, the *Maynard* Court said, has long been 'a great public institution, giving character to our whole civil polity.' " *Id.,* at 213, 8 S.Ct. 723. This idea has been reiterated even as the institution has evolved in substantial ways over time, superseding rules related to parental consent, gender, and race once thought by many to be essential. . . . Marriage remains a building block of our national community.

For that reason, just as a couple vows to support each other, so does society pledge to support the couple, offering symbolic recognition and material benefits to protect and nourish the union. Indeed, while the States are in general free to vary the benefits they confer on all married couples, they have throughout our history made marriage the basis for an expanding list of governmental rights, benefits, and responsibilities. These aspects of marital status include: taxation; inheritance and property rights; rules of intestate succession; spousal privilege in the law of evidence; hospital access; medical decisionmaking authority; adoption rights; the rights and benefits of survivors; birth and death certificates; professional ethics rules; campaign finance restrictions; workers' compensation benefits; health insurance; and child custody, support, and visitation rules. . . . Valid marriage under state law is also a significant status for over a thousand provisions of federal law. See *Windsor,* 570 U.S., at ___–___, 133 S.Ct., at 2690–2691. The States have contributed to the fundamental character of the marriage right by placing that institution at the center of so many facets of the legal and social order.

There is no difference between same- and opposite-sex couples with respect to this principle. Yet by virtue of their exclusion from that institution, same-sex couples are denied the constellation of benefits that the States have linked to marriage. This harm results in more than just material burdens. Same-sex couples are consigned to an instability many opposite-sex couples would deem intolerable in their own lives. As the State itself makes marriage all the more precious by the significance it attaches to it, exclusion from that status has the effect of teaching that gays and lesbians are unequal in important respects. It demeans gays and lesbians for the State to lock them out of a central institution of the Nation's society. Same-sex couples, too, may aspire to the transcendent purposes of marriage and seek fulfillment in its highest meaning.

. . .

The right to marry is fundamental as a matter of history and tradition, but rights come not from ancient sources alone. They rise, too, from a better informed understanding of how constitutional imperatives define a liberty that remains urgent in our own era. Many who deem same-sex marriage to be wrong reach that conclusion based on decent and honorable religious or philosophical premises, and neither they nor their beliefs are disparaged here. But when that sincere, personal opposition becomes enacted law and public policy, the necessary consequence is to put the imprimatur of the State itself on an exclusion that soon demeans or stigmatizes those whose own liberty is then denied. Under the Constitution, same-sex couples seek in marriage the same legal treatment as opposite-sex couples, and it would disparage their choices and diminish their personhood to deny them this right.

The right of same-sex couples to marry that is part of the liberty promised by the Fourteenth Amendment is derived, too, from that Amendment's guarantee of the equal protection of the laws. The Due Process Clause and the Equal Protection Clause are connected in a profound way, though they set forth independent principles. Rights implicit in liberty and rights secured by equal protection may rest on different precepts and are not always co-extensive, yet in some instances each may be instructive as to the meaning and reach of the other. In any particular case one Clause may be thought to capture the essence of the right in a more accurate and comprehensive way, even as the two Clauses may converge in the identification and definition of the right. See *M.L.B.,* 519 U.S., at 120–121, 117 S.Ct. 555; *id.,* at 128–129, 117 S.Ct. 555 (KENNEDY, J., concurring in judgment); *Bearden v. Georgia,* 461 U.S. 660, 665, 103 S.Ct. 2064, 76 L.Ed.2d 221 (1983). This interrelation of the two principles furthers our understanding of what freedom is and must become.

. . .

Indeed, in interpreting the Equal Protection Clause, the Court has recognized that new insights and societal understandings can reveal unjustified inequality within our most fundamental institutions that once passed unnoticed and unchallenged. To take but one period, this occurred with respect to marriage in the 1970's and 1980's. Notwithstanding the gradual erosion of the doctrine of coverture . . . invidious sex-based classifications in marriage remained common through the mid-20th century. See App. to Brief for Appellant in *Reed v. Reed,* O.T. 1971, No. 70–4, pp. 69–88 (an extensive reference to laws extant as of 1971 treating women as unequal to men in marriage). These classifications denied the equal dignity of men and women. One State's law, for example, provided in 1971 that "the husband is the head of the family and the wife is subject to him; her legal civil existence is merged in the husband, except so far as the law recognizes her separately, either for her own protection, or for her benefit." Ga.Code Ann. § 53–501 (1935). Responding to a new awareness, the Court invoked equal protection principles to invalidate laws imposing sex-based inequality on marriage. See, *e.g.,* Kirchberg v. Feenstra, 450 U.S. 455, 101 S.Ct. 1195, 67 L.Ed.2d 428 (1981); Wengler v. Druggists Mut. Ins. Co., 446 U.S. 142, 100 S.Ct. 1540, 64 L.Ed.2d 107 (1980); Califano v. Westcott, 443 U.S. 76, 99 S.Ct. 2655, 61 L.Ed.2d 382 (1979); Orr v. Orr, 440 U.S. 268, 99 S.Ct. 1102, 59 L.Ed.2d 306 (1979); Califano v. Goldfarb, 430 U.S. 199, 97 S.Ct. 1021, 51 L.Ed.2d 270 (1977) (plurality opinion); Weinberger v. Wiesenfeld, 420 U.S. 636, 95 S.Ct. 1225, 43 L.Ed.2d 514 (1975); Frontiero v. Richardson, 411 U.S. 677, 93 S.Ct. 1764, 36 L.Ed.2d 583 (1973). Like *Loving* and *Zablocki,* these precedents show the Equal Protection Clause can help to identify and correct inequalities in the institution of marriage, vindicating precepts of liberty and equality under the Constitution.

. . .

These considerations lead to the conclusion that the right to marry is a fundamental right inherent in the liberty of the person, and under the Due Process and Equal Protection Clauses of the Fourteenth Amendment couples of the same-sex may not be deprived of that right and that liberty. The Court now holds that same-sex couples may exercise the fundamental right to marry. No longer may this liberty be denied to them. *Baker v. Nelson* must be and now is overruled, and the State laws challenged by Petitioners in these cases are now held invalid to the extent they exclude same-sex couples from civil marriage on the same terms and conditions as opposite-sex couples.

. . .

Finally, it must be emphasized that religions, and those who adhere to religious doctrines, may continue to advocate with utmost, sincere conviction that, by divine precepts, same-sex marriage should not be condoned. The First Amendment ensures that religious organizations and persons are given proper protection as they seek to teach the principles that are so fulfilling and so central to their lives and faiths, and to their own deep aspirations to continue the family structure they have long revered. The same is true of those who oppose same-sex marriage for other reasons. In turn, those who believe allowing same-sex marriage is proper or indeed essential, whether as a matter of religious conviction or secular belief, may engage those who disagree with their view in an open and searching debate. The Constitution, however, does not permit the State to bar same-sex couples from marriage on the same terms as accorded to couples of the opposite sex.

. . .

No union is more profound than marriage, for it embodies the highest ideals of love, fidelity, devotion, sacrifice, and family. In forming a marital union, two people become something greater than once they were. As some of the petitioners in these cases demonstrate, marriage embodies a love that may endure even past death. It would misunderstand these men and women to say they disrespect the idea of marriage. Their plea is that they do respect it, respect it so deeply that they seek to find its fulfillment for themselves. Their hope is not to be condemned to live in loneliness, excluded from one of civilization's oldest institutions. They ask for equal dignity in the eyes of the law. The Constitution grants them that right. The judgment of the Court of Appeals for the Sixth Circuit is reversed.

It is so ordered.

■ Chief Justice ROBERTS, with whom Justice SCALIA and Justice THOMAS join, dissenting.

Petitioners make strong arguments rooted in social policy and considerations of fairness. They contend that same-sex couples should be allowed to affirm their love and commitment through marriage, just like opposite-sex couples. That position has undeniable appeal; over the past six years, voters and legislators in eleven States and the District of Columbia have revised their laws to allow marriage between two people of the same-sex. But this Court is not a legislature. Whether same-sex marriage is a good idea should be of no concern to us. Under the Constitution, judges have power to say what the law is, not what it should be. The people who ratified the Constitution authorized courts to exercise "neither force nor will but merely judgment." The Federalist No. 78, p. 465 (C. Rossiter ed. 1961) (A. Hamilton) (capitalization altered). Although the policy arguments for extending marriage to same-sex couples may be compelling, the legal arguments for requiring such an extension are not. The fundamental right to marry does not include a right to make a State change its definition of marriage. And a State's decision to maintain the meaning of marriage that has persisted in every culture throughout human history can hardly be called irrational. In short, our Constitution does not enact any one theory of marriage. The people of a State are free to expand marriage to include same-sex couples, or to retain the historic definition.

Today, however, the Court takes the extraordinary step of ordering every State to license and recognize same-sex marriage. Many people will rejoice at this decision, and I begrudge none their celebration. But for those who believe in a government of laws, not of men, the majority's approach is deeply disheartening. Supporters of same-sex marriage have achieved considerable success persuading their fellow citizens—through the democratic process—to adopt their view. That ends today. Five lawyers have closed the debate and enacted their own vision of marriage as a matter of constitutional law. Stealing this issue from the people will for many cast a cloud over same-sex marriage, making a dramatic social change that much more difficult to accept.

The majority's decision is an act of will, not legal judgment. The right it announces has no basis in the Constitution or this Court's precedent. The majority expressly disclaims judicial "caution" and omits even a pretense of humility, openly relying on its desire to remake society according to its own "new insight" into the "nature of injustice." *Ante,* at 2598, 2605. As a result, the Court invalidates the marriage laws of more than half the States and orders the transformation of a social institution that has formed the basis of human society for millennia, for the Kalahari Bushmen and the Han Chinese, the Carthaginians and the Aztecs. Just who do we think we are?

It can be tempting for judges to confuse our own preferences with the requirements of the law. But as this Court has been reminded throughout our history, the Constitution "is made for people of fundamentally differing views." *Lochner v. New York,* 198 U.S. 45, 76, 25 S.Ct. 539, 49 L.Ed. 937 (1905) (Holmes, J., dissenting). Accordingly, "courts are not concerned with the wisdom or policy of legislation." *Id.,* at 69, 25 S.Ct. 539 (Harlan, J., dissenting). The majority today neglects that restrained conception of the judicial role. It seizes for itself a question the Constitution leaves to the people, at a time when the people are engaged in a vibrant debate on that question. And it answers that question based not on neutral principles of constitutional law, but on its own "understanding of what freedom is and must become." *Ante,* at 2603. I have no choice but to dissent. Understand well what this dissent is about: It is not about whether, in my judgment, the institution of marriage should be changed to include same-sex couples. It is instead about whether, in our democratic republic, that decision should rest with the people acting through their elected representatives, or with five lawyers who happen to hold commissions authorizing them to resolve legal disputes according to law. The Constitution leaves no doubt about the answer.

. . .

The majority purports to identify four "principles and traditions" in this Court's due process precedents that support a fundamental right for same-sex couples to marry. *Ante,* at 2599. In reality, however, the majority's approach has no basis in principle or tradition, except for the unprincipled tradition of judicial policymaking that characterized discredited decisions such as *Lochner v. New York,* 198 U.S. 45, 25 S.Ct. 539, 49 L.Ed. 937. Stripped of its shiny rhetorical gloss, the majority's argument is that the Due Process Clause gives same-sex couples a fundamental right to marry because it will be good for them and for society. If I were a legislator, I would certainly consider that view as a matter of social policy. But as a judge, I find the majority's position indefensible as a matter of constitutional law.

. . .

The legitimacy of this Court ultimately rests "upon the respect accorded to its judgments." *Republican Party of Minn. v. White,* 536 U.S. 765, 793, 122 S.Ct. 2528, 153 L.Ed.2d 694 (2002) (KENNEDY, J., concurring). That respect flows from the perception—and reality—that we exercise humility and restraint in deciding cases according to the Constitution and law. The role of the Court envisioned by the majority today, however, is anything but humble or restrained. Over and over, the majority exalts the role of the judiciary in delivering social change. In the majority's telling, it is the courts, not the people, who are responsible for making "new dimensions of freedom . . . apparent to new generations," for providing "formal discourse" on social issues, and for ensuring "neutral discussions, without scornful or disparaging commentary." *Ante,* at 2596–2597.

Nowhere is the majority's extravagant conception of judicial supremacy more evident than in its description—and dismissal—of the public debate regarding same-sex marriage. Yes, the majority concedes, on one side are thousands of years of human history in every society known to have populated the planet. But on the other side, there has been "extensive litigation," "many thoughtful District Court decisions," "countless studies, papers, books, and other popular and scholarly writings," and "more than 100" *amicus* briefs in these cases alone. *Ante,* at 2597, 2597–2598, 2605. What would be the point of allowing the democratic process to go on? It is high time for the Court to decide the meaning of marriage, based on five lawyers' "better informed understanding" of "a liberty that remains urgent in our own era." *Ante,* at 2602. The answer is surely there in one of those *amicus* briefs or studies.

Those who founded our country would not recognize the majority's conception of the judicial role. They after all risked their lives and fortunes for the precious right to govern themselves. They would never have imagined yielding that right on a question of social policy to unaccountable and unelected judges. And they certainly would not have been satisfied by a system empowering judges to override policy judgments so long as they do so after "a quite extensive discussion." *Ante,* at 2596. In our democracy, debate about the content of the law is not an exhaustion requirement to be checked off before courts can impose their will. "Surely the Constitution does not put either the legislative branch or the executive branch in the position of a television quiz show contestant so that when a given period of time has elapsed and a problem remains unresolved by them, the federal judiciary may press a buzzer and take its turn at fashioning a solution." Rehnquist, The Notion of a Living Constitution, 54 Texas L. Rev. 693, 700 (1976). As a plurality of this Court explained just last year, "It is demeaning to the democratic process to presume that voters are not capable of deciding an issue of this sensitivity on decent and rational grounds." *Schuette v. BAMN,* 572 U.S. ___, ___–___, 134 S.Ct. 1623, 1637, 188 L.Ed.2d 613 (2014).

The Court's accumulation of power does not occur in a vacuum. It comes at the expense of the people. And they know it. Here and abroad, people are in the midst of a serious and thoughtful public debate on the issue of same-sex marriage. They see voters carefully considering same-sex marriage, casting ballots in favor or opposed, and sometimes changing their minds. They see political leaders similarly reexamining their positions, and either reversing course or explaining adherence to old convictions confirmed anew. They see governments and businesses modifying policies and practices with respect to same-sex couples, and participating actively in the civic discourse. They see countries overseas democratically accepting profound social change, or declining to do so. This deliberative process is making people take seriously questions that they may not have even regarded as questions before.

When decisions are reached through democratic means, some people will inevitably be disappointed with the results. But those whose views do not prevail at least know that they have had their say, and accordingly are—in the tradition of our political culture—reconciled to the result of a fair and honest debate. In addition, they can gear up to raise the issue later, hoping to persuade enough on the winning side to think again. "That is exactly how our system of government is supposed to work." *Post,* at 2627 (SCALIA, J., dissenting).

. . .

Federal courts are blunt instruments when it comes to creating rights. They have constitutional power only to resolve concrete cases or controversies; they do not have the flexibility of legislatures to address concerns of parties not before the court or to anticipate problems that may arise from the exercise of a new right. Today's decision, for example, creates serious questions about religious liberty. Many good and decent people oppose same-sex marriage as a tenet of faith, and their freedom to exercise religion is—unlike the right imagined by the majority— actually spelled out in the Constitution. Amdt. 1.

Respect for sincere religious conviction has led voters and legislators in every State that has adopted same-sex marriage democratically to include accommodations for religious practice. The majority's decision imposing same-sex marriage cannot, of course, create any such accommodations. The majority graciously suggests that religious believers may continue to "advocate" and "teach" their views of marriage. *Ante,* at 27. The First Amendment guarantees, however, the freedom to "*exercise*" religion. Ominously, that is not a word the majority uses.

Hard questions arise when people of faith exercise religion in ways that may be seen to conflict with the new right to same-sex marriage—when, for example, a religious college provides married student housing only to opposite-sex married couples, or a religious adoption agency declines to place children with same-sex married couples. Indeed, the Solicitor General candidly acknowledged that the tax exemptions of some religious institutions would be in question if they opposed same-sex marriage. See Tr. of Oral Arg. on Question 1, at 36–38. There is little doubt that these and similar questions will soon be before this Court. Unfortunately, people of faith can take no comfort in the treatment they receive from the majority today.

■ Justice SCALIA, with whom Justice THOMAS joins, dissenting.

I join THE CHIEF JUSTICE's opinion in full. I write separately to call attention to this Court's threat to American democracy.

. . .

Today's decree says that my Ruler, and the Ruler of 320 million Americans coast-to-coast, is a majority of the nine lawyers on the Supreme Court. The opinion in these cases is the furthest extension in fact—and the furthest extension one can even imagine—of the Court's claimed power to create "liberties" that the Constitution and its Amendments neglect to mention. This practice of constitutional revision by an unelected committee of nine, always accompanied (as it is today) by extravagant praise of liberty, robs the People of the most important liberty they asserted in the Declaration of Independence and won in the Revolution of 1776: the freedom to govern themselves.

. . .

But what really astounds is the hubris reflected in today's judicial Putsch. The five Justices who compose today's majority are entirely comfortable concluding that every State violated the Constitution for all of the 135 years between the Fourteenth Amendment's ratification and Massachusetts' permitting of same-sex marriages in 2003. [Footnote omitted] They have discovered in the Fourteenth Amendment a "fundamental right" overlooked by every person alive at the time of ratification, and almost everyone else in the time since. They see what lesser legal minds—minds like Thomas Cooley, John Marshall Harlan, Oliver Wendell Holmes, Jr., Learned Hand, Louis Brandeis, William Howard Taft, Benjamin Cardozo, Hugo Black, Felix Frankfurter, Robert Jackson, and Henry Friendly—could not. They are certain that the People ratified the Fourteenth Amendment to bestow on them the power to remove questions from the democratic process when that is called for by their "reasoned judgment." These Justices *know* that limiting marriage to one man and one woman is contrary to reason; they *know* that an institution as old as government itself, and accepted by every nation in history until 15 years ago, [footnote omitted] cannot possibly be supported by anything other than ignorance or bigotry. And they are willing to say that any citizen who does not agree with that, who adheres to what was, until 15 years ago, the unanimous judgment of all generations and all societies, stands against the Constitution.

■ Justice THOMAS, with whom Justice SCALIA joins, dissenting.

The Court's decision today is at odds not only with the Constitution, but with the principles upon which our Nation was built. Since well before 1787, liberty has been understood as freedom from government action, not entitlement to government benefits. The Framers created our Constitution to preserve that understanding of liberty. Yet the majority invokes our Constitution in the name of a "liberty" that the Framers would not have recognized, to the detriment of the liberty they sought to protect. Along the way, it rejects the idea—captured in our Declaration of Independence—that human dignity is innate and suggests instead that it comes from the Government. This distortion of our Constitution not only ignores the text, it inverts the relationship between the individual and the state in our Republic. I cannot agree with it.

. . .

Even if the doctrine of substantive due process were somehow defensible—it is not—petitioners still would not have a claim. To invoke the protection of the Due Process Clause at all—whether under a theory of "substantive" or "procedural" due process—a party must first identify a deprivation of "life, liberty, or property." The majority claims these state laws deprive petitioners of "liberty," but the concept of "liberty" it conjures up bears no resemblance to any plausible meaning of that word as it is used in the Due Process Clauses. As used in the Due Process Clauses, "liberty" most likely refers to "the power of locomotion, of changing situation, or removing one's person to whatsoever place one's own inclination may direct; without imprisonment or restraint, unless by due course of law." 1 W. Blackstone, Commentaries on the Laws of England 130 (1769) (Blackstone). That definition is drawn from the historical roots of the Clauses and is consistent with our Constitution's text and structure. . . . Even assuming that the "liberty" in those Clauses encompasses something more than freedom from physical restraint, it would not include the types of rights claimed by the majority. In the American legal tradition, liberty has long been understood as individual freedom *from* governmental action, not as a right *to* a particular governmental entitlement.

. . .

Petitioners cannot claim, under the most plausible definition of "liberty," that they have been imprisoned or physically restrained by the States for participating in same-sex relationships. To the contrary, they have been able to cohabitate and raise their children in peace. They have been able to hold civil marriage ceremonies in States that recognize same-sex marriages and private religious ceremonies in all States. They have been able to travel freely around the country, making their homes where they please. Far from being incarcerated or physically restrained, petitioners have been left alone to order their lives as they see fit. Nor, under the broader definition, can they claim that the States have restricted their ability to go about their daily lives as they would be able to absent governmental restrictions. Petitioners do not ask this Court to order the States to stop restricting their ability to enter same-sex relationships, to engage in intimate behavior, to make vows to their partners in public ceremonies, to engage in religious wedding ceremonies, to hold themselves out as married, or to raise children. The States have imposed no such restrictions. Nor have the States prevented petitioners from approximating a number of incidents of marriage through private legal means, such as wills, trusts, and powers of attorney.

Instead, the States have refused to grant them governmental entitlements. Petitioners claim that as a matter of "liberty," they are entitled to access privileges and benefits that exist solely *because of* the government. They want, for example, to receive the State's *imprimatur* on their marriages—on state issued marriage licenses, death certificates, or other official forms. And they want to receive various monetary benefits, including reduced inheritance taxes upon the death of a spouse, compensation if a spouse dies as a result of a work-related injury, or loss of consortium damages in tort suits. But receiving governmental recognition and benefits has nothing to do with any understanding of "liberty" that the Framers would have recognized.

. . .

Our Constitution—like the Declaration of Independence before it—was predicated on a simple truth: One's liberty, not to mention one's dignity, was something to be shielded from—not provided by—the State. Today's decision casts that truth aside. In its haste to reach a desired result, the majority misapplies a clause focused on "due process" to afford substantive rights, disregards the most plausible understanding of the "liberty" protected by that clause, and distorts the principles on which this Nation was founded. Its decision will have inestimable consequences for our Constitution and our society. I respectfully dissent.

. . .

■ Justice ALITO, with whom Justice SCALIA and Justice THOMAS join, dissenting.

. . .

Today's decision usurps the constitutional right of the people to decide whether to keep or alter the traditional understanding of marriage. The decision will also have other important consequences. It will be used to vilify Americans who are unwilling to assent to the new orthodoxy. In the course of its opinion, the majority compares traditional marriage laws to laws that denied equal treatment for African-Americans and women. *E.g., ante,* at 2598–2599. The implications of this analogy will be exploited by those who are determined to stamp out every vestige of dissent. Perhaps recognizing how its reasoning may be used, the majority attempts, toward the end of its opinion, to reassure those who oppose same-sex marriage that their rights of conscience will be protected. *Ante,* at 2606–2607. We will soon see whether this proves to be true. I assume that those who cling to old beliefs will be able to whisper their thoughts in the recesses of their homes, but if they repeat those views in public, they will risk being labeled as bigots and treated as such by governments, employers, and schools.

The system of federalism established by our Constitution provides a way for people with different beliefs to live together in a single nation. If the issue of same-sex marriage had been left to the people of the States, it is likely that some States would recognize same-sex marriage and others would not. It is also possible that some States would tie recognition to protection for conscience rights. The majority today makes that impossible. By imposing its own views on the entire country, the majority facilitates the marginalization of the many Americans who have traditional ideas. Recalling the harsh treatment of gays and lesbians in the past, some may think that turnabout is fair play. But if that sentiment prevails, the Nation will experience bitter and lasting wounds.

Today's decision will also have a fundamental effect on this Court and its ability to uphold the rule of law. If a bare majority of Justices can invent a new right and impose that right on the rest of the country, the only real limit on what future majorities will be able to do is their own sense of what those with political power and cultural influence are willing to tolerate. Even enthusiastic supporters of same-sex marriage should worry about the scope of the power that today's majority claims.

Today's decision shows that decades of attempts to restrain this Court's abuse of its authority have failed. A lesson that some will take from today's decision is that preaching about the proper method of interpreting the Constitution or the virtues of judicial self-restraint and humility cannot compete with the temptation to achieve what is viewed as a noble end by any practicable means. I do not doubt that my colleagues in the majority sincerely see in the Constitution a vision of liberty that happens to coincide with their own. But this sincerity is cause for concern, not comfort. What it evidences is the deep and perhaps irremediable corruption of our legal culture's conception of constitutional interpretation.

Most Americans—understandably—will cheer or lament today's decision because of their views on the issue of same-sex marriage. But all Americans, whatever their thinking on that issue, should worry about what the majority's claim of power portends.

PROBLEM TWO

Tim, Gina and Gabriel met during their first year of college. They quickly became friends and together they moved into a house they jointly rented not far from the city center where their college was located. Upon graduation each of them took a job but they shared all expenses pertaining to the house and commingled their resources into one jointly held account. Gina was intimate with both Tim and Gabriel; eventually the three of them began to share the same bed in their common home. After ten years together they decided they wanted to marry each other so they applied for a marriage license for them all at the county where they resided. The Domestic Relations Clerk denied them the license even though they were of sufficient age, unmarried, not related to one another, and possessed the proper capacity. Do you think the action of the Clerk is impacted by *Obergefell*? How do you think a judge is likely to rule?

D. ANNULMENT AND ITS EFFECTS

1. THE VOID-VOIDABLE DISTINCTION

An annulment action is brought to declare the legal invalidity of a particular union from its inception. A divorce action seeks to terminate a valid marriage as of a specific date after it came into legally recognized existence. Despite the simplicity of this conceptual framework, our legal treatment of annulment has been the subject of much confusion.

Some of the confused and confusing development surrounding the action for annulment can be attributed to suspicion and lack of understanding of the ecclesiastical law from which it derives. The problems were further exacerbated from an early time by inconsistent use of terms. Coke and Blackstone, the two most venerated commentators on the common law, applied the term "divorce" to all forms of disestablishment of the marriage relationship. The reason lay not in their lack of analytical capacity, but in the fact that English courts often used "divorce" to describe the situation in which the ecclesiastical courts were prepared to say that a marriage never had occurred (annulment), the case in which a separation of the parties would be decreed for grave reasons such as adultery or cruelty (the separation from bed and board, or divorce *a mensa et thoro*), and the case in which the marriage was terminated and the parties were free to remarry afterward (the divorce *a vinculo matrimonii*). This confusion of terminology can be found occasionally even today. *See, e.g.*, VA. CODE ANN. § 20–39 (2016).

The distinction between void and voidable unions is of considerable importance in most jurisdictions. Under the purist approach, a void marriage, which usually offends some strong public policy of the state, needs no formal judicial action or declaration to establish its invalidity. It can be attacked by third persons, and the challenge may be instituted even after death of the parties. Cohabitation between them following removal of the impediment that caused their union to be void will not serve to "ratify" and thereby validate the original marriage (though in some jurisdictions a new common-law marriage may take place). In states that recognize the void marriage concept in this "pure" form, courts nevertheless will entertain annulment actions in such cases in order to accord certainty to wealth transactions or legal relationships. However, some states now require an action for annulment or declaration of invalidity to establish the nullity of what most jurisdictions would regard as void marriages. Other jurisdictions provide for at least limited ratification of what traditionally would be a void (and thus not ratifiable) marriage on removal of the disqualifying impediment.

A voidable marriage typically reflects encroachment on some lesser public policy. Such a union can be ratified by conduct of the parties after removal of the legal impediment that made it vulnerable and unless it is judicially annulled in timely fashion (before ratification, death of a party, or tolling of the action under an applicable statute of limitation), it is valid from its inception. Under the doctrine of "relation back," however, a voidable marriage that has been annulled by a court is deemed to be void *ab initio*. The harshness of such a rule, which at one time could affect legitimacy of children and property rights of the parties, led to widespread adoption of various types of ameliorative statutes. *See* Uniform Marriage and Divorce Act § 208 alt. B, *infra*. Some jurisdictions even provide that a party can sue for divorce on a ground that conceptually should be the basis for annulment (for example, conduct or conditions dating from before the marriage).

Annulment provides an illustration of how the law in practice does not necessarily mirror the law as described in the books. Annulments sometimes have been granted on the joint request of parties who had no children and whose union was of short duration, even though the legal basis for such a ruling was highly tenuous. Historically this reflected both the difficulty of obtaining a divorce under the fault system and the widely held view that annulment was more socially acceptable than divorce. Also, annulment can be desirable for a person whose religious tenets are opposed to divorce. Attitudes about divorce have changed considerably with the advent of no-fault "breakdown" grounds, but the historic view of annulment as the less controversial alternative may be the major reason for its retention today when a persuasive case can be made that the action—at least when it involves only a voidable union—has become an anachronism.

UNIFORM MARRIAGE AND DIVORCE ACT (2015)

§ 207. Prohibited Marriages

(a) The following marriages are prohibited:

(1) a marriage entered into prior to the dissolution of an earlier marriage of one of the parties;

(2) a marriage between an ancestor and a descendant, or between a brother and a sister, whether the

relationship is by the half or the whole blood, or by adoption;

(3) a marriage between an uncle and a niece or between an aunt and a nephew, whether the relationship is by the half or the whole blood, except as to marriages permitted by the established customs of aboriginal cultures.

(b) Parties to a marriage prohibited under this section who cohabit after removal of the impediment are lawfully married as of the date of removal of the impediment.

(c) Children born of a prohibited marriage are legitimate.

§ 208. Declaration of Invalidity

(a) The [______] court shall enter its decree declaring the invalidity of a marriage entered into under the following circumstances:

(1) a party lacked capacity to consent to the marriage at the time the marriage was solemnized, either because of mental incapacity or infirmity or because of the influence of alcohol, drugs, or other incapacitating substances, or a party was induced to enter into a marriage by force or duress, or by fraud involving the essentials of marriage;

(2) a party lacks the physical capacity to consummate the marriage by sexual intercourse, and at the time the marriage was solemnized the other party did not know of the incapacity;

(3) a party [was under the age of 16 years and did not have the consent of his parents or guardian and judicial approval or] was aged 16 or 17 years and did not have the consent of his parents or guardian or judicial approval; or

(4) the marriage is prohibited.

(b) A declaration of invalidity under subsection (a)(1) through (3) may be sought by any of the following persons and must be commenced within the times specified, but in no event may a declaration of invalidity be sought after the death of either party to the marriage:

(1) for a reason set forth in subsection (a)(1), by either party or by the legal representative of the party who lacked capacity to consent, no later than 90 days after the petitioner obtained knowledge of the described condition;

(2) for the reason set forth in subsection (a)(2), by either party, no later than one year after the petitioner obtained knowledge of the described condition;

(3) for the reason set forth in subsection (a)(3), by the underaged party, his parent or guardian, prior to the time the underaged party reaches the age at which he could have married without satisfying the omitted requirement.

Alternative A

[(c) A declaration of invalidity for the reason set forth in subsection (a)(4) may be sought by either party, the legal spouse in case of a bigamous marriage, the [appropriate state official], or a child of either party, at any time prior to the death of one of the parties.]

Alternative B

[(c) A declaration of invalidity for the reason set forth in subsection (a)(4) may be sought by either party, the legal spouse in case of a bigamous marriage, the [appropriate state official] or a child of either party, at any time, not to exceed 5 years following the death of either party.]

(d) Children born of a marriage declared invalid are legitimate.

(e) Unless the court finds, after a consideration of all relevant circumstances, including the effect of a retroactive decree on third parties, that the interests of justice would be served by making the decree not retroactive, it shall declare the marriage invalid as of the date of the marriage. The provisions of this Act relating to property rights of the spouses, maintenance, support, and custody of children on dissolution of marriage are applicable to non-retroactive decrees of invalidity.

NOTES

Fraud. Under UMDA § 208(a)(1), *supra*, a marriage may be declared invalid, and thus annulled, if "a party was induced to enter [the] marriage by . . . fraud involving the *essentials* of marriage." The case of Meagher v. Maleki, 31 Cal.Rptr.3d 663 (Cal. Ct. App. 2005), illuminates the limits typically placed upon "the essentials of marriage." In *Meagher*, the wife, Meagher, sought an annulment of her marriage to Maleki and the restitution of property from him. During their courtship, Maleki falsely represented himself to her as a successful businessman and persuaded Meagher to invest substantial sums of her own money in a series of joint investments with Maleki that Maleki largely controlled. Once the couple married, and the true picture of Maleki's diminished finances and deceit became known to Meagher, Meagher sought annulment on the grounds that Maleki married her "just for money" and that she relied on false representations by Maleki that he was wealthy and could take care of her. The trial court agreed, "concluding that 'there was never a marriage' and that a judgment of nullity should be entered, and therefore that all the assets at issue were Meagher's sole and separate property." *Id.* at 666.

On appeal, the California Court of Appeal first reviewed the types of fraud that historically had been found to go to "the essentials of marriage," matters such as "[lying] about [one's] marital history, or . . . conceal[ing] an intention not to have sexual relations with [one's spouse], [or] not to live with [one's spouse] after the marriage, or not to discontinue an intimate relationship with a third party." *Id.* at 668–69. The court then reversed the trial court's grant of an annulment, rejecting the notion that Maleki's "financial fraud . . . is 'at least as contrary to the essence of marriage' as the types of fraud that have been held sufficient to justify annulment. . . . [Instead,] the cases are entirely to the contrary. Accordingly, we agree with Maleki that the fraud established in this case, as a matter of law, was not of the type that constitutes an adequate basis for granting an annulment." *Id.* at 669.

Reinstatement. One thorny question raised by annulment is whether a spousal support award that terminated upon remarriage may be reinstated upon annulment of the later marriage. Some states now permit spousal maintenance awards to be reinstated by statute. *See* UTAH CODE ANN. § 30–3–5(9) (2016), which provides that:

> Unless a decree of divorce specifically provides otherwise, any order of the court that a party pay alimony to a former spouse automatically terminates upon the remarriage or death of that former spouse. However, if the remarriage is annulled and found to be void *ab initio*, payment of alimony shall resume if the party paying alimony is made a party to the action of annulment and his rights are determined.

In the absence of such a clear statutory directive, courts have taken a number of approaches to reinstatement. The Superior Court of Connecticut, in Fredo v. Fredo, 894 A.2d 399 (Conn. Super. Ct. 2005), describes the range of approaches taken by various jurisdictions:

> [T]he case-by-case approach is the least desirable option. By its very nature, it provides the least certainty and guidance to litigants. . . . Adoption of the case-by-case approach would eviscerate the clear intent of the agreement and deprive the parties of the finality and certainty for which they bargained. A review of the cases that have adopted this approach demonstrates the breadth of the considerations that a court might consider . . . length of the subsequent marriage; whether the alimony recipient receives support as a result of the annulled marriage; the degree to which the payor spouse is prejudiced by the revival of the alimony obligation; the circumstances surrounding the annulment; any changes in the parties' respective financial circumstances. . . . Far from creating a bright line, this approach establishes no line. It vests far too much discretion in a court on an issue which the parties, by the terms of their agreement, decided for themselves . . .

[and] does little to assist family law litigants in their efforts to plan and move on with the very real lives that they lead. . . .

This leaves the court with one of the two remaining alternative approaches: the automatic termination approach or the void/voidable approach. Under the automatic termination approach, the recipient's right to alimony under the decree would be extinguished, in any and all events, upon the occurrence of the ceremonial marriage with her subsequent husband. Under the void/voidable approach, the recipient's right to alimony under the decree is revivable only if the annulled subsequent marriage is determined to be void (as opposed to voidable). . . .

This court joins those courts that have adopted the automatic termination approach. . . . By entering into another marriage, the alimony recipient has made an election to look to another for support. That election in no way hinged on how the later marriage worked out. That the subsequent marriage may later be determined not to be valid does not detract from such a result any more than would the untimely death of the recipient's new spouse or a sudden breakdown in their relationship. . . .

Interests of finality and certainty are furthered only by the automatic termination approach. Upon the recipient's remarriage, the obligor has every right to reorder their life and commit to things which theretofore might not have been practical or possible. . . . If "remarriage" referred only to a valid second marriage, the alimony obligor would be placed in the untenable position of never being certain that the financial responsibility for his former wife would not shift back to him.

Other practical considerations warrant adoption of the automatic termination approach. The obligor may not, indeed likely would not, have access to the facts which form the basis for the claimed annulment and, moreover, would certainly lack standing in an annulment proceeding to be heard on the issue of the validity of the subsequent marriage. . . .

Is the obligor, a nonparty to the annulment proceedings, collaterally bound thereby? And if not, how does the obligor, a stranger to the facts underlying the annulment, go about uncovering them in his effort to attack the annulment decree collaterally? Moreover, any approach other than the automatic termination approach would allow for the unseemly possibility that the alimony recipient may have rights of support from two spouses (resurrecting the alimony obligation under the existing decree, and creating new obligations from the subsequent spouse in the annulment/dissolution proceeding.) Even if a court were not inclined to allow the existence of dual support orders, the recipient would be in the enviable position of choosing the source of support which she prefers. . . . Furthermore, if the subsequent marriage is determined to be void and, therefore, a nullity ab initio, the

> terminating event (remarriage) would be deemed not to have occurred. Under these facts, absent application of the automatic termination approach, the obligor not only remains obligated to continue paying in the future—he arguably remains obligated to pay an arrearage which accrued back to the date of the remarriage which "never took place." . . .
>
> All of these issues arise because the recipient, as here, made an election to look elsewhere for her support. The obligor "has a right to assume the validity of the second marriage and to arrange his affairs accordingly. When his former wife voluntarily accepts the risk of a subsequent marriage, he should not be held accountable for her gullibility, mistake or misfortune." . . . For all of the reasons previously indicated, this court finds that the occurrence of the defendant's ceremonial marriage to her new spouse constituted a remarriage within the meaning of the agreement and decree.

In McConkey v. McConkey, 215 S.E.2d 640 (Va. 1975), the Virginia Supreme Court also opted for a bright-line rule, holding that "[t]o require the former husband to proceed during [the ex-wife's subsequent marriage] at his peril in making financial commitments that could be suddenly disrupted, through no fault of his, would be to penalize him for events beyond his control." *Id.*

As the *Fredo* court noted, other courts adopt the case-by-case approach. In *In re* Marriage of Cargill and Rollins, 843 P.2d 1335 (Colo. 1993), the Supreme Court of Colorado allowed the resumption of a prior spousal support obligation, looking to factors such as

> the length of the second marriage, whether the annulment of the second marriage was proper and should bind the first spouse, whether maintenance is being paid (or is more than theoretically payable) from the invalidated marriage, the circumstances of the parties, and whether the payor spouse would suffer substantial prejudice by reinstating maintenance payments. In sum, the district court should be guided by its role as a court of equity in such matters.

Id. at 1343

In Joye v. Yon, 547 S.E.2d 888 (S.C. Ct. App. 2001), the South Carolina Court of Appeals held that alimony would be restored after an absolutely void marriage (the alimony recipient's putative husband had never been divorced from his prior wife), specifically rejecting the argument that "remarriage" could include such a union for determining alimony termination. The court found no indication in the record that the first husband (the alimony payor) had changed his financial position in reliance upon his wife's void union, and the time lapse was not great. However, the Supreme Court of South Carolina reversed and remanded the case, holding that

> the case by case approach affords the Court the most appropriate method for resolving this novel issue. Just as the family court employs principles of equity in determining support and

> maintenance, equitable distribution, and child custody, so should it embrace these same principles in determining whether payor spouse's periodic alimony obligation is revived after payee spouse's subsequent marriage is annulled.
>
> Restricting family courts to the rigid void/voidable [marriage] approach or the automatic termination approach could produce unjust results. For example, payee spouse remarries, and ten years later, she discovers that her present marriage was bigamous. If the state employs the void/voidable approach, former payor spouse's support and maintenance is revived regardless of the change of circumstances and the amount of time payee spouse had to determine that her second marriage was void *ab initio*. Equity *may* deem this result unfair. Another example would be a payee spouse being fraudulently induced into a subsequent marriage. She quickly discovers the fraud, brings an annulment action, and her subsequent marriage is void. Under the automatic termination approach, the family court judge would be barred from reinstating periodic alimony. Equity *may* also deem this result unfair, as the payee spouse's subsequent marriage was short-lived, and the payor spouse would likely not be prejudiced if he resumed making the alimony payments. A case by case approach provides the family court judge with the tools to avoid these potentially inequitable results.

Joye v. Yon, 586 S.E.2d 131, 134 (S.C. 2003).

A factor that has influenced some courts in the past is whether state law provides for a possible support award to a spouse in an annulment action. The problem can arise both with regard to judicial decrees for alimony and provisions of separation and property settlement agreements. How would you word a decree or contractual provision to deal effectively with it?

2. PUTATIVE MARRIAGE

750 ILLINOIS COMPILED STATUTES ANN. (2016)

§ 305. Putative Spouse

Any person, having gone through a marriage ceremony, who has cohabited with another to whom he is not legally married in the good faith belief that he was married to that person is a putative spouse until knowledge of the fact that he is not legally married terminates his status and prevents acquisition of further rights. A putative spouse acquires the rights conferred upon a legal spouse, including the right to maintenance following termination of his status, whether or not the marriage is prohibited, under Section 212, or declared invalid, under Section 301. If there is a legal spouse or other putative spouse, rights acquired by a putative spouse do not supersede the rights of the legal spouse or those acquired by other putative spouses, but the court shall apportion property, maintenance and support rights among the claimants as appropriate in the circumstances and in the interests of justice. This

Section shall not apply to common law marriages contracted in the State after June 30, 1905.

Williams v. Williams

Nevada Supreme Court, 2004
97 P.3d 1124

■ PER CURIAM.

This is a case of first impression involving the application of the putative spouse doctrine in an annulment proceeding. Under the doctrine, an individual whose marriage is void due to a prior legal impediment is treated as a spouse so long as the party seeking equitable relief participated in the marriage ceremony with the good-faith belief that the ceremony was legally valid. A majority of states recognize the doctrine when dividing property acquired during the marriage, applying equitable principles, based on community property law, to the division. However, absent fraud, the doctrine does not apply to awards of spousal support. While some states have extended the doctrine to permit spousal support awards, they have done so under the authority of state statutes.

We agree with the majority view. Consequently, we adopt the putative spouse doctrine in annulment proceedings for purposes of property division and affirm the district court's division of the property. However, we reject the doctrine as a basis of awarding equitable spousal support. Because Nevada's annulment statutes do not provide for an award of support upon annulment, we reverse the district court's award of spousal support. On August 26, 1973, appellant Richard E. Williams underwent a marriage ceremony with respondent Marcie C. Williams. At that time, Marcie believed that she was divorced from John Allmaras. However, neither Marcie nor Allmaras had obtained a divorce. Richard and Marcie believed they were legally married and lived together, as husband and wife, for 27 years. In March 2000, Richard discovered that Marcie was not divorced from Allmaras at the time of their marriage ceremony.

In August 2000, Richard and Marcie permanently separated. In February 2001, Richard filed a complaint for an annulment. Marcie answered and counterclaimed for one-half of the property and spousal support as a putative spouse. In April 2002, the parties engaged in a one-day bench trial to resolve the matter. At trial, Richard testified that had he known Marcie was still married, he would not have married her. He claimed that Marcie knew she was not divorced when she married him or had knowledge that would put a reasonable person on notice to check if the prior marriage had been dissolved. Specifically, Richard stated that Marcie should not have relied on statements from Allmaras that he had obtained a divorce because Marcie never received any legal notice of divorce proceedings. In addition, Richard claimed that in March 2000, when Marcie received a social security check in the name of Marcie

Allmaras, Marcie told him that she had never been divorced from Allmaras. Marcie denied making the statement.

Marcie testified that she believed she was not married to her former husband, John Allmaras, and was able to marry again because Allmaras told her they were divorced. Marcie further testified that in 1971, she ran into Allmaras at a Reno bus station, where he specifically told her that they were divorced and he was living with another woman. According to Marcie, she discovered she was still married to Allmaras during the course of the annulment proceedings with Richard. Marcie testified that if she had known at any time that she was still married to Allmaras, she would have obtained a divorce from him.

During the 27 years that the parties believed themselves to be married, Marcie was a homemaker and a mother. From 1981 to 1999, Marcie was a licensed child-care provider for six children. During that time, she earned $460 a week. At trial, Marcie had a certificate of General Educational Development (G.E.D.) and earned $8.50 an hour at a retirement home. She was 63 years old and lived with her daughter because she could not afford to live on her own. Both parties stipulated to the value of most of their jointly-owned property. At the time of the annulment proceeding, the parties held various items in their joint names, including bank accounts, vehicles, life insurance policies, a Sparks home, a radiator business, and a motorcycle.

The district court found that Marcie had limited ability to support herself. The district court also concluded that both parties believed they were legally married, acted as husband and wife, and conceived and raised two children. Marcie stayed home to care for and raise their children. Based upon these facts, the district court granted the annulment and awarded Marcie one-half of all the jointly-held property and spousal support. The district court did not indicate whether its award was based on the putative spouse doctrine or an implied contract and quantum meruit theory. The final judgment divided the parties' property so that each received assets of approximately the same value. It also ordered Richard to pay Marcie the sum of $500 per month for a period of four years as "reimbursement and compensation for the benefit received by [Richard] by way of [Marcie's] forgoing a career outside the home in order to care for [Richard] and their children." Richard timely appealed the district court's judgment.

A marriage is void if either of the parties to the marriage has a former husband or wife then living. Richard and Marcie's marriage was void because Marcie was still married to another man when she married Richard. Although their marriage was void, an annulment proceeding was necessary to legally sever their relationship. An annulment proceeding is the proper manner to dissolve a void marriage and resolve other issues arising from the dissolution of the relationship.

First, Richard contends that Marcie is not entitled to one-half of their joint property because their marriage was void. Richard asserts that application of the putative spouse doctrine and quasi-community property principles was improper. Alternatively, Richard argues that if the district court relied on implied contract and quantum meruit theories, the district court should have divided the parties' residence according to this court's decision in *Sack v. Tomlin*, which would provide Richard with 67 percent of the assets instead of 50 percent.

Second, Richard argues that the district court erred in awarding spousal support. Richard contends support is not permitted, absent statutory authority, under the putative spouse doctrine and that there is no basis in Nevada law for awarding compensation for services rendered during the marriage under a theory of quantum meruit. Because the record does not reflect the basis for the district court's decision, resolution of Richard's contentions requires us to address the putative spouse doctrine.

Under the putative spouse doctrine, when a marriage is legally void, the civil effects of a legal marriage flow to the parties who contracted to marry in good faith. That is, a putative spouse is entitled to many of the rights of an actual spouse. A majority of states have recognized some form of the doctrine through case law or statute.[7] States differ, however, on what exactly constitutes a "civil effect." The doctrine was developed to avoid depriving innocent parties who believe in good faith that they are married from being denied the economic and status-related benefits of marriage, such as property division, pension, and health benefits.

The doctrine has two elements: (1) a proper marriage ceremony was performed, and (2) one or both of the parties had a good-faith belief that there was no impediment to the marriage and the marriage was valid and proper. "Good faith" has been defined as an "honest and reasonable belief that the marriage was valid at the time of the ceremony." Good faith is presumed. The party asserting lack of good faith has the burden of proving bad faith. Whether the party acted in good faith is a question of fact. Unconfirmed rumors or mere suspicions of a legal impediment do not vitiate good faith " 'so long as no certain or authoritative knowledge of some legal impediment comes to him or her.' " However, when a person receives reliable information that an impediment exists, the individual cannot ignore the information, but instead has a duty to investigate further. Persons cannot act " 'blindly or without reasonable precaution.' " Finally, once a spouse learns of the impediment, the putative marriage ends.

We have not previously considered the putative spouse doctrine, but we are persuaded by the rationale of our sister states that public policy supports adopting the doctrine in Nevada. Fairness and equity favor recognizing putative spouses when parties enter into a marriage ceremony in good faith and without knowledge that there is a factual or legal impediment to their marriage. Nor does the doctrine conflict with

---

[7] Christopher L. Blakesley, *The Putative Marriage Doctrine,* 60 TUL. L. REV. 1 (1985).

Nevada's policy in refusing to recognize common-law marriages or palimony suits. In the putative spouse doctrine, the parties have actually attempted to enter into a formal relationship with the solemnization of a marriage ceremony, a missing element in common-law marriages and palimony suits. As a majority of our sister states have recognized, the sanctity of marriage is not undermined, but rather enhanced, by the recognition of the putative spouse doctrine. We therefore adopt the doctrine in Nevada.

We now apply the doctrine to the instant case. The district court found that the parties obtained a license and participated in a marriage ceremony on August 26, 1973, in Verdi, Nevada. The district court also found that Marcie erroneously believed that her prior husband, Allmaras, had terminated their marriage by divorce and that she was legally able to marry Richard. In so finding, the district court also necessarily rejected Richard's argument that Marcie acted unreasonably in relying on Allmaras' statements because she had never been served with divorce papers and that she had a duty to inquire about the validity of her former marriage before marrying Richard.

Although Richard's and Marcie's testimony conflicted on this issue, judging the credibility of the witnesses and the weight to be given to their testimony are matters within the discretion of the district court. "This court reviews district court decisions concerning divorce proceedings for an abuse of discretion. Rulings supported by substantial evidence will not be disturbed on appeal." Substantial evidence is that which a sensible person may accept as adequate to sustain a judgment. We apply the same standard in annulment proceedings. The district court was free to disregard Richard's testimony, and substantial evidence supports the district court's finding that Marcie did not act unreasonably in relying upon Allmaras' representations. The record reflects no reason for Marcie to have disbelieved him and, thus, no reason to have investigated the truth of his representations. Although older case law suggests that a party cannot rely on a former spouse's representation of divorce, more recent cases indicate this is just a factor for the judge to consider in determining good faith. We conclude that the district court did not err in finding that Marcie entered into the marriage in good faith. She therefore qualifies as a putative spouse. We now turn to the effect of the doctrine on the issues of property division and alimony.

Community property states that recognize the putative spouse doctrine apply community property principles to the division of property, including determinations of what constitutes community and separate property. Since putative spouses believe themselves to be married, they are already under the assumption that community property laws would apply to a termination of their relationship. There is no point, therefore, in devising a completely separate set of rules for dividing property differently in a putative spouse scenario. We agree with this reasoning.

In some states, courts apply community property principles to divide property acquired during the purported marriage. In other states, the property is considered to be held under joint tenancy principles and is divided equally between the parties. Regardless of the approach, all states that recognize the putative spouse doctrine divide assets acquired during the marriage in an equitable fashion. We conclude that the application of community property principles to a putative marriage, as indicated in *Sanguinetti v. Sanguinetti,* is the better approach to the division of property in such cases.[25] In this case, the district court treated the parties' property as quasi-community property and equally divided the joint property between the parties. Substantial evidence supports the district court's division, and we affirm the district court's distribution of the property.

States are divided on whether spousal support is a benefit or civil effect that may be awarded under the putative spouse doctrine. Although some states permit the award of alimony, they do so because their annulment statutes permit an award of rehabilitative or permanent alimony. At least one state, however, has found alimony to be a civil effect under the putative spouse doctrine even in the absence of a specific statute permitting an award of alimony.[28]

Nevada statutes do not provide for an award of alimony after an annulment. Thus, the cases in which alimony was awarded pursuant to statute are of little help in resolving this issue. In those cases, state legislatures had codified the putative spouse doctrine and specifically indicated that issues such as property division and alimony were to be resolved in the same manner as if the void marriage had been valid. Absent such a determination by the Nevada Legislature, we must look to the cases in which courts have either refused to award alimony in the absence of statutory authority, despite recognizing the doctrine for other purposes, or awarded spousal support based on the putative spouse doctrine.

In *McKinney v. McKinney,* the Georgia Supreme Court summarily stated that alimony is not available in an equitable action for annulment because the right to alimony depends upon a valid marriage. . . . [T]he Georgia Supreme Court does appear to have relied on the putative spouse doctrine in dividing the parties' property since it discussed concepts of good faith. . . .

---

[25] Different rules may apply when one of the parties qualifies as a putative spouse and the other does not. When a person enters into the relationship with knowledge of an impediment and knowledge the marriage is not valid, some states have found the person who acted in bad faith is not entitled to benefit from the marriage. We do not reach this issue because the facts of this case involve two innocent putative spouses.

[28] *Cortes v. Fleming,* 307 So. 2d 611 (La. 1974). While the Louisiana Supreme Court did not rely on a statute specifically granting a putative spouse the right to alimony in its decision, the court did use an annulment statute as a basis of the award. The court indicated the term "civil effect" in the annulment statute was broad enough to include alimony. Nevada does not have similar language in its annulment statutes.

The California Supreme Court followed the same rationale in *Sanguinetti,* noting that a putative spouse has no right to an allowance of alimony. However, the California Supreme Court found that a putative spouse could maintain a claim under quantum meruit for the reasonable value of the services that the putative spouse rendered to the marriage if there was fraud or fault (such as cruelty) committed by the party opposing alimony.

In a similar case, *Kindle v. Kindle*, the Florida Court of Appeals upheld an award of alimony when the husband failed to disclose his previous marriage and was not divorced when he entered into a second marriage ceremony.... At the time the couple married, Preston was already married, but he never disclosed this to Kikeu.... The court further stated that "[i]t would be grossly inequitable to deny alimony to a putative wife of a twenty-year marriage because the husband fraudulently entered into a marriage ceremony." *Sanguinetti* and *Kindle,* however, are distinguishable from the instant case. In those cases, the courts found fraud, bad faith or bad conduct, such as cruelty, to support the award of equitable alimony. In the instant case, Richard and Marcie each acted in good faith. Neither Richard nor Marcie knowingly defrauded the other, and there is no evidence of misconduct or bad faith.

We can find no case, and Marcie has cited to none, in which spousal support was awarded to a putative spouse absent statutory authority, fraud, bad faith or bad conduct. Although one commentator favors such awards on the theory that the purpose of the putative spouse doctrine is to fulfill the reasonable expectations of the parties, we are unaware of any court adopting such a standard.

The putative spouse doctrine did not traditionally provide for an award of spousal support. Extensions of the doctrine have come through statute or findings of fraud and bad faith. As neither is present in this case, we decline to extend the doctrine to permit an award of spousal support when both parties act in good faith. Richard and Marcie's marriage was void, and there was no showing of bad faith or fraud by either party. Absent an equitable basis of bad faith or fraud or a statutory basis, the district court had no authority to grant the spousal support award, and we reverse that part of the judgment awarding spousal support.

NOTES

The putative spouse doctrine safeguards the economic interests of a party who cohabited in a good faith belief that the marriage was valid, not only upon divorce but upon death. In Estate of Leslie, 689 P.2d 133, 144–45 (Cal. 1984), the Supreme Court of California determined that where "the couple involved . . . lived together for a substantial period of time, conducting themselves as husband and wife throughout their union [which occurs in most putative spouse cases], . . . [that t]o deny one of their members an intestate share of the decedent's separate property . . . leads to unjust results. Therefore, this court holds that a surviving putative spouse is entitled to succeed to a share of the decedent's separate property. Similar reasoning supports the conclusion that a surviving putative spouse is entitled to first preference for" the right to administer the estate.

Other approaches to dealing with economic entitlement include common-law marriage, the presumption of validity of the most recent union, and ameliorative statutes that confer certain incidents of marriage such as legitimacy of offspring. Until recently the putative marriage doctrine existed largely in community property states. Inclusion of optional Section 209 in the Uniform Marriage and Divorce Act has led to more widespread adoption. *See* Unif. Marriage and Divorce Act, References and Annotations, "Table of Jurisdictions Wherein Act has been Adopted" (2015). A form of the "putative spouse" test, dealing with cases of ceremonialized marriages that are invalidated because of an unknown impediment, is contained in the federal Social Security law. 42 U.S.C.A. § 416(h)(1)(B)(i) (2012).

For a detailed examination of the putative marriage doctrine and its effects, *see* Monica Hof Wallace, *The Pitfalls of a Putative Marriage and the Call for a Putative Divorce*, 64 LA. L. REV. 71 (2003).

E. DETERMINING LEGAL ELIGIBILITY

States impose a number of different requirements for couples to marry, sometimes called impediments to marriage. These frequently concern age, the degree of relatedness by blood or legal relationship, mental capacity, and gender. *See Grounds for Divorce, 50 State Statutory Survey*, 0080 SURVEYS 9 (West 2007).

1. MINIMUM AGE REQUIREMENTS

Moe v. Dinkins

United States District Court, Southern District of New York, 1981
533 F. Supp. 623

■ MOTLEY, DISTRICT JUDGE.

Plaintiffs Maria Moe, Raoul Roe and Ricardo Roe seek a judgment declaring unconstitutional, and enjoining the enforcement of, the parental consent requirement of New York Domestic Relations Law §§ 15.2 and 15.3. Section 15.2 provides that all male applicants for a marriage license between ages 16 and 18 and all female applicants between ages 14 and 18 must obtain "written consent to the marriage from both parents of the minor or minors or such as shall then be living. . . ." Section 15.3 requires that a woman between ages 14 and 16 obtain judicial approval of the marriage, as well as the parental consent required by Section 15.2. This action is now before the court on plaintiffs' motion for summary judgment declaring Section 15 unconstitutional and enjoining its enforcement. . . .

Plaintiff Raoul Roe was eighteen years old when this action was commenced. Plaintiff Maria Moe was fifteen years old. Plaintiff Ricardo Roe is their one year old son who was born out of wedlock. Plaintiffs live together as an independent family unit. In late November, 1978, Maria became pregnant by Raoul and in April, 1979, they moved into an apartment together. Maria requested consent from her mother, a widow, to marry Raoul, but Mrs. Moe refused, allegedly because she wishes to continue receiving welfare benefits for Maria. Maria and Raoul continue to be prevented from marrying because of Mrs. Moe's failure to give consent to the marriage as required by Section 15. Maria and Raoul allege that they wish to marry in order to cement their family unit and to remove the stigma of illegitimacy from their son, Ricardo. In addition, Cristina Coe and Pedro Doe have moved to intervene as plaintiffs and additional class representatives in this action . . . and for an order allowing them to proceed with this action under pseudonyms and without appointment of a guardian ad litem.

For the reasons discussed below, the motion for intervention is granted. Plaintiffs' motion for summary judgment declaring Section 15 unconstitutional is denied. This court holds that the parental consent requirement of Section 15 does not violate plaintiffs' constitutional rights.

Proposed plaintiff-intervenor Cristina Coe is fifteen years old. Proposed plaintiff-intervenor Pedro Doe is seventeen years old. Cristina is eight months pregnant with Pedro's child. Cristina and Pedro reside in the home of Pedro's father and step-mother. In January 1981, when Cristina discovered she was pregnant, she and Pedro informed Cristina's mother of their desire to have their child and to marry. Mrs. Coe refused to give Cristina her consent to marry and arranged for Cristina to have an abortion. Cristina refused to keep the appointments her mother made for her at the abortion clinic. Consequently, Mrs. Coe told Cristina she wanted to have nothing more to do with her and that she was leaving the country to live in the Dominican Republic.

Cristina and Pedro wish to marry to express their commitment to and caring for each other, to legitimate their relationship, and to raise their child in accord with their beliefs in a traditional family setting sanctioned by law. They wish to marry before their child is born so that he or she will never have the stigma of illegitimacy attached to his or her life. However, Cristina and Pedro are precluded from petitioning for judicial approval to obtain a marriage license by operation of Section 15 because Mrs. Coe, Cristina's custodial parent, refuses to consent to the marriage. . . .

The claims of Cristina and Pedro present the same legal issue presented by the present plaintiffs—whether the parental consent requirement of Section 15 is constitutional. Like plaintiffs Maria Moe and Raoul Roe, Cristina and Pedro wish to marry in order to cement their family unit and raise their child without the stigma of illegitimacy. Like

Maria and Raoul, Cristina and Pedro are prevented from marrying by the parental veto imposed by Section 15. Intervention will not result in any delay or prejudice to the rights of the original parties or to the orderly process of this court. In addition, plaintiffs argue that the intervention of Pedro and Cristina will present the court with a more complete picture of the impact of Section 15's parental consent requirement and will add to the representativeness of the named class members. Section 15 requires that Maria, who is now sixteen, must have parental consent to obtain a marriage license. Section 15 requires that Cristina must obtain judicial approval to marry, but precludes her from petitioning for judicial approval unless her parent has consented. While Maria has already borne a child, Cristina is now expecting a baby and is thus in a position to totally avoid the stigma of illegitimacy for her child.

Defendants object to the intervention of Cristina and Pedro . . . [and] contend that Cristina and Pedro do not belong in the plaintiff class because New York law provides them with a means to obtain a marriage license without Cristina's mother's consent. Defendants state that under the New York Social Services Law a child less than eighteen years old may be declared abandoned by his or her parent. In that case, defendants contend, the Surrogate may grant letters of guardianship for the purpose of consenting to the teenager's marriage if marriage would be in the teenager's best interests. Defendants' contention is contrary to the ruling of the Court of Appeals in Moe v. Dinkins, *supra*, 635 F.2d at 1049, that in New York "the consent of a court-appointed guardian cannot bypass the statutory requirement of parental consent, regardless of the unfairness created by a refusal to grant permission." In that decision, the Court of Appeals rejected each of the alternative constructions of Section 15 posed by defendants which might allow an exception to the parental consent requirement. . . .

Plaintiffs contend that Section 15 of the New York Domestic Relations Law,[1] requiring parental consent for the marriage of minors between the ages of fourteen and eighteen, deprives them of the liberty which is guaranteed to them by the Due Process Clause of the Fourteenth Amendment to the Federal Constitution.

---

[1] The pertinent parts of Section 15 are as follows: (2) If it shall appear upon an application of the applicant as provided in this section or upon information required by the clerk that the man is under eighteen years of age and is not under sixteen years of age, or that the woman is under the age of eighteen and not under fourteen years of age, then the town or city clerk before he shall issue a license shall require the written consent to the marriage from both parents of the minor or minors or such as shall then be living, or if the parents of both are dead, then the written consent of the guardians of such minor or minors. . . . If the marriage of the parents of such a minor has been dissolved by decree of divorce or annulment, the consent of the parent to whom the court which granted the decree has awarded custody of such minor shall be sufficient. If there is no parent or guardian of the minor or minors living to their knowledge then the town or city clerk shall require the written consent for the marriage of the person under whose care and government the minor or minors may be before a license shall be issued. N.Y. Dom. Rel. Law § 15 (14 McKinney). [As of 2012, § 15 applies "If . . . *either party* is at least sixteen years of age but under eighteen years of age" (italics added).]

A review of Supreme Court decisions defining liberties guaranteed by the Fourteenth Amendment reveals that activities relating to child-rearing and education of children, procreation, abortion, family relations, contraception, and, most recently, marriage, are constitutionally protected rights of individual privacy embodied within the concept of liberty which the Due Process Clause of the Fourteenth Amendment was designed to protect. However, [none of these decisions] arose in the context of state regulation of marriages of minors. In that respect, this is a case of first impression.

While it is true that a child, because of his minority, is not beyond the protection of the Constitution, the Court has recognized the State's power to make adjustments in the constitutional rights of minors. . . . This power to adjust minors' constitutional rights flows from the State's concern with the unique position of minors. In Bellotti v. Baird, 443 U.S. 622 (1979), the Court noted "three reasons justifying the conclusion that the constitutional rights of children cannot be equated with those of adults: the peculiar vulnerability of children; their inability to make critical decisions in an informed and mature manner; and the importance of the parental role in child-rearing." Likewise, marriage occupies a unique position under the law. It has been the subject of extensive regulation and control, within constitutional limits, in its inception and termination and has "long been regarded as a virtually exclusive province of the State." Sosna v. Iowa, 419 U.S. 393, 404 (1975).

While it is evident that the New York law before this court directly abridges the right of minors to marry, *in the absence of parental consent*, the question is whether the State interests that support the abridgement can overcome the substantive protection of the Constitution. The unique position of minors and marriage under the law leads this court to conclude that Section 15 should not be subjected to strict scrutiny, the test which the Supreme Court has ruled must be applied whenever a state statute burdens the exercise of a fundamental liberty protected by the Constitution. Applying strict scrutiny would require determination of whether there was a compelling state interest and whether the statute had been closely tailored to achieve that state interest. The compelling state purpose necessitated by application of the strict scrutiny test "would cast doubt on a network of restrictions that the States have fashioned to govern marriage and divorce." Zablocki v. Redhail, 434 U.S. at 399 (Powell, J., concurring). It is this court's view that Section 15 should be looked at solely to determine whether there exists a rational relation between the means chosen by the New York legislature and the legitimate state interests advanced by the State.

The State interests advanced to justify the parental consent requirement of Section 15 include the protection of minors from immature decision-making and preventing unstable marriages. The State possesses paternalistic power to protect and promote the welfare of children who lack the capacity to act in their own best interest. The State interests in mature decision-making and in preventing unstable marriages are legitimate under its *parens patriae* power.

An age attainment requirement for marriage is established in every American jurisdiction. The requirement of parental consent ensures that at least one mature person will participate in the decision of a minor to marry. That the State has provided for such consent in Section 15 is rationally related to the State's legitimate interest in light of the fact that minors often lack the "experience, perspective and judgment" necessary to make "important, affirmative choices with potentially serious consequences." Bellotti v. Baird, *supra*, 443 U.S. at 635–36. Yet, plaintiffs fault the parental consent requirement of Section 15 as possibly arbitrary, suggesting that courts, as non-interested third parties, are in a better position to judge whether a minor is prepared for the responsibilities that attach to marriage. Although the possibility for parents to act in other than the best interest of their child exists, the law presumes that the parents "possess what the child lacks in maturity" and that "the natural bonds of affection lead parents to act in the best interest of their children." Parham v. J.R., 442 U.S. 584, 610 (1979) (procedure for voluntary commitment of children under eighteen to state hospitals by their parents held constitutional). "That the governmental power should supercede parental authority in all cases because some parents" may act in other than the best interest of their children is "repugnant to the American tradition." Id. at 602–03. . . .

Plaintiffs also contend that Section 15 denied them the opportunity to make an individualized showing of maturity and denies them the only means by which they can legitimize their children and live in the traditional family unit sanctioned by law. On the other hand, New York's Section 15 merely delays plaintiffs' access to the institution of marriage. Moreover, the prohibition does not bar minors whose parents consent to their child's marriage. Assuming *arguendo* that the illegitimacy of plaintiff Moe's child and plaintiff Coe's yet unborn child is a harm, it is not a harm inflicted by Section 15. It is merely an incidental consequence of the lawful exercise of State power. The illegitimacy of plaintiffs' children, like the denial of marriage without parental consent, is a temporary situation at worst. A subsequent marriage of the parents legitimatizes the child, thereby erasing the mark of illegitimacy. The rights or benefits flowing from the marriage of minors are only temporarily suspended by Section 15. Any alleged harm to these rights and benefits is not inflicted by Section 15, but is simply an incidental consequence of the valid exercise of State power.

The fact that the State has elected to use a simple criterion, age, to determine probable maturity in the absence of parental consent, instead of requiring proof of maturity on a case by case basis, is reasonable, even if the rule produces seemingly arbitrary results in individual cases. "Simply because the decision of a parent is not agreeable to a child or because there is a [possible stigmatization of the child] does not automatically transfer power to make the decision from parents to some other agency or officer of the state." Parham v. J.R., 442 U.S. at 603. . . .

This court concludes that Section 15's requirement of parental consent is rationally related to the State's legitimate interests in mature decision-making with respect to marriage by minors and preventing unstable marriages. It is also rationally related to the State's legitimate interest in supporting the fundamental privacy right of a parent to act in what the parent perceives to be the best interest of the child free from state court scrutiny. Section 15, therefore, does not offend the constitutional rights of minors but represents a constitutionally valid exercise of state power.

Accordingly, plaintiffs' motion for summary judgment in their favor is denied and summary judgment is entered in favor of defendants.

NOTES

Judge Motley's decision was upheld in Moe v. Dinkins, 669 F.2d 67 (2d Cir. 1982), *cert. denied,* 459 U.S. 827 (1982). In a short Per Curiam opinion the Court of Appeals concluded that:

> Judge Motley was correct in testing the constitutionality of New York Domestic Relations Law § 15 by determining whether there exists a rational relation between the means chosen by the New York legislature and legitimate state interests in adopting and enforcing the restriction. In light of New York's important interest in promoting the welfare of children by preventing unstable marriages among those lacking the capacity to act in their best interests, we agree . . . that the New York statutory scheme passed constitutional muster.

Problems regarding the minimum age for marriage today reflect influences as varying as medieval feudalism and contemporary wisdom about the capacity of adolescents. It is usually stated that the common law set the age of consent to marry at 14 for males and 12 for females. *See* SIR FREDERICK POLLOCK AND FREDERICK WILLIAM MAITLAND, HISTORY OF ENGLISH LAW 389–90 (1968); HENRY SWINBURNE, TREATISE OF SPOUSALS, OR MATRIMONIAL CONTRACTS §§ 8–9 (2010).

In this country, state legislatures typically establish one age at which a person is deemed fully competent to marry and another at which marriage can take place with parental consent. *See Marriage Age Requirements*, 50 State Statutory Surveys: Family Law: Marriage, 0080 SURVEYS 22 (West 2007). The ages for marrying once were different for women and men in many jurisdictions, though this had largely changed even before similar discrimination in the context of child support provisions was declared unconstitutional in Stanton v. Stanton, 429 U.S. 501 (1977). Age can be an important factor for many legal concerns, ranging from juvenile court jurisdiction to eligibility for drivers' licenses. However, after ratification of the 26th Amendment in 1971, which lowered the voting age to 18 in federal elections, many states acted to remove many disabilities of infancy at least by that age. (There has been a subsequent movement toward fixing a higher minimum age for purchase of alcohol.)

Problems about marriage capacity that reached the courts under this system often centered on whether (a) a marriage below the permitted age with parental consent, or (b) a marriage without parental consent but within the age range when parental consent would validate the union, is void, voidable, or valid. Some courts drew from the common law rules to determine that above age 12 or 14 (or perhaps even 7) the marriage is at most voidable. And some held that marriage without parental consent at an age when the applicable statute would permit marriage with such consent creates a perfectly valid union.

Thus, a key concern exists in some jurisdictions with regard to underage marriages that are never annulled but are ignored by the parties when they subsequently marry another. If the first union is not void, then the second marriage may produce a bigamous union.

2. KINSHIP

Some restriction of sexual intercourse between closely related persons exists in nearly every society. Criminal prohibitions are found in all states of this country, with possible penalties ranging from a year to life imprisonment. *See* 52 Am. Jur. 2d Marriage § 53 (2012). This reflects variations both in the inclusiveness of specific prohibitions and differences in public policy concerning such bans. Parties who marry in the face of specific incest prohibitions typically find that their unions will be treated as either voidable or void depending on the closeness of their kinship.

The usually accepted reasons for barring sexual intercourse or marriage between close relatives are:

(1) negative eugenics, through which it is sought to limit the number of offspring with genetically undesirable traits;

(2) religious doctrine;

(3) minimizing internal family pressures and sexual competition and thus promoting family harmony;

(4) widely accepted social taboos; and

(5) protecting young and dependent females against sexual imposition.

Differences in how closely related persons who can marry may be can stem from differing views as to what interests are of greatest import. Genetic concerns, for example, could be satisfied through limiting sexual intercourse only between consanguineous, or blood, relatives. And since the utilitarian goal of eugenics is to guard against procreation of defective children, it is logical for kinship bans to be related to the chance that the offspring will receive an identical genetic contribution from each parent.

Difficulties arise because geneticists disagree in their assessments of the relative dangers of inbreeding.

Moreover, if minimizing family tensions is a crucial goal, then most restrictions on affinity, or legal relationships, would be included in marriage bans. *See* William Saletan, *The Love that Dare not Speak its Name: What's Wrong with Marrying Your Cousin?*, SLATE MAGAZINE, Apr. 10, 2002, *available at* http://www.slate.com/articles/news_and_politics/frame_game/2002/04/the_love_that_dare_not_speak_its_surname.html. In theory, the interest in preserving family harmony should take into consideration the decreased importance of the nuclear family and the increased likelihood that extended kin groups will be living in the same household. Adoption poses relatively new challenge to this framework. Adoptive relationships can exist independently of affinity or consanguinity. *See infra*, Section (E)(2), NOTES, "Relationship through adoption."

CALIFORNIA FAMILY CODE (2016)

§ 2200. Incestuous marriages

Marriages between parents and children, ancestors and descendants of every degree, and between siblings of the half as well as the whole blood, and between uncles or aunts and nieces or nephews, are incestuous, and void from the beginning, whether the relationship is legitimate or illegitimate.

GEORGIA CODE ANN. (2016)

§ 19–3–3. Degrees of relationship within which marriage prohibited

(a) Any person who marries a person to whom he knows he is related, either by blood or by marriage, as follows:

  (1) Father and daughter or stepdaughter;

  (2) Mother and son or stepson;

  (3) Brother and sister of the whole blood or the half blood;

  (4) Grandparent and grandchild;

  (5) Aunt and nephew; or

  (6) Uncle and niece shall be punished by imprisonment for not less than one nor more than three years.

(b) Marriages declared to be unlawful under subsection (a) of this Code section shall be void from their inception.

NOTES

Another statutory approach defines the prohibition in terms of degrees of kinship between the parties, almost universally using the civil law definition. This requires counting back to the nearest common ancestor in the ascending line of the parties, then descending to the person whose kin relationship degree is in question. Each link in the chain, both ascending and descending, counts as a degree; thus, uncle and niece are related within three degrees (*i.e.*, the common ancestor is the niece's grandfather / uncle's father; two ascending links are required to reach the grandfather from the niece, and one descending link to reach the uncle from the grandfather). In some jurisdictions the degrees of relationship within which marriage is prohibited extend further than the degree of relatedness to which criminal sanctions against incestuous sexual intercourse attach. What are the possible legal implications of this?

Some states mandate that parties seeking marriage licenses be advised of the benefits and availability of genetic counseling or, in some instances, receive such counseling. *See, e.g.*, ME. REV. STAT. tit. 19, § 652(6) (2011), stating that "[a] marriage license may not be issued to [first cousins] . . . unless the clerk has received from the parties the physician's certificate of genetic counseling required by [statute]."

Singh v. Singh

Supreme Court of Connecticut, 1990
569 A.2d 1112

■ HEALEY, ASSOCIATE JUSTICE.

This is an appeal from the trial court's denial of the plaintiff's and the defendant's motion to open the 1984 judgment of annulment of their 1983 marriage in Connecticut. We transferred this case from the Appellate Court to this court pursuant to Practice Book § 4023. We find no error. . . .

The parties, David Singh (husband) and Seoranie Singh (wife), were married on January 13, 1983, in Hartford. In their complaint, seeking an annulment, they alleged that their 1983 marriage was entered into "upon the mistaken belief by both parties that they were not related," but "they [had only] recently discovered that they are uncle and niece." There were no issue of this marriage. In 1984, the court, Hon. Simon Cohen, state trial referee, rendered judgment of annulment declaring the marriage null and void after finding, inter alia, that "[t]he marriage was entered into upon the mistaken belief by both parties that they were legally qualified to marry," but that "[both parties] have recently discovered that they are uncle and niece."

Thereafter, in November, 1988, both parties filed a motion to open the judgment. That motion alleged that, although the judgment found that they were uncle and niece and, therefore, not legally qualified to marry, in fact, since the wife's mother is the husband's half sister, the wife is the husband's half niece and not his niece. The parties also maintained that they sought the annulment only because of the advice of counsel that their marriage was, "without question," incestuous and void under our statutory scheme. See General Statutes §§ 46b–21,[1] 53a–191.[2] In view of the fact that our statute concerning kindred who may not marry does not mention "half nieces" or "half uncles" and no Connecticut decision extends the scope of the law's prohibition to relatives of the half blood, the parties claimed that the marriage "might well be deemed lawful and valid." They further alleged that they were remarried in August, 1988, in California where, citing People v. Baker, 442 P.2d 675 (Cal. 1968), they assert that the California Supreme Court has determined that marriages between uncles and nieces of the half blood are not proscribed by that state's incest statute.[3]

The trial court, Kline, J., denied the motion to open the judgment of annulment. In doing so, it found that the wife was the daughter of her husband's half sister and that this half sister and the husband were descended from a common mother but different fathers. It noted that while there were some Connecticut cases implicating the statute, there were no Connecticut cases specifically addressing the question whether persons of the half blood fall within the statutorily prohibited degrees of whole blood relationships. Further, the trial court not only said that a number of cases in other jurisdictions indicated that marriage or sexual intercourse between an uncle and niece of the half blood could be incestuous, but also opined that the texts seemed to be uniform that both at common law and by statute prohibited degrees of relationship by blood included persons of the half blood as well as of the whole blood. The court also stated that these authorities uniformly held that there is no distinction between the whole blood and half blood in computing the degrees within which marriages are prohibited as incestuous. The trial court also concluded that not only consanguinity but also the degree of the relationship between the parties was a basis for prohibiting certain marriages. Because § 46b–21 prohibits marriages between stepparents and stepchildren, the court inferred that it was not the actual blood relationship that appeared to concern the legislature but rather the degree or distance of the relationship between the parties indicating a legislative intent to prevent not only marriages of the whole blood but also those of the half blood. The trial court accordingly denied the motion to open and set aside the judgment of annulment. This appeal followed.

[1] General Statutes § 46b–21 provides: " . . . KINDRED WHO MAY NOT MARRY. No man may marry his mother, grandmother, daughter, granddaughter, sister, aunt, niece, stepmother or stepdaughter, and no woman may marry her father, grandfather, son, grandson, brother, uncle, nephew, stepfather or stepson. Any marriage within these degrees is void."

[2] General Statutes § 53a–191 provides: "INCEST: CLASS D FELONY. (a) A person is guilty of incest when such person marries a person whom such person knows to be related to such person within any of the degrees of kindred specified in section 46b–21. "(b) Incest is a class D felony."

[3] Despite this second marriage, the parties went on to contend in their motion to open that they would still face a "painful two year separation" unless the annulment judgment was opened [since the wife, a Guyanese citizen, could not apply for an "adjustment status" if the marriage were annulled. As a consequence, she would have to return to Guyana and wait two years before reapplying].

The issue to be decided is whether a marriage between persons related to one another as half uncle and half niece is incestuous under our statutory scheme and, therefore, void. See General Statutes §§ 46b–21, 53a–191. The parties maintain that such a marriage is not incestuous under our statutory law. . . . The determination of this question involves the interrelation and judicial interpretation of two statutes, §§ 46b–21 and 53a–191. This case, unlike State v. Skinner, 43 A.2d 76 (Conn. 1945), or State v. Moore, 262 A.2d 166 (Conn. 1969), to which counsel have referred, does not come before us on appeal from a conviction of the crime of incest. These cases, however, are instructive on the issue to be resolved in this case.

Historically, marriage between certain relatives "has been disfavored by all nations during all ages." Although incest was punished by the ecclesiastical courts in England, it was not an indictable offense at common law and punishment was left entirely to the ecclesiastical courts. . . . In 1540, during the reign of Henry VIII, a statute was passed regulating the degrees of relationship within which marriage was illegal. See 32 Henry 8, c. 38. That statute limited the prohibitions against marriage to relatives closer than first cousins, and although the ecclesiastical courts approved of the statute, the courts continued to make no distinction between relatives by consanguinity or affinity. "Consanguinity" is a blood relationship. It is the connection or relation of persons descended from the same stock or common ancestor. Black's Law Dictionary (5th Ed.). It is distinguished from "affinity" which, in turn, is the connection existing in consequence of a marriage between each of the married persons and the kindred of the other spouse.

The initial departure of the American jurisdictions from the English law was to declare incest a crime. The crime of incest is purely statutory, and most states have a statute making it a crime. The statutes delineating incestuous relationships departed from the ecclesiastical law in two respects. The majority of states extended the criminal prohibitions to first cousins and beyond while other states imposed criminal penalties only where the relationship was that of consanguinity. As will be seen, Connecticut's incest statute followed the former course. While these statutes may vary in detail, they generally define incest as marriage or sexual intercourse between persons too closely related in consanguinity or affinity to be entitled to marry legally.

In Connecticut, incest has been a crime since the incest statute was enacted in 1702. . . . The 1702 act[6] prohibited marriages between persons

---

[6] "The Acts and Laws of His Majesty's Colony of Connecticut in New England, Revision of 1702" . . . provides in part: "That no man shall marry any woman within the degrees hereafter named in this Act, That is to say, No man shall marry his . . . Brothers Daughter, Sisters Daughter . . . ; and if any man shall hereafter marry, or have carnal copulation with any woman, who is within the degrees before recited in this Act, every such Marriage shall be, and is hereby declared to be null and void; and all Children that shall hereafter be born of such Incestuous Marriage or Copulation, shall be for ever disabled to Inherit by Descent, or by being generally named in any Deed or Will, by Father or Mother." (Spelling as in original.)

within certain degrees of kinship including that of uncle and niece. *Catalano v. Catalano, supra*; *Gould v. Gould, supra*. In the 1875 revision, the language describing the degree of relationship, now appearing in § 46b–21, was adopted. General Statutes (1875 Rev.) § 1; *Catalano v. Catalano, supra*. There has been no substantive change in the language since that time. Thus, since 1702, our incest statute has interdicted marriage between persons related by either consanguinity or affinity.

Initially, the parties claim that the trial court erred by adhering to a line of cases dating from the interpretations of the incest statute during the reign of Henry VIII citing to the English statute of 32 Henry 8, c. 38. They concede that "[d]espite notable changes in sexual mores and in the very conditions which underlie the incest taboo itself, which have intervened since the time of Henry VIII, most Courts considering [the] question have been satisfied to mechanically reproduce the precedents of several hundred years ago." They, nevertheless, urge "a more modern approach to the construction of our incest statute" and maintain that they "rely upon a line of cases placing more emphasis on the rights of criminal defendants, and the importance of preserving bona fide marriages against the undue extension of statutory categories." They claim that there are several compelling reasons for the statutory construction that they urge: (1) the plain language of § 46b–21 favors the construction allowing uncle-niece marriages between relatives of the half blood; (2) undue judicial extension of the prohibitions contained in § 46b–21 may lead to unfair prosecutions for the crime of incest under § 53a–191; (3) an unwarranted extension of the incest prohibition to include uncles and nieces of the half blood is inconsistent with proper respect for the preservation of bona fide marriages; and (4) since the prohibition of "uncle-niece marriages, especially those between relatives of half blood, are not the object of universal condemnation, the Court will not be at odds with 'natural law' if it adopts the construction [advocated] by [the parties]." We are not persuaded by any of these claims.

It is clear that § 46b–21 does not contain any language that expressly distinguishes between relatives of the whole blood and the half blood. It is also clear that although § 46b–21 is a civil statute, its interrelationship with § 53a–191, the criminal statute prohibiting incest, is such that both statutes may fairly be said to be *in pari materia* and so § 46b–21 is to be construed in this case in harmony with the law of which it forms a part. The infusion into § 53a–191 of the degrees of relationship set out in § 46b–21 as the predicate for the commission of the crime of incest invokes the rule of strict construction that is applied to criminal statutes. The United States Supreme Court has said: "That criminal statutes are to be construed strictly is a proposition which calls for the citation of no authority. But this does not mean that every criminal statute must be given the narrowest possible meaning in complete disregard of the purpose of the legislature." United States v. Bramblett, 348 U.S. 503, 509–10 (1955). The same court also said: "No rule of construction, however, requires that a penal statute be strained and distorted in order to exclude conduct clearly intended to be within its scopeCnor does any rule require that the act be given the 'narrowest meaning.' It is sufficient if the words are given their fair meaning in accord with the evident intent of [the legislature]." United States v. Raynor, 302 U.S. 540, 552 (1938). We have said: "Strict construction does not mean that a statute must be read in isolation. 'In construing a statute, common sense must be used, and courts will assume that the legislature intended to accomplish a reasonable and rational result.' . . . 'The rule of strict construction does not require that the narrowest technical meaning be given to the words employed in a criminal statute in disregard of their context and in frustration of the obvious legislative intent.' " (Citations omitted.) In re Luis R., 528 A.2d 1146 (Conn. 1987). Such authority demonstrates that the rule of strict construction of penal statutes is not without limitation; the doctrine of strict construction is only one of the aids which is to be used in the construction of penal statutes. Other aids include such things as the statutory language itself, legislative history where available, the furthering of the policy and purposes fairly apparent from the statute which include the mischief sought to be proscribed and related statutes.

In our analysis, it is proper to explore further the state of the law as it was at the time that our incest statute was enacted in 1702. . . . [On this basis, it] is fair to assume that, when the incest statute was enacted in 1702, the framers were aware of [early English cases discussing the prohibition of marriage within certain degrees] and adopted the interpretation of the ecclesiastical law as it then existed in England, thus treating the relation of the half blood like that of the whole blood.

There has been no substantive change since that time in our incest statute insofar as the degree of consanguinity within which marriage is proscribed. That is not without significance. Indeed, implicating the issue before us, in 1961, we said: "It has been the declared public policy of this state continuously since 1702 to prohibit marriages of uncle and niece and declare them void." Catalano v. Catalano, *supra*, 170 A.2d 726. Our decisional law under the incest statute has been sparse. In *Catalano*, we held invalid a marriage between an uncle and a niece under our statutory scheme although the marriage was valid in Italy where it was performed. In that case, we noted that the "generally accepted rule" was that a marriage valid where the ceremony was performed was valid everywhere. Id., at 726. . . .

Besides *Catalano*, two other cases merit discussion. In State v. Skinner, 43 A.2d 76 (1945), we held that the relationship of brother and half-sister was comprehended within the degrees of relationship forbidding marriage under the incest statute. In that case, we rejected the defendant brother's claim that the relationship of half-sister did not come within the statutory prohibition. Id. In doing so, we pointed out that the defendant "admitted in his brief that all the cases which [his counsel] have found are to the contrary and that public policy would indicate that relationship of the half blood should be included in the prohibition of the incest statute." Id. After referring to several cases from other jurisdictions that directly held that "brother" includes a brother of the half blood and that "sister" includes a sister of the half blood, we said: "In view of the purpose of the statute . . . its language, and the soundness of the decisions we have cited, we hold that the word sister, as used in the statute, applies to and includes a half sister." Id.

In State v. Moore, 262 A.2d 166 (1969), the defendant had been found guilty of incest[12] where the parties involved were the defendant and the nineteen year old daughter of the defendant's brother-in-law, that is, the daughter of the defendant's wife's brother. In reversing the incest conviction in *Moore*, we observed that the trial court "extended the meaning of § 46–1 (now § 46b–21) beyond its fair import." Id. In doing so, we referred to *Skinner*, pointing out that the relationship in that case contained the element of consanguinity and we also noted that that element appeared in all the relationships enumerated in § 46–1 (now § 46b–21) except the relationship of stepmother or stepdaughter and stepfather or stepson. Id. *Moore* then goes on to say: "The question at once arises as to why, in its enumeration of relationships which do not include the element of consanguinity, the General Assembly saw fit to include only those of stepparent or a stepchild. In the application of the criminal law, it would be an unwarranted extension and presumption to assume that by specifying those relationships the legislature has intended to include others which lack the element of consanguinity. Had the legislative intent been to include what, in this case, would commonly be called a relationship of niece-in-law and uncle-in-law, it would have been a simple matter to say." Id. Therefore, the *Moore* court opined that, absent such a declaration, the trial court's construction "amounted to an unwarranted extension of its expressed meaning and intent." Id.

The parties stress that *Moore* is very supportive of their position. We do not agree for several reasons. First, the fact pattern in *Moore* was different from that in both *Skinner* and *Catalano*, as in the latter two cases, unlike *Moore*, a blood relationship was involved. Second, in *Moore*, we referred to *Skinner*, noting that, in *Skinner*, we not only pointed out that the relationship in that case "is embraced within the meaning of the statute" but also that in that relationship there was the element of consanguinity. *State v. Moore, supra.* In *Moore*, the element of consanguinity was absent but that of affinity was present. Moreover, in *Moore*, we did not qualify our holding in *Skinner* but acknowledged its viability. Finally, in *Moore*, we were not called upon to decide whether the statute proscribed marriage between two persons where each was a

[12] General Statutes § 53–223, at the time of *State v. Moore*, 262 A.2d 166 (Conn. 1969), provided: "Every man and woman who marry or carnally know each other, being within any of the degrees of kindred specified in section 46–1, shall be imprisoned in the State Prison not more than 10 years."

relative of the half blood although *Skinner*, fairly read, was a step in that direction.

Nor do we overlook, in reaching our conclusion, those cases that the parties urge us to rely upon in reaching "a more modern approach" to the construction of our incest statute. This approach, they claim, is one which places more emphasis on the rights of criminal defendants as well as "preserving bona fide marriages against the undue extension of statutory categories." They cite the following cases: *People v. Baker*, *supra*; People v. Womack, 334 P.2d 309 (Cal. Ct. App. 1959); and State v. Bartley, 263 S.W. 95 (Mo. 1924). . . .

The parties place the greatest stress on *People v. Baker*, *supra*. A close reading of that case demonstrates that it is clearly inapposite. That case was an incest prosecution against Baker who had had sexual relations with his niece who was related to him by the half blood; that is, her mother was the defendant's half sister. The trial court found him guilty of incest. His principal claim on appeal was that the prohibition in California Penal Code § 285 against fornication by an uncle and his niece did not apply where they were related by the half blood. That statute provided in part: "Persons being within the degrees of consanguinity within which marriages are declared by law to be incestuous and void . . . who commit fornication . . . with each other . . . are punishable by imprisonment. . . ." California Civil Code § 59 provided: "Marriages between parents and children, ancestors and descendants of every degree, and between brothers and sisters of the half as well as the whole blood, and between uncles and nieces or aunts and nephews, are incestuous, and void from the beginning, whether the relationship is legitimate or illegitimate." (Emphasis added.) The *Baker* court reversed the conviction. In doing so, it reasoned that the phrase "of the half as well as the whole blood" obviously referred to brothers and sisters and could not be interpreted also to modify "uncles and nieces" under established tenets of statutory construction. Moreover, by including relationships between brothers and sisters of the half blood and not so specifying as to more distant relatives, the *Baker* court reasoned that the legislature evinced the intention to exclude such persons from the statutory prohibition. *People v. Baker*, *supra*. In recognizing that various state statutes differ, it acknowledged that the more common type of statute extended the prohibition to uncles and nieces of the half blood even where half blood relationships were not mentioned. The manifest dissimilarity of the California statute in *Baker* from our statutes affords little support for the claims of the parties in this case. Indeed, *Baker* itself expressly points this up when, after stating that incest is governed by specific statutes in the various states, it says that "the relevant decisions must be considered in the context of the statutory scheme peculiar to the particular state." Id., 442 P.2d 675. We agree. . . .

Connecticut has its statutory scheme in place to implement its policy of delineating the relationships between persons under our jurisdiction who may properly enter into marriage. It has been for many years and still remains the declared public policy of the state. See *Catalano v. Catalano, supra*. The degrees of relationship within which marriages are prohibited are not, from what we have already said, words of art. Fairly read, the prohibition against intermarriage of those related by consanguinity can be understood to extend to those of the half blood as well as of the whole blood. In *Skinner*, which predated the case before us by a generation, we held that the words "brother" and "sister" included those of the half blood. "According to the common meaning of the word ['uncle'], it includes the half-brother of the [mother] and there is no distinction between the whole and half blood." 90 C.J.S. 1025. We believe that the same can be said of the term "niece," that is, that it comprehends the half blood as well as the whole blood. In doing so, we accord to each word its common meaning without frustrating legislative intent but rather enhancing it. Other courts have had no difficulty concluding that their statutes, although silent on the half blood matter, comprehend that relationship in "uncle-niece" incest cases. *See, e.g.,* State v. Lamb, 227 N.W. 830 (Iowa 1929); Commonwealth v. Ashey, *supra*, 142 N.E. at 788. In giving a statute its full meaning where that construction is in harmony with the context and policy of the statute, "there is no canon against using common sense in construing laws as saying what they obviously mean." Roschen v. Ward, 279 U.S. 337, (1929); Donnelley v. United States, 276 U.S. 505 (1928).

In conclusion, a marriage between persons related to one another as half-uncle and half-niece is void under General Statutes §§ 46b–21 and 53a–191 as incestuous.

NOTES

Relationship through adoption. Many prohibitions on intermarriage based on kinship (or criminal incest penalties) address only relationships by consanguinity or affinity. In State v. Geile, 747 S.W.2d 757 (Mo. Ct. App. 1988), the Missouri Court of Appeals, Eastern District, held that Missouri's statutory prohibition of marriage between uncle and niece did not extend to such a relationship when created only through adoption. The applicable statute made no specific reference to adoption.

Some states have begun to include persons related only through adoption, particularly siblings, within marriage bans. Such a prohibition was held unconstitutional by the Supreme Court of Colorado in Israel v. Allen, 577 P.2d 762 (Colo. 1978). The parents of the siblings by adoption had married when wife's daughter was 13 and husband's son was 18. The families had been living in different states beforehand. After the marriage, the husband adopted his new wife's daughter.

Colorado's statute, based on the Uniform Marriage and Divorce Act § 207 (2015), explicitly prohibited:

COLO. REV. STAT. (2016)

§ 14–10–111(g)(II). Declaration of invalidity

> A marriage between an ancestor and a descendant, or between a brother and a sister, whether the relationship is by the half or the whole blood . . .

The *Israel* court stated that:

> At the outset, there is an issue as to whether or not marriage is a fundamental right in Colorado. If it is, defendant must show a compelling state interest in order to justify the unequal treatment of adopted brothers and sisters under the statute. Since we find, however, that the provision prohibiting marriage between adopted children fails even to satisfy minimum rationality requirements, we need not determine whether a fundamental right is infringed by this statute.

Israel v. Allen, 577 P.2d 762, 764 (Colo. 1978). The court severed the adoption restriction from the prohibition against intermarriage by brother and sister related by whole or half blood.

Should it make a difference if the adoption proceeding that creates the sibling relationship takes place after one or both of the two individuals reach adulthood? After only one reaches adulthood?

PROBLEM THREE

Michael Brady has three sons: Greg, Peter, and Robert. Mr. Brady meets Caroline Martin, they fall deeply in love, and the two get married. Caroline and her three daughters, Marcia, Jan, and Cindy, move in with Mr. Brady and his sons forming the Brady Bunch. Marcia and Greg are both 16 when their parents marry, and the two start to bond over midnight snacks and chores. Greg and Marcia have fallen in love, and now they want to marry! The pair have just turned 18. Can Greg marry Marcia in any state? Now assume that Michael and Caroline loved each other's kids so much that they adopted them. Does this change the result under the laws of any state?

3. MENTAL INCAPACITY

Edmunds v. Edwards

Supreme Court of Nebraska, 1980
287 N.W.2d 420

■ BRODKEY, JUSTICE.

This case involves an action brought in the District Court for Douglas County on May 23, 1977, by Renne Edmunds, guardian of the estate of Harold Edwards (hereinafter referred to as Harold), against Inez Edwards (nee Ryan, hereinafter referred to as Inez), to annul the marriage of his ward Harold to Inez, which occurred on May 10, 1975. In his petition, the guardian alleged that the marriage was void for the reason that Harold did not have the mental capacity to enter into a marriage contract on that date, which allegation was specifically denied by Inez. In its order entered on November 27, 1978, following trial of the matter, the District Court found that Harold was mentally retarded, as that phrase is commonly used in medical science, but not to a degree which, under the law of the State of Nebraska, is of such a nature as to render him mentally incompetent to enter into the marriage relation, and that at the time of the marriage between Harold and Inez, Harold had sufficient capacity to understand the nature of the marriage contract and the duties and responsibilities incident to it, so as to be able to enter into a valid and binding marriage contract. The court therefore found that the marriage of Harold and Inez, which occurred on May 10, 1975, was, in fact and in law, a valid marriage and continues to exist as a valid marriage under the laws of the State of Nebraska. . . . The guardian has appealed. . . .

Harold was born on August 7, 1918, and was institutionalized at the Beatrice State Home as mentally retarded on September 25, 1939. He was a resident at the Beatrice State Home for a period of approximately 30 years. It was during this period that he first met Inez, who was also a patient of the home, and Bill Lancaster, who lived with Harold in Omaha after their release from the Beatrice State Home, and who has continued to reside with Harold and Inez since their marriage. Harold was placed in Omaha on November 14, 1969, and started a new life under the auspices of the Eastern Nebraska Community Office of Retardation (ENCOR), which was established in 1968 to provide alternatives for institutionalization of retarded persons at the Beatrice State Home and to assist in the normalization of the retarded in local communities. After coming to Omaha, Harold obtained employment as a food service worker in the Douglas County Hospital on February 16, 1970, and lived in a staffed ENCOR apartment from that time until shortly before his marriage in 1975. As will later be made apparent, he has functioned satisfactorily in that employment, and has received promotions and salary increases since commencing on that job. While under the auspices of ENCOR, Harold and Inez developed a romantic interest in each other and eventually decided to get married. The date of the marriage was postponed in order to afford the couple the opportunity to have premarital sex counseling and marriage counseling from the pastor of their church in Omaha. They were married by Reverend Verle Holsteen, pastor of the First Baptist Church in Omaha, Nebraska, and their friends, staff members of ENCOR, and out-of-state relatives attended the wedding in that church. The guardian did not bring this action to annul the marriage for a period of approximately 2 years after the date of the marriage ceremony. . . .

According to testimony in the record, mental retardation refers basically to delayed intellectual function and developmental delays usually associated from the time early in life and persisting throughout life. There are various degrees of mental retardation according to the official diagnostic system or nomenclature of the American Medical Association. Those degrees are mild, moderate, severe, and profound. . . . The expert medical witnesses for both parties agree that Harold falls within the classification of mild mental retardation.

The guardian first called his medical expert, Dr. Robert Mitchell, a psychologist connected with Creighton University in Omaha. Dr. Mitchell expressed the opinion that he did not believe Harold was competent to enter into a valid marriage, but admitted on cross-examination that being mildly mentally retarded did not automatically preclude a person from marriage. He also testified that he had asked Harold during his examinations and consultations what marriage meant, to which Harold responded "For life," and also "You stay married forever." . . . Dr. Mitchell also testified: "It is much better, I think, to refer to Mr. Edwards as a person who is fifty-nine years of age who is not as bright as most people. But he has had fifty-nine years of experience, and he is an adult, and physiologically he is matured, as well."

The medical expert witness called by the defendant was Dr. Frank J. Menolascino, a psychiatrist specializing in the field of mental retardation, and author of numerous books and articles upon the subject. He was well acquainted with Harold, having first met him in 1959 when he was doing work at the Beatrice State Home, and had seen Harold many times since that time. He had examined Harold in December 1977, and again in July 1978, during the week Dr. Menolascino testified. He testified that Harold was not functioning below the mildly retarded range and that the tests reflected that a great deal of Harold's difficulty appeared to be primarily a lack of training. . . . Dr. Menolascino was asked: "Doctor, do you believe that you have an opinion as to whether Mr. Edwards was capable of understanding the nature of a marriage within the paradigm you have discussed in May of 1975?" and he answered: "Yes, he was able to." . . . On cross-examination Dr. Menolascino was asked: "In your opinion, do you think that Harold Edwards understands the fact that he is liable for Mrs. Edwards' bills if she goes to a store and runs up some bills?" to which he replied: "Yes." He was then asked: "Do you think he understands the fact that if he gets a divorce he might have to pay alimony?" His reply to that question was: "I am not sure. I am not sure. . . ."

In addition to the medical witnesses who testified, there was also evidence adduced from various lay witnesses. Renne Edmunds, the guardian, testified that he first met Harold about April 8, 1975, although the date of the inception of the guardianship was October 18, 1972. At that time Harold was already under the care and guidance of ENCOR. Edmunds testified: "It was my conclusion that he [Harold] could not not only manage a fund of thirty thousand, he couldn't manage the small purchases, as well." He testified that he refused to pay certain expenses of the wedding because they were not compensable from guardianship funds. He admits that he was told about the marriage taking place, and that he had filed no action to prevent the marriage, which took place May 10, 1975. His annulment action was filed approximately 2 years later. Harry John Naasz, an adviser for ENCOR, who was Harold's supervisor, testified that he had assisted Harold in making preparations for the marriage including obtaining of blood tests and the marriage certificate. He had discussed the forthcoming wedding with Harold: "Can you tell us what you discussed concerning the marriage? A. We discussed what it would mean, what it would mean living together, sharing their lives. Q. And what did Harold express to you? A. He wanted to get married. Q. What did he say that led you to believe that he might understand marriage? A. He mentioned to me that he understood, too that it was a commitment to each other, that Inez would be living there." Mr. Naasz did admit in his testimony that at the beginning he did have some question in his mind about whether Harold understood marriage. He later referred the couple for marriage counseling.

David Bones, an employee of Planned Parenthood in Omaha and Council Bluffs, and also an ordained minister in the United Methodist Church, testified with reference to premarital sex counseling he had given to Harold and Inez on April 16, 1975. . . . Bones testified that he basically completed his premarital sex course with Harold and Inez and that Harold appeared to understand it and nodded his head.

Reverend Verle Holsteen, who was the pastor of the First Baptist Church on Park Avenue in Omaha, and who was the officiating officer at the marriage between Harold and Inez, testified that he had known Inez since 1971 and Harold since 1974, and they attended his church regularly. He gave them premarital counseling and recalls having had three sessions with them. He asked Harold if he understood what they were talking about and Harold said yes. Reverend Holsteen performed the wedding ceremony and attended the reception which was held at the First Baptist Church parlor. . . . Reverend Holsteen testified on cross-examination: "I felt that Harold understood that if things followed through that he would be married to Inez." He was asked whether he had some doubt in his mind as to whether Harold understood what a marriage contract was all about and he replied: "By observing him I would say that he would not understand as much as other people what a marriage contract would be about. But I recognized, and I stand by this, that they would get along well together." On redirect-examination he was asked: "Reverend, your testimony is, you did have some concern initially about his capacity? A. Yes, I did. Q. And is it also, then, your testimony that after talking to Harold and Inez your reservations were resolved? . . . A. I would say yes, they were resolved."

Also testifying at the trial was Elizabeth Cartwright, an employee of ENCOR, who monitors Harold and Inez' finances. She testified that when Harold gets paid at the Douglas County Hospital he signs his check, takes it to the bank, deposits all the money except $40, and gives Inez

$20 and he keeps $20. She does not have to go to the bank with him. Elizabeth Cartwright also testified that Inez is quite a bit sharper than Harold and she helps him around. She also testified about an incident involving the loss of Harold's wedding ring. She stated: "Just recently Harold lost his wedding band and he called me up at work and was very much upset and stated that he lost his wedding band, and he said to me that it was exchanged to him on his wedding day, Inez gave it to him, he wanted another wedding band. So in talking with Inez and Harold they came to the conclusion that they would purchase another one at Crossroads, and they withdrew money from their savings account for the first time and purchased a wedding band. Harold selected it." She also testified, however, that Harold cannot figure his finances and needs assistance.

The final witness offering testimony at the trial was John Taylor, personnel director for the Civil Service Commission for Douglas County. He testified that Harold was first employed by the Douglas County Hospital on February 16, 1970, in the food service department, and that Harold has been promoted since and has received pay increases since February 1970, reflecting good job performance. Neither party to the marriage testified at the trial.

We now examine some established rules of law which we believe are applicable to this case. We first consider the nature of the marriage contract. Section 42–101, R.R.S.1943, provides: "In law, marriage is considered a civil contract, to which the consent of the parties capable of contracting is essential." Although by statute, marriage is referred to as a "civil contract," we have held: "That it is not a contract resembling in any but the slightest degree, except as to the element of consent, any other contract with which the courts have to deal, is apparent upon a moment's reflection.... What persons establish by entering into matrimony, is not a contractual relation, but a social *status*; and the only essential features of the transactions are that the participants are of legal capacity to assume that status, and freely consent so to do." University of Michigan v. McGuckin, 89 N.W. 778 (Neb. 1902). Also, in Willits v. Willits, 107 N.W. 379 (Neb. 1906), we stated that while our law defines marriage as a civil contract, it differs from all other contracts in its consequences to the body politic, and for that reason in dealing with it or with the status resulting therefrom the state never stands indifferent, but is always a party whose interest must be taken into account.

Another statutory provision of which we must take cognizance in this appeal is section 42–103, R.R.S.1943, which provides: "Marriages are void ... (2) when either party, at the time of marriage, is insane or mentally incompetent to enter into the marriage relation...." This statute was reiterated, and other applicable rules with reference to competency to enter into a marriage relationship were reviewed in Homan v. Homan, 147 N.W.2d 630 (Neb. 1967), wherein we stated: "The petition alleged that the ward was mentally incompetent at the time of the marriage. By statute a marriage is void 'when either party is insane or an idiot [a term that encompassed both profound and severe mental retardation] at the time of marriage, and the term idiot shall include all persons who from whatever cause are mentally incompetent to enter into the marriage relation.' §§ 42–103, R.S.Supp., 1965.

"A marriage contract will not be declared void for mental incapacity to enter into it unless there existed at the time of the marriage such a want of understanding as to render the party incapable of assenting thereto." Fischer v. Adams, 38 N.W.2d 337. Mere weakness or imbecility of mind is not sufficient to void a contract of marriage unless there be such a mental defect as to prevent the party from comprehending the nature of the contract and from giving his fee [sic] and intelligent consent to it. . . . A marriage is valid if the party has sufficient capacity to understand the nature of the contract and the obligations and responsibilities it creates. *Fischer v. Adams, supra*; Kutch v. Kutch, 129 N.W. 169. . . .

"A marriage is presumed valid, and the burden of proof is upon the party seeking annulment. *Adams v. Scott*, supra."

It is the general rule that the existence of a valid marriage is a question of fact. In this case the trier of fact was the court and the court had all the foregoing evidence, summarized above, before it. Concededly, much of the evidence with reference to the capacity of Harold to enter into the marriage contract was conflicting and disputed. An action to annul a marriage, being an action in equity, is governed by the provisions of section 25–1925, R.R.S.1943, which provides: "In all appeals from the district court to the Supreme Court in suits in equity, wherein review of some or all of the findings of fact of the district court is asked by the appellant, it shall be the duty of the Supreme Court to retry the issue or issues of fact involved in the finding or findings of fact complained of upon the evidence preserved in the bill of exceptions, and upon trial de novo of such question or questions of fact, reach an independent conclusion as to what finding or findings are required under the pleadings and all the evidence, without reference to the conclusion reached in the district court or the fact that there may be some evidence in support thereof." However, it is also the well-established rule that where the evidence on material questions of fact is in irreconcilable conflict, this court will, in determining the weight of the evidence, consider the fact that the trial court observed the witnesses and their manner of testifying, and therefore must have accepted one version of the facts rather than the opposite. This rule has been applied both in annulment actions and in divorce actions.

Applying this rule to the present case, we conclude, therefore, that the trial court was correct in dismissing the guardian's petition to annul the marriage of his ward, and that its action in this regard should be and hereby is affirmed.

NOTES

Would it be better policy to use a test that gauges whether a party with mental deficiency or disability understands the nature of marriage, or a test as to that person's ability to function effectively as a spouse or a parent? Should the law differentiate its test for marital capacity between a physically robust party who suffers from feeblemindedness at a young age, and an older person who suffers from senility that cannot be reversed?

Temporary mental incapacity can affect the validity of a marriage if the condition exists at the time of the ceremony and ratification does not take place after the disability has terminated. In Mahan v. Mahan, 88 So. 2d 545 (Fla. 1956), a wife sought annulment of her marriage on the ground that at the time of the ceremony she was so intoxicated by "alcoholic stimulants" that she was not in possession of her mental faculties and was incapable of forming conscious consent to the marriage. The husband answered that he could neither admit nor deny the allegations because at the time of the alleged marriage he was so intoxicated that he could not state whether he was ever married. There was corroboration of the intoxication of both parties by witnesses who traveled with them when the marriage occurred, and there was evidence that the marriage was not followed by cohabitation. Annulment was granted, the court finding the evidence sufficient to establish that at the time of the marriage the wife was incapable of entering a binding agreement.

For a celebrated example of a couple who annulled their "Vegas" marriage because they failed to achieve a meeting of the minds about their marriage contract, *see* Spears v. Alexander, Case No. D311371, Dept. J (Clark Co. Dist. Ct., Nev., Jan. 5, 2004), *available at* http://www.thesmokinggun.com/documents/crime/britney-spears-files-annulment. The court found that when Britney Spears wed her high-school sweetheart, Jason Alexander, at the Little White Wedding Chapel in Las Vegas:

> [she] lacked understanding of her actions to the extent that she was incapable of agreeing to the marriage because . . . the Plaintiff and Defendant did not know each others [*sic*] likes and dislikes, each others [*sic*] desires to have or not have children, and each others [*sic*] desires as to State of residency. Upon learning of each others [*sic*] desires, they are so incompatible that there was a want of understanding of each others [*sic*] actions in entering into this marriage. . . . [T]here was no meeting of the minds in entering into this marriage contract and in a court of equity there is cause for declaring the contract void.

CHAPTER III

SPOUSES: CHANGING ROLES, RIGHTS, AND DUTIES

A. TWO PERSONS, NOT ONE

Our law long imposed substantial disabilities on women. Some of these may be traced to the necessities of military organization, to which so much of the social structure in the early feudal period was subservient. Others can be accounted for only by reference to scriptural texts that allotted women a subordinate position in the scheme of human affairs. From the very beginning, English law drew a distinction between the single woman (feme sole) and the married woman (feme covert) with respect to their capacities and what was called their "abilities." The feme sole was conceded a legal capacity a little less than that of a male (she was excluded from public functions) but in the exercise of private rights she was almost completely competent. The feme covert not only had greatly reduced legal capacity, but her competence to transact in the sphere of private law was almost totally suspended during coverture. One of the earliest sources of English law explains that the married woman is *sub virga*—under the rod of her husband—attributing to him an authority and power of command that lingered in the criminal law of this century in the doctrine of spousal immunity and retained a qualified recognition in statutes that proclaimed the husband to be the head of the family. But the most important result of this ancient conception was the control that the husband was permitted to assume over the wife's realty. If the wife at time of marriage was seised of an estate of inheritance in land, the husband, upon the marriage, became seised of the freehold *jure uxoris* (in the right of the wife), managed and controlled the property, and took the rents and profits during their joint lives. If the wife at the time of marriage had an estate for life or for the life of another, the husband became seised of such estate in the right of his wife and was entitled to profits. In addition, upon marriage the wife's earnings and services became the property of her husband. She lost her legal identity, as a result of which, she lost the ability to contract alone with third parties. To these rights the courts eventually applied theories of guardianship and devised means to prevent alienation without the wife's consent. Personal property that the wife had possessed in her own right vested immediately and absolutely in the husband, with the exception of certain personal "paraphernalia," like jewelry and clothing.

The correlative duties upon the husband were: (1) he was liable for his wife's prenuptial debts and torts, although he was discharged if there was no recovery for these during coverture; (2) as to the property of which the husband was seised during the marriage, the wife received a life interest in some fraction of the husband's property, as a result of which he could not alienate her interest without her consent, protecting her from her husband's creditors; and (3) he was liable to maintain his wife, but this was limited to necessaries suitable to the couple's station in life. If the wife incurred debts for such necessaries the husband was obliged to pay the debts, at first only if agency or ratification could be established, but eventually on the theory that such purchases were made for his use.

The status of the married woman was affected even more profoundly through the law's absorption of the biblical concept that upon marriage man and woman became one flesh.[1] In the hands of the temporal courts this notion was translated into the proposition that man and wife are one person—a notion hardly consistent with the theory of guardianship and the wife's situation of being *sub potestate*, a patent recognition of the individual identities of the spouses. Nevertheless, a variety of rules came to be justified on the "one person" theory. Some of the oldest of these rules related to the matter of rank or condition; for example, a bondwoman marrying a freeman acquired freedom during coverture. In the case of feoffments (conveyance of real estate) to husband and wife they did not take by moieties, but both were seised by the entireties. Similarly, the incapacity of husband and wife to contract with each other was explained on the theory that they were but one person in the law.[2]

It was not feasible to introduce the "one person" theory into the field of procedure. The solutions found in respect of real actions reflect the substantive law; that is to say, although the wife's capacities were suspended, she possessed nevertheless an ultimate proprietary right. Consequently, action for the recovery of land was given to husband and wife and neither could sue without the other. Conversely, it was against husband and wife that action must be brought to recover land that was held in the right of the wife. The development of delictual (tortious, wrongful, or criminally liable) actions also forced the recognition of the wife's identity. From time immemorial, the married woman had been deemed capable of committing wrongs. In respect of crimes she was almost completely *sui juris*. Consequently, when tort actions developed the law was not prepared to acquit her of delictual liability. To provide an adequate remedy against one whom law and custom had made judgment proof, it was early established that the action must lie against husband and wife. The husband might answer alone, but the wife could not. In the course of time the notion of the wife's subjection to her husband caused some alteration in older conceptions of liability—for example, a presumption arose that tortious acts of a feme covert were done at the coercion or instigation of the husband. But the manner of bringing an action remained the same.

The rules about joinder also applied in cases of torts done to the wife's person, though where the action was founded on the special

[1] Genesis 2:24; Matthew 19:5–6; Mark 10:8.

[2] *See* Williams, *The Legal Unity of Husband and Wife*, 10 MOD.L.REV. 16 (1947).

damage done to the husband, he alone could bring the action. Classical examples of the latter are alienation of affections, enticement and criminal conversation, all of which were originally founded on an interference with a husband's property right.

The rigors of the complex of rules respecting the feme covert that developed at common law were eventually relaxed in certain particulars through various expedients that the Court of Chancery took under its protective wing. These related to matters of property and were possible only because of the trust device. The intervention of Chancery was based not so much upon a fixed design of extending the married woman's rights as upon a policy of enabling a person (usually a father) who gave or settled property on a woman even though she was married, to insure that she would have the property as her own and be able to deal with it independently of her husband. The prudent settlor would convey the property to a trustee, in whom legal title was vested, to hold for the benefit of the woman in accordance with the terms of the trust, upon which her actual powers of disposition also depended. Chancery by degrees worked out the idea that a trustee must deal with the property in accordance with the woman's directions. Eventually it also became settled that it was not necessary that property be vested in trustees, but if it be given or devised to a feme covert for her separate use, the husband would be held to be trustee for her. In the latter half of the eighteenth century, a further safeguard against overreaching by the husband was perfected by means of the clause introduced into wills and settlements known as the restraint on anticipation, whereby the married woman could neither alienate her property nor charge it with her debts.[3]

The equitable separate estate of married women was introduced into America during the colonial period, and after the Revolution there was wholesale reception of the English rules. But this institution was predicated upon the possession in the settlor or testator of a respectable corpus of property and consequently was less adapted to the needs of a democratic society than it had been to the order of things in England. The social ferment that characterized the first half of the 19th century in America exemplified by extension of political democracy, anti-slavery agitation, the "rise of the common man," the beginnings of organized labor, the movement for agrarian reform and expansion of public education, inevitably swept into its wake the emancipation of married women. Paul E. Kerry, *Mary Wollstonecraft on Reason, Marriage, Family Life and the Development of Virtue in* A Vindication of the Rights of Women, 30 BYU J. PUB. L. 1 (2015). Abetted by sympathetic males and able and articulate female reformers, a relatively brief period of polemics and propaganda resulted in the initial married woman's property statute in the state of Mississippi (1839). This act was permissive, but in Maine, the first northern state to pass such legislation (1844), the statute was

[3] This was abolished by § 1, Married Women (Restraint upon Anticipation) Act, 1949, 12, 13 & 14 Geo. 6 c. 78.

mandatory. The objective of the reformers was that all property a woman should bring to her marriage and any she might thereafter acquire should be her sole and separate property, not subject to the disposal or control of the husband. Early statutes in some states, such as Massachusetts, fell short of this, but as the movement gained momentum over a period of some forty years the substance of that objective was achieved.

By the twentieth century, every state had enacted some statutory recognition of the economic independence of wives. The property acts made explicit the wife's power to contract (in some states exclusive of her husband), to engage in business or employment in her own right, to make wills, to sue or be sued, and to be held fully responsible in her independent capacity for her tort or criminal actions. *See, e.g.*, Mass. Gen. Laws ch. 209 (2016). Between spouses, these statutes also permitted each spouse to have an independent identity, allowing them to directly convey land to one another and eventually to sue each other for injury.

This early patchwork of state statutes granting married women a minor degree of financial independence remained the law until a series of gender-based discrimination challenges equalized the status of married women and men. In 1979, the United States Supreme Court in *Orr v. Orr* struck down an Alabama state statute authorizing alimony awards from former husbands to former wives, but not from wives to husbands. The gender classification was unconstitutional because it violated equal protection. *Orr* signaled the end of many gender-based distinctions in how we regulate family and property. Since *Orr*, the Supreme Court has subjected statutes that discriminate solely on the basis of gender to heightened scrutiny, requiring these statues to show "an exceedingly persuasive justification." Mississippi University for Women v. Hogan, 458 U.S. 718, 724 (1982). This ultimately led to spouses having equal rights in property held in the entirety, and to the abolition of the common law doctrine of necessaries—which required a husband to pay for his wife's necessaries, but not vice versa—or the doctrine's equal application to both spouses.

The property acts, while advancing the status of wives in some significant respects, did nothing to give wives any interest in the husband's earnings or property owned by him. In fact, the protections wives enjoyed under the early common law—namely, a life estate in the husband's property, giving her considerable protection from the husband's creditors—fell away. The property acts also had no effect on whether husbands would be the head of the household or on who would hold title to property acquired during the marriage. Where the husband titled property in his name, in common law property states, he alone had the right to manage or alienate that property; by contrast, in community property states, both spouses had rights of management in the community property.

Therefore, because many wives were not employed outside of the home and brought little separate property into the marriage, the property acts did not greatly improve the economic position of married women. Elizabeth R. Carter, *The Illusion of Equality: The Failure of the Community Property Reform to Achieve Management Equality*, 48 IND. L. REV. 853 (2015). As Chapter 5 will demonstrate, the economic position of wives would materially improve when notions of economic partnership during the marriage began to appear in divorce proceedings. For a sensitive appraisal of family law in the second half of the 20th century, *see* Michael Grossberg, *How to Give the Present a Past? Family Law in the United States 1950–2000*, in CROSS CURRENTS: FAMILY LAW AND POLICY IN THE UNITED STATES AND ENGLAND (2001).

PROBLEM ONE

When she marries, Wendy owns 100 acres of Blackacre that she was given by her father on her 18th birthday, a diamond necklace valued at $10,000, and $25,000 in stock. Her husband, Hunter, owns nothing but is dashingly handsome. During the marriage, Wendy cares for the couple's two children at home and Hunter joins a real estate firm, for which he eventually becomes the owner. This business is now worth $100,000. Using Hunter's earnings the couple purchases a home, titled in Hunter's name, and makes investments, all in his name. The investments and house together are valued at $250,000. At common law, before the Married Women Property Acts (MWPA), who owns what? Who manages it? What happens with the debt? After the MWPA, in common law property states, what happens? After the MWPA, what happens to this property in community property states? Who owns what? Who manages it? What happens with the debt?

B. NAMES IN THE FAMILY

1. A MARRIED WOMAN'S NAME

Stuart v. Board of Supervisors of Elections

Court of Appeals of Maryland, 1972
295 A.2d 223

■ MURPHY, CHIEF JUDGE.

Mary Emily Stuart and Samuel H. Austell, Jr., were married in Virginia on November 13, 1971 and shortly thereafter, took up residence in Columbia, Howard County, Maryland. In accordance with the couple's oral antenuptial agreement, Stuart continued, after the marriage, to use and be exclusively known by her birth given ("maiden") name and not by the legal surname of her husband.

On March 2, 1972, Stuart undertook to register to vote in Howard County in her birth given name. After disclosing to the registrar that she was married to Austell but had consistently and nonfraudulently used her maiden name, she was registered to vote in the name of Mary Emily Stuart. On March 16, 1972 the Board of Supervisors of Elections for Howard County notified Stuart by letter that since under Maryland law "a woman's legal surname becomes that of her husband upon marriage," she was required by Maryland Code, Article 33, § 3–18(c) to complete a "Request for Change of Name" form or her registration would be cancelled. Stuart did not complete the form and her registration was cancelled on April 4, 1972.

Stuart promptly challenged the Board's action. . . . [S]he maintained that she was properly registered to vote in her birth given name, that being her true and correct name; that under the English common law, in force in Maryland, a wife could assume the husband's name if she desired, or retain her own name, or be known by any other name she wished, so long as the name she used was not retained for a fraudulent purpose; and that since the only name she ever used was Mary Emily Stuart the Board had no right to cancel her voter registration listed in that name. . . .

Evidence was adduced showing that the oral antenuptial agreement between Stuart and Austell that she would retain her maiden name was a matter of great importance to both parties. Stuart testified that her marriage to Austell was "based on the idea that we're both equal individuals and our names symbolize that." . . .

There was evidence showing that the practice of the Board requiring a married woman to use the surname of her husband dated back to 1936; that the practice was a uniform one throughout the State and was adopted to provide some trail of identification to prevent voter fraud; that if a married woman could register under different names the identification trail would be lost; and that the only exception permitted to the requirement that married women register under their husbands' surnames was if the name was changed by court order.

By opinion filed May 10, 1972, Judge Mayfield concluded "that a person may adopt and use any name chosen in the absence of fraudulent intent or purpose;" that the use by Stuart of her maiden name was without fraudulent intent or purpose; that it is the law of Maryland that "the use by the wife of the husband's surname following marriage, while the same have been initially based upon custom and usage, is now based on the common law of England, which law has been duly adopted as the law of this State;" that under the provisions of the Code, Article 33, § 3–18(a)(3) clerks of courts, as therein designated, are required to notify Boards of Supervisors of Elections of the "present names" of females over the age of eighteen years residing within the State "whose names have been changed by marriage;" that by subsection (c) of § 3–18, the Boards, upon being advised of a "change of name by marriage," are required to give notification "that such . . . change of name by marriage . . . has been reported to the board, and shall require the voter to show cause within two weeks . . . why his registration should not be cancelled"; that § 3–18 appeared "to be in conformity with the common law," as espoused in such cases as People ex rel. Rago v. Lipsky, 63 N.E.2d 642 (1945) and Forbush v. Wallace, 341 F. Supp. 217 (M.D.Ala.1971), aff'd per curiam 405 U.S. 970 (1972);* that the "statutory requirements [of § 3–18] are in accordance with the law which says that upon marriage the wife takes the surname of her husband;" that the provisions of § 3–18 do not deprive Stuart of her right to use her maiden name, nor of her right to vote, but require only that she "register to vote under her 'legal' name, . . . based upon the broad general principle of the necessity for proper record keeping and the proper and most expedient way of identifying the person who desires to vote."[1]

From the court's order denying her petitions to correct the voter registry and to restore her name thereto, Stuart has appealed. She claims on appeal, as she did below, that a woman's surname upon marriage does not become that of her husband by operation of the common law in force in Maryland and that nothing in the provisions of § 3–18(a)(3) and (c) mandates a contrary result.

What constitutes the correct legal name of a married woman under common law principles is a question which has occasioned a sharp split of authorities, crystallized in the conflicting cases of State ex rel. Krupa v. Green, 177 N.E.2d 616 (1961), relied upon by Stuart, and People ex rel. Rago v. Lipsky, supra, adopted by the lower court as its principal authority for denying the petitions. *Green* approved the voter registration of a married woman in her birth given name which she had openly, notoriously and exclusively used subsequent to her marriage, and held that she could use that name as a candidate for public office. The court held:

> "It is only *by custom*, in English speaking countries, that a woman, upon marriage, adopts the surname of her husband in place of the surname of her father." Id.(Emphasis in original.)

---

* [The three-judge District Court in *Forbush* upheld the constitutionality of Alabama's regulation requiring a married woman to use her husband's surname in obtaining a driver's license. The U.S. Supreme Court affirmance was without opinion and was based upon Alabama common law.—*EDS.*]

[1] In pertinent part, § 3–18(a)(3) and (c) provides:

"(a) *Reports to be made by certain public agencies.* Reports to the board shall be made by the several officials in Baltimore City at least once each month, and in the several counties, by the last days of January and July in each year, as follows:

. . .

"(3) The clerk of the circuit court for each county shall file with said respective boards the former and present names of all female residents of said city or county, as the case may be, over the age of twenty-one years, whose names have been changed by marriage since the date of the last such report. . . .

"(c) *Notification to show cause before cancellation.* Whenever the . . . change of name by marriage . . . is reported as above provided, the board shall cause to be mailed to the address of such voter . . . a notification that such . . . change of name by marriage . . . has been reported to the board, and shall require the voter to show cause within two weeks . . . why his registration should not be cancelled. . . ."

Lipsky refused to allow a married woman to remain registered to vote under her birth given name on the basis of

> "the long-established custom, policy and rule of the common law among English-speaking peoples whereby a woman's name is changed by marriage and her husband's surname becomes *as a matter of law* her surname." Id. at 645 (Emphasis supplied.) . . .

We think the lower court was wrong in concluding that the principles enunciated in *Lipsky* represent the law of Maryland. We have heretofore unequivocally recognized the common law right of any person, absent a statute to the contrary, to "adopt any name by which he may become known, and by which he may transact business and execute contracts and sue or be sued." Romans v. State, 16 A.2d 642, 646. In the context of the name used in an automobile liability insurance contract, we approved the consistent nonfraudulent use by a married woman of a surname other than that of her lawful husband in Erie Insurance Exchange v. Lane, 227 A.2d 231. Citing with approval Everett v. Standard Acc. Ins. Co., 187 P. 996 (1919), we summarized its holding as follows:

> "The court . . . held that because the insured had been known as Everett for twenty-two years before the policy was issued, a representation that his name was Everett was not a misrepresentation, although his name before had been Cowie, since a man may lawfully change his name without resorting to legal proceedings and by general usage or habit acquire another." Erie, 227 A.2d at 236.

If a married woman may lawfully adopt an assumed name without legal proceedings, then we think Maryland law manifestly permits a married woman to retain her birth given name by the same procedure of consistent, nonfraudulent use following her marriage. In so concluding, we note that there is no statutory requirement in the Code . . . that a married woman adopt her husband's surname. Consistent with the common law principle, we hold that a married woman's surname does not become that of her husband where, as here, she evidences a clear intent to consistently and nonfraudulently use her birth given name subsequent to her marriage. Thus, while under *Romans*, a married woman may choose to adopt the surname of her husband—this being the long-standing custom and tradition which has resulted in the vast majority of married women adopting their husbands' surnames as their own—the mere fact of the marriage does not, as a matter of law, operate to establish the custom and tradition of the majority as a rule of law binding upon all. . . .

Under the common law of Maryland, as derived from the common law of England, Mary Emily Stuart's surname thus has not been changed by operation of law to that of Austell solely by reason of her marriage to him. On the contrary, because of her exclusive, consistent, nonfraudulent use of her maiden name, she is entitled to use the name Mary Emily Stuart unless there is a statute to the contrary. . . .

Nothing in the language of § 3–18(a)(3) or (c) purports to compel *all* married women to register to vote in their husbands' surname. Since Mary Emily Stuart did not undergo a "change of name by marriage," this Section merely requires her to show cause to the Board that she consistently and nonfraudulently used her birth given name rather than her husband's surname following marriage.

In light of our disposition of the common law issue, we find it unnecessary to reach the constitutional issues raised by the appeal.

Order dismissing petitions vacated. . . .

NOTES

During Marriage. When a married woman adopts her husband's surname, there are differing views about what she should do if she wishes to resume her former name during the intact marriage. Under the common law doctrine it would seem that she need not resort to judicial action. But in order to foster certainty and to avoid repeated explanations to various agencies or other entities, many women prefer to utilize the name change provisions generally provided by state statutes. *See, e.g.,* VA. CODE ANN. § 8.01–217 (West 2016). So long as the change is not designed to accomplish a fraudulent purpose, such statutes should be applicable. *See In re* Miller, 243 S.E.2d 464 (Va. 1978).

The California Attorney General published an opinion stating that a person has the freedom to change his or her name and to use whatever name he or she selects, subject only to qualifications as to fraud. Nonetheless, the Attorney General admitted that use of statutory procedures are often beneficial since this procedure would provide an official document. *See* Opinion N. 00–205, Cal. Atty. Gen., recited in 83 Op. Atty Gen. Cal. 136 (2000).

After Divorce. It is common today that statutes specifically authorize a woman who took her husband's name at marriage to resume her birth name after divorce. *See* Ohio Rev. Code Ann. § 3105.16 (West 2016) ("When a divorce is granted the court of common pleas shall, if the person so desires, restore any name that the person had before the marriage."). Although some trial courts have balked at restoring a divorced woman's surname, ostensibly out of concern about possible detriment to her children, appellate courts have taken a less restrictive view. In *In re Marriage of Malloy*, a trial court denied an ex-wife's request after divorce to resume her birth name because she failed to request the name change early in the divorce proceeding and because the change "might be confusing to" her child. 778 N.W.2d 66 (Iowa Ct. App. 2009). The Iowa Court of Appeals reversed, noting that Iowa courts have previously rejected the notion that a parent and child must have the same last name. *See also* Fortune v. Fortune, 61 So. 3d 441, 447 (Fla. Dist. Ct. App. 2011), *reh'g denied* (June 2, 2011); B.J.D. v. L.A.D., 23 S.W.3d 793 (Mo. Ct. App. 2000); Collins v. Collins, 2011 WL 1944276 (Ohio Ct. App. 2011).

2. NAMES FOR CHILDREN

Henne v. Wright

United States Court of Appeals, 8th Circuit, 1990
904 F.2d 1208, *cert. denied*, 498 U.S. 1032 (1991)

■ BRIGHT, SENIOR CIRCUIT JUDGE.

. . .

Plaintiffs brought this action under 42 U.S.C. § 1983 individually and as next friends to their daughters alleging that Neb.Rev.Stat. § 71–640.01 (1986) unconstitutionally infringes their fundamental fourteenth amendment right to choose surnames for their daughters other than those prescribed. The defendants appeal, contending that the district court erred in the following respects: (1) plaintiffs lack standing; (2) plaintiffs failed to join certain parties necessary for a just adjudication under Fed.R.Civ.P. 19(a); and (3) Neb.Rev.Stat. § 71–640.01 does not unconstitutionally infringe a fundamental right. We reject defendants' first two contentions but are persuaded by the third and therefore reverse.

On April 4, 1985, Debra Henne gave birth to Alicia Renee Henne at a hospital in Lincoln, Nebraska. Following Alicia's birth, Debra completed a birth certificate form at the request of a hospital employee. Debra listed Gary Brinton as the father and entered the name Alicia Renee Brinton in the space provided for the child's name. Brinton, also present at the hospital, completed and signed a paternity form. At the time of the birth, Debra was still married to Robert Henne. Although Debra and Robert Henne had filed for a divorce prior to Alicia's birth, the decree dissolving the marriage did not become final until after the birth. As a result of her marital status, hospital personnel, acting on instructions from the Department of Health, informed Debra that she could not surname her daughter "Brinton." Debra then filled out a second birth certificate form, entering the child's name as Alicia Renee Henne and leaving blank the space provided for the father's name. Robert Henne has never claimed to be Alicia's father and, pursuant to the divorce decree, pays no child support for her.

Almost three years later, on February 4, 1988, Debra Henne went in person to the Bureau of Vital Statistics of the Nebraska Department of Health and requested that Alicia's surname be changed to Brinton and that Gary Brinton be listed on the birth certificate as the father. Debra produced a signed statement personally acknowledging Gary Brinton as Alicia's biological father. She also presented a signed acknowledgement of paternity from Gary Brinton and a letter from him requesting that the birth certificate be changed. Personnel at the Bureau of Vital Statistics, acting indirectly at the direction of defendants Cooper and Wright, denied Debra's request. Other than her visit to the Bureau of Vital

Statistics and this action, Debra has made no attempt to change Alicia's surname.

On June 17, 1988, at St. Elizabeth's Hospital in Lincoln, Nebraska, Linda Spidell gave birth to a daughter, Quintessa Martha Spidell. Linda wished to give Quintessa the surname "McKenzie," the same surname as her other two children, who were born in California. Hospital personnel, acting upon instructions from the Department of Health, informed Linda that Quintessa could not be surnamed McKenzie and that if Linda did not complete the birth certificate form the hospital would enter Quintessa's last name as Spidell. Linda completed the form, entering "Spidell" as Quintessa's surname and leaving blank the space provided for the father's name. Linda surnamed her other children McKenzie simply because she liked that name and not because of any familial connection. For that reason, and because she wishes all three children to share the same name, she wants Quintessa surnamed McKenzie. Linda was not married at the time of Quintessa's birth or at the time of this action and there has been no judicial determination of paternity. At trial, however, both Linda and Ray Duffer, who lives with Linda and her children, testified that Duffer is Quintessa's biological father. Other than this action, Linda has made no attempt to change Quintessa's surname. . . .

Debra Henne brought this suit on behalf of herself and her minor child Alicia Renee Henne in federal district court against defendants [Gregg F.] Wright and [Stanley S.] Cooper in their official capacities, alleging that Neb.Rev.Stat. § 71–640.01, as implemented and enforced by defendants, violated the Federal Constitution. Linda Spidell later intervened as an additional plaintiff on her own behalf and on behalf of her minor child Quintessa Martha Spidell.

Following a bench trial, the court ruled that the constitutional right to privacy protects a parent's right to name his or her child. The court did not specifically identify the appropriate level of scrutiny by which to examine Neb.Rev.Stat. § 71–640.01. The court held that the justifications for the statute asserted by the defendants failed to satisfy even a minimal level of constitutional scrutiny. . . .

Defendants contend that the district court erred in holding Neb.Rev.Stat. § 71–640.01[5] unconstitutional. The district court held that

[5] Section 71–640.01 states: The information pertaining to the name of an infant born in this state and reported on a birth certificate, filled out and filed pursuant to sections 71–601 to 71–648, shall comply with the following: (1) If the mother was married at the time of either conception or birth of the child, or at any time between conception and birth, the name of such mother's husband shall be entered on the certificate as the father of the child and the surname of the child shall be entered on the certificate as being (a) the same as that of the husband, unless paternity has been determined otherwise by a court of competent jurisdiction, (b) the surname of the mother, (c) the maiden surname of the mother, or (d) the hyphenated surname of both parents; (2) If the mother was not married at the time of either conception or birth of the child, or at any time between conception and birth, the name of the father shall not be entered on the certificate without the written consent of the mother and the person named as the father, in which case and upon the written request of both such parents the surname of the child shall be that of the father or the hyphenated surname of both parents; (3) In any case in which

an extension of the fourteenth amendment right of privacy protects a parent's right to name his or her child and that the statute failed to survive even minimal scrutiny. We determine that the fourteenth amendment right of privacy does not protect the specific right at issue here and that the statute rationally furthers legitimate state interests.

This case presents the issue whether a parent has a fundamental right to give a child a surname at birth with which the child has no legally established parental connection. We frame the issue this way because each plaintiff wishes to enter on her daughter's birth certificate a surname proscribed by section 71–640.01. Debra Henne wishes to enter the surname of the alleged father (Brinton) without first obtaining a judicial determination of paternity. Linda Spidell wishes to enter a surname (McKenzie) with which her daughter has no connection other than that Linda has already given that name to her two other children. We note, however, that while section 71–640.01 requires that a child have some legally established parental connection to the surname entered on the birth certificate,[6] it does not prevent either plaintiff from ever giving her daughter the desired surname.[7] The district court overlooked this important distinction in characterizing the issue as whether parents generally possess a fundamental right to name a child. This case does not present that broad issue.

Whether there is a fundamental right to give a child a surname at birth with which the child has no legally established parental connection will dictate the appropriate level of constitutional scrutiny for evaluating Neb.Rev.Stat. § 71–640.01. Specifically, if the statute significantly infringes a right deemed fundamental under the fourteenth amendment right of privacy then we must rigorously scrutinize the asserted justifications for the statute. Otherwise, we analyze the statute under the highly deferential rational basis standard of review applicable to

---

paternity of a child is determined by a court of competent jurisdiction, the name of the father shall be entered on the certificate in accordance with the finding of the court and the surname of the child may be entered on the certificate the same as the surname of the father; (4) In all other cases, the surname of the child shall be the legal surname of the mother; and (5) If the father is not named on the certificate, no other information about the father shall be entered thereon.

[6] Thus, Alicia Henne could have been given her mother's surname, her mother's maiden surname or the surname of the presumed father, but not the surname of the alleged father without a judicial determination of paternity. Neb.Rev.Stat. § 71–640.01(1). Quintessa Spidell could have been given her mother's surname, id. § 71–640.01(4), the surname of a person named as the father if that person requested so in writing, id. § 71–640.01(2), or the surname of a person found by a court of competent jurisdiction to be the father, id. § 71–640.01(3).

[7] Debra Henne could enter the surname Brinton on her daughter's birth certificate by obtaining a judicial determination of paternity on the part of Gary Brinton. Neb.Rev.Stat. § 71–640.01(1)(a). Linda Spidell could enter the surname McKenzie on her daughter's birth certificate only by first changing her own surname to McKenzie. Nebraska law provides a procedure, however, whereby either child's name could later be changed. Neb.Rev.Stat. §§ 61–101 to 61–104 (1986). See also Spatz v. Spatz, 199 Neb. 332, 258 N.W.2d 814 (1977). Moreover, under Nebraska law any civil action can be brought in forma pauperis if necessary. Neb.Rev.Stat. §§ 25–2301 to 25–2310 (1986 & Supp.1988).

most economic and social legislation challenged under the fourteenth amendment.

We now turn to the question whether the right at issue is fundamental. A long line of Supreme Court cases have established that "liberty" under the fourteenth amendment encompasses a right of personal privacy to make certain decisions free from intrusive governmental regulation absent compelling justification. See, e.g., Zablocki v. Redhail, 434 U.S. at 374 (fundamental right to marriage); Moore v. City of East Cleveland, 431 U.S. 494 (1977) (fundamental right to live with relatives); Roe v. Wade, 410 U.S. 113 (1973) (fundamental right to an abortion); Loving v. Virginia, 388 U.S. 1 (1967) (fundamental right to interracial marriage). Two of the earliest right to privacy cases, Meyer v. Nebraska, 262 U.S. 390 (1923) (fundamental right to instruct a child in a foreign language), and Pierce v. Society of Sisters, 268 U.S. 510 (1925) (fundamental right to send child to a non-public school), established the existence of a fundamental right to make child rearing decisions free from unwarranted governmental intrusion. See Roe v. Wade, 410 U.S. at 153. Meyer and Pierce do not, however, establish an absolute parental right to make decisions relating to children free from government regulation. See Prince v. Massachusetts, 321 U.S. 158 (1944) ("[N]either rights of religion nor rights of parenthood are beyond limitation."); Stanley v. Illinois, 405 U.S. 645, 652 (1972) (state has legitimate interest in separating neglectful parents from child); Jehovah's Witnesses v. King County Hosp., 278 F. Supp. 488, 504 (W.D.Wash.1967) (three judge panel) (state may intervene in parents' religiously motivated decision refusing medically necessary blood transfusion for children), aff'd, 390 U.S. 598 (1968) (per curiam).

In determining whether a right not enumerated in the Constitution qualifies as fundamental, we ask whether the right is "deeply rooted in this Nation's history and tradition," Moore v. City of East Cleveland, 431 U.S. at 503. We proceed cautiously in this area of the law, ever mindful that the judiciary "is the most vulnerable and comes nearest to illegitimacy when it deals with judge-made constitutional law having little or no cognizable roots in the language or even the design of the Constitution." Id. at 544, (White, J., dissenting).

While Meyer and Pierce extended constitutional protection to parental decisions relating to child rearing, the parental rights recognized in those cases centered primarily around the training and education of children. . . . By contrast, the parental decision in this case relates to the choice of a child's surname. This subject possesses little, if any, inherent resemblance to the parental rights of training and education recognized by Meyer and Pierce. Thus, as the district court rightly recognized, constitutional protection for the right to choose a non-parental surname at birth must flow, if at all, from an extension of Meyer and Pierce. Furthermore, any logical extension of Meyer and Pierce has to be grounded in the tradition and history of this nation. See Moore v.

City of East Cleveland, 431 U.S. at 503; Bowers v. Hardwick, 478 U.S. 186, 192 (1986). Given this standard, we necessarily conclude that plaintiffs have presented no fundamental right.

The custom in this country has always been that a child born in lawful wedlock receives the surname of the father at birth, see, e.g., Secretary of the Commonwealth v. City of Lowell, 366 N.E.2d 717, 725 (1977); . . . and that a child born out of wedlock receives the surname of the mother at birth, see, e.g., Buckley v. State, 98 So. 362, 363 (1923). . . .

While some married parents now may wish to give their children the surname of the mother or a hyphenated surname consisting of both parents' surname, and some unmarried mothers may wish to give their children the surname of the father, we can find no American tradition to support the extension of the right of privacy to cover the right of a parent to give a child a surname with which that child has no legally recognized parental connection. Plaintiffs therefore have not asserted a right that is fundamental under the fourteenth amendment right of privacy and Neb.Rev.Stat. § 71–640.01 need only rationally further legitimate state interests to withstand constitutional scrutiny.

The district court in this case held that section 71–640.01 failed to survive even minimal scrutiny. Other federal courts reviewing statutes restricting the choice of surnames have taken similar positions. Nevertheless, for the reasons discussed below, we determine that the Nebraska statute passes minimal scrutiny, i.e., the rational basis test.

A law must be upheld under the rational basis test unless it bears no rational relation to a legitimate state interest. . . .

We determine that the law rationally furthers at least three legitimate state interests: the state's interest in promoting the welfare of children, the state's interest in insuring that the names of its citizens are not appropriated for improper purposes and the state's interest in inexpensive and efficient record keeping. Specifically, a reasonable legislature could believe that in most cases a child's welfare is served by bearing a surname possessing a connection with at least one legally verifiable parent. Furthermore, the legislature could reasonably perceive that in the absence of a law such as section 71–640.01, the name of a non-parent could be improperly appropriated to achieve a deliberately misleading purpose, such as the creation of a false implication of paternity. Finally, the legislature could reasonably conclude that it is easier and cheaper to verify and index the birth records of a person who has a surname in common with at least one legally verifiable parent. The district court's review of the evidence buttresses this conclusion. 711 F. Supp. at 515.[8] Although the Nebraska legislature could perhaps tailor

[8] The district court noted that the defendants offered evidence that section 71–640.01 promotes inexpensive and efficient indexing and access of birth records. Nevertheless, the court stated that

> "[i]n keeping with the admonishment of [Stanley v. Illinois, 405 U.S. 645, 656 (1972)], I find that the state's interest in efficiency and cost savings loses its legitimacy when

the statute to more closely serve these purposes, we cannot say that section 71–640.01 bears no rational relationship to the state's legitimate interests. We therefore reject plaintiffs' contention that Neb.Rev.Stat. § 71–640.01 unconstitutionally restricts their parental rights.

[T]he district court's judgment is reversed.

■ ARNOLD, CIRCUIT JUDGE, concurring in part and dissenting in part.

. . .

The fundamental right of privacy, in my view, includes the right of parents to name their own children, and the State has shown no interest on the facts of these cases sufficiently compelling to override that right.

A few salient facts are worth repeating. Debra Henne wants to give her daughter the surname of the little girl's father. The father is willing. He has acknowledged his fatherhood. The man to whom Ms. Henne was married when the baby was born has no objection. Linda Spidell wants to name her daughter "McKenzie," which is neither her name nor the name of the child's father. The choice is not so eccentric as it seems, however: Ms. Spidell's two other children are named "McKenzie," and it is quite natural to desire that all of one's three children have the same surname. Again, no one with a personal interest objects. Ray Duffer, the man who lives with Ms. Spidell, is the child's father, and "McKenzie" is fine with him.

The government, in the person of the State of Nebraska, says no to both mothers. The most plausible reason it offers is administrative convenience.[9] Records are easier to keep and use if every person has the surname of "at least one legally verifiable parent." Ante, at 1215. This interest is legitimate, and the statute under challenge is rationally related to it. If the appropriate level of constitutional scrutiny were the rational-basis test, I would agree that the law is valid. But if a fundamental right is at stake, the State must show a compelling interest, which it has wholly failed to do. So the case comes down to this: Do parents have a fundamental right to name their own children?

The question could well be analyzed as a First Amendment issue. What I call myself or my child is an aspect of speech. When the State says I cannot call my child what I want to call her, my freedom of expression, both oral and written, is lessened. And if the First Amendment is at stake, everyone would concede that the State could not win without

compared to the constitutional right at issue here." 711 F. Supp. at 515. In Stanley, the Supreme Court in effect ruled that the state's interests in administrative efficiency did not withstand heightened scrutiny. Here, however, defendants need only demonstrate that the law rationally furthers legitimate state interests.

9 It is also true, as the Court says, ante, at 1215, that allowing an unfettered choice of surname could enable parents to imply falsely that someone was the father of the child. In the example I put at the oral argument, I would have an interest in keeping a stranger from naming her child "Richard S. Arnold, Jr.," and the State would have an interest in defending my reputation against such a false implication. Nothing of the kind is involved in the present cases. Moreover, the State might have an interest in the matter if the child's parents could not agree on a surname. Again, no such issue is presented by these cases.

showing a compelling interest. But the parties have not presented the case in First Amendment terms. So we address the case in terms of the right of privacy. . . . The right of privacy is not the beneficiary of explicit textual protection in the federal Constitution. It is an unenumerated right. . . . Government might protect or recognize rights, but rights, some of them anyway, existed before government and independently of it, and would continue to exist after government had been destroyed. The source of rights was not the State, but, as the Declaration of Independence put it, the "Creator." . . .

The real question is, not whether there is a right of privacy (see also the Fourth Amendment for a modicum of textual support), but how do you tell what it includes? The limits of the right remain controversial, and no doubt they will continue to be tested by litigation. Precedent tells us at least this much, though: family matters, including decisions relating to child rearing and marriage, are on almost everyone's list of fundamental rights. See, e.g., Zablocki v. Redhail, 434 U.S. 374 (1978), and the other cases cited by the Court, ante, at 1214. The right to name one's child seems to me, if anything, more personal and intimate, less likely to affect people outside the family, than the right to send the child to a private school, Pierce v. Society of Sisters, 268 U.S. 510 (1925), or to have the child learn German, Meyer v. Nebraska, 262 U.S. 390 (1923). We know, moreover, from Roe v. Wade, 410 U.S. 113 (1973), that these women had a fundamental right to prevent their children from being born in the first place. It is a bizarre rule of law indeed that says they cannot name the children once they are born. If there was ever a case of the greater including the less, this ought to be it.

So I do not see the right being claimed here as an "extension" of prior cases. It is rather well within the principle of those cases. A person's name is, in a sense, her identity, her personality, her being. I take it the Court would not deny a citizen the right to choose her own name, absent some compelling governmental interest. No more should we deny her the right to choose her child's name. The child has, at birth, no will of her own, and her parents should be allowed to speak for her. There is something sacred about a name. It is our own business, not the government's.

Having labeled the present claim as an "extension" of existing law, the Court goes on to say that extensions may be permitted only if they are "deeply rooted in this Nation's history and tradition," Moore v. City of East Cleveland, supra, 431 U.S. at 503. It then asks whether there is an "American tradition to support the extension of the right of privacy to cover the right of a parent to give a child a surname with which that child has no legally recognized parental connection." Having satisfied itself that there is no such tradition, the Court rejects what it characterizes as an "extension" of the right of privacy.

As is often the case, how one phrases a question has a great deal to do with the answer one gets. To illustrate the point, I refer to some aspects of tradition about names that the Court does not mention. In the beginning, surnames were unknown. They "were not considered of controlling importance until the reign of Queen Elizabeth, 1558–1603." Note, *What's in a Name?*, 2 N.Y. L. REV. 1, 1 (1924). "The surname, in its origin, was not, as a rule, inherited from the father, but was either voluntarily adopted by the son or conferred upon him by his neighbors . . ." Ibid.[10] Fundamentally, names were not inherited. They were something people chose for themselves. "There [was] no such thing as the 'legal name' of a person in the sense that he may not lawfully adopt or acquire another. By the common law a man [sic] may name himself, or change his name at will, and this without solemnity or formality of any kind; or he may acquire a name by reputation, general usage or habit." Id. at 2 (citations omitted). Even after statutes were passed to provide a fixed procedure for changing one's name, the statutes were treated as merely supplementary to the common law. One could use the statute if desired, but the old do-it-yourself right simply to assume a new name still existed. Smith v. United States Cas. Co. 90 N.E. 947, 950 (1910).

The early tradition, then, did not restrict one's own choice of a surname. "You could freely select any name you chose, whether it was your parents' surname or not. . . ." Names were people's own business, not the government's. One's name did not have to be that of a legally recognized parent. . . .

[O]n the question of tradition, . . . it may fairly be asked, whether any tradition that once existed still obtains. There is good evidence that the answer is yes. See, e.g., Hauser v. Callaway, 36 F.2d 667, 669 (8th Cir.1929) ("A man's name for all practical and legal purposes is the name by which he is known and called in the community where he lives and is best known."). The most recent case on the point I have found, Walker v. Jackson, 391 F. Supp. 1395, 1402 (E.D.Ark.1975) (three-judge court) (Webster, Henley, and Eisele, JJ.), squarely holds that under the common law of Arkansas—which has not been changed by statute—a person can change his name at will in the absence of fraud.

So far as the choice of one's own name is concerned, then, it seems well established that the tradition, still extant, is a complete absence of statutory prohibition. Certainly there is no pattern of positive law denying such a right of self-determination. I take it that the Court would concede that there is a fundamental right to choose one's own name. There is no "societal tradition of enacting laws *denying* [this] interest," Michael H. v. Gerald D., 491 U.S. 110 (1989) (plurality opinion) (emphasis in original), and that seems to be the standard that has recently attracted more votes than any other on the Supreme Court.

---

[10] The older authorities on names uniformly refer to "fathers," "sons," and what "a man" might choose for a name. I take it everyone would concede today that mothers, daughters, and women in general are legally entitled to the benefit of whatever tradition was formerly expressed in male terms.

This Court, however, phrases the question more narrowly: is there a tradition supporting "the right of a parent to give a child a surname with which that child has no legally recognized parental connection"? I grant that there is no such tradition: what the plaintiffs in this case want to do is unusual. Few parents, no doubt, have done or wanted to do it in the past, and few would want to do it now. But, by the same token, there is no solid tradition of legislation denying any such right, and under Michael H., supra, that is the relevant question. In the absence of any tradition either way on the precise point, we should look, I submit, to the tradition we do have. People may choose or change their own names without leave of government. It is only a small step to extend the same right to their children's names. Children are, during infancy anyway, simply legal extensions of their parents for many purposes.

So I would hold that the right asserted here is fundamental, and that the State has no interest compelling enough to override it in the circumstances of this case. In attempting to do so, the State intrudes intolerably into what should be a private decision, one of the basic liberties of the citizen. . . .

NOTES

Naming conventions for children have changed dramatically over time from a near-uniform preference for the father's last name to more modern preferences for the mother's last name—especially when the child is a nonmarital child—or to hyphenated names, evidencing a connection to both kin networks. For a clever personal account of a child's experience with a hyphenated name, now trendy with celebrity children like Shiloh Jolie-Pitt, *see* Rebecca Tuhus-Dubrow, *Children of the Hyphens, the Next Generation*, N.Y. TIMES, Nov. 2, 2011 at E–1.

A number of jurisdictions have expressly rejected the historical "presumption that a child bears the surname of his father [as] outdated." *In re* Marriage of Gulsvig, 498 N.W.2d 725, 729 (Iowa 1993). Instead, these jurisdictions focus on the child's best interests in determining the child's last name, guided by a "non-exhaustive list of considerations:"

> (1) convenience for the child to have the same name as or a different name from the custodial parent; (2) identification of the child as part of a family unit; (3) assurances by the mother that she would not change her name if she married or remarried if the child maintains the mother's surname; (4) avoiding embarrassment, inconvenience, or confusion for the custodial parent or the child; (5) the length of time the surname has been used; (6) parental misconduct, such as support or nonsupport or maintaining or failing to maintain contact with the child; (7) the degree of community respect associated with the present or changed name; (8) a positive or adverse effect a name change may have on the bond between the child and either parent or the parents' families; (9) any delay in requesting or objecting to name change; (10) the preference of the child if the child is of sufficient maturity to express a

> meaningful preference; (11) motivation of the parent seeking the change as an attempt to alienate the child from the other parent; (12) and any other factor relevant to the child's best interest.

Montgomery v. Wells, 708 N.W.2d 704, 708–9 (Iowa Ct. App. 2005). Thus, for example, where the mother of a nonmarital child is on the cusp of remarrying and changing her own last name, the court found that it would be in the child's best interest for the child to carry the father's name because the child "will at least have a familial-name identity to one of his parents." *Id.* at 710.

By contrast, when a child has carried the mother's surname for the first 18 months of his life, was baptized with her name, she will be his primary caretaker, she and the child's half-sibling have the same last name, and she has said she will not change her name even if she remarries, then it is in the child's best interest to have her name. *See* Workman v. Olszewski, 993 P.2d 667 (Mont. 1999). In reaching this decision, the Montana Supreme Court rejected as improper a societal preference for preserving the male's lineage through use of the father's surname, stating that any test must be gender neutral and based solely on what is in the best interest of the child.

Some courts have emphasized that "lip-service to the best interests of the child should not be used as a subterfuge to nevertheless perpetuate the paternal preference." Hamby v. Jacobson, 769 P.2d 273, 277 (Utah Ct. App. 1989). In a similar vein, other courts have emphasized that neither parent should have a "superior right to determine a child's surname." *In re* A.C.S., 171 P.3d 1148, 1151 (Alaska 2007). Often the mother of a nonmarital child will unilaterally decide what to name the child. But, in an initial naming dispute, the relevant question should solely be what name would best serve the child's interests. As the Supreme Court of Alaska recently held, in such cases the father should bear no special burden to show that giving the child a hyphenated surname of both parents would be in the child's best interest. *Id.*

In determining a child's best interests, some courts place greater emphasis on the preference of the custodial parent as to the child's name, given the general responsibility of custodial parents "for major life decisions concerning the child." Cormier v. Quist, 933 N.E.2d 153, 155 (Mass. Ct. App. 2010). In some jurisdictions there is a clear presumption in favor of the custodial parent's naming preference, placing the burden of rebutting that presumption on the non-custodial parent. Holst-Knudsen v. Mikisch, 39 A.3d 222, 228 (N.J. Ct. App. 2012). *See also* Ronan v. Adely, 861 A.2d 822 (N.J. 2004).

In Marriage of Gulsvig illustrates the high emotions that sometimes surround a child's name. 498 N.W.2d 725 (Iowa 1993). In *Gulsvig*, a mother after her divorce to the child's father, acting alone, changed the child's name on the birth certificate to the last name of her second husband. The Supreme Court of Iowa held that it was in the best interests of the child to retain the mother's new surname. The court noted that the mother said she would retain her name if she again remarried. Further, the court read her openness to generous visitation by the father as indicating that she wanted him to have strong ties with the child. The parents were awarded joint custody in the divorce, with the mother having primary physical care of the child. Harris, J. dissented, stating although he did not object to the majority's disapproval of the outdated rule giving fathers virtually absolute power to append their surname to a child, he believed that in the absence of an agreement between the parents, they should select a surname used by one of them during their relationship. In a separate dissent, Snell, J. argued for a "more stringent [legal standard] than what is applied by the majority of courts" today:

> In name change cases involving minors, the noncustodial father's name is entitled to be given significant consideration and a change is not warranted unless there is clear and convincing evidence that it is in the child's best interests to change its name. . . .
>
> No name change case has been cited and I have found none in the United States that has sanctioned the stripping of a father's name from his child when he is without fault and the placing of another man's name on the child with whom the child has no biological or legal relationship. I do not believe a divorced father, who is without fault, should have to face the distinct possibility of losing not only the custody of his children but of having his name forever excised from their being. To approve [the mother's] unilateral and deceitful act on the principle of promoting family unity is not an affirmation of the equality of women, which I support, but an assault on the dignity of man. The noncustodial father's role is reduced to that of an anonymous sperm donor, finance provider and unwelcome visitor. At once, history is ignored, custom rejected and genealogy abjured.

Id. at 733.

In many disputes parents are fighting over which of their last names the child will bear. In other cases, one parent may object to the child bearing that parent's last name. In *Scoggins v. Trevino*, the Texas Court of Appeals found that substantial evidence supported the change of a nonmarital child's name to the father's last name over the father's objection. 200 S.W.3d 832 (Tex. Ct. App. 2006). Using a twelve-factor best-interests test, the court found that: the child's mother and nonmarital father had an ongoing romantic relationship for more than a decade since the child's birth; that the child recognized the father as her father; that sharing the father's name would be more likely to identify the child with her family unit than would the mother's name; that bearing the father's name would not adversely affect the bond between the child and either of her parents; that the child preferred to bear the father's name; and that she understood the significance of last names.

C. SUPPORT DURING MARRIAGE

McGuire v. McGuire

Supreme Court of Nebraska, 1953
59 N.W.2d 336

■ MESSMORE, JUSTICE.

The plaintiff, Lydia McGuire, brought this action in equity in the district court for Wayne County against Charles W. McGuire, her husband, as defendant, to recover suitable maintenance and support money, and for costs and attorney's fees. Trial was had to the court and a decree was rendered in favor of the plaintiff.

The district court decreed that the plaintiff was legally entitled to use the credit of the defendant and obligate him to pay for certain items in the nature of improvements and repairs, furniture, and appliances for the household in the amount of several thousand dollars; required the defendant to purchase a new automobile with an effective heater within 30 days; ordered him to pay travel expenses of the plaintiff for a visit to each of her daughters at least once a year; that the plaintiff be entitled in the future to pledge the credit of the defendant for what may constitute necessaries of life; awarded a personal allowance to the plaintiff in the sum of $50 a month; awarded $800 for services for the plaintiff's attorney; and as an alternative to part of the award so made, defendant was permitted, in agreement with plaintiff, to purchase a modern home elsewhere.

The defendant filed a motion for new trial which was overruled. From this order the defendant perfected appeal to this court. . . .

The record shows that the plaintiff and defendant were married in Wayne, Nebraska, on August 11, 1919. At the time of the marriage the defendant was a bachelor 46 or 47 years of age and had a reputation for more than ordinary frugality, of which the plaintiff was aware. She had visited in his home and had known him for about 3 years prior to the marriage. After the marriage the couple went to live on a farm of 160 acres located in Leslie precinct, Wayne County, owned by the defendant and upon which he had lived and farmed since 1905. . . . The plaintiff had been previously married. Her first husband died in October 1914, leaving surviving him the plaintiff and two daughters. He died intestate, leaving 80 acres of land in Dixon County. The plaintiff and each of the daughters inherited a one-third interest therein. At the time of the marriage of the plaintiff and defendant the plaintiff's daughters were 9 and 11 years of age. By working and receiving financial assistance from the parties to this action, the daughters received a high school education in Pender. . . . Both . . . daughters are married and have families of their own. On April 12, 1939, the plaintiff transferred her interest in the 80-acre farm to her two daughters. The defendant signed the deed. At the time of trial plaintiff was 66 years of age and the defendant nearly 80 years of age. No children were born to these parties. The defendant had no dependents except the plaintiff. The plaintiff testified that she was a dutiful and obedient wife, worked and saved, and cohabited with the defendant until the last 2 or 3 years. She worked in the fields, did outside chores, cooked, and attended to her household duties such as cleaning the house and doing the washing. For a number of years she raised as high as 300 chickens, sold poultry and eggs, and used the money to buy clothing, things she wanted, and for groceries. She further testified that the defendant was the boss of the house and his word was law; that he would not tolerate any charge accounts and would not inform her as to his finances or business; and that he was a poor companion. The defendant did not complain of her work, but left the impression to her that she had not done enough. On several occasions the plaintiff asked the defendant for money. He would give her very small amounts, and for the last 3 or 4 years he had not given her any money nor provided her with clothing, except a coat about 4 years previous. The defendant had purchased the groceries the last 3 or 4 years, and permitted her to buy groceries, but he paid for them by check. There is apparently no complaint about the groceries the defendant furnished. The defendant had not taken her to a motion picture show during the past 12 years. They did not belong to any organizations or charitable institutions. . . . For the past 4 years or more, the defendant had not given the plaintiff money to purchase furniture or other household necessities. Three years ago he did purchase an electric, wood-and-cob combination stove which was installed in the kitchen, also linoleum floor covering for the kitchen. The plaintiff further testified that the house is not equipped with a bathroom, bathing facilities, or inside toilet. The kitchen is not modern. She does not have a kitchen sink. Hard and soft water is obtained from a well and cistern. She has a mechanical Servel refrigerator, and the house is equipped with electricity. There is a pipeless furnace which she testified had not been in good working order for 5 or 6 years, and she testified she was tired of scooping coal and ashes. She had requested a new furnace but the defendant believed the one they had to be satisfactory. She related that the furniture was old and she would like to replenish it, at least to be comparable with some of her neighbors; that her silverware and dishes were old and were primarily gifts, outside of what she purchased; that one of her daughters was good about furnishing her clothing, at least a dress a year, or sometimes two; that the defendant owns a 1929 Ford coupé equipped with a heater which is not efficient, and on the average of every 2 weeks he drives the plaintiff to Wayne to visit her mother; and that he also owns a 1927 Chevrolet pickup which is used for different purposes on the farm. The plaintiff was privileged to use all of the rent money she wanted to from the 80-acre farm, and when she goes to see her daughters, which is not frequent, she uses part of the rent money for that purpose, the defendant providing no funds for such use. The defendant ordinarily raised hogs on his farm, but the last 4 or 5 years has leased his farm land to tenants, and he generally keeps up the fences and the buildings. At the present time the plaintiff is not able to raise chickens and sell eggs. She has about 25 chickens. The plaintiff has had three abdominal operations for which the defendant has paid. She selected her own doctor, and there were no restrictions placed in that respect. When she has requested various things for the home or personal effects, defendant has informed her on many occasions that he did not have the money to pay for the same. She would like to have a new car. She visited one daughter in Spokane, Washington, in March 1951 for 3 or 4 weeks, and visited the other daughter living in Fort Worth, Texas, on three occasions for 2 to 4 weeks at a time. She had visited one of her daughters when she was living in Sioux City some weekends. The plaintiff further testified that she had very little funds, possibly $1,500 in the bank which was chicken money and money which her father furnished her, he having departed this life a few years ago; and that use of the telephone was restricted, indicating that defendant did not desire that she make long distance calls, otherwise she had free access to the telephone.

It appears that the defendant owns 398 acres of land with 2 acres deeded to a church, the land being of the value of $83,960; that he has bank deposits in the sum of $12,786.81 and government bonds in the amount of $104,500; and that his income, including interest on the bonds and rental for his real estate, is $8,000 or $9,000 a year. [There are some savings bonds listed in Charles's and Lydia's name in the amount of $2,500, while others are held in the name of Charles only, with no beneficiary.] The plaintiff has a bank account of $5,960.22. This account includes deposits of some $200 and $100 which the court required the defendant to pay his wife as temporary allowance during the pendency of these proceedings. One hundred dollars was withdrawn on the date of each deposit.

The defendant assigns as error that the decree is not supported by sufficient evidence; that the decree is contrary to law; that the decree is an unwarranted usurpation and invasion of defendant's fundamental and constitutional rights; and that the court erred in allowing fees for the plaintiff's attorney.

While there is an allegation in the plaintiff's petition to the effect that the defendant was guilty of extreme cruelty towards the plaintiff, and also an allegation requesting a restraining order be entered against the defendant for fear he might molest plaintiff or take other action detrimental to her rights, the plaintiff made no attempt to prove these allegations and the fact that she continued to live with the defendant is quite incompatible with the same. . . .

[T]here are no cases cited by the plaintiff and relied upon by her from this jurisdiction or other jurisdictions that will sustain the action such as she has instituted in the instant case. . . .

[In] Anshutz v. Anshutz, 16 N.J.Eq. 162, . . . it was said that while a wife had no right to the interference of the court for her maintenance until her abandonment or separation, there might be an abandonment or separation, within the sound construction of the statute, while the parties continued to live under the same roof, as where the husband utterly refused to have intercourse with his wife, or to make any provision for her maintenance, and thus he might seclude himself in a portion of his house, take his meals alone or board elsewhere than in his house, and so as effectively separate himself from his wife and refuse to provide for her as in case of actual abandonment, although in whatever form it might exist it must be an abandonment.

There are also several cases, under statutes of various states, in which separate maintenance was refused the wife, where the husband and wife were living in the same house. These cases are to the effect that it is an indispensable requirement of a maintenance statute that the wife should be living separate and apart from her husband without her fault. . . .

In the instant case the marital relation has continued for more than 33 years, and the wife has been supported in the same manner during this time without complaint on her part. The parties have not been separated or living apart from each other at any time. In the light of the cited cases it is clear, especially so in this jurisdiction, that to maintain an action such as the one at bar, the parties must be separated or living apart from each other.

The living standards of a family are a matter of concern to the household, and not for the courts to determine, even though the husband's attitude toward his wife, according to his wealth and circumstances, leaves little to be said in his behalf. As long as the home is maintained and the parties are living as husband and wife it may be said that the husband is legally supporting his wife and the purpose of the marriage relation is being carried out. Public policy requires such a holding. It appears that the plaintiff is not devoid of money in her own right. She has a fair-sized bank account and is entitled to use the rent from the 80 acres of land left by her first husband, if she so chooses.

Reversed and remanded with directions to dismiss.

■ YEAGER, JUSTICE (dissenting).

In the light of what the decisions declare to be the basis of the right to maintain an action for support, is there any less reason for extending the right to a wife who is denied the right to maintenance in a home occupied with her husband than to one who has chosen to occupy a separate abode?

If the right is to be extended only to one who is separated from the husband equity and effective justice would be denied where a wealthy husband refused proper support and maintenance to a wife physically or mentally incapable of putting herself in a position where the rule could become available to her.

It is true that in all cases examined which uphold the right of a wife to maintain an action in equity for maintenance the parties were living apart, but no case has been cited or found which says that separation is a condition precedent to the right to maintain action in equity for maintenance. Likewise none has been cited or found which says that it is not. . . .

I think however that the court was without proper power to make any of the awards contained in the decree for the support and maintenance of the plaintiff except the one of $50 a month.

From the cases cited herein it is clear that a husband has the obligation to furnish to his wife the necessaries of life. These decisions make clear that for failure to furnish them the wife may seek allowances for her support and maintenance. However neither these decisions nor any others cited or found support the view contended for by plaintiff that the court may go beyond this and impose obligations other than that of payment of money for the proper support and maintenance of the wife. . . .

NOTES

Option of Divorce. Unsurprisingly, it is difficult for most students in the first decades of the 21st century to identify with life in rural Nebraska in the middle of the 20th century. Even so, the facts and the holding of the decision serve as a reminder of why there eventually arose a reform of marital property and divorce law. A glimpse into this history may be found in Martha Fineman, *Implementing Equality: Ideology, Contradiction and Social Change. A Study of Rhetoric and Results in the Regulation of the Consequences of Divorce*, 1983 WIS. L. REV. 789, 855. Divorce would not have been an option for the wife in *McGuire* because of the lack of any grounds. Prior to 1969, fault-based divorce was required. The facts do not suggest that the husband committed adultery, desertion or even cruelty, judged by the local standards at the time. With the advent of no-fault divorce the wife would have had more options, such as irreconcilable differences. And if the wife had killed her husband so as to inherit his wealth she would be barred from inheritance because of state statutes and public policy. *See* Carla Spivak, *Killers Shouldn't Inherit from Their Victims-Or Should They?*, 48 GA. L. REV. 145 (2013).

Spousal Support Duties. At common law, a husband was responsible for necessary goods and services furnished to his wife by third parties. This doctrine of "necessaries" was accepted widely in this country until equal protection challenges, discussed *infra*, led to the abrogation of the doctrine in some states, and the codification of it in gender-neutral terms in others.

Notwithstanding *McGuire*'s noninterference principle, some states make the failure to provide support a crime. *See* VA. CODE ANN. § 20–61 (2016) ("Any spouse who without cause deserts or willfully neglects or refuses or fails to provide for the support and maintenance of his or her spouse . . . shall be guilty of a misdemeanor. . . .").

Other states direct spouses to support one another during the intact marriage. *See* N.Y. FAM. CT. ACT § 412(c) (McKinney 2016) ("A married person is chargeable with the support of his or her spouse and, except where the parties have entered into an agreement pursuant to section four hundred twenty-five of this article providing for support, the court, upon application by a party, shall make its award for spousal support pursuant to the provisions of this part.").

For a historical background of this type of legislation, *see* 3 CHESTER G. VERNIER, AMERICAN FAMILY LAWS 102–08 (1935). For a modern description, *see* Marie T. Reilly, *Me and You Against the World: Marriage and Divorce from Creditors' Perspective*, in RECONCEIVING THE FAMILY: CRITIQUE ON THE AMERICAN LAW INSTITUTE'S PRINCIPLES OF THE LAW OF FAMILY DISSOLUTION 195, n. 30 (Robin Fretwell Wilson ed. 2006); Jay M. Zitter, *Necessity in Action Against Husbands for Necessaries,* 19 A.L.R.4th 432 (2008).

A Gender-Based Duty of Support? The doctrine of necessaries was challenged on grounds that imposing liability on husbands, but not wives, violates equal protection principles. For example, in *Connor v. Southwest Florida Regional Medical Center,* the Supreme Court of Florida held that its application to husbands, but not wives, constituted a denial equal protection. 668 So.2d 175 (Fla. 1995).

Some jurisdictions responded by abrogating the necessaries doctrine. In *Connor,* while the court could have extended duties of support to wives, it refused to impose such a duty where none had previously existed, absent a directive from the legislature. Adopting this same reasoning, the Vermont Supreme Court also completely abolished the necessaries doctrine. *See* Med. Ctr. Hosp. of Vermont v. Lorrain, 675 A.2d 1326 (Vt. 1996).

Other jurisdictions reacted by applying the doctrine equally to both spouses. *See, e.g.*, Richland Memorial Hospital v. Burton, 318 S.E.2d 12 (S.C. 1984) (construing the state's necessaries statute to apply equally to both wives and husbands); N.C. Baptist Hospitals v. Harris, 354 S.E.2d 471 (N.C. 1987). In Virginia, the supreme court first held that imposing financial responsibility on a husband but not a wife constituted gender-based discrimination under both the state and federal constitutions. *See* Schilling v. Bedford County Memorial Hospital, Inc., 303 S.E.2d 905 (Va. 1983). The Virginia legislature responded by enacting a statute applying the necessaries doctrine equally to both spouses:

VIRGINIA CODE (2016)

§ 55–37. Spouse not responsible for other spouse's contracts, etc.; mutual liability for necessaries; responsibility of personal representative

Except as otherwise provided in this section, a spouse shall not be responsible for the other spouse's contract or tort liability to a third party, whether such liability arose before or after the marriage. The doctrine of necessaries as it existed at common law shall apply equally to both spouses, except where they are permanently living separate and apart, but shall in no event create any liability between such spouses as to each other. No lien arising out of a judgment under this section shall attach to the judgment debtors' principal residence held by them as tenants by the entireties or that was held by them as tenants by the entireties prior to the death of either spouse where the tenancy terminated as a result of the death of either spouse.

Are there good reasons to maintain the "necessaries doctrine" today or should it be abolished entirely, even if it does not discriminate based on gender? As a practical matter, widespread use of the joint credit card may have diminished the number of cases that otherwise might arise.

Family Expense Statutes. Family expense statutes are an additional, though limited, method for enforcing support obligations. Many were enacted in the 1920s and 1930s for the benefit of creditors, allowing them to collect on debts incurred for necessary family expenses by executing against either spouse's property. While these statutes encompass a variety of expenses, medical expenses are commonly included. For example, the Minnesota Statute provides:

MINNESOTA STAT. (2015)

§ 519.05. Liability of husband and wife

(a) A spouse is not liable to a creditor for any debts of the other spouse. Where husband and wife are living together, they shall be jointly and severally liable for necessary medical services that have been furnished to either spouse, including any claims arising under section 246.53, 256B.15, 256D.16, or 261.04, and necessary household articles and supplies furnished to and used by the family. Notwithstanding this paragraph, in a proceeding under chapter 518 the court may apportion such debt between the spouses.

(b) Either spouse may close a credit card account or other unsecured consumer line of credit on which both spouses are contractually liable, by giving written notice to the creditor.

Medicaid Benefits. In the modern state, the obligation of spouses to support one another often arises in the context of long-term care. In the United States, Medicaid, a federal and state program, may be available to provide state support for nursing care, but only if the applicant meets rigorous financial needs tests, which examine both resources and income. These requirements focus not only on the resources and income of the spouse who will be in long-term care, the "institutionalized" spouse, but on the financial resources of the spouse who will remain in the "community."

In an effort to thwart the ability of wealthy couples to place the burden of long-term care on the state, federal regulations deem all property owned by both spouses, however held (individually or jointly), to be available to the institutionalized spouse when determining eligibility for state support. The state takes a "snapshot" of the couple's resources on the date the institutionalized spouse permanently enters the long-term care facility. At one time, the couple's residence was exempt from this snapshot, whatever its value. After the Deficit Reduction Act of 2005, however, home equity in excess of $500,000 (in some states up to $750,000) now counts in the snapshot calculation.

Federal rules police transfers from the institutionalized spouse to individuals or trusts in the five years preceding their Medicaid application and may deny coverage to individuals as a result of transfers made during the five-year "look-back" period. Impermissible transfers would be included in the snapshot. Federal rules also deal with how to treat transfers of promissory notes, loans, and mortgages.

Federal legislation strives to be fair to the community spouse, so that use of the couple's assets and income for the care of the institutionalized spouse does not lead to the "pauperization" of the community spouse. *See* H.R. Rep. No. 100–105[II], 100th Cong. (2d Sess. 1965). Thus, federal rules allow the community spouse to keep their own separate income, although it is counted when deciding whether the institutionalized spouse is eligible for Medicaid. In addition, the community spouse is permitted to retain some of the couple's property, up to an amount known as the Community Spouse Resource Allowance (CSRA). The CSRA equals one-half of the couple's countable resources, which in 2013 cannot be less than $23,184 or more than $115,920. *See* Martin J. Hagan, *Spousal Rights and Responsibilities*, HAGANLAW.NET (July 3, 2012), http://haganlaw.net/?page_id=321; John A. Miller, *Medicaid Spend Down, Estate Recovery and Divorce: Doctrine, Planning and Policy*, 23 ELDER L. J. 41 (2015); Raymond C. O'Brien, *Selective Issues in Effective Medicaid Estate Recovery Statutes*, 65 CATH. U. L. REV. 27, 41–43 (2015); RAYMOND C. O'BRIEN AND MICHAEL T. FLANNERY, THE FUNDAMENTALS OF ELDER LAW 563–601 (2015); Raymond C. O'Brien, *Integrating Marital Property in a Spouse's Elective Share*, 59 CATH U. L. REV. 617, 704–707 (2010).

Federal rules also provide that the community spouse should share in the institutionalized spouse's income when necessary for their self-support. This amount, known as the Minimum Monthly Needs Allowance (MMNA), is currently set at a maximum of $2,980.50 per month. Medicaid, *2016 SSI and Spousal Impoverishment Standards*, https://www.medicaid.gov/medicaid/eligibility/downloads/2016-ssi-and-spousal-impoverishment-standards.pdf. The MMNA may be satisfied by the community spouse's income if sufficient. Where the community spouse's income falls short, the community spouse first receives a "credit" for income generated by the couple's property—calculated as 1/12 of 1.5% of the CSRA. If this amount is still insufficient, then the community spouse may be brought up to the MMNA by the institutionalized spouse's income, for example, by capturing a portion of the institutionalized spouse's retirement or social security benefits. Federal law presumes that the institutionalized spouse's income has, in fact, been made available to the community spouse before any adjustment may be made to bring the community spouse up to the MMNA.

Federal law permits either spouse to establish that the community spouse needs more income than the MMNA provides due to "exceptional circumstances resulting in significant financial duress." 42 U.S.C. § 1396–r5(e)(2)(B) (2012). Courts are loathe to consider voluntary choices, such as private school tuition for a child, as creating significant financial duress. Instead, courts have emphasized that the financial duress must be "thrust upon the community spouse by circumstances over which he or she has no control." *In the* Matter of Gomprecht, 652 N.E.2d 936, 938 (N.Y. 1995). The maintenance of a Manhattan apartment as well as a house in East Hampton would not qualify because the community spouse "essentially sought to maintain her prior lifestyle and have the public subsidize it." *Id.* at 939. In *Gomprecht*, the court reversed a trial court order to the community spouse in the amount of $3,339.26.

D. TESTIMONIAL PRIVILEGE, TORTS, AND CRIMES BETWEEN SPOUSES

1. TESTIMONIAL PRIVILEGE

Federal common law recognizes two distinct forms of marital privilege: (1) the privilege against adverse spousal testimony, which gives the testifying witness the privilege to refuse to testify against a spouse, even about non-confidential communications or acts; and (2) the confidential marital communications privilege which may be asserted by either spouse to bar the testimony of the other regarding marital communications made in confidence. 3 JACK B. WEINSTEIN AND MARGARET A. BERGER, WEINSTEIN'S FEDERAL EVIDENCE § 505.03[1] (Joseph M. McLaughlin ed., 2d ed. 2010).

Trammel v. United States

Supreme Court of the United States, 1980
445 U.S. 40

■ BURGER, CHIEF JUSTICE

We granted certiorari to consider whether an accused may invoke the privilege against adverse spousal testimony so as to exclude the voluntary testimony of his wife. . . .

On March 10, 1976, petitioner Otis Trammel was indicted with two others, Edwin Lee Roberts and Joseph Freeman, for importing heroin into the United States from Thailand and the Philippine Islands and for conspiracy to import heroin in violation of 21 U.S.C.A. §§ 952(a), 962(a), and 963. The indictment also named six unindicted co-conspirators, including petitioner's wife Elizabeth Ann Trammel. According to the indictment, petitioner and his wife flew from the Philippines to California in August 1975, carrying with them a quantity of heroin. Freeman and Roberts assisted them in its distribution. Elizabeth Trammel then travelled to Thailand where she purchased another supply of the drug. On November 3, 1975, with four ounces of heroin on her person, she boarded a plane for the United States. During a routine customs search in Hawaii, she was searched, the heroin was discovered, and she was arrested. After discussions with Drug Enforcement Administration agents, she agreed to cooperate with the Government.

Prior to trial on this indictment, petitioner moved to sever his case from that of Roberts and Freeman. He advised the court that the

Government intended to call his wife as an adverse witness and asserted his claim to a privilege to prevent her from testifying against him. At a hearing on the motion, Mrs. Trammel was called as a Government witness under a grant of use immunity. She testified that she and petitioner were married in May 1975 and that they remained married.[1] She explained that her cooperation with the Government was based on assurances that she would be given lenient treatment. She then described in considerable detail, her role and that of her husband in the heroin distribution conspiracy. After hearing this testimony, the District Court ruled that Mrs. Trammel could testify in support of the Government's case to any act she observed during the marriage and to any communication "made in the presence of a third person;" however, confidential communications between petitioner and his wife were held to be privileged and inadmissible. The motion to sever was denied.

At trial, Elizabeth Trammel testified within the limits of the court's pretrial ruling; her testimony, as the Government concedes, constituted virtually its entire case against petitioner. He was found guilty on both the substantive and conspiracy charges. . . .

In the Court of Appeals petitioner's only claim of error was that the admission of the adverse testimony of his wife, over his objection, contravened this Court's teaching in Hawkins v. United States, 358 U.S. 74 (1958). . . .

The privilege claimed by petitioner has ancient roots. Writing in 1628, Lord Coke observed that "it hath been resolved by the Justices that a wife cannot be produced either against or for her husband." 1 Coke, A Commentarie upon Littleton 6b (1628). See, generally, 8 J. Wigmore, Evidence § 2227, (McNaughton rev. 1961). This spousal disqualification sprang from two canons of medieval jurisprudence: first, the rule that an accused was not permitted to testify in his own behalf because of his interest in the proceeding; second, the concept that husband and wife were one, and since the woman had no recognized separate legal existence, the husband was that one. From those two now long-abandoned doctrines, it followed that what was inadmissible from the lips of the defendant-husband was also inadmissible from his wife.

Despite its medieval origins, this rule of spousal disqualification remained intact in most common-law jurisdictions well into the 19th century . . . [I]t was not until 1933, in Funk v. United States, 290 U.S. 371, that this Court abolished the testimonial disqualification in the federal courts, so as to permit the spouse of a defendant to testify in the defendant's behalf. *Funk*, however, left undisturbed the rule that either spouse could prevent the other from giving adverse testimony. The rule thus evolved into one of privilege rather than one of absolute disqualification.

---

[1] In response to the question whether divorce was contemplated, Mrs. Trammel testified that her husband had said that "I would go my way and he would go his."

The modern justification for this privilege against adverse spousal testimony is its perceived role in fostering the harmony and sanctity of the marriage relationship. Notwithstanding this benign purpose, the rule was sharply criticized. Professor Wigmore termed it "the merest anachronism in legal theory and an indefensible obstruction to truth in practice." The Committee on the Improvement of the Law of Evidence of the American Bar Association called for its abolition. 63 American Bar Association Reports, at 594–595 (1938). In its place, Wigmore and others suggested a privilege protecting only private marital communications, modeled on the privilege between priest and penitent, attorney and client, and physician and patient.[5]

These criticisms influenced the American Law Institute, which, in its 1942 Model Code of Evidence, advocated a privilege for marital confidences, but expressly rejected a rule vesting in the defendant the right to exclude all adverse testimony of his spouse. See American Law Institute, Model Code of Evidence, Rule 215 (1942). In 1953 the Uniform Rules of Evidence, drafted by the National Conference of Commissioners on Uniform State Laws, followed a similar course; it limited the privilege to confidential communications and "abolishe[d] the rule, still existing in some states, and largely a sentimental relic, of not requiring one spouse to testify against the other in a criminal action." See Rule 23(e) and comments. Several state legislatures enacted similarly patterned provisions into law.

In Hawkins v. United States, 358 U.S. 74 (1958), this Court considered the continued vitality of the privilege against adverse spousal testimony in the federal courts. There the District Court had permitted petitioner's wife, over his objection, to testify against him. With one questioning concurring opinion, the Court held the wife's testimony inadmissible. . . . Also rejected was the Government's suggestion that the Court modify the privilege by vesting it in the witness spouse, with freedom to testify or not independent of the defendant's control. The Court viewed this proposed modification as antithetical to the widespread belief, evidenced in the rules then in effect in a majority of the States and in England, "that the law should not force or encourage testimony which might alienate husband and wife, or further inflame existing domestic differences." *Hawkins,* then, left the federal privilege for adverse spousal testimony where it found it, continuing "a rule which bars the testimony of one spouse against the other unless both consent." Id., at 78. Accord, Wyatt v. United States, 362 U.S. 525, 528 (1960)[7] . . . .

---

[5] This Court recognized just such a confidential marital communications privilege in Wolfle v. United States, 291 U.S. 7 (1934), and in Blau v. United States, 340 U.S. 332 (1951). In neither case, however, did the Court adopt the Wigmore view that the communications privilege be substituted *in place of* the privilege against adverse spousal testimony. The privilege as to confidential marital communications is not at issue in the instant case; accordingly, our holding today does not disturb *Wolfle* and *Blau.*

[7] The decision in *Wyatt* recognized an exception to *Hawkins* for cases in which one spouse commits a crime against the other. 362 U.S., at 526. This exception placed on the ground of necessity, was a longstanding one at common law. See Lord Audley's Case, 123 Eng.Rep. 1140

The Federal Rules of Evidence acknowledge the authority of the federal courts to continue the evolutionary development of testimonial privileges in federal criminal trials "governed by the principles of the common law as they may be interpreted . . . in the light of reason and experience." Fed.Rule Evid. 501. Cf. Wolfle v. United States, supra, at 12 (1934). The general mandate of Rule 501 was substituted by the Congress for a set of privilege rules drafted by the Judicial Conference Advisory Committee on Rules of Evidence and approved by the Judicial Conference of the United States and by this Court. That proposal defined nine specific privileges, including a husband-wife privilege which would have codified the *Hawkins* rule and eliminated the privilege for confidential marital communications. See Fed.Rule of Evid., Proposed Rule 505. In rejecting the proposed rules and enacting Rule 501, Congress manifested an affirmative intention not to freeze the law of privilege. Its purpose rather was to "provide the courts with the flexibility to develop rules of privilege on a case-by-case basis," 120 Cong.Rec. 40891 (1974) (statement of Rep. Hungate), and to leave the door open to change. Although Rule 501 confirms the authority of the federal courts to reconsider the continued validity of the *Hawkins* rule, the long history of the privilege suggests that it ought not to be casually cast aside. That the privilege is one affecting marriage, home, and family relationships—already subject to much erosion in our day—also counsels caution. . . .

Since 1958, when *Hawkins* was decided, support for the privilege against adverse spousal testimony has been eroded further. Thirty-one jurisdictions, including Alaska and Hawaii, then allowed an accused a privilege to prevent adverse spousal testimony. The number has now declined to 24. In 1974, the National Conference on Uniform State Laws revised its Uniform Rules of Evidence, but again rejected the *Hawkins* rule in favor of a limited privilege for confidential communications. See Uniform Rules of Evidence, Rule 504. That proposed rule has been enacted in Arkansas, North Dakota, and Oklahoma—each of which in 1958 permitted an accused to exclude adverse spousal testimony. The trend in state law toward divesting the accused of the privilege to bar adverse spousal testimony has special relevance because the law of marriage and domestic relations are concerns traditionally reserved to the states. See Sosna v. Iowa, 419 U.S. 393, 404 (1975). Scholarly criticism of the *Hawkins* rule has also continued unabated. . . .

It is essential to remember that the *Hawkins* privilege is not needed to protect information privately disclosed between husband and wife in the confidence of the marital relationship—once described by this Court as "the best solace of human existence." Stein v. Bowman, 13 Pet., at 223. Those confidences are privileged under the independent rule protecting confidential marital communications. The *Hawkins* privilege is invoked,

(1931); 8 Wigmore § 2239. It has been expanded since then to include crimes against the spouse's property, and in recent years crimes against children of either spouse, United States v. Allery, 526 F.2d 1362 (C.A.8 1975). Similar exceptions have been found to the confidential marital communications privilege.

not to exclude private marital communications but rather to exclude evidence of criminal acts and of communications made in the presence of third persons.

No other testimonial privilege sweeps so broadly. The privileges between priest and penitent, attorney and client, and physician and patient limit protection to private communications. These privileges are rooted in the imperative need for confidence and trust. The priest-penitent privilege recognizes the human need to disclose to a spiritual counselor, in total and absolute confidence, what are believed to be flawed acts or thoughts and to receive priestly consolation and guidance in return. The lawyer-client privilege rests on the need for the advocate and counselor to know all that relates to the client's reasons for seeking representation if the professional mission is to be carried out. Similarly, the physician must know all that a patient can articulate in order to identify and to treat disease; barriers to full disclosure would impair diagnosis and treatment.

The *Hawkins* rule stands in marked contrast to these three privileges. Its protection is not limited to confidential communications; rather it permits an accused to exclude all adverse spousal testimony. As Jeremy Bentham observed more than a century and a half ago, such a privilege goes far beyond making "every man's house his castle," and permits a person to convert his house into "a den of thieves." 5 Rationale of Judicial Evidence 340 (1827). It "secures, to every man, one safe and unquestionable and ever ready accomplice for every imaginable crime." Id., at 338.

The ancient foundations for so sweeping a privilege have long since disappeared. Nowhere in the common-law world—indeed in any modern society—is a woman regarded as chattel or demeaned by denial of a separate legal identity and the dignity associated with recognition as a whole human being. Chip by chip, over the years those archaic notions have been cast aside so that "[n]o longer is the female destined solely for the home and the rearing of the family, and only the male for the marketplace and the world of ideas." Stanton v. Stanton, 421 U.S. 7, 14, 15 (1975).

The contemporary justification for affording an accused such a privilege is also unpersuasive. When one spouse is willing to testify against the other in a criminal proceeding—whatever the motivation—their relationship is almost certainly in disrepair; there is probably little in the way of marital harmony for the privilege to preserve. In these circumstances, a rule of evidence that permits an accused to prevent adverse spousal testimony seems far more likely to frustrate justice than to foster family peace.[12] Indeed, there is reason to believe that vesting

---

[12] It is argued that abolishing the privilege will permit the Government to come between husband and wife, pitting one against the other. That, too, misses the mark. Neither *Hawkins,* nor any other privilege, prevents the Government from enlisting one spouse to give information

the privilege in the accused could actually undermine the marital relationship. For example, in a case such as this, the Government is unlikely to offer a wife immunity and lenient treatment if it knows that her husband can prevent her from giving adverse testimony. If the Government is dissuaded from making such an offer, the privilege can have the untoward effect of permitting one spouse to escape justice at the expense of the other. It hardly seems conducive to the preservation of the marital relation to place a wife in jeopardy solely by virtue of her husband's control over her testimony.

Our consideration of the foundations for the privilege and its history satisfy us that "reason and experience" no longer justify so sweeping a rule as that found acceptable by the Court in *Hawkins*. Accordingly, we conclude that the existing rule should be modified so that the witness spouse alone has a privilege to refuse to testify adversely; the witness may be neither compelled to testify nor foreclosed from testifying. This modification—vesting the privilege in the witness spouse—furthers the important public interest in marital harmony without unduly burdening legitimate law enforcement needs. Here, petitioner's spouse chose to testify against him. That she did so after a grant of immunity and assurances of lenient treatment does not render her testimony involuntary. Accordingly, the District Court and the Court of Appeals were correct in rejecting petitioner's claim of privilege, and the judgment of the Court of Appeals is affirmed.

NOTES

MARYLAND CODE, COURTS AND JUDICIAL PROCEEDINGS (2016)

§ 9–106. Spousal privilege

Charges not subject to privilege

(a) The spouse of a person on trial for a crime may not be compelled to testify as an adverse witness unless the charge involves:

- (1) The abuse of a child under 18; or
- (2) Assault in any degree in which the spouse is a victim if:
  - (i) The person on trial was previously charged with assault in any degree or assault and battery of the spouse;
  - (ii) The spouse was sworn to testify at the previous trial; and
  - (iii) The spouse refused to testify at the previous trial on the basis of the provisions of this section.

Spouses who are assault victims

(b) (1) If the spouse of a person on trial for assault in any degree in which the spouse was a victim is sworn to testify at the trial

---

concerning the other or to aid in the other's apprehension. It is only the spouse's testimony in the courtroom that is prohibited.

and refuses to testify on the basis of the provisions of this section, the clerk of the court shall make and maintain a record of that refusal, including the name of the spouse refusing to testify.

(2) When an expungement order is presented to the clerk of the court in a case involving a charge of assault in any degree, the clerk shall check the record to determine whether the defendant's spouse refused to testify on the basis of the provisions of this section.

(3) If the record shows such refusal, the clerk shall make and maintain a separate record of the refusal, including the defendant's name, the spouse's name, the case file number, a copy of the charging document, and the date of the trial in which the spouse refused to testify.

(4) The separate record specified under paragraph (3) of this subsection:

(i) Is not subject to expungement under Title 10, Subtitle 1 of the Criminal Procedure Article; and

(ii) Shall be available only to the court, a State's Attorney's office, and an attorney for the defendant.

Federal Privileges. As stated in the Introduction to this section, federal common law recognizes two distinct forms of marital privilege: (1) the privilege against adverse spousal testimony, at issue in *Trammel*, which gives the testifying witness the privilege to refuse to testify against a spouse, even about non-confidential communications or acts; and (2) the confidential marital communications privilege, which may be asserted by either spouse to bar the testimony of the other regarding marital communications made in confidence.

Trammel holds that with the privilege against adverse spousal testimony, only the testifying-spouse may assert the privilege. The Supreme Court has made clear that this privilege is only applicable in trials "where life or liberty is at stake," such as criminal proceedings. Hawkins v. United States, 358 U.S. 74, 77 (1958).

However, with the confidential marital communications privilege, either spouse may assert the privilege, which applies to both criminal and civil matters. 3 JACK B. WEINSTEIN AND MARGARET A. BERGER, WEINSTEIN'S FEDERAL EVIDENCE § 505.09 (Joseph M. McLaughlin ed., 2d ed. 2010). This privilege applies not only during the marriage but "afterward" also, with the result that communications between spouses during the marriage remain privileged after dissolution of the marriage by death or divorce—in the absence of some statutory exception. *See* C. MCCORMICK, EVIDENCE § 66, at 145 (E. Cleary 2d ed. 1972); WEINSTEIN AND BERGER, *supra*, § 505.09.

One requirement for asserting the confidential marital communications privilege is that the communication be private and confidential. Emails sent between spouses over an employer's email system have been found not to qualify, where one of the spouses had no reasonable expectation of privacy. *In re* Reserve Fund Sec. & Derivative Litig., 275 F.R.D. 154 (S.D.N.Y. 2011).

State Privileges. Spousal privileges also exist under state law. All states recognize the confidential marital communications privilege. *See* Mikah K. Story, *Twenty-First Century Pillow-Talk*, 58 SANTA CLARA L. Rev. 275, 281 & n.40 (2006). As of 2006, thirty-two U.S. jurisdictions recognized the privilege against adverse spousal testimony. With the recognition of same-sex marriage in nine jurisdictions, married same-sex couples receive the benefit of these privileges, just as heterosexual spouses do. Some states extend immunity from compelled testimony to couples in civil unions or domestic partnerships. *See* N.J. STAT. ANN. § 37:1–32(o) (West 2016).

In some states, the spousal testimony privilege disqualifies a spouse from testifying without the consent of the other spouse.

COLORADO REV. STAT. (2016)

§ 13–90–107. Who may not testify without consent—definitions

(1) There are particular relations in which it is the policy of the law to encourage confidence and to preserve it inviolate; therefore, a person shall not be examined as a witness in the following cases:

(a) (I) . . . [A] husband shall not be examined for or against his wife without her consent nor a wife for or against her husband without his consent; nor during the marriage or afterward shall either be examined without the consent of the other as to any communications made by one to the other during the marriage; but this exception does not apply to a civil action or proceeding by one against the other, a criminal action or proceeding for a crime committed by one against the other. . . . However, this exception shall not attach if the otherwise privileged information is communicated after the marriage.

Under this statute, a wife could block her new husband from testifying as to her care and treatment of her child in a custody dispute with her ex-husband. *See In re* Marriage of Bozarth, 779 P.2d 1346, 1347 (Colo. 1989).

Unlike *Bozarth* and *Trammel*, in some cases both spouses want to avoid the state's compulsion that one of them testify in a proceeding against the other. But as Colorado's law illustrates, state legislatures often limit the spousal privilege when one spouse is suing the other or faces criminal prosecution, including for domestic violence in the marriage. *See also* Commonwealth v. Kirkner, 805 A.2d 514 (Pa. 2002) (noting that the state statute eliminated the spousal privilege in criminal proceedings for bodily injury between husband and wife); Rogers v. State, 189 P.3d 265, 265–66 (Wyo. 2008) ("We conclude that a victim spouse may be compelled by the State of Wyoming to testify against his or her spouse when that spouse is charged with a crime against the victim spouse.").

Some states will respect the spousal privilege, even in cases of violence by one spouse against the other, but only if the necessary evidence cannot "be obtained from less intrusive sources." State v. Mauti, 208 N.J. 519, 523

(2012) (finding that the state did not satisfy its three-part burden to pierce the spousal privilege and compel a wife to testify against her husband in a sexual assault case).

Spousal privilege is frequently unavailable in cases of child abuse. For example, in Daniels v. State, 681 P.2d 341 (Alaska Ct. App. 1984), the grand jury subpoenaed a wife to testify about allegations that her husband sexually abused a foster daughter in their care. She refused, claiming spousal privilege. The trial court properly held that her testimony fell within an exception to the spousal privilege, found her in contempt of court, and put her in jail.

For more on spousal privileges, *see* MICHAEL T. FLANNERY & RAYMOND C. O'BRIEN, THE SEXUAL EXPLOITATION OF CHILDREN 491–493 (2016); Erin R. Collins, *The Evidentiary Rules of Engagement in the War Against Domestic Violence*, 90 N.Y.U. L. REV. 397 (2015); Leigh Goodmark, *"Law and Justice are not Always the Same": Creating Community-Based Justice Gorums for People Subjected to Intimate Partner Abuse,* 42 FLA. ST. U. L. REV. 707 (2015); Daniel A. Howwitz, *Twelve Angry Hours: Improving Domestic Violence Holds in Tennessee Without Rick of Violating the Constitution,* 10 TENN. J. L. & POL'Y 215 (2015); John E.B. Myers, *"Testifying" in Family Court*, 46 MCGEORGE L. REV. 499 (2014).

2. SEXUAL ASSAULT OR RAPE

Warren v. State

Supreme Court of Georgia, 1985
336 S.E.2d 221

■ SMITH, JUSTICE.

"When a woman says I do, does she give up her right to say I won't?" This question does not pose the real question because rape and aggravated sodomy are not sexual acts of an ardent husband performed upon an initially apathetic wife,[3] they are acts of violence that are accompanied with physical and mental abuse and often leave the victim with physical and psychological damage that is almost always long lasting.[4] Thus we find the more appropriate question: When a woman says "I do" in Georgia does she give up her right to State protection from

[3] Georgia has recognized both spouses' right to say "I won't" under the domestic law, by providing that before refusal of sexual intercourse rose to the level of cruel treatment in divorce, the refusal had to be "a denial, that . . . was wilful, persistent and without justification and done with an intent to cast him off as a husband completely and forever." Harkness v. Harkness, 184 S.E.2d 566 (Ga. 1971).

[4] "When you have been intimately violated by a person who is supposed to love and protect you, it can destroy your capacity for intimacy with anyone else. Moreover, many wife victims are trapped in a reign of terror and experience repeated sexual assaults over a period of years. When you are raped by a stranger you have to live with a frightening memory. When you are raped by your husband, you have to live with your rapist." National Center on Women and Family Law, Clearing House Review, November, 1984, citing Dr. David Finkelhor's testimony and statement in support of H.B. 516 to remove spousal exemption to sexual assault offenses to the Judiciary Committee, New Hampshire State Legislature (Mar. 25, 1981), p. 745.

the violent acts of rape and aggravated sodomy performed by her husband? The answer is no.[5] We affirm.

The appellant, Daniel Steven Warren, was indicted by a Fulton County Grand Jury for the rape and aggravated sodomy of his wife. They were living together as husband and wife at the time. The appellant filed a pre-trial general demurrer and motion to dismiss the indictment. After a hearing, the motions were denied. The appellant sought and was issued a certificate of immediate review and filed an application for an interlocutory appeal which was granted by this court.

The appellant asserts that there exists within the rape statute an implicit marital exclusion that makes it legally impossible for a husband to be guilty of raping his wife.

Until the late 1970's there was no real examination of this apparently widely held belief. Within the last few years several jurisdictions have been faced with similar issues and they have decided that under certain circumstances a husband can be held criminally liable for raping his wife. What is behind the theory and belief that a husband could not be guilty of raping his wife? There are various explanations for the rule and all of them flow from the common law attitude toward women, the status of women and marriage. Perhaps the most often used basis for the marital rape exemption is the view set out by Lord Hale in 1 Hale P.C. 629. It is known as Lord Hale's contractual theory. The statement attributed to Lord Hale used to support the theory is: "but a husband cannot be guilty of a rape committed by himself upon his lawful wife, for by their mutual matrimonial consent and contract the wife hath given up herself in this kind unto her husband which she cannot retreat."

There is some thought that the foundation of his theory might well have been the subsequent marriage doctrine of English law, wherein the perpetrator could, by marrying his victim, avoid rape charges. It was thus argued as a corollary, rape within the marital relationship would result in the same immunity.[7] Another theory stemming from medieval times is that of a wife being the husband's chattel or property. Since a married woman was part of her husband's property, nothing more than a chattel, rape was nothing more than a man making use of his own property. A third theory is the unity in marriage or unity of person theory that held the very being or legal existence of a woman was suspended during marriage, or at least was incorporated and consolidated into that of her husband. In view of the fact that there was only one legal being, the husband, he could not be convicted of raping himself.

---

[5] It would be incongruous to find both spouses have a right under the domestic law to refuse a normal and mutual satisfying function of married life, and at the same time find that wives have no protection under the criminal law in the event their husbands engage in the violent conduct defined as rape.

[7] The laws in America changed that doctrine, "[t]he general rule apart from statute is that the subsequent marriage of the parties is no bar to a prosecution for rape. [Cit.] . . . " 9 A.L.R. 339.

These three theories have been used to support the marital rape exemption. Others have tried to fill the chasm between these three theories with justifications for continuing the exemption in the face of changes in the recognition of women, their status, and the status of marriage. Some of the justifications include: Prevention of fabricated charges; Preventing wives from using rape charges for revenge; Preventing state intervention into marriage so that possible reconciliation will not be thwarted. A closer examination of the theories and justifications indicates that they are no longer valid, if they ever had any validity.

Hale's implied consent theory was created[8] at a time when marriages were irrevocable and when all wives promised to "love, honor, and obey" and all husbands promised to "love, cherish, and protect until death do us part." Wives were subservient to their husbands, her identity was merged into his, her property became his property, and she took his name for her own.

There have been dramatic changes in women's rights and the status of women and marriage. Today our State Constitution provides that, "no person shall be deprived of life, *liberty,* or property except by due process," (Emphasis supplied.) Art. 1, § 1, Para. 1, and "protection to *person* and property is the paramount duty of government and shall be impartial and complete. No person shall be denied the equal protection of the laws." (Emphasis supplied.) Art. 1, § 2, Para. 2. Our State Constitution also provides that each spouse has a right to retain his or her own property. Art. 1, § 1, Para. 27. Our statutory laws provide that, "[t]he rights of citizens include, *without limitation,* the following: (1) The right of *personal security,* [and] (2) The right of *personal liberty . . .* " (Emphasis supplied.) OCGA § 1–2–6. Women in Georgia "are entitled to the privilege of the elective franchise and have the right to hold any civil office or perform any civil function as fully and completely as do male citizens." OCGA § 1–2–7. Couples who contemplate marriage today may choose either spouse's surname or a combination of both names for their married surname, OCGA § 19–3–33.1. No longer is a wife's domicile presumed to be that of her husband, OCGA § 19–2–3 and no longer is the husband head of the family with the wife subject to him. OCGA § 19–3–8. Marriages are revocable without fault by either party, OCGA § 19–5–3(13); either party, not just the husband, can be required to pay alimony upon divorce, OCGA § 19–6–1; and both parties have a joint and several duty to provide for the maintenance, protection, and education of their children, OCGA § 19–7–2. Couples may write antenuptial agreements in which they are able to decide, prior to marriage, future settlements,

---

[8] Hale cited no legal authority for his proposition, "[t]hus the marital exemption rule expressly adopted by many of our sister states has its ORIGIN in a bare, extra-judicial declaration made some 300 years ago. Such a declaration cannot itself be considered a definite and binding statement of the common law, although legal commentators have often restated the rule since the time of Hale without evaluating its merits, [cits.]" State v. Smith, 426 A.2d 38, 41 (N.J. 1981).

OCGA § 19–3–62; and our legislature has recognized that there can be violence in modern family life and it has enacted special laws to protect family members who live in the same household from one another's violent acts, Ga.L.1981, 880; OCGA § 19–13–1 et seq.

Today, many couples write their own marriage vows in which they specifically decide the terms of their marriage contract. Certainly no normal woman who falls in love and wishes " 'to marry, establish a home and bring up children' . . . a central part of the *liberty* protected by the Due Process Clause, [Cits.]" (Emphasis supplied.) Zablocki v. Redhail, 434 U.S. 374 (1978), would knowingly include an irrevocable term to her revocable marriage contract that would allow her husband to rape her. Rape "is highly reprehensible, both in a moral sense and in its almost total contempt for the personal integrity and autonomy of the female victim. . . . Short of homicide, it is the 'ultimate violation of self.' " Coker v. Georgia, 433 U.S. 584, 599, 97 S.Ct. 2861, 2869 (1977). It is incredible to think that any state would sanction such behavior by adding an implied consent term *to all marriage contracts* that would leave *all* wives with no protection under the law from the "ultimate violation of self," Coker, supra, 97 S.Ct. at 2869, simply because they choose to enter into a relationship that is respected and protected by the law. The implied consent theory to spousal rape is without logical meaning, and *obviously conflicts* with our Constitutional and statutory laws and our regard for all citizens of this State.

One would be hard pressed to argue that a husband can rape his wife because she is his chattel. Even in the darkest days of slavery when slaves were also considered chattel, rape was defined as "the carnal knowledge of a female whether free or slave, forcibly and against her will." Georgia Code, § 4248, p. 824 (1863). Both the chattel and unity of identity rationales have been cast aside. "No where in the common law world—[or] in any modern society—is a woman regarded as chattel or demeaned by denial of a separate legal identity and the dignity associated with recognition as a whole human being." Trammel v. United States, 445 U.S. 40, 52 (1980).

We find that none of the theories have any validity. The justifications likewise are without efficacy. There is no other crime we can think of in which *all of the victims are denied protection* simply because someone might fabricate a charge; there is no evidence that wives have flooded the district attorneys with revenge filled trumped-up charges, and once a marital relationship is at the point where a husband rapes his wife, state intervention is needed for the wife's protection.

There never has been an expressly stated marital exemption included in the Georgia rape statute. Furthermore, our statute never included the word "unlawful" which has been widely recognized as signifying the incorporation of the common law spousal exclusion. Commonwealth v. Chretien, 417 N.E.2d 1203, 1208 (Mass. 1981). A reading of the statute indicates that there is no marital exclusion. "A person commits the offense of rape when he has carnal knowledge of a female forcibly and against her will." OCGA § 16–6–1. We need not decide whether or not a common law marital exemption became part of our old statutory rape law, because the rape statute that was similar to the common law definition[12] was specifically repealed in 1968, and our new broader statute, OCGA § 16–6–1, was enacted in its place which plainly on its face includes a husband.[13]

The appellant contends that there is an implicit marital exclusion within the aggravated sodomy statute that makes it legally impossible for a husband to be guilty of an offense of aggravated sodomy performed upon his wife. Sodomy was originally defined as "the carnal knowledge and connection against the order of nature by man with man, or in the same unnatural manner with woman." Laws 1833, Cobb's 1851 Digest, p. 787. The punishment for sodomy was "imprisonment at labor in the penitentiary for and during the natural life of the person convicted of this detestable crime." Laws 1833, Id.

Under the original rape and sodomy statutes, a man accused of rape could defend by alleging that the victim consented. If the consent could be proven, he could not be guilty of rape, because the third element of the offense "against her will" would be missing. One accused of sodomy could not defend by alleging consent, as lack of consent was not an element of the offense, and "[w]here a man and a woman voluntarily have carnal knowledge and connection against the order of nature with each other, they are both guilty of sodomy, . . . " Comer v. State, 94 S.E. 314 (Ga. App. 1917). Thus an allegation of consent would only go to show the other party's guilt. "One who voluntarily participates in an unnatural act of sexual intercourse with another is also guilty of sodomy. One who does not so participate is not guilty." Perryman v. State, 12 S.E.2d 388 (Ga. App. 1940).

In 1968 the sodomy statute was specifically repealed, and two new offenses were enacted, sodomy and aggravated sodomy. There can be no common law marital exemption under the aggravated sodomy statute based on "implied consent," when the statute was enacted in 1968 and when there clearly was no marital exemption for sodomy based on "consent" under the original sodomy statute. The appellant contends that if we find no marital exemptions under the rape and aggravated sodomy statutes it would be a new interpretation of the criminal law, and to apply the statutes to him would deprive him of his due process rights. "All the Due Process Clause requires is that the law give sufficient warning that

---

[12] "Rape is the carnal knowledge of a female, forcibly and against her will."

[13] When our Criminal Code was revised, the drafters relied upon the Illinois Criminal Code and the Model Penal Code. Both Codes included within their rape statutes an explicit marital exemption. "A male person . . . who has sexual intercourse with a female, not his wife, by force and against her will commits rape." Ill.Rev.Stat. § 11.1; "A male who has sexual intercourse with a female not his wife is guilty of rape if; . . . " Section 213.1 Model Penal Code. Our Legislature could have, but did not, include the words "not his wife." They chose instead to add the words "A person," which broadens the statute and which is in keeping with the enunciated purposes of the code. OCGA § 16–1–2.

men may conduct themselves so as to avoid that which is forbidden. [Cit.]" Rose v. Locke, 423 U.S. 48 (1975). Both the rape and aggravated sodomy statutes are broadly written and they are plain on their face. This is a first application of these statutes to this particular set of facts, this is not an unforeseeable judicial enlargement of criminal statutes that are narrowly drawn. . . .

Judgment affirmed.

NOTES

Unlike Georgia, which had no express marital exemption, a number of states did have such exemptions at one time. Today, more than half the jurisdictions in the United States have abolished the marital rape exemption, permitting a spouse to be convicted of a sexual crime against his or her spouse. However, as of 2011, courts in 23 states have upheld the marital rape exemption, so that a spouse may not be charged with a sexual crime against the other spouse under any circumstances. Michael G. Walsh, Annotation, *Criminal Responsibility of Husband for Rape, or Assault to Commit Rape, on Wife*, 24 A.L.R.4th 105, 108–11, § 4(b) (1983) (current through 2016).

Many states abolished the marital rape exception with specific legislation. *See, e.g.*, ARK. CODE ANN. § 5–14–103 (2016). In State v. Willis, 394 N.W.2d 648 (Neb. 1986), the Supreme Court of Nebraska held that whatever basis may have existed under the common law for the marital rape exception, it was abrogated when the legislature enacted its new sexual assault law. *See generally* Ruthy Lowenstein Lazar, *The "Vindictive Wife": The Credibility of Complaints in Cases of Wife Rape*, 25 S. CAL. REV. L. & SOC. JUST. 1 (2015); Timothy S. Mehok, Recent Developments: Leleux v. United States*: The Fifth Circuit Takes a Look at Federal Tort Claims in the Context of Sexual Battery*, 75 TUL. L. REV. 549 (2000).

In some states, the marital rape exemption was deemed as unconstitutional and abolished. In People v. Liberta, 474 N.E.2d 567 (N.Y. 1984), the New York Court of Appeals struck down both the marital and gender exemptions in that State's criminal rape statute. The case involved a defendant husband who had been judicially ordered to move out and remain away from the marital home. Although the court found that under such a protective order he was statutorily "not married" at the time of the rape, it nevertheless concluded that the marital exemption for rape was unconstitutional. In doing so, they specifically rejected several possible rationales in support of the exemption. These included possible fabrication of complaints by vindictive wives, the right of marital privacy, the interest in promoting reconciliation between parties, and the argument that marital rape is less serious than other rapes and therefore is adequately dealt with under other statutes such as those on assault. The court concluded:

> The question . . . is whether the Legislature would prefer to have statutes which cover forcible rape and sodomy, with no exemption for married men who rape or sodomize their wives and no exception made for females who rape males, or instead to have no

> statutes proscribing forcible rape and sodomy. In any case where a court must decide whether to sever an exemption or instead declare an entire statute a nullity it must look at the importance of the statute, the significance of the exemption within the overall statutory scheme, and the effects of striking down the statute. . . . Forcible sexual assaults have historically been treated as serious crimes and certainly remain so today. . . . Statutes prohibiting such behavior are of the utmost importance, and to declare such statutes a nullity would have a disastrous effect on the public interest and safety. The inevitable conclusion is that the Legislature would prefer to eliminate the exemptions and thereby preserve the statutes. Accordingly we choose the remedy of striking the marital exemption . . . and the gender exemption . . . , so that it is now the law of this State that any person who engages in sexual intercourse or deviate sexual intercourse with any other person by forcible compulsion is guilty of either rape in the first degree or sodomy in the first degree. Because the statutes under which the defendant was convicted are not being struck down, his conviction is affirmed.

Id. at 579.

Other states limited prosecution to spouses who used force, threat, or intimidation to accomplish the rape, or to instances when the couple was living apart or the rape caused serious physical injury. *See, e.g.*, VA. CODE ANN. § 18.2–61(B) (West 2016).

3. CRIMES INVOLVING SPOUSAL PROPERTY

Cladd v. State

Supreme Court of Florida, 1981
398 So.2d 442

■ ALDERMAN, JUSTICE.

The sole issue presented for review is whether a husband, who is physically but not legally separated from his wife, can be guilty of burglary when he enters premises, possessed only by the wife and in which he has no ownership or possessory interest, without the wife's consent and with intent to commit an offense therein. . . . We hold that the Second District [Court of Appeal] correctly decided that, under the particular facts of this case, the defendant could be guilty of burglary of his estranged wife's apartment. . . .

The factual situation is narrow. The defendant and his wife had been separated for approximately six months, although there was no formal separation agreement or restraining order. He had no ownership or possessory interest in his wife's apartment and had at no time lived there. One morning, he broke through the locked door of her apartment with a crowbar, struck her, and attempted to throw her over the second floor stair railing. The next morning, he again attempted to break into her apartment but left when the police arrived.

The defendant was charged with burglary and attempted burglary.[2] Although conceding that his wife did not in fact consent to his entry into her apartment, he moved to dismiss the charges on the basis that since the victim was his wife, he was licensed or invited to enter her apartment as a matter of law. He then contended that, if he had the right to enter the apartment, he could not be guilty of burglary or attempted burglary. Relying upon Vazquez v. State [350 So.2d 1094 (Fla.App.1977)], the trial court dismissed the charges. The State appealed, and the Second District, expressly disagreeing with the rationale of the Third District in *Vazquez,* reversed. The Second District held that although each spouse may have the legal right to the other's company, this does not include the right to break and enter the other's apartment *with intent to commit an offense therein.*

In *Vazquez,* the Third District held that since the husband in that case had the legal right to be with his wife, he could not be guilty of burglary when he broke into her apartment. Judge Haverfield, however, expressing the view later adopted by the Second District, dissented to the reversal of the burglary conviction. Pointing out that the victim's wife had the sole possessory rights to the apartment and that defendant had gained entrance only by actually breaking down the door and finding that the evidence was sufficient to sustain the burglary conviction, he concluded that the wife's apartment was not a marital abode and defendant no longer had a legal right to be there.

Later, in Wilson v. State, 359 So.2d 901 (Fla. 3d DCA), cert. denied, 365 So.2d 716 (Fla.1978), the Third District addressed the issue of whether entry into a father-in-law's home, where defendant's wife was temporarily residing, with intent to assault her constituted burglary. Distinguishing *Vazquez* on the basis that, in *Wilson,* the premises were possessed by the wife's father, the Third District affirmed defendant's burglary conviction and said that the husband's legal right to be with his wife did not establish consent where the wife was living in premises which were not solely possessed by her. The right of consortium alone was not sufficient to give the husband a right of entry into these premises. Yet, the legal right of consortium was the basis upon which the Third District premised its determination of implied consent in *Vazquez.*

We reject the defendant's contention that the marriage relationship and the right of consortium deriving therefrom preclude the State from ever establishing the nonconsensual entry requisite to the crime of burglary, and we disapprove the Third District's contrary ruling in

---

[2] Burglary means entering or remaining in a structure or a conveyance with the intent to commit an offense therein, unless the premises are at the time open to the public or the defendant is licensed or invited to enter or remain. Section 810.02, Florida Statutes (1977). It is a crime that involves primarily the invasion of possessory property rights of another. Cannon v. State, 102 Fla. 928, 136 So. 695 (1931).

Vazquez. Since burglary is an invasion of the possessory property rights of another, where premises are in the sole possession of the wife, the husband can be guilty of burglary if he makes a nonconsensual entry into her premises with intent to commit an offense, the same as he can be guilty of larceny of his wife's separate property. In State v. Herndon, 158 Fla. 115, 27 So.2d 833 (1946), discussing a wife's separate property rights, we held that a husband could be charged with the larceny of his wife's separate property, and we explained:

> In a society like ours, where the wife owns and holds property in her own right, where she can direct the use of her personal property as she pleases, where she can engage in business and pursue a career, it would be contrary to every principle of reason to hold that a husband could ad lib appropriate her property. If the common-law rule was of force, the husband could collect his wife's pay check, he could direct its use, he could appropriate her separate property and direct the course of her career or business if she has one. We think it has not only been abrogated by law, it has been abrogated by custom, the very thing out of which the common law was derived.

27 So.2d at 835. The defendant's consortium rights did not immunize him from burglary where he had no right to be on the premises possessed solely by his wife independent of an asserted right to consortium.

The defendant's estranged wife was in sole possession of the premises into which he broke with intent to assault her. The district court correctly reversed the trial court's dismissal of the burglary and attempted burglary charges. . . .

■ BOYD, JUSTICE, dissenting.

Under long-established principles of Anglo-American law, one of the essential incidents of the marital state is the right of spouses to the company and comfort of one another. This right is referred to as the right of consortium. Consortium is so basic as an incident of marriage that it should not be undermined except by a clear legislative statement of the public policy of this state. The legislature should reconcile the matter of consortium rights with the elements of any crime, and should do so very carefully when dealing in the context of a crime carrying a possible sentence of life imprisonment. See § 810.02(2), Fla.Stat. (1977). . . .

The legislature has met a number of times since the principles of the *Vazquez* and *Wilson* cases were announced. I believe the fact that the legislature failed to modify or clarify the burglary statute in response to the judicial development of these principles indicates that the legislative intent was properly derived in those cases. . . .

■ ENGLAND, JUSTICE, dissenting.

Like an anxious Pandora endeavoring to stuff the ills of the world back into her box, the majority endeavors to confine interspousal crimes to the factual situation of this case. As Pandora and the world sadly learned, however, once the box is opened there is no way to contain the ephemeral evils which escape. The majority today holds that one spouse may commit burglary against another. This new common law doctrine has emanations which go far beyond this case. This becomes evident when the case is viewed preliminarily from the perspective of what is *not* here involved.

First, this is not a prosecution for assault. Any discussion with regard to the husband's physical abuse or intended physical abuse of his wife is extraneous to the legal question presented. Mr. Cladd may or may not be prosecuted for his violent acts toward his wife's person. Whether that occurs is beside the point.

Second, this case does not involve spouses who are divorced, legally separated, or already in court in a pending dissolution proceeding. The husband and wife here are married, and there is no objective, legal manifestation that their marriage or interpersonal relations are being unwound. That they live apart, it will be seen, is quite irrelevant to the legal issue posed.

Third, this case does not entail a situation where separately-owned property, purchased or inherited by the wife, was established as a residence apart from her husband's. The record here only shows that Mrs. Cladd's living accommodations were separate from her husband's. We do not know who purchased the furnishings and fixtures, whether they came from a residence which had been occupied jointly, or even whether the separate abode was a second or alternative home.

When these matters are removed from the *legal* considerations, this case boils down to a husband's uninvited entry onto premises which the wife occupies away from the marital home. This situation is legally indistinguishable from other situations in which a separate residence is maintained by one or both spouses and in which one is temporarily residing, such as a summer home, a winter ski lodge, a vacation cottage at the seashore, a temporary, rented, haven from marital incompatibility, a remote wing or separate building on jointly occupied property (such as a studio-garage in which one spouse alone works), or even a separate bedroom in which one spouse may be seeking a retreat in the marital home. The record of this proceeding nowhere indicates that the wife had a separate possessory interest in the property she placed in her separate facility. We do not know whether the six-month separation of these spouses was the result of estrangement, a mutually agreed-upon cooling off period, a segregated vacation plan, or some other reason. Mr. Cladd here, I submit, was simply charged with illegal entry into a place where his wife claimed sanctuary from their common residence. The manner of entry and the purpose for entry may prompt judicial concerns for the wife's welfare, but the parties' motives or state of mind will prove an unreliable touchstone for criminal prosecutions of this sort, I predict.

The effect of today's decision is to bring prosecuting attorneys into marital disputes in a way which is unprecedented in Florida or elsewhere. I confess I am not comfortable with the Third District's analysis of the basis for rejecting burglary prosecutions in these situations—a right of cohabitation or consortium. Those concepts connote marital harmony, and here we have obvious discord. I am quite comfortable, however, with the thought that our criminal courts should not be involved, in fact or as a threat, in domestic disputes which involve an invasion of one spouse's claim of separateness or privacy. Personal assaults, I repeat, are different, and in those cases perhaps different considerations should pertain.

NOTES

American Law Institute's Model Penal Code § 223.1(4) provides that: "It is not a defense that a theft was from the actor's spouse, except that misappropriation of household and personal effects, or other property normally accessible to both spouses, is theft only if it occurs after the parties have ceased living together."

Other cases have held that a husband cannot steal from his wife or burglarize her home. *See* State v. Weitzel, 112 Ohio App. 300, 168 N.E.2d 550 (1960). However, where a couple has been estranged for years, a husband was properly convicted of burglary of the home he jointly owned with his wife when the burglary occurred after the two had lived separately for 12 years. *See* State v. Herrin, 6 Ohio App.3d 68, 453 N.E.2d 1104, 1106 (1982).

For additional commentary, *see* John M. Leventhal, *Spousal Rights or Spousal Crimes: Where and When Are the Lines to be Drawn?,* 2006 UTAH L. REV. 351, 378 ("The trend to make acts of malicious mischief by an offending spouse unlawful is a sound policy. Once the property is destroyed, the ownership rights of the innocent spouse cannot be redeemed or restored as in the case of larceny. Further, the destruction of property is an act of intimidation and an effort to exert power and control. The criminalization of malicious mischief is an important and necessary tool in combating domestic violence.").

4. INSTITUTIONAL RESPONSES TO VIOLENCE BETWEEN SPOUSES

State ex rel. Williams v. Marsh

Supreme Court of Missouri, En Banc, 1982
626 S.W.2d 223

■ HIGGINS, JUDGE.

Denise Williams petitions this court for a writ of mandamus to compel the trial court to issue an order of protection, an order restraining her husband from entering her dwelling and a temporary order of custody as authorized by The Adult Abuse Act, §§ 455.010–.085, RSMo Supp.1980. In a separate action she appeals the trial court's dismissal of her petition filed under Chapter 455, RSMo Supp.1980. The appeal was consolidated with the mandamus action because both present the same issues concerning the trial court's determination that Chapter 455, RSMo Supp.1980 violates a number of provisions of the Missouri and United States Constitutions. The preliminary writ is made peremptory; the judgment of dismissal is reversed, and the cause is remanded for further proceedings consistent with the writ herein issued.

After a hearing on plaintiff's petition for an *ex parte* order of protection, the trial court found: plaintiff, Denise Williams, and respondent, Edward M. Williams were married; one child was born of the marriage; the couple had been living separately for approximately five months prior to the hearing, plaintiff having custody of the child; respondent's home address was unknown although his place of employment was known[1] and his estimated wages were $1,000 per month; during the separation respondent provided no support or maintenance to plaintiff or the child with the exception of a small amount of clothing for the child; plaintiff leased or rented her residence individually; on November 13, 1980, and on numerous previous occasions, respondent (a 230 lbs., former Golden Gloves boxer) "intentionally, knowingly and wilfully beat petitioner . . . causing . . . serious physical injury . . . requiring petitioner to be hospitalized . . . " for 12 days. The court concluded: respondent was a former adult household member whose actions constituted abuse; he had purposely placed petitioner in apprehension of immediate physical injury; and thus plaintiff had "shown an unqualified right to the temporary relief available under §§ 455.035 and 455.045."

The court dismissed the petition because it held the Adult Abuse Act, in general and specifically §§ 455.035, .045 and .085, RSMo Supp.1980 unconstitutional, and thus unenforceable.

The Adult Abuse Act was adopted by the Missouri Legislature on June 13, 1980, and became effective August 13, 1980. It was adopted by the Missouri Legislature as a result of an increased awareness nationally of the prevalence of domestic violence and of the need to protect the victims of that violence. It is part of a nationwide trend to legislate in this area. Existing remedies such as peace bonds, regular criminal process, and tort law have proved to be less than adequate in aiding the victims of abuse and in preventing further abuse.

An adult who is abused by a present or former adult household member, may petition the circuit court for relief under the Act. Two types of relief are available: *ex parte* orders issued without notice to the respondent or a hearing, and orders issued after notice and an on record hearing. Violation of an *ex parte* order of protection of which the respondent has notice or of a full order of protection is declared to be a

[1] All attempts to notify respondent husband of this appeal have failed; communication by mail sent to him at his alleged place of employment has been returned.

class C misdemeanor for which the respondent may be arrested without a warrant. . . .

The trial court held that plaintiff had "an unqualified right to the . . . relief available under the Act." This ruling confers upon the plaintiff standing to argue in support of the Act because from it she derives an actual and justiciable interest susceptible of protection. . . .

The trial court ruled that the Act violates Mo.Const. art. III, § 23, which provides that "[n]o bill shall contain more than one subject which shall be clearly expressed in its title . . . " because it contains provisions relating to children, i.e., custody and support, rather than relating exclusively to adults, and thus contains more than one subject. The title of Senate Bill 524 is "an Act relating to the abuse of adults by an adult household member, with penalty provisions." The test to determine if a title violates § 23 is whether "all of the provisions of the statute fairly relate to the same subject, have a natural connection therewith or are the incidents or the means to accomplish its purpose." State ex rel. Jardon v. Industrial Development Authority, 570 S.W.2d 666, 677 (Mo.banc 1978). The subject of the Act is adult abuse; the purpose of the Act is to protect household members by preventing further violence. The question is whether the child custody provisions fairly relate to the subject of adult abuse and promote the purpose of the Act.

Studies have shown that the victim of adult abuse is usually a woman. In a large percentage of families, children have been present when the abuse occurred. In one study, fifty-four percent of the battered women interviewed reported that their husbands had committed acts of violence against their children as well as against them. Even if the child is not physically injured, he likely will suffer emotional trauma from witnessing violence between his parents. Abuse appears to be perpetuated through the generations; an individual who grows up in a home where violence occurs is more likely either to abuse others as an adult or to be a victim of abuse. Adult abuse, therefore, is a problem affecting not only the adult members of a household but also the children. The most compelling reason for an abused woman to remain in the home subject to more abuse is her financial dependency; this is particularly true for the women with children. The orders pertaining to child custody, support, and maintenance are all fairly related to and serve the purpose of aiding victims of domestic violence and preventing future incidents of adult abuse.

The court held that §§ 455.035–.045 of the Act facially violate the due process guarantees of U.S. Const., amend. XIV and Mo. Const. art. I, § 10 by permitting a respondent to be deprived of constitutionally protected interests prior to notice or an adversary hearing. The trial court found the *ex parte* orders of protection constitutionally infirm because the Act, on its face, may be applied to exclude a respondent from his home or from contact with his children for a fifteen day period prior to notice or hearing. The trial judge concedes that the goal of the statute is legitimate and important, but nevertheless ruled it unconstitutional because of its impact on important personal rights. He reached this conclusion by finding: that the facts upon which an *ex parte* order may be issued are not easily verifiable and thus not appropriate for presentation by affidavit to the court, as required by Mitchell v. W.T. Grant Co., 416 U.S. 600, 617–18 (1974); and that there is no procedure by which the respondent can dissolve the *ex parte* orders. Fuentes v. Shevin, 407 U.S. 67, 86 (1972).

Sections 455.020–.035, RSMo Supp.1980 set out the procedure for obtaining an *ex parte* order of protection. The person seeking an order of protection files a verified petition with the clerk of the circuit court or, if the court is unavailable, with "any available circuit or associate circuit judge in the city or county having jurisdiction. . . ." The judge may grant the *ex parte* orders only "for good cause shown" which is defined as "[a]n immediate and present danger of abuse to the petitioner." "Abuse" is defined as "inflicting, other than by accidental means, or attempting to inflict physical injury, on an adult or purposely placing another adult in apprehension of immediate physical injury." Section 455.010(1), RSMo Supp.1980. Three orders may be issued *ex parte:* restraining the respondent from further acts of abuse; restraining the respondent from entering the family dwelling unit; and granting temporary custody of any minor children. The statute permits an order restraining the respondent from entering the family dwelling unit to issue in favor of a spouse who otherwise has no property interest in the home. An *ex parte* order of protection remains in effect until the hearing, which is to be held "[n]ot later than fifteen days after the filing of a petition. . . ." Sections 455.035–.045, RSMo Supp.1980.

The due process guarantee is intended to protect an individual against arbitrary acts of the government. Furthermore, it protects the right to use and enjoy one's property without governmental interference. Before the guarantee of due process comes into play, however, there must be a deprivation by the government of a constitutionally protected interest. Mathews v. Eldridge, 424 U.S. 319, 332 (1976). The interests which are subject to temporary deprivation through the issuance of an *ex parte* order constitute significant liberty and property interests falling "within the purview of the Due Process Clause."[8] See Fuentes v. Shevin, 407 U.S. at 90. . . . Thus the procedures available under the Act must meet the constitutional standard.

Notice and an opportunity to be heard must be provided by the state in a meaningful manner prior to deprivation of a protected interest. This rule is not necessarily applied when there is only a temporary taking, as is the case here. Due process is a flexible concept; the same procedures

[8] Defendant contends that two interests are involved; in his home and in custody of the children. In some cases there may be a third protected interest—the liberty interest of a respondent in his reputation. See Taub, supra note 2, at 104–06. Any one of these interests may be sufficient to warrant procedural safeguards required by the Due Process Clause.

need not be applied in all instances. The extent and nature of procedures depends upon weighing of the private interests affected and the governmental functions involved. The United States Supreme Court in Mathews v. Eldridge identified a third factor to be considered in the balancing formula; the risk of erroneous deprivation using the existing procedures. . . .

The first factor is the private interest affected. The respondent has two private interests at stake; a property interest in one's home and a liberty interest in custody of one's children. These interests are significant, the importance of which has been emphasized by the United States Supreme Court. See cases, supra.

The second factor in the balancing formula is the governmental interest. The Adult Abuse Act is an exercise of the state's police power. Through the procedures established to aid victims of domestic violence, the legislature promotes the general health, welfare, and safety of its citizens. The magnitude of the problem of domestic violence is evidenced by statistics compiled by the FBI in 1973 which indicate that one-fourth of all homicides in the United States occur within the family. The petitioner's interests which are protected by the state in furthering its interests are the same as those of the respondent. The parties, irrespective of marital status, may own or rent the dwelling jointly, although under the Act this is not required. If it becomes unsafe for both parties to remain in the home, one may need to be excluded. The choice is reduced to the victim of the abuse leaving or the court ordering the abuser to leave. Parents may have an equal interest in maintaining custody of their children.[10] Both interests are important and have been accorded deference by the courts.

The Missouri Legislature has established a mechanism whereby the state can intervene when abuse of one adult by another household member occurs or is threatened and thus prevent further violence. State legislatures have broad power to enact laws to protect the general health, welfare, and safety. States also have been given deference in adopting reasonable summary procedures when acting under their police power.

The third factor in the test in Mathews v. Eldridge is "the fairness and reliability of the existing pretermination procedures, and the probable value, if any, of additional procedural safeguards." . . .

An *ex parte* order of protection is analogous to a temporary restraining order because both are injunctions issued prior to notice or hearing. *Ex parte* orders restraining acts of abuse or entrance into the dwelling are issued upon a showing of "an immediate and present danger of abuse to the petitioner." Section 455.035, RSMo Supp.1980. As in a proceeding to obtain any other restraining order, the petitioner must

---

[10] This differs from those cases where the state is attempting to remove children from the custody of the natural parent, see, e.g., Stanley v. Illinois, 405 U.S. 645 (1972), and vest custody in the court. Here, one parent retains custody.

satisfy the court that grounds exist to justify granting this order.[11] This will, in most instances, require the petitioner to appear personally before the court at which time the credibility of the petitioner can be tested.[12] In addition, the judge may be able to see first hand "the evidence of violence manifested in burns, cuts, bruises, and fractures." Boyle v. Boyle, supra note 4, slip op. at 7. If the petitioner is unable to appear because of injuries, this may be alleged and proof thereof will allow the court to determine that there is "[a]n immediate and present danger of abuse."

A protection order, if granted, remains in effect until the hearing which is to be held "[n]ot later than fifteen days after the filing of a petition." Section 455.040.1, RSMo Supp.1980. This sets a maximum period that the order could be effective without some hearing. Nothing in the statute suggests that the respondent could not obtain an earlier hearing. Concerning other restraining orders, Rule 92.02(b) provides that a party against whom a temporary restraining order has been issued may, upon two days' (or shorter time if the court so prescribes) notice to the opposing party, receive a hearing on the order. This rule is equally applicable to orders issued under the Act. The statute requires that the petition, notice of the hearing date, and any *ex parte* order of protection be served upon the respondent. Section 455.040.2, RSMo Supp.1980. The court at the same time may include in the notice information regarding the respondent's right to request an earlier hearing and the procedure to be followed.

The Supreme Court in Fuentes v. Shevin, outlined categories of cases where outright seizures have been allowed. 407 U.S. at 91. The first is where seizure has been directly necessary to secure an important governmental or general public interest; the second is where there has been a special need for prompt action; the third is where the state has kept strict control over its monopoly of legitimate force: there is a government official responsible for determining that seizure was necessary under standards set out in "narrowly drawn statutes."

The Act meets the foregoing standards. The Act is directly necessary to secure important governmental interests, i.e., protection of victims of abuse and prevention of further abuse. The situation where the challenged Act is to be applied are those where prompt action is necessary, i.e., when there is "[a]n immediate and present danger of abuse"Cthe only time the *ex parte* order may be issued. The government has kept strict control over its powers. Only a judge in his discretion, may issue the *ex parte* orders. This differs from the procedure where "[p]rivate parties, serving their own private advantage, may unilaterally invoke

[11] The determination made by the court in adult abuse cases is also analogous to a probable cause determination for issuance of a warrant "on oath or affirmation of the complainant." Rule 21.04. See Rule 21.05. The forms issued by this Court for seeking relief under the Act similarly require verification and as such are affidavits of facts upon which the Court may act. Sections 455.020, 455.025, RSMo. See also Order, Supreme Court of Missouri, en banc, August 8, 1980.

[12] Judge Marsh, in this case, conducted an *ex parte* hearing on Mrs. Williams' petition.

state power to replevy goods from another" disapproved in Fuentes v. Shevin, supra at 93. Under the Adult Abuse Act, the petitioner requests the court to act on his or her behalf. The court, not the clerk, must issue the order and the orders are not to be issued routinely but only after the petitioner has filed a verified petition showing good cause. . . .

The interests and procedures considered, these *ex parte* order provisions comply with due process requirements because they are a reasonable means to achieve the state's legitimate goal of preventing domestic violence, and afford adequate procedural safeguards prior to and after any deprivation occurs. . . .

■ BARDGETT, JUDGE, concurring in part.

I concur in the result reached and in the principal opinion except for that portion upholding the constitutionality of § 455.085.3 which makes the violation of an order of protection a crime—a class C misdemeanor.

This is not a criminal case and the question whether the misdemeanor conviction of one for violation of a protective order could be constitutionally upheld ought, in my opinion, await that kind of case. My reservations about this matter flow from the fact that the conduct of a spouse does not become a crime unless and until the judge so declares and then only with respect to that one person. This *law* does not prohibit certain conduct as criminal generally but rather leaves it to a judge to decide whether certain conduct, if engaged in in the future, will be criminal only as to a particular person. Certain acts of an abusive type are criminal by general law—assault and battery—and are a crime regardless of who commits them, but that is not the case under § 455.085.3. I have no particular difficulty with contempt proceedings which may involve incarceration for the violation of an injunctive order—an order of protection—but that is not a crime.

The statute does not make the act of entering one's home a crime. The only time that act becomes a criminal act is when, and if, a judge declares it to be criminal by prohibiting it in a protective order with respect to a particular person. Thus, § 455.085.3 delegates to a judge the power to say what conduct constitutes a crime and whether or not certain conduct, if engaged in by a particular person, will be a crime. . . .

I believe it highly questionable whether a crime can, under our Constitution, be so personalized; nevertheless, the issue of the constitutionality of § 455.085.3 is unnecessary to the adjudication of this case. I therefore reserve judgment on that matter until the case occurs in which that issue is decisive. I concur in all other aspects of the principal opinion.

■ WELLIVER, JUDGE, dissenting.

. . .

When we permit child custody, support and maintenance provisions, usually found in Chapter 452, to be hidden behind the newly created term which we now denominate as "Adult Abuse", when we permit the orders contemplated by the act to be entered without notice or hearing, and, when we permit circuit judges to define the elements of crime on a case by case basis without notice or hearing, then we by judicial interpretation have rendered a nullity: (1) the long established rule of statutory construction that penal statutes must be strictly construed against the state, (2) the constitutional prohibition, Mo. Const. art. III, § 23, that "[n]o bill shall contain more than one subject which shall be clearly expressed in its title . . . ," and (3) due process of law, U.S. Const.Amend. XIV, Mo. Const. art. I, § 10.

The Adult Abuse Act exhibits the fullest potential for creating nine new evils for every evil it would seek by its terms to correct.

NOTES

Other Statutes and Challenges. Protective orders are available in all fifty states and the District of Columbia. DIANE KIESEL, DOMESTIC VIOLENCE: LAW, POLICY, & PRACTICE 1077 (2007); Protective Orders, 50 State Statutory Surveys: Family Law: General, 0080 SURVEYS 19 (West 2007). A temporary order, resulting from an *ex parte* hearing like the one challenged in *Marsh*, generally will precede a final protective order, the hearing for which must occur within a short time-frame, such as twenty days. *See, e.g.*, MONT. CODE ANN. § 40–15–202 (West 2015). The respondent must be given notice and an opportunity to appear. *See, e.g.*, MO. STAT. ANN. § 455.040(2) (West 2016).

Typically, a final protective order can last up to one year, although in some states, the order runs for as long as three years. *See Protective Orders, 50 State Statutory Surveys: Family Law: General*, Westlaw, 0080 SURVEYS 19; KY. REV. STAT. ANN. § 403.740(4) (West 2016). Many statutes provide that the final order may be extended "upon a showing of good cause for additional periods of time not to exceed one (1) year each." WYO. CODE ANN. § 35–21–106(b) (West 2016).

The relief granted in protective orders differs dramatically from jurisdiction to jurisdiction. In some states, the final protective order can authorize counseling; grant temporary custody, visitation, and child support for minor children; can award the possession of certain personal property; and prohibit the abuser from possessing firearms or accessing certain records. *See, e.g.*, 750 ILL. COMP. STAT. § 60/214 (West 2016). One significant variation among the states is whether violation of a protective order requires mandatory jail time, which is authorized in a handful of states. *See, e.g.*, HAW. REV. STAT. § 586–11(b) (West 2016) (requiring not less than 48-hours in jail for the first conviction of violating the protective order, with lengthening jail sentences for subsequent convictions).

Most protective order statutes authorize any adult household member to apply for an order, whether married or cohabiting. *See, e.g.*, ARK. CODE ANN. § 9–15–201 (West 2016). Many permit domestic violence shelter workers to apply on behalf of the victim. *See id.* § 9–15–201(d)(4) (allowing an application on behalf of a minor). Some statutes allow a person with whom the respondent has had a child to apply for an order of protection, even if the two parents do not live together. *See, e.g.*, CAL. FAM. CODE § 6211(d) (West 2016).

With increased recognition of dating violence, a number of states also permit persons in dating or engagement relationships to apply for orders. *See id.* § 6211(c). Of course, when teens are involved, an order of protection as to one often means that public or private schools may be involved. Connecticut law requires that the court transmit a copy of any such order to the school. *See, e.g.*, CONN. GEN. STAT. § 46b–15(g) (2015).

Most statutes require the issuing court to forward a copy of the order to local or state law enforcement officials. Registries of protective orders are available online in some states. *See, e.g.*, LA. REV. STAT. ANN. § 46:2136.2 (2015).

The scope of domestic violence statutes has increased in response to varying circumstances. In *H.E.S. v. J.C.S.*, the New Jersey Supreme Court was asked to review the procedural and substantive due process issues raised by the state's Domestic Violence Act. 815 A.2d 405 (N.J. 2003). Specifically, the court was asked to decide if video surveillance by one spouse of the other spouse's bedroom can constitute a domestic violence offence, and concluded that it did. Even though the complainant did not know of the existence of the video camera, the "totality of the circumstances" indicated that using the surveillance, the respondent was able to use private conversations to "track [complainant's] every move" and therefore constituted harassment. Respondent's actions also constituted stalking because he purposefully acted against a specific person over a period of time and such a course of action could reasonably cause a person fear bodily injury. There have been similar cases. *See, e.g.*, People v. Sullivan, 53 P.3d 1181 (Colo. Ct. App. 2002) (placement of a global positioning system in plaintiff's care can constitute stalking). *See also* United States v. Al-Zubaidy, 283 F.3d 804 (6th Cir. 2002) (Violence Against Women Act's provision against interstate stalking is constitutional); Smith v. Martens, 106 P.3d 28 (Kan. 2005) (state stalking statute is constitutional); Tracey B. Carter, *Local, State, and Federal Responses to Stalking: Are Anti-Stalking Laws Effective?*, 22 WM. & MARY J. WOMEN & L. 333 (2016); Melissa Knight, *Stalking and Cyberstalking in the United States and Rural South Dakota: Twenty-Four Years After the First Legislation,* 59 S. D. L. REV. 392 (2014).

Domestic violence will often constitute a separate crime. *See, e.g., Domestic Violence, 50 State Statutory Surveys: Criminal Laws: Crimes*, 0030 Surveys 7 (West 2015); *See also* Thomas L. Hafemeister, *If All You Have Is A Hammer: Society's Ineffective Response to Intimate Partner Violence*, 60 CATH. U. L. REV. 919, 976–977 (2011).

Remedies for Failure of Officials to Act. In Nearing v. Weaver, 670 P.2d 137 (Or. 1983), the Supreme Court of Oregon held that police officers can be held liable in tort to individuals intended to be beneficiaries of the state's Family Abuse Prevention Act who suffer resulting psychic or physical harm. This case is in the minority.

Most decisions find the police not liable for failure to protect members of the public. Some suits are brought under 42 U.S.C. § 1983, alleging that the state's failure to protect deprived the victim of his or her rights under color of state law. These claims sometimes fail because the state is found to lack a duty to protect the victim. *See* Howard v. Bayes, 378 F. Supp.2d 753 (2005). In *Hayes*, officers responded to a series of emergency calls at the apartment of a woman who was later beaten to death by her boyfriend. Her estate charged that the officers failed to protect her. The court concluded, however, that "[w]hile [the victim] has a substantive due process right to her life, [the officer] did not violate that right; rather, it was [her boyfriend] that killed [her] and is responsible for her death." *Id.* at 760. *See also* Estate of Jennifer Vordermann v. City of Edgerton, 2010 WL 3788669 (W.D. Wis. 2010) (rejecting § 1983 claims brought by murdered woman's mother, alleging that the return by the police of a handgun to the woman, ultimately used by her husband to kill her, constituted an affirmative act creating a danger to her, in violation of her due process rights).

Courts have found that the state has no duty even in the face of state statutes directing the police to enforce protective orders. *See* Town of Castle Rock v. Gonzales, 545 U.S. 748 (2005). In a 7–2 decision, the United States Supreme Court ruled that the town could not be made liable under the 14th Amendment. Writing for the majority, Justice Scalia pointed out that:

> The procedural component of the Due Process Clause does not protect everything that might be described as a "benefit": "To have a property interest in a benefit, a person clearly must have more than an abstract need or desire" and "more than a unilateral expectation of it.

Id. at 756.

Notwithstanding the limits of private lawsuits to change police conduct, some "law enforcement agencies with functioning systems to gather and analyze data about lawsuits have used that information to reduce the likelihood of misconduct." Joanna C. Schwartz, *Myths and Mechanics of Deterrence: The Role of Lawsuits in Law Enforcement Decisionmaking*, 57 UCLA L. REV. 1023, 1023 (2010). As to police protection and liability in general, *see* Edward J. Hanlon, *Proof of Equal Protection Violation By Municipal Police Departments in Failing to Protect Victims of Domestic Violence*, 28 AM. JUR. PROOF OF FACTS 3d 1 (West 2016); Atinuke O. Awoyomi, Note, *The State-Created Danger Doctrine in Domestic Violence Cases: Do We Have a Solution in* Okin v. Village of Cornwall-on-Hudson Police Department?, 20 COLUM. J. GENDER & L. 1 (2011); Niji Jain, *Engendering Fairness in Domestic Violence Arrests: Improving Police Accountability Through the Equal Protection Clause*, 60 EMORY L. J. 1011 (2011); Licia A. Eaton, Annotation, *Liability of Municipality or Other Governmental Unit for Failure to Provide Police Protection From Crime*, 90 A.L.R. 5th 273 (West 2001); Richard Emery and Ilann Margalit Maazel, *Why Civil Rights Lawsuits Do Not Deter Police Misconduct: The Conundrum of Indemnification and a Proposed Solution*, 28 FORD. URB. L. J. 587 (2000).

Some states provide detailed rules regarding police handling of domestic violence cases. *See e.g.*, MASS. GEN. LAWS 209A § 6 (2016). Advocacy groups have sought to enforce the detailed rules about the handling of domestic violence cases with injunctive relief. In New York, twelve "battered wives" asserted that probation and Family Court nonjudicial personnel had engaged in "a pattern of conduct calculated (1) to deter battered wives from filing petitions for orders of protection against their offending husbands, (2) to block them from meaningful access to Family Court judges empowered to issue temporary orders of protection, and (3) by failing to advise the wives that the defendants proffer of counseling is voluntary, to dissuade complainants from pursuing their legal remedies." Bruno v. Codd, 393 N.E.2d 976, 977 (N.Y. 1979). In its opinion, the New York Court of Appeals noted that 40% of all police night calls in New York City are said to involve problems of battered or threatened wives. Although the court dismissed the claims, the concerted action ultimately resulted in a consent judgment with the police. *See* 4 FAM.L.REP. 3095 (July 18, 1978).

Battered Women's Syndrome. Another legal problem raised by domestic violence is whether a victim who subsequently kills his or her abuser should be allowed to raise the abuse as a defense or present evidence of it to mitigate the sentence. Courts are split on this issue. *See e.g.*, Jozsef Meszaros, *Achieving Peace of Mind: The Benefits of Neurobiological Evidence for Battered Women Defendants*, 23 YALE J.L. & FEMINISM 117 (2011); Douglas A. Orr, Weiand v. State*, and Battered Spouse Syndrome: The Toothless Tigress Can Now Roar*, 2 FLA. COASTAL L. J. 125 (2000); Myrna S. Raider, *The Admissibility of Prior Acts of Domestic Violence: Simpson and Beyond (People v. Simpson: Perspectives on the Implications for the Criminal Justice System)*, 69 U.S.C. L. REV. 1463 (1996).

Although domestic violence is commonly discussed in terms of "battered wives," men are also assaulted by intimate partners. *See e.g.*, Michele C. Black, et al., *The National Intimate Partner and Sexual Violence Survey: 2010 Summary Report*, NATIONAL CENTER FOR INJURY PREVENTION AND CONTROL, CENTERS FOR DISEASE CONTROL AND PREVENTION (2011); Mary Z. Silverzweig, *Domestic Terrorism: The Debate and Gender Divides*, 12 J. L. & FAM. STUD. 251 (2010). Same-sex partners also experience domestic violence in their relationships. *See e.g.*, Shannon Little, *Challenging Changing Legal Definitions of Family in Same-Sex Domestic Violence*, 19 HASTINGS WOMEN'S L. J. 259 (2008). For an interesting article arguing that syndrome evidence should be permitted to be used by all victims of domestic violence, *see* Hope Toffee, *Crazy Women, Unharmed Men, and Evil Children: Confronting the Myths about Battered People Who Kill Their Abusers, and the Argument for Extending Battering Syndrome Self-Defenses to All Victims of Domestic Violence,* 70 S. CAL. L. REV. 337–80 (1996).

Federal Response to Domestic Violence. In 1994 Congress passed the Violence Against Women Act (VAWA), Pub. L. No. 103–322, §§ 40001–40703, 108 Stat. 1796, 1902–55. VAWA encouraged the states to implement programs addressing domestic violence, but also created criminal sanctions for interstate domestic violence. VAWA also created a federal civil rights remedy for a person victimized by gender-motivated violence, which would allow the victim to be compensated and receive punitive damages. In 2000, the United States Supreme Court held that the civil rights provision of VAWA was an invalid exercise of Congress's power under the Commerce

Clause and Section 5 of the 14th Amendment. *See* United States v. Morrison, 529 U.S. 598 (2000).

Nonetheless, that aspect of VAWA that makes it a federal crime to commit interstate domestic violence has been held to be constitutional. *See e.g.,* United States v. Lankford, 196 F.3d 563 (5th Cir. 1999); United States v. Page, 167 F.3d 325 (6th Cir.1999), *cert. denied*, 528 U.S. 1003 (1999). For a review, *see* CLARE DALTON and ELIZABETH M. SCHNEIDER, BATTERED WOMEN AND THE LAW 953–91 (2001); Judith Resnick, *The Programmatic Judiciary: Lobbying, Judging, and Invalidating the Violence Against Women Act*, 74 S. CAL. L. REV. 269 (2000); Elizabeth Villiers Gemmette, *Filling in the Silence: Domestic Violence, Literature and Law*, 32 LOY. U. CHI. L. J. 91 (2000).

VAWA has been amended since its enactment to provide better services to domestic violence victims. *See* 18 U.S.C. §§ 2261–2266 (2006). The amended provisions offer victims increased legal services, counseling, and tracking of perpetrators, while offering police and law enforcement personnel educational programs. VAWA has been reauthorized twice since its enactment, in 2000 and 2005, but expired in 2011. *See* U.S. DEPT. OF JUSTICE, *The History of the Violence Against Women Act* 4–5 (accessed Feb. 18, 2013) *available at* http://www.ncdsv.org/images/OVW_HistoryVAWA.pdf. In 2013, Congress reauthorized VAWA (*see* Violence Against Women Reauthorization Act of 2013, Pub. L. No. 113–4, 127 Stat. 54 (2013)).

Other Initiatives. A number of approaches are being tried for dealing with the serious and often devastating problem of domestic violence. Some cities have developed community response initiatives, which bring together various criminal justice and social service agencies and implement coordinated strategies to reduce domestic violence. The city of Duluth, Minnesota, for example, requires police officers responding to domestic violence calls to obtain information from the victim about history of abuse; instructs probation officers to provide information about a defendant's abuse history during sentencing hearings; sentences repeat violent offenders to increased surveillance; and implements a special prosecution policy for domestic violence victims who used violence against their abusers. *See* ELLEN PENSE AND MARTHA MCMAHON, A COORDINATED COMMUNITY RESPONSE TO DOMESTIC VIOLENCE (1997), *available at* http://praxis international.org/library/coordinated-community-response-ccr/.

Domestic violence shelters have become widespread. Usually dependent on community or private donations for financial support, they can offer the battered spouse an immediate, practical alternative of safety and the possibility of counseling before a reunion, if indeed the latter goal is selected. In England the movement toward establishing such refuges was given impetus by the 1974 book, SCREAM QUIETLY OR THE NEIGHBOURS WILL HEAR, by Erin Pizzey. Special training for police officers to deal with the problems of violence is also a prevalent governmental response.

Some victims' advocates also call for jurisdictions to adopt mandatory arrest and no-drop policies in order to ensure that law enforcement officers treat domestic violence seriously and that victims are protected. These policies are controversial, however. Critics contend that mandatory arrest rules may cause victims not to call the police if they do not want their abuser arrested, and victims who have used violence themselves risk being arrested along with the abuser. For competing views on mandatory arrest and no-drop initiatives, *see, e.g.,* G. Kristian Miccio, *A House Divided: Mandatory Arrest, Domestic Violence, and the Conservation of the Battered Women's Movement*, 42 HOUS. L. REV. 237 (2005); Emily J. Sack, *Battered Women and the State: The Struggle for the Future of Domestic Violence Policy*, 2004 WIS. L. REV. 1657; Machaela M. Hoctor, Comment, *Domestic Violence as a Crime Against the State: The Need for Mandatory Arrest in California*, 85 CALIF. L. REV. 643 (1997) (arguing that domestic violence is an offense against the state as well as against the individual victim); Kevin Walsh, *Domestic Violence and the Law: The Mandatory Arrest Law: Police Reaction*, 16 PACE L. REV. 97 (1995) (observing that police officers benefit from mandatory arrest laws, which provide clarity and predictability); Angela Corsilles, Note, *No-Drop Policies in the Prosecution of Domestic Violence Cases: Guarantee to Action or Dangerous Solution?*, 63 FORDHAM L. REV. 853 (1994). *See also* Cheryl Hanna, *No Right to Choose: Mandated Participation in Domestic Violence Prosecutions*, 109 HARV. L. REV. 1849 (1996).

5. TORT ACTIONS BETWEEN SPOUSES

Bozman v. Bozman

Maryland Court of Appeals, 2003
830 A.2d 450

■ BELL, CHIEF JUDGE.

Whether the common-law doctrine of interspousal tort immunity shall remain viable in Maryland is the issue we decide in this appeal. The Circuit Court for Baltimore County dismissed the complaint alleging malicious prosecution filed by William E. Bozman, the petitioner, against Nancie L. Bozman, the respondent, a judgment which the Court of Special Appeals affirmed. We shall reverse the judgment of the intermediate appellate court and, as urged by the petitioner, abrogate the doctrine of interspousal immunity.

The petitioner and the respondent were married in this State on August 16, 1968. On February 24, 2000, the petitioner initiated divorce proceedings against the respondent. As grounds, he pled adultery. The parties were divorced on March 12, 2001.

Shortly before the divorce was finalized, on January 20, 2001, the petitioner filed in the Circuit Court for Baltimore County a complaint sounding in malicious prosecution against the respondent. In that complaint, which consisted of one count, the petitioner alleged that, as a result of criminal charges, which the respondent brought against him on February 17, 2000, May 3, 2000 and July 19, 2000, he was arrested and charged with stalking, harassment and multiple counts of violation of a Protective Order. The petitioner further alleged that the charges were brought without probable cause, were deliberately fabricated to ensure that the petitioner would be arrested, and were in retaliation for the petitioner's initiation of the divorce proceedings and his unwillingness to make concessions in those proceedings. The respondent moved to dismiss the complaint. She argued, in support of that motion, *inter alia,* that the action was barred based upon the common law doctrine of interspousal tort immunity.

The Circuit Court granted the respondent's Motion to Dismiss, but with leave to amend. Thereafter, the petitioner filed an Amended Complaint. As she had done earlier, the respondent filed a motion to dismiss, relying, also as she had done before, on the doctrine of interspousal immunity. Responding to the motion to dismiss and relying on this Court's decision in Lusby v. Lusby, 390 A.2d 77 (Md. 1978), in which the Court held that interspousal immunity was not a defense to a tort action between spouses where the conduct constituting the tort was "outrageous [and] intentional," *id.*, the petitioner argued that the defense was inapplicable under the facts he alleged; his multiple incarcerations and his being subjected to house arrest were sufficiently outrageous and intentional as to fall within the *Lusby* rule. Altogether, the petitioner claims, as a result of the respondent's false accusations, that he was incarcerated on five separate occasions, for periods ranging between one (1) and ten (10) days, and placed on home detention, which required that he wear an ankle monitoring bracelet for approximately eight (8) months.

On the same day that a hearing on the motion to dismiss was held, the petitioner filed a Second Amended Complaint. That complaint reiterated the allegations of the earlier complaint as Count I and added a second malicious prosecution count. That second malicious prosecution count alleged that, on February 2, 2001, the respondent filed, against the petitioner, additional charges of violating an *ex parte* order, which although ultimately dismissed, again resulted in the petitioner's incarceration and incurring an expense to be released. As he did in the initial complaint, the petitioner claimed that the respondent fabricated the charges, although, on this occasion, the momentum was different; it was in response to the initial malicious prosecution action and the respondent's inability to "prevail in her position" in the divorce proceedings. The petitioner specifically alleged that the dismissal of the charges referred to in Count II, one of the elements of a successful malicious prosecution action, occurred after the parties were divorced. Thus, he argued that that count was not subject to the interspousal immunity defense.

The trial court granted the respondent's Motion to Dismiss, ruling that the action was barred by the doctrine of interspousal immunity. The petitioner noted a timely appeal to the Court of Special Appeals. In the intermediate appellate court, the petitioner challenged the trial court's dismissal of Count I of the Second Amended Complaint, arguing that it was error in light of this Court's decision in *Lusby,* because malicious prosecution is an outrageous, intentional tort to which interspousal immunity is not a defense. As to the dismissal of Count II of the Second Amended Complaint, the petitioner submitted that, not only was the conduct outrageous and intentional, but the cause of action for the malicious prosecution alleged in that count arose after the parties were legally divorced. Consequently, he argues, the doctrine of interspousal immunity is rendered inapplicable to that count, as well.

To be sure, the Court of Special Appeals "questioned the continued viability of" the doctrine of interspousal immunity. Bozman v. Bozman, 806 A.2d 740, 747 (Md. App. 2002), citing Boblitz v. Boblitz, 462 A.2d 506 (Md. 1983). Characterizing it as an "antiquated doctrine" and stating that it "runs counter to present-day norms," *id.*, the intermediate appellate court commented:

> "We recognize that the doctrine may serve some practical purpose of preventing spouses from instituting suits in tort as a means of gaining an advantage in pending divorce proceedings or for some other improper reason. We remain unconvinced, however, that retention of this doctrine best reflects the will of the people of this State as evidence by, among other reforms, enactment of the Equal Rights Amendment in 1972."

Id. Nevertheless, it recognized that:

> "Regardless, we are bound to follow the dictates of the law as it presently exists in Maryland. The law is that interspousal immunity may be raised as a defense to a viable cause of action alleging an intentional tort so long as the tort is not 'outrageous,' as that term is used in *Lusby* and Doe [v. Doe, 747 A.2d 617]."

Id. at 747.

Therefore, the Court of Special Appeals addressed the issue that lay at the heart of the case, as submitted to it, the quality of the respondent's conduct and, more generally, the nature of the tort of malicious prosecution. More specifically, the court considered whether the tort, or at least the conduct that constituted the tort, came within the term, "outrageous," as defined in, and contemplated by, *Lusby*. It concluded:

> "Without minimizing in any way the harsh consequences to appellant wrought by appellee's behavior in this case, we cannot say that it is of comparable character to that addressed by the Court in *Lusby*. Appellee's actions in the instant case no doubt caused appellant to suffer significant humiliation and hardship. But they did not involve extreme violence of the most personal and invasive sort, the threat of death and a display of the means by which to carry out that threat, or the physical and psychic trauma that the victim in *Lusby* endured. . . ."

Id. at 748. Accordingly, the intermediate appellate court held that "malicious prosecution is not so outrageous as to bring it within the narrow exception to the doctrine of interspousal immunity." The court affirmed the trial court's dismissal of Count I of the Second Amended Complaint. *Id.* at 741. . . .

We granted both petitions. Bozman v. Bozman, 813 A.2d 257 (Md. 2002). We agree with the Court of Special Appeals, that the interspousal immunity doctrine is an antiquated rule of law which, in our view, runs counter to prevailing societal norms and, therefore, has lived out its usefulness. Accordingly, we shall answer the petitioner's first question in the affirmative and, so, complete the abrogation of the doctrine from the common law of this State. As a result, we need not, and shall not, address the other questions raised by the petitioner's petition or the respondent's cross-petition. . . .

The doctrine of interspousal immunity in tort cases is a rule of law existing in the common law of Maryland. Doe, supra, 747 A.2d at 619 ("Prior to *Lusby,* the doctrine of interspousal immunity in tort cases was clearly recognized as part of the common law of this state."). In *Boblitz,* we noted that it is a rule of "ancient origin" and created "exclusively from judicial decisions." 462 A.2d at 507. "The rule at common law [was] that a married woman cannot maintain an action against her husband for injuries caused by his negligent or tortious act." David v. David, 157 A. 755, 756 (Md. 1932).

The rationale underlying the interspousal immunity rule has been discussed in our cases. In *David,* the Court stated: "The reason usually given for that rule is the presumed legal identity of the husband and wife." *Id.* at 534, 157 A. at 756, quoting *Philips v. Barnet*, 1 QB 436 (1876). A more complete statement of the rationale was provided in Lusby, 390 A.2d at 78–79, with attribution to Blackstone, (1 W. Blackstone, Commentaries, Book 1, Ch. 15, p. 442, 443):

> "By marriage, the husband and wife are one person in the law: that is, the very being of legal existence of the woman is suspended during the marriage, or at least is incorporated and consolidated into that of the husband: under whose wing, protection, and cover, she performs everything; and is therefore called in our law french a *feme-covert, foemina viro co-operta;* is said to be a *covert-baron,* or under the protection and influence of her husband, her *baron,* or *lord;* and her condition during her marriage is called *coverture.* Upon this principle, of a union of person in husband and wife, depend almost all the legal rights, duties and disabilities, that either of them acquire by the marriage."
>
> "He adds, in discussing the consequences of this union of husband and wife, 'If the wife be injured in her person or her property, she can bring no action for redress without her husband's concurrence, and in his name, as well as her own: neither can she be sued without making the husband a defendant.' "

The first breach of the interspousal immunity doctrine in Maryland occurred with our decision in *Lusby*. There, the wife brought a tort action against her husband for damages. As reported by the Court (390 A.2d at 77):

> "She alleged that while she was operating her motor vehicle on a public highway the husband 'pulled alongside of [her] in his pick-up truck and pointed a highpowered rifle at her.' She attempted to flee by increasing the speed of her car. She claimed that then 'another truck occupied by two (2) men, whose identities are unknown to [her] and who, [t]hereinafter are referred to [in the declaration] as John Doe and Richard Roe, cut and forced her off the road, nearly causing a collision.' . . . After she stopped her car, the husband 'approached her automobile with a rifle pointed at her, opened her left door, ordered her to move over, forced his way into the automobile and began to drive the automobile.' They were followed by Doe in the husband's truck and Roe in the second truck. Thereafter, the wife 'was forced to enter [the husband's] truck with [the husband] and Richard Roe.' John Doe drove the wife's vehicle and the second truck was left parked. She alleged that her husband then struck her, 'tore [her] clothes off and did forcefully and violently, despite [her] desperate attempts to protect herself, carnally know [her] against her will and without her consent.' She further claimed that, with the aid and assistance of her husband, both Doe and Roe attempted to rape her. She said that following those events her husband 'and his two companions released [her] and [her husband] told [her] that he would kill her if she informed anyone of the aforesaid events; and that he has continued to harass and threaten [her].' "

Id. at 77–78. On these facts, the Court held, "under the facts and circumstances of this case, amounting to an outrageous, intentional tort, a wife may sue her husband for damages." *Id.* at 77.

In rendering our decision, we stated, having noted the Legislature's inaction with regard to amending the Married Women's Act to ameliorate the effect of the interspousal immunity defense and the purpose of statutory construction in the interpretation of statutes:

> "For purposes of our decision here today . . . we need not be involved with statutory construction nor need we be involved with our prior cases other than for dicta appearing in them to the effect that one spouse may not sue another for tort. None of our prior cases has involved an intentional tort."

Id. at 89.

Merely five years after *Lusby,* we were asked "to reexamine the interspousal immunity rule . . . and to declare that rule to be no longer viable in tort cases involving personal injury to a spouse resulting from the negligence of the other spouse." Boblitz, supra, 462 A.2d at 506. In that case, a wife sued her husband for injuries she sustained almost a year before the marriage, as a result, she alleged, of his negligence in the operation of an automobile. Pleading the parties' marital status and relying on *Hudson,* the husband moved for summary judgment, arguing that the wife's alleged cause of action had been extinguished by the marriage. *Id.* at 506. The motion was granted and we issued the writ of certiorari to review the question previously stated. *Id.* at 506. We reversed the summary judgment, in the process abrogating the interspousal immunity rule in this State as to cases sounding in negligence. *Id.* at 522. We explained:

> "We share the view now held by the vast majority of American States that the interspousal immunity rule is unsound in the circumstances of modern life in such cases as the subject. It is a vestige of the past. We are persuaded that the reasons asserted for its retention do not survive careful scrutiny. They furnish no reasonable basis for denial of recovery for tortious personal injury. We find no subsisting public policy that justifies retention of a judicially created immunity that would bar recovery for injured victims in such cases as the present."

Id. . . . at 521. (citation omitted) . . .

On two occasions in the last twenty-five years, this court has done an analysis of the interspousal immunity doctrine and its rational underpinnings, the reasons or justification offered for its existence and continued viability, and, on each occasion, found the doctrine and the foundation on which it was built to be lacking. We found the trend and, indeed, the great weight of authority, to be to move away from the doctrine and in favor of changing the common law to abolish it, either fully or partially. The majority of the States, we discovered, were of the view that the doctrine was outdated and served no useful purpose, that "there presently exists no cogent or logical reason why the doctrine of interspousal tort immunity should be continued." *Merenoff,* 388 A.2d at 962. As we have seen, this Court, in *Boblitz* expressed its adherence to this majority view, characterizing the doctrine as "unsound in the circumstances of modern life" and "a vestige of the past," for which "the reasons asserted for its retention do not survive careful scrutiny." 462 A.2d at 521. We continue of that view and, the trend toward abrogation having continued and the weight of authority having grown larger, we are fortified in that view. . . .

California abrogated the doctrine in intentional tort cases in 1962. The respondent has not provided any demonstrative evidence that any of the questions or problems she posits as possible and, indeed, "undoubtedly will arise" have arisen in California or any where else for that matter. Moreover, the other States that have fully abrogated the doctrine or in cases of intentional torts, some quite a long time ago, e.g. Brown v. Brown, supra, 89 A. 889 (1914); Gilman v. Gilman, 95 A. 657

(N.H. 1915); Crowell v. Crowell, 105 S.E. 206 (N.C. 1920); Penton v. Penton, 135 So. 481 (Ala. 1931); Pardue v. Pardue, 166 S.E. 101 (S.C. 1932), provide an accurate barometer of what can be expected after abrogation and what they reveal is far different from the picture the respondent paints.

The overwhelming weight of authority supports the petitioner's argument that the interspousal immunity doctrine should be abrogated. Joining the many of our sister States that have already done so, we abrogate the interspousal immunity rule, a vestige of the past, whose time has come and gone, as to all cases alleging an intentional tort. As we did in Boblitz, 462 A.2d at 522, we shall apply the abrogation to this case and to all causes of action accruing after the date of the filing of this opinion.

JUDGMENT OF THE COURT OF SPECIAL APPEALS REVERSED. CASE REMANDED TO THAT COURT, WITH INSTRUCTIONS TO REVERSE THE JUDGMENT OF THE CIRCUIT COURT FOR BALTIMORE COUNTY AND REMAND THE CASE TO THAT COURT FOR PROCEEDINGS CONSISTENT WITH THIS OPINION. COSTS IN THIS COURT AND IN THE COURT OF SPECIAL APPEALS TO BE PAID BY THE RESPONDENT.

NOTES

The slow erosion of the doctrine of interspousal immunity began with the property acts described in Chapter 3, *supra*, which erased the legal "unity" of husband and wife as to property held by women during marriage. Because the property acts gave wives the same rights as husbands to hold property, wives were permitted to bring an action against others, including husbands, for tortious acts affecting the wife's *property*. The property acts, however, did not affect the underlying rationale for interspousal immunity for *personal* torts committed by one spouse against the other.

As *Bozman* notes, one rationale for the continuing vitality of interspousal immunity for personal torts was legal unity of husband and wife. Other courts, however, explained the doctrine in terms of (1) the peace and harmony of the marital home, which would be shattered by litigation between the spouses; and (2) the potential for fraud and collusion between the spouses if insurance coverage was available to pay any damages. *See* Merenoff v. Merenoff, 388 A.2d 951 (N.J. 1978) (rejecting both rationales).

In the face of nearly unanimous criticism by the courts and commentators, an overwhelming majority of U.S. jurisdictions have abolished interspousal immunity through legislation or judicial decision. *See* N.C. GEN. STAT. ANN. § 52–5 (2015) ("A husband and wife have a cause of action against each other to recover damages sustained to their person or property as if they were unmarried."); Asplin v. Amica Mut. Ins. Co., 394 A.2d 1353 (R.I. 1978) (abrogating immunity in motor vehicle torts because there is no longer any family harmony to disrupt when one spouse has died). It is important to note, however, that just because the bar to spousal immunity has been eliminated, this "does *not* mean, however, that the marital relationship itself now gives rise to duties that are actionable in tort." Lasater v. Guttmann, 5 A.3d 79, 93 (Md. Ct. App. 2010) (rejecting claims by a wife against her husband for conversion, intentional infliction of emotional distress, breach of fiduciary duty, and fraud as a result of his imprudent spending of the couple's money).

A handful of jurisdictions today still retain some bar to suits between spouses. *See* Jill Elaine Hasday, *The Canon of Family Law*, 57 STAN. L. REV. 825, fn. 32 (2004) (observing that "spouses can sue each other only for negligent torts [in Delaware], or only for intentional torts [in Utah], or only for torts arising from a motor vehicle accident [in Nevada and Vermont], or only for torts that do not implicate 'marital or nuptial privileges, consensual acts and simple, common domestic negligence,' [in New Jersey] or only for torts that do not involve 'personal injuries between married persons [that] will not justify a recovery of damages,' [in Massachusetts] and that some states do not allow interspousal suits unless the parties were separated at the time the tort occurs or had filed for divorce prior to the suit [citing Georgia and Louisiana]"). *See also Modern Status of Interspousal Tort Immunity in Personal Injury and Wrongful Death Actions*, 92 A.L.R.3d 901 (originally published in 1979).

Concerns about collusion between spouses when any damages would ultimately be paid by an insurer led many insurers to include a "family exclusion" or "household exclusion" in their automobile or homeowner's liabilities policies. Those clauses have received mixed treatment by the courts, some of which *see* them as a valid exercise of the insurer's contractual rights to limit liability, while others treat them as against public policy. *See* JOHN D. GREGORY, PETER N. SWISHER, AND ROBIN FRETWELL WILSON, UNDERSTANDING FAMILY LAW § 7.02 (4th ed. 2013).

For a discussion of a proposed balance between spouses viewed as individuals and spouses viewed as family members, *see* Benjamin Shmueli, *Tort Litigation Between Spouses: Lets Meet Somewhere in the Middle,* 15 HARV. NEGOT. L. REV. 195 (2010); for a discussion of how the family model has changed during recent decades, *see* William N. Eskridge, Jr., *Family Law Pluralism: The Guided-Choice Regime of Menus, Default Rules, and Overdrive Rules*, 100 GEO. L. J. 1881 (2012); and for using spousal torts as a better means of addressing injury than divorce, *see* Pamela Laufer-Ukeles, *Reconstructing Fault: The Case for Spousal Torts*, 79 U. CINN. L. REV. 207 (2010).

E. THIRD PARTY INTERFERENCE WITH THE RELATIONSHIP

A number of actions have been available in the past to deal with disruption of the marriage relationship by a third party, or with harm to one spouse stemming from a third party's injury to the other spouse. Often the major concern at the outset had to do with economic incidents, though there also was concern about pride and personal affront. One should question seriously whether such actions are consistent with today's social habits as well as our concepts of individual rights. As explained below, some such actions have been abolished by a significant number of jurisdictions.

Alienation of Affections and Criminal Conversation. The purpose of an alienation of affections action is to provide redress against a third party who causes one spouse to lose affections for the other. Criminal conversation is a civil action that originally was available against a man who had sexual intercourse with the wife of the plaintiff. Proof of loss of affections or marital breakup was unnecessary because the early rationale for the action was that the husband might be the presumed father of any children produced by such an extramarital liaison, or that questions might be raised as to the legitimacy of his own offspring. Such actions were also said to be grounded on the common law notion of a husband having a property right in the person of his wife. *See* Albertini v. Veal, 357 S.E.2d 716, 718 (S.C. App.1987). The action remained long after those conceptual underpinnings were forgotten, and jurisdictions where it has been retained generally have extended it to wives as well as husbands. As explained in Oppenheim v. Kridel, 140 N.E. 227 (N.Y. 1923):

> [W]hatever reasons there were for giving the husband at common law the right to maintain an action for adultery committed with his wife exist today in behalf of the woman for a like illegal act committed by her husband. If he had feelings and honor which were hurt by such improper conduct, who will say today that she has not the same, perhaps even a keener sense of the wrong done to her and to the home? If he considered it a defilement of the marriage bed, why should she not view it in the same light? The statements that he had a property interest in her body and a right to the personal enjoyment of his wife are archaic, unless used in a refined sense worthy of the times, and which give to the wife the same interest in her husband.

Id. at 229.

Because an action for alienation of affections or criminal conversation is brought by a spouse against a third party, courts look to interference with the marriage. The Utah Supreme Court allowed a suit by a husband against his now ex-wife's paramour when he learned the wife had begun an affair with a man before marriage and continued it throughout the 25-year marriage, and that two of the wife's children had been fathered by the paramour. The court allowed the former husband to bring suit against the paramour on the grounds of alienation of affections and intentional infliction of emotional distress. Heiner v. Simpson, 23 P.3d 1041 (Utah 2001). Likewise, in *Osborne v. Payne*, the Kentucky Supreme Court allowed a suit against a priest for the tort of outrageous conduct when the wrongdoer's conduct amounted to intentional infliction of emotional distress in. There the court permitted a husband's claim for outrage when they had gone to a priest for counseling and without the husband's knowledge or consent, the priest engaged in a sexual relationship with the wife. Osborne v. Payne, 31 S.W.3d 911 (Ky. 2000).

Many of the "anti-heart balm statutes," discussed in Chapter 2, eliminated civil damage actions for alienation of affections or criminal conversation, based on their susceptibility to the same abuses ascribed to breach of promise to marry and seduction actions. In Louisiana alienation of affections was never actionable. Moulin v. Monteleone, 115 So. 447 (La. 1927). Some courts have abolished the action without specific legislation.

Attempts to "relabel" an abolished action generally have not been successful in the courts. For example, in Speer v. Dealy, 495 N.W.2d 911 (Neb. 1993), the Supreme Court of Nebraska rejected a husband's action for tortious interference with the marital contract and intentional infliction of emotional distress against his wife's co-worker, with whom the wife allegedly was romantically involved. The court held that the husband could not recover on either theory because both were in essence claims for either alienation of affections or criminal conversation that had been abolished by statute.

Even though only a handful of states retain this cause of action, electronic communication creates the possibility that an individual residing in a state that has abolished the action may find himself or herself subject to suit in another state. For example, the Mississippi Supreme Court ruled that Mississippi—which recognizes alienation of affections actions—could exercise personal jurisdiction over a Louisiana resident who allegedly interfered with a Mississippi couple's marriage. Knight v. Woodfield, 50 So.3d 995 (Miss. 2011). In *Knight*, a husband sued his ex-wife's paramour in a Mississippi court, alleging that the defendant caused his loss of consortium through his text and email communications with the plaintiff's wife. The defendant resided in Louisiana and moved to dismiss the complaint for lack of personal jurisdiction. The supreme court ruled that Mississippi courts could exercise personal jurisdiction because (1) the state's long-arm statute extends to nonresidents who commit torts within the state; (2) the defendant's "actions of emailing, calling, and sending text messages" to the plaintiff's wife were sufficient minimum contacts to establish personal jurisdiction; and (3) Mississippi's "strong interest" in adjudicating disputes concerning the marriage relationship and providing relief to wronged spouses meant that exercising personal jurisdiction over a nonresident defendant would not violate "traditional notions of fair play and substantial justice." *Id.* at 1000–01.

Loss of Consortium. At common law, a husband had an action for the loss of his wife's services when she was injured by the tort of a third party. As in the case of other interferences with family relations, the loss that he sustained was gradually considered to include many other incidents such as the companionship and attentions of the spouse (consortium). Although a right to services might have to be alleged as a technical requirement, an actual showing of loss of services became relatively unimportant. Today, damages for the action generally reflect both tangible and intangible losses of such things as love and affection, society and companionship, sexual relations, material services, financial support, aid and assistance, and felicity. Clark v. Ark-La-Tex Auction, Inc., 593 So. 2d 870, 879 (La. Ct. App. 1992). And though the action originally had been developed in connection with intentional torts such as assault and battery, it was extended in this country to injury from negligent harms early in the present century. This is the strong majority position today.

A few states forbid the action by statute. *See* VA. CODE ANN. § 55–36 (West 2016); KAN. STAT. ANN. § 23–2605 (2015) (but permitting wrongful death actions).

Although originally based on a husband's property right, jurisdictions recognizing recovery for loss of consortium today generally have extended it to wives. D. Richard Joslyn, *Wife's Right of Action for Loss of Consortium*, 36 A.L.R.3d 900 (Originally Published in 1971). Most courts generally limit recovery to legally married couples. Vanhooser v. Superior Court, 206 Cal.App.4th 921, 933 (Cal. Ct. App. 2012) ("[T]he right to recover for loss of consortium is founded on the relationship of marriage, and absent such a relationship the right does not exist."). In such jurisdictions, spouses cannot recover for injuries that occurred before the couple married. *Id. See also* Rodgers v. Duffy, 95 A.D.3d 864 (N.Y. Ct. App. 2012) (no recovery for injuries prior to marriage); Holmes v. Maimonides Med. Ctr., 95 A.D.3d 831 (N.Y. Ct. App. 2012).

However, a few jurisdictions allow recovery by a cohabitant or fiancée. Dunphy v. Gregor, 642 A.2d 372 (N.J. 1994) (permitting recovery for the emotional distress by a cohabitant-fiancée who witnessed the accident). The New Hampshire Supreme Court allowed a cohabitant of seven years to go forward with a suit for negligent infliction of emotional distress against the driver who killed her partner in a motorcycle accident. Under New Hampshire law, closely related individuals are permitted to bring such claims. Graves v. Estabrook, 818 A.2d 1255 (N.H. 2003). The court concluded that "to foreclose [an unmarried cohabitant] from making a claim based upon emotional harm because her relationship with the injured person does not carry a particular label is to work a potential injustice . . . where the emotional injury is genuine and substantial and is based upon a relationship of significant duration that . . . is deep, lasting and genuinely intimate." *Id.* at 1261–62. Moreover, the court inferred from the couple's "lengthy cohabitation" that they "enjoyed mutual dependence, common contributions to a life together, emotional reliance on each other and attended to life's mundane requirements together." *Id.* at 1262.

Loss of Consortium for Wrongful Divorce? In Prill v. Hampton, 453 N.W.2d 909 (Wis. App.1990), a former wife sought to recover damages for loss of consortium after divorce and for "wrongful divorce" on the theory that her divorce was the direct result of injuries sustained by the husband as a result of the defendant's negligence in a motor vehicle accident. The Court of Appeals of Wisconsin found that "public policy considerations, including uncertainty of claims and unmanageable societal costs, require that damages for consortium be terminated when the marital relationship terminates." As to the action for "wrongful divorce," they stated that:

> This type of claim has not been recognized in the past and we refuse to recognize it now. We conclude that sound public policy reasons preclude claims that a spouse's injuries caused a divorce.
>
> Failure of a marriage is rarely attributable to a single cause. In some instances, there may be evidence that the spouse's injuries were, in part, the cause of the marriage's failure. For the jury to properly assess the amount of damages, however, it is necessary to show both a causal relationship and the extent or degree this factor played in the failure of the marriage. Such an inquiry would open to scrutiny very personal issues, not only of the spouse claiming damages, but also of the injured spouse. This factor, along with the difficulty of the jury in determining the extent to which any single cause may have contributed to the failure of the marriage, requires that such claims be rejected.

Id. at 914–15. The court added that the claim also could be regarded as essentially an alienation of affections action, which has been legislatively abolished.

Medical Treatment. It is a widely accepted practice in the medical community to obtain consent from one spouse for life-sustaining procedures required by the other, who is incapable of fully understanding the nature of the proposed treatment and the alternatives to it. This occurs despite sparse precedent about the degree of authority that a spouse can exercise in such instances without formal appointment as a guardian or authorization under a health care power of attorney or advance directive. Are there potential conflicts of interest in such an approach? Similar questions can arise when it is deemed necessary for someone to make a "substituted judgment" as to what the currently incompetent patient (including one in a persistent vegetative state) would have chosen under the circumstances. One can argue that a spouse is best prepared make this substituted judgment in light of understandings based on the couple's intimate relationship. But in many cases it is the spouse who most likely will be affected financially by a decision to prolong care. Should this possibility affect who should decide when a patient is unable to make decisions for herself?

Widely enacted health care decision-making statutes allow competent persons to make advance declarations as to the kinds of treatments the individual is willing to have performed, if the declarant later becomes incompetent. *See, e.g.*, ALAN MEISEL AND KATHY L. CERMINARA, THE RIGHT TO DIE: THE LAW OF END-OF-LIFE DECISIONMAKING (3d ed., 2004); *Right to Die: Durable Power of Attorney, Euthanasia, Living Wills, 50 State Statutory Surveys: Civil Laws: Rights And Privileges*, 0020 SURVEYS 27 (West 2007). Some of those statutes provide a list of persons authorized to make such decisions if a person did not execute a declaration while competent. The patient's spouse appears high in the hierarchy of "designated decision makers" in such laws . *See, e.g.*, VA. CODE ANN. § 54.1–2986 (West 2016). Louisiana allows decision making by a spouse only if the couple is "not judicially separated," and the decision maker has neither been convicted of violence against the patient or violated a domestic protective order. *See* LA. STAT. ANN. 40:1151.1(13) (West 2015). Would you include such qualifications, or would you expand them in any way?

A Duty to Seek Medical Assistance? Whether one spouse has any special duty to seek medical assistance for the other has been raised in several criminal prosecutions that involved unusual fact situations. In State v. Morgan, 936 P.2d 20 (Wash. App. 1997), a husband was convicted for manslaughter based on his failure to summon aid for his wife, who died of a drug overdose. The court stated that the Washington statute on family nonsupport makes it a crime for one to willfully fail "to provide necessary food, clothing, shelter, or medical attendance to his or her spouse. . . . The violation of this statutory duty could provide the recklessness necessary for a manslaughter charge." *See supra,* Section C, NOTES for similar statutes. The court found also that the husband had a duty under the circumstances independent of the statute, concluding that:

> [The husband] had a . . . natural duty to provide medical help to his wife, and a duty to summon aid for someone he helped place in danger. His violation of this duty amounted to recklessness and was sufficient basis for the manslaughter charge.

Morgan, 936 P.2d at 23. *See also* People v. Oliver, 210 Cal.App.3d 138, 258 Cal.Rptr. 138 (1989); and State v. Mally, 366 P.2d 868 (Mont. 1961); Skylarsky v. New Hope Guild Center, 9 Misc. 3d 1108(A) (N.Y. Sup. 2005). However, the duty does not extend to instances in which one spouse acts in good faith at the request of a competent spouse. "It would be an unwarranted extension of the spousal duty of care to impose criminal liability for failure to summon medical for a competent spouse who has made a rational decision to eschew medical assistance." *See* People v. Robbins, 83 A.D.2d 271, 271 (N.Y. App. Div. 1981). For further examination of this doctrine, *see* Commonwealth v. Konz, 450 A.2d 638 (Pa. 1982); Robbins v. Stephanski, 83 A.D.2d 271 (N.Y. App. Div. 1981).

Case on Point, Terri Schiavo. The contest between Michael Schiavo, Terri Schiavo's husband, and Terri Schiavo's parents over who should have the authority to remove Terri's artificial nutrition and hydration sparked intense national debate. The contest concerned who should make the medical decisions when the incapacitated person has not made his or her wishes known. Consistently, Terri Schiavo's husband maintained the position Terri had told him she would not want to continue living in a persistent vegetative state.

Terri Schiavo's case precipitated a string of legal actions. First, the Florida legislature enacted "Terri's Law," which gave Florida's governor the ability to issue a one-time stay preventing the removal of a feeding tube. Then, in Bush v. Schiavo, 885 So.2d 321 (Fla. 2004), the Florida Supreme Court struck Terri's Law as an unconstitutional violation of the separation of powers. The United States Supreme Court refused to hear an appeal brought by Governor Bush in January 2005. Bush v. Schiavo, 543 U.S. 1121 (2005) (denying certiorari).

One day before Terri's feeding tube was to be removed at the request of her husband, a Florida Circuit Judge ordered a temporary stay upon a motion of her parents alleging that Terri's husband was not acting in Terri's best interests because of his personal involvement with another woman. The court eventually rejected the parents' assertion and lifted the stay. Terri's feeding tube was removed on March 18, 2005.

Sensing that the federal courts would not intervene to overrule the husband's decision, the United States Senate and House of Representatives passed emergency legislation overnight "for the relief of the parents of" Terri Schiavo. The president signed the legislation—the Schiavo Bill—during the pre-dawn hours on March 21, 2005. In essence, the federal legislation sought to provide Terri's parents a federal cause of action, regardless of whether there still remained state causes of action, and to issue injunctive relief to safeguard Terri's rights to continued medical treatment. In spite of this federal statute, the federal district court refused to issue injunctive relief—most importantly to reinsert the feeding tube. Terri's parents appealed again to the Florida Supreme Court and the United States Supreme Court. Both courts declined to intervene and Terri Schiavo died on March 31, 2005, thirteen days after her feeding tube was removed. Terri's husband ordered an autopsy on his wife to discover the extent of her brain damage, and then cremated her body over the objections of her parents. *See* Laura Stanton, *The Battle over Terri Schiavo*, WASH. POST, Apr. 1, 2005, at A13. For a concise summary of the facts concerning the Schiavo case, *see* Kathy L. Cerminara, *Theresa Marie Schiavo's Long Road to Peace*, 30 DEATH STUD. 101 (2006).

The legal struggle between Terri's spouse and parents sparked intense legal, medical and religious controversy. *See, e.g.*, Sandra H. Johnson, *Nothing's Settled*, 41(1) HASTINGS CENTER REPORT 50 (2011); Timothy E. Quill, *Terri Schiavo—A Tragedy Compounded*, 352 NEW ENG. J. MED. 1630 (2005); Paul R. McHugh, *Annihilating Terri Schiavo*, in THE MIND HAS MOUNTAINS: REFLECTIONS ON SOCIETY AND PSYCHIATRY 98 (2006); Editorial, *Extraordinary Means*, COMMONWEAL, Apr. 8, 2005, at 5. The cost in Medicaid dollars of caring for persons such as Terri Schiavo was hotly debated. *See, e.g.*, Jonathan Weisman and Ceci Connolly, *Schiavo Case Puts Face on Rising Medical Costs*, WASH. POST, Mar. 28, 2005, at A13. But the most significant impact of Terri's case may be the intense interest in advance medical planning by citizens who wish to avoid placing themselves or their families in similar circumstances. *See, e.g.*, Lois Shepherd, *Shattering the Neutral Surrogate Myth in End-of-Life Decisionmaking: Terri Schiavo and Her Family*, 35 CUMBERLAND L. REV. 575 (2005).

For a comprehensive summary of end-of-life decision making for family members who did not provide specific advance directives, *see* Sandra H. Johnson, Quinlan *and* Cruzan: *Beyond the Symbols*, in HEALTH LAW AND BIOETHICS: CASES IN CONTEXT (Sandra H. Johnson, Joan H. Krause, Richard S. Saver, and Robin Fretwell Wilson, eds., 2009).

CHAPTER IV

MATRIMONIAL BREAKDOWN: GROUNDS AND JURISDICTION FOR DISSOLUTION

A. THE PERSPECTIVE OF HISTORY

The development of divorce jurisdiction in America proceeded along highly diverse lines and was influenced in significant measure by English law. During the colonial period, couples in England could petition an ecclesiastical court for a judicial separation, called a divorce *a mensa et thoro*, which permitted them to live separately, but not to remarry. The inability to remarry reflected the idea that marriage was a sacrament, or a covenant between the couple and the creator, and therefore—unlike an ordinary contract—was indissoluble. English law also allowed for absolute divorce, known as divorce *a vincula matrimonii*, if the couple secured a private bill from Parliament dissolving the marriage, after which all economic incidents of the marriage (such as the duty to support one's spouse) would disappear and the parties would be free to remarry. However, such private bills were "rarely sought and even more rarely granted." Charles J. Reid, Jr., *Marriage: Its Relationship to Religion, Law, and the State*, in SAME-SEX MARRIAGE AND RELIGIOUS LIBERTY: EMERGING CONFLICTS 157, 161 (Douglas Laycock, Anthony R. Picarello, and Robin Fretwell Wilson, eds., 2008). The English split in approach carried over to the colonies:

> The New England colonies treated divorce as a civil matter and began granting divorces during the seventeenth century. The southern colonies followed the ecclesiastical law pattern and generally refused to permit divorce.

Ann L. Estin, *Family Law Federalism: Divorce and the Constitution*, 16 WM. & MARY BILL RTS. J. 381, 383–84 (2007).

By the time of the founding, the jurisdiction of ecclesiastical courts over divorce "had been abolished" in the United States. Reid, *supra*, at 162. In the Republic, the legislative divorce, an imitation of the English parliamentary divorce, was universal. Only a few states, notably Virginia in 1827 and Maryland in 1830, undertook any early attempt to require judicial or quasi-judicial preliminaries to divorce. Once divorce matters became a judicial function, states with a chancery tradition committed jurisdiction to equity courts, while in New England, common law or probate courts had jurisdiction over divorce matters.

Confusion between the two actions, judicial separation and absolute divorce, was widespread. Many states recognized both actions and developed procedures to convert judicial separation into absolute divorce. As legislatures backed away from the process of granting divorces by private bill and gave courts authority to dissolve marriages on proof of certain conduct regarded as antisocial at that time, the grounds for divorce proliferated. These statutory grounds were sometimes stated with specificity, such as attempting to end the life of the other spouse "by poison or any other means showing malice." TENN. CODE ANN. § 36–4–101 (2016). In other jurisdictions, the grounds were more omnibus, as in Rhode Island where, in addition to a number of specific fault grounds, divorce may be still granted "for any other gross misbehavior and wickedness, in either of the parties, repugnant to and in violation of the marriage covenant." R.I. GEN. LAWS ANN. § 15–5–2 (2015).

In addition to widespread legislative variation among the states, states developed an elaborate body of judicially created defenses to rebut the claimed ground for divorce. Condonation, connivance, and recrimination are still important in some jurisdictions.

Significant differences among the states in access to divorce frequently prompted couples to travel to states that were less hostile to divorce. This "migratory divorce" placed pressure on the states to adopt uniform legislation about marriage and divorce, although that movement that eventually "petered out" without real reform. NELSON M. BLAKE, THE ROAD TO RENO: A HISTORY OF DIVORCE IN THE UNITED STATES 145 (1962). Variations in state law led to efforts over more than sixty years to "empower Congress to regulate marriage and divorce," an effort that gained no real traction. *Id.* Today, the significant differences in state regulation of marriage and divorce raise the possibility of forum-shopping, whether to escape unfavorable financial terms upon divorce or to dissolve a marriage more quickly in one jurisdiction than it could be dissolved in another. *See infra* Section C, "The Jurisdictional Jumble."

In the 1960s, pressure built in state legislatures for reform of the Kafkaesque process of proving fault in order to obtain a divorce. There was growing belief that our divorce laws reflected outdated mores and that many divorce courts had become infested with perjured testimony and collusive actions, often overlooked by judges who felt divorce could be a desirable social goal. At that time, if two parties wanted a divorce and were willing to fib a bit, they could be divorced in many jurisdictions through an uncontested proceeding. But if one spouse wished to thwart or substantially delay the other's divorce desires, this could readily be achieved through contesting the action.

The basic approach of the divorce reform movement that began in the 1960s was to deemphasize the role of fault, at least in determining whether to dissolve a marriage. In the place of fault should be some reasonably simple and non-traumatic method for pronouncing the last legal rites over marriages that were in fact dead. Emphasis shifted from fixing blame or inflicting punishment to determining whether a union had broken down to the point that there was little or no hope for repair.

Approaches that were offered ranged from "living apart" grounds with short enough separation periods to be workable, to new no-fault causes for divorce such as irremediable breakdown or irreconcilable differences that rendered the marriage no longer tenable. Some jurisdictions substituted the term "dissolution" for "divorce" to symbolize the magnitude of the break with past practices and to skirt any vestiges of social criticism that sometimes accompanied divorce in the past.

Opponents of the new approach argued that making divorce too easy posed a threat to marriage as an institution; proponents countered that cultural factors, not divorce law, account for marital breakdown. Decades later, the belief that divorce had become too readily available precipitated a substantial divorce reform movement in some jurisdictions. *See infra* Section B(1), NOTES. Although divorce reform is by no means finished, divorce now can be obtained far more freely.

For further review and analysis of divorce in this country, *see* Deborah Dinner, *The Divorce Bargain: The Fathers' Rights Movement and Family Inequalities,* 102 VA. L. REV. 79 (2016); Allison Anna Tait, *Divorce Equality*, 90 WASH. L. REV. 1245 (2015) (examining issues pertinent to same-sex couples divorcing); J. Herbie DiFonzo and Ruth C. Stern, *The Winding Road from Form to Function: A Brief History of Contemporary Marriage*, 21 J. AM. ACAD. MATRIMONIAL LAW 1 (2008); Mae Kuykendall, *Emerson Family Values: Claims to Duration and Renewal in American Narratives of Divorce, Love and Marriage*, 18 HASTINGS WOMEN'S L. J. 69 (2007); Robert R. Rains, *Disability and Family Relationships: Marriage Penalties and Support Anomalies*, 22 GA. ST. U. L. REV. 561 (2006); Laura Rosenbury, *Two Ways to End a Marriage: Divorce or Death*, 2005 UTAH L. REV. 1227; Barbara Stark, *Rhetoric, Divorce and International Human Rights: The Limits of Divorce Reform for the Protection of Children*, 65 LA. L. REV. 1433 (2005).

B. GROUNDS AND DEFENSES

Approximately one-third of the states have eliminated all fault grounds and replaced them with some form of no-fault grounds, such as irretrievable breakdown. *See Grounds for Divorce, 50 State Statutory Surveys: Family Law: Divorce and Dissolution*, 0080 SURVEYS 9 (West 2007). In fact, every state has some form of "no fault" ground, although Missouri requires an agreement between the parties to use this ground. MO. REV. STAT. § 452.320 (2015).

Notwithstanding the presence of a no-fault ground for divorce in every state, fault continues to matter in a significant number of jurisdictions, either as a ground for divorce or as a factor in deciding the financial terms of the divorce. Given the migratory nature of our population, it is important for attorneys to have a practical understanding of the fault system regardless of their own state's grounds, although no attempt is made here to review the many peculiar rules surrounding fault grounds.

1. THE FAULT SCHEME

UTAH CODE ANN. (2016)

§ 30–3–1. Procedure–Residence–Grounds

(1) Proceedings in divorce are commenced and conducted as provided by law for proceedings in civil causes, except as provided in this chapter.

(2) The court may decree a dissolution of the marriage contract between the petitioner and respondent on the grounds specified in Subsection (3) in all cases where the petitioner or respondent has been an actual and bona fide resident of this state and of the county where the action is brought, or if members of the armed forces of the United States who are not legal residents of this state, where the petitioner has been stationed in this state under military orders, for three months next prior to the commencement of the action.

(3) Grounds for divorce:

(a) impotency of the respondent at the time of marriage;

(b) adultery committed by the respondent subsequent to marriage;

(c) willful desertion of the petitioner by the respondent for more than one year;

(d) willful neglect of the respondent to provide for the petitioner the common necessaries of life;

(e) habitual drunkenness of the respondent;

(f) conviction of the respondent for a felony;

(g) cruel treatment of the petitioner by the respondent to the extent of causing bodily injury or great mental distress to the petitioner;

(h) irreconcilable differences of the marriage;

(i) incurable insanity; or

(j) when the husband and wife have lived separately under a decree of separate maintenance of any state for three consecutive years without cohabitation.

(4) A decree of divorce granted under Subsection (3)(j) does not affect the liability of either party under any provision for separate maintenance previously granted.

(5) (a) A divorce may not be granted on the grounds of insanity unless:

(i) the respondent has been adjudged insane by the appropriate authorities of this or another state prior to the commencement of the action; and

(ii) the court finds by the testimony of competent witnesses that the insanity of the respondent is incurable.

[Provisions (5)(b)–(e) make special rules for divorce sought on grounds of insanity, including appointment of a guardian ad litem, an investigation by the county attorney into the merits of the case, and examination by physicians of the respondent's mental condition.]

NOTES

Multiple Grounds. Often a divorce statute becomes a hodgepodge of grounds, some of which would be better incorporated into suits for annulment (*e.g.*, § 3(a) above), and some of which encompass all of the other grounds (*e.g.*, § 3(h) above). The explanation is that the statute has a long history with varying permutations. *See generally* J. Thomas Oldham, *Why a New Uniform Equitable Distribution Jurisdiction Act is Needed to Reduce Forum Shopping in Divorce Litigation*, 49 FAM. L. Q. 359 (2015) (proposing legislation to make it disadvantageous for one party to petition for a divorce in a state with favorable grounds).

Insanity as a Ground. Insanity has long been an enumerated ground for divorce in some jurisdictions. Many of those provisions, however, required that the condition must be so extreme, the prognosis so bleak, or the length of institutionalization so great that the ground was of little practical use. Some jurisdictions that have shifted almost entirely to a no-fault "breakdown" ground nevertheless retain insanity as a separate cause, as Utah does. *See* § 5, *supra*. *See also* CAL. FAM. CODE § 2312 (West 2016). The generally accepted reason for retaining insanity as a fault grounds is concern about whether no-fault grounds should be applicable in the case of an insane spouse. This reticence stems in part from the need to provide financial support for the insane spouse. Thus, California law provides that dissolution on the grounds of insanity does not relieve a spouse from "any obligation imposed by the law as a result of the marriage for the support of the spouse who lacks legal capacity to make decisions." *Id.* at § 2313.

NEW YORK DOMESTIC RELATIONS LAW (McKinney 2016)

§ 170. Action for divorce

An action for divorce may be maintained by a husband or wife to procure a judgment divorcing the parties and dissolving the marriage on any of the following grounds:

(1) The cruel and inhuman treatment of the plaintiff by the defendant such that the conduct of the defendant so endangers the physical or mental well being of the plaintiff as renders it unsafe or improper for the plaintiff to cohabit with the defendant.

(2) The abandonment of the plaintiff by the defendant for a period of one or more years.

(3) The confinement of the defendant in prison for a period of three or more consecutive years after the marriage of plaintiff and defendant.

(4) The commission of an act of adultery, provided that adultery for the purposes of articles ten, eleven, and eleven-A of this chapter, is hereby defined as the commission of an act of sexual intercourse, oral sexual conduct or anal sexual conduct, voluntarily performed by the defendant, with a person other than the plaintiff after the marriage of plaintiff and defendant. Oral sexual conduct and anal sexual conduct include, but are not limited to, sexual conduct as defined in subdivision two of section 130.00 [sexual contact between two persons] and subdivision three of section 130.20 [sexual contact with an animal or deceased human] of the penal law.

(5) The husband and wife have lived apart pursuant to a decree or judgment of separation for a period of one or more years after the granting of such decree or judgment, and satisfactory proof has been submitted by the plaintiff that he or she has substantially performed all the terms and conditions of such decree or judgment.

(6) The husband and wife have lived separate and apart pursuant to a written agreement of separation, subscribed by the parties thereto and acknowledged or proved in the form required to entitle a deed to be recorded, for a period of one or more years after the execution of such agreement and satisfactory proof has been submitted by the plaintiff that he or she has substantially performed all the terms and conditions of such agreement. Such agreement shall be filed in the office of the clerk of the county wherein either party resides. In lieu of filing such agreement, either party to such agreement may file a memorandum of such agreement, which memorandum shall be similarly subscribed and acknowledged or proved as was the agreement of separation and shall contain the following information: (a) the names and addresses of each of the parties, (b) the date of marriage of the parties, (c) the date of the agreement of separation and (d) the date of this subscription and acknowledgment or proof of such agreement of separation.

(7) The relationship between husband and wife has broken down irretrievably for a period of at least six months, provided that one party has so stated under oath. No judgment of divorce shall be granted under this subdivision unless and until the economic issues of equitable distribution of marital property, the payment or waiver of spousal support, the payment of child support, the payment of counsel and experts' fees and expenses

as well as the custody and visitation with the infant children of the marriage have been resolved by the parties, or determined by the court and incorporated into the judgment of divorce.

§ 173. Jury trial

In an action for divorce there is a right to trial by jury of the issues of the grounds for granting the divorce.

§ 200. Action for separation

An action may be maintained by a husband or wife against the other party to the marriage to procure a judgment separating the parties from bed and board, forever, or for a limited time, for any of the following causes:

1. The cruel and inhuman treatment of the plaintiff by the defendant such that the conduct of the defendant so endangers the physical or mental well being of the plaintiff as renders it unsafe or improper for the plaintiff to cohabit with the defendant.
2. The abandonment of the plaintiff by the defendant.
3. The neglect or refusal of the defendant-spouse to provide for the support of the plaintiff-spouse where the defendant-spouse is chargeable with such support under the provisions of section thirty-two of this chapter or of section four hundred twelve of the family court act.
4. The commission of an act of adultery by the defendant; except where such offense is committed by the procurement or with the connivance of the plaintiff or where there is voluntary cohabitation of the parties with the knowledge of the offense or where action was not commenced within five years after the discovery by the plaintiff of the offense charged or where the plaintiff has also been guilty of adultery under such circumstances that the defendant would have been entitled, if innocent, to a divorce, provided that adultery for the purposes of this subdivision is hereby defined [as in § 170(4) above].
5. The confinement of the defendant in prison for a period of three or more consecutive years after the marriage of plaintiff and defendant.

NOTES

Dual Actions. Note that New York still maintains both actions for judicial separation in § 200 (divorce *a mensa et thoro* or divorce from bed and board), and absolute divorce in § 170 (divorce *a vinculo matrimonii*). Other states, like Virginia, also do this. *See* VA. CODE. ANN. §§ 20–91, 20–95 (2016). Like New York, some states once provided substantially different grounds for the two actions. The practical effect of having two separate actions was that the "innocent" party who did not wish to remarry (or have his or her spouse remarry) could elect between the procedures. Today, states that continue to recognize both actions often provide that either party may merge a decree for judicial separation into a decree for absolute divorce once the requisite statutory period has elapsed. *See, e.g.*, VA. CODE ANN. § 20–121 (2016). Are there any good reasons for maintaining the two actions today, particularly under a statute like New York's that has overlapping grounds?

Two Kinds of No-Fault Divorce. In 2010, New York joined 48 other states in providing "unilateral" no-fault divorce. *See* N.Y. DOM. REL. LAW § 170(7) (2016), which allows the court, in the absence of an agreement by both parties about the financial terms of the divorce, to set those terms. Prior to 2010, New York permitted only "bilateral" no-fault divorce, meaning that the parties could not escape the marriage if they could not agree on the financial terms and, in the case of minor children, custody and child support. *See id.* § 170(6). *See also* Robin Fretwell Wilson, *Often, There is Fault*, N.Y. TIMES.COM, http://roomfordebate.blogs.nytimes.com/2010/06/15/is-new-york-ready-for-no-fault-divorce/#robin (June 15, 2010). Today, only Missouri continues to require "bilateral" no-fault divorce. *See* MO. REV. STAT. § 452.320 (West 2016).

A number of attempts to add unilateral no-fault divorce to New York law before 2010 failed, at least in part because women's groups argued that requiring bilateral agreement gave women, often the weaker-earning spouse, a stronger bargaining position in the divorce. *See* Marcia Pappas, *Reject Divorce on Demand*, N.Y. TIMES.COM, http://roomfordebate.blogs.nytimes.com/2010/06/15/is-new-york-ready-for-no-fault-divorce/#marcia (June 15, 2010).

Fault Combined with No-Fault. New York's extensive list of "fault" grounds, together with New York's two "no-fault" grounds, raise the question: Must the party seeking a divorce choose one or the other, or can the party choose both fault and no-fault grounds when petitioning for a divorce? Is it possible for one party to choose one ground and the other party another? In Ebbert v. Ebbert, 459 A.2d 282 (N.H. 1983), the trial court had approved a master's recommendation on cross libels for divorce that two decrees be awarded, one based on adultery and the other on irreconcilable differences. In overruling this decision, the Supreme Court of New Hampshire explained that the addition of "irreconcilable differences" as a ground did not repeal the original thirteen grounds based on fault, and held that:

> [A] party who seeks a divorce on a fault ground cannot be denied the opportunity to litigate on that basis merely because the other party has advanced irreconcilable differences as grounds for divorce.

Id. at 284.

Under the circumstances, this holding would seem to require that the trial court determine whether breakdown of the marriage was caused by adultery or irreconcilable differences. Is such an approach consistent with one motivating rationale for adding a no-fault ground—namely, to lessen the bitterness that may be abetted by the divorce process?

Some state statutes that mix both fault and no-fault grounds permit a court to make a finding of "fault" for alimony purposes without having to award the divorce on such a ground. *See, e.g.*, VA. CODE ANN. § 20–107.1(E) (2016). Such a finding is crucial because fault is an important consideration in the financial terms of the divorce. Approximately half of the states allow marital or economic fault to be considered in the division of marital property or an award of spousal support, thus making fault of one or both of the parties a significant factor. For analysis and a list of specific states, *see* Linda A. Elrod and Robert G. Spector, *Review of the Year in Family Law: Working Toward More Uniformity in Laws Relating to Families*, 44 FAM. L.Q. 514, chart 4 (2011). For example, the potential recipient's adultery is a complete bar to alimony, without regard to any other facts of the case, in a number of states like Georgia, North Carolina, and South Carolina. *See* GA. CODE. ANN. § 19–6–1(b) (2016); N.C. GEN. STAT. ANN. § 50–16.3A(a) (2016); S.C. CODE ANN. § 20–3–130 (2016).

Although many states have eradicated fault grounds, a raging debate continues over whether fault should matter when couples divorce, as New York's recent reform illustrates. *See Is New York Ready for No-Fault Divorce?*, N.Y. TIMES.COM, http://roomfordebate.blogs.nytimes.com/2010/06/15/is-new-york-ready-for-no-fault-divorce/ (June 15, 2010). *Compare* AMERICAN LAW INSTITUTE, *Principles of the Law of Family Dissolution* § 1, t. 2 (2011) (rejecting any fault other than economic misconduct) *with* Barbara Bennett Woodhouse (with comments by Katharine T. Bartlett), *Sex, Lies, and Dissipation: The Discourse of Fault in a No-Fault Era*, 82 GEO. L. J. 2525, 2567–68 (1994) (arguing that the law should "reclaim[ ] the power of fault" and "reward family-centric, caring conduct, rather than turn a blind eye to abuse and exploitation"), *and* Lynn D. Wardle, *Beyond Fault and No-Fault in the Reform of Marital Dissolution Law*, in RECONCEIVING THE FAMILY: CRITIQUE ON THE AMERICAN LAW INSTITUTE'S PRINCIPLES OF THE LAW OF FAMILY DISSOLUTION 9 (Robin Fretwell Wilson, ed., 2006) (arguing that fault is integral to marital dissolution decisions and proceedings and thus it is "irrational and impractical" for the law to ignore fault).

Proving Adultery. Adultery was universally included as a ground in fault-based divorce laws. New York long maintained adultery as the only ground for divorce in the state, although New York's liberal approach to annulment was used to expand access to marital dissolution.

The major problem that adultery presents is the matter of proof. It may be proven with direct evidence (*e.g.*, photographic evidence) or indirect, circumstantial evidence showing an opportunity and an inclination to commit adultery. *See, e.g.*, Panhorst v. Panhorst, 390 S.E.2d 376 (S.C. Ct. App.1990). From a practical point of view, the evidence often is either too ample or too meager.

The first situation involves the collusive divorce in which evidence has been "staged" for ultimate presentation to an ostensibly unsuspecting referee or judge. This sort of deviousness dated back to the days of Chancellor Kent, who acknowledged having "had occasion to believe, in the exercise of a judicial cognizance over numerous cases of divorce, that the sin of adultery was sometimes committed on the part of the husband for the very purpose of divorce." 2 KENT, COMMENTARIES ON AMERICAN LAW 106 (13th ed.1884). Years later, another New York judge described to a committee on matrimonial law reform the sameness of the circumstantial evidence of adultery that reached his court regularly, noting:

> She is always in a sheer pink robe. It's never blue—always pink. And he is always in his shorts when they catch them.

N.Y. HERALD TRIBUNE, Oct. 1, 1965, p. 19, col. 4.

Today, circumstantial evidence may be used to prove adultery, but it must do more than simply establish a strong suspicion of guilt. *See, e.g.*, Coe v. Coe, 303 S.E.2d 923 (Va. 1983) (requiring clear and convincing evidence based upon proven facts and reasonable inferences). Thus, for example, in Clark v. Clark, 361 S.E.2d 328 (S.C. 1987), a husband received an anonymous telephone call about his wife's relationship with her male business partner, prompting the husband to hire a private investigator. Husband and investigator entered the wife's antique store early one morning, hiding out in an upstairs room. When the wife and partner appeared several hours later, they "dragged a mattress into an upstairs room and closed and locked the door. Husband heard sounds through the door which he described as 'love-making going-on.' " *Id.* at 415–16. When the husband kicked in the door ten minutes later, "[w]ife and her partner were standing in the room, naked." Husband's complaint for divorce on the grounds of adultery was ultimately upheld as being based on sufficient evidence.

Just as proof may be too ample, it also may be too meager. Proof by circumstantial evidence raises the potential for a mistaken finding. This is of particular concern where adultery continues to be a crime. In such jurisdictions, the evidence must be nearly as strong as criminal evidence. *See* VA. CODE ANN. § 18.2–365 (2016) (criminalizing adultery); Phipps v. Phipps, 188 S.E. 168 (Va. 1936) (requiring "strict, satisfactory, and conclusive" evidence to prove adultery). At least one court has held that neither judge nor jury should presume that two people must be engaging in sexual intercourse just because they live in the same residence. Hughes v. Hughes, 531 S.E.2d 654 (Va. Ct. App. 2000).

The trial court is accorded considerable discretion in weighing evidence of adultery, placing a premium on prevailing at the trial level. Consider *McElveen v. McElveen*, in which the husband appealed a trial court award of alimony to his ex-wife. McElveen v. McElveen, 506 S.E.2d 1 (S.C. Ct. App. 1998). Husband presented circumstantial evidence that his wife committed adultery and was therefore barred from alimony. Telephone records showed six hundred phone calls between wife and her paramour, some lasting hours and at very early and late times. However, when wife took weekend trips, no phone calls were made. She paid for such trips with her father's credit card and later demanded that the hotel delete records of her stay. The overnight registry was altered with a name and license plate similar to the paramour's, showing a guest who arrived 18 minutes after wife. Wife also gave her paramour a Valentine's Day cake. Notwithstanding such facts, the trial court concluded that husband had not proven adultery by "a clear preponderance of the evidence." *McElveen*, 506 S.E.2d at 7. The South Carolina Court of Appeals affirmed. While it found this to be was an "extremely close case," husband failed to establish his wife's adultery because the circumstantial evidence was not so convincing as to exclude any other reasonable hypothesis. *Id.* at 9. Although husband's evidence showed wife's opportunity to commit adultery, the evidence did not connect wife to the alteration of the hotel records, and the paramour denied being with wife on weekends. Further, regarding inclination, husband showed "virtually no evidence of a romantic or sexual relationship" between wife and paramour. *Id.* at 8. The appellate court deferred to the trial court's decision to award alimony, noting that the trial judge was in a better position to assess credibility.

What precisely counts as adultery has occupied a number of courts and legislatures. New York's statute counts as adultery any "act of sexual intercourse, oral sexual conduct, or anal sexual conduct, voluntarily performed by the defendant." *See* § 170(4), *supra*. By contrast, the New Hampshire Supreme Court has ruled that the state's adultery ground excludes all non-coital sex acts. Therefore, sexual contact between persons of the same gender cannot constitute adultery, and neither can any act between persons of the opposite gender that does not include intercourse. *In re* Blanchflower, 834 A.2d 1010 (N.H. 2003).

Corroboration. In divorce actions, corroboration by evidence other than testimony of the parties is sometimes required in order to lessen the potential for collusion. *See, e.g.*, VA. CODE ANN. § 20–99 (2016). In Graham v. Graham, 172 S.E.2d 724 (Va. 1970), husband sued wife for divorce, alleging that she willfully deserted him. Wife cross-claimed for divorce on the grounds of cruelty and constructive desertion. A third party testified that wife had physically left the marital home; she justified her departure because of husband's alleged cruelty, established only by the testimony of the spouses. The court denied a divorce to either party, pointing out that wife was justified in leaving home because of husband's conduct, but a fault-based divorce could not be granted to her because there was no corroboration as required by statute. As a consolation, the parties eventually would be able to dissolve their marriage legally by satisfying the no-fault "living apart" ground for divorce.

Brady v. Brady

Court of Appeals of New York, 1985
476 N.E.2d 290

■ WACHTLER, CHIEF JUDGE.

Plaintiff Edward Brady has brought this matrimonial action against his wife, defendant Dorothy Brady, seeking a divorce and sale of the marital residence. The complaint alleged, as grounds for obtaining a divorce, that Mrs. Brady committed acts constituting cruel and inhuman treatment and constructively abandoned plaintiff by refusing to engage in sexual relations with him (see, Domestic Relations Law § 170). The question presented is what conduct constitutes cruel and inhuman treatment in a "long-term" marriage so as to give rise to a cause of action for divorce. More specifically, we must determine whether the principles set forth in Hessen v. Hessen, 33 N.Y.2d 406, 308 N.E.2d 891, with respect to the necessary showing of cruel and inhuman treatment in a long-term marriage, are still to be followed.

The parties were married in 1956 and have four children, who were born between 1957 and 1966. From May 1977 to September 1979, Mr. Brady lived in the marital residence on an infrequent basis and since September or October 1979 he has not resided there at all. Mr. Brady commenced this action for a divorce in 1981. His verified complaint set forth two causes of action, one for constructive abandonment and the other for cruel and inhuman treatment. Among the allegations relating to the claim of cruel and inhuman treatment were that Mrs. Brady, during 1976, struck him with objects, including a lamp and a vase, threatened him with a knife, attempted to choke him and frequently berated him. Her answer denied all of these allegations and set forth counterclaims for maintenance and child support, but not for a judgment of divorce.

At trial, plaintiff, with minimal corroboration, testified to the allegations in the complaint. Mrs. Brady, supported in much of her testimony by one of the Brady children, again denied the charges of constructive abandonment and cruel and inhuman treatment, and stated that she did not seek a divorce. The trial court, although apparently rejecting most of plaintiff's specific claims of cruel and inhuman treatment, granted him a divorce on that cause of action. The court termed the marriage a "dead" one, and concluded that based on the marital breakdown and the separation of the parties further cohabitation was improper. The court also awarded custody of the remaining infant child to Mrs. Brady, granted her exclusive use and occupancy of the marital residence until the emancipation of this child, at which time the residence would be sold, provided for the distribution of other marital property, and ordered plaintiff to make payments to her for maintenance and child support.

The Appellate Division, 101 A.D.2d 797, unanimously modified the trial court judgment. The court found that plaintiff had not made out a cause of action for divorce based on cruel and inhuman treatment, and thus deleted the portions of the judgment granting plaintiff a divorce and ordering the sale of the marital residence upon the emancipation of the remaining infant child. We now affirm.

Prior to the 1966 amendments to the Domestic Relations Law, the sole ground for divorce in this State was adultery. The 1966 reforms added five additional grounds, one of which was, and remains, "The cruel and inhuman treatment of the plaintiff by the defendant such that the conduct of the defendant so endangers the physical or mental wellbeing of the plaintiff as renders it unsafe or improper for the plaintiff to cohabit with the defendant" (Domestic Relations Law § 170[1], added by L.1966, ch. 254).

In Hessen v. Hessen, 308 N.E.2d 891, *supra*, we held that a plaintiff seeking a divorce under the cruel and inhuman treatment subdivision must show serious misconduct, and not mere incompatibility. Subsequent cases have established that a plaintiff, relying on this subdivision, must generally show a course of conduct by the defendant spouse which is harmful to the physical or mental health of the plaintiff and makes cohabitation unsafe or improper. The subdivision requires a finding of fault and thus a showing of irreconcilable or irremediable differences is insufficient by itself.

In *Hessen,* we also noted that the determination of whether conduct constituted cruel and inhuman treatment would depend, in part, on the length of the parties' marriage, because what might be considered substantial misconduct in the context of a marriage of short duration, might only be "transient discord" in that of a long-term marriage. Thus, courts in this State have required a high degree of proof of cruel and inhuman treatment where there is a marriage of long duration and an isolated act of mistreatment will rarely suffice.

At the time the *Hessen* case was decided, only a wife was able to collect alimony following a divorce. If, however, her "misconduct" entitled the husband to obtain a divorce on a ground such as cruel and inhuman treatment, she was precluded under Domestic Relations Law § 236 from receiving alimony or exclusive possession of the marital home.[1] Thus, the effect of granting a husband a divorce on the ground of his wife's cruel and inhuman treatment was a potential financial catastrophe to the wife. In *Hessen,* we noted that this negative effect could be particularly harmful where the defendant, as was the case therein, was a "dependent older woman" and this fact served as one of the bases for requiring a higher degree of proof of cruel and inhuman treatment in a long-term marriage.

In 1980, the Equitable Distribution Law was enacted and Domestic Relations Law § 236 was amended to provide, in part, that either spouse could be required to pay alimony ("maintenance"), and to eliminate the rule that misconduct by a spouse precludes receiving an award of alimony or exclusive possession of the marital home. The change with respect to the person who could be required to pay alimony was constitutionally required in light of the Supreme Court's 1979 decision in Orr v. Orr, 440 U.S. 268,, which held that the Alabama statutory scheme which imposed alimony obligations on husbands only violated the equal protection clause of the 14th Amendment to the United States Constitution. Plaintiff argues that the *Hessen* rule, as to long-term marriages, was designed to protect only women and thus can no longer be followed in view of the *Orr* decision. He also argues that there is no longer any reason to require a higher showing of misconduct in a long-term marriage as the

[1] The only exception to this rule was where the plaintiff had waived his rights under that provision of the Domestic Relations Law and authorized the trial court to make such awards (*Hessen v. Hessen*, 308 N.E.2d 891; *Barry v. Barry*, 93 A.D.2d 797).

spouse against whom the divorce is granted can receive alimony payments and exclusive possession of the marital home, and thus there is no danger that granting a divorce will be financially ruinous to a "dependent older woman".

If the evidentiary requirement set forth in *Hessen* with respect to marriages of long duration were applied only where the plaintiff was the husband, then there would likely be an equal protection violation. *Hessen,* however, has been and should be followed whether the plaintiff is the husband or the wife. Thus, plaintiff's constitutional argument is without merit. Plaintiff's contention that the rationale for the *Hessen* rule has been eliminated by the 1980 amendments to Domestic Relations Law § 236 is also unconvincing. That financial problems could have faced a middle aged woman against whom a cruelty divorce was granted was merely one of the bases for requiring a higher degree of proof of cruel and inhuman treatment in a long-term marriage. The fundamental reason for such a rule was, and remains, the commonsense notion that the conduct which a plaintiff alleges as the basis for a cause of action must be viewed in the context of the entire marriage, including its duration, in deciding whether particular actions can properly be labeled as cruel and inhuman.

Therefore, we reaffirm the holding in *Hessen* that whether a plaintiff has established a cause of action for a cruelty divorce will depend, in part, on the duration of the marriage in issue. The existence of a long-term marriage does not, of course, serve as an absolute bar to the granting of a divorce for cruel and inhuman treatment, and even in such a marriage "substantial misconduct" might consist of one violent episode such as a severe beating.

It is not clear which, if any, of plaintiff's allegations were credited by the trial court. The trial court did conclude that plaintiff had not made a sufficient showing of cruel and inhuman treatment under *Hessen* in view of the duration of the marriage (26 years), but concluded that "the *[Hessen]* rule must be considered as no longer retaining its authority". The court went on to find that the Bradys' marriage was a "dead" one, and, "in its discretion", granted Mr. Brady a divorce on his cause of action for cruel and inhuman treatment. While the trial court does have broad discretion as to whether to grant a cruelty divorce, such a divorce cannot be granted simply because the court concludes that there is a "dead marriage". . . .

NOTES

What Constitutes "Cruelty?" Before enactment of no-fault "breakdown" grounds, nothing contributed more to the relaxation of the old stern standards about how divorce laws should be administered than judicial manipulation of the term "cruelty." Cruelty first became a divorce ground in our country at a time when a woman, as the old phrase had it, was "under the rod of her husband," and consequently was supposed to be subject to his discipline. These ideas of subjection survived long after the passage of Married Women's Property Acts and affected judicial thinking about what conduct properly could be denominated cruel. This conservatism sometimes was abetted by statutory terms; many state legislatures, spendthrift with adjectives, had stipulated that the ground must involve extreme cruelty, intolerable cruelty, or cruel, barbarous and inhuman treatment. The looser, modern interpretations came in spite of such statutory exhortations.

Not only do statutory terms vary, but courts may express greatly differing opinions as to what will constitute "cruelty" under similarly worded statutes. Some may require physical violence, while mental cruelty is enough for others. In Farrar v. Farrar, 553 S.W.2d 741 (Tenn. 1977), the evidence presented by plaintiff to establish cruelty included an extramarital affair of the defendant.

Whether mental cruelty should be a ground for divorce without proof of physical injury figured prominently in some jurisdictions. Some courts required a physical manifestation of mental cruelty. *See, e.g., In re* Henry, 37 A.3d 320 (N.H. 2012) (upholding a trial court's determination that wife offered sufficient evidence to prove cruelty where she introduced email messages, voicemail messages, and testimony from several family members corroborating her claim that husband's conduct caused her to experience depression, insomnia, and weight loss). Eventually most courts found ways to handle the problem, just as they had found ways in the evolution of tort law to permit recovery of damages for emotional harm alone. *See, e.g.,* HOMER H. CLARK, JR, THE LAW OF DOMESTIC RELATIONS IN THE UNITED STATES § 13.4 (2d ed. 1988).

Lord Reid captured the difficulty in defining cruelty in Williams v. Williams, [1964] A.C. 698, 1963, 2 All E.R. 994, H.L., which involved a question of whether insanity could be a defense to cruelty:

> To my mind, "cruelty" is a word that can take its meaning from its context: often it connotes blameworthiness but quite often it does not. Let me give one or two examples. Even in comparatively recent times practically everyone, including men of the highest integrity and intelligence who were quite as civilised as any of us, firmly believed that persecution in one form or another was not only excusable but was a moral duty. Few would deny that their acts were cruel, but I do not see how we can reasonably blame them for not having anticipated modern ideas. And is it a misuse of language to call a cat cruel? Again, when we speak of the cruel sea no doubt we personify the sea but do we blame it? So the law cannot just take "cruelty" in its ordinary or popular meaning, because that is too vague: we must decide what, if any, mental state is a necessary ingredient.

What Constitutes "Constructive Abandonment?" In *Brady*, the New York Court of Appeals did not address the husband's second grounds for fault-based divorce: constructive abandonment as a result of the refusal to have sex. Although not developed in *Brady*, this cause of action frequently arises, but requires a significant showing to make it out. In Virginia, for example, the deserting spouse must completely abandon marital duties so that the marriage becomes well near "intolerable and impossible to be endured." Chandler v. Chandler, 112 S.E. 856 (Va. 1922). Refusing to have sex alone is not enough, but will suffice if the refusing spouse abandons other marital duties. Jamison v. Jamison, 352 S.E.2d 719 (Va. Ct. App. 1987).

Other states require the abandonment of sex to last for a significant period of time. In C.W. v. G.W., 906 N.Y.S.2d 771 (N.Y. Sup. Ct. 2006), wife sued for divorce on constructive abandonment grounds, alleging that husband refused to have sexual relations for 1.5 years. In New York, to show constructive abandonment on this basis, the abandoned spouse must prove that the abandoning spouse willfully and unjustifiably refused to have sexual relations for at least one year, despite repeated requests to resume relations from the abandoned spouse. In *C.W.*, husband underwent treatment for prostate cancer in 2002, leading to erectile dysfunction, which continued even after his cancer treatment ended. The trial court rejected wife's claim, crediting husband's account that they had had sex on one occasion during the year, relying in part on a conversation between husband and his physician in which husband said "he is perfectly responsive to" the Viagra dosage the physician had prescribed. *Id.* at *4.

Like other states, New York also recognizes a second basis for constructive abandonment—the failure to engage in social relations with one's spouse. This may take the form of refusing to have meals together, to speak more than sporadically, to sleep in the same bedroom, or to celebrate holidays and birthdays together. *Id.* at *5. In *C.W.*, the court rejected the wife's claim of constructive abandonment on this ground because the undisputed evidence showed that the couple traveled and attended family functions, birthdays, graduations, and medical appointments together, and continued daily conversation.

In re Dube

Supreme Court of New Hampshire, 2012
44 A.3d 556

■ CONBOY, JUDGE.

The respondent, Jeannie Dube, appeals the final decree in the divorce action initiated by the petitioner, Eric Dube. She argues that the Derry Family Division (Moore, J.) erred when it granted Eric a fault-based divorce. . . . We affirm in part and reverse in part.

The trial court found the following facts. The parties were married in 1997. During their marriage, they purchased a home in Candia, where they lived with their son and one of Eric's children from a previous marriage. In addition, Eric's parents lived in an in-law apartment over the garage of the marital home.

In the later years of their marriage, the parties began to experience marital difficulties. They demonstrated little to no affection toward one another, and Jeannie refused to be intimate with Eric. On November 30, 2008, Jeannie learned that Eric had engaged in a single instance of adultery. Three days later, on December 3, 2008, while the pair discussed their marriage during a telephone conversation, Jeannie told Eric that she was going to kill the parties' minor child, Eric's child from a previous relationship, and Eric's parents. She also told him that she was going to burn down the marital residence. Following their conversation, Jeannie "doused the marital residence and garage with gasoline and attempted to ignite it with a lighter." In addition, she "destroyed a portion of the marital residence and property with an ax[ ]," and then chased Eric's father around the house with the ax, as he tried to prevent her from lighting the gasoline. Consequently, the next day, Eric obtained a restraining order against Jeannie. As a result of her actions, Jeannie was charged with two counts of attempted murder, one count of attempted arson, and one count of criminal mischief.

On December 9, 2008, Eric filed for divorce, claiming irreconcilable differences caused the breakdown of the parties' marriage. *See* RSA 458:7–a (Supp.2011). Thereafter, he amended his divorce petition and added an alternate ground for divorce, claiming Jeannie "ha[d] so treated [him] as seriously to injure health or endanger reason." RSA 458:7, V (2004). After he amended his petition, but prior to the final hearing, Jeannie was convicted of one count of attempted arson and one count of criminal mischief and was subsequently sentenced to two to four years at the New Hampshire State Prison for Women. As a result, during the final divorce hearing, Eric asked the court to consider that Jeannie's "conviction of a crime punishable by prison for more than one year constitute[d] fault grounds that caused the breakdown of the marriage.' " *See* RSA 458:7, IV (2004).

Following the final hearing, the trial court granted Eric a decree of divorce "on the grounds of [Jeannie's] conviction of a crime and imprisonment for more than one year." [In addition, the court ordered Eric an unequal division of the marital property, adopted the parties' stipulated parenting plan, which awarded Eric decision-making and residential responsibility for their minor son, and denied Jeannie's request for alimony, finding it "unwarranted."] This appeal followed.

We first address Jeannie's contention that the trial court erred in granting Eric a fault-based divorce on the grounds of her conviction and subsequent imprisonment. She asserts that Eric is not an "innocent party" because he committed adultery, and, therefore, he is precluded from obtaining a fault-based divorce.

RSA 458:7 (2004) provides in pertinent part:

> A divorce from the bonds of matrimony shall be decreed in favor *of the innocent party* for any of the following causes. . .
>
> II. Adultery of either party. . . .
>
> IV. Conviction of either party, in any state or federal district, of a crime punishable with imprisonment for more than one year and actual imprisonment under such conviction.

V. When either party has so treated the other as seriously to injure health or endanger reason.

RSA 458:7, II, IV–V (emphasis added). Although the trial court did not make a specific finding that Eric was an "innocent party," because it granted a divorce on fault grounds, we assume it made such a finding. *See* Dombrowski v. Dombrowski, 559 A.2d 828 (N.H. 1989). We will affirm the trial court's factual findings unless the evidence does not support them or they are legally erroneous. *In the* Matter of Hampers & Hampers, 911 A.2d 14 (N.H. 2006).

In Rockwood v. Rockwood, 194 A.2d 771 (N.H. 1963), we considered whether the husband, who was found guilty of adultery, was "the innocent party" and therefore entitled to a divorce. We determined that "innocent" meant "free from guilt." *Id.* (quotations omitted). We then explained that a spouse cannot be "the innocent party" if he "is guilty of an offense against the other spouse, which would be grounds for divorce." *Id.*; *see* Schwarz v. Schwarz, 427 S.W.2d 734, 739 (Mo. Ct. App.1968) ("[T]he conduct of one party will not prevent him from being adjudged an innocent party unless it be such as to entitle the other party, prima facie, to a divorce." (quotation omitted)).

Here, the record does not support the trial court's implicit finding that Eric was "the innocent party." Eric does not dispute his infidelity; yet, he contends that he is still an "innocent party" because Jeannie's conduct, and not his adultery, was the primary cause of the marital breakdown. Eric argues that the parties' agreement to "work through" the affair constituted Jeannie's condonation of his adultery, thus restoring his status as an "innocent party." The affirmative defense of condonation "is the forgiveness of an antecedent matrimonial offense on condition that it shall not be repeated." Tibbetts v. Tibbetts, 248 A.2d 75 (N.H. 1968) (quotations omitted). Under the doctrine, "[i]f either party to a marriage thinks proper to forgive the infidelity of the other, it cannot afterwards be set up as a ground of divorce, without evidence of a [further] injury." Quincy v. Quincy, 10 N.H. 272, 273 (1839).

The record, however, does not support Eric's assertion that Jeannie condoned his infidelity. While she may have agreed to work on their marriage, her conduct in the days immediately following his disclosure does not support a finding that Jeannie forgave Eric's adultery. Two days after his disclosure, Eric received numerous voicemail messages from Jeannie who was "irate" and at times "just screaming and yelling." On the third day after his disclosure, she threatened and attempted to kill his family and destroy the marital home. Moreover, during the divorce hearing, Jeannie stated, "I don't think forgiveness was the question at the time. It was what did I—what do I need to do to—if—what did I miss, what did I need to do was what we were—what we were trying to find out." Thus, the doctrine of condonation is inapplicable here, and therefore, Eric cannot claim the status of an "innocent party."

Because we conclude that Eric is not entitled to a fault-based divorce, we need not address Jeannie's alternative argument that the cause of the marital breakdown could not have been her conviction since she had not yet been convicted when the divorce petition was filed or amended prior to the final hearing. Nevertheless, we affirm the trial court's decision dissolving the parties' marriage. The record supports a dissolution based upon irreconcilable differences. *See* RSA 458:7–a. Accordingly, we reverse the trial court's decision to the extent that it granted Eric a fault-based divorce; otherwise, we affirm the trial court's decision to grant a divorce. . . .

■ DALIANIS, C.J., and LYNN, J., concurred.

NEW YORK DOMESTIC RELATIONS LAW (2016)

§ 171. When divorce denied, although adultery proved

In either of the following cases, the plaintiff is not entitled to a divorce, although the adultery is established:

1. Where the offense was committed by the procurement or with the connivance of the plaintiff.
2. Where the offense charged has been forgiven by the plaintiff. The forgiveness may be proven, either affirmatively, or by the voluntary cohabitation of the parties with the knowledge of the fact.
3. Where there has been no express forgiveness, and no voluntary cohabitation of the parties, but the action was not commenced within five years after the discovery by the plaintiff of the offense charged.
4. Where the plaintiff has also been guilty of adultery under such circumstances that the defendant would have been entitled, if innocent, to a divorce.

NOTES

Defenses to Fault Grounds. *Dube* raises two of the classic defenses to fault-based divorce: recrimination and condonation. It illustrates that defenses to fault-based divorce remain robust in those jurisdictions that still recognize both fault and no-fault grounds for divorce—although the primary effect of the defenses may be to allow the couples to escape the marriage on no-fault grounds only.

Recrimination. Recrimination long has been the most criticized of the defenses to fault. When divorce could be granted only on the basis of fault, this doctrine meant that if each party establishes that the other has committed a marital fault, both would be precluded from obtaining a divorce. A variety of theories were advanced in support of the defense: (1) the "clean hands" doctrine; (2) the theory that the parties are *in pari delicto*; (3) that there has been a breach of mutually dependent covenants; (4) the theory of compensation; and (5) that divorce is a remedy only for an innocent spouse.

In such instances of dual fault, the parties could not escape the marriage, and so would have to choose between living separately while remaining married or living together and probably hating it.

Elaborate rules of gamesmanship developed around the defense over time. In some jurisdictions, some grounds were considered of lesser magnitude than others—*e.g.*, mental cruelty versus adultery—and only grounds of equal severity would negate one another. Similarly, in some jurisdictions, a ground for judicial separation (divorce *a mensa et thoro*) would not offset a ground for absolute divorce (divorce *a vinculo matrimonii*).

In other jurisdictions, courts introduced the idea of "comparative rectitude"—sometimes even in the face of apparently contrary statutes. The classic example of this is De Burgh v. De Burgh, 250 P.2d 598 (Cal. 1952), in which Justice Traynor established four guidelines for deciding whether to credit a defense of recrimination: (1) The "likelihood that the marriage can be saved," considering its length, the parties' temperaments, and the "seriousness and frequency of their marital misconduct . . . and the likelihood of its recurrence," among other things. (2) "The effect of the marital conflict upon the parties," especially whether continued cohabitation would pose a "serious hazard to the health of either party." (3) "The effect of the marital conflict upon third parties," such as children or even the community if marriage becomes "discredit[ed]." (4) "Comparative guilt," such as whether one party's transgression is unequal in gravity, frequency, or effect to the other's transgression. *Id.* at 606. Thus, where a wife sued for divorce because her husband was frequently intoxicated, "inflicted physical injury" on her, "boasted of his relations with other women," criticized her daughter, and spent lavishly on himself, wife was entitled to a fault-based divorce despite his claim of recrimination. *Id.* at 599. Husband urged that wife's transgressions negated his because she had "unjustly accused him of dishonesty and homosexuality," charges that she shared with his business associates. *Id.*

With the advent of no-fault divorce, many states eliminated recrimination as a defense. *See, e.g.,* N.J. REV. STAT. § 2A:34–7 (2016).

Condonation. Condonation is one spouse's forgiveness of the other's marital misconduct that would amount to a fault ground. Condonation can take place through specific agreement or continued cohabitation after knowledge of the offense. In *Dube*, the court rejected the husband's reliance on the affirmative defense of condonation. Although the wife had agreed to work through the adultery, the supreme court determined that "her conduct in the days immediately following his disclosure does not support a finding that [she] forgave [his] adultery." *Id.* at 559. Without this forgiveness, the wife had not condoned the husband's adultery, and so he was not restored to the "status of an innocent party." *Id.*

Condonation is widely said to be conditional on the offending party thenceforth treating the forgiving party with "conjugal kindness" and promising not to repeat the violation; breaking this condition can "revive" the original divorce ground. *See, e.g., In re* Marriage of Hightower, 358 Ill.App.3d 165 (2005). Although some courts occasionally have indicated that "a new ground" revives the old one, this is conceptually inaccurate because no such revival would be necessary if a new ground exists and can be proved. The more typical (and insidious) use of the doctrine allows for revival through misconduct falling short of a divorce ground or in cases of insufficient proof to establish the new violation as a ground.

Collusion and Connivance. Two other classic defenses are collusion and connivance. Collusion really is less a defense for the parties than a means for courts to deny a divorce to persons who fabricate evidence because both want a divorce and they have no grounds. During the time when only fault-based divorce was available, collusion often took the form of staged adultery, as described earlier in the chapter. Today, collusion may take the form of the parties representing to the court that they have satisfied any requisite "living apart" period of time for a no-fault divorce.

Unlike collusion, connivance involves one party's "corrupt consent" to the other's misconduct, constituting a divorce ground. *See* N.Y. DOM. REL. LAW § 171(1), *supra*; Gutzwiller v. Gutzwiller, 74 A.2d 325 (N.J. Ct. App. 1950). So, for example, where a wife sends her husband and his girlfriend a note and flowers while the two are spending an amorous weekend at a swanky resort, then wife is barred from divorcing him on the grounds of adultery due to her connivance. *See* Hollis v. Hollis, 427 S.E.2d 233 (Va. Ct. App. 1993).

Statute of Limitations and Waiting Periods. Some states provide statutes of limitation for certain grounds, such as adultery or desertion. For example, the New York statute above requires a suit to be instituted "within five years after the discovery by the plaintiff" of the adultery. N.Y. DOM. REL. LAW § 171(3) (McKinney 2106). Virginia provides a one-year limit from the commencement of the desertion before commencing a petition for divorce. *See* VA. CODE. ANN. § 20–93 (2016).

The Move Toward Covenant Marriage. Since 1997, three states, led first by Louisiana, have enacted legislation giving couples an opportunity to enter into "covenant marriages" rather than the standard marriage—which some pundits have described as "marriage and marriage lite" or "high test" and "regular" marriage. *See, e.g.*, STEVEN NOCK, LAURA SANCHEZ, AND JAMES WRIGHT, COVENANT MARRIAGE: THE MOVEMENT TO RECLAIM TRADITION IN AMERICA xii (2008); Ellen Goodman, *Covenant Marriage*, WASH. POST, Aug. 16, 1997, at A24. If a couple elects a covenant marriage, they sign a declaration of intent stating that they have received premarital counseling, promise to take reasonable efforts to preserve the marriage if marital difficulties arise, and intend to remain married for the rest of their lives. They thus limit the divorce grounds to those associated with fault or agree to lengthened time frames for no-fault divorce, although some statutes have shortened time frames in cases of domestic violence. *See* LA. REV. STAT. ANN. § 9:307 (2015). For general comment on such legislation, *see* Kimberly Diane White, *Covenant Marriage: An Unnecessary Second Attempt at Fault-Based Divorce*, 61 ALA. L. REV. 869 (2010); Katherine Shaw Spaht, *Covenant Marriage Seven Years Later: Its as Yet Unfulfilled Promise*, 65 LA. L. REV. 605–34 (2005); Chauncey E. Brummer, *The Shackles of Covenant Marriage: Who Holds the Key to Wedlock?*, 102 W. VA. L. REV. 339 (2003); NOCK,

SANCHEZ, AND WRIGHT, *supra*; Melissa S. LaBauve, *Covenant Marriages: A Guise for Lasting Commitment?* 43 LOY. L. REV. 421 (1997); Bruce Nolan, *Bishops Back Off Covenant Marriage,* NEW ORLEANS TIMES-PICAYUNE, Oct. 30, 1997 at A1.

2. NO-FAULT DIVORCE

Generally classified as falling within the ambit of "breakdown" or "no fault" divorce grounds are:

(1) incompatibility, sometimes known as incompatibility of temperament;

(2) separation for a specific time period pursuant to agreement between the spouses, generally termed "voluntary separation;"

(3) separation for a specific time period under breakdown circumstances, whether or not both the parties desired or agreed to live apart, and without regard to the circumstances under which the separation commenced;

(4) a general category of laws that require no specific period of separation but requires proof of "irretrievable breakdown," "irreconcilable differences," or some similarly phrased condition that ostensibly denotes that the marriage is dead. There may be crossbreeding between this ground and (3) to require a short separation period or to provide that such a separation creates a presumption that irretrievable breakdown has occurred;

(5) provisions allowing for dissolution based on longstanding absence of one spouse under conditions by which his or her death is presumed.

Although the category (1) ground had a long history, its use and availability were quite limited until recently and is still not very popular. Effectiveness and usage of category (2) and (3) grounds has depended on the length of the separation required. Today's typical "separation" statute requires at least six months or a year of living apart. *See Grounds for Divorce, 50 State Statutory Surveys: Family Law: Divorce And Dissolution*, 0080 SURVEYS 9 (West 2007). Category (4) grounds were introduced in California and Iowa in 1970; the approach was embraced at the same time in the initial version of the Uniform Marriage and Divorce Act. Category (5) includes the so-called "Enoch Arden laws."

When a divorce ground is premised on a period of separation, the issue arises as to whether the intent to terminate the marriage must coincide with the time specified for the separation. For example, in Sinha v. Sinha, 526 A.2d 765 (Pa. 1987), the state's statute required a three-year period of separation to dissolve the marriage and the issue before the court was whether the statute required an intent to dissolve the marriage prior to the three-year period. The husband and wife had been married in India, and then the husband came to America seeking an advanced degree. Even though the husband and wife corresponded regularly, the husband filed for divorce in 1979 but voluntarily dismissed the petition. In 1980, he filed for a divorce a second time on the ground that the couple had lived separate and apart for three years and the marriage was irretrievably broken. The court refused to allow the divorce based on physical separation alone, holding that at least one of the parties must have the intent to dissolve the marriage and communicate that intent to the other spouse prior to the commencement of the three-year period. Although states today typically requires separation of six months to a year, some states still require the couple to separate for three years. *See, e.g.*, TEX. FAM. CODE ANN. § 6.006 (2015); *Grounds for Divorce, 50 State Statutory Surveys: Family Law: Divorce And Dissolution*, 0080 SURVEYS 9 (West 2007).

UNIFORM MARRIAGE AND DIVORCE ACT (1973)

§ 302. [Dissolution of Marriage; Legal Separation]

(a) The [ ] court shall enter a decree of dissolution of marriage if: . . .

(2) the court finds that the marriage is irretrievably broken, if the finding is supported by evidence that (i) the parties have lived separate and apart for a period of more than 180 days next preceding the commencement of the proceeding, or (ii) there is serious marital discord adversely affecting the attitude of one or both of the parties toward the marriage;

(3) the court finds that the conciliation provisions of Section 305 either do not apply or have been met;

(4) to the extent it has jurisdiction to do so, the court has considered, approved, or provided for child custody, the support of any child entitled to support, the maintenance of either spouse, and the disposition of property; or has provided for a separate, later hearing to complete these matters.

(b) If a party requests a decree of legal separation rather than a decree of dissolution of marriage, the court shall grant the decree in that form unless the other party objects.

§ 305. [Irretrievable Breakdown]

(a) If both of the parties by petition or otherwise have stated under oath or affirmation that the marriage is irretrievably broken, or one of the parties has so stated and the other has not denied it, the court, after hearing, shall make a finding whether the marriage is irretrievably broken.

(b) If one of the parties has denied under oath or affirmation that the marriage is irretrievably broken, the court shall consider all relevant factors, including the circumstances that gave rise to filing the petition and the prospect of reconciliation, and shall:

(1) make a finding whether the marriage is irretrievably broken; or

(2) continue the matter for further hearing not fewer than 30 nor more than 60 days later, or as soon thereafter as the matter may be reached on the court's calendar, and may suggest to the parties that they seek counseling. The court, at the request of either party shall, or on its own motion may, order a conciliation conference. At the adjourned hearing the court shall make a finding whether the marriage is irretrievably broken.

(c) A finding of irretrievable breakdown is a determination that there is no reasonable prospect of reconciliation.

NOTES

This version of section 302 was contained in the UNIFORM MARRIAGE AND DIVORCE ACT (UMDA) as approved by the American Bar Association (ABA) House of Delegates in February, 1974. The first version promulgated in 1970 did not contain a specific period of separation or allow a showing of "serious marital discord." Between the original promulgation of the UMDA and the changes just mentioned, the Family Law Section of the ABA proposed a revised version of the UMDA which would have provided for one year of separation or "serious marital misconduct" affecting the physical or mental health of the petitioner. For the full text of the proposed revised statute, *see* 7 FAM. L.Q. 135 (1973). Ironically, it is the less restrictive early version of the UMDA that has served widely as a model for state legislation on the subject.

CALIFORNIA FAMILY CODE (2016)

§ 2310. Grounds for dissolution or legal separation

Dissolution of the marriage or legal separation of the parties may be based on either of the following grounds, which shall be pleaded generally:

(a) Irreconcilable differences, which have caused the irremediable breakdown of the marriage.

(b) Permanent legal incapacity to make decisions.

§ 2311. Irreconcilable differences defined

Irreconcilable differences are those grounds which are determined by the court to be substantial reasons for not continuing the marriage and which make it appear that the marriage should be dissolved.

Palermo v. Palermo

Supreme Court of New York, 2011
35 Misc.3d 1211(A)

■ DOLLINGER, JUSTICE.

In this matter, a husband seeks to dismiss his wife's claim for a divorce based on an irretrievable breakdown of their marriage, even though he has not lived with her for almost a decade. The facts require an examination as to whether a party's sworn allegation of an irretrievable breakdown for a period in excess of six months is a sufficient basis for establishing one of the two indispensable requirements for a divorce under DRL § 170(7).

The couple were married in 1977. In September 2000, the wife moved out of the marital residence. In 2001, the wife commenced a divorce action against the husband on grounds of cruel and inhuman treatment and a jury returned a verdict of no cause for action. In February 2011, the wife again filed a verified complaint, this time on the grounds that the marital relationship had broken down for a period in excess of six months. The husband answered, denying the allegations, and asserting an affirmative defense that the couple had lived separate and apart for a period of at least 10 years. The husband then moved to dismiss the wife's complaint, arguing that the statute of limitations had expired on her claims, that they were barred by *res judicata,* and that the complaint failed to state a cause of action. The wife cross-moved to replead the claim under DRL § 170(7) to include the specific allegation that the marriage was irretrievably broken for a period of greater than six months. This court needs to decide whether the verified statement of "irretrievable breakdown" of a marriage, in itself, without a trial, provides the necessary predicate to granting a divorce under the Domestic Relations Law.

Since 1966 when New York repealed its "adultery-only" divorce laws, the state has permitted divorce on the basis of fault (adultery, abandonment, cruel and inhuman treatment, and/or extended incarceration), and no-fault (living apart pursuant to either an agreement or judgment of separation). *Gleason v. Gleason,* 26 N.Y.2d 28, 308 N.Y.S.2d 347, 256 N.E.2d 513 (1970); DRL § 170. By enacting the no-fault provision, the legislature recognized "that it is socially and morally undesirable to compel a couple whose marriage is dead to remain subject to its bond." *Gleason* at 39, 308 N.Y.S.2d 347, 256 N.E.2d 513. *See also Covington v. Walker,* 3 N.Y.3d 287, 290, 786 N.Y.S.2d 409, 819 N.E.2d 1025 (2004) ("dead marriages . . . should be terminated for the mutual protection and well being of the parties and, in most instances, their children;" *quoting* 1966 Report of the Joint Leg. Comm. on Matrimonial and Family Laws); *Christian v. Christian,* 42 N.Y.2d 63, 69, 396 N.Y.S.2d 817, 365 N.E.2d 849 (1977) (the legislature intended the no-fault provisions to allow couples "to extricate themselves from a perpetual state of marital limbo); *Scully v. Haar,* 67 A.D.3d 1331, 1336, 889

N.Y.S.2d 806 (4th Dep't 2009). The *Gleason* decision is important to the current question because it recognizes that the state legislature could fashion divorce remedies based on both parties consent to end their marriage without further testimony or evidence as to their private intentions.

In this case, the question is whether the state legislature provided the same relief-divorce-based on the intentions of just one of the two partners to the marriage, without any inquiry into their intent or conduct by enacting DRL § 170(7). In 2010, the legislature took the next step and sought to bring New York's divorce laws into the 21st Century by enacting a new no-fault provision which lessened the essential proof necessary to provide the grounds for a divorce. Instead of requiring couples to wait a year after they had expressed their "mutual contemporaneous intent" that their marriage was dead (as required by subdivisions 5 and 6 of Section 170) the legislature:

(a) removed the objective waiting period of one year and the need for a writing signed by both parties; and,

(b) permitted one party to be granted the divorce immediately upon a sworn declaration that the marriage was "irretrievably broken for a period in excess of six months." DRL § 170(7).

Read in this fashion, the legislature no longer requires evidence of the "mutual contemporaneous intention" as required by the two previous no-fault grounds. Under DRL § 170(7), one partner alone can declare the marriage is "dead" if sworn to under oath, in accordance with the statutory language.

While a strict reading of the statute suggests that the declaration alone provides the basis for a divorce, the husband in this case argues that something more is required. The husband contends that he is entitled to a trial on this provision. His argument relies on *Strack v. Strack,* 31 Misc.3d 258, 916 N.Y.S.2d 759 (Sup.Ct. Essex Cty. 2011). Citing the Domestic Relations Law provision for a right to trial by jury, the court concluded that:

> [T]he legislature failed to include anything in the Domestic Relations Law § 170(7) to suggest that the grounds contained therein are exempt from this right to trial. Had it intended to abolish the right to a trial for the grounds contained in the Domestic Relations Law, it would explicitly have done so.

Id. at 263, 916 N.Y.S.2d 759. The court concluded that the question of whether a breakdown is irretrievable is a question of fact to be determined at trial.

In view of the *Strack* decision, there is an apparent collision of the no-fault entitlement under DRL § 170(7), and the trial right under DRL § 173. This court must resolve the statutory contradiction. In doing so, the primary consideration is to ascertain the history and object of the enactment, in light of the facts which were found by the legislature to prompt its enactment. *Malkin v. Wilkins,* 22 A.D.2d 497, 257 N.Y.S.2d 288 (4th Dep't 1965).This court must also consider "the mischief sought to be remedied by the new legislation, and . . . should construe the act in question so as to suppress the evil and advance the remedy." McKinney's Statutes § 95. *See also, Lincoln First Bank v. Rupert,* 60 A.D.2d 193, 400 N.Y.S.2d 618 (4th Dep't 1977) *(the evils the present act was intended to meet must be considered).*[4] The "evil" posed by the lack of a no-fault provision based on one party's sworn declaration was discussed forty years ago by the court of Appeals in *Gleason*: the need for the courts, in a fault-based divorce environment, to probe the inner-life of a marriage to objectively determine its viability. The legislative history of New York's newest no-fault statute demonstrates the legislature's recognition of this "evil" and the proposed "remedy." It is apparent that the legislature intended to provide estranged couples a simple and incontestable basis for ending their marriage, and avoid the squabbling over issues that flow from the other objective grounds in DRL § 170. The Senate sponsor's memorandum contains the following: They [couples] are forced to invent false justifications to legally dissolve their marriages. False accusations and the necessity to hold one partner at fault often result in conflict within the family. The conflict is harmful to the partners and destructive to the emotional well being of children. Prolonging the divorce process adds additional stress to an already difficult situation.

> This legislation enables parties to legally end a marriage which is, in reality, already over and cannot be salvaged. Its intent is to lessen the disputes that often arises between the parties and to mitigate the potential harm to them and their children caused by the current process. Because a resolution of all the major issues must be reached before a divorce judgment is granted, this legislation safeguards the parties' rights and economic interests.

Sponsor's Memorandum to S.3980A, enacted into law as Chapter 384 of the Laws of 2010.

In view of this intent, this court declines to follow the logic or holding of *Strack.* DRL § 173 states that there is a right to trial by jury "of the grounds for granting the divorce." *See Mandel v. Mandel,* 109 Misc.2d 1, 439 N.Y.S.2d 576 (Sup.Ct. Queens Cty.1981). Under DRL § 170(7), the grounds cannot be disputed. Either a party swears the marriage is irretrievably broken or they do not. The grounds are established by the oath; there is no legislative requirement of a judicial finding on the reliability or veracity of the oath. While the right to trial set forth in DRL § 173 could be read to require a trial solely on the question of whether the party has properly sworn to the irretrievable breakdown of their marriage, it leads to a counterproductive, if not absurd, result: a jury trial on the question of whether the party has properly sworn to the irretrievable breakdown, a fact which is readily apparent to the court upon a review of the face of the pleadings. This court declines to interpret these two statutes in such a fashion when to do so creates the exact problem that DRL § 170(7) was designed to avoid.

The *Strack* court, obviously looking ahead to the proof problems that such a trial might encompass, acknowledges the substantial uncertainty that its ruling creates. The court states that "whether a marriage is irretrievable need not necessarily be viewed by both parties." *Strack* at 263, 916 N.Y.S.2d 759. The court asserts that the marriage may still be broken down, "even though one of the parties continues to believe that the breakdown is not irretrievable and/or that there is still some possibility of reconciliation." *Id.* The recitation of the purpose of the hearing underscores the uncertainty. The reference "viewed by both parties" clearly suggests that both parties can, at the required trial, testify on their subjective "views" of whether the marriage is so broken as to be irretrievable. This raises a myriad of questions. How far "broken" does the marriage have to be to be irretrievable? What proof is necessary? Is the court empowered to decide that a marriage can be repaired even if one party states, under oath, that it is their "view" that the marriage can not be repaired? Does the court, in deciding whether a marriage is irretrievable, decide the sincerity—or veracity—of a spouse who states, under oath, that he or she no longer wants to be married? Is any court prepared to state: "the court finds that even though one party says that they want to be divorced, I find that the marriage is not broken?" How will the court determine whether a spouse's belief that marriage is broken is justified? What facts are necessary to establish that a spouse has a good faith belief that the marriage is broken? Is reconciliation a factor? What proof is required to show some possibility of reconciliation? How significant does the "possibility of reconciliation" have to be for the court to conclude that it is significant enough to decline to grant the divorce? Is the court required to find that one spouse is telling the truth about the "possibility of reconciliation" while making the corollary decision that the other is not being truthful when he or she says that reconciliation is not possible?

If this litany of evidentiary complications is allowed to arise, one conclusion is readily apparent: the evil that this legislation was designed to eliminate-public trials on fault-will continue into future divorce cases. By merely permitting one party in a divorce to inquire about a spouse's "belief" about their marriage or their "views" of "the possibility of reconciliation," the New York courts will be plunged into an endless evaluation of people's beliefs and inner most perceptions of their marriages because, as the court in *Strack* even admitted, there are no objective specific standards for evaluating the "possibility of reconciliation." If the *Strack* decision governs future divorce litigation, the courts will be invading, in an incalculable manner, the inner privacy of married couples. These issues surely were not within the scope of the legislature's intentions when the professed target of this new law was to reduce inner family turmoil, and the gut-wrenching pain of trials under the fault provisions of DRL § 170. The legislature never intended to have these personal issues probed by judges or juries and this court declines to read the trial right under DRL § 173 to negate the legislature's design. Having observed a contortion of litigants testify, and often exaggerate the facts underlying the grievances against their spouses, this court will not unleash a new waive of inquiry by opposing litigants, their attorneys, and judges, against the privacy of couples seeking to end their marriage without acrimony and discord. This court will not read the new law in such a fashion to let a jury decide whether a spouse is being truthful when asked about reconciling a marriage that they have already sworn under oath is irretrievably broken.

The wisdom of the state legislature's determination to permit divorce on the subjective sworn testimony of one of the marriages partners is demonstrated by an examination of our sister states who have experimented with no-fault based on objective facts adduced at a hearing. These decisions indicate that while other state legislatures have attempted to permit couples to leave their personal lives behind when seeking a divorce, the need for an objective standard-presented during hearings and trials-ushers the courts into the inner most privacy of couples, whose lives are many times already marred by conflict and turmoil. In Massachusetts, for example, the legislature permits divorce upon "irretrievable breakdown of the marriage," but added two restrictions, neither of which are found in New York's statute. First, unlike New York, the "irretrievable breakdown" must exist for six months from the filing of the complaint seeking divorce. (This "six month" objective period is dated from the complaint. In New York, the six months can precede the filing of the complaint and one party can attest to the existence of the six month period.) Second, the Massachusetts statute requires that a court hold a hearing to determine if there has been a continuous "irretrievable breakdown" of the marriage for the six months since the date of the filing of the complaint. Massachusetts courts have grappled with the amount of proof necessary to establish an "irretrievable breakdown" and have sought to avoid probing into the private of couples whose marriages have, at least in one partner's eyes, failed. In *Caffyn v. Caffyn,* 441 Mass. 487, 806 N.E.2d 415 (Ma.2004), the state's highest court, held that its no-fault statute did not "contain a requirement that a spouse plead or enumerate any objective factors that would lead a court to the conclusion that a marriage is irretrievably broken." *Id.* at 421. The court added that:

> [T]he legislature implicitly recognized that the parties to a marriage should be able to make personal and unavoidably subjective decisions about marriage and divorce free from the overwhelming state control.

Id. at 422. Thus, in Massachusetts, even though the state legislature required a hearing on the existence of irretrievable breakdown, the courts have acknowledged that "subjective declarations" of the breakdown are sufficient to establish grounds and those subjective marital decisions need not be "objectively documented, tested and proven." *Id.* The court in *Caffyn* cited a California court's determination that "the prima facie case for dissolution should be satisfied by the declaration of petitioner that he or she sincerely believes that the marriage is irreparably broken down." *Id.*

The Massachusetts example is echoed in other states. Even though states claim to be "no-fault" jurisdictions, the legislatures have, in almost all cases, like Massachusetts, added requirements that the courts make findings that irreconcilable differences exist or an irretrievable breakdown has occurred before a divorce can be granted. Under these mandatory trial statutes, the state courts are caught in an convoluted conundrum—they must find either a subjective or objective basis that these predicates occur, but with little statutory definition or guidance, they tend to shy away from invading intimate marriage issues. California's legislature requires a finding of "irreconcilable differences" but the courts have acknowledged that a "subjective" judgment by either partner can be sufficient to support the finding. *See, In re Marriage of Walton,* 28 Cal.App.3d 108, 117, 104 Cal.Rptr. 472 (1972), *quoting In re Marriage of McKim,* 6 Cal.3d 673, 100 Cal.Rptr. 140, 493 P.2d 868 (1971) (in deciding whether evidence supports findings "that irreconcilable differences do exist and that the marriage has broken down irremediably and should be dissolved," the court must necessarily "depend to a considerable extent upon the subjective state of mind of the parties"). Connecticut also requires a "finding" by the court that the marriage has "broken down irretrievably" but the legislature never defined "irretrievably" and the courts have considered subjective evidence from a single party effective. As one Connecticut court noted, there need not be objective guidelines for determining that a marriage is irretrievably broken:

> We decline . . . to circumscribe this delicate process of fact-finding by imposing the constraint of guidelines on an inquiry that is necessarily individualized and particularized . . .
>
> *Joy v. Joy,* 178 Conn. 254, 423 A.2d 895 (App.Ct.Conn.1979), *quoted in Eversman v. Eversman,* 4 Conn.App. 611, 496 A.2d 210, 212 (App.Ct.Conn.1985). *See also Mattson v. Mattson,* 376 A.2d 473, 475 (Me.1977) (The term "irreconcilable marital differences" is one that necessarily lacks precision and should not be circumscribed by a strict definition); Matter of the Marriage of Dunn, 13 Or.App. 497, 511 P.2d 427 (1973) (irreconcilable within Oregon law need not necessarily be so viewed by both parties, it may, under certain circumstances, be unilaterally viewed as well).In this court's view, New York's statute, permits the divorce solely on the basis of the sworn statement without the need for a "finding," extending no-fault beyond that permitted in other states, even though these states

> have invoked the "irretrievable breakdown" standard. In most cases, these other states require the courts to find, as an objective fact, that the marriage is "irretrievably broken down." Pennsylvania, for example, permits a divorce upon the grounds of "irretrievably broken," but the legislature permits the opposing party to obtain a hearing if they deny that allegation and allege that counseling may repair the marriage. *Wetzel v. Heiney,* 17 A3d 405 (Superior Ct. Pa.2011), *citing* 23 Pa.C.S. § 3301(d); *see also* 23 Pa. Con. Stat. § 3103 (2011) (definition of irretrievable breakdown as "estrangement due to marital difficulties with no reasonable prospect of reconciliation"). Other state legislatures have imposed, by express statutory language, this same requirement that the court find, as a matter of law and fact, that a marriage is irretrievably broken before a judgment of divorce can be granted. *Szramkowski v. Szramkowski,* 2010 Mo.App. LEXIS 784 (Ct.App.Mo.2010) (Missouri statute requires court to find that a marriage is irretrievably broken before divorce is granted), *citing* Mo.Rev.Stat. § 452.305.1(2); *Bodine v. Bodine,* 2010 WL 2836995, 2010 Ariz.App. Unpub. LEXIS 896 (Ct.App.Ar.2010) (divorce for irretrievable breakdown goes forward if one party swears to it under oath and the other does not deny, but, if denied, then a hearing and specific finding required, *citing* A.R.S. § 25–316.A); *Robins v. Robins,* 2010 WL 4643835, 2010 Wash.App. LEXIS 2567 (Ct.App.Wa.2010) (if the parties agree that marriage is irretrievably broken, then divorce goes forward, but if no agreement, then court must find irretrievable breakdown to grant divorce, *citing* RCW 26.09.30(3)(a)(c); *Wagner v. Wagner,* 275 Neb. 693, 749 N.W.2d 137 (Neb.2008) (Nebraska statute requires the court, after a hearing, to make a finding that the marriage is irretrievably broken), *citing* Neb.Rev.Stat. § 42–361(1); *see also Butler v. Butler,* 642 N.W.2d 646 (Ct.App.Wisc.2002) (court required to find irretrievable breakdown and "no prospect for reconciliation" to justify divorce under Wisc. Stat. § 767.12[2][b]); *Cowsert v. Cowsert,* 78 Mich.App. 129, 259 N.W.2d 393 (Mich.App.Ct.1977) because the legislature called for evidence to be tried in open court, no-fault divorce in Michigan is not automatic and requires a hearing).

Further evidence of the wisdom of New York's legislative purpose is found in Georgia, where its legislature simply permitted divorce upon "irretrievable differences." The legislature did not define that term. The state's highest court then judicially defined "irretrievably broken" as a marriage "where either or both parties are unable or refuse to cohabit and there are no prospects for a reconciliation." *McCoy v. McCoy,* 281 Ga. 604, 642 S.E.2d 18 (Ga.2007), citing *Harwell v. Harwell,* 233 Ga. 89, 209 S.E.2d 625 (1974) and OGCA § 19–5–3(13). The court in *Harwell* added the "no prospects for reconciliation" verbiage, even though it was not included in the statute. OGCA § 19–5–3(13). Later, in *McCoy* the court moved away from the decision in *Harwell*. In *McCoy,* the court held that the mere "prospects for reconciliation" are not sufficient to deny a divorce and added that if the legislature wanted to make "irretrievable breakdown" consensual, the legislature would have required that the parties agree the marriage was irretrievable broken. In essence, under current Georgia law (post *McCoy*), the allegation of "irretrievable breakdown"—without both parties admitting that reconciliation is unlikely—is sufficient for granting a divorce. The Georgia history of interpreting its "irretrievable breakdown" statute illustrates the wisdom of the New York legislature and a cautions New York courts considering a requirement that the subjective declaration of irretrievable breakdown should be subject to the trial requirements of DRL § 173. Any judicial finding of irretrievable breakdown requires judicial inquiry into a myriad of personal and private issues regarding the intimacy of a married couple. These determinations are inherently subjective and intensely personal. As Georgia's judiciary found, the courts are not equipped to venture into the depths of married life and objectify what is intensely personal.

New York's legislature, faced with a choice between "some fault" and no-fault as the grounds for granting a divorce, chose no-fault and forever eliminated the prospects that a partner to a marriage would be required to point a finger at the other during a trial and say "you are at fault for our marriage's demise." In this case, the court of Appeals has the final word. The simple fact is that the larger public interest demonstrated by the present legislation requires that there be a legal termination of dead marriages. *Gleason v. Gleason,* 26 N.Y.2d 28, 308 N.Y.S.2d 347, 256 N.E.2d 513 (1970). This court finds that the legislature transformed the Court of Appeals's logic in *Gleason* into the public policy and law of this state in enacting DRL § 170(7).

This opinion constitutes the decision of the court and the parties will submit an order on consent and attach this decision to it.

NOTES

Just as courts often had a difficult time in defining adultery, cruelty and abandonment, the no-fault "incompatibility" ground offered similar perplexities. One of the earliest no-fault grounds introduced in this country, incompatibility, failed to become the majority no-fault ground. The lack of definition, as well as guidelines for its application, no doubt contributed to its lack of acceptance.

A Right to Remain Married? Definitional difficulties are compounded by the reluctance of parties to accede to a system that allows one party to end the marriage when the other thinks the couple is compatible and is willing to work to keep the marriage intact. *See, e.g.,* Schachter v. Schachter, 726 N.E.2d 224 (Ill. Ct. App. 1999), *cert. denied*, 526 U.S. 1005 (1999), where former husband argued that the no-fault ground deprived him of the liberty interest of sustaining his marriage and caring for his children, and that the state divided his property and income without a proper hearing to establish a reason for doing so.

An Economic Calamity for Women? Concerns also arose that "easy divorce" disproportionately impacted women, who would be unable to provide for their children after divorce or would be more likely to live in poverty. An oft-cited (and oft-criticized) study by Dr. Lenore Weitzman in 1985 estimated that women experienced a 73% reduction in their standard of living after divorce, compared to a 42% reduction for divorced men. *See* LENORE WEITZMAN, THE DIVORCE REVOLUTION (1985). Later studies have confirmed the disparity in economic well-being after divorce, but disputed the degree of decline. Not surprisingly, some women's groups opposed New York's addition of a unilateral no-fault divorce ground for economic reasons. *See* Marcia Pappas, *Divorce New York Style*, THE NEW YORK TIMES, February 19, 2006 *available at* http://www.nytimes.com/2006/02/19/opinion/nyregion opinions/19LIpappas.html ("The problem with unilateral no-fault divorce is that it hurts women by removing the incentive for the moneyed spouse (who is usually the husband) to make a settlement. Instead of negotiating with a dependent spouse—whose only leverage for avoiding an impoverished post-divorce life for herself and her children may be her assent, or lack of it, to divorce—the husband can simply go to court and obtain an uncontested divorce.").

Concerns about the economic fall-out of divorce for women and children are not without basis. For example, the report on Marital Events from the United States Census Bureau found that in 2009, "[w]omen who divorced in the past 12 months were more likely to receive public assistance than recently divorced men (23 percent versus 15 percent, respectively) . . . and reported less income . . . (27 percent of [divorced] women . . . compared with 17 percent of recently divorced men.) Similarly, women who divorced in the past 12 months were more likely than recently divorced men to be in poverty (22 percent compared with 11 percent, respectively)." U.S. DEP'T OF COMMERCE, BUREAU OF THE CENSUS, ACS–13 10, MARITAL EVENTS OF AMERICANS: 2009 (2011).

Notwithstanding the impact on women, studies show that women file for divorce more often than men. *See, e.g.*, Margaret F. Brinig and Douglas W. Allen, *"These Boots Are Made for Walking:" Why Most Divorce Filers Are Women*, 2 AM. L. & ECON. REV. 126, 126–27 (2000) (suggesting that women seek divorce because they are not emotionally satisfied).

Concerns About Children. Resistance to easy divorce also reflects growing social science evidence that divorce often harms children. *See* JUDITH S. WALLERSTEIN ET AL., THE UNEXPECTED LEGACY OF DIVORCE: A 25 YEAR LANDMARK STUDY (2000); ELIZABETH MARQUARDT, BETWEEN TWO WORLDS: THE INNER LIVES OF CHILDREN AND DIVORCE (2005). A burgeoning literature examines whether outcomes for children of divorce are different than for children raised in intact families. *See* Lynn D. Wardle, *The Fall of Marital Family Stability and the Rise of Juvenile Delinquency*, 10 J. L. & FAM. STUD. 83 (2007). *See also* Robin Fretwell Wilson, *Evaluating Marriage: Does Marriage Matter to the Nurturing of Children*, 42 SAN DIEGO L. REV. 847, 851 n.14 (2005) (discussing two studies that conclude "that marriage matters to how children thrive and to the extent to which their parents are willing to invest in them").

Undercutting Reconciliation and Marriage. Other critiques of no-fault divorce have also developed. Some scholars argue that quick and easy divorce hinders any early reconciliation. *See, e.g.*, William J. Doherty et. al., *Interest in Marital Reconciliation Among Divorcing Parents*, 49 FAM. CT. REV. 313, 320 (2011) (conducting a meta-analysis of divorcing spouses' views on reconciliation and concluding that "divorce professionals may have given up on marital reconciliation prematurely in the 1970s"). Additionally, some commentators assert that no-fault divorce devalued marriage and family. *See* Raymond C. O'Brien, *The Reawakening of Marriage*, 102 W. VA. L. REV. 339 (1999); Patrick F. Fagan, et al., *Marriage Still the Safest Place for Women and Children*, Heritage Found. Backgrounder (The Heritage Found., D.C.), March, 9, 2004, at 1–4, *available at*: http://www.heritage.org/Research/Family/bg1732.cfm; W. BRADFORD WILCOX, WHY MARRIAGE MATTERS: THIRTY CONCLUSIONS FROM THE SOCIAL SCIENCES (2011).

Recent reforms in a pair of states show continued experimentation by the states with no-fault divorce. In 2007, New Jersey's governor signed into law a bill that changed immediately the waiting period for a no-fault divorce from 18 months to 6 months in cases of irreconcilable differences. N.J. STAT. ANN. § 2A:34–2 (2016). The same year, Louisiana lengthened the waiting period for no-fault divorce from 6 months to one year when couples have children, but otherwise allowed childless couples to divorce more quickly—a two-track system that essentially follows an approach taken in other countries. LA. CIV. CODE ANN. art. 103.1 (2015). *See also* VA. CODE ANN. § 20–91(9) (2016). Louisiana's law provided prompter exits in instances of domestic violence or child abuse—responding in part to the hardships that result when divorce is too hard to obtain.

C. THE JURISDICTIONAL JUMBLE

This chapter has explored substantive differences in how states regulate marriage and divorce. These substantive differences give rise to another set of thorny jurisdictional and procedural questions, such as: When does a state have jurisdiction to grant a divorce? If one state issues a divorce decree, must every other state recognize that decree as valid, even if another state's divorce laws are stricter? Must both spouses appear at the divorce proceeding in order for a court to grant a divorce or divide property and award alimony? These questions continue to be salient as Americans become increasingly mobile and divorce remains a staple of modern society.

1. QUALIFYING DOMESTIC DIVORCE DECREES FOR FULL FAITH AND CREDIT: THE SIGNIFICANCE OF DOMICILE

Traditionally, a court had jurisdiction to hear a divorce action only if the petitioner was domiciled in that state. Under English common law, a married woman lacked capacity to bring suit in her own name and she took her husband's domicile—meaning that husbands could generally control where couples were domiciled and therefore what state could hear divorce actions. The Married Women's Property Acts helped to equalize this control by granting married women the power to sue and to obtain separate domicils. Consequently, either spouse could move from the state of the marital home and seek divorce in another state.

From roughly the beginning of the 20th century, the rules about divorce jurisdiction were a mixture of full faith and comity. An overarching question was whether an *ex parte* divorce decree was entitled to the Full Faith and Credit required by Article IV, Section 1 of the U.S. Constitution. The United States Supreme Court addressed this question in two successive cases involving the same underlying facts. The first case, *Williams v. North Carolina (I)*, addresses when a state is required to give Full Faith and Credit to a divorce decree issued in another state.

Williams v. North Carolina (I)

Supreme Court of the United States, 1942
317 U.S. 287

■ DOUGLAS, JUSTICE.

Petitioners were tried and convicted of bigamous cohabitation under § 4342 of the North Carolina Code, 1939, and each was sentenced for a term of years to a state prison. The judgment of conviction was affirmed by the Supreme Court of North Carolina. 220 N.C. 445, 17 S.E.2d 769. The case is here on certiorari.

Petitioner Williams was married to Carrie Wyke in 1916 in North Carolina and lived with her there until May, 1940. Petitioner Hendrix was married to Thomas Hendrix in 1920 in North Carolina and lived with him there until May, 1940. At that time petitioners went to Las Vegas, Nevada and on June 26, 1940, each filed a divorce action in the Nevada court. The defendants in those divorce actions entered no appearance nor were they served with process in Nevada. In the case of defendant Thomas Hendrix service by publication was had by publication of the summons in a Las Vegas newspaper and by mailing a copy of the summons and complaint to his last post office address. In the case of defendant Carrie Williams a North Carolina sheriff delivered to her in North Carolina a copy of the summons and complaint. A decree of divorce was granted petitioner Williams by the Nevada court on August 26, 1940, on the grounds of extreme cruelty, the court finding that "the plaintiff has been and now is a bona fide and continuous resident of the County of Clark, State of Nevada, and had been such resident for more than six weeks immediately preceding the commencement of this action in the manner prescribed by law." The Nevada court granted petitioner Hendrix a divorce on October 4, 1940, on the grounds of willful neglect and extreme cruelty and made the same finding as to this petitioner's bona fide residence in Nevada as it made in the case of Williams. Petitioners were married to each other in Nevada on October 4, 1940. Thereafter they returned to North Carolina where they lived together until the indictment was returned. Petitioners pleaded not guilty and offered in evidence exemplified copies of the Nevada proceedings, contending that the divorce decrees and the Nevada marriage were valid in North Carolina as well as in Nevada.... [The trial court convicted the petitioners.] The Supreme Court of North Carolina in affirming the judgment held that North Carolina was not required to recognize the Nevada decrees under the full faith and credit clause of the Constitution (Art. IV, § 1) by reason of Haddock v. Haddock, 201 U.S. 562....

The *Haddock* case involved a suit for separation and alimony brought in New York by the wife on personal service of the husband. The husband pleaded in defense a divorce decree obtained by him in Connecticut where he had established a separate domicil. This Court held that New York, the matrimonial domicil where the wife still resided, need not give full faith and credit to the Connecticut decree, since it was obtained by the husband who wrongfully left his wife in the matrimonial domicil, service on her having been obtained by publication and she not having entered an appearance in the action. But we do not agree with the theory of the *Haddock* case that, so far as the marital status of the parties is concerned, a decree of divorce granted under such circumstances by one state need not be given full faith and credit in another.

Article IV, § 1 of the Constitution not only directs that "Full Faith and Credit shall be given in each State to the public Acts, Records, and Judicial Proceedings of every other State" but also provides that "Congress may by general Laws prescribe the Manner in which such Acts, Records and Proceedings shall be proved, and the Effect thereof." Congress has exercised that power. By the Act of May 26, 1790, c. 11, 28 U.S.C. § 687, 28 U.S.C.A. § 687, Congress has provided that judgments "shall have such faith and credit given to them in every court within the United States as they have by law or usage in the courts of the State from which they are taken." Chief Justice Marshall stated in Hampton v. M'Connel, 3 Wheat. 234, 235, that "the judgment of a state court should have the same credit, validity, and effect, in every other court in the United States, which it had in the state where it was pronounced, and that whatever pleas would be good to a suit thereon in such state, and none others, could be pleaded in any other court in the United States." That view has survived substantially intact. Fauntleroy v. Lum, 210 U.S. 230.... [T]his Court has been reluctant to admit exceptions in case of *judgments* rendered by the courts of a sister state, since the "very purpose" of Art. IV, § 1 was "to alter the status of the several states as independent foreign sovereignties, each free to ignore obligations created under the laws or by the judicial proceedings of the others, and to make them integral parts of a single nation." ...

The historical view that a proceeding for a divorce was a proceeding in rem (2 Bishop, Marriage & Divorce, 4th Ed., § 164) was rejected by the

Haddock case. We likewise agree that it does not aid in the solution of the problem presented by this case to label these proceedings as proceedings in rem. Such a suit, however, is not a mere in personam action. Domicil of the plaintiff, immaterial to jurisdiction in a personal action, is recognized in the *Haddock* case and elsewhere (Beale, Conflict of Laws, § 110.1) as essential in order to give the court jurisdiction which will entitle the divorce decree to extraterritorial effect, at least when the defendant has neither been personally served nor entered an appearance. . . . [T]he decrees in this case like other divorce decrees are more than in personam judgments. They involve the marital status of the parties. Domicil creates a relationship to the state which is adequate for numerous exercises of state power. . . . Each state as a sovereign has a rightful and legitimate concern in the marital status of persons domiciled within its borders. The marriage relation creates problems of large social importance. Protection of offspring, property interests, and the enforcement of marital responsibilities are but a few of commanding problems in the field of domestic relations with which the state must deal. Thus it is plain that each state by virtue of its command over its domiciliaries and its large interest in the institution of marriage can alter within its own borders the marriage status of the spouse domiciled there, even though the other spouse is absent. There is no constitutional barrier if the form and nature of the substituted service (*see* Milliken v. Meyer, supra, 311 U.S. at page 463) meet the requirements of due process. . . . It therefore follows that, if the Nevada decrees are taken at their full face value (as they must be on the phase of the case with which we are presently concerned), they were wholly effective to change in that state the marital status of the petitioners and each of the other spouses by the North Carolina marriages. Apart from the requirements of procedural due process (Atherton v. Atherton, supra, 181 U.S. at page 172) not challenged here by North Carolina, no reason based on the Federal Constitution has been advanced for the contrary conclusion. But the concession that the decrees were effective in Nevada makes more compelling the reasons for rejection of the theory and result of the *Haddock* case.

This Court stated in Atherton v. Atherton, supra, 181 U.S. at page 162, that "A husband without a wife, or a wife without a husband, is unknown to the law." But if one is lawfully divorced and remarried in Nevada and still married to the first spouse in North Carolina, an even more complicated and serious condition would be realized. We would then have what the Supreme Court of Illinois declared to be the "most perplexing and distressing complication in the domestic relations of many citizens in the different states." Dunham v. Dunham, 162 Ill. 589, 607, 44 N.E. 841, 847. Under the circumstances of this case, a man would have two wives, a wife two husbands. The reality of a sentence to prison proves that that is no mere play on words. Each would be a bigamist for living in one state with the only one with whom the other state would permit him lawfully to live. Children of the second marriage would be bastards in one state but legitimate in the other. And all that would flow from the legalistic notion that where one spouse is wrongfully deserted he retains power over the matrimonial domicil so that the domicil of the other spouse follows him wherever he may go, while if he is to blame, he retains no such power. . . .

Moreover, so far as state power is concerned no distinction between a matrimonial domicil and a domicil later acquired has been suggested or is apparent. See Mr. Justice Holmes dissenting, Haddock v. Haddock, supra, 201 U.S. at page 631; Goodrich, *Matrimonial Domicile*, 27 Yale L.Journ. 49. It is one thing to say as a matter of state law that jurisdiction to grant a divorce from an absent spouse should depend on whether by consent or by conduct the latter has subjected his interest in the marriage status to the law of the separate domicil acquired by the other spouse. Beale, Conflict of Laws, § 113.11; Restatement [First], Conflict of Laws, § 113. But where a state adopts, as it has the power to do, a less strict rule, it is quite another thing to say that its decrees affecting the marital status of its domiciliaries are not entitled to full faith and credit in sister states. Certainly if decrees of a state altering the marital status of its domiciliaries are not valid throughout the Union even though the requirements of procedural due process are wholly met, a rule would be fostered which could not help but bring "considerable disaster to innocent persons" and "bastardize children hitherto supposed to be the offspring of lawful marriage," (Mr. Justice Holmes dissenting in Haddock v. Haddock, supra, 201 U.S. at page 628), or else encourage collusive divorces. Beale, Constitutional Protection of Decrees for Divorce, 19 Harv.L.Rev. 586, 596. These intensely practical considerations emphasize for us the essential function of the full faith and credit clause in substituting a command for the former principles of comity. . . .

It is objected, however, that if such divorce decrees must be given full faith and credit, a substantial dilution of the sovereignty of other states will be effected. For it is pointed out that under such a rule one state's policy of strict control over the institution of marriage could be thwarted by the decree of a more lax state. But such an objection goes to the application of the full faith and credit clause to many situations. It is an objection in varying degrees of intensity to the enforcement of a judgment of a sister state based on a cause of action which could not be enforced in the state of the forum. Mississippi's policy against gambling transactions was overriden in *Fauntleroy v. Lum*, supra, when a Missouri judgment based on such a Mississippi contract was enforced by this Court. Such is part of the price of our federal system.

This Court, of course, is the final arbiter when the question is raised as to what is a permissible limitation on the full faith and credit clause. . . . But the question for us is a limited one. In the first place, we repeat that in this case we must assume that petitioners had a bona fide domicil in Nevada, not that the Nevada domicil was a sham. We thus have no question on the present record whether a divorce decree granted by the courts of one state to a resident as distinguished from a domiciliary is entitled to full faith and credit in another state. Nor do we reach here the question as to the power of North Carolina to refuse full faith and credit to Nevada divorce decrees because, contrary to the findings of the Nevada court, North Carolina finds that no bona fide domicil was acquired in Nevada. In the second place, the question as to what is a permissible limitation on the full faith and credit clause does not involve a decision on our part as to which state policy on divorce is the more desirable one. It does not involve selection of a rule which will encourage on the one hand or discourage on the other the practice of divorce. That choice in the realm of morals and religion rests with the legislatures of the states. Our own views as to the marriage institution and the avenues of escape which some states have created are immaterial. It is a Constitution which we are expounding—a Constitution which in no small measure brings separate sovereign states into an integrated whole through the medium of the full faith and credit clause. Within the limits of her political power North Carolina may, of course, enforce her own policy regarding the marriage relation—an institution more basic in our civilization than any other. But society also has an interest in the avoidance of polygamous marriages (Loughran v. Loughran, 292 U.S. 216, 223) and in the protection of innocent offspring of marriages deemed legitimate in other jurisdictions. And other states have an equally legitimate concern in the status of persons domiciled there as respects the institution of marriage. So when a court of one state acting in accord with the requirements of procedural due process alters the marital status of one domiciled in that state by granting him a divorce from his absent spouse, we cannot say its decree should be excepted from the full faith and credit clause merely because its enforcement or recognition in another state would conflict with the policy of the latter. . . .

Haddock v. Haddock is overruled. The judgment is reversed and the cause is remanded to the Supreme Court of North Carolina for proceedings not inconsistent with this opinion.

[The concurring opinion of JUSTICE FRANKFURTER and the dissenting opinion of JUSTICE MURPHY have been omitted.]

NOTES

Divorce Jurisdiction. Under *Williams (I)*, if an issuing court has proper jurisdiction, states are required to give full faith and credit to the issuing court's divorce decree. The Supreme Court emphasized the importance of achieving finality in judgments, a common theme in full faith and credit jurisprudence, including divorce. The principle of finality is generally founded in equity and common sense. *See, e.g.,* Weston v. Jones, 603 N.W.2d 706 (S.D. 1999) (when husband actively participated in an Indian tribal court's divorce court, he was estopped from later attacking the judgment on jurisdictional grounds). The Supreme Court also underscored practical considerations in our inter-state system that demand finality in

Williams (I). Therefore, although divorce is clearly a state law issue, and states retain considerable discretion to develop laws consistent with their own social policies and conceptions of marriage, a state cannot deny the validity of a sister-state's divorce decree because it disagrees with the other state's divorce laws.

***Ex Parte* Divorce.** Divorce proceedings may be conducted *ex parte* (without one of the spouses appearing in the proceeding) if the court has jurisdiction and requirements for due process are satisfied. *Williams (I)* explains that the nature of divorce permits *ex parte* divorce decrees. Divorce involves a status, and the state's unquestioned interest in the marital status of its domiciliaries gives a state the power to alter the marital status of one of its domiciliaries, even in the absence of the other spouse.

Notice. In *Williams (I)*, the petitioners "notified" their respective spouses of their divorce petitions by publishing a notice in a Nevada newspaper. The Supreme Court assumed that this notice met due process requirements because North Carolina had not challenged due process. An elementary and fundamental requirement of due process in any proceeding which is to be accorded finality is notice that is reasonably calculated, under all the circumstances, to apprise interested parties of the pendency of the action and afford them an opportunity to present their objections. The individual states have enacted various procedures for giving notice to an absent spouse in an *ex parte* divorce action, including constructive service through publication. As pointed out in Mullane v. Central Hanover Bank & Trust Co., 339 U.S. 306, 315 (1950), however:

> It would be idle to pretend that publication alone, as prescribed here, is a reliable means of acquainting interested parties of the fact that their rights are before the courts. . . .

State courts continue to wrestle with the Due Process Clause and with United States Supreme Court decisions when considering divorce jurisdiction. For example, in Von Schack v. Von Schack, 893 A.2d 1004 (Me. 2006), the Maine Supreme Judicial Court, in a case of first impression in the state, held that a divorcing resident's out-of-state spouse need not have minimum contacts with Maine in order for the state to enter a divorce judgment. Nonetheless, the out-of-state spouse must have notice of the proceeding and the divorce judgment must not involve property, parental rights, or support issues. *See also* Humphreys v. Humphreys, 123 S.E. 554, 556 (Va. 1924) ("The public policy of the state of Virginia, as evidenced by its legislation with reference to divorces granted by its courts, and otherwise, favors the recognition, on the ground of comity, of the Nevada divorce as granted.").

The Superior Court of New Jersey, Appellate Division, held that e-mail notice could serve to show due diligence to notify the other spouse of a pending divorce action. The court vacated a default judgment of divorce when the husband had the wife's e-mail address but did not notify her of his divorce petition via the e-mail address which he had or any other means reasonably calculated to reach her. *See* Modan v. Modan, 742 A.2d 611 (N.J. Ct. App. 2000).

The Aftermath of *Williams (I)*. Following the Supreme Court's decision in *Williams (I)*, the State of North Carolina brought another action against the same parties, this time challenging whether the parties were validly domiciled in Nevada when Nevada granted the divorce decree.

Williams v. North Carolina (II)

Supreme Court of the United States, 1945
325 U.S. 226

■ FRANKFURTER, JUSTICE.

This case is here to review judgments of the Supreme Court of North Carolina, affirming convictions for bigamous cohabitation, assailed on the ground that full faith and credit, as required by the Constitution of the United States, was not accorded divorces decreed by one of the courts of Nevada. Williams v. North Carolina [I], 317 U.S. 287, decided an earlier aspect of the controversy. . . . The record then before us did not present the question whether North Carolina had the power "to refuse full faith and credit to Nevada divorce decrees because, contrary to the findings of the Nevada court, North Carolina finds that no bona fide domicil was acquired in Nevada." Williams v. North Carolina, supra, 317 U.S. at page 302. This is the precise issue which has emerged after retrial of the cause following our reversal. Its obvious importance brought the case here. . . .

The implications of the Full Faith and Credit Clause, Article IV, Section 1 of the Constitution, first received the sharp analysis of this Court in Thompson v. Whitman, 18 Wall. 457. Theretofore, uncritical notions about the scope of that Clause had been expressed in the early case of Mills v. Duryee, 7 Cranch 481. The "doctrine" of that case, as restated in another early case, was that "the judgment of a state court should have the same credit, validity, and effect in every other court in the United States, which it had in the state where it was pronounced." Hampton v. McConnel, 3 Wheat. 234, 235. This utterance, when put to the test, as it was in *Thompson v. Whitman*, supra, was found to be too loose. *Thompson v. Whitman* made it clear that the doctrine of *Mills v. Duryee* comes into operation only when, in the language of Kent, "the jurisdiction of the court in another state is not impeached, either as to the subject matter or the person." Only then is "the record of the judgment . . . entitled to full faith and credit." . . .

Under our system of law, judicial power to grant a divorce—jurisdiction, strictly speaking—is founded on domicil. Bell v. Bell, 181 U.S. 175; Andrews v. Andrews, 188 U.S. 14. The framers of the Constitution were familiar with this jurisdictional prerequisite, and since 1789 neither this Court nor any other court in the English-speaking world has questioned it. Domicil implies a nexus between person and place of such permanence as to control the creation of legal relations and responsibilities of the utmost significance. . . . Divorce, like marriage, is of concern not merely to the immediate parties. It affects personal rights of the deepest significance. It also touches basic interests of society. Since divorce, like marriage, creates a new status, every consideration of policy makes it desirable that the effect should be the same wherever the question arises.

It is one thing to reopen an issue that has been settled after appropriate opportunity to present their contentions has been afforded to all who had an interest in its adjudication. This applies also to jurisdictional questions. After a contest these cannot be relitigated as between the parties. Forsyth v. Hammond, 166 U.S. 506, 517; Chicago Life Ins. Co. v. Cherry, 244 U.S. 25, 30; Davis v. Davis, supra. But those not parties to a litigation ought not to be foreclosed by the interested actions of others; especially not a State which is concerned with the vindication of its own social policy and has no means, certainly no effective means, to protect that interest against the selfish action of those outside its borders. The State of domiciliary origin should not be bound by an unfounded, even if not collusive, recital in the record of a court of another State. As to the truth or existence of a fact, like that of domicil, upon which depends the power to exert judicial authority, a State not a party to the exertion of such judicial authority in another State but seriously affected by it has a right, when asserting its own unquestioned authority, to ascertain the truth or existence of that crucial fact. . . .[6]

All the world is not party to a divorce proceeding. What is true is that all the world need not be present before a court granting the decree and yet it must be respected by the other forty-seven States provided—and it is a big proviso—the conditions for the exercise of power by the divorce-decreeing court are validly established whenever that judgment is elsewhere called into question. In short, the decree of divorce is a conclusive adjudication of everything except the jurisdictional facts upon which it is founded, and domicil is a jurisdictional fact. To permit the necessary finding of domicil by one State to foreclose all States in the protection of their social institutions would be intolerable. . . .

The problem is to reconcile the reciprocal respect to be accorded by the members of the Union to their adjudications with due regard for another most important aspect of our federalism whereby "the domestic relations of husband and wife . . . were matters reserved to the States". . . . The rights that belong to all the States and the obligations which membership in the Union imposes upon all, are made effective because this Court is open to consider claims, such as this case presents, that the courts of one State have not given the full faith and credit to the judgment of a sister State that is required by Art. IV, § 1 of the Constitution. . . .

---

[6] We have not here a situation where a State disregards the adjudication of another State on the issue of domicil squarely litigated in a truly adversary proceeding.

What is immediately before us is the judgment of the Supreme Court of North Carolina. 224 N.C. 183, 29 S.E.2d 744. We have authority to upset it only if there is want of foundation for the conclusion that that Court reached. The conclusion it reached turns on its finding that the spouses who obtained the Nevada decrees were not domiciled there. The fact that the Nevada court found that they were domiciled there is entitled to respect, and more. The burden of undermining the verity which the Nevada decrees import rests heavily upon the assailant. . . .

When this case was first here, North Carolina did not challenge the finding of the Nevada court that petitioners had acquired domicils in Nevada. . . . Upon retrial, however, the existence of domicil in Nevada became the decisive issue. The judgments of conviction now under review bring before us a record which may be fairly summarized by saying that the petitioners left North Carolina for the purpose of getting divorces from their respective spouses in Nevada and as soon as each had done so and married one another they left Nevada and returned to North Carolina to live there together as man and wife. Against the charge of bigamous cohabitation under § 14–183 of the North Carolina General Statutes, petitioners stood on their Nevada divorces and offered exemplified copies of the Nevada proceedings. . . .

The scales of justice must not be unfairly weighted by a State when full faith and credit is claimed for a sister-State judgment. But North Carolina has not so dealt with the Nevada decrees. She has not raised unfair barriers to their recognition. North Carolina did not fail in appreciation or application of federal standards of full faith and credit. Appropriate weight was given to the finding of domicil in the Nevada decrees, and that finding was allowed to be overturned only by relevant standards of proof. There is nothing to suggest that the issue was not fairly submitted to the jury and that it was not fairly assessed on cogent evidence. . . .

[What the record] shows is that petitioners, long-time residents of North Carolina, came to Nevada, where they stayed in an auto-court for transients, filed suits for divorce as soon as the Nevada law permitted, married one another as soon as the divorces were obtained, and promptly returned to North Carolina to live. . . . It would be highly unreasonable to assert that a jury could not reasonably find that the evidence demonstrated that petitioners went to Nevada solely for the purpose of obtaining a divorce and intended all along to return to North Carolina. Such an intention, the trial court properly charged, would preclude acquisition of domicils in Nevada. See Williamson v. Osenton, 232 U.S. 619. . . .

In seeking a decree of divorce outside the State in which he has theretofore maintained his marriage, a person is necessarily involved in the legal situation created by our federal system whereby one State can grant a divorce of validity in other States only if the applicant has a bona fide domicil in the State of the court purporting to dissolve a prior legal marriage. The petitioners therefore assumed the risk that this Court would find that North Carolina justifiably concluded that they had not been domiciled in Nevada. Since the divorces which they sought and received in Nevada had no legal validity in North Carolina and their North Carolina spouses were still alive, they subjected themselves to prosecution for bigamous cohabitation under North Carolina law. . . . In vindicating its public policy and particularly one so important as that bearing upon the integrity of family life, a State in punishing particular acts may provide that "he who shall do them shall do them at his peril and will not be heard to plead in defense good faith or ignorance." . . . Mistaken notions about one's legal rights are not sufficient to bar prosecution for crime.

We conclude that North Carolina was not required to yield her State policy because a Nevada court found that petitioners were domiciled in Nevada when it granted them decrees of divorce. North Carolina was entitled to find, as she did, that they did not acquire domicils in Nevada and that the Nevada court was therefore without power to liberate the petitioners from amenability to the laws of North Carolina governing domestic relations. And, as was said in connection with another aspect of the Full Faith and Credit Clause, our conclusion "is not a matter to arouse the susceptibilities of the states, all of which are equally concerned in the question and equally on both sides." Fauntleroy v. Lum, 210 U.S. 230.

As for the suggestion that *Williams v. North Carolina [I]*, supra, foreclosed the Supreme Court of North Carolina from ordering a second trial upon the issue of domicil, it suffices to refer to our opinion in the earlier case.

Affirmed.

[The concurring opinion of JUSTICE MURPHY and the dissenting opinions of JUSTICES BLACK, DOUGLAS, and RUTLEDGE are omitted.]

NOTES

Jurisdictional Challenges. *Williams (II)* offers a potential route for states to refuse to enforce a sister state's divorce decree—the second court may be able to reexamine whether the first court had proper jurisdiction to grant the divorce. In *Williams*, if the parties were not validly domiciled in Nevada, then the Nevada court lacked jurisdiction to hear the dispute. If the Nevada court lacked jurisdiction to hear the dispute, then any ruling the Nevada court issued would have no effect within Nevada. Under 28 U.S.C.A. § 1738 (2012), judgments "shall have the same full faith and credit in every court within the United States . . . as they have by law or usage in the courts of such State . . . from which they are taken." Therefore, North Carolina, a sister state, would accord the ruling "the same full faith and credit" as Nevada by also giving the ruling no effect. North Carolina, therefore, would not be obliged to recognize the divorce decree. The Supreme Court followed the rule that divorce jurisdiction requires that at least one of the spouses be domiciled or reside in the forum state. THE RESTATEMENT (SECOND) OF CONFLICT OF LAWS § 72, proposes a slightly different rule:

> A state has power to exercise judicial jurisdiction to dissolve the marriage of spouses, neither of whom is domiciled in the state, if either spouse has such a relationship to the state as would make it reasonable for the state to dissolve the marriage.

The comments to Section 72 clarify that the "reasonable" relationship giving rise to divorce jurisdiction will usually include a spouse's residence in the forum state. *Id.* at cmt. b. Furthermore, the comments clarify that a state's finding that jurisdiction is appropriate based on a "reasonable" relationship with one of the spouses will not immunize a judgment from being collaterally attacked on jurisdictional grounds. *Id.* at cmt. c.

Annulment Jurisdiction and Choice of Law. In contrast to divorce, jurisdiction to annul a marriage may not require domicile. Justice Traynor gave an oft-cited rationale for the relaxed requirement: in annulment actions, the forum court will always apply the law of the state where the marriage was celebrated, not the forum's own law. Whealton v. Whealton, 432 P.2d 979 (Cal. 1967). By contrast, the forum state generally applies forum law to a divorce proceeding. This choice-of-law rule is justified because at least one spouse must be a domicil or resident of the forum state.

Jurisdictional Challenges to Bilateral Divorce Decrees. Bilateral (as opposed to *ex parte*) divorce proceedings result in divorce decrees that generally are not vulnerable to attack for want of jurisdiction. The United States Supreme Court established this rule in Sherrer v. Sherrer, 334 U.S. 343 (1948). In *Sherrer*, a married couple was domiciled in Massachusetts. Wife traveled to Florida with her paramour, Phelps, remained there for the statutorily required 90 days, and then sued husband for divorce. Husband went to Florida and appeared, participating in the court proceedings, but did not contest jurisdiction. The Florida court granted the divorce and dissolved the marriage. Wife and Phelps returned to Massachusetts, where they remained. Husband then sued Phelps for alienation of affections and also sought a Massachusetts decree that wife had deserted him and that his land should therefore be declared free of wife's dower rights. The Massachusetts probate court found that wife had gone to Florida solely to obtain a divorce, never intending to make Florida her permanent home. The state supreme court affirmed.

The U.S. Supreme Court overturned the Massachusetts decisions and ruled that the Florida divorce decree was immune from attack—whether or not Florida had proper jurisdiction when it entered the divorce decree. Unlike in *Williams (II)*, both spouses to the marriage participated in the Florida divorce proceeding, and so *res judicata* applied. Chief Justice Vinson, writing for the Court, explained:

> It is one thing to recognize as permissible the judicial reexamination of findings of jurisdictional fact where such findings have been made by a court of a sister State which has entered a divorce decree in *ex parte* proceedings. It is quite another thing to hold that the vital rights and interests involved in divorce litigation

> may be held in suspense pending the scrutiny by courts of sister States of findings of jurisdictional fact made by a competent court in proceedings conducted in a manner consistent with the highest requirements of due process and in which the defendant has participated. We do not conceive it to be in accord with the purposes of the full faith and credit requirement to hold that a judgment rendered under the circumstances of this case may be required to run the gantlet of such collateral attack in the courts of sister States before its validity outside of the State which rendered it is established or rejected. That vital interests are involved in divorce litigation indicates to us that it is a matter of greater rather than lesser importance that there should be a place to end such litigation. And where a decree of divorce is rendered by a competent court under the circumstances of this case, the obligation of full faith and credit requires that such litigation should end in the courts of the State in which the judgment was rendered.

Id. at 355–56.

Jurisdictional Challenges by a Third Party. In 1951, the United States Supreme Court applied *Sherrer*'s rule to bar a collateral attack from a third party in Johnson v. Muelberger, 340 U.S. 581 (1951). *Johnson* involved a daughter who attacked a Florida divorce decree ending her deceased father's marriage to her mother. After the Florida divorce, the father had remarried. After his death, the father's current wife elected, under New York law, to take one-third of his estate. Daughter sued in New York, attacking the Florida divorce decree on the ground that Florida lacked jurisdiction. The New York Court of Appeals held that the Florida decree bound only the parties themselves, and that under Florida law, the child could attack the decree collaterally in Florida. The Supreme Court reversed, ruling that New York cannot permit an attack by reason of the Full Faith and Credit Clause. The father had a chance to challenge Florida's jurisdiction during the proceeding filed by the mother, and therefore the divorce decree was immune from attack, whether by him or his daughter.

Special Appearance to Contest Jurisdiction. Procedural rules in some states allow a defendant to appear specially to contest jurisdiction without participating so as to invoke the *Sherrer* rule. In *Kulko v. Superior Court, infra,* the husband uses this procedure successfully to challenge the court's jurisdiction.

Sosna v. Iowa

Supreme Court of the United States, 1975
419 U.S. 393

■ REHNQUIST, JUSTICE.

Appellant Carol Sosna married Michael Sosna on September 5, 1964, in Michigan. They lived together in New York between October 1967 and August 1971, after which date they separated but continued to live in New York. In August 1972, appellant moved to Iowa with her three children, and the following month she petitioned the District Court of Jackson County, Iowa, for a dissolution of her marriage. Michael Sosna, who had been personally served with notice of the action when he came to Iowa to visit his children, made a special appearance to contest the jurisdiction of the Iowa court. The Iowa court dismissed the petition for lack of jurisdiction, finding that Michael Sosna was not a resident of Iowa and appellant had not been a resident of the State of Iowa for one year preceding the filing of her petition. In so doing the Iowa court applied the provisions of Iowa Code § 598.6 requiring that the petitioner in such an action be "for the last year a resident of the state." . . .

The statutory scheme in Iowa, like those in other States, sets forth in considerable detail the grounds upon which a marriage may be dissolved and the circumstances in which a divorce may be obtained. Jurisdiction over a petition for dissolution is established by statute in "the county where either party resides," Iowa Code § 598.2, and the Iowa courts have construed the term "resident" to have much the same meaning as is ordinarily associated with the concept of domicile. Korsrud v. Korsrud, 45 N.W.2d 848 (Iowa 1951). Iowa has recently revised its divorce statutes, incorporating the no-fault concept, but it retained the one-year durational residency requirement. The imposition of a durational residency requirement for divorce is scarcely unique to Iowa, since 48 States impose such a requirement as a condition for maintaining an action for divorce. As might be expected, the periods vary among the States and range from six weeks to two years. The one-year period selected by Iowa is the most common length of time prescribed.

Appellant contends that the Iowa requirement of one year's residence is unconstitutional for two separate reasons: *first*, because it establishes two classes of persons and discriminates against those who have recently exercised their right to travel to Iowa . . . and, *second*, because it denies a litigant the opportunity to make an individualized showing of bona fide residence and therefore denies such residents access to the only method of legally dissolving their marriage. Boddie v. Connecticut, 401 U.S. 371 (1971).

State statutes imposing durational residency requirements were of course invalidated when imposed by States as a qualification for welfare payments, for voting, and for medical care. . . . What those cases had in common was that the durational residency requirements they struck down were justified on the basis of budgetary or record-keeping considerations which were held insufficient to outweigh the constitutional claims of the individuals. But Iowa's divorce residency requirement is of a different stripe. Appellant was not irretrievably foreclosed from obtaining some part of what she sought, as was the case with the welfare recipients in *Shapiro*, the voters in *Dunn*, or the indigent patient in *Maricopa County*. She would eventually qualify for the same sort of adjudication which she demanded virtually upon her arrival in the State. Iowa's requirement delayed her access to the courts, but, by fulfilling it, a plaintiff could ultimately obtain the same opportunity for adjudication which she asserts ought to be hers at an earlier point in time.

Iowa's residency requirement may reasonably be justified on grounds other than purely budgetary considerations or administrative convenience. *Cf.* Kahn v. Shevin, 416 U.S. 351 (1974). A decree of divorce is not a matter in which the only interested parties are the State as a sort of "grantor," and a plaintiff such as appellant in the role of "grantee." Both spouses are obviously interested in the proceedings, since it will affect their marital status and very likely their property rights. Where a married couple has minor children, a decree of divorce would usually include provisions for their custody and support. With consequences of such moment riding on a divorce decree issued by its courts, Iowa may insist that one seeking to initiate such a proceeding have the modicum of attachment to the State required here.

Such a requirement additionally furthers the State's parallel interests in both avoiding officious intermeddling in matters in which another State has a paramount interest, and in minimizing the susceptibility of its own divorce decrees to collateral attack. A State such as Iowa may quite reasonably decide that it does not wish to become a divorce mill for unhappy spouses who have lived there as short a time as appellant had when she commenced her action in the state court after having long resided elsewhere. Until such time as Iowa is convinced that appellant intends to remain in the State, it lacks the "nexus between person and place of such permanence as to control the creation of legal relations and responsibilities of the utmost significance." Williams v. North Carolina [II], 325 U.S. 226 (1945). Perhaps even more importantly, Iowa's interests extend beyond its borders and include the recognition of its divorce decrees by other States under the Full Faith and Credit Clause of the Constitution, Art. IV, § 1. . . . Where a divorce decree is entered after a finding of domicile in *ex parte* proceedings,[20] this Court has held that the finding of domicile is not binding upon another State and may be disregarded in the face of "cogent evidence" to the contrary. Williams [I], supra, 325 U.S. at 236. For that reason, the State asked to enter such a decree is entitled to insist that the putative divorce plaintiff satisfy something more than the bare minimum of constitutional requirements before a divorce may be granted. The State's decision to exact a one-year residency requirement as a matter of policy is therefore

[20] . . . Our Brother Marshall argues in dissent that the Iowa durational residency requirement "sweeps too broadly" since it is not limited to *ex parte* proceedings and could be narrowed by a waiver provision. But Iowa's durational residency requirement cannot be tailored in this manner without disrupting settled principles of Iowa practice and pleading. Iowa's rules governing special appearances made it impossible for the state court to know, either at the time a petition for divorce is filed or when a motion to dismiss for want of jurisdiction is filed, whether or not a defendant will appear and participate in the divorce proceedings. Iowa Rules of Civil Procedure 66, 104. The fact that the state legislature might conceivably adopt a system of waivers and revise court rules governing special appearances does not make such detailed rewriting appropriate business for the federal judiciary.

buttressed by a quite permissible inference that this requirement not only effectuates state substantive policy but likewise provides a greater safeguard against successful collateral attack than would a requirement of bona fide residence alone. This is precisely the sort of determination that a State in the exercise of its domestic relations jurisdiction is entitled to make.

We therefore hold that the state interest in requiring that those who seek a divorce from its courts be genuinely attached to the State, as well as a desire to insulate divorce decrees from the likelihood of collateral attack, requires a different resolution of the constitutional issue presented than was the case in *Shapiro*, supra, *Dunn*, supra, and *Maricopa County*, supra.

Nor are we of the view that the failure to provide an individualized determination of residency violates the Due Process Clause of the Fourteenth Amendment. . . . An individualized determination of physical presence plus the intent to remain, which appellant apparently seeks, would not entitle her to a divorce even if she could have made such a showing.[22] For Iowa requires not merely "domicile" in that sense, but residence in the State for a year in order for its courts to exercise their divorce jurisdiction.

In *Boddie v. Connecticut, supra*, this Court held that Connecticut might not deny access to divorce courts to those persons who could not afford to pay the required fee. Because of the exclusive role played by the State in the termination of marriages, it was held that indigents could not be denied an opportunity to be heard "absent a countervailing state interest of overriding significance." 401 U.S., at 377. But the gravamen of appellant Sosna's claim is not total deprivation, as in *Boddie*, but only delay. The operation of the filing fee in *Boddie* served to exclude forever a certain segment of the population from obtaining a divorce in the courts of Connecticut. No similar total deprivation is present in appellant's case, and the delay which attends the enforcement of the one-year durational residency requirement is, for the reasons previously stated, consistent with the provisions of the United States Constitution.

Affirmed.

■ MR. JUSTICE MARSHALL, with whom MR. JUSTICE BRENNAN joins, dissenting.

. . .

[T]he previous decisions of this Court make it plain that the right of marital association is one of the most basic rights conferred on the individual by the State. . . . I think it is clear beyond cavil that the right

[22] In addition to a showing of residence within the State for a year, Iowa Code § 598.6 requires any petition for dissolution to state "that the maintenance of the residence has been in good faith and not for the purpose of obtaining a marriage dissolution only." In dismissing appellant's petition in state court, Judge Keck observed that appellant had failed to allege good-faith residence.

to seek dissolution of the marital relationship is of such fundamental importance that denial of this right to the class of recent interstate travelers penalizes interstate travel within the meaning of *Shapiro, Dunn*, and *Maricopa County*. . . . I would scrutinize Iowa's durational residency requirement to determine whether it constitutes a reasonable means of furthering important interests asserted by the State. . . .

The Court's third justification seems to me the only one that warrants close consideration. Iowa has a legitimate interest in protecting itself against invasion by those seeking quick divorces in a forum with relatively lax divorce laws, and it may have some interest in avoiding collateral attacks on its decree in other States. These interests, however, would adequately be protected by a simple requirement of domicile—physical presence plus intent to remain—which would remove the rigid one-year barrier while permitting the State to restrict the availability of its divorce process to citizens who are genuinely its own. . . .

[The dissenting opinion of JUSTICE WHITE has been omitted.]

2. COMITY FOR DECREES OF FOREIGN COUNTRIES

The Full Faith and Credit Clause applies only to judgments rendered by United States courts. U.S. courts are not constitutionally obliged to enforce judgments from courts in foreign countries. In practice, however, courts often choose to accept foreign courts' judicial decrees as a matter of comity, or discretion, as *Perrin* illustrates.

Perrin v. Perrin

United States Court of Appeals, Third Circuit, 1969
408 F.2d 107

■ MARIS, JUDGE.

This is an appeal by the defendant husband from a judgment of the District Court of the Virgin Islands granting to the plaintiff wife a divorce and the custody of their minor son, Daniel, now 9 years old. The parties, who were married in New York on September 10, 1954, are Swiss citizens. On February 8, 1967 the present plaintiff filed a petition in a court of the State of Chihuahua, Mexico, praying for a divorce from her husband, the present defendant. The plaintiff appeared personally in the Mexican proceeding. The defendant appeared by a duly empowered attorney at law and filed a consenting answer. On February 23, 1967 the Mexican court entered a decree of divorce, dissolving the marriage and awarding custody of the minor child to the defendant. . . .

In the latter part of November, 1967, the defendant arrived in St. Thomas from Martinique on the motor vessel Jolly Rover to engage in the charter business for the tourist season. The defendant had just returned from Switzerland where the minor child had been living with the defendant's parents and he brought the minor child to St. Thomas with him. . . . On January 29, 1968 the plaintiff filed . . . a complaint . . . against the defendant . . . praying for an absolute divorce and again seeking the custody of the minor child. A motion to dismiss this complaint for lack of jurisdiction of the subject matter and persons of the plaintiff and minor child was filed by the defendant and on March 7, 1968 was denied. . . .

The defendant's motion to dismiss the complaint was based, inter alia, upon the proposition that the court lacked jurisdiction of the subject matter because there was no existing marriage between the parties to dissolve, the marriage having been terminated a year previously by the Mexican divorce decree, an authenticated copy of which was annexed to the motion. In her brief opposing the motion the plaintiff attacked the validity of the Mexican divorce decree on the ground that neither party was domiciled in Mexico at the time it was rendered and that the Mexican court, therefore, lacked jurisdiction to render it. Thus was raised the question of the validity of the Mexican decree or, more precisely, the question whether the plaintiff can be heard to attack in this proceeding the validity of the Mexican decree which she herself had sought and obtained and in the entry of which the defendant had acquiesced. . . .

It is true, as the plaintiff now argues, that domicile is regarded as the basis for jurisdiction to grant a divorce in the *United States*. Granville-Smith v. Granville-Smith, 1955, 349 U.S. 1. It is likewise true that a divorce decree may be collaterally attacked for lack of domiciliary jurisdiction, Williams [II] 1945, 325 U.S. 226, if the defendant was not personally served and did not appear. But it is equally well settled that if the defendant was personally served or did actually appear in the action he is estopped from impeaching the resulting divorce decree, whether the domiciliary jurisdiction was contested by the defendant, Sherrer v. Sherrer, 1948, 334 U.S. 343, or was admitted by him, Coe v. Coe, 1948, 334 U.S. 378.

The *Sherrer* and *Coe* cases involved . . . the full faith and credit clause of the federal Constitution. Here, however, we are dealing with a decree of a foreign state as to which the principles of comity, rather than full faith and credit, apply. Ordinarily, the recognition in the United States of such a foreign decree will depend upon whether at least one of the spouses was domiciled in the foreign state when the decree of divorce was rendered. Certainly "mail order" divorce decrees in which neither spouse has appeared personally in the foreign jurisdiction are not recognized here, and this appears to be equally true in the case of *ex parte* divorce decrees in which an absent defendant is served only extraterritorially or constructively and does not actually appear or file an answer in the action.

In the Mexican proceeding involved in the present case, however, as in the *Coe* case, a bilateral divorce is involved. For here, as there, the plaintiff was personally present in the foreign state and appeared in the foreign court and the defendant appeared in that court by counsel and filed a consenting answer. In Rosenstiel v. Rosenstiel, 1965, 209 N.E.2d 709, *cert. den.* 384 U.S. 971, the Court of Appeals of New York was presented with the question whether such a bilateral divorce granted in the State of Chihuahua, Mexico, was entitled to recognition in New York State. In speaking for the Court of Appeals in that case Judge Bergan said, *inter alia*:

> "There is squarely presented to this court now for the first time the question whether recognition is to be given by New York to a matrimonial judgment of a foreign country based on grounds not accepted in New York, where personal jurisdiction of one party to the marriage has been acquired by physical presence before the foreign court; and jurisdiction of the other has been acquired by appearance and pleading through an authorized attorney although no domicile of either party is shown within that jurisdiction; and 'residence' has been acquired by one party through a statutory formality based on brief contact.
>
> "In cases where a divorce has been obtained without any personal contact with the jurisdiction by either party or by physical submission to the jurisdiction by one, with no personal service of process within the foreign jurisdiction upon, and no appearance or submission by, the other, decision has been against the validity of the foreign decree (Caldwell v. Caldwell, 81 N.E.2d 60 (N.Y. 1948); Rosenbaum v. Rosenbaum, 130 N.E.2d 902 (N.Y. 1955)).
>
> "Although the grounds for divorce found acceptable according to Mexican law are inadmissible in New York, and the physical contact with the Mexican jurisdiction was ephemeral, there are some incidents in the Mexican proceedings which are common characteristics of the exercise of judicial power.
>
> "The former husband was physically in the jurisdiction, personally before the court, with the usual incidents and the implicit consequences of voluntary submission to foreign sovereignty. Although he had no intention of making his domicile there, he did what the domestic law of the place required he do to establish a 'residence' of a kind which was set up as a statutory prerequisite to institute an action for divorce. This is not our own view in New York of what a bona fide residence is or should be, but it is that which the local law of Mexico prescribes.
>
> "Since he was one party to the two-party contract of marriage he carried with him legal incidents of the marriage itself, considered as an entity, which came before the court when he personally appeared and presented his petition. In a highly mobile era such as ours, it is needful on pragmatic grounds to regard the marriage itself as moving from place to place with

either spouse, a concept which underlies the decision in Williams [I], 317 U.S. 287, p. 304.

"The voluntary appearance of the other spouse in the foreign court by attorney would tend to give further support to an acquired jurisdiction there over the marriage as a legal entity. In theory jurisdiction is an imposition of sovereign power over the person. It is usually exerted by symbolic and rarely by actual force, e.g., the summons as a symbol of force; the attachment and the civil arrest, as exerting actual force.

"But almost universally jurisdiction is acquired by physical and personal submission to judicial authority and in legal theory there seems to be ground to admit that the Mexican court at Juarez acquired jurisdiction over the former marriage of the defendant.

"It is true that in attempting to reconcile the conflict of laws and of State interests in matrimonial judgments entered in States of the United States, where the Constitution compels each to give full faith and credit to the judgments of the others, a considerable emphasis has been placed on domicile as a prerequisite to that compulsory recognition. . . . But domicile is not intrinsically an indispensable prerequisite to jurisdiction (cf. Stimson, *Jurisdiction in Divorce Cases: The Unsoundness of the Domiciliary Theory*, 42 AMER.BAR ASSN.J. 222 (1956); Griswold, Divorce Jurisdiction and Recognition of Divorce Decrees—A Comparative Study, 65 Harv. L. Rev. 193, 228).

"The duration of domicile in sister States providing by statute for a minimal time to acquire domicile as necessary to matrimonial action jurisdiction is in actual practice complied with by a mere formal gesture having no more relation to the actual situs of the marriage or to true domicile than the formality of signing the Juarez city register. The difference in time is not truly significant of a difference in intent or purpose or in effect.

"The State or country of the true domicile has the closest real public interest in a marriage but, where a New York spouse goes elsewhere to establish a synthetic domicile to meet technical acceptance of a matrimonial suit, our public interest is not affected differently by a formality of one day than by a formality of six weeks.

"Nevada gets no closer to the real public concern with the marriage than Chihuahua . . . "

With these views we agree and we think that the case is ruled in principle by the *Coe* case. We find it impossible to believe that six weeks residence by Mr. Coe gave Nevada a greater or more real concern with his marriage than a day or two's residence in Chihuahua by Mrs. Perrin gave to that Mexican State. Although we recognize that there is a divergence of view on this question among American jurisdictions, we hold, as did the Court of Appeals of New York in that case, that "A balanced public policy now requires that recognition of the bilateral Mexican divorce be given rather than withheld and such recognition as a matter of comity offends no public policy" of this Territory. We are the more persuaded to this result in this case because the party who seeks to attack the Mexican decree is not the defendant in that case but rather the plaintiff who procured it upon her representation to the Mexican court that she resided in the City of Juarez. It follows that the plaintiff may not in this proceeding be heard to deny the validity of the Mexican divorce decree. Since by the terms of that decree her marriage with the defendant was dissolved on February 23, 1967, no marriage status remained to be terminated when the present complaint was filed. . . .

The decree of the District Court will be reversed. . . .

NOTES

As the *Perrin* court notes, foreign judgments—unlike sister-state judgments—fall outside the purview of the Full Faith and Credit Clause. Absent a treaty or presidential order, American courts have discretion and can choose not to recognize a foreign judgment based on faulty jurisdiction, disagreements about law or policy, or other such reasons. *See, e.g.*, Robert C. Casad, *Issue Preclusion and Foreign Country Judgments: Whose Law?*, 70 IOWA L. REV. 53 (1984). But, states often choose to recognize foreign judgments, such as divorce decrees, as a matter of comity. THE RESTATEMENT (2D) OF CONFLICT OF LAWS § 98 adopts a general policy favoring recognition: "A valid judgment rendered in a foreign nation after a fair trial in a contested proceeding will be recognized in the United States so far as the immediate parties and the underlying cause of action are concerned."

In Dart v. Dart, 597 N.W.2d 82 (Mich. 1999), *cert. denied*, 529 U.S. 1018 (2000), the wife was present and represented by counsel at an English proceeding which granted a decree of divorce and ordered a property division in accordance with English law, which looks to the wife's financial needs in regard to large assets rather than the equitable division of marital assets. She later petitioned an American court to deny comity to the English decree, arguing that the property distribution was repugnant to Michigan due process of law. The court rejected her appeal and gave comity to the English decree.

While American courts often choose to recognize foreign divorce decrees, a court may decline to give comity to a foreign judgment if the foreign proceeding violates American due process or sharply departs from a state's public policy. In Jewell v. Jewell, 751 A.2d 735 (R.I. 2000), husband filed for divorce in Rhode Island in December, 1995, but then filed another petition for divorce in the Dominican Republic in May, 1997. The latter court granted an *ex parte* divorce, and husband subsequently remarried in the Dominican Republic. On wife's petition, the Rhode Island family court issued a restraining order to prevent husband from obtaining a foreign divorce.

Husband appealed, arguing that the Rhode Island courts should recognize the foreign divorce decree. The Rhode Island Supreme Court disagreed:

> [W]e unequivocally refuse to recognize the Dominican Republic divorce, or to accord it any comity whatsoever. The *ex parte* divorce issued by the Dominican Republic, purportedly dissolving the marriage of two people, neither of whom had any connection to that forum, is void as a matter of law as repugnant to the public policy of this state, and we decline to accord it comity. This fly-by-day divorce that was pronounced on May 26, 1997, after Paul flew into the country in the morning, made a brief appearance with counsel, and departed the same day, is a sham, particularly where neither party was a resident of the Dominican Republic nor maintained any other legitimate connection to that forum.

Id. at 739.

3. EQUITABLE ESTOPPEL AND LACHES

Two other claims may be made to avoid the effect of a divorce decree: that the defendant is equitably estopped from seeking a divorce by the lapse of time or may not deny the validity of a prior divorce decree due to their own actions during a later marriage.

Equitable Estoppel. In Kazin v. Kazin, 405 A.2d 360 (N.J. 1979), the plaintiff sought a divorce decree and alimony from Michael Kazin, her second husband. She married Kazin after obtaining a divorce from her first husband in a Mexican court. Kazin claimed she was estopped from seeking divorce and alimony from him because her dissolution of the prior marriage was invalid due to lack of jurisdiction since the divorce was obtained in Mexico. Consequently, he argued she was still married to her first husband and thus their subsequent marriage was invalid. Mr. Kazin was not only aware of plaintiff's attempt to obtain a divorce from her first husband, but had also participated in a meeting between his wife and her prior husband pertaining to the divorce and had accompanied his wife while she was traveling to Mexico to obtain the divorce. The Supreme Court of New Jersey held that Mr. Kazin was estopped from denying the validity of his current marriage because he participated in the divorce proceedings dissolving his wife's prior marriage, and she detrimentally relied on the validity of that divorce and thus the validity of her second marriage. As the court noted:

> The equitable rule precluding individuals from attacking foreign divorce decrees "[has] not [been] limited to situations of what might be termed 'true estoppel' where one party induces another to rely to his damage upon certain representations . . . ", Restatement (Second) of Conflict of Laws § 74, Comment b (1971), but has also encompassed situations sometimes termed "quasi-estoppel" where an individual is not permitted to "blow both hot and cold," taking a position inconsistent with prior

> conduct, if this would injure another, regardless of whether that person has actually relied thereon.
>
> In the overwhelming majority of cases, estoppel has been applied to thwart a spouse from attacking his or her own divorce. Estoppel has also been applied, however, in situations analogous to that presented in this case, to prevent an individual from attacking his spouse's prior divorce. . . .

Id. at 366.

A similar attack occurred in *In re* Goode, 997 P.2d 244 (Or. Ct. App. 2000). *Goode* involved a Columbian woman who was married to a Columbian man when the two obtained a Dominican Republic divorce in 1984. The woman then moved to Oregon where she and a second man married. Nonetheless, six years after her marriage to the second husband she obtained an Oregon divorce from the first husband again. She then re-married the second husband in Oregon. A few years passed and she petitioned the Oregon court for a divorce from her second husband and he responded that their first marriage in 1984 was void because she was still married to the first husband then. He argued that the woman's first divorce should be denied comity and thus she was still married to the first husband at the time of her purported marriage to the second. His argument was that comity should not be granted by Oregon because neither of the parties was domiciled in the Dominican Republic at the time of the divorce and thus granting comity would reward forum-shopping. Furthermore, the woman should be estopped from asserting the validity of the divorce in 1984 since her divorce from the same marriage six years later in Oregon was premised on her own recognition that she was still married. The court rejected the man's arguments and awarded comity to the 1984 divorce. The court reasoned that estoppel is an equitable doctrine and because the man promoted and encouraged the Dominican Republic divorce, he should not be able to later claim the divorce was invalid in his own suit.

Laches. The passage of time will also sometimes bar a divorce action or a defense to it, but the defense requires a significant showing of prejudice to the party who did not act with delay. In Staley v. Staley, 248 A.2d 655 (Md. 1968), the wife left Maryland and obtained an *ex parte* Nevada divorce from her first husband, H_1, on January 20, 1965. The following day she married her second husband, H_2, and one day after that returned with him to Maryland. H_1 was aware of the divorce during the month of the decree and some two months later learned of her remarriage. Wife and H_1 were in court together a number of times afterward concerning child custody, which was awarded to H_1 with visitation rights in wife. Some eighteen months after the Nevada decree, H_1 brought an action for divorce based on desertion. Wife asserted that H_1 was guilty of laches and, following a trial court's award of divorce, she appealed, asserting laches again and questioning whether H_1 had sustained his burden of proof as to the Nevada court's lack of jurisdiction.

Affirming the decision of the trial court, the Court of Appeals noted that the defense of laches requires both the plaintiff's negligence or lack of diligence in asserting his rights *and* prejudice or injury to the defendant; since wife had remarried one day after being divorced, she did not suffer prejudice as the result of action or inaction by H_1. The court also rejected wife's argument that her relations with her children were prejudiced by the husband's delay because they would know that she had been living in adultery for eighteen months, saying: "By her own acts she created the domestic situation which she now decries and must suffer the consequences."

In Bartsch v. Bartsch, 132 S.E.2d 416 (Va. Ct. App. 1963), the Virginia Court of Appeals, reversing a lower court decision that had set aside a Nevada *ex parte* divorce decree, held that W_1 was barred by laches from asserting invalidity even for lack of jurisdiction. The divorce was granted in 1939 but the attack came after the husband's death in 1960. The court noted, without being explicit, that there was prejudice to W_2 who, along with W_1, sought to participate in the husband's estate. Some emphasis was placed on the fact that W_1 waited until the death of the husband, who was obviously a key witness, to bring the action.

4. THE DOCTRINE OF DIVISIBLE DIVORCE

Vanderbilt v. Vanderbilt

Supreme Court of the United States, 1957
354 U.S. 416

■ BLACK, JUSTICE.

Cornelius Vanderbilt, Jr., petitioner, and Patricia Vanderbilt, respondent, were married in 1948. They separated in 1952 while living in California. The wife moved to New York where she has resided since February 1953. In March of that year the husband filed suit for divorce in Nevada. This proceeding culminated, in June 1953, with a decree of final divorce which provided that both husband and wife were "freed and released from the bonds of matrimony and all the duties and obligations thereof. . . ."[1] The wife was not served with process in Nevada and did not appear before the divorce court.

In April 1954, Mrs. Vanderbilt instituted an action in a New York court praying for separation from petitioner and for alimony. The New York court did not have personal jurisdiction over him, but in order to satisfy his obligations, if any, to Mrs. Vanderbilt, it sequestered his property within the State. He appeared specially and, among other defenses to the action, contended that the Full Faith and Credit Clause

[1] It seems clear that in Nevada the effect of this decree was to put an end to the husband's duty to support the wife-provided, of course, that the Nevada courts had power to do this. *Sweney v. Sweeney*, 42 Nev. 431, 438–439, 179 P. 638, 639–640; *Herrick v. Herrick*, 55 Nev. 59, 68, 25 P.2d 378, 380. *See Estin v. Estin*, 334 U.S. 541.

of the United States Constitution compelled the New York court to treat the Nevada divorce as having ended the marriage and as having destroyed any duty of support which he owed the respondent. While the New York court found the Nevada decree valid and held that it had effectively dissolved the marriage, it nevertheless entered an order, under § 1170–b of the New York Civil Practice Act, directing petitioner to make designated support payments to respondent. 207 Misc. 294, 138 N.Y.S.2d 222. The New York Court of Appeals upheld the support order. Petitioner then applied to this Court for certiorari contending that § 1170–b, as applied, is unconstitutional because it contravenes the Full Faith and Credit Clause. . . .

In Estin v. Estin, 334 U.S. 541, this Court decided that a Nevada divorce court, which had no personal jurisdiction over the wife, had no power to terminate a husband's obligation to provide her support as required in a pre-existing New York separation decree. . . . Since the wife was not subject to its jurisdiction, the Nevada divorce court had no power to extinguish any right which she had under the law of New York to financial support from her husband. It has long been the constitutional rule that a court cannot adjudicate a personal claim or obligation unless it has jurisdiction over the person of the defendant. Here, the Nevada divorce court was as powerless to cut off the wife's support right as it would have been to order the husband to pay alimony if the wife had brought the divorce action and he had not been subject to the divorce court's jurisdiction. Therefore, the Nevada decree, to the extent it purported to affect the wife's right to support, was void and the Full Faith and Credit Clause did not obligate New York to give it recognition. . . .

Affirmed.

[The dissenting opinion of JUSTICE FRANKFURTER is omitted.]

NOTES

Divisible Divorce. In *Vanderbilt*, the Supreme Court upheld New York's order granting wife support from her husband, even though husband had obtained a divorce decree in Nevada, on the grounds that Nevada—lacking personal jurisdiction over wife—could not terminate her right to support. This ruling illustrates the concept of divisible divorce.

As explained *supra*, a divorce decree changes the spouses' legal status, or *res*, and therefore can be accomplished through an *ex parte* hearing. Incidents of a person's status as married or divorced (*e.g.*, spousal support, alimony, child support, or child custody) are distinct, however. Each of these is divisible because each conceivably could be established or litigated in separate states under separate rules; enforcement or recognition is likewise distinct for each.

Usually the concept of divisible divorce is addressed in the context of claims to separate the fact of divorce from property or support rights—say, for example, whether a court has jurisdiction over a physically absent spouse so as to allow for a property settlement that would comply with due process requirements. *See, e.g.*, Dawson-Austin v. Austin, 968 S.W.2d 319 (Tex. 1998), *cert. denied*, 525 U.S. 1067 (1999), where the court held there was no minimum contact by absent-wife with Texas and hence no personal jurisdiction over her when the only basis claimed for jurisdiction was assets that petitioning husband moved to the state. In Isaacs v. Isaacs, 79 S.E. 1072 (Va. 1913), a Virginia court gave the wife a judicial separation (in contrast to an absolute divorce) and placed a lien on her husband's property to secure alimony payments it awarded to her. Subsequently, husband petitioned a Kentucky court to issue an absolute divorce, so that the divorce would erase the duty to pay the alimony ordered by the Virginia court. Courts in both states had personal jurisdiction over the spouses. Wife sued in Virginia to collect alimony under the Virginia order. The Virginia court recognized the Kentucky decree as a final dissolution of the marriage, but refused to give it effect with regards to alimony because Virginia had awarded alimony before the Kentucky divorce proceeding was initiated. Similarly, in Newport v. Newport, 245 S.E.2d 134 (Va. 1978), the spouses resided in Virginia, but husband received an *ex parte* divorce decree from Nevada, which he argued precluded wife from receiving alimony. In rejecting husband's argument, the Supreme Court of Virginia stated:

> [T]he duty of a husband to support his wife is a moral as well as a legal obligation; it is a marital duty, in the performance of which the public as well as the parties are interested; it is a duty which is an incident to the marriage state and arises from the relation of the marriage; and it is an inherent right which may be asserted in a divorce suit or in an independent suit therefor.
>
> The right of a wife to support is of such importance to the community, as well as to the parties, that it survives an absolute divorce obtained by her husband in an *ex parte* proceeding in another state. Thus we affirm the decree of the lower court which accorded full faith and credit to the Nevada divorce decree insofar as that decree terminated the marital status of appellant and appellee; decreed that the Nevada court was without power to adjudicate the question of alimony; and held that the Nevada decree did not terminate appellee's right to support by appellant.

Id. at 139.

Divisible Divorce and "Sit-Tight" Spouses. Because a court can dissolve a marriage when only one spouse is a domiciliary or a resident of the state, a spouse who "sits tight" at home must then second-guess whether the other spouse will establish a true domicile elsewhere to secure a divorce. In order to divorce, there also must be proper service of process upon the absent spouse. *See, e.g.*, Raymond v. Raymond, 36 S.W.3d 733 (Ark. 2001). Even though one spouse may petition for divorce, the other spouse has a number of options about how to respond. In Snider v. Snider, 551 S.E.2d 693 (W.Va. 2001), the West Virginia Supreme Court reaffirmed the divisible divorce concept in a suit by the husband to dismiss West Virginia's jurisdiction over him concerning issues of alimony and equitable division of property. As in *Vanderbilt*, he argued that because Illinois already dissolved his marriage, West Virginia no longer had jurisdiction to adjudge the wife's personal rights to support or property distribution. But the court held that because he had maintained a marital residence in West Virginia, owned real estate there, secured a loan from a state bank, and lived in that property when residing in the state, there were sufficient minimum contacts for West Virginia courts to exercise jurisdiction over him to resolve the wife's claims, even though his divorce in Illinois was entitled to recognition. Note, however, that some states require that to award property or support after an earlier decree from another state, the action must be initiated within two years after the domiciliary receives notice of the earlier decree. *See, e.g.*, VA. CODE ANN. § 20–107.3(J) (2016).

In re Marriage of Laine, 120 P.3d 802 (Kan. Ct. App. 2005), involved another set of sit-tight facts. The husband and wife had resided in Texas but then the husband moved to Kansas where he established residency and a new life. The wife filed for divorce in Texas and the husband responded there. At that time, the Texas court enjoined the husband from filing any other action concerning the marriage until the Texas court had the opportunity to rule. In spite of this, the husband filed for a divorce in Kansas and petitioned for an award of property he had acquired in Kansas. The Kansas court awarded him a divorce and various pension and investment funds. The wife did not appear in the Kansas proceedings, but did appeal, arguing that Texas had personal jurisdiction over both of the parties and that Texas alone had the right to award the divorce and divide any and all marital property. On appeal, the Kansas court agreed with the wife and set aside the husband's Kansas divorce and division of marital property. Thus, the wife's choice to sit tight provided Texas with sole jurisdiction.

D. SPECIAL PROBLEMS OF SERVICE OF PROCESS

Kulko v. Superior Court of California

Supreme Court of the United States, 1978
436 U.S. 84

■ MARSHALL, JUSTICE.

The issue before us is whether, in this action for child support, the California state courts may exercise *in personam* jurisdiction over a nonresident, nondomiciliary parent of minor children domiciled within the State. For reasons set forth below, we hold that the exercise of such jurisdiction would violate the Due Process Clause of the Fourteenth Amendment.

[Ezra Kulko and Sharon Kulko Horn—both New York domiciliaries—married in California in 1959 during a short trip through that state. Sharon returned to New York following the marriage, and Ezra returned to New York as well after completing military service abroad. The Kulkos gave birth to two children in New York and the family remained there until 1972, when the couple separated.

Sharon subsequently moved to California. Sharon and Ezra signed a separation agreement in New York in September 1972, which provided that the children would live with Ezra in New York during the school year and visit Sharon in California for holidays and summers. Ezra agreed to pay Sharon $3,000 per year in child support, to cover the children's expenses while they visited her in California. Sharon immediately obtained a divorce decree in Haiti, which incorporated the separation agreement's terms.

In December 1973, the couple's daughter requested to move to California with Sharon, and Ezra bought his daughter a one-way plane ticket to California, where she commenced living with her mother during the school year and spending vacations with her father. In January 1976, the couple's son also took up residence with Sharon. Less than a month later, Sharon sued Ezra in California to obtain a California judgment establishing the Haitian divorce; to modify the previous separation agreement and award Sharon full custody; and to increase Ezra's child support obligation.] Ezra appeared specially and moved to quash service of the summons on the ground that he was not a resident of California and lacked sufficient "minimum contacts" with the State under International Shoe Co. v. Washington, 326 U.S. 310, 316 (1945), to warrant the State's assertion of personal jurisdiction over him. . . .

The trial court summarily denied the motion to quash, and [Ezra] sought review in the California Court of Appeal by petition for a writ of mandate. [Ezra] did not contest the court's jurisdiction for purposes of the custody determination, but, with respect to the claim for increased support, he renewed his argument that the California courts lacked personal jurisdiction over him. The appellate court affirmed the denial of [Ezra's] motion to quash, reasoning that, by consenting to his children's living in California, [Ezra] had "caused an effect in th[e] state" warranting the exercise of jurisdiction over him. 133 Cal.Rptr. 627, 628 (1976). . . .

[The California Supreme Court] noted first that the California Code of Civil Procedure demonstrated an intent that the courts of California utilize all bases of *in personam* jurisdiction "not inconsistent with the Constitution." Agreeing with the court below, the Supreme Court stated that, where a nonresident defendant has caused an effect in the State by an act or omission outside the State, personal jurisdiction over the defendant in causes arising from that effect may be exercised whenever "reasonable." It went on to hold that such an exercise was "reasonable" in this case because [Ezra] had "purposely availed himself of the benefits and protections of the laws of California" by sending Ilsa to live with her mother in California. While noting that [Ezra] had not, "with respect to his other child, Darwin, caused an effect in [California]"—since it was [Sharon] who had arranged for Darwin to fly to California in January 1976—the court concluded that it was "fair and reasonable for defendant to be subject to personal jurisdiction for the support of both children, where he has committed acts with respect to one child which confers [*sic*] personal jurisdiction and has consented to the permanent residence of the other child in California." . . .

We have concluded that jurisdiction by appeal does not lie, but, treating the papers as a petition for a writ of certiorari, we hereby grant the petition and reverse the judgment below.

The Due Process Clause of the Fourteenth Amendment operates as a limitation on the jurisdiction of state courts to enter judgments affecting rights or interests of nonresident defendants. *See* Shaffer v. Heitner, 433 U.S. 186, 198–200 (1977). It has long been the rule that a valid judgment imposing a personal obligation or duty in favor of the plaintiff may be entered only by a court having jurisdiction over the person of the defendant. Pennoyer v. Neff, 95 U.S. 714, 732–733, (1878); International Shoe Co. v. Washington, supra, 326 U.S., at 316. The existence of personal jurisdiction, in turn, depends upon the presence of reasonable notice to the defendant that an action has been brought. Mullane v. Central Hanover Trust Co., 339 U.S. 306, 313–314 (1950), and a sufficient connection between the defendant and the forum State as to make it fair to require defense of the action in the forum. In this case, [Ezra] does not dispute the adequacy of the notice that he received, but contends that his connection with the State of California is too attenuated, under the standards implicit in the Due Process Clause of the Constitution, to justify imposing upon him the burden and inconvenience of defense in California.

The parties are in agreement that the constitutional standard for determining whether the State may enter a binding judgment against [Ezra] here is that set forth in this Court's opinion in International Shoe Co. v. Washington, supra: that a defendant "have certain minimum contacts with [the forum state] such that the maintenance of the suit does not offend 'traditional notions of fair play and substantial justice.' " . . . [A]n essential criterion in all cases is whether the "quality and nature" of the defendant's activity is such that it is "reasonable" and "fair" to require him to conduct his defense in that State. . . .

Like any standard that requires a determination of "reasonableness," the "minimum contacts" test of *International Shoe* is not susceptible of mechanical application; rather, the facts of each case must be weighed to determine whether the requisite "affiliating circumstances" are present. Hanson v. Denckla, 357 U.S. 235, 246 (1958). We recognize that this determination is one in which few answers will be written "in black and white. The greys are dominant and even among them the shades are innumerable." Estin v. Estin, 334 U.S. 541, 545 (1948). But we believe that the California Supreme Court's application of the minimum contacts test in this case represents an unwarranted extension of *International Shoe* and would, if sustained, sanction a result that is neither fair, just, nor reasonable.

In reaching its result, the California Supreme Court did not rely on [Ezra's] glancing presence in the State some 13 years before the events that led to this controversy, nor could it have. [Ezra] has been in California on only two occasions, once in 1959 for a three-day military stopover on his way to Korea, *see* p. 1694, supra, and again in 1960 for a 24-hour stopover on his return from Korean service. To hold such temporary visits to a State a basis for the assertion of *in personam* jurisdiction over unrelated actions arising in the future would make a mockery of the limitations on state jurisdiction imposed by the Fourteenth Amendment. Nor did the California court rely on the fact that [Ezra] was actually married in California on one of his two brief visits. We agree that where two New York domiciliaries, for reasons of convenience, marry in the State of California and thereafter spend their entire married life in New York, the fact of their California marriage by itself cannot support a California court's exercise of jurisdiction over a spouse who remains a New York resident in an action relating to child support.

Finally, in holding that personal jurisdiction existed, the court below carefully disclaimed reliance on the fact that [Ezra] had agreed at the time of separation to allow his children to live with their mother three months a year and that he had sent them to California each year pursuant to this agreement. As was noted below, to find personal jurisdiction in a State on this basis, merely because the mother was residing there, would discourage parents from entering into reasonable visitation agreements. Moreover, it could arbitrarily subject one parent to suit in any State of the Union where the other parent chose to spend time while having custody of their offspring pursuant to a separation agreement.[6] As we have emphasized,

> "The unilateral activity of those who claim some relationship with a nonresident defendant cannot satisfy the requirement of contact with the forum State. . . . [I]t is essential in each case that there be some act by which the defendant purposefully avails [him]self of the privilege of conducting activities within the forum State. . . ." Hanson v. Denckla, supra, 357 U.S., at 253.

The "purposeful act" that the California Supreme Court believed did warrant the exercise of personal jurisdiction over appellant in California was his "actively and fully consent[ing] to Ilsa living in California for the school year . . . and . . . sen[ding] her to California for that purpose." We cannot accept the proposition that [Ezra's] acquiescence in Ilsa's desire to live with her mother conferred jurisdiction over [Ezra] in the California courts in this action. A father who agrees, in the interests of family harmony and his children's preferences, to allow them to spend more time in California than was required under a separation agreement

---

[6] Although the separation agreement stated that [Sharon] resided in California and provided that child-support payments would be mailed to her California address, it also specifically contemplated that [Sharon] might move to a different State. The agreement directed [Ezra] to mail the support payments to [Sharon]'s San Francisco address or "any other address which the Wife may designate from time to time in writing."

can hardly be said to have "purposefully availed himself" of the "benefits and protection" of California's laws. *See* Shaffer v. Heitner, supra, 433 U.S., at 216.[7]

Nor can we agree with the assertion of the court below that the exercise of *in personam* jurisdiction here was warranted by the financial benefit [Ezra] derived from his daughter's presence in California for nine months of the year. This argument rests on the premise that, while [Ezra's] liability for support payments remained unchanged, his yearly expenses for supporting the child in New York decreased. But this circumstance, even if true, does not support California's assertion of jurisdiction here. Any diminution in [Ezra's] household costs resulted, not from the child's presence in California, but rather from her absence from [Ezra's] home. Moreover, an action by appellee Horn to increase support payments could now be brought, and could have been brought when Ilsa first moved to California, in the State of New York; a New York court would clearly have personal jurisdiction over [Ezra] and, if a judgment were entered by a New York court increasing [Ezra's] child support obligations, it could properly be enforced against him in both New York and California. Any ultimate financial advantage to [Ezra] thus results not from the child's presence in California but from [Sharon's] failure earlier to seek an increase in payments under the separation agreement. The argument below to the contrary, in our view, confuses the question of [Ezra's] liability with that of the proper forum in which to determine that liability. . . .

In light of our conclusion that [Ezra] did not purposefully derive benefit from any activities relating to the State of California, it is apparent that the California Supreme Court's reliance on [Ezra's] having caused an "effect" in California was misplaced. This "effects" test is derived from the American Law Institute's Restatement (Second) of Conflicts § 37 (1971), which provides:

> "A state has power to exercise judicial jurisdiction over an individual who causes effects in the state by an act done elsewhere with respect to any cause of action arising from these effects unless the nature of the effects and of the individual's relationship to the state make the exercise of such jurisdiction unreasonable."

While this provision is not binding on this Court, it does not in any event support the decision below. As is apparent from the examples accompanying § 37 in the Restatement, this section was intended to reach wrongful activity outside of the State causing injury within the State, see, e.g., Comment *a,* p. 157 (shooting bullet from one State into

[7] The court below stated that the presence in California of [Ezra]'s daughter gave [Ezra] the benefit of California's "police and fire protection, its school system, its hospital services, its recreational facilities, its libraries and museums. . . ." 564 P.2d, at 356. But, in the circumstances presented here, these services provided by the State were essentially benefits to the child, not the father, and in any event were not benefits that [Ezra] purposefully sought for himself.

another), or commercial activity affecting state residents, ibid. Even in such situations, moreover, the Restatement recognizes that there might be circumstances that would render "unreasonable" the assertion of jurisdiction over the nonresident defendant.

The circumstances in this case clearly render "unreasonable" California's assertion of personal jurisdiction. . . . There is no claim that [Ezra] has visited physical injury on either property or persons within the State of California. *Compare* Hess v. Pawloski, 274 U.S. 352 (1927). The cause of action herein asserted arises, not from the defendant's commercial transactions in interstate commerce, but rather from his personal, domestic relations. . . . Furthermore, the controversy between the parties arises from a separation that occurred in the State of New York; [Sharon] seeks modification of a contract that was negotiated in New York and that she flew to New York to sign. . . .

Finally, basic considerations of fairness point decisively in favor of [Ezra's] State of domicile as the proper forum for adjudication of this case, whatever the merits of [Sharon's] underlying claim. It is [Ezra] who has remained in the State of the marital domicile, whereas it is [Sharon] who has moved across the continent. . . .

In seeking to justify the burden that would be imposed on [Ezra] were the exercise of *in personam* jurisdiction in California sustained, [Sharon] argues that California has substantial interests in protecting the welfare of its minor residents and in promoting to the fullest extent possible a healthy and supportive family environment in which the children of the State are to be raised. These interests are unquestionably important. But while the presence of the children and one parent in California arguably might favor application of California law in a lawsuit in New York, the fact that California may be the " 'center of gravity' " for choice of law purposes does not mean that California has personal jurisdiction over the defendant. . . .

California's legitimate interest in ensuring the support of children resident in California without unduly disrupting the children's lives, moreover, is already being served by the State's participation in the Uniform Reciprocal Enforcement of Support Act of 1968. This statute provides a mechanism for communication between court systems in different States, in order to facilitate the procurement and enforcement of child-support decrees where the dependent children reside in a State that cannot obtain personal jurisdiction over the defendant. California's version of the Act essentially permits a California resident claiming support from a nonresident to file a petition in California and have its merits adjudicated in the State of the alleged obligor's residence, without either party having to leave his or her own State. Cal.Code Civ.Proc. § 1650 et seq. New York State is a signatory to a similar act. Thus, not only may [Sharon] here vindicate her claimed right to additional child support from her former husband in a New York court, but the uniform acts will facilitate both her prosecution of a claim for additional support and collection of any support payments found to be owed by [Ezra].[15]

It cannot be disputed that California has substantial interests in protecting resident children and in facilitating child-support actions on behalf of those children. But these interests simply do not make California a "fair forum," Shaffer v. Heitner, supra, 433 U.S., at 215, in which to require [Ezra], who derives no personal or commercial benefit from his child's presence in California and who lacks any other relevant contact with the State, either to defend a child-support suit or to suffer liability by default. . . .

Accordingly, we conclude that the [Ezra]'s motion to quash service, on the ground of lack of personal jurisdiction, was erroneously denied by the California courts. The judgment of the California Supreme Court is, therefore,

Reversed.

[The dissenting opinion of JUSTICE BRENNAN has been omitted.]

NOTES

"Tag" Jurisdiction. In *Kulko*, the Supreme Court overturned the California court's ruling that the state could exercise personal jurisdiction over the non-resident defendant, on the grounds that his due process rights were violated. In another case involving slightly different facts—the defendant was served with process while in the forum state of California—the Supreme Court reached the opposite conclusion, holding that California could exercise personal jurisdiction. *See* Burnham v. Superior Court of California, 495 U.S. 604 (1990). *Burnham* involved a married couple who resided in New Jersey for ten years. When the couple decided to separate, they agreed that wife would move to California with their two children, and also agreed to file for no-fault divorce in the future. Husband remained in New Jersey. A few months later, wife sued for fault-based divorce in California. When husband visited California for business and to see the children, he was served with wife's divorce petition and a summons.

Husband entered a special appearance to contest jurisdiction. His motion to quash the service was denied in the state courts, and the Supreme Court held that exercise of personal jurisdiction based on his in-state service was proper, comporting with traditional notions of fair play and substantial justice. In an opinion by Justice Scalia, the Court stated:

> Among the most firmly established principles of personal jurisdiction in American tradition is that the courts of a State have jurisdiction over nonresidents who are physically present in the State. The view developed early that each State had the power to hale before its courts any individual who could be found within its

---

[15] Thus, it cannot here be concluded, as it was in *McGee v. International Life Insurance Co.*, 355 U.S., at 223–224, with respect to actions on insurance contracts, that resident plaintiffs would be at a "severe disadvantage" if *in personam* jurisdiction over out-of-state defendants were sometimes unavailable.

borders, and that once having acquired jurisdiction over such a person by properly serving him with process, the State could retain jurisdiction to enter judgment against him, no matter how fleeting his visit. . . .

It goes too far to say, as petitioner contends, that *Shaffer* [*v. Heitner*, 433 U.S. 186 (1977)] compels the conclusion that a State lacks jurisdiction over an individual unless the litigation arises out of his activities in the State. *Shaffer* . . . involved jurisdiction over an absent defendant. . . . The logic of *Shaffer*'s holding—which places all suits against absent nonresidents on the same constitutional footing . . . does not compel the conclusion that physically present defendants must be treated identically to absent ones. As we have demonstrated at length, our tradition has treated the two classes of defendants quite differently, and it is unreasonable to read *Shaffer* as casually obliterating that distinction. *International Shoe* confined its 'minimum contacts' requirement to situations in which the defendant 'be not present within the territory of the forum,' " 326 U.S., at 316, and nothing in *Shaffer* expands that requirement beyond that.

It is fair to say, however, that while our holding today does not contradict *Shaffer*, our basic approach to the due process question is different. We have conducted no independent inquiry into the desirability or fairness of the prevailing in-state service rule, leaving that judgment to the legislatures that are free to amend it; for our purposes, its validation is its pedigree, as the phrase "traditional notions of fair play and substantial justice" makes clear. *Shaffer* did conduct such an independent inquiry, asserting that " 'traditional notions of fair play and substantial justice' can be as readily offended by the perpetuation of ancient forms that are no longer justified as by the adoption of new procedures that are inconsistent with the basic values of our constitutional heritage." 433 U.S., at 212. Perhaps that assertion can be sustained when the "perpetuation of ancient forms" is engaged in by only a very small minority of the States. Where, however, as in the present case, a jurisdictional principle is both firmly approved by tradition and still favored, it is impossible to imagine what standard we could appeal to for the judgment that it is "no longer justified." While in no way receding from or casting doubt upon the holding of *Shaffer* or any other case, we reaffirm today our time-honored approach. . . . For new procedures, hitherto unknown, the Due Process Clause requires analysis to determine whether "traditional notions of fair play and substantial justice" have been offended. International Shoe, 326 U.S., at 316. But a doctrine of personal jurisdiction that dates back to the adoption of the Fourteenth Amendment and is still generally observed unquestionably meets that standard.

Id. at 610–622.

"Family law" long-arm statutes. Many states have added specific family law provisions to their "long-arm" statutes. KAN. STAT. ANN. § 60–308(b)(1)(H) (2015) extends jurisdiction for maintenance, child support, and property settlement obligations to any person who lives in a marital relationship in Kansas—including spouses who move to another state, if one spouse continues to reside in Kansas. Like Kansas, other states' long-arm statutes often refer to the "matrimonial domicile" at the commencement of—or preceding—the divorce action as the basis for jurisdiction. *See, e.g.*, GA. CODE ANN. § 9–10–91 (2016); Cooke v. Cooke, 594 S.E.2d 370 (Ga. 2004) (finding that an ex-resident was subject to the state's jurisdiction in a divorce action because the couple's marital domicile was Georgia for a five-year period).

In the absence of specific statutory reference to a long-arm statute, courts safeguard due process requirements through minimum contact requirements. *See, e.g.*, Sherlock v. Sherlock, 545 S.E.2d 757 (N.C. Ct. App. 2001), where the court found sufficient minimum contacts where husband administered his important legal, civic, personal, and financial affairs primarily from North Carolina. But in Bushelman v. Bushelman, 629 N.W.2d 795 (Wisc. 2001), the court held that a non-resident husband's consent to his wife and children living in Wisconsin, and his phone calls and letters to them, as well as his visits with them in the state, did not confer minimum contacts for personal jurisdiction.

For a summary of states' long-arm statutes, including specific family law provisions, *see Personal Jurisdiction Statutes, 50 State Statutory Surveys: Civil Laws: Civil Procedure*, 0020 SURVEYS 10 (West 2012).

PROBLEM ONE

Harry and Wendy met at a party in D.C. (a jurisdiction which recognizes common law marriage) in 2012. They fell in love almost immediately and Harry moved into Wendy's apartment within a few months. Wendy and Harry were deliriously in love and Wendy would frequently tell her friends, "I'm so lucky to have met my husband, Harry." Harry would glow when Wendy said that and often return the compliment saying, "And I'm so lucky to have the wife I have." When Harry presented Wendy with a gorgeous ring the next Valentine's Day and promised to always be faithful to her, Wendy was ecstatic and promised she would wear the ring always. The following year, Wendy and Harry set up a joint bank account together. They eventually were able to buy a car with money from that account. Sadly, the very next year, Harry faced charges of fraud. He was convicted and sentenced to fifteen years in prison. Soon after Harry went in jail in D.C., Wendy packed all her clothes and personal items into the car and moved to Virginia. Using the rest of the money in her joint bank account with Harry, Wendy made a down payment on a small house off the bay in Reedville, Virginia. Disappointed in Harry, but determined to get on with her life, Wendy filed for divorce in Virginia.

Although Harry is still in prison in D.C., he gets his mother to pay for an attorney to appear for him in the Virginia divorce proceeding. But after the court enters a decree awarding Wendy a divorce and giving her the car and house in Virginia, Harry is devastated. Harry calls his divorce attorney and demands to know how the Virginia Court could enter a divorce decree against him when he is in jail in D.C. and has never been to Virginia. Explain why the Virginia court was able to enter the decree and what remedies were properly given in the divorce proceeding.

i) Assume Harry did not have a lawyer. However, Harry gets out from jail on probation for good behavior. He goes to Virginia to see his mom and Wendy serves Harry while he is there. Because he is on probation, Harry has to go back to D.C., where he gets a job making minimum wage. Harry is unable to be in Virginia for the divorce proceeding. Will Wendy be able to obtain a divorce decree now? If so, what remedies will she be able to obtain through the divorce?

ii) Now assume Harry has never been to VA but Wendy properly served him while he was in jail in D.C. Can the Virginia court grant a divorce decree? If so, what remedies will be available to Wendy?

PROBLEM TWO

Assume same facts as in Problem 1, but due to overcrowding, Harry is soon transferred to a North Carolina prison. While in North Carolina, Harry becomes increasingly frustrated with the fact that Wendy no longer visits and doesn't accept his calls. Harry believes Wendy, who moved to Virginia after Harry was sent to prison, has met a new boyfriend. Harry decides to file for divorce. Harry also wants alimony from Wendy because he never has enough money to buy ramen and cigarettes from commissary. However, Harry is unable to serve Wendy because he lacks an address or email. Will Harry be able to obtain a divorce decree? What remedies would be available in this North Carolina divorce?

PROBLEM THREE

Assume Harry obtains his divorce from the North Carolina court, as in Problem 2, and there is no Virginia divorce awarded to Wendy. Harry turned out to be a model inmate and is released from prison early. Harry struggles to get back on his feet at first. He moves back to Virginia with his mother, where he eventually finds employment at an upscale restaurant. In short order, Harry becomes a partner in the restaurant and is able to buy his own house as well as a 1959 convertible Ford Thunderbird, a car he has always admired. Wendy, who stumbles on Harry on Facebook, notices that he seems to be doing well even as her fortunes have plummeted. Wendy decides to petition for alimony in Virginia. Will she be successful? How might this affect the house in Virginia?

PROBLEM FOUR

Assume the same facts as in 2 and 3 but imagine that Harry was able to properly and personally serve Wendy with notice of the North Carolina divorce. The North Carolina court decided that neither party would get alimony and the issue was not reserved. How does that change the result?

E. FEDERALISM, MEDIATION, AND MALPRACTICE

As the preceding sections illustrate, divorce raises complicated problems within our federal system. Justice Frankfurter articulated the issues in his concurring opinion in *Williams (I)*:

> In a country like ours where each state has the constitutional power to translate into law its own notions of policy concerning the family institution, and where citizens pass freely from one state to another, tangled marital situations, like the one immediately before us, inevitably arise. They arose before and after the decision in the *Haddock* case, 201 U.S. 562, and will, I daresay, continue to arise no matter what we do today. For these complications cannot be removed by any decisions this Court can make—neither the crudest nor the subtlest juggling of legal concepts could enable us to bring forth a uniform national law of marriage and divorce.

Williams v. North Carolina (I), 317 U.S. 287, 304 (1942). Are there ways to simplify the divorce process given the variety of state divorce laws and the need to protect due process?

Should Divorce Become a Federal Issue? Some commentators suggest that the federal government take over the entire divorce mechanism and provide uniformity throughout the states. *See, e.g.*, Ann L. Estin, *Family Law Federalism: Divorce and the Constitution*, 16 WM. & MARY BILL RTS. J. 381 (2007). History and the resurgence of federalism, however, mitigate against such proposals. *See generally* Ronald M. Jacobs, *Defining the Line Between State and Federal Governance*, 69 GEO. WASH. L. REV. 135 (2001); Ernest A. Young, *Dual Federalism, Concurrent Jurisdiction, and the Foreign Affairs Exception*, 69 GEO. WASH. L. REV. 139 (2001); Linda H. Elrod, *Epilogue: Of Families, Federalization, and a Quest for Policy*, 33 FAM. L. Q. 843 (1999); STANLEY ELKINS AND ERIC MCKITRICK, THE AGE OF FEDERALISM (1993); Ankenbrandt v. Richards, 504 U.S. 689 (1992) (affirming the domestic relations exception to federal subject matter jurisdiction).

Should Divorces be Mediated? A more feasible approach to simplifying the divorce process is a trend towards mediation and avoiding attorneys in the process. Mediation may facilitate custody and visitation issues. *See generally Mediation Requirements,* 50 STATE STATUTORY SURVEYS, 0080 SURVEYS 12 (West 2012); Marsha B. Freeman, *Divorce Mediation: Sweeping Conflicts Under the Rug, Time to Cleans House*, 78 U. DET. L. REV. 67 (2000); Judge Diane K. Vescovo, Allen S. Blair and Hayden D. Lait, *Ethical Dilemmas in Mediation,* 31 U. MIAMI L. REV. 59 (2000).

Legal Misconduct in Divorce Proceedings. Divorce has become a matter of negotiation rather than litigation in many instances, as the material in the following chapters will reveal. Not surprisingly, disputes have reached the courts concerning what roles non-lawyers may play (*e.g.*, selling divorce forms or helping complete them) without running afoul of proscriptions against unauthorized legal practice. Lawyer misconduct during divorce proceedings has precipitated even more lawsuits, with allegations such as: (1) misuse of the legal process, Caudle v. Mendel, 994 P.2d 372 (Alaska 1999); (2) having sexual relationships with clients in a divorce action, *In re* Halverson, 998 P.2d 833 (Wisc. 2000); *see also In re* Tsoutsouris, 748 N.E.2d 856 (Ind. 2001); (3) equitable indemnity, Gursey Schneider & Co. v. Wasser, Rosenson & Carter, 90 Cal.App.4th 1367 (2001); (4) malpractice, Fang v. Bock, 28 P.3d 456 (Mont. 2001); (5) intentional infliction of emotional distress, Gaspard v. Beadle, 36 S.W.3d 229 (Tex. Ct. App. 2001). For a general review of the attorney-client role in the process of divorce, *see* Patrick Ziepolt & Margaret Christensen, *Developments in Professional Responsibility*, 47 IND. L. REV. 1153 (2014); Carrie J. Menkel-Meadow, *When Winning Isn't Everything: The Lawyer as Problem Solver*, 28 HOFSTRA L. REV. 905 (2000); Marianne M. Jennings, *Moral Disengagement and Lawyers: Codes, Ethics, Conscience, and Some Great Movies*, 37 DUQ. L. REV. 637 (2000).

In re Belding

Supreme Court of South Carolina, 2003
589 S.E.2d 197

■ PER CURIAM:

Todd Hunnicutt ("Mr. Hunnicutt") and Elizabeth Hunnicutt ("Ms. Hunnicutt") were having marital problems. According to Respondent, in the late summer of 2000, Mr. Hunnicutt approached Respondent and told him that he and his wife were undergoing a "Gestalt" method of therapy. Mr. Hunnicutt asked Respondent to create a fictitious set of divorce documents to "shock" his wife as prescribed by the therapy. According to this method, Ms. Hunnicutt would be "shocked" into mending the marriage upon seeing the fictitious documents. As requested, Respondent prepared the documents. He drafted a Summons and Complaint titled *Elizabeth Stenzel Hunnicutt v. A. Todd Hunnicutt.* The documents bore a fictitious docket number with the last three digits handwritten, a fictitious filing stamp for the Clerk of Court of Newberry County, and the signature of "Mark J. Taylor," as Respondent purported to be. Respondent continued to draft documents that appeared authentic. He drafted a fictitious Consent Order to Change Venue from Newberry to Lexington County. On the document, Respondent signed the names "Mark J. Taylor" and "Warren Powell." He also signed "J. M. Rucker" in the block designated "presiding judge." Respondent then drafted a letter on his own letterhead, which purported to be written to Taylor, indicating that he, Respondent, was now representing Mr. Hunnicutt in the divorce.

Respondent then prepared a false "Defendant's First Set of Interrogatories and First Request for Production." He signed his assistant's name to the certificate of mailing, purporting proper service of the Interrogatories. He then drafted a fictitious Request for Hearing form, bearing "Mark J. Taylor" as counsel for Ms. Hunnicutt. Respondent then prepared a handwritten letter on his letterhead addressed to "Todd" and attached a fictitious settlement agreement bearing the false docket numbers. The documents are entirely false and were never filed in any court. Respondent gave the documents to Mr. Hunnicutt. Ms. Hunnicutt found the documents in the trunk of Mr. Hunnicutt's car and was confused because she had not initiated the divorce action as suggested in the documents. She faxed the documents to a cousin in Missouri. The Missouri attorney confirmed that the documents appeared authentic and that a divorce action appeared to be underway. The Missouri attorney contacted Taylor and Judge Rucker, neither of whom knew about the matter. In turn, Taylor and Judge Rucker contacted the Commission on Lawyer Conduct. The Attorney General's Office joined this matter with the Jennifer Carmen matter and issued formal charges accordingly.

In 1997, Jennifer Carmen ("Ms. Carmen") hired Respondent in an action to increase child support payments from her former husband. Respondent brought the action in Lexington County Family Court. Ms. Carmen's former husband, Mark Carmen ("Mr. Carmen"), who was represented by Nancy M. Young ("Young"), counterclaimed for additional visitation with the couple's son. Respondent told Ms. Carmen that a hearing would take place on June 29, 1998. The Lexington County docketing clerk sent Respondent a Notice of Hearing indicating that the hearing had been set for June 23, 1998. Respondent failed to send Ms. Carmen a copy of the Notice, and he did not inform her of the change. As a result, Ms. Carmen and Respondent were not present at the June 23 hearing.

After the June 23 hearing, Young called Respondent and offered to settle the case. Respondent was unaware that he had missed the hearing. Young presented Respondent with an offer that would increase visitation rights for Mr. Carmen and would increase child support for Ms. Carmen. Respondent told her that he would call Ms. Carmen to obtain her consent to settle the matter. He was unable to reach Ms. Carmen and obtain her approval. Nevertheless, he called Young and accepted the offer to settle. On June 26, 1998, Mr. Carmen contacted Ms. Carmen to ask her when he could pick up their son. Ms. Carmen did not know about the June 23 hearing or the subsequent settlement agreement. She contacted Respondent to find out about the status of her case. Respondent assured her that he would call the court to find out the results of the hearing. He admitted to missing the hearing date and encouraged her to agree to the terms of the proposed settlement. He reiterated that the settlement terms were consistent with what a judge would order, but Ms. Carmen refused to consent to the proposed settlement.

In late July 1998, Ms. Carmen went to Respondent's office to retrieve her file. The file contained a copy of the settlement agreement that she never signed. On July 29, 1998, Young filed a Motion to Compel

Settlement. Respondent received a copy of this Motion and informed Ms. Carmen that a hearing on the Motion was set for September 4, 1998. On August 4, 1998, Respondent filed a Motion to be Relieved as Counsel in the case. He did not notify Ms. Carmen that he had filed this Motion. On September 4, 1998, Respondent and Ms. Carmen attended the scheduled hearing. The court was the first to inform Ms. Carmen of Respondent's Motion to be Relieved as Counsel. She agreed to find another counsel. Judge Sawyer issued an Order granting Young's Motion to Compel Settlement but ruled that the issues of reasonableness and fairness would be heard *de novo* on November 17, 1998. After Respondent was relieved as counsel, Ms. Carmen hired Kenneth H. Lester ("Lester") to represent her at the November hearing. Lester also helped negotiate a settlement that was more advantageous to Ms. Carmen than the settlement that Respondent negotiated for her. Lester's fees totaled approximately $7,000.

We hold that Respondent's conduct constituted a violation of Rules 1.1 (competence), 1.2 (scope of representation), 1.4 (communication), 1.16 (terminating representation), 4.1 (truthfulness and statements to others), and 8.4(a), (d), and (e) (misconduct) of the *Rules of Professional Conduct,* Rule 407, SCACR, and warrants discipline in accordance with Rule 7(a)(3) (definite suspension from the practice of law) of the *Rules for Lawyer Disciplinary Enforcement,* Rule 413, SCACR. We hold that Respondent violated Rule 4.1, which states that a lawyer shall not knowingly, "make a false statement of material fact or law to a third person" or "fail to disclose a material fact to a third person when disclosure is necessary to avoid assisting a criminal or fraudulent act by a client, unless disclosure is prohibited by Rule 1.6."

This Court has recently heard two cases involving lawyers who engaged in conduct similar to Respondent's conduct. In *In the Matter of Mozingo,* 330 S.C. 67, 497 S.E.2d 729 (1998), this Court disbarred an attorney for signing Chief Justice Toal's name on a falsified document. The attorney represented his client in an action to reduce or eliminate child support and alimony payments. To help the client appease his family, the attorney signed Justice Toal's name to a letter stating that the court had received the client's Motion and was in the process of eliminating the requirement that his wages be garnished. *In the Matter of Walker,* 305 S.C. 482, 409 S.E.2d 412 (1991), a client hired an attorney to expunge the client's record. Two years later, the client saw his attorney at a party. The attorney told the client that he "was a free man" when in fact the attorney had done nothing to expunge his client's record. To support his misrepresentation, the attorney signed a circuit court judge's name to a false order and gave it to the client. The client, concerned that the document did not appear to be properly filed, went to the Clerk of Court to file it. The Clerk rejected the order because the signature had been forged. The attorney argued that the only reason that he signed the judge's name was so that client could see how the order would appear.

The attorney was indefinitely suspended. Chief Justice Gregory dissented, stating that the attorney should have been disbarred.

In the present case, Respondent drafted false documents that included names of real lawyers and a judge. He argues that he never intended for the documents to be presented as if they were authentic, yet the record indicates that he made a conscious effort to make the documents appear authentic. Respondent further argues that he has not violated Rule 4.1 because he lacked the intent to commit criminal forgery as defined by the Court of Appeals in *State v. Wescott,* 316 S.C. 473, 477, 450 S.E.2d 598, 601 (Ct.App.1994). We disagree. Rule 4.1 does not require that criminal conduct be shown in order to justify a sanction. Whether Respondent committed criminal forgery is a collateral determination that is not dispositive of a determination of Respondent's misconduct under Rule 4.1.

This Court generally imposes severe sanctions for attorneys who sign another's name without authorization. However, we elect to impose a less severe sanction for this violation because we find that the facts of *Mozingo* and *Walker* are distinguishable from the present case. In both *Mozingo* and *Walker,* attorneys actively presented false documents as if the documents were authentic. In this case, the documents were never presented as authentic; rather, Ms. Hunnicutt found the documents in Mr. Hunnicutt's car. The Attorney General's Office presented no direct evidence that Respondent used these documents to facilitate fraud upon the court. Nevertheless, the documents appear authentic and Respondent signed the names of real people, including a family court judge. This Court will impose substantial sanctions upon any attorney who signs the name of a judge, regardless of the use made of the document.

We hold that Respondent violated Rule 1.2(a), which provides that "[a] lawyer shall abide by a client's decision whether to accept an offer of settlement." This Court has frequently held that failing to receive a client's consent before entering into a contract is a violation of Rule 1.2. *See In the Matter of Edens* 344 S.C. 394, 544 S.E.2d 627 (2001) (attorney refinanced loan without client's consent); *In the Matter of Lewis,* 344 S.C. 1, 542 S.E.2d 713 (2001) (in approximately fifty-one instances, attorney signed settlement agreements without client's consent). In this case, Respondent accepted Young's offer to settle without consulting Ms. Carmen and obtaining her consent. Respondent denies that he and Young entered into a binding settlement agreement. Nevertheless, Young prepared an agreement, and the court granted a Motion to Compel settlement. That Respondent attempted to reach Ms. Carmen when Young proposed the settlement demonstrates that he knew he needed his client's consent in order to proceed, yet he proceeded anyway.

We also hold that Respondent violated Rule 1.4(a) and (b). Rule 1.4(a) states that "[a] lawyer shall keep a client reasonably informed about the status of a matter." Respondent admits that he failed to inform his client about the September 23, 2003 hearing. Rule 1.4(b) states that "[a] lawyer shall explain a matter to the extent reasonably necessary to permit the client to make informed decisions regarding the representation." Respondent failed to inform Ms. Carmen about the settlement negotiations. He also failed to properly inform Ms. Carmen of her rights and options upon his Motion to be Relieved as Counsel.

We hold that Respondent violated Rule 1.16, which states that "[u]pon termination of representation, a lawyer shall take steps to the extent reasonably practicable to protect a client's interests, such as giving reasonable notice to the client." This Court has reiterated the policy considerations of proper notice upon intention to withdraw as counsel. In *Ex Parte Strom*, this Court held that "[s]trong policy considerations dictate that a client and the court must be unequivocally informed when an attorney intends to withdraw from representing a party, for whatever reason." 343 S.C. 257, 259, 539 S.E.2d 699, 701 (2000). Respondent's notice was less than "unequivocal." Ms. Carmen was entitled to notice that Respondent's Motion to be Relieved as Counsel had been filed. Upon learning that he missed the June 23, 1998 hearing, Respondent engaged in a charade to conceal his mistakes. Rather than trying to mitigate the damage he caused to his client, Respondent orchestrated an unauthorized settlement. When his client would not consent to that settlement he attempted to be relieved as counsel. We believe that when an attorney attempts to cover up bad acts in lieu of continuing to remain an active advocate for his client, he subjects himself to substantial sanctions.

Consequently, we suspend Respondent for one year, effective as of the date of this opinion, and order him to pay the costs of the disciplinary proceedings. Within fifteen days of the date of this opinion, Respondent shall file an affidavit with the Clerk of Court showing that he has complied with Rule 30, RLDE, of Rule 413, SCACR.

■ TOAL, C.J., WALLER, BURNETT, PLEICONES, JJ., and Acting Justice REGINALD I. LLOYD, concur.

CHAPTER V

MARITAL BREAKDOWN: RESOLVING THE FINANCIAL CONCERNS

A. ALIMONY AND PROPERTY DISTRIBUTION: THE BASIC FRAMEWORKS

1. INTRODUCTION

Originally, support during marriage was the responsibility of the husband in return for the wife's services and sometimes the economic dowry the wife brought to the marriage. Likewise, awarding alimony after marriage originated in English law as a continuing duty of support owed by husband to wife during a period of separation "from bed and board" described by the ecclesiastical courts as a divorce "*a mensa et thoro*." During this period of support, neither party could remarry because the bond of matrimony was indissoluble and still intact; thus support was part of the continuing duty owed by the husband to his wife. Today, support or maintenance awards during periods of physical and legal separation mirror this practice, but awards are made without reference to gender. Whenever a couple was able to obtain a Parliamentary divorce, one which allowed for the bond of matrimony to be severed absolutely (divorce "*a vincula*"), each spouse was able to marry another person and technically the prior marriage and support duty of the prior spouse ceased. This complete cessation of marriage and support—a "clean break"—occurs infrequently in modern society and legislatures and courts grapple with two distinct elements of financial concern: (1) distribution of marital assets, and (2) providing for alimony, or what the American Law Institute (ALI) now terms "compensatory spousal payments." A third financial concern, child support, addressed later in this chapter, completes the legal spectrum of financial concerns that must be resolved.

In making distributions of marital property and/or awarding alimony, American jurisdictions may be grouped under two general classifications: (1) common law or equitable property states, and (2) community property states. More often than not, these two overlap in approach so that any precise delineation is impossible. Nonetheless, the common law property states traditionally recognize title—ownership—in one of the marital partners; equitable principles are then used to apportion that property between both parties. Community property states tend to disregard title in one partner, presuming instead that everything acquired with spousal labor during the marriage is the property of the community in which each spouse has an undivided one-half interest without regard to equitable principles. Again, the two systems often overlap depending on state statutes and the considerable discretion of the trial court.

The material presented below offers two statutory models. New York is representative of the common law property states' acknowledgment of ownership through title. The legislature adopted a list of equitable factors to guide the court in fairly apportioning marital assets and, if necessary, awarding alimony, which was premised upon the marriage itself. Equitable distribution has actually decreased the importance of alimony, which had been utilized to provide support for a former spouse who lacked title over property. Divorce courts are given more authority to make division of property and support awards based on factors approved by the legislature, thus providing at least a basis for uniformity within the jurisdiction. Issues such as fault, duration of any award, and whether to treat things like income-producing education and goodwill as property continue to challenge common law property states.

The second statutory approach typifies community property states. Most often identified with California, nine American states and Puerto Rico historically have followed the community property system of wealth transfer. These nine states are Arizona, California, Idaho, Louisiana, Nevada, New Mexico, Texas, Washington, and Wisconsin. *See* Richard A. Leitner, *Marital Property, 50 State Statutory Survey: Family Law: Divorce and Dissolution*, 0080 SURVEYS 10 (2007). This system originated with the Visigoth tribes in Europe and then the Spanish conquerors occupying parts of the United States. Title is unimportant; all property acquired during marriage is presumed to be community property. In a pure community property state, community property will be divided equally upon divorce. Spousal support is allowed but only in those instances to redress loss of earning capacity, expectations, or the destruction or concealment of community assets.

Particular attention should be given to the ability of adult parties at the time of their marriage to structure the outcome of property distribution upon any separation or divorce through contractual provisions pursuant to state laws patterned after the Uniform Premarital and Marital Agreement Act. Fairness, full disclosure, and the ability of attorneys to structure parties' expectations at the beginning of marriage may limit what the parties can decide by contract. Increasingly, periods of nonmarital cohabitation precede the marriage and this, too, may deserve incorporation into marital agreements.

Finally, modern courts give the parties wide latitude to order economic affairs between themselves as long as the arrangement does not impinge on the rights of children. Thus, parties may enter into post-nuptial agreements or separation agreements in contemplation of divorce. In such instances, attorneys and mediators serve as negotiators with the various statutory models operating as default rules. Such negotiation involves expertise in taxation, bankruptcy, torts, contracts, federal and state enforcement techniques, and of course professional responsibility.

2. APPROACH OF A COMMON LAW PROPERTY/EQUITABLE DISTRIBUTION STATE

All common law property states have enacted statutory lists of equitable distribution factors to accommodate the fact that title to property may be held in the name of one spouse even though it was acquired during marriage as a result of marital labor. *See* Linda A. Elrod and Robert G. Spector, *Review of the Year in Family Law: Working Toward More Uniformity in Laws Relating to Families*, 44 FAM. L.Q. 514, chart 5 (2011). The factors are to be utilized by trial judges in a fair allocation of property, but preference among the factors is missing, giving judges immense discretion. This promotes unpredictability in distribution. *See, e.g.,* Marsha Garrison, *How Do Judges Decide Divorce Cases? An Empirical Analysis of Discretionary Decision Making*, 74 N.C. L. REV. 401 (1996) and CYNTHIA LEE STARNES, THE MARRIAGE BUYOUT: THE TROUBLED TRAJECTORY OF U.S. ALIMONY LAW (2014). For a state court analysis, *see* Charles P. Kindregan, Jr. & Monroe L. Inker, *A Quarter Century of Allocating Spousal Property Interests: The Massachusetts Experience*, 33 SUFF. L. REV. 11 (1999). Duration of marriage, contributions made to the acquisition of marital property, and economic circumstances of the parties at the commencement of the marriage are among the most common factors in any statute. *See* ALI, PRINCIPLES OF THE LAW OF FAMILY DISSOLUTION: ANALYSIS AND RECOMMENDATIONS § 4:09, REPORTER'S NOTES, COMMENT A (2000). *See also* David N. Hofstein, Scott J.G. Finger, & Charles J. Meyer, *Equitable Distribution Involving Large Marital Estates,* 26 J. AM. ACAD. MATRIM. LAW 311 (2014). The New York state statute, *infra*, listing factors considered in equitable distribution is a prime example of one state's common law approach. The proportion of divorces in New York where alimony was awarded declined from 21 percent to 12 percent after the state adopted its equitable distribution statute. *See* Marsha Garrison, *Good Intentions Gone Awry: The Impact of New York's Equitable Distribution Law on Divorce Outcomes*, 57 BROOK. L. REV. 621, 697 (1991).

The statute is offered to provide an exploration of a common law approach to two of the three financial concerns of this chapter: marital property, spousal support, and child support. Specific definitions of what constitutes marital property and issues concerning child support will be discussed specifically *infra.*

NEW YORK DOMESTIC RELATIONS LAW (McKinney 2016)

§ 236, Part B

NEW ACTIONS OR PROCEEDINGS

Maintenance and distributive award.

1. Definitions. Whenever used in this part, the following terms shall have the respective meanings hereinafter set forth or indicated:

a. The term "maintenance" shall mean payments provided for in a valid agreement between the parties or awarded by the court in accordance with the provisions of subdivision six of this part, to be paid at fixed intervals for a definite or indefinite period of time, but an award of maintenance shall terminate upon the death of either party or upon the recipient's valid or invalid marriage, or upon modification pursuant to paragraph (b) of subdivision nine of section two hundred thirty-six of this part or section two hundred forty-eight of this chapter.

b. The term "distributive award" shall mean payments provided for in a valid agreement between the parties or awarded by the court, in lieu of or to supplement, facilitate or effectuate the division or distribution of property where authorized in a matrimonial action, and payable either in a lump sum or over a period of time in fixed amounts. Distributive awards shall not include payments which are treated as ordinary income to the recipient under the provisions of the United States Internal Revenue Code.

c. The term "marital property" shall mean all property acquired by either or both spouses during the marriage and before the execution of a separation agreement or the commencement of a matrimonial action, regardless of the form in which title is held, except as otherwise provided in agreement pursuant to subdivision three of this part. Marital property shall not include separate property as hereinafter defined.

d. The term separate property shall mean:

(1) property acquired before marriage or property acquired by bequest, devise, or descent, or gift from a party other than the spouse;

(2) compensation for personal injuries;

(3) property acquired in exchange for or the increase in value of separate property, except to the extent that such appreciation is due in part to the contributions or efforts of the other spouse;

(4) property described as separate property by written agreement of the parties pursuant to subdivision three of this part. . . .

2. Matrimonial actions. Except as provided in subdivision five of this part, the provisions of this part shall be applicable to actions for an annulment or dissolution of a marriage, for a divorce, for a separation, for a declaration of the nullity of a void marriage, for a declaration of the validity or nullity of a foreign judgment of divorce, for a declaration of the validity or nullity of a marriage, and to proceedings to obtain

maintenance or a distribution of marital property following a foreign judgment of divorce, commenced on and after the effective date of this part. Any application which seeks a modification of a judgment, order or decree made in an action commenced prior to the effective date of this part shall be heard and determined in accordance with the provisions of part A of this section.

3. Agreement of the parties. [Permitting enforcement of certain prenuptial agreements, discussed *infra*]. . . .

4. Compulsory financial disclosure. a. In all matrimonial actions and proceedings in which alimony, maintenance or support is in issue, there shall be compulsory disclosure by both parties of their respective financial states. No showing of special circumstances shall be required before such disclosure is ordered. A sworn statement of net worth shall be provided upon receipt of a notice in writing demanding the same, within twenty days after the receipt thereof. In the event said statement is not demanded, it shall be filed with the clerk of the court by each party, within ten days after joinder of issue, in the court in which the proceeding is pending. As used in this part, the term "net worth" shall mean the amount by which total assets including income exceed total liabilities including fixed financial obligations. It shall include all income and assets of whatsoever kind and nature and wherever situated and shall include a list of all assets transferred in any manner during the preceding three years, or the length of the marriage, whichever is shorter; provided, however that transfers in the routine course of business which resulted in an exchange of assets of substantially equivalent value need not be specifically disclosed where such assets are otherwise identified in the statement of net worth. All such sworn statements of net worth shall be accompanied by a current and representative paycheck stub and the most recently filed state and federal income tax returns including a copy of the W–2(s) wage and tax statement(s) submitted with the returns. In addition, both parties shall provide information relating to any and all group health plans available to them for the provision of care or other medical benefits by insurance or otherwise for the benefit of the child or children for whom support is sought, including all such information as may be required to be included in a qualified medical child support order as defined in section six hundred nine of the employee retirement income security act of 1974 (29 USC 1169) including, but not limited to: (i) the name and last known mailing address of each party and of each dependent to be covered by the order; (ii) the identification and a description of each group health plan available for the benefit or coverage of the disclosing party and the child or children for whom support is sought; (iii) a detailed description of the type of coverage available from each group health plan for the potential benefit of each such dependent; (iv) the identification of the plan administrator for each such group health plan and the address of such administrator; (v) the identification numbers for each such group health plan; and (vi) such other information

as may be required by the court. Noncompliance shall be punishable by any or all of the penalties prescribed in section thirty-one hundred twenty-six of the civil practice law and rules, in examination before or during trial.

b. As soon as practicable after a matrimonial action has been commenced, the court shall set the date or dates the parties shall use for the valuation of each asset. The valuation date or dates may be anytime from the date of commencement of the action to the date of trial.

5. Disposition of property in certain matrimonial actions. a. Except where the parties have provided in an agreement for the disposition of their property pursuant to subdivision three of this part, the court, in an action wherein all or part of the relief granted is divorce, or the dissolution, annulment or declaration of the nullity of a marriage, and in proceedings to obtain a distribution of marital property following a foreign judgment of divorce, shall determine the respective rights of the parties in their separate or marital property, and shall provide for the disposition thereof in the final judgment.

b. Separate property shall remain such.

c. Marital property shall be distributed equitably between the parties, considering the circumstances of the case and of the respective parties.

d. In determining an equitable disposition of property under paragraph c, the court shall consider:

(1) the income and property of each party at the time of marriage, and at the time of the commencement of the action;

(2) the duration of the marriage and the age and health of both parties;

(3) the need of a custodial parent to occupy or own the marital residence and to use or own its household effects;

(4) the loss of inheritance and pension rights upon dissolution of the marriage as of the date of dissolution;

(5) any award of maintenance under subdivision six of this part;

(6) any equitable claim to, interest in, or direct or indirect contribution made to the acquisition of such marital property by the party not having title, including joint efforts or expenditures and contributions and services as a spouse, parent, wage earner and homemaker, and to the career or career potential of the other party;

(7) the liquid or non-liquid character of all marital property;

(8) the probable future financial circumstances of each party;

(9) the impossibility or difficulty of evaluating any component asset or any interest in a business, corporation or profession, and the economic desirability of retaining such asset or interest intact and free from any claim or interference by the other party;

(10) the tax consequences to each party;

(11) the wasteful dissipation of assets by either spouse;

(12) any transfer or encumbrance made in contemplation of a matrimonial action without fair consideration;

(13) any other factor which the court shall expressly find to be just and proper.

e. In any action in which the court shall determine that an equitable distribution is appropriate but would be impractical or burdensome or where the distribution of an interest in a business, corporation or profession would be contrary to law, the court in lieu of such equitable distribution shall make a distributive award in order to achieve equity between the parties. The court in its discretion, also may make a distributive award to supplement, facilitate or effectuate a distribution of marital property.

f. In addition to the disposition of property as set forth above, the court may make such order regarding the use and occupancy of the marital home and its household effects as provided in section two hundred thirty-four of this chapter, without regard to the form of ownership of such property.

g. In any decision made pursuant to this subdivision, the court shall set forth the factors it considered and the reasons for its decision and such may not be waived by either party or counsel.

h. In any decision made pursuant to this subdivision the court shall, where appropriate, consider the effect of a barrier to remarriage, as defined in subdivision six of section two hundred fifty-three of this article, on the factors enumerated in paragraph d of this subdivision. . . .

PROBLEM ONE

Ken, a singer, and Kimber, a model and designer, started dating in April of 2013. Their whirlwind romance garnered a joint fan base and swept social media by storm. Busy falling in love with his eventual wife, Ken did not release an album in 2013. Kimber did not take a hiatus, she continued to work on a new clothing line and make promotional appearances. In August of 2014, just two months later, Kimber tells Ken that she is pregnant. Ken, still head over heels with Kimber, proposed to her with a $50,000 engagement ring. In a lavish ceremony that broke social media records, Ken and Kimber married on January 1st, 2015. Living up to their means, their net worths are a meager $1 million each on the day they marry. The happy couple purchased their first home together in September of 2014, and titled it in Kimber's name alone. Their 9,000 sq. ft. mansion cost $2 million, into which Ken and Kimber each contributed $1 million. Kimber delivers healthy twin infants in 2015. From 2014 to 2016, Kimber doubled her net worth every year, while Ken stumbled. In January of 2017, Ken gets laryngitis. It shatters his music career permanently, and his music-sharing venture Typhoon goes under, wiping out his earnings. To Kimber's disdain, Ken files for bankruptcy. Relying on Kimber to support their lavish lifestyle, Ken becomes a stay-at-home dad. He takes the kids to school, cooks their meals, and tucks them into bed while Kimber goes to gala after gala. To date in 2016, Kimber has earned a total of $120 million. This year, she started squirreling away earnings, and has $60 million in her bank account. Ken is destitute. If the couple divorces, Kimber wants to know how much exposure she has because she married "the bum." How would you predict a judge would equitably divide property under the New York statute?

3. APPROACH OF A COMMUNITY PROPERTY STATE

Ruggles v. Ruggles

Supreme Court of New Mexico, 1993
860 P.2d 182

■ MONTGOMERY, JUSTICE.

We . . . revisit a subject of recurring concern in our case law: the proper treatment, in a proceeding to dissolve a marriage, of the spouses' community property interest in an employer-sponsored retirement plan. We deem this subject to involve an issue of substantial public interest. . . . This Court discussed the subject most recently in Schweitzer v. Burch, 103 N.M. 612, 711 P.2d 889 (1985), in which we said (in what we shall see below was essentially dictum): "[U]pon dissolution of marriage, unless both parties agree otherwise, the trial court *must* divide community property retirement benefits on a 'pay as it comes in' basis." *Id.* at 615, 711 P.2d at 892 (emphasis added).

In the cases now under review, our Court of Appeals, in two 2-to-1 opinions by different panels, faithfully followed the *Schweitzer* "pay as it comes in" rule and held in effect that a nonemployee spouse is entitled, on dissolution of the marriage, to no monetary benefits representing his or her community interest in a retirement plan when the employee spouse has not yet retired. The nonemployee spouse's only entitlement on dissolution, the Court of Appeals held, is to an order that he or she will eventually, when the employee spouse actually retires and begins to receive payment of the pension provided for under the plan, receive payments of his or her share as they "come in." This is true even though the employee spouse's interest at the time of dissolution is, as it was in *Ruggles,* fully vested and matured. Ruggles v. Ruggles, 114 N.M. 63, 68–70, 834 P.2d 940, 945–47 (Ct.App.1992). . . .

We now withdraw *Schweitzer*'s rigid "pay as it comes in" mandate and return to the more flexible pre-*Schweitzer* formulations that permitted a trial court to award to a nonemployee spouse in a marital dissolution all or a portion of his or her community interest in a retirement plan. We hold that the preferred method of dealing with these community assets is to treat them as all other community assets are treated on dissolution—namely, to value, divide, and distribute them (or other assets with equivalent value) to the divorcing spouses. We realize that in some cases, given the innumerable variations in pension plans and the infinite variety in the circumstances of individual divorcing couples, it will not be possible or practicable to achieve this preferred method of distribution and that other methods, including the "reserved jurisdiction" or "pay as it comes in" method, will have to be utilized. In cases such as the two before us, in which the employee spouse's interest is vested and matured, the desirability and feasibility of an immediate distribution to the nonemployee spouse are at their zenith. Consequently, we hold that in such cases the trial court should adopt as its first priority the making of a "lump sum" or other equivalent distribution to the nonemployee spouse. The Court of Appeals having ruled otherwise in these cases, its decisions are reversed and each case is remanded to the respective trial court for further proceedings consistent with this opinion. . . .

Joseph and Nancy Ruggles were married on April 4, 1959. At the time of their marriage, Joseph was employed by Sandia Corporation ("Sandia") in Albuquerque, New Mexico. He began employment with Sandia on May 26, 1958, and remained continuously employed there through the time of trial. Sandia maintained a retirement plan for its employees, under which Joseph's interest was fully vested and matured at the time of trial;[2] he had become eligible to retire after thirty years' employment. The trial court found that as of the date of trial, June 28, 1988, Joseph would have been entitled to receive a pension of $1,570.71 per month had he elected to retire on that date. However, as of the date of trial he had not decided to retire and did not know when he would retire; he speculated that he might retire at age 63. At the time of trial he was 50.

The parties stipulated that as of June 28, 1988, Nancy owned a 48% interest in Joseph's Sandia pension benefits. Although they had entered into a comprehensive marital settlement agreement (discussed below), the agreement did not specifically provide when Nancy was to begin receiving her interest in the pension plan nor the specific dollar amount she was to receive, and these issues were disputed at trial. The court ruled that Nancy was entitled to receive 48% of $1,570.71, or $753.94, directly from Joseph, effective June 28, 1988, and continuing each month thereafter until Joseph's retirement from Sandia. At that time Nancy could receive her $753.94 directly from Sandia pursuant to a qualified

[2] An employee's interest is "vested" when he or she has the right to receive retirement benefits at normal or early retirement, whether or not the employee continues to work for the employer until retirement. Steven R. Brown, *Berry v. Berry and the Division of Pension Benefits in Divorce and Post-Judgment Partition Actions,* 13 Community Prop.J., April 1986, at 30, 34. An employee generally becomes 100% vested after some minimum number of years of employment, but the vesting rate varies greatly among retirement plans. An employee's interest has "matured" when the employee is actually eligible to retire and receive benefits. *See id.* at 33. The maturity date is generally determined by the employee's age and years of employment. Phoebe Carter & John Myers, *Division and Distribution of the Community Interest in Defined Benefit Pensions: Schweitzer Reconsidered,* 18 N.M. L.Rev. 95, 100–01 (1988).

domestic relations order ("QDRO").[3] The court also found that, if Joseph retired at the time of trial (at age 50), the then present value of the benefits he would receive from Sandia was $269,854.00; that if he retired at age 55, the present value of the benefits would be $182,000.00; and that if he retired at age 65, the present value would be $48,000.00. The court summed up these findings by declaring: "The present value of Joseph Ruggles's Sandia pension benefits drops every day that passes before retirement . . . " The trial court ruled that the agreement was not ambiguous and applied it in accordance with Nancy's contention: that she was entitled to receive $753.94 per month from Joseph commencing June 28, 1988, representing her interest in the Sandia pension benefits that Joseph would receive if he elected to retire at that time.

Joseph appealed to the Court of Appeals, arguing generally that the trial court's rulings contravened basic principles of community property law and misapplied the parties' MSA. The Court of Appeals agreed and reversed the trial court's judgment. In reaching its decision, the Court of Appeals first considered the parties' MSA. Although the Court agreed with the trial court that the agreement was unambiguous, it disagreed with the trial court as to the meaning of the agreement and concluded that the parties had agreed that Nancy would not receive her share of Joseph's benefits until he actually retired. Ruggles, 114 N.M. at 66–67, 834 P.2d at 943–44. The Court then stated that, while the MSA was binding on the parties, the trial court had discretion to modify it to ensure "fairness." It identified the fairness in question as "the equalized division of community property upon divorce." *Id.* at 67, 834 P.2d at 944.

The Court of Appeals then went on to discuss the trial court's order that Joseph pay Nancy her share of the retirement benefits before he actually retired. The Court gave three reasons for rejecting Nancy's argument that Joseph should not be able to time his retirement to deprive her of her share of their community property. First, the Court said that Nancy's position was contrary to *Schweitzer,* which requires distribution of retirement benefits on a "pay as it comes in basis." *Id.* at 69, 834 P.2d at 946. The Court's second reason was that delaying Nancy's receipt of benefits until Joseph actually retired did not deprive her of any rights because her rights derived from the community's rights; since the community's right to the benefits was always subject to Joseph's decision on when to retire, so too was her community interest upon dissolution of the marriage. *Id.* at 69–70, 834 P.2d at 946–47. Finally . . . the Court said

---

[3] A QDRO is a mechanism by which a nonemployee spouse can receive his or her community share of an employee spouse's retirement benefits directly from the employer. QDRO's were created by the Retirement Equity Act of 1984, Pub.L. No. 98–397, 98 Stat. 1426 ("REA"). The REA created a limited exception to the broad antiassignment provisions of the Employee Retirement Income Security Act of 1974 ("ERISA") and the Internal Revenue Code of 1954 ("IRC") to allow state courts, by order, to assign plan benefits if the state court order is a "qualified domestic relations order," or QDRO. Section 104, 98 Stat. at 1433 (amendment to ERISA) (codified as amended at 29 U.S.C. § 1056(d) (1988 & Supp. III 1991)); § 204, 98 Stat. at 1445 (amendment to IRC) (codified as amended at IRC §§ 401(a)(13), 414(p) (1988 & Supp. III 1991)).

that Joseph's postponement of retirement did not wholly delay Nancy's receipt of benefits since Nancy could immediately begin to receive a portion of her share of benefits directly from Sandia through a QDRO, which the trial court had found would amount to $182.98 per month. *Id.* at 70, 834 P.2d at 947. The Court remanded the case to the trial court with instructions to enter a QDRO for the amount Nancy could immediately begin receiving from Sandia.

Upon Nancy's petition, we granted certiorari. . . .

In LeClert v. LeClert, 80 N.M. 235, 236, 453 P.2d 755, 756 (1969), this Court first held that retirement benefits are a form of employee compensation and are community property to the extent they are attributable to employment during coverture. In that case we affirmed an order directing payment to the nonemployee spouse of one-half of the community share of the employee spouse's (the husband's) military retirement benefits *as received.* The husband had been ordered to retire from the military, so there was no issue over whether his benefits were vested or matured. We commented: "[The husband's] retirement pay to which he was to become entitled [on retirement] cannot be considered a mere expectancy. . . ." *Id.*

Several years after deciding *LeClert,* we issued our opinion in Copeland v. Copeland, 91 N.M. 409, 575 P.2d 99 (1978), which remained the leading case . . . until it was modified in *Schweitzer. Copeland* involved the division and distribution of vested but unmatured retirement benefits. We first concluded that unmatured benefits are community property subject to division *upon dissolution,* 91 N.M. at 412, 575 P.2d at 102, reasoning that it would be inequitable to consider such benefits to be a mere expectancy simply because they are subject to divestment by death, *see id.* at 411–12, 575 P.2d at 101–02. We noted that "[t]he cases are in agreement that at the time of the divorce the court must place a value on the pension rights and include it in the entire assets, then make a distribution of the assets equitably." *Id.* at 413, 575 P.2d at 103. Relying on cases from other community property jurisdictions, we pointed out that a determination of the discounted present value of the benefits at dissolution depends on a variety of factors, including, in addition to the possibility of the employee spouse's death, the possibility of termination of employment, the length of time remaining before the employee becomes eligible to retire and his or her interest matures, and the community's investment, if any, in the pension plan. *Id.* Quoting from *Wilder,* we recognized that "[t]here can be no set rule for determining every case and as in all other cases of property distribution, the trial court must exercise a wise and sound discretion." Copeland, 91 N.M. at 413, 575 P.2d at 103 (quoting *Wilder,* 534 P.2d at 1358).

We continued in *Copeland:*

> It would appear that a flexible approach to this problem is needed. The trial court should make a determination of the

> present value of the unmatured pension benefits with a division of assets which includes this amount, or divide the pension on a "pay as it comes in" system. This way, if the community has sufficient assets to cover the value of the pension, an immediate division would make a final disposition; but, if the pension is the only valuable asset of the community and the employee spouse could not afford to deliver either goods or property worth the other spouse's interest, then the trial court may award the non-employee spouse his/her portion as the benefits are paid.

Id. at 414, 575 P.2d at 104.

However, quoting from *In re Marriage of Brown,* 544 P.2d at 567, we cautioned that the trial court should observe "the fundamental principle that property attributable to community earnings must be divided equally *when the community is dissolved.*" 91 N.M. at 411, 575 P.2d at 101 (emphasis added). . . .

In 1985, this Court decided *Schweitzer* and in the process announced an abrupt departure from the principles of *Copeland* and its progeny. The issue was whether a beneficiary of the estate of a previously divorced nonemployee spouse, who upon her divorce had been awarded a share of her husband's monthly retirement benefit on a "pay as it comes in" basis, was entitled to continue to receive the benefits, which purportedly had been devised to the beneficiary by the decedent. In other words, was a deceased former spouse's right to receive her share of community property retirement benefits a devisable property right?

We answered that it was not. We held that community property retirement benefits that are awarded on a "pay as it comes in" basis are only inheritable or devisable up to the amount of the community contributions, if any, to the plan. An order dividing benefits on a "pay as it comes in" basis terminates, we held, on the death of either spouse unless the amount contributed by the community, if any, has not yet been paid out in benefits. Schweitzer, 103 N.M. at 615, 711 P.2d at 892.

There was thus no issue in *Schweitzer* about how a nonemployee spouse's community interest in a retirement plan should be distributed, or otherwise dealt with, upon divorce. Nevertheless, the Court stated: "We now modify *Copeland* prospectively to hold that upon dissolution of marriage, unless both parties agree otherwise, the trial court must divide community property retirement benefits on a 'pay as it comes in' basis." *Id.* After stating the actual holding of the case—that an order dividing benefits on a "pay as it comes in" basis terminates upon the death of either spouse (unless any amount contributed by the community has not yet been paid out in benefits)—the Court went on to explain the rationale for requiring distribution of all community retirement benefits on a "pay as it comes in" basis. We said that the reason for this requirement is to assure equity and fairness. Otherwise, the court could award a "lump sum" benefit in one case which would grant to the non-employee spouse an amount that might not ever be received if either spouse died before the projected benefits had been paid out; and on a "pay as it comes in" basis in another case, which would operate to the benefit of the employee spouse whose retirement income would not have to be divided after the non-employee spouse's death. The inequality would be compounded if the employee spouse died first, having received only a portion of his or her divided share but having paid the ex-spouse the present value of all of his or her estimated lifetime share under the lump sum decree. . . .

Schweitzer firmly committed New Mexico to the "reserved jurisdiction" method of distributing the community interest in retirement benefits. The other principal method of distributing these benefits is the "lump sum" or "cash value" method. Under the lump sum method, retirement plan benefits are awarded to the employee spouse at the time of dissolution and assets of equivalent value are awarded to the nonemployee spouse. *See* L. Glenn Hardie, *Pay Now or Later: Alternatives in the Disposition of Retirement Benefits on Divorce*, 53 CAL.ST.B.J. 106, 107 (1978). Under the reserved jurisdiction method, the court does not distribute the community interests at the time of dissolution, but reserves jurisdiction to distribute the benefits when the employee spouse actually receives them. *Id.; see also* Barbara A. DiFranza and Donald W. Parkyn, *Dividing Pensions on Marital Dissolution*, 55 CAL. ST. B. J. 464, 466–68 (1980) (describing both methods and referring to lump sum method as "present cash value" method).

With respect to the specific issue involved in this case—whether a nonemployee spouse should receive her community interest in a retirement plan, or begin to receive it, upon dissolution when the employee spouse's interest is vested and matured, or should be required to wait until retirement benefits are actually paid before receiving, or beginning to receive, her share—only three of the eight community property states appear to have expressly considered the issue. All three of those states have ruled that, when the employee spouse's interest is vested and matured, the nonemployee spouse is entitled upon dissolution to immediate distribution of her share of retirement benefits: Arizona—Koelsch v. Koelsch, 148 Ariz. 176, 713 P.2d 1234 (1986) (en banc); California—Gillmore v. Gillmore (*In re* Marriage of Gillmore), 29 Cal.3d 418, 174 Cal.Rptr. 493, 629 P.2d 1 (1981); and Nevada—Gemma v. Gemma, 105 Nev. 458, 778 P.2d 429 (1989). Rulings in the other community property jurisdictions are somewhat ambivalent on whether courts should follow one method or the other, and in any event none appears to have addressed the precise issue considered in this case.[10]

[10] The Texas Supreme Court has announced a clear preference for the "if, as, and when received" method of distributing retirement benefits, reasoning that it avoids the difficulties of computing present value. *Cearley v. Cearley,* 544 S.W.2d 661, 666 (Tex.1976). However, the court apparently has never *required* use of that method, and at least one appellate court has affirmed a trial court's lump sum distribution of retirement benefits. *See May v. May,* 716 S.W.2d 705, 711–12 (Tex.Ct.App.1986). Both Idaho and Washington recognize discretion in their

In re Marriage of Gillmore is a leading case. There, the California Supreme Court held that the nonemployee spouse can immediately receive her community interest in the benefits from the employee spouse. The court stated, "A unilateral choice to postpone retirement cannot be manipulated so as to impair a spouse's interest in . . . retirement benefits." Gillmore, 629 P.2d at 4. The court reasoned that the nonemployee spouse's interest would be impaired because she would be deprived of immediate enjoyment and management of her community property. *Id.* at 4 n. 4 (recognizing that "the timing of receipt and the control of an asset are important aspects of its value"). The court also said that the employee spouse cannot force the nonemployee spouse to share in the risk that the benefits could be forfeited if the employee spouse dies before retirement. *Id.* at 4.

The Arizona Supreme Court followed *Gillmore,* to a considerable extent, in *Koelsch.* In an extensive discussion covering various aspects of the subject considered in this opinion, the Arizona court held that a nonemployee spouse's community interest in an employee spouse's matured retirement plan, when the employee wants to continue working, is to be valued and paid, or commenced to be paid, upon dissolution. The court recognized, however, that the trial court retains considerable discretion in selecting the appropriate method of payment. The court expressed a preference for the lump sum distribution method as providing a clean break between the parties and an unencumbered pension plan to the employee, as well as relieving the court of any further supervision over the parties' relationship. Koelsch, 148 Ariz. at 183, 713 P.2d at 1241.

The court continued that the nonemployee spouse's lump sum interest in the plan can be satisfied in several ways: by an award of cash or property equal to the value of the interest or by an installment obligation, which may or may not correspond with the amount the nonemployee spouse would receive if the employee spouse were to retire, and which may be secured by a lien on some or all of the employee spouse's separate property and may bear interest. *Id.* at 183, 713 P.2d at 1241. Further, "[i]f the lump sum method would be impossible or inequitable, the court can order that the non-employee spouse be paid a monthly amount equal to his or her share of the benefit which would be received if the employee spouse were to retire." *Id.* at 185, 713 P.2d at 1243.

> For the reasons that appear below, we agree with *Koelsch* that the lump sum method is the preferable one for satisfying the nonemployee spouse's claim to her community interest in her spouse's retirement plan, and that the trial court should have discretion in implementing that method, alone or in combination with other methods, including in an appropriate

---

trial courts to make either a lump sum or a deferred distribution. . . . In Louisiana, trial courts similarly have flexibility to select an equitable method for distributing retirement benefits. . . .

case the reserved jurisdiction method, in distributing the nonemployee spouse's interest upon dissolution. . . .

Before applying the principles reviewed thus far in this opinion, we pause to remind ourselves of some equally important—indeed, fundamental—principles of community property law in New Mexico (and, so far as we are aware, in all other community property jurisdictions). First, it is axiomatic that each spouse in a marriage has a present, vested, one-half interest in the spouses' community property. This has been the law in this state at least since Beals v. Ares, 25 N.M. 459, 492–93, 185 P. 780, 790 (1919). The proposition has been reiterated countless times in our case law. . . .

Second . . . one of the chief incidents of community property lies in the district court's duty on dissolution to divide the property equally. Other cases, of course, can be cited to the same effect. . . .

Third, almost as a corollary to the rule requiring equal division of the community property on divorce, we have recognized the desirability of granting each spouse complete and immediate control over his or her share of the community property in order to ease the transition of the parties after dissolution. Hertz v. Hertz, 99 N.M. 320, 330, 657 P.2d 1169, 1179 (1983) (quoting Cunningham v. Cunningham, 96 N.M. 529, 531, 632 P.2d 1167, 1169 (1981)). In *Hertz* we reversed a trial court's order granting the divorcing spouses' residence to the husband and ordering him to pay the wife her community share of the residence through installments over a ten-year period. We held that the trial court erred in refusing to give the wife " 'complete and immediate control' of her interest in the community property." *Id.* at 330, 657 P.2d at 1169. Similarly, in Chrane v. Chrane, 98 N.M. 471, 649 P.2d 1384 (1982), we reversed a trial court's award to the wife of a life estate in the divorcing parties' residence. We reasoned that the effect of the court's award was to divest the husband of his equity in the property. *Id.* at 472, 649 P.2d at 1385. We accordingly directed the court on remand to order sale of the house and distribution of the proceeds to the parties within a reasonable time or to "make such other disposition of the home as will result in the husband receiving, within a reasonable time, his share of the value of the home." *Id.*

Immediately distributing community property on dissolution is of signal importance, not only because it eases the parties' transition following dissolution, but also because it furthers the important goal of minimizing future contact and conflict between divorcing spouses. Any court order that postpones distribution, thereby financially linking the parties to one another following a judgment of dissolution, invites future strife when one of the parties seeks to enforce the order. In the context of distribution of retirement benefits, several courts and commentators have identified severance of the parties' interest as an advantage of the lump sum distribution method over the reserved jurisdiction method.

Koelsch, 148 Ariz. at 183, 713 P.2d at 1241 ("provides a clean break between the parties"). . . .

With these principles in mind, we now apply them to the issues in these cases. . . . As noted above, the Court's concern in *Schweitzer* over the lump sum method was twofold: First, the court could award a "lump sum" benefit in one case which would grant to the non-employee spouse an amount that might not ever be received if either spouse died before the projected benefits had been paid out; and on a "pay as it comes in" basis in another case, which would operate to the benefit of the employee spouse whose retirement income would not have to be divided after the non-employee spouse's death.

Thus, the Court focused its concern over the lump sum method on the potential inequality arising from the risk of forfeiture borne by the employee spouse: If he lived longer than his life expectancy, he would realize benefits in excess of those distributed to his ex-spouse on dissolution; if he died before retirement or before living out his life expectancy, with no ability to alienate or transmit at death the value of his pension rights, he would receive less than the value of the rights transferred to his former spouse at the time of divorce. As the Court of Appeals put it in *Ruggles* below, this Court in *Schweitzer* "was most concerned with the possibility of the employee spouse bearing all the risk of forfeiture and desired instead for both parties to bear the risk . . . [The Supreme Court determined] that it is preferable for both spouses to bear the risk of forfeiture equally . . . " 114 N.M. at 69, 834 P.2d at 946.

But we think it impossible to devise a system that, in all cases, will result in both spouses bearing the risk of forfeiture equally. Although this is the professed goal of the reserved jurisdiction or "pay as it comes in" method, its achievement of that goal is illusory. For, while the nonemployee spouse risks losing everything if her husband dies prematurely (*i.e.,* before retirement), the employee spouse walks away from the marriage dissolution secure in the knowledge that, if he lives past retirement, he will eventually have a pension to protect him in his retirement years. In the meantime, he has a *job*. He has a source of income (probably amounting to considerably more than the amount he would receive as a retirement pension) and the relative comfort of knowing that his income will probably increase, his eventual pension will probably increase, and upon retirement he will receive a guaranteed lifetime annuity. The nonemployee spouse, to be sure, has some of the same expectations as her former husband; depending on how long he lives and when he chooses to retire, she will eventually share in his pension (to the extent, probably, determined years before at the time of divorce). In the meantime, she may lack employment, and her future security depends entirely on when her ex-spouse decides to retire. The goals of effecting a clean break between the parties and of disentangling them from one another financially have been subverted, and the court has the prospect of relitigating the parties' precise shares of the pension payments when the employee decides to retire.

This is not an equal sharing of the risk.... In *Ruggles,* for the reasons and subject to the principles discussed below, we reverse the Court of Appeals and remand the case to the trial court to decide the parties' dispute over their marital settlement agreement. If the court finds that the parties agreed on when and how Nancy's share of Joseph's retirement benefits was to be paid to her, then that agreement should, of course, be enforced. We agree with *Schweitzer* that the rule for distribution of a nonemployee spouse's interest in a retirement plan, whatever the rule is, should be applied only in the absence of an agreement between the spouses on the subject. However, if the parties did not agree one way or the other on when and how Nancy was to receive her interest in Joseph's retirement plan, the court should reinstate its judgment awarding Nancy $753.94 per month as her community interest in Joseph's retirement plan. At the same time, we agree with the Court of Appeals that $182.98 of this amount should be paid directly by Joseph's employer, Sandia, through a QDRO. The court should enter such a QDRO, reduce Joseph's monthly obligation accordingly, and provide for Nancy's full entitlement to be paid to her on Joseph's actual retirement through an increased QDRO.

We acknowledge that this resolution of the parties' dispute does not comport with what we have described as the preferred method of satisfying a nonemployee spouse's community interest in an employee spouse's retirement plan—namely, a lump sum distribution, through other assets (including an installment obligation secured by a lien on other assets and bearing interest) and utilizing a QDRO to the maximum extent available, equal to the present cash value of her interest in the plan. However, Nancy has raised no issue about the court's failure to make a lump sum distribution, and Joseph has at no point contended that such a distribution was preferable to the manner in which the trial court divided the pension benefits. In any event, the parties' other assets have been divided pursuant to their MSA, and it would seem unwise to attempt to unscramble the eggs at this point. On remand, however, either party may request the court to revisit the questions of present-value determination and distribution, and the court may exercise its sound discretion in deciding how to deal with any such request....

We agree with the Court of Appeals that the MSA, fairly construed, reflects the parties' understanding that Joseph would continue working until well after the divorce. We further agree that the parties did not provide in their MSA, expressly or by implication, that Joseph would pay Nancy $753.94 per month from and after the dissolution of their marriage. However, we do not agree that the absence of such a provision from their written agreement necessarily means that the parties agreed that Nancy would not begin to receive any portion of her community share of Joseph's retirement plan until he actually retired. Unlike both the trial court and the Court of Appeals, we believe the MSA is ambiguous on this point and that further proceedings are necessary to resolve the ambiguity. If it cannot be resolved as an evidentiary or factual matter, then it follows that the parties made no agreement on the issue—their agreement simply failed to cover the point, and Nancy's entitlement to her share of Joseph's retirement benefits must be decided under the principles outlined previously in this opinion. . . .

We therefore remand *Ruggles* to the trial court with directions to consider extrinsic evidence of the parties' intent as to distribution of Nancy's community share of the Sandia benefits . . . The trial court might determine that the parties reached no agreement on this issue—that is, that they did not consider it and therefore did not agree on how to resolve it . . . The court should then utilize the lump sum method to the extent feasible, as previously discussed, except that the court should not apply the lump sum method arbitrarily and without regard for the equities of the situation obtaining at that time. It is the burden of the party contesting the lump sum method to adduce a sufficient basis for denying a lump sum award. In the absence of findings to justify such a denial, the denial might well constitute an abuse of the trial court's discretion. With appropriate findings, the trial court may, as we have discussed, utilize other methods, in combination with or apart from the lump sum method.

Finally, we wish to comment on the Court of Appeals' statement in *Ruggles* that "the trial court had discretion to modify the terms of the agreement to assure fairness." 114 N.M. at 67, 834 P.2d at 944. The Court cited Brister v. Brister, 92 N.M. 711, 594 P.2d 1167 (1979), and Wolcott v. Wolcott, 101 N.M. 665, 687 P.2d 100 (Ct.App.1984), as support for this statement. Neither case supports the proposition that a court dividing community property in a dissolution proceeding has authority to modify the parties' agreed-upon division to assure "fairness." *Brister* involved modification of an award of alimony, as expressly permitted by statute. Brister, 92 N.M. at 713–14, 594 P.2d at 1169–70 (relying on NMSA 1978 § 40–4–7(B)(2)) . . . We are inclined to agree with Joseph that a voluntary property settlement between divorcing spouses, dividing their community property as they see fit, is sacrosanct and cannot be upset by the court granting the divorce, absent fraud, duress, mistake, breach of fiduciary duty, or other similar equitable ground for invalidating an agreement. . . .

The decisions of the Court of Appeals in these cases are reversed, and each case is remanded to the district court where it arose for further proceedings consistent with this opinion.

CALIFORNIA FAMILY CODE (2016)

§ 2550. Manner of division of community estate

Except upon the written agreement of the parties, or on oral stipulation of the parties in open court, or as otherwise provided in this division, in a proceeding for dissolution of marriage or for legal separation of the parties, the court shall, either in its judgment of dissolution of the marriage, in its judgment of legal separation of the parties, or at a later time if it expressly reserves jurisdiction to make such a property division, divide the community estate of the parties equally.

§ 2551. Characterization of liabilities; confirmation or assignment

For the purposes of division and in confirming or assigning the liabilities of the parties for which the community estate is liable, the court shall characterize liabilities as separate or community and confirm or assign them to the parties in accordance with Part 6 (commencing with Section 2620).

§ 2552. Valuation of assets and liabilities

(a) For the purpose of division of the community estate upon dissolution of marriage or legal separation of the parties, except as provided in subdivision (b), the court shall value the assets and liabilities as near as practicable to the time of trial.

(b) Upon 30 days' notice by the moving party to the other party, the court for good cause shown may value all or any portion of the assets and liabilities at a date after separation and before trial to accomplish an equal division of the community estate of the parties in an equitable manner.

§ 2553. Powers of court

The court may make any orders the court considers necessary to carry out the purposes of this division.

§ 2554. Failure to agree to voluntary division of property; submission to arbitration

(a) Notwithstanding any other provision of this division, in any case in which the parties do not agree in writing to a voluntary division of the community estate of the parties, the issue of the character, the value, and the division of the community estate may be submitted by the court to arbitration for resolution pursuant to Chapter 2.5 (commencing with Section 1141.10) of Title 3 of Part 3 of the Code of Civil Procedure, if the total value of the community and quasi-community property in controversy in the opinion of the court does not exceed fifty thousand dollars ($50,000). The decision of the court regarding the value of the community and quasi-community property for purposes of this section is not appealable.

(b) The court may submit the matter to arbitration at any time it believes the parties are unable to agree upon a division of the property.

§ 2556. Community property or debts; continuing jurisdiction

In a proceeding for dissolution of marriage, for nullity of marriage, or for legal separation of the parties, the court has continuing jurisdiction to award community estate assets or community estate liabilities to the parties that have not been previously adjudicated by a judgment in the proceeding. A party may file a postjudgment motion or order to show cause in the proceeding in order to obtain adjudication of any community estate asset or liability omitted or not adjudicated by the judgment. In these cases, the court shall equally divide the omitted or unadjudicated community estate asset or liability, unless the court finds upon good cause shown that the interests of justice require an unequal division of the asset or liability.

§ 2602. Additional award or offset against existing property; award of amount determined to have been misappropriated

As an additional award or offset against existing property, the court may award, from a party's share, the amount the court determines to have been deliberately misappropriated by the party to the exclusion of the interest of the other party in the community estate.

PROBLEM TWO

Bobby and Betty met on the beach in Malibu, California. Bobby was a "career lifeguard" and Betty was an aspiring actress. After a whirlwind romance of six months, they were wed at Our Lady of Malibu Church and moved into a bungalow in Venice, California. Betty ignored the advice of her agent and she and Bobby never signed a prenup agreement. Nonetheless, Betty followed the agent's advice otherwise and soon became a famous star on a well-established soap opera filmed in nearby Hollywood. Between endorsements, commercial roles, and her presence on daytime television, Betty was soon making seven figures, which enabled her and Bobby to purchase a large home in Malibu, create a substantial retirement account, and a Build diversified investment portfolio. All of these assets were titled in Betty's name, another recommendation of her agent. After nearly ten years of marriage, Bobby was still working as a lifeguard. And alas, on one of the four days a year when it was cloudy at Malibu, he returned home early one afternoon to find Betty entertaining a gentleman in the couple's marital bedroom. Bobby was more livid than hurt and he rushed from the home and straight to the nearest family law attorney he could find. Bobby explained what he had just witnessed and frantically exclaimed: "How much am I going to get if we divorce?"

The marital assets were in a community property state, California. How would you respond to Bobby's question?

B. TEMPORARY (PENDENTE LITE) ALIMONY

Alimony today is often called spousal support or maintenance. *See, e.g.*, ARIZ. REV. STAT. ANN. § 25–319 (2016) (using the term maintenance). Alimony originally arose from a husband's duty to support his wife during the marriage and included support when the couple received a divorce from bed and board (which, as Chapter 4 noted, was also called a divorce *a mensa et thoro*). Alimony was later available after absolute divorce as well (also called divorce *a vinculo matrimonii*).

Today, spouses may receive support during the divorce proceeding, still widely known as alimony *pendente lite,* to provide for living expenses during the action. For example, in Alaska the court may award a spouse reasonable expenses, which could include medical expenses. *See, e.g.,* ALASKA STAT. ANN. § 25.24.140 (2015). Some states explicitly authorize *pendente lite* support to assist with attorney's fees and other costs of maintaining or defending the action. *See, e.g.,* FLA. STAT. ANN. § 61.071 (2016) (allowing the award of suit money). *See generally* Alimony, Maintenance, and Other Spousal Support, tbl.1 titled "State by State Analysis," *50 State Statutory Surveys: Family Law: Divorce and Dissolution*, 0080 SURVEYS 11 (2012).

Some jurisdictions recognize an action for legal separation, independent of divorce, and treat requests for alimony after a legal separation in the same manner as requests for alimony *pendente lite. See, e.g.,* OHIO REV. CODE ANN. § 3105.18 (2013). In some jurisdictions, support may be awarded during separation based on equitable principles rather than statute. *See* Rodgers v. Rodgers, 349 So.2d 540 (Miss. 1977). Because an action for judicial separation is distinct from an action for absolute divorce, the payment of support to a separated spouse is technically not alimony *pendente lite.*

UNIFORM MARRIAGE AND DIVORCE ACT (1973)

§ 304. [Temporary Order or Temporary Injunction]

(a) In a proceeding for dissolution of marriage or for legal separation, or in a proceeding for disposition of property or for maintenance or support following dissolution of the marriage by a court which lacked personal jurisdiction over the absent spouse, either party may move for temporary maintenance or temporary support of a child of the marriage entitled to support. The motion shall be accompanied by an affidavit setting forth the factual basis for the motion and the amounts requested.

(b) As a part of a motion for temporary maintenance or support or by independent motion accompanied by affidavit, either party may request the court to issue a temporary injunction for any of the following relief:

(1) restraining any person from transferring, encumbering, concealing, or otherwise disposing of any property except in the usual course of business or for the necessities of life, and, if so restrained, requiring him to notify the moving party of any proposed extraordinary expenditures made after the order is issued;

(2) enjoining a party from molesting or disturbing the peace of the other party or of any child;

(3) excluding a party from the family home or from the home of the other party upon a showing that physical or emotional harm would otherwise result;

(4) enjoining a party from removing a child from the jurisdiction of the court; and

(5) providing other injunctive relief proper in the circumstances.

(c) The court may issue a temporary restraining order without requiring notice to the other party only if it finds on the basis of the moving affidavit or other evidence that irreparable injury will result to the moving party if no order is issued until the time for responding has elapsed.

(d) A response may be filed within [20] days after service of notice of motion or at the time specified in the temporary restraining order.

(e) On the basis of the showing made and in conformity with Sections 308 and 309, the court may issue a temporary injunction and an order for temporary maintenance or support in amounts and on terms just and proper in the circumstance.

(f) A temporary order or temporary injunction:

(1) does not prejudice the rights of the parties or the child which are to be adjudicated at subsequent hearings in the proceeding;

(2) may be revoked or modified before final decree on a showing by affidavit of the facts necessary to revocation or modification of a final decree under Section 316;

(3) terminates when the final decree is entered or when the petition for dissolution or legal separation is voluntarily dismissed.

NOTES

At one time, alimony payments could go only to the wife, reflecting then-prevalent stereotypes of roles within marriage. Such limitations generally were removed even before the U.S. Supreme Court's decision in Orr v. Orr, 440 U.S. 268 (1979), which set aside an Alabama statute that allowed only husbands, but not wives, to be required to pay alimony upon divorce.

Despite the fact that alimony *pendente lite* is considered to be in some sense a continuation of the duty of support between spouses during the intact marriage, from a strategic standpoint some attorneys express concern that the amount judicially fixed *pendente lite* may influence the level of any eventual award of permanent alimony. States like Colorado provide that the *pendente lite* amount will not determine the amount of alimony payable after divorce and "should not prejudice the right of either party" in the permanent order. COLO. REV. STAT. ANN. § 14–10–114(2)(d) (2016). This approach reflects the fact that alimony *pendente lite* is awarded "under different standards and for different reasons than" the permanent award. *Id.* Generally, the *pendente lite* amount reflects the recipient's need for support during the proceeding, but is not a hearing on the merits as to entitlement to alimony after divorce. *Id.* at (2)(a) (establishing a rebuttable presumption in favor of alimony *pendente lite* when the "combined annual gross income of the two parties is seventy-five thousand dollars or less," the amount of which follows a statutory formula). New York also provides a formula for determining the amount of *pendente lite* alimony. *See* N.Y. DOM. REL. § 236(b)(5–a) (McKinney 2016).

The basis for concern about the *pendente lite* amount dictating or influencing a later award has lessened with the Uniform Marriage and Divorce Act (UMDA) approach to alimony described in the next section, which determines the division of property before deciding whether alimony is necessary.

Like § 304 of the UMDA, some jurisdictions authorize the award of child support *pendente lite* in any proceeding where child support is at issue. *See, e.g.,* CAL. FAM. CODE § 3600 (2016).

C. PERMANENT ALIMONY

The number of spouses receiving alimony after dissolution has declined over time, with only a small percentage of divorced spouses being awarded alimony and even fewer actually receiving it. *See* Cynthia Lee Starnes, *Mothers as Suckers: Pity, Partnership, and Divorce Discourse*, 90 IOWA L. REV. 1513, 1516 n.7 (2005). *See also* Patricia A. Cain, *Taxing Families Fairly*, 48 SANTA CLARA L. REV. 805, 827 n.85 (2008); Jana B. Singer, *Divorce, Reform and Gender Justice*, 82 GEO. L. J. 2423, 2426 n.14 (1994); Marsha Garrison, *Good Intentions Gone Awry: The Impact of New York's Equitable Distribution Law on Divorce Outcomes*, 57 BROOK. L. REV. 621 (1991). From 1996 to 2006, the number of individuals reporting that they received alimony fell by 17%. *See* U.S. Dept. of Commerce, Bureau of the Census, *Statistical Abstract of the United States: 2012* (131st ed.), Table 542: Number of People With Income by Specified Sources of Income: 2009 (2011), *available at* https://www2.census.gov/library/publications/2011/compendia/statab/131ed/2012-statab.pdf. By 2009, only 349,000 individuals reported alimony payments as income from their former spouses. *Id.* The number of individuals reporting alimony may have decreased because many jurisdictions now prefer to award time-limited alimony, rather than permanent periodic alimony, believing that time-limited alimony will encourage the recipient to become self-supporting. *See, e.g., In re* Marriage of Rodriguez, 834 N.E.2d 71, 75 (Ill. 2005) ("The purpose of a time limit on the award is generally intended to motivate the recipient spouse to take the steps necessary to attain self-sufficiency."). *See also* Allison Anna Tait, *Divorce Equality*, 90 WASH. L. REV. 1245 (2015) (discussing alimony when same-sex couples divorce).

Time-limited alimony is discussed in Part D, *infra*.

NOTES

Some states severely restrict the instances in which fault would matter to an alimony award. For instance, CALIFORNIA FAMILY CODE § 4324 provides that when one spouse attempts to murder the other (the "injured spouse"), the injured spouse cannot be made to pay alimony *pendente lite* or permanent alimony to the other, and neither can the injured spouse be made to pay the other's "medical, life, or other insurance benefits or payments." However, in response to a high profile case in which a woman was ordered to pay her husband alimony despite his later conviction for raping her (for which he was on trial during the divorce proceeding), the California Assembly enacted Assembly Bill No. 1522. It expands the grounds for non-payment of alimony to include conviction for a violent sexual felony. *See* 2011 California Assembly Bill No. 1522, California 2011–2012 Regular Session; Juju Chang and Alyssa Litoff, *Sexual Assault Victim Ordered to Pay Alimony to Attacker Fights to Change California Law*, ABC NEWS (Apr. 5 2012), http://abcnews.go.com/US/sexual-assault-victim-ordered-pay-alimony-attacker-fights/story?id=16075409.

A number of states attach special significance to adultery. *See, e.g.*, S.C. CODE ANN. § 20–3–130(c)(10) (2016) (treating adultery as a factor in awarding alimony when it is the grounds for divorce or affects the economic circumstances of the parties). In these states, adultery may operate to bar alimony completely. *See, e.g.*, S.C. CODE ANN. § 20–3–130(a) (2016) (providing that no alimony may be awarded to a spouse who commits adultery before specified events, such as the court's entry of an order approving the couple's marital settlement agreement).

In some states, like South Carolina, adultery both bars alimony to the recipient and may increase the amount due from the payor. Other states, like Kentucky, make adultery meaningful only when committed by the potential recipient. *See, e.g.*, Platt v. Platt, 728 S.W.2d 542 (Ky. Ct. App. 1987) (stating that adultery by the higher earning spouse may not be used to grant a greater amount of alimony than what would be statutorily permitted).

The American Law Institute allies itself with those states rejecting marital misconduct, arguing that tort law is a better remedy to address pain, suffering, and emotional loss during marriage. *See* ALI, PRINCIPLES OF THE LAW OF FAMILY DISSOLUTION: ANALYSIS AND RECOMMENDATIONS: CH. 1, TOPIC 2 (2000). In part, the ALI's rejection of fault rests on the fact that when adultery acts as a complete bar to alimony, a needy spouse may have no source of support. Although the ALI rejects fault generally as a consideration, it would allow consideration of economic misconduct in the awarding of alimony. As the Reporters for the PRINCIPLES explain, "[d]ivorce also imposes emotional losses and emotional gains, but these PRINCIPLES do not recognize these as an element of awards," because "[t]he pains and joys that individuals find from divorce are not commensurable with its financial costs. . . ." *Id.* at § 5.02, cmt. b at 790.

For an argument that the ALI's "attempt to separate emotional and personal aspects of a marriage from financial ones" is "deeply flawed" because "finances . . . are an avenue through which spouses express emotions," *see* Katharine B. Silbaugh, *Money as Emotion in the Distribution of Wealth at Divorce*, in RECONCEIVING THE FAMILY: CRITIQUE ON THE AMERICAN LAW INSTITUTE'S *PRINCIPLES OF THE LAW OF FAMILY DISSOLUTION* 234, 234 (Robin Fretwell Wilson, ed., 2006). For an argument suggesting that all fault may be appropriately considered, *see* Carl E. Schneider, *Marriage, Morals, and the Law: No Fault Divorce and Moral Discourse*, 1994 UTAH L. REV. 503. *See also* Chapter 4(B)(1), "The Fault Scheme," NOTES.

NEW YORK DOMESTIC RELATIONS LAW, § 236–(6) (McKinney Supp. 2016)

. . .

6. Post-divorce maintenance awards. a. Except where the parties have entered into an agreement pursuant to subdivision three of this part providing for maintenance, in any matrimonial action the court may order maintenance in such amount as justice requires, having regard for the standard of living of the parties established during the marriage, whether the party in whose favor maintenance is granted lacks sufficient property and income to provide for his or her reasonable needs and whether the other party has sufficient property or income to provide for the reasonable needs of the other and the circumstances of the case and of the respective parties. Such order shall be effective as of the date of the application therefor, and any retroactive amount of maintenance due shall be paid in one sum or periodic sums, as the court shall direct, taking into account any amount of temporary maintenance which has been paid. In determining the amount and duration of maintenance the court shall consider:

(1) the income and property of the respective parties including marital property distributed pursuant to subdivision five of this part;

(2) the length of the marriage;

(3) the age and health of both parties;

(4) the present and future earning capacity of both parties;

(5) the need of one party to incur education or training expenses;

(6) the existence and duration of a pre-marital joint household or a pre-divorce separate household;

(7) acts by one party against another that have inhibited or continue to inhibit a party's earning capacity or ability to obtain meaningful employment. Such acts include but are not limited to acts of domestic violence as provided in section four hundred fifty-nine-a of the social services law;

(8) the ability of the party seeking maintenance to become self-supporting and, if applicable, the period of time and training necessary therefor;

(9) reduced or lost lifetime earning capacity of the party seeking maintenance as a result of having foregone or delayed education, training, employment, or career opportunities during the marriage;

(10) the presence of children of the marriage in the respective homes of the parties;

(11) the care of the children or stepchildren, disabled adult children or stepchildren, elderly parents or in-laws that has inhibited or continues to inhibit a party's earning capacity;

(12) the inability of one party to obtain meaningful employment due to age or absence from the workforce;

(13) the need to pay for exceptional additional expenses for the child/children, including but not limited to, schooling, day care and medical treatment;

(14) the tax consequences to each party;

(15) the equitable distribution of marital property;

(16) contributions and services of the party seeking maintenance as a spouse, parent, wage earner and homemaker, and to the career or career potential of the other party;

(17) the wasteful dissipation of marital property by either spouse;

(18) the transfer or encumbrance made in contemplation of a matrimonial action without fair consideration;

(19) the loss of health insurance benefits upon dissolution of the marriage, and the availability and cost of medical insurance for the parties; and

(20) any other factor which the court shall expressly find to be just and proper.

b. In any decision made pursuant to this subdivision, the court shall set forth the factors it considered and the reasons for its decision and such may not be waived by either party or counsel.

c. The court may award permanent maintenance, but an award of maintenance shall terminate upon the death of either party or upon the recipient's valid or invalid marriage, or upon modification pursuant to paragraph b of subdivision nine of this part or section two hundred forty-eight of this chapter.

d. In any decision made pursuant to this subdivision the court shall, where appropriate, consider the effect of a barrier to remarriage, as defined in subdivision six of section two hundred fifty-three of this article, on the factors enumerated in paragraph a of this subdivision.

Rainwater v. Rainwater

Court of Appeals of Arizona, 1993
869 P.2d 176

■ FIDEL, CHIEF JUSTICE.

Sam Rainwater ("husband") appeals from the trial court's award of spousal maintenance to Barbara Rainwater ("wife") until her death or remarriage.

In June of 1988, wife petitioned the superior court to dissolve the parties' twenty-two-year marriage. Resolving all other issues by stipulation, the parties went to trial on the single issue of appropriate spousal maintenance for wife.

Wife through much of the parties' marriage worked full time outside the home. At the time of dissolution, wife, a forty-one-year-old secretary, was working toward a Bachelor of Arts degree, but neither party showed the extent to which her earning capacity would be enhanced by that degree. Weighing wife's needs in the context of her marital standard of living, the trial court found that wife "would not be able to meet her reasonable needs . . . nor enjoy the standard of living established during the marriage based on reasonably anticipated income from her investments and her employment." Finding that husband's earnings exceeded his needs, the trial court awarded wife $1900 per month for three years or until one year after completion of her B.A. degree, whichever should first occur, and $1200 per month thereafter till her death or remarriage.

Husband argues that the trial court erred by entering an award that would allow his able-bodied former wife "to live off his labors forever." He argues that, in the absence of evidence that wife is permanently unable to become self-sustaining, Arizona public policy permits only a fixed-term award to assist her in transition to an independent life. Wife responds that our maintenance law requires a case-by-case determination, that it is flexible enough to permit an indefinite award when justified by statutorily enumerated considerations, and that those considerations support indefinite maintenance in this case.

We turn to husband's claim that the 25–319(B)[1] balance is weighted by public policy in favor of maintenance that is transitional,

[1] The factors listed in section 25–319(B) are [the standard of living during the marriage; the duration; the age, employment history, earning ability and the physical and emotional condition of the party seeking maintenance; the ability of the spouse to meet maintenance request; comparative financial resources, including earning ability; the contribution of the spouse seeking maintenance to the other spouse, including any reduction in career opportunity to further the other spouse; the ability of both spouses to contribute to mutual child education costs; the financial resources of the party seeking maintenance (including marital property apportioned) and the ability to meet needs independently; the time necessary to acquire

rehabilitative, and limited in term. We agree up to a point. Citing Schroeder v. Schroeder, 161 Ariz. 316, 778 P.2d 1212 (1989), husband emphasizes the supreme court's statement that:

> the current aim [of spousal maintenance] is to achieve independence for both parties and to require an effort toward independence by the party requesting maintenance. The temporary award of maintenance in its present form reflects both of these values. In most cases of temporary maintenance, the key issue for the parties and the court will be whether that independence will be achieved by a good faith effort.

Id. at 321, 778 P.2d at 1217. This general statement is best examined in the context of the facts.

In *Schroeder,* the trial court had initially awarded wife four years of spousal maintenance, but later extended maintenance until her death or remarriage or the further order of the court. *Id.* at 317, 778 P.2d at 1213. The supreme court upheld the modified award. The court explained that maintenance awards are modifiable both in amount *and* in duration, unless the parties have expressly agreed to the contrary and the trial court has so ordered. *Id.* at 323, 778 P.2d at 1219. The wife in *Schroeder* was fifty and had worked primarily as a homemaker before her twenty-eight-year marriage ended. Although the initial award of four years' duration was "intended to support [wife's] transitional growth of earning capacity," *id.,* by the time of the petition for modification, wife had only found relatively unlucrative work as a filing clerk, and her expenses had increased to include chemotherapy treatment for cancer. Because time had disproved the trial court's apparent initial expectation that four years of transitional support would enable wife to become self-supporting, the supreme court concluded that the evidence now justified an indefinite maintenance award. *Id. Schroeder* indeed recognizes the transition toward independence as a principal objective of maintenance under 25–319(B). But *Schroeder* also reaffirms the trial court's discretion to award indefinite maintenance when it appears from the evidence that independence is unlikely to be achieved. Additionally, *Schroeder* shows that assessing the likelihood of a successful transition to independence requires a prediction that may vary not only from case to case, but from time to time within a case.

The crux of husband's argument is that indefinite maintenance can be awarded only to a spouse who is "permanently unable to be self-sustaining." The principal flaw in this argument is husband's failure to define "self-sustaining" by reference to any standard of living. The evidence certainly suggests that wife can be self-sustaining beyond the minimal subsistence level. Yet the trial court expressly found that wife's "reasonably anticipated income" would not meet her "reasonable needs",

sufficient education or training to find employment; and any "Excessive or abnormal expenditures, destruction, concealment or fraudulent disposition of community, joint tenancy and other property held in common"].

when those needs were determined by reference to "the standard of living established during the marriage."

Marital standard of living has long been listed by our legislature among the factors pertinent to the duration and amount of spousal maintenance. And though Arizona courts have stated that public policy favors fixed-term maintenance as a means to promote a diligent effort to become self-sustaining, we have repeatedly cautioned that this goal "must be balanced with some realistic appraisal of the probabilities that the receiving spouse will in fact subsequently be able to support herself in some reasonable approximation of the standard of living established during the marriage." Sommerfield v. Sommerfield, 121 Ariz. 575, 578, 592 P.2d 771, 774 (1979). . . .

We do not suggest that at the end of every marriage, the party of lesser earning capacity is entitled to enough support to maintain the standard of living achieved during the marriage. First of all, divorce often requires a lesser standard of living for both parties. The statute requires consideration of "[t]he ability of the spouse from whom maintenance is sought to meet his or her needs while meeting those of the spouse seeking maintenance." A.R.S. § 25–319(B)(4). Second, there will be case-to-case variance in the degree to which the marital standard of living may be seen as a product of the marriage. For this reason, such factors as length of the marriage, the receiving spouse's contributions to the education and earning capacity of the paying spouse, and the receiving spouse's reduction in income or career opportunities for the benefit of the family home and children bear heavily on the trial court's effort to establish an equitable award.

In this case, the parties had a marriage of long duration, to which wife contributed financially and by assuming the role of primary caretaker for the family home and children. She contributed to husband's support as he worked toward an engineering degree, and she contributed socially and emotionally to his professional advancement once his formal education was complete. The parties had achieved a relatively high standard of living by the last years of their marriage, which the trial court properly regarded as a product of their sustained *common* efforts for 23 years. The trial court built an incentive toward independence into its maintenance award by reducing wife's monthly payment from $1900 to $1200 after the expiration of a reasonable period for getting her B.A. degree. But the trial court also concluded—and the evidence permits the conclusion—that wife could not foreseeably expect to maintain her standard of living without ongoing support from husband at a level reasonably within his ability to provide. Under all of these circumstances, we find that the trial court properly balanced the many relevant factors of 25–319(B), and we find no abuse of discretion in the trial court's award.

We add that our decision is strongly affected by the presumptive modifiability of spousal maintenance awards. *See* Schroeder, 161 Ariz. at

323, 778 P.2d at 1219 (spousal maintenance orders are presumed to be modifiable in amount and duration upon a showing of substantial and continuing change in circumstances affecting the purposes of the original decree). . . .

For the reasons stated above, we affirm the trial court's order of spousal maintenance.

NOTES

Tests for Awarding Permanent Alimony. Some jurisdictions direct the court to award permanent alimony when the equities involved merit such an award. *See, e.g.*, MD. CODE ANN., FAM. LAW, § 11–106(c) (2016) (allowing permanent alimony when the parties' "respective standards of living . . . will be unconscionably disparate"). Other jurisdictions so favor a permanent award that they direct the court to "order a permanent award leaving its order open for later modification" if "there is some uncertainty as to the necessity of a permanent award." *See, e.g.,* MINN. STAT. ANN. § 518.552(3) (2016).

Other jurisdictions express a preference for permanent alimony only when the marriage lasted a significant amount of time. Effective March 1, 2012, Massachusetts permits a court to "order alimony for an indefinite length of time for marriages . . . longer than 20 years." MASS. GEN. LAWS ANN. ch. 208 § 49 (2016).

Theories Supporting the Payment of Alimony. The duty to pay alimony after a divorce can be supported by a number of theories of marriage. Traditionally, the husband owed a duty to his wife to support her after divorce when the marriage ended due to his fault. One way to explain the obligation to pay alimony after divorce is that marriage is a contract between the spouses to support one another until death. Thus, when one spouse "breaches" the contract by committing a fault that ends the marriage before death, the other could recover on the contract for support in the form of alimony. Lynn D. Wardle, *Beyond Fault and No-Fault in the Reform of Marital Dissolution Law*, in RECONCEIVING THE FAMILY: CRITIQUE ON THE AMERICAN LAW INSTITUTE'S *PRINCIPLES OF THE LAW OF FAMILY DISSOLUTION* 9 (Robin Fretwell Wilson, ed., 2006). Others explain the obligation as "founded in the law of tort—the 'duty is to make pecuniary amends for the consequences of an illicit act.'" Katherine Shaw Spaht, *Postmodern Marriage as Seen through the Lens of the ALI's "Compensatory Payments,"* in RECONCEIVING THE FAMILY, *supra,* at 256–7 (citing French Civ. Code art. 1382, which corresponds to LA. CIV. CODE art. 2315); JILL ELAINE HASDAY, FAMILY LAW'S LOOSE CANON: FAMILY LAW REIMAGINED (2014).

With the universal embrace of no-fault divorce, an obligation to pay support after the marriage ends becomes harder to explain. One explanation maintains that marriage is a partnership in which both parties seek to maximize the partnership's value. Often, one party sacrifices in order to better the position of the other while furthering the partnership as a whole. Under this theory, alimony is owed in order to properly split the assets of the partnership. An alternative theory, proposed by Professor Ira Ellman, a reporter for the ALI PRINCIPLES, is based on maximizing sharing behavior in marriage. This theory requires alimony to compensate a spouse for losses in earning capacity flowing from the allocation of marital duties, such as when one party works in the home caring for the children. *See* Ira Mark Ellman, *The Theory of Alimony*, 77 CAL. L. REV. 1, 81 (1989).

The ALI PRINCIPLES also reconceptualize alimony "as compensation for loss rather than relief of need." ALI, PRINCIPLES OF THE LAW OF FAMILY DISSOLUTION: ANALYSIS AND RECOMMENDATIONS § 5.02 cmt. a at 789 (2000). In rejecting theories of alimony based on need or contract, one reporter for the ALI PRINCIPLES commented elsewhere that "there is also a widespread *intuition* that marriage alone does not create an obligation of one spouse to provide the other with post marital support, the way that parentage alone creates the child support obligation. . . . [T]he sense that one spouse has an obligation to meet the other's post-dissolution needs arises from the recognition that the need results *at least in part from an unfair distribution of the financial losses arising from the marital failure.* Alimony thus becomes a remedy for unfair loss allocation. . . ." Ira Mark Ellman, *Brigette M. Bodenheimer Memorial Lecture on the Family: Inventing Family Law*, 32 U.C. DAVIS L. REV. 855, 878, 870 (1999).

Multiple forms of alimony. In *Rainwater*, the trial court directed Mr. Rainwater to pay a time-limited form of alimony called rehabilitative alimony, explained in the next section, after which a permanent award would begin. This "stacking" of forms of alimony is explicitly authorized by statute in a number of jurisdictions. *See, e.g.,* S.C. CODE ANN. § 20–3–130(b)(6) (2016) (authorizing the court to "grant more than one form of support").

D. REHABILITATIVE (TRANSITIONAL) ALIMONY

Murphy v. Murphy

Supreme Court of Maine, 2003
816 A.2d 814

■ CLIFFORD, JUSTICE.

Michael J. Murphy appeals and Stephanie Murphy cross-appeals from a divorce judgment entered in the District Court (Bangor, *Russell, J.*). Michael contends that the trial court erred in awarding transitional spousal support to cover Stephanie's dental and medical expenses. Michael also challenges the amount of the spousal support. Stephanie contends that the trial court erred in its determination and valuation of marital property, its division of marital property, and its failure to order Michael to pay her legal fees. We affirm the judgment.

The parties met and began living together over twenty-six years ago in New York. In 1980, they moved to Massachusetts and purchased a home as joint tenants. Michael worked for New England Electric for about ten years. During this time, the parties held themselves out as married. On July 5, 1985, their son Brendon was born, and the parties agreed that Stephanie would stay at home and take care of him.

Stephanie also home schooled Brendon. After approximately ten years in Massachusetts, Michael accepted a job with an engineering firm in Maine. Two years later, the parties bought the current marital home in Hampden using about $25,000 realized from the sale of their Massachusetts home. In 1993, Stephanie decided that they needed to be married because she was concerned that if anything happened to Michael she and Brendon would not be taken care of, so the couple married in October of 1993. In 1995, Michael started his own engineering consultant business. Stephanie helped Michael with the management of this business for about one year. In the fall of 1998, Stephanie began work as a psychiatric technician at Acadia Hospital. She was trained at the hospital and currently works full time. The divorce proceeding was commenced in September of 2000. Prior to the trial, the couple sold real estate they owned in Brewer, and the net proceeds of approximately $4600 went to Stephanie.

After the parties separated, Michael and Brendon continued to live in the marital home in Hampden. The parties agreed that after the divorce, Brendon would continue to live with Michael, but would visit Stephanie whenever Brendon wanted and the parties would share parental rights and responsibilities. Stephanie lives in an apartment and shares expenses with a domestic partner, who earns approximately $28,000 a year. Stephanie previously took a sign language course and would like to go to college to earn a degree so that she could become an American sign language interpreter. She would be able to take some electives near where she lives, but would have to attend the University of Southern Maine for two years to take the core courses in sign language.

Stephanie testified that she is in need of a substantial amount of dental work. She estimated that the cost of the extractions and bridge work needed would be about $11,250. Stephanie also testified that she would like to continue in therapy to treat her depression, for which she takes prescription medication. . . .

[T]he court concluded that Michael had nonmarital assets of approximately $355,000, and Stephanie had none. Michael received approximately $78,300 and Stephanie $18,600 from the court's initial division of the marital estate, but to ensure a more equitable division, the court ordered Michael to pay Stephanie $50,000.

The court found Stephanie's earning potential is approximately $18,000, and Michael's earning capacity to be about $90,000 a year. Although Stephanie has less income potential than Michael, given Stephanie and her partner's combined income, the court concluded that she could "maintain a reasonable standard of living without general support." Taking into account Stephanie's medical, dental, and educational needs, as well as her attorney fees obligation, the court awarded her transitional spousal support in the amount of $60,000. . . .

In contending that the trial court erred in awarding Stephanie transitional spousal support to cover her dental and medical expenses,

Michael argues that those two categories do not fall within the definition of transitional support. We disagree.

Issues regarding spousal support are within the sound discretion of the trial court. Noyes v. Noyes, 662 A.2d 921, 922 (Me.1995). Title 19–A M.R.S.A. § 951–A(2) (Supp. 2002), lists the five possible types of spousal support that a trial court may award, including general support and transitional support.[2] There is a rebuttable presumption that general support will not be awarded when the marriage is less than ten years in duration.[3] 19–A M.R.S.A. § 951–A(2)(A). . . .

Transitional support, "may be awarded to provide for a spouse's transitional needs, including, *but not limited to:* (1) Short-term needs resulting from financial dislocations associated with the dissolution of the marriage; or (2) Reentry or advancement in the work force, including, but not limited to, physical or emotional rehabilitation services, vocational training and education." 19–A M.R.S.A. § 951–A(2)(B) (emphasis added). In determining an award of spousal support, the court must consider a number of factors, which include "health and disabilities of each party," and "any other factors the court considers appropriate."[4]

The court's transitional support award in this case is based partly on Stephanie's health issues, her desire to receive counseling, her need for dental work, her obligation to pay attorney fees, and her need for more

---

[2] Title 19–A M.R.S.A. § 951–A (2) in pertinent part provides as follows:

2. Types of spousal support. The court may, after consideration of all factors set forth in subsection 5, award or modify spousal support for one or more of the following reasons.

A. General support may be awarded to provide financial assistance to a spouse with substantially less income potential than the other spouse so that both spouses can maintain a reasonable standard of living after the divorce.

(1) There is a rebuttable presumption that general support may not be awarded if the parties were married for less than 10 years as of the date of the filing of the action for divorce. There is also a rebuttable presumption that general support may not be awarded for a term exceeding 1/2 the length of the marriage if the parties were married for at least 10 years but not more than 20 years as of the date of the filing of the action for divorce.

(2) If the court finds that a spousal support award based upon a presumption established by this paragraph would be inequitable or unjust, that finding is sufficient to rebut the applicable presumption.

[3] Although Stephanie contends that she is entitled to an award of general support, the length of the marriage was eight years, and the trial court was not compelled to find that she overcame the presumption. *See* 19–A M.R.S.A. § 951–A(2).

[4] Title 19–A M.R.S.A. § 951–A provides as follows:

5. Factors. The court shall consider the following factors when determining an award of spousal support;

[The length of the marriage; each party's: ability to pay, age, employment history and potential, income history and potential, education and training, retirement and health benefits, health and disabilities, contribution as a homemaker, and contribution to other party's education and earning potential; the tax consequences of marital property division including the sale of the marital home, and of alimony; marital misconduct resulting in diminution of marital property or income; the standard of living during the marriage; ability of the party seeking support to become self-supporting; the effect of 1) actual or potential income from property awarded during dissolution, and 2) child support for children of the marriage, on a party's need for spousal support; and any other factors the court considers appropriate.]

education and training. Michael challenges the court's consideration of Stephanie's counseling and dental work and contends that these items are not "transitional needs." The spousal support statute, however, does not specifically define the limits of "transitional needs," but rather provides that transitional needs "includ[e] but [are] not limited to" two broad categories. 19–A M.R.S.A. § 951–A (2)(B). Moreover, in determining an award of alimony, the court is required to consider the factors listed in § 951–A (5), including the health of the parties. 19 M.R.S.A. § 951–A (5)(I). Accordingly, the transitional alimony award based in part on Stephanie's need for counseling and dental work is well within the trial court's discretion. *See* Noyes, 662 A.2d at 922.

Spousal Support-Amount

Michael also argues that the trial court's award of $60,000 for transitional spousal support was excessive and beyond its discretion, contending that the evidence supports a transitional award of no more than $27,700. We disagree.

Stephanie has demonstrated a need for dental work, the need for legal representation in connection with this appeal, and that she will have to limit her work hours to accommodate her class schedule, and will be required to move to or commute to USM for two years. Furthermore, the statute provides that in determining an award of spousal support, the court must consider, among other factors, the income potential of the parties, their age, their standard of living, training and education, and their ability to pay spousal support. 19–A M.R.S.A. § 951–A(5). Contrary to Michael's contention, the transitional award of $60,000 was reasonable, was in keeping with the purpose of transitional support and well within the trial court's discretion. *See* Noyes, 662 A.2d at 922.

Attorney fees

Attorney fees awards in divorce actions are reviewed by this Court only for an abuse of discretion. Warner, 2002 ME 156, & 54, 807 A.2d 607. Title 19–A M.R.S.A. § 952(3) (1998) provides that "[w]hen making a final decree, the court may order a party to pay reasonable attorney[ ] fees. Attorney[ ] fees awarded in the nature of support may be payable immediately or in installments." *Id.* This Court has previously recognized that the legislature has given trial courts broad discretion in determining whether or not to award attorney fees to a party in a divorce action. Rosen v. Rosen, 651 A.2d 335, 336 (Me. 1994).

The trial court based its $60,000 transitional support award to Stephanie in part on her need to pay her divorce attorney. The court declined to directly award either party counsel fees, and determined that the parties should be responsible for their own attorney fees. Stephanie argues that Michael is in a better financial position and is more able to pay attorney fees. In *Rosen,* we said the parties' financial position is not the only factor to consider in determining an award of attorney fees. Rosen, 651 A.2d at 336–37. Rather, all relevant factors must be considered to reach a fair and just award. *Id.* at 336. As the trial court considered Stephanie's need to pay her attorney in awarding her transitional spousal support, the court did not abuse its discretion by failing to award her attorney fees directly.

The entry is: Judgment affirmed.

NOTES

The *Murphy* decision illustrates the direction legislatures and courts have taken during the last forty years, that is, away from permanent alimony. At an earlier time, courts were willing to order permanent alimony until death, remarriage, or a significant involuntary change of circumstances that made payment unnecessary or impossible. *See, e.g.*, Olsen v. Olsen, 557 P.2d 604 (Idaho 1976).

The Role of Cohabitation. Like the couple in *Murphy,* many couples today cohabit prior to marriage, raising the question of whether to take into account the duration of the cohabitation. At the time of the *Murphy* decision, Maine law established a rebuttable presumption that permanent alimony would not exceed "1/2 the length of the marriage if the parties were married for at least 10 years," but not run "more than 20 years," unless the time limit would result in an "inequitable or unjust" award. ME. REV. STAT. ANN. tit. 19–A § 951–A(2) (2016). Stephanie contended that she qualified for permanent alimony after an eight year marriage, but received no credit for cohabiting with Michael for more than a decade. *But see* Collins v. Wassell, 323 P.3d 1216 (Haw. 2014) (holding that premarital cohabitation could be taken into consideration when dividing the marital estate).

Duration. A number of jurisdictions presumptively measure the duration of time-limited alimony by the marriage's length. Massachusetts now limits transitional alimony to three years from the date of the parties' divorce and specifically directs that at the end of the three years, the court may not "modify or extend transitional alimony or replace transitional alimony with another form of alimony." MASS. GEN. LAW ANN. CH. 208 § 52 (2016).

One influential law reform group, the American Academy of Matrimonial Lawyers (AAML), made recommendations in 2007 as to how long and in what amount alimony should be awarded after dissolution. Under the AAML guidelines, the income of the parties and the length of the marriage presumptively dictate the award. The duration of alimony payments is calculated by multiplying the length of the marriage by a multiplier. The multiplier is based on the duration of the marriage: 0 to 3 years results in a multiplier of (.3); 3 to 10 years, (.5); 10 to 20 years, (.75); and marriages over 20 years result in permanent alimony. *See* REPORT OF THE AMERICAN ACADEMY OF MATRIMONIAL LAWYERS ON CONSIDERATIONS WHEN DETERMINING ALIMONY, SPOUSAL SUPPORT OR MAINTENANCE (2007). Using *Murphy* as an example, Stephanie's alimony would last for 4 years (as the next NOTE explains, Michael would pay Stephanie $23,400 for 4 years, for a total of $93,600) because the marriage lasted for 8 years. However, if Stephanie received credit for the entire duration of the relationship, which lasted more than 20 years, she would receive $1,950 a month until she remarried or died.

Some jurisdictions have adopted graduated time limits for alimony keyed to the marriage's length. Massachusetts statutorily specifies that for any marriage less than 5 years, alimony cannot extend longer than half of the total months married. *See* MASS. GEN. LAWS ANN. ch. 208, § 49 (2016). In a marriage of 5 to 10 years, alimony shall not be longer than 60% of the months married; if 10 to 15 years, no longer than 70%; and if 15 to 20 years, no more than 80%. *Id.* However, the court may deviate from the defined time limits "upon written finding by the court." *Id.*

Amount Due. The AAML guidelines also provide guidance as to the presumptive amount of any award. The amount is calculated by starting with 30% of the payor's gross income and subtracting 20% of the payee's gross income. However, the alimony payment can never exceed 40% of the combined gross income of the two parties. Using this formula to calculate alimony due in the *Murphy* case, Michael, as the payor, has an income of $90,000, generating $27,000 as available for alimony. Twenty percent of Stephanie's $18,000 (or $3,600) in earnings is subtracted, yielding a $23,400 payment; this amount is less than the cap of 40% of the couple's combined income ($43,200)—meaning that Michael would pay Stephanie alimony of $23,400 annually (or $1,950 a month).

Some jurisdictions have taken this formulaic approach, while preserving a modicum of discretion. *See* MASS. GEN. LAWS ANN. ch. 208, § 53 (2016) (providing that "the amount of alimony should generally not exceed the recipient's need or 30 to 35 per cent of the difference between the parties' gross incomes").

Rehabilitative Alimony. In *Murphy*, the time-limited alimony award challenged by Michael included Stephanie's medical and dental expenses. More typical, however, are time-limited "rehabilitative" alimony awards designed to promote the recipient's "reentry or advancement in the work force," and so may include support for the recipient's "vocational training and education." ME. REV. STAT. ANN. tit. 19–A § 951–A(2)(B) (2016). In fact, this was the kind of award that Mr. Rainwater urged the court to make in *Rainwater* rather than awarding permanent alimony.

By its very nature, rehabilitative alimony is measured by the time needed to secure the necessary vocational training or education. Thus, many jurisdictions specify that rehabilitative alimony will end not only upon the "remarriage of the recipient" or death of either spouse, but also "the occurrence of a specific event in the future," such as completion of a training program or the running of five years, whichever comes first. *See* MASS. GEN. LAWS ANN. ch. 208 § 50(a) (2016).

Other Forms of Time-Limited Alimony. Some jurisdictions recognize that the financial needs of spouses may be greater during the divorce process and immediately thereafter and therefore provide for alimony over very short time frames. This gap-bridging or transitional alimony "smooth[es] the transition between a higher standard of marital living and the standard that a spouse can provide for herself" shortly after divorce. Bell v. Bell, 68 So.3d 321, 327 (Fla.Ct. App. 2011). "Bridge-the-gap alimony is most appropriately awarded in instances where the receiving spouse is already employed, possesses adequate employment skills, and requires no further rehabilitation other than a brief time to ease the transition to single life." *Id.* Massachusetts allows the court to award transitional alimony for no "longer than 3 years from the date of the parties' divorce." MASS. GEN. LAWS ANN. ch. 208, § 55(a) (2016). Transitional alimony cannot be replaced with another form of alimony if the recipient continues to be financially stressed after the alimony ceases. *Id.* at (b).

Attorney's Fees. Payment of attorney's fees in divorce cases is of considerable importance, as *Murphy* illustrated. Other courts have also considered financial need in awarding fees. *See, e.g.,* Pfohl v. Pfohl, 345 So.2d 371 (Fla. 1977) (finding that the trial judge was well within his discretion in awarding $30,000 in attorney's fees to the husband given the wife's grossly disproportionate wealth). Similarly, in Brady v. Brady, 39 S.W.3d 557 (Mo. Ct. App. 2001), the court ordered the husband to pay the wife's attorney's fees in light of her financial constraints and his marital misconduct. Some awards of attorney's fees reflect the complexity and duration of the case. For example, in *Ex Parte* James, 764 S.2d 557 (Ala.1999), the Alabama Supreme Court affirmed the trial court's award of $100,000 to the wife's attorney to be taken off the top of the marital estate, which had been divided two-thirds/one-third between the husband and the wife, given the length and complexity of the divorce. Other jurisdictions will award fees especially where one party's conduct during the litigation prolonged final resolution. *See, e.g.,* Anderson v. Tolbert, 473 S.E.2d 456 (S.C. Ct. App. 1996) (requiring husband to reimburse wife for attorney's fees incurred due to his uncooperativeness).

Some jurisdictions provide factors to guide a court when awarding attorney's fees. *See, e.g.,* Glasscock v. Glasscock, 403 S.E.2d. 313 (S.C. 1991) (considering the nature, extent, and difficulty of the case; the time necessarily devoted to it; counsel's professional standing; any contingency of compensation; the beneficial results; and the customary legal fees for similar services). A court's decision to award attorney's fees will not be disturbed absent an abuse of discretion. Banker v. Banker, 474 S.E.2d 465 (W. Va. 1996).

Generally, attorneys may not use contingency fee arrangements for work in securing a divorce. *See* ABA MODEL RULES OF PROFESSIONAL CONDUCT RULE 1.5(d)(1). "The rule against contingent fees in domestic relations cases . . . is deep seated and well established. The policy reasons include a belief that this kind of fee might induce lawyers to discourage reconciliation and encourage bitter and wounding court battles." 7 N.Y. JUR. 2D ATTORNEYS AT LAW § 211 (2012).

Discrepancies Between the Sexes. Historically, it was customary for husbands but not wives to pay alimony, but a decision by the United States Supreme held that an Alabama statute authorizing awards against husbands only was unconstitutional discrimination. Orr v. Orr, 440 U.S. 268 (1979). Although the law today is gender neutral, it is overwhelmingly the case that alimony awards run from husbands to wives. *See* Anita Raghavan,

Men Receiving Alimony Want a Little Respect: Modern Males Say Living off the Ex-Wife is No Cause for Shame, WALL ST. J., April 1, 2008, at A1. In 2011, men represented only 3.16% of all alimony recipients. U.S. DEPT. OF COMMERCE, BUREAU OF THE CENSUS, CURRENT POPULATION SURVEY, 2011 ANNUAL SOCIAL AND ECONOMIC SUPPLEMENT, Table 4 (2011). The Census Bureau's *Current Population Survey* is based upon a monthly survey of 57,000 U.S. households that are carefully and scientifically selected to represent the nation as a whole. Of the households surveyed in March, 2011 in which an adult reported receiving alimony income, 96.86% of recipients were women and only 3.14% of recipients were men. *Id.* For more on the gender divide, *see* Alicia Brokars Kelly, *The Marital Partnership Pretense and Career Assets: the Ascendency of Self Over the Marital Community*, 81 B.U.L. REV. 59 (2001); Anne Lawton, *The Meritocracy Myth and the Illusion of Equal Employment Opportunity*, 85 MINN. L. REV. 587 (2000); Ann Estin, *Love and Obligation: Family Law and the Romance of Economics*, 36 WILLIAM AND MARY L. REV. 989 (1995); Jana Singer, *Alimony and Efficiency: The Gendered Costs and Benefits of the Economic Justification for Alimony*, 82 GEO. L. J. 2423 (1994); Milton C. Regan, Jr., *Spouses and Strangers: Divorce Obligations and Property Rhetoric*, 82 GEO. L. J. 2303 (1994).

Some statutes direct the trial judge to consider the non-monetary contributions of homemakers. *See, e.g.*, W. VA. CODE ANN. § 48–7–103 (2012). *See also* Katharine Silbaugh, *Turning Labor Into Love: Housework and the Law*, 92 NORTHWESTERN. U. L. REV. 1 (1996).

E. TERMINATION

Traditionally alimony terminated upon remarriage of recipient or death of either party, unless the parties otherwise agreed. *See, e.g.*, CAL. FAM. CODE § 4337 (2016). With the rise of cohabitation, an increasing number of jurisdictions have had to decide whether cohabitation by the recipient will also constitute a terminating event, either as a matter of law or private agreement.

Bell v. Bell

Supreme Judicial Court of Massachusetts, 1984
468 N.E.2d 859

■ O'CONNOR, JUSTICE.

The plaintiff appealed to the Appeals Court from the dismissal of her contempt complaint against her former husband for his failure to continue support payments allegedly owed to her under a judgment of divorce. The Appeals Court, by a two-to-one decision, reversed the judgment of the Probate Court. Bell v. Bell, 16 Mass.App.Ct. 188, 197, 459 N.E.2d 109 (1983). . . . We affirm the judgment of the Probate Court.

The judgment of divorce was entered on April 28, 1976, effective as of November 28, 1975. It incorporated a separation agreement that provided in part that the defendant would make significant monthly alimony payments to the plaintiff for a period of fifteen years following the entry of a final judgment of divorce or until the "happening of the following contingencies: 1) the [w]ife's death, 2) the [w]ife's remarriage, and/or 3) [the w]ife's living together with a member of the opposite sex, so as to give the outward appearance of marriage at any time prior to May 1, 1981, whichever of the . . . three contingencies happens first." The controversy concerns the interpretation and application of the third contingency provision (cohabitation clause). After a trial of the contempt matter, the judge made written findings and rulings. Based on his subsidiary findings with respect to the conduct of the plaintiff, we conclude that she "liv[ed] together with a member of the opposite sex, so as to give the outward appearance of marriage . . . prior to May 1, 1981."[1] It follows that the judge correctly ruled that the defendant's obligation to pay alimony had terminated and the contempt complaint was properly dismissed.

The judge found that following the judgment of divorce the plaintiff resided at the marital home in Cohasset on a regular basis until March, 1978. From March, 1978, until that summer she resided part of the time at the Cohasset home and part of the time in an apartment leased by a man identified as "J.R." From June, 1978, through October, 1979, she resided on a regular basis with J.R. in his apartment, and from October, 1979, to June, 1980, she resided with him at his apartment "for the most part." The judge also found that "[d]uring the period of time from June, 1978 through May, 1981, the plaintiff on a regular basis cohabited with J.R. . . . during which time they shared the same bedroom."

In addition, the judge made numerous detailed findings which we summarize briefly. The apartment lease stood solely in J.R.'s name. The plaintiff's name did not appear on the door or on the mailbox and she received her mail elsewhere. J.R. paid the rent and the plaintiff purchased the food and did most of the cooking and cleaning. Part of the furniture in the apartment was his and part of it was hers. They maintained separate bank accounts and never commingled assets. They took trips together and divided the costs. They socialized together. The plaintiff never represented to anyone that she was married to J.R. She never used his surname.

The cohabitation clause in question allowed the termination of alimony payments in the event that the plaintiff lived with a man "so as to give the outward appearance of marriage." It focused on the possibility of the plaintiff's sharing a home with a man, and it contemplated that that might occur in either of two ways: in a way that would create the appearance that the plaintiff and the man were married, or in a way that would not create such an appearance. Clearly, the parties thought that a man and a woman could live together in a way that would normally be associated with being married without their actually being married and

---

[1] We consider the cohabitation clause to be unambiguous as applied to the facts of this case, and therefore we do not rely on parol evidence or on findings of the judge to determine the intent of the parties.

without claiming or acknowledging a marriage relationship. It is difficult to conceive of what conduct the parties contemplated if that conduct did not at least include the plaintiff's sharing a bedroom with a man on a regular basis for approximately three years.

The Appeals Court held that it was the intention of the parties that alimony might be terminated only on the death or remarriage of the plaintiff, or "in circumstances so closely like marriage as to result in Mrs. Bell acquiring significant actual support or a new right to support from a man prior to the specified date in 1981." Bell v. Bell, supra at 194, 459 N.E.2d 109. The Appeals Court correctly noted that, in the absence of a formally solemnized marriage, the plaintiff could not become entitled to support from a man except by a contract providing for it. Thus, in effect, the Appeals Court interpreted the separation agreement to provide for the termination of alimony in less than fifteen years only if the plaintiff died or remarried or, irrespective of appearances, if she actually received significant financial support from a man other than the defendant, or entered into a contract for support.

The plain language of the agreement cannot properly be ignored. The clause in question does not mention support or the plaintiff's continuing need for it in the absence of a new source. It would have been relatively easy for the parties to have expressly provided for the termination of alimony in the event of the plaintiff's being substantially supported by another man or becoming contractually entitled to such support. There was no need to subtly express that thought by a reference to the plaintiff's living with a man so as to give the outward appearance of marriage. The language is better suited, and we think was employed, to provide for termination of the plaintiff's right to alimony if she were to remarry or were to live as though she were remarried.

In arriving at its interpretation of the cohabitation clause as relieving the defendant of his alimony obligation only if the plaintiff were to receive substantial support or were to become contractually entitled to receive support from another man, the Appeals Court relied in part on a provision in the separation agreement that "neither the [h]usband nor the [w]ife will hereafter interfere with the personal liberty of the other, and each may lead his or her life free from any criticism or restraint by the other." Bell v. Bell, supra at 194, 459 N.E.2d 109. The court reasoned that, if the defendant were entitled to terminate alimony payments in response to the plaintiff's arrangement with J.R., the defendant could coerce the plaintiff's conduct in a way that was inconsistent with the intent of the parties as expressed in their agreement. Id. at 194–195, 459 N.E.2d 109. It is true that the disputed clause, as we interpret it, might give the plaintiff reason not to live with a man so as to give the outward appearance of marriage. It is also true that the provision permitting a termination of alimony in the event of the plaintiff's remarriage might give her reason to decide against remarriage. We think, however, that it is clear that the parties did not intend by the noninterference provision to preclude the defendant from possibly influencing the plaintiff's choices by terminating alimony payments in the event she were to remarry or were to live with a man in the manner of a married couple. Termination of alimony payments in such circumstances cannot be considered interference with the plaintiff's personal liberty or "criticism or restraint" within the meaning of the agreement.

Finally, the plaintiff argues that "[c]ohabitation clauses which operate to bar the receipt of support payments by the wife upon the commencement of a non-marital relationship with a man, unfairly discriminate against women, both pursuant to the equal protection clause of the United States Constitution and the Massachusetts Equal Rights Amendment." The plaintiff's argument challenging the constitutionality of the provision appears for the first time on appeal to this court. Because this argument was not raised below, we decline to consider it.

Judgment of the Probate Court affirmed.

■ WILKINS, JUSTICE (dissenting, with whom LIACOS and ABRAMS, JUSTICES, join).

The opinion of the Appeals Court presents a reasonable interpretation of the separation agreement, certainly a view preferable to that expressed in the opinion of this court. The court's opinion gives no effect to the provision in the separation agreement that neither party will "interfere with the personal liberty of the other, and each may lead his or her life free from any criticism or restraint of the other." We would reverse the judgment of the trial court by focusing on the crucial language of the separation agreement, and would thus ignore the details of the private arrangements between Mrs. Bell and J.R. that have influenced the opinion of this court and the majority and dissenting opinions of the Justices of the Appeals Court.

The question for decision is what the parties meant by the phrase "(3) [the w]ife's living together with a member of the opposite sex, so as to give the outward appearance of marriage at any time prior to May 1, 1981 . . . " We know that the wife's living with a man would not alone terminate the husband's alimony obligation. The living together must have the appearance of marriage and that appearance must be outward. The court is wrong, therefore, in relying exclusively on the fact of "[Mrs. Bell's] sharing a bedroom with [J.R.] on a regular basis for approximately three years." That fact presents no outward appearance of anything. It was a private matter.

The significant point is that all the facts concerning the conduct and relationship of the wife and J.R. are equally consistent with a couple's not being married as they are with a couple's being married.[1] Couples,

[1] There is one fact which, if true, might indicate that Mrs. Bell and J.R. did not give the outward appearance of marriage. She testified that, during the entire time she had known J.R., she had dated other men and that she and J.R. had no arrangement by which she could not go out with other men. The opinion of the court ignores both this testimony concerning outward

married and unmarried, share or do not share living and travel expenses when they live together. In today's society, for better or for worse, unmarried couples live together and, from that fact alone, no conclusion can fairly be drawn that such couples are married or that they give the outward appearance of marriage. The fact of sharing a bedroom over a period of time is thus inconclusive on the question of an outward appearance of marriage.

The disputed language would apply, however, if Mrs. Bell were to have held herself out as married to J.R. That fact would have given the outward appearance of marriage. The facts in this case incontestably show that Mrs. Bell made no such representation. It is not for us to apply our moral judgment to conclude that the sharing of a bedroom over a period of time should be treated as giving an outward appearance of marriage when in fact, in today's world, such a sharing of a bedroom gives no such appearance.

■ ABRAMS, JUSTICE (dissenting).

I cannot share the court's certitude that the plaintiff and her former husband agreed that his obligation to pay alimony would terminate if she shared a bedroom with another man "on a regular basis." A separation agreement incorporated in a judgment of divorce is not an ordinary contract, but a judicially sanctioned contract setting forth the allocation between former spouses of rights, responsibilities, and resources. Although wives today may be less economically dependent on their husbands than was the case in the past, it remains true that the typical alimony recipient is a woman who has sacrificed her earning capacity to her marriage and who, as an equitable and practical matter, must look to her former husband for financial support following a separation or divorce. Such women have little bargaining power and to a large extent must rely on judicial supervision to ensure that their entitlement to support is not made contingent on unjust and unreasonable conditions. See Knox v. Remick, 371 Mass. 433, 436–437, 358 N.E.2d 432 (1976). By giving its imprimatur to an interpretation of the Bells' separation agreement that hinges the plaintiff's entitlement to support on her conformity to life-style requirements imposed by the defendant, the court encourages economically-dominant husbands to meddle arbitrarily with the postdivorce lives of their wives, and thereby sends an unfortunate message to probate judges charged with scrutinizing such separate agreements to ensure that the agreements are "fair and reasonable." Knox v. Remick, supra at 436, 358 N.E.2d 432.

To be sure, there is nothing unreasonable about provisions allowing the defendant and others similarly situated to discontinue support payments in circumstances where the recipient's need is eliminated or met by another source. As construed by the court, the separation

---

conduct and the trial judge's failure to consider it. The trial judge simply found that "on rare occasions [Mrs. Bell] brought someone other than J.R. to . . . cocktail parties" at J.R.'s apartment.

agreement and divorce judgment terminated the plaintiff's right to support solely because of her involvement in a relationship that does not have the defendant's approval, without any inquiry into its effect on her need for support and without reciprocal restraint on her husband.

Such a purely punitive elimination of support cannot be reconciled with the agreement's guarantee that "each [spouse] may lead his or her life free from any . . . restraint by the other." But even if, as the court decides, the unjustified limitation on the plaintiff's personal life imposed by a cutoff of support in the circumstances of this case is not plainly inconsistent with the terms of the Bells' agreement, public policy considerations should operate to preclude the result reached by the court. It is well established that a contractual restraint on fundamental private rights is subversive of public policy if it is "more onerous in its nature than is reasonably necessary for the proper fulfillment" of its purposes. Gleason v. Mann, 312 Mass. 420, 423–424, 425, 45 N.E.2d 280 (1942) (agreement that bound woman "to live a life of celibacy" unenforceable on public policy grounds where obligation "could be of no benefit" to employer). Compare Whitinsville Plaza, Inc. v. Kotseas, 378 Mass. 85, 102–103, 390 N.E.2d 243 (1979). By interpreting and enforcing the clause at issue here so as to give judicial sanction to a termination of support, the court allies itself with alimony payors who exercise their economic power in a manner that unreasonably interferes with the private, autonomous lives of the spouse from whom they have been divorced. I dissent.

NOTES

In the *Bell* case, the court had to construe an inartfully drafted cohabitation provision in a separation agreement that was incorporated into the divorce decree. In other cases, husbands have also lost support payments because of cohabitation. *See, e.g.,* Baker v. Baker, 566 N.W.2d 806 (N.D. 1997) (upholding the termination of alimony when recipient husband "cohabit[ed] in an 'informal marital relationship,'" which the divorce agreement treated as a ground for termination, because although girlfriend maintained a separate residence 50 miles away, she spent the night three fourths of the time at husband's residence).

Statutory Responses. A growing number of jurisdictions specifically address cohabitation as a terminating event in their alimony statutes. For example, South Carolina provides that alimony will end after the recipient cohabits continuously for 90 days. *See* S.C. CODE ANN. § 20–3–130 (2016). This necessarily raises the question of what will count as cohabitation. In Massachusetts, permanent alimony can be suspended, reduced, or terminated if the recipient maintains a "common household . . . with another person for a continuous period of at least 3 months." MASS. GEN. LAWS ANN. ch. 208 § 49 (2016). A common household results when two parties "share a primary residence together with or without others," and may be established by the couple's statements to third parties about the relationship, their "economic interdependence," "collaborative roles," benefit from the relationship, and reputation in the community as a couple. *Id.* If the relationship later dissolves, the prior alimony obligation may be reinstated but cannot "extend beyond the termination date of the original order." *Id.* Continuous cohabitation could be easily avoided by asking one's live-in partner to exit periodically—prompting some states to provide specific rules to aggregate periods of cohabitation when it appears the recipient is attempting to "game the system." *See* S.C. CODE ANN. § 20–3–130 (2016).

Some jurisdictions make no durational requirement. *See, e.g.*, 31 L.P.R.A. § 385 (2013) ("Alimony shall be revoked through judicial decision if . . . the divorced spouse entitled to such alimony contracts a new marriage or lives in public concubinage."). Moreover, because alimony awards extend court supervision into the couple's future, a material change in circumstances can justify modification or even termination of support, as Section F explains.

Cohabitation, however, does require some semblance of a spousal relationship. *See* Myers v. Myers, 266 P.3d 806 (Utah 2011) (holding that a woman who moved in with her parents and their teenage foster son was not cohabitating with the foster son in "a relationship 'akin' to a marriage").

Termination of Other Forms of Alimony. Certain forms of alimony follow a different pattern because of the nature of the award. Reimbursement alimony compensates the recipient for finite investments made during the marriage, for example in the other person's career or in childcare. Such awards terminate "upon the death of the recipient or a date certain;" but does not end on the payor's death; it becomes a debt of the estate. MASS. GEN. LAWS ANN. ch. 208, § 51(a) (2016). Because the award compensates for a specific investment, it cannot be modified. *See, e.g.,* MASS. GEN. LAWS ANN. ch. 208, § 51(b) (2016).

Security for Alimony Payments. Some states authorize courts to order that a life insurance policy be maintained for the benefit of a supported spouse as long as alimony is due. *See, e.g.*, N.Y. DOM. REL. LAW § 236(B)(8)(a) (2016). Likewise, for time-limited "transitional" alimony, Massachusetts allows a court to provide "reasonable security for payment of sums due to the recipient in the event of the payor's death during the alimony term." MASS. GEN. LAW ANN. 208 § 52 (2016). The court must consider the payor's age, insurability, the cost of the insurance, policies maintained during the marriage, and the amount and duration of the alimony. *See* MASS. GEN. LAW ANN. 208, § 55 (2016).

F. MODIFICATION

Naylor v. Naylor

Supreme Court of Utah, 1985
700 P.2d 707

■ DURHAM, JUSTICE.

This is an appeal from an order granting the respondent's motion to modify a decree of divorce. The appellant claims that the trial judge erred

(1) in extending the period for the payment of temporary alimony, (2) in finding a material change in circumstances warranting an increase in alimony and child support, and (3) in awarding attorney fees to the respondent. We affirm.

The parties were divorced in 1978 after eleven and a half years of marriage. At the time he filed for divorce, the appellant had recently completed his medical training and had just become a practicing surgeon. The respondent was, and still is, a hairdresser. The findings of fact accompanying the original decree, which was entered pursuant to the written stipulation and property settlement of the parties, stated that the appellant had net earnings at that time of $2,600 per month and that the respondent had net earnings of $702 per month. The decree awarded alimony to the respondent in the amount of $500 per month for five years and child support in the amount of $250 per month until the child reaches age 21 or leaves the home or until a court-ordered modification, whichever occurs first.

In 1981, the respondent filed this action for modification of the decree, and the matter was tried in 1983. At the time of the hearing, the appellant had become a shareholder in his medical practice corporation and was earning a base salary of $5,000 per month (gross) plus annual bonuses. The trial court found that the appellant's net income after taxes had increased to $75,000 since the time of the divorce.

After trial, the district court found that, at the time of the original divorce, the respondent had an expectancy that in the five-year period for which the alimony was awarded she would be able to establish herself as a hairdresser and have an increase in income sufficient to meet her financial needs, which expectancy has not been fulfilled as her current income is only $720 per month.

The court also found that the living expenses of the respondent and the parties' child had increased from $1,450 at the time of the divorce to $2,180 at the time of the modification hearing, due to increases in the cost of living and the fact that the child had become a teenager with significantly greater financial needs. Finally, the court found, "[The respondent] needs and [the appellant] has the ability to pay an increased and extended alimony award and increased [child] support award." Consequently, the decree was modified to extend the payment of alimony through 1987 (an additional four years) and to increase the amount by $100 per month beginning in December 1982. The trial court also increased the amount of child support from $250 per month to $400 per month.

The appellant argues that the trial court exceeded its power in modifying the term of temporary alimony awarded in the original divorce decree even if a substantial change in relevant circumstances had occurred. This argument is contrary to the legislative mandate to the district courts and to the principles of equity followed by this Court. Section 30–3–5(1), U.C.A., 1953 (Supp.1983), states: "The court shall have continuing jurisdiction to make such subsequent changes or new orders with respect to the support and maintenance of the parties, the custody of the children and their support and maintenance, or the distribution of the property as shall be reasonable and necessary." The language of the statute makes it clear that the appellant's position that the trial court lacked power or jurisdiction to modify an alimony award is without merit. This Court rejected a similar argument respecting a stipulated settlement requiring periodic payments in Callister v. Callister, 1 Utah 2d 34, 261 P.2d 944 (1953):

> We further hold that these [monthly payment] provisions are not an inseparable part of the agreement relating to division of property and that by approval of the agreement in the decree the court did not divest itself of jurisdiction under the statute to make such subsequent changes and orders with respect to alimony payments as might be reasonable and proper, based upon change of circumstances. We hold this to be true even though the provisions of the agreement should be interpreted to mean that the parties intended to stipulate for a fixed and unalterable amount of monthly alimony. The object and purpose of the statute is to give the courts power to enforce, after divorce, the duty of support which exists between a husband and wife or parent and child. Legislators who enacted the law were probably aware of a fact, which is a matter of common knowledge to trial courts, that parties to divorce suits frequently enter into agreements relative to alimony or for child support which, if binding upon the courts, would leave children or divorced wives inadequately provided for. It is therefore reasonable to assume that *the law was intended to give the courts power to disregard the stipulations or agreement of the parties in the first instance and enter judgment for such alimony or child support as appears reasonable, and to thereafter modify such judgments when change of circumstances justifies it, regardless of attempts of the parties to control the matter by contract.*

Id. at 41, 261 P.2d at 948–49 (emphasis added). *See also* Mitchell v. Mitchell, Utah, 527 P.2d 1359, 1360 (1974); Georgedes v. Georgedes, Utah, 627 P.2d 44, 46 (1981). Thus, the trial court in this case clearly had the power to modify the alimony provision of the decree.

The appellant's second claim of error challenges the equity of the result of the hearing below and the adequacy of the evidence to support the trial court's finding of a substantial change in circumstances. On a petition for a modification of a divorce decree, the threshold requirement for relief is a showing of a substantial change of circumstances occurring since the entry of the decree and not contemplated in the decree itself. Lea v. Bowers, Utah, 658 P.2d 1213, 1215 (1983). *See also* Kessimakis v. Kessimakis, Utah, 580 P.2d 1090, 1091 (1978). We note first that the record amply supports the trial court's finding on the change of circumstances question: the appellant's net income has more than doubled since the time of the divorce, even without the inclusion of the income being diverted into pension and profit sharing. The respondent's income, on the other hand, has remained approximately the same in dollar amounts, thereby actually decreasing in real value, contrary to the parties' expectation that it would increase. The fact that this expectation, which was a predicate for the original support order, has not been fulfilled constitutes a material change in circumstances. The age and cost of supporting the parties' child has also clearly changed substantially since the time of the divorce.

Concerning the equities of the modification ordered by the trial judge, we note that the evidence at the hearing established the following, in addition to the specific facts included in the trial court's findings: the respondent supported the parties during the appellant's four-year medical school course and continued to contribute to their support after he began to earn modest amounts as an intern and resident; the respondent has a high school degree; she was not employed as a hairdresser during the marriage, but had just completed her training and was beginning a career in that field at the time of the divorce; she agreed to the limited term of alimony because she anticipated that her work would be more remunerative than it has in fact been; and in order to support herself and the parties' child, she has had to borrow over $13,000 since the divorce, in addition to her earnings and the amounts provided by the appellant. In view of the totality of the circumstances of the parties, we are unable to say that the modification ordered by the trial judge constituted an abuse of his discretion or was so unfair or inequitable as to be arbitrary and capricious. On the contrary, the increases awarded (an additional $100 per month for an extended term of four more years, and an additional $150 per month in child support) seem entirely appropriate, given the relative situations of the parties.

Therefore, we affirm the order of the trial judge in its entirety and further award to the respondent her costs and attorney fees in connection with this appeal in an amount to be determined by the trial court.

UNIFORM MARRIAGE AND DIVORCE ACT (1973)

§ 316. [Modification and Termination of Provisions for Maintenance, Support and Property Disposition]

(a) . . . [T]he provisions of any [divorce] decree respecting maintenance or support may be modified only as to installments accruing subsequent to the motion for modification and only upon a showing of changed circumstances so substantial and continuing as to make the terms unconscionable. . . .

NOTES

Test for Modification. While the UMDA adopts a heightened standard for modification, in most states modification of alimony requires that the moving party must show a material change in the circumstances of one or both parties that was not reasonably contemplated when the award was made. *See generally* Alimony, Maintenance, and Other Spousal Support, tbl.1 titled "State by State Analysis," *50 State Statutory Surveys: Family Law: Divorce and Dissolution*, 0080 SURVEYS 11 (2012).

Additionally, some states allow for modification when an anticipated future event does not occur through no fault of the parties. *See, e.g.*, VA. CODE ANN. § 20–109 (2016). Examples of material change include changes in the payor's ability to pay that are beyond the payor's control and changes in the recipient's need beyond the recipient's control. Factors considered may include the cost of living, change in cost of supporting children, and illness, including mental or physical injury. Occasionally, couples will have an agreement delineating modification. Typically, however, courts are left to their own discretion.

Agreements Not to Modify Support. Some jurisdictions permit the spouses to "agree in writing if properly approved by the court to make the payment of alimony . . . nonmodifiable and not subject to subsequent modification by the court." S.C. CODE ANN. § 20–3–130(G) (2016).

The Importance of Reserving Jurisdiction. Some jurisdictions simply do not allow a court to award alimony if it was not awarded in the original decree. *See, e.g.*, Arbuckle v. Ciccotelli, 857 A.2d 324 (Vt. 2004). Therefore, as the Vermont Supreme Court stressed:

> [A] court may award maintenance in a nominal amount, to preserve the court's ability to modify the award later in the event of a "real, substantial, and unanticipated change in circumstances." Absent such preservation, the court cannot order maintenance at a later time, even if the financial situation of one of the spouses would warrant it.

Id. at 326.

In fact, where a divorce decree is silent as to alimony, two different risks arise. First, for the potential recipient, he or she may forever lose the ability to seek alimony. Thus, if a party does not intend this result, he or she should reserve the right to seek alimony in the future. *See* Perry v. Perry, 120 S.E.2d 385 (Va. 1961). Second, if alimony is not addressed explicitly, a potential payor also faces a risk: namely, that the other party will seek alimony at a later date. Thus, if a party does not intend this result, he or she should secure an explicit waiver in any divorce settlement agreement or decree.

Rehabilitative Alimony. Jurisdictions generally authorize courts to review rehabilitative alimony awards for whether they should be extended or modified for a change of circumstances. In some jurisdictions, this authority simply derives from the fact that "all maintenance awards are reviewable," unless the court's jurisdiction over the award has been properly removed. *In re* Marriage of Rodriguez, 834 N.E.2d 71, 75 (Ill. Ct. App. 2005). Other jurisdictions regulate the ability to extend or change rehabilitative awards by statute. So, for example, Massachusetts allows the rehabilitative award to be extended beyond the initial five year term "upon a showing of compelling circumstances" that "(1) unforeseen events prevent[ed] the recipient spouse from being self-supporting at the end of the term with due consideration to the length of the marriage;" "(2) . . . that the recipient tried to become self-supporting; and (3) the payor is able to pay without undue burden"—unless the recipient first remarries. MASS. GEN. LAWS ANN. ch. 208, § 50 (2016). The court is also permitted to modify rehabilitative alimony based "upon material change of circumstance within the rehabilitative period." MASS. GEN. LAWS ANN. ch. 208 § 50(c) (2016).

Notwithstanding the general ability to modify a rehabilitative award, an "overwhelming majority of jurisdictions that have considered the issue" have concluded that "rehabilitative maintenance awards cannot be modified after the term of rehabilitative maintenance has expired." Arbuckle v. Ciccotelli, 857 A.2d 324, 325 (Vt. 2004). This is so because "support requirements may be modified [only] so long as the duty to support exists, but not thereafter." *Id.* at 326. Moreover, it is only fair that "[o]nce a divorce decree is final and the maintenance order has expired, neither the parties nor the court should be burdened by the inevitable uncertainty that would flow from a perpetually unresolved maintenance award." *Id.* at 327. Of course, a court may always reserve jurisdiction to revisit the need for support after the end of the original award and the parties would have notice of this.

Just because a court has authority to extend or modify a rehabilitative award does not mean a court will necessarily do so. As the court explained in Rickenbach v. Kosinski, 32 So.3d 732 (Fla. Ct. App. 2010), "[r]ehabilitative alimony is essentially a projection based upon certain assumptions and probabilities. If these assumptions and probabilities develop as predicted within the projected term, the spouse should be able to support himself or herself when the alimony ends. . . . In order to be entitled to a modification, either to extend the rehabilitative period or to convert the rehabilitative alimony to permanent alimony, the petitioner must show why the original plan of rehabilitation did not work out. . . . [A] party seeking an extension or conversion of rehabilitative alimony must show only that he or she has not been rehabilitated despite reasonable and diligent efforts." *Id.* at 735–36. *See generally* Russell G. Donaldson, *Power to Modify Spousal Support Award for a Limited Term*, 62 A.L.R. 4TH 180 (2011). One of the more extreme remedies available after such a showing is, in some jurisdictions, conversion of the time-limited alimony into a permanent award. *Id.* (remanding to the trial court for a determination of whether conversion was warranted if the recipient must "continue to depend upon the support of the former husband or wife").

No Modification of Finite Awards. Certain forms of alimony may not be modified or escaped. For example, Massachusetts provides that reimbursement alimony, once ordered, cannot be modified. MASS. GEN. LAWS ANN. ch. 208, § 51(b) (2016). Neither can transitional alimony be modified for an increase in needs. *See* MASS. GEN. LAWS ANN. ch. 208, § 52 (2016). Some jurisdictions specifically authorize lump-sum awards, which can be paid "in one installment, or periodically," but because they represent a "finite total sum," they terminate "only upon the death of the supported spouse" and may not be modified for a change of circumstances. S.C. CODE ANN. § 20–3–130(b)(2) (2016).

Typical Modification Scenarios. There are some typical scenarios in which a payor or recipient may ask the court to modify a spousal support award. The first instance occurs when the payor's ability to pay increases. Jurisdictions take two different approaches. One approach is to cap the amount of support at the standard of living enjoyed during the marriage. *See, e.g., In re* Marriage of Hoffmeister, 236 Cal. Rptr. 543 (Cal. Ct. App. 1987). *But see In re* Marriage of Smith, 274 Cal. Rptr. 911 (Cal. Ct. App. 1990) (holding that there is no duty to maintain the level of support enjoyed during the marriage if the paying spouse worked excessively to provide that level). The other approach is to allow for a modification sharing the post-marriage wealth. *See, e.g.,* Naylor v. Naylor, 700 P.2d 707 (Utah 1985); Siegel v. Siegel, 102 Cal. Rptr. 613 (Cal. Ct. App. 1972).

A second instance occurs when the payor's ability to pay decreases. If the ability to pay decreases through no fault of the payor, then the award may be modified. *See, e.g.,* Smith v. Smith, 419 A.2d 1035 (Me. 1980). However, if the payor's own actions result in the decreased ability to pay, the reason for those actions matters. If the decreased ability to pay is due to a remarriage, courts are split on whether to permit modification. *Compare* Cowie v. Cowie, 564 So.2d 533 (Fla. Dist. Ct. App. 1990) (payor's trouble paying alimony due to new marriage and purchase of new home did not merit modification) *with* Lewis v. Lewis, 248 P.2d 1061 (Idaho 1952) (considering responsibility to second family in modification of support).

If the reason for the decrease is a voluntary change of jobs to a lower paying position, then the court is unlikely to modify the award. *See, e.g.,* Storey v. Storey, 862 A.2d 551 (N.J. Ct. App. 2004). If the payor takes early retirement, he or she is likely to be required to maintain the pre-retirement support amount. *See, e.g.,* Acker v. Acker, 904 So.2d 384 (Fla. 2005).

The third common situation in which one party seeks modification is when the recipient's need increases. When the greater need results from an increased cost of living due to the parties' children, the court is likely to modify an award. *See, e.g.,* Naylor v. Naylor, 700 P.2d 707 (Utah 1985). Likewise, if the increased need results from physical ailments of the recipient, the court is likely to modify an award to provide greater support. *See, e.g.*, Schaff v. Schaff, 449 N.W.2d 570 (N.D. 1989) (where wife, who suffered from systemic lupus erythematosus, in which the body attacks its own organs, an increase in alimony after disease progressed was warranted). However, if need is elevated due to a voluntary change in lifestyle, the spousal support award is unlikely to be modified. *See, e.g.,* Sistrunk v. Sistrunk, 235 So.2d 53 (Fla. Ct. App. 1970) (refusing to increase support when supported spouse left gainful employment to further education).

A fourth common situation is when the recipient's need decreases. Frequently, the event precipitating a request to modify alimony is the recipient's cohabitation with another, discussed *infra*. *See, e.g.,* ARIZ. REV. STAT. ANN. § 25–317 (2016). *See also* Alimony, Maintenance, and Other Spousal Support, tbl.1 titled "State by State Analysis," *50 State Statutory Surveys: Family Law: Divorce and Dissolution*, 0080 SURVEYS 11 (2012).

Cohabitation as Grounds for Modification. A material change in circumstances can always justify modification or even termination of support. In modification cases premised on cohabitation, whether courts ask if the cohabitation has had a financial impact is central. *See* Jill Bornstein, *At a Crossroad: Anti-Same-Sex Marriage Policies and Principles of Equity: The Effect of Same-Sex Cohabitation on Alimony Payments to an Ex-Spouse*, 84 CHI.-KENT L. REV. 1027 (2010). The ALI PRINCIPLES take the position that the establishment of a domestic partnership, or the continuous maintenance of a common household with a partner, are bases upon which the court may suspend payments of support unless it "would work a substantial injustice." *See* ALI, PRINCIPLES OF THE LAW OF FAMILY DISSOLUTION: ANALYSIS AND RECOMMENDATIONS § 5.09 (2000). While the PRINCIPLES leave states the discretion to define how long a common household must be maintained, the reporters' comments suggest that two years would be appropriate when the couple has a child in common, and three years without. The reporters urge that the durational requirement "be long enough to make it likely that the parties have established a life together as a couple . . . [with] some significant impact on the circumstances of one or both parties." *Id.* at cmt. (d).

By contrast, some states make cohabitation with another person, regardless of their sex, grounds for modification, whatever the length of the relationship, as Georgia does:

> Subsequent to a final judgment of divorce awarding periodic payment of alimony for the support of a spouse, the voluntary cohabitation of such former spouse with a third party in a meretricious relationship shall also be grounds to modify provisions made for periodic payments of permanent alimony for the support of the former spouse. As used in this subsection, the word "cohabitation" means dwelling together continuously and openly in a meretricious relationship with another person, regardless of the sex of the other person. In the event the petitioner does not prevail in the petition for modification on the ground set forth in this subsection, the petitioner shall be liable for reasonable attorney's fees incurred by the respondent for the defense of the action.

GA. CODE ANN. § 19–6–19(b) (2016).

G. DIVIDING PROPERTY UPON DIVORCE

UNIFORM MARRIAGE AND DIVORCE ACT (1973)

Alternative A

§ 307. [Disposition of Property.]

(a) In a proceeding for dissolution of a marriage, legal separation, or disposition of property following a decree of dissolution of marriage or legal separation by a court which lacked personal jurisdiction over the absent spouse or lacked jurisdiction to dispose of the property, the court, without regard to marital misconduct, shall, and in a proceeding for legal separation may, finally equitably apportion between the parties the property and assets belonging to either or both however and whenever acquired, and whether the title thereto is in the name of the husband or wife or both. In making apportionment the court shall consider the duration of the marriage, and prior marriage of either party, antenuptial agreement of the parties, the age, health, station, occupation, amount and sources of income, vocational skills, employability, estate, liabilities, and needs of each of the parties, custodial provisions, whether the apportionment is in lieu of or in addition to maintenance, and the opportunity of each for future acquisition of capital assets and income. The court shall also consider the contribution or dissipation of each party in the acquisition, preservation, depreciation, or appreciation in value of the respective estates, and the contribution of a spouse as a homemaker or to the family unit.

(b) In a proceeding, the court may protect and promote the best interests of the children by setting aside a portion of the jointly and separately held estates of the parties in a separate fund or trust for the support, maintenance, education, and general welfare of any minor, dependent, or incompetent children of the parties.

Alternative B

§ 307. [Disposition of Property.]

In a proceeding for dissolution of the marriage, legal separation, or disposition of property following a decree of dissolution of the marriage or legal separation by a court which lacked personal jurisdiction over the absent spouse or lacked jurisdiction to dispose of the property, the court shall assign each spouse's separate property to that spouse. It also shall divide community property, without regard to marital misconduct, in just proportions after considering all relevant factors including:

(1) contribution of each spouse to acquisition of the marital property, including contribution of a spouse as homemaker;

(2) value of the property set apart to each spouse;

(3) duration of the marriage; and

(4) economic circumstances of each spouse when the division of property is to become effective, including the desirability of awarding the family home or the right to live therein for a reasonable period to the spouse having custody of any children.

NEW YORK DOMESTIC RELATIONS LAW, § 236.B.5 (McKinney Supp. 2016)

(For the text of this statute, see *supra*.)

NOTES

Four Steps. When courts divide the couple's property and debts at divorce, they follow four steps. First, the court must determine what property is divisible—often called marital or community property—and the value of that property. Any property that is non-divisible—called separate property—is then simply assigned to its owner. Second, guided by statutory factors, the court must arrive at a fractional split of the divisible property. Third, the court must assign each piece of the divisible property to one party or the other. Typically, the assignment of assets results in a split that does not match the fractional split arrived at in step 2. Thus, the fourth step requires the court to use "offsets"—such as a monetary payment or a lien on divisible property from one party to the other—to arrive at the fractional division determined in step 2.

In the UMDA, Alternatives A and B take very different approaches to steps 1 and 2 of this four-step process.

What Gets Divided and Who Bears the Burden of Proof. In step 1, states that follow UMDA Alternative A have historically been called common law property or equitable distribution states. Under Alternative A, the court equitably apportions all "property and assets belonging to either or both however and whenever acquired," however titled. Montana is an example of a state that follows this approach. *See* MONT. CODE ANN. § 40–4–202 (2015).

States that follow Alternative B are commonly referred to as community property states. Under Alternative B, the court divides the couple's "community property," which generally includes property acquired by labor during the marriage. Louisiana follows such an approach. *See* LA. CIV. CODE ANN. art. 2338 (2016) ("The community property comprises: property acquired during the existence of the legal regime through the effort, skill, or industry of either spouse; property acquired with community things or with community and separate things, unless classified as separate property under Article 2341; property donated to the spouses jointly; natural and civil fruits of community property; damages awarded for loss or injury to a thing belonging to the community; and all other property not classified by law as separate property."). Because so much turns on whether a specific piece of property is part of the divisible property, who bears the burden of proof matters significantly. In South Carolina, for example, the party seeking to avoid division must prove that a specific item is excluded from the divisible property as separate. *See, e.g.*, Pruitt v. Pruitt, 697 S.E.2d 702 (S.C. Ct. App. 2010).

For a comparison of approaches in all fifty states, *see* Linda A. Elrod & Robert G. Spector, *Review of the Year in Family Law: Working Toward More Uniformity in Laws Relating to Families*, 44 FAM. L.Q. 514, chart 5 (2011).

The Fractional Split. In step 2, under UMDA Alternative A, the court arrives at a fractional split by considering a range of factors from duration of the marriage to whether the property division is in lieu of alimony or in addition to it.

Under UMDA Alternative B, the court divides the community property in "just proportions after considering all relevant factors," including those listed. Wisconsin generally follows this approach. *See* WIS. STAT. ANN. § 767.61 (2015–2016) (allowing a departure from equal division after considering a host of factors).

Unlike the UMDA approaches, some states give little discretion to the court when determining the fractional split under step 2. This is true in what would otherwise be common law property states, *see, e.g.,* Arneault v. Arneault, 639 S.E.2d 720 (W.Va. 2006), and community property states, *see, e.g.,* CAL. FAM. CODE § 2550 (2016). These states strongly favor a 50–50 split in longer marriages.

Property Division as Enacted. States have borrowed liberally from the stylized approaches in UMDA Alternatives A and B. Many states have enacted statutes that merge both approaches. Thirty-four states today divide only community or marital property—mirroring Alternative B. *See* Linda A. Elrod & Robert G. Spector, *Review of the Year in Family Law: Working Toward More Uniformity in Laws Relating to Families*, 44 FAM. L.Q. 514, chart 5 (2011). Thirty-seven states set forth statutory factors on how to divide the divisible assets—mirroring Alternative A. *Id.*

Characterization of Certain Property. States are split over whether and how to divide certain kinds of property acquired before the marriage or during it. One such split concerns the increase in value during the marriage of property that is clearly the separate property of one spouse. Some states condition division of the increased value on (A) the use of marital funds to "reduce[ ] indebtedness against separate property, extinguish[ ] liens, or otherwise increase[ ]" the separate property's net value or (B) the increased value resulting from "work performed" by one or both parties during the marriage. W. VA. CODE ANN. § 48–1–233 (2016). Other states assess whether the increased value is due to passive gains or the active labor of one of the parties. *See, e.g.,* VA. CODE ANN. § 20–107.3(A)(1) (2016).

States also split on whether to divide any income generated by separate property. Some jurisdictions treat that income as divisible property. *See, e.g.,* Friebel v. Friebel, 510 N.W.2d 767 (Wis. Ct. App. 1993) (dividing income generated from investments of gifts from one spouse's parents). Other jurisdictions treat the income generated by separate property as separate property. *See, e.g.,* ARIZ. REV. STAT. ANN. § 25–213 (2016) (treating as separate "[a] spouse's real and personal property," including all property owned before marriage or acquired by "gift, devise or descent, and the increase, rents, issues and profits of that property").

Another split between the states concerns the treatment of gifts between spouses during the marriage. Some states make a non-interspousal gift separate property of the recipient, but make gifts between spouses divisible. *See, e.g.,* WIS. STAT. ANN. § 767.61 (2015–2016). In North Carolina, a gift from one spouse to the other is separate property of the recipient "only if such an intention is stated in the conveyance." N.C. GEN. STAT. ANN. § 50–20 (2016).

When Does the Accrual of Marital Property End? Some statutes provide that specific events will cut off the accrual of marital property. For example, in South Carolina, marital property no longer accrues after the earliest of (a) a *pendente lite* order, (b) the formal signing of a settlement agreement, or (c) the permanent divorce order. *See* S.C. CODE ANN. § 20–3–630 (2016).

However, because of the lack of clarity in some statutes, questions have been raised about when a couple ceases to accrue marital property. In Portner v. Portner, 460 A.2d 115, 120 (N.J. 1983), the Supreme Court of New Jersey held that "for purposes of the equitable distribution of marital assets, a marriage is deemed to end on the day a valid complaint for divorce is filed that commences a proceeding culminating in a final judgment of divorce." In Anglin v. Anglin, 607 N.E.2d 777 (N.Y. 1992), the Court of Appeals of New York construed N.Y. DOMESTIC RELATIONS LAW § 236(B)(1)(c) to mean that a separation action does not, ipso facto, terminate the marital economic partnership and, therefore, does not preclude the subsequent accrual of marital property. Courts frequently have to address what happens with "dueling divorces" when couples file a divorce action and discontinue that action, only to later file for the ultimate dissolution of the marriage. In Mesholam v. Mesholam, 892 N.E.2d 846 (N.Y. 2008), the court held that the husband's pension should be valued through the date he filed a second valid divorce action, rather than the date on which wife filed an earlier, discontinued divorce action.

In Dobbyn v. Dobbyn, 471 A.2d 1068 (Md. 1984), the parties agreed that the date on which the petition was filed would determine what constituted marital property. However, they disagreed on the date that should be used for establishing the value of assets such as securities, options, and commodities. The Court of Special Appeals of Maryland held that "securities, stocks, bonds, options, commodities, and reserve funds . . . are to be valued as of the earlier time of either liquidation or . . . the date the parties were granted an absolute divorce." *Id.* at 1074.

Premarital Cohabitation. Should property acquired by a couple during a period of premarital cohabitation be treated as separate or marital property if that couple later marries and then divorces? In states that follow UMDA Alternative A, like Montana, all property is divided whether acquired during the marriage or before it, allowing premarital property to be divided. *See, e.g., In re* Marriage of Funk, 270 P.3d 39 (Mont. 2012). *See also* Northrop v. Northrop, 622 N.W.2d 219 (N.D. 2001). Increasingly, in states that follow Alternative B, which divides only community or marital property acquired during the marriage, a judge may consider the cohabitation prior to marriage when apportioning the marital estate. *See, e.g.*, Matter of Marriage of Dubnicay, 830 P.2d 608 (Or. 1992) (dividing assets acquired during cohabitation as marital property because the couple comingled their assets). Other courts take the position that the period of cohabitation and any assets acquired should not be considered in dividing assets at the end of the marriage. *See, e.g., In re* Marriage of Crouch, 410 N.E.2d 580 (Ill. 1980).

Hardy v. Hardy

Court of Appeals of South Carolina, 1993
429 S.E.2d 811

■ GARDNER, JUSTICE.

The parties were married in 1957 and of the marriage two children were born, both now emancipated. At the time of the institution of the divorce, the wife was 57 years of age and the husband 58 years of age. At the time of the divorce, Mr. Hardy owed in his name approximately $32,000 (exclusive of medical expenses); Mrs. Hardy owed in her name about $2,800.

The appealed order provided in pertinent part:

> The Court is of the opinion that each party should be required to satisfy all indebtedness in their respective names, or for which they have been the primary payor in the past with the exception of real estate mortgages and car payments which will be paid by the party receiving the property . . .

We hold that the trial judge failed to recognize that the law relating to marital debts was materially impacted by S.C. Code Ann. section 20–7–472 (Supp.1991), which provides in pertinent part:

> In making apportionment, the court must give weight in such proportion as it finds appropriate to all of the following factors:
>
> * * *
>
> (13) liens and any other encumbrances upon the marital property, which themselves must be equitably divided, or upon the separate property of either of the parties, *and any other existing debts incurred by the parties or either of them during the course of the marriage;* [Emphasis ours.]
>
> * * *
>
> (15) such other relevant factors as the trial court shall expressly enumerate in its order.

We hold that section 20–7–472 creates a presumption that a debt of either spouse incurred prior to marital litigation is a marital debt and must be factored in the totality of equitable apportionment. The presumption is rebuttable. For purposes of equitable distribution, "marital debt" is debt incurred for the joint benefit of the parties regardless of whether the parties are legally jointly liable for the debt or whether one party is legally individually liable. *See* Geer v. Geer, 84 N.C.App. 471, 353 S.E.2d 427 (1987). *See also* Allen v. Allen, 287 S.C. 501, 339 S.E.2d 872 (Ct.App.1986).

In the equitable division of a marital estate, the estate which is to be equitably divided by the family court judge is the net estate, i.e., provision for the payment of marital debts must be apportioned as well as the apportionment of property itself. We hold this to be implicit in the above statute. We hold, therefore, that basically the same rules of fairness and equity which apply to the equitable division of marital property also apply to the division of marital debts.

We hold that the burden of proving a spouse's debt as non-marital rests upon that party who makes such assertion. If the trial judge finds that a spouse's debt was not made for marital purposes, we hold that it need not be factored in the court's equitable apportionment of the marital estate and the trial judge may require payment by the spouse who created the debt for non-marital purposes.

We hold that the words "in such proportion as it finds appropriate," as used in section 20–7–472 accord much discretion to the trial judge in providing for the payment of marital debts as a consideration in the equitable division of the marital estate.

In the instant case, the trial judge failed to recognize that section 20–7–472 creates a presumption that all debts regardless of who created them are marital debts; additionally, the trial judge failed to make a determination that the husband's debts were non-marital. We, accordingly, reverse that portion of the appealed order which requires each spouse to satisfy the debts which were in his or her name and remand this issue for determination in accordance with this decision. Upon remand, the trial court shall concurrently distribute the marital assets and the marital debts. . . .

NOTES

Often, when a married couple files for divorce, the only "property" consists of debt. *Hardy* directs the court to equitably divide the marital property, using South Carolina's statutory factors, at the same time that it equitably divides the marital debt. But note that the trial judge has significant discretion on both scores, and could divide property in a different fraction than used to divide debt. *See* Bursum v. Bursum, 102 P.3d 651 (N.M. Ct. App. 2004).

Other states provide less discretion. Just as California, a community property state, provides that assets should be divided equally, so must debt. But if community debts exceed community assets, then the court may assign the excess debt as it deems "just and equitable, taking into account factors such as the parties' relative ability to pay." CAL. FAM. CODE § 2622 (2016).

The American Law Institute anchors a third approach, which is to distribute "net shares" of the marital estate equal in value, although not necessarily identical in kind. ALI, PRINCIPLES OF THE LAW OF FAMILY DISSOLUTION: ANALYSIS AND RECOMMENDATIONS § 4.09 (2000). Net shares are arrived at by taking the total value of assets and subtracting the total value of debts and distributing the remainder. Like California, the ALI proposes that courts have significant discretion when marital debts exceed marital assets, permitting the court to assign the excess unequally if a significant disparity exists between the spouses in their financial capacity, their participation in the decision to incur the debt, their consumption of the goods and services the debt supported, or some combination of these factors. *Id.*

What Counts as Marital Debt. *Hardy* treated as marital debt any debt incurred for the joint benefit of the parties, however held. Other states examine whether the debt benefits the community's dependents. *See* Bustos v. Gilroy, 751 P.2d 188. (N.M. Ct. App. 1988) (treating as a community debt attorney fees for wife in custody dispute against husband while she lived apart from him because outcome of attorney's work benefitted the couple's child). Other courts take a more black-and-white approach, looking only to whether the debt was incurred during the marriage. *See, e.g., In re* Marriage of Scoffield, 852 P.2d 664 (Mont. 1993).

Direct Payments of Debts to Third Parties. States often authorize orders directing one party to make payments to third parties, like a mortgage company. *See* N.Y. DOM. REL. § 236 ("In any action where the court has ordered . . . a distributive award . . . the court may direct that a payment be made directly to the other spouse or a third person for . . . rental or mortgage amortization or interest payments, insurances, taxes, repairs or other carrying charges on premises occupied by the other spouse, or for both payments to the other spouse and to such third persons."). Such orders do not change whether creditors have recourse against both spouses for payment in the case of joint debts.

Mahoney v. Mahoney

Supreme Court of New Jersey, 1982
453 A.2d 527

■ PASHMAN, JUSTICE.

Once again the Court must interpret this state's law regarding the distribution of marital property upon divorce. The question here is whether the defendant has the right to share the value of a professional business (M.B.A.) degree earned by her former husband during their marriage. The Court must decide whether the plaintiff's degree is "property" for purposes of N.J.S.A. 2A:34–23, which requires equitable distribution of "the property, both real and personal, which was legally and beneficially acquired . . . during the marriage." If the M.B.A. degree is not property, we must still decide whether the defendant can nonetheless recover the money she contributed to her husband's support while he pursued his professional education. For the reasons stated below, we hold that the plaintiff's professional degree is not property and therefore reject the defendant's claim that the degree is subject to equitable distribution. To this extent, we concur in the reasoning of the Appellate Division. Notwithstanding this concurrence, we reverse the judgment of the Appellate Division, which had the effect of denying the defendant any remedial relief for her contributions toward her husband's professional education and remand for further proceedings.

When the parties married in Indiana in 1971, plaintiff, Melvin Mahoney, had an engineering degree and defendant, June Lee Mahoney, had a bachelor of science degree. From that time until the parties separated in October 1978 they generally shared all household expenses. The sole exception was the period between September 1975 and January 1977, when the plaintiff attended the Wharton School of the University of Pennsylvania and received an M.B.A. degree. During the 16-month period in which the plaintiff attended school, June Lee Mahoney contributed about $24,000 to the household. Her husband made no financial contribution while he was a student. Melvin's educational expenses of about $6,500 were paid for by a combination of veterans' benefits and a payment from the Air Force. After receiving his degree, the plaintiff went to work as a commercial lending officer for Chase Manhattan Bank.

Meanwhile, in 1976 the defendant began a part-time graduate program at Rutgers University, paid for by her employer, that led to a master's degree in microbiology one year after the parties had separated. June Lee worked full-time throughout the course of her graduate schooling.

In March 1979, Melvin Mahoney sued for divorce; his wife filed a counterclaim also seeking a divorce. In May 1980, the trial court granted dual judgments of divorce on the ground of 18 months continuous separation. At the time of trial, plaintiff's annual income was $25,600 and defendant's income was $21,000. No claim for alimony was made. The parties owned no real property and divided the small amount of their personal property by agreement.

The only issue at trial was the defendant's claim for reimbursement of the amount of support she gave her husband while he obtained his M.B.A. degree. Defendant sought 50% of the $24,000 she had contributed to the household during that time, plus one-half of the $6,500 cost of her husband's tuition.

The trial court decided that defendant should be reimbursed, 175 N.J.Super. 443, 419 A.2d 1149 (Ch.Div.1980), holding that "the education and degree obtained by plaintiff, under the circumstances of this case, constitute a property right . . . " However, the court did not attempt to determine the value of plaintiff's M.B.A. degree. Instead, finding that in this case "[t]o ignore the contributions of the sacrificing spouse would be . . . an unjust enrichment of the educated spouse," *id.* at 446, 419 A.2d 1149, the court ordered the award of a "reasonable sum as a credit [for] . . . the maintenance of the household and the support of plaintiff during the educational period." *Id.* at 447. Plaintiff was ordered to reimburse his wife in the amount of $5,000, to be paid at the rate of $100 per month. The court did not explain why it chose this amount. Plaintiff appealed to the Appellate Division, which reversed the award. . . .

This Court . . . has never subjected to equitable distribution an asset whose future monetary value is as uncertain and unquantifiable as a professional degree or license. The Appellate Division discussed at some length the characteristics that distinguish professional licenses and degrees from other assets and interests, including intangible ones, that courts equitably distribute as marital property. Quoting from *In re* Marriage of Graham, 194 Colo. 429, 574 P.2d 75, 77 (1978), in which the Colorado Supreme Court held that an M.B.A. degree is not subject to equitable distribution, the court stated:

> An educational degree, such as an M.B.A., is simply not encompassed even by the broad views of the concept of "property." It does not have an exchange value or any objective transferable value on an open market. It is personal to the holder. It terminates on death of the holder and is not inheritable. It cannot be assigned, sold, transferred, conveyed, or pledged. An advanced degree is a cumulative product of many years of previous education, combined with diligence and hard work. It may not be acquired by the mere expenditure of money. It is simply an intellectual achievement that may potentially assist in the future acquisition of property. In our view, it has none of the attributes of property in the usual sense of that term. [182 N.J.Super. at 605, 442 A.2d 1062]

A professional license or degree is a personal achievement of the holder. It cannot be sold and its value cannot readily be determined. A professional license or degree represents the opportunity to obtain an amount of money only upon the occurrence of highly uncertain future events. By contrast, the vested but unmatured pension at issue in *Kikkert, supra*, entitled the owner to a definite amount of money at a certain future date.

The value of a professional degree for purposes of property distribution is nothing more than the possibility of enhanced earnings that the particular academic credential will provide. In Stern v. Stern, 66 N.J. 340, 345, 331 A.2d 257 (1975), we held that a lawyer's

> earning capacity, even where its development has been aided and enhanced by the other spouse . . . should not be recognized as a separate, particular item of property within the meaning of N.J.S.A. 2A:34–23. Potential earning capacity . . . should not be deemed property as such within the meaning of the statute.[3]

Equitable distribution of a professional degree would similarly require distribution of "earning capacity" income that the degree holder might never acquire. The amount of future earnings would be entirely speculative. Moreover, any assets resulting from income for professional services would be property acquired *after* the marriage; the statute restricts equitable distribution to property acquired *during* the marriage. N.J.S.A. 2A:34–23.

Valuing a professional degree in the hands of any particular individual at the start of his or her career would involve a gamut of calculations that reduces to little more than guesswork. As the Appellate Division noted, courts would be required to determine far more than what the degree holder could earn in the new career. The admittedly speculative dollar amount of

[3] A professional degree should not be equated with goodwill which, as we noted in *Stern*, may, in a given case, add economic worth to a property interest. Stern v. Stern, 66 N.J. at 346–47 n. 5, 331 A.2d 257 (1975).

> earnings in the "enhanced" career [must] be reduced by the . . . income the spouse should be assumed to have been able to earn if otherwise employed. In our view [this] is ordinarily nothing but speculation, particularly when it is fair to assume that a person with the ability and motivation to complete professional training or higher education would probably utilize those attributes in concomitantly productive alternative endeavors. [182 N.J.Super. at 609, 442 A.2d 1062]

Even if such estimates could be made, however, there would remain a world of unforeseen events that could affect the earning potential—not to mention the actual earnings—of any particular degree holder.

> A person qualified by education for a given profession may choose not to practice it, may fail at it, or may practice in a specialty, location or manner which generates less than the average income enjoyed by fellow professionals. The potential worth of the education may never be realized for these or many other reasons. An award based upon the prediction of the degree holder's success at the chosen field may bear no relationship to the reality he or she faces after the divorce. [DeWitt v. DeWitt, 98 Wis.2d 44, 296 N.W.2d 761, 768 (Ct.App.1980) (footnote omitted)]

Moreover, the likelihood that an equitable distribution will prove to be unfair is increased in those cases where the court miscalculates the value of the license or degree. . . . The finality of property distribution precludes any remedy for such unfairness. "Unlike an award of alimony, which can be adjusted after divorce to reflect unanticipated changes in the parties' circumstances, a property division may not [be adjusted]." *Id.* . . .

Even if it were marital property, valuing educational assets in terms of their cost would be an erroneous application of equitable distribution law. As the Appellate Division explained, the cost of a professional degree "has little to do with any real value of the degree and fails to consider at all the nonfinancial efforts made by the degree holder in completing his course of study." 182 N.J.Super. at 610, 442 A.2d 1062. See also DeWitt, supra, 296 N.W.2d at 767. Once a degree candidate has earned his or her degree, the amount that a spouse—or anyone else—paid towards its attainment has no bearing whatever on its value. The cost of a spouse's financial contributions has no logical connection to the value of that degree. . . .

This Court does not support reimbursement between former spouses in alimony proceedings as a general principle. Marriage is not a business arrangement in which the parties keep track of debits and credits, their accounts to be settled upon divorce. Rather, as we have said, "marriage is a shared enterprise, a joint undertaking . . . in many ways it is akin to a partnership." Rothman v. Rothman, 65 N.J. 219, 229, 320 A.2d 496 (1974); see also Jersey Shore Medical Center-Fitkin Hospital v. Estate of

Baum, 84 N.J. 137, 141, 417 A.2d 1003 (1980). But every joint undertaking has its bounds of fairness. Where a partner to marriage takes the benefits of his spouse's support in obtaining a professional degree or license with the understanding that future benefits will accrue and inure to both of them, and the marriage is then terminated without the supported spouse giving anything in return, an unfairness has occurred that calls for a remedy.

In this case, the supporting spouse made financial contributions towards her husband's professional education with the expectation that both parties would enjoy material benefits flowing from the professional license or degree. It is therefore patently unfair that the supporting spouse be denied the mutually anticipated benefit while the supported spouse keeps not only the degree, but also all of the financial and material rewards flowing from it.

Furthermore, it is realistic to recognize that in this case, a supporting spouse has contributed more than mere earnings to her husband with the mutual expectation that both of them—she as well as he—will realize and enjoy material improvements in their marriage as a result of his increased earning capacity. Also, the wife has presumably made personal financial sacrifices, resulting in a reduced or lowered standard of living. Additionally, her husband, by pursuing preparations for a future career, has foregone gainful employment and financial contributions to the marriage that would have been forthcoming had he been employed. He thereby has further reduced the level of support his wife might otherwise have received, as well as the standard of living both of them would have otherwise enjoyed. In effect, through her contributions, the supporting spouse has consented to live at a lower material level while her husband has prepared for another career. She has postponed, as it were, present consumption and a higher standard of living, for the future prospect of greater support and material benefits. The supporting spouse's sacrifices would have been rewarded had the marriage endured and the mutual expectations of both of them been fulfilled. The unredressed sacrifices—loss of support and reduction of the standard of living—coupled with the unfairness attendant upon the defeat of the supporting spouse's shared expectation of future advantages, further justify a remedial reward. In this sense, an award that is referable to the spouse's monetary contributions to her partner's education significantly implicates basic considerations of marital support and standard of living—factors that are clearly relevant in the determination and award of conventional alimony.

To provide a fair and effective means of compensating a supporting spouse who has suffered a loss or reduction of support, or has incurred a lower standard of living, or has been deprived of a better standard of living in the future, the Court now introduces the concept of reimbursement alimony into divorce proceedings. The concept properly accords with the Court's belief that regardless of the appropriateness of permanent alimony or the presence or absence of marital property to be equitably distributed, there will be circumstances where a supporting spouse should be reimbursed for the financial contributions he or she made to the spouse's successful professional training. Such reimbursement alimony should cover *all* financial contributions towards the former spouse's education, including household expenses, educational costs, school travel expenses and any other contributions used by the supported spouse in obtaining his or her degree or license.

This result is consistent with the remedial provisions of the matrimonial statute. N.J.S.A. 2A:34–23. A basic purpose of alimony relates to the quality of economic life to which one spouse is entitled and that becomes the obligation of the other. Alimony has to do with support and standard of living. We have recently recognized the relevance of these concepts in accepting the notion of rehabilitative alimony, which is consonant with the basic underlying rationale that a party is entitled to continue at a customary standard of living inclusive of costs necessary for needed educational training. Lepis v. Lepis, 83 N.J. 139, 155 n. 9, 416 A.2d 45.

The statute recognizes that alimony should be tailored to individual circumstances, particularly those relating to the financial status of the parties. . . . The Court does not hold that every spouse who contributes toward his or her partner's education or professional training is entitled to reimbursement alimony. Only monetary contributions made with the mutual and shared expectation that both parties to the marriage will derive increased income and material benefits should be a basis for such an award. For example, it is unlikely that a financially successful executive's spouse who, after many years of homemaking, returns to school would upon divorce be required to reimburse her husband for his contributions toward her degree. Reimbursement alimony should not subvert the basic goals of traditional alimony and equitable distribution.

In proper circumstances, however, courts should not hesitate to award reimbursement alimony. Marriage should not be a free ticket to professional education and training without subsequent obligations. This Court should not ignore the scenario of the young professional who after being supported through graduate school leaves his mate for supposedly greener pastures. One spouse ought not to receive a divorce complaint when the other receives a diploma. Those spouses supported through professional school should recognize that they may be called upon to reimburse the supporting spouses for the financial contributions they received in pursuit of their professional training. And they cannot deny the basic fairness of this result.[5]

[5] This decision recognizes the fairness of an award of reimbursement alimony for past contributions to a spouse's professional education that were made with the expectation of mutual economic benefit. We need not in the present posture of this case determine the degree of finality or permanency that should be accorded an award of reimbursement alimony as compared to conventional alimony. As noted, an award of reimbursement alimony combines elements relating to the support, standard of living and financial expectations of the parties

As we have stated, reimbursement alimony will not always be appropriate or necessary to compensate a spouse who has contributed financially to the partner's professional education or training. "Rehabilitative alimony" may be more appropriate in cases where a spouse who gave up or postponed her own education to support the household requires a lump sum or a short-term award to achieve economic self-sufficiency. . . . However, rehabilitative alimony would not be appropriate where the supporting spouse is unable to return to the job market, or has already attained economic self-sufficiency.

Similarly, where the parties to a divorce have accumulated substantial assets during a lengthy marriage, courts should compensate for any unfairness to one party who sacrificed for the other's education, not by reimbursement alimony but by an equitable distribution of the assets to reflect the parties' different circumstances and earning capacities. In *Rothman, supra*, the Court explicitly rejected the notion that courts should presume an equal division of marital property. 65 N.J. at 232 n. 6, 320 A.2d 496. "Rejecting any simple formula, we rather believe that each case should be examined as an individual and particular entity." *Id.* If the degree-holding spouse has already put his professional education to use, the degree's value in enhanced earning potential will have been realized in the form of property, such as a partnership interest or other asset, that is subject to equitable distribution. *See* Stern, supra, 65 N.J. at 346–47, 331 A.2d 257.

The degree holder's earning capacity can also be considered in an award of permanent alimony.[6] . . . Even though the enhanced earning potential provided by a degree or license is not "property" for purposes of N.J.S.A. 2A:34–23, it clearly should be a factor considered by the trial judge in determining a proper amount of alimony. If the degree holder's actual earnings turn out to diverge greatly from the court's estimate, making the amount of alimony unfair to either party, the alimony award can be adjusted accordingly.

We stated in *Stern, supra*, that while earning potential should not be treated as a separate item of property,

> [p]otential earning capacity is doubtless a factor to be considered by a trial judge in determining what distribution will

with notions of marital fairness and avoidance of unjust enrichment. We must also recognize that, while these cases frequently illustrate common patterns of human behavior and experience among married couples, circumstances vary among cases. Consequently, it would be unwise to attempt to anticipate all of the ramifications that flow from our present recognition of a right to reimbursement alimony. We therefore leave for future cases questions as to whether and under what changed circumstances such awards may be modified or adjusted.

[6] It should be noted that alimony is not generally available for a self-supporting spouse under the laws of Minnesota, *see DeLa Rosa, supra*, 309 N.W.2d at 758, or Kentucky, *see Inman, supra*, 578 S.W.2d at 270, two states that have treated professional licenses as property. Those states are thus handicapped in their ability to do equity in situations where little or no marital property has been accumulated and the supporting spouse does not qualify for maintenance unless they treat professional licenses as property.

be "equitable" and it is even more obviously relevant upon the issue of alimony. [66 N.J. at 345, 331 A.2d 257]

We believe that *Stern* presents the best approach for achieving fairness when one spouse has acquired a professional degree or license during the marriage. Courts may not make any permanent distribution of the value of professional degrees and licenses, whether based upon estimated worth or cost. However, where a spouse has received from his or her partner financial contributions used in obtaining a professional degree or license with the expectation of deriving material benefits for both marriage partners, that spouse may be called upon to reimburse the supporting spouse for the amount of contributions received.

In the present case, the defendant's financial support helped her husband to obtain his M.B.A. degree, which assistance was undertaken with the expectation of deriving material benefits for both spouses. Although the trial court awarded the defendant a sum as "equitable offset" for her contributions, the trial court's approach was not consistent with the guidelines we have announced in this opinion. Therefore, we are remanding the case so the trial court can determine whether reimbursement alimony should be awarded in this case and, if so, what amount is appropriate.

The judgment of the Appellate Division is reversed and the cause remanded for further proceedings not inconsistent with this opinion.

CALIFORNIA FAMILY CODE (2016)

§ 2641. Community contributions to education or training

(a) "Community contributions to education or training" as used in this section means payments made with community or quasi-community property for education or training or for the repayment of a loan incurred for education or training, whether the payments were made while the parties were resident in this state or resident outside this state.

(b) Subject to the limitations provided in this section, upon dissolution of marriage or legal separation of the parties:

> (1) The community shall be reimbursed for community contributions to education or training of a party that substantially enhances the earning capacity of the party. The amount reimbursed shall be with interest at the legal rate, accruing from the end of the calendar year in which the contributions were made.
>
> (2) A loan incurred during marriage for the education or training of a party shall not be included among the liabilities of the community for the purpose of division pursuant to this division but shall be assigned for payment by the party.

(c) The reimbursement and assignment required by this section shall be reduced or modified to the extent circumstances render such a disposition unjust, including, but not limited to, any of the following:

(1) The community has substantially benefited from the education, training, or loan incurred for the education or training of the party. There is a rebuttable presumption, affecting the burden of proof, that the community has not substantially benefited from community contributions to the education or training made less than 10 years before the commencement of the proceeding, and that the community has substantially benefited from community contributions to the education or training made more than 10 years before the commencement of the proceeding.

(2) The education or training received by the party is offset by the education or training received by the other party for which community contributions have been made.

(3) The education or training enables the party receiving the education or training to engage in gainful employment that substantially reduces the need of the party for support that would otherwise be required.

(d) Reimbursement for community contributions and assignment of loans pursuant to this section is the exclusive remedy of the community or a party for the education or training and any resulting enhancement of the earning capacity of a party. However, nothing in this subdivision limits consideration of the effect of the education, training, or enhancement, or the amount reimbursed pursuant to this section, on the circumstances of the parties for the purpose of an order for support pursuant to Section 4320.

(e) This section is subject to an express written agreement of the parties to the contrary.

NOTES

Like *Mahoney*, nearly every state takes the position that occupational licenses and educational degrees are not property that can be divided on divorce "because their value is inextricably intertwined with spousal skills or earning capacity, or post-marital spousal labor," as does the American Law Institute. ALI, PRINCIPLES OF THE LAW OF FAMILY DISSOLUTION: ANALYSIS AND RECOMMENDATIONS § 4.07, Comments and Illustrations, Comment B (2000). But "a spouse is entitled at divorce to reimbursement for the financial contributions made to the other spouse's education or training" under defined circumstances which allow for calculation. *Id.* at § 5.12(1). The argument for this approach is that relief should come from alimony. *See, e.g.*, Wilson v. Wilson, 388 N.W.2d 432 (Minn. Ct. App. 1986). For a general discussion of property dissolution and ongoing support obligations, *see* Ann Laquer Estin, *Love and Obligation: Family Law and the Romance of Economics*, 36 WM. & MARY L. REV. 989, 1066 (1995).

Goodwill is another intangible asset. *See, e.g.*, Piscopo v. Piscopo, 557 A.2d 1040 (N.J. Ct. App.1989) (holding that celebrity's goodwill was marital property subject to division based on the celebrity's past earning capacity which likely will continue). Goodwill has been defined as the excess value of the business's market value over its asset value. *See generally* Grace Blumberg, *Intangible Assets: Recognition and Valuation in* 2 VALUATION AND DISTRIBUTION OF MARITAL PROPERTY § 23.05[1] (Matthew Bender 1996). Other courts decline to treat goodwill as marital property in the absence of a sale of the asset, treating it instead as earning potential when applied to professional persons. *See, e.g., In re* Marriage of Talty, 652 N.E.2d 330 (Ill. 1995) and Sorensen v. Sorensen, 839 P.2d 774 (Utah 1992). Some courts make a distinction between goodwill held by individuals, which is not property but can be an equitable factor, and the goodwill of a company, which is marital property. *See, e.g., In re* Marriage of Schneider, 824 N.E.2d 177 (Ill. 2005). Other courts distinguish between professional goodwill that can be sold and professional goodwill that cannot. *See, e.g., In re* McReath v. McReath, 789 N.W.2d 89 (Wis. Ct. App. 2010).

A personal injury award is tangible but personal to the victim, raising the question whether it should be part of the divisible property. The Nebraska Supreme Court represents the majority approach, holding that any decision should be based on an analysis of the underlying purposes of the award rather than the mechanical approach that treats personal injury awards as entirely marital property. Compensation for pain, suffering, disfigurement, disability, or loss of post-divorce earnings should not be considered marital property but the burden is upon the victim to demonstrate that the award was for these reasons. If the award is to compensate for anything that would diminish the marital partnership, the award is marital property. *See* Parde v. Parde, 602 N.W.2d 657 (Neb. 1999).

By contrast, a New York decision held that an increase in the value of a career, in this instance, of an opera singer, could be subject to equitable distribution because the other spouse's contribution and efforts led to the increase. The court said things of value acquired during marriage are marital property even if they do not share the attributes of traditional property (capacity to transfer, sale or assign). *See* Elkus v. Elkus, 572 N.Y.S. 2d 901 (Ct. App. 1991).

O'Brien v. O'Brien

Court of Appeals of New York, 1985
66 N.Y.2d 576

■ SIMONS, JUDGE.

In this divorce action, the parties' only asset of any consequence is the husband's newly acquired license to practice medicine. The principal issue presented is whether that license, acquired during their marriage, is marital property subject to equitable distribution under Domestic Relations Law § 236(B)(5). . . .

Plaintiff and defendant married on April 3, 1971. At the time both were employed as teachers at the same private school. Defendant had a bachelor's degree and a temporary teaching certificate but required 18 months of postgraduate classes at an approximate cost of $3,000, excluding living expenses, to obtain permanent certification in New York. She claimed, and the trial court found, that she had relinquished the opportunity to obtain permanent certification while plaintiff pursued his education. At the time of the marriage, plaintiff had completed only three and one-half years of college but shortly afterward he returned to school at night to earn his bachelor's degree and to complete sufficient premedical courses to enter medical school. In September 1973 the parties moved to Guadalajara, Mexico, where plaintiff became a full-time medical student. While he pursued his studies defendant held several teaching and tutorial positions and contributed her earnings to their joint expenses. The parties returned to New York in December 1976 so that plaintiff could complete the last two semesters of medical school and internship training here. After they returned, defendant resumed her former teaching position and she remained in it at the time this action was commenced. Plaintiff was licensed to practice medicine in October 1980. He commenced this action for divorce two months later. At the time of trial, he was a resident in general surgery.

During the marriage both parties contributed to paying the living and educational expenses and they received additional help from both of their families. They disagreed on the amounts of their respective contributions but it is undisputed that in addition to performing household work and managing the family finances defendant was gainfully employed throughout the marriage, that she contributed all of her earnings to their living and educational expenses and that her financial contributions exceeded those of plaintiff. The trial court found that she had contributed 76% of the parties' income exclusive of a $10,000 student loan obtained by defendant. Finding that plaintiff's medical degree and license are marital property, the court received evidence of its value and ordered a distributive award to defendant.

Defendant presented expert testimony that the present value of plaintiff's medical license was $472,000. Her expert testified that he had arrived at this figure by comparing the average income of a college graduate and that of a general surgeon between 1985, when plaintiff's residency would end, and 2012, when he would reach age 65. After considering Federal income taxes, an inflation rate of 10% and a real interest rate of 3% he capitalized the difference in average earnings and reduced the amount to present value. He also gave his opinion that the present value of defendant's contribution to plaintiff's medical education was $103,390. Plaintiff offered no expert testimony on the subject.

The court, after considering the life-style that plaintiff would enjoy from the enhanced earning potential his medical license would bring and defendant's contributions and efforts toward attainment of it, made a distributive award to her of $188,800, representing 40% of the value of the license, and ordered it paid in 11 annual installments . . . [but awarded no maintenance]. The court also directed plaintiff to maintain a life insurance policy on his life for defendant's benefit for the unpaid balance of the award and it ordered plaintiff to pay defendant's counsel fees of $7,000 and her expert witness fee of $1,000. It did not award defendant maintenance.

The Equitable Distribution Law contemplates only two classes of property: marital property and separate property (Domestic Relations Law§ 236[B][1][c], [d]). The former, which is subject to equitable distribution, is defined broadly as "*all* property acquired by either or both spouses during the marriage and before the execution of a separation agreement or the commencement of a matrimonial action, *regardless of the form in which title is held*" (Domestic Relations Law§ 236[B][1][c] [emphasis added]; *see* § 236[B][5][b], [c]). Plaintiff does not contend that his license is excluded from distribution because it is separate property; rather, he claims that it is not property at all but represents a personal attainment in acquiring knowledge. . . . [T]he New York Legislature deliberately went beyond traditional property concepts when it formulated the Equitable Distribution Law. Instead, our statute recognizes that spouses have an equitable claim to things of value arising out of the marital relationship and classifies them as subject to distribution by focusing on the marital status of the parties at the time of acquisition. . . . [T]he Legislature . . . left it to the courts to determine what interests come within the terms of section 236(B)(1)(c).

We made such a determination in Majauskas v. Majauskas, 61 N.Y.2d 481, 474 N.Y.S.2d 699, 463 N.E.2d 15, holding there that vested but unmatured pension rights are marital property subject to equitable distribution ... Section 236 provides that in making an equitable distribution of marital property, "the court shall consider: . . . (6) any equitable claim to, interest in, or direct or indirect contribution made to the acquisition of such marital property by the party not having title, including joint efforts or expenditures and contributions and services as a spouse, parent, wage earner and homemaker, and *to the career or career potential* of the other party [and] . . . (9) the impossibility or difficulty of evaluating any component asset or any interest in a business, corporation or *profession*" (Domestic Relations Law § 236[B][5][d][6], [9] [emphasis added]). Where equitable distribution of marital property is appropriate but "the distribution of an interest in a business, corporation or *profession* would be contrary to law" the court shall make a distributive award in lieu of an actual distribution of the property (Domestic Relations Law § 236[B][5][e] [emphasis added]). The words mean exactly what they say: that an interest in a profession or professional career potential is marital property which may be represented by direct or indirect contributions of the non-title-holding spouse, including financial contributions and nonfinancial contributions made by caring for the home and family. . . .

Equitable distribution was based on the premise that a marriage is, among other things, an economic partnership to which both parties contribute as spouse, parent, wage earner or homemaker. Consistent with this purpose, and implicit in the statutory scheme as a whole, is the view that upon dissolution of the marriage there should be a winding up of the parties' economic affairs and a severance of their economic ties by an equitable distribution of the marital assets. . . .

The determination that a professional license is marital property is also consistent with the conceptual base upon which the statute rests. As this case demonstrates, few undertakings during a marriage better qualify as the type of joint effort that the statute's economic partnership theory is intended to address than contributions toward one spouse's acquisition of a professional license. Working spouses are often required to contribute substantial income as wage earners, sacrifice their own educational or career goals and opportunities for child rearing, perform the bulk of household duties and responsibilities and forego the acquisition of marital assets that could have been accumulated if the professional spouse had been employed rather than occupied with the study and training necessary to acquire a professional license. In this case, nearly all of the parties' nine-year marriage was devoted to the acquisition of plaintiff's medical license and defendant played a major role in that project. . . . The Legislature has decided, by its explicit reference in the statute to the contributions of one spouse to the other's profession or career, that these contributions represent investments in the economic partnership of the marriage and that the product of the parties' joint efforts, the professional license, should be considered marital property. . . .

Plaintiff's principal argument, adopted by the majority below, is that a professional license is not marital property because it does not fit within the traditional view of property as something which has an exchange value on the open market and is capable of sale, assignment or transfer. The position does not withstand analysis for at least two reasons. First, as we have observed, it ignores the fact that whether a professional license constitutes marital property is to be judged by the language of the statute which created this new species of property previously unknown at common law or under prior statutes. Thus, whether the license fits within traditional property concepts is of no consequence. Second, it is an overstatement to assert that a professional license could not be considered property even outside the context of section 236(B). A professional license is a valuable property right, reflected in the money, effort and lost opportunity for employment expended in its acquisition, and also in the enhanced earning capacity it affords its holder, which may not be revoked without due process of law. That a professional license has no market value is irrelevant. Obviously, a license may not be alienated as may other property and for that reason the working spouse's interest in it is limited. The Legislature has recognized that limitation, however, and has provided for an award in lieu of its actual distribution (*see*, Domestic Relations Law § 236[B][5][e]).

Plaintiff also contends that alternative remedies should be employed, such as an award of rehabilitative maintenance or reimbursement for direct financial contributions. The statute does not expressly authorize retrospective maintenance or rehabilitative awards and we have no occasion to decide in this case whether the authority to do so may ever be implied from its provisions. It is sufficient to observe that normally a working spouse should not be restricted to that relief because to do so frustrates the purposes underlying the Equitable Distribution Law. Limiting a working spouse to a maintenance award, either general or rehabilitative, not only is contrary to the economic partnership concept underlying the statute but also retains the uncertain and inequitable economic ties of dependence that the Legislature sought to extinguish by equitable distribution. Maintenance is subject to termination upon the recipient's remarriage and a working spouse may never receive adequate consideration for his or her contribution and may even be penalized for the decision to remarry if that is the only method of compensating the contribution. As one court said so well, "[t]he function of equitable distribution is to recognize that when a marriage ends, each of the spouses, based on the totality of the contributions made to it, has a stake in and right to a share of the marital assets accumulated while it endured, not because that share is needed, but because those assets represent the capital product of what was essentially a partnership entity" (Wood v. Wood, 119 Misc.2d 1076, 1079, 465 N.Y.S.2d 475). The Legislature stated its intention to eliminate such inequities by providing that a supporting spouse's "direct or indirect contribution" be recognized, considered and rewarded (Domestic Relations Law § 236[B][5][d][6]).

Turning to the question of valuation, it has been suggested that even if a professional license is considered marital property, the working spouse is entitled only to reimbursement of his or her direct financial contributions. . . . By parity of reasoning, a spouse's down payment on real estate or contribution to the purchase of securities would be limited to the money contributed, without any remuneration for any incremental value in the asset because of price appreciation. Such a result is completely at odds with the statute's requirement that the court give full consideration to both direct and indirect contributions "made to the acquisition of such marital property by the party not having title, including joint *efforts* or expenditures and *contributions and services as a spouse, parent,* wage earner *and homemaker*" (Domestic Relations Law 236[B][5][d][6] [emphasis added]). If the license is marital property, then the working spouse is entitled to an equitable portion of it, not a return of funds advanced. Its value is the enhanced earning capacity it affords the holder and although fixing the present value of that enhanced earning capacity may present problems, the problems are not insurmountable. Certainly they are no more difficult than computing tort damages for wrongful death or diminished earning capacity resulting from injury and they differ only in degree from the problems presented when valuing a professional practice for purposes of a distributive award, something the courts have not hesitated to do. The trial court retains the flexibility and discretion to structure the distributive award equitably, taking into consideration factors such as the working spouse's need for immediate payment, the licensed spouse's current ability to pay and the income tax consequences of prolonging the period of payment, and once it has received evidence of the present value of the license and the working spouse's contributions toward its acquisition and considered the remaining factors mandated by the statute, it may then make an appropriate distribution of the marital property including a distributive award for the professional license if such an award is warranted. When other marital assets are of sufficient value to provide for the supporting spouse's equitable portion of the marital property, including his or her contributions to the acquisition of the professional license, however, the court retains the discretion to distribute these other marital assets or to make a distributive award in lieu of an actual distribution of the value of the professional spouse's license. . . .

Accordingly, in view of our holding that plaintiff's license to practice medicine is marital property, the order of the Appellate Division should be modified, with costs to defendant, by reinstating the judgment and the case remitted to the Appellate Division for determination of the facts, including the exercise of that court's discretion and, as so modified, affirmed. . . .

■ MEYER, JUDGE (concurring).

I concur in Judge Simons' opinion but write separately to point up for consideration by the Legislature the potential for unfairness involved in distributive awards based upon a license of a professional still in training. . . .

The present case points up the problem. A medical license is but a step toward the practice ultimately engaged in by its holder, which follows after internship, residency and, for particular specialties, board certification. Here it is undisputed that plaintiff was in a residency for general surgery at the time of the trial, but had the previous year done a residency in internal medicine. Defendant's expert based his opinion on the difference between the average income of a general surgeon and that of a college graduate of plaintiff's age and life expectancy, which the trial judge utilized, impliedly finding that plaintiff would engage in a surgical practice despite plaintiff's testimony that he was dissatisfied with the general surgery program he was in and was attempting to return to the internal medicine training he had been in the previous year. . . .

The equitable distribution provisions of the Domestic Relations Law were intended to provide flexibility so that equity could be done. But if the assumption as to career choice on which a distributive award payable over a number of years is based turns out not to be the fact (as, for example, should a general surgery trainee accidentally lose the use of his hand), it should be possible for the court to revise the distributive award to conform to the fact. . . .

NOTES

As noted above, nearly every state excludes professional income-enhancing degrees from classification as marital property—a fact that has not escaped the notice of New York courts: "It may be doubted whether an innovation which has attracted so little imitation, and so little praise, will endure forever." Holterman v. Holterman, 814 N.E.2d 765, 781 (N.Y. 2004) (Smith, J., dissenting). Nonetheless, New York's approach has been reaffirmed repeatedly. In McSparron v. McSparron, 662 N.E.2d 745 (N.Y. 1995), the court held that the value of a newly earned professional license may be measured by comparing average lifetime income of college graduates and the lifetime earnings of persons with such a license and then reducing the difference to its present value. *Id.* at 751. In *Holterman, supra*, the court upheld an award to wife of 35% "of husband's enhanced earning capacity as a physician practicing medicine in New York," given the parties' "19-year marriage, wife's employment and monetary contributions during husband's final two years of medical school, the parties' mutual decision that wife would forgo her career to take care of the children and home, the gross disparity in the parties' current and probable future incomes, the fact that husband was 44 years of age and wife was 46 years of age at the time of trial and husband's good health in contrast to wife's chronic health difficulties."

In order for a degree to be property subject to division upon divorce, the non-degree earning spouse must contribute in a meaningful way to the attainment of the degree during marriage—not before the marriage or after separation. *See* Gandhi v. Gandhi, 283 A.D.2d 782 (N.Y. 2001).

In re Marriage of Brown

Supreme Court of California, 1976
544 P.2d 561

■ TOBRINER, JUSTICE.

Since French v. French (1941) 17 Cal.2d 775, 778, 112 P.2d 235, California courts have held that nonvested pension rights are not property, but a mere expectancy, and thus not a community asset subject to division upon dissolution of a marriage. . . . Upon reconsideration of this issue, we have concluded that *French v. French* should be overruled and that the subsequent decisions which rely on that precedent should be disapproved. As we shall explain, the *French* rule cannot stand because nonvested pension rights are not an expectancy but a contingent interest in property; furthermore, the *French* rule compels an inequitable division of rights acquired through community effort. Pension rights, whether or not vested, represent a property interest; to the extent that such rights derive from employment during coverture, they comprise a community asset subject to division in a dissolution proceeding.

Before we turn to the facts of this appeal we must devote a few words to terminology. Some decisions that discuss pension rights, but do not involve division of marital property, describe a pension right as "vested" if the employer cannot unilaterally repudiate that right without terminating the employment relationship. As we explain later, we believe that these decisions correctly define the point at which a pension right becomes a property interest. In divorce and dissolution cases following *French v. French*, however, the term "vested" has acquired a special meaning; it refers to a pension right which is not subject to a condition of forfeiture if the employment relationship terminates before retirement. We shall use the term "vested" in this latter sense as defining a pension right which survives the discharge or voluntary termination of the employee.

As so defined, a vested pension right must be distinguished from a "matured" or unconditional right to immediate payment. Depending upon the provisions of the retirement program, an employee's right may vest after a term of service even though it does not mature until he reaches retirement age and elects to retire. Such vested but immature rights are frequently subject to the condition, among others, that the employee survive until retirement.

The issue in the present case concerns the nonvested pension rights of respondent Robert Brown. General Telephone Company, Robert's employer, maintains a noncontributory pension plan in which the rights of the employees depend upon their accumulation of "points," based upon a combination of the years of service and the age of the employee. Under this plan, an employee who is discharged before he accumulates 78 points forfeits his rights; an employee with 78 points can opt for early retirement at a lower pension, or continue to work until age 63 and retire at an increased pension.

Gloria and Robert Brown married on July 29, 1950. When they separated in November of 1973, Robert had accumulated 72 points under the pension plan, a substantial portion of which is attributable to his work during the period when the parties were married and living together.[3] If he continues to work for General Telephone, Robert will accumulate 78 points on November 30, 1976. If he retires then, he will receive a monthly pension of $310.94; if he continues his employment until normal retirement age his pension will be $485 a month.

Relying on the *French* rule, the trial court held that since Robert had not yet acquired a "vested" right to the retirement pension, the value of his pension rights did not become community property subject to division by the court. It divided the remaining property, awarding Gloria the larger share but directing her to pay $1,742 to Robert to equalize the value received by each spouse. The court also awarded Gloria alimony of

[3] Since it concluded that nonvested pension rights are not divisible as a community asset, the trial court did not determine what portion of Robert's pension rights is owned by the community.

$75 per month. Gloria appeals from the portion of the interlocutory judgment that declares that Robert's pension rights are not community property and thus not subject to division by the court.

As we have stated, the fundamental theoretical error which led to the inequitable division of marital property in the present case stems from the seminal decision of French v. French, supra, 17 Cal.2d 775, 112 P.2d 235. Mrs. French claimed a community interest in the prospective retirement pay of her husband, an enlisted man in the Fleet Reserve. The court noted that "under the applicable statutes the [husband] will not be entitled to such pay until he completes a service of 14 years in the Fleet Reserve and complies with all the requirements of that service." (P. 778, 112 P.2d p. 236.) It concluded that "At the present time, his right to retirement pay is an expectancy which is not subject to division as community property." (*Ibid.*)

In 1962 the Court of Appeal in Williamson v. Williamson, 203 Cal.App.2d 8, 21 Cal.Rptr. 164, explained the *French* rule, asserting that "To the extent that payment is, at the time of the divorce, subject to conditions which may or may not occur, the pension is an expectancy, not subject to division as community property."

Subsequent cases, however, have limited the sweep of *French*, holding that a vested pension is community property even though it has not matured or is subject to conditions within the employee's control. But although we have frequently reiterated the *French* rule in dictum, we have not previously had occasion to reexamine the merits of that rule.

Throughout our decisions we have always recognized that the community owns all pension rights attributable to employment during the marriage. The *French* rule, however, rests on the theory that nonvested pension rights may be community, but that they are not property; classified as mere expectancies, such rights are not assets subject to division on dissolution of the marriage. We have concluded, however, that the *French* court's characterization of nonvested pension rights as expectancies errs. The term expectancy describes the interest of a person who merely foresees that he might receive a future beneficence, such as the interest of an heir apparent, or of a beneficiary designated by a living insured who has a right to change the beneficiary.[6] As these examples demonstrate, the defining characteristic of an expectancy is that its holder has no *enforceable right* to his beneficence.

Although some jurisdictions classify retirement pensions as gratuities, it has long been settled that under California law such benefits "do not derive from the beneficence of the employer, but are

[6] The cases discussing the interest of an insurance beneficiary clarify the distinction between an expectancy and a contractual right. "The interest of a beneficiary designated by an insured who has the right to change the beneficiary is, like that of a legatee under a will, a mere expectancy of a gift at the time of the insured's death." (*Grimm v. Grimm* (1945) 26 Cal.2d 173, 175–176, 157 P.2d 841, 842.) But if the holder acquires a contractual right to be named as beneficiary of the policy, his interest is no longer an expectancy, but a property right. (See *Page v. Washington Mut. Life Ass'n* (1942) 20 Cal.2d 234, 242, 125 P.2d 20.).

properly part of the consideration earned by the employee." *In re Marriage of Fithian, supra,* 10 Cal. 3d 592, 596. Since pension benefits represent a form of deferred compensation for services rendered, the employee's right to such benefits is a contractual right, derived from the terms of the employment contract. Since a contractual right is not an expectancy but a chose in action, a form of property, we held in Dryden v. Board of Pension Commissioners, 6 Cal.2d 575, 579, 59 P.2d 104 (1936), that an employee acquires a property right to pension benefits when he enters upon the performance of his employment contract.

Although *Dryden* involved an employee who possessed vested pension rights, the issue of nonvested rights came before us in Kern v. City of Long Beach, 29 Cal.2d 848, 179 P.2d 799 (1947). There a city employee contended that the city's repeal of a pension plan unconstitutionally impaired the obligation of contract. The city defended on the ground that the employee's pension rights had not vested at the time of the abrogation of the plan.

Ruling in favor of the employee, we stated in *Kern* that: "[T]here is little reason to make a distinction between the periods before and after the pension payments are due. It is true that an employee does not earn the right to a full pension until he has completed the prescribed period of service, but he has actually earned some pension rights as soon as he has performed substantial services for his employer. [Citations omitted.] He . . . has then earned certain pension benefits, the payment of which is to be made at a future date . . . [T]he mere fact that performance is in whole or in part dependent upon certain contingencies does not prevent a contract from arising, and the employing governmental body may not deny or impair the contingent liability any more than it can refuse to make the salary payments which are immediately due. Clearly, it cannot do so after all the contingencies have happened, and in our opinion it cannot do so at any time after a contractual duty to make salary payments has arisen, since a part of the compensation which the employee has at that time earned consists of his pension rights." (29 Cal.2d at p. 855, 179 P.2d at p. 803.)

Since we based our holding in *Kern* upon the constitutional prohibition against impairment of contracts, a prohibition applicable only to public entities, the private employer in Hunter v. Sparling (1948) 87 Cal.App.2d 711, 197 P.2d 807 contended that it could repudiate an employee's nonvested pension rights without liability. Rejecting that contention, the Court of Appeal cited the language from *Kern* quoted above and concluded that once the employee performed services in reliance upon the promised pension, he could enforce his right to a pension either under traditional contract principles of offer, acceptance and consideration or under the doctrine of promissory estoppel. In subsequent years the courts have repeatedly reaffirmed that a nonvested pension right is nonetheless a contractual right, and thus a property right. . . .

In other situations when community funds or effort are expended to acquire a conditional right to future income, the courts do not hesitate to treat that right as a community asset.[9] For example, in Waters v. Waters (1946) 75 Cal.App.2d 265, 170 P.2d 494, the attorney husband had a contingent interest in a suit pending on appeal at the time of the divorce; the court held that his fee, when and if collected, would be a community asset. Indeed in the several recent pension cases the courts have asserted that vested but immature pensions are community assets although such pensions are commonly subject to the condition that the employee survive until retirement.

We conclude that French v. French, and subsequent cases erred in characterizing nonvested pension rights as expectancies and in denying the trial courts the authority to divide such rights as community property. This mischaracterization of pension rights has, and unless overturned, will continue to result in inequitable division of community assets. Over the past decades, pension benefits have become an increasingly significant part of the consideration earned by the employee for his services. As the date of vesting and retirement approaches, the value of the pension right grows until it often represents the most important asset of the marital community. A division of community property which awards one spouse the entire value of this asset, without any offsetting award to the other spouse, does not represent that equal division of community property contemplated by Civil Code section 4800.

The present case illustrates the point. Robert's pension rights, a valuable asset built up by 24 years of community effort, under the *French* rule would escape division by the court as a community asset solely because dissolution occurred two years before the vesting date. If, as is entirely likely, Robert continues to work for General Telephone Company for the additional two years needed to acquire a vested right, he will then enjoy as his separate property an annuity created predominantly through community effort. This "potentially whimsical result," as the Court of Appeal described a similar division of community property in In re Marriage of Peterson, 41 Cal.App.3d 642, 651, 115 Cal.Rptr. 184 (1974), cannot be reconciled with the fundamental principle that property attributable to community earnings must be divided equally when the community is dissolved.

Respondent does not deny that if nonvested pension rights are property, the *French* rule results in an inequitable division of that property. He maintains, however, that any inequity can be redressed by an award of alimony to the nonemployee spouse. Alimony, however, lies within the discretion of the trial court; the spouse "should not be dependent on the discretion of the court . . . to provide her with the equivalent of what should be hers as a matter of absolute right." (In re

[9] See Thiede, The Community Property Interest of the Non-Employee Spouse in Private Employee Retirement Benefits (1975) 9 U.S.F.L.Rev. 635, 656–661; Note, Retirement Pay: A Divorce in Time Saved Mine (1973) 24 Hastings L.J. 347, 354–356.

Marriage of Peterson, supra, 41 Cal.App.3d 642, 651, 115 Cal.Rptr. 184, 191.) Respondent and amicus further suggest that a decision repudiating the *French* rule would both impose severe practical burdens upon the courts and restrict the employee's freedom to change his place or terms of employment. We shall examine these contentions and point out why they do not justify a continued refusal by the courts to divide nonvested pension rights as a community asset.

In dividing nonvested pension rights as community property the court must take account of the possibility that death or termination of employment may destroy those rights before they mature. In some cases the trial court may be able to evaluate this risk in determining the present value of those rights. But if the court concludes that because of uncertainties affecting the vesting or maturation of the pension that it should not attempt to divide the present value of pension rights, it can instead award each spouse an appropriate portion of each pension payment as it is paid.[10] This method of dividing the community interest in the pension renders it unnecessary for the court to compute the present value of the pension rights, and divides equally the risk that the pension will fail to vest.

As respondent points out, an award of future pension payments as they fall due will require the court to continue jurisdiction to supervise the payments of pension benefits. Yet this obligation arises whenever the court cannot equitably award all pension rights to one spouse, whether or not such rights are vested; the claim of mere administrative burden surely cannot serve as support for an inequitable substantive rule which distinguishes between vested and nonvested rights. Despite the administrative burden such an award imposes, courts in the past have successfully divided *vested* pension rights by awarding each spouse a share in future payments. Courts can divide nonvested pension rights in like fashion. Moreover, the practical consequence of the *French* rule has been historically that the court must often award alimony to the spouse who, deprived of any share in the nonvested pension rights, lacks resources to purchase the necessities of life. Judicial supervision of alimony awards, undertaken in the past, entails far more onerous a burden than supervision of future pension payment.

As to the claim that our present holding will infringe upon the employee's freedom of contract, we note that judicial recognition of the nonemployee spouse's interest in vested pension rights has not limited the employee's freedom to change or terminate his employment, to agree to a modification of the terms of his employment (including retirement

[10] Our suggestion in *Phillipson v. Board of Administration, supra*, 3 Cal.3d 32, 46, 89 Cal.Rptr. 61, 473 P.2d 765, that when feasible the trial court should award the employee all pension rights and compensate his spouse with other property of equal value, was not intended to tie the hands of the trial court. That court retains the discretion to divide the community assets in any fashion which complies with the provisions of Civil Code section 4800.

benefits), or to elect between alternative retirement programs.[12] We do not conceive that judicial recognition of spousal rights in nonvested pensions will change the law in this respect. The employee retains the right to decide, and by his decision define, the nature of the retirement benefits owned by the community.

Robert finally contends that any decision overruling French v. French should be given purely prospective effect. Although as we explain our decision cannot be accorded complete retroactivity without upsetting final judgments of long standing, we believe the decision may properly govern any case in which no final judgment dividing the marital property has been rendered. . . .

We conclude that our decision today should not apply retroactively to permit a nonemployee spouse to assert an interest in nonvested pension rights when the property rights of the marriage have already been adjudicated by a decree of dissolution or separation which has become final as to such adjudication, unless the decree expressly reserved jurisdiction to divide such pension rights at a later date. Our decision will apply retroactively, however, to any case in which the property rights arising from the marriage have not yet been adjudicated, to such rights if such adjudication is still subject to appellate review, or if in such adjudication the trial court has expressly reserved jurisdiction to divide pension rights. . . .

In sum, we submit that whatever abstract terminology we impose, the joint effort that composes the community and the respective contributions of the spouses that make up its assets, are the meaningful criteria. The wife's contribution to the community is not one whit less if we declare the husband's pension rights not a contingent asset but a mere "expectancy." Fortunately we can appropriately reflect the realistic situation by recognizing that the husband's pension rights, a contingent interest, whether vested or not vested, comprise a property interest of the community and that the wife may properly share in it.

The judgment of the superior court is reversed and the cause remanded for further proceedings consistent with the views expressed herein.

NOTES

At one point in time, the most significant asset owned by a married couple was the family residence, followed by the retirement pension jointly funded by the employed spouse and that spouse's employer. The *Brown* decision illustrates the court's willingness to value and divide the spouse's

---

[12] In *Phillipson v. Board of Administration, supra*, 3 Cal.3d 32, 89 Cal.Rptr. 61, 473 P.2d 765, the employee had absconded with most of the community assets; the trial court to equalize the division of community property awarded the spouse all of the employee's pension rights. Under those special circumstances we held that since the employee no longer enjoyed a beneficial interest in the rights, the divorce court could control the employee's election between alternative benefit programs. (3 Cal.3d at p. 48, 89 Cal.Rptr. 61, 473 P.2d 765.)

nonvested pension because of the presence of a contractual obligation and past payments made to the fund. The court's willingness to take into consideration the conditional element surrounding the pension is reminiscent of a prior decision, *Ruggles*, when a New Mexico court held that conditionality is acceptable as long as it is borne by both of the parties to the marriage. *See* Ruggles v. Ruggles, 860 P.2d 182, 194 (1993). For a discussion of this point, *see, e.g.*, James R. Ratner, *Distribution of Marital Assets in Community Property Jurisdictions: Equitable Doesn't Equal Equal,* 72 LA. L. REV. 21 (2011).

Stock Options. Nonvested stock options are considered marital property subject to division upon divorce if they are evidenced by a contract giving the employee the option to exercise the option during or after the marital period. Examples include Hiett v. Hiett, 158 S.W.3d 720 (Ark. Ct. App. 2004) (stock options may be considered as divisible property and also for payment of support); *In re* Valence, 798 A.2d 35 (N.H. 2002) (nonvested stock options are marital property if they are defined by contractual rights); and Otley v. Otley, 810 A.2d 1 (Md. 2002) (stock options earned during marriage but payable after divorce are nonetheless marital property). Other courts evaluate whether the stock option rewards the employee for past services rendered during the marriage or is, instead, designed to reward services in the future. *See In re* Marriage of Miller, 915 P.2d 1314, 1319 (Colo. 1996):

> [W]e conclude that to the extent an employee stock option is granted in consideration of past services, the option may constitute marital property when granted. *See* Grubb, 745 P.2d at 665; *see also In re* Marriage of Short, 890 P.2d 12, 16 (Wash. 1995). On the other hand, an employee stock option granted in consideration of future services does not constitute marital property until the employee has performed those future services.

Id.

Deferred and Accelerated Compensation. These benefits are marital property if earned, although not received, during the marriage. A separation incentive bonus that became available to an employee after entry of the divorce decree but before property division was completed was separate property because the benefit did not accrue during the marriage. Sharber v. Sharber, 35 S.W.3d 841 (Ky. Ct. App. 2001).

Accrued Leave. Sick leave benefits are accumulated by the employee during employment in exchange for services rendered and are thus marital property for those periods employed, but the cash value is limited to any employee contractual terms. Purpura v. Kelly, 913 So.2d 110 (Fla. Ct. App. 2005).

Life Insurance. Courts have held that a term life insurance policy is nonmarital property, *see* Estate of Logan, 236 Cal.Rptr. 368 (1987), but the Maryland Court of Special Appeals has ruled that an irrevocable life insurance trust established by a man during his marriage for wife's benefit is marital property subject to equitable division upon divorce. Caccamise v. Caccamise, 747 A.2d 221 (Md. 2000).

Severance Pay. Severance pay received after separation is marital property if based on services performed during marriage or under a contractual agreement, but nonmarital property if meant to compensate the employee for loss of employment after separation. *See* Marriage of Wright, 189 Cal.Rptr. 336 (1983). If, however, a severance package enhances the employee's retirement pay based on total number of years in service, some of which were worked during the marriage, a court may divide the enhanced retirement pay as a form of deferred compensation. *See, e.g., In re* Marriage of Gram, 30 Cal. Rptr. 2d 792, 793 (1994).

Cost of Living Adjustments to Pension Benefits. Moore v. Moore, 553 A.2d 20 (N.J. 1989), holds that cost of living increases should be included in division of marital property if the benefits are not specifically attributable to post-separation employment.

Disability Payments. The American Law Institute recommends that "[d]isability pay and workers' compensation payments are marital property to the extent they replace income or benefits the recipient would have earned during the marriage but for the qualifying disability or injury." ALI, PRINCIPLES OF THE LAW OF FAMILY DISSOLUTION: ANALYSIS AND RECOMMENDATIONS § 4.08(2)(b) (2000). Many state court decisions take this approach. *See, e.g.,* Beckley v. Beckley, 822 N.E.2d 158 (Ind. 2005) (disability payments paid as compensation for lost wages are subject to division as marital property); Metz v. Metz, 61 P.3d 383 (Wyo. 2003) (to be divisible, a disability payment must be a substitute for income earned during the marital period). Other courts hold that disability payments are marital property. *See, e.g.,* Walswick-Boutwell v. Boutwell, 663 N.W.2d 20, 23 (Minn. Ct. App. 2003).

Mansell v. Mansell

Supreme Court of the United States, 1989.
490 U.S. 581

■ MARSHALL, JUSTICE delivered the opinion of the Court.

In this appeal, we decide whether state courts, consistent with the federal Uniformed Services Former Spouses' Protection Act, 10 U.S.C. § 1408 (1982 ed. and Supp. V) (Former Spouses' Protection Act or Act), may treat, as property divisible upon divorce, military retirement pay waived by the retiree in order to receive veterans' disability benefits. We hold that they may not.

Members of the Armed Forces who serve for a specified period, generally at least 20 years, may retire with a pension. . . . Veterans who became disabled as a result of military service are eligible for disability benefits. . . . The amount of disability benefits a veteran is eligible to receive is calculated according to the seriousness of the disability and the degree to which the veteran's ability to earn a living has been impaired. §§ 314 and 355.

In order to prevent double dipping, a military retiree may receive disability benefits only to the extent that he waives a corresponding amount of his military retirement pay. § 3105.[1] Because disability benefits are exempt from federal, state, and local taxation, § 3101(a), military retirees who waive their retirement pay in favor of disability benefits increase their after-tax income. Not surprisingly, waivers of retirement pay are common. . . .

California treats military retirement payments as community property to the extent they derive from military service performed during the marriage. *See, e.g.,* Casas v. Thompson, 42 Cal.3d 131, 139, 228 Cal.Rptr. 33, 37–38, 720 P.2d 921, 925, cert. denied, 479 U.S. 1012, 107 S.Ct. 659, 93 L.Ed.2d 713 (1986).

In McCarty v. McCarty, 453 U.S. 210, 101 S.Ct. 2728, 69 L.Ed.2d 589 (1981), we held that the federal statutes then governing military retirement pay prevented state courts from treating military retirement pay as community property. We concluded that treating such pay as community property would do clear damage to important military personnel objectives. We reasoned that Congress intended that military retirement pay reach the veteran and no one else. . . .

In direct response to *McCarty,* Congress enacted the Former Spouses' Protection Act, which authorizes state courts to treat "disposable retired or retainer pay" as community property. 10 U.S.C. § 1408(c)(1).[2] " 'Disposable retired or retainer pay' " is defined as "the total monthly retired or retainer pay to which a military member is entitled," minus certain deductions. § 1408(a)(4) (1982 ed., Supp. V). Among the amounts required to be deducted from total pay are any amounts waived in order to receive disability benefits. § 1408(a)(4)(B).

The Act also creates a payments mechanism under which the Federal Government will make direct payments to a former spouse who presents, to the Secretary of the relevant military service, a state-court order granting her a portion of the military retiree's disposable retired or retainer pay. This direct payments mechanism is limited in two ways. § 1408(d). First, only a former spouse who was married to a military member "for a period of 10 years or more during which the member performed at least 10 years of service creditable in determining the member's eligibility for retired or retainer pay," § 1408(d)(2), is eligible to receive direct community property payments. Second, the Federal Government will not make community property payments that exceed 50 percent of disposable retired or retainer pay. § 1408(e)(1).

Appellant Gerald E. Mansell and appellee Gaye M. Mansell were married for 23 years and are the parents of six children. Their marriage

---

[1] For example, if a military retiree is eligible for $1500 a month in retirement pay and $500 a month in disability benefits, he must waive $500 of retirement pay before he can receive any disability benefits.

[2] The language of the Act covers both community property and equitable distribution States, as does our decision today. Because this case concerns a community property State, for the sake of simplicity we refer to § 1408(c)(1) as authorizing state courts to treat "disposable retired or retainer pay" as community property.

ended in 1979 with a divorce decree from the Merced County, California, Superior Court. At that time, Major Mansell received both Air Force retirement pay and, pursuant to a waiver of a portion of that pay, disability benefits. Mrs. Mansell and Major Mansell entered into a property settlement which provided, in part, that Major Mansell would pay Mrs. Mansell 50 percent of his total military retirement pay, including that portion of retirement pay waived so that Major Mansell could receive disability benefits. In 1983, Major Mansell asked the Superior Court to modify the divorce decree by removing the provision that required him to share his total retirement pay with Mrs. Mansell. The Superior Court denied Major Mansell's request without opinion.

Major Mansell appealed to the California Court of Appeal, Fifth Appellate District, arguing that both the Former Spouses' Protection Act and the antiattachment clause that protects a veteran's receipt of disability benefits, 38 U.S.C. § 3101(a) (1982 ed. and Supp. IV),[4] precluded the Superior Court from treating military retirement pay that had been waived to receive disability benefits as community property. Relying on the decision of the Supreme Court of California in Casas v. Thompson, supra, the Court of Appeal rejected that portion of Major Mansell's argument based on the Former Spouses' Protection Act. *Casas* held that after the passage of the Former Spouses' Protection Act, federal law no longer pre-empted state community property law as it applies to military retirement pay. The *Casas* court reasoned that the Act did not limit a state court's ability to treat total military retirement pay as community property and to enforce a former spouse's rights to such pay through remedies other than direct payments from the Federal Government. 42 Cal.3d, at 143–151, 228 Cal.Rptr., at 40–46, 720 P.2d, at 928–933. The Court of Appeal did not discuss the antiattachment clause, 38 U.S.C. § 3101(a).[6] The Supreme Court of California denied Major Mansell's petition for review. We noted probable jurisdiction, and now reverse.

Because domestic relations are preeminently matters of state law, we have consistently recognized that Congress, when it passes general legislation, rarely intends to displace state authority in this area. Thus we have held that we will not find preemption absent evidence that it is " 'positively required by direct enactment.' " *Hisquierdo, supra*, at 581, 99 S.Ct. at 808 (quoting Wetmore v. Markoe, 196 U.S. 68, 77, 25 S.Ct. 172, 176, 49 L.Ed. 390 (1904)). The instant case, however, presents one of

[4] That clause provides that veterans' benefits "shall not be assignable except to the extent specifically authorized by law, and . . . shall be exempt from the claim[s] of creditors, and shall not be liable to attachment, levy, or seizure by or under any legal or equitable process whatever, either before or after receipt by the [veteran]." 38 U.S.C. § 3101(a) (1982 ed. and Supp. IV).

[6] Because we decide that the Former Spouses' Protection Act precludes States from treating as community property retirement pay waived to receive veterans disability benefits, we need not decide whether the anti-attachment clause, § 3101(a), independently protects such pay. *See, e.g., Rose v. Rose*, 481 U.S. 619, 107 S.Ct. 2029, 95 L.Ed.2d 599 (1987); *Wissner v. Wissner*, 338 U.S. 655, 70 S.Ct. 398, 94 L.Ed. 424 (1950).

those rare instances where Congress has directly and specifically legislated in the area of domestic relations.

It is clear from both the language of the Former Spouses' Protection Act, and its legislative history, that Congress sought to change the legal landscape created by the *McCarty* decision. Because pre-existing federal law, as construed by this Court, completely pre-empted the application of state community property law to military retirement pay, Congress could overcome the *McCarty* decision only by enacting an affirmative grant of authority giving the States the power to treat military retirement pay as community property.

The appellant and appellee differ sharply on the scope of Congress' modification of *McCarty*. Mrs. Mansell views the Former Spouses' Protection Act as a complete congressional rejection of *McCarty's* holding that state law is pre-empted; she reads the Act as restoring to state courts all pre-*McCarty* authority. Major Mansell, supported by the Solicitor General, argues that the Former Spouses' Protection Act is only a partial rejection of the *McCarty* rule that federal law preempts state law regarding military retirement pay.

Where, as here, the question is one of statutory construction, we begin with the language of the statute. Mrs. Mansell's argument faces a formidable obstacle in the language of the Former Spouses' Protection Act. Section 1408(c)(1) of the Act affirmatively grants state courts the power to divide military retirement pay, yet its language is both precise and limited. It provides that "a court may treat disposable retired or retainer pay . . . either as property solely of the member or as property of the member and his spouse in accordance with the law of the jurisdiction of such court." § 1408(c)(1). The Act's definitional section specifically defines the term "disposable retired or retainer pay" to exclude, *inter alia,* military retirement pay waived in order to receive veterans' disability payments. § 1408(a)(4)(B).[9] Thus, under the Act's plain and precise language, state courts have been granted the authority to treat disposable retired pay as community property; they have not been granted the authority to treat total retired pay as community property.

Mrs. Mansell attempts to overcome the limiting language contained in the definition, § 1408(a)(4)(B), by reading the Act as a garnishment statute designed solely to set out the circumstances under which, pursuant to a court order, the Federal Government will make direct payments to a former spouse. According to this view, § 1408(a)(4)(B) defines "[d]isposable retired or retainer pay" only because payments under the federal direct payments mechanism are limited to amounts defined by that term.

The garnishment argument relies heavily on the Act's savings clause. That clause provides:

[9] Although the Solicitor General has filed an *amicus* brief supporting Major Mansell, his initial *amicus* brief, filed before the Court noted jurisdiction, supported Mrs. Mansell.

> "Nothing in this section shall be construed to relieve a member of liability for the payment of alimony, child support, *or other payments* required by a court order on the grounds that payments made out of disposable retired or retainer pay under this section have been made in the maximum amount permitted under [the direct payments mechanism]. Any such unsatisfied obligation of a member may be enforced by any means available under law other than the means provided under this section in any case in which the maximum amount permitted under . . . [the direct payments mechanism] has been paid." § 1408(e)(6) (emphasis added).

Mrs. Mansell argues that, because the savings clause expressly contemplates "other payments" in excess of those made under the direct payments mechanism, the Act does not "attempt to tell the state courts what they may or may not do with the underlying property." For the reasons discussed below, we find a different interpretation more plausible. In our view, the savings clause serves the limited purpose of defeating any inference that the federal direct payments mechanism displaced the authority of state courts to divide and garnish property not covered by the mechanism. . . .

First, the most serious flaw in the garnishment argument is that it completely ignores § 1408(c)(1). Mrs. Mansell provides no explanation for the fact that the defined term—"disposable retired or retainer pay"—is used in § 1408(c)(1) to limit specifically and plainly the extent to which state courts may treat military retirement pay as community property.

Second, the view that the Act is solely a garnishment statute and therefore not intended to pre-empt the authority of state courts is contradicted not only by § 1408(c)(1), but also by the other subsections of § 1408(c). Sections 1408(c)(2), (c)(3), and (c)(4) impose new substantive limits on state courts' power to divide military retirement pay. Section 1408(c)(2) prevents a former spouse from transferring, selling, or otherwise disposing of her community interest in the military retirement pay.[10] Section 1408(c)(3) provides that a state court cannot order a military member to retire so that the former spouse can immediately begin receiving her portion of military retirement pay. And § 1408(c)(4) prevents spouses from forum shopping for a State with favorable divorce laws.[12] Because each of these provisions pre-empts state law, the argument that the Act has no pre-emptive effect of its own must fail.[13]

---

[10] The Senate Report expressly contemplates that § 1408(c)(2) will preempt state law. S.Rep. No. 97–502, p. 16 (1982).

[12] A state court may not treat disposable retirement pay as community property unless it has jurisdiction over the military member by reason of (1) residence, other than by military assignment in the territorial jurisdiction of the court, (2) domicile, or (3) consent. § 1408(c)(4). . . .

[13] That Congress intended the substantive limits in § 1408(c)(1) to be, to some extent, distinct from the limits on the direct payments mechanism contained in § 1408(d) is demonstrated by the legislative compromise that resulted in the direct payments mechanism

Significantly, Congress placed each of these substantive restrictions on state courts in the same section of the Act as § 1408(c)(1). We think it unlikely that every subsection of § 1408(c), except § 1408(c)(1), was intended to pre-empt state law.

In the face of such plain and precise statutory language, Mrs. Mansell faces a daunting standard. She cannot prevail without clear evidence that reading the language literally would thwart the obvious purposes of the Act. The legislative history does not indicate the reason for Congress' decision to shelter from community property law that portion of military retirement pay waived to receive veterans' disability payments. But the absence of legislative history on this decision is immaterial in light of the plain and precise language of the statute; Congress is not required to build a record in the legislative history to defend its policy choices.

Because of the absence of evidence of specific intent in the legislative history, Mrs. Mansell resorts to arguments about the broad purposes of the Act. But this reliance is misplaced because, at this general level, there are statements that both contradict and support her arguments. . . .

Thus, the legislative history, read as a whole, indicates that Congress intended both to create new benefits for former spouses and to place limits on state courts designed to protect military retirees. Our task is to interpret the statute as best we can, not to second guess the wisdom of the congressional policy choice. . . . Given Congress' mixed purposes, the legislative history does not clearly support Mrs. Mansell's view that giving effect to the plain and precise language of the statute would thwart the obvious purposes of the Act.

We realize that reading the statute literally may inflict economic harm on many former spouses. But we decline to misread the statute in order to reach a sympathetic result when such a reading requires us to do violence to the plain language of the statute and to ignore much of the legislative history. Congress chose the language that requires us to decide as we do, and Congress is free to change it.

For the reasons stated above, we hold that the Former Spouses' Protection Act does not grant state courts the power to treat, as property divisible upon divorce, military retirement pay that has been waived to receive veterans disability benefits. The judgment of the California Court of Appeal is hereby reversed and the case is remanded for further proceedings not inconsistent with this opinion.

---

being available only to former spouses who had been married to the military retiree for 10 years or more. § 1408(d)(2). . . .

■ JUSTICE O'CONNOR, with whom JUSTICE BLACKMUN joins, dissenting.

. . .

Under the Court's reading of the Act as precluding the States from characterizing gross retirement pay as community property, a military retiree has the power unilaterally to convert community property into separate property and increase his after-tax income, at the expense of his ex-spouse's financial security and property entitlements. To read the statute as permitting a military retiree to pocket 30 percent, 50 percent, even 80 percent of gross retirement pay by converting it into disability benefits and thereby to avoid his obligations under state community property law, however, is to distort beyond recognition and to thwart the main purpose of the statute, which is to recognize the sacrifices made by military spouses and to protect their economic security in the face of a divorce. Women generally suffer a decline in their standard of living following a divorce. See Weitzman, *The Economics of Divorce: Social and Economic Consequences of Property, Alimony and Child Support Awards*, 28 UCLA L. REV. 1181, 1251 (1981). Military wives face special difficulties because "frequent change-of-station moves and the special pressures placed on the military spouse as a homemaker make it extremely difficult to pursue a career affording economic security, job skills and pension protection." S.Rep. No. 97–502, at 6, U.S. Code Cong. & Admin.News 1982, p. 1601. The average military couple married for 20 years moves about 12 times, and military wives experience an unemployment rate more than double that of their civilian counterparts. . . . Reading the Act as not precluding States from characterizing retirement pay waived to receive disability benefits as property divisible upon divorce is faithful to the clear remedial purposes of the statute in a way that the Court's interpretation is not.

The conclusion that States may treat gross military retirement pay as property divisible upon divorce is not inconsistent with 38 U.S.C. § 3101(a) (1982 ed., Supp. V). This anti-attachment provision provides that veterans' disability benefits "shall not be liable to attachment, levy, or seizure by or under any legal or equitable process whatever, either before or after receipt by the beneficiary." Gaye Mansell acknowledges, as she must, that § 3101(a) precludes her from garnishing under state law Major Mansell's veterans' disability benefits in satisfaction of her claim to a share of his gross military retirement pay, just as § 1408(c)(1) precludes her from invoking the federal direct payments mechanism in satisfaction of that claim. To recognize that § 3101(a) protects the funds from a specific source, however, does not mean that § 3101(a) prevents Gaye Mansell from recovering her 50 percent interest in Major Mansell's gross retirement pay out of any income or assets he may have *other* than his veterans' disability benefits. So long as those benefits themselves are protected, calculation of Gaye Mansell's entitlement on the basis of Major Mansell's gross retirement pay does not constitute an "attachment" of his veterans' disability benefits. Section 3101(a) is designed to ensure that the needs of disabled veterans and their families are met, see *Rose v. Rose*, 481 U.S. 619, 634, 107 S.Ct. 2029, 2038, 95 L.Ed.2d 599 (1987), without interference from creditors. That purpose is fulfilled so long as the benefits themselves are protected by the anti-attachment provision.

In sum, under the Court's interpretation of the Former Spouses' Protection Act, the former spouses Congress sought to protect risk having their economic security severely undermined by a unilateral decision of their ex-spouse to waive retirement pay in lieu of disability benefits. It is inconceivable that Congress intended the broad remedial purposes of the statute to be thwarted in such a way. . . .

It is now once again up to Congress to address the inequity created by the Court in situations such as this one. But because I believe that Congress has already expressed its intention that the States have the authority to characterize waived retirement pay as property divisible upon divorce, I dissent.

NOTES

When confronting the dilemma presented by the federal Uniformed Services Former Spouses' Protection Act, some state courts have been willing to compensate the former non-electing spouse with divisible assets not associated with the military disability payments. *See, e.g.*, Surratt v. Surratt, 148 S.W.3d 761 (Ark. Ct. App. 2004); *In re* Marriage of Lodeski, 107 P.3d 1097 (Colo. Ct. App. 2004); Whitfield v. Whitfield, 862 A.2d 1187 (N.J. Super. 2004). Thus, if there is alternative property, courts may diminish or eliminate the hardship presented by the election. Such an approach is not prohibited by the statute. Likewise, when an active duty soldier elected to take a "CSB/Redux Bonus" after fifteen years of military service, knowing that this would reduce the military pension, the former non-electing spouse had a right to share in the bonus to the extent that the former spouse's award of the pension would be reduced. Boedeker v. Larson, 605 S.E.2d 764 (Va. Ct. App. 2004). Some state courts have used a similar approach when contemplating the loss of future Social Security benefits. *See, e.g.*, Depot v. Depot, 893 A.2d 995 (Me. 2006).

For a description of all military benefits and an appraisal of the difficulties posed by the Uniformed Services Former Spouses' Protection Act, *see* James E. Kirchner, *Division of Military Retirement Pay*, 43 FAM. L. Q. 367, 368 (2009) ("Unfortunately, there is no uniform treatment among the fifty states for pensions in general or for military retirement in particular. Thus, implementation of the Act is dependent upon diverse perceptions of both the nature of military retirement benefits and the complex interrelationship of those benefits with Veterans Administration benefits, Social Security benefits, and the original intent of Congress in its passage of the Act. This lack of uniformity or consistency among the states arises primarily because the specific terminology of the Act.").

Boggs v. Boggs

Supreme Court of the United States, 1997
520 U.S. 833

■ KENNEDY, JUSTICE delivered the opinion of the Court.

We consider whether the Employee Retirement Income Security Act of 1974 (ERISA), 88 Stat. 832, as amended, 29 U.S.C. § 1001 et seq., pre-empts a state law allowing a nonparticipant spouse to transfer by testamentary instrument an interest in undistributed pension plan benefits. Given the pervasive significance of pension plans in the national economy, the congressional mandate for their uniform and comprehensive regulation, and the fundamental importance of community property law in defining the marital partnership in a number of States, the question is of undoubted importance. We hold that ERISA pre-empts the state law.

Isaac Boggs worked for South Central Bell from 1949 until his retirement in 1985. Isaac and Dorothy, his first wife, were married when he began working for the company, and they remained husband and wife until Dorothy's death in 1979. They had three sons. Within a year of Dorothy's death, Isaac married Sandra, and they remained married until his death in 1989. Upon retirement, Isaac received various benefits from his employer's retirement plans. One was a lump-sum distribution from the Bell System Savings Plan for Salaried Employees (Savings Plan) of $151,628.94, which he rolled over into an Individual Retirement Account (IRA). He made no withdrawals and the account was worth $180,778.05 when he died. He also received 96 shares of AT & T stock from the Bell South Employee Stock Ownership Plan (ESOP). In addition, Isaac enjoyed a monthly annuity payment during his retirement of $1,777.67 from the Bell South Service Retirement Program.

The instant dispute over ownership of the benefits is between Sandra (the surviving wife) and the sons of the first marriage. The sons' claim to a portion of the benefits is based on Dorothy's will. Dorothy bequeathed to Isaac one-third of her estate, and a lifetime usufruct in the remaining two-thirds. A lifetime usufruct is the rough equivalent of a common-law life estate. See La. Civ. Code Ann., Art. 535 (1980). She bequeathed to her sons the naked ownership in the remaining two-thirds, subject to Isaac's usufruct. All agree that, absent pre-emption, Louisiana law controls and that under it Dorothy's will would dispose of her community property interest in Isaac's undistributed pension plan benefits. A Louisiana state court, in a 1980 order entitled "Judgment of Possession," ascribed to Dorothy's estate a community property interest in Isaac's Savings Plan account valued at the time at $21,194.29.

Sandra contests the validity of Dorothy's 1980 testamentary transfer, basing her claim to those benefits on her interest under Isaac's will and 29 U.S.C. § 1055. Isaac bequeathed to Sandra outright certain real property including the family home. His will also gave Sandra a lifetime usufruct in the remainder of his estate, with the naked ownership interest being held by the sons. Sandra argues that the sons' competing claim, since it is based on Dorothy's 1980 purported testamentary transfer of her community property interest in undistributed pension plan benefits, is pre-empted by ERISA. The Bell South Service Retirement Program monthly annuity is now paid to Sandra as the surviving spouse.

After Isaac's death, two of the sons filed an action in state court requesting the appointment of an expert to compute the percentage of the retirement benefits they would be entitled to as a result of Dorothy's attempted testamentary transfer. They further sought a judgment awarding them a portion of: the IRA; the ESOP shares of AT & T stock; the monthly annuity payments received by Isaac during his retirement; and Sandra's survivor annuity payments, both received and payable.

In response, Sandra Boggs filed a complaint in the United States District Court for the Eastern District of Louisiana, seeking a declaratory judgment that ERISA pre-empts the application of Louisiana's community property and succession laws to the extent they recognize the sons' claim to an interest in the disputed retirement benefits. The District Court granted summary judgment against Sandra Boggs. 849 F. Supp. 462 (1994). It found that, under Louisiana community property law, Dorothy had an ownership interest in her husband's pension plan benefits built up during their marriage. The creation of this interest, the court explained, does not violate 29 U.S.C. § 1056(d)(1), which prohibits pension plan benefits from being "assigned" or "alienated," since Congress did not intend to alter traditional familial and support obligations. In the court's view, there was no assignment or alienation because Dorothy's rights in the benefits were acquired by operation of community property law and not by transfer from Isaac. Turning to Dorothy's testamentary transfer, the court found it effective because "[ERISA] does not display any particular interest in preserving maximum benefits to any particular beneficiary." 849 F. Supp., at 465.

A divided panel of the Fifth Circuit affirmed. . . .

[The court noted that there was a split between holdings of the Fifth and Ninth Circuits. The former includes the community property states of Louisiana and Texas, while the latter includes the community property states of Arizona, California, Idaho, Nevada, and Washington.]

We now reverse. . . . This case lies at the intersection of ERISA pension law and state community property law. None can dispute the central role community property laws play in the nine community property States. It is more than a property regime. It is a commitment to the equality of husband and wife and reflects the real partnership inherent in the marital relationship. State community property laws, many of ancient lineage, "must have continued to exist through such lengths of time because of their manifold excellences and are not lightly to be abrogated or tossed aside." 1 W. de Funiak, Principles of Community Property 11 (1943). . . .

The nine community property States have some 80 million residents, with perhaps $1 trillion in retirement plans. See Brief for Estate Planning, Trust and Probate Law Section of the State Bar of California as *Amicus Curiae* 1. This case involves a community property claim, but our ruling will affect as well the right to make claims or assert interests based on the law of any State, whether or not it recognizes community property. Our ruling must be consistent with the congressional scheme to assure the security of plan participants and their families in every State. In enacting ERISA, Congress noted the importance of pension plans in its findings and declaration of policy, explaining: "[T]he growth in size, scope, and numbers of employee benefit plans in recent years has been rapid and substantial; . . . the continued well-being and security of millions of employees and their dependents are directly affected by these plans; . . . they are affected with a national public interest [and] they have become an important factor affecting the stability of employment and the successful development of industrial relations. . . ." 29 U.S.C. § 1001(a).

ERISA is an intricate, comprehensive statute. Its federal regulatory scheme governs employee benefit plans, which include both pension and welfare plans. All employee benefit plans must conform to various reporting, disclosure and fiduciary requirements, see §§ 1021–1031, 1101–1114, while pension plans must also comply with participation, vesting, and funding requirements, see §§ 1051–1086. The surviving spouse annuity and QDRO provisions, central to the dispute here, are part of the statute's mandatory participation and vesting requirements. These provisions provide detailed protections to spouses of plan participants which, in some cases, exceed what their rights would be were community property law the sole measure.

ERISA's express pre-emption clause states that the Act "shall supersede any and all State laws insofar as they may now or hereafter relate to any employee benefit plan. . . ." § 1144(a). We can begin, and in this case end, the analysis by simply asking if state law conflicts with the provisions of ERISA or operates to frustrate its objects. We hold that there is a conflict, which suffices to resolve the case. We need not inquire whether the statutory phrase "relate to" provides further and additional support for the pre-emption claim. Nor need we consider the applicability of field pre-emption. . . .

We first address the survivor's annuity and then turn to the other pension benefits. Sandra Boggs, as we have observed, asserts that federal law pre-empts and supersedes state law and requires the surviving spouse annuity to be paid to her as the sole beneficiary. We agree.

The annuity at issue is a qualified joint and survivor annuity mandated by ERISA. Section 1055(a) provides: "Each pension plan to which this section applies shall provide that—§ (1) in the case of a vested participant who does not die before the annuity starting date, the accrued benefit payable to such participant shall be provided in the form of a qualified joint and survivor annuity.' " ERISA requires that every qualified joint and survivor annuity include an annuity payable to a nonparticipant surviving spouse. The survivor's annuity may not be less than 50% of the amount of the annuity which is payable during the joint lives of the participant and spouse. § 1055(d)(1). Provision of the survivor's annuity may not be waived by the participant, absent certain limited circumstances, unless the spouse consents in writing to the designation of another beneficiary, which designation also cannot be changed without further spousal consent, witnessed by a plan representative or notary public. § 1055(c)(2). Sandra Boggs, as the surviving spouse, is entitled to a survivor's annuity under these provisions. She has not waived her right to the survivor's annuity, let alone consented to having the sons designated as the beneficiaries.

Respondents say their state-law claims are consistent with these provisions. Their claims, they argue, affect only the disposition of plan proceeds after they have been disbursed by the Bell South Service Retirement Program, and thus nothing is required of the plan. . . . [The Court disagreed, stating the goal of the qualified joint and survivor annuity provisions is to ensure income to surviving spouses.]

ERISA's solicitude for the economic security of surviving spouses would be undermined by allowing a predeceasing spouse's heirs and legatees to have a community property interest in the survivor's annuity. Even a plan participant cannot defeat a nonparticipant surviving spouse's statutory entitlement to an annuity. It would be odd, to say the least, if Congress permitted a predeceasing nonparticipant spouse to do so. Nothing in the language of ERISA supports concluding that Congress made such an inexplicable decision. Testamentary transfers could reduce a surviving spouse's guaranteed annuity below the minimum set by ERISA (defined as 50% of the annuity payable during the joint lives of the participant and spouse). In this case, Sandra's annuity would be reduced by approximately 20%, according to the calculations contained in the sons' state-court filings. . . . States are not free to change ERISA's structure and balance. Louisiana law, to the extent it provides the sons with a right to a portion of Sandra Boggs' § 1055 survivor's annuity, is pre-empted.

Beyond seeking a portion of the survivor's annuity, respondents claim a percentage of: the monthly annuity payments made to Isaac Boggs during his retirement; the IRA; and the ESOP shares of AT & T stock. As before, the claim is based on Dorothy Boggs' attempted testamentary transfer to the sons of her community interest in Isaac's undistributed pension plan benefits. Respondents argue further—and somewhat inconsistently—that their claim again concerns only what a plan participant or beneficiary may do once plan funds are distributed, without imposing any obligations on the plan itself. Both parties agree that the ERISA benefits at issue here were paid after Dorothy's death, and thus this case does not present the question whether ERISA would permit a nonparticipant spouse to obtain a devisable community property interest in benefits paid out during the existence of the community between the participant and that spouse.

A brief overview of ERISA's design is necessary to put respondents' contentions in the proper context. The principal object of the statute is to protect plan participants and beneficiaries. . . . Section 1001(c) explains that ERISA contains certain safeguards and protections which help guarantee the "equitable character and the soundness of [private pension] plans" in order to protect "the interests of participants in private pension plans and their beneficiaries." The general policy is implemented by ERISA's specific provisions. . . .

ERISA confers beneficiary status on a nonparticipant spouse or dependent in only narrow circumstances delineated by its provisions. For example, as we have discussed, § 1055(a) requires provision of a surviving spouse annuity in covered pension plans, and, as a consequence the spouse is a beneficiary to this extent. Section 1056's QDRO provisions likewise recognize certain pension plan community property interests of nonparticipant spouses and dependents. A QDRO is a type of domestic relations order which creates or recognizes an alternate payee's right to, or assigns to an alternate payee the right to, a portion of the benefits payable with respect to a participant under a plan. § 1056(d)(3)(B)(i). A domestic relations order, in turn, is any judgment, decree, or order that concerns "the provision of child support, alimony payments, or marital property rights to a spouse, former spouse, child, or other dependent of a participant" and is "made pursuant to a State domestic relations law (including a community property law)." § 1056(d)(3)(B)(ii). A domestic relations order must meet certain requirements to qualify as a QDRO. See §§ 1056(d)(3)(C)–(E). QDRO's, unlike domestic relations orders in general, are exempt from both the pension plan anti-alienation provision,' 1056(d)(3)(A), and ERISA's general pre-emption clause, § 1144(b)(7). In creating the QDRO mechanism Congress was careful to provide that the alternate payee, the "spouse, former spouse, child, or other dependent of a participant," is to be considered a plan beneficiary. §§ 1056(d)(3)(K), (J). These provisions are essential to one of REA's central purposes, which is to give enhanced protection to the spouse and dependent children in the event of divorce or separation, and in the event of death the surviving spouse. Apart from these detailed provisions, ERISA does not confer beneficiary status on nonparticipants by reason of their marital or dependent status.

Even outside the pension plan context and its anti-alienation restriction, Congress deemed it necessary to enact detailed provisions in order to protect a dependent's interest in a welfare benefit plan. Through a § 1169 "qualified medical child support order" a child's interest in his or her parent's group health care plan can be enforced. . . . The surviving spouse annuity and QDRO provisions, which acknowledge and protect specific pension plan community property interests, give rise to the strong implication that other community property claims are not consistent with the statutory scheme. ERISA's silence with respect to the right of a nonparticipant spouse to control pension plan benefits by testamentary transfer provides powerful support for the conclusion that the right does not exist. . . .

We conclude the sons have no claim under ERISA to a share of the retirement benefits. To begin with, the sons are neither participants nor beneficiaries. A "participant" is defined as an "employee or former employee of an employer, or any member or former member of an employee organization, who is or may become eligible to receive a benefit." § 1002(7). A "beneficiary" is a "person designated by a participant, or by the terms of an employee benefit plan, who is or may become entitled to a benefit thereunder." § 1002(8). Respondents' claims are based on Dorothy Boggs' attempted testamentary transfer, not on a designation by Isaac Boggs or under the terms of the retirement plans. They do not even attempt to argue that they are beneficiaries by virtue of the judgment of possession qualifying as a QDRO. . . .

Respondents and their *amicus* in effect ask us to ignore § 1002(8)'s definition of "beneficiary" and, through case law, create a new class of persons for whom plan assets are to be held and administered. The statute is not amenable to this sweeping extratextual extension. It is unpersuasive to suggest that third parties could assert their claims without being counted as "beneficiaries." A plan fiduciary's responsibilities run only to participants and beneficiaries. § 1104(a)(1). Assets of a plan are held for the exclusive purposes of providing benefits to participants and beneficiaries and defraying reasonable expenses of administration. § 1103(c)(1). Reading ERISA to permit nonbeneficiary interests, even if not enforced against the plan, would result in troubling anomalies. Either pension plans would be run for the benefit of only a subset of those who have a stake in the plan or state law would have to move in to fill the apparent gaps between plan administration responsibilities and ownership rights, resulting in a complex set of requirements varying from State to State. Neither result accords with the statutory scheme.

The conclusion that Congress intended to pre-empt respondents' nonbeneficiary, nonparticipant interests in the retirement plans is given specific and powerful reinforcement by the pension plan anti-alienation provision. Section 1056(d)(1) provides that "[e]ach pension plan shall provide that benefits provided under the plan may not be assigned or alienated." Statutory anti-alienation provisions are potent mechanisms to prevent the dissipation of funds. In Hisquierdo we interpreted an anti-alienation provision to bar a divorced spouse's interest in her husband's retirement benefits. See 439 U.S., at 583–590, 99 S.Ct., at 809–813. ERISA's pension plan anti-alienation provision is mandatory and contains only two explicit exceptions, see §§ 1056(d)(2), (d)(3)(A), which are not subject to judicial expansion. See Guidry v. Sheet Metal Workers Nat. Pension Fund, 493 U.S. 365, 376, 110 S.Ct. 680, 687, 107 L.Ed.2d 782 (1990). The anti-alienation provision can "be seen to bespeak a pension law protective policy of special intensity: Retirement funds shall remain inviolate until retirement." J. Langbein & B. Wolk, Pension and Employee Benefit Law 547 (2d ed.1995).

Dorothy's 1980 testamentary transfer, which is the source of respondents' claimed ownership interest, is a prohibited "assignment or alienation." An "assignment or alienation" has been defined by regulation, with certain exceptions not at issue here, as "[a]ny direct or indirect arrangement whereby a party acquires from a participant or beneficiary" an interest enforceable against a plan to "all or any part of a plan benefit payment which is, or may become, payable to the participant or beneficiary." 26 CFR § 1.401(a)–3(c)(1)(ii). Those requirements are met. Under Louisiana law community property interests are enforceable against a plan. See Eskine v. Eskine, 518 So.2d 505, 508 (La.1988). If respondents' claims were allowed to succeed they would have acquired, as of 1980, an interest in Isaac's pension plan at the expense of plan participants and beneficiaries.

As was true with survivors' annuities, it would be inimical to ERISA's purposes to permit testamentary recipients to acquire a competing interest in undistributed pension benefits, which are intended to provide a stream of income to participants and their beneficiaries. See *Guidry, supra*, at 376, 110 S.Ct., at 687 ("[The anti-alienation provision] reflects a considered congressional policy choice, a decision to safeguard a stream of income for pensioners ... and their dependents ..."). Pension benefits support participants and beneficiaries in their retirement years, and ERISA's pension plan safeguards are designed to further this end. See § 1001(c). Besides the anti-alienation provision, Congress has enacted other protective measures to guarantee that retirement funds are there when a plan's participants and beneficiaries expect them. There are, for instance, minimum funding standards for pension plans and a pension plan termination insurance program which guarantees benefits in the event a plan is terminated before being fully funded. See §§ 1082, 1301–1461. Under respondents' approach, retirees could find their retirement benefits reduced by substantial sums because they have been diverted to testamentary recipients. Retirement benefits and the income stream provided for by ERISA-regulated plans would be disrupted in the name of protecting a nonparticipant spouses' successors over plan participants and beneficiaries. Respondents' logic would even permit a spouse to transfer an interest in a pension plan to creditors, a result incompatible with a spendthrift provision such as § 1056(d)(1). . . .

The same reasoning applies here. If state law is not pre-empted, the diversion of retirement benefits will occur regardless of whether the interest in the pension plan is enforced against the plan or the recipient of the pension benefit. The obligation to provide an accounting, moreover, as with the probate proceedings referred to in Free, is itself a burden of significant proportions. Under respondents' view, a pension plan participant could be forced to make an accounting of a deceased spouse's community property interest years after the date of death. If the couple had lived in several States, the accounting could entail complex, expensive, and time-consuming litigation. Congress could not have intended that pension benefits from pension plans would be given to accountants and attorneys for this purpose.

Respondents contend it is anomalous and unfair that a divorced spouse, as a result of a QDRO, will have more control over a portion of his or her spouse's pension benefits than a predeceasing spouse. Congress thought otherwise. The QDRO provisions, as well as the surviving spouse annuity provisions, reinforce the conclusion that ERISA is concerned with providing for the living. The QDRO provisions protect those persons who, often as a result of divorce, might not receive the benefits they otherwise would have had available during their retirement as a means of income. In the case of a predeceased spouse, this concern is not implicated. The fairness of the distinction might be debated, but Congress has decided to favor the living over the dead and we must respect its policy.

The axis around which ERISA's protections revolve is the concepts of participant and beneficiary. When Congress has chosen to depart from this framework, it has done so in a careful and limited manner. Respondents' claims, if allowed to succeed, would depart from this framework, upsetting the deliberate balance central to ERISA. It does not matter that respondents have sought to enforce their rights only after the retirement benefits have been distributed since their asserted rights are based on the theory that they had an interest in the undistributed pension plan benefits. Their state-law claims are pre-empted. The judgment of the Fifth Circuit is

Reversed.

■ The dissenting opinion of JUSTICE BREYER, with whom JUSTICE O'CONNOR, THE CHIEF JUSTICE and JUSTICE GINSBURG join in part, is omitted.

NOTES

Because the vast majority of pensions are encompassed by ERISA, federal law is an important element of any state's marital property award. In order to provide payment from a covered plan to an alternate payee, the federal requirements for a Qualified Domestic Relations Order (QDRO) must be satisfied. *See* Howard A. Massler, *Qualified Domestic Relations Orders*, in 3 VALUATION AND DISTRIBUTION OF MARITAL PROPERTY § 47–1 (Matthew Bender 1996). Most jurisdictions have liberally construed the criteria by which a domestic relations order will qualify as a QDRO. *See, e.g.*, Stewart

v. Thorpe Holding Co. Profit Sharing Plan, 207 F.3d 1143 (9th Cir. 2000), *rev. denied* 531 U.S. 1074 (2001).

Social Security benefits differ from pensions. In Boulter v. Boulter, 930 P.2d 112 (Nev. 1997), the court held that Social Security benefits could not be divided by a divorce decree, stating that "Congress' clear and stringent interpretation of the prohibition on transfer or assignment of benefits [under the Social Security Act] compels us to strictly interpret the clause to prohibit voluntary as well as involuntary transfer or assignments." Although state courts may not treat federal Social Security benefits as divisible marital property, this is one example of when they can anticipate the economic worth of the benefits that were earned during the marriage, which can then be a factor in dividing the couple's other divisible marital property. *See* Depot v. Depot, 893 A.2d 995 (Me. 2006).

H. SUPPORT FOR CHILDREN

1. BIOLOGICAL AND STATUTORILY ADOPTED CHILDREN SUPPORT OBLIGATION

UNIFORM MARRIAGE AND DIVORCE ACT (1973)

§ 309. [Child Support]

In a proceeding for dissolution of marriage, legal separation, maintenance, or child support, the court may order either or both parents owing a duty of support to a child to pay an amount reasonable or necessary for his support, without regard to marital misconduct, after considering all relevant factors including:

(1) the financial resources of the child;

(2) the financial resources of the custodial parent;

(3) the standard of living the child would have enjoyed had the marriage not been dissolved;

(4) the physical and emotional condition of the child and his educational needs; and

(5) the financial resources and needs of the noncustodial parent.

Voishan v. Palma

Court of Appeals of Maryland, 1992
609 A.2d 319

■ CHASANOW, JUDGE.

John and Margaret Voishan were divorced on June 26, 1981, by decree of the Circuit Court for Anne Arundel County. Margaret was awarded custody of their two daughters and John was ordered to pay $250 per week toward the girls' support. Over four years later, an order dated October 7, 1985 increased the amount of John's obligation for the support of both children to $1400 per month. The circuit court's order also awarded John certain detailed visitation rights.

On March 8, 1991, the circuit court's intercession was again sought to address John's request to find Margaret in contempt for violating the visitation order as well as Margaret's motion to modify child support. . . . [The circuit court] entered an order finding that Margaret was not in contempt of court [and] increased John's child support obligation for the one daughter who was still a minor from $700 per month to $1550 per month. John then appealed the modification of child support to the Court of Special Appeals. Because of the important issues raised on appeal, this Court granted certiorari before consideration by the intermediate appellate court. . . .

This dispute requires the Court, for the first time, to address Maryland Code, (1984, 1991 Repl.Vol.) Family Law Article §§ 12–201 *et seq.* (the "guidelines").[1] The General Assembly enacted these guidelines in 1989 to comply with federal law and regulations. *See* 42 U.S.C. §§ 651–667 (1982 & 1984 Supp. II) and 45 C.F.R. § 302.56 (1989). The federal mandate required that the guidelines be established and "based on specific descriptive and numeric criteria and result in a computation of the support obligation." *Id.* When drafting the guidelines, the Maryland Senate Judicial Proceedings Committee had before it *Development of Guidelines For Child Support Orders: Advisory Panel Recommendations and Final Report,* U.S. Department of Health and Human Services' Office of Child Support Enforcement. This report explained that the need for the guidelines was threefold: (1) to "remedy a shortfall in the level of awards" that do not reflect the actual costs of raising children, (2) to "improve the consistency, and therefore the equity, of child support awards," and (3) to "improve the efficiency of court processes for adjudicating child support. . . ."

After considering several different models recommended by the Advisory Panel on Child Support Guidelines, the General Assembly chose to base Maryland's guidelines on the Income Shares Model. *See* Senate Judicial Proceedings Committee, *Bill Analysis,* Senate Bill 49 (1989). The conceptual underpinning of this model is that a child should receive the same proportion of parental income, and thereby enjoy the standard of living, he or she would have experienced had the child's parents remained together. *Id. See also* Robert G. Williams, *Child Support Guidelines: Economic Basis and Analysis of Alternative Approaches*, IMPROVING CHILD SUPPORT PRACTICE I–12 to I–13 (A.B.A.1986). Accordingly, the model establishes child support obligations based on estimates of the percentage of income that parents in an intact household typically spend on their children. *Id.* Consistent with this model, the legislature constructed the schedule in § 12–204(e),

[1] Unless otherwise specified, all statutory references are to Maryland Code, (1984, 1991 Repl.Vol.) Family Law Article.

which sets forth the basic child support obligation for any given number of children based on combined parental income.

Following the Income Shares Model, Maryland's guidelines first require that the trial judge determine each parent's monthly "adjusted actual income." Section 12–201(d) states:

> " 'Adjusted actual income' means actual income minus:
>
> (1) preexisting reasonable child support obligations actually paid;
>
> (2) except as provided in § 12–204(a)(2) of this subtitle, alimony or maintenance obligations actually paid; and
>
> (3) the actual cost of providing health insurance coverage for a child for whom the parents are jointly and severally responsible."

After determining each parent's monthly "adjusted actual income," the judge then adds these two amounts together to arrive at the monthly "combined adjusted actual income" of the parents. *See* § 12–201(e). Having calculated the combined adjusted actual income of the parents, the judge can then determine whether that figure falls within the range of incomes found in the schedule of § 12–204(e). If the figure is within the schedule, the judge then locates the corresponding "basic child support obligation" for the given number of children. Where the monthly income falls between two amounts set forth in the schedule, § 12–204(c) dictates that the basic child support obligation is the same as the obligation specified for the next highest income level. The judge then divides this basic child support obligation between the parents in proportion to each of their adjusted actual incomes. § 12–204(a). The judge must then add together any work-related child care expenses, extraordinary medical expenses, and school and transportation expenses and allocate this total between the parents in proportion to their adjusted actual incomes. § 12–204(g)–(i). The amount of child support computed in this manner[2] is presumed to be correct, although this presumption may be rebutted by evidence that such amount would be unjust and inappropriate in a particular case. § 12–202(a)(2). In the instant case, evidence was presented at the March 8, 1991 hearing that John now earns $145,000 per year, while Margaret's annual income is $30,000. John does not contend that his actual income should be reduced by any expenses identified in § 12–201(d). Therefore, he computes a "combined adjusted actual income" of $175,000 a year or $14,583 per month in his argument to this Court. This combined income exceeds $10,000 per month, which

[2] This is the proper procedure for cases other than shared physical custody cases. § 12–204(k). Where the parents share physical custody of the child, as defined by § 12–201(i), the judge shall multiply the basic child support obligation by one and one-half to determine the "adjusted basic child support obligation." *See* §§ 12–201(j) and 12–204(f). The judge then divides that amount "between the parents in proportion to their respective adjusted actual incomes." § 12–204(*l*)(1). After that, the judge calculates which parent owes payment to the other by applying the provisions of § 12–204(*l*)(2)–(5).

is the highest income provided for in § 12–204(e). The legislature addressed this situation in § 12–204(d), which says: "If the combined adjusted actual income exceeds the highest level specified in the schedule in subsection (e) of this section, the court may use its discretion in setting the amount of child support. . . ."

John contends that the $1550 monthly child support award is inconsistent with the spirit and intent behind the Income Shares Model, and concludes that Judge Thieme abused his discretion in awarding that amount. John maintains that Judge Thieme accurately found that the parties' earnings created a ratio of 83 to 17 for John's and Margaret's respective percentages of their $175,000 combined annual income. John contends, however, that Judge Thieme erred in the manner in which he applied these percentages to arrive at the amount of $1550 per month for John's share of the obligation. Judge Thieme examined expense sheets for each of the parties and concluded that the "reasonable expenses of the child" were $1873 each month. The judge then calculated 83% of that figure and rounded John's share of the obligation down to $1550.

John argues here, as he did below, that a "reasonable approach" would have been for the trial judge to assume that the maximum basic child support obligation listed in the schedule is not only applicable to combined monthly incomes of $10,000, but also applies to those in excess of $10,000 per month. Under the schedule in § 12–204(e), the maximum basic child support obligation of $1040 per month is presumptively correct for parties who have a combined monthly income of $10,000. John argues that $1040 per month should also provide the presumptively correct basic child support obligation for all combined monthly incomes over $10,000. While we believe that $1040 could provide the presumptive *minimum* basic award for those with combined monthly incomes above $10,000, we do not believe that the legislature intended to cap the basic child support obligation at the upper limit of the schedule. *See, e.g.,* Hinshelwood v. Hinshelwood, 564 So.2d 141 (Fla. 5th DCA 1990); In re Marriage of Van Inwegen, 757 P.2d 1118, 1120 (Colo.App.1988). Had the legislature intended to make the highest award in the schedule the presumptive basic support obligation in all cases with combined monthly income over $10,000, it would have so stated and would not have granted the trial judge discretion in fixing those awards. Further, John's proposed approach creates an artificial ceiling and itself defeats the guidelines' policy that the child enjoy a standard of living consonant with that he or she would have experienced had the parents remained married. We are unpersuaded by John's argument that the legislature meant for all children whose parents earn more than $10,000 per month to have the same standard of living as those whose parents earn $10,000 per month.

Alternatively, John argues that Judge Thieme should have extrapolated from the guidelines to determine what the support obligation would have been had the schedule extended up to the parties' $14,583 monthly income. John notes that at the upper levels in the guidelines, the basic child support obligation for one child increases by $5 for every $100 rise in combined adjusted actual income. Extrapolating on that basis, John argues that the basic child support obligation would be $1270 per month ($4583/100 x $5 plus $1040). John also acknowledges that under the guidelines, in addition to the basic child support obligation—whatever that is computed to be, he has an obligation to pay 83% of the additional work-related child care expenses which, in the instant case, are $400 per month. *See* § 12–204(g). Taking 83% of the $1270 basic child support obligation plus 83% of the $400 work-related child care expenses, John argues, renders his portion of his daughter's support to be $1386 per month. Although slightly more generous than his earlier argument, which would leave the judge with no discretion, John's second contention is essentially that this Court should significantly restrict the judicial discretion granted by § 12–204(d) and allow judges very little latitude in deviating from the extrapolation method. John asks this Court to hold that Judge Thieme abused his discretion when he set the award $164 higher than the amount computed by John's strict extrapolation theory. While we believe that the trial judge should consider the underlying policies of the guidelines and strive toward congruous results, we think that Judge Thieme did not abuse his discretion in fixing the amount of this award.

The legislature has clearly enunciated that the policies of the guidelines are those embodied in the Income Shares Model. John also argues that this model relies on the assumption that the percentage of income expended on children decreases as parental income increases, and therefore the General Assembly could not have intended to permit an award in this case to exceed 10.4% of combined monthly income, the percentage represented by the schedule's maximum support obligation for one child. The legislative history, however, indicates that the General Assembly did not intend to impose a maximum percentage of income or any similar restraint on the judge's discretion in setting awards where the parents' combined adjusted actual income exceeds $10,000 per month. In the hearings on the guidelines, the General Assembly was asked repeatedly to circumscribe the discretion granted in § 12–204(d). The Fair Family Law Association of Maryland testified that "[t]he proposed statute leaves families with income above $10,000 a month ($120,000 a year) with absolutely no guidelines," and suggested that the schedule be amended to provide that "for family incomes greater than $10,000 per month the basic child support obligation shall be the same percentage of total family income as for income of $10,000 per month [10.4% for one child]." Senate Judicial Proceedings Committee, S.B. 49 Bill File (1989). Several members of Family Law Section of the Montgomery County Bar Association testified that "[l]eaving the amount of child support in upper income cases to the discretion of the court will not help us to predict results or settle cases. . . . We suggest that the table be extended, or that guidelines of some sort be provided." *Id.* Notwithstanding these pleas, the General Assembly did not change § 12–

204(d) or address any specific comment to these concerns. Rather, it chose to rely on judicial discretion. We agree with the Attorney General's conclusion in its amicus curiae brief that

> "[i]mplicit in this judgment is the view that at very high income levels, the percentage of income expended on children may not necessarily continue to decline or even remain constant because of the multitude of different options for income expenditure available to the affluent. The legislative judgment was that at such high income levels judicial discretion is better suited than a fixed formula to implement the guidelines' underlying principle that a child's standard of living should be altered as little as possible by the dissolution of the family."

While the legislature specifically rejected the request for more explicit formulae for incomes above the schedule, the general principles from which the schedule was derived should not be ignored. *See* § 12–202(a), which provides that "in *any* proceeding to establish or modify child support . . . the court shall use the child support guidelines set forth in this subtitle." (emphasis added). To effectuate the legislative intent to improve the consistency of child support awards, trial judges should bear in mind the guidelines' underlying principles when deciding matters within their discretion. Extrapolation from the schedule may act as a "guide," but the judge may also exercise his or her own independent discretion in balancing

> "the best interests and needs of the child with the parents' financial ability to meet those needs. Factors which should be considered when setting child support include the financial circumstances of the parties, their station in life, their age and physical condition, and expenses in educating the children." (Citations omitted).

Unkle v. Unkle, 305 Md. 587, 597, 505 A.2d 849, 854 (1986). These principles expressed in the pre-guidelines *Unkle* decision are consistent with the underlying concept that the child's needs be met as they would have been absent the parents' divorce.

While we reject John's argument that Judge Thieme abused his discretion because he placed too *little* reliance on John's suggested mechanical extrapolation from the schedule, we also decline to adopt the position taken by the Maryland Chapter of the American Academy of Matrimonial Lawyers (the AAML) in their amicus curiae brief. The AAML basically argues that Judge Thieme abused his discretion because he placed too *much* reliance on a mechanical application of the guidelines. The AAML contends that the economic data from which the figures in the schedule were derived did not include empirical evidence of the actual household expenditures for children of high income parents. Because the research and data used in constructing the Income Shares Model did not contemplate these high-range combined parental incomes, the AAML argues, the model provides *no* assistance in calculating the proper amount of child support. Thus, the AAML concludes, "the trial court erred when it applied a rigid formula (relative percentage of parents' income). . . ."

In support of this conclusion, the AAML points out that the legislature did not include in § 12–204(d) the phrase which appears in § 12–204(a)(1), (g)(1), (h), and (i)—"shall be divided between the parents in proportion to their adjusted actual incomes." While the argument is not expressly articulated, the AAML seems to suggest that Judge Thieme should not have divided the child support obligation in an 83 to 17 ratio. We believe that Judge Thieme acted properly in apportioning the obligation based upon the parties' respective percentages of their combined adjusted actual income. Moreover this action was consonant with the principle, expressed in the Income Shares Model as well as pre-guidelines caselaw, that each parent "share the responsibility for parental support in accordance with their respective financial resources." Rand v. Rand, 280 Md. 508, 517, 374 A.2d 900, 905 (1977). Finally, Judge Thieme did not look only to the parties' incomes and calculate a particular percentage thereof. Rather, he determined the reasonable needs of the child and then calculated each parent's proportionate share.

The Court in *Rand* declined to "mandate any specific formula by which the chancellor is to calculate the amount of support to be charged against each parent" and left to the chancellor's discretion the manner of assessing financial resources. *Id.* The legislature has modified *Rand*'s holding, as § 12–201 now defines the manner in which the trial judge should determine each party's "adjusted actual income." This would seem to be the initial step in *any* proceeding to establish or modify child support, as the judge must first determine whether the parents' combined adjusted actual income falls within, above, or below the schedule range. Although § 12–204(d) itself does not contain specific language requiring that the judge divide the child support obligation "between the parents in proportion to their adjusted actual incomes," this principle certainly underlies the Income Shares Model. Consequently, we believe that Judge Thieme properly calculated the support obligation and divided it between the parties in proportion to their incomes. . . .

While awards made under § 12–204(d) will be disturbed only if there is a clear abuse of discretion, a reviewing court must also be mindful that the federal call for child support guidelines was motivated in part by the need to improve the consistency of awards. Thus, the trial judge has somewhat more latitude than that argued by John, but not the unguided discretion of pre-guidelines cases as advocated by the AAML. Rather, we agree with the Attorney General's position that the guidelines do establish a rebuttable presumption that the maximum support award under the schedule is the minimum which should be awarded in cases above the schedule.[5] Beyond this the trial judge should examine the

---

[5] The Maryland guidelines were "patterned after the Colorado child support guidelines." Senate Judicial Proceedings Committee, *Floor Report,* Senate Bill 49 (1989). While it appears

needs of the child in light of the parents' resources and determine the amount of support necessary to ensure that the child's standard of living does not suffer because of the parents' separation. Further, the judge should give some consideration to the Income Shares method of apportioning the child support obligation. Consequently, we conclude that Judge Thieme properly exercised his discretion in receiving evidence of the parents' financial circumstances, considering the needs of the child, and then apportioning the "reasonable expenses of the child." . . .

JUDGMENT OF THE CIRCUIT COURT FOR ANNE ARUNDEL COUNTY AFFIRMED. COSTS TO BE PAID BY APPELLANT.

■ MCAULIFFE, JUDGE, (concurring).

I concur in the result. I do not believe that the legislature intended to authorize trial judges to ignore basic policy decisions made by the legislature with respect to the equitable establishment of child support, or to authorize virtually unlimited discretion as soon as the combined adjusted actual income of the parties exceeds $10,000 per month. . . .

I believe the Income Shares Model adopted by the legislature provides informed guidance for the fixing of child support obligations even when the combined adjusted actual income exceeds $10,000 per month, while still granting the discretion referred to in § 12–204(d) of the Family Law Article, Maryland Code (1991 Repl.Vol.). The schedule of basic child support obligations, based upon data that the legislature found acceptable, shows that above the poverty level the percentage of parental income dedicated to child-rearing expenses decreases as the parental income increases. I do not agree with the father that the curve which can be plotted from the schedule must be projected to establish child support obligations beyond the limits of the schedule; that argument is contrary to the express intention of the legislature to grant a measure of discretion to the court when incomes exceed the highest income listed on the schedule. But that does not mean that the entire concept of the schedule, or its underlying data, should be jettisoned as soon as the upper limit of the schedule is passed. The legislative objective may be carried forward by using the schedule to establish presumptive maximum and minimum amounts for basic child support.

Specifically, I suggest that the amount calculated in accordance with the schedule for child support when the combined income equals $10,000 per month should serve as the presumptive floor for awards based upon combined income in excess of that amount. It makes no sense to hold the parents who would be required to provide $1,040 per month for the

---

the Colorado Supreme Court has not yet spoken on the issue, that state's intermediate appellate court has repeatedly held that in cases above the schedule "there is a rebuttable presumption that the basic child support obligation at the uppermost level of the guidelines is the *minimum* presumptive amount of support." *In re Marriage of LeBlanc,* 800 P.2d 1384, 1388 (Colo.App.1990) (emphasis in original). Further, that court has held that it is an abuse of discretion for a trial judge to mechanically extrapolate from the guidelines without making a determination regarding the needs of the child. *In re Marriage of Van Inwegen,* 757 P.2d 1118, 1121 (Colo.App.1988).

support of a child when their combined monthly income is $10,000 would be permitted to pay less if their income were $10,050 per month. Similarly, I believe the presumptive maximum base payment for one child should be 10.4 percent of the combined income of the parents, which is the percentage that the maximum scheduled payment bears to the maximum combined income ($1,040 to $100,000). . . .

Applying these principles to this case, the presumptive minimum base payment would be $1,040 (the payment established by the schedule for $10,000), and the presumptive maximum would be $1,517 (10.4 percent of combined income of $14,583). Adding $400 of child care expenses to the presumptive maximum figure produces a total of $1,917, and multiplying that amount by 83 percent to arrive at the contribution to be made by the father produces a total presumptive maximum payment of $1,591. The monthly payment ordered in this case was $1,550. Although calculated by a method which I believe is at variance with the approach intended by the legislature, the payment ordered here falls within the range of discretion which I believe the legislature intended to grant to trial judges, and I would therefore affirm the decision in this case.

NOTES

Child Support Calculators. For websites that will perform child support calculations using certain assumptions about income and expenses, *see* http://www.divorcenet.com. Child support calculators may also be found at http://www.divorcesource.com and http://www.adrr.com/law1/csp11.htm. For a list of child support oversight entities, *see* National Conference of State Legislatures, *State Child Support Oversight Entities*, *available at* http://www.ncsl.org/issues-research/human-services/state-child-support-oversight-entities.aspx (current as of August 2016).

Three Child Support Models. The Income Shares Model, or variations of it, have been adopted by an overwhelming majority of states. In addition to the Income Shares Model, there are two other models used across the country, the "Obligor Model" and the Delaware "Melson" Model. *See* LAURA W. MORGAN, CHILD SUPPORT GUIDELINES: INTERPRETATION AND APPLICATION § 1.03[a] (1996 ed. & Supp. 2010) (providing state-by-state comparison of support guideline models). However, studies show that, outside low-income groups, there is little or no difference in the amount of child support awarded under each model. *See* Laura W. Morgan and Mark C. Lino, *A Comparison of Child Support Awards Calculated under States' Child Support Guidelines with Expenditures on Children Calculated by the U.S. Department of Agriculture*, 33 FAM. L. Q. 191 (1999).

The Income Shares Model uses both parents' income to arrive at a presumptive basic child support amount that is supposed to approximate the standard of living that a child would have had if the parents had not divorced. The basic child support amount is derived by taking the parents' combined gross incomes and then finding the corresponding amount on the state's child support guideline chart. Added to that basic amount are actual expenses for childcare and healthcare, yielding the total child support amount due. Each parent shares responsibility for the total child support amount pro rata, based on his or her fractional share of the couples' combined gross income. They also share pro rata any extraordinary out-of-pocket medical care expenses. The non-custodial parent pays his or her fractional share to the custodial parent, and the custodial parent simply retains his or her fractional share.

The second model, the "Obligor Model," simply requires non-custodial parents to pay as child support a percentage of net income, which varies from state to state. By its very nature, that percentage considers neither the custodial parent's resources nor the child's extraordinary expenses. This model is easier to understand and implement, however.

The third model, used in only three states, is called the Delaware "Melson" model. It requires that a parent devote his or her income to meeting the child's basic needs before retaining any income for him or herself beyond the parent's subsistence needs. In other words, all of a parent's income beyond a subsistence amount must be shared with the child, who then benefits from the absent parent's often higher standard of living. Delaware, Hawaii, and Montana presently use this approach. *See* LAURA W. MORGAN, CHILD SUPPORT GUIDELINES: INTERPRETATION AND APPLICATION § 3.02[b] (1996 ed. & Supp. 2010).

What Constitutes Income for Child Support Purposes. Whatever model a state uses, state guidelines define what counts as "income," which has been described as the "most important piece of information" in arriving at the total amount due. L. Gold-Bikin & L. Hammond (U.S. Dep't of Health & Human Svcs., Ofc. of Child Support Enforcement,) *Determination of Income*, in CHILD SUPPORT GUIDELINES: THE NEXT GENERATION 29 (1994). In all jurisdictions, a broad range of financial resources count as income when calculating the total support due, including: deferred compensation, severance pay, disability payments, personal injury awards, retirement income, certain gifts, loans, and inheritances, and Social Security benefits. *See* JOHN DEWITT GREGORY, PETER SWISHER, & ROBIN FRETWELL WILSON, UNDERSTANDING FAMILY LAW (4th ed. 2013).

High-Income Parents. Courts may only depart from the presumptive child support amount under state guidelines if the award would be "unjust or inappropriate." *See, e.g.*, VA. CODE ANN. § 20–108.1 (2016). What constitutes an appropriate child support award for children of high-income parents is a contentious issue. The Illinois Court of Appeals upheld an $8,500 a month award for the child of a professional basketball player, concluding that although the child's living expenses were $1,000 a month, the child would have enjoyed a higher standard of living if the parents lived together. *In re* Keon C., 800 N.E.2d 1257 (Ill. Ct. App. 2003). By contrast, the Minnesota Court of Appeals upheld a trial court's decision not to deviate from a presumptive $1000 monthly support amount, despite the fact that the father's monthly gross income of $116,000 dwarfed the mother's meager resources. State v. Hall, 418 N.W.2d 187 (Minn. Ct. App. 1988). For additional examples, *see Alimony, Maintenance, and Other Spousal Support,* tbl.1 titled "State by State Analysis", *50 State Statutory Surveys: Family Law: Divorce and Dissolution*, 0080 SURVEYS 11 (2012).

Low-Income Parents. Parents are not relieved of the responsibility to support their children due to their low income. State child support guidelines often require a minimum amount of support to be paid—in effect imputing a minimum income to the low-income parent. *See* VA. CODE ANN. § 20–108.1 (2016). The presumption that parents should pay something is so strong that even a parent's disability payments count as gross income available for child support. For instance, in Commonwealth. *ex rel.* Morris v. Morris, 984 S.W.2d 840 (Ky. 1998), the court held that a statute allowing Social Security Supplemental Security Income benefits to be included in calculations of gross income did not interfere with federal anti-attachment statutes.

Under-Employed Parents. Because the child support owed depends heavily on a parent's income, courts often must consider whether a parent is earning up to his or her potential. When a parent is voluntarily unemployed or underemployed, many states provide that the presumptive basic child support amount, derived from the parent's *actual* combined income, may be departed from if the presumptive amount would be "unjust or inappropriate" when considering the child's best interest and other factors. One explicit factor supporting deviation is when a party is:

> [V]oluntarily unemployed or voluntarily under-employed; provided that income may not be imputed to the custodial parent when a child is not in school, child care services are not available and the cost of such child care services are not included in the computation and provided further, that any consideration of imputed income based on a change in a party's employment shall be evaluated with consideration of the good faith and reasonableness of employment decisions made by the party.

VA. CODE ANN. § 20–108.1 (2016).

In Broadhead v. Broadhead, 655 S.E.2d 748 (Va. Ct. App. 2008), a father lost his job in the financial industry, took a lower-paying job, and petitioned for a reduction in child support. The trial court found that the father was voluntarily underemployed, imputed income to him, and required him to pay $800 in support. The father appealed, and the appellate court reversed and remanded, directing the trial court to consider "all of the relevant factors, particularly whether father's efforts to find a position were reasonable and whether other positions . . . were available to father, utilizing his education and experience, at a pay level comparable to his former positions." *Id.* at 183.

Just as income may be imputed to the non-custodial parent, it can be imputed to the custodial parent. In Engle v. Engle, 539 S.E.2d 712 (S.C. Ct. App. 2000), the custodial mother held a master's degree in education but left a good job at Furman University to go back to graduate school. The court imputed income to her as a result of her voluntary decision.

Nash v. Mulle

Supreme Court of Tennessee, 1993
846 S.W.2d 803

■ DAUGHTREY, JUSTICE.

The essential facts in this case are not in dispute. What is contested is the extent of the child support obligation of Charles Mulle, who fathered Melissa Alice Matlock as the result of an extramarital affair with the appellant, Helen Nash, in 1981 but has since had nothing to do with mother or child. After an order was entered establishing his paternity in 1984, the Juvenile Court also ordered him to pay $200.00 each month in child support, in addition to other specified expenses. In 1990, Helen Nash filed this action seeking an increase in the amount of his payments because of Charles Mulle's dramatically increased income.[1] The Juvenile Court then ordered Mulle to pay $3,092.62 per month, with $1,780.17 reserved for a trust fund established for Melissa's college education. The Court of Appeals reversed, limiting the award to $1,312.00 per month, or exactly 21 percent of $6,250.00, the top monthly income to which the child support guidelines explicitly apply. The Court of Appeals also disallowed the trust, finding that it improperly extended the parental duty of support beyond the age of majority. Because the facts are not disputed, we review de novo the questions of law presented on appeal.

Child support in Tennessee is statutorily governed by T.C.A. § 36–5–101. Section 36–5–101(e)(1) provides that "[i]n making its determination concerning the amount of support of any minor child . . . of the parties, the court shall apply as a rebuttable presumption the child support guidelines as provided in this subsection." The General Assembly adopted the child support guidelines promulgated by the Tennessee Department of Human Services in order to maintain compliance with the Family Support Act of 1988, codified in various sections of 42 U.S.C.[2] While they add a measure of consistency to child support awards statewide, the guidelines provide more than simple percentages to be applied against the net incomes of non-custodial parents. They also embody "the rules promulgated by the Department of Human Services in

---

[1] Mr. Mulle's income has risen substantially since the original award, thus justifying this review under T.C.A. § 36–5–101(a), which permits a change in child support only "upon a showing of a substantial and material change of circumstances." Whereas his income when the first award was made was approximately $30,000.00 annually, his gross annual income has risen considerably. In 1988 his gross income was approximately $192,000.00; in 1989, he earned approximately $292,000.00; and in 1990, his income was approximately $260,000.00. These figures contrast with Ms. Nash's 1989 gross annual income of approximately $42,000.00. In its calculation under the guidelines, the Juvenile Court increased Mulle's payments to reflect a more appropriate contribution in light of his present earnings.

[2] Under 42 U.S.C. §§ 651, 652, and 654, a "state plan" is essential in order to assure the state's receipt of federal money for child support enforcement. 42 U.S.C. § 667(a) requires that "[e]ach state, as a condition for having its State plan approved . . . must establish guidelines for child support award amounts within the state."

compliance with [the] requirements [of the Family Support Act of 1988]."[3] Hence, the purposes, premises, guidelines for compliance, and criteria for deviation from the guidelines carry what amounts to a legislative mandate.

The first issue presented concerns the proper measure of child support to be awarded in this case in view of the fact that Charles Mulle's monthly income exceeds $6,250.00. The guidelines apply in all cases awarding financial support to a custodial parent for the maintenance of a child, whether or not the child is a welfare recipient, and whether or not the child's parents are married. The guidelines are based, however, on several goals; they make many assumptions; and they permit deviation in circumstances that do not always comport with the assumptions. In studying the goals, premises, and criteria for deviation, we are convinced that the guidelines permit a monthly award greater than $1,312.00 without a specific showing of need by the custodial parent.

One major goal expressed in the guidelines is "[t]o ensure that when parents live separately, the economic impact on the child(ren) is minimized and to the extent that either parent enjoys a higher standard of living, the child(ren) share(s) in that higher standard." Tenn.Comp.R. and Regs. ch. 1240–2–4–.02(2)(e). This goal becomes significant when, as here, one parent has vastly greater financial resources than the other. It reminds us that Tennessee does not define a child's needs literally, but rather requires an ward to reflect both parents' financial circumstances. This goal is consistent with our long-established common law rule, which requires that a parent must provide support "in a manner commensurate with his means and station in life." Evans v. Evans, 125 Tenn. 112, 119, 140 S.W. 745, 747 (1911).

The guidelines are currently structured to require payment by the non-custodial parent of a certain percentage of his or her net income, depending upon the number of children covered by the support order (21 percent for one child, 32 percent for two children, etc.). The statute promulgating the use of the guidelines creates a "rebuttable presumption" that the scheduled percentages will produce the appropriate amounts to be awarded as monthly child support.[4] However, they are subject to deviation upward or downward when the assumptions on which they are based do not pertain to a particular situation. For example, one assumption on which the percentages are based is that the "children are living primarily with one parent but stay overnight with the other parent as often as every other weekend . . . two weeks in the summer and two weeks during holidays. . . ."[5] The criteria for deviation provide that when this level of visitation does not occur, child support should be adjusted upward to provide for the additional support required of the custodial parent. Additionally, "[e]xtraordinary educational

[3] Tenn.Comp.R. and Regs. ch. 1240–2–4–.01(6) (1989).

[4] T.C.A. § 36–5–101(a)(2); Tenn.Comp.R. & Regs. ch. 1240–2–4–.02(8).

[5] Tenn.Comp.R. & Regs. ch. 1240–2–4–.02(7).

expenses and extraordinary medical expenses not covered by insurance" are given as reasons for deviation. The guidelines thus recognize that "unique case circumstances will require a court determination on a case-by-case basis."

Among the "unique cases" specifically anticipated in the guidelines are those cases in which the income of the parent paying support exceeds $6,250.00 per month. In the criteria for deviation the guidelines provide that among the "cases where guidelines are neither appropriate nor equitable" are those in which "the net income of the obligor exceeds $6,250 per month." In the present case, the Juvenile Court calculated Charles Mulle's net monthly income to be $14,726.98, a figure well above the $6,250.00 figure justifying deviation from the guidelines. Yet the total award of $3,092 ordered by the trial judge is exactly 21 percent of Mulle's monthly income.

Obviously, to treat the monthly income figure of $6,250.00 as a cap and automatically to limit the award to 21 percent of that amount for a child whose non-custodial parent makes over $6,250.00 may be "neither appropriate nor equitable." Such an automatic limit fails to take into consideration the extremely high standard of living of a parent such as Charles Mulle, and thus fails to reflect one of the primary goals of the guidelines, i.e., to allow the child of a well-to-do parent to share in that very high standard of living. On the other hand, automatic application of the 21 percent multiplier to every dollar in excess of $6,250.00 would be equally unfair.

We conclude that the courts below found themselves at such polar extremes in this case due to a misreading of the criteria for deviation in the guidelines. The Juvenile Court placed the burden "on Mr. Mulle to convince the Court of the inequity or inappropriateness of the guidelines in this case," i.e., to prove that the court should award less than 21 percent of his income in excess of $6,250.00. That court ultimately found that Mulle had shown no "extraordinary burden" on his budget or other reason justifying deviation downward from the presumptive award of 21 percent, and awarded that amount. The Court of Appeals, on the other hand, held that "to obtain support larger than 21% of $6,250.00 for one child, the [custodial parent] has the burden of showing such need." Thus, to receive more than $1,312.00 per month for the child, Helen Nash would have to demonstrate exactly why the additional money was required. Rather than adopting either of these diametrically opposed approaches, we conclude that the trial court should retain the discretion to determine—as the guidelines provide, "on a case-by-case basis"—the appropriate amount of child support to be paid when an obligor's net income exceeds $6,250.00 per month, balancing both the child's need and the parents' means.

The guidelines' very latitude reflects this need for an exercise of discretion. Twenty-one percent of an enormous monthly income may provide far more money than most reasonable, wealthy parents would allot for the support of one child. However, it would also be unfair to require a custodial parent to prove a specific need before the court will increase an award beyond $1,312.00. At such high income levels, parents are unlikely to be able to "itemize" the cost of living. Moreover, most parents living within their means would not be able to present lists of expenditures made in the mere anticipation of more child support. Until the guidelines more specifically address support awards for the children of high-income parents, we are content to rely on the judgment of the trial courts within the bounds provided them by those guidelines. In this case, although the child support award may be appropriate, we think it expedient to remand this case to the Juvenile Court, thus providing the trial judge an opportunity to reconsider his opinion in light of the fact that he is not limited to the $1,312.00 cap imposed by the Court of Appeals, nor is he bound to award 21 percent of Charles Mulle's full net income, but may exercise his discretion as the facts warrant.

As he did before the Court of Appeals, Charles Mulle contends that the establishment of an educational trust fund for his daughter unlawfully requires him to support her past her minority. Citing Garey v. Garey, 482 S.W.2d 133 (Tenn.1972), and Whitt v. Whitt, 490 S.W.2d 159, 160 (Tenn.1973), he argues that the trust fund is incompatible with Tennessee case law. In *Garey*, this Court held that "[b]y lowering the age of majority from 21 to 18 years of age the Legislature has completely emancipated the minor from the control of the parents and relieved the parents of their attendant legal duty to support the child." 482 S.W.2d at 135. Because the trust fund is intended for Melissa's college education, her father insists that it unlawfully requires post-minority support.

We conclude, to the contrary, that the establishment of the trust fund in this case does not conflict with the holding in *Garey*. Although child support payments may not extend beyond the child's minority (except in extraordinary circumstances involving physical or mental disability), the benefits from such payments can. Hence, it is consistent with established rules of Tennessee law to hold, as we do here, that funds ordered to be accumulated during a child's minority that are in excess of the amount needed to supply basic support may be used to the child's advantage past the age of minority.

In reaching this conclusion, we must recognize the obvious fact that responsible parents earning high incomes set aside money for their children's future benefit and often create trusts for that purpose. They save for unforeseen emergencies; they accumulate savings for trips and other luxuries; and they may, and usually do, save for their children's college educations. Melissa's mother has expressed her intention to send her daughter to college. As all parents realize, however, the goal of sending a child to college often requires the wise management of money through savings. For a child of Melissa's age, assumed to begin college in the fall of 2000, it has been estimated that a parent must invest $457.00 per month for a public college education, or $964.00 per month for a private education, in order to save the $61,571.00 or $129,893.00, respectively, that will be required to fund a college education beginning that year.[11] Lacking the resources to write a check for the full amount of college tuition, room, board, and other expenses when that time arrives, Helen Nash must accumulate these savings over the course of the child's minority, or be forced to borrow the money later on. Such savings in this case would inevitably deplete Melissa's child support award. While in many cases parents undergo serious financial sacrifices to make college possible for their children, in this case, as the Juvenile Court found, Charles Mulle's income can afford Melissa a high standard of living that also includes savings for college.

We believe that an approach that refuses to recognize the laudable goal of post-secondary education and instead provides only for the child's immediate needs, would not be a responsible approach. If the most concerned, caring parents do not operate in such a haphazard way, surely the courts cannot be expected to award child support in such a fashion. Thus, we conclude that establishing a program of savings for a college education is a proper element of child support when, as in this case, the resources of the non-custodial parent can provide the necessary funds without hardship to that parent.

Moreover, the use of a trust fund for just such a purpose is explicitly approved by the guidelines. In the section on criteria for deviation, the guidelines provide: There are . . . cases where guidelines are neither appropriate nor equitable when a court so finds. Guidelines are inappropriate in cases including but not limited to, the following: (a) In cases where the net income of the obligor . . . exceeds $6,250 per month. *These cases may require such things as the establishment of educational or other trust funds* for the benefit of the child(ren) or other provisions as may be determined by the court. Tenn.Comp.R. & Regs., ch. 1240–2–4–.04(2)(a) (emphasis added). Thus, the guidelines specifically recommend a trust fund in cases in which a large cash award may be inappropriate. Moreover, the guidelines do not limit expenditures from such trusts to the child's minority. We defer to the policy judgment of the legislature in adopting the guidelines and uphold the use of the trust in this case.

In addition to adhering to the guidelines and providing a mechanism for this laudable use of savings, a trust fund for college education achieves several other goals. First, in a case such as this one involving a large difference in the parents' incomes, the trust allows for equitable contributions from each parent while avoiding an immediate cash windfall to one of them. When a large award given to a custodial parent with a much lower income would result in a windfall to the custodial parent, a trust fund helps to ensure that money earmarked for the child actually inures to the child's benefit. Thus, the trust fund is properly used to minimize unintended benefits to the custodial parent.

---

[11] *See The Tennessean*, Nov. 14, 1992, at 1E, col. 4.

We also note the need for a trust as protection for the child of an uncaring non-custodial parent. When the Supreme Court of Washington upheld an order requiring a parent to fund the college education of his three sons, it noted "the long standing special powers the courts have had (in equity, regardless of legislation) over the children of broken homes to assure that their disadvantages are minimized." Childers v. Childers, 89 Wash.2d 592, 575 P.2d 201, 207 (1978). Later, quoting Esteb v. Esteb, 138 Wash. 174, 184, 244 P. 264, 267 (1926), the *Childers* court continued, "Parents, when deprived of the custody of their children very often refuse to do for such children what natural instinct would ordinarily prompt them to do." 575 P.2d at 208. When a non-custodial parent has shown normal parental concern for a child, a trust fund may be unnecessary to ensure that his or her feelings are reflected in spending. However, when a non-custodial parent shows a lack of care, the court may step in and require the parent to support his or her child. The establishment of a trust is simply one discretionary mechanism used in the endeavor.

Thus, Charles Mulle's argument that the absence of a relationship with Melissa obviates the need to fund her college education is simply backwards. Child support is designed to prevent a non-custodial parent from shirking responsibility for the child he or she willingly conceived. It is precisely when natural feelings of care and concern are absent, and no parent-child relationship has been developed, that the court must award child support in a manner that best mirrors what an appropriate contribution from an interested parent would be. In fact, at least one court has gone beyond the acknowledgment of this lack of parental interest, and has spoken in terms of compensating the child for the parent's lack of concern. In Cohen v. Cohen, 193 Misc. 106, 82 N.Y.S.2d 513, 514 (1948), the court stated that the non-custodial parent "should be obliged to make up for his neglect, and to contribute towards his son's education as much as lies within his power." While we do not adhere to this compensatory view of child support, we do believe that an appropriate child support award should reflect an amount that would normally be spent by a concerned parent of similar resources.

We thus find no merit to Charles Mulle's complaint that the order deprives him of the freedom to decide his daughter's educational fate, arguing that a requirement is being imposed upon him that does not exist for married parents. He contends in his brief that "some parents plan for the future education of their children and some do not"; he argues that "[s]urely a divorce decree or a paternity order should not give children rights that children who are living with their parents who are married do not have." This argument overlooks the obvious fact that divorced and unmarried parents face a substantial loss of parental autonomy whenever a court must step in to exercise responsibility for their children in the absence of parental cooperation. Married parents may choose to rear their children in an extravagant or miserly fashion; they may send their children to expensive private schools and universities; or they may require their children to make their ways in the world at age 18. Nevertheless, when children become the subject of litigation, courts must judge the children's needs. Long-standing Tennessee law requires the courts to evaluate children's needs not in terms of life's essentials, but in terms of the parents' "means and station in life." *See* Atchley v. Atchley, 29 Tenn.App. 124, 127, 194 S.W.2d 252, 253 (1945) (citing Evans v. Evans, supra, 140 S.W. at 747). The guidelines' requirement that child support allow a child to share in the higher standard of living of a high-income parent continues this objective. Thus, Mulle's complaint about the alleged unfairness of the court's judgment concerning the benefits his standard of living should afford Melissa is misplaced.

Moreover, as the court stated in *Atchley*, "[r]eason, as well as the public policy of this state, favorable as it is to higher learning, permits no other conclusion. The high esteem in which college training is held in this state is unmistakably indicated by the numerous colleges found in the various parts of this state." 29 Tenn.App. at 129, 194 S.W.2d at 254 (citing Jackman v. Short, 165 Or. 626, 109 P.2d 860 (1941)). When the Illinois court in Maitzen v. Maitzen, 24 Ill.App.2d 32, 163 N.E.2d 840, 845 (1959), required a parent to provide a college education to a child over the age of majority in the absence of legislative approval, it stated in a similar vein: The public policy of this state, that a college education be given children whenever possible, is evidenced by the many institutions of higher education maintained by the state . . . A divorced parent should not . . . expect his children to rely on the bounty of others when he has ample means to provide for them. *Id.*, 163 N.E.2d at 845 (citing state and federal college aid statutes) . . . The Washington Supreme Court likewise reasoned in *Childers*, saying, "[The fact that] it is the public policy of the state that a college education should be had, if possible, by all its citizens, is made manifest by the fact that the state of Washington maintains so many institutions of higher learning at public expense." *Id.* 575 P.2d at 206. Given the public policy favoring higher education in Tennessee, likewise evidenced by our many colleges and universities, it would be highly improper in this case to cast the burden of Melissa's higher education entirely on her mother, or on the "bounty of the state," when her father can provide for her education without unduly burdening himself.

In ruling the trust in this case illegal because it "has no relation to the support of the child during minority," the Court of Appeals relied for authority on prior Tennessee case law discussed earlier in this section, as well as cases from other jurisdictions, primarily Illinois and Hawaii. But, the Tennessee precedents predate the enactment of the Child Support Guidelines, which specifically authorize the use of trusts in cases involving non-custodial parents with high income, without limiting expenditures to the beneficiary's minority. Moreover the courts and legislatures of many other states have approved the funding of a college education by non-custodial parents who can afford such an expense.

Indeed, several courts have done so without explicit statutory permission. In Pennsylvania, for example, the rule that a parent owes no duty of support for a child's college education is subject to an important exception. A parent may be ordered to provide such support if that parent has the "earning capacity or income to enable him to do so without undue hardship to himself." *See* Commonwealth v. Thomas, 243 Pa.Super. 599, 364 A.2d 410, 411 (1976); *see also* Brake v. Brake, 271 Pa.Super. 314, 413 A.2d 422 (1979). Therefore, in appropriate cases, the Pennsylvania courts require college support, even though the age of majority in that jurisdiction is 18.[12] An Alabama court, similarly, has required the establishment of a trust during a child's minority for educational expenses incurred after the age of majority. *See* Armstrong v. Armstrong, 391 So.2d 124, 126 (Ala.Civ.App.1980). The Iowa Supreme Court decreed in Hart v. Hart, 239 Iowa 142, 30 N.W.2d 748 (1948), that a non-custodial parent should provide his sons with four-year college educations despite the fact that college funding would likely require support beyond the 21-year-old age of majority in existence at that time.[13] New Hampshire courts also have the discretion to award college support past the age of majority. *See* Gnirk v. Gnirk, 134 N. 199, 589 A.2d 1008, 1011–12 (1991). These courts have used their equitable powers to require wealthy non-custodial parents to fund their children's college educations past the age of majority.

In yet other states, the authority of the courts to require non-custodial parents to fund a college education for their children is provided by statute. In Washington, after the child support statute was amended to include support for "dependents," the Washington Supreme Court declared that a college education could be included in the duty of support in cases where it "works the parent no significant hardship and . . . the child shows aptitude." Childers v. Childers, supra, 575 P.2d at 207. Oregon, similarly, allows courts to award support to children until the age of 21, three years past the age of majority, if they attend school. *See* Or.Rev.Stat. § 107.108 (1991); *In the* Matter of the Marriage of Wiebe, 113 Or.App. 535, 537, 833 P.2d 333, 334 (1992). Indiana allows child support for college expenses if the parent has the financial ability and the child has the aptitude. Ind.Code § 31–1–11.5–12(b) (1991); *see also* Martin v. Martin, 495 N.E.2d 523 (Ind.1986).

Other legislatures have taken the lead from court decisions allowing college support and now statutorily provide for such support. For example, Illinois has codified prior case law that had established a parent's duty to provide for his or her child's education whether the child was of minority or majority age. Ill.Ann.Stat. ch. 40, para. 513 (Smith-Hurd (1980)) (codifying Maitzen v. Maitzen, 24 Ill.App.2d 32, 163 N.E.2d 840 (1959)). In addition, a New York statute permits an award for post-

[12] 23 Pa.Cons.Stat.Ann. § 4321.

[13] Iowa Code § 599.1 (1981) now makes the age of majority 18. In 1972 the age was reduced to 19 from 21, and a year later the age was reduced again to 18 (*see* historical notes).

secondary educational expenses when the court determines that the award is appropriate in light of "the circumstances of the case and of the respective parties and the best interests of the child and as justice requires." N.Y.Jud.Law § 413(1)(c)(7) (McKinney 1992). New York's statute replaces years of case law holding that a college education could be a "special circumstance" meriting support past minority. *See* Gamble v. Gamble, 71 A.D.2d 649, 418 N.Y.S.2d 800 (1979); Brundage v. Brundage, 100 A.D.2d 887, 889, 474 N.Y.S.2d 546, 549 (1984); Shapiro v. Shapiro, 116 Misc.2d 40, 45, 455 N.Y.S.2d 157, 160–61 (1982). Thus, whether based on statute or rooted in the courts' equitable powers in family matters, the efforts of these states to provide for the college educations of children with wealthy parents persuade us that reason and public policy permit the use of a trust fund in this case.

In light of the guidelines' explicit provision for the use of trusts in cases involving high-income parents, the goals promoted by the use of a trust in this instance, and the reasoned support of other state courts and legislatures, we find the use of an educational trust in this case to be proper. As noted in Section I, however, there remains the question of the level at which the trust should be funded in this case. We therefore reverse the judgment of the Court of Appeals, and remand the case to the Juvenile Court for calculation of an award in accordance with this opinion. . . .

NOTES

When Does the Duty of Support to a Child End? Absent a written agreement to the contrary, a parent's obligation to support his or her child usually ends when the child reaches the age of majority (commonly age 18), graduates from high school, or becomes legally emancipated by marrying, joining the military, or becoming otherwise self-sufficient. *See* LAURA W. MORGAN, CHILD SUPPORT GUIDELINES: INTERPRETATION AND APPLICATION tbl. 4–6 (1996 ed. & Supp. 2010) (giving state-by-state comparison). Most jurisdictions require parents to provide support beyond the legal age of majority if the child is unable by reason of mental or physical handicap or disability to become self-supporting. *See, e.g.,* Eccleston v. Bankosky, 780 N.E.2d 1266, 1274 (Mass. 2003). For more information on the termination of support, *see* generally National Conference of State Legislatures, *Termination of Support—Age of Majority, available at* http://www.ncsl.org/issues-research/human-services/termination-of-child-support-age-of-majority.aspx (current as of August 2016); National Conference of State Legislatures, *Termination of Child Support- Exception for Adult Children with Disabilities, available at* http://www.ncsl.org/issues-research/human-services/termination-of-child-support-exception-for-adult.aspx (current as of August 2016); National Conference of State Legislatures, *Termination of Support—College Support Beyond the Age of Majority, available at* http://www.ncsl.org/issues-research/human-services/termination-of-support-college-support.aspx (current as of August 2016).

Statutory Requirements to Pay for College. Before widespread legislative action lowered the age of majority to 18, many states had developed rules requiring contribution to college education in accordance with a child's scholarly ability and a parent's financial ability to pay. Some jurisdictions required a parent to seek and receive an order for the other parent to contribute to the child's education *before* the child had reached majority. With the lowering of the majority age, some courts held that their power to require such contribution ended at the age when most college students entered their first year. *Compare Ex Parte* Barnard, 581 So.2d 489 (Ala. 1991) (denying mother's petition for post-minority education support because the court lacked jurisdiction over two of the three children who had reached the age of majority before the petition was filed) *with Ex Parte* Bayliss, 550 So.2d 986 (Ala. 1989) (where application is made before child attains the age of majority, trial court may award support for post-minority education out of the property and income of either or both parents).

Some state legislatures, such as Washington's, adopted legislation specifically dealing with post-minority educational support. *See* WASH. REV. CODE ANN. § 26.19.090 (2016) ("When considering whether to order support for postsecondary educational expenses, the court shall determine whether the child is in fact dependent and is relying upon the parents for the reasonable necessities of life, [exercising] its discretion when determining whether and for how long to award postsecondary educational support based upon consideration of [listed] factors."). By 2010, twelve states had enacted statutes expressly authorizing courts to award support for college expenses. *See* LAURA W. MORGAN, CHILD SUPPORT GUIDELINES: INTERPRETATION AND APPLICATION tbl. 4–6.1 (1996 ed. & Supp. 2010) (listing Alabama, Connecticut, Hawaii, Illinois, Indiana, Iowa, Massachusetts, Missouri, New York, North Dakota, Oregon, and Washington). Many of these statutes have encountered constitutional challenges, which have had varying success in court. The Supreme Court of Pennsylvania held that a statute allowing a court to order separated, divorced, or unmarried parents to provide equitably for their children's college educations while imposing no obligation on married parents was an unconstitutional violation of equal protection because the state had no legitimate purpose for discriminating between children of unmarried parents and children of married parents. *See* Curtis v. Kline, 666 A.2d 265 (Pa. 1995).

By contrast, in LeClair v. LeClair, 624 A.2d 1350, 1357 (N.H. 1993), the Supreme Court of New Hampshire upheld a statute authorizing a greater child support contribution for a child after the parents' divorce, even though another statute provides for termination of child support when a child finishes high school. Reasoning that children of divorced parents suffer economic disadvantages, the court found that requiring parents to contribute to their children's education fosters the state goal of having an educated population. *See also In re* McGinley, 19 P.3d 954 (Or. Ct. App. 2001). The New Hampshire legislature subsequently repealed the statute and expressly provided that child support orders may not require contributions to an "adult child's college expenses." N.H. REV. STAT. ANN. § 461–A:14 (2016).

When State Statutes are Silent on College Expenses. For jurisdictions with statutes that impose no explicit duty to pay for post-secondary education, states are divided on whether and to what extent parents with the financial ability to pay for their children's college expenses may be required to by courts.

In *In re* Marriage of Plummer, 735 P.2d 165 (Colo. 1987), the court reversed a trial court order requiring a father to continue paying support for his twenty-one-year-old daughter while in her third year of college. The court reasoned that no duty exists "to require an award of child support payments when a capable, able-bodied young adult chooses to attend college after reaching the age of majority." *Id.* at 167.

Other jurisdictions allow a child support award to encompass post-secondary support if "the characteristics of the child indicate that he or she will benefit from college, . . . demonstrates the ability to do well, or at least make satisfactory grades, . . . the child cannot otherwise go to school, . . . and the parent has the financial ability to help pay." West v. West, 419 S.E.2d 804, 806 n.2 (S.C. Ct. App. 1992). Some courts consider the child's ability to fund such education through scholarships, financial aid, employment, or the child's own funds, in addition to each parent's financial circumstances and the child's educational potential. *See, e.g.*, *In re* Marriage of Steele, 502 N.W.2d 18 (Iowa Ct. App. 1993); *In re* Marriage of Murphy, 592 N.W.2d 681 (Iowa 1999); Passemato v. Passemate, 691 N.E.2d 549 (Mass. 1998).

Like express statutory provisions authorizing payment for post-secondary educational expenses, orders to pay such expenses under the state's general child support provisions have also been challenged on constitutional grounds. *See, e.g.,* Webb v. Sowell, 692 S.E.2d 543 (S.C. 2010), *overruled by* McLeod v. Starnes, 723 S.E.2d 198 (S.C. 2012).

In jurisdictions where the court has no power to award post-majority child support, most states permit the parents to extend the support obligation contractually. *See, e.g.,* H.P.A. v. S.C.A., 704 P.2d 205 (Alaska 1985); Nichols v. Tedder, 547 So.2d 766 (Miss. 1989). For general commentary, *see* Laurie S. Kohn, *Money Can't Buy You Love*, 81 BROOK. L. REV. 53 (2015) (concluding that the state's prioritization of the father's breadwinning role over the caretaking role can result in paternal absence and the perpetuation of gender inequality); and Margaret Ryznar, *The Obligations of High-Income Parents*, 43 HOFSTRA L. REV. 481 (2014); Lindsay Cohen, *Daddy Will You Buy Me a College Education? Children of Divorce and the Constitutional Implications of Noncustodial Parents Providing for Higher Education*, 66 MO. L. REV. 187 (2001); Judith G. McMullen, *Father (or Mother) Knows Best: An Argument Against Including Post-Majority Educational Expenses in Court-Ordered Child Support*, 34 IND. L. REV. 343 (2001).

Interpreting Contractual Agreements and Orders to Pay for College. Often upon divorce, parents agree to share certain expenses for children, including college, raising difficult contractual questions when one party later refuses payment. In Gimlett v. Gimlett, 629 P.2d 450, 451 (Wash. 1981), the Supreme Court of Washington interpreted the terms of a decree requiring support "until said children are emancipated." The question was whether the term "emancipate" meant attaining majority or ceasing to be dependent. While recognizing that support can be granted after majority, the judge examined the original decree and concluded that emancipation meant reaching the age of majority, 18. In a later decision in the same jurisdiction, the phrase "so long as the children remain dependent" did not operate to automatically end the support obligations at majority. *See In re* Marriage of Anderson, 746 P.2d 1220, 1221 (Wash. Ct. App. 1987).

In *In re* Marriage of Baumgartner, 912 N.E.2d 783 (Ill. Ct. App. 2009), the father filed a motion to amend a judgment for dissolution requiring the father to pay for post-secondary expenses until his son turned twenty-three years old. The petition was initially filed when his twenty year-old son was incarcerated for a sex crime for three years. The father contended that incarceration emancipated his son and that the divorce judgment conditioned payment of higher-education expenses on his son's "desire and ability to further his education." Because his son graduated at the bottom of his high school class, failed out of community college, and, as a sex offender, was prohibited from being in the vicinity of public or private schools, the father argued it is unlikely that the son would undertake any form of higher education prior to his twenty-third birthday. The Circuit Court terminated the ex-husband's obligation, citing the child's emancipation due to incarceration. The ex-wife appealed. The Court of Appeals reversed, holding that incarceration does not extinguish a parent's duty to support their child, but merely decreases it. In the dissent's view, however:

> [The child] is not a minor. Nor is he a delinquent. He is a 22-year-old adult. He was 20 when he was convicted of a felony and sentenced to three years in prison. The judgment order in this case provides that the obligation to pay Max's educational expenses is conditioned on "the child's desire and ability to further his education." No evidence concerning Max's desire and ability to further his education was received by the trial court. In my view the record reflects Max abandoned any pursuit of a higher education when he pled guilty to two felonies involving sexual abuse of a child. An adult's abandonment of education can be an emancipating event. . . .

Id. at 301.

What is an Educational Expense? Often parties agree that a parent's support obligation will encompass "reasonable necessaries of the child's college expenses" or the amount necessary for the child to attend high school and four years of college. Entrekin v. Entrekin, 627 So.2d 955, 957 (Ala. Ct. App. 1993). Similarly, the Supreme Court of Mississippi has held that a parent may be held responsible for the child's college education, to include car insurance and sorority fees, even though the child has substantial financial assets of her own when the question of college support was reserved in the couple's divorce settlement agreement. *See* Saliba v. Saliba, 753 So.2d 1095 (Miss. 2000).

When such contractual provisions for post-majority support are incorporated into a divorce decree, some jurisdictions allow those terms to be enforced as part of the court decree itself, even though the children have reached the age of majority. *See* Jameson v. Jameson, 306 N.W.2d 240 (S.D. 1981). There is some risk, however, that contractual promises may be merged into a final decree, with the result that the contract cannot be separately enforced. Thus, in Noble v. Fisher, 894 P.2d 118 (Idaho 1995), neither statutes nor case law in Idaho imposed a duty to support a child while in college. Because the father's promise to pay half of college expenses appeared in a separation agreement that was merged into the divorce decree, it was unenforceable as a separate contract.

The Trust Device. In *In re* Paternity of Tukker M.O., 544 N.W.2d 417 (Wis. 1996), the Supreme Court of Wisconsin held that the state's child support guidelines did not preclude the family court's establishment in a paternity proceeding of both a trust fund to pay for a child's post-minority higher education expenses and a discretionary fund from which the mother could withdraw funds without court approval when monthly child support needs were not met. The father was a professional athlete with a high current income.

In re Barrett

Supreme Court of New Hampshire, 2004
150 N.H. 520

■ DALIANIS, JUDGE.

The respondent, John T. Coyne, appeals an order recommended by a Marital Master (*Harriet J. Fishman*, Esq.) and approved by the Portsmouth Family Division (*DeVries*, J.). We vacate and remand.

The record supports the following facts. Coyne and the petitioner, Susan C. Barrett, were divorced on August 22, 1996, in the Commonwealth of Pennsylvania. The parties agreed to share joint legal custody of their two daughters, Kathryn and Jacqueline, with Barrett having primary physical custody. Additionally, Coyne was ordered to pay child support. Barrett and the children moved to New Hampshire in 1998. At approximately the same time, Coyne ceased communication with them, although he continued to pay child support. Kathryn attended Winnacunnet High School, a public secondary school in Hampton, during her freshman year. Kathryn had been diagnosed in 1997 with attention deficit disorder and she suffered emotional problems due to her estranged relationship with Coyne. As a result of both conditions, she failed her freshman year. Although Barrett met with the Winnacunnet administration, Kathryn was neither coded for special education nor provided with other assistance.

In order to help her daughter, Barrett decided to enroll her in private school. Kathryn took summer courses and qualified for acceptance as a sophomore at Tilton School (Tilton), a private secondary school. Despite the high cost of private school, Barrett believed that unless Kathryn attended private school she would continue to fail. When requested by Tilton to provide financial information, Coyne submitted the necessary forms without objection. Because of Coyne's and Barrett's financial status, Tilton did not give Kathryn significant financial aid. Kathryn's grades improved upon her enrollment at Tilton and she passed both her sophomore and junior years. In 2002 Barrett suffered financial difficulties and asked Coyne to pay for Kathryn's tuition to enable her to attend Tilton in her senior year. Coyne refused Barrett's request.

Barrett filed a motion in the Portsmouth Family Division seeking an order that Coyne contribute financially towards Kathryn's senior year at Tilton. The trial court initially found, on October 2, 2002, that Coyne "[did] not have the ability to pay" any amount towards Kathryn's senior year at Tilton. Barrett filed a motion for reconsideration, arguing that Coyne's ability to pay was greater than that presented to the court because Coyne had failed to include his current wife's income in his financial statements. The trial court reconsidered and ordered Coyne to pay $8,000 of Kathryn's school tuition.

On appeal, Coyne argues that the trial court erred in applying an "ability to pay" standard when ordering him to pay for Kathryn's private school tuition in addition to child support. We will uphold the trial court's decision unless it is unsupported by the evidence or tainted by an error of law. . . .

[T]he award of private secondary education expenses for a minor child is an issue of first impression for this court. Two statutes are relevant to our analysis: (1) RSA 458:17, I (1992), which provides that "the court shall make such . . . decree in relation to the support, education, and custody of the children as shall be most conducive to their benefit and may order a reasonable provision for their support and education"; and (2) RSA chapter 458–C (Supp. 2002), the child support guidelines, adopted by the legislature "to establish a uniform system to be used in the determination of the amount of child support," RSA 458–C:1. . . .

There exists an inconsistency between RSA 458:17, I, and RSA chapter 458–C. RSA 458:17, I, on its face appears to authorize an award of education expenses in addition to an award for child support. RSA chapter 458–C, adopted after RSA 458:17, I, however, purports to allow for deviations from the child support guidelines only when "the application of the guidelines would be unjust or inappropriate," RSA 458–C:4, II, IV, because of "special circumstances," RSA 458–C:5, which include "ongoing extraordinary . . . education expenses," RSA 458–C:5, I(a). . . . When interpreting two statutes that deal with a similar subject matter, we construe them so that they do not contradict each other, and so that they lead to reasonable results and effectuate the legislative purpose of each statute. *Id.* . . .

Under normal circumstances a trial court need not consider private secondary education expenses when determining a non-custodial parent's child support obligation because all children are entitled to a public education. Instead, it is only when the trial court finds that "special circumstances" exist that it may require an obligor parent to contribute to private or specialized education. RSA 458:5, I(a). So, while RSA 458:17, I, read separately from the rest of the child support scheme, on its face would appear to authorize an award of private secondary education expenses in addition to the amount awarded under the child support guidelines, such a deviation, absent "special circumstances," would be inconsistent with the child support guidelines. *See* RSA 458–C:5. Therefore, a trial court may deviate from the child support guidelines to account for private secondary education expenses only after a finding that "the application of the guidelines would be unjust or inappropriate," RSA 458–C:4, II, IV, because of "special circumstances," RSA 458–C:5. . . .

Therefore, when making a finding that "special circumstances" exist that warrant a deviation from the child support guidelines so as to require a non-custodial parent to contribute toward private secondary education expenses, the trial court must find that both the child has a demonstrated "special need" and the non-custodial parent has "an ability to pay." Furthermore, when determining whether a demonstrated "special need" exists, the trial court may consider such factors as: (1) the child's attendance at private school prior to the separation and divorce; (2) the availability of satisfactory public education, including special education; (3) the child's academic performance; (4) the child's family and/or religious tradition; and (5) the child's particular emotional and/or physical needs. . . .

In this case the trial court required Coyne to contribute to the cost of Kathryn's private education without a finding of "special circumstances." We hold that this was error and remand for consideration of whether Kathryn's private education expenses constitute "special circumstances."

Additionally, Coyne argues that the trial court may not consider his current wife's income when determining whether to order him to contribute towards Kathryn's tuition. Coyne points to RSA 458–C:2, IV(b), which provides that when determining the gross income of a parent, that parent's spouse's income "shall not be considered as gross income to the parent unless the parent resigns from or refuses employment or is voluntarily unemployed or underemployed," and contends that, because neither condition is present in this case, such income may not, therefore, be considered. The circumstances in this case, however, deal, not with determining Coyne's gross income, but rather with determining whether to allow for a deviation from the child support guidelines. RSA 458–C:5, I(c) expressly allows the trial court to consider "[t]he economic consequences of the presence of stepparents." Therefore, upon remand the trial court may consider Coyne's current wife's income for the purpose of determining whether "special circumstances" exist so as to justify a deviation from the child support guidelines. *See* RSA 458–C:5, I(c).

Finally, we turn to Coyne's arguments that the trial court is precluded from awarding Barrett private secondary education expenses because she: (1) failed to pursue certain State and federal remedies; and (2) failed to inform Coyne of her decision to send Kathryn to private school, thus eliminating his ability to pursue those remedies. . . . [I]n evaluating the placement of a child in private school, the court should determine whether "special circumstances" warrant such placement and may consider the "availability of satisfactory public education, including special education" in its analysis of "special needs."

As to the latter argument . . . there exist statutory periods within which to pursue certain "special education" remedies. Coyne contends that because Barrett failed to inform him of her decision to place Kathryn in private school, she eliminated his ability to pursue those remedies on Kathryn's behalf, since by the time he knew of such placement the statutory periods had expired. We begin by noting that Coyne and Barrett share joint legal custody of Kathryn. "Legal custody refers to the responsibility for making major decisions affecting the child's welfare," 59 Am. Jur. 2d Parent and Child § 26 (2002), and legal custodians are entitled to make the major decisions regarding the health, education and religious upbringing of the child, Chandler v. Bishop, 142 N.H. 404, 412, 702 A.2d 813 (1997). Thus, either Barrett or Coyne is entitled to bring a petition for "special education" on behalf of Kathryn, if they are unable to make a joint decision. . . .

Though the trial court found that Coyne had knowledge of Kathryn's attendance at Tilton, it did not specify whether that knowledge arose within the relevant statutory time period. It is clear from the limited record available to us that Coyne knew of Kathryn's attendance at Tilton because he filled out the forms to determine her financial aid. Though it is not clear from the record exactly when he filled out those forms, we infer from the trial court's ruling denying him relief that his knowledge must have arisen within the relevant statutory time period. Coyne does not argue that the lack of a record has prejudiced him. The trial court did not commit any legal error and Coyne has presented us with no basis to overturn its ruling.

Coyne also argues that his rights to due process and equal protection under the law were violated by the trial court's order. Because Coyne's constitutional arguments were not adequately briefed and argued, we decline to address them. State v. Schultz, 141 N.H. 101, 104, 677 A.2d 675 (1996).

Vacated and remanded.

■ BRODERICK, C.J., and NADEAU and DUGGAN, JJ., concurred; BROCK, C.J., retired, specially assigned under RSA 490:3, concurred.

NOTES

Child support guidelines invest the court with significant discretion to make awards. Before majority, most child support guidelines yield a presumptive amount due, out of which would be paid educational costs. Many couples will stipulate to paying for secondary school expenses in their divorce settlement agreement, especially if the child attended a private school during the couple's intact relationship. Those agreements are likely to be accepted by the court in its final decree, although care must be taken that the agreement can be enforced after the divorce if it is merged into the final decree.

CALIFORNIA FAMILY CODE (2016)

§ 3901. Duration of duty of support

(a) The duty of support imposed by Section 3900 continues as to an unmarried child who has attained the age of 18 years, is a full-time high school student, and who is not self-supporting, until the time the child completes the 12th grade or attains the age of 19 years, whichever occurs first.

(b) Nothing in this section limits a parent's ability to agree to provide additional support or the court's power to inquire whether an agreement to provide additional support has been made.

2. STEPCHILDREN SUPPORT OBLIGATION

VERMONT STATUTES ANN. (2016)

Title 15, § 296 Liability of stepparents

A stepparent has a duty to support a stepchild if they reside in the same household and if the financial resources of the natural or adoptive parents are insufficient to provide the child with a reasonable subsistence consistent with decency and health. The duty of a stepparent to support a stepchild under this section shall be coextensive with and enforceable according to the same terms as the duty of a natural or adoptive parent to support a natural or adoptive child including any such duty of support as exists under the common law of this state, for so long as the marital bond creating the step relationship shall continue.

NOTES

Given the many blended families today, courts often grapple with the support that parents provide to other children who are not the subject of the order at issue. This scenario commonly arises when a parent remarries and lives with stepchildren or when a parent later has a child with a new partner. Most states have statutes that recognize the reduced resources that such parents have, either directly or indirectly. In Virginia, for example, gross income of the non-custodial parent is reduced by the guideline amount for the number of stepchildren being supported, as well as any "actual monetary support for other family members or former family members" that the obligor is already paying. VA. CODE ANN. § 20–108.1 (2016). However, some courts have held that when no legal duty exists for a parent to support stepchildren—either by statute like Vermont's or by contract, as authorized in California—the presence of stepchildren does not necessarily entitle a parent to a reduction in support that would otherwise be owed.

Stahl v. Department of Social and Health Services

Court of Appeals of Washington, 1986
717 P.2d 320

■ COLEMAN, JUDGE.

Department of Social and Health Services (DSHS) appeals a summary judgment determining that Mr. Stahl had no obligation to support his stepchildren after he separated from his wife. We reverse.

William Lester Stahl married on July 9, 1974. His wife was the custodial parent of three children by a former marriage. The family lived together until Mr. and Mrs. Stahl separated in October 1981. Mrs. Stahl filed for dissolution of the marriage on October 16, 1981. The marriage was dissolved on February 14, 1983. Mrs. Stahl applied for and began receiving public assistance benefits from DSHS in March 1982. As a condition precedent to receiving assistance, she assigned to DSHS all of her right, title, and interest in any support owing for the children. Mrs. Stahl received assistance through February 1983.

In August 1982, Mr. Stahl was served with a Notice and Finding of Financial Responsibility by DSHS. Mr. Stahl was granted an administrative hearing. The decision of the administrative law judge and of the review examiner was that Mr. Stahl was obligated to support his stepchildren until his marriage to their mother was dissolved. Mr. Stahl petitioned for judicial review of the DSHS decision. On summary judgment, the superior court reversed the DSHS decision, holding that (1) there were no genuine issues of material fact; (2) Mr. Stahl was a custodial stepparent from the time of his marriage to the date he and his wife separated; and (3) Mr. Stahl became a noncustodial stepparent upon his separation from his wife and had no obligation to support her children following the separation. The court also determined that Mr. Stahl would be awarded his reasonable attorney's fees for the judicial review.

The parties agree that there are no genuine issues of material fact. The only issue on appeal is the legal question of when a stepparent's obligation of support terminates. The statute dealing with family support provides:

> The expenses of the family and the education of the children, including stepchildren, are chargeable upon the property of both husband and wife, or either of them, and in relation thereto they may be sued jointly or separately: *Provided*, That with regard to

> stepchildren, the obligation shall cease upon the termination of the relationship of husband and wife.

RCW 26.16.205.

In *State v. Gillaspie,* 8 Wash.App. 560, 507 P.2d 1223 (1973), this court interpreted a criminal nonsupport statute containing the same proviso that is in RCW 26.16.205. Mr. Gillaspie argued that when he separated from his wife, there was a "termination of the relationship of husband and wife" as provided in the statute. The *Gillaspie* court disagreed, stating:

> We believe that the legislative words, "termination of the relationship of husband and wife", as commonly understood, mean a legal end to the marriage either by divorce or death, and that the intent of the legislature was to give stepchildren the same status as natural children in the operation of the statute.

Gillaspie, at 562–63, 507 P.2d 1223.

Respondent contends, however, that *Gillaspie* is no longer correct in light of the Supreme Court's holding in Van Dyke v. Thompson, 97 Wash.2d 726, 630 P.2d 420 (1981). In *Van Dyke,* the court examined the common law and statutory bases for a stepparent's duty of support. Under the common law, only stepparents in loco parentis were required to contribute to the needs of a child. *Taylor v. Taylor*, 58 Wash.2d 510, 364 P.2d 444 (1961). The *Van Dyke* court examined the support obligation created by RCW 26.16.205 and determined that the Legislature did not intend to extend this obligation to noncustodial stepparents. Respondent argues that *Van Dyke* overruled *Gillaspie sub silentio* and determined that common law principles apply to a stepparent's obligation of support. Respondent's argument is without merit. The *Gillaspie* court found that the Legislature intended to alter the common law obligation of *custodial* stepparents, making them liable for support until the legal termination of the marriage. *Van Dyke,* which determined that the Legislature did not intend to alter the common law obligation of *noncustodial* stepparents, did not overrule *Gillaspie.*

There is further authority to support DSHS's interpretation of the statute in Groves v. Department of Social & Health Servs., 42 Wash.App. 84, 709 P.2d 1213 (1985). In *Groves,* the marriage lasted only a short time before the parties separated. The husband argued that he should not be required to support the stepchildren after the separation. The court disagreed, holding that once the parties married, "Groves thereupon became obligated to support his stepchildren. That obligation continued until the marriage was legally dissolved." *Groves,* at 86, 709 P.2d 1213. Respondent concedes that *Groves* is directly contrary to his position, but asks that we decline to follow it. Because we believe that both *Gillaspie* and *Groves* were correctly decided, we adhere to those decisions.

The judgment of the trial court is reversed.

■ SCHOLFIELD, Acting C.J., and GROSSE, J., concur.

3. EQUITABLE CHILD SUPPORT OBLIGATION

M.H.B. v. H.T.B

Supreme Court of New Jersey, 1985
498 A.2d 775

■ PER CURIAM.

The members of the Court being equally divided, the judgment of the Appellate Division is affirmed.

■ HANDLER, J., concurring.

We have recently recognized that upon a divorce, one spouse may be obligated under principles of equitable estoppel to provide financial support for his or her stepchildren who are the children of the other spouse. Miller v. Miller, 97 N.J. 154, 167, 478 A.2d 351 (1984). In this appeal, we consider the circumstances that can give rise to an equitable estoppel forbidding a divorced stepparent from denying the validity of a previous voluntary commitment to provide financial support for a stepchild. The child in this case was born while the defendant was married to the child's mother. However, the defendant knew shortly after the child's birth that he probably was not her natural father. Nevertheless, throughout the marriage and for five years following the divorce, the defendant consistently conducted himself as the child's father, successfully gained the child's love and affection, and established himself as the little girl's parental provider of emotional and material support. Under such circumstances, I believe that the stepfather is obligated to provide continuing financial support for his stepchild.

The parties in this case (referred to by their initials or first names in order to protect the child who is the object of the controversy) were married in 1966. The couple settled in New Jersey where, during their first five years together, they conceived two sons, G.B. and M.B. The marriage turned sour during 1975, however, and sometime thereafter the plaintiff-wife, Marilyn, had a brief extra-marital affair. In 1977, while still married to the defendant-husband, Henry, Marilyn gave birth to a daughter, K.B.

Three months later, Henry first learned that he might not be K.B.'s biological father. He discovered a letter, or a diary entry, implicating Marilyn's former paramour as K.B.'s natural father. Henry then confronted Marilyn with this evidence of her infidelity, and moved out of the family residence. Following this separation, the marriage continued for almost three years. After living for six months in the same town as the rest of his family, however, Henry moved twice, first to California and then to Wisconsin, where he continues to live. During this period of separation, Henry maintained close bonds with all of the children, K.B. as well as the two sons, through phone calls, letters, gifts, and visits.

Marilyn also moved several times with the children. Between March and September 1978, she cohabitated with her erstwhile paramour, K.B.'s purported natural father, whom she briefly considered marrying. In December 1978, however, Marilyn brought herself and the children to Henry's home in Wisconsin, and for six months the parties attempted to reconcile their differences. Henry then professed to Marilyn that he would always love K.B., and that he did not want the child's illegitimacy to interfere with the couple's future together. . . . [I]n June 1979, the couple signed a separation agreement covering financial support obligations, child custody, and visitation. Marilyn assumed custody of all three children, then ages 2, 7, and 10, and Henry undertook to pay $600 per month as family support, based on his annual income of over $34,000 at a time when Marilyn had no income. Marilyn thereafter moved back to New Jersey with all three children. . . .

In March 1980, the couple obtained a divorce in Wisconsin under terms established by an extensive written settlement agreement. The parties, Henry as well as Marilyn, stipulated that all three children were born of the marriage. They further agreed that Marilyn would have custody of the children during the school year, and that Henry would get custody during the three summer months. Although at this point Henry earned about $51,000 each year while Marilyn still had no income, Henry promised only to continue paying $200 per month per child in Marilyn's custody. These payments would have totaled about $5,400 annually if three children had lived with their mother for nine months each year; however, by the parties' agreement, M.B. lived with his father for most of the post-divorce period, and therefore Henry's annual support obligation came to about $3,600. No alimony was awarded, and the couple's remaining, limited assets were divided in half.

All three minor children remained objects of Henry's affection, attention, and solicitude throughout the post-divorce period. In particular, Henry expressed interest in and concern for K.B. As found by the trial judge,

> K.B. bears Henry's surname, is registered on all of her records as bearing his surname, knows no other father, and is ignorant of the facts surrounding her paternity. Henry made innumerable representations to K.B. and to the world that he was her father. . . . The testimony related many tender moments between father and daughter. He sent her roses on her birthdays and comforted her in his bed during thunder and lightening storms.

Thus, Henry treated K.B. exactly as he treated his own son G.B., who was also in Marilyn's custody. Both K.B. and G.B. received Christmas gifts in 1979, 1980, and 1981. Further, Henry willingly provided child support payments on behalf of both children through the end of 1981. Based on all of the evidence, the trial judge concluded that Henry had become K.B.'s "psychological, if not biological parent."

Then, in March of 1981, Henry remarried. The following summer, both K.B. and G.B. visited and remained with Henry. By September 1981, however, Marilyn and Henry's second wife did not get along. The relationship between Marilyn and Henry deteriorated and Henry began withholding child support payments.

In January 1982 Henry petitioned a Wisconsin court to grant him custody of all three children, including K.B. The Wisconsin judge transferred the case to the New Jersey courts based on the children's best interests and the absence of local jurisdictional prerequisites. Marilyn filed a separate complaint, in March 1982, in New Jersey, seeking to retain custody of G.B. and K.B., and to obtain an increase in child support. Consistent with the petition he had filed in Wisconsin, Henry filed a counterclaim requesting custody of these children, K.B. as well as G.B. Later, by a pre-trial motion, Henry amended his counterclaim, claiming, in the alternative, that he should be under no duty to provide child support for K.B., and seeking to litigate the issue of the child's paternity. This was the first time that Henry had ever attempted to repudiate his paternal relationship with K.B. Without conceding Henry's right to contest paternity, Marilyn consented to allow the completion of Human Leucocyte Analysis blood test in December 1982. The results of the test excluded Henry as K.B.'s biological father.

A plenary hearing on the custody and support applications took place over several days in April and May of 1983. In addition to the foregoing facts, including Henry's knowledge in 1977 that he might not be K.B.'s natural father, the trial judge found that

> [i]t is clear Henry intended to be K.B.'s father and that she relied on that fact. . . . Even Henry's [second] wife . . . described Henry's relationship with K.B. as that of "a loving father-daughter relationship." . . . K.B. relied upon Henry's representations and has treated H.B. as her father, giving to him and receiving back from him all of the love and affection that the parent-child relationship should naturally evoke.
>
> Henry is certainly K.B.'s psychological, if not biological parent. . . . Henry is the only father K.B. knows or has ever known. . . . To permit Henry now to repudiate his intent to support K.B . . . would cause irreparable harm to the child.

Based on these findings, the trial judge concluded that the doctrine of equitable estoppel was applicable to preclude Henry from denying the duty to provide child support on behalf of K.B. This aspect of his decision was affirmed by a divided court in the Appellate Division, and presents the sole issue on the appeal that Henry filed with this Court as of right under *R.* 2:2–1(a).

The framework for analysis of the issue on this appeal is provided by Miller v. Miller, 97 N.J. 154, 478 A.2d 351 (1984). In that case, the Court recognized that the doctrine of equitable estoppel could properly be applied in the context of a matrimonial controversy in which the interests of individual children were at stake. Because we were dealing with responsibilities that may flow from familial relationships that are inherently complicated and subtle, we acknowledged that the application of equitable principles called for great sensitivity, caution, and flexibility.

The *Miller* case involved two girls whose mother remarried after divorcing their father. During the mother's second marriage the defendant, her second husband, assumed sole responsibility for the girls' financial support, as well as other parental privileges and obligations. He also discouraged his wife and stepchildren from maintaining any personal or financial relationship with the children's natural father. The second marriage ended in divorce after seven years, at which time the mother sought to receive continuing child support from the girls' stepfather.

The Court ruled in *Miller* that, before a duty of child support could be imposed based on equitable considerations, it must first be shown that, by a course of conduct, the stepparent affirmatively encouraged the child to rely and depend on the stepparent for parental nurture and financial support. We specifically recognized that such conduct could interfere with the children's relationship to their natural father. Under the facts, we held that the stepfather would be equitably estopped to deny his duty to continue to provide child support on behalf of his stepchildren, if it could be shown that the children would suffer financial harm if the stepparent were permitted to repudiate the parental obligations he had assumed. We further held that the natural father could continue to be legally liable for the support of these children.

Applying the principles set forth in *Miller,* the evidence in this case compels the imposition of equitable estoppel to prevent Henry from denying the duty to provide financial support for K.B. Henry's actions throughout the marriage and following the divorce constituted a continuous course of conduct toward the child that was tantamount to a knowing and affirmative representation that he would support her as would a natural father. By both deed and word, Henry repeatedly and consistently recognized and confirmed the parent-child relationship between himself and K.B. He acted in every way like a father toward his own child. He also stipulated to the child's paternity. At the time of his divorce he promised to pay child support, which obligation was incorporated into the judgment of divorce.

The volitional nature of Henry's conduct is underscored by Henry's persistent attempts to gain custody of K.B., efforts that he continued on appeal from the trial court's award of custody to Marilyn. He thus sought child custody even after blood tests conclusively demonstrated that, biologically, he was not K.B.'s father. Consequently, there can be no suggestion that Henry's prior actions were merely accidental or inadvertent. His actions attest to the previously well-developed father-daughter bond, and convey all possible indicia of an affirmative and purposeful representation of continuing support, which constitutes a primary element of equitable estoppel.

There was clearly reasonable reliance upon Henry's purposeful conduct. The obvious expectations engendered by Henry's conduct were that K.B. fully accepted and reasonably believed Henry to be her father. Significantly, the court found that Henry became K.B.'s psychological father, a finding that imports much more than mere affection. *See generally* Goldstein, Freud & Solnit, *Beyond the Best Interests of the Child* 9–28 (1973).... The parent-child bond thus serves to anchor the material and financial, as well as emotional, support that are vital to the well-being of a child. In this frame of reference, the critical factor is K.B.'s total filial dependence on Henry. Were Henry permitted to disavow the parent-child relationship that he created and fostered and to repudiate the parental responsibility that flowed from that relationship, K.B. would suffer demonstrable harm fully commensurate with her dependent condition. The detrimental character of reliance in such situations has led courts to impose an estoppel against a man whose wife gives birth to another man's child if the husband then knowingly "represents himself to both the child and the community as the natural father. . . ."

Defendant cites two reasons why he should not be responsible for his stepchild's financial support. He urges that the New Jersey Parentage Act, requires that if a man is found not to be a child's biological father, then he cannot be held liable to support that child, at least if the biological father may be identified. Defendant also contends that *Miller* stands for the proposition that Marilyn had a duty to bring the purported natural father into court and that, because she did not, we should remand to consider whether that person should be liable for K.B.'s support. Neither argument is persuasive.

With respect to the argument based on the New Jersey Parentage Act, N.J.S.A. 9:17–45a provides that "a man alleged . . . to be the father [of a child] . . . or any person with an interest recognized as justiciable by the court may bring . . . an action . . . for the purpose of determining the existence or nonexistence of the parent and child relationship." N.J.S.A. 9:17–45d further provides that "[r]egardless of its terms, an agreement, other than an agreement approved by the court in accordance with [N.J.S.A. 9:17–48c] between an alleged or presumed father and the mother of the child, shall not bar an action under this section." Henry alleges that these provisions shield him, as a stepparent, from child support obligations.

The statute, however, draws a distinction between paternity and the duty of support. The statute also recognizes the need for flexibility in determining child support. Thus, under N.J.S.A. 9:17–53c, after a court determines paternity and clarifies birth records, "[t]he judgment or order may contain any other provision directed against the *appropriate* party to the proceeding, concerning the duty of support, the custody . . . of the child, visitation privileges . . . or any other matter *in the best interests of the child.*" (Emphasis added.) This provision assures that in custody and support cases the children's best interests trump any determination of parentage. Clearly the Legislature did not intend to preclude the equitable imposition of a duty of child support upon a stepparent when the evidence assessed in accordance with principles of equity demand that result.

With respect to the other contention, in *Miller* there was undisputed evidence of a pre-existing and continuing relationship between the natural father and the daughters prior to the mother's remarriage to the defendant stepfather. There was also considerable testimony regarding the continuing viability of that relationship. In this case, by contrast there is no competent evidence as to K.B.'s natural parentage. Moreover, the uncontroverted testimony revealed no contact whatsoever between K.B. and her alleged natural father, nor any inkling on K.B.'s part that Henry was not her actual father. In addition there was evidence in *Miller* that the natural father had acknowledged in the past his financial ability and willingness to support his daughters. There is no comparable evidence in this case.

We recognized in *Miller* that a natural parent ordinarily is the primary source of financial support of a child, and that such a legal obligation is not abrogated by imposing a current obligation of child support upon a stepparent under principles of equitable estoppel. In that case, the Court felt it would be in the best interests of the child to consider whether the natural father, if available, should be made to honor his legal obligation to support his children. In this case, the circumstances are markedly different because no person, other than Henry, has ever emerged in K.B.'s life as her father.

A determination to affix a present obligation upon a stepfather does not in any way mean that we exonerate or condone a biological father who abdicates his responsibility to support his child. I fully acknowledge the statutory and common law requirement that the primary responsibility of child raising and support is that of the natural parent. Consequently, any decision to impose liability for child support on a stepparent must recognize the exceptional nature of such relief, as we have done in this case.

Notwithstanding the existence of exceptional circumstances and an equitable basis to impose a child support obligation on a child's stepparent, that relief remains mutable; it is subject to changing circumstances as these may affect the child's best interests. Indeed, in appropriate cases a stepparent, or any other person entitled to represent the interest of the child, may demonstrate the existence of changed circumstances justifying the assumption of liability for child support by the biological parent. That assumption of child support will be required if changed circumstances show that it would be in the best interest of the child, fair to the stepparent, and legally just as to the biological father.

The record in this case, however, does not present these issues, and hence we cannot deal with them further.

For the reasons expressed, I would affirm the judgment below. Chief Justice Wilentz and Justice O'Hern join in this opinion.

■ POLLOCK, J., (concurring in part and dissenting in part).

. . . Today's concurring opinion . . . would impose on a stepparent a duty of support not on the basis of estoppel but of a perceived emotional bonding between stepparent and child. From that premise, the opinion then proceeds to force the facts of the present case within its expanded interpretation of *Miller*.

I believe that the expansion of the *Miller* opinion is unwise and unnecessary. I further believe that the better practice would be to remand the matter to the Chancery Division for reconsideration in light of *Miller*. Pending that determination, I would continue to require Henry to support K.B. . . .

Notwithstanding the contentions of the concurring opinion to the contrary, the record is devoid of any proof that Henry directly interfered with the natural father's relationship with K.B. In this regard, the facts of the present case differ from those in *Miller,* where the stepparent actively interfered with the natural parent's attempt to support his children. For example, the stepfather in *Miller* tore up the natural father's support checks, which eventually induced the natural father to discontinue his support payments. Here, the natural father has never claimed K.B. as his child and has been content to allow Henry to support her. The tragic fact is that neither Henry nor the natural father has spent much time with K.B.

Although the concurrence purports to rely on *Miller v. Miller, supra,* it actually stands the *Miller* opinion on its head. *Miller* recognized "that in appropriate cases, the doctrine of equitable estoppel may be invoked to impose on a stepparent the duty to support a stepchild after a divorce from the child's natural parent." We admonished, however, that the doctrine was to be invoked "cautiously."

Accordingly, we held that a stepparent could be equitably estopped from denying an obligation to support a stepchild on proof of three conditions. First, the stepparent must have made a representation to either the children or the natural parent that he or she would provide support. Second, that representation must have been relied on by either the children or the natural parent. We declined to rely on these two conditions alone to establish estoppel because such a rule would penalize a "stepparent who tried to create a warm family atmosphere with his or her stepchildren." Consistent with that concern, we imposed a third condition, one that required a showing that "the children will suffer future financial detriment as a result of the stepparent's representation or conduct that caused the children to be cut off from their natural parent's financial support." Such financial detriment could be shown if the custodial parent cannot locate or does not know the whereabouts of the natural parent, or cannot obtain legal jurisdiction over the natural parent, and the natural parent's unavailability is attributable to the actions of the stepparent. Thus, a stepparent is responsible for the unavailability of a natural parent only when he or she takes "positive action interfering with the natural parent's support obligation." *Id.* at 170, 478 A.2d 351. Accordingly, in *Miller,* we remanded the matter to the trial court to determine whether the stepfather had detrimentally affected his stepchildren's ability to obtain future support by interfering with the children's relationship with the natural father. . . .

I continue to be counselled by *Miller's* warning not to impose a child-support obligation on a stepfather merely because he developed a close relationship with the stepchildren. Without further proof, I would not alter *Miller's* requirement that when the natural parent can be located and is financially able, he or she remains principally responsible to pay permanent child support.

The concurring opinion in the present case reflects the understandable desire to spare K.B. the painful knowledge that Henry is not her biological father. As painful as that discovery may be, however, it is inevitable that one day K.B. will learn the facts. For example, Marilyn has already revealed to G.B. and M.B., K.B.'s stepbrothers, the identity of K.B.'s natural father. In addition, Marilyn advises that she intends to inform K.B. at a later date that Henry is not her natural father. As well-intentioned as the concurrence may be, it cannot spare K.B. whatever anguish she will feel when she learns the identity of her natural father.

This case stands in stark contrast to *Miller,* where the evidence was that the stepparent actively resisted the natural father's attempt to maintain relations with his children. Here, the whereabouts of the natural father are known; he is in the next town. Most importantly, Henry has not done anything to interfere directly with the natural father's relationship with K.B. On the present record, the absence of financial support from the natural father is as attributable to his insouciance as it is to Henry's conduct.

In seeking an appropriate judicial response, I am guided, as are the concurring justices, by the best interests of the child. Like my colleagues who join in the concurring opinion, I believe that Henry is obliged to provide support for K.B., but I would require Henry to meet that obligation only until such time as a support order may be entered against the natural father. . . .

NOTES

Not all courts are willing to hold that a man of dubious parentage may, through a course of conduct, become equitably estopped from refusing to pay child support. For example, in K.B. v. D.B., 639 N.E.2d 725 (Mass. Ct. App.

1994), the facts illustrate how a man and a woman married and three years later a daughter was born. The couple had separated for a time at the start of their marriage and remained estranged after the wife admitted to a sexual relationship with another man. Hence, the husband doubted that he was the father of the girl but allowed his name to be placed on the birth certificate and for seven years supported the girl as a part of the family. He gave her presents, called her his daughter, and fostered a family relationship. Eventually, a court-ordered paternity test confirmed that the man could not be the father of the girl and when he and his wife divorced, he refused to pay child support. The court discusses the rationale for equitable estoppel, specifically that the man should not be able to change the fact that he voluntarily held a child out as his own and now seeks to disown the child to avoid paying child support. But in this case, the court holds that the man never truly voluntarily held himself out as the child's father. Instead, he consistently sought paternity testing and did all he could to prevent the birth of the girl and the establishment of paternity in himself. Lacking a voluntary assumption of parenthood, the man is not estopped from withholding child support.

By contrast, in S.R.D. v. T.L.B., 174 S.W.3d 502 (Ky. Ct. App. 2005), the court held that an ex-husband who held himself out for nine years as the father of a daughter born during his marriage was equitably estopped from denying paternity and child support obligations. He possessed constructive knowledge for over six years that he may not have been the father before seeking the paternity test that excluded him. Moreover, by holding himself out as the child's father for nine years, he prevented her from forming a relationship with her biological father, causing emotional and, potentially, financial detrimental reliance.

Equitable estoppel also has a role to play in child custody determinations. If a parent voluntarily allows a non-parent to assume the role of a parent, when is the parent equitably estopped from denying that non-parent a continuing parent-child relationship with a child? For commentary, *see, e.g.,* Samuel Johnson, Comment, *Are You My Mother? A Critique of the Requirements for De Facto parenthood in Maine Following the Law Court's Decision in Pitts v. Moore*, 67 ME. L. REV. 353 (2015); Gargi Sen & Tiffanie Tam, *Child Custody, Visitation & Termination of Parental Rights*, 16 GEO. J. GENDER & L. 41, 60–65 (2015); Kerry Abrams & R. Kent Piacenti, *Immigration Family Values*, 100 VA. L. REV. 629 (2014); Katherine T. Bartlett, *Prioritizing Past Caretaking in Child-Custody Decisionmaking*, 77 LAW & CONTEMP. PROBS. 29 (2014); Nancy D. Polikoff, *From Third Parties to Parents: The Case of Lesbian Couples and Their Children*, 77 LAW & CONTEMP. PROBS. 195 (2014).

I. FEDERALIZATION OF CHILD SUPPORT

Kansas v. United States

Tenth Circuit Court of Appeals, 2000
214 F.3d 1196

■ SEYMOUR, CHIEF JUDGE.

[The state of Kansas brought this action for declarative and injunctive relief following changes effectuated by the Personal Responsibility and Work Opportunity Reconciliation Act (PRWORA). The changes required state child support enforcement laws (IV-D) programs to meet certain federally-mandated standards in order for the state to receive block grants for the Temporary Assistance to Needy Families (TANF) program. TANF is a welfare program through which the states receive federal money and distribute it within the state to needy families.]

Kansas argues that the amended IV-D program requirements are too onerous and expensive, necessitate too much manpower, and encroach upon its ability to determine its own laws. Because of the amount of money at stake, Kansas contends it is being coerced into implementing the program requirements in violation of two provisions of the United States Constitution, specifically the Spending Clause of Article 1, § 8 and the Tenth Amendment. These claims are essentially mirror images of each other: if the authority to act has been delegated by the Constitution to Congress, then it may act pursuant to Article I; if not, the power has been reserved to the states by the Tenth Amendment. *See* New York v. United States, 505 U.S. 144, 156, 112 S.Ct. 2408, 120 L.Ed.2d 120 (1992). Because the legislation at issue was enacted pursuant to Congress' spending power, we will address the issue as arising under the Spending Clause.

A. *Spending Clause Challenges Generally*

Congress' spending power enables it "to further broad policy objectives by conditioning receipt of federal moneys upon compliance by the recipient with federal statutory and administrative directives." Fullilove v. Klutznick, 448 U.S. 448, 474, 100 S.Ct. 2758, 65 L.Ed.2d 902 (1980). The most instructive case on the Spending Clause issue is South Dakota v. Dole, 483 U.S. 203, 107 S.Ct. 2793, 97 L.Ed.2d 171 (1987), in which the Supreme Court upheld a legislative provision directing the Secretary of Transportation to withhold federal highway money from states refusing to raise their legal drinking age to 21.

The Court in *Dole* recognized four general restrictions on Congress' exercise of power under the Spending Clause. First, Congress' object must be in pursuit of "the general welfare." *Id.* at 207, 107 S.Ct. 2793. In considering whether an expenditure falls into this category, courts should defer substantially to the judgment of Congress. *See, e.g.,* Helvering v. Davis, 301 U.S. 619, 640–41, 57 S.Ct. 904, 81 L.Ed. 1307

(1937). Second, if Congress desires to place conditions on the state's receipt of federal funds, it must do so unambiguously so that states know the consequences of their decision to participate. *See* Dole, 483 U.S. at 207, 107 S.Ct. 2793. Third, the conditions must be related to the federal interest in the particular program. *See id.* The required degree of this relationship is one of reasonableness or minimum rationality. *See* New York, 505 U.S. at 167, 112 S.Ct. 2408 (conditions must "bear some relationship to the purpose of the federal spending"); *id.* at 172, 112 S.Ct. 2408 (conditions imposed are "reasonably related to the purpose of the expenditure"). Fourth, there can be no independent constitutional bar to the conditions. *See* Dole, 483 U.S. at 208, 107 S.Ct. 2793. The Tenth Amendment itself does not act as a constitutional bar; rather, the fourth restriction stands for the more general proposition that Congress may not induce the states to engage in activities that would themselves be unconstitutional. *See id.* at 210, 107 S.Ct. 2793.

Kansas does not seriously argue that the IV-D conditions in the PRWORA violate the four restrictions outlined in *Dole.* The first two restrictions are easily dispensed with. As the district court noted in its opinion below, the "general welfare" test is substantially deferential to Congress, and can clearly be met here.[4] And although contending that some of the requirements associated with the computerized database are vague, Kansas fails to assert that the alleged ambiguity resulted in its inability to exercise its choice to accept the funds knowingly and "cognizant of the consequences of . . . participation," as required by *Dole. Id.* at 207, 107 S.Ct. 2793 (citing Pennhurst State Sch. & Hosp. v. Halderman, 451 U.S. 1, 17, 101 S.Ct. 1531, 67 L.Ed.2d 694 (1981)). The PRWORA unambiguously attaches its many conditions to the TANF and IV-D funds, and Kansas does not claim it accepted the money without knowledge of those conditions.

Regarding the third *Dole* requirement, under which the conditions must be related to the federal interest in the program, Kansas asserts that the IV-D conditions are not sufficiently related to the larger TANF

---

[4] In its brief to this court, Kansas tries to downplay the seriousness of the problem of unpaid child support, perhaps in an attempt to argue that the general welfare requirement is not met. Kansas makes numerous references to "the perceived need to crack down on the elusive and rumored population of 'deadbeat dads' " "believed to be running from state to state," and the "rare" "so-called dead-beat dads allegedly fleeing from State to State," *Plaintiff's Br.* at 8, 10, 19, 29. These characterizations do nothing to advance Kansas' argument. Congress made clear that non-payment of child support, particularly in interstate cases, is a widespread problem which has significant deleterious effects on children, particularly those in low-income families. The changes in IV–D's requirements were made in response to the widespread belief that the system of pursuing child support across state lines was "far too sluggish to be effective" and "universally regarded as broken." H.R. Rep. No. 104–651, at 1405, *reprinted in* 1996 U.S.C.C.A.N. 2183, 2464. For example, Congress found that in 1992 only 54% of single-parent families with children had a child support order established and, of that 54%, only about one-half received the full amount due. 42 U.S.C. § 601 note. Only 18% of the cases enforced through the public child support enforcement system resulted in a collection. *Id.* Interstate cases represent almost 30% of all child support orders, yet yield only 10% of collections. *See* H.R. Rep. No. 104–651, at 1405, *reprinted in* 1996 U.S.C.C.A.N. 2183, 2464. While lawyers may legitimately debate the application of the laws which address the non-payment of child support, no one is served by denying the existence of the problem.

program. This contention is based on Justice O'Connor's dissent in *Dole,* in which she argued for a closer correlation between the funding condition and the federal interest, stating that the drinking age condition was "far too over and under-inclusive" in addressing the problem of drunk driving. *Id.* at 214–15, 218, 107 S.Ct. 2793 (O'Connor, J., dissenting). The majority in *Dole,* however, endorsed a much less demanding test and determined that the drinking age condition was reasonably related to the highway program because of the connection between the drinking age and highway fatalities.

The TANF program, which provides financial support for low-income families, is clearly related to the IV-D program and its requirements, which assist low-income families in collecting child support from absent parents. *See* H.R.Rep. No. 104–651, at 1410 (1996), *reprinted in,* 1996 U.S.C.C.A.N. 2183, 2469 (noting IV-D complements the TANF program because establishing paternity and collecting child support may enable families to reduce dependence on the welfare system). Indeed, child support enforcement was conceived of as a related component of the AFDC system. *See* S.Rep. No. 93–1356 (1974), *reprinted in,* 1974 U.S.C.C.A.N. 8133, 8145–48 (discussing the interrelationship between the welfare system and non-support of children by absent parents). It is no coincidence that the AFDC/TANF and the child support programs are both set forth in the same subchapter of the Social Security Act, which bears the heading "Grants to States for Aid and Services to Needy Families with Children and for Child-Welfare Services."[5]

Finally, Kansas makes a few cursory arguments to the effect that the United States is requiring it to violate the privacy and procedural due process rights of its citizens. These claims center around the requirements that the state keep a directory of new hires, and that it take automatic enforcement action against those parents found to be in arrears on child support. Neither of these arguments is developed in the brief, and neither appears to have merit. In fact, Congress has expressly required participating states to adopt safeguards to protect against the unauthorized use or disclosure of confidential information handled by a state child support enforcement agency. *See* 42 U.S.C. § 654(26). Moreover, the states are free to adopt other measures to protect the information they receive.

In general, Kansas bears a very heavy burden in seeking to have the PRWORA declared unconstitutional. There are no recent relevant instances in which the Supreme Court has invalidated a funding condition . . . On the other hand, there have been many cases in which the Supreme Court has upheld conditions placed on the receipt of federal funds. . . .

---

[5] As stated previously, child support enforcement falls under Subchapter IV, Part D of the statute. The TANF program is contained in Subchapter IV, Part A.

Federal courts of appeal have been similarly reluctant to invalidate funding conditions. For example, in Schweiker, 655 F.2d 401, the D.C. Circuit upheld Congress' conditioning of Medicaid funds on state implementation of a provision in the Supplemental Security Income program. *See also* California v. United States, 104 F.3d 1086 (9th Cir.1997) (upholding conditioning receipt of Medicaid funds on agreement to provide emergency medical services to illegal aliens); Padavan v. United States, 82 F.3d 23, 28–29 (2d Cir.1996) (same); Planned Parenthood v. Dandoy, 810 F.2d 984 (10th Cir.1987) (upholding Medicaid funding condition which required changes in state law regarding the provision of family planning advice to minors) (per curiam); New Hampshire v. Marshall, 616 F.2d 240 (1st Cir.1980) (upholding requirements in the Federal Unemployment Tax Act).

Virginia v. Riley, 106 F.3d 559 (4th Cir.1997) (en banc) (per curiam) (superseded by statute), represents the rare case in which a federal court invalidated a funding condition. In *Riley,* the Fourth Circuit found that conditions in the Individuals with Disabilities Education Act were not sufficiently clear and unambiguous to satisfy *Dole's* second requirement. Specifically, the court objected to conditions requiring every state to provide a free, appropriate education to learning disabled students, which the United States Department of Education later interpreted to apply even where school authorities had expelled a student for behavioral problems unrelated to the learning disability. Because we have determined that the conditions at issue in the present case do not violate *Dole's* ambiguity restriction, however, *Riley* is inapposite.

B. Coercion Theory

In addition to the four categorical restrictions, the Court in *Dole* articulated a fifth, indistinct limit on the spending power: "[I]n some circumstances the financial inducement offered by Congress might be so coercive as to pass the point at which 'pressure turns into compulsion.' " Dole, 483 U.S. at 211, 107 S.Ct. 2793 (quoting Steward Mach. Co. v. Davis, 301 U.S. 548, 590, 57 S.Ct. 883, 81 L.Ed. 1279 (1937)). It is this coercion theory upon which Kansas primarily relies. The crux of Kansas' argument is that the size of its IV-D and TANF grants, totalling over $130 million, leaves it no choice but to accept the PRWORA's many requirements. In this connection, Kansas correctly argues that the Court in *Dole* specifically pointed out that the federal government there was only threatening to withhold 5% of South Dakota's federal highway funds:

> When we consider . . . that all South Dakota would lose if she adheres to her chosen course as to a suitable minimum drinking age is 5% of the funds otherwise obtainable under specified highway grant programs, the argument as to coercion is shown to be more rhetoric than fact.

Id.

This passage does not get Kansas far. It is merely an instance in which the Court acknowledged circumstances *not* sufficient to constitute coercion. In fact, the cursory statements in *Steward Machine* and *Dole* mark the extent of the Supreme Court's discussion of a coercion theory.[7] The Court has never employed the theory to invalidate a funding condition, and federal courts have been similarly reluctant to use it. "The coercion theory has been much discussed but infrequently applied in federal case law, and never in favor of the challenging party." Nevada v. Skinner, 884 F.2d 445, 448 (9th Cir.1989). Most of the treatment given the theory in the federal courts has been negative.

The boundary between incentive and coercion has never been made clear, and courts have found no coercion in situations where similarly large amounts of federal money were at stake. For example, numerous courts have upheld conditions on Medicaid grants even where the removal of Medicaid funding would devastate the state's medical system. In Schweiker, 655 F.2d 401, Oklahoma argued that the threat of losing all Medicaid funding was so drastic that it had no choice but to comply in order to prevent the collapse of its medical system. The D.C. Circuit stated: "[t]he courts are not suited to evaluating whether the states are faced here with an offer they cannot refuse or merely with a hard choice. . . . We therefore follow the lead of other courts that have explicitly declined to enter this thicket when similar funding conditions have been at issue." *Id.* at 414. *See also* California, 104 F.3d 1086 (conditioning receipt of Medicaid funds); Padavan, 82 F.3d at 28–29 (same); Planned Parenthood v. Dandoy, 810 F.2d 984 (upholding Medicaid funding condition). *But see* Virginia v. Riley, 106 F.3d at 561 (noting in dicta that a "substantial constitutional question under the Tenth Amendment would be presented," if the provision were not already being struck down on ambiguity grounds, because it "resembles impermissible coercion").

In any event, the coercion theory is unclear, suspect, and has little precedent to support its application. Indeed, in *Steward Machine,* the first case to articulate the coercion theory, the Court minimized its force, observing, "to hold that motive or temptation is equivalent to coercion is to plunge the law in endless difficulties. The outcome of such a doctrine is the acceptance of a philosophical determinism by which choice becomes impossible." 301 U.S. at 589–90, 57 S.Ct. 883. For all these reasons, we hold that the conditioning of TANF funds on Kansas' compliance with the requirements contained in IV-D does not present a situation of impermissible coercion. . . .[8]

---

[7] The Court also acknowledged the coercion theory in passing in *College Sav. Bank v. Florida Prepaid Postsecondary Educ. Expense Bd.,* 527 U.S. 666, 119 S.Ct. 2219, 2231, 144 L.Ed.2d 605 (1999). The Court merely quoted the language from *Dole* and *Steward Machine* but did not have an occasion to apply it.

[8] Moreover, IV–D contains a "safety valve" provision which allows states to be exempted from requirements that will not increase the effectiveness and efficiency of their CSE programs.

Kansas has invited us to forge new ground in Spending Clause jurisprudence by invalidating the child support enforcement conditions Congress attached to its social welfare funding program. In doing so, it asks that we expand the concept of "coercion" as it applies to relations between the state and federal governments, and find a large federal grant accompanied by a set of conditional requirements to be coercive because of the powerful incentive it creates for the states to accept it. We decline the invitation. In this context, a difficult choice remains a choice, and a tempting offer is still but an offer. If Kansas finds the IV-D requirements so disagreeable, it is ultimately free to reject both the conditions and the funding, no matter how hard that choice may be. *See* Kathleen M. Sullivan, Unconstitutional Conditions, 102 HARV. L.REV. 1413, 1428 (May 1989) (discussing the resilience of the argument that "offers of conditioned benefits expand rather than contract the options of the beneficiary class, and so present beneficiaries with a free choice"). Put more simply, Kansas' options have been increased, not constrained, by the offer of more federal dollars.

The requirements contained in IV-D represent a reasoned attempt by Congress to ensure that its grant money is used to further the state and federal interest in assisting needy families, in part through improved child support enforcement. This is a valid exercise of Congress' spending power, and the requirements do not render the PRWORA unconstitutional.

We AFFIRM the judgment of the district court.

NOTES

Federal Involvement. In 2015, only 65% of child support due was actually collected by recipients. U.S. DEP'T OF HEALTH & HUMAN SERVICES, ADMINISTRATION FOR CHILDREN & FAMILIES, OFFICE OF CHILD SUPPORT ENFORCEMENT, *Child Support Enforcement FY 2015: Preliminary Report* (2015), at http://www.acf.hhs.gov/css/resource/fy-2015-preliminary-data-report.

Given federal welfare programs to support needy families, like TANF, it is not surprising that federal involvement in the area of child support enforcement has increased significantly during the past four decades. While cases like *Kansas* grapple with federal regulations that primarily impact individuals on public assistance, we will see later in this chapter that states have also put in place a number of mechanisms to assist individuals who are not on public assistance to recover child support due. Federal attempts to increase child support enforcement stretch back for decades.

The Child Support and Establishment of Paternity amendments of 1974 and 1975 to Title IV of the Social Security Act added sharper teeth to the existing state law framework for support enforcement. The stated purposes of that legislation were "enforcing the support obligations owed by absent parents to their children, locating absent parents, establishing paternity,

---

See 42 U.S.C. § 666(d). In light of this, Kansas' prediction that it will be forced to labor under a cumbersome and byzantine set of regulations appears to be overstated.

and obtaining child support. . . ." 42 U.S.C.A. § 651 (2016). A separate organizational unit, established by the Secretary of the Department of Health and Human Services, was charged with monitoring state performance under these duties. 42 U.S.C.A. § 653 (2016).

A key feature of the law was a waiver of sovereign immunity by the United States with regard to child support or alimony payments due from federal employees, including service persons, thereby making it possible to subject federal salaries to garnishment proceedings. *Id.* at § 659. Another provision authorized suits in federal court to enforce such orders. *Id.* at § 652(a)(8). Under another provision, states could establish a mechanism for referring certain delinquent, court-ordered support payments to the Secretary of the Treasury for collection when they have been assigned to a state with an approved plan and diligent efforts to collect have been made. *Id.* at § 652(b); *see also* 26 U.S.C.A. § 6305 (2016).

Even though the 1974 and 1975 acts operate within the sphere of state-federal cooperation, as many public assistance programs do, they nevertheless constituted a substantial federal step into the family law field. In this regard, the acts' provisions on what a state plan for child and spousal support must include is of special impact. *See* 42 U.S.C.A. § 654 (2016). The goal of paring welfare expenditures has obviously provided the basis for such a role.

The Child Support Enforcement Amendments of 1984 took a further step toward dealing with child support on a national basis by effectively requiring states to enact more stringent enforcement legislation. Pub. L. No. 98–378, 98 Stat. 1305 (1984). Key among the latter is the establishment of nonbinding support guidelines to be made available to judges, discussed above.

The Family Support Act of 1988 introduced further changes, many of which benefited persons not on public assistance. Pub. L. No. 100–485, 102 Stat. 2343 (1988). The 1988 Act made adherence to established support guidelines the rule rather than an exception—by creating the rebuttable presumption that requires a specific finding that a given application of the guidelines would be "unjust or inappropriate in a particular case," discussed extensively above in order to depart from the guidelines. The 1988 Act introduced "performance standards" for state paternity establishment programs and required wage withholding to begin sooner after default. Automatic tracking and monitoring systems were made mandatory, and beginning in 1992 states had to meet federal standards for establishing paternity for nonmarital children. The 1988 Act created a special Commission on Interstate Child Support Enforcement.

A stream of federal legislation designed to increase the receipt of past due child support followed these initial acts. The Omnibus Budget Reconciliation Act of 1990, 42 U.S.C. §§ 664, 666 (2016), required the Internal Revenue Service to collect child support arrearages of $500 or more when requested by a state. The Child Support Recovery Act of 1992, 18 U.S.C. § 228 (2016) and 42 U.S.C. § 3796cc (2016), criminalized the willful failure to pay child support for a child in another state, where past-due support was unpaid for over one year or exceeded $5,000. The Full Faith and Credit for Child Support Orders Act of 1994 (FFCCSOA), 28 U.S.C. § 1738B (2011), required each state to enforce the child support orders of other states and prohibited modification of the orders from other states unless certain jurisdictional requirements were met. The Bankruptcy Reform Act of 1994, 11 U.S.C. § 523(a)(5), (15) (2016), enabled a person who was due alimony and child support to prevent discharge of those obligations by the obligor in bankruptcy. The Personal Responsibility and Work Opportunity Reconciliation Act of 1996 (PRWORA), 42 U.S.C. §§ 652–666 (2016), the subject of the *Kansas* suit, mandated the creation of state and federal child support case registries, as well as a registry of new hires by employers which would then be cross-referenced against the child support registries. PRWORA also required the adoption of the Uniform Interstate Family Support Act, discussed *infra*, and authorized liens on professional and occupational licenses, while expanding the services of the Federal Parent Locator Service.

PRWORA ended the federal government's Aid to Families with Dependent Children program that provided income to poor children and their parent or parents, and replaced it with TANF, which gives capped block grants to the states to assist low-income families. The states may also receive block grants for child care and social services as well as high performance grants for success in reducing the number of nonmarital children and placing welfare recipients in paid employment. *See generally* Louis Kaplow & Steven Shavell, *Fairness Versus Welfare*, 114 HARV. L. REV. 961–1388 (2001); Cary LaCheen, *Using Title II of the Americans With Disabilities Act on Behalf of Clients in TANF Programs*, 8 GEO. J. ON POVERTY L. & POL'Y 1 (2001); Parvin R. Huda, *Singled Out: A Critique of the Representation of Single Motherhood in Welfare Discourse*, 7 WM. & MARY J. WOMEN AND L. 341 (2001); THOMAS MASSARO, CATHOLIC SOCIAL TEACHING AND UNITED STATES WELFARE REFORM (1998).

More recently, the Deadbeat Parents Punishment Act of 1998, 18 U.S.C. § 228 (2016), amended the Child Support Recovery Act of 1992 to provide harsher punishment for chronic failure to pay child support. Pub. L. No. 102–2521, 106 Stat. 3403 (1992). Later, in 2005, Congress reauthorized TANF in the Deficit Reduction Act of 2005 and imposed new, more restrictive enforcement measures on the states. For example, the 2005 Act reduced the threshold for denying a passport to an applicant as a result of child support arrearages. The Deficit Reduction Act of 2005, Pub. L. No. 109–171, 120 Stat. 4 (2005). It also created an additional fee when the state assists with child support collection, which may be paid by the state or passed onto the child support recipient. *Id.* at § 7310.

Coercion Analysis. The coercion claim raised in *Kansas* also figured prominently in the 2012 U.S. Supreme Court ruling on the constitutionality of the federal health care reform law, the Patient Protection and Affordable Care Act (ACA). The Supreme Court upheld parts of the ACA, while striking others as unconstitutional. *See* Nat'l Fed'n of Indep. Bus. v. Sebelius, 132 S.Ct. 2566 (2012). The Court held that it is unconstitutional coercion, in violation of the Tenth Amendment, for the federal government to withhold all current federal Medicaid funding if a state fails to comply with the ACA's Medicaid expansion. As Chief Justice Roberts noted, "Nothing in our opinion precludes Congress from offering funds under the ACA to expand the availability of health care, and requiring that states accepting such funds comply with the conditions on their use. What Congress is not free to do is to penalize states that choose not to participate in that new program by taking away their existing Medicaid funding." *Id.* at 2607.

Courts have not yet had the opportunity to determine how this analysis applies to similar federal child support enforcement laws. Unlike the penalty discussed in *Kansas*, federal Medicaid funds make up as much as 20% or more of a state's budget, which, had the Medicaid expansion penalties been upheld, would have left states without any meaningful option except to adopt the ACA's federal Medicaid expansion. The funding at issue in *Kansas* was a significantly smaller part of the state's budget and so constitute the kind of impermissible coercion at issue in *Sebelius*.

J. THE SCOPE OF PREMARITAL CONTRACTING

Spouses and prospective spouses often enter into three very different types of contracts: Premarital contracts in contemplation of marriage; marital agreements made during the intact relationship; and separation agreements or divorce settlement agreements when dissolving the couple's marriage. As Professor Brian Bix explains:

> Premarital agreements, also called "antenuptial" and "prenuptial" agreements, are entered into when marriage is imminent, to settle, create, or modify certain rights between the parties during their marriage, upon the death of one of the partners, or upon divorce. . . .
>
> "[M]arital agreements" cover[ ] any agreement between the spouses entered after marriage, but not in contemplation of separation or imminent divorce. This usually means an agreement which purports to affect significantly the property rights of the spouses during the marriage or after, or alimony claims after divorce. . . .
>
> Separation agreements are agreements entered into when legal separation or divorce is imminent, with the purpose of settling the terms of the dissolution. In the vast majority of divorces, an estimated 75 percent, the terms of divorce are settled by the parties "in the shadow of the law" [by the couple's agreement].

Brian Bix, *The ALI Principles and Agreements: Seeking a Balance between Status and Contract*, in RECONCEIVING THE FAMILY: CRITIQUE ON THE AMERICAN LAW INSTITUTE'S PRINCIPLES OF THE LAW OF FAMILY DISSOLUTION 372, 382, 387 (Robin Fretwell Wilson, ed., 2006).

This Section primarily explores premarital agreements. Section K will discuss marital and divorce settlement agreements. Premarital agreements long were used primarily by wealthy (and often older) persons to assure that their separate estates would be passed along family or other lines of their choice. However, objection to some of the economic and legal incidents of marriage also led to far greater use of premarital agreements. Other factors that contributed to their increased use include (1) female and male role changes regarding property management and career choices, (2) popular awareness that marriages may not last for life, and therefore it may be advisable to plan for dissolution before the tensions of marital discord make negotiating more difficult, (3) desire of the parties to retain their separate identities, and (4) clearer delineation and expansion of the permissible legal scope of such contracts.

Lawyers typically view premarital agreements as dealing largely with matters of property and alimony. Agreements drafted by the individual parties address other matters ranging from their proposed relationships with third persons (including other family members) to their personal habits. Because not all such provisions are legally enforceable, problems of interpretation and even overall validity of such agreements may arise when a marriage breaks down.

Although not discussed further here, many of the subjects touched on as possible items for inclusion in premarital agreements might just as easily be included in contracts between cohabitants. The California Supreme Court's decision in *Marvin v. Marvin* makes it important to consider the potential legal impact of cohabitation in the absence of an express agreement. Notably, the American Academy of Matrimonial Lawyers is in the process of creating a model cohabitation agreement. *See* http://www.AAML.org.

Many older cases focus on whether premarital agreements that seem unfair or seem to have resulted from overreaching conduct should be invalidated. Some of these decisions now appear to be obsolete because of their presumptions concerning relative disabilities and disadvantages based on sex. A newer group of cases centers on the permissible scope of the parties' rearrangement of the traditional legal incidents of marriage, as well as whether and when there should be economic obligations after dissolution.

Statutes based on the Uniform Premarital Agreement Act (UPAA) and the newer Uniform Premarital and Marital Agreements Act (UPMAA), both put forward by the National Conference of Commissioners on Uniform State Laws (NCCUSL), have given parties great latitude to order their marital rights and duties by contract in advance of (and during) marriage. Because of the variation in approaches, it is important to understand the differing frameworks that continue to coexist.

The UPAA, promulgated in 1983, has been adopted by 24 states and the District of Columbia (Arizona, Arkansas, California, Connecticut, Delaware, Florida, Hawaii, Idaho, Illinois, Indiana, Iowa, Kansas, Maine, Montana, Nebraska, Nevada, New Mexico, North Carolina,

Oregon, Rhode Island, South Dakota, Texas, Utah, and Virginia) and has been proposed as legislation in Mississippi, Missouri, South Carolina, and West Virginia.

The UPAA provided a framework for evaluating only premarital agreements. More recently, in 2012, NCCUSL released the UPMAA to bring premarital and marital agreements into a single framework for deciding questions of enforcement. The UPMAA replaces the UPAA and so is the focus of this Section. The UPMAA has been adopted by Colorado and North Dakota. *See* West's C.R.S.A. §§ 14–2–301 to 14–2–311 (2016); West's NORTH DAKOTA CENTURY CODE ANN. 14–03.2–01 to 14–03.2–11 (2016).

UNIFORM PREMARITAL AND MARITAL AGREEMENTS ACT (2012)

SECTION 1. SHORT TITLE. This [act] may be cited as the Uniform Premarital and Marital Agreements Act.

SECTION 2. DEFINITIONS. In this [act]:

(1) "Amendment" means a modification or revocation of a premarital agreement or marital agreement.

(2) "Marital agreement" means an agreement between spouses who intend to remain married which affirms, modifies, or waives a marital right or obligation during the marriage or at separation, marital dissolution, death of one of the spouses, or the occurrence or nonoccurrence of any other event. The term includes an amendment, signed after the spouses marry, of a premarital agreement or marital agreement.

(3) "Marital dissolution" means the ending of a marriage by court decree. The term includes a divorce, dissolution, and annulment.

(4) "Marital right or obligation" means any of the following rights or obligations arising between spouses because of their marital status:

(A) spousal support;

(B) rights to property, including characterization, management, and ownership;

(C) responsibility for liabilities;

(D) rights to property and responsibility for liabilities at separation, marital dissolution, or death of a spouse; or

(E) allocation and award of attorney's fees and costs.

(5) "Premarital agreement" means an agreement between individuals who intend to marry which affirms, modifies, or waives a marital right or obligation during the marriage or at separation, marital dissolution, death of one of the

spouses, or the occurrence or nonoccurrence of any other event. The term includes an amendment, signed before the individuals marry, of a premarital agreement.

(6) "Property" means anything that may be the subject of ownership, whether real or personal, or legal or equitable, or any interest therein.

(7) "Record" means information that is inscribed on a tangible medium or that is stored in an electronic or other medium and is retrievable in perceivable form.

(8) "Sign" means with present intent to authenticate or adopt a record:

(A) to execute or adopt a tangible symbol; or

(B) to attach to or logically associate with the record an electronic symbol, sound, or process.

(9) "State" means a state of the United States, the District of Columbia, Puerto Rico, the United States Virgin Islands, or any territory or insular possession subject to the jurisdiction of the United States.

SECTION 3. SCOPE.

(a) This [act] applies to a premarital agreement or a marital agreement signed on or after [the effective date of this [act]].

(b) This [act] does not affect any right, obligation, or liability arising under a premarital agreement or marital agreement signed before [the effective date of this [act]].

(c) This [act] does not apply to:

(1) an agreement between spouses affirming, modifying, or waiving marital rights or obligations which requires court approval to become effective; or

(2) an agreement between spouses intending to obtain a marital dissolution or court-decreed separation which resolves their marital rights or obligations and is signed when a proceeding for marital dissolution or court-decreed separation is anticipated or pending.

(d) The application of this [act] to the waiver of a marital right or obligation in a transfer or conveyance of property by a spouse to a third party does not adversely affect the rights of a bona fide purchaser for value.

SECTION 4. GOVERNING LAW. The validity, enforceability, interpretation, and construction of a premarital agreement or marital agreement are determined:

(1) by the law of the jurisdiction designated in the agreement if the jurisdiction has a significant relationship to the

agreement or either party, and the designated law is not contrary to a fundamental public policy of this state; or

(2) absent an effective designation described in paragraph (1), by the law of this state, including the choice of law rules of this state.

SECTION 5. PRINCIPLES OF LAW AND EQUITY. Unless displaced by the provisions of this Act, principles of law and equity supplement the provisions of this Act.

SECTION 6. FORMATION REQUIREMENTS. A premarital agreement or marital agreement must be in a record signed by both parties. The agreement is enforceable without consideration.

SECTION 7. WHEN AGREEMENT EFFECTIVE. A premarital agreement is effective on marriage. A marital agreement is effective on signing by both parties.

SECTION 8. VOID MARRIAGE. If a marriage is determined to be void, a premarital agreement or marital agreement is enforceable to the extent necessary to avoid an inequitable result.

SECTION 9. ENFORCEMENT.

(a) A premarital agreement or marital agreement is unenforceable if a party against whom enforcement is sought proves any of the following:

(1) the party's consent to the agreement was involuntary or the result of duress;

(2) the party did not have access to independent legal representation under subsection (b);

(3) unless the party had independent legal representation at the time the agreement was signed, the agreement did not include a notice of waiver of rights under subsection (c) or an explanation in plain language of the marital rights or obligations being modified or waived by the agreement; or

(4) before signing the agreement, the party did not receive adequate financial disclosure under subsection (d).

(b) Access to independent legal representation under this section requires that:

(1) the party had a reasonable time both to:

(A) decide whether to retain an independent lawyer before signing a premarital agreement or marital agreement and

(B) locate an independent lawyer, obtain advice, and consider the advice provided; and

(2) if the other party was represented by a lawyer, either the party had the financial ability to retain a lawyer or the other party agreed to pay the reasonable fees and expenses of representation.

(c) A notice of waiver of rights under this section requires language, conspicuously displayed, substantially similar to the following, as applicable to the agreement:

If you sign this agreement, you may be:

Giving up your right to be supported by the person you are marrying or to whom you are married.

Giving up your right to ownership or control of money and property.

Agreeing to pay bills and debts of the person you are marrying or to whom you are married.

Giving up your right to money and property if your marriage ends or the person to whom you are married dies.

Giving up your right to have your legal fees paid.

(d) Adequate financial disclosure under this section requires that:

(1) the party received a reasonably accurate description and good faith estimate of value of the property, liabilities, and income of the other party;

(2) the party expressly waived, in a separate signed record, the right to financial disclosure beyond the disclosure provided; or

(3) the party had adequate knowledge or a reasonable basis for having adequate knowledge of the information required to be disclosed in subsection (d)(1).

(e) If a premarital agreement or marital agreement modifies or eliminates spousal support and the modification or elimination causes a party to the agreement to be eligible for support under a program of public assistance at the time of separation or marital dissolution, a court, on request of that party, may require the other party to provide support to the extent necessary to avoid that eligibility.

(f) A court may refuse to enforce a term of a premarital agreement or marital agreement if, in the context of the agreement taken as a whole[:]

[(1)] the term was unconscionable at the time of signing [; or

(2) enforcement of the term would result in substantial hardship for a party because of a material change in

circumstances arising since the agreement was signed].

(g) The court shall decide a question of unconscionability [or substantial hardship] under subsection (f) as a matter of law.

SECTION 10. UNENFORCEABLE TERMS.

(a) In this section, "custodial responsibility" includes physical or legal custody, parenting time, access, visitation, or other custodial right or duty with respect to a child.

(b) A term in a premarital or marital agreement is not enforceable to the extent that it:

(1) adversely affects a child's right to support;

(2) limits or restricts a remedy available to a victim of domestic violence under law of this state other than this [act];

(3) purports to modify the grounds for a court-decreed separation or marital dissolution available under law of this state other than this [act]; or

(4) penalizes a party for initiating a legal proceeding leading to a court-decreed separation or marital dissolution.

(c) A term in a premarital agreement or marital agreement that defines the rights or duties of the parties regarding custodial responsibility is not binding on a court.

SECTION 11. LIMITATION OF ACTION. A statute of limitations applicable to an action asserting a claim for relief under a premarital agreement or marital agreement is tolled during the marriage of the parties to the agreement, but equitable defenses limiting the time for enforcement, including laches and estoppel, are available to either party.

[Omitting Sections 12 through 15 addressing effective date, repeal of prior acts, electronic signatures, and uniformity of construction]

NOTES

The UPMAA uses a single framework for deciding questions of enforcement of premarital and marital agreements. NCCUSL expanded the UPMAA to encompass both types of agreements because most states have laws concerning the creation and enforcement of premarital agreements, but few states have case law or legislation on the creation and enforcement of marital agreements. Moreover, NCCUSL worried that laws governing the enforcement of premarital agreements varied from state to state, creating uncertainty when couples move between states.

The UPMAA provides five notable grounds for challenging marital and premarital agreements. *See* Turney P. Berry & Barbara A. Atwood, *The*

Uniform Premarital and Marital Agreements Act, 151 TRUSTS. & EST. 13–14 (Sept. 2012). First, no agreement may be enforced against a party if that individual did not have access to independent legal representation. UPMAA § 9(a)(2). Second, no agreement may be enforced against a party who lacked adequate financial disclosure unless the party waives financial disclosure or receives an explanation in plain language of the rights being modified or waived. § 9(a)(3). Third, no agreement may be enforced against a party who did not receive adequate financial disclosure. § 9(a)(4). Fourth, no agreement may be enforced against a party whose consent was involuntary or resulted from duress. § 9(a)(1). Fifth, Section 9(f)(1), like the UPAA before it, would permit courts to refuse to enforce an agreement if it is unconscionable at the time of signing. The UPMAA creates a sixth optional ground for invalidating the agreement—namely, when enforcement would create a substantial hardship due to a material change in circumstances after signing. § 9(f)(2).

Like the UPAA before it, the UPMAA makes unenforceable any agreement that contains certain provisions. No agreement may be enforced if it adversely affects child support or purports to dictate any custody arrangements. UPMAA §§ 10(b)(1); § 10(c). The UPMAA further bars enforcement of an agreement that limits remedies (a) in the event of domestic violence, (b) penalizes a party for filing for divorce, or (c) modifies the grounds for dissolution under state law, limiting access to divorce. Thus, an agreement would be unenforceable if the parties sought to mimic with their private agreement a "covenant marriage" by setting a minimum length of time prior to filing for divorce. §§ 10(b)(2)–(4).

Other noticeable changes from the UPAA include an expanded definitions section, a more explicit notice of waiver section with specific suggested text, and detailed requirements for independent legal representation and adequate financial disclosure.

In addition to NCCUSL, the American Law Institute has made recommendations in its PRINCIPLES OF THE LAW OF FAMILY DISSOLUTION to govern premarital agreements. The ALI provisions specifically state that they could be applicable to domestic partnerships and civil unions. *See generally* ALI, PRINCIPLES OF THE LAW OF FAMILY DISSOLUTION: ANALYSIS AND RECOMMENDATIONS, Chapter 7 (2000). Both the NCCUSL and ALI recommendations would require that for a premarital agreement to be valid, it must (1) be in writing and signed by both of the parties; (2) that the agreement may affect the property of the parties in the context of marital dissolution or death, even allowing the parties to eliminate support obligations; (3) result from voluntary actions; (4) be based on full and fair disclosure with reasonable opportunity to adequately acquire knowledge of the property or financial obligations of the other party; and (5) if the subsequent marriage is declared void, the agreement is enforceable only to the extent necessary to avoid an inequitable result. *See, e.g.*, Jeffrey A. Parness, *Parentage Prenups and Midnups,* 31 GA. ST. U. L. REV. 343 (2015). Additionally, the UPAA and UPMAA create a rebuttable presumption that the agreement is valid. The ALI takes the position that the agreement is presumptively valid only if the agreement was entered into (1) at least 30 days prior to the actual marriage, partnership or union; (2) both parties were advised to obtain independent counsel and had opportunity to do so; and (3) if there was no independent counsel obtained, the agreement is written in such a way that persons of ordinary intelligence with no legal training could understand any adverse consequences that would occur because of the agreement. ALI PRINCIPLES §§ 7.04, 7.05, 7.04(c). Attorneys representing couples or persons executing the agreements must be careful to provide full and adequate disclosure, the opportunity to consult with legal counsel, address the possibility of future events, and consider the timing of the agreement in reference to the wedding or similar ceremony. Failure to be attentive to these issues may result in disciplinary or malpractice action against the attorney. *See, e.g.,* Antone v. Mirviss, 694 N.W.2d 564 (Minn. Ct. App. 2005) (successfully suing attorney for malpractice sixteen years after drafting a faulty premarital agreement), *rev'd for other grounds,* 720 N.W.2d 331 (Minn. 2006).

Blige v. Blige

Supreme Court of Georgia, 2008
656 S.E.2d 822

■ SEARS, CHIEF JUSTICE.

Meagan Taylor Blige filed a complaint for divorce against Willie Alonzo Blige in 2005. The trial court set aside the parties' antenuptial agreement based on Mr. Blige's failure to make a fair and complete disclosure of his assets, income, and liabilities, and the jury returned a verdict awarding Ms. Blige $160,000 representing her equitable interest in the marital home. Mr. Blige filed an application for discretionary review, which this Court granted pursuant to its pilot project in family law cases. We have determined that the trial court did not err in setting aside the antenuptial agreement for non-disclosure and that the jury did not err in awarding Ms. Blige $160,000 as her equitable interest in the marital property. Accordingly, we affirm.

The Bliges had a child together in 1994 and married in 2000. They did not live together before the marriage. The day before the wedding, Mr. Blige took his bride-to-be to an office building to meet with an attorney he had hired for her. The attorney handed her a fully drafted antenuptial agreement, read through it with her, and asked her to sign it, which she did. Mr. Blige signed the antenuptial agreement later, and the parties were married the following day as scheduled.

The antenuptial agreement provided that Mr. Blige would retain as his sole and separate property 19.5 acres of land in Bryan County that he had previously purchased "together with any house or structure which may be situated upon said property." There was no house or structure situated on the property when the parties married, but Mr. Blige had hidden away $150,000 in cash that he planned to use to build a home there after the wedding. Ms. Blige knew Mr. Blige worked as a delivery truck driver and approximately what he made. However, Mr. Blige never told Ms. Blige about the $150,000 in cash, and she had no knowledge of the money from any other source.

On July 26, 2005, Ms. Blige filed a complaint for divorce in the Bryan County Superior Court. In his answer and counterclaim, Mr. Blige sought enforcement of the antenuptial agreement. Ms. Blige moved to have it set aside for failure to comply with the legal requirements for antenuptial agreements, and the trial court conducted a pretrial evidentiary hearing on the issue. After hearing from both Mr. Blige and Ms. Blige, the trial court found as fact that Mr. Blige failed to make a fair and clear disclosure of his income, assets, and liabilities to Ms. Blige before the execution of the antenuptial agreement. On November 7, 2006, the trial court entered an order setting aside the antenuptial agreement, and a jury trial on property division ensued.

The evidence before the jury showed that Mr. Blige put the $150,000 in cash he had concealed from Ms. Blige toward the construction of an enormous home on the Bryan County property. The cost to complete the construction of the home was approximately $280,000, and by the time of trial, it was worth approximately $375,000 to $400,000. At the conclusion of the evidence, the jury returned a verdict awarding Mr. Blige the Bryan County property and house minus $160,000 to be paid to Ms. Blige representing her equitable interest in the marital property. The jury assigned each party the debts held in his or her own name and held that Mr. Blige would be responsible for the mortgage on the house. On February 15, 2007, the trial court entered a final judgment and decree of divorce incorporating the jury's equitable division of the marital property. Mr. Blige appealed.

Until 1982, antenuptial agreements were unenforceable in Georgia divorce proceedings as being contrary to public policy. Then, in *Scherer v. Scherer,* this Court concluded that Georgia courts were no longer justified in applying a rule of per se invalidity to antenuptial agreements entered into in contemplation of divorce. At the same time, we recognized the importance of marriage as a social institution and the vital public policy interests that can be undermined by antenuptial agreements. Accordingly, we held that antenuptial agreements would henceforth be enforceable in Georgia divorce proceedings, but only if certain prerequisites are met.

Taking the law of other jurisdictions as our guide, we devised a three-part test for determining whether a particular antenuptial agreement is enforceable under Georgia law. We held that the party seeking enforcement bears the burden of proof to demonstrate that: (1) the antenuptial agreement was not the result of fraud, duress, mistake, misrepresentation, or nondisclosure of material facts; (2) the agreement is not unconscionable; and (3) taking into account all relevant facts and circumstances, including changes beyond the parties' contemplation when the agreement was executed, enforcement of the antenuptial agreement would be neither unfair nor unreasonable. The

Scherer test, as refined and clarified by our later case law, continues to govern the enforceability of antenuptial agreements.

The three-part test we adopted in *Scherer* is consistent with the standards governing the enforcement of antenuptial agreements that prevail throughout most of the nation today. As one commentator has explained:

> Generally accepted guidelines for analyzing antenuptial agreements determine whether they are enforceable. The contract must meet the usual requirements of offer, acceptance, and consideration, and there is often an implied, sometimes express, requirement of fundamental fairness. The agreement cannot violate a statute or clear public policy. If the circumstances have changed beyond the parties' contemplation at the time they entered into the agreement, it may not be enforceable. Usually both parties must fully disclose their assets at the time of the agreement. . . .

We evaluate a trial court's determination regarding the enforceability of an antenuptial agreement under the familiar abuse of discretion standard of review.

On appeal, Mr. Blige contends the trial court erred in setting aside the antenuptial agreement under the first prong of the *Scherer* test, i.e., the agreement must not be the result of fraud, duress, mistake, misrepresentation, or nondisclosure of material facts. To satisfy the first prong of the *Scherer* test, the party seeking enforcement must show both that there was "a full and fair disclosure of the assets of the parties prior to the execution of the [antenuptial] agreement," and that the party opposing enforcement entered into the antenuptial agreement "[freely], voluntarily, and with full understanding of its terms after being offered the opportunity to consult with independent counsel." Thus, Georgia law, like that of virtually every other State in the Union, imposes an affirmative duty of disclosure on both parties to an antenuptial agreement. In essence, the law writes into every antenuptial agreement a provision requiring both parties to disclose all material facts. Absent "full and fair disclosure" of the parties' financial condition prior to execution, enforcement of the antenuptial agreement would violate Georgia public policy.

The trial court specifically found that Mr. Blige did not make a "fair and clear disclosure of his income, assets and liabilities before the parties signed [the] antenuptial agreement" as required by the first prong of the *Scherer* test. The evidence presented at the pretrial hearing showed that at the time of the parties' marriage, Mr. Blige made his living as a vending and delivery person for Savannah Coca-Cola. His base pay was $10 an hour. A year before the nuptials, Mr. Blige purchased 19.5 acres of land in rural Bryan County for $85,000. He owned no other property. Ms. Blige did not live with Mr. Blige before the marriage, and it was undisputed that he never told her prior to the execution of the antenuptial agreement that he had $150,000 in cash in his possession. To the contrary, there are indications in the record that Mr. Blige actively hid his true financial status from Ms. Blige before the marriage and for some time thereafter. Thus, the evidence in the record amply supports the trial court's finding that Mr. Blige failed to disclose a fact material to the antenuptial agreement-i.e., the $150,000 in cash he had hidden away-and therefore did not make a full and fair disclosure of his financial status before the signing of the antenuptial agreement as required by the first prong of the *Scherer* test.

Mr. Blige claims that in spite of his nondisclosure of the $150,000 in cash, the trial court was required to enforce the ante nuptial agreement under our recent decision in *Mallen v. Mallen*. However, *Mallen* is easily distinguishable on the facts, at least with respect to the disclosure requirement. First, in *Mallen,* the trial court, after hearing all the evidence, exercised its discretion to uphold the antenuptial agreement, while here, the trial court exercised its discretion to do the opposite. Second, in *Mallen,* the parties attached financial disclosure statements to the antenuptial agreement itself that accurately reflected their assets and liabilities and that clearly revealed the tremendous disparity between the net worths of the prospective spouses (approximately $10,000 versus at least $8.5 million); there was no exchange of financial disclosure statements between the Bliges. Third, the Mallens had lived together for four years before the execution of the antenuptial agreement, and we specifically held that Ms. Mallen "was aware from the standard of living they enjoyed that he [i.e., Mr. Mallen] received significant income from his business and other sources." By contrast, Ms. Blige never moved in with Mr. Blige, even after the marriage, and there was nothing in Mr. Blige's lifestyle to indicate that he might have enormous sums of cash stashed away somewhere.

Mr. Blige argues that *Mallen* requires trial courts to enforce an antenuptial agreement, even where the spouse seeking enforcement did not make a full and fair disclosure, if the spouse resisting enforcement failed to "exercise reasonable diligence in ascertaining the assets" of the other before the execution of the antenuptial agreement. Thus, according to Mr. Blige, *Mallen* recognized a generalized "duty to . . . inquir[e]" into the financial status of one's prospective spouse, and absent such inquiry, a challenge to the enforceability of the antenuptial agreement is barred.

Mr. Blige's reading of *Mallen* turns *Scherer's* disclosure requirement on its head. *Mallen* did not purport to overrule the portion of the first prong of the *Scherer* test that asks whether the antenuptial agreement was "obtained through . . . nondisclosure of material facts." In *Mallen* itself, both the majority and dissenting opinions directly quoted this portion of the decision in *Scherer*. In decisions rendered both before and after *Mallen,* we have repeatedly recognized that *Scherer* imposes an affirmative duty of full and fair disclosure of all material facts on parties entering into an antenuptial agreement. As noted above, this is the prevailing rule throughout the United States.

To support his claim that *Mallen* created a "duty of inquiry," Mr. Blige relies on a single passage from *Mallen* quoting a New Jersey trial court's [description of a California case that has] . . . never once been relied on or even cited by any California appellate court[.] . . . [W]hile California, like Georgia, does not consider individuals planning to wed to be in a "fiduciary" or "confidential" relationship, California law nevertheless imposes an affirmative duty of disclosure as part of its test for determining the enforceability of antenuptial agreements. . . .

While . . . we agree . . . that the "better rule" is that the "burden is not on either party to inquire, but on each to inform, for it is only by requiring full disclosure of the amount, character, and value of the parties' respective assets that courts can ensure intelligent waiver of the statutory (and other) rights involved," and that "[w]hen a spouse has a duty to fully and completely disclose his financial wealth[,] we would eviscerate and render meaningless that duty if we imposed upon the other spouse a duty to investigate." In short, the "duty of inquiry" envisioned by Mr. Blige is incompatible with the duty of full and fair disclosure recognized by *Scherer* and its progeny.

Finally, in *Mallen,* we did not rest our decision upholding the trial court's enforcement of the antenuptial agreement on Ms. Mallen's failure to inquire into Mr. Mallen's financial status prior to the execution of the antenuptial agreement. Instead, we concluded that the omission of Mr. Mallen's income from the financial statement he attached to the antenuptial agreement was not material given the unique circumstances of that case. We emphasized the fact that Ms. Mallen had lived with Mr. Mallen for four years before she signed the antenuptial agreement, that the financial disclosure statement Mr. Mallen attached to the antenuptial agreement revealed him to be a wealthy man with significant income-producing assets, and that Ms. Mallen was well aware from the standard of living they enjoyed prior to the marriage that Mr. Mallen received substantial income from the business bearing his name and other sources.

The evidence supports the trial court's finding that Mr. Blige failed to make a full and fair disclosure of his assets, income, and liabilities to Ms. Blige prior to the execution of the antenuptial agreement, and nothing in *Mallen* or Ms. Blige's actions or inactions prior to the execution of the antenuptial agreement excuses Mr. Blige's nondisclosure. Accordingly, the trial court properly held that Mr. Blige failed to establish the first prong of the *Scherer* test, and it did not abuse its discretion in setting aside the antenuptial agreement.

Mr. Blige also contends the evidence presented at trial does not support the jury's verdict awarding Ms. Blige $160,000 for her equitable interest in the marital property. We have independently reviewed the record on appeal, and it supports the jury's verdict. This argument is meritless.

Judgment affirmed. All the Justices concur.

NOTES

Frequently, the question before the court is not whether there is no disclosure, as in *Blige,* but whether the disclosure was adequate. As to the latter, Section (9)(d) of the UPMAA fills an important gap by providing guidance as to what would be considered adequate disclosure. It requires a reasonably accurate description and good faith estimate of value of the property, liabilities, and income of the other party. UPMAA § (9)(d). *In Blige* and *Mallen,* the nature of the required disclosure changed based on the circumstances surrounding the disclosure—specifically, whether the couple cohabited before marrying. Rather than bearing the burden of showing that disclosure was unnecessary given the circumstances, better practice suggests that each party should attach his or her financials or latest tax return to the agreement as exhibits.

Just as the required disclosure may change with circumstances, so might the standards of fairness. In Rosenberg v. Lipnick, 389 N.E.2d 385, 388–89 (Mass. 1979), the foundational case in Massachusetts for determining the validity of premarital agreements, the court states "[i]t is clear that the reasonableness of any monetary provision in an antenuptial contract cannot ultimately be judged in isolation. Rather, reference may appropriately be made to such factors as the parties' respective worth, the parties' respective ages, the parties' respective intelligence, literacy, and business acumen, and prior family ties or commitments. . . ."

As the next case illustrates, an agreement may ultimately be seen as fair if the weaker earning party is capable of self-support and receives something of value from the marriage, even if considerably less than what the background law would provide.

Biliouris v. Biliouris

Appeals Court of Massachusetts, 2006
852 N.E.2d 687

■ SMITH, JUSTICE.

In his findings in support of judgments of divorce nisi, a judge of the Probate and Family Court concluded, inter alia, that an antenuptial agreement executed by the parties was fair and reasonable at the time of its execution, was not the product of coercion or duress, and was not unconscionable at the time of its enforcement. On appeal, the wife challenges the judge's rulings concerning the enforceability of the antenuptial agreement as well as other aspects of the divorce judgments, including the judge's apparent determination that the husband's medical office building was not a marital asset subject to equitable division pursuant to G.L. c. 208, § 34. We conclude that the judge did not err in upholding the antenuptial agreement but we vacate so much of the judgments as allow the husband to retain title to the medical office building property and remand the matter to the Probate and Family Court in order that the judge may further articulate the rationale for his decision with respect to that property and enter a new (or, if appropriate, revised) order pertaining thereto.

1. *Background and proceedings.* At the time the parties began their dating relationship in mid-1991, the husband, a physician, was thirty-one years of age and the wife, a home economics teacher, was thirty-five years of age. The wife had three children by an earlier marriage. In late September or early October, 1992, the wife learned that she was pregnant and shortly thereafter informed the husband of the pregnancy. Upon receipt of the news, the husband told the wife that he would not marry her unless she signed an antenuptial agreement (agreement). Thereafter, the husband's attorney prepared an agreement that the husband presented to the wife.[1] The wife sought the assistance of counsel who, upon review of the draft agreement, advised the wife not to sign it.

On December 31, 1992, the wife met at a restaurant with the husband and his attorney to discuss the agreement,[2] and immediately thereafter went to a bank where, in the presence of a notary, the parties executed the agreement. On the same date, the parties also signed the exhibits pages listing the parties' assets that were attached to the agreement.

The husband's premarital assets (including stocks, mutual funds, a lot of land in West Barnstable, and a one-bedroom rental condominium in the Allston section of Boston) were worth $986,000; the wife's premarital assets (including her interests in a pending lawsuit and a home in Sandwich in which the parties were then living) were worth $100,000. The parties' financial statements (portions of which were attached to the agreement) reflect that at the time the agreement was executed the husband's gross income was $6,400 per week and the wife's gross income $1,675 per week.[3]

The antenuptial agreement . . . provides generally that the individual property of each party, as well as the appreciation thereon,

---

[1] The husband testified that he raised the subject of an antenuptial agreement shortly after learning of the wife's pregnancy and that he presented the wife with the draft agreement approximately two months prior to the parties' wedding on January 2, 1993. The wife testified that the husband broached the subject of an antenuptial agreement in November, 1992, but that she did not see the agreement until approximately one week before the parties' wedding.

[2] It is undisputed that the wife, who at times was crying at the meeting, stated initially that she did not wish to sign the agreement. The husband testified that there were no negotiations concerning the terms of the agreement.

[3] The wife's income consisted of her salary as a teacher ($660 per week) as well as Social Security and workers' compensation benefits ($500 per week and $515 per week, respectively) she received on behalf of the three children of her first marriage after the death of her first husband in 1992.

shall remain the party's sole and exclusive property, and that neither party shall have a claim to alimony from the other.[4]

During their ten-year marriage, the parties had two children. By agreement, the wife was a "stay-at-home" mother and was the "primary caretaker of the home" while the husband ran his medical practice. In 1995, the parties sold their home in Sandwich[5] and built a new home, title to which they held as tenants by the entirety, in West Barnstable. The cost of the West Barnstable home (excluding the land) was either $500,000 or $600,000. The husband paid the mortgage on the home (granted in 1999) as well as other extraordinary expenses, and in addition, contributed initially $700 per month (later $1,000 per month) toward the operating expenses of the household. The wife contributed $4,365[6] per month toward the operating expenses of the house. At the time of the divorce, the West Barnstable house was worth $1,075,000 and carried a mortgage of $86,000. During the marriage the parties enjoyed an upper middle class standard of living.[7]

---

[4] The agreement provides, inter alia:

"1. Except as otherwise may be expressly provided elsewhere in this Agreement, the individual property of each of the parties, both real and personal, now owned by him or her, or which he or she may hereafter acquire or become entitled to, shall remain and be the sole and exclusive property of the owner, subject to his or her individual control and use as if he or she were unmarried. Neither shall acquire by reason of the marriage any interest in the separate property, now or hereafter acquired, of the other or the right to the control thereof, or any interest in the income or any increase in value arising therefrom. . . .

"2. In the event that the marriage of [the husband] and [the wife] shall terminate by reason of their divorce, or if action for legal separation is initiated by either of them, the parties hereby agree that, in view of their respective ages, existing families and issue, and individual assets and income available to each therefrom, neither party shall make any claim against the other for alimony, separate maintenance, or support, or a division or assignment of income or assets of the other as a part of, or in lieu of, such alimony under the laws of the Commonwealth of Massachusetts or any other jurisdiction.

"3. Each party hereby acknowledges that the agreements contained herein shall constitute a reasonable resolution of any rights they may acquire in the income, asset, or estate of the other in all foreseeable circumstances, including legal separation and termination of the marriage by divorce, giving consideration to their current and future ages, the length of the marriage, and other factors cognizable under Massachusetts General Laws, Chapter 208, Section 34, or similar laws of other jurisdictions."

[5] At the time of the marriage, title to the home was in the wife's name. Shortly after the marriage the wife conveyed the property to herself and the husband as tenants by the entirety and the husband contributed $7,500 to the home (roughly the same amount as the wife's down payment on the home).

[6] This figure was reduced at some point when the wife's oldest child from her previous marriage became emancipated and the wife stopped receiving Social Security benefits on his behalf.

[7] At the time of the divorce, the wife was employed part-time as a teacher's assistant at an elementary school at a salary of $236.40 per week. The wife also received Social Security benefits on behalf of one remaining eligible child of her first marriage in the amount of $255.80 per week and workers' compensation benefits on behalf of her three older children in the amount of $604.65 per week. Although the judge found that the husband's income as reflected on his financial statement was $2,302.60 per week, the judge stated that it is unlikely that the husband, who did not work on Fridays, was suffering the loss he was claiming from his medical practice. The husband presently lives with a female companion who is the facility manager at his medical office clinic and who earns approximately $60,000 per year.

In November, 2001, the husband filed a complaint for divorce, which was amended in August, 2002, to include a provision requesting that the court enforce the terms of the parties' antenuptial agreement. . . . The wife filed an answer and counterclaim requesting, inter alia, that she be granted a divorce on the grounds of cruel and abusive treatment or irretrievable breakdown of the marriage.

After a trial, the judge found that the antenuptial agreement was free from fraud, both parties having fully disclosed their assets at the time of execution, and neither party having unfairly taken "advantage of the confidential and emotional relationship that the party had with the other." The judge further found that the parties had adequate opportunity to consult with independent counsel prior to signing the agreement, that the agreement indicated what rights the parties were giving up, that the wife (who had been through a prior divorce) would be aware of what rights she might have had absent the existence of an agreement, and that there had been "an adequate waiver." Continuing, the judge found "that the [w]ife did not suffer from any duress and was not coerced into signing the agreement at the time of" its execution. Finally, the judge determined that the agreement was fair and reasonable at the time of its execution and was "not an unconscionable agreement" at the time of its enforcement.

By the terms of the judgment of divorce nisi (dated April 11, 2003) that was entered on the husband's complaint, the parties were awarded joint legal and shared physical custody of the parties' two minor children. The husband was allowed to retain his interests in assets worth approximately $1,962,000 (including his interest in the medical office building),[8] while the wife was allowed to retain her interest in assets worth approximately $105,000. In addition, the judge awarded the wife, after adjustment, eighty percent of the equity in the West Barnstable home (based on the wife's "contribution" or payment of eighty percent of the household's operating expenses)[9] and most of the contents of the home. The judge also awarded the wife $750 per week as child support and directed the husband to maintain his existing medical insurance for the benefit of the wife, the children of the marriage, and the wife's

---

[8] The judge found that the bulk of the assets could be traced to the husband's premarital assets.

[9] As we have stated, the West Barnstable home was worth $1,075,000 at the time of trial. Because the home had been built on a lot for which the husband had paid $93,700 prior to the marriage, the judge deducted that amount from the value of the property (resulting in a sum of $981,300). The judge determined that the husband was entitled to twenty percent of the $981,300 value of the property (based on his twenty percent "contribution" or payment of the household's operating expenses), or $196,260, as well as reimbursement for his payment of $19,543 toward the college costs of one of the wife's children from her first marriage. The judge ordered the husband to transfer his interest in the West Barnstable property to the wife and to pay off the existing mortgage on the property before May 1, 2003. In consideration of the transfer, the judge ordered the wife to execute an unassignable noninterest bearing promissory note in the amount of $309,503 ($93,700 plus $196,260 plus $19,543), secured by a first mortgage, which was to "be due and payable [to the husband] upon the emancipation of the children [of the marriage], the sale of the real estate, or the [w]ife's remarriage, whichever first occurs."

children from her first marriage for so long as they qualify. . . . The judge dismissed the wife's counterclaim for divorce. . . . [T]he judge denied the wife's motions for new trial and to alter and amend judgment and findings of fact. . . . The wife has appealed from the judgments of divorce nisi and the orders denying her postjudgment motions. . . .

The wife argues initially that she was under duress at the time she executed the antenuptial agreement and "was coerced into signing it due to the circumstances in which she found herself."[10] More specifically, the wife asserts that the evidence at trial established that the husband wanted to have children, but given the wife's age, he was concerned that she could not bear children or carry them to term. The wife asserts that there was an oral agreement between the parties where, as a "precondition" of the husband's agreeing to marry her, she would have to become pregnant (which she did).[11] Continuing, the wife asserts that the husband's proposal of an *additional* condition (i.e., the execution of the antenuptial agreement), after she had become pregnant, was coercive in and of itself.

The problem with the wife's argument is that the judge made no finding that any such oral agreement existed between the parties. (The husband vigorously disputed at trial that there was such an agreement.) Indeed, the judge denied the wife's motion to amend findings of fact in which she sought to include findings with respect to the alleged oral agreement.

The wife also asserts, apparently apart from her argument concerning the alleged oral agreement between the parties, that the fact that she found herself, a pregnant single mother, presented with an agreement shortly before her scheduled wedding date and being told that if she did not sign the agreement there would be no wedding, is by its very nature coercive.[12]

It is settled that a person who enters into a contract "under the influence of such fear as precludes him from exercising free will and judgment" may avoid the contract on the grounds of duress. Coveney v. President & Trustees of the College of the Holy Cross, 388 Mass. 16, 22, 445 N.E.2d 136 (1983), quoting from Avallone v. Elizabeth Arden Sales Corp., 344 Mass. 556, 561, 183 N.E.2d 496 (1962). . . . "Coercion sufficient to avoid a contract need not, of course, consist of physical force or threats of it. Social or economic pressure illegally or immorally applied may be sufficient." International Underwater Contractors, Inc. v. New England Tel. & Tel. Co., 8 Mass.App.Ct. 340, 342, 393 N.E.2d 968 (1979), quoting

[10] In her brief and in her oral argument to this court, the wife made no attempt to distinguish legally between the terms "coercion" and "duress" and appears to use them synonymously. See *Delaney v. Chief of Police of Wareham,* 27 Mass.App.Ct. 398, 406, 539 N.E.2d 65 n.7 (1989).

[11] The wife claims, in essence, a "prior agreement to marry" where she "completed her obligation [thereunder] by becoming pregnant."

[12] The wife makes no argument on appeal that her religious or moral beliefs contributed to the alleged coercive atmosphere at the time the antenuptial agreement was executed.

from Struck Constr. Co. v. United States, 96 Ct.Cl. 186, 220 (1942). Here, we perceive nothing in the record that would cause us to disturb the judge's finding that the wife's execution of the antenuptial agreement was not the product of coercion or duress.

Even were we to assume that the wife was presented with a draft of the antenuptial agreement only one week prior to the parties' wedding . . . she still had sufficient time to review it, and did in fact seek the advice of independent counsel as to its terms. As we have stated, the wife rejected counsel's opinion that she should not sign the agreement. The wife also acknowledged at trial that prior to executing the agreement and in response to a question posed by the notary, she informed the notary that her signing of the agreement was her "free act and deed." While the wife's pregnancy coupled with the husband's insistence that there would be no marriage unless she signed the antenuptial agreement presented the wife with a difficult choice, those factors cannot be said, in the circumstances presented here, to have divested the wife of her free will and judgment.

Other jurisdictions have reached the same result on somewhat similar facts. See, e.g., Kilborn v. Kilborn, 628 So.2d 884, 885 (Ala.Civ.App.1993) (no error in the trial judge's determination that an antenuptial agreement was valid and enforceable and not the product of coercion where the wife, though pregnant, signed the agreement after full disclosure and against the advice of counsel); Hamilton v. Hamilton, 404 Pa.Super. 533, 537, 591 A.2d 720 (1991) (antenuptial agreement not signed under duress where the wife, although "pregnant, unemployed, and probably frightened," was represented by counsel and signed the agreement against his advice).[13] To the extent the wife appeared to suggest at oral argument that duress or coercion may have resulted in

[13] For additional cases upholding, against claims of coercion, duress, or undue influence, a trial judge's determination that an antenuptial agreement executed by a woman who was pregnant was valid, see *In re Marriage of Dawley,* 17 Cal.3d 342, 355, 131 Cal.Rptr. 3, 551 P.2d 323 (1976); *Herrera v. Herrera,* 895 So.2d 1171, 1173, 1175 (Fla.App.2005); *Mallen v. Mallen,* 280 Ga. 43, 45–46, 622 S.E.2d 812 (2005); *Osorno v. Osorno,* 76 S.W.3d 509, 511 (Tex.App.2002) (reasoning that because duress consists of a threat to do something a party has no legal right to do, and because the father had no legal duty to marry the pregnant mother, "[h]is threat to do something he had the legal right to do is insufficient to invalidate the premarital agreement"). Other appellate cases we have located in our research, in which courts have found coercion or duress (or that genuine issues of material fact existed as to whether there was coercion) in circumstances where, among other factors, an antenuptial agreement was executed by a pregnant woman, are distinguishable from the case at bar. In *Holler v. Holler,* 364 S.C. 256, 266–268, 612 S.E.2d 469 (Ct.App.2005), the court, in concluding that the wife, who was from the Ukraine, did not enter into the premarital agreement freely and voluntarily, noted that not only was the wife pregnant at the time she executed the premarital agreement, but her visa was about to expire (thus requiring her to leave the United States unless she married), she could not understand the agreement, and she had no money of her own to retain or consult with an attorney or a translator. In *Williams v. Williams,* 617 So.2d 1032, 1035 (Ala.1992), the court held that summary judgment was inappropriate as the testimony in the case created genuine issues of material fact as to whether, among other things, the "the father's conditioning the marriage on the pregnant mother's signing the antenuptial agreement, joined with the mother's moral objection to abortion and the importance of legitimacy in a small town, created a coercive atmosphere in which the mother had no viable alternative to accepting the father's condition for marriage, i.e., signing the agreement."

this case from the prospect of her being a single mother and the economic circumstances that may flow therefrom, the husband testified that he informed the wife that even if she did not sign the agreement he would act as a father to the child and would support the child financially. In any event, even if the husband did not make that statement, a court may enter an order for the support of a child born out of wedlock pursuant to G.L. c. 209C, § 9.[14]

b. *Validity of alimony waiver.* The wife argues next that under the circumstances known and reasonably to be anticipated by the parties at the time of the execution of the antenuptial agreement, the waiver of alimony provision, as to her, was neither fair nor reasonable when it was made.[15]

"Antenuptial agreements that waive alimony are not 'per se against public policy and may be specifically enforced.'" Austin v. Austin, 445 Mass. at 603–604, 839 N.E.2d 837, quoting from Osborne v. Osborne, 384 Mass. 591, 598, 428 N.E.2d 810 (1981). Vakil v. Vakil, 66 Mass.App.Ct. at 536, 849 N.E.2d 233. As we have stated, however, to be enforceable, an agreement must be valid at the time of execution. "In order [for such an agreement] to be valid at the time of execution, the judge must determine whether '(1) [the agreement] contains a fair and reasonable provision as measured at the time of its execution for the party contesting the agreement; (2) the contesting party was fully informed of the other party's worth prior to the agreement's execution, or had, or should have had, independent knowledge of the other party's worth; and (3) a waiver by the contesting party is set forth.'" Austin v. Austin, 445 Mass. at 604, 839 N.E.2d 837, quoting from DeMatteo v. DeMatteo, 436 Mass. at 26, 762 N.E.2d 797.

In determining whether an agreement was fair and reasonable at the time of execution, reference may be made to numerous factors, including "the parties' respective worth . . . ages . . . intelligence, literacy, and business acumen, and prior family ties or commitments." Rosenberg v. Lipnick, 377 Mass. 666, 672, 389 N.E.2d 385 (1979). Austin v. Austin, 445 Mass. at 604, 839 N.E.2d 837. See DeMatteo v. DeMatteo, 436 Mass.

[14] There is no merit in the wife's additional arguments that she had no way to verify the husband's disclosures concerning the existence and values of his assets in exhibit A to the parties' agreement (or to correct errors concerning her own assets listed in exhibit B). . . . As to the former point, the wife does not argue that the husband's disclosures were incorrect in any material respect, and in fact, her attorney stated at trial: "We'll stipulate that the [husband's] assets as listed, we have no reason to dispute their value except [in minor respects] for the ring. . . ." [T]he wife indicated during cross-examination at trial that the assets and values in exhibit B were substantially correct. . . .

[15] The wife made clear at oral argument that she was challenging the fairness and reasonableness of the agreement at the time of its execution and not its conscionability at the time of enforcement (the so-called "second look" during which a judge determines whether "due to circumstances occurring during the course of the marriage, enforcement . . . would leave the contesting spouse 'without sufficient property, maintenance, or appropriate employment to support' herself." *DeMatteo v. DeMatteo,* 436 Mass. at 37, 762 N.E.2d 797, quoting from 1 Clark, Jr., Domestic Relations in the United States § 1.9 [2d ed.1987]. *Austin v. Austin,* 445 Mass. at 604, 839 N.E.2d 837. *Korff v. Korff,* 64 Mass.App.Ct. 94, 97, 831 N.E.2d 385 [2005]).

at 30, 762 N.E.2d 797 (reasonableness of the monetary provision in an antenuptial agreement "cannot ultimately be judged in isolation"). "It is only where the contesting party is essentially stripped of substantially all marital interests," and indeed, the terms of the agreement "essentially vitiate the very status of marriage," that an agreement is not fair and reasonable. *Id.* at 31, 762 N.E.2d 797.

Here, the judge did not err in concluding that the waiver of alimony provision of the antenuptial agreement was fair and reasonable at the time of its execution. The wife was an educated professional who had a demonstrated earning capacity at the time she executed the agreement in 1992. Although the parties agreed that the wife would leave her job in order to be a "stay-at-home" mother, there is nothing in the record to suggest that the wife would be incapable of working and earning income to support herself in the event of a divorce in the future.[16] Moreover, as we have discussed, the agreement provided that the wife's separate premarital property (valued at approximately $100,000), and any appreciation thereon, would remain her property and not be incorporated into the marital estate subject to division.

The agreement (in the absence of any limitation or provision to the contrary) also permitted the wife an interest in marital assets accrued by the parties during the marriage. As the husband owned no home at the time the agreement was executed (and was residing with the wife and her three children in the wife's home in Sandwich), and as the agreement specifically provided "that, in the event of their marriage, the parties *expect to reside* together *in a location,* style and manner mutually suitable to them"[ ](emphasis supplied), it was reasonably foreseeable that the parties would acquire a home in which to raise the combined families and that at least some portion of this asset would be available for the wife's support if the parties ultimately divorced. See Austin v. Austin, 445 Mass. at 606, 839 N.E.2d 837. In the circumstances presented, the parties' agreement cannot be said to have vitiated the very status of marriage. If the terms of the agreement were unsatisfactory to the wife, she was "free not to marry." DeMatteo v. DeMatteo, 436 Mass. at 33, 762 N.E.2d 797. . . .

So ordered.

NOTES

A Classic Example of Four-Step Property Division and the Importance of Offsets. In *Biliouris*, the court split the couple's nearly $1,000,000 in marital property 80–20 with 80% going to the wife. It awarded the house to the wife—presumably so that she and the couple's children could

[16] The wife had shown the ability to work full time prior to the parties' marriage (and shortly thereafter) notwithstanding the fact that she had three children under the age of eleven from her first marriage. The wife was also receiving at the time she executed the agreement $1,015 per week for the benefit of her children by her first marriage and anticipated receiving substantial sums for their benefit for many years to come. See note 3, *supra*.

continue to live in the same residence after the divorce—and gave the husband his 20% in the form of an unassignable, non-interest bearing promissory note. Notice that the note, from wife to husband, was to "be due and payable [to the husband] upon the emancipation of the children [of the marriage], the sale of the real estate, or the [w]ife's remarriage, whichever first occurs." It is typical for a court to use a promissory note from the lower-income spouse to the higher-income spouse when dividing a significant asset that cannot be easily sold—or should not be sold because it will continue to serve as a residence for the children. The promissory note the husband receives earns no interest, has no monthly payments, and has no date certain by which he will receive his money.

A Floor to "Fair and Reasonable." Like many premarital agreements, the Bilouris' agreement waived alimony and provided that premarital, separate property would remain separate. But, the agreement did not alter the norm of sharing with respect to marital assets "accrued by the parties during the marriage." The fact that the couple continued to jointly share rights in the marital property ultimately supported the court's conclusion that the agreement was fair and reasonable at the time of execution. Why? The court notes that the agreement did not strip the wife of "substantially all marital interests." If the agreement had altered the equitable distribution rule, too, in addition to waiving alimony, one wonders whether such a one-sided agreement would then have "essentially vitiate[d] the very status of marriage," making it unenforceable.

Just as *Biliouris* implies that there is a floor to fair and reasonableness, at the time of execution, so does the UPMAA. It explicitly provides that an alimony waiver cannot be enforced if doing so would "cause a party . . . to be eligible for support under a program for public assistance at the time of dissolution." UPMAA § 9(e).

Two Time Frames for Measuring Fairness. Early in the decision, the *Biliouris* court noted that a premarital agreement must be "valid at the time of execution" and "fair and reasonable at the time of divorce." Biliouris v. Biliouris, 852 N.E.2d 687, 692 (Mass. 2006). The court spent the majority of its decision examining whether the terms were fair and reasonable at the time of enforcement. The UPMAA gives states the option to evaluate the premarital agreement for fairness at *both* signing *and* enforcement, but states have to specifically elect the latter. UPMAA § 9(f). Note, however, NCCUSL suggests that adopting jurisdictions closely evaluate whether a substantial hardship at the time of enforcement should be an escape hatch.

Procedural Fairness. In *Biliouris*, the wife's claim of coercion or duress gained little traction because she had sufficient time to review the agreement, even if just one week, and she in fact received the advice of independent counsel. Contrast this with the premarital agreement entered into by famed baseball player Barry Bonds. In 1988, on the cusp of spring training, Bonds entered into a premarital agreement with his fiancé, Sun, a Swedish model whose native language was Swedish. The couple signed the agreement and flew to Las Vegas, where they married the next day. Bonds petitioned for divorce six years later after the couple had two children. Sun sought spousal support, which she ultimately received, and division of the couple's community property, as to which the premarital agreement purported to waive her interest. The California Supreme Court rejected Sun's request to invalidate the agreement. The court placed significant weight on freedom of contract and the need of couples contemplating marriage to be able to rely on any agreement reached. The court relied on evidence that Sun knew about the agreement for more than a week before signing it, that Bonds' attorney had advised her that she could seek independent legal advice but she did not, and that Sun's command of the English language allowed her to understand what was at stake. *See In re* Marriage of Bonds, 24 Cal.4th 1 (Cal. 2000).

In response to the *Bonds* decision, the California legislature enacted CALIFORNIA FAMILY CODE § 1615 requiring for enforcement of a premarital agreement, among other things, a seven-day waiting period before signing and that the party be "proficient in the language in which the explanation of the party's rights was conducted and in which the agreement was written."

Stregack v. Moldofsky

Supreme Court of Florida, 1985
474 So.2d 206

■ MCDONALD, JUSTICE.

We have for review Moldofsky v. Stregack, 449 So.2d 918 (Fla. 3d DCA 1984), which directly and expressly conflicts with Coleman v. Estate of Coleman, 439 So.2d 1016 (Fla. 1st DCA 1983). . . . The issue here is whether a surviving spouse may challenge an antenuptial agreement based upon fraudulent nondisclosure of assets by a decedent spouse, in light of section 732.702, Florida Statutes (1983), which requires no disclosure for a valid antenuptial agreement in probate. We quash *Moldofsky* because nondisclosure in any form cannot invalidate an antenuptial agreement in probate proceedings of a deceased spouse.

When Manuel Moldofsky died, his will contained no provision for his wife, Sally Moldofsky, beyond a reference to an antenuptial agreement between them. Mrs. Moldofsky filed a notice of elective share after the circuit court probate division admitted the will to probate. Susan Stregack, Mr. Moldofsky's daughter and personal representative of his estate, moved to strike the notice of elective share based upon an antenuptial agreement executed by the parties, in which Mr. and Mrs. Moldofsky waived all rights in each other's estate. Mrs. Moldofsky then filed an action in the circuit court general jurisdiction division seeking cancellation of the antenuptial agreement for fraud. The probate court struck Moldofsky's motion for elective share. Following this order, the trial court dismissed on mootness and res judicata grounds the pending action to cancel the antenuptial agreement.

The district court reversed both orders on appeal. While acknowledging that section 732.702 eliminated the disclosure requirement for an antenuptial agreement to be valid in probate, the district court held that a surviving spouse could challenge an antenuptial agreement for fraudulent nondisclosure by the deceased spouse. The district court declined to follow the contrary holding in *Coleman*.

In Del Vecchio v. Del Vecchio, 143 So.2d 17 (Fla.1962), this Court held that a valid antenuptial agreement must either contain fair and reasonable provisions for the spouse waiving his or her rights or else the spouse obtaining the waiver of rights must make a full and fair disclosure of assets to the other spouse. Id. at 20. The legislature changed this rule by enacting subsection 732.702(2), which provides: "Each spouse shall make a fair disclosure to the other of his or her estate if the agreement, contract, or waiver is executed after marriage. *No disclosure shall be required for an agreement, contract, or waiver executed before marriage.*" (Emphasis added). We held this statute constitutional against access to courts, due process, and equal protection challenges. Estate of Roberts, 388 So.2d 216 (Fla.1980).

Relying on subsection 732.702(2), the *Coleman* court affirmed the denial of a surviving spouse's motion to amend pleadings and attack an otherwise valid antenuptial agreement for nondisclosure by the decedent spouse before execution of the antenuptial agreement. *Coleman* held that nondisclosure, however pled, could not constitute a basis for invalidating an antenuptial agreement in probate proceedings because the statute required no disclosure in such cases. 439 So.2d at 1018–19. In the present case, on the other hand, the district court interpreted subsection 732.702(2) to eliminate the disclosure duty before marriage, but not the duty that any disclosure be made truthfully. According to the third district, fraudulent nondisclosure would provide a basis to challenge the antenuptial agreement because the surviving spouse's signature was "otherwise improperly obtained" under Roberts. 388 So.2d at 217. We disagree.

Nondisclosure, whether fraudulent or not, is precisely what the legislature intended to eliminate from consideration on the validity of antenuptial agreements. Many older Florida residents want to marry again but also want to keep their assets separate. Often this is the desire of both parties contemplating marriage. Section 732.702 allows complete control over assets accumulated over a lifetime without fear that a partial disclosure before marriage may trigger an unwanted disposition of those assets. We cannot accept the district court decision which rewards the totally silent spouse and punishes the spouse who attempts some disclosure.

We also reject the argument that fraudulent nondisclosure may render the surviving spouse's signature improperly obtained. The quoted language from *Roberts* would apply where the surviving spouse had been misled about what he or she was signing, i.e., a marriage license application instead of an antenuptial agreement. Such fraud could provide grounds to set aside an antenuptial agreement.

[Dissenting and Concurring Opinions Omitted]

NOTES

Premarital Agreements in Probate. In *Stregack*, the surviving spouse sought to avoid enforcement of the premarital agreement upon the death of her husband. In the absence of the agreement, she would receive an elective share. In non-community property states, such as Florida, each spouse may devise his or her property in its entirety to whomever he or she wishes. *See* Raymond C. O'Brien, *Integrating Marital Property Into A Spouse's Elective Share,* 59 CATH. L. REV. 617, 702–715 (2010). However, with the exception of one state (Georgia), if the decedent does not provide a certain amount of property for the surviving spouse, the surviving spouse can petition to take a forced elective share, which is generally one-half to one-third of the estate after accounting for nonprobate transfers which often can form the bulk of an estate. *See* Robin Fretwell Wilson, *Privatizing Family Law in the Name of Religion*, 18(4) WM. & MARY BILL RTS. J. 925, 941–42 (2010).

The UPMAA contemplates the enforcement of premarital agreements upon death if, for instance, there is an adequate waiver of rights or representation by independent legal counsel. This waiver has to be conspicuous but may be as simple as the model text in the UPMAA: "If you sign this agreement you may be giving up your right to money and property if your marriage ends or the person to whom you are married dies." Query whether this text is sufficient to alert a prospective spouse that he or she is losing the right to an elective share.

As the next statute illustrates, many parties enter into premarital agreements not to change the economic effects of death or divorce, but to impose certain religious or moral obligations on the other spouse at the time of dissolution. The statute below, informally known as New York's "get statute," is a response to efforts by Jewish women to enforce premarital promises by their husbands to grant them a traditional Jewish divorce, called a "get," at the same time that the state civilly dissolves the couple's marriage.

NEW YORK DOMESTIC RELATIONS LAW (McKinney 2016)

§ 253. Removal of barriers to remarriage

1. This section applies only to a marriage solemnized in this state or in any other jurisdiction by a person specified in subdivision one of section eleven of this chapter.

2. Any party to a marriage defined in subdivision one of this section who commences a proceeding to annul the marriage or for a divorce must allege, in his or her verified complaint: (i) that, to the best of his or her knowledge, that he or she has taken or that he or she will take, prior to the entry of final judgment, all steps solely within his or her power to remove any barrier to the defendant's remarriage following the annulment or divorce; or (ii) that the defendant has waived in writing the requirements of this subdivision.

3. No final judgment of annulment or divorce shall thereafter be entered unless the plaintiff shall have filed and served a sworn statement:

(i) that, to the best of his or her knowledge, he or she has, prior to the entry of such final judgment, taken all steps solely within his or her power to remove all barriers to the defendant's remarriage following the annulment or divorce; or (ii) that the defendant has waived in writing the requirements of this subdivision.

4. In any action for divorce based on subdivisions five and six of section one hundred seventy of this chapter in which the defendant enters a general appearance and does not contest the requested relief, no final judgment of annulment or divorce shall be entered unless both parties shall have filed and served sworn statements: (i) that he or she has, to the best of his or her knowledge, taken all steps solely within his or her power to remove all barriers to the other party's remarriage following the annulment or divorce; or (ii) that the other party has waived in writing the requirements of this subdivision.

5. The writing attesting to any waiver of the requirements of subdivision two, three or four of this section shall be filed with the court prior to the entry of a final judgment of annulment or divorce.

6. As used in the sworn statements prescribed by this section "barrier to remarriage" includes, without limitation, any religious or conscientious restraint or inhibition, of which the party required to make the verified statement is aware, that is imposed on a party to a marriage, under the principles held by the clergyman or minister who has solemnized the marriage, by reason of the other party's commission or withholding of any voluntary act. Nothing in this section shall be construed to require any party to consult with any clergyman or minister to determine whether there exists any such religious or conscientious restraint or inhibition. It shall not be deemed a "barrier to remarriage" within the meaning of this section if the restraint or inhibition cannot be removed by the party's voluntary act. Nor shall it be deemed a "barrier to remarriage" if the party must incur expenses in connection with removal of the restraint or inhibition and the other party refuses to provide reasonable reimbursement for such expenses. "All steps solely within his or her power" shall not be construed to include application to a marriage tribunal or other similar organization or agency of a religious denomination which has authority to annul or dissolve a marriage under the rules of such denomination.

7. No final judgment of annulment or divorce shall be entered, notwithstanding the filing of the plaintiff's sworn statement prescribed by this section, if the clergyman or minister who has solemnized the marriage certifies, in a sworn statement, that he or she has solemnized the marriage and that, to his or her knowledge, the plaintiff has failed to take all steps solely within his or her power to remove all barriers to the defendant's remarriage following the annulment or divorce, provided that the said clergyman or minister is alive and available and competent to testify at the time when final judgment would be entered.

8. Any person who knowingly submits a false sworn statement under this section shall be guilty of making an apparently sworn false statement in

the first degree and shall be punished in accordance with section 210.40 of the penal law.

9. Nothing in this section shall be construed to authorize any court to inquire into or determine any ecclesiastical or religious issue. The truth of any statement submitted pursuant to this section shall not be the subject of any judicial inquiry, except as provided in subdivision eight of this section.

NOTES

Jewish Premarital Contracts. Even before the "get statute," in Avitzur v. Avitzur, 446 N.E.2d 136 (N.Y. 1983), the court enforced the terms of a Jewish premarital agreement, the "ketubah." The agreement required the parties go before a religious tribunal, called a "Beth Din," to obtain a religious divorce, the "get." The court found the obligation to go before the Beth Din to be based in contract and thus enforceable. For a further discussion of *Avitzur*, *see generally* David Novak, *Jewish Marriage and Civil Law: A Two Way Street?*, 68 GEO. WASH. L. REV. 1059 (2000); Jesse Choper, *A Century of Religious Freedom*, 88 CAL. L. REV. 1709 (2000); Lisa Zornberg, *Beyond the Constitution: Is the New York Get Legislation Good Law*, 15 PACE L. REV. 703 (1995). New York enacted the "get" statute in the same year as *Avitzur*; some question its constitutionality. *See* Michael A. Helfand & Barak D. Richman, *The Challenge of Co-Religionist Commerce*, 64 DUKE L. J. 769 (2015).

Outside New York, in Victor v. Victor, 866 P.2d 899 (Ariz. Ct. App. 1993), an Arizona Court of Appeals held that a ketubah, which set forth the husband's financial obligations to his wife under Jewish law, was not an enforceable premarital agreement pursuant to which the husband could be ordered to obtain a get. However, in Scholl v. Scholl, 621 A.2d 808 (Del. Fam. 1992), a Delaware Family Court determined that an order to enforce a stipulation of settlement between the parties in which the husband agreed to cooperate in obtaining an Orthodox get (he had obtained a get from a Conservative body but his wife was Orthodox) would not be an excessive entanglement with religion. For a discussion of the issues with judicial enforcement and review of religious disputes, *see* Shiva Falsafi, *Religion, Women, and the Holy Grail of Legal Pluralism,* 35 CARDOZO L. REV. 1881 (2014).

Islamic Premarital Contracts. The dual nature of marriage as civil *and* religious also figures in Islamic marriages. In Aziz v. Aziz, 488 N.Y.S.2d 123 (1985), the court found enforceable the secular terms of a "mahr" which is a payment received by a party for marrying—that is often deferred in whole or part until the time of divorce or death. As a part of a religious ceremony under Islamic law, the husband usually agrees to pay the wife the mahr, which operates like a dowry. However, in *In re* Marriage of Obaidi & Qayoum, 226 P.3d 787, 790 (Wash. Ct. App. 2010), *reconsideration denied* (Apr. 21, 2010), *review denied*, 238 P.3d 503 (Wash. 2010), the court declined to enforce a mahr because it did not meet the requirements for enforceability for all premarital agreements, requirements that are "neutral principles of contract law." For more discussion on Islamic mahrs and whether they should be treated as premarital agreements, *see* Nathan B. Oman, *Bargaining in the Shadow of God's Law: Islamic Mahr Contracts and the Perils of Legal Specialization*, 45 WAKE FOREST L. REV. 579 (2010). For a discussion of the impact on women and children of such agreements, *see* Robin Fretwell Wilson, *The Perils of Privatized Marriage*, in MARRIAGE AND DIVORCE IN A MULTI-CULTURAL CONTEXT: RECONSIDERING THE BOUNDARIES OF CIVIL LAW AND RELIGION (Joel A. Nichols, ed., Cambridge University Press, 2011). *See generally*, Mohammad H. Fadel, *Religious Law, Family Law and Arbitration: Sharia and Halakha in America*, 90 CHI-KENT L. REV. 163 (2015); and James A. Sonnne, *Domestic Application of Sharia and the Exercise of Ordered Liberty*, 45 SETON HALL L. REV. 717 (2015).

Bad-Boy Clauses. Just as religious adherent may want religious obligations to govern their relationships, so may some couples seek to have moral obligations apply to their relationships. With the embrace of no-fault divorce, some couples sign premarital agreements designed to reintroduce the concept of fault. In Diosdado v. Diosdado, the couple's premarital agreement provided for liquidated damages if either spouse engaged in sexual activity outside of the marriage. 118 Cal. Rptr.2d 494 (2002). The court refused to enforce the agreement, saying it was contrary to California's no-fault divorce laws because it "attempts to impose [a liquidated damages] premium for the 'emotional angst' caused by [the husband's] breach of his promise of sexual fidelity." *Id.* at 474. *See also In re* Marriage of Cooper, 769 N.W.2d 582, 586 (Iowa 2009).

K. MARITAL CONTRACTS AND DIVORCE SETTLEMENT AGREEMENTS

As noted above, a marital agreement is any agreement entered into during the marriage, but not in anticipation of divorce or separation. A separation agreement occurs in anticipation of divorce or separation to specify the terms for dissolution outside of a formal hearing by the court.

Pacelli v. Pacelli

Superior Court of New Jersey, 1999
725 A.2d 56

■ D'ANNUNZIO, J.A.D.

At issue is the enforceability of a mid-marriage agreement resolving issues of equitable distribution and alimony in the event of a divorce. This appears to be a case of first impression in New Jersey. The trial court, after a plenary trial, determined that the agreement was enforceable. An order entered on October 25, 1996 memorialized that determination. Thereafter, on July 9, 1997, the court entered a judgment of divorce. The wife, defendant Francesca Pacelli, appeals.

The parties were married in June 1975. The husband, plaintiff Antonio Pacelli, was forty-four years of age at that time; defendant was twenty. Defendant had been born in Italy, but migrated to the United

States when she was fourteen. Plaintiff was a builder and a real estate developer. He also owned a restaurant at the time of the marriage. Plaintiff testified that he was worth three million dollars when the parties married, but he presented no documents to support that statement.

Two children were born of the marriage. Tony was born in 1976 and Franco was born in 1977. The family lived in a very substantial home in Passaic County and enjoyed a high standard of living. Their income tax returns showed a gross income of $540,000 in 1984 and $476,000 in 1985. Defendant contributed no income to the family.

In mid-1985, plaintiff informed defendant that he would divorce her unless she agreed to certain terms regarding their economic relationship. To punctuate his demand, plaintiff moved out of the marital bedroom and into an apartment above their garage. At or about the time he made this demand on defendant, plaintiff sought the advice of matrimonial counsel Barry Croland. Croland testified that he advised plaintiff of his economic exposure for equitable distribution and alimony. According to Croland, plaintiff admitted to a net worth of $4.7 million in 1985, $1.7 million more than he had when he married defendant. Croland informed plaintiff that any agreement between plaintiff and defendant, to be enforceable, had to be fair and made only after full disclosure of relevant information regarding the parties' assets. Croland also informed plaintiff that defendant should be represented by counsel.

The record establishes that defendant did not want a divorce. Upon being informed of plaintiff's demand and suggestion that she should retain counsel, defendant consulted matrimonial lawyer, Gary Skoloff, in July 1985. Skoloff advised defendant of her rights in the event of a divorce. Defendant's next contact with Skoloff was in the fall of 1985. At that time, she informed Skoloff that plaintiff was going to pay her $500,000 in the event of a future divorce, as full satisfaction of plaintiff's equitable distribution and alimony obligations. Skoloff advised her not to sign such an agreement and that if she divorced plaintiff in 1985, a judge would award her much more than $500,000 in equitable distribution and alimony. Defendant did not take Skoloff's advice. Defendant informed Skoloff that she wanted to preserve the marriage and did not want her children to grow up in a broken family. Skoloff testified that defendant told him that she would sign anything in an effort to preserve the marriage.

Thereafter, Skoloff received a form of agreement drafted by Croland and the family's tax returns for four years, through 1984. Croland also provided Skoloff with financial statements. Skoloff testified that the agreement was not negotiable and it was presented as an agreement to be signed as is, otherwise there would be a divorce. Defendant signed the agreement in February 1986 and plaintiff signed it in March 1986. The parties resumed their marriage until 1994, when plaintiff filed a complaint for divorce. In 1994, plaintiff's assets totaled $14,291,500. He had a net worth of $11,241,500.

The issues are: whether the agreement was the result of coercion or duress and, therefore, unenforceable; and whether the agreement was unfair and, therefore, unenforceable. Regarding the fairness issue, a subsidiary issue is whether the agreement should be measured for fairness as the facts were in 1985 or as the facts were in 1994 when plaintiff filed his divorce complaint. Defendant also contends that in 1989, she and the plaintiff agreed to nullify the agreement and that plaintiff and she signed a paper to that effect. Defendant could not produce the signed paper at the trial, contending that plaintiff had stolen it from her and destroyed it.

The trial court, in a comprehensive letter opinion, summarized the evidence, made specific findings of fact and determined that the agreement was not the result of coercion or duress, that it was fair as measured in 1985, and that defendant's contention that the parties had nullified the agreement was not credible. . . .

Pre-nuptial agreements made in contemplation of marriage are enforceable if they are fair and just. D'Onofrio v. D'Onofrio, 200 N.J.Super. 361, 366–67, 491 A.2d 752 (App.Div.1985); DeLorean v. DeLorean, 211 N.J.Super. 432, 435, 511 A.2d 1257 (Ch.Div.1986); Marschall v. Marschall, 195 N.J.Super. 16, 28, 477 A.2d 833 (Ch.Div.1984). Agreements made at the end of a marriage in contemplation of a divorce and to fix each party's economic rights on entry of a divorce judgment are enforceable if "fair and equitable." Lepis v. Lepis, 83 N.J. 139, 148–49, 416 A.2d 45 (1980); Petersen v. Petersen, 85 N.J. 638, 642, 428 A.2d 1301 (1981); Berkowitz v. Berkowitz, 55 N.J. 564, 569, 264 A.2d 49 (1970); Schlemm v. Schlemm, 31 N.J. 557, 581–82, 158 A.2d 508 (1960). . . .

We are persuaded that the mid-marriage agreement in the present case differs from pre-nuptial agreements and property settlement agreements made at a marriage's termination. It was entered into before the marriage lost all of its vitality and when at least one of the parties, without reservation, wanted the marriage to survive. Plaintiff also wanted to continue the marriage, but only on his terms.

Here, unlike the pre-nuptial bride, Francesca Pacelli had entered into the legal relationship of marriage when her husband presented her with his ultimatum. Moreover, the marriage had produced two children. Thus, defendant faced a more difficult choice than the bride who is presented with a demand for a pre-nuptial agreement. The cost to Francesca would have been the destruction of a family and the stigma of a failed marriage. She testified on several occasions that she signed the agreement to preserve the family and to make sure that her sons were raised in an intact family.

The mid-marriage agreement in this case also differs from a property settlement agreement made when the marriage has died. In that case, as Judge Lesemann perceptively observed in *Marschall,* each party, recognizing that the marriage is over, can look to his or her economic rights; the relationship is adversarial. Our point is that the context in which plaintiff made his demand was inherently coercive. Defendant's access to eminent counsel is of little relevance because her decision was dictated not by a consideration of her legal rights, but by her desire to preserve the family.

We have found no decision in New Jersey or other jurisdictions addressing the enforceability of this type of agreement. Courts have addressed "reconciliation" agreements, however.

Nicholson v. Nicholson, 199 N.J.Super. 525, 489 A.2d 1247 (App.Div.1985), involved a reconciliation agreement made after the couple had separated due to the husband's second episode of infidelity. As consideration for resumption of the marriage, the wife demanded and received a conveyance of the marital home from the husband. Previously, the couple had held title as tenants by the entirety. Twelve years later, the couple divorced and the trial court determined that the home was not subject to equitable distribution, thereby enforcing the reconciliation agreement.

On appeal, we observed that "[i]n some circumstances a reconciliation agreement will be enforced if it is fair and equitable." Nicholson, supra, 199 N.J.Super. at 530, 489 A.2d 1247. A prerequisite to enforcement is a requirement that "the marital relationship has deteriorated at least to the brink of an indefinite separation or a suit for divorce." *Id.* at 531, 489 A.2d 1247. Under such circumstances a "promise that induces a reconciliation will be enforced if it is fair and equitable." *Ibid.* We summarized additional factors that must be considered by the trial court in evaluating such an agreement:

> Before a reconciliation agreement will be enforced, the court must determine that the promise to resume marital relations was made when the marital rift was substantial. If the agreement was oral and enforcement is sought of a promise to convey real estate, there must also be compliance with the statute of frauds. *Carlsen,* 49 *N.J.Super.* at 134–138 [139 A.2d 309]. The court may have to resolve disputes over the terms of the agreement. *Carlsen,* 49 *N.J.Super.* at 138–139 [139 A.2d 309]; Schichtel v. Schichtel, 3 Ark.App. 36, 621 S.W.2d 504, 507–508 (1981). The court must consider whether the circumstances under which the agreement was entered into were fair to the party charged. D'Arc v. D'Arc, 164 N.J.Super. 226, 238–239 [395 A.2d 1270] (Ch.Div.1978), *rev'd in part, aff'd. in part,* 175 N.J.Super. 598 [421 A.2d 602] (App.Div.1980), *cert. denied,* 85 N.J. 487 [427 A.2d 579] (1981), *cert. denied,* 451 U.S. 971, 101 S.Ct., 2049, 68 L.Ed.2d 350 (1981). The terms of the agreement

> must have been conscionable when the agreement was made. *See* Wertlake v. Wertlake, 137 N.J.Super. 476, 482 [349 A.2d 552] (App.Div.1975). The party seeking enforcement must have acted in good faith. *See* Marshall v. Marshall, [166 W.Va. 304] 273 S.E.2d 360 (W.Va.Ct.App.1981). *Cf.* Sullivan v. Sullivan, 79 Ill.App.2d 194, 223 N.E.2d 461 (1967) (court will not enforce conveyance made in exchange for wife's fraudulent promise to return home). Changed circumstances must not have rendered literal enforcement inequitable.

[*Id.* at 532, 489 A.2d 1247.] We remanded to the trial court for further consideration.

Two of our observations in *Nicholson* are particularly relevant in the present case. In *Nicholson,* we required a showing that the marital relationship had genuinely deteriorated "to the brink of an indefinite separation or a suit for divorce." Here, the testimony of plaintiff and his lawyer establish that plaintiff's primary interest was financial. Plaintiff wanted an agreement that would limit his exposure to his wife's economic demands. Plaintiff testified on direct that

> I felt uncomfortable if I didn't have-I had to have an agreement, because I was involved in so many of these deals, and I just wanted to operate with a clear head. And I didn't want to have to worry about any day this thing could blow up, and I could be in a real bind.

Plaintiff returned to this theme later in his direct examination:

> Well, I just wasn't comfortable, you know, knowing that the marriage is always on a-sort of on the rocks. And I wanted to put everything in its [perspective]. I wanted to know that if I was going to go into a deal, I could not worry about, you know, getting involved in all kinds of legal stuff.

Plaintiff stated that the *DeLorean* case, involving a pre-nuptial agreement "gave me an idea to use some kind of an agreement to . . . keep the marriage intact, and still operate and being able to do business."

Plaintiff's lawyer, Croland, testified that plaintiff's purpose "was to stay married, that's what he wanted." But he wanted to understand his financial exposure in the event of a divorce. Croland also testified that during their initial conference Pacelli stated that he had "new deals coming his way," and he was concerned that his wife "not share beyond a certain point."

The evidence, therefore, supports an inference that the marital "crisis" was artificial, created by plaintiff to take advantage of his wife's dedication to the marriage and her family.

The second relevant standard in *Nicholson* is that the agreement must be fair and equitable when made *and* when it is sought to be enforced. We will allude to this standard later in this opinion.

The majority view in other jurisdictions is that "[a]n agreement the object of which is to restore marital relations after a separation has taken place will generally be upheld." 17 *C.J.S. Contracts,* § 236 (1963). According to Annotation, *Validity and enforceability of agreement designed to prevent divorce, or avoid or end separation,* 11 A.L.R. 277 (1921), a "contract between a husband and wife, made when the spouses are separated for legal cause, and providing for the payment of a consideration for their reunion, is, by weight of authority, enforceable by either spouse." The annotation offers the policy reasons for the majority and minority views:

> In most jurisdictions, an agreement of that character is held not only to be unobjectionable in this respect, but to promote the stability of the relation, as it purports to do. On the other hand, several courts have considered such an agreement as mischievous, because it offers an inducement for domestic discord to persons who are willing to occupy this vantage ground for the purpose of obtaining pecuniary or other concessions.

[Ibid.]

Flansburg v. Flansburg, 581 N.E.2d 430 (Ind.App.1991), is an example of the majority view regarding reconciliation agreements. There, the court affirmed enforcement of a reconciliation agreement made after the wife had filed a petition for dissolution of the marriage. The court concluded that "it was entirely appropriate for the trial court to apply the law of antenuptial contracts" to the reconciliation agreement. 581 N.E.2d at 433. The court cited a number of opinions from other jurisdictions recognizing the validity of reconciliation agreements and treating them "in much the same way as antenuptial agreements." *Id.* at 434. . . .

In Hoyt v. Hoyt, 213 Tenn. 117, 372 S.W.2d 300 (1963), the Supreme Court of Tennessee held that a reconciliation agreement made after the wife had filed a divorce action was not void or contrary to public policy. In a comprehensive opinion the court reviewed authorities representing the minority and majority views. It analogized the reconciliation agreement to antenuptial agreements and property settlements made in conjunction with a pending or contemplated divorce proceeding. 372 S.W.2d at 303–04.

Mathie v. Mathie, 12 Utah 2d 116, 363 P.2d 779 (1961) articulated some of the concerns on which the minority view is founded. The court noted that reconciliation agreements "between spouses to fix their property rights inter se during coverture are generally not held to be so absolute as to prevent a court under its equity powers in divorce actions from doing that which justice and equity require for the interest and welfare of the parties." 363 P.2d at 782–83. The court then stated:

> Some cases which contain language to the effect that agreements of that kind are valid state that they should be favored because they tend to encourage reconciliation and

> preservation of the family. But it is obvious that this is a two-edged sword. Other well-considered cases disavow such contracts, reasoning that the rights and duties in the marriage relationship are fixed by law and that the parties should not be encouraged to abrogate or avoid them *by using family strife to bargain themselves into positions of advantage;* that doing so bears the seeds of further strife; whereas there should be a forgetting and forgiveness of past difficulties and a fresh re-establishment of the obligations and duties of the marriage as originally intended.

[363 P.2d at 783 (Emphasis added)]. . . .

We are persuaded that placing a mid-marriage agreement in the same category as a pre-nuptial agreement is inappropriate. As previously indicated, the dynamics and pressures involved in a mid-marriage context are qualitatively different. Similarly, there are significant differences between a mid-marriage agreement and a property settlement agreement made in the context of termination of the marriage. In the latter circumstances, knowing that the marriage is over, though one party may wish to continue it, each party can pursue his or her economic self interest. Mid-marriage agreements closely resemble so-called reconciliation agreements. We must be aware, however, that such circumstances are pregnant with the opportunity for one party to use the threat of dissolution "to bargain themselves into positions of advantage." Mathie, supra, 363 P.2d at 783.

We need not decide whether such agreements are so inherently and unduly coercive that they should not be enforced, though we conclude that, at the very least, they must be closely scrutinized and carefully evaluated. In the present case, we conclude that the terms were not fair and just.

Defendant contends that the fairness of the agreement must be measured as of 1994 when plaintiff sought to enforce it. At that time, plaintiff's net worth was approximately $11,000,000. Defendant's argument relies in part on the Uniform Premarital Agreement Act, N.J.S.A. 37:2–31 to –41. It provides that an agreement is not enforceable if it was "unconscionable at the time enforcement was sought." N.J.S.A. 37:2–38b. The Act, however, only applies to premarital agreements and, consequently, it does not control the present case.

Defendant limits her attack on the agreement's fairness to the circumstances existing in 1994. We conclude, however, that the agreement was unfair in 1986, when it was signed. . . . We conclude that in 1985 the marital estate was $3,000,000. . . . Thus, the $540,000 provided in the agreement was 18% of the marital estate. Plaintiff's lawyer, Croland, testified that he had advised plaintiff that he could expect "the probable range of equitable distribution could be somewhere around . . . one-third. Could be less, it could be more." Skoloff testified that an equitable distribution range would be between thirty and forty percent of post-marital assets. Thus, the $500,000 buy out was approximately half of a potential equitable distribution award, using the low end of the range.

The $500,000 also purchased defendant's waiver of alimony. An alimony award in 1985 would have been substantial, perhaps approaching six figures. Plaintiff's annual income in 1984 and 1985 averaged $500,000. The parties lived well. They lived in an expensive home, drove luxury automobiles and vacationed at some of the most desirable destinations. Plaintiff estimated that defendant spent $20,000 to $30,000 per year on clothing from stores such as Bergdorf Goodman. Their son, Tony, went to Deerfield Academy, and Franco went to Choate. . . .

Defendant argues that the agreement should be measured for fairness in 1994, when plaintiff sought to enforce it. In *Nicholson, supra,* we observed that in evaluating a reconciliation agreement "[c]hanged circumstances must not have rendered literal enforcement inequitable." 199 N.J.Super. at 532, 489 A.2d 1247. We are persuaded that the close scrutiny and careful evaluation of mid-marriage agreements also requires consideration of the agreement's impact when enforced. This is so for at least two reasons. A marriage may survive for many years after such an agreement, as in this case. During that time, the family may continue to prosper, due in part to the contribution of a spouse, such as defendant, in her capacity as mother, homemaker and helpmate. It may be inequitable to preclude her participation in post-agreement wealth.

Moreover, post-agreement prosperity may elude the parties. A family's assets may be worth less at the time of enforcement than when the agreement was executed. In that case, enforcement of the agreement may be inequitable to the obligor.

It is apparent that the agreement is also unfair when measured in 1994. At that time, plaintiff's net worth exceeded $11,000,000, and post-marital assets were $8,000,000. Thus, $540,000 is approximately seven percent of the 1994 assets. The parties built a home at the Saint Andrews Club in Florida after executing the agreement. It is in joint names and defendant is entitled to one-half of the $1,200,000 equity, or $600,000. Even considering this asset, defendant's distribution is less than fifteen per cent of the marital estate. In light of the inherently coercive circumstances leading to the agreement, the result is unfair, inequitable and unenforceable. The trial court, on remand, must make determinations regarding equitable distribution and alimony, and other ancillary economic issues, if any. . . .

[Court reversed and remanded.]

NOTES

Enforcement of Marital Agreements, Generally. Typically, marital agreements seek to modify specific economic rights between the spouses that would otherwise govern in the event of divorce or death, just as the Pacellis' agreement sought to do. Courts take a hard look at marital agreements because many parties value the intact marriage and, therefore, cannot freely bargain. Additionally, some states impose different, heightened requirements on marital agreements, as opposed to premarital agreements, for the simple reason that many state laws based on the older UPAA apply only "to premarital agreements but, by [their] own terms, [do] not apply to marital agreements." Brian Bix, *The ALI Principles and Agreements: Seeking a Balance between Status and Contract*, in RECONCEIVING THE FAMILY: CRITIQUE ON THE AMERICAN LAW INSTITUTE'S PRINCIPLES OF THE LAW OF FAMILY DISSOLUTION 372, 382 (Robin Fretwell Wilson, ed., 2006). The more recent UPMAA would impose the same requirements on both marital and premarital agreements, and may ultimately help to erase this different treatment.

Thirty years after the UPAA and thirty-five years after the UMDA, inconsistent judicial precedent persists regarding the enforceability of postnuptial agreements. *See* Sean Hannon Williams, *Postnuptial Agreements*, 2007 WIS. L. REV. 827. The Massachusetts Supreme Court concluded that postnuptial agreements could be sanctioned if, at a minimum: "(1) each party has had an opportunity to obtain separate legal counsel of each party's own choosing; (2) there was no fraud or coercion in obtaining the agreement; (3) all assets were fully disclosed by both parties before the agreement was executed; (4) each spouse knowingly and explicitly agreed in writing to waive the right to a judicial equitable division of assets and all marital rights in the event of a divorce; and (5) the terms of the agreement are fair and reasonable at the time of execution and at the time of divorce." Ansin v. Craven-Ansin, 929 N.E.2d 955, 963–64 (Mass. 2010). However, some jurisdictions find postnuptial agreements to be contrary to public policy, except in limited instances, and will therefore not enforce them. *See, e.g.,* OHIO REV. CODE ANN. § 3103.06 (2016) (stating that "a husband and wife cannot, by any contract with each other, alter their legal relations, except that they may agree to an immediate separation and make provisions for the support of either of them and their children during the separation"). This approach is so ingrained in some jurisdictions that even when a couple signs a written postnuptial agreement modifying their premarital agreement, the court will not enforce it. *See, e.g.,* Hoffman v. Dobbins, 2009 WL 3119635 (Ohio Ct. App. 2009).

Reconciliation Agreements. Reconciliation agreements frequently operate to salvage a marriage, if only for a period of time. The law tends to favor such agreements as being consistent with public policy. *See* Louis I. Parley, *Post-Marital Agreements*, 8 J. AM. ACAD. MATRIM. LAW 125 (1992). Nonetheless, they receive the same scrutiny as any other marital agreement.

As *Pacelli* shows, some reconciliation agreements are entered into before the parties even file for divorce, and the consideration for the agreement is the decision not to file. Far more often, reconciliation agreements are entered into after the parties have already filed for divorce, raising the question of the reconciliation's impact on any agreement already reached by the parties, specifically, a separation agreement or divorce settlement agreement.

Reconciliation (with or without a written agreement) after the execution of a separation agreement or divorce settlement agreement may affect the enforceability of the separation or settlement agreement. *See generally* Brett R. Turner, *Reconciliation as a Defense to the Validity of Separation Agreements*, 15(10) DIVORCE LITIG. 180 (2003). Historically, in order to enter into a separation agreement, the parties had to be physically separated and remain so. If the parties reconciled, then the agreement became void due to lack of physical separation. *See, e.g., In re* Wilson, 66 A.D.2d 893 (N.Y. Ct. App. 1978).

Courts today focus on the intent of the parties when reconciling; specifically, whether they mean to abrogate the separation or settlement agreement or duties under it that have yet to be performed, called executory provisions. In Brazina v. Brazina, the court stated:

> [T]he modern view is that the executory provisions of a property settlement agreement are deemed to be abrogated by a subsequent reconciliation of the parties, unless it can be shown by the party seeking to enforce the agreement that the parties intended . . . [for] the executed provisions . . . [to be] unaffected by the reconciliation. . . . The philosophy underpinning the theory of abrogation is that, since the policy of courts is to encourage and strengthen the bond of marriage, it is the presumed intent of the parties at the time of the reconciliation to resume the marital relationship in all respects and abrogate any prior agreements restricting or inhibiting the rights of one of the spouses, unless they indicate otherwise at the time of the reconciliation.

558 A.2d 69, 72 (N.J. Ch. Div. 1989). While many states presume that the reconciling parties intend to abrogate the separation or settlement agreement, the presumption may be rebutted with factors showing that the parties intended to keep the agreement intact. Such factors include the parties continuing to make payments under the terms of the separation or settlement agreement, such as mortgage or child support payments; continuing to keep separate residences, bank accounts, and mailing addresses; and filing separate tax returns. *See* Pugsley v. Pugsley, 288 A.D.2d 284 (N.Y. Ct. App. 2001). Additionally, the agreement may specifically state that it is the parties' intent *not* to abrogate the agreement even in the event of reconciliation. *Id.*

Other jurisdictions make the opposite presumption—namely, that the parties intend to keep the separation or settlement agreement intact and so will only invalidate that agreement if it is shown that the parties intend this result. In Muchesko v. Muchesko, the court stated:

> To effect a revocation of a settlement agreement, the parties must intend to resume married life "completely and entirely" and not just temporarily or for a trial period. . . . Reconciliation is the voluntary resumption of a marital relationship in the fullest sense, and is a state of mind to be determined by the evidence. . . . In determining

> whether a reconciliation has occurred, courts look at whether the parties have resumed cohabiting, sexual relations, and the maintenance of joint affairs as husband and wife.

955 P.2d 21, 26 (Ariz. Ct. App. 1997).

Courts sometimes struggle to define reconciliation. Typically, a remarriage constitutes reconciliation. *See, e.g.,* Ray v. Ohio National Insurance Co., 537 So.2d 915 (Ala. 1989). Moreover, if parties resume a marriage-like relationship, the court often will find reconciliation. *See, e.g.,* Rudansky v. Rudansky, 223 A.D.2d 500 (N.Y. Ct. App. 1996) (finding reconciliation where the parties are "living together and resuming marital relations, their selling of their separate apartments and purchase of a new apartment, plaintiff's quitting her job and resuming a role as a housewife such as by traveling with and attending defendant's social and business gatherings, defendant's giving plaintiff a weekly allowance to pay for their joint household expenses, and their filing of joint tax returns and stating thereon that they were married"). However, sexual relations and cohabitation alone may not be enough to establish reconciliation. *See, e.g.*, N.C. GEN. STAT. ANN. § 52–10.2 (2016) ("Isolated incidents of sexual intercourse between the parties shall not constitute resumption of marital relations."); Pugsley v. Pugsley, 288 A.D.2d 284 (N.Y. Ct. App. 2001) ("[C]ohabitation alone does not by itself destroy the validity of the separation agreement.").

PROBLEM THREE

One day before marrying while vacationing, Harry and Wilma sign a prenup that provides: "If we, Harry and Wilma, divorce, we agree to split all property acquired during the marriage 50–50." The happily married couple returns from their vacation. Harry goes back to his stockbroker job, where his is racking in the money: about a million dollars a year. Wilma quits her job and since she has spare time, she tries her hand at inventing. The first few gadgets that Wilma invents don't turn out to work very well, but eventually Wilma comes up with a wildly successful kitchen gadget. Wilma's kitchen gadget gets picked up by several kitchen supply ware stores and becomes an important feature in every kitchen. Wilma makes about 25 million dollars on her very first invention. Not long after her invention success, Wilma and Harry have a child, named Charlie. Wilma loves her son Charlie but finds the day to day duties of caring for him boring after the excitement of her life as a successful inventor. Wilma decides that she wants a divorce. However, she is worried that now that she has 25 million from her successful invention, Harry will ask for alimony and she will have to give him half of her 25 million. Wilma feels that she earned that 25 million herself, and in any event Harry makes enough as a stockbroker to support himself. Wilma desperately wants to get out of her marriage, but she doesn't want to do so at the cost of her invention fortune. Wilma asks Harry to sign a new agreement saying that he will waive property distribution and not ask for alimony if they divorce. Harry is devastated that Wilma, who he thought was happy, is considering a divorce. Harry agrees that he won't ask for property distribution or alimony, but Wilma wants him to sign the new agreement. Harry cannot face the prospect of them divorcing and doesn't want to sign the agreement. He cries and begs Wilma to reconsider. She won't so eventually Harry agrees to sign the agreement as is. Now that Wilma has the agreement, she feels more secure, so she decides not to file for divorce immediately. At first, Harry is glad, but over the next year their marriage deteriorates. Wilma is clearly not very interested in her family life and Harry is broken hearted and begins to resent Wilma for making him sign the agreement. A year later, neither of them really likes the other anymore, and they agree to divorce. They decide that they will share custody of Charlie. What will happen with the terms of the agreement?

Johnston v. Johnston

Court of Appeals of Maryland, 1983
465 A.2d 436

■ COUCH, JUDGE.

Although the parties have raised four issues in this case, the issue, as we see it, is whether a separation agreement approved and incorporated but not merged in a divorce decree may be collaterally attacked. For reasons to be discussed herein, we hold that it may not be where, as here, its validity is conclusively established by the decree which operates as *res judicata*.

The parties hereto were married in June of 1948 and lived together 23 years prior to separating in June of 1971. During the marriage, four children were born all of whom have now reached their majority. Subsequent to their separation, each party retained counsel and negotiated an agreement the purpose of which was "to effect a final and permanent settlement of their respective property rights." The agreement was executed by the parties in February of 1973 and provided, *inter alia*, for the support and maintenance of Mrs. Johnston and the four children, the transfer of certain property interests, the execution of testamentary designations, and the creation of various trusts. The agreement was made in contemplation of divorce proceedings and provided:

> "This agreement shall be offered in evidence in any such suit, and if acceptable to the court, shall be incorporated by reference in the decree that may be granted therein. *Notwithstanding such incorporation, this agreement shall not be merged in the decree, but shall survive the same and shall be binding and conclusive on the parties for all time.*" (Emphasis supplied).

The agreement also provided:

> "No modification or waiver of any of the terms of this agreement shall be valid unless in writing and executed with the same formality as this agreement."

Mr. Johnston filed a "Bill of Complaint for Divorce A *Vinculo Matrimonii*" in the Circuit Court for Baltimore City, specifically requesting "[t]hat the Agreement of the parties dated February 16, 1973 be incorporated by reference in any decree that may be granted herein." A "Decree of Divorce" was entered June 27, 1973, stating in relevant part:

> "It is further ADJUDGED, ORDERED AND DECREED that the Plaintiff provide for maintenance, and support of Defendant and of the infant children of the parties, all as provided in the Agreement between the parties dated February 16, 1973 and filed in this cause of action, *said Agreement being hereby approved and made a part hereof as if fully set forth herein. . . .*" (Emphasis added).

In May, 1981, Mr. Johnston filed a "Petition to Set Aside and Void Agreement" on the basis that "consultations [with professionals] ha[d] disclosed that [he] suffered from a mental disease and/or mental defect during the negotiations and subsequent execution of the aforesaid Agreement which severely impaired [his] mental competency at that time." The petition further asserted that Mr. Johnston's mental incompetency justified the voiding of the separation agreement. Mrs. Johnston in turn filed a "Motion to Strike and Motion Raising Preliminary Objection" contending that the four children were necessary parties as they were affected by the agreement, the allegations in the petition were insufficient to advise her of the nature of Mr. Johnston's mental disease or defect, that Mr. Johnston had failed to state whether he is presently mentally competent, and that she and other members of the family have relied upon and continue to rely upon the terms of the agreement. She also asserted that the relief requested should be denied because of laches and public policy. In addition, Mrs. Johnston argued that Mr. Johnston was actually seeking to have the enrolled decree set aside but had failed to allege "fraud, mistake or irregularity" as required by Maryland Rule 625.[1] . . .

[The chancellor granted Mrs. Johnston's motion to strike, ruling: not to bifurcate the agreement, that there must be a showing of fraud, mistake, or irregularity, that there was no fraud, mistake or irregularity, and that the children were parties. The Appellate Court affirmed.]

We believe that the threshold issue, which neither the chancellor nor the intermediate appellate court discussed, is whether the separation agreement merged in the decree so as to be superseded by the decree.[3] The decree expressly approved and incorporated the agreement. However, the agreement explicitly provided that it was not to merge in

---

[1] Md. Rule 625a states:

"For a period of thirty days after the entry of a judgment, or thereafter pursuant to motion filed within such period, the court shall have revisory power and control over such judgment. After the expiration of such period the court shall have revisory power and control over such judgment, only in case of fraud, mistake or irregularity."

[3] "Merger" is defined as the "[s]ubstitution of rights and duties under judgment or decree for those under property settlement agreement." Black's Law Dictionary 892 (5th ed. 1979); *Flynn v. Flynn*, 42 Cal.2d 55, 265 P.2d 865, 866 (1954) (en banc); *Roesbery v. Roesbery*, 88 Idaho 514, 401 P.2d 805, 807 (1965).

the decree but was to survive the decree. As observed by the Supreme Court of Arizona in McNelis v. Bruce, 90 Ariz. 261, 367 P.2d 625, 631 (1961) (en banc):

> "It is the rule that the mere approval of a property settlement in the divorce decree does not operate to make it a part of an enforceable as a decree. If the language of the agreement shows an intent to make it part of the divorce decree and the agreement is actually incorporated in the decree, the provisions of the agreement may be enforced as an order of the court. As soon as a property settlement agreement is incorporated into the decree the agreement is superceded by the decree and the obligations imposed are not those imposed by contract but are those imposed by the decree since the contract is merged in the decree." (Citations omitted).

The language of the agreement in *McNelis* was similar to that in the instant case, providing: " 'This agreement shall be offered in evidence in such action and if acceptable to the court shall be incorporated by reference in any decree that may be granted herein. Notwithstanding such incorporation, this agreement shall not be merged in the decree but shall survive the same and shall be binding and conclusive upon the parties for all time.' " *Id.* 367 P.2d at 631–32.

In determining whether the agreement merged in the decree so as to be modifiable by the court, the court looked to the intent of the parties, stating in pertinent part:

> "The foregoing clause manifests the intention of the parties to the agreement. It was not disapproved by the court but rather adopted as part of the agreement; it therefore must be taken as speaking the intention of not only the parties but of the court that the agreement was not to be merged in the judgment." *Id.* 367 P.2d at 632.

The Supreme Court of California has also had occasion to discuss the issue of merger:

> "Merger is the substitution of rights and duties under the judgment or the decree for those under the agreement or cause of action sued upon. The question as to what extent, if any, a merger has occurred, when a separation agreement has been presented to the court in a divorce action, arises in various situations. Thus, it may be necessary to determine whether or not contempt will lie to enforce the agreement, whether or not other judgment remedies, such as execution or a suit on the judgment, are available, whether or not an action may still be maintained on the agreement itself, and whether or not there is an order of the court that may be modified. . . .
>
> In any of these situations it is first necessary to determine whether the parties and the court intended a merger. If the

agreement is expressly set out in the decree, and the court orders that it be performed, it is clear that a merger is intended. On the other hand, the parties may intend only to have the validity of the agreement established, and not to have it become a part of the decree enforceable as such. Whether or not a merger is intended, the agreement may be incorporated into the decree either expressly or by reference. If a merger is not intended, the purpose of incorporation will be only to identify the agreement so as to render its validity res judicata in any subsequent action based upon it. If a merger is intended, the purpose of incorporation is, of course, to make the agreement an operative part of the decree." Flynn v. Flynn, 42 Cal.2d 55, 265 P.2d 865, 866 (1954) (en banc) (numerous citations omitted).

The agreement in *Flynn* provided that it could be approved by the court and incorporated in the decree. However, there was no provision, as in the instant case, that it would not merge. The decree ratified, approved, and incorporated the agreement. The court concluded that the parties and the court had clearly intended the agreement to merge in the decree and, accordingly, the court had jurisdiction to modify the provision for monthly payments.

In our view, where, as in the instant case, the agreement provides that it shall be *incorporated but not merged* in the decree, it is patent that the parties did not intend merger and the agreement survives as a separate and independent contractual arrangement between the parties. On the other hand, where, as in *Flynn* supra, the agreement does not include a non-merger clause and it is incorporated in the decree, the agreement is superseded by the decree. See also Wallace v. Wallace, 1 Hawaii Ct.App. 315, 619 P.2d 511, 513 (1980); Bowman v. Bennett, 250 N.W.2d 47, 50 (Iowa 1977). The agreement, once incorporated and merged in the decree, is enforceable through contempt proceedings and may be modified by the court. See, e.g., Early v. Early, 6 Ariz.App. 110, 430 P.2d 456, 460–61 (1967); *Flynn*, supra. It has also been stated that where the court incorporates the agreement as a whole, including the non-merger clause, the court approves the clause against merger so that the contract survives.

It is undisputed that pursuant to Maryland Rule S77 b[5] a separation agreement may be incorporated in the divorce decree. Moreover, there are numerous cases previously decided by this Court that firmly establish that once incorporated, the contractual provisions become part of the decree, modifiable by the court where appropriate and enforceable through contempt proceedings. . . . It is significant to note that the issue

[5] Md.Rule S77 b provides:

"A deed, agreement or settlement between husband and wife as described in Art. 16, Sec. 28 of the Annotated Code of Maryland may be received in evidence and made a part of the record in an action for divorce, annulment or alimony and may be incorporated, insofar as the court may deem proper, into the decree."

of merger has simply never arisen as none of the incorporated agreements contained a non-merger clause. On the other hand, it appears to be well established that separation agreements not incorporated in divorce decrees remain separate enforceable instruments. For example, we have observed that:

> "A support or property agreement is not invalid nor unenforceable merely because it is not embodied in the divorce decree, if not in conflict with such decree. If the divorce decree does not provide for alimony, it does not terminate liability of the husband to make the payments provided for by a separation agreement. A support or property agreement is not affected by the subsequent decree of divorce, if such settlement is neither incorporated in the decree, disapproved by the decree, nor superseded by provisions of the decree." Shacter v. Shacter, 251 Md. 304, 307–08, 247 A.2d 268, 270 (1968) (quoting 1 Nelson on Divorce, Ch. 13, § 13.54 (2d ed. 1945)).

In *Shacter*, the separation agreement was not incorporated as there were no grounds for divorce. However, its validity was clearly recognized as the court entered judgment for the wife against the husband in the amount due under the agreement. . . .

In our view, the cases from other jurisdictions as well as the various treatises concerning the doctrine of merger, as discussed hereinabove at length, are very persuasive. On the basis of such authority, we hold that where the parties intend a separation agreement to be incorporated but not merged in the divorce decree, the agreement remains a separate, enforceable contract and is not superseded by the decree. In the case *sub judice*, the agreement expressly provided that it was to be incorporated but not merged in the decree. The decree approved the agreement as a whole and made it a part of the decree as if it were *fully* set forth, thus approving the non-merger clause. Accordingly, the agreement remained an independent contract which in some instances could be attacked separately from the decree and thus the trial judge erred in granting the motion to strike on the basis that the requirements of Md.Rule 625 had not been met. . . .

Although the parties in the instant case have not precisely raised the issue of *res judicata*, we believe that in the interests of judicial economy it is appropriate for us to address it as it is dispositive of the matter before us. . . .

In the instant case, the separation agreement was executed "[w]hereas the Husband desire[d] to make provision for the Wife's and children's support and maintenance, and the parties desire[d] to effect a final and permanent settlement of their respective property rights." Both parties were represented by competent counsel at the time of the execution of the agreement as well as during the divorce proceeding. The agreement, consisting of 17 pages and numerous exhibits, was submitted to the court for its approval. By its own terms, it was to be incorporated in the decree only if it were acceptable to the court. Mr. Johnston testified at the divorce hearing and was questioned by the chancellor regarding the separation agreement. . . .

The divorce decree expressly approved the agreement, which was filed as an exhibit, and ordered, at the request of the parties, that it be sealed due to the confidential nature of various matters and facts contained therein.

In our view the property rights of the parties were determined in the divorce proceeding. Moreover, the approval and incorporation of the agreement conclusively established the validity of the agreement and precludes a collateral attack by either party. . . .

For the reasons stated herein, we conclude that where, as in the instant case, the property settlement agreement is presented to the court for approval and is approved by the court and incorporated in the divorce decree, the validity of the agreement is conclusively established and the doctrine of *res judicata* operates so as to preclude a collateral attack on the agreement.

In accordance with the above, we hold that Mrs. Johnston's motion to strike was properly granted by the chancellor although for reasons different from those assigned by the Court of Special Appeals.

NOTES

Problems remain in some jurisdictions about whether (or how) divorce settlement agreements can be modified after divorce and the means available for enforcing their terms through judicial action. However, the larger movement toward private ordering in family law has created pressure for such agreements to retain their contractual integrity even after they have been incorporated into judicial decrees. This interplay of decree and contract sometimes has the effect of permitting modification of the decree only in accordance with the terms of the contract or by subsequent agreement between the parties. At the same time, there has been movement towards providing for increased enforcement of divorce settlement agreements through such judicial remedies as contempt, as discussed *infra*.

Does the Agreement Continue as a Separate Contract? A key question raised by the use of separation or divorce settlement agreements is whether their inclusion in a divorce decree, either by reference or by specific incorporation of the agreement, in whole or part, subsumes the agreement into the decree, extinguishing its separate contractual identity. If subsumed, the contract's executory portions may be subject to statutory rules about future modification or termination of alimony, among other questions. *See* Noble v. Fisher, 894 P.2d 118 (Idaho 1995). If it is not merged, then, as the Court of Special Appeals of Maryland in Mendelson v. Mendelson, 75 Md.App. 486, 541 A.2d 1331 (1988), relying on *Johnston,* held:

> an agreement for spousal support that is not merged into the divorce decree remains entirely contractual and passes beyond the

> court's power to modify it for any reason—other than the one provided for in the contract—once the decree is enrolled.

Id. at 1337. The Maryland legislature has since provided by statute that parties may "specifically state[ ] that the provisions with respect to spousal support are not subject to any court modification." MD. CODE ANN., FAM. LAW § 8–103 (2016).

Inconsistent use of terminology, by courts and legislatures as well as lawyers, has caused much confusion. The terms "incorporate," "merge," "ratify," and "affirm" have produced the most difficulty. In some jurisdictions they have become words of art, to be used according to the result desired. In others, some of the terms may be interchangeable.

In some jurisdictions, the difference between merger and incorporation is vast. In Virginia, for example, whether a divorce settlement agreement is incorporated into a final decree or merged into it has important implications for enforcement of promises. As the court explained in Hering v. Hering:

> the Supreme Court of Virginia draw[s] a distinction among situations where an agreement is affirmed, where it is incorporated into a decree, or where, as here, the agreement is "affirmed, ratified, incorporated, but not merged" into the final decree. . . . [I]f the court accepts the agreement, its decree may merely approve . . . without incorporating its provisions into the decree or ordering payment or compliance with its terms. In that situation, the decree merely constitutes judicial approval of a private bilateral contract and the provisions of the support agreement do not have the full force and effect of a court's decree and are not enforceable by the court's contempt powers. The court also has the option to incorporate by reference the child support provisions, in whole or in part, as part of the final decree, and retain jurisdiction to enforce compliance through its contempt powers.

533 S.E.2d 631, 633–34 (2000).

Sometimes parties make no mention of the terms of their settlement agreement to the court at the time of divorce and simply intend to enforce the agreement as an ordinary contract. In a variation of this, practiced regularly in some jurisdictions in the past, parties ask the court to pass on the fairness of their agreement without jeopardizing its separate contractual nature. This procedure developed out of concern for insuring against future invalidation of an agreement for unconscionability or other reason. The court's validation was particularly important in jurisdictions that only permitted alimony awards to be made at the time of the divorce; if a settlement agreement in such a state were set aside after divorce, there would be no avenue for seeking a judicial award of alimony after the fact.

For a discussion of some of the problems of separation agreements and private ordering versus public policy, and negotiation in the context of separation and divorce, *see* Brian Bix, *The ALI Principles and Agreements: Seeking a Balance between Status and Contract*, in RECONCEIVING THE FAMILY: CRITIQUE ON THE AMERICAN LAW INSTITUTE'S PRINCIPLES OF THE LAW OF FAMILY DISSOLUTION 372 (Robin Fretwell Wilson, ed., 2006); Richard

A. Corwin, *Ethical Considerations: the Attorney-Client Relationship*, 75 TUL. L. REV. 1327 (2001); Martha M. Ertman, *Marriage as a Trade: Bridging the Private/Public Distinction*, 36 HARV. C.R.-C.L. L. REV. 79 (2001); Brian H. Bix, *State of the Union: The States' Interest in the Marital Status of Their Citizens*, 55 U. MIAMI L. REV. 1 (2000).

UNIFORM MARRIAGE AND DIVORCE ACT (1973)

§ 306. [Separation Agreement]

(a) To promote amicable settlement of disputes between parties to a marriage attendant upon their separation or the dissolution of their marriage, the parties may enter into a written separation agreement containing provisions for disposition of any property owned by either of them, maintenance of either of them, and support, custody, and visitation of their children.

(b) In a proceeding for dissolution of marriage or for legal separation, the terms of the separation agreement, except those providing for the support, custody, and visitation of children, are binding upon the court unless it finds, after considering the economic circumstances of the parties and any other relevant evidence produced by the parties, on their own motion or on request of the court, that the separation agreement is unconscionable.

(c) If the court finds the separation agreement unconscionable, it may request the parties to submit a revised separation agreement or may make orders for the disposition of property, maintenance, and support.

(d) If the court finds that the separation agreement is not unconscionable as to disposition of property or maintenance, and not unsatisfactory as to support:

(1) unless the separation agreement provides to the contrary, its terms shall be set forth in the decree of dissolution or legal separation and the parties shall be ordered to perform them, or

(2) if the separation agreement provides that its terms shall not be set forth in the decree, the decree shall identify the separation agreement and state that the court has found the terms not unconscionable.

(e) Terms of the agreement set forth in the decree are enforceable by all remedies available for enforcement of a judgment, including contempt, and are enforceable as contract terms.

(f) Except for terms concerning the support, custody, or visitation of children, the decree may expressly preclude or limit modification of terms set forth in the decree if the separation agreement so provides. Otherwise, terms of a separation agreement set forth in the decree are automatically modified by modification of the decree.

NOTES

The UMDA provides one model for evaluating the fairness of a divorce settlement agreement privately entered into by the parties. Notice that the UMDA would leave questions of alimony to the parties, but that questions of child support, visitation, and custody would always remain within the purview of the court. Like marital agreements, separation or divorce settlement agreements were regarded with suspicion, if not hostility, by the courts not long ago. This suspicion reflected the then strong public policy against encouraging divorce. *See, e.g.,* Glickman v. Collins, 533 P.2d 204 (1975). With the introduction of no-fault divorce grounds—particularly those requiring the parties to live separately for a specified period—separation and divorce settlement agreements gained increasing popularity and legislatures began to enact statutes facilitating their use. Persons contemplating divorce may, on separating, execute an agreement that will govern their economic relationship during the period before divorce, as well as afterward.

L. TAX ISSUES AND INCIDENTS

A course in family law does not provide time for detailed coverage of taxation. Some basic rules and issues need to be understood, however, if only to alert practitioners about the need to seek advice from a tax expert. *See, e.g.,* Kathleen DeLaney Thomas, *Taxing Compensatory Stock Rights Transferred in Divorce*, 93 N.C. L. REV. 741 (2015); Joanne Ross Wilder, *Divorce and Taxes: Fifty Years of Changes,* 24 J. AM. ACAD. MATRIM. LAW 489 (2012); Michelle Drumbl, *Decoupling Taxes & Marriage: Beyond Innocence and Income Splitting*, 4 COLUM. J. TAX. L. 94 (Dec. 2012).

This Section highlights five tax consequences of divorce: tax consequences of alimony, of child support payments, of property settlement payments, of claiming a child as a dependent, and of the parties' post-divorce filing status. For clarity, this Section refers to the person making some form of payment, such as alimony or child support, as the "payor," and the person receiving the payment as the "recipient."

Tax Consequences of Alimony Payments. Alimony and separate maintenance payments are considered "income," meaning that the recipient of these payments must report these amounts. INTERNAL REVENUE CODE (IRC) §§ 61(a)(8), 71(a). Correspondingly, the spouse making alimony or maintenance payments may deduct these amounts "above-the-line," reducing the payor's gross income. IRC § 215. Note the combined effect of this treatment: receiving alimony payments may put the recipient into a higher tax bracket while making alimony payments may shift the payor into a lower bracket.

The IRC defines an "alimony or separate maintenance payment" as (1) a cash payment that (2) is received under a divorce or separation agreement when (3) the agreement does not indicate that the payment should not be reported as gross income and deducted as alimony, where (4) the payor and recipient do not reside in the same household, and (5) the payor would not continue to be liable for the amounts after the recipient's death. IRC § 71(b).

IRC Section 71(f) contains provisions designed to prevent "excess front-loading" of alimony payments. A special set of recapture rules limits the extent to which a payor can compress several years' worth of alimony payments into just a few years, and enjoy the high deductions in these early years. Under Section 71(f), if it is determined that the payor has made "excess alimony payments," the payor must recompute the deduction and include the amount defined as "excess" as income in later years, and the recipient receives a later-year deduction to make up for the excess income included in the prior year.

Tax Consequences of Child Support Payments. Child support payments are not included in gross income. IRC § 71(c). Because the parent-child relationship does not end at divorce, child support payments merely reflect ongoing parental support.

Tax Consequences of Property Settlements. Unlike alimony payments, property settlements are neither includible in the recipient's gross income nor deductible by the payor. IRC Section 1041 provides that no gain or loss will be recognized on property transferred between spouses or former spouses if the transfer is incident to divorce. Instead, a transfer between spouses (or former spouses) will be treated like a gift, in that the transferee's basis in the property will be the adjusted basis of the transferor.

Special IRC provisions govern tax consequences related to the marital home. If one spouse transfers the title to the couple's home as part of a divorce settlement to the other spouse, the recipient will be able to include the time that the transferor owned the house for purposes of excluding up to $250,000 of gain on the sale of a principal residence under Section 121. IRC § 121(d)(3)(A); Treas. Reg. § 1.121–4(b)(1).

Who Can Claim a Child as a Dependent? Upon divorce, one spouse will be able to claim the couple's child as a dependent, giving the claimant an additional exemption. IRC §§ 151–152. In general, the custodial parent—meaning the parent with whom the child lives for a greater part of the calendar year—may claim this exemption. IRC § 152(c)(4)(B); Treas. Reg. § 1.152–4(d).

The IRC provides that the custodial parent receives the exemption, regardless of whether the noncustodial parent provided a greater amount of financial support for the child. However, taxpayers can use the release provision in Section 152(e) to shift the exemption to the non-custodial parent, which would allow the divorced parents, as an economic unit, to pay less in taxes. To claim the dependent, the non-custodial parent must attach IRS Form 8332 to the tax return. A court order, divorce decree, or separation agreement will not be accepted as a written declaration for purposes of the exemption release if the decree or agreement was entered into after tax year 2008. Treas.Reg. § 1.152–4(e)(ii).

Filing Status. If the spouses have a child in common, under IRC Section 2(b), one party can file as "head of household" if the "qualifying child" lives in the home for more than one-half of the taxable year. The head of household status allows this party to benefit from a lower tax rate than filing as an unmarried individual. *Compare* IRC § 1(b) *with*

§ 1(c). In order to use the head of household status, the child must be a dependent without regard to Section 153(e), meaning that one cannot claim head of household if he or she is the non-custodial parent. Conversely, the custodial parent can claim head of household even if he or she releases the exemption to the non-custodial parent.

M. DISCHARGE IN BANKRUPTCY

The Bankruptcy Code permits individuals to file for bankruptcy under Chapters 7, 11, 12 and 13. 11 U.S.C. §§ 109(b)–(e). This discussion focuses on individuals who have filed for bankruptcy under Chapter 7. The desire to give debtors a "fresh start" is one of the primary policies underlying bankruptcy law. Ordinarily, a "fresh start" entails a discharge of most pre-bankruptcy debts, releasing the debtor from continued personal liability on those debts. 11 U.S.C. § 524 (2005). However, countervailing policy concerns demand that debtors remain liable for certain debts after bankruptcy—foremost among these debts are obligations to pay child support, spousal support, and, more recently, any other obligation incurred at divorce. 11 U.S.C. § 523(a) (providing exceptions from discharge in Chapters 7, 11, 12 and 13 cases).

Congress and the courts have long deemed the duties of support that a debtor owes to the debtor's present or former family members as deserving no discharge. *See generally* Wetmore v. Markoe, 196 U.S. 68, 77 (1904); Shine v. Shine, 802 F.2d 583, 585–588 (1st Cir. 1986); *In re* Johnson, 445 B.R. 50, 59 (Bankr. D. Mass. 2011) *amended in part,* 09–19214–JNF, 2011 WL 1467913 (Bankr. D. Mass. Apr. 18, 2011). Section 523(a)(5) of the Bankruptcy Code provides that an individual debtor may not receive discharge "for any domestic support obligation," whether future payments or accrued arrearages. The obligation, however, may be stayed during the bankruptcy proceeding's pendency if the property that the creditor is attempting to reach is part of the debtor's estate. *See generally* MARGARET HOWARD, BANKRUPTCY: CASES AND MATERIALS 689–90 (5th ed. 2012).

In 1994, Congress extended the non-discharge policy to both property settlement debts and "hold harmless" agreements, making both non-dischargeable. *See* CHARLES J. TABB, THE LAW OF BANKRUPTCY § 10.20, 990–992 (2d. ed. 2009). Under a "hold harmless" arrangement, the debtor spouse agrees to pay certain marital debts, such as a mortgage on the marital home, directly to a third party, and to hold the non-debtor spouse harmless from those debts. *See* DOUGLAS G. BAIRD, THE ELEMENTS OF BANKRUPTCY 18–19 (4th ed. 2006). In 2005, Congress further strengthened the property settlement provisions by removing previously available affirmative defenses and making "all property settlements arising out of separation or divorce non-dischargeable." *See* TABB, *supra* at 991. Today, Section 523(a)(15) prevents the discharge of any debt:

> to a spouse, former spouse, or child of the debtor and not of the kind described in [section (a)(5)] that is incurred by the debtor in the course of a divorce or separation or in connection with a separation agreement, divorce decree or other order of a court of record, or a determination made in accordance with State or territorial law by a governmental unit.

Together, Sections 523(a)(5) and (a)(15) shield support obligations and debts incurred at divorce from discharge. *See, e.g.,* § 727(b) (exception to discharge under Chapter 7); *see also* §§ 1141, 1228(a), 1228(b) and 1328(b). Sections 523(a)(5) and (a)(15) work "in tandem" with a number of other Bankruptcy Code provisions addressing the automatic stay and issues of exemption and priority, as well as a number of other matters. Specifically:

> [Section] 362(b)(2), excepting from the automatic stay actions to establish paternity, to obtain or modify a support order, or to collect spousal or child support from non-state property; § 507(a)(1), providing first priority for domestic support obligations; § 522(c), making exempt property liable for nondischargeable support obligations; § 522(f)(1)(A), barring avoidance of judicial liens that secure domestic support obligations; and § 547(c)(7), excepting payments for domestic support obligations from preference avoidance.
>
> [In addition,] debtors must be current on domestic support obligations in order to confirm any reorganization plan, §§ 1129(a)(14), 1225(a)(7), [and] 1325(a)(8), or to receive a discharge in Chapters 12 or 13, §§ 1225(a) [and] 1328(a); information about pending bankruptcy cases must be sent to support claimants, as well as to state child support agencies, §§ 704(a)(10), 1106(a)(8), 1202(b)(6), [and] 1302(b)(6); and a debtor's failure to pay postpetition support obligations may constitute cause for conversion or dismissal of a case under Chapters 11, 12 and 13, §§ 1112(b)(4)(P), 1208(c)(10) [and] 1307(c)(11).

HOWARD, *supra*, 689–90.

Prior to the revision of Section 523(a)(15) in 2005 to eliminate affirmative defenses to property settlement obligations to the non-discharge of property settlement agreements, a significant amount of litigation in bankruptcy concerned the proper classification of a debt as either a support obligation or a property settlement. *See generally* Sheryl Scheible, *Defining "Support" Under Bankruptcy Law: Revitalization of the "Necessaries" Doctrine*, 41 VAND. L. REV. 1 (1988).

Whether a debt stems from a support obligation under Section 523(a)(5) or is a property settlement under Section 523(a)(15) can sometimes be relevant today. This is so because Section 523(a)(5) support obligations are not discharged in Chapter 13 proceedings and may also be enforced against exempt property, such as the homestead. *See* Howard, *supra.* Section 523(a)(15) debts arising from divorce enjoy neither benefit. *Id.*

N. SPECIAL PROBLEMS OF ENFORCEMENT

Hicks on Behalf of Feiock v. Feiock

Supreme Court of the United States, 1988
485 U.S. 624

■ WHITE, JUSTICE delivered the opinion of the Court.

. . .

On January 19, 1976, a California state court entered an order requiring respondent, Phillip Feiock, to begin making monthly payments to his ex-wife for the support of their three children. Over the next six years, respondent only sporadically complied with the order, and by December 1982 he had discontinued paying child support altogether. His ex-wife sought to enforce the support orders. On June 22, 1984, a hearing was held in California state court on her petition for ongoing support payments and for payment of the arrearage due her. The court examined respondent's financial situation and ordered him to begin paying $150 per month commencing on July 1, 1984. . . .

Respondent apparently made two monthly payments but paid nothing for the next nine months. He was then served with an order to show cause why he should not be held in contempt on nine counts of failure to make the monthly payments ordered by the court. At a hearing on August 9, 1985, petitioner made out a *prima facie* case of contempt against respondent by establishing the existence of a valid court order, respondent's knowledge of the order, and respondent's failure to comply with the order. Respondent defended by arguing that he was unable to pay support during the months in question. This argument was partially successful, but respondent was adjudged to be in contempt on five of the nine counts. He was sentenced to five days in jail on each count, to be served consecutively, for a total of 25 days. This sentence was suspended, however, and respondent was placed on probation for three years. As one of the conditions of his probation, he was ordered once again to make support payments of $150 per month. As another condition of his probation, he was ordered, starting the following month, to begin repaying $50 per month on his accumulated arrearage, which was determined to total $1650.

At the hearing, respondent had objected to the application of Cal.Civ.Proc.Code Ann.§ 1209.5 (1982) against him, claiming that it was unconstitutional under the Due Process Clause of the Federal Constitution because it shifts to the defendant the burden of proving inability to comply with the order, which is an element of the crime of contempt.[1] This objection was rejected, and he renewed it on appeal. The intermediate state appellate court agreed with respondent and annulled the contempt order, ruling that the state statute purports to impose "a mandatory presumption compelling a conclusion of guilt without independent proof of an ability to pay," and is therefore unconstitutional because "the mandatory nature of the presumption lessens the prosecution's burden of proof." 180 Cal.App.3d 649, 654, 225 Cal.Rptr. 748, 751 (1986). In light of its holding that the statute as previously interpreted was unconstitutional, the court went on to adopt a different interpretation of that statute to govern future proceedings: "For future guidance, however, we determine the statute in question should be construed as authorizing a permissive inference, but not a mandatory presumption." The court explicitly considered this reinterpretation of the statute to be an exercise of its "obligation to interpret the statute to preserve its constitutionality whenever possible." The California Supreme Court denied review, but we granted certiorari.

Three issues must be decided to resolve this case. First is whether the ability to comply with a court order constitutes an element of the offense of contempt or, instead, inability to comply is an affirmative defense to that charge. Second is whether § 1209.5 requires the alleged contemnor to shoulder the burden of persuasion or merely the burden of production in attempting to establish his inability to comply with the order. Third is whether this contempt proceeding was a criminal proceeding or a civil proceeding, i.e., whether the relief imposed upon respondent was criminal or civil in nature.

Petitioner argues that the state appellate court erred in its determinations on the first two points of state law. . . . Although petitioner marshals a number of sources in support of the contention that the state appellate court misapplied state law on these two points, the California Supreme Court denied review of this case and we are not free in this situation to overturn the state court's conclusions of state law. . . . The fact that this proceeding and the resultant relief were judged to be criminal in nature as a matter of state law is thus not determinative of this issue. . . .

The question of how a court determines whether to classify the relief imposed in a given proceeding as civil or criminal in nature, for the purposes of applying the Due Process Clause and other provisions of the Constitution, is one of long standing, and its principles have been settled at least in their broad outlines for many decades. When a State's proceedings are involved, state law provides strong guidance about whether or not the State is exercising its authority "in a nonpunitive, noncriminal manner," and one who challenges the State's classification

---

[1] California Civ.Proc.Code Ann. § 1209.5 (1982) states that "[w]hen a court of competent jurisdiction makes an order compelling a parent to furnish support . . . for his child, proof that . . . the parent was present in court at the time the order was pronounced and proof of noncompliance therewith shall be prima facie evidence of a contempt of court."

of the relief imposed as "civil" or "criminal" may be required to show "the clearest proof" that it is not correct as a matter of federal law. Nonetheless, if such a challenge is substantiated, then the labels affixed either to the proceeding or to the relief imposed under state law are not controlling and will not be allowed to defeat the applicable protections of federal constitutional law. This is particularly so in the codified laws of contempt, where the "civil" and "criminal" labels of the law have become increasingly blurred.[4]

Instead, the critical features are the substance of the proceeding and the character of the relief that the proceeding will afford. "If it is for civil contempt the punishment is remedial, and for the benefit of the complainant. But if it is for criminal contempt the sentence is punitive, to vindicate the authority of the court." Gompers v. Bucks Stove & Range Co., 221 U.S. 418, 441, 31 S.Ct. 492, 498, 55 L.Ed. 797 (1911). The character of the relief imposed is thus ascertainable by applying a few straightforward rules. If the relief provided is a sentence of imprisonment, it is remedial if "the defendant stands committed unless and until he performs the affirmative act required by the court's order," and is punitive if "the sentence is limited to imprisonment for a definite period." *Id.*, at 442, 31 S.Ct. at 498. If the relief provided is a fine, it is remedial when it is paid to the complainant, and punitive when it is paid to the court, though a fine that would be payable to the court is also remedial when the defendant can avoid paying the fine simply by performing the affirmative act required by the court's order. These distinctions lead up to the fundamental proposition that criminal penalties may not be imposed on someone who has not been afforded the protections that the Constitution requires of such criminal proceedings, including the requirement that the offense be proved beyond a reasonable doubt. . . .[5]

Shillitani v. United States, 384 U.S. 364, 86 S.Ct. 1531, 16 L.Ed.2d 622 (1966), adheres to these same principles. There two men were adjudged guilty of contempt for refusing to obey a court order to testify under a grant of immunity. Both were sentenced to two years of imprisonment, with the proviso that if either answered the questions before his sentence ended, he would be released. The penalties were upheld because of their "conditional nature," even though the underlying proceeding lacked certain constitutional protections that are essential in criminal proceedings. Any sentence "must be viewed as remedial," and

---

[4] California is a good example of this modern development, for although it defines civil and criminal contempts in separate statutes, compare Cal.Civ.Proc.Code Ann. § 1209 (Supp.1988) with Cal.Penal Code Ann. § 166 (1970), it has merged the two kinds of proceedings under the same procedural rules. See Cal.Civ.Proc.Code Ann. §§ 1209–1222 (1982 and Supp.1988).

[5] We have recognized that certain specific constitutional protections, such as the right to trial by jury, are not applicable to those criminal contempts that can be classified as petty offenses, as is true of other petty crimes as well. *Bloom v. Illinois*, 391 U.S. 194, 208–210, 88 S.Ct. 1477, 1485–1486, 20 L.Ed.2d 522 (1968). This is not true, however, of the proposition that guilt must be proved beyond a reasonable doubt. *Id.*, at 205, 88 S.Ct. at 1484.

hence civil in nature, "if the court conditions release upon the contemnor's willingness to [comply with the order]." By the same token, in a civil proceeding the court "may also impose a determinate sentence *which includes a purge clause.*" (emphasis added). "On the contrary, a criminal contempt proceeding would be characterized by the imposition of an unconditional sentence for punishment or deterrence."

In repeatedly stating and following the rules set out above, the Court has eschewed any alternative formulation that would make the classification of the relief imposed in a State's proceedings turn simply on what their underlying purposes are perceived to be. Although the purposes that lie behind particular kinds of relief are germane to understanding their character, this Court has never undertaken to psychoanalyze the subjective intent of a State's laws and its courts, not only because that effort would be unseemly and improper, but also because it would be misguided. In contempt cases, both civil and criminal relief have aspects that can be seen as either remedial or punitive or both: when a court imposes fines and punishments on a contemnor, it is not only vindicating its legal authority to enter the initial court order, but it also is seeking to give effect to the law's purpose of modifying the contemnor's behavior to conform to the terms required in the order. As was noted in *Gompers:*

> "It is true that either form of [punishment] has also an incidental effect. For if the case is civil and the punishment is purely remedial, there is also a vindication of the court's authority. On the other hand, if the proceeding is for criminal contempt and the [punishment] is solely punitive, to vindicate the authority of the law, the complainant may also derive some incidental benefit from the fact that such punishment tends to prevent a repetition of the disobedience. But such indirect consequences will not change [punishment] which is merely coercive and remedial, into that which is solely punitive in character, or *vice versa.*" 221 U.S., at 443, 31 S.Ct. at 498.

For these reasons, this Court has judged that conclusions about the purposes for which relief is imposed are properly drawn from an examination of the character of the relief itself.

There is yet another reason why the overlapping purposes of civil and criminal contempt proceedings have prevented this Court from hinging the classification on this point. If the definition of these proceedings and their resultant relief as civil or criminal is made to depend on the federal courts' views about their underlying purposes, which indeed often are not clearly articulated in any event, then the States will be unable to ascertain with any degree of assurance how their proceedings will be understood as a matter of federal law. The consequences of any such shift in direction would be both serious and unfortunate. Of primary practical importance to the decision in this case is that the States should be given intelligible guidance about how, as a matter of federal constitutional law, they may lawfully employ presumptions and other procedures in their contempt proceedings. It is of great importance to the States that they be able to understand clearly and in advance the tools that are available to them in ensuring swift and certain compliance with valid court orders—not only orders commanding payment of child support, as in this case, but orders that command compliance in the more general area of domestic relations law, and in all other areas of the law as well. . . .

[C]ertainly the fact that a contemnor has his sentence suspended and is placed on probation cannot be decisive in defining the civil or criminal nature of the relief, for many convicted criminals are treated in exactly this manner for the purpose (among others) of influencing their behavior. What is true of the respondent in this case is also true of any such convicted criminal: as long as he meets the conditions of his informal probation, he will never enter the jail. Nonetheless, if the sentence is a determinate one, then the punishment is criminal in nature, and it may not be imposed unless federal constitutional protections are applied in the contempt proceeding.[8]

The proper classification of the relief imposed in respondent's contempt proceeding is dispositive of this case. As interpreted by the state court here, § 1209.5 requires respondent to carry the burden of persuasion on an element of the offense, by showing his inability to comply with the court's order to make the required payments. If applied in a criminal proceeding, such a statute would violate the Due Process Clause because it would undercut the State's burden to prove guilt beyond a reasonable doubt. If applied in a civil proceeding, however, this particular statute would be constitutionally valid, and respondent conceded as much at the argument.[9]

The state court found the contempt proceeding to be "quasi-criminal" in nature without discussing the point. There were strong indications that the proceeding was intended to be criminal in nature, such as the notice sent to respondent, which clearly labeled the proceeding as "criminal in nature," and the participation of the District Attorney in the case. Though significant, these facts are not dispositive of the issue before us, for if the trial court had imposed only civil coercive remedies, as surely it was authorized to do, then it would be improper to invalidate that

---

[8] This does not even suggest, of course, that the State is unable to suspend the sentence imposed on either a criminal contemnor or a civil contemnor in favor of a term of informal probation. That action may be appropriate and even most desirable in a great many cases, especially when the order that has been disobeyed was one to pay a sum of money. This also accords with the repeated emphasis in our decisions that in wielding its contempt powers, a court "must exercise 'the least possible power adequate to the end proposed.' " *Shillitani v. United States*, 384 U.S. 364, 371, 86 S.Ct. 1531, 1536, 16 L.Ed.2d 622 (1966), quoting *Anderson v. Dunn*, 6 Wheat. 204, 231 (1821).

[9] Our precedents are clear, however, that punishment may not be imposed in a civil contempt proceeding when it is clearly established that the alleged contemnor is unable to comply with the terms of the order. *United States v. Rylander*, 460 U.S. 752, 757, 103 S.Ct. 1548, 1552, 75 L.Ed.2d 521 (1983); *Shillitani*, supra, at 371, *Oriel*, 278 U.S., at 366, 49 S.Ct. at 175.

result merely because the Due Process Clause, as applied in *criminal* proceedings, was not satisfied. It also bears emphasis that the purposes underlying this proceeding were wholly ambiguous. Respondent was charged with violating nine discrete prior court orders, and the proceeding may have been intended primarily to vindicate the court's authority in the face of his defiance. On the other hand, as often is true when court orders are violated, these charges were part of an ongoing battle to force respondent to conform his conduct to the terms of those orders, and of future orders as well.

Applying the traditional rules for classifying the relief imposed in a given proceeding requires the further resolution of one factual question about the nature of the relief in this case. Respondent was charged with nine separate counts of contempt, and was convicted on five of those counts, all of which arose from his failure to comply with orders to make payments in past months. He was sentenced to five days in jail on each of the five counts, for a total of 25 days, but his jail sentence was suspended and he was placed on probation for three years. If this were all, then the relief afforded would be criminal in nature.[11] But this is not all. One of the conditions of respondent's probation was that he begin making payments on his accumulated arrearage, and that he continue making these payments at the rate of $50 per month. At that rate, all of the arrearage would be paid before respondent completed his probation period. Not only did the order therefore contemplate that respondent would be required to purge himself of his past violations, but it expressly states that "[i]f any two payments are missed, whether consecutive or not, the entire balance shall become due and payable." What is unclear is whether the ultimate satisfaction of these accumulated prior payments would have purged the determinate sentence imposed on respondent. Since this aspect of the proceeding will vary as a factual matter from one case to another, depending on the precise disposition entered by the trial court, and since the trial court did not specify this aspect of its disposition in this case, it is not surprising that neither party was able to offer a satisfactory explanation of this point at argument. If the relief imposed here is in fact a determinate sentence with a purge clause, then it is civil in nature.

---

[11] That a determinate sentence is suspended and the contemnor put on probation does not make the remedy civil in nature, for a suspended sentence, without more, remains a determinate sentence, and a fixed term of probation is itself a punishment that is criminal in nature. A suspended sentence with a term of probation is not equivalent to a conditional sentence that would allow the contemnor to avoid or purge these sanctions. A determinate term of probation puts the contemnor under numerous disabilities that he cannot escape by complying with the dictates of the prior orders, such as: any conditions of probation that the court judges to be reasonable and necessary may be imposed; the term of probation may be revoked and the original sentence (including incarceration) may be reimposed at any time for a variety of reasons without all the safeguards that are ordinarily afforded in criminal proceedings; and the contemnor's probationary status could affect other proceedings against him that may arise in the future (for example, this fact might influence the sentencing determination made in a criminal prosecution for some wholly independent offense).

The state court did not pass on this issue because of its erroneous view that it was enough simply to aver that this proceeding is considered "quasi-criminal" as a matter of state law. And, as noted earlier, the court's view on this point, coupled with its view of the Federal Constitution, also led it to reinterpret the state statute, thus softening the impact of the presumption, in order to save its constitutionality. Yet the Due Process Clause does not necessarily prohibit the State from employing this presumption as it was construed by the state court, *if* respondent would purge his contempt judgment by paying off his arrearage. In these circumstances, the proper course for this Court is to vacate the judgment below and remand for further consideration of § 1209.5 free from the compulsion of an erroneous view of federal law. If on remand it is found that respondent would purge his sentence by paying his arrearage, then this proceeding is civil in nature and there was no need for the state court to reinterpret its statute to avoid conflict with the Due Process Clause.[13]

We therefore vacate the judgment below and remand for further proceedings consistent with this opinion.

■ JUSTICE O'CONNOR, with whom THE CHIEF JUSTICE and JUSTICE SCALIA join, dissenting.

. . .

In my view, the proceeding is civil as a matter of federal law. Therefore, the Due Process Clause of the Fourteenth Amendment does not prevent the trial court from applying a legislative presumption that the parent remained capable of complying with the order until the time of the contempt proceeding. . . .

The California Court of Appeal has erected a substantial obstacle to the enforcement of child support orders. As petitioner vividly describes it, the judgment turns the child's support order into "a worthless piece of scrap." The judgment hampers the enforcement of support orders at a time when strengthened enforcement is needed. "The failure of enforcement efforts in this area has become a national scandal. In 1983, only half of custodial parents received the full amount of child support ordered; approximately 26% received some lesser amount, and 24% received nothing at all." Brief for Women's Legal Defense Fund et al. as *Amici Curiae* 26 (footnote omitted). The facts of this case illustrate how easily a reluctant parent can evade a child support obligation. Congress recognized the serious problem of enforcement of child support orders

---

[13] Even if this relief is judged on remand to be criminal in nature because it does not allow the contemnor to purge the judgment by satisfying the terms of the prior orders, this result does not impose any real handicap on the States in enforcing the terms of their orders, for it will be clear to the States that the presumption established by § 1209.5 can be imposed, consistent with the Due Process Clause, in any proceeding where the relief afforded is civil in nature as defined by this Court's precedents. In addition, the state courts remain free to decide for themselves the state law issues we have taken as having been resolved in this case by the court below, and to judge the lawfulness of statutes that impose similar presumptions under the provisions of their own state constitutions.

when it enacted the Child Support Enforcement Amendments of 1984. The California legislature responded to the problem by enacting the presumption described in § 1209.5. Now, says petitioner, the California Court of Appeal has sabotaged the California legislature's effort.

Contempt proceedings often will be useless if the parent seeking enforcement of valid support orders must prove that the obligor can comply with the court order. The custodial parent will typically lack access to the financial and employment records needed to sustain the burden imposed by the decision below, especially where the noncustodial parent is self-employed, as is the case here. Serious consequences follow from the California Court of Appeal's decision to invalidate California's statutory presumption that a parent continues to be able to pay the child support previously determined to be within his or her means. . . .

The linchpin of the Court of Appeal's opinion is its determination that the contempt proceeding against respondent was criminal in nature. . . . The characterization of a state proceeding as civil or criminal for the purpose of applying the Due Process Clause of the Fourteenth Amendment is itself a question of federal law. The substance of particular contempt proceedings determines whether they are civil or criminal, regardless of the label attached by the court conducting the proceedings. Civil contempt proceedings are primarily coercive; criminal contempt proceedings are punitive. As the Court explained in *Gompers:* "The distinction between refusing to do an act commanded,Cremedied by imprisonment until the party performs the required act; and doing an act forbidden,Cpunished by imprisonment for a definite term; is sound in principle, and generally, if not universally, affords a test by which to determine the character of the punishment." Failure to pay alimony is an example of the type of act cognizable in an action for civil contempt.

Whether a particular contempt proceeding is civil or criminal can be inferred from objective features of the proceeding and the sanction imposed. The most important indication is whether the judgment inures to the benefit of another party to the proceeding. A fine payable to the complaining party and proportioned to the complainant's loss is compensatory and civil. Because the compensatory purpose limits the amount of the fine, the contemnor is not exposed to a risk of punitive sanctions that would make criminal safeguards necessary. By contrast, a fixed fine payable to the court is punitive and criminal in character.

An analogous distinction can be drawn between types of sentences of incarceration. Commitment to jail or prison for a fixed term usually operates as a punitive sanction because it confers no advantage on the other party. But if a contemnor is incarcerated until he or she complies with a court order, the sanction is civil. Although the imprisonment does not compensate the adverse party directly, it is designed to obtain compliance with a court order made in that party's favor. . . .

Several peculiar features of California's contempt law make it difficult to determine whether the proceeding in this case was civil or criminal. All contempt proceedings in California courts are governed by the same procedural rules. Because state law provides that defendants in civil contempt proceedings are entitled to most of the protections guaranteed to ordinary criminal defendants, the California courts have held that civil contempt proceedings are quasi-criminal under state law. Therefore, indications that the California Superior Court conducted respondent's hearing as a criminal proceeding do not conclusively demonstrate for purposes of federal due process analysis that respondent was tried for criminal contempt.

Certain formal aspects of the proceeding below raise the possibility that it involved criminal contempt. The orders to show cause stated that "[a] contempt proceeding is criminal in nature" and that a violation would subject the respondent to "possible penalties." The orders advised respondent of his right to an attorney. During the hearing, the trial judge told respondent that he had a constitutional right not to testify. Finally, the judge imposed a determinate sentence of five days in jail for each count of contempt, to be served consecutively. See Cal.Civ.Proc. Code Ann. § 1218 (1982) (contempt may be punished by a fine not exceeding $500, or imprisonment not exceeding five days, or both); cf. Cal.Civ.Proc.Code Ann.§ 1219 (1982) (contempt may be punished by imprisonment until an act is performed, if the contempt is the omission to perform the act).

Nevertheless, the substance of the proceeding below and the conditions on which the sentence was suspended reveal that the proceeding was civil in nature. Mrs. Feiock initiated the underlying action in order to obtain enforcement of the child support order for the benefit of the Feiock children. The California District Attorney conducted the case under a provision of the URESA that authorizes him to act on Mrs. Feiock's behalf. As the very caption of the case in this Court indicates, the District Attorney is acting on behalf of Mrs. Feiock, not as the representative of the State of California in a criminal prosecution. Both of the provisions of California's enactment of the URESA that authorize contempt proceedings appear in a chapter of the Code of Civil Procedure entitled "Civil Enforcement." It appears that most States enforce child and spousal support orders through civil proceedings like this one, in which the burden of persuasion is shifted to the defendant to show inability to comply. J. Atkinson, Modern Child Custody Practice 556 (1986); H. Krause, Child Support in America 65 (1981); Annot., 53 A.L.R.2d 591, 607–616 (1957 and Supp.1987).

These indications that the proceeding was civil are confirmed by the character of the sanction imposed on respondent. The California Superior Court sentenced respondent to a fixed term of 25 days in jail. Without more, this sanction would be punitive and appropriate for a criminal contempt. But the court suspended the determinate sentence and placed respondent on three years' informal probation on the conditions that he comply with the support order in the future and begin to pay on the arrearage that he had accumulated in the past. These special conditions aim exclusively at enforcing compliance with the existing child support order.

Our precedents indicate that such a conditional sentence is coercive rather than punitive. Thus in *Gompers,* we observed that civil contempt may be punished by an order that "the defendant stand committed *unless* and until he performs the affirmative act required by the court's order." 221 U.S., at 442, 31 S.Ct. at 498 (emphasis added). . . Respondent's prison sentence is coercive rather than punitive because it effectively "conditions release upon the contemnor's willingness to [comply]." *Id.*, at 370, 86 S.Ct. at 1535.

It is true that the order imposing the sentence does not expressly provide that, *if* respondent is someday incarcerated and *if* he subsequently complies, he will be released immediately. The parties disagree about what will happen if this contingency arises, and there is no need to address today the question of whether the failure to grant immediate release would render the sanction criminal. In the case before us respondent carries something even better than the "keys to the prison" in his own pocket: as long as he meets the conditions of his informal probation, he will never enter the jail.

It is critical that the only conditions placed on respondent's probation, apart from the requirement that he conduct himself generally in accordance with the law, are that he cure his past failures to comply with the support order and that he continue to comply in the future.* The sanction imposed on respondent is unlike ordinary criminal probation because it is collateral to a civil proceeding initiated by a private party, and respondent's sentence is suspended on the condition that he comply with a court order entered for the benefit of that party. This distinguishes respondent's sentence from suspended criminal sentences imposed outside the contempt context.

This Court traditionally has inquired into the substance of contempt proceedings to determine whether they are civil or criminal, paying particular attention to whether the sanction imposed will benefit another party to the proceeding. In this case, the California Superior Court suspended respondent's sentence on the condition that he bring himself into compliance with a court order providing support for his children, represented in the proceeding by petitioner. I conclude that the

* Unlike the Court, I find no ambiguity in the court's sentencing order that hints that respondent can purge his jail sentence by paying off the arrearage alone. The sentencing order suspends execution of the jail sentence and places respondent on probation on the conditions that he *both* make future support payments at $150 per month *and* pay $50 per month on the arrearage. If respondent pays off the arrearage before the end of his probation period, but then fails to make a current support payment, the suspension will be revoked and he will go to jail. See *People v. Chagolla*, 151 Cal.App.3d 1045, 199 Cal.Rptr. 181 (1984) (explaining that if a court suspends a sentence on conditions, and any condition is violated, the court *must* reinstate the original sentence).

proceeding in this case should be characterized as one for civil contempt, and I would reverse the judgment below.

NOTES

Post-Script to *Feiock* and the Inability to Pay. After *Feiock* was remanded, the California Court of Appeal held that the proceedings against the father were criminal in nature but that the statute did not create a mandatory presumption of ability to pay but rather made inability to pay an affirmative defense in a contempt proceeding. *In re* Feiock, 215 Cal.App.3d 141 (1989). The court said:

> Court decisions have long upheld the constitutionality of legislation making issues such as inability to pay matters of defense. As noted in Martin v. Ohio [480 U.S. 228, 235], "[T]he common law rule was that affirmative defenses . . . were matters for the defendant to prove. 'This was the rule when the Fifth Amendment was adopted, and it was the American rule when the Fourteenth Amendment was ratified.' " Thus, there is no constitutional impediment to making inability to pay an affirmative defense, at least if there is some rational basis for doing so.
>
> Common sense dictates that the contemnor raise inability to pay. The contemnor is the person in the best position to know whether inability to pay is even a consideration in the proceeding and also has the best access to evidence on the issue, particularly in cases of self-employment. Considerations of policy and convenience have led courts to sanction placement of the burden of establishing a defense on defendants under similar circumstances.
>
> Making inability to pay a matter of defense does not place too harsh a burden on the contemnor. Since inability to pay goes to the heart of the contempt, the contemnor's task is merely to raise the issue of his ability to pay. The petitioner's burden then remains to prove the contempt beyond a reasonable doubt, including ability to pay. (People v. Figueroa (1986) 41 Cal.3d 714, 721, 224 Cal.Rptr. 719, 715 P.2d 680) It also eliminates the district attorney's concern that proof of the contempt would be unreasonably difficult if ability to pay were an element, yet minimizes the prospect that a truly indigent contemnor will end up in what is tantamount to debtor's prison.

Id. at 147–48.

Right to Counsel. Although civil contemnors may face incarceration for failing to pay their child support orders, the United States Supreme Court held in Turner v. Rogers, 131 S.Ct. 2507 (2011), that the Due Process Clause does not automatically require a state to provide free counsel to an indigent, non-custodial parent. However, the Due Process Clause does require that "the [s]tate must nonetheless have in place alternative procedures that assure a fundamentally fair determination of the critical incarceration-related question, whether the supporting parent is able to comply with the support order." *Id.* at 2512. The procedural safeguards designed to reduce the risk of an erroneous deprivation of liberty include: notice to the defendant that his ability to pay is a critical issue in the contempt proceeding; use of a form to elicit relevant financial information; an opportunity for the defendant to answer questions regarding his financial situation; and a court's express finding that the defendant does indeed have the ability to pay. *Id.* at 2519. The Court's enumeration of acceptable safeguards was not exhaustive; rather, the Court noted that "sometimes assistance other than purely legal assistance (here, say, that of a neutral social worker) can prove constitutionally sufficient." *Id.*

Past-Due Support as a Final Judgment. Most states treat past-due installments of both child support and alimony as final judgments. *See, e.g.,* Britton v. Britton, 671 P.2d 1135 (N.M. 1983). This means that the past due amount may not be modified retroactively and may be enforced by execution without any additional legal action. *See* HOMER H. CLARK, JR., THE LAW OF DOMESTIC RELATIONS IN THE UNITED STATES 672, 725 (2d ed. 1988).

Additional Enforcement Mechanisms. As noted earlier, in 2015, only 65% of child support due was actually collected by recipients. U.S. DEP'T OF HEALTH & HUMAN SERVICES, ADMINISTRATION FOR CHILDREN & FAMILIES, OFFICE OF CHILD SUPPORT ENFORCEMENT, *Child Support Enforcement FY 2015: Preliminary Report* (2015), at http://www.acf.hhs.gov/css/resource/fy-2015-preliminary-data-report. Enforcing support obligations is a priority for both the federal and state governments, which have put in place a number of measures to enforce these obligations. In addition to contempt proceedings discussed in *Feiock*, states principally utilize three different enforcement measures: a) liens, garnishments and attachments of property, b) actions affecting state licenses, or c) actions affecting state tax returns. *See, e.g., License Restrictions For Failure to Pay Child Support,* NATIONAL CONFERENCE OF STATE LEGISLATURES, STATE-BY-STATE LICENSE RESTRICTIONS CHART (2014), at http://www.ncsl.org/research/human-services/license-restrictions-for-failure-to-pay-child-support.aspx#1.

Liens, Garnishments and Attachments. Liens upon an obligor's property are commonly used to secure compliance with support obligations. *See generally* JEFFREY BALL & VIRGINIA SABLAN, EFFECTIVE USE OF LIENS IN CHILD SUPPORT CASES (1990). Courts have broad discretion regarding liens; they may order an obligor to provide security for future payments or may impose a lien as a response to an obligor's non-payment. *See, e.g.,* N.C. GEN. STAT. § 50–16.7(e) (2016). Wage garnishment is another commonly utilized enforcement method. A federal law requires that all states include in any support order the ability to withhold wages when payments go into arrears. 42 U.S.C. §§ 666(a)(8), (b)(2), (b)(3) (2016). Private settlement agreements that are not incorporated or merged into a divorce decree are exempt, however. Income withholding may commence when the obligor is in arrears by one month's support. 42 U.S.C.A. § 666(b)(3)(B) (2016). The state must make income withholding available when the recipient receives welfare benefits, although the state can also assist non-welfare recipients. Arrearages can be enforced against the deceased obligor's estate. *See, e.g.,* Estate of Carpenter v. Carpenter, 220 S.W.3d 263 (Ar. 2005).

Licenses. Several state statutes also permit state agencies to refuse, suspend, or revoke a delinquent obligor's state-issued license. These statutes are an especially potent means for enforcing support obligations, as they reach any state-issued license including driver's and professional licenses, such as state bar membership. *See, e.g.,* TEX. FAM. CODE ANN. § 232.003 (2016). *See also* State Department of Revenue v. Beans, 965 P.2d 725 (Alaska 1998) (finding constitutional a state statute suspending driver's license of delinquent child support obligor to the extent it is applied to obligors who have the ability to pay).

Tax Returns and Credit Reports. Under federal law, a state may intercept the federal tax refund of any individual with arrearages of $500 or greater, although interception requires notice and the ability to contest it. *See* 42 U.S.C. § 664 (2016). Interception is available both for welfare and non-welfare recipients. Only arrearages, not current support, may be collected through the intercept. States must also report arrearages to credit agencies.

Interstate Enforcement. The Full Faith and Credit Clause of the United States Constitution renders one state's judgments enforceable throughout the United States. Uniform laws have been proposed—and in many jurisdictions enacted—to aid in the enforcement of state court judgments and do so in two primary ways: streamlining the recognition of another state's judgment and eliminating an obligor's ability to escape an obligation simply by crossing state lines. For example, the Uniform Law's Enforcement of Foreign Judgments Act simplifies the registration process required for one state to recognize the judgment of another. The Uniform Interstate Family Support Act (UIFSA) limits an obligor's ability to escape an obligation simply by crossing state lines by expanding personal jurisdiction to its constitutional limits and authorizing income tax refund intercepts. For further discussion of numerous child support enforcement mechanisms, *see* JOHN DEWITT GREGORY, PETER SWISHER, & ROBIN FRETWELL WILSON, UNDERSTANDING FAMILY LAW § 9.06(f) (4th ed. 2013).

Federal legislation requires that every state adopt UIFSA. Pub. L. No. 104–193, 110 Stat. 2105 § 321, codified at 42 U.S.C. § 666(f) (2011). Collection for child support has increased due to federal efforts and concomitant efforts to strengthen interstate collection. For example, the Full Faith and Credit for Child Support Orders Act (FFCCSOA) requires states to enforce child support orders of other states and prohibits modification of those orders unless certain requirements are satisfied. 28 U.S.C. § 1738B (2011). For an example of state enforcement using the FFCCSOA, *see* Auclair v. Bolderson, 6 A.D.3d 892, 775 N.Y.S.2d 121 (2004) (a state must have continuing jurisdiction under the legislation or, if there is no continuing jurisdiction, have personal jurisdiction over the parties).

Non-Payment as a Federal Crime. Federal law makes the willful failure to pay child support a federal crime. *See* Child Support Recovery Act of 1992, 18 U.S.C. § 228. To be criminally liable, the obligor's child must reside in another state and the support obligation must have resulted from a court or administrative order. *Id.* at § 228(f)(3). The willful failure to pay child support of more than $5,000 is punishable by fines and/or imprisonment for up to six months. *Id.* at § 228(a)(1), (c)(1).

CHAPTER VI

PARENT AND CHILD: LEGAL AND BIOLOGICAL RELATIONSHIPS

A. ESTABLISHING LEGAL PARENTAGE

Reese v. Muret

Supreme Court of Kansas, 2007
150 P.3d 309

■ ROSEN, JUSTICE delivered the opinion of the court.

This is a paternity action in the context of a probate case. Heather S. Reese (formerly Waldschmidt) (Heather) seeks a determination that she is the child of Wade Samuel Waldschmidt, Jr. (Sam). Sam's spouse, Sandra Waldschmidt (Sandra) opposed Heather's claim as a child in Samuel's intestate estate and filed a motion for genetic testing. Heather filed a paternity action pursuant to the Kansas Parentage Act, claiming that Sam was her presumptive father. Sandra intervened in the paternity action and moved for genetic testing. The district court denied Sandra's motions in both the probate and paternity actions, and she brings this appeal, claiming that In re Marriage of Ross, 245 Kan. 591, 783 P.2d 331 (1989), does not apply to genetic testing in paternity cases brought by adults for the purpose of determining inheritance.

Sam married Deloris Hibbs (Deloris) on June 1, 1970. On January 25, 1971, Deloris gave birth to a daughter named Heather Shea Waldschmidt (Heather). Heather's birth certificate named Sam as her father. Deloris and Sam divorced on July 12, 1972. The divorce pleadings acknowledged Heather as a child of the union. The district court ordered Sam to pay child support and granted Sam visitation with Heather.

In November 1972, Sam filed a motion to terminate his child support payments, alleging that Deloris "took the minor child of said parties and disappeared." Sam's motion further alleged that Deloris was unfit and that he should have custody of Heather. In December 1972, the district court entered an order terminating Sam's child support until Deloris could show just cause to have the child support reinstated. Deloris never reinstated Sam's child support obligation, but Sam's Aunt Irene provided financial assistance to Deloris and Heather.

After the divorce, Sam had little contact with Heather. Sam saw Heather at Waldschmidt family gatherings for Thanksgiving and Christmas but did not attempt to have a relationship with her. However,

Heather was very close to members of Sam's family including his mother, Margaret; his brother, David; and his Aunt Irene. Heather was also close to her Waldschmidt cousins. Although Heather did not have a relationship with Sam, she always considered him to be her father.

Sam married Sandra Woodard in October 1976. According to Sandra, Sam said that Heather was not his child. Sam and Sandra had no children. They separated in September 1988 and divorced in 1990. Sandra moved back in with Sam in 1994, moved out again in 1995, and remarried him in 1996. After their remarriage, Sandra did not live with Sam, but visited him occasionally on weekends.

Before Sandra moved back in with Sam in 1994, he executed a will leaving everything to his sisters, Camille and Anna Jane. On December 10, 2002, Sam visited with an attorney about his estate. Sam told the attorney that he had a daughter. The attorney perceived that there was tension between Sam and Sandra regarding Sam's daughter, but Sam did not explain the situation. On or about December 13, 2002, Sam committed suicide.

On December 18, 2002, Heather petitioned the district court to appoint administrators for Sam's estate. Sandra responded to Heather's petition, denying that Heather was Sam's daughter and requesting the court to appoint her as the administrator for Sam's estate. Sandra also filed a petition in the probate action for genetic testing to determine whether Sam was Heather's biological father. The district court appointed an attorney, who was a disinterested third party, as the administrator of Sam's estate. In response to Sandra's motion for genetic testing, Heather filed a paternity action pursuant to the Kansas Parentage Act, seeking a determination that Sam was Heather's father. The petition alleged that Sam was Heather's presumed father because she was born during her mother's marriage to Sam, Sam had acknowledged his paternity in the divorce pleadings, and Sam was ordered to pay child support on Heather's behalf. Sandra filed a motion to intervene and a motion for genetic testing. Over Heather's objection, the district court granted Sandra's motion to intervene pursuant to K.S.A. 60–224(b).

Heather objected to Sandra's motions for genetic testing. The district court then ordered a *Ross* hearing to determine whether it was in Heather's best interests to grant Sandra's motions. The parties agreed to submit the evidence for the *Ross* hearing based on stipulated depositions and exhibits rather than conducting an evidentiary hearing. Based on this evidence, the district court held that it was not in Heather's best interests to conduct genetic testing and denied Sandra's motion. Sandra filed a motion for an interlocutory appeal in the paternity action and requested a ruling on her petition for genetic testing in the probate action. The district court denied Sandra's petition for genetic testing in the probate action and granted her request for an interlocutory appeal in the paternity action. Sandra filed a notice of appeal in both actions. The appeals were consolidated and transferred to this court on our motion pursuant to K.S.A. 20–3018(c).

The matter was originally set for oral argument on December 5, 2005. However, upon finding a copy of Sam's will in the record, we remanded the matter to the district court for a determination of the validity of Sam's will. Thereafter, Sam's sister, Camille Pond, petitioned the district court to admit a copy of Sam's will to probate. After an evidentiary hearing, the district court denied Camille's petition to probate Sam's will because she had failed to overcome the presumption that Sam had destroyed or revoked his original will. Following the district court's refusal to probate Sam's will, we reinstated Sandra's appeal.

Sandra argues that the district court improperly applied the ruling of Ross, 245 Kan. 591, 783 P.2d 331, in determining whether to order genetic testing in a probate action and in a parentage action brought by an adult for the purposes of applying the probate code. According to Sandra, *Ross* is inapplicable to a probate case and inapplicable to adults. We analyze this issue as a question of law subject to de novo review because it involves stipulated facts and statutory interpretation. See In re Harris Testamentary Trust, 275 Kan. 946, 951, 69 P.3d 1109 (2003); In re Estate of Antonopoulos, 268 Kan. 178, 180, 993 P.2d 637 (1999).

The fundamental rule of statutory construction is that the intent of the legislature governs. Legislative intent is first determined by considering the language in the statute. When a statute is plain and unambiguous, the court must give effect to the intention of the legislature as expressed, rather than determine what the law should or should not be. In re Conservatorship of Huerta, 273 Kan. 97, 105, 41 P.3d 814 (2002).

Because this action arises out of the administration of a decedent's estate, we will begin our analysis with the probate code, K.S.A. 59–101 *et seq.* K.S.A. 59–501 defines children for purposes of intestate succession, stating:

> " 'Children' means biological children, including a posthumous child; children adopted as provided by law; and children whose parentage is or has been determined under the Kansas parentage act or prior law."

When Heather filed the petition to administer Sam's estate, she asserted her interest in Sam's estate as a biological child because none of the other possible definitions in K.S.A. 59–501 applied. As long as Heather's claim to Sam's estate was based on her being Sam's biological child, the genetic connection between Heather and Sam was in issue. Under this scenario, Sandra correctly argues that *Ross* is inapplicable to an intestate claim based on the biological definition of child because genetic testing is the only conclusive means of establishing biological parentage.

However, K.S.A. 59–501 does not limit the definition of children to biological offspring. Rather, the definition of children is much broader, requiring the probate court to treat any person as a child if such person's parentage is or has been determined under the Kansas Parentage Act. K.S.A. 59–501(a). Heather invoked the Kansas Parentage Act as the basis for her inheritance claim under K.S.A. 59–501 when she filed her petition to determine paternity under the Act. We note that K.S.A. 59–501(a) does not require a determination under the Kansas Parentage Act to occur prior to a probate proceeding. Rather, the legislature acknowledged that proceedings under the Kansas Parentage Act may occur simultaneously with probate proceedings by incorporating the phrase "whose parentage is or has been determined" in the definition of children. See K.S.A. 59–501(a).

The probate code treats a determination of parentage pursuant to the Kansas Parentage Act as conclusive. See K.S.A. 59–501(a). Once paternity is established in accordance with the Kansas Parentage Act, the probate code provides no mechanism for challenging that paternity determination. Because Heather eliminated the issue of biological parentage in the probate action by filing her paternity action and the probate code does not authorize genetic testing to challenge a paternity determination under the Kansas Parentage Act, there is no statutory basis for Sandra's motion for genetic testing in the probate case. Although Sandra correctly argues that *Ross* does not apply to an order for genetic testing under the probate code, the district court properly denied Sandra's motion because there was no statutory basis for the motion.

Pursuant to the Kansas Parentage Act, a man is presumed to be the father of a child born while the man is married to the child's mother. K.S.A. 38–1114(a)(1). A child or a person on behalf of the child may file an action at any time to establish paternity when there is a presumption of paternity. K.S.A. 38–1115(a)(1). However, a presumption based on genetic test results must relate to genetic testing that occurs prior to the filing of the paternity action. See K.S.A. 38–1114(a)(5); In re Estate of Foley, 22 Kan.App.2d 959, 925 P.2d 449 (1996). The child, the child's mother, and the presumptive father are parties to the paternity action. K.S.A. 38–1117(a). K.S.A. 38–1118(a) requires the district court to order genetic testing when any party requests genetic testing. However, the *Ross* court tempered the statutory requirement of K.S.A. 38–1118(a), by requiring the district court to conduct a hearing prior to issuing an order for genetic testing to determine whether genetic testing is in the best interests of the child. Ross, 245 Kan. at 602, 783 P.2d 331. Since *Ross* was decided in 1989, the legislature has not amended the statute to reverse the limitation imposed by *Ross*.

In *Ross,* the child, R.A.R., was born during the marriage of his mother Sylvia to Robert. When Sylvia and Robert divorced, Sylvia alleged that Robert was R.A.R.'s father. Robert was granted joint custody and ordered to pay child support. Two years later, Sylvia filed a petition pursuant to the Kansas Parentage Act to establish Charles as R.A.R.'s biological father. Sylvia wanted Charles to be named R.A.R.'s father so he could consent to R.A.R.'s adoption by Sylvia's current husband. To establish Charles as R.A.R.'s biological parent, Sylvia requested an order compelling all of the parties to submit to genetic testing. The district court ordered the genetic testing pursuant to K.S.A. 38–1118(a) and admitted the results over Robert's and Charles's objections. Based on the results of the genetic testing, the district court determined that Charles was R.A.R.'s biological father and ordered him to pay child support. Nevertheless, the district court determined that it was in R.A.R.'s best interest to maintain his relationship with Robert, so the court continued the joint custody arrangement between Sylvia and Robert.

The *Ross* court reversed the district court's order for genetic testing and the order establishing Charles as R.A.R.'s biological father. 245 Kan. at 602, 783 P.2d 331. Noting that "the ancient presumption of the legitimacy of a child born in wedlock is one of the strongest presumptions known to the law," the *Ross* court held that the district court must conduct a hearing to determine whether it is in the child's best interests to perform genetic testing and determine the child's biological paternity as opposed to his presumptive paternity. 245 Kan. at 596, 602, 783 P.2d 331.

Sandra argues that *Ross* only applies to minor children. However, in Ferguson v. Winston, 27 Kan.App.2d 34, 35, 36, 996 P.2d 841 (2000), the Court of Appeals applied *Ross* to a paternity proceeding involving an adult child. In *Ferguson,* the child, Michael, was born to Debra while she was living with Dale. Debra and Dale married after Michael's birth, and Debra recognized Dale as Michael's father for a period of 14 years. During Debra and Dale's divorce proceedings, Debra asserted for the first time that Dale was not Michael's biological father. In response, Dale filed a paternity action pursuant to the Kansas Parentage Act, seeking a determination that Michael was his son. Michael became an adult during the pendency of the paternity proceedings but was not made a party to the action and was not represented by a guardian ad litem. Without conducting a *Ross* hearing, the district court ordered genetic testing and summarily determined that Dale was not Michael's biological father.

The *Ferguson* court reversed the district court's decision, concluding that the district court committed both legal and procedural errors. 27 Kan.App.2d at 36, 996 P.2d 841. The *Ferguson* court determined that Dale is Michael's presumptive father based on K.S.A. 38–1114. Because of the presumption that Michael is Dale's son, the *Ferguson* court held that the district court erroneously considered genetic test results obtained without the benefit of a *Ross* hearing to determine whether it was in Michael's best interests to shift paternity from the presumptive father to the biological father. 27 Kan.App.2d at 36–37, 996 P.2d 841. The

Ferguson court also held that the district court erred when it treated the genetic test results as conclusive on the issue of paternity, stating:

> "If DNA evidence is conclusive on the issue of paternity, we could simply do away with the judicial process in paternity cases. If the DNA test is conclusive, the paternity of children will be left for resolution by the scientists, and judges will become superfluous in that regard. We do not perceive the law to require or to recommend that result, and we hold that DNA evidence is not conclusive on the issue of paternity. On remand, if the trial court decides the DNA evidence is in Michael's best interests, it must still consider any other evidence offered before making a final decision." 27 Kan.App.2d at 38, 996 P.2d 841.

The *Ferguson* court further concluded that the district court violated Michael's constitutional right to due process by proceeding without joining Michael as a party or protecting his interests by appointing a guardian ad litem on his behalf. 27 Kan.App.2d at 38–39, 996 P.2d 841. Ordering that Michael be joined as a party and represented by counsel on remand, the *Ferguson* court suggested that the district court and the parties give "special attention" to Michael's wishes. 27 Kan.App.2d at 40, 996 P.2d 841.

Sandra attempts to distinguish *Ferguson* by arguing that it did not involve a question of intestate succession. Sandra further argues that *Ferguson* does not apply because, unlike Michael, Heather was an adult when the action was filed. Sandra also points to Heather's representation by counsel and asserts that Heather waived her right to a *Ross* hearing when she filed the paternity action. Sandra focuses on the following excerpt from *Ferguson:* "The facts which underlie this action give it a somewhat bizarre tilt and certainly create questions as to the relevance of the entire proceedings. To begin with, there is an obvious question as to just why this is being litigated. Michael became an adult during the litigation, and it is apparent there were and are no issues of child custody or child support being litigated." 27 Kan.App.2d at 35, 996 P.2d 841.

Sandra's attempt to factually distinguish *Ferguson* overlooks the legal foundation of the *Ferguson* court's holding. Both the *Ross* and *Ferguson* courts were concerned with the purpose for determining a child's biological paternity when there was already a presumptive father. Ross, 245 Kan. at 601, 783 P.2d 331; Ferguson, 27 Kan.App.2d at 35–36, 996 P.2d 841. Like the *Ross* court, the *Ferguson* court focused on the legal presumption of paternity that existed prior to the commencement of the paternity action. Ross, 245 Kan. at 596, 602, 783 P.2d 331; Ferguson, 27 Kan.App.2d at 36, 996 P.2d 841. The *Ferguson* court expressed this focus by stating that the "relevance, in a legal sense, of who is Michael's biological father is questionable." 27 Kan.App.2d at 35–36, 996 P.2d 841.

We believe the *Ross* and *Ferguson* analysis applies in this case. The relevance of who is Heather's biological father is questionable given the strong presumption that Sam was her father. The presumption of Sam's paternity existed for many years prior to the filing of this paternity action. Although the *Ferguson* court found the facts in that case were "somewhat bizarre" because it was litigated even though there were no issues regarding support or custody and the child had become an adult, this case demonstrates a set of circumstances in which an adult child may be forced to establish paternity pursuant to the Kansas Parentage Act even though a strong presumption of paternity already exists. *Ross* and *Ferguson* support the protection of presumptive paternity over biological paternity when it is in the child's best interests. We believe that protection extends to both minor and adult children.

Extending *Ross* to adult children accomplishes the legislature's intent as stated in the plain language of the statutory scheme. K.S.A. 38–1114 establishes six presumptions of paternity. If two presumptions conflict, the court must determine which presumption is founded on "weightier considerations of policy and logic, including the best interests of the child" before deciding which presumption controls. K.S.A. 38–1114(c). If any one of the presumptions arise, that presumption is a sufficient basis for an order requiring a man to support a child. K.S.A. 38–1114(e).

Without a *Ross* hearing to determine whether genetic testing is in the child's best interests, genetic testing becomes conclusive on the issue of paternity regardless of whether any other presumptions apply. As a result, denying adult children the protection of a *Ross* hearing is tantamount to rewriting the Kansas Parentage Act because it eliminates all of the other paternal presumptions besides genetic testing. If the legislature intended for genetic testing to be conclusive for determining the paternity of an adult child, it could have included language limiting the remaining presumptions to minor children. However, the Kansas Parentage Act does not include such limiting language in the statutory scheme. See K.S.A. 38–1114. The *Ferguson* court recognized the legislature's intent to treat all children the same, regardless of age, when it specifically held that genetic testing is not conclusive on the issue of paternity and ordered the district court to consider all of the evidence available before deciding Michael's paternity if it determined that genetic testing was in Michael's best interests. Ferguson, 27 Kan.App.2d at 38, 996 P.2d 841.

Extending *Ross* to adult children also furthers the purpose of the Kansas Parentage Act by protecting an adult child's right to inherit from his or her presumptive parent. The *Ross* court noted that the purpose of the Kansas Parentage Act is to provide for the "equal beneficial treatment of children." 245 Kan. at 597, 783 P.2d 331. The Kansas Parentage Act requires courts to act in the child's best interests "when imposing legal obligations or conferring legal rights" on the parent/child relationship. 245 Kan. at 597, 783 P.2d 331. The *Ross* court construed the Kansas Parentage Act to recognize that "every child has an interest not only in obtaining support, but also in inheritance rights, family bonds, and accurate identification of his parentage." 245 Kan. at 597, 783 P.2d 331. While the court does not need to protect a child's right to support after emancipation, the need to protect a child's right to inherit, the child's family bonds, and the accurate identification of the child's parentage are not limited to the child's period of minority.

Finally, extending *Ross* to adult children recognizes the public policy that paternity is both broader and deeper than genetics. The recognition of family identity extends beyond the years of a child's minority. Every adult continues to be someone's son or daughter for purposes of family identification, family bonding, and inheritance. The parental relationship continues to exist regardless of whether the bonds are close, strained, or nonexistent. The presumptions of paternity set forth in K.S.A. 38–1114(a) were instituted to protect and maintain the concept of family identity. Intruding upon this concept can cause emotional damage to children of all ages, not only to minors. See Ross, 245 Kan. at 602, 783 P.2d 331 (noting that "[t]he shifting of paternity from the presumed father to the biological father could easily be detrimental to the emotional and physical well-being of *any* child" [emphasis added]); Ferguson, 27 Kan.App.2d at 39, 996 P.2d 841 (concluding that children have a fundamental liberty interest in maintaining familial relationships).

This case illustrates the importance of protecting the presumption of paternity. Although the ultimate issue in this case involves the division of a decedent's estate, the resolution of that issue turns on the legal designation of paternity for a child born with a presumptive father. Heather was born during Sam's and Deloris' marriage. Sam's name appears on Heather's birth certificate. Heather was identified with Sam's familial name and included in the membership of Sam's family. Although her relationship with Sam was externally distant, she always believed he was her father. Sandra is attempting to vitiate a legal parent and child relationship that had not been questioned while Sam was alive. Requiring the district court to conduct genetic testing without determining whether it is in Heather's best interest would allow Sandra to accomplish after Sam's death that which could not be accomplished during Sam's lifetime. We cannot support a policy which gives anyone an opportunity to legally undermine a child's lifelong understanding of his or her parental heritage after his or her presumptive parents are deceased.

Sandra relies on Tedford v. Gregory, 125 N.M. 206, 959 P.2d 540 (Ct.App.1998), for the proposition that courts should only consider the best interests of the child when the action involves a minor. In *Tedford,* an adult child filed a paternity action against her purported natural father even though the adult child had a presumptive father who had raised and supported her since her birth. The adult child filed the action seeking retroactive child support from the date of her birth. After ordering genetic testing, which revealed that the purported natural father was the adult child's biological father, the district court granted the adult child's paternity action and awarded her $50,000 in retroactive child support. Noting that case law in other jurisdictions was limited to actions involving minor children, the *Tedford* court upheld the district court's ruling, concluding that the best interest of the child standard did not apply to adult children in paternity actions. 125 N.M. at 211, 959 P.2d 540. The *Tedford* court reasoned that the putative father was not the proper party to assert the best interest of the child standard because the standard could not be invoked on behalf of someone other than the child. 125 N.M. at 212, 959 P.2d 540.

Applying the *Tedford* court's reasoning to this case does not support Sandra's argument for two reasons. First, *Tedford,* which is not controlling precedent, was decided before *Ferguson,* which is controlling precedent. Second, Heather invoked the application of the best interests standard. Under the *Tedford* court's reasoning, Heather is the proper party to invoke the standard. *Tedford* does not persuade us to allow anyone to bypass the best-interest standard simply because the child has reached the age of majority.

We cannot subvert the presumption of paternity in favor of biology without requiring a court to consider whether it is in the child's best interests regardless of the child's age. Interpretation of the relevant statutes, controlling precedent, and public policy support the district court's decision to hold a *Ross* hearing in Heather's paternity action. Sandra's appeal is limited to the legal application of *Ross* to an adult child's paternity action in the context of a probate case. Sandra does not contest the district court's determination that it is not in Heather's best interests to conduct genetic testing. Thus, we affirm the district court's well-reasoned opinion denying Sandra's motions for genetic testing in both the probate and paternity cases and remand the matter for further proceedings.

■ ALLEGRUCCI, J., not participating.

■ LOCKETT, J., Retired, assigned.

NOTES

Establishing legal parentage under the Uniform Parentage Act begins with a series of presumptions. The Act provides detailed provisions for voluntary acknowledgement of paternity (Article 3), presumptions of paternity (Article 2 § 204), and genetic testing procedures (Article 5). Article 6 of the Act establishes procedures for adjudicating parentage and challenging acknowledgements and presumptions. These presumptions may be rebutted, as *Reese* illustrates, when it can be demonstrated that rebuttal is in the child's best interest, regardless of the child's age. Additional decisions emphasize the determinative effect of the presumption of paternity and the best interest of the child. *See, e.g.*, N.J. Div. of Youth and Fam. Servs. v. D.S.H., 40 A.3d 734, (N.J. Ct. App. 2012) (holding that presumption of paternity occurred because man was recorded as the father on the child's birth certificate); D.H. v. R.R., 964 N.E.2d 950 (Mass. 2012) (holding voluntary acknowledgement of paternity by a paramour-mother and alleged father is ineffective to establish paternity of third party if the mother is married to another man at the time of the child's birth). Without the benefit of statutory presumptions of paternity, courts have been willing to apply a common law doctrine of paternity by estoppel. *See, e.g.*, K.E.M. v. P.C.S., 38 A.3d 798 (Pa. 2012) (holding that the husband's continued marriage to the mother of a child, despite her disclosure that he was not the father of the child, resulted in his duty to support the child because this was in the child's best interest). For more commentary, *see*, Linda D. Elrod., *Family Law*, 1 KAN. LAW & PRAC., § 7:6 (2015) (discussing the 1973 Uniform Parentage Act and more recent revisions in the context of presumptions of paternity and the best interest of the child); Rebecca Moulton. Student Note, *Who's Your Daddy?: The Inherent Unfairness of the Marital Presumption for Children of Unmarried Parents*, 47 FAM. CT. REV. 698 (2009); Angela Chesney Herrington, Comment, *For Love or Money: Kansas Supreme Court's Problematic Acceptance of the "Best Interests of the Child" Standard in an Intestate Claim [Reese v. Muret, 150 P.3d 309 (Kan. 2007)]*, WASHBURN L. J. 177 (2007); Jane C. Murphy, *Legal Images of Fatherhood: Welfare Reform, Child Support Enforcement and Fatherless Children*, 81 NOTRE DAME L. REV. 325 (2005).

If rebuttal of any presumption of paternity is permitted by a court, then genetic testing may be utilized to establish parentage. Article 5 of the Uniform Parentage Act addresses the requirements for voluntary genetic testing, and alternatively, when genetic testing is ordered by a court. Indigent parties may seek state assistance in paying for paternity testing. *See, e.g.,* Little v. Streater, 452 U.S. 1 (1981). When testing specimens are not available from a man who may be the father of a child, a court may, for good cause and under circumstances the court considers to be just, order relatives of the man to submit specimens for testing. In some cases this has involved exhuming a body from the grave. *See, e.g., In re* Estate of Kingsbury, 946 A.2d 389 (Me. 2008); *but see* Will of Janis, 157 Misc.2d 999, 600 N.Y.S.2d 416 (N.Y. Sur. 1993). Autopsy specimens may also be used for genetic testing. *See In re* Poldrugovaz, 50 A.D.3d 117, 851 N.Y. S.2d 254 (App. Div. 2008). For commentary, *see* Dylan R. Boyd, Note, *Raising the Dead: An Examination of In re* Kingsbury *and Maine's Law Regarding Intestate Succession and Posthumous Paternity Testing*, 61 ME. L. REV. 567 (2009).

UNIFORM PARENTAGE ACT OF 2000 (AMENDED 2002)

§ 201. Establishment of a Parent-Child Relationship

(a) The mother-child relationship is established between a woman and a child by:

(1) the woman's having given birth to the child [except as otherwise provided in [Article] 8];

(2) an adjudication of the woman's maternity; [or]

(3) adoption of the child by the woman [; or

(4) an adjudication confirming the woman as a parent of a child born to a gestational mother if the agreement was

validated under [Article] 8 or is enforceable under other law].

(b) The father-child relationship is established between a man and a child by:

(1) an unrebutted presumption of the man's paternity of the child under Section 204;

(2) an effective acknowledgement of paternity by the man under [Article] 3, unless the acknowledgement has been rescinded or successfully challenged;

(3) an adjudication of the man's paternity;

(4) adoption of the child by the man; [or]

(5) the man's having consented to assisted reproduction by a woman under [Article] 7 which resulted in the birth of the child [; or

(6) an adjudication confirming the man as a parent of a child born to a gestational mother if the agreement was validated under [Article] 8 or is enforceable under other law]. . . .

§ 204. Presumption of Paternity

(a) A man is presumed to be the father of a child if:

(1) he and the mother of the child are married to each other and the child is born during the marriage;

(2) he and the mother of the child were married to each other and the child is born within 300 days after the marriage is terminated by death, annulment, declaration of invalidity, or divorce [, or after a decree of separation];

(3) before the birth of the child, he and the mother of the child married each other in apparent compliance with the law, even if the attempted marriage is or could be declared invalid, and the child is born during the invalid marriage or within 300 days after its termination by death, annulment, declaration of invalidity, or divorce [, or after a decree of separation];

(4) after the birth of the child, he and the mother of the child married each other in apparent compliance with law, whether or not the marriage is or could be declared invalid, and he voluntarily asserted his paternity of the child, and:

(A) the assertion is in a record filed with [state agency maintaining birth records];

(B) he agreed to be and is named as the child's father on the child's birth certificate; or

(C) he promised in a record to support the child as his own; or

(5) for the first two years of the child's life, he resided in the same household with the child and openly help out the child as his own.

(b) A presumption of paternity established under this section may be rebutted only by adjudication under [Article] 6.

NOTES

For general commentary on the Uniform Parentage Act, *see* Douglas NeJaime, *Marriage Equality and the New Parenthood*, 129 HARV. L. REV. 1185 (2016); Jeffrey A. Parness, *Choosing Among Imprecise American State Parentage Laws*, 76 LA. L. REV. 481 (2015); Kerry Abrams & Brandon L. Garrett, *DNA and Distrust*, 91 NOTRE DAME L. REV. 757 (2015); Melissa Murray, *Family Law's Doctrines*, 163 U. PA. L. REV. 1985 (2015); Lynda Wray Black, *The Birth of a Parent: Defining Parentage for Lenders of Genetic Material*, 92 NEB. L. REV. 799 (2014); Mary Patricia Byrn, *Which Came First the Parent or the Child?*, 62 RUTGERS L. REV. 305 (2010); W. Nicholson Price II, *Am I My Son? Human Clones and the Modern Family*, 11 COLUM. SCI. & TECH. L. REV. 119 (2010); Robin Fretwell Wilson, *Trusting Mothers: A Critique of the American Law Institute's Treatment of De Facto Parents*, 38 HOFSTRA L. REV. 1103 (2010).

B. PROTECTION OF PUTATIVE FATHERS

Stanley v. Illinois

Supreme Court of the United States, 1972
405 U.S. 645

■ WHITE, JUSTICE delivered the opinion of the Court.

Joan Stanley lived with Peter Stanley intermittently for 18 years during which time they had three children. When Joan Stanley died, Peter Stanley lost not only her but also his children. Under Illinois law the children of unwed fathers become wards of the State upon the death of the mother. Accordingly, upon Joan Stanley's death, in a dependency proceeding instituted by the State of Illinois, Stanley's children were declared wards of the State and placed with court appointed guardians. Stanley appealed, claiming that he had never been shown to be an unfit parent and that since married fathers and unwed mothers could not be deprived of their children without such a showing, he had been deprived of the equal protection of the laws guaranteed him by the Fourteenth Amendment. The Illinois Supreme Court accepted the fact that Stanley's own unfitness had not been established but rejected the equal protection claim, holding that Stanley could properly be separated from his children upon proof of the single fact that he and the dead mother had not been married. Stanley's actual fitness as a father was irrelevant. In re Stanley, 45 Ill.2d 132, 256 N.E.2d 814 (1970).

Stanley presses his equal protection claim here. The State continues to respond that unwed fathers are presumed unfit to raise their children and that it is unnecessary to hold individualized hearings to determine whether particular fathers are in fact unfit parents before they are separated from their children.

At the outset we reject any suggestion that we need not consider the propriety of the dependency proceeding that separated the Stanleys because Stanley might be able to regain custody of his children as a guardian or through adoption proceedings. The suggestion is that if Stanley has been treated differently from other parents, the difference is immaterial and not legally cognizable for the purposes of the Fourteenth Amendment. This Court has not, however, embraced the general proposition that a wrong may be done if it can be undone. . . .

It is clear, moreover, that Stanley does not have the means at hand promptly to erase the adverse consequences of the proceeding in the course of which his children were declared wards of the State. It is first urged that Stanley could act to adopt his children. . . . Insofar as we are informed, Illinois law affords him no priority in adoption proceedings. It would be his burden to establish not only that he would be a suitable parent but also that he would be the most suitable of all who might want custody of the children. Neither can we ignore that in the proceedings from which this action developed, the "probation officer," the assistant state's attorney, and the judge charged with the case, made it apparent that Stanley, unmarried and impecunious as he is, could not now expect to profit from adoption proceedings.

Before us, the State focuses on Stanley's failure to petition for "custody and control"—the second route by which, it is urged, he might regain authority for his children. Passing the obvious issue whether it would be futile or burdensome for an unmarried father—without funds and already once presumed unfit—to petition for custody, this suggestion overlooks the fact that legal custody is not parenthood or adoption. A person appointed guardian in an action for custody and control is subject to removal at any time without such cause as must be shown in a neglect proceeding against a parent. Ill.Rev.Stat., c. 37, § 705–8. He may not take the children out of the jurisdiction without the court's approval. He may be required to report to the court as to his disposition of the children's affairs. Ill.Rev.Stat., c. 37, § 705–8. Obviously then, even if Stanley were a mere step away from "custody and control," to give an unwed father only "custody and control" would still be to leave him seriously prejudiced by reason of his status.

We must therefore examine the question which Illinois would have us avoid: Is a presumption which distinguishes and burdens all unwed fathers constitutionally repugnant? We conclude that as a matter of due process of law, Stanley was entitled to a hearing on his fitness as a parent before his children were taken from him and that by denying him a hearing and extending it to all other parents whose custody of their children is challenged the State denied Stanley the equal protection of the law guaranteed by the Fourteenth Amendment.

Illinois has two principal methods of removing non-delinquent children from the homes of their parents. In a dependency proceeding it may demonstrate that the children are wards of the State because they have no surviving parent or guardian. In a neglect proceeding it may show that children should be wards of the State because the present parent(s) or guardian does not provide suitable care.

The State's right—indeed duty—to protect minor children through a judicial determination of their interests in a neglect proceeding is not challenged here. Rather we are faced with a dependency statute which empowers state officials to circumvent neglect proceedings on the theory that an unwed father is not a "parent" whose existing relationship with his children must be considered. "Parents," says the State, "means the father and mother of a legitimate child, or the survivor of them, or the natural mother of an illegitimate child, and includes any adoptive parent," Ill.Rev.Stat., c. 37, § 701–14, but the term does not include unwed fathers. . . .

The private interest here, that of a man in the children he has sired and raised, undeniably warrants deference and, absent a powerful countervailing interest, protection. It is plain that the interest of a parent in the companionship, care, custody, and management of his or her children "come[s] to this Court with a momentum for respect lacking when appeal is made to liberties which derive merely from shifting economic arrangements." Kovacs v. Cooper, 336 U.S. 77, 95 (1949) (concurring opinion).

The Court has frequently emphasized the importance of the family. The rights to conceive and to raise one's children have been deemed "essential," Meyer v. Nebraska, 262 U.S. 390, 399 (1923), "basic civil rights of man," Skinner v. Oklahoma, 316 U.S. 535, 541 (1942), and "[r]ights far more precious . . . than property rights," May v. Anderson, 345 U.S. 528, 533 (1953). "It is cardinal with us that the custody, care and nurture of the child reside first in the parents, whose primary function and freedom include preparation for obligations the state can neither supply nor hinder." Prince v. Massachusetts, 321 U.S. 158, 166 (1944). The integrity of the family unit has found protection in the Due Process Clause of the Fourteenth Amendment, Meyer v. Nebraska, supra, at 399, the Equal Protection Clause of the Fourteenth Amendment, Skinner v. Oklahoma, supra, at 541, and the Ninth Amendment, Griswold v. Connecticut, 381 U.S. 479, 496 (1965) (Goldberg, J., concurring).

Nor has the law refused to recognize those family relationships unlegitimized by a marriage ceremony. The Court has declared unconstitutional a state statute denying natural, but illegitimate, children a wrongful death action for the death of their mother, emphasizing that such children cannot be denied the right of other children because familial bonds in such cases were often as warm, enduring, and important as those arising within a more formally organized family unit. Levy v. Louisiana, 391 U.S. 68, 71–72 (1968).

These authorities make it clear that, at the least, Stanley's interest in retaining custody of his children is recognizable and substantial.

For its part, the State has made its interest quite plain: Illinois has declared that the aim of the Juvenile Court Act is to protect "the moral, emotional, mental and physical welfare of the minor and the best interests of the community" and to "strengthen the minor's family ties whenever possible, removing him from the custody of his parents only when his welfare or safety or the protection of the public cannot be adequately safeguarded without removal. . . ." Ill.Rev.Stat., c. 37, §§ 701–702. These are legitimate interests well within the power of the State to implement. We do not question the assertion that neglectful parents may be separated from their children.

But we are here not asked to evaluate the legitimacy of the state ends, but rather to determine whether the means used to achieve these ends are constitutionally defensible. What is the state interest in separating children from fathers without a hearing designed to determine whether the father is unfit in a particular disputed case? We observe that the State registers no gain towards its declared goals when it separates children from the custody of fit parents. Indeed, if Stanley is a fit father, the State spites its own articulated goals when it needlessly separates him from his family.

In Bell v. Burson, 402 U.S. 535 (1971), we found a scheme repugnant to the Due Process Clause because it deprived a driver of his license without reference to the very factor (there fault in driving, here fitness as a parent) which the State itself deemed fundamental to its statutory scheme. Illinois would avoid the self-contradiction which rendered the Georgia license suspension system invalid by arguing that Stanley and all other unmarried fathers can reasonably be presumed to be unqualified to raise their children.

It may be, as the State insists, that most unmarried fathers are unsuitable and neglectful parents.[6] It may also be that Stanley is such a parent and that his children should be placed in other hands. But all unmarried fathers are not in this category; some are wholly suited to have custody of their children.[7] This much the State readily concedes,

---

6 The State speaks of "the general disinterest of putative fathers in their illegitimate children" and opines "In most instances the natural father is a stranger to his children."

7 See *In re Mark T.*, 8 Mich.App. 122, 154 N.W.2d 27 (1967). There a panel of the Michigan Court of Appeals in unanimously affirming a circuit court's determination that the father of an illegitimate son was best suited to raise the boy, said:

> "The appellants' presentation in this case proceeds on the assumption that placing Mark for adoption is inherently preferable to rearing by his father, that uprooting him from the family which he knew from birth until he was a year and a half old, secretly institutionalizing him and later transferring him to strangers is so incontrovertibly

and nothing in this record indicates that Stanley is or has been a neglectful father who has not cared for his children. Given the opportunity to make his case, Stanley may have been seen to be deserving of custody of his offspring. Had this been so, the State's statutory policy would have been furthered by leaving custody in him. . . .

[I]t may be argued that unmarried fathers are so seldom fit that Illinois need not undergo the administrative inconvenience of inquiry in any case, including Stanley's. The establishment of prompt efficacious procedures to achieve legitimate state ends is a proper state interest worthy of cognizance in constitutional adjudication. But the Constitution recognizes higher values than speed and efficiency. Indeed, one might fairly say of the Bill of Rights in general, and the Due Process Clause in particular, that they were designed to protect the fragile values of a vulnerable citizenry from the overbearing concern for efficiency and efficacy which may characterize praiseworthy government officials no less, and perhaps more, than mediocre ones.

Procedure by presumption is always cheaper and easier than individualized determination. But when, as here, the procedure forecloses the determinative issues of competence and care, when it explicitly disdains present realities in deference to past formalities, it needlessly risks running roughshod over the important interests of both parent and child. It therefore cannot stand.[9]

Bell v. Burson held that the State could not, while purporting to be concerned with fault in suspending a driver's license, deprive a citizen of his license without a hearing which would assess fault. Absent fault, the State's declared interest was so attenuated that administrative convenience was insufficient to excuse a hearing where evidence of fault could be considered. That drivers involved in accidents, as a statistical matter, might be very likely to have been wholly or partially at fault did

---

better that no court has the power even to consider the matter. Hardly anyone would even suggest such a proposition if we were talking about a child born in wedlock.

"We are not aware of any sociological data justifying the assumption that an illegitimate child reared by his natural father is less likely to receive a proper upbringing than one reared by his natural father who was at one time married to his mother, or that the stigma of illegitimacy is so pervasive it requires adoption by strangers and permanent termination of a subsisting relationship with the child's father." *Id.*, at 39.

[9] We note in passing that the incremental cost of offering unwed fathers an opportunity for individualized hearings on fitness appears to be minimal. If unwed fathers, in the main, do not care about the disposition of their children, they will not appear to demand hearings. If they do care, under the scheme here held invalid, Illinois would admittedly at some later time have to afford them a properly focused hearing in a custody or adoption proceeding.

Extending opportunity for hearing to unwed fathers who desire and claim competence to care for their children creates no constitutional or procedural obstacle to foreclosing those unwed fathers who are not so inclined. The Illinois law governing procedure in juvenile cases, Ill.Rev.Stat., c. 37, § 704–1 et seq., provides for personal service, notice by certified mail or for notice by publication when personal or certified mail service cannot be had or when notice is directed to unknown respondents under the style of "all whom it may concern." Unwed fathers who do not promptly respond cannot complain if their children are declared wards of the State. Those who do respond retain the burden of proving their fatherhood.

not foreclose hearing and proof in specific cases before licenses were suspended.

We think the Due Process Clause mandates a similar result here. The State's interest in caring for Stanley's children is *de minimis* if Stanley is shown to be a fit father. It insists on presuming rather than proving Stanley's unfitness solely because it is more convenient to presume than to prove. Under the Due Process Clause that advantage is insufficient to justify refusing a father a hearing when the issue at stake is the dismemberment of his family.

The State of Illinois assumes custody of the children of married parents, divorced parents, and unmarried mothers only after a hearing and proof of neglect. The children of unmarried fathers, however, are declared dependent children without a hearing on parental fitness and without proof of neglect. Stanley's claim in the state courts and here is that failure to afford him a hearing on his parental qualifications while extending it to other parents denied him equal protection of the laws. We have concluded that all Illinois parents are constitutionally entitled to a hearing on their fitness before their children are removed from their custody. It follows that denying such a hearing to Stanley and those like him while granting it to other Illinois parents is inescapably contrary to the Equal Protection Clause

The judgment of the Supreme Court of Illinois is reversed and the case is remanded to that court for proceedings not inconsistent with this opinion.

■ MR. CHIEF JUSTICE BURGER, with whom MR. JUSTICE BLACKMUN, concurs, dissenting. . . .

No due process issue was raised in the state courts; and no due process issue was decided by any state court. . . .

All of those persons in Illinois who may have followed the progress of this case will, I expect, experience no little surprise at the Court's opinion handed down today. Stanley will undoubtedly be surprised to find that he has prevailed on an issue never advanced by him. . . .

In regard to the only issue which I consider properly before the Court, I agree with the State's argument that the Equal Protection Clause is not violated when Illinois gives full recognition only to those father-child relationships that arise in the context of family units bound together by legal obligations arising from marriage or from adoption proceedings. Quite apart from the religious or quasi-religious connotations which marriage has—and has historically enjoyed—for a large proportion of this Nation's citizens, it is in law an essentially contractual relationship, the parties to which have legally enforceable rights and duties, with respect both to each other and to any children born to them. Stanley and the mother of these children never entered such a relationship. The record is silent as to whether they ever privately exchanged such promises as would have bound them in marriage under the common law. . . . In any event, Illinois has not recognized common law marriages since 1905. . . . Stanley did not seek the burdens when he could have freely assumed them.

Where there is a valid contract of marriage, the law of Illinois presumes that the husband is the father of any child born to the wife during the marriage; as the father, he has legally enforceable rights and duties with respect to that child. When a child is born to an unmarried woman, Illinois recognizes the readily identifiable mother, but makes no presumption as to the identity of the biological father. It does, however, provide two ways, one voluntary and one involuntary, in which that father may be identified. First, he may marry the mother and acknowledge the child as his own; this has the legal effect of legitimating the child and gaining for the father full recognition as a parent. Ill.Rev.Stat., c. 3, § 12–8. Second, a man may be found to be the biological father of the child pursuant to a paternity suit initiated by the mother; in this case, the child remains illegitimate, but the adjudicated father is made liable for the support of the child until the latter attains age 18 or is legally adopted by another. . . .

Stanley argued before the Supreme Court of Illinois that the definition of "parents," set out in Ill.Rev.Stat., c. 37, § 701–14, as including "the father and mother of a legitimate child, or the survivor of them, or the natural mother of an illegitimate child, [or] . . . any adoptive parent,"[3] violates the Equal Protection Clause in that it treats unwed mothers and unwed fathers differently. Stanley then enlarged upon his equal protection argument when he brought the case here; he argued before this Court that Illinois is not permitted by the Equal Protection Clause to distinguish between unwed fathers and any of the other biological parents included in the statutory definition of legal "parents."

The Illinois Supreme Court correctly held that the State may constitutionally distinguish between unwed fathers and unwed mothers. Here, Illinois' different treatment of the two is part of that State's statutory scheme for protecting the welfare of illegitimate children. In almost all cases, the unwed mother is readily identifiable, generally from hospital records and alternatively by physicians or others attending the child's birth. Unwed fathers, as a class are not traditionally quite so easy to identify and locate. Many of them either deny all responsibility or exhibit no interest in the child or its welfare; and, of course, many unwed fathers are simply not aware of their parenthood.

---

[3] The Court seems at times to ignore this statutory definition of "parents," even though it is precisely that definition itself whose constitutionality has been brought into issue by Stanley. In preparation for finding a purported similarity between this case and Bell v. Burson, 402 U.S. 535 (1971), the Court quotes the legislatively declared aims of the Juvenile Court Act to "strengthen the minor's family ties whenever possible, removing him from the custody of his *parent* only when his welfare or the safety or the protection of the public cannot be adequately safeguarded without removal." (Emphasis added.) The Court then goes on to find a "self-contradiction" between that stated aim and the Act's non-recognition of unwed fathers. There is, of course, no such contradiction. The word "parent" in the statement of legislative purpose obviously has the meaning given to it by the definitional provision of the Act.

Furthermore, I believe that a State is fully justified in concluding, on the basis of common human experience, that the biological role of the mother in carrying and nursing an infant creates stronger bonds between her and the child than the bonds resulting from the male's often casual encounter. This view is reinforced by the observable fact that most unwed mothers exhibit a concern for their offspring either permanently or at least until they are safely placed for adoption, while unwed fathers rarely burden either the mother or the child with their attentions or loyalties. Centuries of human experience buttress this view of the realities of human conditions and suggest that unwed mothers of illegitimate children are generally more dependable protectors of their children than are unwed fathers. While these, like most generalizations, are not without exceptions, they nevertheless provide a sufficient basis to sustain a statutory classification whose objective is not to penalize unwed parents but to further the welfare of illegitimate children in fulfillment of the State's obligations as *parens patriae*.

Stanley depicts himself as a somewhat unusual unwed father, namely, as one who has always acknowledged and never doubted his fatherhood of these children. He alleges that he loved, cared for, and supported these children from the time of their birth until the death of their mother. He contends that he consequently must be treated the same as a married father of legitimate children. Even assuming the truth of Stanley's allegations, I am unable to construe the Equal Protection Clause as requiring Illinois to tailor its statutory definition of "parents" so meticulously as to include such unusual unwed fathers, while at the same time excluding those unwed, and generally unidentified, biological fathers who in no way share Stanley's professed desires.

Indeed, the nature of Stanley's own desires is less than absolutely clear from the record in this case. Shortly after the death of the mother, Stanley turned these two children over to the care of a Mr. and Mrs. Ness; he took no action to gain his own recognition as a father, through adoption, or as a legal custodian, through a guardianship proceeding. Eventually it came to the attention of the State that there was no living adult who had any legally enforceable obligation for the care and support of the children; it was only then that the dependency proceeding here under review took place and that Stanley made himself known to the juvenile court in connection with these two children.[4] Even then, however, Stanley did not ask to be charged with the legal responsibility for the children. He asked only that such legal responsibility be given to no one else. He seemed, in particular, to be concerned with the loss of the

[4] As the majority notes, Joan Stanley gave birth to three children during the 18 years Peter Stanley was living "intermittently" with her. At oral argument, we were told by Stanley's counsel that the oldest of these three children had previously been declared a ward of the court pursuant to a neglect proceeding which was "proven against" Stanley at a time, apparently, when the juvenile court officials were under the erroneous impression that Peter and Joan Stanley had been married.

welfare payments he would suffer as a result of the designation of others as guardians of the children.

Not only, then, do I see no ground for holding that Illinois' statutory definition of "parents" on its face violates the Equal Protection Clause; I see no ground for holding that any constitutional right of Stanley has been denied in the application of that statutory definition in the case at bar. . . .

Lehr v. Robertson

Supreme Court of the United States, 1983
463 U.S. 248

■ STEVENS, JUSTICE.

The question presented is whether New York has sufficiently protected an unmarried father's inchoate relationship with a child whom he has never supported and rarely seen in the two years since her birth. The appellant, Jonathan Lehr, claims that the Due Process and Equal Protection Clauses of the Fourteenth Amendment, as interpreted in Stanley v. Illinois, 405 U.S. 645, 92 S.Ct. 1208, 31 L.Ed.2d 551 (1972), and Caban v. Mohammed, 441 U.S. 380, 99 S.Ct. 1760, 60 L.Ed.2d 297 (1979), give him an absolute right to notice and an opportunity to be heard before the child may be adopted. We disagree.

Jessica M. was born out of wedlock on November 9, 1976. Her mother, Lorraine Robertson, married Richard Robertson eight months after Jessica's birth.[1] On December 21, 1978, when Jessica was over two years old, the Robertsons filed an adoption petition in the Family Court of Ulster County, New York. The court heard their testimony and received a favorable report from the Ulster County Department of Social Services. On March 7, 1979, the court entered an order of adoption. In this proceeding, appellant contends that the adoption order is invalid because he, Jessica's putative father, was not given advance notice of the adoption proceeding.[3]

The State of New York maintains a "putative father registry." A man who files with that registry demonstrates his intent to claim paternity of a child born out of wedlock and is therefore entitled to receive notice of any proceeding to adopt that child. Before entering Jessica's adoption order, the Ulster County Family Court had the putative father registry examined. Although appellant claims to be Jessica's natural father, he had not entered his name in the registry.

In addition to the persons whose names are listed on the putative father registry, New York law requires that notice of an adoption proceeding be given to several other classes of possible fathers of children

[1] Although both Lorraine and Richard Robertson are appellees in this proceeding, for ease of discussion the term "appellee" will hereafter be used to identify Lorraine Robertson.

[3] Appellee has never conceded that appellant is Jessica's biological father, but for purposes of analysis in this opinion it will be assumed that he is.

born out of wedlock—those who have been adjudicated to be the father, those who have been identified as the father on the child's birth certificate, those who live openly with the child and the child's mother and who hold themselves out to be the father, those who have been identified as the father by the mother in a sworn written statement, and those who were married to the child's mother before the child was six months old. Appellant admittedly was not a member of any of those classes. He had lived with appellee prior to Jessica's birth and visited her in the hospital when Jessica was born, but his name does not appear on Jessica's birth certificate. He did not live with appellee or Jessica after Jessica's birth, he has never provided them with any financial support, and he has never offered to marry appellee. Nevertheless, he contends that the following special circumstances gave him a constitutional right to notice and a hearing before Jessica was adopted.

On January 30, 1979, one month after the adoption proceeding was commenced in Ulster County, appellant filed a "visitation and paternity petition" in the Westchester County Family Court. In that petition, he asked for a determination of paternity, an order of support, and reasonable visitation privileges with Jessica. Notice of that proceeding was served on appellee on February 22, 1979. Four days later appellee's attorney informed the Ulster County Court that appellant had commenced a paternity proceeding in Westchester County; the Ulster County judge then entered an order staying appellant's paternity proceeding until he could rule on a motion to change the venue of that proceeding to Ulster County. On March 3, 1979, appellant received notice of the change of venue motion and, for the first time, learned that an adoption proceeding was pending in Ulster County. On March 7, 1979, appellant's attorney telephoned the Ulster County judge to inform him that he planned to seek a stay of the adoption proceeding pending the determination of the paternity petition. In that telephone conversation, the judge advised the lawyer that he had already signed the adoption order earlier that day. According to appellant's attorney, the judge stated that he was aware of the pending paternity petition but did not believe he was required to give notice to appellant prior to the entry of the order of adoption.

Thereafter, the Family Court in Westchester County granted appellee's motion to dismiss the paternity petition, holding that the putative father's right to seek paternity " . . . must be deemed severed so long as an order of adoption exists." Appellant did not appeal from that dismissal.[6] On June 22, 1979, appellant filed a petition to vacate the order of adoption on the ground that it was obtained by fraud and in violation of his constitutional rights. . . .

Appellant has now invoked our appellate jurisdiction. He offers two alternative grounds for holding the New York statutory scheme

[6] Without trying to intervene in the adoption proceeding, appellant had attempted to file an appeal from the adoption order. That appeal was dismissed.

unconstitutional. First, he contends that a putative father's actual or potential relationship with a child born out of wedlock is an interest in liberty which may not be destroyed without due process of law; he argues therefore that he had a constitutional right to prior notice and an opportunity to be heard before he was deprived of that interest. Second, he contends that the gender-based classification in the statute, which both denied him the right to consent to Jessica's adoption and accorded him fewer procedural rights than her mother, violated the Equal Protection Clause.

The Due Process Claim. . . .

The intangible fibers that connect parent and child have infinite variety. They are woven throughout the fabric of our society, providing it with strength, beauty, and flexibility. It is self-evident that they are sufficiently vital to merit constitutional protection in appropriate cases. In deciding whether this is such a case, however, we must consider the broad framework that has traditionally been used to resolve the legal problems arising from the parent-child relationship.

In the vast majority of cases, state law determines the final outcome. Rules governing the inheritance of property, adoption, and child custody are generally specified in statutory enactments that vary from State to State. Moreover, equally varied state laws governing marriage and divorce affect a multitude of parent-child relationships. The institution of marriage has played a critical role both in defining the legal entitlements of family members and in developing the decentralized structure of our democratic society.[12] In recognition of that role, and as part of their general overarching concern for serving the best interests of children, state laws almost universally express an appropriate preference for the formal family.

In some cases, however, this Court has held that the Federal Constitution supersedes state law and provides even greater protection for certain formal family relationships. In those cases, as in the state cases, the Court has emphasized the paramount interest in the welfare of children and has noted that the rights of the parents are a counterpart of the responsibilities they have assumed. . . . There are also a few cases in which this Court has considered the extent to which the Constitution affords protection to the relationship between natural parents and children born out of wedlock. In some we have been concerned with the rights of the children. In this case, however, it is a parent who claims that the state has improperly deprived him of a protected interest in liberty. This Court has examined the extent to which a natural father's biological relationship with his illegitimate child receives protection under the Due Process Clause in precisely three cases: Stanley v. Illinois, 405 U.S. 645, 92 S.Ct. 1208, 31 L.Ed.2d 551 (1972), Quilloin v. Walcott,

[12] See Hafen, Marriage, Kinship and Sexual Privacy, 81 MICH. L. REV. 463, 479–481 (1983) (hereinafter Hafen).

434 U.S. 246, 98 S.Ct. 549, 54 L.Ed.2d 511 (1978), and Caban v. Mohammed, 441 U.S. 380, 99 S.Ct. 1760, 60 L.Ed.2d 297 (1979).

Stanley involved the constitutionality of an Illinois statute that conclusively presumed every father of a child born out of wedlock to be un unfit person to have custody of his children. The father in that case had lived with his children all their lives and had lived with their mother for eighteen years. There was nothing in the record to indicate that Stanley had been a neglectful father who had not cared for his children. 405 U.S., at 655, 92 S.Ct., at 1214. Under the statute, however, the nature of the actual relationship between parent and child was completely irrelevant. Once the mother died, the children were automatically made wards of the state. Relying in part on a Michigan case[14] recognizing that the preservation of "a subsisting relationship with the child's father" may better serve the child's best interest than "uprooting him from the family which he knew from birth," the Court held that the Due Process Clause was violated by the automatic destruction of the custodial relationship without giving the father any opportunity to present evidence regarding his fitness as a parent.

Quilloin involved the constitutionality of a Georgia statute that authorized the adoption of a child born out of wedlock over the objection of the natural father. The father in that case had never legitimated the child. It was only after the mother had remarried and her new husband had filed an adoption petition that the natural father sought visitation rights and filed a petition for legitimation. The trial court found adoption by the new husband to be in the child's best interests, and we unanimously held that action to be consistent with the Due Process Clause.

Caban involved the conflicting claims of two natural parents who had maintained joint custody of their children from the time of their birth until they were respectively two and four years old. The father challenged the validity of an order authorizing the mother's new husband to adopt the children; he relied on both the Equal Protection Clause and the Due Process Clause. Because this Court upheld his equal protection claim, the majority did not address his due process challenge. The comments on the latter claim by the four dissenting Justices are nevertheless instructive, because they identify the clear distinction between a mere biological relationship and an actual relationship of parental responsibility.

Justice Stewart correctly observed:

> "Even if it be assumed that each married parent after divorce has some substantive due process right to maintain his or her parental relationship, cf. Smith v. Organization of Foster Families, 431 U.S. 816, 862–863 [97 S.Ct. 2094, 2119, 53 L.Ed.2d 14] (opinion concurring in judgment), it by no means follows that each unwed parent has any such right. *Parental*

[14] *In re Mark T.*, 8 Mich.App. 122, 154 N.W.2d 27 (1967).

> *rights do not spring full-blown from the biological connection between parent and child.* They require relationships more enduring." 441 U.S., at 397, 99 S.Ct., at 1770 (emphasis added).[16] In a similar vein, the other three dissenters in *Caban* were prepared to "assume that, *if and when one develops,* the relationship between a father and his natural child is entitled to protection against arbitrary state action as a matter of due process." Caban v. Mohammed, 441 U.S. 380, 414, 99 S.Ct. 1760, 1779, 60 L.Ed.2d 297 (emphasis added).

The difference between the developed parent-child relationship that was implicated in *Stanley* and *Caban,* and the potential relationship involved in *Quilloin* and this case, is both clear and significant. Where an unwed father demonstrates a full commitment to the responsibilities of parenthood by "com[ing] forward to participate in the rearing of his child," Caban, 441 U.S., at 392, 99 S.Ct., at 1768, his interest in personal contact with his child acquires substantial protection under the due process clause. At that point it may be said that he "act[s] as a father toward his children." But the mere existence of a biological link does not merit equivalent constitutional protection. The actions of judges neither create nor sever genetic bonds. "[T]he importance of the familial relationship, to the individuals involved and to the society, stems from the emotional attachments that derive from the intimacy of daily association, and from the role it plays in 'promot[ing] a way of life' through the instruction of children as well as from the fact of blood relationship." Smith v. Organization of Foster Families for Equality and Reform, 431 U.S. 816, 844, 97 S.Ct. 2094, 2109–2110, 53 L.Ed.2d 14 (1977) (quoting Wisconsin v. Yoder, 406 U.S. 205, 231–233, 92 S.Ct. 1526, 1541–1542, 32 L.Ed.2d 15 (1972)).

The significance of the biological connection is that it offers the natural father an opportunity that no other male possesses to develop a relationship with his offspring. If he grasps that opportunity and accepts some measure of responsibility for the child's future, he may enjoy the

---

[16] In the balance of that paragraph Justice Stewart noted that the relation between a father and his natural child may acquire constitutional protection if the father enters into a traditional marriage with the mother or if "the actual relationship between father and child" is sufficient.

> "The mother carries and bears the child, and in this sense her parental relationship is clear. The validity of the father's parental claims must be gauged by other measures. By tradition, the primary measure has been the legitimate familial relationship he creates with the child by marriage with the mother. By definition, the question before us can arise only when no such marriage has taken place. In some circumstances the actual relationship between father and child may suffice to create in the unwed father parental interests comparable to those of the married father. Cf. Stanley v. Illinois, supra. But here we are concerned with the rights the unwed father may have when his wishes and those of the mother are in conflict, and the child's best interests are served by a resolution in favor of the mother. It seems to me that the absence of a legal tie with the mother may in such circumstances appropriately place a limit on whatever substantive constitutional claims might otherwise exist by virtue of the father's actual relationship with the children."

Ibid.

blessings of the parent-child relationship and make uniquely valuable contributions to the child's development.[18] If he fails to do so, the Federal Constitution will not automatically compel a state to listen to his opinion of where the child's best interests lie.

In this case, we are not assessing the constitutional adequacy of New York's procedures for terminating a developed relationship. Appellant has never had any significant custodial, personal, or financial relationship with Jessica, and he did not seek to establish a legal tie until after she was two years old.[19] We are concerned only with whether New York has adequately protected his opportunity to form such a relationship.

The most effective protection of the putative father's opportunity to develop a relationship with his child is provided by the laws that authorize formal marriage and govern its consequences. But the availability of that protection is, of course, dependent on the will of both parents of the child. Thus, New York has adopted a special statutory scheme to protect the unmarried father's interest in assuming a responsible role in the future of his child.

After this Court's decision in *Stanley*, the New York Legislature appointed a special commission to recommend legislation that would accommodate both the interests of biological fathers in their children and the children's interest in prompt and certain adoption procedures. The commission recommended, and the legislature enacted, a statutory adoption scheme that automatically provides notice to seven categories of putative fathers who are likely to have assumed some responsibility for the care of their natural children.[20] If this scheme were likely to omit

---

[18] Of course, we need not take sides in the ongoing debate among family psychologists over the relative weight to be accorded biological ties and psychological ties, in order to recognize that a natural father who has played a substantial role in rearing his child has a greater claim to constitutional protection than a mere biological parent. New York's statutory scheme reflects these differences, guaranteeing notice to any putative father who is living openly with the child, and providing putative fathers who have never developed a relationship with the child the opportunity to receive notice simply by mailing a postcard to the putative father registry.

[19] This case happens to involve an adoption by the husband of the natural mother, but we do not believe the natural father has any greater right to object to such an adoption than to an adoption by two total strangers. If anything, the balance of equities tips the opposite way in a case such as this. In denying the putative father relief in *Quilloin*, we made an observation equally applicable here:

> "Nor is this a case in which the proposed adoption would place the child with a new set of parents with whom the child had never before lived. Rather, the result of the adoption in this case is to give full recognition to a family unit already in existence, a result desired by all concerned, except appellant. Whatever might be required in other situations, we cannot say that the State was required in this situation to find anything more than that the adoption, and denial of legitimation, were in the 'best interests of the child.' " 434 U.S., at 255, 98 S.Ct., at 555.

[20] In a report explaining the purpose of the 1976 Amendments to § 111–a of the New York Domestic Relations Law, the temporary state commission on child welfare that was responsible for drafting the legislation stated, in part:

> "The measure will dispel uncertainties by providing clear constitutional statutory guidelines for notice to fathers of out-of-wedlock children. It will establish a desired finality in adoption proceedings and will provide an expeditious method for child placement agencies of identifying those fathers who are entitled to notice through the

many responsible fathers, and if qualification for notice were beyond the control of an interested putative father, it might be thought procedurally inadequate. Yet, as all of the New York courts that reviewed this matter observed, the right to receive notice was completely within appellant's control. By mailing a postcard to the putative father registry, he could have guaranteed that he would receive notice of any proceedings to adopt Jessica. The possibility that he may have failed to do so because of his ignorance of the law cannot be a sufficient reason for criticizing the law itself. The New York legislature concluded that a more open-ended notice requirement would merely complicate the adoption process, threaten the privacy interests of unwed mothers, create the risk of unnecessary controversy, and impair the desired finality of adoption decrees. Regardless of whether we would have done likewise if we were legislators instead of judges, we surely cannot characterize the state's conclusion as arbitrary.[22]

Appellant argues, however, that even if the putative father's opportunity to establish a relationship with an illegitimate child is adequately protected by the New York statutory scheme in the normal case, he was nevertheless entitled to special notice because the court and the mother knew that he had filed an affiliation proceeding in another court. This argument amounts to nothing more than an indirect attack on the notice provisions of the New York statute. The legitimate state interests in facilitating the adoption of young children and having the adoption proceeding completed expeditiously that underlie the entire statutory scheme also justify a trial judge's determination to require all interested parties to adhere precisely to the procedural requirements of the statute. The Constitution does not require either a trial judge or a litigant to give special notice to nonparties who are presumptively capable of asserting and protecting their own rights. Since the New York statutes adequately protected appellant's inchoate interest in establishing a relationship with Jessica, we find no merit in the claim

---

creation of a registry of such fathers within the State Department of Social Services. Conversely, the bill will afford to concerned fathers of out-of-wedlock children a simple means of expressing their interest and protecting their rights to be notified and have an opportunity to be heard. It will also obviate an existing disparity of Appellate Division decisions by permitting such fathers to be petitioners in paternity proceedings.

"The measure is intended to codify the minimum protections for the putative father which *Stanley* would require. In so doing it reflects policy decisions to (a) codify constitutional requirements; (b) clearly establish, as early as possible in a child's life, the rights, interests and obligations of all parties; (c) facilitate prompt planning for the future of the child and permanence of his status; and (d) through the foregoing, promote the best interest of children."

[22] Nor can we deem unconstitutionally arbitrary the state courts' conclusion that appellant's absence did not distort its analysis of Jessica's best interests. The adoption does not affect Jessica's relationship with her mother. It gives legal permanence to her relationship with her adoptive father, a relationship they had maintained for 21 months at the time the adoption order was entered. Appellant did not proffer any evidence to suggest that legal confirmation of the established relationship would be unwise; he did not even know the adoptive father.

that his constitutional rights were offended because the family court strictly complied with the notice provisions of the statute.

The Equal Protection Claim. . . .

The legislation at issue in this case, sections 111 and 111a of the New York Domestic Relations Law, is intended to establish procedures for adoptions. Those procedures are designed to promote the best interests of the child, protect the rights of interested third parties, and ensure promptness and finality. To serve those ends, the legislation guarantees to certain people the right to veto an adoption and the right to prior notice of any adoption proceeding. The mother of an illegitimate child is always within that favored class, but only certain putative fathers are included. Appellant contends that the gender-based distinction is invidious.

As we noted above, the existence or non-existence of a substantial relationship between parent and child is a relevant criterion in evaluating both the rights of the parent and the best interests of the child. In Quilloin v. Walcott, supra, we noted that the putative father, like appellant, "ha[d] never shouldered any significant responsibility with respect to the daily supervision, education, protection, or care of the child. Appellant does not complain of his exemption from these responsibilities. . . ." 434 U.S., at 256, 98 S.Ct., at 555. We therefore found that a Georgia statute that always required a mother's consent to the adoption of a child born out of wedlock, but required the father's consent only if he had legitimated the child, did not violate the Equal Protection Clause. Because, like the father in *Quilloin,* appellant has never established a substantial relationship with his daughter, the New York statutes at issue in this case did not operate to deny appellant equal protection.

We have held that these statutes may not constitutionally be applied in that class of cases where the mother and father are in fact similarly situated with regard to their relationship with the child. In Caban v. Mohammed, the Court held that it violated the Equal Protection Clause to grant the mother a veto over the adoption of a four-year-old girl and a six-year-old boy, but not to grant a veto to their father, who had admitted paternity and had participated in the rearing of the children. The Court made it clear, however, that if the father had not "come forward to participate in the rearing of his child, nothing in the Equal Protection Clause [would] preclude[ ] the State from withholding from him the privilege of vetoing the adoption of that child." 441 U.S., at 392, 99 S.Ct., at 1768.

Jessica's parents are not like the parents involved in *Caban.* Whereas appellee had a continuous custodial responsibility for Jessica, appellant never established any custodial, personal, or financial relationship with her. If one parent has an established custodial relationship with the child and the other parent has either abandoned or never established a relationship, the Equal Protection Clause does not prevent a state from according the two parents different legal rights.

The judgment of the New York Court of Appeals is Affirmed.

■ JUSTICE WHITE, with whom JUSTICE MARSHALL and JUSTICE BLACKMUN join, dissenting.

. . .

It is axiomatic that "[t]he fundamental requirement of due process is the opportunity to be heard 'at a meaningful time and in a meaningful manner.'" Mathews v. Eldridge, 424 U.S. 319, 333, 96 S.Ct. 893, 902, 47 L.Ed.2d 18 (1976), quoting Armstrong v. Manzo, 380 U.S. 545, 552, 85 S.Ct. 1187, 1191, 14 L.Ed.2d 62 (1965). As Jessica's biological father, Lehr either had an interest protected by the Constitution or he did not.[1] If the entry of the adoption order in this case deprived Lehr of a constitutionally protected interest, he is entitled to notice and an opportunity to be heard before the order can be accorded finality.

According to Lehr, he and Jessica's mother met in 1971 and began living together in 1974. The couple cohabited for approximately 2 years, until Jessica's birth in 1976. Throughout the pregnancy and after the birth, Lorraine acknowledged to friends and relatives that Lehr was Jessica's father; Lorraine told Lehr that she had reported to the New York State Department of Social Services that he was the father.[2] Lehr visited Lorraine and Jessica in the hospital every day during Lorraine's confinement. According to Lehr, from the time Lorraine was discharged from the hospital, until August, 1978, she concealed her whereabouts from him. During this time Lehr never ceased his efforts to locate Lorraine and Jessica and achieved sporadic success until August, 1977, after which time he was unable to locate them at all. On those occasions when he did determine Lorraine's location, he visited with her and her children to the extent she was willing to permit it. When Lehr, with the aid of a detective agency, located Lorraine and Jessica in August, 1978, Lorraine was already married to Mr. Robertson. Lehr asserts that at this time he offered to provide financial assistance and to set up a trust fund for Jessica, but that Lorraine refused. Lorraine threatened Lehr with arrest unless he stayed away and refused to permit him to see Jessica. Thereafter Lehr retained counsel who wrote to Lorraine in early December, 1978, requesting that she permit Lehr to visit Jessica and threatening legal action on Lehr's behalf. On December 21, 1978, perhaps

---

[1] The majority correctly assumes that Lehr is in fact Jessica's father. Indeed, Lehr has admitted paternity and sought to establish a legal relationship with the child. It is also noteworthy that the mother has never denied that Lehr is the father.

[2] Under 18 NYCRR § 369.2(b), recipients of public assistance in the Aid to Families with Dependent Children program are required as a condition of eligibility to provide the name and address of the child's father. Lorraine apparently received public assistance after Jessica's birth; it is unclear whether she received public assistance after that regulation went into effect in 1977.

as a response to Lehr's threatened legal action, appellees commenced the adoption action at issue here. . . .

Lehr's version of the "facts" paints a far different picture than that portrayed by the majority. The majority's recitation, that "[a]ppellant has never had any significant custodial, personal, or financial relationship with Jessica, and he did not seek to establish a legal tie until after she was two years old," obviously does not tell the whole story. Appellant has never been afforded an opportunity to present his case. The legitimation proceeding he instituted was first stayed, and then dismissed, on appellees' motions. Nor could appellant establish his interest during the adoption proceedings, for it is the failure to provide Lehr notice and an opportunity to be heard there that is at issue here. We cannot fairly make a judgment based on the quality or substance of a relationship without a complete and developed factual record. This case requires us to assume that Lehr's allegations are true—that but for the actions of the child's mother there would have been the kind of significant relationship that the majority concedes is entitled to the full panoply of procedural due process protections.[3]

I reject the peculiar notion that the only significance of the biological connection between father and child is that "it offers the natural father an opportunity that no other male possesses to develop a relationship with his offspring." A "mere biological relationship" is not as unimportant in determining the nature of liberty interests as the majority suggests.

"[T]he usual understanding of 'family' implies biological relationships, and most decisions treating the relation between parent and child have stressed this element." Smith v. Organization of Foster Families, supra, 431 U.S., at 843, 97 S.Ct., at 2109. The "biological connection" is itself a relationship that creates a protected interest. Thus the "nature" of the interest is the parent-child relationship; how well-developed that relationship has become goes to its "weight," not its "nature."[4] Whether Lehr's interest is entitled to constitutional protection does not entail a searching inquiry into the quality of the relationship but a simple determination of the *fact* that the relationship exists—a fact that even the majority agrees must be assumed to be established.

---

[3] In response to our decision in Caban v. Mohammed, 441 U.S. 380, 99 S.Ct. 1760, 60 L.Ed.2d 297 (1979), the statute governing the persons whose consent is necessary to an adoption has been amended to include certain unwed fathers. The State has recognized that an unwed father's failure to maintain an actual relationship or to communicate with a child will not deprive him of his right to consent if he was "prevented from doing so by the person or authorized agency having lawful custody of the child." N.Y. DOM. REL. LAW § 111(1)(d) (as amended by Chap. 575, L.1980). Thus, even the State recognizes that before a lesser standard can be applied consistent with due process requirements, there must be a determination that there was no significant relationship and that the father was not prevented from forming such a relationship.

[4] The majority's citation of *Quilloin* and *Caban* as examples that the Constitution does not require the same procedural protections for the interests of all unwed fathers is disingenuous. Neither case involved notice and opportunity to be heard. In both, the unwed fathers were notified and participated as parties in the adoption proceedings.

Beyond that, however, because there is no established factual basis on which to proceed, it is quite untenable to conclude that a putative father's interest in his child is lacking in substance, that the father in effect has abandoned the child, or ultimately that the father's interest is not entitled to the same minimum procedural protections as the interests of other putative fathers. Any analysis of the adequacy of the notice in this case must be conducted on the assumption that the interest involved here is as strong as that of *any* putative father. That is not to say that due process requires actual notice to every putative father or that adoptive parents or the State must conduct an exhaustive search of records or an intensive investigation before a final adoption order may be entered. The procedures adopted by the State, however, must at least represent a reasonable effort to determine the identity of the putative father and to give him adequate notice.

In this case, of course, there was no question about either the identity or the location of the putative father. The mother knew exactly who he was and both she and the court entering the order of adoption knew precisely where he was and how to give him actual notice that his parental rights were about to be terminated by an adoption order.[5] Lehr was entitled to due process, and the right to be heard is one of the fundamentals of that right, which "has little reality or worth unless one is informed that the matter is pending and can choose for himself whether to appear or default, acquiesce or contest." Schroeder v. City of New York, 371 U.S. 208, 212, 83 S.Ct. 279, 282, 9 L.Ed.2d 255 (1962), quoting Mullane v. Central Hanover Trust Co., 339 U.S. 306, 314, 70 S.Ct. 652, 657, 94 L.Ed. 865 (1950).

The State concedes this much but insists that Lehr has had all the process that is due to him. It relies on § 111–a, which designates seven categories of unwed fathers to whom notice of adoption proceedings must be given, including any unwed father who has filed with the State a notice of his intent to claim paternity. The State submits that it need not give notice to anyone who has not filed his name, as he is permitted to do, and who is not otherwise within the designated categories, even if his identity and interest are known or are reasonably ascertainable by the State.

I am unpersuaded by the State's position. In the first place, § 111–a defines six categories of unwed fathers to whom notice must be given even though they have not placed their names on file pursuant to the section. Those six categories, however, do not include fathers such as

[5] Absent special circumstances, there is no bar to requiring the mother of an illegitimate child to divulge the name of the father when the proceedings at issue involve the permanent termination of the father's rights. Likewise, there is no reason not to require such identification when it is the spouse of the custodial parent who seeks to adopt the child. Indeed, the State now requires the mother to provide the identity of the father if she applies for financial benefits under the Aid to Families with Dependent Children Program. The state's obligation to provide notice to persons before their interests are permanently terminated cannot be a lesser concern than its obligation to assure that state funds are not expended when there exists a person upon whom the financial responsibility should fall.

Lehr who have initiated filiation proceedings, even though their identity and interest are as clearly and easily ascertainable as those fathers in the six categories. Initiating such proceedings necessarily involves a formal acknowledgment of paternity, and requiring the State to take note of such a case in connection with pending adoption proceedings would be a trifling burden, no more than the State undertakes when there is a final adjudication in a paternity action. Indeed, there would appear to be more reason to give notice to those such as Lehr who acknowledge paternity than to those who have been adjudged to be a father in a contested paternity action.

The State asserts that any problem in this respect is overcome by the seventh category of putative fathers to whom notice must be given, namely those fathers who have identified themselves in the putative father register maintained by the State. Since Lehr did not take advantage of this device to make his interest known, the State contends, he was not entitled to notice and a hearing even though his identity, location and interest were known to the adoption court prior to entry of the adoption order. I have difficulty with this position. First, it represents a grudging and crabbed approach to due process. The State is quite willing to give notice and a hearing to putative fathers who have made themselves known by resorting to the putative fathers' register. It makes little sense to me to deny notice and hearing to a father who has not placed his name in the register but who has unmistakably identified himself by filing suit to establish his paternity and has notified the adoption court of his action and his interest. I thus need not question the statutory scheme on its face. Even assuming that Lehr would have been foreclosed if his failure to utilize the register had somehow disadvantaged the State, he effectively made himself known by other means, and it is the sheerest formalism to deny him a hearing because he informed the State in the wrong manner.

No state interest is substantially served by denying Lehr adequate notice and a hearing. The State no doubt has an interest in expediting adoption proceedings to prevent a child from remaining unduly long in the custody of the State or foster parents. But this is not an adoption involving a child in the custody of an authorized state agency. . . .

The State's undoubted interest in the finality of adoption orders likewise is not well served by a procedure that will deny notice and a hearing to a father whose identity and location are known. As this case well illustrates, denying notice and a hearing to such a father may result in years of additional litigation and threaten the reopening of adoption proceedings and the vacation of the adoption. . . .

Because in my view the failure to provide Lehr with notice and an opportunity to be heard violated rights guaranteed him by the Due Process Clause, I need not address the question whether § 111–a violates the Equal Protection Clause by discriminating between categories of unwed fathers or by discriminating on the basis of gender.

Respectfully, I dissent.

NOTES

The number of nonmarital sexual liaisons, including nonmarital partners, has expanded expeditiously since *Stanley* and *Lehr* were decided, thereby multiplying the number of putative fathers. The issue remains the same: How to balance the parental rights of a putative father against the necessity of an orderly and prompt process of support, adoption, and paternity affecting the rights of a child. In addition, as we will discuss *infra*, assisted reproductive technology expands the possibilities of birth; modern petitions to establish paternity or maternity often involve donated sperm, eggs, or embryos. *See, e.g.*, Breit v. Mason, 718 S.E.2d 482 (Va. Ct. App. 2011) (holding that sperm donor may petition for parentage when he and mother acknowledged his paternity of the resulting child). For commentary on the rights of all putative fathers, *see, e.g.*, Josh Gupta-Kagan, *Stanley v. Illinois's Untold Story*, 24 WM. & MARY BILL RTS. J. 773 (2016); Erin E. Gibbs, *Preserving Your Right to Parent: The Supreme Court of North Carolina Addresses Unmarried Fathers' Due Process Rights in In re Adoption of S.D.W.*, 94 N.C. L. REV. 723 (2016); Ivy Waisbord, Note, *Amending State Putative Father Registries: Affording More Rights and Protections to America's Unwed Fathers*, 44 HOFSTRA L. REV. 565 (2015); Dara E. Purvis, *Expectant Fathers, Abortion, and Embryos*, 43 J.L. MED. & ETHICS 330 (2015); Michael J. Higdon, *Marginalized Fathers and Demonized Mothers: A Feminist Look at the Reproductive Freedom of Unmarried Men*, 66 ALA. L. REV. 507 (2015); Claire Huntington, *Postmarital Family Law: A Legal Structure for Nonmarital Families*, 67 STAN. L. REV. 167 (2015); Mary D. Fan, *Sex, Privacy, and Public Health in a Casual Encounters Culture*, 45 U.C. DAVIS L. REV. 531 (2011); Elizabeth F. Emens, *Intimate Discrimination: The State's Role in the Accidents of Sex and Love*, 122 HARV. L. REV. 1307 (2009); Browne Lewis, *Two Fathers, One Dad: Allocating the Parental Obligations Between the Men Involved in the Artificial Insemination Process*, 13 LEWIS & CLARK L. REV. 949 (2009); Lee-Ford Tritt, *Sperms and Estates: An Unadulterated Functionally Based Approach to Parent-Child Property Succession*, 62 SMU L. REV. 3767 (2009); James G. Dwyer, *A Constitutional Birthright: The State, Parentage, and the Rights of Newborn Persons*, 56 UCLA L. REV. 755 (2009).

Even after *Stanley* and *Lehr*, courts continue to grapple with allegations that fathers were denied Due Process protection when children they fathered were placed for adoption by biological mothers without obtaining the biological father's permission or termination of parental rights. *See, e.g., In re* Adoption of B.Y., 356 P.3d 1215 (Utah 2015) (discussing *Lehr* and holding that a putative father's failure to comply with statutory procedures because of a private agreement with infant's mother forfeits his right to parentage of child); *In re* Adoption of S.D.W., 758 S.E.2d 374, 396 (NC 2014) (discussing *Lehr* and holding that, "Because of his passivity in the face of ample evidence that Welker may have become pregnant with his child and given birth, Johns does not fall into the class of protected fathers who may claim a liberty interest in developing a relationship with a child, and thus he was not deprived of due process."); *In re* Doe, 304 P.3d 1202 (Idaho 2013) (discussing *Lehr* and holding that father's Due Process rights as to an infant were forfeited when he did not comply with statutory requirements to establish a paternity claim).

Article 4 of the Uniform Parentage Act establishes provisions for a registry of paternity. In accordance with the Act, a man may register with a state agency maintaining the registry. Once registered, the man will be notified of a proceeding for adoption or termination of parental rights regarding a child that he may have fathered. (Sections 402 & 403). Information in the registry is confidential (Section 412), and no fee may be charged for the service (Section 416). If a father-child relationship has not been established for a child under one year of age, anyone petitioning to adopt the child or to terminate parental rights of the child must obtain a certificate of search of the registry of paternity (Section 421). This certificate must be filed with the court before termination of parental rights, or adoption of the child may be concluded (Section 422).

C. PROTECTION OF CHILDREN

Michael H. v. Gerald D.

Supreme Court of the United States, 1989
491 U.S. 110

■ SCALIA, JUSTICE delivered the plurality opinion of the Court.

Under California law, a child born to a married woman living with her husband is presumed to be a child of the marriage. Cal.Evid.Code Ann. § 621 (West Supp.1989). The presumption of legitimacy may be rebutted only by the husband or wife, and then only in limited circumstances. The instant appeal presents the claim that this presumption infringes upon the due process rights of a man who wishes to establish his paternity of a child born to the wife of another man, and the claim that it infringes upon the constitutional right of the child to maintain a relationship with her natural father.

The facts of this case are, we must hope, extraordinary. On May 9, 1976, in Las Vegas, Nevada, Carole D., an international model, and Gerald D., a top executive in a French oil company, were married. The couple established a home in Playa del Rey, California, in which they resided as husband and wife when one or the other was not out of the country on business. In the summer of 1978, Carole became involved in an adulterous affair with a neighbor, Michael H. In September 1980, she conceived a child, Victoria D., who was born on May 11, 1981. Gerald was listed as father on the birth certificate and has always held Victoria out to the world as his daughter. Soon after delivery of the child, however, Carole informed Michael that she believed he might be the father.

In the first three years of her life, Victoria remained always with Carole, but found herself within a variety of quasi-family units. In

October 1981, Gerald moved to New York City to pursue his business interests, but Carole chose to remain in California. At the end of that month, Carole and Michael had blood tests of themselves and Victoria, which showed a 98.07% probability that Michael was Victoria's father. In January 1982, Carole visited Michael in St. Thomas, where his primary business interests were based. There Michael held Victoria out as his child. In March, however, Carole left Michael and returned to California, where she took up residence with yet another man, Scott K. Later that spring, and again in the summer, Carole and Victoria spent time with Gerald in New York City, as well as on vacation in Europe. In the fall, they returned to Scott in California.

In November 1982, rebuffed in his attempts to visit Victoria, Michael filed a filiation action in California Superior Court to establish his paternity and right to visitation. In March 1983, the court appointed an attorney and guardian ad litem to represent Victoria's interests. Victoria then filed a cross-complaint asserting that if she had more than one psychological or *de facto* father, she was entitled to maintain her filial relationship, with all of the attendant rights, duties, and obligations, with both. In May 1983, Carole filed a motion for summary judgment. During this period, from March through July 1983, Carole was again living with Gerald in New York. In August, however, she returned to California, became involved once again with Michael, and instructed her attorneys to remove the summary judgment motion from the calendar.

For the ensuing eight months, when Michael was not in St. Thomas he lived with Carole and Victoria in Carole's apartment in Los Angeles and held Victoria out as his daughter. In April 1984, Carole and Michael signed a stipulation that Michael was Victoria's natural father. Carole left Michael the next month, however, and instructed her attorneys not to file the stipulation. In June 1984, Carole reconciled with Gerald and joined him in New York, where they now live with Victoria and two other children since born into the marriage.

In May 1984, Michael and Victoria, through her guardian ad litem, sought visitation rights for Michael *pendente lite*. To assist in determining whether visitation would be in Victoria's best interests, the Superior Court appointed a psychologist to evaluate Victoria, Gerald, Michael, and Carole. The psychologist recommended that Carole retain sole custody, but that Michael be allowed continued contact with Victoria pursuant to a restricted visitation schedule. The court concurred and ordered that Michael be provided with limited visitation privileges *pendente lite*.

On October 19, 1984, Gerald, who had intervened in the action, moved for summary judgment on the ground that under Cal.Evid.Code § 621 there were no triable issues of fact as to Victoria's paternity. This law provides that "the issue of a wife cohabiting with her husband, who is not impotent or sterile, is conclusively presumed to be a child of the marriage." The presumption may be rebutted by blood tests, but only if a motion for such tests is made, within two years from the date of the child's birth, either by the husband or, if the natural father has filed an affidavit acknowledging paternity, by the wife.

On January 28, 1985, having found that affidavits submitted by Carole and Gerald sufficed to demonstrate that the two were cohabiting at conception and birth and that Gerald was neither sterile nor impotent, the Superior Court granted Gerald's motion for summary judgment, rejecting Michael's and Victoria's challenges to the constitutionality of § 621. The court also denied their motions for continued visitation pending the appeal under Cal.Civ.Code § 4601, which provides that a court may, in its discretion, grant "reasonable visitation rights . . . to any . . . person having an interest in the welfare of the child." Cal.Civ.Code Ann. § 4601 (West Supp.1989). It found that allowing such visitation would "violat[e] the intention of the Legislature by impugning the integrity of the family unit."

On appeal, Michael asserted, *inter alia,* that the Superior Court's application of § 621 had violated his procedural and substantive due process rights. Victoria also raised a due process challenge to the statute, seeking to preserve her *de facto* relationship with Michael as well as with Gerald. She contended, in addition, that as § 621 allows the husband and, at least to a limited extent, the mother, but not the child, to rebut the presumption of legitimacy, it violates the child's right to equal protection. Finally, she asserted a right to continued visitation with Michael under § 4601. After submission of briefs and a hearing, the California Court of Appeal affirmed the judgment of the Superior Court and upheld the constitutionality of the statute. It interpreted that judgment, moreover, as having denied permanent visitation rights under § 4601, regarding that as the implication of the Superior Court's reliance upon § 621 and upon an earlier California case, Vincent B. v. Joan R., 126 Cal.App.3d 619, 179 Cal.Rptr. 9 (1981), which had held that once an assertion of biological paternity is "determined to be legally impossible" under § 621, visitation against the wishes of the mother should be denied under § 4601. . . .

Before us, Michael and Victoria both raise equal protection and due process challenges. We do not reach Michael's equal protection claim, however, as it was neither raised nor passed upon below.

The California statute that is the subject of this litigation is, in substance, more than a century old. California Code of Civ.Proc. § 1962(5), enacted in 1872, provided that "[t]he issue of a wife cohabiting with her husband, who is not impotent, is indisputably presumed to be legitimate. . . ." In 1955, the legislature amended the statute by adding the preface: "Notwithstanding any other provision of law." In 1965, when California's Evidence Code was adopted, the statute was codified as § 621, with no substantive change except replacement of the word "indisputably" with "conclusively." When California adopted the Uniform Parentage Act . . . it amended § 621 by replacing the word "legitimate" with the phrase "a child of the marriage" and by adding nonsterility to nonimpotence and cohabitation as a predicate for the presumption. In 1980, the legislature again amended the statute to provide the husband an opportunity to introduce blood-test evidence in rebuttal of the presumption . . . and in 1981 amended it to provide the mother such an opportunity. In their present form, the substantive provisions of the statute are as follows:

"§ 621. Child of the marriage; notice of motion for blood tests

"(a) Except as provided in subdivision (b), the issue of a wife cohabiting with her husband, who is not impotent or sterile, is conclusively presumed to be a child of the marriage.

"(b) Notwithstanding the provisions of subdivision (a), if the court finds that the conclusions of all the experts, as disclosed by the evidence based upon blood tests performed pursuant to Chapter 2 (commencing with Section 890) of Division 7 are that the husband is not the father of the child, the question of paternity of the husband shall be resolved accordingly.

"(c) The notice of motion for blood tests under subdivision (b) may be raised by the husband not later than two years from the child's date of birth.

"(d) The notice of motion for blood tests under subdivision (b) may be raised by the mother of the child not later than two years from the child's date of birth if the child's biological father has filed an affidavit with the court acknowledging paternity of the child. . . .

We address first the claims of Michael. At the outset, it is necessary to clarify what he sought and what he was denied. California law, like nature itself, makes no provision for dual fatherhood. Michael was seeking to be declared *the* father of Victoria. The immediate benefit he evidently sought to obtain from that status was visitation rights. See Cal.Civ.Code Ann. § 4601 (West 1983) (parent has statutory right to visitation "unless it is shown that such visitation would be detrimental to the best interests of the child"). But if Michael were successful in being declared the father, other rights would follow-most importantly, the right to be considered as the parent who should have custody, Cal.Civ.Code Ann. § 4600 (West 1983), a status which "embrace[s] the sum of parental rights with respect to the rearing of a child, including the child's care; the right to the child's services and earnings; the right to direct the child's activities; the right to make decisions regarding the control, education, and health of the child; and the right, as well as the duty, to prepare the child for additional obligations, which includes the teaching of moral standards, religious beliefs, and elements of good citizenship." 4 California Family Law § 60.02[1][b] (C. Markey ed. 1987).All parental rights, including visitation, were automatically denied by denying

Michael status as the father. While Cal.Civ.Code Ann. § 4601 places it within the discretionary power of a court to award visitation rights to a nonparent, the Superior Court here, affirmed by the Court of Appeal, held that California law denies visitation, against the wishes of the mother, to a putative father who has been prevented by § 621 from establishing his paternity.

Michael raises two related challenges to the constitutionality of § 621. First, he asserts that requirements of procedural due process prevent the State from terminating his liberty interest in his relationship with his child without affording him an opportunity to demonstrate his paternity in an evidentiary hearing. We believe this claim derives from a fundamental misconception of the nature of the California statute. While § 621 is phrased in terms of a presumption, that rule of evidence is the implementation of a substantive rule of law. California declares it to be, except in limited circumstances, *irrelevant* for paternity purposes whether a child conceived during, and born into, an existing marriage was begotten by someone other than the husband and had a prior relationship with him. . . . Of course the conclusive presumption not only expresses the State's substantive policy but also furthers it, excluding inquiries into the child's paternity that would be destructive of family integrity and privacy.[3]

This Court has struck down as illegitimate certain "irrebuttable presumptions. . . ." A conclusive presumption does, of course, foreclose the person against whom it is invoked from demonstrating, in a particularized proceeding, that applying the presumption to him will in fact not further the lawful governmental policy the presumption is designed to effectuate. But the same can be said of any legal rule that establishes general classifications, whether framed in terms of a presumption or not. In this respect there is no difference between a rule which says that the marital husband shall be irrebuttably presumed to be the father, and a rule which says that the adulterous natural father shall not be recognized as the legal father. *Both* rules deny someone in Michael's situation a hearing on whether, in the particular circumstances of his case, California's policies would best be served by giving him parental rights. Thus . . . our "irrebuttable presumption" cases must ultimately be analyzed as calling into question not the adequacy of procedures but . . . the adequacy of the "fit" between the classification and the policy that the classification serves. We therefore reject Michael's procedural due process challenge and proceed to his substantive claim.

Michael contends as a matter of substantive due process that, because he has established a parental relationship with Victoria, protection of Gerald's and Carole's marital union is an insufficient state

[3] In those circumstances in which California allows a natural father to rebut the presumption of legitimacy of a child born to a married woman, *e.g.*, where the husband is impotent or sterile, or where the husband and wife have not been cohabiting, it is more likely that the husband already knows the child is not his, and thus less likely that the paternity hearing will disrupt an otherwise harmonious and apparently exclusive marital relationship.

interest to support termination of that relationship. This argument is, of course, predicated on the assertion that Michael has a constitutionally protected liberty interest in his relationship with Victoria. . . .

Thus, the legal issue in the present case reduces to whether the relationship between persons in the situation of Michael and Victoria has been treated as a protected family unit under the historic practices of our society, or whether on any other basis it has been accorded special protection. We think it impossible to find that it has. In fact, quite to the contrary, our traditions have protected the marital family (Gerald, Carole, and the child they acknowledge to be theirs) against the sort of claim Michael asserts. . . .

We have found nothing in the older sources, nor in the older cases, addressing specifically the power of the natural father to assert parental rights over a child born into a woman's existing marriage with another man. [T]he evidence shows that even in modern times-when . . . the rigid protection of the marital family has in other respects been relaxed-the ability of a person in Michael's position to claim paternity has not been generally acknowledged. For example, [in] a 1957 annotation on the subject . . . [n]ot a single decision is set forth specifically according standing to the natural father, and "express indications of the nonexistence of any . . . limitation" upon standing were found only "in a few jurisdictions."

Moreover, even if it were clear that one in Michael's position generally possesses, and has generally always possessed, standing to challenge the marital child's legitimacy, that would still not establish Michael's case. . . . What Michael asserts here is a right to have himself declared the natural father *and thereby to obtain parental prerogatives.* What he must establish, therefore, is not that our society has traditionally allowed a natural father in his circumstances to establish paternity, but that it has traditionally accorded such a father parental rights, or at least has not traditionally denied them. . . . What counts is whether the States in fact award substantive parental rights to the natural father of a child conceived within, and born into, an extant marital union that wishes to embrace the child. We are not aware of a single case, old or new, that has done so. This is not the stuff of which fundamental rights qualifying as liberty interests are made. . . .

We have never had occasion to decide whether a child has a liberty interest, symmetrical with that of her parent, in maintaining her filial relationship. We need not do so here because, even assuming that such a right exists, Victoria's claim must fail. Victoria's due process challenge is, if anything, weaker than Michael's. Her basic claim is not that California has erred in preventing her from establishing that Michael, not Gerald, should stand as her legal father. Rather, she claims a due process right to maintain filial relationships with both Michael and Gerald. This assertion merits little discussion, for, whatever the merits of the guardian ad litem's belief that such an arrangement can be of great psychological benefit to a child, the claim that a State must recognize multiple fatherhood has no support in the history or traditions of this country. Moreover, even if we were to construe Victoria's argument as forwarding the lesser proposition that, whatever her status vis-à-vis Gerald, she has a liberty interest in maintaining a filial relationship with her natural father, Michael, we find that, at best, her claim is the obverse of Michael's and fails for the same reasons.

Victoria claims in addition that her equal protection rights have been violated because, unlike her mother and presumed father, she had no opportunity to rebut the presumption of her legitimacy. We find this argument wholly without merit. We reject, at the outset, Victoria's suggestion that her equal protection challenge must be assessed under a standard of strict scrutiny because, in denying her the right to maintain a filial relationship with Michael, the State is discriminating against her on the basis of her illegitimacy. See Gomez v. Perez, 409 U.S. 535, 538, 93 S.Ct. 872, 875, 35 L.Ed.2d 56 (1973). Illegitimacy is a legal construct, not a natural trait. Under California law, Victoria is not illegitimate, and she is treated in the same manner as all other legitimate children: she is entitled to maintain a filial relationship with her legal parents.

We apply, therefore, the ordinary "rational relationship" test to Victoria's equal protection challenge. The primary rationale underlying § 621's limitation on those who may rebut the presumption of legitimacy is a concern that allowing persons other than the husband or wife to do so may undermine the integrity of the marital union. When the husband or wife contests the legitimacy of their child, the stability of the marriage has already been shaken. In contrast, allowing a claim of illegitimacy to be pressed by the child-or, more accurately, by a court-appointed guardian ad litem-may well disrupt an otherwise peaceful union. Since it pursues a legitimate end by rational means, California's decision to treat Victoria differently from her parents is not a denial of equal protection.

The judgment of the California Court of Appeal is *Affirmed.*

■ JUSTICE O'CONNOR, with whom JUSTICE KENNEDY joins, concurring in part [omitted].

■ JUSTICE BRENNAN, with whom JUSTICE MARSHALL and JUSTICE BLACKMUN join, dissenting.

In a case that has yielded so many opinions as has this one, it is fruitful to begin by emphasizing the common ground shared by a majority of this Court. Five Members of the Court refuse to foreclose "the possibility that a natural father might ever have a constitutionally protected interest in his relationship with a child whose mother was married to, and cohabiting with, another man at the time of the child's conception and birth." Five Justices agree that the flaw inhering in a conclusive presumption that terminates a constitutionally protected interest without any hearing whatsoever is a *procedural* one. Four Members of the Court agree that Michael H. has a liberty interest in his relationship with Victoria, and one assumes for purposes of this case that he does.

In contrast, only one other Member of the Court fully endorses Justice SCALIA's view of the proper method of analyzing questions arising under the Due Process Clause. Nevertheless, because the plurality opinion's exclusively historical analysis portends a significant and unfortunate departure from our prior cases and from sound constitutional decisionmaking, I devote a substantial portion of my discussion to it.

Once we recognized that the "liberty" protected by the Due Process Clause of the Fourteenth Amendment encompasses more than freedom from bodily restraint, today's plurality opinion emphasizes, the concept was cut loose from one natural limitation on its meaning. This innovation paved the way, so the plurality hints, for judges to substitute their own preferences for those of elected officials. Dissatisfied with this supposedly unbridled and uncertain state of affairs, the plurality casts about for another limitation on the concept of liberty.

It finds this limitation in "tradition." Apparently oblivious to the fact that this concept can be as malleable and as elusive as "liberty" itself, the plurality pretends that tradition places a discernible border around the Constitution. The pretense is seductive; it would be comforting to believe that a search for "tradition" involves nothing more idiosyncratic or complicated than poring through dusty volumes on American history. . . . Indeed, wherever I would begin to look for an interest "deeply rooted in the country's traditions," one thing is certain: . . . reasonable people can disagree about the content of particular traditions, and because they can disagree even about which traditions are relevant to the definition of "liberty," the plurality has not found the objective boundary that it seeks.

Even if we could agree, moreover, on the content and significance of particular traditions, we still would be forced to identify the point at which a tradition becomes firm enough to be relevant to our definition of liberty and the moment at which it becomes too obsolete to be relevant any longer. The plurality supplies no objective means by which we might make these determinations. Indeed, as soon as the plurality sees signs that the tradition upon which it bases its decision (the laws denying putative fathers like Michael standing to assert paternity) is crumbling, it shifts ground and says that the case has nothing to do with that tradition, after all. "[W]hat is at issue here," the plurality asserts after canvassing the law on paternity suits, "is not entitlement to a state pronouncement that Victoria was begotten by Michael." But that is precisely what is at issue here, and the plurality's last-minute denial of this fact dramatically illustrates the subjectivity of its own analysis. . . .

It is not that tradition has been irrelevant to our prior decisions. Throughout our decisionmaking in this important area runs the theme that certain interests and practices-freedom from physical restraint, marriage, childbearing, childrearing, and others-form the core of our definition of "liberty." Our solicitude for these interests is partly the result of the fact that the Due Process Clause would seem an empty promise if it did not protect them, and partly the result of the historical and traditional importance of these interests in our society. In deciding cases arising under the Due Process Clause, therefore, we have considered whether the concrete limitation under consideration impermissibly impinges upon one of these more generalized interests.

Today's plurality, however, does not ask whether parenthood is an interest that historically has received our attention and protection; the answer to that question is too clear for dispute. Instead, the plurality asks whether the specific variety of parenthood under consideration-a natural father's relationship with a child whose mother is married to another man-has enjoyed such protection. If we had looked to tradition with such specificity in past cases, many a decision would have reached a different result. Surely the use of contraceptives by unmarried couples, or even by married couples, the freedom from corporal punishment in schools, the freedom from an arbitrary transfer from a prison to a psychiatric institution, and even the right to raise one's natural but illegitimate children, were not "interest[s] traditionally protected by our society," at the time of their consideration by this Court. If we had asked, therefore, in *Eisenstadt, Griswold, Ingraham, Vitek,* or *Stanley* itself whether the specific interest under consideration had been traditionally protected, the answer would have been a resounding "no. . . ."

The plurality's interpretive method is more than novel; it is misguided. It ignores the good reasons for limiting the role of "tradition" in interpreting the Constitution's deliberately capacious language. In the plurality's constitutional universe, we may not take notice of the fact that the original reasons for the conclusive presumption of paternity are out of place in a world in which blood tests can prove virtually beyond a shadow of a doubt who sired a particular child and in which the fact of illegitimacy no longer plays the burdensome and stigmatizing role it once did. Nor, in the plurality's world, may we deny "tradition" its full scope by pointing out that the rationale for the conventional rule has changed over the years, as has the rationale for Cal.Evid.Code Ann. § 621 (West Supp.1989); instead, our task is simply to identify a rule denying the asserted interest and not to ask whether the basis for that rule-which is the true reflection of the values undergirding it-has changed too often or too recently to call the rule embodying that rationale a "tradition." Moreover, by describing the decisive question as whether Michael's and Victoria's interest is one that has been "traditionally *protected by* our society," rather than one that society traditionally has thought important (with or without protecting it), and by suggesting that our sole function is to "*discern* the society's views," the plurality acts as if the only purpose of the Due Process Clause is to confirm the importance of interests already protected by a majority of the States. Transforming the protection afforded by the Due Process Clause into a redundancy mocks those who, with care and purpose, wrote the Fourteenth Amendment.

In construing the Fourteenth Amendment to offer shelter only to those interests specifically protected by historical practice, moreover, the plurality ignores the kind of society in which our Constitution exists. We are not an assimilative, homogeneous society, but a facilitative, pluralistic one, in which we must be willing to abide someone else's unfamiliar or even repellent practice because the same tolerant impulse protects our own idiosyncracies. Even if we can agree, therefore, that "family" and "parenthood" are part of the good life, it is absurd to assume that we can agree on the content of those terms and destructive to pretend that we do. In a community such as ours, "liberty" must include the freedom not to conform. The plurality today squashes this freedom by requiring specific approval from history before protecting anything in the name of liberty.

The document that the plurality construes today is unfamiliar to me. It is not the living charter that I have taken to be our Constitution; it is instead a stagnant, archaic, hidebound document steeped in the prejudices and superstitions of a time long past. *This* Constitution does not recognize that times change, does not see that sometimes a practice or rule outlives its foundations. . . .

We must first understand the nature of the challenged statute: it is a law that stubbornly insists that Gerald is Victoria's father, in the face of evidence showing a 98 percent probability that her father is Michael. What Michael wants is a chance to show that he is Victoria's father. By depriving him of this opportunity, California prevents Michael from taking advantage of the best-interest standard embodied in § 4601 of California's Civil Code, which directs that *parents* be given visitation rights unless "the visitation would be detrimental to the best interests of the child."

As interpreted by the California courts, however, § 621 not only deprives Michael of the benefits of the best-interest standard; it also deprives him of any chance of maintaining his relationship with the child he claims to be his own. When, as a result of § 621, a putative father may not establish his paternity, neither may he obtain discretionary visitation rights as a "nonparent" under § 4601. Justice STEVENS' assertion to the contrary is mere wishful thinking. In concluding that the California courts afford putative fathers like Michael a meaningful opportunity to show that visitation rights would be in the best interests of their children, he fastens upon the words "in the circumstances of this case. . . ."

The question before us, therefore, is whether California has an interest so powerful that it justifies granting Michael *no* hearing before terminating his parental rights. "Many controversies have raged about the cryptic and abstract words of the Due Process Clause but there can be no doubt that at a minimum they require that deprivation of life, liberty or property by adjudication be preceded by notice and opportunity for hearing appropriate to the nature of the case." Mullane v. Central Hanover Bank & Trust Co., 339 U.S. 306, 313, 70 S.Ct. 652, 656, 94 L.Ed. 865 (1950). When a State seeks to limit the procedures that will attend the deprivation of a constitutionally protected interest, it is only the State's interest in streamlining procedures that is relevant. . . .

The purported state interests here, however, stem primarily from the State's antagonism to Michael's and Victoria's constitutionally protected interest in their relationship with each other and not from any desire to streamline procedures. Gerald D. explains that § 621 promotes marriage, maintains the relationship between the child and presumed father, and protects the integrity and privacy of the matrimonial family. It is not, however, § 621, but the best-interest principle, that protects a stable marital relationship and maintains the relationship between the child and presumed father. These interests are implicated by the determination of who gets parental rights, *not* by the determination of who is the father; in the hearing that Michael seeks, parental rights are not the issue. Of the objectives that Gerald stresses, therefore, only the preservation of family privacy is promoted by the refusal to hold a hearing itself. Yet § 621 furthers even this objective only partially.

Gerald D. gives generous proportions to the privacy protected by § 621, asserting that this provision protects a couple like Gerald and Carole from answering questions on such matters as "their sexual habits and practices with each other and outside their marriage, their finances, and their thoughts, beliefs, and opinions concerning their relationship with each other and with Victoria." Yet invalidation of § 621 would not, as Gerald suggests, subject Gerald and Carole to public scrutiny of all of these private matters. . . . In this day and age . . . proving paternity by asking intimate and detailed questions about a couple's relationship would be decidedly anachronistic. Who on earth would choose this method of establishing fatherhood when blood tests prove it with far more certainty and far less fuss? The State's purported interest in protecting matrimonial privacy thus does not measure up to Michael's and Victoria's interest in maintaining their relationship with each other.

Make no mistake: to say that the State must provide Michael with a hearing to prove his paternity is not to express any opinion of the ultimate state of affairs between Michael and Victoria and Carole and Gerald. In order to change the current situation among these people, Michael first must convince a court that he is Victoria's father, and even if he is able to do this, he will be denied visitation rights if that would be in Victoria's best interests. It is elementary that a determination that a State must afford procedures before it terminates a given right is not a prediction about the end result of those procedures.

The atmosphere surrounding today's decision is one of make-believe. Beginning with the suggestion that the situation confronting us here does not repeat itself every day in every corner of the country moving on to the claim that it is tradition alone that supplies the details of the liberty that the Constitution protects, and passing finally to the notion that the Court always has recognized a cramped vision of "the family," today's decision lets stand California's pronouncement that Michael-whom blood tests show to a 98 percent probability to be Victoria's father-is not Victoria's father. When and if the Court awakes to reality, it will find a world very different from the one it expects.

■ JUSTICE WHITE, with whom JUSTICE BRENNAN joins, dissenting [omitted].

NOTES

Seemingly, the holding in *Michael H.* is contrary to the Court's holding in *Lehr, supra.* But note the factual dissimilarity. In *Lehr*, the child was born to an unmarried woman, whereas in *Michael H.* the child was born into an ongoing marriage between the mother and her husband. The Court's preference for marital status is the basis of the majority opinion, and the reason why the decision is so often criticized by the dissent and commentators. More recent judicial decisions continue to reference the controversial holding of *Michael H. See, e.g.,* Bryan M. v. Anne B., 874 N.W.2d 824 (Neb. 2016) (holding that changing family patterns did not abolish the need to petition for paternity within the state's statute of limitations); *In re* Parenting of K.P., 124 P.3d 109 (Mont. 2005) (holding that *Michael H.* prohibited a challenge to a husband's paternity only when state law did not provide otherwise, but when a state allows a challenge to be established by the preponderance of the evidence, state policy permits a challenge to a husband's paternity); People *ex rel.* Shockley v. Hoyle, 789 N.E.2d 1282 (Ill. Ct. App. 2003) (holding that the ruling in *Michael H.* only applies when there is an intact family unit to support, such as a marriage). The decision continues to generate controversy and discussion. *See, e.g.,* Vanessa S. Browne-Barbour, *"Mama's Baby, Papa's Maybe": Disestablishment of Paternity*, 48 AKRON L. REV. 263, 275–277 (2015); Steven G. Calabresi & Sofia M. Vickery, *On Liberty and the Fourteenth Amendment: The Original Understanding of the Lockean Natural Rights Guarantees,* 93 TEX. L. REV. 1299, 1323 (2015); Gautam Bhatia, *The Politics of Statutory Interpretation: The Hayekian Foundations of Justice Antonin Scalia's Jurisprudence*, 42 HAST. CONST. L. Q. 525, 541 (2015).

Gomez v. Perez

Supreme Court of the United States, 1973
409 U.S. 535

■ PER CURIAM.

The issue presented by this appeal is whether the laws of Texas may constitutionally grant legitimate children a judicially enforceable right to support from their natural fathers and at the same time deny that right to illegitimate children.

In 1969, appellant filed a petition in Texas District Court seeking support from appellee on behalf of her minor child. After a hearing, the state trial judge found that appellee is "the biological father" of the child, and that the child "needs the support and maintenance of her father," but concluded that because the child was illegitimate "there is no legal obligation to support the child and the Plaintiff take nothing." The Court of Civil Appeals affirmed this ruling over the objection that this illegitimate child was being denied equal protection of law. 466 S.W.2d 41. The Texas Supreme Court refused application for a Writ of Error. . . .

In Texas, both at common law and under the statutes of the State, the natural father has a continuing and primary duty to support his legitimate children. That duty extends even beyond dissolution of the marriage, and is enforceable on the child's behalf in civil proceedings and, further, is the subject of criminal sanctions. The duty to support exists despite the fact that the father may not have custody of the child. The Court of Civil Appeals has held in this case that nowhere in this elaborate statutory scheme does the State recognize any enforceable duty on the part of the biological father to support his illegitimate children and that, absent a statutory duty to support, the controlling law is the Texas common-law rule that illegitimate children, unlike legitimate children, have no legal right to support from their fathers. It is also true that fathers may set up illegitimacy as a defense to prosecutions for criminal nonsupport of their children.

In this context, appellant's claim on behalf of her daughter that the child has been denied equal protection of the law is unmistakably presented. Indeed, at argument here, the attorney for the State of Texas, appearing as *amicus curiae,* conceded that but for the fact that this child is illegitimate she would be entitled to support from appellee under the laws of Texas.

We have held that under the Equal Protection Clause of the Fourteenth Amendment a State may not create a right of action in favor of children for the wrongful death of a parent and exclude illegitimate children from the benefit of such a right. Levy v. Louisiana, 391 U.S. 68 (1968). Similarly, we have held that illegitimate children may not be excluded from sharing equally with other children in the recovery of workmen's compensation benefits for the death of their parent. Weber v. Aetna Casualty & Surety Co., 406 U.S. 164 (1972). Under these decisions, a State may not invidiously discriminate against illegitimate children by denying them substantial benefits accorded children generally. We therefore hold that once a State posits a judicially enforceable right on behalf of children to needed support from their natural fathers there is no constitutionally sufficient justification for denying such an essential right to a child simply because its natural father has not married its mother. For a State to do so is "illogical and unjust." *Weber v. Aetna Casualty & Surety Co., supra,* at 175. We recognize the lurking problems with respect to proof of paternity. Those problems are not to be lightly brushed aside, but neither can they be made into an impenetrable barrier that works to shield otherwise invidious discrimination.

The judgment is reversed and the case remanded for further proceedings not inconsistent with this opinion.

■ [The dissenting opinion of JUSTICE STEWART, in which JUSTICE REHNQUIST joined, is omitted.]

NOTES

In the past, states traditionally treated marital children differently from nonmarital children. *See, e.g.*, Zepeda v. Zepeda, 190 N.E.2d 849 (Ill. Ct. App. Ct. 1963) (discussing the social evolutions of words, such as changing "bastard" to "illegitimate"). States tasked with providing a mechanism for establishing a support obligation from a living parent, or for the administration of a decedents' estate, seek an orderly process that is both speedy and efficient. As *Gomez* demonstrates, when assigning a support obligation, nonmarital children have increasingly been granted the constitutional right to equal treatment as marital children. Four years after *Gomez*, in an action to permit a nonmarital child inheritance from a putative father's estate, the Court held that any state classification based on illegitimacy must be based on factors substantially related to permissible state interests. *See* Trimble v. Gordon, 430 U.S. 762 (1977). In *Trimble*, the Court ruled that the Illinois statute was unconstitutional as applied to nonmarital children because it required, prior to inheritance, that the father not only acknowledge the child, but also that the father marry the mother. The next year, in 1978, the Court held that state procedures that require the paternity of a nonmarital child to be judicially established within two years after the child's birth are rationally related to the state's interest in administration of an estate. *See* Lalli v. Lalli, 439 U.S. 259 (1978). In 1988, the Court revisited the issue again, holding that a Pennsylvania statute that required a nonmarital child to initiate a petition of support within six years of birth, as compared to "at any time" by a marital child, was unconstitutional. When judged under a heightened level of scrutiny, the Court ruled that the state statute was not reasonably related to avoiding stale or fraudulent claims. *See* Clark v. Jeter, 486 U.S. 456 (1988). For general commentary, *see* Katharine K. Baker, *Legitimate Families and Equal Protection*, 6 B.C. L. REV. 1647 (2015); Clare Huntington, *Family Law and Nonmarital Families,* 53 FAM. CT. REV. 233 (2015); Serena Mayeri, Essay, *Marital Supremacy and the Constitution of the Nonmarital Family*, 103 CAL. L. REV. 1277 (2015); Allison Anna Tait, *A Tale of Three Families: Historical Households, Earned Belonging, and Natural Connections,* 63 HASTINGS L. J. 1345 (2012); and Solangel Maldonado, *Illegitimate Harm: Law, Stigma, and Discrimination Against Nonmarital Children*, 63 FLA. L. REV. 345 (2011).

Cleo A.E. v. Rickie Gene E.

Supreme Court of Appeals of West Virginia, 1993
438 S.E.2d 886

■ WORKMAN, CHIEF JUSTICE.

The Child Advocate Office ("CAO") brought this appeal to challenge the voluntary bastardization of a minor child. Having examined the record in this matter in conjunction with the issue presented, this Court concludes that the best interests of the child standard precludes the parties from entering into a stipulation which has as its effect the bastardization of a child born to the parties during their marriage.

Cleo and Rickie E. were married on May 24, 1981, in Mason County, West Virginia. Cleo and Rickie E. had two children—Sheila E. on January 19, 1981, and Amber Dawn E. ("Amber Dawn") on July 9, 1983. Cleo and Rickie E. last cohabitated in July 1985 and Cleo E. filed for a divorce on July 10, 1986. Through the final order of divorce, which was entered by the Mason County Circuit Court on August 11, 1986, Cleo E. was awarded custody of both children. No child support was awarded, however, based on the fact that Cleo E. had not made a request for support during the divorce proceedings.

On July 2, 1987, Cleo and Rickie E. entered into a written agreement whereby Rickie E. agreed to pay Cleo E. $250 per month for child support. The record bears no indication that this agreement was ever ratified by the circuit court, but the parties do not dispute the document's existence. In late 1991, the CAO located Rickie E. in Marion County, Florida, through its efforts to collect child support. The CAO filed a petition in the Circuit Court of Cabell County, West Virginia, on February 13, 1992, pursuant to the Uniform Reciprocal Enforcement of Support Act ("URESA"), WEST VIRGINIA CODE §§ 48A–7–1 to –41 (1992 & Supp.1993) to collect support payments.

On May 21, 1992, a hearing was held before the Circuit Court for the Fifth Judicial Circuit in Marion County, Florida, on the URESA petition. Rickie E. appeared and challenged the petition's claim that he was the father of Amber Dawn.[1] He requested that HLA blood testing be performed to determine whether he was in fact the natural father of Amber Dawn. The Florida court ordered Rickie E. to pay $31.24 per week to the court as temporary support. Following the submission of briefs on the issue of whether Rickie E. could properly challenge the paternity of a child conceived during marriage in the Florida court, a second hearing was held on September 15, 1992, in Florida. At this hearing the court ruled that Rickie E. was the father of Amber Dawn and entered an order requiring Rickie E. to pay $62.40 per week to the court beginning September 7, 1992, for support arrearages which totaled $18,074 as of December 31, 1991. The Florida court reserved jurisdiction to modify

[1] Rickie E. claims that he learned through hearsay in late 1991 or early 1992 that a cousin of his was the true father of Amber Dawn.

both support and arrears retroactively upon its receipt of a modified final order of divorce from a West Virginia court.[2]

An amended final order of divorce was entered in West Virginia by the Mason County Circuit Court on October 26, 1992. The order referenced and attached a stipulation which set forth, inter alia, that Rickie E. was not the natural father of Amber Dawn.[3] It is unclear whether the circuit court held an actual hearing on this matter, but its order provides no reasoning for its decision to approve an amendment to the final order of divorce which had as its primary objective the bastardization of one of the children born to the parties during their marriage. The CAO brings this appeal seeking to have the amended final order of divorce set aside.

The CAO premises its position on the "nearly universal concept that a child born in wedlock is presumptively legitimate." As this Court explained in Michael K.T. v. Tina L.T., 182 W.Va. 399, 387 S.E.2d 866 (1989): "Historically, society has frowned upon the bastardization of children. Thus, many states like West Virginia view a child as being presumptively legitimate if the child was born or conceived during a marriage." Id. at 402, 387 S.E.2d at 869. Recognizing that this presumption of legitimacy is rebuttable, we ruled in Michael K.T. that blood test evidence offered to disprove paternity should only be admitted after an in camera hearing has been held and various factors considered to determine "whether the equities surrounding the particular facts and circumstances of the case warrant admission of blood test results." See id. at 404, 387 S.E.2d at 871 and Syl. Pt. 2, in part. This Court further instructed in syllabus point four of Michael K.T. that "[a] guardian ad litem should be appointed to represent the interests of the minor child whenever an action is initiated to disprove a child's paternity." Id. at 400, 387 S.E.2d at 867.

The CAO argues that the guidelines established in Michael K.T. regarding the admissibility of blood test evidence should be extended to cases such as this which involve a stipulated disavowal of paternity. In Michael K.T., we instructed courts to consider these factors: (1) the length of time following when the putative father first was placed on notice that he might be the biological father before he acted to contest paternity; (2) the length of time during which the individual desiring to challenge paternity assumed the role of father to the child; (3) the facts surrounding the putative father's discovery of nonpaternity; (4) the

[2] The order of the Circuit Court of Marion County, Florida, dated September 15, 1992, does not state any reason for its finding that Rickie E. is the father of Amber Dawn. However, because the Florida court reserved jurisdiction to modify its order regarding both support and arrears retroactively upon its receipt of a modified final order from a West Virginia court, the implication is that the court thought that only the West Virginia courts would have jurisdiction to make such a finding. See W.Va.Code § 48A–7–26 (URESA permits court to adjudicate paternity issue "if both of the parties are present at the hearing or the proof required in the case indicates that the presence of either or both of the parties is not necessary").

[3] The stipulation was signed by Rickie E. on October 2, 1992, in Florida and by Cleo E. on October 26, 1992, in West Virginia.

nature of the father/child relationship; (5) the age of the child; (6) the harm which may result to the child if paternity were successfully disproved; (7) the extent to which the passage of time reduced the chances of establishing paternity and a child support obligation in favor of the child; and (8) all other factors which may affect the equities involved in the potential disruption of the parent/child relationship or the chances of undeniable harm to the child. Id. at 405, 387 S.E.2d at 872.

We determine initially that the parties to a domestic proceeding cannot by stipulation agree to bastardize children born during their marriage. Our conclusion is not founded on the traditional arguments against bastardization: the social stigma imposed on the child and the financial burden imposed on the state. As we discussed in Michael K.T., "[t]hese two historical bases for opposing bastardization have been significantly vitiated given the modernization of society and legislation drafted to address the problems of bastardization." 182 W.Va. at 402–03, 387 S.E.2d at 869. Rather, we are once again guided by the cardinal principle that "the best interests of the child is the polar star by which decisions must be made which affect children." Id. at 405, 387 S.E.2d at 872. Furthermore, a child has a right to an establishment of paternity and a child support obligation, and a right to independent representation on matters affecting his or her substantial rights and interests.

Because it appears that consideration of Amber Dawn's best interests were totally ignored in the proceedings below, we conclude that a court cannot properly adjudicate the issue of paternity based on a stipulation between the parties. Given the serious and long-lasting effects of bastardization, resolution of the paternity issue should be accomplished with the active participation of the court, rather than involvement that is limited to reviewing a previously-executed document. This is necessary to guarantee that the issue of paternity is not used as a bargaining tool, perhaps to secure a favorable monetary award or some other preferred attainment. But, more importantly, it is required to secure proper consideration of the facts of the case in light of the best interests of the child and with due regard to the rights of the child. Accordingly, the guidelines which this Court identified in Michael K.T., regarding the admission of blood test evidence on the issue of paternity, should similarly be utilized when making a ruling which has as its effect the bastardization of a minor child. See 182 W.Va. at 405, 387 S.E.2d at 872.

This case demonstrates vividly the need for a court-appointed attorney to represent the interests of a child whose paternity is at issue. Not only were the interests of Amber Dawn unrepresented during the drafting of the stipulation, but the court's approval of the document was also apparently made without any consideration for its impact upon her. Further, a hearing should have been held for the presentation of evidence on the factors enumerated in Michael K.T. such as: the length of time following when Rickie E. allegedly learned that he was not the natural father of Amber Dawn and when he took action to disprove paternity; the period of time during which Rickie E. assumed the role of father to Amber Dawn and the nature of their relationship; the harm which might result through disestablishment of paternity; and the extent to which the passage of time reduced the possibility that paternity can be established and child support obtained. See id.

Although historically courts have addressed issues affecting children primarily in the context of competing adults' rights, the present trend in courts throughout the country is to give greater recognition to the rights of children, including their right to independent representation in proceedings affecting substantial rights. Consequently, we extend our previous ruling in Michael K.T. regarding the appointment of a guardian ad litem.[4] A guardian ad litem should be appointed to represent the interests of a minor child whenever the issue of disproving paternity is involved in a proceeding, regardless of whether the proceeding was initiated for the sole purpose of disproving paternity.[5] Furthermore, if paternity of a child is abrogated, the guardian ad litem should seek to establish legal paternity and child support.[6]

The CAO suggests that a finding of fraud against Cleo E. is necessary to overcome the res judicata doctrine established by this Court in State ex. rel. West Virginia Dep't of Health and Human Resources v. Cline, 185 W.Va. 318, 406 S.E.2d 749 (1991). We ruled in Cline in syllabus point two that "[a]n adjudication of paternity, which is expressed in a divorce order, is res judicata as to the husband and wife in any subsequent proceeding." 185 W.Va. at 319, 406 S.E.2d at 750 (quoting Syl. Pt. 1, in part, Nancy Darlene M. v. James Lee M., Jr., 184 W.Va. 447, 400 S.E.2d 882 (1990)). The Cline decision also referenced this Court's statement in Michael K.T. that "absent evidence of fraudulent conduct which prevented the putative father from questioning paternity, this Court will not sanction the disputation of paternity through blood test

---

4 In response to the Michael K.T. decision the Legislature amended West Virginia Code § 48–2–11 (Supp.1993) to include subsection (b) which reads as follows: If, in an action for divorce or annulment, either party shall allege that a person, other than the husband, is the father of a child born during the marriage of the parties, the court shall appoint a competent attorney to act as guardian ad litem on behalf of the child. The attorney shall be appointed without motion and prior to an entry of any order requiring blood testing. W.Va.Code § 48–2–11(b).

5 This Court's decision in Michael K.T. arguably permits the appointment of a guardian ad litem presently in such cases given the directive contained therein that "a guardian ad litem should be appointed to represent the interests of the minor child whenever the issue of disproving paternity is raised outside of a proceeding contemplated by W.Va.Code § 48A–6–1." 182 W.Va. at 406, 387 S.E.2d at 873. Because, however, the issue of Amber Dawn's paternity was resolved through a stipulation rather than any specific court proceeding, we resolve any potential confusion by creating a separate syllabus point addressing this issue; in actuality, our ruling regarding the required appointment of a guardian ad litem is more of a clarification than an extension.

6 In Michael K.T., we pointed out that the fees of a guardian ad litem in a divorce or related domestic relations action should be paid by the party most able to bear that cost. 182 W.Va. at 406, 387 S.E.2d at 873. In the event paternity is disproved, the court should appoint the guardian for the child, and the guardian should act expeditiously to establish actual paternity and to obtain entry of a child support award.

evidence if there has been more than a relatively brief passage of time." 185 W.Va. at 321, 406 S.E.2d at 752 (quoting Michael K.T., 182 W.Va. at 405, 387 S.E.2d at 872). Certainly, evidence of fraud on the part of Cleo E. of withholding information from Rickie E. concerning the identity of Amber Dawn's biological father would be relevant on remand if the circuit court is required to rule on blood testing, or ultimately, when it makes its ruling regarding the paternity of Amber Dawn.

Based on the foregoing, the decision of the Circuit Court of Mason County is hereby reversed and remanded for additional proceedings consistent with this opinion.

NOTES

The emphasis of this decision is on the child's best interest, including the child's right to legitimacy and to independent representation in proceedings affecting substantial rights. The court rejected the parents' stipulated disavowal of paternity, holding that a child has a right to an establishment of paternity and a child support obligation. With continuing advances in assisted reproductive technology, the *Cleo* decision establishes the parameters of contests between the rights of genetic donors, functional parents, birth mothers, birth fathers, gestational carriers, and persons intending to be parents of the resulting child. For commentary, *see,* Brandon James Hoover, *Establishing the Best Answer to Paternity Disestablishment*, 37 OHIO N.U. L. REV. 145 (2011); Laurence C. Nolan, *Legal Strangers and the Duty of Support: Beyond the Biological Tie—But How Far Beyond the Biological Tie?,* 41 SANTA CLARA L. REV. 1 (2000); Susan Frelich Appleton, *Parents by the Numbers*, 37 HOFSTRA L. REV. 11 (2008).

D. CHILDREN OF ASSISTED REPRODUCTIVE TECHNOLOGY

1. ESTABLISHING PARENTAGE THROUGH CONSENT

Buzzanca v. Buzzanca

Court of Appeal, Fourth District, Division 3, California, 1998
61 Cal. App. 4th 1410

■ SILLS, PRESIDING JUSTICE.

Jaycee was born because Luanne and John Buzzanca agreed to have an embryo genetically unrelated to either of them implanted in a woman—a surrogate—who would carry and give birth to the child for them. After the fertilization, implantation and pregnancy, Luanne and John split up, and the question of who are Jaycee's lawful parents came before the trial court. Luanne claimed that she and her erstwhile husband were the lawful parents, but John disclaimed any responsibility, financial or otherwise. The woman who gave birth also appeared in the case to make it clear that she made no claim to the child. The trial court then reached an extraordinary conclusion: Jaycee had *no* lawful parents. First, the woman who gave birth to Jaycee was not the mother; the court had—astonishingly—already accepted a stipulation that neither she nor her husband were the "biological" parents. Second, Luanne was not the mother. According to the trial court, she could not be the mother because she had neither contributed the egg nor given birth. And John could not be the father, because, not having contributed the sperm, he had no biological relationship with the child.

We disagree. Let us get right to the point: Jaycee never would have been born had not Luanne and John both agreed to have a fertilized egg implanted in a surrogate.

The trial judge erred because he assumed that legal motherhood, under the relevant California statutes, could *only* be established in one of two ways, either by giving birth or by contributing an egg. He failed to consider the substantial and well-settled body of law holding that there are times when *fatherhood* can be established by conduct apart from giving birth or being genetically related to a child. The typical example is when an infertile husband consents to allowing his wife to be artificially inseminated. As our Supreme Court noted in such a situation over 30 years ago, the husband is the "lawful father" because he *consented* to the procreation of the child. (See People v. Sorensen (1968) 68 Cal.2d 280, 284–286, 66 Cal.Rptr. 7, 437 P.2d 495.)

The same rule which makes a husband the lawful father of a child born because of his consent to artificial insemination should be applied here—by the same parity of reasoning that guided our Supreme Court in the first surrogacy case, Johnson v. Calvert (1993) 5 Cal.4th 84, 19 Cal.Rptr.2d 494, 851 P.2d 776—to both husband and wife. Just as a husband is deemed to be the lawful father of a child unrelated to him when his wife gives birth after artificial insemination, so should a husband *and* wife be deemed the lawful parents of a child after a surrogate bears a biologically unrelated child on their behalf. In each instance, a child is procreated because a medical procedure was initiated and consented to by intended parents. The only difference is that in this case—unlike artificial insemination—there is no reason to distinguish between husband and wife. We therefore must reverse the trial court's judgment and direct that a new judgment be entered, declaring that both Luanne and John are the lawful parents of Jaycee.[1]

John filed his petition for dissolution of marriage on March 30, 1995, alleging there were no children of the marriage. Luanne filed her response on April 20, alleging that the parties were expecting a child by way of surrogate contract. Jaycee was born six days later. In September 1996 Luanne filed a separate petition to establish herself as Jaycee's mother. Her action was consolidated into the dissolution case. In

1 . . . When we refer to artificial insemination in this opinion we are only referring to the heterologous variety.

February 1997, the court accepted a stipulation that the woman who agreed to carry the child, and her husband, were not the "biological parents" of the child.[2] At a hearing held in March, based entirely on oral argument and offers of proof, the trial court determined that Luanne was not the lawful mother of the child and therefore John could not be the lawful father or owe any support. . . .

Perhaps recognizing the inherent lack of appeal for any result which makes Jaycee a legal orphan, John now contends that the surrogate is Jaycee's legal mother; and further, by virtue of that fact, the surrogate's husband is the legal father. His reasoning goes like this: Under the Uniform Parentage Act (the Act), and particularly as set forth in section 7610 of California's Family Code, there are only two ways by which a woman can establish legal motherhood, i.e., giving birth or contributing genetically. Because the genetic contributors are not known to the court, the only candidate left is the surrogate who must therefore be deemed the lawful mother. And, as John's counsel commented at oral argument, if the surrogate and her husband cannot support Jaycee, the burden should fall on the taxpayers.

The law doesn't say what John says it says. It doesn't say: "The legal relationship between mother and child shall be established only by either proof of her giving birth or by genetics." The statute says "may," not "shall," and "under this part," *not* "by genetics." Here is the complete text of section 7610: "The parent and child relationship may be established as follows: [¶] (a) Between a child and the natural mother, it may be established by proof of her having given birth to the child, or under this part. [¶] (b) Between a child and the natural father, it may be established under this part. [¶] (c) Between a child and an adoptive parent, it may be established by proof of adoption."

The statute thus contains no direct reference to genetics (i.e., blood tests) at all. The *Johnson* decision teaches us that genetics is simply *subsumed* in the words "under this part." In that case, the court held that genetic consanguinity was equally "acceptable" as "proof of maternity" as evidence of giving birth. (Johnson v. Calvert, supra, 5 Cal.4th at p. 93, 19 Cal.Rptr.2d 494, 851 P.2d 776.)

It is important to realize, however, that in construing the words "under this part" to include genetic testing, the high court in *Johnson* relied on several statutes in the Evidence Code (former Evid.Code,

---

2 John's attorney was present at the hearing when the court accepted the stipulation that the surrogate was not the "biological" parent of Jaycee. He made no objection. Yet in the respondent's brief on appeal and in oral argument, he has argued that the surrogate is the lawful mother of Jaycee by virtue of the biological connection of having given birth.

One reaction to this inconsistency might be to hold, simply, that John is barred from arguing the point that the surrogate is the lawful mother because he did not object to the surrogate being let off the hook when he had the chance at the trial level. We reject that course of analysis because in this case of first impression it would be an intellectual cheat. Particularly in matters regarding children and parental responsibilities, courts must be wary of allowing lawyers from trying to cleverly (or inadvertently) maneuver a case into a posture where the court's decision does not reflect the underlying legal reality.

§§ 892, 895, and 895.5) all of which, by their terms, only applied to *paternity*. (See Johnson v. Calvert, supra, 5 Cal.4th at pp. 90–92, 19 Cal.Rptr.2d 494, 851 P.2d 776.) It was only by a "parity of reasoning" that our high court concluded those statutes which, on their face applied only to men, were also "dispositive of the question of maternity." (5 Cal.4th at p. 92, 19 Cal.Rptr.2d 494, 851 P.2d 776.)

The point bears reiterating: It was only by a parity of reasoning from statutes which, on their face, referred only to *paternity* that the court in *Johnson v. Calvert* reached the result it did on the question of *maternity*. Had the *Johnson* court reasoned as John now urges us to reason—by narrowly confining the means under the Uniform Parentage Act by which a woman could establish that she was the lawful mother of a child to texts which on their face applied only to motherhood (as distinct from fatherhood)—the court would have reached the opposite result.[5]

In addition to blood tests there are several other ways the Act allows paternity to be established. Those ways are not necessarily related at all to any biological tie. Thus, under the Act, paternity may be established by:

> marrying, remaining married to, or attempting to marry the child's mother when she gives birth (see § 7611, subds. (a) & (b));
>
> marrying the child's mother after the child's birth and either consenting to being named as the father on the birth certificate (' 7611, subd. (c)(1)) or making a written promise to support the child (see § 7611, subd. (c)(2)).

A man may also be deemed a father under the Act in the case of artificial insemination of his wife, as provided by section 7613 of the

---

[5] In *In re Marriage of Moschetta* (1994) 25 Cal.App.4th 1218, 1224–1226, 30 Cal.Rptr.2d 893, the court refused to apply certain *presumptions* regarding paternity found in the Act to overcome the claim of a woman who was both the genetic and birth mother. Relying on *In re Zacharia D.* (1993) 6 Cal.4th 435, 24 Cal.Rptr.2d 751, 862 P.2d 751, we observed that there may be times when the Act cannot be applied in a gender interchangeable manner. (See *Moschetta, supra,* 25 Cal.App.4th at p. 1225, fn. 8, 30 Cal.Rptr.2d 893.)

It made sense in *Moschetta* not to apply the paternity statutes cited by the father to the biologically unrelated intended mother because those statutes merely embody presumptions. The statutes were: (1) the presumption that a child of a wife cohabiting with her husband at the time of birth is conclusively presumed to be a child of the marriage unless the husband is impotent or sterile (see Fam.Code, § 7540), and (2) the presumption that a man is the natural father if he receives the child into his home and openly holds out the child as his own (Fam.Code, § 7611, subd. (d)). We rejected application of these presumptions because, even assuming they could be applied to a woman, they were only presumptions and, just like a paternity case, could be overcome by blood tests showing an actual genetic relationship. (*Moschetta, supra,* 25 Cal.App.4th at pp. 1225–1226, 30 Cal.Rptr.2d 893.) Most fundamentally, as we pointed out on page 1226, 30 Cal.Rptr.2d 893 of the opinion, the presumptions were inapposite because they arose out of the "old law of illegitimacy" and were designed as evidentiary devices to make a determination of a child's biological father.

Moschetta thus cannot be read for the proposition that statutes which are part of the Act and refer to an individual of one sex can never be applied to an individual of another. For one reason, *Moschetta* never said that. For another, such a broad proposition would contradict the rationale used by a higher court in *Johnson*.

Family Code.[6] To track the words of the statute: "If, under the supervision of a licensed physician and surgeon and with the consent of her husband, a wife is inseminated artificially with semen donated by a man not her husband, the husband is treated in law as if he were the natural father of a child thereby conceived."[7]

As noted in *Johnson,* "courts must construe statutes in factual settings not contemplated by the enacting legislature." (Johnson v. Calvert, supra, 5 Cal.4th at p. 89, 19 Cal.Rptr.2d 494, 851 P.2d 776.) So it is, of course, true that application of the artificial insemination statute to a gestational surrogacy case where the genetic donors are unknown to the court may not have been contemplated by the legislature. Even so, the two kinds of artificial reproduction are *exactly* analogous in this crucial respect: Both contemplate the procreation of a child by the consent to a medical procedure of someone who intends to raise the child but who otherwise does not have any biological tie.

If a husband who consents to artificial insemination under section 7613 is "treated in law" as the father of the child by virtue of his consent, there is no reason the result should be any different in the case of a married couple who consent to in vitro fertilization by unknown donors and subsequent implantation into a woman who is, as a surrogate, willing to carry the embryo to term for them. The statute is, after all, the clearest expression of past legislative intent when the legislature did contemplate a situation where a person who caused a child to come into being had no biological relationship to the child.

Indeed, the establishment of fatherhood and the consequent duty to support when a husband consents to the artificial insemination of his wife is one of the well-established rules in family law. The leading case in the country (so described by a New York family court in Adoption of Anonymous (1973) 74 Misc.2d 99, 345 N.Y.S.2d 430, 433) is People v. Sorensen, supra, 68 Cal.2d 280, 66 Cal.Rptr. 7, 437 P.2d 495, in which our Supreme Court held that a man could even be *criminally* liable for failing to pay for the support of a child born to his wife during the

---

[6] California Family Code section 7613 is California's enactment of the artificial insemination provision of section 5 of the Uniform Parentage Act.

[7] The entire statute reads as follows: "If, under the supervision of a licensed physician and surgeon and with the consent of her husband, a wife is inseminated artificially with semen donated by a man not her husband, the husband is treated in law as if he were the natural father of a child thereby conceived. The husband's consent must be in writing and signed by him and his wife. The physician and surgeon shall certify their signatures and the date of the insemination, and retain the husband's consent as part of the medical record, where it shall be kept confidential and in a sealed file. However, the physician and surgeon's failure to do so does not affect the father and child relationship. All papers and records pertaining to the insemination, whether part of the permanent record of a court or of a file held by the supervising physician and surgeon or elsewhere, are subject to inspection only upon an order of the court for good cause shown. [ ] (b) The donor of semen provided to a licensed physician and surgeon for use in artificial insemination of a woman other than the donor's wife is treated in law as if he were not the natural father of a child thereby conceived."

California's Family Code section 7613 varies from the promulgated version in that it omits the word "married" in subdivision (b) in front of the word "woman," a textual indication that the California Legislature contemplated use of artificial insemination by single women.

marriage as a result of artificial insemination using sperm from an anonymous donor.

In *Sorensen,* the high court emphasized the role of the husband in *causing* the birth, even though he had no biological connection to the child: "[A] reasonable man who . . . actively participates and consents to his wife's artificial insemination in the hope that a child will be produced whom they will treat as their own, *knows that such behavior carries with it the legal responsibilities of fatherhood and criminal responsibility for nonsupport.*"(*Id.* at p. 285, 66 Cal.Rptr. 7, 437 P.2d 495, emphasis added.) The court went on to say that the husband was "directly responsible" for the "existence" of the child and repeated the point that "without defendant's active participation and consent the child would not have been procreated." (*Ibid.*)

Sorensen expresses a rule universally in tune with other jurisdictions. "Almost exclusively, courts which have addressed this issue have assigned parental responsibility to the husband based on conduct evidencing his consent to the artificial insemination." In re Baby Doe (1987) 291 S.C. 389, 353 S.E.2d 877, 878; accord, Gursky v. Gursky (1963) 39 Misc.2d 1083, 242 N.Y.S.2d 406, 411–412 [even though child was not technically "legitimate" under New York law at the time, husband's conduct in consenting to the artificial insemination properly invoked application of the doctrine of equitable estoppel requiring him to support the child]; Anonymous v. Anonymous (1964) 41 Misc.2d 886, 246 N.Y.S.2d 835, 836–837 [following *Gursky*]; K.S. v. G.S. (1981) 182 N.J.Super. 102, 440 A.2d 64, 68 [because husband did not offer clear and convincing evidence that he had *withdrawn* his consent to artificial insemination procedure, he was bound by initial consent given earlier and accordingly held to be lawful father of the child]; . . . One New York family court even went so far as to hold the lesbian partner of a woman who was artificially inseminated responsible for the support of two children where the partner had dressed as a man and the couple had obtained a marriage license and a wedding ceremony had been performed prior to the inseminations. (Karin T. v. Michael T. (1985) 127 Misc.2d 14, 484 N.Y.S.2d 780.) Echoing the themes of causation and estoppel which underlie the cases, the court noted that the lesbian partner had "by her course of conduct in this case . . . brought into the world two innocent children" and should not "be allowed to benefit" from her acts to the detriment of the children and public generally. (484 N.Y.S.2d at p. 784.)

Indeed, in the one case we are aware of where the court did not hold that the husband had a support obligation, the reason was *not* the absence of a biological relationship as such, but because of actual lack of consent to the insemination procedure. (See In re Marriage of Witbeck-Wildhagen (1996) 281 Ill.App.3d 502, 217 Ill.Dec. 329, 331–332, 667 N.E.2d 122, 125–126 [it would be "unjust" to impose support obligation on husband who never consented to the artificial insemination].)

It must also be noted that in applying the artificial insemination statute to a case where a party has caused a child to be brought into the world, the statutory policy is really echoing a more fundamental idea—a sort of *grundnorm* to borrow Hans Kelsen's famous jurisprudential word—already established in the case law. That idea is often summed up in the legal term "estoppel." Estoppel is an ungainly word from the Middle French (from the word meaning "bung" or "stopper") expressing the law's distaste for inconsistent actions and positions—like consenting to an act which brings a child into existence and then turning around and disclaiming any responsibility.

While the *Johnson v. Calvert* court was able to predicate its decision on the Uniform Parentage Act rather than making up the result out of whole cloth, it is also true that California courts, prior to the enactment of the Act, had based certain decisions establishing paternity merely on the common law doctrine of estoppel. . . . [This was] the basis for establishing paternity and its concomitant responsibility as far back as the 1961 decision of Clevenger v. Clevenger (1961) 189 Cal.App.2d 658, 662, 11 Cal.Rptr. 707 (husband who took illegitimate child into his home and held child out as his own "estopped" to assert illegitimacy and "avoid liability for its support").

There is no need in the present case to predicate our decision on common law estoppel alone, though the doctrine certainly applies. The estoppel concept, after all, is *already* inherent in the artificial insemination statute. . . .

John argues that the artificial insemination statute should not be applied because, after all, his wife did not give birth. But for purposes of the statute with its core idea of estoppel, the fact that Luanne did not give birth is irrelevant. The statute contemplates the establishment of lawful fatherhood in a situation where an intended father has no biological relationship to a child who is procreated as a result of the father's (as well as the mother's) *consent* to a medical procedure. . . .

The legal paradigm adopted by the trial court, and now urged upon us by John, is one where all forms of artificial reproduction in which intended parents have no biological relationship with the child result in legal parentlessness. It means that, absent adoption, such children will be dependents of the state. One might describe this paradigm as the "adoption default" model: The idea is that by not specifically addressing some permutation of artificial reproduction, the Legislature has, in effect, set the default switch on adoption. The underlying theory seems to be that when intended parents resort to artificial reproduction without biological tie the Legislature wanted them to be *screened* first through the adoption system. (Thus John, in his brief, argues that a surrogacy contract must be "subject to state oversight.")

The "adoption default" model is, however, inconsistent with both statutory law and the Supreme Court's *Johnson* decision. As to the statutory law, the Legislature has already made it perfectly clear that public policy (and, we might add, common sense) favors, whenever possible, the establishment of legal parenthood with the concomitant responsibility. Family Code section 7570, subdivision (a) states that "There is a compelling state interest in establishing paternity for all children." The statute then goes on to elaborate why establishing paternity is a good thing: It means someone besides the taxpayers will be responsible for the child: "Establishing paternity is the first step toward a child support award, which, in turn, provides children with equal rights and access to benefits. . . ." (*Ibid.*) In light of this strong public policy, the statutes which follow section 7570, subdivision (a) seek to provide a "simple system allowing for the establishment of voluntary paternity." (See Fam.Code, § 7570, subd. (b).)

Section 7570 necessarily expresses a legislative policy applicable to maternity as well. It would be lunatic for the Legislature to declare that establishing paternity is a compelling state interest yet conclude that establishing maternity is not. The obvious reason the Legislature did not include an explicit parallel statement on "maternity" is that the issue almost never arises except for extraordinary cases involving artificial reproduction.

Very plainly, the Legislature has declared its preference for assigning *individual* responsibility for the care and maintenance of children; not leaving the task to the taxpayers. That is why it has gone to considerable lengths to insure that parents will live up to their support obligations. (Cf. Moss v. Superior Court (1998) 17 Cal.4th 396, 424, 71 Cal.Rptr.2d 215, 950 P.2d 59 [noting legislative priority put on child support obligations].) The adoption default theory flies in the face of that legislative value judgment.

As this court noted in Jaycee B. v. Superior Court (1996) 42 Cal.App.4th 718, 731, 49 Cal.Rptr.2d 694, the *Johnson* court had occasion, albeit in dicta, to address "pretty much the exact situation before us." The language bears quoting again: "In what we must hope will be the extremely rare situation in which neither the gestator nor the woman who provided the ovum for fertilization is willing to assume custody of the child after birth, a rule recognizing the intending parents as the child's legal, natural parents should best promote certainty and stability." (Johnson v. Calvert, supra, 5 Cal.4th at pp. 94–95, 19 Cal.Rptr.2d 494, 851 P.2d 776.) This language quite literally describes precisely the case before us now: Neither the woman whose ovum was used nor the woman who gave birth have come forward to assume custody of the child after birth.

John now argues that the Supreme Court's statement should be applied only in situations, such as that in the *Johnson* case, where the intended parents have a genetic tie to the child. The context of the *Johnson* language, however, reveals a broader purpose, namely, to emphasize the intelligence and utility of a rule that looks to intentions. . . .

The *Johnson* court had just enunciated its conclusion that in cases of "genetic consanguinity" and "giving birth" the intended mother is to be held the lawful mother.[13] The court then found "support" for its conclusions in the writings of several legal commentators (*id.* at p. 93, 19 Cal.Rptr.2d 494, 851 P.2d 776), the first of whom, Professor Hill, had made the point that the intended parents are the " 'first cause, or prime movers, of the procreative relationship.' " (*Id.* at p. 94, 19 Cal.Rptr.2d 494, 851 P.2d 776, quoting Hill, What Does It Mean to Be a "Parent"? The Claims of Biology as the Basis for Parental Rights (1991) 66 N.Y.U.L.Rev. 353, 415.) The court then quoted two more law review articles, both of which emphasized the same theme as Professor Hill.[14] This laid the foundation for the court's next point, which was that people who " 'choose' " to bring a child into being are likely to have the child's best interest at heart, which the court immediately juxtaposed against the surrogate's position which would result in a woman becoming the legal mother *against* her expectations. Then came the sentence which we have already quoted addressing the "extremely rare situation" where—as is precisely the case before us now—neither the woman who has given birth nor the woman who provided the ovum were "willing to assume custody of the child after birth"—and therefore recognizing intentions as the best rule to promote certainty and stability for the child. (*Id.* at pp. 94–95, 19 Cal.Rptr.2d 494, 851 P.2d 776.)

In context, then, the high court's considered dicta is directly applicable to the case at hand. The context was not limited to just *Johnson*-style contests between women who gave birth and women who contributed ova, but to any situation where a child would not have been born " 'but for the efforts of the intended parents.' " (*Id.* at p. 94, 19 Cal.Rptr.2d 494, 851 P.2d 776, quoting Hill, *op. cit., supra,* 66 N.Y.U.L.Rev. at p. 415.)

Finally, in addition to its contravention of statutorily enunciated public policy and the pronouncement of our high court in *Johnson,* the adoption default model ignores the role of our dependency statutes in protecting children. Parents are not screened for the procreation of their *own* children; they are screened for the adoption of *other* people's children. It is the role of the dependency laws to protect children from neglect and abuse from their own parents. The adoption default model is essentially an exercise in circular reasoning, because it assumes the idea

[13] This rule, incidentally, has the salutary effect of working both ways. Thus if an intended mother who could carry a baby to term but had no suitable eggs was implanted with an embryo in which the egg was from a donor who did not intend to parent the child, the law would still reflect the intentions of the parties rather than some arbitrary or imposed preference.

[14] The *Johnson* court quoted Professor Schulz to the effect that " 'intentions that are voluntarily chosen, deliberate, express and bargained-for ought presumptively to determine legal parenthood' " (*Johnson v. Calvert, supra,* 5 Cal.4th at p. 94, 19 Cal.Rptr.2d 494, 851 P.2d 776, quoting Schultz, *Reproductive Technology and Intent-Based Parenthood: An Opportunity for Gender Neutrality* (1990) Wis.L.Rev. 297, 323) and a Yale Law Journal Note that the " '[m]ental concept of the child *is a controlling factor of its creation*' " (*Johnson v. Calvert, supra,* 5 Cal.4th at p. 94, 19 Cal.Rptr.2d 494, 851 P.2d 776, quoting Note, *Redefining Mother: A Legal Matrix for New Reproductive Technologies* (1986) 96 YALE L. J. 187, 196 (our emphasis).)

that it seeks to prove; namely, that a child who is born as the result of artificial reproduction is somebody else's child from the beginning.

In the case before us, there is absolutely no dispute that Luanne caused Jaycee's conception and birth by initiating the surrogacy arrangement whereby an embryo was implanted into a woman who agreed to carry the baby to term on Luanne's behalf. In applying the artificial insemination statute to a gestational surrogacy case where the genetic donors are unknown, there is, as we have indicated above, no reason to distinguish *between* husbands and wives. Both are equally situated from the point of view of consenting to an act which brings a child into being. Accordingly, Luanne should have been declared the lawful mother of Jaycee. . . .

Even though neither Luanne nor John are biologically related to Jaycee, they are still her lawful parents given their initiating role as the intended parents in her conception and birth. And, while the absence of a biological connection is what makes this case extraordinary, this court is hardly without statutory basis and legal precedent in so deciding. Indeed, in both the most famous child custody case of all time,[19] and in our Supreme Court's *Johnson v. Calvert* decision, the court looked to *intent to parent* as the ultimate basis of its decision.[20] Fortunately, as the *Johnson* court also noted, intent to parent " 'correlate[s] significantly' " with a child's best interests. (Johnson v. Calvert, supra, 5 Cal.4th at p. 94, 19 Cal.Rptr.2d 494, 851 P.2d 776, quoting Schultz, *op. cit. supra,* Wis.L.Rev., at p. 397.) That is far more than can be said for a model of the law that renders a child a legal orphan.[21]

Again we must call on the Legislature to sort out the parental rights and responsibilities of those involved in artificial reproduction. No matter what one thinks of artificial insemination, traditional and gestational surrogacy (in all its permutations), and—as now appears in the not-too-distant future, cloning and even gene splicing—courts are still going to be faced with the problem of determining lawful parentage. A child cannot be ignored. Even if all means of artificial reproduction were outlawed with draconian criminal penalties visited on the doctors and parties involved, courts will still be called upon to decide who the

---

[19] See I Kings 3:25–26 (dispute over identity of live child by two single women, each of whom had recently delivered a child but one child had died, resolved by novel evidentiary device designed to ferret out intent to parent).

[20] While in each case intent to parent was used as a tie-breaker as between two claimants who either had or claimed a biological connection, it is still undeniable that, when push came to shove, the court employed a legal idea that was *unrelated* to any necessary biological connection.

[21] It is significant that even if the *Johnson* majority had adopted the position of Justice Kennard advocating best interest as the more flexible and better rule (see *id.* at p. 118, 19 Cal.Rptr.2d 494, 851 P.2d 776 (dis. opn. of Kennard, J.)) there is no way the trial court's decision could stand. Luanne has cared for Jaycee since infancy; she is the only parent Jaycee has ever known. It would be unthinkable, given the facts of this case and her role as caregiver for Jaycee, for Luanne not to be declared the lawful mother under a best interest test.

As for the father, John would not be the first man whose responsibility was based on having played a role in causing a child's procreation, regardless of whether he really wanted to assume it.

lawful parents really are and who—other than the taxpayers—is obligated to provide maintenance and support for the child. These cases will not go away. . . .

In re M.J.

Supreme Court of Illinois, 2003
787 N.E.2d 144

■ KILBRIDE, JUSTICE delivered the opinion of the court.

Appellant, Alexis Mitchell, brought this action against appellee, Raymond Banary, her former paramour, seeking to establish paternity and to impose support obligations for twin boys conceived through artificial insemination by an anonymous donor. The circuit court of Cook County dismissed Alexis' suit. The appellate court affirmed. 325 Ill.App.3d 826, 259 Ill.Dec. 641, 759 N.E.2d 121. We allowed Alexis' petition for leave to appeal. . . . We now affirm in part, reverse in part, and hold that the Illinois Parentage Act does not bar common law claims for child support. . . .

Alexis is a single woman who was 40 years old at the time of the filing of her complaint, and Raymond is a male who was 57 years old at the time of the filing of the complaint. Alexis and Raymond first met in 1986 and began an intimate relationship lasting 10 years. When they met, Raymond introduced himself to Alexis as "Jim Richardson" and told her that he was divorced. During their 10-year relationship, the parties discussed marriage. Alexis and Raymond are of different races and, according to Alexis, Raymond told her that he would have to wait until retirement to marry because his community would not accept a mixed-race marriage. Raymond promised Alexis that upon his retirement, they would move to another community and be married.

The parties also discussed Alexis' desire to have children with Raymond. Despite their attempts to conceive, Alexis did not become pregnant, and it became apparent that Raymond could not father children. In 1991, Raymond suggested to Alexis that she become artificially inseminated by an anonymous donor as a means to have their child. Artificial insemination by a donor is also known as heterologous artificial insemination. Alexis claims that Raymond promised her that he would provide financial support for any child born by means of artificial insemination. However, Raymond's written consent to the procedure was never obtained. Alexis contends that Raymond orally consented to the procedure and that but for Raymond's promise to support the children, Alexis would not have completed the procedure.

According to Alexis, with Raymond's continuing consent and active encouragement, she attempted to become pregnant through artificial insemination. Raymond provided financial assistance for the insemination procedure; accompanied Alexis to the doctor's office for examinations; injected Alexis with medication designed to enhance her fertility; and participated in selecting the donor so that the offspring would appear to be a product of their relationship.

On the fifth attempt, Alexis became pregnant and gave birth to twin boys in 1993. Raymond participated in selecting names for the children. After the births, Raymond acknowledged the children as his own. He also provided support for them in the form of monthly payments of cash and the purchase of food, clothing, furniture, toys, and play equipment. In her complaint, Alexis further describes many family vacations with Raymond to 10 different states and Mexico, and alleges that Raymond also paid for the children's medical, travel, and entertainment expenses. In 1996, Alexis discovered that Raymond was not named Jim Richardson and that he was married. Upon discovering Raymond's true name and marital status, Alexis ended their relationship. Since 1996, Raymond has provided no financial support for the children.

Alexis filed a three-count complaint against Raymond seeking to establish paternity and impose a support obligation for the benefit of the twin boys. In the first two counts, Alexis sought to impose child support obligations by invoking common law theories of breach of an oral agreement and promissory estoppel. In the remaining count of her complaint, Alexis sought a declaration of paternity and establishment of child support pursuant to the Illinois Parentage Act (750 ILCS 40/1 *et seq.* (West 1998)).

Raymond filed a motion to dismiss, arguing that Alexis' common law claims, contained in counts I and II, were unenforceable under the provisions of the Frauds Act (740 ILCS 80/0.01 *et seq.* (West 1998)) and contravened Illinois public policy. Raymond also argued that all three counts should be dismissed pursuant to section 2–615 of the Code (735 ILCS 5/2–615 (West 1998)) because Alexis failed to set forth a legally recognized basis for the imposition of a father-child relationship or for child support under the Illinois Parentage Act (750 ILCS 40/1 *et seq.* (West 1998)).

The circuit court granted Raymond's motion and dismissed Alexis' complaint. The circuit court interpreted the Illinois Parentage Act as requiring that a husband consent in writing before he is treated in law as the natural father of a child conceived to his wife by means of artificial insemination. The circuit court commented that it would not be rational that unmarried couples would have fewer safeguards in such a matter. The circuit court therefore held that Alexis' common law theories were not actionable because the Illinois Parentage Act expressly requires written consent. The circuit court did not refer to the Frauds Act in its dismissal of the complaint.

Alexis appealed the circuit court's decision, and the appellate court majority determined that Alexis' common law theories for child support fail because the Illinois Parentage Act governs artificial insemination and requires that the "husband's consent must be in writing." The appellate court held that written consent is required before an unmarried man becomes legally obligated to support a child born as a result of artificial insemination. Based on its decision, the appellate court did not reach the issue concerning the Frauds Act. . . .

In construing a statute, this court must give effect to the intent of the legislature. Antunes v. Sookhakitch, 146 Ill.2d 477, 484, 167 Ill.Dec. 981, 588 N.E.2d 1111 (1992). To ascertain legislative intent, we must examine the language of the entire statute and consider each part or section in connection with every other part or section. Castaneda v. Illinois Human Rights Comm'n, 132 Ill.2d 304, 318, 138 Ill.Dec. 270, 547 N.E.2d 437 (1989). Where the language is clear and unambiguous, we must apply the statute without resort to further aids of statutory construction. Davis v. Toshiba Machine Co., America, 186 Ill.2d 181, 184–85, 237 Ill.Dec. 769, 710 N.E.2d 399 (1999). With these principles in mind, we now turn to the interpretation of the Illinois Parentage Act.

In 1984, the General Assembly enacted the Illinois Parentage Act (750 ILCS 40/1 *et seq.* (West 1998)) "to define the legal relationships of a child born to a wife and husband requesting and consenting to . . . artificial insemination." Pub. Act 83–1026, eff. January 5, 1984. Section 3 of the Illinois Parentage Act provides:

> "(a) If, under the supervision of a licensed physician and with the consent of her husband, a wife is inseminated artificially with semen donated by a man not her husband, the husband shall be treated in law as if he were the natural father of a child thereby conceived. The husband's consent must be in writing executed and acknowledged by both the husband and wife. The physician who is to perform the technique shall certify their signatures and the date of the insemination, and file the husband's consent in the medical record where it shall be kept confidential and held by the patient's physician. However, the physician's failure to do so shall not affect the legal relationship between father and child. All papers and records pertaining to the insemination, whether part of the permanent medical record held by the physician or not, are subject to inspection only upon an order of the court for good cause shown.
>
> (b) The donor of the semen provided to a licensed physician for use in artificial insemination of a woman other than the donor's wife shall be treated in law as if he were not the natural father of a child thereby conceived." 750 ILCS 40/3(a) (West 1998).

Any child born as a result of artificial insemination is considered the legitimate child of the husband and wife consenting to the use of the technique. 750 ILCS 40/2 (West 1998). Our interpretation of the express language of this provision of the statute indicates that the primary purpose of the Illinois Parentage Act is to provide a legal mechanism for a husband and wife to obtain donor sperm for use in artificial insemination and to ensure that a child is considered the legitimate child of the husband and wife requesting and consenting to the artificial technique.

Section 3(b) of the Illinois Parentage Act also provides a statutory vehicle for women to obtain semen for artificial insemination without fear that the donor may claim paternity. 750 ILCS 40/3(b) (West 1998). Additionally, section 3(b) protects sperm donors from claims of paternity and liability for child support. The parties dispute whether, under section 3(a) of the Illinois Parentage Act, the failure to provide written consent will preclude the establishment of a parent-child relationship and the imposition of a support obligation. This court has not conclusively interpreted the written-consent provision of the Act. We have, however, commented that the provision in the Act that "the husband's consent to the [artificial insemination] procedure 'must be in writing' *could be* considered a mandatory requirement for establishing a parent-child relationship pursuant to the statute." (Emphasis added.) In re Marriage of Adams, 133 Ill.2d 437, 444, 141 Ill.Dec. 448, 551 N.E.2d 635 (1990), citing Andrews v. Foxworthy, 71 Ill.2d 13, 21, 15 Ill.Dec. 648, 373 N.E.2d 1332 (1978) (the word "must" is generally construed in a mandatory sense). . . .

The first sentence of section 3(a) provides for the establishment of a parent-child relationship by consent. The second sentence of section 3(a) unequivocally requires that the consent for establishment of a parent-child relationship be in writing. This provision is clearly designed to safeguard rights concerning parentage. In light of the purpose of the written-consent requirement, we must conclude that the written-consent provision of section 3(a) of the Illinois Parentage Act is mandatory. Thus, section 3(a) of the Illinois Parentage Act mandates that written consent be obtained before parental responsibility may be established. Consequently, the failure to provide or obtain written consent will preclude a claim for paternity and child support under the Illinois Parentage Act. Accordingly, the appellate court did not err in affirming the circuit court's dismissal of count III of Alexis' complaint.

We note that the language of the Illinois Parentage Act was largely adopted from section 5 of the Uniform Parentage Act (UPA) (Unif. Parentage Act § 5, 9B U.L.A. 377 (1973)), as approved by the National Conference of Commissioners on Uniform State Laws. The commentary to section 5 of the UPA states:

> "This Act does not deal with the many complex and serious legal problems raised by the practice of artificial insemination. It was though [*sic*] useful, however, to single out and cover in this Act at least one fact situation that occurs frequently. Further consideration of other legal aspects of artificial insemination has been urged on the National Conference of Commissioners on Uniform State Laws and is recommended to state legislators." Unif. Parentage Act § 5, 9B U.L.A. 408, Comment (1973).

At the time the Illinois Parentage Act was enacted, the legislature intended to clarify the legal relationships among the parties involved in the artificial insemination procedure. See L. Smith, The AID Child and In re Marriage of Adams: Ambiguities in the Illinois Parentage Act, 21 Loy. U. Chi. L.J. 1173, 1192–93 (1990). However, as recognized by the commentary to section 5 of the UPA, the artificial insemination legislation "does not deal with the many complex and serious legal problems raised by the practice of artificial insemination." Unif. Parentage Act § 5, 9B U.L.A. 408, Comment (1973). Accordingly, the UPA comment urges that state legislators consider other legal aspects of artificial insemination.

In its current form, the Illinois Parentage Act fails to address the full spectrum of legal problems facing children born as a result of artificial insemination and other modern methods of assisted reproduction. The rapid evolution of assisted reproduction technology will continue to produce legal problems similar to those presented in this case. We urge the Illinois legislature to enact laws that are responsive to these problems in order to safeguard the interests of children born as a result of assisted reproductive technology. The need for reform to the Illinois Parentage Act is clear where, as here, we are compelled to apply the statute, in its current form, to a complex legal situation that the legislature did not anticipate when it passed the Illinois Parentage Act nearly 20 years ago.

Based on our determination that written consent is a prerequisite for invoking the protections of the Illinois Parentage Act, we need not and do not make any determination with regard to whether the Illinois Parentage Act applies to unmarried persons. Section 3(a) of the Illinois Parentage Act is simply not satisfied in this case because written consent was lacking.

Our determination that Alexis may not maintain an action under the Illinois Parentage Act does not end our inquiry. We must now determine whether the Illinois Parentage Act precludes common law claims for child support. Two Illinois appellate court cases have addressed this issue. These cases are In re Marriage of Adams, 174 Ill.App.3d 595, 124 Ill.Dec. 184, 528 N.E.2d 1075 (1988), *rev'd on other grounds,* 133 Ill.2d 437, 141 Ill.Dec. 448, 551 N.E.2d 635 (1990), and In re Marriage of Witbeck-Wildhagen, 281 Ill.App.3d 502, 217 Ill.Dec. 329, 667 N.E.2d 122 (1996). Each case reached a different result based on its unique facts.

In *Adams,* the appellate court held that the Illinois Parentage Act does not bar the imposition of a support obligation under an estoppel or waiver theory and that the failure to execute a written consent did not bar further inquiry into the circumstances surrounding the decision to use artificial insemination. Adams, 174 Ill.App.3d at 610–11, 124 Ill.Dec. 184, 528 N.E.2d 1075. The appellate court affirmed the trial court's finding that there was "actual consent" by the husband to the insemination procedure, who twice attempted to have his vasectomy reversed, had knowledge of and paid for tests and medical bills, accepted joint responsibility for the child, and listed the child as a dependent on his federal income tax return. Adams, 174 Ill.App.3d at 613–15, 124 Ill.Dec. 184, 528 N.E.2d 1075. This court reversed and remanded the cause, on other grounds, holding that Florida law governed because the parties had resided in that state when the procedure was performed. Adams, 133 Ill.2d at 448, 141 Ill.Dec. 448, 551 N.E.2d 635. We did not, however, reach the issue of whether a cause of action for child support could be maintained under common law theories.

In Witbeck v. Wildhagen, 281 Ill.App.3d 502, 217 Ill.Dec. 329, 667 N.E.2d 122, the husband made it clear that he did not consent to the procedure, and the wife acknowledged that he did not consent. Nonetheless, the wife petitioned to have the husband declared the legal father of her child and she sought child support. The appellate court upheld the trial court's finding that the husband did not consent to the insemination procedure since there was no evidence of the husband's consent, written or otherwise. Witbeck v. Wildhagen, 281 Ill.App.3d at 506–07, 217 Ill.Dec. 329, 667 N.E.2d 122. The appellate court specifically stated that it was not deciding whether the failure to obtain written consent would be an absolute bar to the establishment of the father-child relationship where the conduct of the father otherwise demonstrated his consent. Witbeck v. Wildhagen, 281 Ill.App.3d at 506–07, 217 Ill.Dec. 329, 667 N.E.2d 122. The appellate court recognized that this was not a case where the husband was "attempting to evade responsibility for his own actions in helping to conceive or encouraging the conception of a child." Witbeck v. Wildhagen, 281 Ill.App.3d at 507, 217 Ill.Dec. 329, 667 N.E.2d 122. Although the appellate court reached opposite conclusions in *Adams* and *Witbeck v. Wildhagen,* a finding of the existence or nonexistence of consent was based on an examination of the specific facts in each case.

In interpreting the Illinois Parentage Act, this court has specifically noted that "[i]t may be the case that a support obligation will be found even in the absence of a parent-child relationship." In re Marriage of Adams, 133 Ill.2d 437, 445, 141 Ill.Dec. 448, 551 N.E.2d 635 (1990). In *Adams,* this court recognized its duty, in an action where the interests of a minor are at stake, to ensure that the rights of the child are adequately protected. Adams, 133 Ill.2d at 445, 141 Ill.Dec. 448, 551 N.E.2d 635, citing Muscarello v. Peterson, 20 Ill.2d 548, 170 N.E.2d 564 (1960). We also suggested that estoppel might be available to prove consent. Adams, 133 Ill.2d at 448, 141 Ill.Dec. 448, 551 N.E.2d 635

Illinois has articulated its public policy recognizing the right of every child to the physical, mental, emotional, and monetary support of his or her parents. See 750 ILCS 45/1.1 (West 1998). Public policy considerations also seek to prevent children born as a result of assisted reproductive technology procedures from becoming public charges. See Department of Public Aid ex rel. Cox v. Miller, 146 Ill.2d 399, 411–12,

166 Ill.Dec. 922, 586 N.E.2d 1251 (1992) (concluding that the legislature intends to provide parental support for all minor children and commenting that "[l]egislative common sense dictates that if parents do not support their children, an already strained State welfare system must do so"). Illinois has a strong interest in protecting and promoting the welfare of its children. See In re Marriage of Lappe, 176 Ill.2d 414, 431, 223 Ill.Dec. 647, 680 N.E.2d 380 (1997). We believe that, consistently with this important public policy, cases involving assisted reproduction must be decided based on the particular circumstances presented. . . .

We believe that if the legislature had intended to bar common law actions for child support, it would have clearly stated its intent, and we will not imply a legislative intent where none is expressed. See Nottage, 172 Ill.2d at 395, 217 Ill.Dec. 298, 667 N.E.2d 91. We therefore determine that the best interests of children and society are served by recognizing that parental responsibility may be imposed based on conduct evincing actual consent to the artificial insemination procedure.

The courts of other states have reached similar results and have assigned parental responsibility based on conduct evincing consent to the artificial insemination. See Gursky v. Gursky, 39 Misc.2d 1083, 242 N.Y.S.2d 406 (1963) (husband held liable for support of a child conceived by artificial insemination under either the basis of implied consent to support or the application of the doctrine of estoppel); K.S. v. G.S., 182 N.J.Super. 102, 440 A.2d 64 (1981) (oral consent of husband was effective at the time pregnancy occurs unless established by clear and convincing evidence that consent has been revoked or rescinded); In re Marriage of L.M.S., 105 Wis.2d 118, 122–23, 312 N.W.2d 853, 855 (App.1981) (sterile man who suggested to his wife that she become pregnant by another man and promised that he would acknowledge the child as his own has a legal obligation "to support the child for whose existence he is responsible"); In re Baby Doe, 291 S.C. 389, 353 S.E.2d 877 (1987) (husband's consent to artificial insemination may be express, or implied from conduct).

Here, Raymond's *alleged* conduct evinces a powerful case of actual consent. The allegations demonstrate a deliberate course of conduct with the precise goal of causing the birth of these children. In comparison, statutes and case law do not equivocate in imposing child support obligations for other children born out of wedlock. Moreover, a state may not discriminate against a child based on the marital status of the parties at the time of the child's birth. See Miller, 146 Ill.2d at 405, 166 Ill.Dec. 922, 586 N.E.2d 1251; Gomez v. Perez, 409 U.S. 535, 538, 93 S.Ct. 872, 875, 35 L.Ed.2d 56, 60 (1973); Mills v. Habluetzel, 456 U.S. 91, 92, 102 S.Ct. 1549, 1551, 71 L.Ed.2d 770, 773 (1982). Thus, if an unmarried man who biologically causes conception through sexual relations without the premeditated intent of birth is legally obligated to support a child, then the equivalent resulting birth of a child caused by the deliberate conduct of artificial insemination should receive the same treatment in the eyes of the law. Regardless of the method of conception, a child is born in need of support. Under the alleged facts of this case, to hold otherwise would deprive the children of financial support merely because of deception and a technical oversight. Simply put, we cannot accept Raymond's argument that these children and their mother must be left to fend for themselves.

Claims of parentage and support of children produced as a result of assisted reproductive technologies are unique and must be decided based on the particular facts in each case. We hold that the Illinois Parentage Act does not preclude Alexis' claims based on common law theories of oral contract or promissory estoppel. Accordingly, the circuit court erred in dismissing counts I and II of Alexis' complaint on this basis, and the appellate court erred in affirming that order. We make no determination on the merits of Alexis' claims, or Raymond's affirmative defenses, including the Frauds Act, since these claims and defenses must be developed in the circuit court. . . .

For the foregoing reasons, we affirm that part of the appellate court judgment affirming the circuit court's dismissal of count III of Alexis' complaint, we reverse that part of the judgment of the appellate court affirming the dismissal of Alexis' claim for child support under counts I and II, and we remand the cause to the circuit court of Cook County for further proceedings not inconsistent with this opinion.

Judgments affirmed in part and reversed in part; cause remanded.

NOTES

The two prior decisions, *Buzzanca* and *In re* M.J. establish paternity through the consent freely given by persons intending to become parents but without a genetic connection. In neither case was the father genetically connected to the child, hence paternity resulted through statutory means (*Buzzanca*) or common law promissory estoppel (*In re* M.J.). The issue of consensual parenthood has prompted commentary. *See, e.g.*, Leora I. Gabry, *Procreating Without Pregnancy: Surrogacy and the Need for a Comprehensive Regulatory Scheme*, 5 COLUM. J.L. & SOC. PROBS. 415 (2012); Melanie B. Jacobs, *Intentional Parenthood's Influence: Rethinking Procreative Autonomy and Federal Paternity Establishment Policy*, 20 AM. U. J. GENDER SOC. POL'Y & L. 489 (2012).

Statutes, such as the Uniform Parentage Act, and judicial opinions involving ART cannot keep pace with the technological advances in assisted reproductive technology. Even parenthood by consent will not suffice in the near future, as predicted by commentators. *See* Yehezkel Margalit, Orrie Levy, John Loike, *The New Frontier of Advanced Reproductive Technology: Reevaluating Modern Legal Parenthood*, 37 HARV. J. L. & GENDER 107, 116–117 (2014):

> While both case law and academic literature have increasingly relied on intentional parenthood as the preferred model to determine parentage in the context of ARTs, advances in ARTs in the future may require a more nuanced view of the parental paradigms, particularly with respect to same-sex couples. New

technologies may in the future allow two women to create a child with whom they both share an equal genetic link, without requiring any male genetic contribution, or two men to create a child with only a minimal female genetic contribution. By eliminating the potential parental claim of a third biological parent, this technology would bolster the utility of the genetic and gestational paradigms. On the other hand, this technology could allow multiple parties to contribute genetically to a child, necessitating reliance on intentional parenthood.

UNIFORM PARENTAGE ACT OF 2000 (AMENDED 2002)

Section 201. Establishment of Parent-Child Relationship

* * *

(b) The father-child relationship is established between a man and a child by . . .

(2) an effective acknowledgement of paternity by the man under [Article] 3, unless the acknowledgement has been rescinded or successfully challenged . . .

(5) the man's having consented to assisted reproduction by a woman under [Article] 7 which resulted in the birth of a child.

Section 204. Presumption of Paternity

(a) A man is presumed to be the father of a child if . . .

(5) for the first two years of the child's life, he resided in the same household with the child and openly held out the child as his own.

Section 302. Execution of Acknowledgement of Paternity

(a) An acknowledgement of paternity must:

(1) be in a record;

(2) be signed, or otherwise authenticated, under penalty of perjury by the mother and by the man seeking to establish his paternity;

(3) state that the child whose paternity is being acknowledged:

(A) does not have a presumed father, or has a presumed father whose full name is stated; and

(B) does not have another acknowledged or adjudicated father;

(4) state whether there has been genetic testing and, if so, that the acknowledging man's claim of paternity is consistent with the results of the testing; and

(5) state that the signatories understand that the acknowledgement is the equivalent of a judicial

adjudication of paternity of the child and that a challenge to the acknowledgement is permitted only under limited circumstances and is barred after two years.

2. DISPOSITION OF HUMAN GENETIC MATERIALS AT DIVORCE

J.B. v. M.B. and C.C.

Supreme Court of New Jersey, 2001
783 A.2d 707

■ The opinion of the Court was delivered by PORITZ, C.J.

In this case, a divorced couple disagree about the disposition of seven preembryos[1] that remain in storage after the couple, during their marriage, undertook in vitro fertilization procedures. We must first decide whether the husband and wife have entered into an enforceable contract that is now determinative on the disposition issue. If not, we must consider how such conflicts should be resolved by our courts. Although the reproductive technology to accomplish in vitro fertilization has existed since the 1970s, there is little caselaw to guide us in our inquiry.

J.B. and M.B. were married in February 1992. After J.B. suffered a miscarriage early in the marriage, the couple encountered difficulty conceiving a child and sought medical advice from the Jefferson Center for Women's Specialties. Although M.B. did not have infertility problems, J.B. learned that she had a condition that prevented her from becoming pregnant. On that diagnosis, the couple decided to attempt in vitro fertilization at the Cooper Center for In Vitro Fertilization, P.C. (the Cooper Center).

The in vitro fertilization procedure requires a woman to undergo a series of hormonal injections to stimulate the production of mature oocytes[2] (egg cells or ova). The medication causes the ovaries to release multiple egg cells during a menstrual cycle rather than the single egg normally produced. The egg cells are retrieved from the woman's body and examined by a physician who evaluates their quality for fertilization. Egg cells ready for insemination are then combined with a sperm sample and allowed to incubate for approximately twelve to eighteen hours. Successful fertilization results in a zygote[3] that develops into a four-to eight-cell preembryo. At that stage, the preembryos are either returned

---

[1] A preembryo is a fertilized ovum (egg cell) up to approximately fourteen days old (the point when it implants in the uterus). *The American Heritage Stedman's Medical Dictionary* 667 (1995). Throughout this opinion, we use the term "preembryo," rather than "embryo," because preembryo is technically descriptive of the cells' stage of development when they are cryopreserved (frozen).

[2] Oocytes are cells from which an egg or ovum develops. *Id.* at 578.

[3] A zygote is a fertilized ovum before it undergoes cell division. *Id.* at 906.

to the woman's uterus for implantation or cryopreserved at a temperature of –196 C and stored for possible future use.

A limited number of preembryos are implanted at one time to reduce the risk of a multiple pregnancy. Cryopreservation of unused preembryos reduces, and may eliminate, the need for further ovarian stimulation and egg retrieval, thereby reducing the medical risks and costs associated with both the hormone regimen and the surgical removal of egg cells from the woman's body. Cryopreservation also permits introduction of the preembryos into the uterus at the optimal time in the natural cycle for pregnancy. Egg cells must be fertilized before undergoing cryopreservation because unfertilized cells are difficult to preserve and, once preserved, are difficult to fertilize.

The Cooper Center's consent form describes the procedure:

> IVF [or in vitro fertilization] will be accomplished in a routine fashion: that is, ovulation induction followed by egg recovery, insemination, fertilization, embryo development and embryo transfer of up to three or four embryos in the stimulated cycle. With the couple's consent, any "extra" embryos beyond three or four will be cryopreserved according to our freezing protocol and stored at –196 C. Extra embryos, upon thawing, must meet certain criteria for viability before being considered eligible for transfer. These criteria require that a certain minimum number of cells composing the embryo survive the freeze-thaw process. These extra embryos will be transferred into the woman's uterus in one or more future menstrual cycles for the purpose of establishing a normal pregnancy. The physicians and embryologists on the IVF team will be responsible for determining the appropriate biological conditions and the timing for transfers of cryopreserved embryos.

The consent form also contains language discussing the control and disposition of the preembryos:

> The control and disposition of the embryos belongs to the Patient and her Partner. You will be asked to execute the attached legal statement regarding control and disposition of cryopreserved embryos. The IVF team will not be obligated to proceed with the transfer of any cryopreserved embryos if experience indicates the risks outweigh the benefits.

Before undertaking in vitro fertilization in March 1995, the Cooper Center gave J.B. and M.B. the consent form with an attached agreement for their signatures. The agreement states, in relevant part:

> I, J.B. (patient), and M.B. (partner), agree that all control, direction, and ownership of our tissues will be relinquished to the IVF Program under the following circumstances:

> 1. A dissolution of our marriage by court order, unless the court specifies who takes control and direction of the tissues . . . .

The in vitro fertilization procedure was carried out in May 1995 and resulted in eleven preembryos. Four were transferred to J.B. and seven were cryopreserved. J.B. became pregnant, either as a result of the procedure or through natural means, and gave birth to the couple's daughter on March 19, 1996. In September 1996, however, the couple separated, and J.B. informed M.B. that she wished to have the remaining preembryos discarded. M.B. did not agree.

J.B. filed a complaint for divorce on November 25, 1996, in which she sought an order from the court "with regard to the eight[4] frozen embryos." In a counterclaim filed on November 24, 1997, M.B. demanded judgment compelling his wife "to allow the (8) eight frozen embryos currently in storage to be implanted or donated to other infertile couples." J.B. filed a motion for summary judgment on the preembryo issue in April 1998 alleging, in a certification filed with the motion, that she had intended to use the preembryos solely within her marriage to M.B. She stated:

> Defendant and I made the decision to attempt conception through in vitro fertilization treatment. Those decisions were made during a time when defendant and I were married and intended to remain married. Defendant and I planned to raise a family together as a married couple. I endured the in vitro process and agreed to preserve the preembryos for our use in the context of an intact family.

J.B. also certified that "[t]here were never any discussions between the Defendant and I regarding the disposition of the frozen embryos should our marriage be dissolved." M.B., in a cross-motion filed in July 1998, described his understanding very differently. He certified that he and J.B. had agreed prior to undergoing the in vitro fertilization procedure that any unused preembryos would not be destroyed, but would be used by his wife or donated to infertile couples. His certification stated:

> Before we began the I.V.F. treatments, we had many long and serious discussions regarding the process and the moral and ethical repercussions. For me, as a Catholic, the I.V.F. procedure itself posed a dilemma. We discussed this issue extensively and had agreed that no matter what happened the eggs would be either utilized by us or by other infertile couples. In fact, the option to donate [the preembryos] to infertile couples was the Plaintiff's idea. She came up with this idea because she knew of other individuals in her work place who were having trouble conceiving. M.B.'s mother, father, and sister also

[4] As noted above, seven had actually been cryopreserved.

certified that on several occasions during family gatherings J.B. had stated her intention to either use or donate the preembryos.

The couple's final judgment of divorce, entered in September 1998, resolved all issues except disposition of the preembryos. Shortly thereafter, the trial court granted J.B.'s motion for summary judgment on that issue. The court found that the reason for the parties' decision to attempt in vitro fertilization—to create a family as a married couple—no longer existed. J.B. and M.B. had become parents and were now divorced. Moreover, M.B. was not infertile and could achieve parenthood in the future through natural means. The court did not accept M.B.'s argument that the parties undertook the in vitro fertilization procedure to "create life," and found no need for further fact finding on the existence of an agreement between them, noting that there was no written contract memorializing the parties' intentions. Because the husband was "fully able to father a child," and because he sought control of the preembryos "merely to donate them to another couple," the court concluded that the wife had "the greater interest and should prevail."

The Appellate Division affirmed. J.B. v. M.B., 331 N.J.Super. 223, 751 A.2d 613 (2000). The court noted the inconsistency between the trial court's finding that "the parties engaged in IVF to create their child within the context of their marriage" and M.B.'s claim that the couple had entered into an agreement to donate or use, and not to destroy, the preembryos. *Id.* at 228, 751 A.2d 613. Before the Appellate Division, the husband argued that his constitutional right to procreate had been violated by the ruling of the trial court and sought a remand to establish the parties' understanding regarding the disposition of the preembryos. *Ibid.*

The Appellate Division understood this case to "involv[e] an attempt to enforce an alleged agreement to use embryos to create a child." *Id.* at 231, 751 A.2d 613. It initially examined that "attempt" in the context of two fundamental rights, "the right to procreate and the right not to procreate," citing Skinner v. Oklahoma, 316 U.S. 535, 541, 62 S.Ct. 1110, 1113, 86 L. Ed. 1655, 1660 (1942), and Roe v. Wade, 410 U.S. 113, 152–53, 93 S.Ct. 705, 726, 35 L. Ed.2d 147, 176–77 (1973), among other cases. J.B., supra, 331 N.J.Super. at 231–32, 751 A.2d 613. The court found that, on the facts presented, the conflict between those rights was "more apparent than real." *Id.* at 232, 751 A.2d 613. It observed that destruction of the preembryos would not seriously impair M.B.'s constitutional right to procreate since "he retains the capacity to father children." *Ibid.* In contrast, allowing donation or use of the preembryos would impair J.B.'s right not to procreate "[e]ven if [she was] relieved of the financial and custodial responsibility for her child" because she would then have been forced to allow strangers to raise that child. *Ibid.* In those circumstances, and assuming "that the Fourteenth Amendment applies," the court found no impairment of the husband's constitutional rights. *Ibid.*

Nonetheless, the court chose not to decide this case on constitutional grounds. . . . In affirming the judgment of the trial court in favor of J.B., the panel considered the parties' views and the trial court's opinion, and determined that destruction of the preembryos was required.

M.B. contends that the judgment of the court below violated his constitutional rights to procreation and the care and companionship of his children. He also contends that his constitutional rights outweigh J.B.'s right not to procreate because her right to bodily integrity is not implicated, as it would be in a case involving abortion. He asserts that religious convictions regarding preservation of the preembryos, and the State's interest in protecting potential life, take precedence over his former wife's more limited interests. Finally, M.B. argues that the Appellate Division should have enforced the clear agreement between the parties to give the preembryos a chance at life. He believes that his procedural due process rights have been violated because he was not given an opportunity to introduce evidence demonstrating the existence of that agreement, and because summary judgment is inappropriate in a case involving novel issues of fact and law.

J.B. argues that the Appellate Division properly held that any alleged agreement between the parties to use or donate the preembryos would be unenforceable as a matter of public policy. She contends that New Jersey has "long recognized that individuals should not be bound by agreements requiring them to enter into family relationships or [that] seek to regulate personal intimate decisions relating to parenthood and family life." J.B. also argues that in the absence of an express agreement establishing the disposition of the preembryos, a court should not imply that an agreement exists. It is J.B.'s position that requiring use or donation of the preembryos would violate her constitutional right not to procreate. Discarding the preembryos, on the other hand, would not significantly affect M.B.'s right to procreate because he is fertile and capable of fathering another child. . . .

M.B. contends that he and J.B. entered into an agreement to use or donate the preembryos, and J.B. disputes the existence of any such agreement. As an initial matter, then, we must decide whether this case involves a contract for the disposition of the cryopreserved preembryos resulting from in vitro fertilization. We begin, therefore, with the consent form provided to J.B. and M.B. by the Cooper Center. . . . That form states, among other things:

> The control and disposition of the embryos belongs to the Patient and her Partner. You will be asked to execute the attached legal statement regarding control and disposition of cryopreserved embryos.

The attachment, executed by J.B. and M.B., provides further detail in respect of the parties' "control and disposition": I, J.B. (patient), and M.B. (partner) agree that all control, direction, and ownership of our tissues will be relinquished to the IVF Program under the following circumstances:

> 1. A dissolution of our marriage by court order, unless the court specifies who takes control and direction of the tissues, or
>
> 2. In the event of death of both of the above named individuals, or unless provisions are made in a Will, or
>
> 3. When the patient is no longer capable of sustaining a normal pregnancy, however, the couple has the right to keep embryos maintained for up to two years before making a decision [regarding a] "host womb" or
>
> 4. At any time by our/my election which shall be in writing, or
>
> 5. When a patient fails to pay periodic embryo maintenance payment.

The consent form, and more important, the attachment, do not manifest a clear intent by J.B. and M.B. regarding disposition of the preembryos in the event of "[a] dissolution of [their] marriage." Although the attachment indicates that the preembryos "will be relinquished" to the clinic if the parties divorce, it carves out an exception that permits the parties to obtain a court order directing disposition of the preembryos. That reading is consistent with other provisions of the attachment allowing for disposition by a last will and testament "[i]n the event of death," or "by our/my election . . . in writing." Clearly, the thrust of the document signed by J.B. and M.B. is that the Cooper Center obtains control over the preembryos unless the parties choose otherwise in a writing, or unless a court specifically directs otherwise in an order of divorce.

The conditional language employed in the attachment stands in sharp contrast to the language in the informed consents provided by the hospital in Kass v. Kass, 91 N.Y.2d 554, 673 N.Y.S.2d 350, 696 N.E.2d 174 (N.Y.1998). In *Kass,* the New York Court of Appeals enforced a couple's memorialized decision to donate their preembryos for scientific research when they could not agree on disposition. The court found that the parties had signed an unambiguous contract to relinquish control of their preembryos to the hospital for research purposes in the event of a dispute. In that case, the parties executed several forms before undergoing in vitro fertilization. Informed Consent No. 2 stated:

> In the event of divorce, we understand that legal ownership of any stored pre-zygotes[5] must be determined in a property settlement and will be released as directed by order of a court of competent jurisdiction.

---

[5] The term "pre-zygote" is used in the forms and in the opinion of the New York court where this opinion uses the term "preembryo."

Addendum No. 2–1 further elaborated:

In the event that we . . . are unable to make a decision regarding the disposition of our stored, frozen pre-zygotes, we now indicate our desire for the disposition of our pre-zygotes and direct the IVF Program to (choose one):

Our frozen pre-zygotes may be examined by the IVF Program for biological studies and be disposed of by the IVF Program for approved research investigation as determined by the IVF Program.

Moreover, before the parties divorced, they drafted and signed an " 'uncontested divorce' agreement" indicating that their preembryos "should be disposed of [in] the manner outlined in our consent form and [neither party] will lay claim to custody of these pre-zygotes." *Id.* at 177.[6]

The *Kass* court found that the parties had agreed to donate their preembryos for IVF research if they could not together decide on another disposition. The court interpreted the provision of the consent form dealing directly with divorce to indicate only that the parties' agreement would be embodied in a document of divorce, noting that the couple had, indeed, endorsed an " 'uncontested divorce' instrument" ratifying the consent forms they had signed earlier. That holding is based on language entirely different from the language in the form in this case. Here, the parties have agreed that on the dissolution of their marriage the Cooper Center obtains control of the preembryos unless the court specifically makes another determination. Under that provision, the parties have sought another determination from the court.

M.B. asserts, however, that he and J.B. jointly intended another disposition. Because there are no other writings that express the parties' intentions, M.B. asks the Court either to remand for an evidentiary hearing on that issue or to consider his certified statement. In his statement, he claims that before undergoing in vitro fertilization the couple engaged in extensive discussions in which they agreed to use the preembryos themselves or donate them to others. In opposition, J.B. has certified that the parties never discussed the disposition of unused preembryos and that there was no agreement on that issue.

We find no need for a remand to determine the parties' intentions at the time of the in vitro fertilization process. Assuming that it would be possible to enter into a valid agreement at that time irrevocably deciding the disposition of preembryos in circumstances such as we have here, a formal, unambiguous memorialization of the parties' intentions would be required to confirm their joint determination. The parties do not contest the lack of such a writing. We hold, therefore, that J.B. and M.B. never entered into a separate binding contract. . . .

---

[6] Although the agreement was never finalized, it was accepted by the New York court as "reaffirm[ing] the [parties'] earlier understanding. . . . " *Id.* at 181.

In essence, J.B. and M.B. have agreed only that on their divorce the decision in respect of control, and therefore disposition, of their cryopreserved preembryos will be directed by the court. In this area, however, there are few guideposts for decision-making. Advances in medical technology have far outstripped the development of legal principles to resolve the inevitable disputes arising out of the new reproductive opportunities now available. For infertile couples, those opportunities may present the only way to have a biological family. Yet, at the point when a husband and wife decide to begin the in vitro fertilization process, they are unlikely to anticipate divorce or to be concerned about the disposition of preembryos on divorce. As they are both contributors of the genetic material comprising the preembryos, the decision should be theirs to make. . .

But what if, as here, the parties disagree. Without guidance from the Legislature, we must consider a means by which courts can engage in a principled review of the issues presented in such cases in order to achieve a just result. Because the claims before us derive, in part, from concepts found in the Federal Constitution and the Constitution of this State, we begin with those concepts.

Both parties and the ACLU *Amici* invoke the right to privacy in support of their respective positions. More specifically, they claim procreational autonomy as a fundamental attribute of the privacy rights guaranteed by both the Federal and New Jersey Constitutions. Their arguments are based on various opinions of the United States Supreme Court that discuss the right to be free from governmental interference with procreational decisions. See Eisenstadt v. Baird, 405 U.S. 438, 453, 92 S.Ct. 1029, 1038, 31 L. Ed.2d 349, 362 (1972); Griswold v. Connecticut, 381 U.S. 479, 485–86, 85 S.Ct. 1678, 1682, 14 L. Ed.2d 510, 515–16 (1965); Skinner v. Oklahoma, 316 U.S. 535, 541, 62 S.Ct. 1110, 1113, 86 L. Ed. 1655, 1660 (1942). . . .

This Court also has recognized the fundamental nature of procreational rights. In *In re Baby M,* we considered a custody dispute between a father and a surrogate mother. 109 N.J. 396, 537 A.2d 1227 (1988). Although the case involved the enforceability of a surrogacy contract, the father asserted that his right to procreate supported his claim for custody of Baby M. We held that the right to procreate was not implicated by the custody battle, which dealt with parental rights after birth. We observed, however, that "the rights of personal intimacy, of marriage, of sex, of family, of procreation . . . are fundamental rights protected by both the federal and state Constitutions." *Id.* at 447, 537 A.2d 1227; *see also* In re Grady, 85 N.J. 235, 247–48, 426 A.2d 467 (1981) (recognizing that decisions in *Griswold* and *Eisenstadt* ended "any doubt about a personal right to prevent conception," and holding that "an individual's constitutional right of privacy includes the right to undergo sterilization voluntarily"); *cf.* Schroeder v. Perkel, 87 N.J. 53, 66, 432 A.2d 834 (1981) (allowing recovery against defendants whose negligent diagnosis deprived mother of right to choose not to conceive child with genetic defect).

Those decisions provide a framework within which disputes over the disposition of preembryos can be resolved. In *Davis, supra,* for example, a divorced couple could not agree on the disposition of their unused, cryopreserved preembryos. 842 *S.W.*2d at 589. The Tennessee Supreme Court balanced the right to procreate of the party seeking to donate the preembryos (the wife), against the right not to procreate of the party seeking destruction of the preembryos (the husband). *Id.* at 603. The court concluded that the husband's right would be significantly affected by unwanted parenthood "with all of its possible financial and psychological consequences." *Ibid.* In his case, that burden was the greater because, as a child, he had been separated from his parents after they divorced and his mother suffered a nervous breakdown. *Id.* at 603–04. Because of his personal experiences, the husband was "vehemently opposed to fathering a child that would not live with both parents." *Id.* at 604.

Against that interest, the court weighed the wife's "burden of knowing that the lengthy IVF procedures she underwent were futile, and that the preembryos to which she contributed genetic material would never become children." *Ibid.* Although that burden was not insignificant, the court found that it did not outweigh the father's interest in avoiding procreation. *Ibid.* The court held that the scales "[o]rdinarily" would tip in favor of the right not to procreate if the opposing party could become a parent through other reasonable means. *Ibid.*

We agree with the Tennessee Supreme Court that "[o]rdinarily, the party wishing to avoid procreation should prevail." *Ibid.* Here, the Appellate Division succinctly described the "apparent" conflict between J.B. and M.B.:

> In the present case, the wife's right not to become a parent seemingly conflicts with the husband's right to procreate. The conflict, however, is more apparent than real. Recognition and enforcement of the wife's right would not seriously impair the husband's right to procreate. Though his right to procreate using the wife's egg would be terminated, he retains the capacity to father children.

[J.B., supra, 331 N.J.Super. at 232, 751 A.2d 613.]

In other words, M.B.'s right to procreate is not lost if he is denied an opportunity to use or donate the preembryos. M.B. is already a father and is able to become a father to additional children, whether through natural procreation or further in vitro fertilization. In contrast, J.B.'s right not to procreate may be lost through attempted use or through donation of the preembryos. Implantation, if successful, would result in the birth of her biological child and could have life-long emotional and psychological repercussions. . . .[7]

The court below "conclude[d] that a contract to procreate is contrary to New Jersey public policy and is unenforceable." 331 N.J.Super. at 234, 751 A.2d 613. That determination follows the reasoning of the Massachusetts Supreme Judicial Court in *A.Z. v. B.Z.,* wherein an agreement to compel biological parenthood was deemed unenforceable as a matter of public policy. 431 Mass. 150, 725 N.E.2d 1051, 1057–58 (2000). The Massachusetts court likened enforcement of a contract permitting implantation of preembryos to other contracts to enter into familial relationships that were unenforceable under the laws of Massachusetts, *i.e.,* contracts to marry or to give up a child for adoption prior to the fourth day after birth. *Id.* at 1058. In a similar vein, the court previously had refused to enforce a surrogacy contract without a reasonable waiting period during which the surrogate mother could revoke her consent, and a contract to abandon or to prevent marriage. *Id.* at 1059. Likewise, the court declined to enforce a contract that required an individual to become a parent. *Id.* at 1058.

As the Appellate Division opinion in this case points out, the laws of New Jersey also evince a policy against enforcing private contracts to enter into or terminate familial relationships. 331 N.J.Super. at 234–35, 751 A.2d 613. New Jersey has, by statute, abolished the cause of action for breach of contract to marry. N.J.S.A. 2A:23–1. Private placement adoptions are disfavored, Sees v. Baber, 74 N.J. 201, 217, 377 A.2d 628 (1977), and may be approved over the objection of a parent only if that parent has failed or is unable to perform "the regular and expected parental functions of care and support of the child." N.J.S.A. 9:3–46; *see* N.J.S.A. 9:3–48 (stating statutory requirements for private placement adoption).

That public policy also led this Court to conclude in *Baby M, supra,* that a surrogacy contract was unenforceable. 109 N.J. at 433–34, 537 A.2d 1227. We held that public policy prohibited a binding agreement to require a surrogate, there the biological mother, to surrender her parental rights. *Id.* at 411, 537 A.2d 1227. The contract in *Baby M* provided for a $10,000 payment to the surrogate for her to be artificially inseminated, carry the child to term, and then, after the child's birth, relinquish parental rights to the father and his wife. *Id.* at 411–12, 537

[7] The legal consequences for J.B. also are unclear. *See N.J.A.C.* 8:2–1.4(a) (stating "the woman giving birth shall be recorded as a parent"). We note without comment that a recent case before the Chancery Division in Bergen County concluded that seventy-two hours must pass before a non-biological surrogate mother may surrender her parental rights and the biological mother's name may be placed on the birth certificate. *A.H.W. v. G.H.B.,* 339 *N.J.Super.* 495, 505, 772 *A.*2d 948 (2000). In Arizona, an appellate court determined that a statute allowing a biological father but not a biological mother to prove paternity violated the Equal Protection Clause. *Soos v. Superior Court,* 182 *Ariz.* 470, 897 *P.*2d 1356, 1361 (1995). In California, the legal mother is the person who "intended to bring about the birth of a child that she intended to raise as her own." *Johnson v. Calvert,* 5 *Cal.*4th 84, 19 *Cal.Rptr.*2d 494, 851 *P.*2d 776, 782 (Cal.1993), *cert. denied,* 510 *U.S.* 874, 114 *S.Ct.* 206, 126 *L. Ed.*2d 163, *and cert. dismissed, Baby Boy J. v. Johnson,* 510 *U.S.* 938, 114 *S.Ct.* 374, 126 *L. Ed.*2d 324 (1993).

A.2d 1227. The surrogate mother initially surrendered the child to the father, but subsequently reconsidered her decision and fled with Baby M. In an action by the father to enforce the surrogacy contract, we held that the contract conflicted with "(1) laws prohibiting the use of money in connection with adoptions; (2) laws requiring proof of parental unfitness or abandonment before termination of parental rights is ordered or an adoption is granted; and (3) laws that make surrender of custody and consent to adoption revocable in private placement adoptions." *Id.* at 423, 537 A.2d 1227. Our decision was consistent with the policy expressed earlier in *Sees, supra,* that consent to terminate parental rights was revocable in all but statutorily approved circumstances. 74 N.J. at 212, 377 A.2d 628.

Enforcement of a contract that would allow the implantation of preembryos at some future date in a case where one party has reconsidered his or her earlier acquiescence raises similar issues. If implantation is successful, that party will have been forced to become a biological parent against his or her will. We note disagreement on the issue both among legal commentators and in the limited caselaw on the subject. *Kass, supra,* held that "[a]greements between progenitors, or gamete donors, regarding disposition of their prezygotes should generally be presumed valid and binding, and enforced in a dispute between them. . . ." 673 N.Y.S.2d 350, 696 N.E.2d at 180. The New York court emphasized that such agreements would "avoid costly litigation," "minimize misunderstandings and maximize procreative liberty by reserving to the progenitors the authority to make what is in the first instance a quintessentially personal private decision."; see also New York State Task Force on Life and the Law, *Executive Summary of Assisted Reproductive Technologies: Analysis and Recommendations for Public Policy* (last modified Aug. 1999) http://www.health.ny.gov/regulations/task_force/reports_publications/execsum.htm (stating that "[i]ndividuals or couples who have excess embryos no longer desired for assisted reproduction have a strong interest in controlling the fate of those embryos"); John A. Robertson, Prior Agreements For Disposition of Frozen Embryos, 51 Ohio St. L.J. 407, 409–18 (1990) (arguing that enforcement of advance directives maximizes reproductive freedom, minimizes disputes, and provides certainty to couples and in vitro fertilization programs); Peter E. Malo, Deciding Custody of Frozen Embryos: Many Eggs Are Frozen But Who Is Chosen?, 3 DePaul J. Health Care L. 307, 332 (2000) (favoring mandatory preembryo disposition agreements). Yet, as discussed above, the Massachusetts Supreme Judicial Court as well as our Appellate Division have declared that when agreements compel procreation over the subsequent objection of one of the parties, those agreements are violative of public policy. A.Z., supra, 725 N.E.2d at 1057–58; J.B., supra, 331 N.J.Super. at 234, 751 A.2d 613; *cf.* Coleman, supra, 84 Minn. L.Rev. at 83–84 (suggesting that party objecting to implantation should prevail against infertile party seeking use of preembryos).

We recognize that persuasive reasons exist for enforcing preembryo disposition agreements. *See* Kass, supra, 673 N.Y.S.2d 350, 696 N.E.2d at 179 (noting "need for clear, consistent principles to guide parties in protecting their interests and resolving their disputes"); *Davis, supra,* 842 *S.W.*2d at 597 (discussing benefit of guidance to parties undertaking in vitro fertilization procedures). We also recognize that in vitro fertilization is in widespread use, and that there is a need for agreements between the participants and the clinics that perform the procedure. We believe that the better rule, and the one we adopt, is to enforce agreements entered into at the time in vitro fertilization is begun, subject to the right of either party to change his or her mind about disposition up to the point of use or destruction of any stored preembryos.

The public policy concerns that underlie limitations on contracts involving family relationships are protected by permitting either party to object at a later date to provisions specifying a disposition of preembryos that that party no longer accepts. Moreover, despite the conditional nature of the disposition provisions, in the large majority of cases the agreements will control, permitting fertility clinics and other like facilities to rely on their terms. Only when a party affirmatively notifies a clinic in writing of a change in intention should the disposition issue be reopened. Principles of fairness dictate that agreements provided by a clinic should be written in plain language, and that a qualified clinic representative should review the terms with the parties prior to execution. Agreements should not be signed in blank . . . or in a manner suggesting that the parties have not given due consideration to the disposition question. Those and other reasonable safeguards should serve to limit later disputes.

Finally, if there is disagreement as to disposition because one party has reconsidered his or her earlier decision, the interests of both parties must be evaluated. Because ordinarily the party choosing not to become a biological parent will prevail, we do not anticipate increased litigation as a result of our decision. In this case, after having considered that M.B. is a father and is capable of fathering additional children, we have affirmed J.B.'s right to prevent implantation of the preembryos. We express no opinion in respect of a case in which a party who has become infertile seeks use of stored preembryos against the wishes of his or her partner, noting only that the possibility of adoption also may be a consideration, among others, in the court's assessment.

Under the judgment of the Appellate Division, the seven remaining preembryos are to be destroyed. It was represented to us at oral argument, however, that J.B. does not object to their continued storage if M.B. wishes to pay any fees associated with that storage. M.B. must inform the trial court forthwith whether he will do so; otherwise, the preembryos are to be destroyed.

The judgment of the Appellate Division is affirmed as modified.

■ VERNIERO, J., concurring.

I join in the disposition of this case and in all but one aspect of the Court's opinion. I do not agree with the Court's suggestion, in *dicta,* that the right to procreate may depend on adoption as a consideration.

I also write to express my view that the same principles that compel the outcome in this case would permit an infertile party to assert his or her right to use a preembryo against the objections of the other party, if such use were the only means of procreation. In that instance, the balance arguably would weigh in favor of the infertile party absent countervailing factors of greater weight. I do not decide that profound question today, and the Court should not decide it or suggest a result, because it is absent from this case.

■ ZAZZALI, J., concurring.

I join in the Court's opinion, except as noted by Justice Verniero's concurring opinion, which I also join. I write separately to note that these difficult disputes all too often prompt dire predictions. And yet, most assuredly, developing technologies will give rise to many more such controversies in the future. The resolution of those controversies depends on the amount of caution, compassion, and common sense we summon up as we balance the competing interests. The significance of those interests underscores the need for continued careful and deliberate decisionmaking, infused with equity, in this developing jurisprudence.

NOTES

The law pertaining to the disposition of human genetic materials at divorce (or termination of a nonmarital relationship) is far from settled. Analysis of state approaches indicates that there are three alternatives when deciding how to dispose of these materials upon any divorce: (1) contractual, (2) balancing of interests, and (3) contemporaneous mutual consent of the divorcing couple. The New Jersey Supreme Court in *J.B. v. M.B. and C.C.* agreed with the Tennessee Supreme Court in stating that ordinarily the party wishing to avoid procreation should prevail, concluding that a person should not be forced to become a parent against his or her will. Likewise, the New Jersey court joined with the Massachusetts Supreme Court in holding that enforcing a contractual approach is against public policy. Nonetheless, the New Jersey court stated its willingness to enforce agreements entered into at the time of the storage of the materials, but only if either of the parties could change his or her mind at the dissolution of the marriage or upon the use or destruction of the materials. Overall, the New Jersey approach favors the balancing of interests.

When the Iowa Supreme Court considered the issue in *In re* Marriage of Witten, 672 N.W.2d 768 (Iowa 2003), the court recognized that the couple had signed a storage agreement for disposal of the human material, but the agreement did not reference divorce, only death. Nonetheless, the court held that the agreement's terms were broad enough to encompass divorce and hence held the agreement applicable. The court considers the three approaches identified as possible among the states, and concludes that agreements between the parties should be enforced as long as neither of the parties has changed his or her mind. If there is a change, then the court holds that the status quo should be maintained. Also, if a stalemate results, the status quo would be maintained. "The practical effect will be that the embryos are stored indefinitely unless both parties can agree to destroy the fertilized eggs. Thus, any expense associated with maintaining the status quo should logically be borne by the person opposing destruction." *Id.* at 783.

The Illinois Appellate Court confronted the disposition of human genetic materials not upon divorce, but upon the dissolution of a nonmarital relationship. Szafranski v. Dunston, 993 N.E.2d 502 (Ill. Ct. App. 2013). The couple signed a cryopreservation agreement that did not address the issue of disposition of the materials should the nonmarital relationship end. Shortly after signing the agreement they deposited sperm and eggs with the clinic the eggs were later fertilized with the sperm. One month later, one of the partners sent the other a text message ending the relationship and three months later filed an injunction to prohibit the use of the embryos at any time in the future. The other party wished to use her eggs, which had been fertilized with the man's sperm but he refused her permission to use them. The court discusses both the *Witten* approach (contemporaneous mutual consent) and the *J.B. v. M.B. and C.C.* approach (balancing approach), but adopts a contractual approach. "Having considered the arguments of the parties and case law from other jurisdictions, we believe that the best approach for resolving disputes over the disposition of pre-embryos created with one party's sperm and another party's ova is to honor the parties' own mutually expressed intent as set forth in their prior agreements." *Id.* at 514. Upon remand the circuit court ruled that the couple had an oral agreement that the girlfriend could use the embryos to have a child. The appellate court affirmed this finding and rejected the counter argument put forth by the boyfriend that there was no oral agreement. *See Szafranski v. Dunston*, 34 N.E.3d 1132 (2015).

For additional commentary and practice guidelines pertaining to disposition of human genetic materials at divorce or dissolution of a relationship *see* Susan L. Crockin & Gary A. Debele, *Ethical Issues in Assisted Reproduction: A Primer for Family Law Attorneys*, 7 J. AM. ACAD. MATRIM. LAW. 289 (2015); Meagan R. Marold, *Ice, Ice, Baby! The Division of Frozen Embryos at the Time of Divorce,* 25 HASTINGS WOMEN'S L.J. 179 (2014); Mary Ziegler, *Abortion and the Constitutional Right (Not) to Procreate*, 48 U. RICH. L. REV. 1263 (2014); Michael T. Flannery, *"Rethinking" Embryo Disposition Upon Divorce*, 29 J. CONTEMP. HEALTH L. & POL'Y 233 (2013).

3. POSTHUMOUS CONCEPTION

Woodward v. Commissioner of Social Security

Massachusetts Supreme Judicial Court, 2002
760 N.E.2d 257

■ MARSHALL, C.J.

The United States District Court for the District of Massachusetts has certified the following question to this court. See S.J.C. Rule 1:03, as appearing in 382 Mass. 700 (1981).

> "If a married man and woman arrange for sperm to be withdrawn from the husband for the purpose of artificially impregnating the wife, and the woman is impregnated with that sperm after the man, her husband, has died, will children resulting from such pregnancy enjoy the inheritance rights of natural children under Massachusetts' law of intestate succession?"

We answer the certified question as follows: In certain limited circumstances, a child resulting from posthumous reproduction may enjoy the inheritance rights of "issue" under the Massachusetts intestacy statute. These limited circumstances exist where, as a threshold matter, the surviving parent or the child's other legal representative demonstrates a genetic relationship between the child and the decedent. The survivor or representative must then establish both that the decedent affirmatively consented to posthumous conception and to the support of any resulting child. Even where such circumstances exist, time limitations may preclude commencing a claim for succession rights on behalf of a posthumously conceived child. Because the government has conceded that the timeliness of the wife's paternity action under our intestacy law is irrelevant to her Federal appeal, we do not address that question today. . . .

The undisputed facts and relevant procedural history are as follows. In January, 1993, about three and one-half years after they were married, Lauren Woodward and Warren Woodward were informed that the husband had leukemia. At the time, the couple was childless. Advised that the husband's leukemia treatment might leave him sterile, the Woodwards arranged for a quantity of the husband's semen to be medically withdrawn and preserved, in a process commonly known as "sperm banking." The husband then underwent a bone marrow transplant. The treatment was not successful. The husband died in October, 1993, and the wife was appointed administratrix of his estate.

In October, 1995, the wife gave birth to twin girls. The children were conceived through artificial insemination using the husband's preserved semen. In January, 1996, the wife applied for two forms of Social Security survivor benefits: "child's" benefits under 42 U.S.C. § 402(d)(1) (1994 &

Supp. V 1999), and "mother's" benefits under 42 U.S.C. § 402(g)(1) (1994).[3]

The Social Security Administration (SSA) rejected the wife's claims on the ground that she had not established that the twins were the husband's "children" within the meaning of the Act. In February, 1996, as she pursued a series of appeals from the SSA decision, the wife filed a "complaint for correction of birth record" in the Probate and Family Court against the clerk of the city of Beverly, seeking to add her deceased husband as the "father" on the twins' birth certificates. In October, 1996, a judge in the Probate and Family Court entered a judgment of paternity and an order to amend both birth certificates declaring the deceased husband to be the children's father. In his judgment of paternity, the Probate Court judge did not make findings of fact, other than to state that he "accepts the [s]tipulations of [v]oluntary [a]cknowledgment of [p]arentage of [the children] . . . executed by [the wife] as [m]other, and [the wife], [a]dministratrix of the [e]state of [the husband], for father." See G.L. c. 209C, § 11.

The wife presented the judgment of paternity and the amended birth certificates to the SSA, but the agency remained unpersuaded. A United States administrative law judge, hearing the wife's claims de novo, concluded, among other things, that the children did not qualify for benefits because they "are not entitled to inherit from [the husband] under the Massachusetts intestacy and paternity laws." The appeals council of the SSA affirmed the administrative law judge's decision, which thus became the commissioner's final decision for purposes of judicial review. The wife appealed to the United States District Court for the District of Massachusetts, seeking a declaratory judgment to reverse the commissioner's ruling.

The United States District Court judge certified the above question to this court because "[t]he parties agree that a determination of these children's rights under the law of Massachusetts is dispositive of the case and . . . no directly applicable Massachusetts precedent exists." We have been asked to determine the inheritance rights under Massachusetts law of children conceived from the gametes of a deceased individual and his or her surviving spouse. We have not previously been asked to consider whether our intestacy statute accords inheritance rights to posthumously conceived genetic children. Nor has any American court of last resort considered, in a published opinion, the question of posthumously

[3] At the time of his death, the husband was a fully insured individual under the United States Social Security Act (Act). Section 402(d)(1) of 42 U.S.C. provides "child's" benefits to dependent children of deceased parents who die fully insured under the Act. See 42 U.S.C. § 402(d)(1); 20 C.F.R. § 404.350. Section 402(g)(1) of 42 U.S.C. provides "mother's" benefits to the widow of an individual who died fully insured under the Act, if, inter alia, she has care of a child or children entitled to child's benefits. See 42 U.S.C. § 402(g)(1); 20 C.F.R. § 404.339 (2001). Thus, the wife's eligibility for Social Security survivor benefits hinges on her children's eligibility for such benefits.

conceived genetic children's inheritance rights under other States' intestacy laws.

This case presents a narrow set of circumstances, yet the issues it raises are far reaching. Because the law regarding the rights of posthumously conceived children is unsettled, the certified question is understandably broad. Moreover, the parties have articulated extreme positions. The wife's principal argument is that, by virtue of their genetic connection with the decedent, posthumously conceived children must *always* be permitted to enjoy the inheritance rights of the deceased parent's children under our law of intestate succession. The government's principal argument is that, because posthumously conceived children are not "in being" as of the date of the parent's death, they are *always* barred from enjoying such inheritance rights.

Neither party's position is tenable. In this developing and relatively uncharted area of human relations, bright-line rules are not favored unless the applicable statute requires them. The Massachusetts intestacy statute does not. Neither the statute's "posthumous children" provision, see G.L. c. 190, § 8, nor any other provision of our intestacy law limits the class of posthumous children to those in utero at the time of the decedent's death. Cf. La. Civ.Code Ann. art. 939 (West 2000) ("A successor must exist at the death of the decedent"). On the other hand, with the act of procreation now separated from coitus, posthumous reproduction can occur under a variety of conditions that may conflict with the purposes of the intestacy law and implicate other firmly established State and individual interests. We look to our intestacy law to resolve these tensions.

We begin our analysis with an overview of Massachusetts intestacy law. In our Commonwealth, the devolution of real and personal property in intestacy is neither a natural nor a constitutional right. It is a privilege conferred by statute. Merchants Nat'l Bank v. Merchants Nat'l Bank, 318 Mass. 563, 573, 62 N.E.2d 831 (1945). Our intestacy statute "excludes all rules of law which might otherwise be operative. It impliedly repealed all preexisting statutes and supersedes the common law." Cassidy v. Truscott, 287 Mass. 515, 521, 192 N.E. 164 (1934).

Section 1 of the intestacy statute directs that, if a decedent "leaves issue," such "issue" will inherit a fixed portion of his real and personal property, subject to debts and expenses, the rights of the surviving spouse, and other statutory payments not relevant here. See G.L. c. 190, § 1. To answer the certified question, then, we must first determine whether the twins are the "issue" of the husband.

The intestacy statute does not define "issue." However, in the context of intestacy the term "issue" means all lineal (genetic) descendants, and now includes both marital and nonmarital descendants. See generally S.M. Dunphy, Probate Law and Practice § 8.5, at 123 (2d ed. 1997 & Supp.2001), and cases cited. See also G.L. c. 4, § 7, Sixteenth ("Issue, as applied to the descent of estates, shall include all the lawful lineal descendants of the ancestor"); Powers v. Wilkinson, 399 Mass. 650, 662, 506 N.E.2d 842 (1987). The term " '[d]escendants' . . . has long been held to mean persons 'who by consanguinity trace their lineage to the designated ancestor.' " Lockwood v. Adamson, 409 Mass. 325, 329, 566 N.E.2d 96 (1991), quoting Evarts v. Davis, 348 Mass. 487, 489, 204 N.E.2d 454 (1965).

The "posthumous children" provision of the intestacy statute, G.L. c. 190, § 8, is yet another expression of the Legislature's intent to preserve wealth for consanguineous descendants. That section provides that "[p]osthumous children shall be considered as living at the death of their parent." The Legislature, however, has left the term "posthumous children" undefined. The Massachusetts intestacy statute originally made no provision for after-born children. See, e.g., St. 1805, c. 90 (approved Mar. 12, 1806). Then in Hall v. Hancock, 15 Pick. 255, 1834 WL 2638 (1834), in the context of a will contest, this court held that a child who was presumptively in utero as of the date of the decedent's death was a child "in being" as of the date of the decedent's death "in all cases where it will be for the benefit of such child to be so considered." *Id.* at 257, 258. Two years later, the Legislature enacted the "posthumous children" provision of the intestacy statute, bringing that devolution mechanism into conformity with our decision concerning wills. See Rev. St. 1836, c. 61, § 13. Despite numerous later amendments to our intestacy laws, the "posthumous children" provision has remained essentially unchanged for 165 years.

The Massachusetts intestacy statute thus does not contain an express, affirmative requirement that posthumous children must "be in existence" as of the date of the decedent's death. The Legislature could surely have enacted such a provision had it desired to do so. Cf. La. Civ.Code Ann. art. 939 (effective July 1, 1999) (West 2000) ("A successor must exist at the death of the decedent"). See also N.D. Cent.Code Ann. 14–18–04 (Michie 1997) ("A person who dies before a conception using that person's sperm or egg is not a parent of any resulting child born of the conception"). We must therefore determine whether, under our intestacy law, there is any reason that children conceived after the decedent's death who are the decedent's direct genetic descendants-that is, children who "by consanguinity trace their lineage to the designated ancestor"-may not enjoy the same succession rights as children conceived before the decedent's death who are the decedent's direct genetic descendants. *Lockwood v. Adamson, supra.*

To answer that question we consider whether and to what extent such children may take as intestate heirs of the deceased genetic parent consistent with the purposes of the intestacy law, and not by any assumptions of the common law. See *Cassidy v. Truscott, supra* at 520–521, 192 N.E. 164. In the absence of express legislative directives, we construe the Legislature's purposes from statutory indicia and judicial decisions in a manner that advances the purposes of the intestacy law.

Houghton v. Dickinson, 196 Mass. 389, 391, 82 N.E. 481 (1907). The question whether posthumously conceived genetic children may enjoy inheritance rights under the intestacy statute implicates three powerful State interests: the best interests of children, the State's interest in the orderly administration of estates, and the reproductive rights of the genetic parent. Our task is to balance and harmonize these interests to effect the Legislature's over-all purposes.

First and foremost we consider the overriding legislative concern to promote the best interests of children. "The protection of minor children, most especially those who may be stigmatized by their 'illegitimate' status . . . has been a hallmark of legislative action and of the jurisprudence of this court." L.W.K. v. E.R.C., 432 Mass. 438, 447–448, 735 N.E.2d 359 (2000). Repeatedly, forcefully, and unequivocally, the Legislature has expressed its will that all children be "entitled to the same rights and protections of the law" regardless of the accidents of their birth. G.L. c. 209C, § 1. See G.L. c. 119, § 1 ("It is hereby declared to be the policy of the commonwealth to direct its efforts, first, to the strengthening and encouragement of family life for the protection and care of children. . . ."). Among the many rights and protections vouchsafed to all children are rights to financial support from their parents and their parents' estates. See G.L. c. 119A, § 1 ("It is the public policy of this commonwealth that dependent children shall be maintained, as completely as possible, from the resources of their parents, thereby relieving or avoiding, at least in part, the burden borne by the citizens of the commonwealth"); G.L. c. 191, § 20 (establishing inheritance rights for pretermitted children); G.L. c. 196, §§ 1–3 (permitting allowances from estate to widows and minor children); G.L. c. 209C, § 14 (permitting paternity claims to be commenced prior to birth). See also G.L. c. 190, §§ 1–3, 5, 7–8 (intestacy rights).

We also consider that some of the assistive reproductive technologies that make posthumous reproduction possible have been widely known and practiced for several decades. See generally Banks, Traditional Concepts and Nontraditional Conceptions: Social Security Survivor's Benefits for Posthumously Conceived Children, 32 Loy. L.A. L. Rev. 251, 267–273 (1999). In that time, the Legislature has not acted to narrow the broad statutory class of posthumous children to restrict posthumously conceived children from taking in intestacy. Moreover, the Legislature has in great measure affirmatively supported the assistive reproductive technologies that are the only means by which these children can come into being. See G.L. c. 46, § 4B (artificial insemination of married woman). *See also* G.L. c. 175, § 47H; G.L. c. 176A, § 8K; G.L. c. 176B, § 4J; G.L. c. 176G, § 4 (insurance coverage for infertility treatments). We do not impute to the Legislature the inherently irrational conclusion that assistive reproductive technologies are to be encouraged while a class of children who are the fruit of that technology are to have fewer rights and protections than other children.

In short, we cannot, absent express legislative directive, accept the commissioner's position that the historical context of G.L. c. 190, § 8, dictates as a matter of law that all posthumously conceived children are automatically barred from taking under their deceased donor parent's intestate estate. We have consistently construed statutes to effectuate the Legislature's overriding purpose to promote the welfare of all children, notwithstanding restrictive common-law rules to the contrary. See, e.g., *L.W.K. v. E.R.C., supra* at 447, 735 N.E.2d 359; Adoption of Tammy, 416 Mass. 205, 210, 619 N.E.2d 315 (1993); Powers v. Wilkinson, 399 Mass. 650, 661–662, 506 N.E.2d 842 (1987); Powers v. Steele, 394 Mass. 306, 310, 475 N.E.2d 395 (1985); Hall v. Hancock, 32 Mass. 255, 15 Pick. 255 (1834). Posthumously conceived children may not come into the world the way the majority of children do. But they are children nonetheless. We may assume that the Legislature intended that such children be "entitled," in so far as possible, "to the same rights and protections of the law" as children conceived before death. See G.L. c. 209C, § 1.

However, in the context of our intestacy laws, the best interests of the posthumously conceived child, while of great importance, are not in themselves conclusive. They must be balanced against other important State interests, not the least of which is the protection of children who are alive or conceived before the intestate parent's death. In an era in which serial marriages, serial families, and blended families are not uncommon, according succession rights under our intestacy laws to posthumously conceived children may, in a given case, have the potential to pit child against child and family against family. Any inheritance rights of posthumously conceived children will reduce the intestate share available to children born prior to the decedent's death. See G.L. c. 190, § 3(1). Such considerations, among others, lead us to examine a second important legislative purpose: to provide certainty to heirs and creditors by effecting the orderly, prompt, and accurate administration of intestate estates. See generally S.M. Dunphy, Probate Law and Practice § 8.1, at 115 (2d ed.1997).

The intestacy statute furthers the Legislature's administrative goals in two principal ways: (1) by requiring certainty of filiation between the decedent and his issue, and (2) by establishing limitations periods for the commencement of claims against the intestate estate. In answering the certified question, we must consider each of these requirements of the intestacy statute in turn.

First, as we have discussed, our intestacy law mandates that, absent the father's acknowledgment of paternity or marriage to the mother, a nonmarital child must obtain a judicial determination of paternity as a prerequisite to succeeding to a portion of the father's intestate estate. Both the United States Supreme Court and this court have long recognized that the State's strong interest in preventing fraudulent claims justifies certain disparate classifications among nonmarital children based on the relative difficulty of accurately determining a child's direct lineal ancestor. See Lowell v. Kowalski, 380 Mass. 663, 668–669, 405 N.E.2d 135 (1980). See also Trimble v. Gordon, 430 U.S. 762, 771, 97 S.Ct. 1459, 52 L.Ed.2d 31 (1977). . . .

We now turn to the second way in which the Legislature has met its administrative goals: the establishment of a limitations period for bringing paternity claims against the intestate estate. Our discussion of this important goal, however, is necessarily circumscribed by the procedural posture of this case and by the terms of the certified question. The certification record discloses that, after one unsuccessful insemination attempt, the wife conceived using her deceased husband's sperm approximately sixteen months after his death. The children were born approximately two years after the husband's death, and the paternity action (in the form of a "complaint for correction of birth record") was filed approximately four months after the children's birth. Both the SSA and the administrative law judge concluded that the wife and the children were not entitled to Social Security survivor benefits because, among other things, the paternity actions were not brought within the one-year period for commencing paternity claims mandated by the intestacy statute. *See* G.L. c. 190, § 7.

Nevertheless, the limitations question is inextricably tied to consideration of the intestacy statute's administrative goals. In the case of posthumously conceived children, the application of the one-year limitations period of G.L. c. 190, § 7 is not clear; it may pose significant burdens on the surviving parent, and consequently on the child. It requires, in effect, that the survivor make a decision to bear children while in the freshness of grieving. It also requires that attempts at conception succeed quickly. Cf. Commentary, Modern Reproductive Technologies: Legal Issues Concerning Cryopreservation and Posthumous Conception, 17 J. Legal Med. 547, 549 (1996) ("It takes an average of seven insemination attempts over 4.4 menstrual cycles to establish pregnancy"). Because the resolution of the time constraints question is not required here, it must await the appropriate case, should one arise.

Finally, the question certified to us implicates a third important State interest: to honor the reproductive choices of individuals. We need not address the wife's argument that her reproductive rights would be infringed by denying succession rights to her children under our intestacy law. Nothing in the record even remotely suggests that she was prevented by the State from choosing to conceive children using her deceased husband's semen. The husband's reproductive rights are a more complicated matter.

In A.Z. v. B.Z., 431 Mass. 150, 725 N.E.2d 1051 (2000), we considered certain issues surrounding the disposition of frozen preembryos. A woman sought to enforce written agreements between herself and her former husband. The wife argued that these agreements permitted her to implant frozen preembryos created with the couple's gametes during the marriage, even in the event of their divorce. We declined to enforce the agreements. Persuasive to us, among other factors, was the lack of credible evidence of the husband's "true intention" regarding the disposition of the frozen preembryos, and the changed family circumstance resulting from the couple's divorce. See *id.* at 158–159, 725 N.E.2d 1051. Recognizing that our laws strongly affirm the value of bodily and reproductive integrity, we held that "forced procreation is not an area amenable to judicial enforcement." *Id.* at 160, 725 N.E.2d 1051. In short, *A.Z. v. B.Z., supra,* recognized that individuals have a protected right to control the use of their gametes.

Consonant with the principles identified in *A.Z. v. B.Z., supra,* a decedent's silence, or his equivocal indications of a desire to parent posthumously, "ought not to be construed as consent." See Schiff, Arising from the Dead: Challenges of Posthumous Procreation, 75 N.C. L.Rev. 901, 951 (1997). The prospective donor parent must clearly and unequivocally consent not only to posthumous reproduction but also to the support of any resulting child. Cf. Paternity of Cheryl, 434 Mass. 23, 37, 746 N.E.2d 488 (2001) ("The law places on men the burden to consider carefully the permanent consequences that flow from an acknowledgment of paternity"). After the donor-parent's death, the burden rests with the surviving parent, or the posthumously conceived child's other legal representative, to prove the deceased genetic parent's affirmative consent to both requirements for posthumous parentage: posthumous reproduction and the support of any resulting child.

This two-fold consent requirement arises from the nature of alternative reproduction itself. It will not always be the case that a person elects to have his or her gametes medically preserved to create "issue" posthumously. A man, for example, may preserve his semen for myriad reasons, including, among others: to reproduce after recovery from medical treatment, to reproduce after an event that leaves him sterile, or to reproduce when his spouse has a genetic disorder or otherwise cannot have or safely bear children. That a man has medically preserved his gametes for use by his spouse thus may indicate only that he wished to reproduce after some contingency while he was alive, and not that he consented to the different circumstance of creating a child after his death. Uncertainty as to consent may be compounded by the fact that medically preserved semen can remain viable for up to ten years after it was first extracted, long after the original decision to preserve the semen has passed and when such changed circumstances as divorce, remarriage, and a second family may have intervened. See Banks, Traditional Concepts and Nontraditional Conceptions: Social Security Survivor's Benefits for Posthumously Conceived Children, 32 Loy. L.A. L. Rev. 251, 270 (1999).

Such circumstances demonstrate the inadequacy of a rule that would make the mere genetic tie of the decedent to any posthumously conceived child, or the decedent's mere election to preserve gametes, sufficient to bind his intestate estate for the benefit of any posthumously conceived child. Without evidence that the deceased intestate parent affirmatively consented (1) to the posthumous reproduction and (2) to support any resulting child, a court cannot be assured that the intestacy statute's goal of fraud prevention is satisfied.

As expressed in our intestacy and paternity laws, sound public policy dictates the requirements we have outlined above. Legal parentage imposes substantial obligations on adults for the welfare of children. Where two adults engage in the act of sexual intercourse, it is a matter of common sense and logic, expressed in well-established law, to charge them with parental responsibilities for the child who is the natural, even if unintended, consequence of their actions. Where conception results from a third-party medical procedure using a deceased person's gametes, it is entirely consistent with our laws on children, parentage, and reproductive freedom to place the burden on the surviving parent (or the posthumously conceived child's other legal representative) to demonstrate the genetic relationship of the child to the decedent and that the intestate consented both to reproduce posthumously and to support any resulting child. . . .

It is undisputed in this case that the husband is the genetic father of the wife's children. However, for the reasons stated above, that fact, in itself, cannot be sufficient to establish that the husband is the children's legal father for purposes of the devolution and distribution of his intestate property. In the United States District Court, the wife may come forward with other evidence as to her husband's consent to posthumously conceive children. She may come forward with evidence of his consent to support such children. We do not speculate as to the sufficiency of evidence she may submit at trial. . . .

For the second time this term, we have been confronted with novel questions involving the rights of children born from assistive reproductive technologies. See Culliton v. Beth Israel Deaconess Med. Ctr., 435 Mass. 285, 756 N.E.2d 1133 (2001). As these technologies advance, the number of children they produce will continue to multiply. So, too, will the complex moral, legal, social, and ethical questions that surround their birth. The questions present in this case cry out for lengthy, careful examination outside the adversary process, which can only address the specific circumstances of each controversy that presents itself. They demand a comprehensive response reflecting the considered will of the people.

In the absence of statutory directives, we have answered the certified question by identifying and harmonizing the important State interests implicated therein in a manner that advances the Legislature's over-all purposes. In so doing, we conclude that limited circumstances may exist, consistent with the mandates of our Legislature, in which posthumously conceived children may enjoy the inheritance rights of "issue" under our intestacy law. These limited circumstances exist where, as a threshold matter, the surviving parent or the child's other legal representative demonstrates a genetic relationship between the child and the decedent. The survivor or representative must then establish both that the decedent affirmatively consented to posthumous conception and to the support of any resulting child. Even where such circumstances exist, time limitations may preclude commencing a claim for succession rights on behalf of a posthumously conceived child. In any action brought to establish such inheritance rights, notice must be given to all interested parties.

NOTES

The *Woodward* decision is unique among state court decisions. *Woodward* interprets the state statute regarding inheritance in such a way as to emphasize the best interest of any posthumously conceived child, rather than deferring to the state legislature. The state intestate statutes provide the mechanism by which a child conceived and born posthumously may receive Social Security benefits from the deceased parent. If the child is unable to inherit, the child is barred from Social Security. Most state courts offer no remedy to the child other than to suggest that the legislature amend the state statute. *See, e.g.,* Finley v. Astrue, 270 S.W.3d 849, 855 (Ark. 2008) ("[We] strongly encourage the General Assembly to revisit the intestate succession statutes to address the issues involved in the instant case and those that have not but will likely evolve."). Seeking to avoid the harsh consequences of state intestate laws, petitioners sought to decouple the federal benefits from state inheritance laws. A unanimous United States Supreme Court held, however, that for purposes of establishing benefits under the Social Security Act, the Commissioner shall apply state intestacy law. Thus, in the context of posthumous conception, if a child is not entitled to inherit from a decedent parent under the state's intestate statute, there is no recourse in the federal Social Security Act. Astrue v. Capato, 132 S.Ct. 2021 (2012). For commentary on the issues involved, *see* Michael T. Flannery, *The Intestacy Rights of a Child Created as an Embryo by In Vitro Fertilization During the Parents' Marriage, but Who is Implanted in the Mother's Womb After the Father's Death:* Finley v. Astrue *(Ark. Sup. Ct. 2008),* LexisNexis Expert Commentary, 2008 Emerging Issues 2060 (May 2008). *See also* Buckley W. Bridges, *Statutory Misconceptions: The Arkansas Supreme Court's Method in* Finley v. Astrue *Sets New Precedent for Uncertainty*, 63 ARK. L. REV. 419 (2010); Raymond C. O'Brien, *The Momentum of Posthumous Conception: A Model Act*, 25 J. CONTEMP. HEALTH L. & POL'Y 332 (2009); Browne C. Lewis, *Dead Men Reproducing: Responding to the Existence of Afterdeath Children*, 16 GEO. MASON L. REV. 403 (2009). There have been some statutory modifications to accommodate the inclusion of posthumously conceived children within intestate succession statutes.

CALIFORNIA PROBATE CODE (2016)

§ 249.5. Posthumous conception; child of decedent deemed born in decedent's lifetime; conditions

For purposes of determining rights to property to be distributed upon the death of a decedent, a child of the decedent conceived and born after the death of the decedent shall be deemed to have been born in the lifetime of the decedent, and after the execution of all of the decedent's testamentary instruments, if the child or his or her representative proves by clear and convincing evidence that all of the following conditions have been satisfied:

(a) The decedent, in writing, specifies that his or her genetic material shall be used for the posthumous conception of a child of the decedent, subject to the following:

(1) The specification shall be signed by the decedent and dated.

(2) The specification may be revoked or amended only by a writing, signed by the decedent and dated.

(3) A person is designated by the decedent to control the use of the genetic material.

(b) The person designated by the decedent to control the use of the genetic material has given written notice by certified mail, return receipt requested, that the decedent's genetic material was available for the purpose of posthumous conception. The notice shall have been given to a person who has the power to control the distribution of either the decedent's property or death benefits payable by reason of the decedent's death, within four months of the date of issuance of a certificate of the decedent's death or entry of a judgement determining the fact of the decedent's death, whichever occurs first.

(c) The child was in utero using the decedent's genetic material and was in utero within two years of the date of issuance of a certificate of the decedent's death or entry of a judgement determining the fact of the decedent's death, whichever event occurs first. This subdivision does not apply to a child who shares all of his or her nuclear genes with the person dating the implanted nucleus as a result of the application of somatic nuclear transfer technology commonly known as human cloning.

UNIFORM PROBATE CODE (2016)

§ 2–120. Child Conceived By Assisted Reproduction Other Than Child Born to Gestational Carrier

* * *

(k) **[When Posthumously Conceived Child Treated as in Gestation.]** If, under this section, an individual is a parent of a child of assisted reproduction who is conceived after the individual's death, the child is treated as in gestation at the individual's death for purposes of Section 2–104(a)(2) if the child is:

(1) in utero not later than 36 months after the individual's death; or

(2) born not later than 45 months after the individual's death.

[Note that Unif. Prob. Code § 2–104(a)(2) requires a child to survive birth by 120 hours to inherit under this section.]

UNIFORM PARENTAGE ACT OF 2000

§ 707. Parental Status of Deceased Individual

If an individual who consented in a record to be a parent by assisted reproduction dies before placement of eggs, sperm, or embryos, the deceased individual is not a parent of the resulting child unless the deceased spouse consented in a record that if assisted reproduction were to occur after death, the deceased individual would be a parent of the child.

4. GESTATIONAL CONTRACTS WITH SURROGATES

Matter of Baby M

Supreme Court of New Jersey, 1988
537 A.2d 1227

■ WILENTZ, C.J.

In this matter the Court is asked to determine the validity of a contract that purports to provide a new way of bringing children into a family. For a fee of $10,000, a woman agrees to be artificially inseminated with the semen of another woman's husband; she is to conceive a child, carry it to term, and after its birth surrender it to the natural father and his wife. The intent of the contract is that the child's natural mother will thereafter be forever separated from her child. The wife is to adopt the child, and she and the natural father are to be regarded as its parents for all purposes. The contract providing for this is called a "surrogacy contract," the natural mother inappropriately called the "surrogate mother."

We invalidate the surrogacy contract because it conflicts with the law and public policy of this State. While we recognize the depth of the yearning of infertile couples to have their own children, we find the payment of money to a "surrogate" mother illegal, perhaps criminal, and potentially degrading to women. Although in this case we grant custody to the natural father, the evidence having clearly proved such custody to be in the best interests of the infant, we void both the termination of the surrogate mother's parental rights and the adoption of the child by the wife/stepparent. We thus restore the "surrogate" as the mother of the child. We remand the issue of the natural mother's visitation rights to the trial court, since that issue was not reached below and the record before us is not sufficient to permit us to decide it *de novo*.

We find no offense to our present laws where a woman voluntarily and without payment agrees to act as a "surrogate" mother, provided that she is not subject to a binding agreement to surrender her child. Moreover, our holding today does not preclude the Legislature from altering the current statutory scheme, within constitutional limits, so as to permit surrogacy contracts. Under current law, however, the surrogacy agreement before us is illegal and invalid.

In February 1985, William Stern and Mary Beth Whitehead entered into a surrogacy contract. It recited that Stern's wife, Elizabeth, was infertile, that they wanted a child, and that Mrs. Whitehead was willing to provide that child as the mother with Mr. Stern as the father.

The contract provided that through artificial insemination using Mr. Stern's sperm, Mrs. Whitehead would become pregnant, carry the child to term, bear it, deliver it to the Sterns, and thereafter do whatever was necessary to terminate her maternal rights so that Mrs. Stern could thereafter adopt the child. Mrs. Whitehead's husband, Richard,[1] was also a party to the contract; Mrs. Stern was not. Mr. Whitehead promised to do all acts necessary to rebut the presumption of paternity under the Parentage Act. N.J.S.A. 9:17–43a(1), –44a. Although Mrs. Stern was not a party to the surrogacy agreement, the contract gave her sole custody of the child in the event of Mr. Stern's death. Mrs. Stern's status as a nonparty to the surrogate parenting agreement presumably was to avoid the application of the baby-selling statute to this arrangement.

Mr. Stern, on his part, agreed to attempt the artificial insemination and to pay Mrs. Whitehead $10,000 after the child's birth, on its delivery to him. In a separate contract, Mr. Stern agreed to pay $7,500 to the Infertility Center of New York ("ICNY"). The Center's advertising campaigns solicit surrogate mothers and encourage infertile couples to consider surrogacy. ICNY arranged for the surrogacy contract by bringing the parties together, explaining the process to them, furnishing the contractual form, and providing legal counsel.

The history of the parties' involvement in this arrangement suggests their good faith. William and Elizabeth Stern were married in July 1974, having met at the University of Michigan, where both were Ph.D. candidates. Due to financial considerations and Mrs. Stern's pursuit of a medical degree and residency, they decided to defer starting a family until 1981. Before then, however, Mrs. Stern learned that she might have multiple sclerosis and that the disease in some cases renders pregnancy

[1] Subsequent to the trial court proceedings, Mr. and Mrs. Whitehead were divorced, and soon thereafter Mrs. Whitehead remarried. Nevertheless, in the course of this opinion we will make reference almost exclusively to the facts as they existed at the time of trial, the facts on which the decision we now review was reached. We note moreover that Mr. Whitehead remains a party to this dispute. For these reasons, we continue to refer to appellants as Mr. and Mrs. Whitehead.

a serious health risk. Her anxiety appears to have exceeded the actual risk, which current medical authorities assess as minimal. Nonetheless that anxiety was evidently quite real, Mrs. Stern fearing that pregnancy might precipitate blindness, paraplegia, or other forms of debilitation. Based on the perceived risk the Sterns decided to forego having their own children. The decision had a special significance for Mr. Stern. Most of his family had been destroyed in the Holocaust. As the family's only survivor, he very much wanted to continue his bloodline.

Initially the Sterns considered adoption, but were discouraged by the substantial delay apparently involved and by the potential problem they saw arising from their age and their differing religious backgrounds. They were most eager for some other means to start a family.

The paths of Mrs. Whitehead and the Sterns to surrogacy were similar. Both responded to advertising by ICNY. The Sterns' response, following their inquiries into adoption, was the result of their longstanding decision to have a child. Mrs. Whitehead's response apparently resulted from her sympathy with family members and others who could have no children (she stated that she wanted to give another couple the "gift of life"); she also wanted the $10,000 to help her family.

Both parties, undoubtedly because of their own self-interest, were less sensitive to the implications of the transaction than they might otherwise have been. Mrs. Whitehead, for instance, appears not to have been concerned about whether the Sterns would make good parents for her child; the Sterns, on their part, while conscious of the obvious possibility that surrendering the child might cause grief to Mrs. Whitehead, overcame their qualms because of their desire for a child. At any rate, both the Sterns and Mrs. Whitehead were committed to the arrangement; both thought it right and constructive.

Mrs. Whitehead had reached her decision concerning surrogacy before the Sterns, and had actually been involved as a potential surrogate mother with another couple. After numerous unsuccessful artificial inseminations, that effort was abandoned. Thereafter, the Sterns learned of the Infertility Center, the possibilities of surrogacy, and of Mary Beth Whitehead. The two couples met to discuss the surrogacy arrangement and decided to go forward. On February 6, 1985, Mr. Stern and Mr. and Mrs. Whitehead executed the surrogate parenting agreement. After several artificial inseminations over a period of months, Mrs. Whitehead became pregnant. The pregnancy was uneventful and on March 27, 1986, Baby M was born.

Not wishing anyone at the hospital to be aware of the surrogacy arrangement, Mr. and Mrs. Whitehead appeared to all as the proud parents of a healthy female child. Her birth certificate indicated her name to be Sara Elizabeth Whitehead and her father to be Richard Whitehead. In accordance with Mrs. Whitehead's request, the Sterns visited the hospital unobtrusively to see the newborn child.

Mrs. Whitehead realized, almost from the moment of birth, that she could not part with this child. She had felt a bond with it even during pregnancy. Some indication of the attachment was conveyed to the Sterns at the hospital when they told Mrs. Whitehead what they were going to name the baby. She apparently broke into tears and indicated that she did not know if she could give up the child. She talked about how the baby looked like her other daughter, and made it clear that she was experiencing great difficulty with the decision. Nonetheless, Mrs. Whitehead was, for the moment, true to her word. Despite powerful inclinations to the contrary, she turned her child over to the Sterns on March 30 at the Whiteheads' home.

The Sterns were thrilled with their new child. They had planned extensively for its arrival, far beyond the practical furnishing of a room for her. It was a time of joyful celebration—not just for them but for their friends as well. The Sterns looked forward to raising their daughter, whom they named Melissa. While aware by then that Mrs. Whitehead was undergoing an emotional crisis, they were as yet not cognizant of the depth of that crisis and its implications for their newly-enlarged family. Later in the evening of March 30, Mrs. Whitehead became deeply disturbed, disconsolate, stricken with unbearable sadness. She had to have her child. She could not eat, sleep, or concentrate on anything other than her need for her baby. The next day she went to the Sterns' home and told them how much she was suffering.

The depth of Mrs. Whitehead's despair surprised and frightened the Sterns. She told them that she could not live without her baby, that she must have her, even if only for one week, that thereafter she would surrender her child. The Sterns, concerned that Mrs. Whitehead might indeed commit suicide, not wanting under any circumstances to risk that, and in any event believing that Mrs. Whitehead would keep her word, turned the child over to her. . . .

The struggle over Baby M began when it became apparent that Mrs. Whitehead could not return the child to Mr. Stern. Due to Mrs. Whitehead's refusal to relinquish the baby, Mr. Stern filed a complaint seeking enforcement of the surrogacy contract. He alleged, accurately, that Mrs. Whitehead had not only refused to comply with the surrogacy contract but had threatened to flee from New Jersey with the child in order to avoid even the possibility of his obtaining custody. The court papers asserted that if Mrs. Whitehead were to be given notice of the application for an order requiring her to relinquish custody, she would, prior to the hearing, leave the state with the baby. And that is precisely what she did. After the order was entered, *ex parte,* the process server, aided by the police, in the presence of the Sterns, entered Mrs. Whitehead's home to execute the order. Mr. Whitehead fled with the child, who had been handed to him through a window while those who came to enforce the order were thrown off balance by a dispute over the child's current name.

The Whiteheads immediately fled to Florida with Baby M. They stayed initially with Mrs. Whitehead's parents, where one of Mrs. Whitehead's children had been living. For the next three months, the Whiteheads and Melissa lived at roughly twenty different hotels, motels, and homes in order to avoid apprehension. From time to time Mrs. Whitehead would call Mr. Stern to discuss the matter; the conversations, recorded by Mr. Stern on advice of counsel, show an escalating dispute about rights, morality, and power, accompanied by threats of Mrs. Whitehead to kill herself, to kill the child, and falsely to accuse Mr. Stern of sexually molesting Mrs. Whitehead's other daughter.

Eventually the Sterns discovered where the Whiteheads were staying, commenced supplementary proceedings in Florida, and obtained an order requiring the Whiteheads to turn over the child. Police in Florida enforced the order, forcibly removing the child from her grandparents' home. She was soon thereafter brought to New Jersey and turned over to the Sterns. The prior order of the court, issued *ex parte,* awarding custody of the child to the Sterns *pendente lite,* was reaffirmed by the trial court after consideration of the certified representations of the parties (both represented by counsel) concerning the unusual sequence of events that had unfolded. Pending final judgment, Mrs. Whitehead was awarded limited visitation with Baby M.

The Sterns' complaint, in addition to seeking possession and ultimately custody of the child, sought enforcement of the surrogacy contract. Pursuant to the contract, it asked that the child be permanently placed in their custody, that Mrs. Whitehead's parental rights be terminated, and that Mrs. Stern be allowed to adopt the child, *i.e.,* that, for all purposes, Melissa become the Sterns' child. The trial took thirty-two days over a period of more than two months. . . . Soon after the conclusion of the trial, the trial court announced its opinion from the bench. 217 N.J.Super. 313, 525 A.2d 1128 (1987). It held that the surrogacy contract was valid; ordered that Mrs. Whitehead's parental rights be terminated and that sole custody of the child be granted to Mr. Stern; and, after hearing brief testimony from Mrs. Stern, immediately entered an order allowing the adoption of Melissa by Mrs. Stern, all in accordance with the surrogacy contract. Pending the outcome of the appeal, we granted a continuation of visitation to Mrs. Whitehead, although slightly more limited than the visitation allowed during the trial.

Although clearly expressing its view that the surrogacy contract was valid, the trial court devoted the major portion of its opinion to the question of the baby's best interests. The inconsistency is apparent. The surrogacy contract calls for the surrender of the child to the Sterns, permanent and sole custody in the Sterns, and termination of Mrs. Whitehead's parental rights, all without qualification, all regardless of any evaluation of the best interests of the child. As a matter of fact the contract recites (even before the child was conceived) that it is in the best interests of the child to be placed with Mr. Stern. In effect, the trial court awarded custody to Mr. Stern, the natural father, based on the same kind of evidence and analysis as might be expected had no surrogacy contract existed. Its rationalization, however, was that while the surrogacy contract was valid, specific performance would not be granted unless that remedy was in the best interests of the child. The factual issues confronted and decided by the trial court were the same as if Mr. Stern and Mrs. Whitehead had had the child out of wedlock, intended or unintended, and then disagreed about custody. . . .

On the question of best interests—and we agree, but for different reasons, that custody was the critical issue—the court's analysis of the testimony was perceptive, demonstrating both its understanding of the case and its considerable experience in these matters. We agree substantially with both its analysis and conclusions on the matter of custody. The court's review and analysis of the surrogacy contract, however, is not at all in accord with ours. The trial court concluded that the various statutes governing this matter, including those concerning adoption, termination of parental rights, and payment of money in connection with adoptions, do not apply to surrogacy contracts. It reasoned that because the Legislature did not have surrogacy contracts in mind when it passed those laws, those laws were therefore irrelevant. . . .

Mrs. Whitehead contends that the surrogacy contract, for a variety of reasons, is invalid. She contends that it conflicts with public policy since it guarantees that the child will not have the nurturing of both natural parents—presumably New Jersey's goal for families. She further argues that it deprives the mother of her constitutional right to the companionship of her child, and that it conflicts with statutes concerning termination of parental rights and adoption. With the contract thus void, Mrs. Whitehead claims primary custody (with visitation rights in Mr. Stern) both on a best interests basis (stressing the "tender years" doctrine) as well as on the policy basis of discouraging surrogacy contracts. She maintains that even if custody would ordinarily go to Mr. Stern, here it should be awarded to Mrs. Whitehead to deter future surrogacy arrangements.

In a brief filed after oral argument, counsel for Mrs. Whitehead suggests that the standard for determining best interests where the infant resulted from a surrogacy contract is that the child should be placed with the mother absent a showing of unfitness. All parties agree that no expert testified that Mary Beth Whitehead was unfit as a mother; the trial court expressly found that she was *not* "unfit," that, on the contrary, "she is a good mother for and to her older children," 217 N.J.Super. at 397, 525 A.2d 1128; and no one now claims anything to the contrary. . . .

The Sterns claim that the surrogacy contract is valid and should be enforced, largely for the reasons given by the trial court. They claim a constitutional right of privacy, which includes the right of procreation, and the right of consenting adults to deal with matters of reproduction as they see fit. . . .

Of considerable interest in this clash of views is the position of the child's guardian *ad litem,* wisely appointed by the court at the outset of the litigation. As the child's representative, her role in the litigation, as she viewed it, was solely to protect the child's best interests. She therefore took no position on the validity of the surrogacy contract, and instead devoted her energies to obtaining expert testimony uninfluenced by any interest other than the child's. We agree with the guardian's perception of her role in this litigation. She appropriately refrained from taking any position that might have appeared to compromise her role as the child's advocate. She first took the position, based on her experts' testimony, that the Sterns should have primary custody, and that while Mrs. Whitehead's parental rights should not be terminated, no visitation should be allowed for five years. As a result of subsequent developments, mentioned infra, her view has changed. She now recommends that no visitation be allowed at least until Baby M reaches maturity. . . .

The trial court, consistent in this respect with its view that the surrogacy contract was valid, did not deal at all with the question of visitation. Having concluded that the best interests of the child called for custody in the Sterns, the trial court enforced the operative provisions of the surrogacy contract, terminated Mrs. Whitehead's parental rights, and granted an adoption to Mrs. Stern. . . .

We have concluded that this surrogacy contract is invalid. Our conclusion has two bases: direct conflict with existing statutes and conflict with the public policies of this State, as expressed in its statutory and decisional law.

One of the surrogacy contract's basic purposes, to achieve the adoption of a child through private placement, though permitted in New Jersey "is very much disfavored." Sees v. Baber, 74 N.J. 201, 217, 377 A.2d 628 (1977). Its use of money for this purpose—and we have no doubt whatsoever that the money is being paid to obtain an adoption and not, as the Sterns argue, for the personal services of Mary Beth Whitehead—is illegal and perhaps criminal. N.J.S.A. 9:3–54. In addition to the inducement of money, there is the coercion of contract: the natural mother's irrevocable agreement, prior to birth, even prior to conception, to surrender the child to the adoptive couple. Such an agreement is totally unenforceable in private placement adoption. Even where the adoption is through an approved agency, the formal agreement to surrender occurs only *after* birth and then, by regulation, only after the birth mother has been counseled. Integral to these invalid provisions of the surrogacy contract is the related agreement, equally invalid, on the part of the natural mother to cooperate with, and not to contest, proceedings to terminate her parental rights, as well as her contractual concession, in aid of the adoption, that the child's best interests would be served by awarding custody to the natural father and his wife—all of this before she has even conceived, and, in some cases, before she has the slightest idea of what the natural father and adoptive mother are like.

The foregoing provisions not only directly conflict with New Jersey statutes, but also offend long-established State policies. These critical terms, which are at the heart of the contract, are invalid and unenforceable; the conclusion therefore follows, without more, that the entire contract is unenforceable.

The surrogacy contract conflicts with: (1) laws prohibiting the use of money in connection with adoptions; (2) laws requiring proof of parental unfitness or abandonment before termination of parental rights is ordered or an adoption is granted; and (3) laws that make surrender of custody and consent to adoption revocable in private placement adoptions.

Our law prohibits paying or accepting money in connection with any placement of a child for adoption. N.J.S.A. 9:3–54a. Violation is a high misdemeanor. N.J.S.A. 9:3–54c. Excepted are fees of an approved agency (which must be a nonprofit entity, N.J.S.A. 9:3–38a) and certain expenses in connection with childbirth. N.J.S.A. 9:3–54b. . . .

The termination of Mrs. Whitehead's parental rights, called for by the surrogacy contract and actually ordered by the court, fails to comply with the stringent requirements of New Jersey law. Our law, recognizing the finality of any termination of parental rights, provides for such termination only where there has been a voluntary surrender of a child to an approved agency or to the Division of Youth and Family Services ("DYFS"), accompanied by a formal document acknowledging termination of parental rights, or where there has been a showing of parental abandonment or unfitness. . . .

The surrogacy contract's invalidity, resulting from its direct conflict with the above statutory provisions, is further underlined when its goals and means are measured against New Jersey's public policy. The contract's basic premise, that the natural parents can decide in advance of birth which one is to have custody of the child, bears no relationship to the settled law that the child's best interests shall determine custody. . . .

The surrogacy contract guarantees permanent separation of the child from one of its natural parents. Our policy, however, has long been that to the extent possible, children should remain with and be brought up by both of their natural parents. . . . This is not simply some theoretical ideal that in practice has no meaning. The impact of failure to follow that policy is nowhere better shown than in the results of this surrogacy contract. A child, instead of starting off its life with as much peace and security as possible, finds itself immediately in a tug-of-war between contending mother and father. . . .

Although the interest of the natural father and adoptive mother is certainly the predominant interest, realistically the *only* interest served, even they are left with less than what public policy requires. They know little about the natural mother, her genetic makeup, and her psychological and medical history. Moreover, not even a superficial attempt is made to determine their awareness of their responsibilities as parents.

Worst of all, however, is the contract's total disregard of the best interests of the child. There is not the slightest suggestion that any inquiry will be made at any time to determine the fitness of the Sterns as custodial parents, of Mrs. Stern as an adoptive parent, their superiority to Mrs. Whitehead, or the effect on the child of not living with her natural mother. This is the sale of a child, or, at the very least, the sale of a mother's right to her child, the only mitigating factor being that one of the purchasers is the father. Almost every evil that prompted the prohibition of the payment of money in connection with adoptions exists here.

The differences between an adoption and a surrogacy contract should be noted, since it is asserted that the use of money in connection with surrogacy does not pose the risks found where money buys an adoption. Katz, "Surrogate Motherhood and the Baby-Selling Laws," 20 Colum.J.L. & Soc.Probs. 1 (1986).

First, and perhaps most important, all parties concede that it is unlikely that surrogacy will survive without money. Despite the alleged selfless motivation of surrogate mothers, if there is no payment, there will be no surrogates, or very few. That conclusion contrasts with adoption; for obvious reasons, there remains a steady supply, albeit insufficient, despite the prohibitions against payment. The adoption itself, relieving the natural mother of the financial burden of supporting an infant, is the equivalent of payment.

Second, the use of money in adoptions does not *produce* the problem—conception occurs, and usually the birth itself, before illicit funds are offered. With surrogacy, the "problem," if one views it as such, consisting of the purchase of a woman's procreative capacity, at the risk of her life, is caused by and originates with the offer of money.

Third, with the law prohibiting the use of money in connection with adoptions, the built-in financial pressure of the unwanted pregnancy and the consequent support obligation do not lead the mother to the highest paying, ill-suited, adoptive parents. She is just as well off surrendering the child to an approved agency. In surrogacy, the highest bidders will presumably become the adoptive parents regardless of suitability, so long as payment of money is permitted.

Fourth, the mother's consent to surrender her child in adoption is revocable, even after surrender of the child, unless it be to an approved agency, where by regulation there are protections against an ill-advised surrender. In surrogacy, consent occurs so early that no amount of advice would satisfy the potential mother's need, yet the consent is irrevocable.

The main difference, that the plight of the unwanted pregnancy is unintended while the situation of the surrogate mother is voluntary and intended, is really not significant. Initially, it produces stronger reactions of sympathy for the mother whose pregnancy was unwanted than for the surrogate mother, who "went into this with her eyes wide open." On reflection, however, it appears that the essential evil is the same, taking advantage of a woman's circumstances (the unwanted pregnancy or the need for money) in order to take away her child, the difference being one of degree.

In the scheme contemplated by the surrogacy contract in this case, a middleman, propelled by profit, promotes the sale. Whatever idealism may have motivated any of the participants, the profit motive predominates, permeates, and ultimately governs the transaction. The demand for children is great and the supply small. The availability of contraception, abortion, and the greater willingness of single mothers to bring up their children has led to a shortage of babies offered for adoption. The situation is ripe for the entry of the middleman who will bring some equilibrium into the market by increasing the supply through the use of money. . . .

The long-term effects of surrogacy contracts are not known, but feared—the impact on the child who learns her life was bought, that she is the offspring of someone who gave birth to her only to obtain money; the impact on the natural mother as the full weight of her isolation is felt along with the full reality of the sale of her body and her child; the impact on the natural father and adoptive mother once they realize the consequences of their conduct. Literature in related areas suggests these are substantial considerations, although, given the newness of surrogacy, there is little information.

The surrogacy contract creates, it is based upon, principles that are directly contrary to the objectives of our laws. It guarantees the separation of a child from its mother; it looks to adoption regardless of suitability; it totally ignores the child; it takes the child from the mother regardless of her wishes and her maternal fitness; and it does all of this, it accomplishes all of its goals, through the use of money.

Beyond that is the potential degradation of some women that may result from this arrangement. In many cases, of course, surrogacy may bring satisfaction, not only to the infertile couple, but to the surrogate mother herself. The fact, however, that many women may not perceive surrogacy negatively but rather see it as an opportunity does not diminish its potential for devastation to other women.

In sum, the harmful consequences of this surrogacy arrangement appear to us all too palpable. In New Jersey the surrogate mother's agreement to sell her child is void. Its irrevocability infects the entire contract, as does the money that purports to buy it. . . .

Both parties argue that the Constitutions—state and federal—mandate approval of their basic claims. The source of their constitutional arguments is essentially the same: the right of privacy, the right to procreate, the right to the companionship of one's child, those rights flowing either directly from the fourteenth amendment or by its incorporation of the Bill of Rights, or from the ninth amendment, or through the penumbra surrounding all of the Bill of Rights. They are the rights of personal intimacy, of marriage, of sex, of family, of procreation. Whatever their source, it is clear that they are fundamental rights protected by both the federal and state Constitutions. The right asserted by the Sterns is the right of procreation; that asserted by Mary Beth Whitehead is the right to the companionship of her child. . . .

The right to procreate very simply is the right to have natural children, whether through sexual intercourse or artificial insemination. It is no more than that. Mr. Stern has not been deprived of that right. Through artificial insemination of Mrs. Whitehead, Baby M is his child. The custody, care, companionship, and nurturing that follow birth are not parts of the right to procreation; they are rights that may also be constitutionally protected, but that involve many considerations other than the right of procreation. To assert that Mr. Stern's right of procreation gives him the right to the custody of Baby M would be to assert that Mrs. Whitehead's right of procreation does *not* give her the right to the custody of Baby M; it would be to assert that the constitutional right of procreation includes within it a constitutionally protected contractual right to destroy someone else's right of procreation.

We conclude that the right of procreation is best understood and protected if confined to its essentials, and that when dealing with rights concerning the resulting child, different interests come into play. There is nothing in our culture or society that even begins to suggest a fundamental right on the part of the father to the custody of the child as part of his right to procreate when opposed by the claim of the mother to the same child. We therefore disagree with the trial court: there is no constitutional basis whatsoever requiring that Mr. Stern's claim to the custody of Baby M be sustained. Our conclusion may thus be understood as illustrating that a person's rights of privacy and self-determination are qualified by the effect on innocent third persons of the exercise of those rights.

Mr. Stern also contends that he has been denied equal protection of the laws by the State's statute granting full parental rights to a husband in relation to the child produced, with his consent, by the union of his wife with a sperm donor. N.J.S.A. 9:17–44. The claim really is that of Mrs. Stern. It is that she is in precisely the same position as the husband in the statute: she is presumably infertile, as is the husband in the statute; her spouse by agreement with a third party procreates with the understanding that the child will be the couple's child. The alleged unequal protection is that the understanding is honored in the statute when the husband is the infertile party, but no similar understanding is honored when it is the wife who is infertile.

It is quite obvious that the situations are not parallel. A sperm donor simply cannot be equated with a surrogate mother. The State has more than a sufficient basis to distinguish the two situations—even if the only difference is between the time it takes to provide sperm for artificial insemination and the time invested in a nine-month pregnancy—so as to justify automatically divesting the sperm donor of his parental rights without automatically divesting a surrogate mother. Some basis for an equal protection argument might exist if Mary Beth Whitehead had contributed her egg to be implanted, fertilized or otherwise, in Mrs. Stern, resulting in the latter's pregnancy. That is not the case here, however. . . .

By virtue of our decision Mrs. Whitehead's constitutional complaint—that her parental rights have been unconstitutionally terminated—is moot. . . .

Under the Parentage Act the claims of the natural father and the natural mother are entitled to equal weight, i.e., one is not preferred over the other solely because it is the father or the mother. N.J.S.A. 9:17–40. The applicable rule given these circumstances is clear: the child's best interests determine custody. . . .

Our reading of the record persuades us that the trial court's decision awarding custody to the Sterns (technically to Mr. Stern) should be affirmed since "its findings . . . could reasonably have been reached on sufficient credible evidence present in the record."

Our custody conclusion is based on strongly persuasive testimony contrasting both the family life of the Whiteheads and the Sterns and the personalities and characters of the individuals. The stability of the Whitehead family life was doubtful at the time of trial. Their finances were in serious trouble (foreclosure by Mrs. Whitehead's sister on a second mortgage was in process). Mr. Whitehead's employment, though relatively steady, was always at risk because of his alcoholism, a condition that he seems not to have been able to confront effectively. Mrs. Whitehead had not worked for quite some time, her last two employments having been part-time. One of the Whiteheads' positive attributes was their ability to bring up two children, and apparently well, even in so vulnerable a household. Yet substantial question was raised even about that aspect of their home life. The expert testimony contained criticism of Mrs. Whitehead's handling of her son's educational difficulties. Certain of the experts noted that Mrs. Whitehead perceived herself as omnipotent and omniscient concerning her children. She knew what they were thinking, what they wanted, and she spoke for them. As to Melissa, Mrs. Whitehead expressed the view that she alone knew what that child's cries and sounds meant. Her inconsistent stories about various things engendered grave doubts about her ability to explain honestly and sensitively to Baby M—and at the right time—the nature of her origin. Although faith in professional counseling is not a *sine qua non* of parenting, several experts believed that Mrs. Whitehead's contempt for professional help, especially professional psychological help, coincided with her feelings of omnipotence in a way that could be devastating to a child who most likely will need such help. In short, while love and affection there would be, Baby M's life with the Whiteheads promised to be too closely controlled by Mrs. Whitehead. The prospects for a wholesome independent psychological growth and development would be at serious risk.

The Sterns have no other children, but all indications are that their household and their personalities promise a much more likely foundation for Melissa to grow and thrive. There *is* a track record of sorts—during the one-and-a-half years of custody Baby M has done very well, and the relationship between both Mr. and Mrs. Stern and the baby has become very strong. The household is stable, and likely to remain so. Their finances are more than adequate, their circle of friends supportive, and their marriage happy. Most important, they are loving, giving, nurturing, and open-minded people. They have demonstrated the wish and ability to nurture and protect Melissa, yet at the same time to encourage her independence. Their lack of experience is more than made up for by a willingness to learn and to listen, a willingness that is enhanced by their professional training, especially Mrs. Stern's experience as a pediatrician. They are honest; they can recognize error, deal with it, and learn from it. They will try to determine rationally the best way to cope with problems in their relationship with Melissa. When the time comes to tell her about her origins, they will probably have found a means of doing so that accords with the best interests of Baby M. All in all, Melissa's future appears solid, happy, and promising with them.

Based on all of this we have concluded, independent of the trial court's identical conclusion, that Melissa's best interests call for custody in the Sterns. . . .

The trial court's decision to terminate Mrs. Whitehead's parental rights precluded it from making any determination on visitation. Our reversal of the trial court's order, however, requires delineation of Mrs. Whitehead's rights to visitation. It is apparent to us that this factually sensitive issue, which was never addressed below, should not be determined *de novo* by this Court. We therefore remand the visitation issue to the trial court for an abbreviated hearing and determination as set forth below. . . .[19]

---

[19] As we have done in similar situations, we order that this matter be referred on remand to a different trial judge by the vicinage assignment judge. The original trial judge's potential "commitment to its findings," New Jersey Div. of Youth & Family Servs. v. A.W., supra, 103 N.J. at 617, 512 A.2d 438, and the extent to which a judge "has already engaged in weighing the evidence," In re Guardianship of R, 155 N.J.Super. 186, 195, 382 A.2d 654 (App.Div.1977), persuade us to make that change. On remand the trial court will consider developments subsequent to the original trial court's opinion, including Mrs. Whitehead's divorce, pregnancy, and remarriage.

We join those who want this litigation to end for the benefit of this child. To spare this two-year-old another sixty to ninety days of litigation, however, at the risk of wrongly deciding this matter, which has life-long consequences for the child and the parties, would be unwise.

We also note the following for the trial court's consideration: First, this is not a divorce case where visitation is almost invariably granted to the non-custodial spouse. To some extent the facts here resemble cases where the non-custodial spouse has had practically no relationship with the child, see Wilke v. Culp, supra, 196 N.J.Super. 487, 483 A.2d 420; but it only "resembles" those cases. In the instant case, Mrs. Whitehead spent the first four months of this child's life as her mother and has regularly visited the child since then. Second, she is not only the natural mother, but also the legal mother, and is not to be penalized one iota because of the surrogacy contract. Mrs. Whitehead, as the mother (indeed, as a mother who nurtured her child for its first four months—unquestionably a relevant consideration), is entitled to have her own interest in visitation considered. Visitation cannot be determined without considering the parents' interests along with those of the child.

In all of this, the trial court should recall the touchstones of visitation: that it is desirable for the child to have contact with both parents; that besides the child's interests, the parents' interests also must be considered; but that when all is said and done, the best interests of the child are paramount.

We have decided that Mrs. Whitehead is entitled to visitation at some point, and that question is not open to the trial court on this remand. The trial court will determine what kind of visitation shall be granted to her, with or without conditions, and when and under what circumstances it should commence. . . .

This case affords some insight into a new reproductive arrangement: the artificial insemination of a surrogate mother. The unfortunate events that have unfolded illustrate that its unregulated use can bring suffering to all involved. Potential victims include the surrogate mother and her family, the natural father and his wife, and most importantly, the child. Although surrogacy has apparently provided positive results for some infertile couples, it can also, as this case demonstrates, cause suffering to participants, here essentially innocent and well-intended.

We have found that our present laws do not permit the surrogacy contract used in this case. Nowhere, however, do we find any legal prohibition against surrogacy when the surrogate mother volunteers, without any payment, to act as a surrogate and is given the right to change her mind and to assert her parental rights. Moreover, the Legislature remains free to deal with this most sensitive issue as it sees fit, subject only to constitutional constraints.

If the Legislature decides to address surrogacy, consideration of this case will highlight many of its potential harms. We do not underestimate the difficulties of legislating on this subject. In addition to the inevitable confrontation with the ethical and moral issues involved, there is the question of the wisdom and effectiveness of regulating a matter so private, yet of such public interest. Legislative consideration of surrogacy may also provide the opportunity to begin to focus on the overall implications of the new reproductive biotechnology—*in vitro* fertilization, preservation of sperm and eggs, embryo implantation and the like. The problem is how to enjoy the benefits of the technology—especially for infertile couples—while minimizing the risk of abuse. The problem can be addressed only when society decides what its values and objectives are in this troubling, yet promising, area.

The judgment is affirmed in part, reversed in part, and remanded for further proceedings consistent with this opinion.

NOTES

Appendixes to the opinion reproduce the agreements between the various parties. Contained in the basic "SURROGATE PARENTING AGREEMENT" are the following provisions:

[4.] (C) William Stern, Natural Father, shall pay the expenses incurred by Mary Beth Whitehead, Surrogate, pursuant to her pregnancy, more specifically defined as follows:

> (1) All medical, hospitalization, and pharmaceutical, laboratory and therapy expenses incurred as a result of Mary Beth Whitehead's pregnancy, not covered or allowed by her present health and major medical insurance, including all extraordinary medical expenses and all reasonable expenses for treatment of any emotional or mental conditions or problems related to said pregnancy, but in no case shall any such expenses be paid or reimbursed after a period of six (6) months have elapsed since the date of the termination of the pregnancy, and this Agreement specifically excludes any expenses for lost wages or other non-itemized incidentals (see Exhibit "B") related to said pregnancy.
>
> (2) William Stern, Natural Father, shall not be responsible for any latent medical expenses occurring six (6) weeks subsequent to the birth of the child, unless the medical problem or abnormality incident thereto was known and treated by a physician prior to the expiration of said six (6) week period and in written notice of the same sent to ICNY, as representative of William Stern by certified mail, return receipt requested, advising of this treatment.
>
> (3) William Stern, Natural Father, shall be responsible for the total costs of all paternity testing. Such paternity testing may, at the option of William Stern, Natural Father, be required prior to release of the surrogate fee from escrow. In the event William Stern, Natural Father, is conclusively determined not to be the biological father of the child as a result of an HLA test, this Agreement will be deemed breached and Mary Beth Whitehead,

Surrogate, shall not be entitled to any fee. William Stern, Natural Father, shall be entitled to reimbursement of all medical and related expenses from Mary Beth Whitehead, Surrogate, and Richard Whitehead, her husband.

(4) Mary Beth Whitehead's reasonable travel expenses incurred at the request of William Stern, pursuant to this Agreement.

5. Mary Beth Whitehead, Surrogate, and Richard Whitehead, her husband, understand and agree to assume all risks, including the risk of death, which are incidental to conception, pregnancy, childbirth, including but not limited to, postpartum complications. A copy of said possible risks and/or complications is attached hereto and made a part hereof (see Exhibit "C").

6. Mary Beth Whitehead, Surrogate, and Richard Whitehead, her husband, hereby agree to undergo psychiatric evaluation by Joan Einwohner, a psychiatrist as designated by William Stern or an agent thereof. William Stern shall pay for the cost of said psychiatric evaluation. Mary Beth Whitehead and Richard Whitehead shall sign, prior to their evaluations, a medical release permitting dissemination of the report prepared as a result of said psychiatric evaluations to ICNY or William Stern and his wife.

7. Mary Beth Whitehead, Surrogate, and Richard Whitehead, her husband, hereby agree that it is the exclusive and sole right of William Stern, Natural Father, to name said child.

8. "Child" as referred to in this Agreement shall include all children born simultaneously pursuant to the inseminations contemplated herein.

9. In the event of the death of William Stern, prior or subsequent to the birth of said child, it is hereby understood and agreed by Mary Beth Whitehead, Surrogate, and Richard Whitehead, her husband, that the child will be placed in the custody of William Stern's wife.

10. In the event that the child is miscarried prior to the fifth (5th) month of pregnancy, no compensation, as enumerated in paragraph 4(A), shall be paid to Mary Beth Whitehead, Surrogate. However, the expenses enumerated in paragraph 4(C) shall be paid or reimbursed to Mary Beth Whitehead, Surrogate. In the event the child is miscarried, dies or is stillborn subsequent to the fourth (4th) month of pregnancy and said child does not survive, the Surrogate shall receive $1,000.00 in lieu of the compensation enumerated in paragraph 4(A). In the event of a miscarriage or stillbirth as described above, this Agreement shall terminate and neither Mary Beth Whitehead, Surrogate, nor William Stern, Natural Father, shall be under any further obligation under this Agreement.

11. Mary Beth Whitehead, Surrogate, and William Stern, Natural Father, shall have undergone complete physical and genetic evaluation, under the direction and supervision of a licensed physician, to determine whether the physical health and well-being of each is satisfactory. Said physical examination shall include testing for venereal diseases, specifically including but not limited to, syphilis, herpes and gonorrhea. Said venereal

disease testing shall be done prior to, but not limited to, each series of inseminations.

12. In the event that pregnancy has not occurred within a reasonable time, in the opinion of William Stern, Natural Father, this Agreement shall terminate by written notice to Mary Beth Whitehead, Surrogate, at the residence provided to the ICNY by the Surrogate, from ICNY, as representative of William Stern, Natural Father.

13. Mary Beth Whitehead, Surrogate, agrees that she will not abort the child once conceived except, if in the professional medical opinion of the inseminating physician, such action is necessary for the physical health of Mary Beth Whitehead or the child has been determined by said physician to be physiologically abnormal. Mary Beth Whitehead further agrees, upon the request of said physician to undergo amniocentesis (see Exhibit "D") or similar tests to detect genetic and congenital defects. In the event said test reveals that the fetus is genetically or congenitally abnormal, Mary Beth Whitehead, Surrogate, agrees to abort the fetus upon demand of William Stern, Natural Father, in which event, the fee paid to the Surrogate will be in accordance to Paragraph 10. If Mary Beth Whitehead refuses to abort the fetus upon demand of William Stern, his obligations as stated in this Agreement shall cease forthwith, except as to obligations of paternity imposed by statute.

14. Despite the provisions of Paragraph 13, William Stern, Natural Father, recognizes that some genetic and congenital abnormalities may not be detected by amniocentesis or other tests, and therefore, if proven to be the biological father of the child, assumes the legal responsibility for any child who may possess genetic or congenital abnormalities. (See Exhibits "E" and "F").

15. Mary Beth Whitehead, Surrogate, further agrees to adhere to all medical instructions given to her by the inseminating physician as well as her independent obstetrician. Mary Beth Whitehead also agrees not to smoke cigarettes, drink alcoholic beverages, use illegal drugs, or take non-prescription medications or prescribed medications without written consent from her physician. Mary Beth Whitehead agrees to follow a prenatal medical examination schedule to consist of no fewer visits than: one visit per month during the first seven (7) months of pregnancy, two visits (each to occur at two-week intervals) during the eighth and ninth months of pregnancy.

Visitation. A visitation plan determined by the New Jersey Superior Court, Bergen County, that Ms. Whitehead Gould is entitled to one eight hour visitation period weekly, with an increase in September 1988 to two days every other week. There is also a provision for visits overnight after a year and for two weeks during summer 1989. *See* 14 FAM. LAW REP. 1276 (Apr. 12, 1988).

Raftopol v. Ramey

Supreme Court of Connecticut, 2011
12 A.3d 783

■ MCLACHLAN, JUDGE.

This appeal raises the question of whether Connecticut law permits an intended parent[1] who is neither the biological[2] nor the adoptive parent of a child to become a legal parent of that child by means of a valid gestational agreement. The use of technology to accomplish reproduction by means other than sexual intercourse no longer may be considered "new" science, and, indeed, the legislature has recognized the validity of such agreements. Moreover, no one can deny that assisted reproductive technology implicates an essential matter of public policy—it is a basic expectation that our legal system should enable each of us to identify our legal parents with reasonable promptness and certainty. Despite the facts that assisted reproductive technology has been available for some time, and that the technology implicates the important issue of the determination of legal parentage, our laws, and the laws of most other states, have struggled unsuccessfully to keep pace with the complex legal issues that continue to arise as a result of the technology. It is our view that our laws should provide an answer to the following two basic questions: (1) who are the legal parents of children born as a result of such technology; and (2) what steps must such persons take to clarify their status as legal parents of such children? Our answers to these questions are limited by the scope of the question presented on appeal, and, even more importantly, by the fact that the broad public policy issues raised by modern reproductive technology and implicated by this appeal more appropriately would be addressed by the legislature. When, as in the present case, however, a statutory scheme is susceptible to an interpretation whereby a child born as a result of a gestational agreement could be deemed to have no legal parent, which rationally could not have been the legislature's intent, the court is bound to interpret the scheme in a manner that confers legal parentage on the intended parents pursuant to the legally valid gestational agreement.

The defendant department of public health (department) appeals from the judgment of the trial court in favor of the plaintiff Shawn Hargon, an intended parent under the gestational agreement. On appeal, the department argues that the trial court lacked subject matter jurisdiction both to terminate the putative parental rights of the

---

[1] I presume, as does the majority, that the gestational agreement is valid.

[2] I note that traditional surrogacy agreements also incorporate the principle that one of the intended parents is not biologically related to the child because the surrogate mother under such arrangements donates her own egg due to the infertility of the intended parent. The only exception to the rule that at least one of the intended parents named in a gestational or a traditional surrogacy agreement is not biologically related to the unborn child would seem to be when a woman is unable to carry and give birth to a child for medical reasons and the egg of the intended mother and the sperm of the intended father are used to create an embryo that is then implanted in the gestational carrier's uterus.

gestational carrier, the defendant Karma A. Ramey, and to declare Hargon a legal parent of the children to whom Ramey gave birth, and, consequently, to order the department to issue a replacement birth certificate pursuant to General Statutes § 7–48a, naming Hargon and the named plaintiff, Anthony Raftopol, the children's biological father, as the children's parents. The department also argues that the trial court improperly concluded that § 7–48a conferred parental status on Hargon solely on the ground that he was an intended parent and party to a valid gestational agreement. We conclude that the trial court had jurisdiction to issue the declaratory judgment. Moreover, we conclude that the trial court's judgment declaring Hargon to be the parent of the children and ordering the department to place his name on the replacement birth certificate is supported by the applicable statutes. Accordingly, we affirm the judgment of the trial court.

The record reflects the following facts, either as found by the trial court or undisputed. The plaintiffs, who were domestic partners living in Bucharest, Romania, entered into a written agreement (gestational agreement), dated July 29, 2007, with Ramey, in which she agreed to act as a gestational carrier for the plaintiffs. Pursuant to the gestational agreement, eggs were recovered from a third party egg donor and fertilized with sperm contributed by Raftopol. Three of the resulting frozen embryos were subsequently implanted in Ramey's uterus. As a result of the procedures, Ramey gave birth to two children on April 19, 2008. DNA testing confirmed that Raftopol was the biological father of the children. Pursuant to the gestational agreement, Ramey had agreed to terminate her parental rights to any children resulting from the procedures, and to sign any forms necessary for the issuance of a replacement birth certificate naming the plaintiffs as the parents of such children. Ramey also had agreed to consent to the adoption of any such children by Hargon and to cooperate fully to obtain this goal.

Prior to the expected delivery date, the plaintiffs brought this action, seeking a declaratory judgment that the gestational agreement was valid, that the plaintiffs were the legal parents of the children and requesting that the court order the department to issue a replacement birth certificate reflecting that they, and not Ramey, were parents of the children. The department responded that the court lacked jurisdiction over the matter because Hargon did not allege that he had conceived the children and because the court lacked jurisdiction to terminate the parental rights of the gestational carrier, the egg donor, and any husbands either may have, which the department argued would be a necessary prerequisite to the declaration that Hargon is a parent of the children. Finally, the department contended that the allegations of the complaint did not sufficiently establish the paternity of the children. Following a hearing, the trial court issued a ruling declaring that: (1) the gestational agreement is valid; (2) Raftopol is the genetic and legal father of the children; (3) Hargon is the legal father of the children; and

(4) Ramey is not the genetic or legal mother of the children. The court therefore ordered the department to issue a replacement birth certificate pursuant to § 7–48a. This appeal followed.

We first turn to the issue of whether the trial court lacked subject matter jurisdiction to declare Hargon a legal parent of the children because Hargon was not biologically related to the children and did not adopt them. Included within this issue is the question of whether the court was required, as a prerequisite to making any determination regarding Hargon's parental status, to terminate Ramey's parental rights, and, if so, whether the court had jurisdiction to terminate those rights. We conclude that: (1) because Ramey did not have any parental rights with respect to the children, the termination of those nonexistent rights was not a necessary prerequisite to a determination of Hargon's parental status with respect to the children; and (2) the court had jurisdiction to issue a declaratory ruling regarding Hargon's parental status.

Preliminarily, we address the department's claim that the trial court lacked subject matter jurisdiction to declare Hargon a parent because the termination of Ramey's parental rights—over which the trial court would have lacked jurisdiction—was a necessary prerequisite to Hargon's acquiring parental status with respect to the children. "[O]nce the question of lack of jurisdiction of a court is raised, [it] must be disposed of no matter in what form it is presented . . . and the court must fully resolve it before proceeding further with the case." (Internal quotation marks omitted.) Golden Hill Paugussett Tribe of Indians v. Southbury, 231 Conn. 563, 570, 651 A.2d 1246 (1995). Because Ramey had no parental rights to terminate, we conclude that the trial court was not deprived of jurisdiction.

Our statutes and case law establish that a gestational carrier who bears no biological relationship to the child she has carried does not have parental rights with respect to that child. We have long recognized that there are three ways by which a person may become a parent: conception, adoption or pursuant to the artificial insemination statutes. See, e.g., Doe v. Doe, 244 Conn. 403, 435, 710 A.2d 1297 (1998); Remkiewicz v. Remkiewicz, 180 Conn. 114, 116–17, 429 A.2d 833 (1980). The definitional section of chapter 803 of the General Statutes, which deals with termination of parental rights and adoption, defines " '[p]arent' " as "a biological or adoptive parent. . . ." General Statutes § 45a–707 (5). The same definitional section defines " '[t]ermination of parental rights' " as "the complete severance by court order of the legal relationship, with all its rights and responsibilities, between the child and the child's *parent* or *parents*. . . ." (Emphasis added.) General Statutes § 45a–707 (8). Reading these two subdivisions of the same statute together suggests that only persons who are biological or adoptive parents have parental rights with respect to the subject children.

In 1975, the legislature provided the third means by which a person may gain parental status. Public Acts 1975, No. 75–233, now codified at General Statutes § 45a–774. Section 45a–774 provides: "Any child or children born as a result of A.I.D. shall be deemed to acquire, in all respects, the status of a naturally conceived legitimate child of the husband and wife who consented to and requested the use of A.I.D." " 'A.I.D.' " is defined as "artificial insemination with the use of donated sperm or eggs from an identified or anonymous donor." General Statutes § 45a–771a (2). " 'Artificial insemination' " is specifically defined to include both "intrauterine insemination and in vitro fertilization. . . ." General Statutes § 45a–771a (1). Accordingly, a child born to a married woman and conceived through artificial insemination by an egg or sperm donor is the child of the wife and husband who requested and consented to the use of A.I.D.

Our decisions prior to the passage of § 7–48a confirm that these three avenues were the exclusive means by which a person could acquire parental status. The question of the meaning of the term parent has most commonly arisen in the context of dissolution actions, when the parties have raised claims relating to custody or support. For example, in Remkiewicz v. Remkiewicz, supra, 180 Conn. at 120, 429 A.2d 833, the attorney general sought an order compelling the defendant husband to pay support for his wife's minor child, Jennifer, who was not the defendant's biological child. Three years prior to the dissolution action, the husband had filed an affidavit of parentage, seeking to change Jennifer's birth certificate to list himself as her father and her name as Jennifer Remkiewicz. Id., at 116, 429 A.2d 833. In affirming the judgment of the trial court denying the motion for an order of support, we framed the issue as "whether the court had any authority to issue such an order as against a husband who was neither the biological nor adoptive parent of the child for whom support was sought." Id., at 116–17, 429 A.2d 833. We began with the proposition that the duty to support "is one imposed on parents." Id., at 117, 429 A.2d 833. We concluded that the defendant was not Jennifer's legal father because he was not her biological father, had not been adjudicated so in a paternity proceeding, and had not adopted her. Id. This rule, we reasoned, was consistent with the legislative intent expressed in the statutory scheme for adoption; see General Statutes c. 803; namely, that "no person shall acquire parental status unless certain formalities are observed. . . . If a stepfather could acquire parental rights through the simple expedient of changing his stepchild's birth certificate, all sorts of mischief could result." *Remkiewicz v. Remkiewicz,* supra, at 120, 429 A.2d 833. . . .

Under any of the three specified ways of acquiring parental status, as set forth both in our statutes and interpretive case law, Ramey is not a parent of the children in the present case. It is undisputed that she is neither the biological nor the adoptive mother to the children. Nor does she fall within the parameters of the artificial insemination statutes.

Accordingly, Ramey did not have parental rights that required termination before Hargon could acquire parental status with respect to the children.

NOTES

The *Raftopol* facts indicate that Shawn Hargon and Anthony Raftopol were domestic partners, a status granting them some of the benefits of marriage in the states that permitted it. After June 26, 2015, same-sex marriage became available to all citizens of the United States, perhaps impacting how these cases will be decided in the future. *See* Obergefell v. Hodges, 135 S.Ct. 2584 (2015).

The facts indicate that Mr. Hargon sought to become a parent to the children born to Karma A. Ramey, even though he had no genetic connection to the child; Anthony Raftopol's sperm was used in conception. Would it have made a difference if he and Mr. Raftopol had been married instead of domestic partners? The court makes no explicit reference to this, perhaps because same-sex marriage was rare at the time of the decision and the same-sex couple was not in fact married. Nonetheless, the court's decision references General Statutes § 45a–774, which provides that any child born shall be a child of the *husband and wife* who consented to the use of assisted reproduction. Because the court holds that the gestational agreement is valid, it would follow that a marriage between persons of the same sex would result in parenthood for the spouse who contributed no genetic material but that resulted in the birth of a child via a valid surrogacy agreement. Commentary following *Obergefell* is still nascent but discussion has started. *See, e.g.*, Deborah A. Widiss, *Non-Marital Families and (or After?) Marriage Equality*, 42 FLA. ST. U. L. REV. 547 (2015); Kenji Yoshino, *A New Birth of Freedom? Obergefell v. Hodges,* 129 HARV. L. REV. 147 (2015); Joanna L. Grossman, *The New Illegitimacy: Tying Parentage to Marital Status for Lesbian Co-Parents*, 20 AM. U. J. GENDER SOC. POL'Y & L. 671 (2012).

There is a contrast between the historic New Jersey decision of *Baby M* and the Connecticut decision of *Raftopol*. They are similar in that both involved surrogacy contracts and both lack clearly defined statutory guidelines. Yet, *Raftopol* involves a same-sex couple seeking to become joint parents, a procedure employed by many same-sex couples today. Perceptions, and thus public policy, have shifted considerably since *Baby M* was decided. Nonetheless, New Jersey courts continue to rule that surrogacy contracts are void. *See* A.G.R. v. D.R.H., No. ED–09–1838–07 (N.J. Super. Ct. Dec. 23, 2009). At least a third of the states have enacted statutes permitting, forbidding, or qualifying gestational agreements. The National Conference of Commissioners on Uniform State Laws, seeking to provide clarity, promulgated the Uniform Status of Children of Assisted Conception Act (9C U.L.A. 363 et seq. (2001)). The Act provides two alternatives for states to consider in reference to gestational agreements: total prohibition, or sanctioning of the agreements with supervisory provisions. Two states were influenced by the Act: New Hampshire, N.H. STAT. ANN. §§ 168–B:1 thru B:32 (2016) (permitting agreements if they have been approved prior to the birth of any child); and Virginia, VA. CODE ANN. § 20–156 et seq. (2016)

(permitting agreements if a married couple fulfills the extensive conditions imposed by the statute). For commentary on surrogacy, *see, e.g.*, Joseph F. Morrissey, *Surrogacy: The Process, The Law, and the Contracts*, 51 WILLAMETTE L. REV. 459 (2015); Yehezkel Margalit, *In Defense of Surrogacy Agreement: A Modern Contract Law Perspective*, 20 WM. & MARY J. WOMEN & L. 423 (2014); Gaia Bernstein, *Unintended Consequences: Prohibitions on Gamete Donor Anonymity and the Fragile Practice of Surrogacy*, 10 IND. HEALTH L. REV. 291 (2013); Paul G. Arshagouni, *Be Fruitful and Multiply, By Other Means, If Necessary: The Time Has Come to Recognize and Enforce Gestational Surrogacy Agreements*, 61 DEPAUL L. REV. 799 (2012); Andrea B. Carroll, *Regulating the Baby Market: A Call for a Ban on Payment of Birth-Mother Living Expenses*, 59 U. KAN. L. REV. 285 (2011); J. Herbie DiFonzo and Ruth C. Stern, *The Children of Baby M*, 39 CAP. U. L. REV. 345 (2011); Linda D. Elrod, *A Child's Perspective of Defining a Parent: The Case for Intended Parenthood*, 25 BYU J. PUB. L. 217 (2011); Deborah L. Forman, *When 'Bad' Mothers Make Worse Law: A Critique of Legislative Limits on Embryo Transfer*, 15 U. PA. J.L. & SOC. CHANGE 273 (2011); J. Brad Reich and Dawn Swink, *Outsourcing Human Reproduction: Embryos & Surrogacy Services in the Cyberprocreation Era*, 14 J. HEALTH CARE L. & POL'Y 241 (2011); and Christine Metteer *Lorillard, Informed Choices and Uniform Decisions: Adopting the ABA's Self-Enforcing Administrative Model to Ensure Successful Surrogacy Arrangements,* 16 CARDOZO J.L. & GENDER 237 (2010); Carla Spivack, *The Law of Surrogate Motherhood in the United States*, 58 AM. J. OF COMP. LAW 97 (2010).

UNIFORM PARENTAGE ACT (AMENDED 2002)

§ 801. Gestational Agreement Authorized

(a) A Prospective gestational mother, her husband if she is married, a donor or the donors, and the intended parents may enter into a written agreement providing that:

  (1) the prospective gestational mother agrees to pregnancy by means of assisted reproduction;

  (2) the prospective gestational mother, her husband if she is married, and the donors relinquish all rights and duties as the parents of a child conceived through assisted reproduction; and

  (3) the intended parents become the parents of the child.

(b) The man and the woman who are the intended parents must both be parties to the gestational agreement.

(c) A gestational agreement is enforceable only if validated as provided in Section 803.

(d) A gestational agreement does not apply to the birth of a child conceived by means of sexual intercourse.

(e) A gestational agreement may provide for payment of consideration.

(f) A gestational agreement may not limit the right of the gestational mother to make decisions to safeguard her health or that of the embryos or fetus. . . .

§ 803. Hearing to Validate Gestational Agreement

(a) If the requirements of subsection (b) are satisfied, a court may issue an order validating the gestational agreement and declaring that the intended parents will be the parents of a child born during the term of the agreement.

(b) The court may issue an order under subsection (a) only on finding that:

(1) the residence requirements of Section 802 have been satisfied and the parties have submitted to the jurisdiction of the court under the jurisdictional standards of this [Act];

(2) unless waived by the court, the [relevant child-welfare agency] has made a home study of the intended parents and the intended parents meet the standards of suitability applicable to adoptive parents;

(3) all parties have voluntarily entered into the agreement and understand its terms;

(4) adequate provision has been made for all reasonable health-care expense associated with the gestational agreement until the birth of the child, including responsibility for those expenses if the agreement is terminated; and

(5) the consideration, if any, paid to the prospective gestational mother is reasonable. . . .

§ 807. Parentage Under Validated Gestational Agreement

(a) Upon birth of a child to a gestational mother, the intended parents shall file notice with the court that a child has been born to the gestational mother within 300 days after assisted reproduction. Thereupon a court shall issue an order:

(1) confirming that the intended parents are the parents of the child;

(2) if necessary, ordering that the child be surrendered to the intended parents; and

(3) directing the [agency maintaining birth records] to issue a birth certificate naming the intended parents as parents of the child.

(b) If the parentage of a child born to a gestational mother is alleged not to be the result of assisted reproduction, the court shall order genetic testing to determine the parentage of the child.

(c) If the intended parents fail to file notice required under subsection (a), the gestational mother or the appropriate State agency may file notice with the court that a child has been born to the gestational mother within 300 days after assisted reproduction. Upon proof of a court order issued pursuant to Section 803 validating the gestational agreement, the court shall order the intended parents are the parents of the child and are financially responsible for the child.

CHAPTER VII

RAISING CHILDREN: COMPETING INTERESTS

A. PARENTAL PREROGATIVES

1. RELIGIOUS LIBERTY

Wisconsin v. Yoder

Supreme Court of the United States, 1972
406 U.S. 205

■ BURGER, CHIEF JUSTICE delivered the opinion of the Court.

[We granted certiorari to review a] Wisconsin Supreme Court holding that respondents' convictions for violating the State's compulsory school-attendance law were invalid under the Free Exercise Clause of the First Amendment to the United States Constitution made applicable to the States by the Fourteenth Amendment. . . . [W]e affirm the judgment of the Supreme Court of Wisconsin.

[Respondents were Wisconsin residents and members of either the Old Order Amish religion or the Conservative Amish Mennonite Church. Their children, ages 14 and 15 were not enrolled in any public or private school, although Wisconsin's compulsory school-attendance law requires parents to cause their children to attend school until they reach age 16. Respondents were convicted of violating the law and fined $5 each.]

The trial testimony showed that respondents believed, in accordance with the tenets of Old Order Amish communities generally, that their children's attendance at high school, public or private, was contrary to the Amish religion and way of life. They believed that by sending their children to high school, they would not only expose themselves to the danger of the censure of the church community, but, as found by the county court, also endanger their own salvation and that of their children. The State stipulated that respondents' religious beliefs were sincere. In support of their position, respondents presented as expert witnesses scholars on religion and education whose testimony is uncontradicted. They expressed their opinions on the relationship of the Amish belief concerning school attendance to the more general tenets of their religion, and described the impact that compulsory high school attendance could have on the continued survival of Amish communities as they exist in the United States today. . . .

Formal high school education beyond the eighth grade is contrary to Amish beliefs, not only because it places Amish children in an environment hostile to Amish beliefs with increasing emphasis on competition in class work and sports and with pressure to conform to the styles, manners, and ways of the peer group, but also because it takes them away from their community, physically and emotionally, during the crucial and formative adolescent period of life. During this period, the children must acquire Amish attitudes favoring manual work and self-reliance and the specific skills needed to perform the adult role of an Amish farmer or housewife. They must learn to enjoy physical labor. Once a child has learned basic reading, writing, and elementary mathematics, these traits, skills, and attitudes admittedly fall within the category of those best learned through example and "doing" rather than in a classroom. And, at this time in life, the Amish child must also grow in his faith and his relationship to the Amish community if he is to be prepared to accept the heavy obligations imposed by adult baptism. In short, high school attendance with teachers who are not of the Amish faith—and may even be hostile to it—interposes a serious barrier to the integration of the Amish child into the Amish religious community. Dr. John Hostetler, one of the experts on Amish society, testified that the modern high school is not equipped, in curriculum or social environment, to impart the values promoted by Amish society.

The Amish do not object to elementary education through the first eight grades as a general proposition because they agree that their children must have basic skills in the "three R's" in order to read the Bible, to be good farmers and citizens, and to be able to deal with non-Amish people when necessary in the course of daily affairs. They view such a basic education as acceptable because it does not significantly expose their children to worldly values or interfere with their development in the Amish community during the crucial adolescent period. While Amish accept compulsory elementary education generally, wherever possible they have established their own elementary schools in many respects like the small local schools of the past. In the Amish belief higher learning tends to develop values they reject as influences that alienate man from God.

On the basis of such considerations, Dr. Hostetler testified that compulsory high school attendance could not only result in great psychological harm to Amish children, because of the conflicts it would produce, but would also, in his opinion, ultimately result in the destruction of the Old Order Amish church community as it exists in the United States today. . . .

[A] State's interest in universal education, however highly we rank it, is not totally free from a balancing process when it impinges on fundamental rights and interests, such as those specifically protected by the Free Exercise Clause of the First Amendment, and the traditional interest of parents with respect to the religious upbringing of their children so long as they, in the words of Pierce [v. Society of Sisters], "prepare [them] for additional obligations." 268 U.S., at 535, 45 S.Ct., at 573.

It follows that in order for Wisconsin to compel school attendance beyond the eighth grade against a claim that such attendance interferes with the practice of a legitimate religious belief, it must appear either that the State does not deny the free exercise of religious belief by its requirement, or that there is a state interest of sufficient magnitude to override the interest claiming protection under the Free Exercise Clause. Long before there was general acknowledgment of the need for universal formal education, the Religion Clauses had specifically and firmly fixed the right to free exercise of religious beliefs, and buttressing this fundamental right was an equally firm, even if less explicit, prohibition against the establishment of any religion by government. The values underlying these two provisions relating to religion have been zealously protected, sometimes even at the expense of other interests of admittedly high social importance. The invalidation of financial aid to parochial schools by government grants for a salary subsidy for teachers is but one example of the extent to which courts have gone in this regard, notwithstanding that such aid programs were legislatively determined to be in the public interest and the service of sound educational policy by States and by Congress. Lemon v. Kurtzman, 403 U.S. 602, 91 S.Ct. 2105, 29 L.Ed.2d 745 (1971).

The essence of all that has been said and written on the subject is that only those interests of the highest order and those not otherwise served can overbalance legitimate claims to the free exercise of religion. We can accept it as settled, therefore, that, however strong the State's interest in universal compulsory education, it is by no means absolute to the exclusion or subordination of all other interests.

We come then to the quality of the claims of the respondents concerning the alleged encroachment of Wisconsin's compulsory school-attendance statute on their rights and the rights of their children to the free exercise of the religious beliefs they and their forbears have adhered to for almost three centuries. In evaluating those claims we must be careful to determine whether the Amish religious faith and their mode of life are, as they claim, inseparable and interdependent. . . . [T]he record in this case abundantly supports the claim that the traditional way of life of the Amish is not merely a matter of personal preference, but one of deep religious conviction, shared by an organized group, and intimately related to daily living. . . . [T]he unchallenged testimony of acknowledged experts in education and religious history, almost 300 years of consistent practice, and strong evidence of a sustained faith pervading and regulating respondents' entire mode of life support the claim that enforcement of the State's requirement of compulsory formal education after the eighth grade would gravely endanger if not destroy the free exercise of respondents' religious beliefs. . . .

We turn . . . to the State's broader contention that its interest in its system of compulsory education is so compelling that even the established religious practices of the Amish must give away. The State advances two primary arguments in support of its system of compulsory education. It notes, as Thomas Jefferson pointed out early in our history, that some degree of education is necessary to prepare citizens to participate effectively and intelligently in our open political system if we are to preserve freedom and independence. Further, education prepares individuals to be self-reliant and self-sufficient participants in society. We accept these propositions.

However, the evidence adduced by the Amish in this case is persuasively to the effect that an additional one or two years of formal high school for Amish children in place of their long-established program of informal vocational education would do little to serve those interests. Respondents' experts testified at trial, without challenge, that the value of all education must be assessed in terms of its capacity to prepare the child for life. It is one thing to say that compulsory education for a year or two beyond the eighth grade may be necessary when its goal is the preparation of the child for life in modern society as the majority live, but it is quite another if the goal of education be viewed as the preparation of the child for life in the separated agrarian community that is the keystone of the Amish faith. See Meyer v. Nebraska, 262 U.S., at 400, 43 S.Ct., at 627, 67 L.Ed. 1042.

The State attacks respondents' position as one fostering "ignorance" from which the child must be protected by the State. No one can question the State's duty to protect children from ignorance but this argument does not square with the facts disclosed in the record. Whatever their idiosyncrasies as seen by the majority, this record strongly shows that the Amish community has been a highly successful social unit without our society, even if apart from the conventional "mainstream." Its members are productive and very law-abiding members of society; they reject public welfare in any of its usual modern forms. The Congress itself recognized their self-sufficiency by authorizing exemption of such groups as the Amish from the obligation to pay social security taxes.[11]

It is neither fair nor correct to suggest that the Amish are opposed to education beyond the eighth grade level. What this record shows is that they are opposed to conventional formal education of the type provided by a certified high school because it comes at the child's crucial

---

[11] Title 26 U.S.C. § 1402(h) authorizes the Secretary of Health, Education, and Welfare to exempt members of "a recognized religious sect" existing at all times since December 31, 1950, from the obligation to pay social security taxes if they are, by reason of the tenets of their sect, opposed to receipt of such benefits and agree to waive them, provided the Secretary finds that the sect makes reasonable provision for its dependent members. The history of the exemption shows it was enacted with the situation of the Old Order Amish specifically in view. H.R.Rep. No. 213, 89th Cong., 1st Sess., 101–102 (1965).

The record in this case establishes without contradiction that the Green County Amish had never been known to commit crimes, that none had been known to receive public assistance, and that none were unemployed.

adolescent period of religious development. Dr. Donald Erickson, for example, testified that their system of learning-by-doing was an "ideal system" of education in terms of preparing Amish children for life as adults in the Amish community. . . .

We must not forget that in the Middle Ages important values of the civilization of the Western World were preserved by members of religious orders who isolated themselves from all worldly influences against great obstacles. There can be no assumption that today's majority is "right" and the Amish and others like them are "wrong." A way of life that is odd or even erratic but interferes with no rights or interests of others is not to be condemned because it is different.

The State, however, supports its interest in providing an additional one or two years of compulsory high school education to Amish children because of the possibility that some such children will choose to leave the Amish community, and that if this occurs they will be ill-equipped for life. The State argues that if Amish children leave their church they should not be in the position of making their way in the world without the education available in the one or two additional years the State requires. However, on this record, that argument is highly speculative. There is no specific evidence of the loss of Amish adherents by attrition, nor is there any showing that upon leaving the Amish community Amish children, with their practical agricultural training and habits of industry and self-reliance, would become burdens on society because of educational shortcomings. Indeed, this argument of the State appears to rest primarily on the State's mistaken assumption, already noted, that the Amish do not provide any education for their children beyond the eighth grade, but allow them to grow in "ignorance." To the contrary, not only do the Amish accept the necessity for formal schooling through the eighth grade level, but continue to provide what has been characterized by the undisputed testimony of expert educators as an "ideal" vocational education for their children in the adolescent years.

There is nothing in this record to suggest that the Amish qualities of reliability, self-reliance, and dedication to work would fail to find ready markets in today's society. Absence some contrary evidence supporting the State's position, we are unwilling to assume that persons possessing such valuable vocational skills and habits are doomed to become burdens on society should they determine to leave the Amish faith, nor is there any basis in the record to warrant a finding that an additional one or two years of formal school education beyond the eighth grade would serve to eliminate any such problem that might exist. . . .

The requirement for compulsory education beyond the eighth grade is a relatively recent development in our history. Less than 60 years ago, the educational requirements of almost all of the States were satisfied by completion of the elementary grades, at least where the child was regularly and lawfully employed. The independence and successful social functioning of the Amish community for a period approaching almost three centuries and more than 200 years in this country are strong evidence that there is at best a speculative gain, in terms of meeting the duties of citizenship, from an additional one or two years of compulsory formal education. Against this background it would require a more particularized showing from the State on this point to justify the severe interference with religious freedom such additional compulsory attendance would entail.

We should also note that compulsory education and child labor laws find their historical origin in common humanitarian instincts, and that the age limits of both laws have been coordinated to achieve their related objectives. In the context of this case, such considerations, if anything, support rather than detract from respondents' position. The origins of the requirement for school attendance to age 16, an age falling after the completion of elementary school but before completion of high school, are not entirely clear. But to some extent such laws reflected the movement to prohibit most child labor under age 16 that culminated in the provisions of the Federal Fair Labor Standards Act of 1938. It is true, then, that the 16-year child labor age limit may to some degree derive from a contemporary impression that children should be in school until that age. But at the same time, it cannot be denied that, conversely, the 16-year education limit reflects, in substantial measure, the concern that children under that age not be employed under conditions hazardous to their health, or in work that should be performed by adults.

The requirement of compulsory schooling to age 16 must therefore be viewed as aimed not merely at providing educational opportunities for children, but as an alternative to the equally undesirable consequence of unhealthful child labor displacing adult workers, or, on the other hand, forced idleness. The two kinds of statutes—compulsory school attendance and child labor laws—tend to keep children of certain ages off the labor market and in school; this regimen in turn provides opportunity to prepare for a livelihood of a higher order than that which children could pursue without education and protects their health in adolescence.

In these terms, Wisconsin's interest in compelling the school attendance of Amish children to age 16 emerges as somewhat less substantial than requiring such attendance for children generally. For, while agricultural employment is not totally outside the legitimate concerns of the child labor laws, employment of children under parental guidance and on the family farm from age 14 to age 16 is an ancient tradition that lies at the periphery of the objectives of such laws. There is no intimation that the Amish employment of their children on family farms is in any way deleterious to their health or that Amish parents exploit children at tender years. Any such inference would be contrary to the record before us. Moreover, employment of Amish children on the family farm does not present the undesirable economic aspects of eliminating jobs that might otherwise be held by adults.

Finally, the State, on authority of Prince v. Massachusetts, argues that a decision exempting Amish children from the State's requirement fails to recognize the substantive right of the Amish child to a secondary education, and fails to give due regard to the power of the State as *parens patriae* to extend the benefit of secondary education to children regardless of the wishes of their parents. Taken at its broadest sweep, the Court's language in *Prince,* might be read to give support to the State's position. However, the Court was not confronted in *Prince* with a situation comparable to that of the Amish as revealed in this record; this is shown by the Court's severe characterization of the evils that it thought the legislature could legitimately associate with child labor, even when performed in the company of an adult. 321 U.S., at 169–170, 64 S.Ct., at 443–444. The Court later took great care to confine *Prince* to a narrow scope in Sherbert v. Verner, when it stated:

> "On the other hand, the Court has rejected challenges under the Free Exercise Clause to governmental regulation of certain overt acts prompted by religious beliefs or principles, for 'even when the action is in accord with one's religious convictions, [it] is not totally free from legislative restrictions.' Braunfeld v. Brown, 366 U.S. 599, 603, 81 S.Ct. 1144, 1146, 6 L.Ed.2d 563. The conduct or actions so regulated have invariably posed some substantial threat to public safety, peace or order. *See, e.g.*, Reynolds v. United States, 98 U.S. 145, 25 L.Ed. 244; Jacobson v. Massachusetts, 197 U.S. 11, 25 S.Ct. 358, 49 L.Ed. 643; Prince v. Massachusetts, 321 U.S. 158, 64 S.Ct. 438, 88 L.Ed. 645. . . ." 374 U.S., at 402–403, 83 S.Ct., at 1793.

This case, of course, is not one in which any harm to the physical or mental health of the child or to the public safety, peace, order, or welfare has been demonstrated or may be properly inferred. The record is to the contrary, and any reliance on that theory would find no support in the evidence.

Contrary to the suggestion of the dissenting opinion of Mr. Justice Douglas, our holding today in no degree depends on the assertion of the religious interest of the child as contrasted with that of the parents. It is the parents who are subject to prosecution here for failing to cause their children to attend school, and it is their right of free exercise, not that of their children, that must determine Wisconsin's power to impose criminal penalties on the parent. The dissent argues that a child who expresses a desire to attend public high school in conflict with the wishes of his parents should not be prevented from doing so. There is no reason for the Court to consider that point since it is not an issue in the case. The children are not parties to this litigation. The State has at no point tried this case on the theory that respondents were preventing their children from attending school against their expressed desires, and indeed the record is to the contrary. The State's position from the outset has been that it is empowered to apply its compulsory-attendance law to

Amish parents in the same manner as to other parents—that is, without regard to the wishes of the child. That is the claim we reject today.

Our holding in no way determines the proper resolution of possible competing interests of parents, children, and the State in an appropriate state court proceeding in which the power of the State is asserted on the theory that Amish parents are preventing their minor children from attending high school despite their expressed desires to the contrary. Recognition of the claim of the State in such a proceeding would, of course, call into question traditional concepts of parental control over the religious upbringing and education of their minor children recognized in this Court's past decisions. It is clear that such an intrusion by a State into family decisions in the area of religious training would give rise to grave questions of religious freedom comparable to those raised here and those presented in Pierce v. Society of Sisters, 268 U.S. 510, 45 S.Ct. 571, 69 L.Ed. 1070 (1925). On this record we neither reach nor decide those issues.

The State's argument proceeds without reliance on any actual conflict between the wishes of parents and children. It appears to rest on the potential that exemption of Amish parents from the requirements of the compulsory-education law might allow some parents to act contrary to the best interests of their children by foreclosing their opportunity to make an intelligent choice between the Amish way of life and that of the outside world. The same argument could, of course, be made with respect to all church schools short of college. There is nothing in the record or in the ordinary course of human experience to suggest that non-Amish parents generally consult with children of ages 14–16 if they are placed in a church school of the parents' faith.

Indeed it seems clear that if the State is empowered, as *parens patriae,* to "save" a child from himself or his Amish parents by requiring an additional two years of compulsory formal high school education, the State will in large measure influence, if not determine, the religious future of the child. Even more markedly than in *Prince,* therefore, this case involves the fundamental interest of parents, as contrasted with that of the State, to guide the religious future and education of their children. The history and culture of Western civilization reflect a strong tradition of parental concern for the nurture and upbringing of their children. This primary role of the parents in the upbringing of their children is now established beyond debate as an enduring American tradition. If not the first, perhaps the most significant statements of the Court in this area are found in Pierce v. Society of Sisters, in which the Court observed:

> "Under the doctrine of Meyer v. Nebraska, 262 U.S. 390, 43 S.Ct. 625, 67 L.Ed. 1042, we think it entirely plain that the Act of 1922 unreasonably interferes with the liberty of parents and guardians to direct the upbringing and education of children under their control. As often heretofore pointed out, rights

> guaranteed by the Constitution may not be abridged by legislation which has no reasonable relation to some purpose within the competency of the State. The fundamental theory of liberty upon which all governments in this Union repose excludes any general power of the State to standardize its children by forcing them to accept instruction from public teachers only. The child is not the mere creature of the State; those who nurture him and direct his destiny have the right, coupled with the high duty, to recognize and prepare him for additional obligations." 268 U.S., at 534–535, 45 S.Ct., at 573.

The duty to prepare the child for "additional obligations," referred to by the Court, must be read to include the inculcation of moral standards, religious beliefs, and elements of good citizenship. *Pierce,* of course, recognized that where nothing more than the general interest of the parent in the nurture and education of his children is involved, it is beyond dispute that the State acts "reasonably" and constitutionally in requiring education to age 16 in some public or private school meeting the standards prescribed by the State.

However read, the Court's holding in *Pierce* stands as a charter of the rights of parents to direct the religious upbringing of their children. And, when the interests of parenthood are combined with a free exercise claim of the nature revealed by this record, more than merely a "reasonable relation to some purpose within the competency of the State" is required to sustain the validity of the State's requirement under the First Amendment. To be sure, the power of the parent, even when linked to a free exercise claim, may be subject to limitation under *Prince* if it appears that parental decisions will jeopardize the health or safety of the child, or have a potential for significant social burdens. But in this case, the Amish have introduced persuasive evidence undermining the arguments the State has advanced to support its claims in terms of the welfare of the child and society as a whole. The record strongly indicates that accommodating the religious objections of the Amish by forgoing one, or at most two, additional years of compulsory education will not impair the physical or mental health of the child, or result in an inability to be self-supporting or to discharge the duties and responsibilities of citizenship, or in any other way materially detract from the welfare of society.

In the face of our consistent emphasis on the central values underlying the Religion Clauses in our constitutional scheme of government, we cannot accept a *parens patriae* claim of such all-encompassing scope and with such sweeping potential for broad and unforeseeable application as that urged by the State.

For the reasons stated we hold, with the Supreme Court of Wisconsin, that the First and Fourteenth Amendments prevent the State from compelling respondents to cause their children to attend formal high school to age 16. Our disposition of this case, however, in no way alters our recognition of the obvious fact that courts are not school boards or legislatures, and are ill-equipped to determine the "necessity" of discrete aspects of a State's program of compulsory education. This should suggest that courts must move with great circumspection in performing the sensitive and delicate task of weighing a State's legitimate social concern when faced with religious claims for exemption from generally applicable educational requirements. It cannot be overemphasized that we are not dealing with a way of life and mode of education by a group claiming to have recently discovered some "progressive" or more enlightened process for rearing children for modern life.

Aided by a history of three centuries as an identifiable religious sect and a long history as a successful and self-sufficient segment of American society, the Amish in this case have convincingly demonstrated the sincerity of their religious beliefs, the interrelationship of belief with their mode of life, the vital role that belief and daily conduct play in the continued survival of Old Order Amish communities and their religious organization, and the hazards presented by the State's enforcement of a statute generally valid as to others. Beyond this, they have carried the even more difficult burden of demonstrating the adequacy of their alternative mode of continuing informal vocational education in terms of precisely those overall interests that the State advances in support of its program of compulsory high school education. In light of this convincing showing, one that probably few other religious groups or sects could make, and weighing the minimal difference between what the State would require and what the Amish already accept, it was incumbent on the State to show with more particularity how its admittedly strong interest in compulsory education would be adversely affected by granting an exemption to the Amish.

Nothing we hold is intended to undermine the general applicability of the State's compulsory school-attendance statutes or to limit the power of the State to promulgate reasonable standards that, while not impairing the free exercise of religion, provide for continuing agricultural vocational education under parental and church guidance by the Old Order Amish or others similarly situated. The States have had a long history of amicable and effective relationships with church-sponsored schools, and there is no basis for assuming that, in this related context, reasonable standards cannot be established concerning the content of the continuing vocational education of Amish children under parental guidance, provided always that state regulations are not inconsistent with what we have said in this opinion.

Affirmed.

■ MR. JUSTICE POWELL and MR. JUSTICE REHNQUIST took no part in the consideration or decision of this case.

■ MR. JUSTICE STEWART with whom MR. JUSTICE BRENNAN joins, concurring. (omitted).

■ MR. JUSTICE WHITE, with whom MR. JUSTICE BRENNAN and MR. JUSTICE STEWART join, concurring. (omitted).

■ MR. JUSTICE DOUGLAS, dissenting in part.

. . .

The Court's analysis assumes that the only interests at stake in the case are those of the Amish parents on the one hand, and those of the State on the other. The difficulty with this approach is that, despite the Court's claim, the parents are seeking to vindicate not only their own free exercise claims, but also those of their high-school-age children.

It is argued that the right of the Amish children to religious freedom is not presented by the facts of the case, as the issue before the Court involves only the Amish parents' religious freedom to defy a state criminal statute imposing upon them an affirmative duty to cause their children to attend high school.

First, respondents' motion to dismiss in the trial court expressly asserts, not only the religious liberty of the adults, but also that of the children, as a defense to the prosecutions. It is, of course, beyond question that the parents have standing as defendants in a criminal prosecution to assert the religious interests of their children as a defense.[1] Although the lower courts and a majority of this Court assume an identity of interest between parent and child, it is clear that they have treated the religious interest of the child as a factor in the analysis.

Second, it is essential to reach the question to decide the case, not only because the question was squarely raised in the motion to dismiss, but also because no analysis of religious-liberty claims can take place in a vacuum. If the parents in this case are allowed a religious exemption, the inevitable effect is to impose the parents' notions of religious duty upon their children. Where the child is mature enough to express potentially conflicting desires, it would be an invasion of the child's rights to permit such an imposition without canvassing his views. As in Prince v. Massachusetts, 321 U.S. 158, 64 S.Ct. 438, 88 L.Ed. 645, it is an imposition resulting from this very litigation. As the child has no other effective forum, it is in this litigation that his rights should be considered. And, if an Amish child desires to attend high school, and is mature enough to have that desire respected, the State may well be able to override the parents' religiously motivated objections. Religion is an

---

[1] Thus, in Prince v. Massachusetts, 321 U.S. 158, 64 S.Ct. 438, 88 L.Ed. 645, a Jehovah's Witness was convicted for having violated a state child labor law by allowing her nine-year-old niece and ward to circulate religious literature on the public streets. There, as here, the narrow question was the religious liberty of the adult. There, as here, the Court analyzed the problem from the point of view of the State's conflicting interest in the welfare of the child. But, as Mr. Justice Brennan, speaking for the Court, has so recently pointed out, "The Court [in *Prince*] implicitly held that the custodian had standing to assert alleged freedom of religion . . . rights of the child that were threatened in the very litigation before the Court and that the child had no effective way of asserting herself." Eisenstadt v. Baird, 405 U.S. 438, 446 n. 6, 92 S.Ct. 1029, 1034, 31 L.Ed.2d 349. Here, as in *Prince,* the children have no effective alternate means to vindicate their rights. The question, therefore, is squarely before us.

individual experience. It is not necessary, nor even appropriate, for every Amish child to express his views on the subject in a prosecution of a single adult. Crucial, however, are the views of the child whose parent is the subject of the suit. Frieda Yoder has in fact testified that her own religious views are opposed to high-school education. I therefore join the judgment of the Court as to respondent Jonas Yoder. But Frieda Yoder's views may not be those of Vernon Yutzy or Barbara Miller. I must dissent, therefore, as to respondents Adin Yutzy and Wallace Miller as their motion to dismiss also raised the question of their children's religious liberty. . . . These children are "persons" within the meaning of the Bill of Rights. We have so held over and over again. . . .

On this important and vital matter of education, I think the children should be entitled to be heard. While the parents, absent dissent, normally speak for the entire family, the education of the child is a matter on which the child will often have decided views. He may want to be a pianist or an astronaut or an oceanographer. To do so he will have to break from the Amish tradition.

It is the future of the student, not the future of the parents, that is imperiled by today's decision. If a parent keeps his child out of school beyond the grade school, then the child will be forever barred from entry into the new and amazing world of diversity that we have today. The child may decide that that is the preferred course, or he may rebel. It is the student's judgment, not his parents', that is essential if we are to give full meaning to what we have said about the Bill of Rights and of the right of students to be masters of their own destiny.[3] If he is harnessed to the Amish way of life by those in authority over him and if his education is truncated, his entire life may be stunted and deformed. The child, therefore, should be given an opportunity to be heard before the State gives the exemption which we honor today.

[3] The court below brushed aside the students' interests with the offhand comment that "[w]hen a child reaches the age of judgment, he can choose for himself his religion." 49 Wis.2d 430, 440, 182 N.W.2d 539, 543. But there is nothing in this record to indicate that the moral and intellectual judgment demanded of the student by the question in this case is beyond his capacity. Children far younger than the 14- and 15-year-olds involved here are regularly permitted to testify in custody and other proceedings. Indeed, the failure to call the affected child in a custody hearing is often reversible error. See, e.g., Callicott v. Callicott, 364 S.W.2d 455 (Tex.Civ.App.) (reversible error for trial judge to refuse to hear testimony of eight-year-old in custody battle). Moreover, there is substantial agreement among child psychologists and sociologists that the moral and intellectual maturity of the 14-year-old approaches that of the adult. See, e.g., J. Piaget, The Moral Judgment of the Child (1948); D. Elkind, Children and Adolescents 75–80 (1970); Kohlberg, Moral Education in the Schools: A Development View, in R. Muuss, Adolescent Behavior and Society 193, 199–200 (1971); W. Kay, Moral Development 172–183 (1968); A. Gesell & F. Ilg, Youth: The Years From Ten to Sixteen 175–182 (1956). The maturity of Amish youth, who identify with and assume adult roles from early childhood, see M. Goodman, The Culture of Childhood 92–94 (1970), is certainly not less than that of children in the general population.

The views of the two children in question were not canvassed by the Wisconsin courts. The matter should be explicitly reserved so that new hearings can be held on remand of the case. . . .[4]

NOTES

The ability of parents to raise their children in accordance with their beliefs is enhanced with options such as homeschooling and state-provided school vouchers. These options will be explored *infra*. As suggested in *Yoder*, however, what if there are significant differences of opinion between the children and their parents regarding educational opportunities? Does the child's prerogative trump those of the parents? *See* Hillel Y. Levin, Allan J. Jacobs, and Kavita Shah Arora, *To Accommodate or Not to Accommodate: (When) Should the State Regulate Religion to Protect the Rights of Children and Third Parties?*, 73 WASH. & LEE L. REV. 915 (2016); Samantha Godwin, *Against Parental Rights*, 47 COLUM. HUM. RTS. L. REV. 1 (2015); Khiara M. Bridges, *Privacy Rights and Public Families*, 34 HARV. J. L. & GENDER 113 (2011); Mary Patricia Byrn and Jenni Vainic Ives, *Which Came First the Parent or the Child?*, 62 RUTGERS L. REV. 305 (2010); Jeffrey Shulman, *What* Yoder *Wrought: Religious Disparagement, Parental Alienation and the Best Interests of the Child*, 53 VILL. L. REV. 173 (2008); Yochai Benkler, *Siren Songs and Amish Children: Autonomy, Information, and Law*, 76 N.Y.U. L. REV. 23 (2001); Emily Buss, *The Adolescent's Stake in the Allocation of Educational Control Between Parent and State*, 67 U. CHI. L. REV. 1233 (2000). When parents divorce, often there are disputes over how to provide for the child's religious education. Increasingly, courts have been guided by a determination of what constitutes the child's best interest. *See, e.g., In re* Kurowski, 161 N.H. 578 (N.H. 2011) (holding that while the facts have religious overtones, the issue lies in resolving a dispute between two parents that have equal constitutional rights, but have been unable to agree on how best to educate their child). *See also* Jordan v. Rea, 221 Ariz. 581 (Ariz. Ct. App. 2009) (determining what the best interest of the child is when both fit parents are unable to agree). *See also* Joshua E. Weishart, *Reconstituting the Right to Education*, 67 ALA. L. REV. 915 (2016) (discussing the right to education and its inability to uphold its protective function).

Smith v. Ricci

Supreme Court of New Jersey, 1982
446 A.2d 501

■ CLIFFORD, JUSTICE.

Appellants challenge a regulation of the State Board of Education (Board) that requires each local school district to develop and implement a family life education program in the public elementary and secondary curricula. N.J.A.C. 6:29–7.1. Appellants contend that such a program

[4] Canvassing the views of all school-age Amish children in the State of Wisconsin would not present insurmountable difficulties. A 1968 survey indicated that there were at that time only 256 such children in the entire State. Comment, 1971 Wis.L.Rev. 832, 852 n. 132.

impinges upon the free exercise of their religion and constitutes an establishment of religion in violation of the United States Constitution. U.S. Const. amend. I. . . . The Board adopted the regulation on August 6, 1980. Appellants then sought review in the Appellate Division, R. 2:2–3(a)(2). Before argument was heard in the Appellate Division we certified the matter directly.

In January 1979 the Board appointed a committee, called the Family Life Committee, to make recommendations concerning the teaching of family life and human sexuality in the public schools. Prior to that time the Board's policy toward sex education was embodied in a resolution that had been adopted in 1967. That policy recommended but did not require that local school boards develop programs for sex education. A survey by the Department of Education, conducted at the Family Life Committee's request, determined that under the "recommended-but-not-required" policy, only 40 per cent of the state's public school pupils were receiving sex education. See Report of the Family Life Committee of the New Jersey State Board of Education, August 1979 (hereinafter Report).

In the Report, the Family Life Committee pointed out several sociological factors and statistics that it believed reinforced the need for sex education. Although the source of these statistics is not given, there is nothing to indicate that they are unreliable nor do appellants dispute them. The Report sets forth the following: in the United States one in five births is to a teenager between 15 and 19; in 1977 one million babies were born to girls between the ages of 10 and 18; in New Jersey in 1977, twelve thousand babies were born to girls between 15 and 19; 60% of these girls were unmarried; of the teenagers who do become pregnant when in school, about 80% drop out and do not return to complete their education; research studies continue to show that babies born to adolescent mothers are more apt to be premature and underweight; babies of low birth weight often suffer from a lag in development through their early years which affects their ability to learn in school; the incidence of venereal disease in both males and females continues to rise. The Committee also cited the results of a 1978 Gallup poll indicating that 77 per cent of the public and 95 per cent of the students favored sex education in the schools. However, the Committee pointed out that no research studies had been found that showed a correlation between teaching about human sexuality and a reduction in teenage pregnancy or venereal disease.

The Committee then made the following recommendations: that the study of family life education as part of the sequential comprehensive kindergarten through twelfth grade curriculum be required; that the State Board's regulation provide for an excusal policy from sections of the curriculum dealing directly with sex education on parental grounds of conscience; that the districts provide appropriate services to assist pregnant teenagers and teenage parents; that the Department of Education be directed to prepare for consideration of the board, administrative code regulations to implement the above recommendations. [Report, supra, at 8–10.]

Thereafter, the Commissioner of Education submitted a proposed regulation to the Board, which considered it at its February 6, 1980 meeting. At this meeting members of the public offered comments, both for and against the proposed regulations. The Board then approved the publication of the proposed regulation. The regulation, along with an invitation for comment, was published in the March 1980 New Jersey Register, 12 N.J.R. 105 (1980).

At its April 8, 1980 meeting the Board again heard extensive public comment on the proposed regulation. Although a variety of objections were raised, the common theme of those opposed to the family life education program was the fear that it would destroy the prerogative of parents to educate their children on matters involving sexual morality, and would inculcate in pupils concepts and attitudes, especially as related to sexuality, that conflict with their parents' views. Those in favor of the program stressed the need for young people to receive information about family life and sexuality, and saw the program as supplementing rather than replacing parental and religious efforts in this area. At the conclusion of this meeting the Board adopted the regulation by a vote of nine to one.

Less than a month later the New Jersey Senate passed a resolution directing the Board to reconsider the Family Life Education regulation. See Senate Resolution No. 24 (May 1, 1980). In response, the Board reviewed the regulations and made some changes at its meeting on June 11, 1980. The revised regulation was published in the July New Jersey Register, 12 N.J.R. 388 (1980), and was adopted at the August 6, 1980 meeting.

The regulation required each local district to institute, by September 1981, a policy that would begin the development of a family life education program. The local programs were to be developed through consultation with and participation of teachers, administrators, parents, pupils in grades nine through twelve, physicians, members of the clergy, and other community members. N.J.A.C. 6:29–7.1(b). Each year the district must give parents an outline of the curriculum and a list of instructional material, and must permit parents to review all the materials prior to their use in the classroom. The regulation also listed the teaching staff members authorized to teach in the program and provided for in-service preparation for those teachers. It also permitted districts to use "resource people," such as physicians, clergymen, attorneys, and psychologists, to assist with the program's development, and required the Department of Education to give technical assistance to local districts in developing their programs.

The regulation devotes one paragraph to defining "family life education programs." It says: (a) As used in this subchapter, "family life education program" means instruction to develop an understanding of the physical, mental, emotional, social, economic, and psychological aspects of interpersonal relationships; the physiological, psychological and cultural foundations of human development, sexuality, and reproduction, at various stages of growth; the opportunity for pupils to acquire knowledge which will support the development of responsible personal behavior, strengthen their own family life now, and aid in establishing strong family life for themselves in the future thereby contributing to the enrichment of the community. [N.J.A.C. 6:29.7.1(a)]

As part of its technical assistance to local districts, the Department of Education has provided the districts with curriculum guidelines that clarify the above definition. These guidelines indicate that although the emphasis of the program is on teaching about human sexuality, that is not its only focus. Other areas of study include such topics as "Family Structure," "Growing Up Emotionally," and "Dating." Although a wide range of physical, psychological, and social phenomena are suggested as appropriate areas of study, the final decision as to what specific topics are appropriate for each district is left to that district. However, local districts must provide a program that satisfies the definition of family life education as given in the regulation.

Finally, the regulation includes an "excusal clause," which states: (i) The local board of education shall establish procedures whereby any pupil, whose parent or guardian presents to the school principal a signed statement that any part of the instruction in family life education is in conflict with his/her conscience, or sincerely held moral or religious beliefs, shall be excused from that portion of the course where such instruction is being given and no penalties as to credit or graduation shall result therefrom. [N.J.S.A. 18A:35–4.6 et seq.] [N.J.A.C. 6:29.7.1(i)][1]

Under the excusal policy a pupil will receive instruction in all aspects of the family life education program unless a parent or guardian objects. In such a case, the pupil will be excused, but only from those parts of the program that the parent finds morally, conscientiously, or religiously objectionable. . . .

Appellants assert that by teaching about human reproduction, sexuality, and the development of personal and social values, the schools will "inhibit the moral concepts held by those students who have received them through their Judeo-Christian and other home teaching." As a result, children will be exposed to attitudes, goals, and values that are contrary to their own and to those of their parents, and will thereby be inhibited in the practice of their religion. We do not question that this argument is sincerely made. Whether or not it is well reasoned we need not now decide, for we believe that the simple fact that parents can remove their children from any objectionable part of the program is dispositive. If the program violates a person's beliefs, that person is not

[1] Even if this paragraph were not included in the regulation, such an excusal policy would be required by statute, N.J.S.A. 18A:35–4.7, the wording of which is nearly identical to that used in the regulation.

required to participate. Where there is no compulsion to participate in this program, there can be no infringement upon appellants' rights freely to exercise their religion. [citations omitted.]

Even though the program permits excusal, appellants argue that it nonetheless inhibits the free exercise of their religion. They assert that requiring pupils affirmatively to assert their objection to the program in front of teachers and peers exerts an intolerable pressure on those pupils such that they may be compelled to abandon their beliefs and to choose not to exercise their option to be excused. Relying on School District of Abington Township v. Schempp, 374 U.S. 203, 83 S.Ct. 1560, 10 L.Ed.2d 844 (1963), they argue that such pressure is constitutionally unacceptable. . . .

Courts in at least two states have addressed the validity of sex education curricula in light of free exercise considerations. In both instances the courts held that where there was adequate provision for excusal on the grounds of conscientiously-held belief, sex education or family life education programs did not offend the Free Exercise Clause. The Supreme Court of Hawaii specifically rejected a Schempp-based coercion argument in Medeiros v. Kiyosaki, supra, 52 Haw. at 442, 478 P.2d at 318, holding that where excusal was permitted, no government compulsion inhibiting religion existed. The California Court of Appeals has also rejected appellant's argument that coercion exists despite an excusal policy. Citizens for Parental Rights v. San Mateo County Bd. of Ed., supra, 51 Cal.App.3d at 17–18, 124 Cal.Rptr. at 81–82.

Indeed, both the Hawaii and California courts pointed out that accepting the argument that public schools may not offer curricula that offend the religious or moral views of a particular group would be tantamount to enshrining that group's views as state policy, thereby violating the Establishment Clause. In Epperson v. Arkansas, 393 U.S. 97, 89 S.Ct. 266, 21 L.Ed.2d 228 (1968) the Supreme Court said, "There is and can be no doubt that the First Amendment does not permit the State to require that teaching and learning must be tailored to the principles or prohibitions of any religious sect or dogma." Id. at 106, 89 S.Ct. at 271, 21 L.Ed.2d at 235. The Court in Epperson held that the prohibition of teaching one point of view (evolution) because it was contrary to the religious views of some constituted an impermissible establishment of religion. Appellants' argument is essentially the same as the one rejected in Epperson.

Thus, appellants' argument based on the Free Exercise Clause is flawed in two ways. First, the regulation, because of the excusal clause, does not inhibit the free exercise of religion. Second, to permit the appellants to control what others may study because the subject may be offensive to appellants' religious or moral scruples would violate the Establishment Clause. . . .

This argument is unpersuasive. There is absolutely nothing in the regulation or in the curriculum guidelines that gives even the slightest indication that the program favors a "secular" view of its subject matter over a "religious" one. The program is, as it must be, neither antagonistic toward religion nor supportive of non-religion. The mention of religion in the classroom is not forbidden. Indeed, it might be entirely appropriate in the context of discussing sexuality for a teacher to mention that different religions have different views as to the morality of certain aspects of sexual behavior and to encourage the students to seek guidance from their parents and clergymen. As one writer has stated, As long as the state does not unfairly represent any moral views that might undercut the teaching of a child's religion, sex is as unobjectionable a classroom subject as lyric passages from the Bible. Further, such a course need not be "dehumanizing," or constitute a "religion of secularism". Competing moral interpretations of sex may still be discussed, provided that one particular interpretation is not stressed to the exclusion of others. [Comment, Sex Education: The Constitutional Limits of State Compulsion, 48 S.Cal.L.Rev. 548, 563 (1970) (footnotes omitted).]

The regulation is barren of any requirement that a point of view, be it secular or religious, must be stressed to the exclusion of others. We therefore hold that this program does not contravene any of the three requirements of the Lemon test and does not constitute an establishment of religion.

Appellants argue that the Board's action in adopting N.J.A.C. 6:29–7.1 violates the Due Process Clause of the Fourteenth Amendment because the Board did not show a reasonable relationship between the goals of the family life education program and the means adopted.

The Board, on the other hand, maintains that the Family Life Committee Report, as well as the testimony of knowledgeable people such as the Commissioner of the Department of Health and the Commissioner of Human Services, supports the view that not only is there a relationship between the program and the reduction of teenage pregnancy, venereal disease, and other social problems, but also the program is necessary if these problems are to be ameliorated.

It is well established that a presumption of reasonableness attaches to the actions of an administrative agency and that the burden of proving unreasonableness falls upon those who challenge the validity of the action. Appellants have offered no evidence to meet that burden but instead merely assert that there are no data that prove that the program will have any effect on the societal ills that it attacks. This bare assertion does not satisfy appellants' burden of proving that the regulation is unreasonable.

In addition, the record reveals a sufficient factual basis for the Board's conclusion that the family life education program is a reasonable, desirable, and necessary method of dealing with readily identifiable educational and social problems. If the Board were required to prove the efficacy of each curricular program before implementing it, the Board's ability to operate would be severely and unnecessarily encumbered. No such proof is required. . . .

The action of the State Board of Education is:

Affirmed.

NOTES

In 1999, Florida became the first state to enact a plan for high school education that targets adolescents in an effort to teach them about marriage and relationship skills. *See* 1998 Fla. Sess. Law Serv. 403 (West) (codified in scattered sections of FLA. STAT. ANN (West Supp. 1999)). The effort is an attempt to reduce the number of divorces. For an analysis of the legislative initiative, *see* Raymond C. O'Brien, *The Reawakening of Marriage*, 102 W. VA. L. REV. 339, 374–380 (1999). The issue concerns the ability of the state to intervene in the parent-child relationship in issues that often involve religion and other parental prerogatives concerning their children's education. Thus, an issue arises contrasting the constitutional rights of the parents and their child's education. A case in Massachusetts was brought by parents on behalf of their elementary school children in opposition of the school's use of textbooks that advocated tolerance of same-sex marriage and homosexuality. The court found that the parents' due process rights in the moral upbringing of their children were not violated because their rights did not extend to determining a public school's curriculum in which the parents had chosen to enroll their children. Parker v. Hurley, 474 F. Supp. 2d 261 (D. Mass 2007); Leebaert v. Harrington, 332 F.3d 134 (2d Cir. 2003). It is arguable that a program that has a form of opt-out or parental notification provision is more likely to survive any constitutional challenge by parents. *Compare* Alfonso v. Fernandez, 167 Misc. 2d 793, 635 N.Y.S.2d 932, (Sup. 1995) (condom distribution program that had no opt-out or required parental permission was held to be unconstitutional) *with* Curtis v. School Committee of Falmouth, 420 Mass. 749, 652 N.E.2d 580 (Mass. 1995) (neither opt-out nor parental permission required where condom program was voluntary and not coercive). States have implemented statutes addressing the inclusion of sex or health education in the school's curriculum. *See, e.g.,* CONN. GEN. STAT. § 10–16b (West 2016) (prescribing minimum core subjects that includes health education); IOWA STAT. § 256.11 (West 2016) (describing the types of instruction necessary for state accreditation, including one unit of health education that includes instruction in the prevention of sexually transmitted diseases); N.Y. EDUC. L. § 3204(5) (McKinney 2016) (but excusing student from required health and hygiene education when it conflicts with the religion of student's parents or guardian). For further commentary, *see* Matthew Lashof-Sullivan, *Sex Education in Schools,* 16 GEO. J. GENDER & L. 263 (2015); Kelly Percival and Emily Sharpe, *Sex Education in Schools*, 13 GEO. J. GENDER & L. 425 (2012); and Jorge O. Elorza, *Secularism and the Constitution: Can Government be Too Secular?* 2 U. PITT. L. REV. 53 (2010).

2. SCHOOL VOUCHERS

Arizona Christian School Tuition Organization v. Winn

Supreme Court of the United States, 2011
563 U.S. 125

■ KENNEDY, JUSTICE delivered the opinion of the Court.

Arizona provides tax credits for contributions to school tuition organizations, or STOs. STOs use these contributions to provide scholarships to students attending private schools, many of which are religious. Respondents are a group of Arizona taxpayers who challenge the STO tax credit as a violation of Establishment Clause principles under the First and Fourteenth Amendments. After the Arizona Supreme Court rejected a similar Establishment Clause claim on the merits, respondents sought intervention from the Federal Judiciary.

To obtain a determination on the merits in federal court, parties seeking relief must show that they have standing under Article III of the Constitution. Standing in Establishment Clause cases may be shown in various ways. Some plaintiffs may demonstrate standing based on the direct harm of what is claimed to be an establishment of religion, such as a mandatory prayer in a public school classroom. See School Dist. of Abington Township v. Schempp, 374 U.S. 203, 224, n. 9, 83 S.Ct. 1560, 10 L.Ed.2d 844 (1963). Other plaintiffs may demonstrate standing on the ground that they have incurred a cost or been denied a benefit on account of their religion. Those costs and benefits can result from alleged discrimination in the tax code, such as when the availability of a tax exemption is conditioned on religious affiliation. See Texas Monthly, Inc. v. Bullock, 489 U.S. 1, 8, 109 S.Ct. 890, 103 L.Ed.2d 1 (1989) (plurality opinion).

For their part, respondents contend that they have standing to challenge Arizona's STO tax credit for one and only one reason: because they are Arizona taxpayers. But the mere fact that a plaintiff is a taxpayer is not generally deemed sufficient to establish standing in federal court. To overcome that rule, respondents must rely on an exception created in Flast v. Cohen, 392 U.S. 83, 88 S.Ct. 1942, 20 L.Ed.2d 947 (1968). For the reasons discussed below, respondents cannot take advantage of *Flast*'s narrow exception to the general rule against taxpayer standing. As a consequence, respondents lacked standing to commence this action, and their suit must be dismissed for want of jurisdiction.

Respondents challenged § 43–1089, a provision of the Arizona Tax Code. See 1997 Ariz. Sess. Laws § 43–1087, codified, as amended, Ariz.Rev.Stat. Ann. § 43–1089 (West Supp.2010). Section 43–1089 allows Arizona taxpayers to obtain dollar-for-dollar tax credits of up to $500 per person and $1,000 per married couple for contributions to STOs. § 43–

1089(A). If the credit exceeds an individual's tax liability, the credit's unused portion can be carried forward up to five years. § 43–1089(D). Under a version of § 43–1089 in effect during the pendency of this lawsuit, a charitable organization could be deemed an STO only upon certain conditions. See § 43–1089 (West 2006). The organization was required to be exempt from federal taxation under § 501(c)(3) of the Internal Revenue Code of 1986. § 43–1089(G)(3) (West Supp.2005). It could not limit its scholarships to students attending only one school. *Ibid.* And it had to allocate "at least ninety per cent of its annual revenue for educational scholarships or tuition grants" to children attending qualified schools. *Ibid.* A "qualified school," in turn, was defined in part as a private school in Arizona that did not discriminate on the basis of race, color, handicap, familial status, or national origin. § 43–1089(G)(2). . . .

Respondents suggest that their status as Arizona taxpayers provides them with standing to challenge the STO tax credit. Absent special circumstances, however, standing cannot be based on a plaintiff's mere status as a taxpayer. This Court has rejected the general proposition that an individual who has paid taxes has a "continuing, legally cognizable interest in ensuring that those funds are not *used* by the Government in a way that violates the Constitution." Hein v. Freedom From Religion Foundation, Inc., 551 U.S. 587, 599, 127 S.Ct. 2553, 168 L.Ed.2d 424 (2007) (plurality opinion). This precept has been referred to as the rule against taxpayer standing.

The doctrinal basis for the rule was discussed in Frothingham v. Mellon, 262 U.S. 447, 43 S.Ct. 597, 67 L.Ed. 1078 (1923) (decided with *Massachusetts v. Mellon*). There, a taxpayer-plaintiff had alleged that certain federal expenditures were in excess of congressional authority under the Constitution. The plaintiff argued that she had standing to raise her claim because she had an interest in the Government Treasury and because the allegedly unconstitutional expenditure of Government funds would affect her personal tax liability. The Court rejected those arguments. The "effect upon future taxation, of any payment out of funds," was too "remote, fluctuating and uncertain" to give rise to a case or controversy. *Id.*, at 487, 43 S.Ct. 597. And the taxpayer-plaintiff's "interest in the moneys of the Treasury," the Court recognized, was necessarily "shared with millions of others." *Ibid.* As a consequence, *Frothingham* held that the taxpayer-plaintiff had not presented a "judicial controversy" appropriate for resolution in federal court but rather a "matter of public . . . concern" that could be pursued only through the political process. *Id.*, at 487–489, 43 S.Ct. 597.

In a second pertinent case, Doremus v. Board of Ed. of Hawthorne, 342 U.S. 429, 72 S.Ct. 394, 96 L.Ed. 475 (1952), the Court considered *Frothingham*'s prohibition on taxpayer standing in connection with an alleged Establishment Clause violation. A New Jersey statute had provided that public school teachers would read Bible verses to their students at the start of each schoolday. A plaintiff sought to have the law enjoined, asserting standing based on her status as a taxpayer. Writing for the Court, Justice Jackson reiterated the foundational role that Article III standing plays in our separation of powers.

" 'The party who invokes the power [of the federal courts] must be able to show not only that the statute is invalid, but that he has sustained or is immediately in danger of sustaining some direct injury as a result of its enforcement, and not merely that he suffers in some indefinite way in common with people generally.' " *Doremus, supra,* at 434, 72 S.Ct. 394 (quoting *Frothingham, supra,* at 488, 43 S.Ct. 597).

The plaintiff in *Doremus* lacked any "direct and particular financial interest" in the suit, and, as a result, a decision on the merits would have been merely "advisory." 342 U.S., at 434–435, 72 S.Ct. 394. It followed that the plaintiff's allegations did not give rise to a case or controversy subject to judicial resolution under Article III. *Ibid.* Cf. School Dist. of Abington Township v. Schempp, 374 U.S., at 224, n. 9, 83 S.Ct. 1560 (finding standing where state laws required Bible readings or prayer in public schools, not because plaintiffs were state taxpayers but because their children were enrolled in public schools and so were "directly affected" by the challenged laws).

In holdings consistent with *Frothingham* and *Doremus,* more recent decisions have explained that claims of taxpayer standing rest on unjustifiable economic and political speculation. When a government expends resources or declines to impose a tax, its budget does not necessarily suffer. On the contrary, the purpose of many governmental expenditures and tax benefits is "to spur economic activity, which in turn *increases* government revenues." DaimlerChrysler, 547 U.S., at 344, 126 S.Ct. 1854. . . .

The primary contention of respondents, of course, is that, despite the general rule that taxpayers lack standing to object to expenditures alleged to be unconstitutional, their suit falls within the exception established by Flast v. Cohen, 392 U.S. 83, 88 S.Ct. 1942, 20 L.Ed.2d 947. It must be noted at the outset that, as this Court has explained, *Flast*'s holding provides a "narrow exception" to "the general rule against taxpayer standing." Bowen v. Kendrick, 487 U.S. 589, 618, 108 S.Ct. 2562, 101 L.Ed.2d 520 (1988).

At issue in *Flast* was the standing of federal taxpayers to object, on First Amendment grounds, to a congressional statute that allowed expenditures of federal funds from the General Treasury to support, among other programs, "instruction in reading, arithmetic, and other subjects in religious schools, and to purchase textbooks and other instructional materials for use in such schools." 392 U.S., at 85–86, 88 S.Ct. 1942. *Flast* held that taxpayers have standing when two conditions are met.

The first condition is that there must be a "logical link" between the plaintiff's taxpayer status "and the type of legislative enactment attacked." *Id.*, at 102, 88 S.Ct. 1942. This condition was not satisfied in *Doremus* because the statute challenged in that case—providing for the recitation of Bible passages in public schools—involved at most an "incidental expenditure of tax funds." Flast, 392 U.S., at 102, 88 S.Ct. 1942. In *Flast,* by contrast, the allegation was that the Federal Government violated the Establishment Clause in the exercise of its legislative authority both to collect and spend tax dollars. *Id.*, at 103, 88 S.Ct. 1942. In the decades since *Flast,* the Court has been careful to enforce this requirement. See Hein, 551 U.S. 587, 127 S.Ct. 2553, 168 L.Ed.2d 424 (no standing under *Flast* to challenge federal executive actions funded by general appropriations); Valley Forge, 454 U.S. 464, 102 S.Ct. 752, 70 L.Ed.2d 700 (no standing under *Flast* to challenge an agency's decision to transfer a parcel of federal property pursuant to the Property Clause).

The second condition for standing under *Flast* is that there must be "a nexus" between the plaintiff's taxpayer status and "the precise nature of the constitutional infringement alleged." 392 U.S., at 102, 88 S.Ct. 1942. This condition was deemed satisfied in *Flast* based on the allegation that Government funds had been spent on an outlay for religion in contravention of the Establishment Clause. *Id.*, at 85–86, 88 S.Ct. 1942. In *Frothingham,* by contrast, the claim was that Congress had exceeded its constitutional authority without regard to any specific prohibition. 392 U.S., at 104–105, 88 S.Ct. 1942. Confirming that *Flast* turned on the unique features of Establishment Clause violations, this Court has "declined to lower the taxpayer standing bar in suits alleging violations of any constitutional provision apart from the Establishment Clause." *Hein, supra,* at 609, 127 S.Ct. 2553 (plurality opinion); see also Richardson, 418 U.S. 166, 94 S.Ct. 2940, 41 L.Ed.2d 678 (Statement and Account Clause); Schlesinger, 418 U.S. 208, 94 S.Ct. 2925, 41 L.Ed.2d 706 (Incompatibility Clause).

After stating the two conditions for taxpayer standing, *Flast* considered them together, explaining that individuals suffer a particular injury for standing purposes when, in violation of the Establishment Clause and by means of "the taxing and spending power," their property is transferred through the Government's Treasury to a sectarian entity. 392 U.S., at 105–106, 88 S.Ct. 1942. As *Flast* put it: "The taxpayer's allegation in such cases would be that his tax money is being extracted and spent in violation of specific constitutional protections against such abuses of legislative power." *Id.*, at 106, 88 S.Ct. 1942. *Flast* thus "understood the 'injury' alleged in Establishment Clause challenges to federal spending to be the very 'extract[ion] and spen[ding]' of 'tax money' in aid of religion alleged by a plaintiff." DaimlerChrysler, 547 U.S., at 348, 126 S.Ct. 1854 (quoting Flast, 392 U.S., at 106, 88 S.Ct. 1942)). "Such an injury," *Flast* continued, is unlike "generalized grievances about the conduct of government" and so is "appropriate for judicial redress." *Id.,* at 106, 88 S.Ct. 1942. . . .

Respondents contend that these principles demonstrate their standing to challenge the STO tax credit. In their view the tax credit is, for *Flast* purposes, best understood as a governmental expenditure. That is incorrect.

It is easy to see that tax credits and governmental expenditures can have similar economic consequences, at least for beneficiaries whose tax liability is sufficiently large to take full advantage of the credit. Yet tax credits and governmental expenditures do not both implicate individual taxpayers in sectarian activities. A dissenter whose tax dollars are "extracted and spent" knows that he has in some small measure been made to contribute to an establishment in violation of conscience. *Flast, supra,* at 106, 88 S.Ct. 1942. In that instance the taxpayer's direct and particular connection with the establishment does not depend on economic speculation or political conjecture. The connection would exist even if the conscientious dissenter's tax liability were unaffected or reduced. See *DaimlerChrysler, supra,* at 348–349, 126 S.Ct. 1854. When the government declines to impose a tax, by contrast, there is no such connection between dissenting taxpayer and alleged establishment. Any financial injury remains speculative. See *supra,* at 1442–1445. And awarding some citizens a tax credit allows other citizens to retain control over their own funds in accordance with their own consciences.

The distinction between governmental expenditures and tax credits refutes respondents' assertion of standing. When Arizona taxpayers choose to contribute to STOs, they spend their own money, not money the State has collected from respondents or from other taxpayers. Arizona's § 43–1089 does not "extrac[t] and spen[d]" a conscientious dissenter's funds in service of an establishment, Flast, 392 U.S., at 106, 88 S.Ct. 1942, or " 'force a citizen to contribute three pence only of his property' " to a sectarian organization, *id.,* at 103, 88 S.Ct. 1942 (quoting 2 Writings of James Madison, *supra,* at 186). On the contrary, respondents and other Arizona taxpayers remain free to pay their own tax bills, without contributing to an STO. Respondents are likewise able to contribute to an STO of their choice, either religious or secular. And respondents also have the option of contributing to other charitable organizations, in which case respondents may become eligible for a tax deduction or a different tax credit. See, *e.g.,* Ariz.Rev.Stat. Ann. § 43–1088 (West Supp.2010). The STO tax credit is not tantamount to a religious tax or to a tithe and does not visit the injury identified in *Flast.* It follows that respondents have neither alleged an injury for standing purposes under general rules nor met the *Flast* exception. Finding standing under these circumstances would be more than the extension of *Flast* "to the limits of its logic." Hein, 551 U.S., at 615, 127 S.Ct. 2553 (plurality opinion). It would be a departure from *Flast's* stated rationale. . . .

If an establishment of religion is alleged to cause real injury to particular individuals, the federal courts may adjudicate the matter. Like other constitutional provisions, the Establishment Clause acquires substance and meaning when explained, elaborated, and enforced in the context of actual disputes. That reality underlies the case-or-controversy requirement, a requirement that has not been satisfied here. . . .

Few exercises of the judicial power are more likely to undermine public confidence in the neutrality and integrity of the Judiciary than one which casts the Court in the role of a Council of Revision, conferring on itself the power to invalidate laws at the behest of anyone who disagrees with them. In an era of frequent litigation, class actions, sweeping injunctions with prospective effect, and continuing jurisdiction to enforce judicial remedies, courts must be more careful to insist on the formal rules of standing, not less so. Making the Article III standing inquiry all the more necessary are the significant implications of constitutional litigation, which can result in rules of wide applicability that are beyond Congress' power to change.

The present suit serves as an illustration of these principles. The fact that respondents are state taxpayers does not give them standing to challenge the subsidies that § 43–1089 allegedly provides to religious STOs. To alter the rules of standing or weaken their requisite elements would be inconsistent with the case-or-controversy limitation on federal jurisdiction imposed by Article III.

The judgment of the Court of Appeals is reversed.

It is so ordered.

. . .

■ JUSTICE KAGAN, with whom JUSTICE GINSBURG, JUSTICE BREYER, and JUSTICE SOTOMAYOR join, dissenting.

Since its inception, the Arizona private-school-tuition tax credit has cost the State, by its own estimate, nearly $350 million in diverted tax revenue. The Arizona taxpayers who instituted this suit (collectively, Plaintiffs) allege that the use of these funds to subsidize school tuition organizations (STOs) breaches the Establishment Clause's promise of religious neutrality. Many of these STOs, the Plaintiffs claim, discriminate on the basis of a child's religion when awarding scholarships. For almost half a century, litigants like the Plaintiffs have obtained judicial review of claims that the government has used its taxing and spending power in violation of the Establishment Clause. Beginning in Flast v. Cohen, 392 U.S. 83, 88 S.Ct. 1942, 20 L.Ed.2d 947 (1968), and continuing in case after case for over four decades, this Court and others have exercised jurisdiction to decide taxpayer-initiated challenges not materially different from this one. Not every suit has succeeded on the merits, or should have. But every taxpayer-plaintiff has had her day in court to contest the government's financing of religious activity.

Today, the Court breaks from this precedent by refusing to hear taxpayers' claims that the government has unconstitutionally subsidized religion through its tax system. These litigants lack standing, the majority holds, because the funding of religion they challenge comes from a tax credit, rather than an appropriation. A tax credit, the Court asserts, does not injure objecting taxpayers, because it "does not extract and spend [their] funds in service of an establishment." *Ante,* at 1447 (internal quotation marks and alterations omitted).

This novel distinction in standing law between appropriations and tax expenditures has as little basis in principle as it has in our precedent. Cash grants and targeted tax breaks are means of accomplishing the same government objective—to provide financial support to select individuals or organizations. Taxpayers who oppose state aid of religion have equal reason to protest whether that aid flows from the one form of subsidy or the other. Either way, the government has financed the religious activity. And so either way, taxpayers should be able to challenge the subsidy.

Still worse, the Court's arbitrary distinction threatens to eliminate *all* occasions for a taxpayer to contest the government's monetary support of religion. Precisely because appropriations and tax breaks can achieve identical objectives, the government can easily substitute one for the other. Today's opinion thus enables the government to end-run *Flast*'s guarantee of access to the Judiciary. From now on, the government need follow just one simple rule—subsidize through the tax system—to preclude taxpayer challenges to state funding of religion.

And that result—the effective demise of taxpayer standing—will diminish the Establishment Clause's force and meaning. Sometimes, no one other than taxpayers has suffered the injury necessary to challenge government sponsorship of religion. Today's holding therefore will prevent federal courts from determining whether some subsidies to sectarian organizations comport with our Constitution's guarantee of religious neutrality. Because I believe these challenges warrant consideration on the merits, I respectfully dissent from the Court's decision. . . .

The majority reaches a contrary decision by distinguishing between two methods of financing religion: A taxpayer has standing to challenge state subsidies to religion, the Court announces, when the mechanism used is an appropriation, but not when the mechanism is a targeted tax break, otherwise called a "tax expenditure."[1] In the former case, but not

---

[1] "Tax expenditures" are monetary subsidies the government bestows on particular individuals or organizations by granting them preferential tax treatment. The co-chairmen of the National Commission on Fiscal Responsibility and Reform recently referred to these tax breaks as "the various deductions, credits and loopholes that are just spending by another name." Washington Post, Feb. 20, 2011, p. A19, col. 3; *see also* 2 U.S.C. § 622(3) (defining "tax expenditures," for purposes of the Federal Government's budgetary process, as "those revenue losses attributable to provisions of the . . . tax laws which allow a special exclusion, exemption, or deduction from gross income or which provide a special credit, a preferential rate of tax, or a deferral of tax liability"); S. Surrey & P. McDaniel, Tax Expenditures 3 (1985) (explaining that

in the latter, the Court declares, the taxpayer suffers cognizable injury. *Ante,* at 1447.

But this distinction finds no support in case law, and just as little in reason. In the decades since *Flast,* no court—not one—has differentiated between appropriations and tax expenditures in deciding whether litigants have standing. Over and over again, courts (including this one) have faced Establishment Clause challenges to tax credits, deductions, and exemptions; over and over again, these courts have reached the merits of these claims. And that is for a simple reason: Taxpayers experience the same injury for standing purposes whether government subsidization of religion takes the form of a cash grant or a tax measure. The only rationale the majority offers for its newfound distinction—that grants, but not tax expenditures, somehow come from a complaining taxpayer's own wallet—cannot bear the weight the Court places on it. If *Flast* is still good law—and the majority today says nothing to the contrary—then the Plaintiffs should be able to pursue their claim on the merits. . . .

Our taxpayer standing cases have declined to distinguish between appropriations and tax expenditures for a simple reason: Here, as in many contexts, the distinction is one in search of a difference. To begin to see why, consider an example far afield from *Flast* and, indeed, from religion. Imagine that the Federal Government decides it should pay hundreds of billions of dollars to insolvent banks in the midst of a financial crisis. Suppose, too, that many millions of taxpayers oppose this bailout on the ground (whether right or wrong is immaterial) that it uses their hard-earned money to reward irresponsible business behavior. In the face of this hostility, some Members of Congress make the following proposal: Rather than give the money to banks via appropriations, the Government will allow banks to subtract the exact same amount from the tax bill they would otherwise have to pay to the U.S. Treasury. Would this proposal calm the furor? Or would most taxpayers respond by saying that a subsidy is a subsidy (or a bailout is a bailout), whether accomplished by the one means or by the other? Surely the latter; indeed, we would think the less of our countrymen if they failed to see through this cynical proposal.

And what ordinary people would appreciate, this Court's case law also recognizes—that targeted tax breaks are often "economically and functionally indistinguishable from a direct monetary subsidy." Rosenberger v. Rector and Visitors of Univ. of Va., 515 U.S. 819, 859, 115 S.Ct. 2510, 132 L.Ed.2d 700 (1995) (THOMAS, J., concurring). Tax credits, deductions, and exemptions provided to an individual or organization have "much the same effect as a cash grant to the [recipient] of the amount of tax it would have to pay" absent the tax break. Regan v.

---

tax expenditures "represent government spending for favored activities or groups, effected through the tax system rather than through direct grants, loans, or other forms of government assistance").

Taxation With Representation of Wash., 461 U.S. 540, 544, 103 S.Ct. 1997, 76 L.Ed.2d 129 (1983). "Our opinions," therefore, "have long recognized . . . the reality that [tax expenditures] are a form of subsidy that is administered through the tax system." Arkansas Writers' Project, Inc. v. Ragland, 481 U.S. 221, 236, 107 S.Ct. 1722, 95 L.Ed.2d 209 (1987) (SCALIA, J., dissenting) (internal quotation marks omitted). Or again: Tax breaks "can be viewed as a form of government spending," Camps Newfound/Owatonna, Inc. v. Town of Harrison, 520 U.S. 564, 589–590, n. 22, 117 S.Ct. 1590, 137 L.Ed.2d 852 (1997), even assuming the diverted tax funds do not pass through the public treasury. And once more: Both special tax benefits and cash grants "represen[t] a charge made upon the state," Nyquist, 413 U.S., at 790–791, 93 S.Ct. 2955 (internal quotation marks omitted); both deplete funds in the government's coffers by transferring money to select recipients. . . .[6]

The majority offers just one reason to distinguish appropriations and tax expenditures: A taxpayer experiences injury, the Court asserts, only when the government "extracts and spends" her very own tax dollars to aid religion. *Ante,* at 1447 (internal quotation marks and alterations omitted). In other words, a taxpayer suffers legally cognizable harm if but only if her particular tax dollars wind up in a religious organization's coffers. *See also* Tr. of Oral Arg. 4 (Solicitor General proposing that the "key point" was: "If you placed an electronic tag to track and monitor each cent that the [Plaintiffs] pay in tax," none goes to religious STOs). And no taxpayer can make this showing, the Court concludes, if the government subsidizes religion through tax credits, deductions, or exemptions (rather than through appropriations). . . .[9]

Today's decision devastates taxpayer standing in Establishment Clause cases. The government, after all, often uses tax expenditures to subsidize favored persons and activities. Still more, the government

[6] The majority observes that special tax benefits may in fact "*increas[e]* government revenues" by "spur[ring] economic activity." *Ante,* at 1443 (internal quotation marks omitted). That may be so in the long run (although the only non-speculative effect is to immediately diminish funds in the public treasury). But as the majority acknowledges, *ibid.,* this possibility holds just as true for appropriations; that is why we (optimistically) refer to some government outlays as "investments." The insight therefore cannot help the majority distinguish between tax expenditures and appropriations.

[9] Even taken on its own terms, the majority's reasoning does not justify the conclusion that the Plaintiffs lack standing. Arizona's tuition-tax-credit program in fact necessitates the direct expenditure of funds from the state treasury. After all, the statute establishing the initiative requires the Arizona Department of Revenue to certify STOs, maintain an STO registry, make the registry available to the public on request and post it on a website, collect annual reports filed by STOs, and send written notice to STOs that have failed to comply with statutory requirements. Ariz.Rev.Stat. Ann. §§ 43–1502(A)–(C), 43–1506 (West Supp.2010). Presumably all these activities cost money, which comes from the state treasury. Thus, on the majority's own theory, the government has "extract[ed] and spen[t]" the Plaintiffs' (along with other taxpayers') dollars to implement the challenged program, and the Plaintiffs should have standing. (The majority, after all, makes clear that nothing in its analysis hinges on the size or proportion of the Plaintiffs' contribution. *Ante,* at 1446.) But applying the majority's theory in this way reveals the hollowness at its core. Can anyone believe that the Plaintiffs have suffered injury through the costs involved in administering the program, but not through the far greater costs of granting the tax expenditure in the first place?

almost *always* has this option. Appropriations and tax subsidies are readily interchangeable; what is a cash grant today can be a tax break tomorrow. The Court's opinion thus offers a roadmap—more truly, just a one-step instruction—to any government that wishes to insulate its financing of religious activity from legal challenge. Structure the funding as a tax expenditure, and *Flast* will not stand in the way. No taxpayer will have standing to object. However blatantly the government may violate the Establishment Clause, taxpayers cannot gain access to the federal courts.

And by ravaging *Flast* in this way, today's decision damages one of this Nation's defining constitutional commitments. "Congress shall make no law respecting an establishment of religion"—ten simple words that have stood for over 200 years as a foundation stone of American religious liberty. Ten words that this Court has long understood, as James Madison did, to limit (though by no means eliminate) the government's power to finance religious activity. The Court's ruling today will not shield all state subsidies for religion from review; as the Court notes, some persons alleging Establishment Clause violations have suffered individualized injuries, and therefore have standing, independent of their taxpayer status. See *ante,* at 1440, 1448–1449. But *Flast* arose because "the taxing and spending power [may] be used to favor one religion over another or to support religion in general," 392 U.S., at 103, 88 S.Ct. 1942, without causing particularized harm to discrete persons. It arose because state sponsorship of religion sometimes harms individuals only (but this "only" is no small matter) in their capacity as contributing members of our national community. In those cases, the *Flast* Court thought, our Constitution's guarantee of religious neutrality still should be enforced.

Because that judgment was right then, and remains right today, I respectfully dissent.

NOTES

Currently, twenty-four states have some type of voucher program or voucher-like program: Alabama, Arizona, Arkansas, Colorado, Florida, Georgia, Indiana, Iowa, Kansas, Louisiana, Mississippi, Montana, Nevada, New Hampshire, North Carolina, Ohio, Oklahoma, Pennsylvania, Rhode Island, South Carolina, Tennessee, Utah, Virginia, and Wisconsin. *See e.g.,* Julie F. Mead, *The Right to an Education or the Right to Shop for Schooling: Examining Voucher Programs in Relation to State Constitutional Guarantees*, 42 FORDHAM URB. L. J. 703 (2015). In April 2003, Colorado became the first state to enact a statewide school voucher program. On June 28, 2004, however, the Colorado Supreme Court declared the voucher program unconstitutional on the ground that it violated the local control requirement under the state's constitution. *See* Owens v. Colo. Cong. of Parents, Teachers and Students, 92 P.3d 933 (Colo. 2004). Likewise, in 2006, the Florida Supreme Court, in a 5 to 2 decision, declared the Florida Opportunity Scholarship Program unconstitutional because it violated the state constitutional requirement for a "uniform, efficient, safe, secure and high quality system of free public schools." *See* Bush v. Holmes, 919 So.2d 392 (2006). Then, in 2009, the Arizona Supreme Court declared the state's special education voucher program unconstitutional because the program aided private schools and religious establishments. *See* Cain v. Horne, 202 P.3d 1178 (Ariz. 2009). The District of Columbia enacted a voucher program titled the District of Columbia Choice Incentive Act of 2003. *See* Pub. L. No. 108–199, § 301, 118 Stat. 126 (2004). In 2009, President Obama and Secretary of Education Arne Duncan announced that the D.C. voucher program would be defunded. However, as part of a federal budget agreement in 2011, funding was restored. *See* www.DCscholarships.com. For commentary on school vouchers, *see* Calvin Massey, *Standing in State Courts, State Law, and Federal Review*, 53 DUQ. L. REV. 401 (2015); Julie F. Mead, *The Right to an Education or the Right to Shop for Schooling: Examining Voucher Programs in Relation to State Constitutional Guarantees*, 42 FORDHAM URB. L. J. 703 (2015); Stephen G. Calabresi & Abe Salander, *Religion and the Equal Protection Clause: Why the Constitution Requires School Vouchers*, 65 FLA. L. REV. 909 (2013); James G. Dwyer, *No Accounting for School Vouchers*, 48 WAKE FOREST L. REV. 361 (2013); Dru Stevenson & Sonny Eckhart, *Standing as Channeling in the Administrative Age*, 53 B.C. L. REV. 1357 (2012).

B. CHILDREN BEYOND PARENTAL CONTROL

L.A.M. v. State

Supreme Court of Alaska, 1976
547 P.2d 827

■ ERWIN, JUSTICE.

L.A.M. seeks review of the superior court's order dated July 26, 1973, declaring her a delinquent child for violation of AS 09.50.010,[2] i.e., willful failure to comply with certain court orders made after a prior adjudication that she was a child in need of supervision.[3]

---

[2] AS 09.50.010 provides in relevant part:

Acts or omissions constituting contempt. The following acts or omissions in respect to a court of justice or court proceedings are contempts of the authority of the court:

. . .

(5) disobedience of a lawful judgment, order, or process of the court. . . .

[3] AS 47.10.290 provides in relevant part:

In this chapter, unless the context otherwise requires . . .

(7) "child in need of supervision" is a minor whom the court determines is within the provisions of (AS 47.10.010(a)(2), (3), (4), and (6)). [Matter in parentheses supplied.]

AS 47.10.010(a)(2), (3) and (6) respectively provide:

[B]y reason of being wayward or habitually disobedient is uncontrolled by his parent, guardian or custodian;

[I]s habitually truant from school or home, or habitually so conducts himself as to injure or endanger the morals or health of himself or others . . .

In order to understand L.A.M.'s arguments and place her situation in context, it will be necessary to set out her history at some length.

L.A.M. was born in Canada in 1958 and was adopted by the M.'s shortly thereafter. The M.'s soon were divorced and Mrs. M. moved with L.A.M. to Alaska. In 1971 Mrs. M. married Mr. C. and retired from work, intending to spend more time with L.A.M. Difficulties arose almost immediately with L.A.M. neglecting to return home after staying with friends. L.A.M. began a consistent pattern of running away in the Spring and Summer of 1972. During this period two petitions were filed seeking to have her declared a child in need of supervision, but in both cases the petitions were dismissed on stipulation and the matter handled informally.[4] On November 2, 1972, a new petition was filed. At the hearing L.A.M. admitted the allegations of the petition and was declared a child in need of supervision. She was ordered detained at the McLaughlin Youth Center pending adjudication.

On December 12, 1972, the disposition hearing was continued and L.A.M. was released to her parents. One week later the court was informed that she had run away. A pick-up order was issued and the minor was brought back to court on December 27, 1972, at which time she was detained pending disposition. The disposition hearing was finally held on January 11, 1973. Upon listening to testimony, the Master for the Family Court filed his recommendation that the minor be "released to her parents." A superior court judge adopted the finding and executed a release.

On March 19, 1973, L.A.M. was brought back to court by an intake officer who informed the court that she had "been a runaway almost constantly since the time the court released her." The intake officer then filed a petition with the court alleging that the minor was a "child in need of supervision" by virtue of having been truant from school in violation of AS 47.10.010(a)(3) and AS 14.30.010 (truancy).[5] At the hearing the court was informed that Mrs. C. had obtained a child psychiatrist who had met with the child and her mother, and together they had worked out some program of counseling. The parties agreed that L.A.M. would be placed in a foster home during a period of counseling and the judge accepted a stipulation to that effect. Having previously explained to L.A.M. that if

---

[4] Children's Rule 4(d) provides:

Informal Disposition. If the intake officer, after investigation, believes that in the best interest of the child the matter should be handled on an informal basis, he may thereafter refrain from filing a petition and shall thereafter on behalf of the court, counsel with the child and parents, guardian or custodian, and with their consent and cooperation establish such informal supervision or disposition of the child matter as the circumstances may require.

[5] AS 14.30.010 provides in relevant part:

When attendance compulsory. (a) Every child between seven and 16 years of age shall attend school at the public school in the district in which the child resides during each school term. Every parent, guardian or other person having the responsibility for or control of a child between seven and 16 years of age shall insure that the child is not absent from attendance.

she violated a court order she could be held in contempt of court and incarcerated, the judge informed the child that she was not to leave the foster home without contacting her psychiatrist, her social worker, or her mother. She agreed. The minor was released from McLaughlin on March 31, 1973, and placed in a foster home. She ran away on April 2, without notification, and was not apprehended until May 4.

[A CINS petition was filed by an intake officer.] The court denied the motion [to dismiss] but permitted the State to file an amended petition alleging as a separate count an act of delinquency predicated upon "criminal contempt."

A petition alleging delinquency was filed on May 23, 1973, at which time a hearing was held. In responding to the petition L.A.M. denied the allegations and requested a trial. Pending trial, she was placed at the Alaska Children's Services receiving home. A written order was entered on June 8, 1973, specifically setting out the conditions under which L.A.M. would reside at the receiving home pending her adjudication hearing. Specifically, it provided that "[T]he child is not to remain away from the Anchorage Children's Christian Home overnight without the permission of the appropriate adult authorities of the home."

[After this order was entered L.A.M. ran away three times for a period of days in two instances and a period of weeks in a third instance.]

On March 18, 1974, Ms. Lankford [of the Division of Corrections Probation Department] filed a further petition seeking revocation of probation. In it she alleged that on February 20, 1974, the minor ran away from the receiving home and remained away until March 16, 1974, when she was apprehended by the police. At the hearing on the petition, held on March 22, 1974, the court found the minor had violated the conditions of her probation and had run away from the receiving home. The court considered the minor's objections presented by her attorney and, after considering the evidence and the argument of the parties, directed that the minor be institutionalized.

L.A.M. seeks to have her adjudication of delinquency set aside on two grounds. She contends that both as a matter of statutory interpretation and constitutional law, a child in need of supervision may not be prosecuted for criminal contempt; or, in the alternative, if such a prosecution is allowable, such prosecution cannot result in incarceration. Upon discussing the nature of contempt in this case, each of these grounds be dealt with in order. . . .

[T]he contempt order issued by the court would obviously be classified as "criminal." Were L.A.M. an adult, her failure to abide by court orders would be characterized as a "crime" under AS 09.50.010(5). Hence, L.A.M. could properly be declared a delinquent under AS 47.10.010(a)(1) after a proceeding in the Children's Court.

L.A.M. grounds her constitutional argument in Breese v. Smith,[9] where this court ruled that the right to liberty set out in Art. I, Sec. 1, of the Alaska State Constitution[10] guarantees every Alaskan regardless of age " . . . total personal immunity from governmental control: the right to be let alone . . . " which L.A.M. contends the supreme court qualified only to the extent that it " . . . must yield when [it] intrudes upon the freedom of others. . . ." Therefore, she continues, a citizen's right to liberty as enunciated in *Breese,* supra, (bolstered by the more recently enacted "right to privacy")[11] cannot be infringed by preventing her from doing anything that does not injure a specific definable victim. Consequently, L.A.M. concludes since her conduct, i.e. running away from home and foster home placement, did not injure anyone (except perhaps herself, which she contends has not been proved), it necessarily follows that it cannot constitutionally be interfered with by the State because there is no compelling state interest to justify such an interference. L.A.M. assumes that the only interest to be protected by legislation in this area is that of the children. This is simply not the case. The parents' interest as well as the State's must be considered.

Proceedings against children alleged to be in need of supervision are in substance and effect custody disputes where the contestants are parent and child, and the parent appeals to the court to vindicate and enforce his custody rights in the child against that child.[13] Viewed in this

---

9 501 P.2d 159, 168–170 (Alaska 1972).

10 Art. I of the declaration of rights of the Alaska Constitution, § 1, provides:

Inherent Rights. This constitution is dedicated to the principles that all persons have a natural right to life, liberty, the pursuit of happiness, and the enjoyment of the rewards of their own industry; that all persons are equal and entitled to equal rights, opportunities, and protection under the law; and that all persons have corresponding obligations to the people and to the State.

11 Alaska Constitution, Art. I, § 22, provides:

Right of Privacy. The right of the people to privacy is recognized and shall not be infringed. The legislature shall implement this section.

13 While there is much discussion of parental rights in reported cases, few cases attempt to define those rights making discussion difficult. A careful review of the literature, including case law, treatise and law review, indicates that the following have been listed as "parental rights" protected to varying degrees by the Constitution:

(1) Physical possession of the child which, in the case of a custodial parent includes the day-to-day care and companionship of the child. In the case of a non-custodial parent, possession is tantamount to the right to visitation.

(2) The right to discipline the child, which includes the right to inculcate in the child the parent's moral and ethical standards.

(3) The right to control and manage a minor child's earnings.

(4) The right to control and manage a minor child's property.

(5) The right to be supported by an adult child.

(6) The right to have the child bear the parent's name.

(7) The right to prevent an adoption of the child without the parents' consent.

Of these so called residual parental rights, those that remain after custody is placed in another include the right to consent to an adoption and to withhold consent to prevent an adoption, the right to visitation and the right to have the child bear the parents' name. See the discussion in Burt, Forcing Protection on Children and Their Parents, 69 Michigan 1259 (1971); Dobson, The Juvenile Court and Parental Rights, 4 Family Law Quarterly 393 (1970). . . .

light, the statutes creating the status "child in need of supervision" provide a judicial remedy and discourage resort to self-help and the attendant risk of violence.[14]

Thus, before L.A.M. can sustain her case that the child in need of supervision procedure, including the invocation of the court's contempt power to enforce orders made pursuant to it, is an unconstitutional invasion of her liberty and privacy, she must first establish that her mother has no legally enforceable right to her custody and the State thus has no right to enforce such an order. We note at the outset, however, that there is more to the parent-child relationship than simple custody. It is love and trust and a responsibility toward each other which cannot be defined legally. It is impossible to discuss severing this relationship without considering the heartache and anguish of the parents who must ultimately live with themselves and the decision after the child reaches adulthood. Further, the consideration of such an issue must accept the limitations of the State to be a parent; good intentions are not adequate substitutes for the day-to-day relationship which we have come to accept as necessary to the growth of children into responsible adults. True, like all legal rights, a parent's right to the custody of his child is not absolute and may be lost through divorce, by conduct depriving the child of the necessities of life, by abandonment, by the child's emancipation or, subject to constitutional limitations, where the welfare of the child requires a limitation or termination of parental rights.

L.A.M. was given an opportunity to show any of the foregoing as a defense to a finding that she was a "child in need of supervision" or, subsequent thereto, to a finding that she had committed criminal contempt of court and was therefore delinquent by violating orders regarding her placement; but she failed to do so.

Runaway children of L.A.M.'s age are generally incapable of providing for or protecting themselves. As a result, police spend a substantial amount of time protecting these youths from those who would prey upon them, as well as protecting the community from those who are ultimately driven to criminal activity to provide themselves with the necessities of life. Various other social agencies also expend considerable efforts attempting to protect and shelter runaways in an effort to provide both an alternative to criminal activities and counseling in lieu of that they received from their parents. Without question these children's matters are of broad public interest and concern. They go to all aspects of the physical and mental well being of such children.

The family, school, social agency and police resources allocated to aid the runaway are enormous. In this case, the child had continuing aid and

[14] By withdrawing court assistance (and police assistance) from embattled parents, the state is not inducing compromise but may encourage violence, since parents have the right under Alaska law to physically control their children. See AS 11.15.110(1) as interpreted in State v. England, 220 Or. 395, 349 P.2d 668 (1960), and compare the civil liability of parents for disciplining their children which is discussed in Hebel v. Hebel, 435 P.2d 8, 14–15 (Alaska 1967).

support of (1) her mother and step-father, (2) a private psychiatrist hired by her mother, (3) counseling with social workers in Division of Family and Children's Services, (4) probation officers in Division of Corrections, (5) school counselors, (6) psychologists and psychiatrists from Langdon Clinic, (7) Alaska Youth Advocates, (8) group home counselors, (9) her court-appointed attorney, and (10) the court. To assert that the State has no interest in this child is to deny that the function of government is to protect its citizens. All of this presupposes the heartache and anguish of the parents, who in the first instance have been unable to deal with this problem but who must also live with the solution.

This court has previously found that there is sufficient State interest to justify restrictive measures on much less substantial grounds. Further, this court has noted that distinct government interests with reference to children may justify legislation that could not properly be applied to adults. The State has a legitimate interest in protecting children from venereal disease, from exposure to the use of dangerous and illicit drugs, from attempted rape, and from physical injury, all of which occurred in this case. Doubtless the State will never be entirely successful in its efforts. It does, however, have the right and obligation to *try* to protect its young people from such conditions. The test set out by this court in Ravin v. State,[24] is whether the means chosen by the State are closely and substantially related to an appropriate government interest. Clearly they are here.

While it may be argued that the necessary "supervision" contemplated by the statute is simply the furnishing of food, clothing, shelter and schooling in lieu of that which would otherwise have been provided by a parent, this argument begs the question, for the purpose of the supervision or treatment contemplated by the creation of the child in need of supervision and its predecessor non-criminal delinquency was reintegration of the child into her family and resumption of parental custody including parental control (cf. AS 47.10.280). Thus, the State's efforts regarding the child are not directed solely at providing an alternate living situation (as they are in a true case of dependency) but at putting the child back in her own home. The reestablishment of her mother's custody and supervision over her and any foster placement is merely a means to that end, not an end in itself. Thus, by rejecting these efforts L.A.M. defeats, or at least slows, this reintegration process and thereby prejudices her mother's right to her custody and control, subjecting herself to the more severe sanction contemplated by AS 09.50.020.

We note that L.A.M.'s primary argument in this case is that as a child in need of supervision whose conduct from the inception of the case to the present has not changed, she may not be placed in a closed setting, i.e. one where the doors may be locked. However, the cases upon which

[24] 537 P.2d 494 (Alaska 1975).

L.A.M. relies proceed to a different point, namely that the child should not be placed in a state training school. In Colorado, California, Illinois and New York, children in need of supervision can at the first instance be placed in juvenile halls or youth centers, i.e. places with locked doors, but cannot be placed at the state training school, i.e. maximum security institutions. The McLaughlin Youth Center in Anchorage is more the equivalent of a juvenile hall than it is a state training school. It should be noted that Alaska has contracts with Colorado and California to place Alaska delinquents who are too sophisticated for McLaughlin in the state institutions in those states. Thus L.A.M. is not to be placed at either the California or Colorado training schools; she is threatened with placement at the McLaughlin Youth Center.

Substantial evidence was introduced during the many hearings of this case regarding the population at the McLaughlin Youth Center. Based upon that evidence, it is clear that the kind of children who are extremely aggressive, and extremely hardened in delinquency, are not treated at McLaughlin Youth Center but are sent outside for placement at schools in Colorado and California under contract with the State of Alaska. While the population at McLaughlin is made up at the present time exclusively of "delinquents," the evidence introduced at trial convinces us that while delinquency in some form is a prerequisite to gaining admission to McLaughlin, it is not the real reason that the child is at McLaughlin. The overwhelming majority of delinquents with strong family ties are treated in the community. Those delinquents who end up at McLaughlin are by and large there for the same reason that L.A.M. may be there, namely an unwillingness to remain at home or a home substitute and heed parental or a custodian's regulations. Based upon the evidence, it appears that L.A.M. and other chronic runaways would not be distinguishable in sophistication, exposure to criminal activity, etc., from the average child in the population at McLaughlin and that therefore the reasoning of the cases cited by L.A.M. should not apply to Alaska.

Whether we characterize L.A.M. as a delinquent child, a child in need of supervision, a dependent child, or merely a child whose custody is disputed in a domestic relations proceeding, the court has authority, upon extending all procedural safeguards, to make orders affecting her custody. It is argued, however, that this is a situation where the court has no power to enforce its order, and thus the court must release L.A.M. This view is contrary to the inherent power of the court to enforce its orders or decrees. While the court may have limitations on its power to act, there are only due process limitations on its authority to compel enforcement of its orders. Hence, we reject the argument that the superior court lacked the authority to enforce specific orders against L.A.M. in this case.

The lower court determined that L.A.M. would not abide by any orders it entered regarding her supervision under AS 47.10.080(j). This behavior constitutes willful criminal contempt of the court's authority; were she an adult, her actions would be characterized as a "crime" under Alaska statutes. She was, therefore, properly declared a delinquent and subject to those sanctions available for the correction of a delinquent minor's behavior. Certainly, conciliation should precede coercion; and if coercion is necessary, mild sanctions should first be tried before more severe sanctions are imposed. However, where mild sanctions fail, the court's orders must be enforced and severe sanctions should be imposed if necessary. In the instant case, all available sanctions, save institutionalization, were tried and found unsuccessful. Thus, the lower court determined that it had no choice but to order L.A.M. institutionalized. . . .

■ BOOCHEVER, JUSTICE, with whom RABINOWITZ, CHIEF JUSTICE, joins, concurring.

I concur in the court's opinion based on the last three paragraphs thereof. I would not reach the other issues discussed in the opinion. Protection of parental rights to care, custody and supervision do not seem to me to be an appropriate rationale for placing a child in an institution. In my opinion, the court's efforts were devoted primarily to furthering the welfare of the child, a subject in which the state does have an interest. There was ample testimony to indicate that L.A.M.'s conduct was harmful to her.[2]

On the basis of the record, I do not believe that we can conclude that police spend countless hours protecting the community from anti-social conduct of runaway children. Recent studies indicate that status offenders (such as runaways) are not a source of general harm to others as contrasted with children who have committed offenses which, if perpetrated by adults, would be crimes. I concur in the opinion since I believe that the state has an interest in the welfare of children justifying the entry of appropriate orders. In cases involving status offenders, only after all else fails, should placement in a closed setting be justified. But under the facts of this case, the trial judge had no alternative.

Matter of Andrew R.

Family Court, Richmond County, New York, 1982
454 N.Y.S.2d 820

■ LEDDY, JR., JUDGE.

In dismissing the instant Person in Need of Supervision (PINS) proceeding this court holds that thirteen-year old Andrew R. was legally justified in resisting his parents' efforts to return him to foster care against his will. Reaching this decision, the court concludes that his placement at Hawthorne Cedar Knolls (Hawthorne) for over seven

---

2 While a runaway, L.A.M. was truant from school; was allegedly the victim of a rape as reported in a call to the police; contracted gonorrhea; suffered an injured jaw and broken teeth from a fall, which injuries had not received medical attention.

months under a so-called voluntary placement without any review by a neutral fact-finder violated his fundamental liberty interest as protected by the due process clause of the Fourteenth Amendment to the United States Constitution.

Andrew is an intelligent, appealing boy who desperately wishes to remain at home on Staten Island. His parents are equally determined to return him to Hawthorne, a residential treatment center, to which he had been sent by them under a so-called voluntary placement instrument. Social Services Law Sec. 384–a. The parent-child conflict culminated in the instant PINS proceeding.

Thus, on August 16, 1982, Andrew's father filed a petition with this court alleging that his son was a Person in Need of Supervision (PINS) in that

> "... he is beyond the lawful control of his parents. Respondent on this date, threatened petitioner with a knife and damaged household property. Respondent had been voluntarily placed with Hawthorne Cedar Knolls from January, 1982 up until about a week ago, at which time he ran away and returned home."

The petition was subsequently amended to add an additional allegation that

"Respondent truanted from school for over two years and truanted while in placement."

A fact-finding hearing was held during which the only witnesses were Andrew and his father. During the hearing, the assistant corporation counsel, representing the petitioner-father, attempted to elicit testimony about additional alleged misbehavior on the part of Andrew other than that specifically set forth in the petition. In offering this testimony, the petitioner argued that it was sufficiently pleaded under the umbrella allegation that Andrew "is beyond the lawful control of his parents". The court sustained the law guardian's objection as a matter of both statutory law and constitutional due process.

Section 732(a) of the Family Court Act provides that a PINS proceeding is initiated by the filing of a petition, alleging that

> "the respondent is an habitual truant or is incorrigible, ungovernable, or habitually disobedient and beyond the lawful control of his parents ... and *specifying the acts on which the allegations are based and the time and place they allegedly occurred;*" (emphasis supplied).

This statutory provision evidences clear legislative intent to accord a PINS respondent adequate notice of the charges. It is consistent with longstanding judicial recognition that a PINS proceeding is quasi-criminal in nature, involving the potential for significant governmental interference in the liberty of the child. FCA Secs. 754; 756. Therefore, the due process rights accorded to a respondent in a juvenile delinquency proceeding apply with equal force to a PINS respondent. . . . Matter of Reynaldo R., 73 Misc.2d 390, 341 N.Y.S.2d 998; Matter of George C., 91 Misc.2d 875, 398 N.Y.S.2d 936.

For these reasons, a general allegation that a respondent is beyond the lawful control of his parents may not be utilized as a predicate to subject the child's life to parental attack.

As was stated in Matter of Reynaldo R., (supra)

> " . . . no petition alleging a person to be in need of supervision can stand unless the acts complained of are set forth in specific terms with dates and frequency, the nature of the behavior and conduct charged. . . . Otherwise, there is a violation of child's constitutional rights to notice of charges against him *in time to prepare for trial, not at the time of trial.* None of these rights can be taken away from children merely because their conduct is noncriminal or the subject of a PINS petition. (Matter of Gault, 387 U.S. 1 [87 S.Ct. 1428, 18 L.Ed.2d 527])" 73 Misc.2d at 394, 341 N.Y.S.2d 998.

In January of 1982, while under the so-called "voluntary placement" Andrew was sent to Hawthorne, a residential treatment center in Hawthorne, New York. At the hearing, the petitioner-father testified that his son agreed to the placement at Hawthorne. Andrew disputed this, maintaining that he never wanted to leave home and that, in effect, he was tricked into going by a promise from his father that his stay would be no longer than a month. The court believes Andrew and concludes that he was induced to go to Hawthorne by a representation that was at least misleading, if not purposely false.

In August of this year, the respondent ran away from Hawthorne and returned home, refusing to return. When pressed by his father to go back to the facility, Andrew reacted with threats against him. On one occasion, he threatened to kill his father. In response thereto, his father handed him a knife and told him to go ahead and do it. Andrew thereupon proceeded to thrust the knife into a household item. While in school at Hawthorne, the respondent cut a number of classes, although he attended his academic subjects for the most part.

Hawthorne is anxious to have Andrew return since it believes that he can be helped by their program. In fact, it was at the urging of Hawthorne personnel that the petitioner initiated this proceeding. It has been apparent at the outset that the petitioner is utilizing the PINS procedure to compel his son's return to Hawthorne.

Stripped of all euphemism, the term "voluntary placement" is dangerously misleading. A review of Sec. 384–a of the Social Services Law reveals that the child is not a party to the instrument effecting the foster care placement. Nor is there a requirement that the wishes of the child be considered or even solicited. It is readily evident, therefore, that there is no reason to assume that any "voluntary placement" is truly voluntary on the part of the child. This is significant since, in this case, there can be no doubt that Andrew's placement at Hawthorne against his will involves a substantial deprivation of liberty. . . .

The deprivation of liberty extends beyond the mere fact of confinement in a residential treatment center. A child so placed loses the daily consortium of family and friends, schoolmates, and participation in community affairs and activities.

In his concurring and dissenting opinion in Parham v. J.R., 442 U.S. 584, 626, 99 S.Ct. 2493, 61 L.Ed.2d 101, Mr. Justice Brennan referred to commitment to a mental institution as involving a "massive curtailment of liberty" since it restricts not only physical liberty but also contacts with "friends, family and community".

Andrew's liberty interest has been further impaired by the fact that he has been sent to a facility that contains both juvenile delinquents and PINS, children who are entitled to treatment measured by their need for rehabilitation. Thus, where there is a commingling of voluntarily placed children, PINS, and juvenile delinquents, it may well be that the "basic care" to which a foster child is entitled is in jeopardy. It is more than ironic that Andrew arrived at Hawthorne by a process that accorded him absolutely no legal rights while others, with whom he came into daily contact, enjoyed all of the procedural and substantive protection that apply to PINS and juvenile delinquency cases.[3] At least in this case, the problem created by this disparity in treatment reaches constitutional dimensions.

New York has virtually ignored the feelings of children who are placed in foster care against their will. Section 358–a of the Social Services Law provides for judicial approval of a voluntary placement instrument in any instance where the child is likely to remain in foster care for in excess of thirty consecutive days. The statute requires that the review proceeding be filed "as soon as practicable, but in no event later than thirty days following removal of the child from the home." SSL Sec. 358–a(1). This should be contrasted with a PINS proceeding where a child is entitled to a probable cause hearing within three days of any remand to a foster care facility, FCA Sec. 739(b). What is critically important, however, is that while SSL Sec. 358–a mandates the filing of a petition within thirty days of the removal from home, there is no statutory time limitation within which the court proceeding must take place. And in Andrew's case, a review of the records of the Family Court Foster Care review term in Manhattan reveals that no petition has yet been filed to review the voluntary placement instrument which is now over seven months old.

---

[3] These include, *inter alia,* the right to counsel, to adequate notice of the charges, to confront and cross-examine witnesses, to the exercise of the privilege against self-incrimination, and to have the stated charges proven beyond a reasonable doubt.

It is apparent that the protection accorded to a child under Sec. 358–a is anywhere from minimal to non-existent. This is consistent with a finding that the statute is, in reality, a "funding device to trigger the flow of Federal dollars" and that the issue at a hearing thereunder is "the voluntariness of a parent's transfer of custody, not whether a placement by the state is in the child's best interests". Sinhogar v. Parry, 53 N.Y.2d 424, 446, 442 N.Y.S.2d 438, 425 N.E.2d 826. (Fuchsberg, J., dissenting.)

To reach a decision in this case, the court need not consider whether New York's statutory scheme for effecting voluntary placements violates the child's right to due process of law. The holding herein must be limited to the facts of this case. Thus, the issue is whether Andrew R., an intelligent youngster, "mature enough to have (his contrary) desire respected" (Wisconsin v. Yoder, 406 U.S. 205, 242, 92 S.Ct. 1526, 1546, 32 L.Ed.2d 15) suffered a constitutionally infirmed deprivation of liberty by being kept in foster care at Hawthorne against his will for over seven months without any hearing or other review by a neutral factfinder. The issue is thus framed since it is fundamental that a child may not be adjudicated a PINS for refusing to comply with a directive that violates his constitutional rights or is otherwise unlawful. Matter of Mary P., 111 Misc.2d 532, 444 N.Y.S.2d 545. . . .

In Parham v. J.R. (supra), the United States Supreme Court held that a child has a substantial liberty interest in not being confined unnecessarily for medical treatment. Accordingly,

> " . . . the risk of error inherent in the parental decision to have a child institutionalized for mental health care is sufficiently great that some kind of inquiry should be made by a 'neutral factfinder' to determine whether the statutory requirements for admission are satisfied. . . . That inquiry must carefully probe the child's background using all available sources, including, but not limited to, parents, schools, and other social agencies. Of course, the review must also include an interview with the child. It is necessary that the decisionmaker have the authority to refuse to admit any child who does not satisfy the medical standards for admission." 442 U.S. 584, 606, 607, 99 S.Ct. 2493, 2506, 2507, 61 L.Ed.2d 101.

As has already been established, Andrew has a liberty interest that suffers substantial infringement by his placement at Hawthorne against his will. For the purposes of this decision, however, it is not necessary to decide whether due process required a formal hearing either before Andrew was placed in foster care or even immediately thereafter.

Given the posture of the case, the court need only decide whether his running away from Hawthorne in August and his refusal to return constitutes PINS behavior. The court concludes that it does not and finds that the failure to afford Andrew any review of his foster care placement by a neutral factfinder for over seven months violated his constitutional right to due process of law. It must follow, therefore, that the boy may not be penalized in any manner whatsoever for running away and staying away from Hawthorne. For the same reasons, his failure to cooperate with the school program at Hawthorne may not subject him to the stigma of a PINS finding.

The court is aware that Andrew made threats against his father as a result of his placement at Hawthorne and in response to his father's desire to implement that placement. And it must be emphasized that this court in no way condones this behavior on Andrew's part. Nevertheless, those threats (and they remained just that) must be evaluated against all the facts in this case. An intelligent, sensitive youngster is placed against his will in a facility that houses juvenile delinquents and PINS and is denied review of that parental decision for over seven months. He lacks the resources to challenge the placement through legal means and resorts to threats to enunciate his liberty interest. On the facts of this case, those threats are more attributable to the failure of the state to provide the boy with an opportunity to be heard rather than PINS intent on his part.

Furthermore, in handing Andrew a knife at a time when the boy threatened to kill him, the petitioner demonstrated remarkably poor judgment. The inappropriate nature of this behavior on the part of the petitioner is exceeded only by his temerity in charging the boy with threatening him with a knife.

> "A parent in a PINS petition has no divine right to be right. Their actions and conduct must be more carefully screened than those of the accused child." Matter of Reynaldo R. (supra), 73 Misc.2d at page 394, 341 N.Y.S.2d 998.

While at Hawthorne, Andrew's attendance at school was less than exemplary. He cut several classes a week even though there is no evidence to controvert his assertion that he was present for his academic subjects. Nevertheless, Andrew's failure to attend school while at Hawthorne must be viewed in the same light as his refusal to stay at that facility. His truancy was simply another manifestation of his deep-seated desire not to be at Hawthorne, a desire that was never evaluated in a manner consistent with constitutional due process. Accordingly, the court cannot find that Andrew had the requisite intent to truant from school or to disobey the mandates of Article 65 of the Education Law.

The court also finds that the petitioner has failed to establish beyond a reasonable doubt that Andrew was sufficiently truant from school prior to placement in order to sustain a finding that he is "incorrigible, ungovernable or habitually disobedient and beyond the lawful control" of his parents. FCA Sec. 712(b). In that regard, it should be noted that the petitioner chose not to allege specifically a violation of Article 65 of the Education Law, preferring instead, to make the allegation of truancy following the assertion that Andrew "is beyond the lawful control of his parents".

Section 3233 of the Education Law makes absence from school for even one day a violation and provides a stated penalty. However, even if measured by the dictates of Article 65 of the Education Law, Andrew's sporadic absences prior to placement cannot support a PINS finding. To interpret Article 65 as justifying state interference in the parent-child relationship as a result of a few absences from school would render the statute unconstitutional as an arbitrary and unreasonable interference in the affairs of both parent and child. In order to sustain a PINS finding on the basis of truancy, there must be a substantial and intentional failure to attend school. Such has not been established here.

For all of the foregoing reasons, the petition is dismissed. Furthermore, incidental to the order of dismissal and at the request of the law guardian, a final order of protection is issued to the child directing the petitioner to cease and desist in his efforts to have Andrew return to Hawthorne under the instant voluntary placement instrument. Since his continued placement there offends his constitutionally protected liberty interests, any attempt by the parents to force his return against his will is conduct that is "offensive" to the child within the meaning of Sec. 759(c) of the Family Court Act. The petitioner is warned that any violation of the order of protection may result in a six-month jail term. . . .

This is a sad commentary on the degree of our society's commitment to treating children with the respect they deserve as citizens. This case demonstrates in graphic terms the need to avoid granting to agencies unfettered discretion over the liberties of children, something that is certain to occur if, as some would have it, PINS cases are removed from the jurisdiction of the Family Court.

NOTES

The Fourteenth Amendment's Due Process Clause provides heightened protection against governmental interference with the fundamental liberty interests of parents exercising authority over their children's care, custody, and control. *See* Troxel v. Granville, 530 U.S. 57, 68 (2000); Bellotti v. Baird, 443 U.S. 622, 634 (1979) (arguing that the constitutional rights of minors may be treated differently because of "the particular vulnerability of children; their inability to make critical decisions in an informed mature manner; and the importance of the parental role in child rearing"). Seeking to escape that authority, children sometimes seek to "divorce" their parents; however, the courts have consistently refused to grant such petitions. *See* Ryan v. Ryan, 677 N.W.2d 899 (Mich. Ct. App. 2004) (holding that parents have a natural right to the custody of their children). To escape parental authority, a minor must petition for and be declared emancipated under the state's emancipation statute. *See, e.g.*, ARK. CODE ANN. § 9–27–362 (2016); AZ. REV. STAT. § 12–2451 (2016); MICH. STAT. ANN. § 722.4a (2016). In addition, see *infra*, Section (G). "Emancipation: 'Divorce' Between Parent and Child?" For commentary on the use of state resources used to support parental rights over their children, *see* Orly Rachmilovitz, *Family*

Assimilation Demands and Sexual Minority Youth, 98 MINN. L. REV. 1374 (2014); John C. Duncan, Jr., *The Ultimate Best Interest of the Child Inures from Parental Reinforcement: The Journey to Family Integrity*, 83 NEB. L. REV. 1240 (2005).

C. NEGLECT (ENDANGERMENT) AND DEPENDENCY

CALIFORNIA WELFARE AND INSTITUTIONS CODE (2016)

§ 300. Children subject to jurisdiction; legislative intent and declarations; guardian defined

A child who comes within any of the following descriptions is within the jurisdiction of the juvenile court which may adjudge that person to be a dependent child of the court:

(a) The child has suffered, or there is a substantial risk that the child will suffer, serious physical harm inflicted nonaccidentally upon the child by the child's parent or guardian. For the purposes of this subdivision, a court may find there is a substantial risk of serious future injury based on the manner in which a less serious injury was inflicted, a history of repeated inflictions of injuries on the child or the child's siblings, or a combination of these and other actions by the parent or guardian which indicate the child is at risk of serious physical harm. For purposes of this subdivision, "serious physical harm" does not include reasonable and age-appropriate spanking to the buttocks where there is no evidence of serious physical injury.

(b) (1) The child has suffered, or there is a substantial risk that the child will suffer, serious physical harm or illness, as a result of the failure or inability of his or her parent or guardian to adequately supervise or protect the child, or the willful or negligent failure of the child's parent or guardian to adequately supervise or protect the child from the conduct of the custodian with whom the child has been left, or by the willful or negligent failure of the parent or guardian to provide the child with adequate food, clothing, shelter, or medical treatment, or by the inability of the parent or guardian to provide regular care for the child due to the parent's or guardian's mental illness, developmental disability, or substance abuse. No child shall be found to be a person described by this subdivision solely due to the lack of an emergency shelter for the family. Whenever it is alleged that a child comes within the jurisdiction of the court on the basis of the parent's or guardian's willful failure to provide adequate medical treatment or specific decision to provide spiritual treatment through prayer, the court shall give deference to the parent's or guardian's medical treatment, nontreatment, or spiritual treatment through prayer alone in accordance with the tenets and practices of a recognized church or religious denomination, by an accredited practitioner thereof, and shall not assume jurisdiction unless necessary to protect the child from suffering serious physical harm or illness. In making its determination, the court shall consider (1) the nature of the treatment proposed by the parent or guardian, (2) the risks to the child posed by the course of treatment or nontreatment proposed by the parent or guardian, (3) the risk, if any, of the course of treatment being proposed by the petitioning agency, and (4) the likely success of the courses of treatment or nontreatment proposed by the parent or guardian and agency. The child shall continue to be a dependent child pursuant to this subdivision only so long as is necessary to protect the child from risk of suffering serious physical harm or illness.

(2) The Legislature finds and declares that a child who is sexually trafficked, as described in Section 236.1 of the Penal Code, or who receives food or shelter in exchange for, or who is paid to perform, sexual acts described in Section 236.1 or 11165.1 of the Penal Code, and whose parent or guardian failed to, or was unable to, protect the child, is within the description of this subdivision, and that this finding is declaratory of existing law. These children shall be known as commercially sexually exploited children.

(c) The child is suffering serious emotional damage, or is at substantial risk of suffering serious emotional damage, evidenced by severe anxiety, depression, withdrawal, or untoward aggressive behavior toward self or others, as a result of the conduct of the parent or guardian or who has no parent or guardian capable of providing appropriate care. No child shall be found to be a person described by this subdivision if the willful failure of the parent or guardian to provide adequate mental health treatment is based on a sincerely held religious belief and if a less intrusive judicial intervention is available.

(d) The child has been sexually abused, or there is a substantial risk that the child will be sexually abused, as defined in Section 11165.1 of the Penal Code, by his or her parent or guardian or a member of his or her household, or the parent or guardian has failed to adequately protect the child from sexual abuse when the parent or guardian knew or reasonably should have known that the child was in danger of sexual abuse.

(e) The child is under the age of five years and has suffered severe physical abuse by a parent, or by any person known by the parent, if the parent knew or reasonably should have known that the person was physically abusing the child. For the purposes of this subdivision, "severe physical abuse" means any of the following: any single act of abuse which causes physical trauma of sufficient severity that, if left untreated, would cause permanent physical disfigurement, permanent physical disability, or death; any single act of sexual abuse which causes significant bleeding, deep bruising, or significant external or internal swelling; or more than one act of physical abuse, each of which causes bleeding, deep bruising, significant external or internal swelling, bone fracture, or unconsciousness; or the willful, prolonged failure to provide adequate food. A child may not be removed from the physical custody of his or her parent or guardian on the basis of a finding of severe physical abuse unless the social worker has made an allegation of severe physical abuse pursuant to Section 332.

(f) The child's parent or guardian caused the death of another child through abuse or neglect.

(g) The child has been left without any provision for support; physical custody of the child has been voluntarily surrendered pursuant to Section 1255.7 of the Health and Safety Code and the child has not been reclaimed within the 14-day period specified in subdivision (e) of that section; the child's parent has been incarcerated or institutionalized and cannot arrange for the care of the child; or a relative or other adult custodian with whom the child resides or has been left is unwilling or unable to provide care or support for the child, the whereabouts of the parent are unknown, and reasonable efforts to locate the parent have been unsuccessful.

(h) The child has been freed for adoption by one or both parents for 12 months by either relinquishment or termination of parental rights or an adoption petition has not been granted.

(i) The child has been subjected to an act or acts of cruelty by the parent or guardian or a member of his or her household, or the parent or guardian has failed to adequately protect the child from an act or acts of cruelty when the parent or guardian knew or reasonably should have known that the child was in danger of being subjected to an act or acts of cruelty.

(j) The child's sibling has been abused or neglected, as defined in subdivision (a), (b), (d), (e), or (i), and there is a

> substantial risk that the child will be abused or neglected, as defined in those subdivisions. The court shall consider the circumstances surrounding the abuse or neglect of the sibling, the age and gender of each child, the nature of the abuse or neglect of the sibling, the mental condition of the parent or guardian, and any other factors the court considers probative in determining whether there is a substantial risk to the child.

It is the intent of the Legislature that this section not disrupt the family unnecessarily or intrude inappropriately into family life, prohibit the use of reasonable methods of parental discipline, or prescribe a particular method of parenting. Further, nothing in this section is intended to limit the offering of voluntary services to those families in need of assistance but who do not come within the descriptions of this section. To the extent that savings accrue to the state from child welfare services funding obtained as a result of the enactment of the act that enacted this section, those savings shall be used to promote services which support family maintenance and family reunification plans, such as client transportation, out-of-home respite care, parenting training, and the provision of temporary or emergency in-home caretakers and persons teaching and demonstrating homemaking skills. The Legislature further declares that a physical disability, such as blindness or deafness, is no bar to the raising of happy and well-adjusted children and that a court's determination pursuant to this section shall center upon whether a parent's disability prevents him or her from exercising care and control. The Legislature further declares that a child whose parent has been adjudged a dependent child of the court pursuant to this section shall not be considered to be at risk of abuse or neglect solely because of the age, dependent status, or foster care status of the parent.

As used in this section, "guardian" means the legal guardian of the child.

In re M.L.

Supreme Court of Pennsylvania, 2000
757 A.2d 849

■ CASTILLE, JUSTICE.

Allowance of appeal was granted in this matter limited to the issue of whether a court may properly adjudge a child to be dependent where the non-custodial parent is ready, willing and able to provide the child with proper parental care and control. The Superior Court affirmed the trial court's finding of dependency in the instant case even though the child's father was available and willing to provide adequate care for the child. We hold that a child, whose non-custodial parent is ready, willing and able to provide adequate care to the child, cannot be found dependent and, therefore, reverse.

Appellant is the natural mother of the child, born February 6, 1995, and R.G. is the child's natural father. The child's parents never married but shared custody of the child from the time of her birth. A January 1997 custody dispute ended with appellant having primary physical custody and the father having partial custody every other weekend. In May of 1996, appellant contacted Cambria County Children and Youth Service (CYS) to complain that the father did not care for the child properly during her weekends with him in that he lacked supplies for the child and did not feed her appropriately.

Then, in August of 1996, appellant began alleging that the father was sexually abusing the child. Between August 1996 and January 1997, appellant subjected the child to six separate physical examinations for possible sexual abuse at either the hospital emergency room or the child's pediatrician's office. Each examining physician reported that the child had diaper rash or normal redness for a child of her age wearing diapers; no signs of sexual abuse were found in any of the examinations. Despite the lack of evidence, appellant continued to allege that the father was sexually abusing the child, leading CYS to file a petition for dependency. Following two evidentiary hearings on February 24 and March 19, 1997, the trial court found, on March 25, 1997, that the child was a dependent child and awarded custody to her father.[4]

The sole issue for our determination is whether the trial court erred in finding that the child was a dependent child when her father was ready, willing and able to provide adequate care to her. Two earlier panels of the Superior Court reached conflicting decisions as to whether a child can be found dependent and then placed in the custody of the non-custodial parent. . . .

A dependent child is defined in pertinent part at 42 Pa.C.S. § 6302 as:

A child who:

(1) is without proper parental care or control, subsistence, education as required by law, or other care or control necessary for his physical, mental or emotional health, or morals;

(2) has been placed for care or adoption in violation of law;

(3) has been abandoned by his parents, guardian, or other custodian;

(4) is without parent, guardian, or legal custodian; . . .

---

[4] The trial court's decision was based upon a finding that appellant suffers from factitious disorder by proxy, that she had repeatedly subjected the child to physical examinations which revealed nothing more than diaper rash, and that appellant's mental illness had the strong potential to escalate to the point where appellant would actually harm the child physically in order to provide substantiation of her abuse allegations against the child's father. Factitious disorder by proxy means, in this case, that appellant transferred to the child her own psychological difficulties such that she claimed that the child was experiencing symptoms of abuse that the child did not actually experience.

A court is empowered by 42 Pa.C.S. § 6341(a) and (c) to make a finding that a child is dependent if the child meets the statutory definition by clear and convincing evidence. If the court finds that the child is dependent, then the court may make an appropriate disposition of the child to protect the child's physical, mental and moral welfare, including allowing the child to remain with the parents subject to supervision, transferring temporary legal custody to a relative or a private or public agency, or transferring custody to the juvenile court of another state. 42 Pa.C.S. § 6351(a).

The definition of a dependent child contained in section 6302 clearly states that a child must lack a parent, guardian or other legal custodian who can provide appropriate care to the child. A child whose non-custodial parent is ready, willing and able to provide such care does not meet this definition. In *Justin S.*, 375 Pa.Super. at 104, 543 A.2d at 1200, the Superior Court stated:

> [I]t is the duty of the trial court to determine whether the non-custodial parent is capable and willing to render proper parental control prior to adjudicating a child dependent. If the court determines that the custodial parent is unable to provide proper parental care and control "at this moment" and that the non-custodial parent is "immediately available" to provide such care, the child is not dependent under the provisions of the Juvenile Act. Consequently, the court must grant custody of the allegedly dependent child to the non-custodial parent. Once custody is granted to the non-custodial parent, "the care, protection, and wholesome mental and physical development of the child" can occur in a family environment as the purpose of the Juvenile Act directs. 42 Pa.C.S. § 6301(b).

We are in accord with the Superior Court's decision in *Justin S.* The plain language of the statutory definition of a dependent child compels the conclusion that a child is not dependent if the child has a parent who is willing and able to provide proper care to the child. When a court adjudges a child dependent, that court then possesses the authority to place the child in the custody of a relative or a public or private agency. Where a non-custodial parent is available and willing to provide care to the child, such power in the hands of the court is an unwarranted intrusion into the family. Only where a child is truly lacking a parent, guardian or legal custodian who can provide adequate care should we allow our courts to exercise such authority. Accordingly, we hold that where a non-custodial parent is ready, willing and able to provide adequate care to a child, a court may not adjudge that child dependent.

Therefore, she does not meet the statutory definition of a dependent child, and the trial court erred in adjudging her dependent. Therefore, the decision of the Superior Court affirming the trial court's finding that the child is a dependent child is reversed.

[The concurring opinion of JUSTICE NEWMAN and the dissenting opinion of JUSTICE CAPPY have not been reproduced. In the latter the Justice stated agreement with the majority's ultimate result that the child should remain with her non-custodial parent but states his belief that the majority "fundamentally misapprehended the nature of dependency proceedings" and its reversal of the decision of the Superior Court violated both the language and intent of the Juvenile Act, 42 Pa.C.S. § 6301 *et seq.*]

NOTES

Often the courts appoint separate counsel to represent a child in any case involving the child's dependency. *See, e.g.,* WASH. REV. CODE 13.34.100(6) (2013), which provides that the appointment of counsel for children, who are the subject of dependency and termination cases, is to be within the trial court's discretion and is not mandatory. The statute has been held to be constitutional in spite of the fact that there is no mandatory appointment of counsel. *See In re* Dependency of MSR, 174 Wash. 2d 1 (Wash. 2012). In holding the statute constitutional, the Washington Supreme Court reviewed two pertinent cases on due process: Mathews v. Eldridge, 424 U.S. 319 (1976), and Lassiter v. Department of Social Services, 452 U.S. 18 (1981). The court concluded that a child's due process rights might be adequately protected through the appointment of a guardian ad litem, a special advocate, or the availability of appellate review. Thus, the mandatory appointment of counsel to represent a child in a dependency proceeding is not required under the Fourteenth Amendment's Due Process Clause. For commentary on attorneys generally and the civil and criminal process, *see* Nadine Frederique, Patricia Joseph, and R. Christopher C. Hild, *What is the State of Empirical Research on Indigent Defense Nationwide? A Brief Overview and Suggestions for Future Research*, 78 ALB. L. REV. 1317 (2014–2015); Raymond C. O'Brien, *Reasonable Efforts and Parent-Child Reunification*, 2013 MICH. ST. L. REV. 1029; Alberto Bernabe, *The Right to Counsel Denied: Confusing the Roles of Lawyers and Guardians*, 43 LOY. U. CHI. L. J. 833 (2012); and Jessica Dixon Weaver, *The Texas Mis-Step: Why the Largest Child Removal in Modern U.S. History Failed*, 16 WM. & MARY J. WOMEN & L. 449 (2010).

In re Juvenile Appeal (83–CD)

Supreme Court of Connecticut, 1983
455 A.2d 1313

■ SPEZIALE, CHIEF JUSTICE.

This is an appeal by the defendant, mother of five children, from the order of the Superior Court for juvenile matters granting temporary custody of her children to the plaintiff commissioner of the department of children and youth services.

The defendant and her six children lived in a small apartment in New Haven. They had been receiving services from the department of children and youth services (hereinafter DCYS) as a protective service family[1] since 1976, and were supported by the Aid to Families with Dependent Children program. Michelle Spicknall, a DCYS caseworker, was assigned to the defendant's case in January 1979. In the next nine months she visited the defendant's home twenty-seven times. She considered the family situation "marginal," but noted that the children were "not abused [or] neglected." It was Spicknall's opinion that the children were very happy and active, and that they had a "very warm" relationship with their mother.

During the night of September 4–5, 1979, the defendant's youngest child, nine month old Christopher, died. The child was brought by ambulance to Yale-New Haven Medical Center where resuscitation was unsuccessfully attempted by his pediatrician, Dr. Robert Murphy. No cause of death could be determined at that time, but the pediatrician noticed some unexplained superficial marks on Christopher's body. Because of Christopher's unexplained death, the plaintiff commissioner of children and youth services seized custody of the defendant's five remaining children on September 5, 1979, under authority of the "96-hour hold" provision of General Statutes § 17–38a(e)[3] which permits summary seizure if the commissioner has probable cause to believe that a child is "suffering from serious physical illness or serious physical injury or is in immediate physical danger from his surroundings, and that immediate removal from such surroundings *is necessary to insure the child's safety. . . .*" (Emphasis added.)

On September 7, 1979, in the Juvenile Court for New Haven, DCYS filed petitions of neglect under General Statutes § 46b–129(a) for each of the defendant's children. Accompanying each petition was an affidavit

[1] A protective services family is one which has come to the attention of DCYS as having a potential for abuse, neglect, abandonment, or sexual exploitation. DCYS then investigates the family and, where appropriate, provides "support systems to bolster family functioning." DCYS: Programs and Priorities, FY 1979.

[3] General Statutes § 17–38a(e) provides: "Agencies or institutions receiving reports of child abuse as provided in this section shall, within twenty-four hours, transfer such information to the commissioner of children and youth services or his agent, who shall cause the report to be investigated immediately. If the investigation produces evidence that the child has been abused in the manner described in subsection (b), he shall take such measures as he deems necessary to protect the child, and any other children similarly situated, including but not limited to the removal of the child or children from his home with the consent of his or their parents or guardian or by order of the superior court. If the commissioner of children and youth services or his designee, after such investigation, has probable cause to believe that the child is suffering from serious physical illness or serious physical injury or is in immediate physical danger from his surroundings, and that immediate removal from such surroundings is necessary to insure the child's safety, the commissioner, or his designee, may authorize any employee of his department or any law enforcement officer to remove the child from such surroundings without the consent of the child's parent or guardian. Such removal and temporary custody shall not exceed ninety-six hours during which time either a petition shall be filed with the superior court or the child shall be returned to his parent or guardian. If the commissioner determines that there are grounds to believe the child may be properly cared for in his own home, the parents or guardian, as the case may be, shall be aided to give such proper care under the supervision of the commissioner. Such supervised custody may be terminated when the commissioner finds a safe environment has been provided the child; but if the commissioner, after a reasonable time, finds this condition cannot be achieved in the child's own home under such supervision, he may petition the superior court for commitment of the child."

for orders of temporary custody asking that the court issue temporary ex parte orders to keep the five children in DCYS custody under authority of § 46b–129(b)(2).[5] The petitions alleged, in addition to Christopher's unexplained death, that the defendant's apartment was dirty, that numerous roaches could be found there, that beer cans were to be found in the apartment, that the defendant had been observed drinking beer, that on one occasion the defendant may have been drunk, that a neighbor reported that the children once had been left alone all night,[6] and that the two older children had occasionally come to school without having eaten breakfast. On the basis of these allegations, on September 7, 1979, the court granted, ex parte, temporary custody to the commissioner pending a noticed hearing on temporary custody set for September 14, 1979, within ten days of the ex parte order as required by § 46b–129(b)(2). The court also set October 1, 1979, for a hearing on the neglect petitions.[7]

At the September 14 temporary custody hearing, DCYS presented testimony of Spicknall confirming and elaborating on the conditions of the defendant's home and on the defendant's beer drinking. Christopher's pediatrician testified concerning Christopher's treatment and physical appearance when the child was brought to the hospital on September 5. The doctor also testified that, although the pathologist's report on the autopsy was not complete,[8] the external marks on Christopher's body were not a cause of death, that no internal injuries were found, and that the child had had a viral lung infection. He also explained, on cross-examination, the term "sudden infant death syndrome" and its pathology. At the conclusion of the state's case, the court found "probable cause" and ordered temporary custody of the children to remain with the plaintiff commissioner of children and youth services.

---

[5] General Statutes § 46b–129(b) provides: "If it appears from the allegations of the petition and other verified affirmations of fact accompanying the petition, or subsequent thereto, that there is reasonable cause to find that the child's or youth's condition or the circumstances surrounding his care require that his custody be immediately assumed to safeguard his welfare, the court shall either (1) issue an order to the parents or other person having responsibility for the care of the child or youth to show cause at such time as the court may designate why the court shall not vest in some suitable agency or person the child's or youth's temporary care and custody pending a hearing on the petition, or (2) vest in some suitable agency or person the child's or youth's temporary care and custody pending a hearing upon the petition which shall be held within ten days from the issuance of such order on the need for such temporary care and custody. The service of such orders may be made by any officer authorized by law to serve process, or by any probation officer appointed in accordance with section 46b–123, investigator from the department of administrative services, state police officer or indifferent person. The expense for any temporary care and custody shall be paid by the town in which such child or youth is at the time residing, and such town shall be reimbursed therefor by the town found liable for his support, except that where a state agency has filed a petition pursuant to the provisions of subsection (a) of this section, the agency shall pay such expense."

[6] The report was allegedly made by an upstairs neighbor of the defendant. At the hearing, the neighbor denied having made such a report at any time.

[7] The hearing on the neglect petitions was continued when additional evidence on the temporary custody petitions was heard on October 1, 1979. It was never rescheduled.

[8] The final autopsy report was not complete at the time of the hearing. Preliminary findings were available, however, and the cause of death could not be determined. No evidence available at the hearing connected the death with any sort of neglect or abuse.

The defendant appealed to this court claiming that General Statutes § 46b–129(b) violates the due process clause of the fourteenth amendment both because it is an impermissible infringement on her right to family integrity, and because the statute is unconstitutionally vague. The defendant also claims error in the trial court's determination that "probable cause" is the standard of proof in a temporary custody proceeding. We conclude that § 46b–129(b) is constitutional; however, we do find that the trial court erred when it decided that "probable cause" is the standard of proof in a temporary custody proceeding. As hereinafter set forth, we hold: (1) that § 46b–129(b) is constitutional because it must be read together with § 17–38a which contains adequate criteria for determining whether temporary custody of children may be taken from the parent by court order; and (2) that the standard of proof applicable to temporary custody proceedings pursuant to § 46b–129(b) is a fair preponderance of the evidence. . . .

Where fundamental rights are concerned we have a two-part test: "[1] regulations limiting these rights may be justified only by a 'compelling state interest,' and . . . [2] legislative enactments must be narrowly drawn to express only the legitimate state interests at stake." Roe v. Wade, 410 U.S. 113, 155, 93 S.Ct. 705, 727, 35 L.Ed.2d 147 (1973). The state has a substantial interest in protecting minor children; intervention in family matters by the state is justified, however, only when such intervention is actually "in the best interests of the child," a standard long used in this state.

Studies indicate that the best interests of the child are usually served by keeping the child in the home with his or her parents. "Virtually all experts, from many different professional disciplines, agree that children need and benefit from continuous, stable home environments." Institute of Judicial Administration—American Bar Association, Juvenile Justice Standards Project, Standards Relating to Abuse and Neglect, p. 45 (Tentative draft, 1977) (IJA–ABA, STDS). The love and attention not only of parents, but also of siblings, which is available in the home environment, cannot be provided by the state. Unfortunately, an order of temporary custody often results in the children of one family being separated and scattered to different foster homes with little opportunity to see each other. Even where the parent-child relationship is "marginal," it is usually in the best interests of the child to remain at home and still benefit from a family environment.[11]

[11] Uninterrupted home life "comports . . . with each child's biological and psychological need for unthreatened and unbroken continuity of care by his parents. No other animal is for so long a time after birth in so helpless a state that its survival depends upon continuous nurture by an adult. Although breaking or weakening the ties to the responsible and responsive adults may have different consequences for children of different ages, there is little doubt that such breaches in the familial bond will be detrimental to a child's well-being." (Footnotes omitted.) Goldstein, "Medical Care for the Child at Risk: On State Supervision of Parental Autonomy," 865 Yale L.J. 645, 649 (1977). Separation from his or her parents for any significant time has damaging effects on a child, even when the parents are minimally supportive of the child's needs. See Goldstein, Freud and Solnit, Before the Best Interests of the Child, pp. 6–12 (1979);

The defendants' challenge to the temporary custody statute, § 46b–129(b), must be addressed in light of the foregoing considerations. The defendant contends that only when the child is "at risk of harm" does the state's interest become a compelling one, justifying even temporary removal of the child from the home. We agree.

In custody proceedings, any criteria used to determine when intervention is permissible must take into account the competing interests involved. The parent has only one interest, that of family integrity; and the state has only one compelling interest, that of protecting minor children. . . . The child, however, has two distinct and often contradictory interests. The first is a basic interest in safety; the second is the important interest, discussed above, in having a stable *family* environment. Connecticut's child welfare statutes recognize both the conflicting interests and the constitutional limitations involved in any intervention situation. Thus, under the criteria of General Statutes § 17–38a(e), summary assumption of temporary custody is authorized only when there is probable cause to believe that "the child is suffering from serious physical illness or serious physical injury or is in *immediate* physical danger from his surroundings, *and* that *immediate* removal from such surroundings is *necessary* to insure the child's safety. . . ." (Emphasis added.)

The language of § 17–38a(e) clearly limits the scope of intervention to cases where the state interest is compelling . . . Intervention is permitted only where "serious physical illness or serious physical injury" is found or where "immediate physical danger" is present. It is at this point that the child's interest no longer coincides with that of the parent, thereby diminishing the magnitude of the parent's right to family integrity; In re Angelia P., 28 Cal.3d 908, 916–17, 171 Cal.Rptr. 637, 623 P.2d 198 (1981); and therefore the state's intervention as parens patriae to protect the child becomes so necessary that it can be considered paramount. Alsager v. District Court, 406 F. Supp. 10, 22–23 (S.D.Iowa 1975). A determination that the state interest is compelling does not alone affirm the constitutionality of the statute. More is needed. The second part of the due process analysis of Roe v. Wade, supra, requires that statutes affecting fundamental rights be "narrowly drawn to express only the legitimate state interests at stake." General Statutes § 17–38a(e) meets this part of the test by requiring, in addition to the compelling need to protect the child, that the assumption of temporary custody by the commissioner be immediately "necessary to insure the child's safety." This phrase requires that various steps short of removal

Wald, "State Intervention on Behalf of 'Neglected' Children: Standards for Removal of Children from Their Homes, Monitoring the Status of Children in Foster Care, and Termination of Parental Rights," 28 Stan.L.Rev. 623 (1976); Goldstein, Freud and Solnit, Beyond the Best Interests of the Child, p. 20 (1973). "Even when placed in good environments, which is often not the case, they suffer anxiety and depression from being separated from their parents, they are forced to deal with new caretakers, playmates, school teachers, etc. As a result they often suffer emotional damage and their development is delayed." Wald, "Thinking About Public Policy Toward Abuse and Neglect of Children," 78 Mich.L.Rev. 645, 662 (1980).

from the home be used when possible in preference to disturbing the integrity of the family. The statute itself mentions supervised in-home custody, but a wide range of other programs short of removal are a part of existing DCYS procedure. See DCYS: Programs and Priorities, FY 1979.

The challenged statute, § 46b–129(b), does not contain the "serious physical illness or serious physical injury" or "immediate physical danger" language of § 17–38a(e). We note, however, that § 46b–129(b) does limit the temporary custody order to those situations in which "the child or youth's condition or the circumstances surrounding his care require that his custody be immediately assumed to safeguard his welfare." It is axiomatic that statutes on a particular subject be "considered as a whole, with a view toward reconciling their separate parts in order to render a reasonable overall interpretation. . . . We must avoid a consequence which fails to attain a rational and sensible result which bears most directly on the object which the legislature sought to obtain." This is no less true when the legislature has chosen to place related laws in different parts of the General Statutes. Therefore, the language limiting coercive intervention in chapter 301 ("Child Welfare"), § 17–38a, must be read as applying equally to such intervention in chapter 815t ("[Family Law] Juvenile Matters"), § 46b–129. Because we hold that General Statutes § 46b–129(b) may be applied only on the basis of the criteria enunciated in § 17–38a, we reject the defendant's claim that § 46b–129(b) is unconstitutional.[12]

---

[12] The American Bar Association Juvenile Justice Standards Project, after a thorough study of the competing individual, societal, and legal interests involved when state intervention into family affairs is contemplated, developed model Standards Relating to Abuse and Neglect (Tentative Draft, 1977). The basic policy assumptions underlying the study mirror our own law, i.e, "[s]tate intervention should promote family autonomy and family life. . . . [B]ut where a child's needs . . . conflict with his/her parents' interests, the child's needs should have priority." ABA Standard 1.5. When interpreting the "at risk" criteria set forth in General Statutes § 17–38a(e), the following guidelines may be considered insofar as they help to define more clearly our own statutes pertaining to temporary custody orders:

"Courts should . . . assume jurisdiction in order to condition continued parental custody upon the parents' accepting supervision or to remove a child from his/her home only when a child is endangered in a manner specified in subsection A.–F.:

"A. a child has suffered, or there is a substantial risk that a child will imminently suffer, a physical harm, inflicted nonaccidentally upon him/her by his/her parents, which causes, or creates a substantial risk of causing disfigurement, impairment of bodily functioning, or other serious physical injury;

"B. a child has suffered, or there is a substantial risk that the child will imminently suffer, physical harm causing disfigurement, impairment of bodily functioning, or other serious physical injury as a result of conditions created by his/her parents or by the failure of the parents to adequately supervise or protect him/her;

"C. a child is suffering serious emotional damage, evidenced by severe anxiety, depression, or withdrawal, or untoward aggressive behavior toward self or others, and the child's parents are not willing to provide treatment for him/her;

"D. a child has been sexually abused by his/her parent or a member of his/her household . . . ;

"E. a child is in need of medical treatment to cure, alleviate, or prevent him/her from suffering serious physical harm which may result in death, disfigurement, or substantial impairment of bodily functions, and his/her parents are unwilling to provide or consent to the medical treatment;

In the instant case, no substantial showing was made at the temporary custody hearing that the defendant's five children were suffering from either serious physical illness or serious physical injury, or that they would be in immediate physical danger if they were returned to the defendant's home. The DCYS caseworker admitted at trial, as did the state's counsel at argument before this court, that without the unexplained death of Christopher there was no reason for DCYS to have custody of the other children. The medical evidence at the hearing indicated no connection between Christopher's death and either the defendant or the conditions in her home. While the final autopsy report was not available at the hearing, the pediatrician testified that the marks on Christopher's body were *not* related to the child's death. There was, therefore, no evidence before the court to indicate whether his death was from natural causes or was the result of abuse. Yet with nothing before it but subjective suspicion, the court granted the commissioner custody of the defendant's other children. It was error for the court to grant to the commissioner temporary custody when no immediate risk of danger to the children was shown.

It appears from this record that DCYS has not heeded the suggestion of this court that the agency bears a responsibility of continuing review of cases it is litigating. In In re Juvenile Appeal (Anonymous), 177 Conn. 648, 662, 420 A.2d 875 (1979), we stated that when the cause for the commitment of children to DCYS custody ends, the state bears the burden of showing the necessity to continue the commitment. Although that holding concerned a parent's petition for revocation of a commitment, implicit in our holding was that the state had a duty to seek the best interests of the child even after adversary proceedings with the parent had begun. In this case, at some time shortly after the orders of temporary custody were granted, the state received the final autopsy report which effectively exonerated the defendant from any wrongdoing in Christopher's death. The reason for the custody order then no longer existed. It was then incumbent on DCYS to reunite the family. "In this situation, the state cannot constitutionally 'sit back and wait' for the parent to institute judicial proceedings. It 'cannot . . . [adopt] for itself an attitude of if you don't like it, sue.'" Duchesne v. Sugarman, 566 F.2d 817, 828 (2d Cir.1977).[13]

"F. a child is committing delinquent acts as a result of parental encouragement, guidance, or approval." ABA Standard 2.1.

[13] We recognize that there are three parties to litigation in the Superior Court for juvenile matters—DCYS, the parent, and the child (through a guardian ad litem appointed pursuant to Practice Book § 484) and that any of these parties could have moved to terminate this litigation in a number of ways. We are saying only that DCYS, acting as parens patriae, had a duty to do so.

This court notes, however, that the defendant mother took no steps either to revoke custody under General Statutes § 46b–129(f) or to pursue a judicial resolution of the neglect petitions. We are even more concerned that the attorney for the children took no steps to protect their interests in family integrity by insisting on a resolution of the neglect petitions, and failed to represent their interests before this court. This court, therefore, is appreciative of the fact that

Petitions for neglect and for temporary custody orders, like the petitions to terminate parental rights in Duchesne v. Sugarman, supra, or in In re Juvenile Appeal (Anonymous), supra, "are particularly vulnerable to the risk that judges or social workers will be tempted, consciously or unconsciously, to compare unfavorably the material advantages of the child's natural parents with those of prospective adoptive parents [or foster parents]." In re Juvenile Appeal (Anonymous), supra, 177 Conn. 672, 420 A.2d 875.

This case clearly shows that these dangers do exist; it is shocking that the defendant's children have been in "temporary" custody for more than three years. This is a tragic and deplorable situation, and DCYS must bear full responsibility for this unwarranted and inexcusable delay. Too often the courts of this state are faced with a situation where, as here, litigation has continued for years while the children, whose interests are supposed to be paramount, suffer in the insecurity of "temporary" placements. The well-known deleterious effects of prolonged temporary placement on the child, which we have discussed above, makes continuing review by DCYS of all temporary custody and commitment cases imperative. Where appropriate, the agency can and must take unilateral action either to reunite families or to terminate parental rights as expeditiously as possible to free neglected children for placement and adoption in stable family settings.

The failure of DCYS properly to administer § 46b–129 does not, however, affect its constitutionality. The statute is constitutional because when it is read together with § 17–38a, as it must be, it is justified by a compelling state interest and is narrowly drawn to express only that legitimate state interest. . . .

NOTES

The Connecticut Supreme Court decision holds that a state may not sit back and wait for a parent to sue the state when a child is involuntarily removed from the parent's custody. Why not? Because the parent has a fundamental Due Process right to the custody of his or her child. *See* Troxel v. Granville, 530 U.S. 57 (2000). But what must the state do to facilitate parent-child reunification? Most often state services consist of drug or alcohol treatment programs, medical services, nutritionists, anger management, vocational counseling, housing, or psychological evaluation. *See, e.g., In re* Dependence of D.C.M., 253 P.3d 112 (Wash. Ct. App. 2011) (listing services available to parents in dependency cases). While parents are receiving reasonable reunification efforts the child is often in foster care, an expensive placement option paid for by the federal government. *See* Raymond C. O'Brien, *Reasonable Efforts and Parent-Child Reunification*, 2013 MICH. ST. L. REV. 1029, 1042–1043. To limit the time a child stays in foster care, in 1997 Congress enacted the Adoption and Safe Families Act.

---

the interests of the children have been ably represented by the Connecticut Civil Liberties Union as amicus curiae on this appeal.

The Act specifies that if a child remains in foster care for fifteen out of the last twenty-two consecutive months, the state no longer has to provide reunification efforts and may terminate parental rights. Pub. L. 105–89, 111 Stat. 2115 (codified as amended in scattered sections of 2, 42 U.S.C.). Therefore, must a state provide for reasonable reunification efforts before it may begin to toll the 22 months and then terminate parental rights? Many states have held that a failure to provide reunification services is not a bar to terminating parental rights as long as the Due Process rights of the parent are protected. *See, e.g., In re* Shirley B., 18 A.3d 40 (Md. 2011) (holding that the state's inability to provide services due to limited state financial resources did not prohibit termination of parental rights). Likewise, the Tennessee Supreme Court has held that, in a parental termination proceeding, "the extent of [the state agency's] efforts to reunify the family is weighed in the court's best-interest analysis, but proof of providing reasonable efforts to reunify the family is not a precondition to termination of parental rights. As with other factual findings made in connection with the best-interest analysis, reasonable efforts must be proven by a preponderance of the evidence, not by clear and convincing evidence." *In re* Kalizah, 455 S.W.3d 533, 555 (Tenn. 2015). Likewise, the Pennsylvania Supreme Court distinguished between the requirements of the Adoption and Safe Families Act and termination of parental rights. The court held that even though other states have included reasonable efforts as an element in their termination provisions, the Pennsylvania legislature has not. Therefore, a parent's rights may be terminated even though reasonable reunification efforts have not been provided to the parents. The only detriment may be a loss in federal funds under the ASFA. *See In re* D.C.D., 105 A.3d 662 (Pa. 2014).

D. PARAMETERS OF CHILD ABUSE

1. ABUSE IN GESTATION

Johnson v. State

Supreme Court of Florida, 1992
602 So.2d 1288

■ HARDING, JUSTICE.

We have for review Johnson v. State, 578 So.2d 419, 420 (Fla. 5th DCA 1991), in which the Fifth District Court of Appeal certified the following question as one of great public importance: WHETHER THE INGESTION OF A CONTROLLED SUBSTANCE BY A MOTHER WHO KNOWS THE SUBSTANCE WILL PASS TO HER CHILD AFTER BIRTH IS A VIOLATION OF FLORIDA LAW? . . .

The issue before the court is whether section 893.13(1)(c)(1), Florida Statutes (1989), permits the criminal prosecution of a mother, who ingested a controlled substance prior to giving birth, for delivery of a controlled substance to the infant during the thirty to ninety seconds following the infant's birth, but before the umbilical cord is severed.

Johnson presents four arguments attacking the applicability of section 893.13(1)(c)(1) to her conviction: 1) the district court's interpretation of the statute violates the legislature's intent; 2) the plain language of the statute prevents her conviction; 3) the conviction violates her constitutional rights of due process and privacy; and 4) the State presented insufficient evidence to show that she intentionally delivered cocaine to a minor. . . . The State contends that the district court correctly found that the statute's plain language prohibits the delivery of the controlled substance to a minor, and that the conviction does not violate Johnson's constitutional rights.

We adopt Judge Sharp's analysis concerning the insufficiency of the evidence to support Johnson's conviction and her analysis concerning the legislature's intent in section 893.13(1)(c)(1). However, we note that Judge Sharp's analysis did not clearly state the rules of statutory construction in the criminal context. Although Judge Sharp correctly applied the rule of strict construction, she failed to apply the other paramount rule of criminal statutory construction, the rule of lenity. § 775.021(1), Fla. Stat. (1989).

The rules of statutory construction require courts to strictly construe criminal statutes, and that "when the language is susceptible to differing constructions, [the statute] shall be construed most favorably to the accused." § 775.021(1). In strictly construing criminal statutes, we have held that only those terms which are " 'clearly and intelligently described in [a penal statute's] very words, as well as manifestly intended by the Legislature' " are to be considered as included in the statute. State v. Wershow, 343 So.2d 605, 608 (Fla.1977), quoting Ex parte Amos, 93 Fla. 5, 112 So. 289 (1927). We find that the legislative history does not show a manifest intent to use the word "delivery" in the context of criminally prosecuting mothers for delivery of a controlled substance to a minor by way of the umbilical cord. This lack of legislative intent coupled with uncertainty that the term "delivery" applies to the facts of the instant case, compels this Court to construe the statute in favor of Johnson. The text of Judge Sharp's dissent is as follows:

Johnson appeals from two convictions for delivering a controlled substance to her two minor children in violation of section 893.13(1)(c)1., Florida Statutes (1989).[1] The state's theory of the case was that Johnson "delivered" cocaine or a derivative of the drug to her two children via

---

[1] Section 893.13(1)(c)1., Florida Statutes (1989) provides as follows: 893.13 Prohibited acts; penalties . . .

> (c) Except as authorized by this chapter, it is unlawful for any person 18 years of age or older to deliver any controlled substance to a person under the age of 18 years, or to use or hire a person under the age of 18 years as an agent or employee in the sale or delivery of such a substance, or to use such person to assist in avoiding detection or apprehension for a violation of this chapter. Any person who violates this provision with respect to: 1. A controlled substance . . . is guilty of a felony of the first degree. . . .

blood flowing through the children's umbilical cords in the sixty-to-ninety second period after they were expelled from her birth canal but before their cords were severed. The application of this statute to this concept of "delivery" presents a case of first impression in this state. Because I conclude that section 893.13(1)(c)1. was not intended to apply to these facts, I would vacate the convictions and remand for the entry of a judgment of acquittal.

The record in this case establishes the following facts. On October 3, 1987, Johnson delivered a son. The birth was normal with no complications. There was no evidence of fetal distress either within the womb or during the delivery. About one and one-half minutes elapsed from the time the son's head emerged from his mother's birth canal to the time he was placed on her stomach and the cord was clamped.

The obstetrician who delivered Johnson's son testified he presumed that the umbilical cord was functioning normally and that it was delivering blood to the baby after he emerged from the birth canal and before the cord was clamped. Johnson admitted to the baby's pediatrician that she used cocaine the night before she delivered. A basic toxicology test performed on Johnson and her son was positive for benzoylecgonine, a metabolite or "breakdown" product of cocaine.

In December 1988, Johnson, while pregnant with a daughter, suffered a crack overdose. Johnson told paramedics that she had taken $200 of crack cocaine earlier that evening and that she was concerned about the effects of the drug on her unborn child. Johnson was then taken to the hospital for observation. Johnson was hospitalized again on January 23, 1989, when she was in labor. Johnson told Dr. Tompkins, an obstetrician, that she had used rock cocaine that morning while she was in labor. With the exception of finding meconium stain fluid in the amniotic sack,[2] there were no other complications with the birth of Johnson's baby daughter. Approximately sixty-to-ninety seconds elapsed from the time the child's head emerged from her mother's birth canal until her umbilical cord was clamped.

The following day, the Department of Health and Rehabilitative Services investigated an abuse report of a cocaine baby concerning Johnson's daughter. Johnson told the investigator that she had smoked pot and crack cocaine three to four times every-other-day throughout the duration of her pregnancy with her daughter. Johnson's mother acknowledged that Johnson had been using cocaine for at least three years during the time her daughter and son were born.

At Johnson's trial, Dr. Tompkins testified that a mother's blood passes nutrients, oxygen and chemicals to an unborn child by a diffusion exchange at the capillary level from the womb to the placenta. The umbilical cord then circulates the baby's blood (including the exchange

---

[2] This condition may indicate that the baby is normal or that its neurological function has been compromised.

from its mother) between the placenta and the child. Metabolized cocaine derivatives in the mother's blood thus diffuse from the womb to the placenta, and then reach the baby through its umbilical cord. Although the blood flow is somewhat restricted during the birthing process, a measurable amount of blood is transferred from the placenta to the baby through the umbilical cord during delivery and after birth.

Dr. Shashi Gore, a pathologist and toxicologist, testified that cocaine has a half life of about one hour. This means that half of the amount of the drug remains in a person's blood stream for about one hour. The remainder gradually decreases over a period of forty-eight to seventy-two hours. The liver metabolizes the cocaine into benzoylecgonine which travels through the kidneys and into the urine until it is voided. When Dr. Gore was asked whether a woman who had smoked cocaine at 10:00 p.m. and again between 6:00 and 7:00 a.m. the following morning and delivered a child at 1:00 p.m. that afternoon would still have cocaine or benzoylecgonine present in her blood stream at the time of delivery, the response was yes. When asked whether a woman who had smoked cocaine sometime the night before delivering a child at 8:00 in the morning would still have cocaine or benzoylecgonine in her system at the time of the child's birth, the response again was yes.

Dr. Stephen Kandall, a neonatologist, testified for the defense that it was impossible to tell whether the cocaine derivatives which appeared in these children's urine shortly after birth were the result of the exchange from the mother to her children before or after they were born because most of it took place from womb to the placenta before the birth process was complete. He also testified that blood flow to the infant from the placenta through the umbilical cord to the child is restricted during contractions. Cocaine also constricts the passage of blood dramatically but benzoylecgonine does not. Dr. Kandall admitted that it is theoretically possible that cocaine or other substances can pass between a mother and her baby during the thirty-to-sixty second period after the child is born and before the umbilical cord is cut, but that the amount would be tiny.

I submit there was no medical testimony adequate to support the trial court's finding that a "delivery" occurred here during the birthing process, even if the criminal statute is applicable. The expert witnesses all testified about blood flow from the umbilical cord to child. But that blood flow is the child's and the placenta through which it flows, is not part of the mother's body. No witness testified in this case that any cocaine derivatives passed from the mother's womb to the placenta during the sixty-to-ninety seconds after the child was expelled from the birth canal. That is when any "delivery" would have to have taken place under this statute, from one "person" to another "person."

Further, there was no evidence that Johnson timed her dosage of cocaine so as to be able to transmit some small amount after her child's birth. Predicting the day or hour of a child's birth is difficult to impossible even for experts. Had Johnson given birth one or two days later, the cocaine would have been completely eliminated, and no "crime" would have occurred. But since she went into labor which progressed to birth after taking cocaine when she did, the only way Johnson could have prevented the "delivery" would have been to have severed the cord before the child was born which, of course, would probably have killed both herself and her child. This illustrates the absurdity of applying the delivery-of-a-drug statute to this scenario.

However, in my view, the primary question in this case is whether section 893.13(1)(c)1. was intended by the Legislature to apply to the birthing process. Before Johnson can be prosecuted under this statute, it must be clear that the Legislature intended for it to apply to the delivery of cocaine derivatives to a newborn during a sixty-to-ninety second interval, before severance of the umbilical cord. I can find no case where "delivery" of a drug was based on an involuntary act such as diffusion and blood flow.[3] Criminal statutes must be strictly—not loosely—construed.

Further, in construing a statute, we must consider its history, the evil to be corrected, the intention of the Legislature, the subject to be regulated and the objects to be attained. Legislative intent is the polestar by which the courts must be guided. Legislative intent may be express or it may be gathered from the purpose of the act, the administrative construction of it, other legislative acts bearing upon the subject, and all the circumstances surrounding and attendant upon it. My review of other pertinent legislative enactments, specifically chapter 415, leads me to conclude in this case that the Legislature expressly chose to treat the problem of drug dependent mothers and newborns as a public health problem and that it considered but rejected imposing criminal sanctions, via section 893.13(1)(c)1.

In 1982, sections 415.501–514 were enacted to deal with the problem of child abuse and neglect. The Legislature determined that because of the impact that abuse or neglect has on a victimized child, siblings, family structure, and inevitably on all citizens of the state, the prevention

[3] As examples of delivery of a controlled substance, see State v. Medlin, 273 So.2d 394 (Fla.1973) (defendant's conviction for delivering a barbiturate affirmed where a defendant gave sixteen-year-old girl a capsule, advising her that it would make her go up and gave her another pill to be taken when she came down); Gelsey v. State, 565 So.2d 876 (Fla. 5th DCA 1990) (defendant's conviction for delivery of a controlled substance affirmed where he met with officers and exchanged crack and cash for powdered cocaine); Roberts v. State, 557 So.2d 685 (Fla. 5th DCA 1990) (defendant's conviction for delivery of cocaine affirmed where he sold one rock of cocaine to undercover officer); Willingham v. State, 541 So.2d 1240 (Fla. 2d DCA), rev. denied, 548 So.2d 663 (Fla.1989) (delivery of cocaine convictions affirmed where defendant offered two pieces of rock cocaine to officer, officer bought one and defendant retained the other); Newman v. State, 522 So.2d 71 (Fla. 4th DCA 1988) (defendant's conviction for trafficking in cocaine by constructive delivery affirmed where cocaine was sampled and cocaine and money not yet exchanged); King v. State, 336 So.2d 1200 (Fla. 2d DCA 1976), cert. denied, 345 So.2d 424 (Fla.), cert. dismissed, King v. Florida, 434 U.S. 802, 98 S.Ct. 30, 54 L.Ed.2d 60 (1977) (defendant guilty of delivery of narcotics by writing prescriptions in bad faith); State v. Vinson, 298 So.2d 505 (Fla. 2d DCA 1974) (physician who issued prescription for drug in bad faith guilty of delivery).

of child abuse and neglect is a priority of this state. § 415.501, Fla. Stat. (1989). To further this end, the Legislature required that a comprehensive approach for the prevention of abuse and neglect of children be developed for the state. Id. The statute defined an "abused or neglected child" as a child whose physical or mental health or welfare was harmed, or threatened with harm, by the acts of omissions of the parent or other person responsible for the child's welfare. As originally defined, "harm" included physical or mental injury, sexual abuse, exploitation, abandonment, and neglect. § 415.503(7), Fla. Stat. (1983)

In 1987, a bill was proposed to broaden the definition of "harm" to include physical dependency of a newborn infant upon certain controlled drugs. However, there was a concern among legislators that this language might authorize criminal prosecutions of mothers who give birth to drug-dependent children. Comment, A Response to "Cocaine Babies"—Amendment of Florida's Child Abuse and Neglect Laws to Encompass Infants Born Drug Dependent, 15 Fla.S.U.L.Rev. 865, 877 (1987).[4] The bill was then amended to provide that no parent of a drug-dependent newborn shall be subject to criminal investigation solely on the basis of the infant's drug dependency. In the words of the sponsor of the House bill:

> This clearly states that the individual would not be subject to any investigation solely upon the basis of the infant's drug dependency.
>
> The prime purpose of this bill is to keep the families intact. It's not for the purpose of investigation. . . .
>
> Again, there is a well-founded anxiety that we are looking to arrest Moms. We're not looking to do that. What we are looking to do is we're looking to intervene on behalf of many different state policies. . . .

The bill was passed by the Legislature and the changes were codified in section 415.503(9)(a)2.

From this legislative history, it is clear that the Legislature considered and rejected a specific statutory provision authorizing criminal penalties against mothers for delivering drug-affected children who received transfer of an illegal drug derivative metabolized by the mother's body, in utero. In light of this express legislative statement, I conclude that the Legislature never intended for the general drug delivery statute to authorize prosecutions of those mothers who take illegal drugs close enough in time to childbirth that a doctor could testify that a tiny amount passed from mother to child in the few seconds before the umbilical cord was cut. Criminal prosecution of mothers like Johnson will undermine Florida's express policy of "keeping families intact" and

[4] The staff analysis of this bill noted that the legislation, as written, provided a likelihood that a parent could be criminally prosecuted under chapter 893 for delivering a drug dependent child.

could destroy the family by incarcerating the child's mother when alternative measures could protect the child and stabilize the family. Comment, A Response to "Cocaine Babies", 15 Fla.S.U.L.Rev. at 881.

In similar cases in which charges have been brought against mothers after delivery of drug-affected newborns, those charges have been dismissed. See People v. Hardy, 188 Mich.App. 305, 469 N.W.2d 50 (1991); People v. Bremer, No. 90–32227–FH (Mich.Cir.Ct. January 31, 1991); State v. Gray, 1990 WL 125695, No. L–89–239 (Ohio Ct.App. August 31, 1990), jurisdictional motion allowed, 57 Ohio St.3d 711, 568 N.E.2d 695 (1991). In People v. Bremer, the defendant was charged with delivery of cocaine to her newborn daughter after urine samples from the defendant and child following birth tested positive for benzoylecgonine. The circuit court concluded that the Michigan Legislature never intended to include the action of the defendant under the delivery statute: To interpret this section to cover ingestion of cocaine by a pregnant woman would be a radical incursion upon existing law. A person may not be punished for a crime unless her acts fall clearly within the language of the statute. The specific language of this act does not allow the strained construction advanced by the prosecution. Neither judges nor prosecutors can make criminal laws. This is the purview of the Legislature. If the Legislature wanted to punish the uterine transfer of cocaine from a mother to her fetus, it would be up to the Legislature to consider the attending public policy and constitutional arguments and then pass its legislation. The Legislature has not done so and the court has no power to make such a law.

The Michigan court also rejected the prosecutor's argument that charging women with delivery of controlled substances to their newborns provides a strong deterrent against unlawful use of drugs by pregnant women and prompts them to drug treatment. The court noted that prosecution of these women would likely have the opposite effect. A woman may abort her child or avoid prenatal care or treatment out of fear of prosecution. Thus the court concluded that the state's interest was better served by making treatment programs available to pregnant addicts rather than driving them away from treatment by criminal sanctions.

In State v. Gray, the defendant was indicted for child endangering based on her use of cocaine during the last trimester of pregnancy. The trial court concluded that the child endangering statute did not apply to this situation and dismissed the charge against her. On appeal, the state of Ohio argued that the trial court had failed to consider the time the fetus is a child and still attached to the mother and the duty of care created at that point. The appellate court concluded that the Ohio General Assembly did not intend to criminalize the passage of harmful substances from a mother to a child in the brief moments from birth to the severance of the umbilical cord. "To construe the statute in this manner would mean that every expectant woman who ingested a substance with the potential of harm to her child, e.g., alcohol or nicotine, would be criminally liable under [the child endangering statute]. We do not believe such result was intended by the General Assembly."

There can be no doubt that drug abuse is one of the most serious problems confronting our society today. National Treasury Employees Union v. Von Raab, 489 U.S. 656, 109 S.Ct. 1384, 1395, 103 L.Ed.2d 685 (1989). Of particular concern is the alarming rise in the number of babies born with cocaine in their systems as a result of cocaine use by pregnant women. Some experts estimate that as many as eleven percent of pregnant women have used an illegal drug during pregnancy, and of those women, seventy-five percent have used cocaine. Report of the American Medical Association Board of Trustees, Legal Interventions During Pregnancy, 264 JAMA 2663 (Nov. 28, 1990). Others estimate that 375,000 newborns per year are born to women who are users of illicit drugs. American Public Health Association 1990 Policy Statement.

It is well-established that the effects of cocaine use by a pregnant woman on her fetus and later on her newborn can be severe. On average, cocaine-exposed babies have lower birth weights, shorter body lengths at birth, and smaller head circumferences than normal infants. 264 JAMA at 2666. Cocaine use may also result in sudden infant death syndrome, neural-behavioral deficiencies as well as other medical problems and long-term developmental abnormalities. American Public Health Association 1990 Policy Statement. The basic problem of damaging the fetus by drug use during pregnancy should not be addressed piecemeal, however, by prosecuting users who deliver their babies close in time to use of drugs and ignoring those who simply use drugs during their pregnancy.

Florida could possibly have elected to make *in utero* transfers criminal. But it chose to deal with this problem in other ways. One way is to allow evidence of drug use by women as a ground for removal of the child to the custody of protective services, as was done in this case. Some states have responded to this crisis by charging women with child abuse and neglect. See In re Baby X, 97 Mich.App. 111, 293 N.W.2d 736 (1980) (newborn suffering from narcotics withdrawal symptoms due to prenatal maternal drug addiction is neglected and within jurisdiction of the probate court); In re Smith, 128 Misc.2d 976, 492 N.Y.S.2d 331 (N.Y.Fam.Ct.1985) (person under Family Court Act includes unborn child who is neglected as the result of mother's conduct); In re Ruiz, 27 Ohio Misc.2d 31, 27 O.B.R. 350, 500 N.E.2d 935 (Com.Pl.1986) (mother's use of heroin close to baby's birth created substantial risk to the health of the child and constituted child abuse).

However, prosecuting women for using drugs and "delivering" them to their newborns appears to be the least effective response to this crisis.[5]

[5] As the AMA Board of Trustees Report notes, possession of illicit drugs already results in criminal penalties and pregnant women who use illegal substances obviously are not deterred by existing sanctions. Thus the goal of deterrence is not served. To punish a person for substance

Rather than face the possibility of prosecution, pregnant women who are substance abusers may simply avoid prenatal or medical care for fear of being detected. Yet the newborns of these women are, as a group, the most fragile and sick, and most in need of hospital neonatal care. A decision to deliver these babies "at home" will have tragic and serious consequences. As the Board of Trustees Reports notes:

> [C]riminal penalties may exacerbate the harm done to fetal health by deterring pregnant substance abusers from obtaining help or care from either the health or public welfare professions, the very people who are best able to prevent future abuse. The California Medical Association has noted:
>
> While unhealthy behavior cannot be condoned, to bring criminal charges against a pregnant woman for activities which may be harmful to her fetus is inappropriate. Such prosecution is counterproductive to the public interest as it may discourage a woman from seeking prenatal care or dissuade her from providing accurate information to health care providers out of fear of self-incrimination. This failure to seek proper care or to withhold vital information concerning her health could increase the risks to herself and her baby.
>
> Florida's Secretary of Health and Rehabilitative Services has also observed that potential prosecution under existing child abuse or drug use statutes already "makes many potential reporters reluctant to identify women as substance abusers." (footnotes omitted)
>
> 264 JAMA at 2669. See also Commonwealth v. Pellegrini, No. 87970 (Mass. Superior Court Oct. 15, 1990) (by imposing criminal sanctions, women may turn away from seeking prenatal care for fear of being discovered, undermining the interests of the state in protecting potential human life). Prosecution of pregnant women for engaging in activities

---

abuse ignores the impaired capacity of these individuals to make rational decisions concerning their drug use. "In all but a few cases, taking a harmful substance such as cocaine is not meant to harm the fetus but to satisfy an acute psychological and physical need for that particular substance. If a pregnant woman suffers from a substance dependency, it is the physical impossibility of avoiding an impact on fetal health that causes severe damage to the fetus, not an intentional or malicious wish to cause harm." 264 JAMA at 2667–2668. Punishment is simply not an effective way of curing a dependency or preventing future substance abuse. Id. at 2667. See also National Treasury Employees Union, 109 S.Ct. at 1396 ("Addicts may be unable to abstain even for a limited period of time, or may be unaware of the 'fade-away affect' of certain drugs."). Stated another way: However the initial use of a drug might be characterized, its continued use by addicts is rarely, if any, truly voluntarily. Drug addiction tends to obliterate rational, autonomous decision making about drug use. Drugs become a necessity for dependent users, even when they would much prefer to escape their addiction. In virtually all instances, a user specifically does not want to harm her fetus, yet she cannot resist the drive to use the drug. Thus it is not plausible to attribute to drug-using women a motive of causing harm to the fetus. Mariner, Glantz and Annas, Pregnancy, Drugs and the Perils of Prosecution, 9 Criminal Justice Ethics 30, 36 (Winter/Spring 1990).

harmful to their fetuses or newborns may also unwittingly increase the incidence of abortion.[6]

Such considerations have led the American Medical Association Board of Trustees to oppose criminal sanctions for harmful behavior by a pregnant woman toward her fetus and to advocate that pregnant substance abusers be provided with rehabilitative treatment appropriate to their specific psychological and physiological needs. 264 JAMA at 2670. Likewise, the American Public Health Association has adopted the view that the use of illegal drugs by pregnant women is a public health problem. It also recommends that no punitive measures be taken against pregnant women who are users of illicit drugs when no other illegal acts, including drug-related offenses, have been committed. See 1990 Policy Statement.

In summary, I would hold that section 893.13(1)(c)1. does not encompass "delivery" of an illegal drug derivative from womb to placenta to umbilical cord to newborn after a child's birth. If that is the intent of the Legislature, then this statute should be redrafted to clearly address the basic problem of passing illegal substances from mother to child in utero, not just in the birthing process. . . .

At oral argument the State acknowledged that no other jurisdiction has upheld a conviction of a mother for delivery of a controlled substance to an infant through either the umbilical cord or an *in utero* transmission; nor has the State submitted any subsequent authority to reflect that this fact has changed. The Court declines the State's invitation to walk down a path that the law, public policy, reason and common sense forbid it to tread. Therefore, we quash the decision below, answer the certified question in the negative, and remand with directions that Johnson's two convictions be reversed.

NOTES

In Whitner v. State, 492 S.E.2d 777 (S.C. 1997), *cert. denied,* 523 U.S. 1145, 118 S.Ct. 1857, 140 L.Ed.2d 1104 (1998), a woman in South Carolina was sentenced to eight years in prison for criminal child neglect when she took crack cocaine during her pregnancy and the child was subsequently stillborn. Subsequently the South Carolina Supreme Court held unconstitutional a public hospital's practice of identifying and testing pregnant women suspected of using controlled substances. If presence of narcotics was discovered, the hospital referred the women to law enforcement officials for eventual prosecution. The court held that such testing violated the Fourth Amendment prohibition of warrantless searches and was not conducted with consent of the women. More recently, the state's supreme court permitted a mother to be charged with "homicide by child

[6] See 264 JAMA at 2667; Rush, Prenatal Care Taking: Limits of State Intervention With and Without Roe, 39 Univ.Fla.L.Rev. 55, 68 n. 38 (1986). A woman could simply "opt out" of the scope of any criminal regulations by terminating the pregnancy through abortion. 39 Univ.Fla.L.Rev. at 68 n. 38.

abuse" when the mother's baby was stillborn. The mother's use of cocaine during pregnancy was deemed to be the cause of the baby's death. South Carolina v. McKnight, 352 S.C. 635, 576 S.E.2d 168 (2003). For a state-by-state analysis of parental drug use as child abuse, *see* Child Welfare Information Gateway, *Parental Drug Use As Child Abuse*, Department of Health and Human Services, Children's Bureau (2015) *available at*: https://www.childwelfare.gov/pubPDFs/drugexposed.pdf. Drug testing with or without knowledge and possibility of third-party notification is of particular concern as the HIV/AIDS pandemic continues. The trend is to read criminal statutes relating to abuse in gestation in the same manner as the *Johnson* decision, thereby barring prosecution of drug-ingesting mothers. *See, e.g.*, Arms v. State, 471 S.W.3d 637 (Ark. 2015) (holding that "The record is completely devoid of any evidence that Arms directly introduced methamphetamine into her baby's system by causing the child to ingest or inhale it" and therefore the state criminal statute was inapplicable); Kilmon v. State, 905 A.2d 306 (Md. 2005) (potential injury to fetus caused by defendant's ingestion of cocaine while pregnant could not form basis for reckless endangerment conviction as to child later born alive).

The Supreme Court of Connecticut, in *In re* Valerie D., 223 Conn. 492, 613 A.2d 748 (1992), held that its state statute allowing termination of parental rights if a child has been denied care necessary for its well being by acts of parental commission or omission, did not authorize termination of parental rights of a mother based on her prenatal conduct of injecting cocaine several hours before onset of labor. Further, where the assertion of custody over the child immediately after birth led directly to the condition supporting termination of parental rights (no ongoing parent-child relationship), the state could not terminate mother's parental rights on that basis.

Fetal Protection. Increasing controversy is developing over how to cope with what some label "fetal abuse". The term describes maternal conduct during pregnancy that would endanger a child's health or development. Most prominent is substance abuse leading to fetal alcohol syndrome or impairment from cocaine. In State ex rel. Angela M.W. v. Kruzicki, 209 Wis.2d 112, 561 N.W.2d 729 (1997), the Supreme Court of Wisconsin held that the definition of "child" in the children's code as a "person who is less than 18 years of age" does not include a viable fetus for purposes of protection and services afforded to children in need. A Circuit Judge had held to the contrary and ordered that the mother be held in protective custody within a hospital so as to isolate her and her baby from cocaine and other drugs which were found within the mother's blood during tests performed while a woman is pregnant. *See, also* Reinesto v. Superior Court, 182 Ariz. 190, 894 P.2d 733 (App.1995) (court refused to criminally prosecute mother for child abuse when she gave birth to a heroin-addicted child); and Pima County Juvenile Severance Action No. S–120171, 183 Ariz. 546, 905 P.2d 555 (App.1995) (fetal abuse cannot be the basis of termination of parental rights).

A few states have modified their child protection laws to provide greater latitude in dealing with substance abuse affecting children immediately after birth. Provisions such as these may be used to intervene after birth for the protection of such children. However, some persons would like to take measures to protect the fetus before birth at least in cases of extreme or well-defined danger. This obviously raises serious legal and ethical questions about the extent to which the state can intervene to regulate maternal life styles and habits. In a widely publicized case in the District of Columbia during 1988, a pregnant woman was convicted of forging some $700 of checks and sentenced to jail during the remainder of her pregnancy. The checks were against an account of her employer, who previously had paid for a private rehabilitation program to help the employee deal with cocaine addiction. The judge explained that even though the offense normally might not have resulted in a jail term, the purpose was to protect the fetus against the mother's cocaine use. *See* WASH. POST, July 23, 1988, page 1, col. 1. The mother remained in jail until she went to the hospital and gave birth to a normal child. Intervention before birth is increasingly disallowed. In an opinion which explores other state practices, the Oklahoma Supreme Court held that a fetus is not a child for purposes of child abuse and neglect law. The court reasoned that even though the child may be the subject of homicide and its biological parents may recover for wrongful death, medical science cannot furnish evidence as to whether a fetus might be mentally, physically, or intellectually deprived within the meaning of the Children's Code. Only if the legislature changes the text of the code would there be applicability to a viable or nonviable fetus. Starks v. State (*In re* Unborn Child), 18 P.3d 342 (Okla.2001).

Authority to take affirmative action before birth has been asserted by some courts in requiring a cesarean section over a mother's objection—cases that also are controversial. *See, e.g.,* Jefferson v. Griffin Spalding County Hospital Authority, 247 Ga. 86, 274 S.E.2d 457 (1981). However, in Matter of A.C., 573 A.2d 1235 (D.C.1990), the D. C. Court of Appeals held that when a pregnant patient with a viable fetus is near death, the decision whether to undergo a cesarean is for the patient to make unless she is incompetent or unable to give informed consent. In the latter instance, according to the court, her decision must be ascertained through substituted judgment. The court explained their view of such a process:

> [T]o determine the subjective desires of the patient, the court must consider the totality of the evidence, focusing particularly on written or oral directions concerning treatment to family, friends, and health-care professionals. The court should also take into account the patient's past decisions regarding medical treatment, and attempt to ascertain from what is known about the patient's value system, goals, and desires what the patient would decide if competent.
>
> After considering the patient's prior statements, if any, the previous medical decisions of the patient, and the values held by the patient, the court may still be unsure what course the patient would choose. In such circumstances the court may supplement its knowledge about the patient by determining what most persons would likely do in a similar situation. When the patient is pregnant, however, she may not be concerned exclusively with her own

> welfare. Thus it is proper for the court, in a case such as this, to weigh (along with all the other factors) the mother's prognosis, the viability of the fetus, the probable result of treatment or non-treatment for both mother and fetus, and the mother's likely interest in avoiding impairment for her child together with her own instincts for survival.
>
> Additionally, the court should consider the context in which prior declarations, treatment decisions, and expressions of personal values were made, including whether statements were made casually or after contemplation, or in accordance with deeply held beliefs. Finally, in making a substituted judgment, the court should become as informed about the patient's condition, prognosis, and treatment options as one would expect any patient to become before making a treatment decision. Obviously, the weight accorded to all of these factors will vary from case to case.

For further commentary on the issue of abuse in gestation, *see* Andrew J. Weisberg, *A Liberal Dilemma: Respecting Autonomy While Also Protecting Inchoate Children from Prenatal Substance Abuse,* 4 WM. & MARY BILL RTS. J. 659 (2016); Michele Goodwin, *Fetal Protection Laws: Moral Panic and the New Constitutional Battlefront,* 102 CAL. L. REV. 781 (2014); Carla-Michelle Adams, *Criminalization in Shades of Color: Prosecuting Pregnant Drug-Addicted Women,* 20 CARDOZO J.L. & GENDER 89 (2013); Seema Mohapatra, *Unshackling Addiction: A Public Health Approach to Drug Use During Pregnancy*, 26 WIS. J.L. GENDER & SOCIETY 241 (2011).

In a related case, the New Mexico Court of Appeals reversed the conviction of a man who had been charged with voluntary manslaughter. He had hit, kicked, and pushed a woman who was twenty-four weeks pregnant. The next day she gave birth to a premature infant who died two days later due to "prematurity and infection due to maternal abdominal blunt force trauma." The appellate court held that the state's statute on child abuse did not intend that a viable fetus be included for purposes of prosecution for child abuse. *See* State v. Mondragon, 203 P.3d 105 (N.M. Ct. App. 2008). For commentary on additional possibilities of abuse by parents, such as childhood obesity or staying with a partner who is abusive, *see* Melissa Mitgang, *Childhood Obesity and State Intervention: An Examination of the Health Risks of Pediatric Obesity and When They Justify State Involvement,* 44 COLUM. J. L. & SOC. PROBS. 553 (2011); Cheryl George, *Parents Super-Sizing Their Children: Criminalizing and Prosecuting the Rising Incidence of Childhood Obesity as Child Abuse*, 13 DEPAUL J. HEALTH CARE L. 33 (2010); Thomas D. Lyon and Mindy B. Mechanic, *Domestic Violence and Child Protection: Confronting the Dilemmas in Moving from Family Court to Dependency Court, in* HANDBOOK OF CHILDREN, CULTURE & VIOLENCE (Nancy Dowd, Dorothy G. Singer & Robin Fretwell Wilson, eds., 2006). Also, parents who have allowed their home to be filled with clutter, debris, and potential safety hazards were not guilty of abuse defined as "withholding necessary and adequate physical care." *See* State v. Baker-Krofft, 239 P.3d 226 (Or. 2010).

2. PROVING ABUSIVE CONDUCT

Sanders v. State

Supreme Court of Georgia, 1983
303 S.E.2d 13

■ BELL, JUSTICE.

Lillian Sanders appeals her conviction and life sentence for the murder of her infant daughter, Cassandra Denise Sanders. There was evidence at trial showing that Cassandra was born September 11, 1981. She was twelve weeks premature and had a low birth weight, a hernia, and anemia. She was hospitalized for treatment of these ailments and was discharged November 6. On November 17 she was treated at a pediatric clinic for fussiness stemming from a suspected allergy, and on November 30 for a cold and a fungus infection. The clinic's record of the November 30 examination had a notation that Cassandra had gained weight, but did not indicate that bruises or other injuries had been found.

At about three p.m. on December 3, 1981 appellant used a neighbor's phone to call the police. She told the police dispatcher her baby was sick, and asked for an ambulance. The dispatcher later said appellant was not sobbing, and her voice seemed normal; appellant's neighbor testified she seemed worried. After making the call Sanders returned to her own home, from which the neighbor then heard crying and hollering. When the county emergency medical service arrived at appellant's residence a few minutes later, the technicians found her holding Cassandra in her arms. One technician asked what the trouble was and she replied the baby had been crying and had just stopped. She also repeatedly told them, "Please don't let my baby die." The technicians gave Cassandra a quick examination and found multiple bruises on her face, neck, chest and abdomen. A patch of skin was missing from her neck, and one side of her head was mushy due to blood and fluid under the skin. The child was gasping for breath, had a high pulse and low respiration, and appeared unconscious. The technicians then took Cassandra and her mother to the emergency room of Archbold Hospital, arriving about 3:20 p.m. At the emergency room Dr. Randolph Malone examined the infant, who had stopped breathing and was being given artificial respiration. At that point she was unconscious and appeared dead. Because she had suffered a severe head injury and had unusual bruise marks around the neck he had the police notified, and he questioned Lillian about what had happened. She told him she didn't know, even though she had been with the baby right until she left to call the ambulance.

Forest Roberts, a child protective services worker with the Thomas County Department of Family and Children Services, was summoned to the hospital and was told that Sanders was suspected of child abuse. She questioned appellant, who first told her that she didn't know what had happened to the baby, that there had been nothing wrong with her earlier, and that she had gone in to check on her and found her like that. She said she might have "popped" her to make her stop crying, but insisted she hadn't hurt her. However, Sanders admitted after more questioning that she hadn't felt well that morning and had been depressed. She had been alone with Cassandra and her older child, Chrishenbo Lashan, that afternoon. The baby had begun to cry so she changed her and gave her some milk. When Roberts asked how the child had gotten its neck bruises appellant maintained she didn't know, but then a few minutes later she said some milk had dried and caked around Cassandra's neck, and that she had scrubbed her neck to remove the milk, and might have bruised and scratched her in the process. Roberts left the room, then returned and told her the child was seriously ill, that it didn't appear she'd gotten that way by herself, and appellant needed to tell her what happened. Lillian said she may have dropped the baby but didn't remember, then she said the baby cried all the time and she must have dropped it. Sanders appeared upset and nervous during this interrogation, but was not hysterically crying or otherwise showing a lot of emotion. While Roberts was questioning Sanders the police arrived. They were present during some of the questioning, and at some point read Sanders *Miranda* warnings. In the course of their interrogation she told them that the child had fallen out of her hands when she reached for something on a table or chest of drawers in the bedroom. She was asked if the child had struck anything except the floor, and she said she hadn't. Her demeanor during this inquiry was confused but otherwise normal, except that a few minutes later she cried.[1]

The baby was pronounced dead at 5:30 that afternoon. Appellant was taken to the police station where shortly after seven that evening she was again questioned after being given *Miranda* warnings, and again she said she'd dropped the baby, that it hadn't hit anything except the floor, and she didn't know how she had been that badly injured. During this interrogation Sanders expressed concern about what would happen to her and asked if she told the truth she would still have to go to court or jail. The police told her they couldn't promise anything, whereupon she volunteered she'd been upset, was pregnant, and didn't want another baby. Sanders consented to a search of her house, during which she pointed out the spot where she claimed the baby had fallen and again denied the baby had hit anything except the floor. Sanders was allowed to go home for the night, but was questioned again at the police station shortly after six p.m. the next day. After being advised a third time about *Miranda* rights, she told the police she'd gone downtown the previous day, leaving Cassandra in her sister's care. When she returned the child had no scratches, bruises, or other apparent injuries. After she related this story, the police then told her she was being charged with murder, and she asked them about securing bond. When queried about

[1] The trial court conducted a *Jackson-Denny* hearing and found by a preponderance of the evidence that Sander's statements given to or in the presence of the police were freely and voluntarily given.

Cassandra's head injury, she said she may have mashed her head while picking her up.

Dr. Larry Howard, forensic pathologist and Director of the State Crime Laboratory, performed the autopsy. He testified that the primary cause of death was a severe crushing type head injury which consisted of a circular skull fracture on the right side of the head. There was severe damage to the brain, including much bleeding into the brain tissue and laceration of the brain by the edges of the skull fracture. There were numerous bruises on the face, chest, and abdomen. The neck had considerable bruising and abrasions which were possible fingernail marks, indicating pressure may have been applied to the neck with a hand. Similar possible fingernail abrasions were found on the chest and the back of the right hand. The upper right arm was broken, probably by someone placing tension on it until it snapped. The liver had been split, which was an injury consistent with a blow to the front of the chest. This injury was at least four and possibly twelve hours older than many of the others, which appeared fresh. Some of the bruises were lined up as if caused by a blunt instrument with several projections, which would have been consistent with the child having been struck by the knuckles of a hand. In his opinion these injuries were not consistent with the child having been dropped on a floor, and he described them as evidencing a typical battered child syndrome. Moreover, he testified they would have been impossible for another young child to inflict.

The defense rested without introducing evidence, and the jury returned a verdict of guilty. Sanders was sentenced to life imprisonment and appealed without having moved for a new trial. . . .

In her second enumeration Sanders claims the state impermissibly placed her character in issue. The record shows that three employees of the Department of Family and Children Services ("the Department") testified for the prosecution. Their combined testimony established certain aspects of appellant's personal history and the fact that appellant had sought the Department's help on several occasions. Specifically, they testified that during the period 1976–81 Sanders had moved several times and had asked the Department for help in locating housing; that she had sought food stamps; that both her children had been problem pregnancies; that appellant's mother had contacted the Department and complained about the quality of care Chrishenbo was receiving and about appellant's attitude toward the child; that Lillian was counseled about child care and a stable living environment; and that appellant's mother's own family had been supervised by the Department for several years. Following this testimony about appellant's background, Dr. Wallace Kennedy, a clinical psychologist, took the stand to testify about the "battering parent syndrome."[2] After his qualifications as an expert in the field of clinical and family psychology and child abuse were established,

---

[2] This term is not Dr. Kennedy's, but clearly represents his concept. See Loebach v. State, 310 N.W.2d 58 (Minn.1981).

Dr. Kennedy constructed a profile of the typical abusive parent.[3] He testified that the characteristics of an adult who abuses a child in a life threatening fashion almost always are, first, that the parent herself is the product of a violent, abusive environment and usually commits violent acts with growing frequency; second, that the parent is under some kind of chronic environmental stress, caused by, for example, money or housing problems, and is frequently a single parent; third, that the parent has a history of poor social judgment, in that she tends to be impulsive or explosive under stress; fourth, that the child she abuses is the product of an unplanned, difficult, and unpleasant pregnancy and is prematurely born; fifth, that the abused child is a chronically difficult child, either sickly or frequently crying. . . .

We have held that under appropriate circumstances a woman who kills her husband or boyfriend and raises the defense of self-defense may, as evidence of whether she acted in fear of her life, have an expert witness describe the "battered woman syndrome", apply that model to the facts, and conclude that the woman falls within the profile. Smith v. State, 247 Ga. 612, 277 S.E.2d 678 (1981).[4] We also observed in *Smith* that it is accepted practice for the state to offer expert opinion testimony that a child is a victim of "battered child syndrome" and that its injuries are not accidental. Id. at 617, 277 S.E.2d 678.[5] In addition, we cited the case of State v. Baker, 120 N.H. 773, 424 A.2d 171 (N.H.1980). In *Baker* the defendant husband claimed his attempt to kill his wife was the result of insanity, but the state contended it was but a single episode in a recurring pattern of domestic violence. Baker called two psychiatrists who testified that in their opinion he was insane at the time of the crime, and the New Hampshire Supreme Court held that the state then could properly call an expert on domestic violence to testify regarding the battered wife syndrome and to give his opinion that mental illness is not an important cause of wife beating. It was also proper, the court ruled, for the state's expert to state his opinion that, based on prior testimony by Baker's wife and daughter that he had physically abused them, Baker's marriage probably fell within the contours of the battered woman

[3] Although Dr. Kennedy indicated he had researched this area and was familiar with the relevant literature, he cited no specific source for his profile and he attempted no showing of its scientific validity.

[4] The other primary issue in *Smith* concerned the admissibility of expert opinion testimony on issues of ultimate fact. Not considered were whether the particular clinical psychologist whom Smith sought to use was qualified to give an opinion in that area (her qualifications were not contested by the state), and whether the state of the art of the study of battered women and the application of diagnostic profiles to particular defendants has reached a scientific stage of verifiable certainty, Harper v. State, 249 Ga. 519(1), 292 S.E.2d 389 (1982).

[5] As support for this principle we cited State v. Wilkerson, 295 N.C. 559, 247 S.E.2d 905 (N.C.1978). However, the Wilkerson court took pains to indicate the limits of the use of the battered child syndrome. Although an expert may diagnose a particular child as a "battered child," explain the use of that term, and give his opinion regarding the usual cause of the syndrome, i.e., that it is usually intentionally inflicted by some physical custodian of the child, the expert may not testify that the injuries were in fact caused by any particular person or class of persons engaged in any particular activity or class of activities, nor may he give his opinion as to the defendant's guilt or innocence. *Wilkerson, Id.* 247 S.E.2d at 911.

syndrome. We have not previously been faced with a case wherein the state has seized the initiative and attempted to use a profile in its case-in-chief as an affirmative weapon against the defendant; however, this question has been confronted by another appellate court, Loebach v. State, 310 N.W.2d 58 (Minn.1981). In that case Loebach appealed his conviction for murdering his infant son. At trial the state had called an expert on child abuse, Dr. Robert ten Bensel, to testify that, based on the child's injuries, in his opinion the child had suffered from nonaccidental physical abuse over a period of time and accordingly was a victim of battered child syndrome. Ten Bensel also testified over objection that battering parents tend to have similar personality traits and personal histories; he described those characteristics but did not suggest Loebach possessed any of them. However, evidence about Loebach's past was introduced through other witnesses. On appeal the Minnesota Supreme Court found that the testimony about Loebach's personal history and personality was nothing more than character evidence, introduced for the purpose of showing Loebach fit within ten Bensel's battering parent profile, and it held that since Loebach had not placed his character in issue, admission of the testimony was error. The court then announced a prospective rule that the prosecution would not be permitted to introduce evidence of the battering parent syndrome or establish a defendant's character as a battering parent unless the defendant first raised that issue. However, the court went on to rule that there was overwhelming evidence of Loebach's guilt without the battering parent testimony, which was only a small percentage of the evidence, and held the error was not prejudicial.

Turning to the instant case, we find that the disputed portion of Dr. Kennedy's testimony clearly implicated Sanders's character. It matters little that, as the state points out, Kennedy never expressly drew the conclusion that appellant fit his profile of battering parents; his construction of the profile, coupled with the previous testimony that appellant possessed many characteristics which Kennedy's profile identified as being shared by the typical battering parent, could lead a reasonable juror to no other inference than that the state was implying that this parent had a history of violent behavior, and, more important, that this parent fit within the syndrome, and had in fact murdered her baby. We hold that unless a defendant has placed her character in issue or has raised some defense which the battering parent syndrome is relevant to rebut, the state may not introduce evidence of the syndrome, nor may the state introduce character evidence showing a defendant's personality traits and personal history as its foundation for demonstrating the defendant has the characteristics of a typical battering parent. Accordingly, the trial court in the instant case erred in admitting the portion of Dr. Kennedy's testimony which was challenged.

However, we find that it is highly probable that the error did not contribute to the verdict, since the evidence of guilt was otherwise overwhelming. Moreover, we find the error was harmless for the additional reason that testimony covering substantially the same area, including the testimony about appellant's personal history and most of Dr. Kennedy's testimony, was introduced without challenge. . . .

Judgment affirmed.

NOTES

The difficulty in proving allegations of abuse continues. To assist in gathering information, the Commonwealth of Massachusetts has a statute that permits evidence to be admitted in a civil proceeding of "out-of-court statements of a child under the age of ten describing any act of sexual contact performed on or with the child." MASS. GEN. LAWS ANN. ch. 233, § 82 (West 2016). The Massachusetts Supreme Judicial Court has ruled that the statute applies whenever the child is under the age of ten when the statements are made, even if the child is over the age of ten when the trial occurs. By allowing the statements to be admissible at a later date, the court found that there would be no incentive on the part of potential perpetrators to delay the trial and prevent the admission of the child's testimony. *See* Adoption of Daisy, 948 N.E.2d 1239 (Mass. 2011). Likewise, New York has, by statute, established a res ipsa loquitor approach to certain types of child abuse, denominating certain injuries as prima facie evidence of abuse or neglect. *See* N.Y. FAM. CT. ACT § 1046(a)(ii) (McKinney 2016):

> "[P]roof of injuries sustained by a child or of the condition of a child of such a nature as would ordinarily not be sustained or exist except by reason of the acts or omissions of the parent or other person responsible for the care of such child shall be prima facie evidence of child abuse or neglect, as the case may be, of the parent or other person legally responsible . . . "

For commentary on resolving allegations of child abuse, *see* MICHAEL T. FLANNERY & RAYMOND C. O'BRIEN, THE SEXUAL EXPLOITATION OF MINORS (2016); Rebevva Naeder, Note, *"I know My Client Would Never Hurt His Daughter, but How Can I Prove It?"*, 80 BROOK. L. REV. (2015); Shireen Y. Husain, *A Voice for the Voiceless: A Child's Right to Legal Representation in Dependency Proceedings*, 79 GEO. WASH. L. REV. 232 (2010); Myrna S. Raeder, *Distrusting Young Children Who Allege Sexual Abuse: Why Stereotypes Don't Die and Ways to Facilitate Child Testimony*, 16 WIDENER L. REV. 239 (2010).

VIRGINIA CODE ANN. (2016)

Court Appointed Special Advocate (CASA)

§ 9.1–151. Court Appointed Special Advocate Program; Appointment of Advisory Committee

A. There is established a Court-Appointed Special Advocate Program (the "Program") that shall be administered by the Department. The Program shall provide services in accordance with this article to children who are subjects of judicial proceedings involving allegations that the child is abused, neglected, in need of services or in need of supervision, and for whom the juvenile and domestic relations district court judge determines such services appropriate. The Department shall adopt regulations necessary and appropriate for the administration of the Program.

B. The Board shall appoint an Advisory Committee to the Court-Appointed Special Advocate Program, consisting of fifteen members, knowledgeable of court matters, child welfare and juvenile justice issues and representative of both state and local interests. The duties of the Advisory Committee shall be to advise the Board on all matters relating to the Program and the needs of the clients served by the Program, and to make such recommendations as it may deem desirable.

§ 9.1–152. Local Court-Appointed Special Advocate Programs; Powers and Duties

A. The Department shall provide a portion of any funding appropriate for this purpose to applicants seeking to establish and operate a local court-appointed special advocate program in their respective judicial districts. Only local programs operate in accordance with this article shall be eligible to receive state funds.

B. Local programs may be established and operated by local boards created for this purpose. Local boards shall ensure conformance to regulations adopted by the Board and my:

1. Solicit and accept financial support from public and private sources.
2. Oversee the financial program management of the local court-appointed special advocate program.
3. Employ and supervise a director who shall serve as a professional liaison to personnel of the court and agencies serving children.
4. Employ such staff as is necessary to the operation of the program.

§ 9.1–153. Volunteer Court-Appointed Special Advocates; Powers and Duties; Assignment; Qualifications; Training

A. Services in each local court-appointed special advocate program shall be provided by volunteer court-appointed special advocates, hereinafter referred to as advocates. The advocate's duties shall include:

1. Investigating the case to which he is assigned to provide independent factual information to the court.
2. Submitting to the court of a written report of his investigation in compliance with the provisions of § 16.1–274. The report may, upon request of the court, include recommendations as to the child's welfare.
3. Monitoring the case to which he is assigned to ensure compliance with the court's orders.

4. Assisting any appointed guardian ad litem to represent the child in providing effective representation of the child's needs and best interests.

5. Reporting a suspected abused or neglected child pursuant to § 63.2–1509.

B. The advocate is not a party to the case to which he is assigned and shall not call witnesses or examine witnesses. The advocate shall not, with respect to the case to which he is assigned, provide legal counsel or advice to any person, appear as counsel in court or in proceedings which are part of the judicial process, or engage in the unauthorized practice of law. The advocate may testify if called as a witness.

C. The program director shall assign an advocate to a child when requested to do so by the judge of the juvenile and domestic relations district court having jurisdiction over the proceedings. The advocate shall continue his association with each case to which he is assigned until relieved of his duties by the court or by the program director.

D. The Department shall adopt regulations governing the qualifications of advocates who for purposes of administering this subsection shall be deemed to be criminal justice employees. The regulations shall require that an advocate be at least twenty-one years of age and that the program director shall obtain with the approval of the court (i) a copy of his criminal history record or certification that no conviction data are maintained on him and (ii) a copy of information from the central registry maintained pursuant to § 63.2–1515 on any investigation of child abuse or neglect undertaken on him or certification that no such record is maintained on him. Advocates selected prior to the adoption of regulations governing qualifications shall meet the minimum requirements set forth in this article.

E. An advocate shall have no associations which create a conflict of interests or the appearance of such a conflict with his duties as an advocate. No advocate shall be assigned to a case of a child whose family has a professional or personal relationship with the advocate. Questions concerning conflicts of interests shall be determined in accordance with regulations adopted by the Department.

F. No applicant shall be assigned as an advocate until successful completion of a program of training required by regulations. The Department shall set standards for both basic and ongoing training.

§ 9.1–154. Immunity

No staff of, or volunteers participating in a program, whether or not compensated, shall be subject to personal liability while acting within the scope of their duties, except for gross negligence or intentional misconduct.

§ 9.1–155. Notice of Hearings and Proceedings

The provision of § 16.1–264 regarding notice to parties shall apply to ensure that an advocate is notified of hearings and other proceedings concerning the case to which he is assigned.

§ 9.1–156. Inspection and Copying of Records by Advocate; Confidentiality of Records

A. Upon presentation by the advocate of the order of his appointment and upon specific court order, any state or local agency, department, authority, or institution, and any hospital, school, physician, or other health or mental health care provider shall permit the advocate to inspect and copy, without the consent of the child or his parents, any records relating to the child involved in the case. Upon the advocate presenting to the mental health provider the order of the advocate's appointment and, upon specific court order, in lieu of the advocate inspecting and copying any related records of the child involved, the mental health care provider shall be available within seventy-two hours to conduct for the advocate a review and an interpretation of the child's treatment records which are specifically related to the investigation.

B. An advocate shall not disclose the contents of any document or record to which he becomes privy, which is otherwise confidential pursuant to the provisions of this Code, except upon order of a court of competent jurisdiction.

§ 9.1–157. Cooperation of State and Local Entities

All state and local departments, agencies, authorities, and institutions shall cooperate with the Department and with each local court-appointed special advocate program to facilitate its implementation of the Program.

3. PARENTAL DISCIPLINE

People v. Jennings

Supreme Court of Colorado, En Banc, 1982
641 P.2d 276

■ DUBOFSKY, JUSTICE.

On July 18, 1979 the defendant, John Jennings, was convicted in Garfield County District Court of child abuse resulting in serious bodily injury under section 18–6–401(1)(c), C.R.S.1973 (1978 Repl. Vol. 8).[1] Subsequently, the trial court granted the defendant's motion to dismiss based on the vagueness of the criminal child abuse statute. The People appealed the trial court's ruling, and we reverse.

The child abuse charge arises from an incident which occurred on August 16, 1978. On that day, the defendant left work at about noon because he felt ill, went home, and dismissed the babysitter who was caring for his stepson, Jason, aged three, and his four-month-old

[1] At the time of the defendant's conviction child abuse resulting in serious bodily injury to the child was a class 3 felony, while all other instances of child abuse were classified as class 2 misdemeanors. Subsequent to the defendant's conviction section 18–6–401(7), C.R.S.1973 (1978 Repl. Vol. 8) was amended to classify the offense of child abuse depending on the state of mind of the defendant and the extent of injury to the victim. For example, subsection 18–6–401(7)(a)(i), C.R.S.1973 (1981 Supp.) provides: "When a person acts knowingly, . . . and the child abuse results in death to the child, it is a class 2 felony."

daughter, Christina. The defendant testified that from the time he arrived home, Christina was "fussy." He attempted to calm her, then lay down and tried to take a nap, but the baby continued to cry. The defendant got up, checked Christina's diaper and tried to give her a bottle. She continued crying. The defendant testified that he was going to pick her up, but instead he struck her on the head with his open hand. The following colloquy regarding the slap took place at trial:

> "Q. Okay. Now, how many times did you hit Christina?
>
> "A. One time.
>
> "Q. Why did you do that?
>
> "A. I don't know.
>
> "Q. Were you trying to punish her?
>
> "A. No, I wasn't trying to punish her.
>
> "Q. Do you think a four-month-old child knows the meaning of discipline?
>
> "A. No.
>
> "Q. Had you intended to slap her?
>
> "A. No. . . .
>
> "Q. Did you mean to hurt her?
>
> "A. No.
>
> "Q. Did it ever occur to you, John, that by hitting a child that young in the face that it might cause serious bodily injury?
>
> "A. I never really gave it that much thought because I never wanted to hit my children anywhere. . . ."

Apparently as a result of the slap, Christina stopped breathing for a time, causing brain damage which resulted in blindness and arrested mental development. After the defendant's trial, on November 3, 1979, Christina died. The defendant stipulated before trial that Christina suffered serious bodily injury as a result of his single slap to her head. The only question for the jury was whether the slap resulting in brain damage constituted felony child abuse, defined under section 18–6–401(1)(c) as "knowingly, intentionally, or negligently, and without justifiable excuse," causing or permitting a child to be "abandoned, tortured, cruelly confined or cruelly punished." In response to the defendant's request for a bill of particulars, the prosecution alleged that the child had been "cruelly punished."

The jury found the defendant guilty of felony child abuse. The defendant filed a new trial motion and renewed his pre-trial motion to dismiss, which the court had taken under advisement. At a hearing on November 6, 1979, the court found the language "cruelly punished" unconstitutionally vague because of the subjective nature of the words "cruel" and "punish. . . ."

The vagueness challenge to the child abuse statute centers on the statutory phrase "cruelly punished."[4] The defendant argues that the words "cruel" and "punish," while they may have generally understood meanings in day-to-day usage, are, in the context of the child abuse statute, unclear and susceptible of subjective interpretation. The defendant contends that the absence of a statutory definition of these words forces jurors to import their subjective impressions as to what punishment is cruel. The defendant cites State v. Meinert, 225 Kan. 816, 594 P.2d 232 (1979), in which the Kansas Supreme Court, interpreting that state's criminal child abuse statute, stated:

> "Some persons do not believe in any form of corporal punishment and to them any such treatment would be unjustified. On the other hand, others may believe any correction, however severe, which produces temporary pain only, and no lasting injury or disfigurement, is justified. The statute can conceivably cover anything from a minor spanking or slapping to severe beating depending upon the personal beliefs of the individual."

594 P.2d at 234–35.

At the outset, we note that the defendant's argument is a broad one, amounting to a contention that in light of the wide divergence in personal views as to what constitutes cruel punishment of a child, a statute which does not define in detail each act proscribed cannot delineate an enforceable standard. We disagree; the prohibition in the child abuse statute against cruel punishment is sufficiently precise to satisfy due process requirements.

This Court has on numerous occasions enunciated the standard a statute challenged on vagueness grounds must satisfy to accord due process. As a preliminary matter, a statute claimed to be impermissibly vague must be closely scrutinized. If a challenged statute is capable of alternate constructions, one of which is constitutional, the constitutional interpretation must be adopted. A penal statute is unconstitutionally vague if it "forbids or requires the doing of an act in terms so vague that men of common intelligence must necessarily guess as to its meaning and differ as to its application. . . ." Connally v. General Construction Co., 269 U.S. 385, 46 S.Ct. 126, 70 L.Ed. 322 (1926); . . . Criminal statutes should be framed with sufficient clarity so as to inform the persons subject to them of the standards of conduct imposed and to give fair warning of which acts are forbidden. The vagueness doctrine also seeks to minimize arbitrary and discriminatory enforcement of laws by providing police and prosecutors with clearly defined standards. Such standards serve as well

---

[4] In People v. Hoehl, 193 Colo. 557, 568 P.2d 484 (1977) we upheld the child abuse statute against a vagueness challenge based on the language of section 18–6–401(1)(a) which provides that a person commits child abuse if he causes or permits a child to be "placed in a situation that may endanger the child's life or health. . . ." We construed the word "may" to mean a reasonable probability that the child's life or health will be endangered from the situation in which the child is placed.

to inform a court and jury whether a crime has been committed and proved.

The vagueness standard, while frequently enunciated, is nevertheless difficult to apply. Here, the defendant's contention is that the distinction between mere "punishment" and "cruel punishment" is impermissibly vague. The distinction between the two centers on the meaning of the word "cruel." Webster's Third New International Dictionary (1961) defines "cruel" as "disposed to inflict pain, especially in a wanton, insensate, or vindictive manner," and "cruelly" as "so as to cause pain or hurt."

That a distinction can be made between permissible punishment and "cruel" punishment is supported by the traditional common law rule concerning parental discipline of children. At common law the parent of a minor child or one standing *in loco parentis* was privileged in using a reasonable amount of force upon a child for purposes of safeguarding or promoting the child's welfare. Bowers v. State, 283 Md. 115, 389 A.2d 341 (Ct.App.1978); Boyd v. State, 88 Ala. 169, 7 So. 268–69 (1890); W. LaFave and A. Scott, Handbook on Criminal Law § 52, at 389–90 (1972); Restatement of Torts (Second) § 147(1); Paulsen, The Legal Framework for Child Protection, 66 Colum.L.Rev. 679 (1966). While at common law the precise test of what constituted permissible force varied from jurisdiction to jurisdiction, as a general proposition, so long as the chastisement was moderate and reasonable in light of the child's age and condition, the misconduct being punished, the kind of punishment inflicted, the degree of harm done to the child and other relevant circumstances, the parent or custodian would incur neither civil nor criminal liability, even though identical behavior against a stranger would be grounds for an action in tort or prosecution for assault and battery or a similar offense.

This common law privilege has been codified in Colorado in section 18–1–703(1)(a), C.R.S.1973 (1978 Repl.Vol. 8), which provides:

> "The use of physical force upon another person which would otherwise constitute an offense is justifiable and not criminal under any of the following circumstances . . .
>
> A parent, guardian or other person entrusted with the care and supervision of a minor or an incompetent person . . . may use reasonable and appropriate physical force upon the minor or incompetent person when and to the extent it is reasonably necessary and appropriate to maintain discipline or promote the welfare of the minor or incompetent person."

The parental privilege to inflict moderate, reasonable and appropriate corporal punishment has never shielded from liability parental acts which cannot be justified as salutary discipline. Before the adoption of statutes specifically proscribing child abuse, "cruel and outrageous" treatment of a child defeated the parental privilege and subjected the parent to the penal sanctions normally applicable to the acts committed. Paulsen, supra, 66 Colum.L.Rev. at 686–87.

This discussion of the common law background to the present child abuse statute illustrates that rather than existing in a vacuum, the parental privilege set out in section 18–1–703(1)(a) and the definition of criminal child abuse in section 18–6–401 codify common law principles concerning the limits of permissible parental chastisement. As the Maryland Court of Appeals said in Bowers v. State, supra:

> "Since the contours of the common law privilege have been subject for centuries to definition and refinement through careful and constant judicial decisionmaking, terms like 'cruel' or 'inhumane' and 'malicious' have acquired a relatively widely accepted connotation in the law."

389 A.2d at 348.

In addition to the criminal sanctions in section 18–6–401, the General Assembly has enacted other statutes to prevent cruelty to children. They evidence the legislature's parallel intent to protect children from unwarranted abuse while permitting parents to discipline those in their charge within the limits of the traditional privilege. For example, Article 10 of the Children's Code, which concerns the reporting of child abuse to the proper authorities, defines abuse in section 19–10–103(1)(a) as "an act or omission . . . which seriously threatens the health or welfare of a child" including:

> "(i) Any case in which a child exhibits evidence of skin bruising, bleeding, malnutrition, failure to thrive, burns, fracture of any bone, subdural hematoma, soft tissue swelling, or death. . . ."

Paragraph (b) of the same subsection provides:

> "Nothing in this subsection (1) shall refer to acts which could be construed to be a reasonable exercise of parental discipline."

Child abuse may also trigger the commencement of proceedings to terminate the parent-child relationship under Article 11 of the Children's Code, sections 19–11–101 through –110. In an action for termination of a parent-child relationship, criteria which support the determination that a parent is unfit include:

> "(b) Conduct towards the child of a physically or sexually abusive nature . . .
>
> (d) A single incident of life-threatening or gravely disabling injury or disfigurement of the child."

Section 19–11–105(2)(b) and (d).

Implicit in our decisions upholding as constitutionally sound the definition of child abuse in the termination of parental rights statute is the proposition that a meaningful distinction can be made between permissible discipline and abusive treatment. See People in the Interest of C.S., Colo., 613 P.2d 1304 (1980); People in the Interest of V.A.E.Y.H.D., 199 Colo. 148, 605 P.2d 916 (1980); People in the Interest of D.A.K., 198 Colo. 11, 596 P.2d 747 (1979). In the context of a termination proceeding where the definition of child abuse is at issue we have recognized that "fundamental fairness does not require a statute to enunciate in all-encompassing examples, or exactly described acts, precisely how poorly a parent can treat a child before risking loss of parental rights." While termination of parental rights actions are civil cases and distinguishable from this criminal prosecution, we scrutinize the child abuse standard at issue in these cases with special care, reasoning that "although no criminal sanction is involved, a serious and substantial parental interest is at stake, which in many, if not most, cases is as important to the parents as their freedom."

Given the statutory and common law context in which the "cruelly punished" language of section 18–6–401 is set, we are satisfied that this language is intelligible and capable of nonarbitrary enforcement. Although the criminal child abuse standard is enunciated in general terms, this is not a fatal flaw. Scientific exactitude in statutory language is not required as long as the statute meets the minimal requirements of due process. . . . The relationship between parents or guardians and children is a delicate and complex one, and standards designed to regulate this relationship must necessarily provide some flexibility while at the same time effectuating the state policy of protecting children from abuse.

The defendant also argues that the mental state requirements in the statute are too broad to have meaning and that even if the mental states can be defined with sufficient clarity, the defendant did not have the mens rea required by the term "punished." At both the time of the defendant's act and when his trial was conducted, section 18–6–401 provided that child abuse is committed when a person "knowingly, intentionally, or negligently, and without justifiable excuse, causes or permits a child to be: . . . (a) cruelly punished."[5] The defendant specifically argues that negligently causing cruel punishment is impossible to understand and therefore unconstitutionally vague. However, in People v. Taggart, Colo., 621 P.2d 1375 (1981), we ruled that the inclusion of "negligently" as a state of mind in section 18–6–401 does not render the child abuse statute unconstitutionally vague:

> "[A] person may negligently cause or permit a child to be placed in a situation so debilitating to the child's physical well-being that a reasonable juror, looking at the effect of the offender's conduct on the child, would consider it torture or cruel punishment. The term 'negligently' is not irreconcilably at odds with 'tortured' and 'cruelly punished', and the statutory definition of child abuse is sufficiently particular as to furnish

---

[5] Section 18–6–401(1) has since been amended to add "recklessly" to the mental states applicable to commission of child abuse.

> adequate notice to potential wrongdoers of the proscribed conduct and to protect against discriminatory enforcement [citations omitted]."

621 P.2d at 1375. See People v. Noble, Colo., 635 P.2d 203, 210 (1981).

In addition, we note that the child abuse statute proscribes acts of mistreatment which include inaction as well as action. The inclusion of a range of states of mind can deal, for example, with a parent who "negligently . . . permits" a child to be abused in some way. See State v. Zobel, 81 S.D. 260, 134 N.W.2d 101 cert. denied, 382 U.S. 833, 86 S.Ct. 74, 15 L.Ed.2d 76 (1965) (father who had never actively mistreated two infant daughters convicted of child abuse for leaving them with his insane wife, who he knew beat them and deprived them of food, and who eventually killed them).

The defendant's argument that "punished" implies a mens rea which he did not possess is also without merit. As we made clear in People v. Taggart, supra:

> " 'Tortured' and 'cruelly punished' do not refer to the *mens rea* of the crime of child abuse. Rather, these words refer to the *actus reus* as measured by the consequences wrought on the child."

621 P.2d at 1383. The defendant's testimony that he did not mean to punish Christina does not preclude a jury from finding that he caused her to be "cruelly punished."

Reversed and remanded for a new trial.

NOTES

There is a fine line separating physical abuse from parental discipline. Often, state statutes will specify appropriate levels of parental discipline. *See, e.g.*, CAL. WELF. AND INST. CODE § 300(a) (2016): "For purposes of this subdivision, 'serious physical harm' does not include reasonable and age-appropriate spanking to the buttocks where there is no evidence of serious physical injury." The issue of what is appropriate is often the subject of litigation. *See, e.g.*, Simons v. State, 803 N.W.2d 587 (N.D. 2011) (holding the 24 "swats" that a father inflicted on his two-year-old son with a wooden back-scratcher during a two-hour "power struggle" because the boy refused to say "yes, sir" was child abuse, not reasonable parental discipline); M.R. v. State, 257 P.3d 1043 (Utah Ct. App. 2011) (holding that a long-term pattern of a father slapping his daughter and calling her names, together with threats to order an exam to prove or disprove her virginity, was unreasonable discipline and abuse); State v. Wade, 245 P.3d 1083 (Kan. Ct. App. 2010) (holding that father was entitled to the common-law defense of parental discipline when charged with battery of his fifteen year-old son); Jaet v. Siso, 2009 WL 35270 (S.D. Fla. 2009) (holding that the father's spanking of his children did not constitute a "grave risk of physical harm" under the Hague Convention on the Civil Aspects of International Child Abduction so as to justify the mother's refusal to return the children to the father in Mexico).

4. CIVIL ENFORCEMENT PROCEDURE

Baltimore City Dept. of Social Services v. Bouknight

Supreme Court of the United States, 1990
493 U.S. 549

■ O'CONNOR, JUSTICE delivered the opinion of the Court.

In this action, we must decide whether a mother, the custodian of a child pursuant to a court order, may invoke the Fifth Amendment privilege against self-incrimination to resist an order of the Juvenile Court to produce the child. We hold that she may not.

Petitioner Maurice M. is an abused child. When he was three months old, he was hospitalized with a fractured left femur, and examination revealed several partially healed bone fractures and other indications of severe physical abuse. In the hospital, respondent Bouknight, Maurice's mother, was observed shaking Maurice, dropping him in his crib despite his spica cast, and otherwise handling him in a manner inconsistent with his recovery and continued health. Hospital personnel notified Baltimore City Department of Social Services (BCDSS) of suspected child abuse. In February 1987, BCDSS secured a court order removing Maurice from Bouknight's control and placing him in shelter care. Several months later, the shelter care order was inexplicably modified to return Maurice to Bouknight's custody temporarily. Following a hearing held shortly thereafter, the Juvenile Court declared Maurice to be a "child in need of assistance," thus asserting jurisdiction over Maurice and placing him under BCDSS's continuing oversight. BCDSS agreed that Bouknight could continue as custodian of the child, but only pursuant to extensive conditions set forth in a court-approved protective supervision order. The order required Bouknight to "cooperate with BCDSS," "continue in therapy," participate in parental aid and training programs, and "refrain from physically punishing [Maurice]." The order's terms were "all subject to the further Order of the Court." Bouknight's attorney signed the order, and Bouknight in a separate form set forth her agreement to each term.

Eight months later, fearing for Maurice's safety, BCDSS returned to Juvenile Court. BCDSS caseworkers related that Bouknight would not cooperate with them and had in nearly every respect violated the terms of the protective order. BCDSS stated that Maurice's father had recently died in a shooting incident and that Bouknight, in light of the results of a psychological examination and her history of drug use, could not provide adequate care for the child. On April 20, 1988, the Court granted BCDSS's petition to remove Maurice from Bouknight's control for placement in foster care. BCDSS officials also petitioned for judicial relief from Bouknight's failure to produce Maurice or reveal where he could be found. The petition recounted that on two recent visits by BCDSS officials to Bouknight's home, she had refused to reveal the location of the child or had indicated that the child was with an aunt whom she would not identify. The petition further asserted that inquiries of Bouknight's known relatives had revealed that none of them had recently seen Maurice and that BCDSS had prompted the police to issue a missing persons report and referred the case for investigation by the police homicide division. Also on April 20, the Juvenile Court, upon a hearing on the petition, cited Bouknight for violating the protective custody order and for failing to appear at the hearing. Bouknight had indicated to her attorney that she would appear with the child, but also expressed fear that if she appeared the State would "snatch the child." The court issued an order to show cause why Bouknight should not be held in civil contempt for failure to produce the child. Expressing concern that Maurice was endangered or perhaps dead, the court issued a bench warrant for Bouknight's appearance.

Maurice was not produced at subsequent hearings. At a hearing one week later, Bouknight claimed that Maurice was with a relative in Dallas. Investigation revealed that the relative had not seen Maurice. The next day, following another hearing at which Bouknight again declined to produce Maurice, the Juvenile Court found Bouknight in contempt for failure to produce the child as ordered. There was and has been no indication that she was unable to comply with the order. The court directed that Bouknight be imprisoned until she "purge[d] herself of contempt by either producing [Maurice] before the court or revealing to the court his exact whereabouts." The Juvenile Court rejected Bouknight's subsequent claim that the contempt order violated the Fifth Amendment's guarantee against self-incrimination. The court stated that the production of Maurice would purge the contempt and that "[t]he contempt is issued not because she refuse[d] to testify in any proceeding . . . [but] because she has failed to abide by the Order of this Court, mainly [for] the production of Maurice M." While that decision was being appealed, Bouknight was convicted of theft and sentenced to 18 months' imprisonment in separate proceedings. The Court of Appeals of Maryland vacated the Juvenile Court's judgment upholding the contempt order. In re Maurice M., 314 Md. 391, 550 A.2d 1135 (1988). The Court of Appeals found that the contempt order unconstitutionally compelled Bouknight to admit through the act of production "a measure of continuing control and dominion over Maurice's person" in circumstances in which "Bouknight has a reasonable apprehension that she will be prosecuted." Chief Justice Rehnquist granted BCDSS's application for a stay of the judgment and mandate of the Maryland Court of Appeals, pending disposition of the petition for a writ of certiorari. We granted certiorari, and we now reverse.

The Fifth Amendment provides that "No person . . . shall be compelled in any criminal case to be a witness against himself." The Fifth Amendment's protection "applies only when the accused is compelled to make a *testimonial* communication that is incriminating." Fisher v.

United States, 425 U.S. 391, 408 (1976); . . . The courts below concluded that Bouknight could comply with the order through the unadorned act of producing the child, and we thus address that aspect of the order. When the government demands that an item be produced, "the only thing compelled is the act of producing the [item]." The Fifth Amendment's protection may nonetheless be implicated because the act of complying with the government's demand testifies to the existence, possession, or authenticity of the things produced. But a person may not claim the Amendment's protections based upon the incrimination that may result from the contents or nature of the thing demanded. Bouknight therefore cannot claim the privilege based upon anything that examination of Maurice might reveal, nor can she assert the privilege upon the theory that compliance would assert that the child produced is in fact Maurice (a fact the State could readily establish, rendering any testimony regarding existence or authenticity insufficiently incriminating.) Rather, Bouknight claims the benefit of the privilege because the act of production would amount to testimony regarding her control over and possession of Maurice. Although the State could readily introduce evidence of Bouknight's continuing control over the child—e.g., the custody order, testimony of relatives, and Bouknight's own statements to Maryland officials before invoking the privilege—her implicit communication of control over Maurice at the moment of production might aid the State in prosecuting Bouknight.

The possibility that a production order will compel testimonial assertions that may prove incriminating does not, in all contexts, justify invoking the privilege to resist production. Even assuming that this limited testimonial assertion is sufficiently incriminating and "sufficiently testimonial for purposes of the privilege," Bouknight may not invoke the privilege to resist the production order because she has assumed custodial duties related to production and because production is required as part of a noncriminal regulatory regime.

The Court has on several occasions recognized that the Fifth Amendment privilege may not be invoked to resist compliance with a regulatory regime constructed to effect the State's public purposes unrelated to the enforcement of its criminal laws. . . .

These principles readily apply to this case. Once Maurice was adjudicated a child in need of assistance, his care and safety became the particular object of the State's regulatory interests. See 314 Md., at 404, 550 A.2d, at 1141; Md.Cts. & Jud. Proc. Code §§ 3–801(e), 3–804(a) (Supp.1989); see also App. 105 ("This court has jurisdiction to require at all times to know the whereabouts of the minor child. We asserted jurisdiction over that child in the spring of 1987 . . . "). Maryland first placed Maurice in shelter care, authorized placement in foster care, and then entrusted responsibility for Maurice's care to Bouknight. By accepting care of Maurice subject to the custodial order's conditions (including requirements that she cooperate with BCDSS, follow a prescribed training regime, and be subject to further court orders), Bouknight submitted to the routine operation of the regulatory system and agreed to hold Maurice in a manner consonant with the State's regulatory interests and subject to inspection by BCDSS. In assuming the obligations attending custody, Bouknight "has accepted the incident obligation to permit inspection." Wilson, 221 U.S. at 382, 31 S.Ct., at 545. The State imposes and enforces that obligation as part of a broadly directed, noncriminal regulatory regime governing children cared for pursuant to custodial orders. See Md.Cts. & Jud.Proc.Code Ann. § 3–802(a) (1984) (setting forth child protective purposes of subtitle, including "provid[ing] for the care, protection, and wholesome mental and physical development of children coming within the provisions of this subtitle"); see also Md.Cts. & Jud.Proc.Code Ann. §§ 3–820(b), (c) (Supp.1989); In re Jessica M., 312 Md. 93, 538 A.2d 305 (1988).

Persons who care for children pursuant to a custody order, and who may be subject to a request for access to the child, are hardly a "selective group inherently suspect of criminal activities." Marchetti, 390 U.S. at 57 (quoting Albertson v. Subversive Activities Control Board, 382 U.S., at 79). The Juvenile Court may place a child within its jurisdiction with social service officials or "under supervision in his own home or in the custody or under the guardianship of a relative or other fit person, upon terms the court deems appropriate." Md.Cts. & Jud.Proc.Code Ann. § 3–820(c)(1)(i) (Supp.1989). Children may be placed, for example, in foster care, in homes of relatives, or in the care of state officials. Even when the court allows a parent to retain control of a child within the court's jurisdiction, that parent is not one singled out for criminal conduct, but rather has been deemed to be, without the State's assistance, simply "unable or unwilling to give proper care and attention to the child and his problems." Md.Cts. & Jud.Proc.Code Ann. § 3–801(e) (Supp.1989); see In re Jertrude O., 56 Md.App. 83, 466 A.2d 885 (1983), cert. denied, 298 Md. 309, 469 A.2d 863 (1984). The provision that authorized the Juvenile Court's efforts to gain production of Maurice reflects this broad applicability. See Md.Cts. & Jud.Proc.Code Ann. § 3–814(c) (1984) ("If a parent, guardian, or custodian fails to bring the child before the court when requested, the court may issue a writ of attachment directing that the child be taken into custody and brought before the court. The court may proceed against the parent, guardian, or custodian for contempt"). This provision "fairly may be said to be directed at . . . parents, guardians, and custodians who accept placement of juveniles in custody." 314 Md., at 418, 550 A.2d, at 1148 (McAuliffe, J., dissenting).

Similarly, BCDSS's efforts to gain access to children, as well as judicial efforts to the same effect, do not "focu[s] almost exclusively on conduct which was criminal." Many orders will arise in circumstances entirely devoid of criminal conduct. Even when criminal conduct may exist, the court may properly request production and return of the child, and enforce that request through exercise of the contempt power, for reasons related entirely to the child's well-being and through measures unrelated to criminal law enforcement or investigation. See Maryland Cts. & Jud.Proc.Code Ann. § 3–814(c) (1984). This case provides an illustration: concern for the child's safety underlay the efforts to gain access to and then compel production of Maurice. Finally, production in the vast majority of cases will embody no incriminating testimony, even if in particular cases the act of production may incriminate the custodian through an assertion of possession, the existence, or the identity of the child. These orders to produce children cannot be characterized as efforts to gain some testimonial component of the act of production. The government demands production of the very public charge entrusted to a custodian, and makes the demand for compelling reasons unrelated to criminal law enforcement and as part of a broadly applied regulatory regime. In these circumstances, Bouknight cannot invoke the privilege to resist the order to produce Maurice.

We are not called upon to define the precise limitations that may exist upon the State's ability to use the testimonial aspects of Bouknight's act of production in subsequent criminal proceedings. But we note that imposition of such limitations is not foreclosed. The same custodial role that limited the ability to resist the production order may give rise to corresponding limitations upon the direct and indirect use of that testimony. The State's regulatory requirement in the usual case may neither compel incriminating testimony nor aid a criminal prosecution, but the Fifth Amendment protections are not thereby necessarily unavailable to the person who complies with the regulatory requirement after invoking the privilege and subsequently faces prosecution. . . .

The judgment of the Court of Appeals of Maryland is reversed and the cases remanded to that court for further proceedings not inconsistent with this opinion.

■ JUSTICE MARSHALL, with whom JUSTICE BRENNAN joins, dissenting.

. . . The State's goal of protecting children from abusive environments through its juvenile welfare system cannot be separated from criminal provisions that serve the same goal. When the conduct at which a civil statute aims—here, child abuse and neglect—is frequently the same conduct subject to criminal sanction, it strikes me as deeply problematic to dismiss the Fifth Amendment concerns by characterizing the civil scheme as "unrelated to criminal law enforcement investigation". A civil scheme that inevitably intersects with criminal sanctions may not be used to coerce, on pain of contempt, a potential criminal defendant to furnish evidence crucial to the success of her own prosecution.

I would apply a different analysis, one that is more faithful to the concerns underlying the Fifth Amendment. This approach would target the respondent's particular claim of privilege, the precise nature of the testimony sought, and the likelihood of self-incrimination caused by this respondent's compliance. "To sustain the privilege, it need only be evident from the implications of the question, in the setting in which it is asked, that a responsive answer to the question or an explanation of why it cannot be answered might be dangerous because injurious disclosure could result." Hoffman v. United States, 341 U.S. 479, 486–487, 71 S.Ct. 814, 818–819, 95 L.Ed.2d 1118 (1951). This analysis unambiguously indicates that Bouknight's Fifth Amendment privilege must be respected to protect her from the serious risk of self-incrimination.

An individualized inquiry is preferable to the Court's analysis because it allows the privilege to turn on the concrete facts of a particular case, rather than on abstract characterizations concerning the nature of a regulatory scheme. Moreover, this particularized analysis would not undermine any appropriate goals of civil regulatory schemes that may intersect with criminal prohibitions. Instead, the ability of a State to provide immunity from criminal prosecution permits it to gather information necessary for civil regulation, while also preserving the integrity of the privilege against self-incrimination. The fact that the State throws a wide net in seeking information does not mean that it can demand from the few persons whose Fifth Amendment rights are implicated that they participate in their own criminal prosecutions. Rather, when the State demands testimony for its citizens, it should do so with an explicit grant of immunity. . . .

Although I am disturbed by the Court's willingness to apply inapposite precedent to deny Bouknight her constitutional right against self-incrimination, especially in light of the serious allegations of homicide that accompany this civil proceeding, I take some comfort in the Court's recognition that the State may be prohibited from using any testimony given by Bouknight in subsequent criminal proceedings (leaving open the question of the "State's ability to use the testimonial aspects of Bouknight's act of production" in such criminal proceedings).[2] Because I am not content to deny Bouknight the constitutional protection required by the Fifth Amendment *now* in the hope that she will not be convicted *later* on the basis of her own testimony, I dissent.

NOTES

Jacqueline L. Bouknight, a 29-year-old woman, was released from prison on November 1, 1995, after 7 1/2 years behind bars for contempt. The

[2] I note, with both exasperation and skepticism about the bona fide nature of the State's intentions, that the State may be able to grant Bouknight use immunity under a recently enacted immunity statute, even though it has thus far failed to do so. See 1989 Md. Laws, Ch. 288 (amending § 9–123). Although the statute applies only to testimony "in a criminal prosecution or a proceeding before a grand jury of the State," Md.Cts. & Jud.Proc.Code Ann. § 9–123(b)(1) (Supp.1989), the State represented to this Court that "[a]s a matter of law, [granting limited use immunity for the testimonial aspects of Bouknight's compliance with the production order] would now be possible". If such a grant of immunity has been possible since July 1989 and the State has refused to invoke it so that it can litigate Bouknight's claim of privilege, I have difficulty believing that the State is sincere in its protestations of concern for Maurice's well-being.

judge said that continued imprisonment was no longer an effective tool to learn the location of her son, Maurice. The son remained missing.

Child Abuse Reporting Statutes. The proliferation of state statutes mandating the reporting of abuse or neglect attest to their popularity; the statutes have also progressively expanded the scope of who must report. For instance, some statutes require anyone who suspects child abuse to report, while other statutes specify a particular class of persons. Still other statutes include a permissive reporting provision, stating that any person not included under the mandatory provision may report suspected abuse. Some persons are exempted from reporting because of state confidential communication privileges normally granted to attorney-client, doctor-patient, and priest-penitent. Nonetheless, with the increase of abuse, some states have abrogated the privilege. For example, GA. CODE ANN. § 19–7–5(g) (Supp. 2016) provides:

> Suspected child abuse which is required to be reported by any person pursuant to this Code section shall be reported notwithstanding that the reasonable cause to believe such abuse has occurred or is occurring is based in whole or in part upon any communication to that person which is otherwise made privileged or confidential by law.

States give reporters immunity from civil or criminal liability for reporting suspected child abuse as long as they act in good faith. Others, who are mandated to report and do not do so, can be found criminally liable and also civilly liable for failure to report under a negligence or malpractice cause of action. For instance: ALA. CODE § 26–14–13 (2016) provides that failure to report is a misdemeanor, punishable by no more than six months in jail or by a fine of not more than $500.00. In a leading case, Landeros v. Flood, 17 Cal.3d 399, 131 Cal.Rptr. 69, 551 P.2d 389 (1976), the California Supreme Court upheld the potential liability of a physician with a duty to report suspected abuse, for negligently failing to diagnose a case of battered child syndrome and subsequently failing to report it. For extensive discussion of reporting requirements, immunity, and defenses, *see* MICHAEL T. FLANNERY & RAYMOND C. O'BRIEN, THE SEXUAL EXPLOTATION OF CHILDREN 395–534 (2016).

Computers, expanded reporting requirements, and the anonymous nature of most reports, must be balanced against individual privacy, the limits of search and seizure, and traditional notions of confidentiality. For instance, if the state has abrogated all confidential communication privileges and requires all persons who suspect abuse of a child to report this suspicion to the authorities, must an ordained member of the clergy report a conversation confined to a sacramental confessional? *See* Raymond C. O'Brien and Michael T. Flannery, *The Pending Gauntlet to Free Exercise: Mandating That Clergy Report Child Abuse*, 25 LOY. L.A. L. REV. 1 (1991); and Raymond C. O'Brien, *Clergy, Sex and the American Way*, 31 PEPPERDINE L. REV. 363, 430–435 (2004). Pertaining to all forms of abuse, is it justifiable to provide for a data bank in each hospital emergency room to obtain computerized information about past reports of actual or possible child abuse of a specific child, or about the number of times a particular child has been brought to the attention of a physician or had suffered physical injury requiring emergency room attention at other facilities?

Finally, modern reporting requirements have embraced dependent adults and the elderly, who often are subjected to abuse. *See, e.g.,* CAL. WELF. AND INST. CODE § 15630 (2016). *See* RAYMOND C. O'BRIEN & MICHAEL T. FLANNERY, THE FUNDAMENTALS OF ELDER LAW 700–727 (2015).

In re Michael C.

Supreme Court of Rhode Island, 1989
557 A.2d 1219

■ KELLEHER, JUSTICE.

The parents of Michael C. are before this court on their respective appeals from a judgment of the Family Court in which the trial justice found that the couple's thirteen-year-old son had been sexually abused by his father[1] and neglected by both parents.

At the Family Court hearing, counsel for the Department of Children and Their Families (DCF), acting pursuant to G.L.1956 (1985 Reenactment) § 9–17–14, called both parents as adverse witnesses. The mother testified that at the time of the events in question she had been married to Michael's father for seven years. The mother would leave for work early in the morning. The father, who had been injured in a work-related incident and was receiving Workers' Compensation benefits, remained at home. Consequently, he had the responsibility of awakening Michael and ensuring his readiness for school.

The mother testified that on two occasions in the spring of 1987 Michael told her that her husband was "after his body." When she relayed this information to her husband, he denied any such intent. Michael was told by his mother to stay away from his father and not to bother him. In his appearance as an adverse witness, the father denied ever having engaged in any sexual activity with Michael. When his wife first told him of Michael's accusations, the father asserted, he thought she was joking. Prior to Michael's testifying, an attorney for DCF and Michael's guardian ad litem explained to the trial justice that Michael had "expressed a great deal of anxiety about testifying in open court." He was described as being "most reticent and embarrassed to testify in open court."

It should be noted at this point that the trial justice decided that Michael's testimony was to be given in camera before him, with a stenographer recording the proceedings. After Michael had been questioned by the trial justice, his testimony was read back to the attorneys for the parents. The attorneys were then permitted to formulate written questions for cross-examination, which would also be

---

[1] Michael was adopted by John C. in May 1984.

posed by the trial justice in camera. The father's attorney submitted some fifty inquiries. The mother's attorney submitted an almost equal number.

Michael told the trial justice of various episodes involving the father's stripping him of his pants and pajamas and stroking his genitalia and, apparently on other occasions, committing what might be described as first-degree sexual assault. When Michael informed the mother of what was occurring, she did not believe him. On cross-examination Michael denied that he complained about his father because he was afraid of being punished for a report card that did not measure up to parental expectations. He also denied that he was attempting to retaliate against the father after he had been punished for beating up a boy in school. The punishment included confinement to his room for a six-week period with the knob on the television set turned to the off position.

The parents, for their part, denied any wrongdoing by either party and described Michael's testimonial efforts as an attempt to gain revenge for his father's "failure to give him a motorcycle" or because of the parental discipline that had been imposed. The trial justice found Michael's testimony to be forthright, clear, and convincing. He rejected the parents' defense of fabrication, and he specifically ruled that the father's testimony was not worthy of belief.

The trial justice found that the father had sexually abused Michael and that the mother was "confused and bewildered . . . and perhaps torn between the love for the child and loyalty to her husband." Consequently the trial justice committed Michael to the custody of DCF after finding that he was an abused and neglected child. He also restrained the father from having any contact with Michael.

In their appeals both the mother and the father claim that the trial justice erred in allowing the in-camera testimony of Michael. They also claim that their due-process rights were violated by the trial justice's technique and their right to confrontation unduly restricted. The father also argues that the trial justice erred in not permitting him to call Michael as an adverse witness.

The mother claims that DCF violated Rule 13(b) of the Rules of Juvenile Proceedings because its petition did not explicitly state the facts on which DCF relied to show that Michael had been abused and neglected. She also faults the trial justice for considering the argument presented by the guardian ad litem who was not present on the first day of the hearing. The DCF sees little merit in these contentions, and neither does this court.

The sole critical issue in this familial dispute concerns the trial justice's refusal to have Michael testify in open court. All the litigants recognize that this court, in In re James A., 505 A.2d 1386 (R.I.1986), approved an approach taken by another Family Court justice who authorized a procedure somewhat similar to that used in the case at bar. Initially the trial justice submitted questions to the child with the attorneys for both parties present. After the child became upset, the trial justice cleared the chambers and continued questioning the child with only the stenographer present. Later the questions and answers were read back, and the attorneys were permitted to formulate follow-up questions. There the father argued before us that this procedure, because it did not permit confrontation, failed to accord him his constitutional right of confrontation.

After noting that there is no constitutional right to confrontation in noncriminal proceedings, this court stated that the issue was whether due process necessitated the father's being permitted to cross-examine. There this court emphasized that such a determination "must be made in light of the particular facts and circumstances of the particular case." This court found no abuse of discretion in the trial justice's decision to protect the child from a potentially "severe psychological trauma" by reason of testifying in court. Here virtually the same procedure was followed. The only significant difference is that Michael was thirteen years of age at the time of the hearing whereas the child in *In re James A.* was five years old. Naturally Michael's mother and father argue that there was no need to protect the sensitivities of a thirteen-year-old boy.

While the trial justice in *In re James A.* expressed concern for the tender years of the child, we are of the belief that a similar trauma may await an adolescent boy when testifying about sexual acts performed upon him by an adult male. However, it was argued that the emotional impact upon an adolescent boy of thirteen, after testifying about sexual acts performed upon him by an adult male, may be substantially less severe than the impact experienced by a younger child testifying about sexual abuse. This concept is highly debatable.

We believe that this issue is best resolved at the trial level where the trial justice is in a position to see and hear the witnesses. Thus such a decision is one that lies within the discretion of the trial justice after consideration of the best interests of the child as weighed against the interests of the parents and the state. The adoption of a special procedure in order to protect a child, if the trial justice deems it appropriate, is a discretionary matter. The record before us discloses no abuse of that discretion.

Proof of the correctness of the trial justice's decision can be found during the cross-examination of the father, when he was asked if he had threatened to punch Michael after Michael had told his mother what was going on at home. After replying in the negative, the father continued, "I threatened to strangle the little bugger if he took a swing at his mother or any other member of the family again. . . . I told him if he ever did it again, I would kill him and put him through the wall because I was furious." We believe that these shocking remarks provide a sufficient evidentiary basis for the trial justice's conclusion that Michael's testimony would be given in camera.

While this controversy was on appeal, counsel were asked to comment on whether the holding in Coy v. Iowa, 487 U.S. 1012, 108 S.Ct. 2798, 101 L.Ed.2d 857 (1988), is applicable to this litigation. Counsel for the parents argued that it is. However, *Coy* has no relevancy to the issues that were pending before the trial justice. *Coy* was a criminal appeal involving the defendant's constitutional right to confront his accusers, two thirteen-year-old girls. Here we are concerned with a civil proceeding in which the petition speaks in terms of the parents' neglect and abuse and seeks a change in the care, custody, and control of Michael from his parents to DCF. In such proceedings the parents have no right to face-to-face confrontation with Michael.

Accordingly the mother's and the father's appeals are denied and dismissed.

NOTES

The preceding case involved child testimony within a civil context of due process in conjunction with an action similar to that defined in CAL. FAM. CODE § 7507 (2016):

> The abuse of parental authority is the subject of judicial cognizance in a civil action brought by the child, or by the child's relative within the third degree, or by the supervisors of the county where the child resides; and when the abuse is established, the child may be freed from the dominion of the parent, and the duty of support and education enforced.

Clearly, the role of the attorneys representing the children and the adults is a crucial one in determining both facts and resolution. *See* Bruce A. Boyer, *Ethical Issues in the Representation of Parents in Child Welfare Cases*, 64 FORDHAM L. REV. 1621 (1996) (argues that zealous parent advocacy can accomplish much for the parents and the children); Marvin R. Ventrell, *Rights & Duties: An Overview of the Attorney-Child Client Relationship*, 26 LOY. U. CHI. L.J. 259 (1995) (argues that children historically have not been given equal advocacy with parents and attorneys have an obligation to promote children's interests); Robin A. Rosencrantz, *Rejecting "Hear No Evil Speak No Evil": Expanding the Attorney's Role in Child Abuse Reporting*, 8 GEO. J. LEGAL ETHICS 327 (1995) (recommends an expanded role for attorneys in child abuse reporting). *See also* Uniform Representation of Children in Abuse, Neglect and Custody Proceedings Act (2006); Barbara Ann Atwood, *Representing Children: The Ongoing Search for Clear and Workable Standards*, 19 J. AM. ACAD. MATRIMONIAL LAWYERS 183 (2005). For further discussion of the child as witness in sexual abuse cases, *see* MICHAEL T. FLANNERY & RAYMOND C. O'BRIEN, THE SEXUAL EXPLOITATION OF CHILDREN 635–644 (2016) (addressing statements made by alleged victims during interviews); Bennett L. Gershman, *Child Witnesses and Procedural Fairness*, 24 AM. J. TRIAL ADVOC. 585 (2001); Randi Mandelbaum, *Revisiting the Question of Whether Young Children in Child Protection Proceedings Should be Represented by Lawyers*, 32 LOY. U. CHI. L. J. 1 (2000); Mary Ann

Mason, *A Judicial Dilemma: Expert Witness Testimony in Child Sex Abuse Cases*, 19 J. PSYCHIATRY & L. 185 (1991); John E.B. Myers, et al., *Expert Testimony in Child Sexual Abuse Litigation*, 68 NEB. L. REV. 1 (1989); John E.B. Myers, *The Child Witness: Techniques for Direct Examination, Cross-Examination, and Impeachment*, 18 PAC. L.J. 801 (1987).

The criminal prosecution of child sexual abuse and the concomitant constitutional guarantee of the Sixth Amendment ("In all criminal prosecutions, the accused shall enjoy the right . . . to be confronted with the witnesses against him.") were the subject of Maryland v. Craig, 497 U.S. 836, 110 S.Ct. 3157, 111 L.Ed.2d 666 (1990). In this case, a six-year-old child had attended a kindergarten and prekindergarten operated by a woman. The woman was charged with child abuse, first and second degree sexual offenses, perverted sexual practices, assault and battery. During the trial the State sought to receive the testimony of the child through a one-way closed circuit television in the presence of the prosecutor and the defense counsel. Nonetheless, the judge, the defendant and the jury remained in the courtroom outside the physical presence of the child.

In her majority opinion, Justice Sandra Day O'Connor weighed the state's interest in protecting children from abuse with the Sixth Amendment's guarantee of the right to confront one's accuser. The Court held that a state's interest in the well-being of child abuse victims may be sufficiently important, in some cases, to outweigh a defendant's right to face his or her accusers in court. Justice O'Connor continued, that the general rules of law that grant protections such as those offered by the Sixth Amendment, "however beneficent in their operation and valuable to the accused, must occasionally give way to considerations of public policy and the necessity of the case." The constitutionally protected interest in confrontation may in fact "disserve" the Confrontation Clause's truth-seeking goal by causing significant emotional distress in the child and inhibiting the child's testimony.

Before the child may be sequestered and the accused denied confrontation with his or her witness accuser, the child must be very susceptible to the trauma of testifying and the state must employ special procedures. In his dissent, Justice Scalia argued the procedure is not permitted by the plain wording of the Constitution, and impliedly, because children are more prone to fantasy, face-to-face confrontation is better to arrive at truth. For further discussion, *see* Hon. Barbara Gilleran-Johnson and Timothy R. Evans, *The Criminal Courtroom: Is It Childproof?*, 26 LOY. U. CHI. L.J. 681 (1995); Robert P. Mosteller, *Remaking Confrontation Clause and Hearsay Doctrine Under the Challenge of Child Sexual Abuse Prosecutions*, 1993 U. ILL. L. REV. 691.

After *Maryland v. Craig*, the United States Congress enacted the Child Victims' and Witnesses' Rights Act, 18 U.S.C.A. § 3509, allowing for a child's testimony to be given beyond the sight of the defendant if any of the following occur: (1) The child is unable to testify because of fear; (2) The child is likely to suffer emotional trauma from testifying; (3) The child suffers from a mental or other infirmity; (4) Conduct of the defendant or defense counsel causes the child to be unable to testify. The federal statute has been found constitutional. *See* United States v. Garcia, 7 F.3d 885 (9th Cir.1993), and United States v. Carrier, 9 F.3d 867 (10th Cir.1993).

For an important discussion of the problem of evaluating the broader danger to other siblings of a victimized child, *see* Robin Fretwell Wilson, *The Cradle of Abuse: Evaluating the Danger Posed by a Sexually Predatory Parent to the Victim's Siblings*, 51 EMORY L. J. 241 (2002).

DeShaney v. Winnebago County DSS

Supreme Court of the United States, 1989
489 U.S. 189

■ REHNQUIST, CHIEF JUSTICE delivered the opinion of the Court.

. . .

The facts of this case are undeniably tragic. Petitioner Joshua DeShaney was born in 1979. In 1980, a Wyoming court granted his parents a divorce and awarded custody of Joshua to his father, Randy DeShaney. The father shortly thereafter moved to Neenah, a city located in Winnebago County, Wisconsin, taking the infant Joshua with him. There he entered into a second marriage, which also ended in divorce.

The Winnebago County authorities first learned that Joshua DeShaney might be a victim of child abuse in January 1982, when his father's second wife complained to the police, at the time of their divorce, that he had previously "hit the boy causing marks and [was] a prime case for child abuse." The Winnebago County Department of Social Services (DSS) interviewed the father, but he denied the accusations, and DSS did not pursue them further. In January 1983, Joshua was admitted to a local hospital with multiple bruises and abrasions. The examining physician suspected child abuse and notified DSS, which immediately obtained an order from a Wisconsin juvenile court placing Joshua in the temporary custody of the hospital. Three days later, the county convened an ad hoc "Child Protection Team"Cconsisting of a pediatrician, a psychologist, a police detective, the county's lawyer, several DSS caseworkers, and various hospital personnelCto consider Joshua's situation. At this meeting, the Team decided that there was insufficient evidence of child abuse to retain Joshua in the custody of the court. The Team did, however, decide to recommend several measures to protect Joshua, including enrolling him in a preschool program, providing his father with certain counselling services, and encouraging his father's girlfriend to move out of the home. Randy DeShaney entered into a voluntary agreement with DSS in which he promised to cooperate with them in accomplishing these goals.

Based on the recommendation of the Child Protection Team, the juvenile court dismissed the child protection case and returned Joshua to the custody of his father. A month later, emergency room personnel called the DSS caseworker handling Joshua's case to report that he had once again been treated for suspicious injuries. The caseworker concluded that there was no basis for action. For the next six months, the caseworker made monthly visits to the DeShaney home, during which she observed a number of suspicious injuries on Joshua's head; she also noticed that he had not been enrolled in school and that the girlfriend had not moved out. The caseworker dutifully recorded these incidents in her files, along with her continuing suspicions that someone in the DeShaney household was physically abusing Joshua, but she did nothing more. In November 1983, the emergency room notified DSS that Joshua had been treated once again for injuries that they believed to be caused by child abuse. On the caseworker's next two visits to the DeShaney home, she was told that Joshua was too ill to see her. Still DSS took no action.

In March 1984, Randy DeShaney beat 4-year-old Joshua so severely that he fell into a life-threatening coma. Emergency brain surgery revealed a series of hemorrhages caused by traumatic injuries to the head inflicted over a long period of time. Joshua did not die, but he suffered brain damage so severe that he is expected to spend the rest of his life confined to an institution for the profoundly retarded. Randy DeShaney was subsequently tried and convicted of child abuse.

Joshua and his mother brought this action under 42 U.S.C. § 1983 in the United States District Court for the Eastern District of Wisconsin against respondents Winnebago County, its Department of Social Services, and various individual employees of the Department. The complaint alleged that respondents had deprived Joshua of his liberty without due process of law, in violation of his rights under the Fourteenth Amendment, by failing to intervene to protect him against a risk of violence at his father's hands of which they knew or should have known. The District Court granted summary judgment for respondents.

The Court of Appeals for the Seventh Circuit affirmed, 812 F.2d 298 (1987), holding that petitioners had not made out an actionable § 1983 claim for two alternative reasons. First, the court held that the Due Process Clause of the Fourteenth Amendment does not require a state or local governmental entity to protect its citizens from "private violence, or other mishaps not attributable to the conduct of its employees." Id., at 301. In so holding, the court specifically rejected the position endorsed by a divided panel of the Third Circuit in Estate of Bailey by Oare v. County of York, 768 F.2d 503, 510–511 (C.A.3 1985), and by dicta in Jensen v. Conrad, 747 F.2d 185, 190–194 (C.A.4 1984), cert. denied, 470 U.S. 1052, 105 S.Ct. 1754, 84 L.Ed.2d 818 (1985), that once the State learns that a particular child is in danger of abuse from third parties and actually undertakes to protect him from that danger, a "special relationship" arises between it and the child which imposes an affirmative constitutional duty to provide adequate protection. Second, the court held, in reliance on our decision in Martinez v. California, 444 U.S. 277, 285, 100 S.Ct. 553, 559, 62 L.Ed.2d 481 (1980), that the causal connection between respondents' conduct and Joshua's injuries was too attenuated to establish a deprivation of constitutional rights actionable under § 1983. The court therefore found it unnecessary to reach the question whether respondents' conduct evinced the "state of mind" necessary to make out a due process claim after Daniels v. Williams, 474 U.S. 327, 106 S.Ct. 662, 88 L.Ed.2d 662 (1986), and Davidson v. Cannon, 474 U.S. 344, 106 S.Ct. 668, 88 L.Ed.2d 677 (1986).

Because of the inconsistent approaches taken by the lower courts in determining when, if ever, the failure of a state or local governmental entity or its agents to provide an individual with adequate protective services constitutes a violation of the individual's due process rights, and the importance of the issue to the administration of state and local governments, we granted certiorari. We now affirm.

The Due Process Clause of the Fourteenth Amendment provides that "[no State shall . . . deprive any person of life, liberty, or property, without due process of law." Petitioners contend that the State deprived Joshua of his liberty interest in "freedom] from . . . unjustified intrusions on personal security," by failing to provide him with adequate protection against his father's violence. The claim is one invoking the substantive rather than procedural component of the Due Process Clause; petitioners do not claim that the State denied Joshua protection without according him appropriate procedural safeguards, but that it was categorically obligated to protect him in these circumstances.

But nothing in the language of the Due Process Clause itself requires the State to protect the life, liberty, and property of its citizens against invasion by private actors. The Clause is phrased as a limitation on the State's power to act, not as a guarantee of certain minimal levels of safety and security. It forbids the State itself to deprive individuals of life, liberty, or property without "due process of law," but its language cannot fairly be extended to impose an affirmative obligation on the State to ensure that those interests do not come to harm through other means. Nor does history support such an expansive reading of the constitutional text. Like its counterpart in the Fifth Amendment, the Due Process Clause of the Fourteenth Amendment was intended to prevent government "from abusing [its] power, or employing it as an instrument of oppression," Davidson v. Cannon, supra, at 348, 106 S.Ct., at 670; . . . Its purpose was to protect the people from the State, not to ensure that the State protected them from each other. The Framers were content to leave the extent of governmental obligation in the latter area to the democratic political processes.

Consistent with these principles, our cases have recognized that the Due Process Clauses generally confer no affirmative right to governmental aid, even where such aid may be necessary to secure life, liberty, or property interests of which the government itself may not deprive the individual. . . .

Petitioners contend, however, that even if the Due Process Clause imposes no affirmative obligation on the State to provide the general public with adequate protective services, such a duty may arise out of certain "special relationships" created or assumed by the State with respect to particular individuals. Petitioners argue that such a "special relationship" existed here because the State knew that Joshua faced a special danger of abuse at his father's hands, and specifically proclaimed, by word and by deed, its intention to protect him against that danger. Having actually undertaken to protect Joshua from this dangerCwhich petitioners concede the State played no part in creatingCthe State acquired an affirmative "duty," enforceable through the Due Process Clause, to do so in a reasonably competent fashion. Its failure to discharge that duty, so the argument goes, was an abuse of governmental power that so "shocks the conscience," Rochin v. California, 342 U.S. 165, 172, 72 S.Ct. 205, 209, 96 L.Ed. 183 (1952), as to constitute a substantive due process violation.

We reject this argument. It is true that in certain limited circumstances the Constitution imposes upon the State affirmative duties of care and protection with respect to particular individuals. In Estelle v. Gamble, 429 U.S. 97, 97 S.Ct. 285, 50 L.Ed.2d 251 (1976), we recognized that the Eighth Amendment's prohibition against cruel and unusual punishment, made applicable to the States through the Fourteenth Amendment's Due Process Clause, Robinson v. California, 370 U.S. 660, 82 S.Ct. 1417, 8 L.Ed.2d 758 (1962), requires the State to provide adequate medical care to incarcerated prisoners. 429 U.S., at 103–104, 97 S.Ct., at 290–291.[5] We reasoned that because the prisoner is unable " 'by reason of the deprivation of his liberty [to] care for himself,' 'it is only' 'just' " that the State be required to care for him. Ibid., quoting Spicer v. Williamson, 191 N.C. 487, 490, 132 SE 291, 293 (1926).

In Youngberg v. Romeo, 457 U.S. 307, 102 S.Ct. 2452, 73 L.Ed.2d 28 (1982), we extended this analysis beyond the Eighth Amendment setting, holding that the substantive component of the Fourteenth Amendment's Due Process Clause requires the State to provide involuntarily committed mental patients with such services as are necessary to ensure their "reasonable safety" from themselves and others. As we explained, "[i]f it is cruel and unusual punishment to hold convicted criminals in unsafe conditions, it must be unconstitutional [under the Due Process Clause] to confine the involuntarily committed—who may not be punished at all—in unsafe conditions."

[5] To make out an Eighth Amendment claim based on the failure to provide adequate medical care, a prisoner must show that the state defendants exhibited "deliberate indifference" to his "serious" medical needs; the mere negligent or inadvertent failure to provide adequate care is not enough. Estelle v. Gamble, 429 U.S., at 105–106, 97 S.Ct., at 291–292. In Whitley v. Albers, 475 U.S. 312, 106 S.Ct. 1078, 89 L.Ed.2d 251 (1986), we suggested that a similar state of mind is required to make out a substantive due process claim in the prison setting. Id., at 326–327, 106 S.Ct., at 1088.

But these cases afford petitioners no help. Taken together, they stand only for the proposition that when the State takes a person into its custody and holds him there against his will, the Constitution imposes upon it a corresponding duty to assume some responsibility for his safety and general well-being. . . . The rationale for this principle is simple enough: when the State by the affirmative exercise of its power so restrains an individual's liberty that it renders him unable to care for himself, and at the same time fails to provide for his basic human needs—e.g., food, clothing, shelter, medical care, and reasonable safety—it transgresses the substantive limits on state action set by the Eighth Amendment and the Due Process Clause. The affirmative duty to protect arises not from the State's knowledge of the individual's predicament or from its expressions of intent to help him, but from the limitation which it has imposed on his freedom to act on his own behalf. . . . In the substantive due process analysis, it is the State's affirmative act of restraining the individual's freedom to act on his own behalf—through incarceration, institutionalization, or other similar restraint of personal liberty—which is the "deprivation of liberty" triggering the protections of the Due Process Clause, not its failure to act to protect his liberty interests against harms inflicted by other means.

The . . . analysis simply has no applicability in the present case. Petitioners concede that the harms Joshua suffered did not occur while he was in the State's custody, but while he was in the custody of his natural father, who was in no sense a state actor. While the State may have been aware of the dangers that Joshua faced in the free world, it played no part in their creation, nor did it do anything to render him any more vulnerable to them. That the State once took temporary custody of Joshua does not alter the analysis, for when it returned him to his father's custody, it placed him in no worse position than that in which he would have been had it not acted at all; the State does not become the permanent guarantor of an individual's safety by having once offered him shelter. Under these circumstances, the State had no constitutional duty to protect Joshua.

It may well be that, by voluntarily undertaking to protect Joshua against a danger it concededly played no part in creating, the State acquired a duty under state tort law to provide him with adequate protection against that danger. . . . But the claim here is based on the Due Process Clause of the Fourteenth Amendment, which, as we have said many times, does not transform every tort committed by a state actor into a constitutional violation. A State may, through its courts and legislatures, impose such affirmative duties of care and protection upon its agents as it wishes. But not "all common-law duties owed by government actors were . . . constitutionalized by the Fourteenth Amendment." Daniels v. Williams, supra, 474 U.S. at 335, 106 S.Ct., at 678. Because, as explained above, the State had no constitutional duty to protect Joshua against his father's violence, its failure to do so—though calamitous in hindsight—simply does not constitute a violation of the Due Process Clause.[10]

Judges and lawyers, like other humans, are moved by natural sympathy in a case like this to find a way for Joshua and his mother to receive adequate compensation for the grievous harm inflicted upon them. But before yielding to that impulse, it is well to remember once again that the harm was inflicted not by the State of Wisconsin, but by Joshua's father. The most that can be said of the state functionaries in this case is that they stood by and did nothing when suspicious circumstances dictated a more active role for them. In defense of them it must also be said that had they moved too soon to take custody of the son away from the father, they would likely have been met with charges of improperly intruding into the parent-child relationship, charges based on the same Due Process Clause that forms the basis for the present charge of failure to provide adequate protection.

The people of Wisconsin may well prefer a system of liability which would place upon the State and its officials the responsibility for failure to act in situations such as the present one. They may create such a system, if they do not have it already, by changing the tort law of the State in accordance with the regular law-making process. But they should not have it thrust upon them by this Court's expansion of the Due Process Clause of the Fourteenth Amendment.

■ JUSTICE BRENNAN, with whom JUSTICE MARSHALL and JUSTICE BLACKMUN join, dissenting.

"The most that can be said of the state functionaries in this case," the Court today concludes, "is that they stood by and did nothing when suspicious circumstances dictated a more active role for them." Because I believe that this description of respondents' conduct tells only part of the story and that, accordingly, the Constitution itself "dictated a more active role" for respondents in the circumstances presented here, I cannot agree that respondents had no constitutional duty to help Joshua DeShaney.

It may well be, as the Court decides, that the Due Process Clause as construed by our prior case creates no general right to basic governmental services. That, however, is not the question presented here; indeed, that question was not raised in the complaint, urged on appeal, presented in the petition for certiorari, or addressed in the briefs on the merits. No one, in short, has asked the Court to proclaim that, as

---

[10] Because we conclude that the Due Process Clause did not require the State to protect Joshua from his father, we need not address respondents' alternative argument that the individual state actors lacked the requisite "state of mind" to make out a due process violation. See Daniels v. Williams, 474 U.S., at 334, n. 3, 106 S.Ct., at 677, n. 3. Similarly, we have no occasion to consider whether the individual respondents might be entitled to a qualified immunity defense, see Anderson v. Creighton, 483 U.S. 635, 107 S.Ct. 3034, 97 L.Ed.2d 523 (1987), or whether the allegations in the complaint are sufficient to support a § 1983 claim against the county and its Department of Social Services under Monell v. New York City Dept. of Social Services, 436 U.S. 658, 98 S.Ct. 2018, 56 L.Ed.2d 611 (1978), and its progeny.

a general matter, the Constitution safeguards positive as well as negative liberties.

This is more than a quibble over dicta; it is a point about perspective, having substantive ramifications. In a constitutional setting that distinguishes sharply between action and inaction, one's characterization of the misconduct alleged under § 1983 may effectively decide the case. Thus, by leading off with a discussion (and rejection) of the idea that the Constitution imposes on the States an affirmative duty to take basic care of their citizens, the Court foreshadows—perhaps even preordains—its conclusion that no duty existed even on the specific facts before us. This initial discussion establishes the baseline from which the Court assesses the DeShaneys' claim that, when a State has—"by word and by deed,"—announced an intention to protect a certain class of citizens and has before it facts that would trigger that protection under the applicable state law, the Constitution imposes upon the State an affirmative duty of protection.

The Court's baseline is the absence of positive rights in the Constitution and a concomitant suspicion of any claim that seems to depend on such rights. From this perspective, the DeShaneys' claim is first and foremost about inaction (the failure, here, of respondents to take steps to protect Joshua), and only tangentially about action (the establishment of a state program specifically designed to help children like Joshua). And from this perspective, holding these Wisconsin officials liable—where the only difference between this case and one involving a general claim to protective services is Wisconsin's establishment and operation of a program to protect children—would seem to punish an effort that we should seek to promote.

I would begin from the opposite direction. I would focus first on the action that Wisconsin *has* taken with respect to Joshua and children like him, rather than on the actions that the State failed to take. Such a method is not new to this Court. Both Estelle v. Gamble, 429 U.S. 97, 97 S.Ct. 285, 50 L.Ed.2d 251 (1976), and Youngberg v. Romeo, 457 U.S. 307, 102 S.Ct. 2452, 73 L.Ed.2d 28 (1982), began by emphasizing that the States had confined J.W. Gamble to prison and Nicholas Romeo to a psychiatric hospital. This initial action rendered these people helpless to help themselves or to seek help from persons unconnected to the government. See Estelle, supra, 429 U.S. at 104, 97 S.Ct., at 291 ("[I]t is but just that the public be required to care for the prisoner, who cannot by reason of the deprivation of his liberty, care for himself"); Youngberg, supra, 457 U.S. at 317, 102 S.Ct., at 2458 ("When a person is institutionalized—and wholly dependent on the State—it is conceded by petitioners that a duty to provide certain services and care does exist"). Cases from the lower courts also recognize that a State's actions can be decisive in assessing the constitutional significance of subsequent inaction. For these purposes, moreover, actual physical restraint is not the only State action that has been considered relevant. See, e.g., White

v. Rochford, 592 F.2d 381 (C.A.7 1979) (police officers violated due process when, after arresting the guardian of three young children, they abandoned the children on a busy stretch of highway at night). . . .

Wisconsin has established a child-welfare system specifically designed to help children like Joshua. Wisconsin law places upon the local departments of social services such as respondent (DSS or Department) a duty to investigate reported instances of child abuse. See Wis.Stat.Ann. § 48.981(3) (1987 and Supp.1988–1989). While other governmental bodies and private persons are largely responsible for the reporting of possible cases of child abuse, see § 48.981(2), Wisconsin law channels all such reports to the local departments of social services for evaluation and, if necessary, further action. § 48.981(3). Even when it is the sheriff's office or police department that receives a report of suspected child abuse, that report is referred to local social services departments for action, see § 48.981(3)(a); the only exception to this occurs when the reporter fears for the child's immediate safety. § 48.981(3)(b). In this way, Wisconsin law invites—indeed, directs—citizens and other governmental entities to depend on local departments of social services such as respondent to protect children from abuse.

The specific facts before us bear out this view of Wisconsin's system of protecting children. Each time someone voiced a suspicion that Joshua was being abused, that information was relayed to the Department for investigation and possible action. When Randy DeShaney's second wife told the police that he had " 'hit the boy causing marks and [was] a prime case for child abuse,' " the police referred her complaint to DSS. When, on three separate occasions, emergency room personnel noticed suspicious injuries on Joshua's body, they went to DSS with this information. When neighbors informed the police that they had seen or heard Joshua's father or his father's lover beating or otherwise abusing Joshua, the police brought these reports to the attention of DSS. And when respondent Kemmeter, through these reports and through her own observations in the course of nearly 20 visits to the DeShaney home, compiled growing evidence that Joshua was being abused, that information stayed within the Department—chronicled by the social worker in detail that seems almost eerie in light of her failure to act upon it. (As to the extent of the social worker's involvement in and knowledge of Joshua's predicament, her reaction to the news of Joshua's last and most devastating injuries is illuminating: "I just knew the phone would ring some day and Joshua would be dead." 812 F.2d 298, 300 (C.A.7 1987).)

Even more telling than these examples is the Department's control over the decision whether to take steps to protect a particular child from suspected abuse. While many different people contributed information and advice to this decision, it was up to the people at DSS to make the ultimate decision (subject to the approval of the local government's Corporation Counsel) whether to disturb the family's current arrangements. When Joshua first appeared at a local hospital with injuries signaling physical abuse, for example, it was DSS that made the decision to take him into temporary custody for the purpose of studying his situation—and it was DSS, acting in conjunction with the Corporation Counsel, that returned him to his father. Unfortunately for Joshua DeShaney, the buck effectively stopped with the Department.

In these circumstances, a private citizen, or even a person working in a government agency other than DSS, would doubtless feel that her job was done as soon as she had reported her suspicions of child abuse to DSS. Through its child-welfare program, in other words, the State of Wisconsin has relieved ordinary citizens and governmental bodies other than the Department of any sense of obligation to do anything more than report their suspicions of child abuse to DSS. If DSS ignores or dismisses these suspicions, no one will step in to fill the gap. Wisconsin's child-protection program thus effectively confined Joshua DeShaney within the walls of Randy DeShaney's violent home until such time as DSS took action to remove him. Conceivably, then, children like Joshua are made worse off by the existence of this program when the persons and entities charged with carrying it out fail to do their jobs.

It simply belies reality, therefore, to contend that the State "stood by and did nothing" with respect to Joshua. Through its child-protection program, the State actively intervened in Joshua's life and, by virtue of this intervention, acquired ever more certain knowledge that Joshua was in grave danger. These circumstances, in my view, plant this case solidly within the tradition of cases like *Youngberg* and *Estelle.*

It will be meager comfort to Joshua and his mother to know that, if the State had "selectively den[ied] its protective services" to them because they were "disfavored minorities," ante, at 1004, n. 3, their § 1983 suit might have stood on sturdier ground. Because of the posture of this case, we do not know why respondents did not take steps to protect Joshua; the Court, however, tells us that their reason is irrelevant so long as their inaction was not the product of invidious discrimination. Presumably, then, if respondents decided not to help Joshua because his name began with a "j," or because he was born in the spring, or because they did not care enough about him even to formulate an intent to discriminate against him based on an arbitrary reason, respondents would not be liable to the DeShaneys because they were not the ones who dealt the blows that destroyed Joshua's life.

I do not suggest that such irrationality was at work in this case; I emphasize only that we do not know whether or not it was. I would allow Joshua and his mother the opportunity to show that respondents' failure to help him arose, not out of the sound exercise of professional judgment that we recognized in *Youngberg* as sufficient to preclude liability, see 457 U.S., at 322–323, 102 S.Ct., at 2461–2462, but from the kind of arbitrariness that we have in the past condemned. . . .

Youngberg's deference to a decisionmaker's professional judgment ensures that once a caseworker has decided, on the basis of her professional training and experience, that one course of protection is preferable for a given child, or even that no special protection is required, she will not be found liable for the harm that follows. (In this way, *Youngberg's* vision of substantive due process serves a purpose similar to that served by adherence to procedural norms, namely, requiring that a State actor stop and think before she acts in a way that may lead to a loss of liberty.) Moreover, that the Due Process Clause is not violated by merely negligent conduct, means that a social worker who simply makes a mistake of judgment under what are admittedly complex and difficult conditions will not find herself liable in damages under § 1983.

As the Court today reminds us, "the Due Process Clause of the Fourteenth Amendment was intended to prevent government 'from abusing [its] power, or employing it as an instrument of oppression.' " My disagreement with the Court arises from its failure to see that inaction can be every bit as abusive of power as action, that oppression can result when a State undertakes a vital duty and then ignores it. Today's opinion construes the Due Process Clause to permit a State to displace private sources of protection and then, at the critical moment, to shrug its shoulders and turn away from the harm that it has promised to try to prevent. Because I cannot agree that our Constitution is indifferent to such indifference, I respectfully dissent.

■ JUSTICE BLACKMUN, dissenting.

Today, the Court purports to be the dispassionate oracle of the law, unmoved by "natural sympathy." But, in this pretense, the Court itself retreats into a sterile formalism which prevents it from recognizing either the facts of the case before it or the legal norms that should apply to those facts. As Justice Brennan demonstrates, the facts here involve not mere passivity, but active state intervention in the life of Joshua DeShaney—intervention that triggered a fundamental duty to aid the boy once the State learned of the severe danger to which he was exposed.

The Court fails to recognize this duty because it attempts to draw a sharp and rigid line between action and inaction. But such formalistic reasoning has no place in the interpretation of the broad and stirring clauses of the Fourteenth Amendment. Indeed, I submit that these clauses were designed, at least in part, to undo the formalistic legal reasoning that infected antebellum jurisprudence, which the late Professor Robert Cover analyzed so effectively in his significant work entitled *Justice Accused* (1975).

Like the antebellum judges who denied relief to fugitive slaves, the Court today claims that its decision, however harsh, is compelled by existing legal doctrine. On the contrary, the question presented by this case is an open one, and our Fourteenth Amendment precedents may be read more broadly or narrowly depending upon how one chooses to read them. Faced with the choice, I would adopt a "sympathetic" reading, one which comports with dictates of fundamental justice and recognizes that compassion need not be exiled from the province of judging. . . .

Poor Joshua! Victim of repeated attacks by an irresponsible, bullying, cowardly, and intemperate father, and abandoned by respondents who placed him in a dangerous predicament and who knew or learned what was going on, and yet did essentially nothing except, as the Court revealingly observes, ante, at 1001, "dutifully recorded these incidents in [their] files." It is a sad commentary upon American life, and constitutional principles—so full of late of patriotic fervor and proud proclamations about "liberty and justice for all," that this child, Joshua DeShaney, now is assigned to live out the remainder of his life profoundly retarded. Joshua and his mother, as petitioners here, deserve—but now are denied by this Court—the opportunity to have the facts of their case considered in the light of the constitutional protection that 42 U.S.C. § 1983 is meant to provide.

E. MEDICAL DECISION MAKING FOR AND BY CHILDREN

1. SPIRITUAL TREATMENT ACCOMMODATION

Hermanson v. State

Supreme Court of Florida, 1992
604 So.2d 775

■ OVERTON, JUSTICE.

. . .

In this tragic case, Amy Hermanson, the daughter of William and Christine Hermanson, died from untreated juvenile diabetes. The Hermansons, members of the First Church of Christ, Scientist, were charged and convicted of child abuse resulting in third-degree murder for failing to provide Amy with conventional medical treatment. The Hermansons received four-year suspended prison sentences on their murder convictions and were ordered to serve fifteen years' probation. The district court, finding that the spiritual treatment accommodation provision of section 415.503(7)(f), Florida Statutes (1985), did not prevent their prosecution and conviction, affirmed the trial court's sentence and certified the above question. In summary, we find that sections 827.04(1) and 415.503(7)(f), when considered together, are ambiguous and result in a denial of due process because the statutes in question fail to give parents notice of the point at which their reliance on spiritual treatment loses statutory approval and becomes culpably negligent. We further find that a person of ordinary intelligence cannot be expected to understand the extent to which reliance on spiritual healing is permitted and the point at which this reliance constitutes a criminal offense under the subject statutes. The statutes have created a trap that the legislature should address. Accordingly, we quash the decision of the district court.

The statutory provisions are critical to the legal and constitutional issues presented in this case. Florida's child abuse statute, section 827.04(1)–(2), Florida Statutes (1985), provides:

> (1) Whoever, willfully or by culpable negligence, deprives a child of, or allows a child to be deprived of, necessary food, clothing, shelter, or medical treatment, or who, knowingly or by culpable negligence, permits physical or mental injury to the child, and in so doing causes great bodily harm, permanent disability, or permanent disfigurement to such child, shall be guilty of a felony of the third degree. . . .
>
> (2) Whoever, willfully or by culpable negligence, deprives a child of, or allows a child to be deprived of, necessary food, clothing, shelter, or medical treatment, or who, knowingly or by culpable negligence, permits physical or mental injury to the child, shall be guilty of a misdemeanor of the first degree. . . .

The third-degree murder provision of section 782.04(4), Florida Statutes (1985), provides that the killing of a human being while engaged in the commission of child abuse constitutes murder in the third degree and is a felony of the second degree. Section 415.503 provides, in part, as follows:

> (1) "Abused or neglected child" means a child whose physical or mental health or welfare is harmed, or threatened with harm, by the acts or omissions of the parent or other person responsible for the child's welfare. . . .
>
> (7) "Harm" to a child's health or welfare can occur when the parent or other person responsible for the child's welfare: . . .
>
> (f) Fails to supply the child with adequate food, clothing, shelter, *or health care,* although financially able to do so or although offered financial or other means to do so; *however, a parent or other person responsible for the child's welfare legitimately practicing his religious beliefs, who by reason thereof does not provide specified medical treatment for a child, may not be considered abusive or neglectful for that reason alone,* but such an exception does not:
>
> 1. Eliminate the requirement that such a case be reported to the department;
>
> 2. Prevent the department from investigating such a case; or
>
> 3. Preclude a court from ordering, when the health of the child requires it, the provision of medical services by a physician, as defined herein, or treatment by a duly accredited practitioner who relies solely on spiritual means for healing in accordance

> with the tenets and practices of a well-recognized church or religious organization.

(Emphasis added)[1]

The religious accommodation provision in section 415.503(7)(f) was initially passed by the legislature in 1975 as section 827.07(2), Florida Statutes (1975), the same chapter that contained the child abuse provision under which the Hermansons were prosecuted. The senate staff analysis of the religious accommodation provision stated that these provisions were "a defense for parents who decline medical treatment for legitimate religious reasons." Staff of Fla. S. Comm. Crim. Just., SB 1186 (1975) Staff Analysis 1 (final May 26, 1975) (available at Fla. Dep't of State, Div. of Archives, Tallahassee, Fla.). In 1983, the Division of Statutory Revision moved the above religious accommodation provision from chapter 827 to chapter 415. . . .

The district court summarized the facts presented at trial as follows:

> In the month or so before her death Amy was having a marked and dramatic weight loss, that she was almost skeletal in her thinness and this was a big change in her appearance. There were great dark circles under her eyes that had never been there before. Her behavior was very different from the usual; she was lethargic and complaining whereas previously she had been bubbly, vivacious, and outgoing. She was seen lying down on the floor to sleep during the day when accompanying her mother to visit music students and lying down on the floor after school at her mother's fine arts academy. She often complained of not feeling well, that her stomach hurt and that she wasn't sleeping well. She was too tired during the day to participate in gym class at school. There was a bluish tint to her skin. Her breath smelled funny, one observer called it a "fruity" odor.
>
> The pathologist who performed the autopsy testified to Amy's skeletal appearance, that her vertebrae and shoulder blades were prominent and her abdomen distended as if she were undernourished. Her eyes were quite sunken, due to the dehydration, although her parents had told the pathologist that on the day before her death she was drinking a lot of fluids but urinating frequently too. They also told him that they had noticed changes in Amy starting about a month previously. Amy had complained of constipation during the last week of her life but at no time seemed feverish although there was intermittent vomiting.
>
> The pathologist opined that the illness was chronic, not acute. According to her parents' talk with the pathologist, Amy seemed incoherent on the evening before her death although the next

---

[1] [The court lists statutes in 27 other states that provide some form of religious exemption.]

> morning she seemed better. The pathologist also testified that vomiting and dehydration are compatible with flu-like symptoms but these, added to a four-week-long history of weight loss with the more severe conditions reported, would not be indicative of flu. Finally, the jury was shown photographs of Amy taken shortly after she died before her body was removed from the home by the paramedics as well as some taken before the autopsy was performed.

Id. at 336–37.

The evidence and the stipulated facts established that the Hermansons treated Amy in accordance with their Christian Science beliefs. On the day of Amy's death, a Christian Science nurse had been summoned to the home to care for her. The nurse testified that Amy was unresponsive and that, when she began vomiting and her condition worsened, she recommended that an ambulance should be called. The Christian Science practitioner who was present advised the nurse that the church headquarters in Boston should be contacted before an ambulance was called. After placing a call to Boston, an ambulance was summoned.

In its argument to the jury, the State asserted that the Hermansons' reliance on Christian Science healing practices under these circumstances constituted culpable negligence. The basis of its argument was that the Hermansons were not legitimately practicing their religious beliefs. Drawing on the evidence that the Christian Science nurse had called an ambulance when Amy began vomiting, the State suggested that the Christian Science Church recognizes conventional medical care and, therefore, the Hermansons had not been legitimately practicing their religious beliefs when they failed to seek medical care before Amy's death. No specific evidence was introduced by either side on the question of when, if at all, the Christian Science faith allows its members to call for medical attention. The Hermansons, on the other hand, argued to the jury that they should not be convicted of a criminal offense because they were "legitimately" practicing their faith in accordance with the accommodation provision of section 415.503(7)(f).

The jury, after one and one-half hours of deliberation, sought the answer to three questions: "(1) As a Christian Scientist do they have a choice to go to a medical doctor if they want to? (2) Or if not, can they call a doctor at a certain point? (3) Do they need permission first?" In response, the court advised the jurors that they must look to the evidence presented during the trial to find the answers. Counsel for both parties had previously agreed to this response by the trial court. The jury found the Hermansons guilty of felony child abuse and third-degree murder, and they were sentenced to four-year suspended prison sentences, with fifteen years' probation, on condition that they provide regular medical examinations and treatment for their surviving children.

On appeal, the district court affirmed, finding that the statutory accommodation section in 415.503(7)(f) applied only to matters contained in chapter 415 and that that provision did not provide any protection from criminal penalties for actual child abuse or neglect in chapters 782 and 827, Florida Statutes (1985). The district court rejected the Hermansons' claim that the evidence did not establish that they had acted willfully or with culpable negligence under the circumstances of this case. The district court agreed with the trial court that, when they returned from Indiana thirty-six hours before Amy's death and had seen that her condition had worsened, the Hermansons were placed on notice "that their attempts at spiritual treatment were unavailing and [that] it was time to call in medical help." The district court concluded that those facts justified the issue's being submitted to the jury and the verdict finding the Hermansons guilty of culpable negligence. The district court also rejected the Hermansons' claim of a due process violation for lack of notice of when their conduct became criminal. In rejecting this contention, the district court relied on the decision of the California Supreme Court in Walker v. Superior Court, 47 Cal.3d 112, 253 Cal.Rptr. 1, 21, 763 P.2d 852, 872 (1988), cert. denied, 491 U.S. 905 (1989), in which that court stated:

> "[T]he law is full of instances where a man's fate depends on his estimating rightly, that is, as the jury subsequently estimates it, some matter of degree . . . 'An act causing death may be murder, manslaughter, or misadventure according to the degree of danger attending it' by common experience in the circumstances known to the actor." (Nash v. United States (1913) 229 U.S. 373, 377; see also Coates v. City of Cincinnati, (1971) 402 U.S. 611, 614.) The "matter of degree" that persons relying on prayer treatment must estimate rightly is the point at which their course of conduct becomes criminally negligent. In terms of notice, due process requires no more.

Hermanson, 570 So.2d at 332.

In this appeal, the Hermansons challenge the district court decision on the following four issues: (1) that the Florida Statutes under which they were convicted did not give them fair warning of the consequences of practicing their religious belief and their conviction was, therefore, a denial of due process; (2) that the Hermansons were entitled to a judgment of acquittal because the evidence presented at trial failed to establish culpable negligence beyond a reasonable doubt; (3) that permitting a jury to decide the reasonableness of the Hermansons in following their religious beliefs was a violation of the First Amendment freedom of religion; and (4) that the trial court erred in not granting a mistrial when the prosecutor stated in closing argument that Christian Science recognizes conventional medical treatment, which was not supported by any evidence in the record. We choose to discuss only the first issue because we find that it is dispositive.

In asserting that they were denied due process, the Hermansons claim that the statutes failed to give them sufficient notice of when their treatment of their child in accordance with their religious beliefs became criminal. They argue that their position is supported by (1) the fact that it took the district court of appeal nine pages to explain how it arrived at its conclusion that the exemption for spiritual treatment was only part of the civil child abuse statute, not the criminal child abuse statute and (2) the trial court's construing the statute differently, holding that they were protected by the provision of section 415.503(7)(f) to the extent of making it a jury issue.

The United States Supreme Court, in United States v. Cardiff, 344 U.S. 174 (1952), stated that confusion in lower courts is evidence of vagueness which violates due process. Furthermore, in Linville v. State, 359 So.2d 450, 453–54 (Fla.1978), we held that due process is lacking where "a man of common intelligence cannot be expected to discern what activity the statute is seeking to proscribe." In State v. McKown, 461 N.W.2d 720 (Minn.Ct.App.1990), aff'd, 475 N.W.2d 63 (Minn.1991), cert. denied, ___ U.S. ___, 112 S.Ct. 882, 116 L.Ed.2d 786 (1992), a child's parents utilized a Christian Science practitioner and a Christian Science nurse, but did not seek conventional medical treatment. The McKowns were indicted for second-degree manslaughter when their child died of untreated diabetes. The issue in that case was whether the child abuse statute, which contained an exception for spiritual treatment similar to the Florida statute, was to be construed in conjunction with a manslaughter statute that was based on culpable negligence resulting in death. In finding a violation of due process, the Minnesota court concluded that there was a "lack of clarity in the relationship between the two statutes." Id. at 723.

> [T]he state would have us conclude that the choice of spiritual treatment, which has been put on legal footing equal to that of orthodox medical care by the child neglect statute, can result in a manslaughter indictment, simply because of its outcome. That is unacceptably arbitrary, and a violation of due process.

Id. at 724. The court further stated:

> Evidence before the trial court suggests that, due to the sensitive nature of this issue, many Christian Scientists, including the McKowns, were specifically aware of the statutory provisions relating to use of spiritual means and prayer. They may have indeed "mapped out" their behavior based upon the statute. While the cases in this area are more likely to involve reliance by the defendant on administrative pronouncements, there is nothing inherent in the concept which would make it inapplicable to an argument of reliance on a specific statutory enactment. The state in this instance has attempted to take away with the one hand—by way of criminal prosecution—that which it apparently granted with the other hand, and upon

> which defendants relied. This it cannot do, and meet constitutional requirements.

Id. at 724–25.

The State, in this instance, relies primarily on the decision of the Supreme Court of California in Walker. In Walker, a child died from untreated meningitis as a result of her mother's reliance on spiritual means in treating the child's illness. The mother, charged with manslaughter and felony child endangerment, argued that a religious accommodation provision found in a California misdemeanor child neglect statute, similar to chapter 415, barred her prosecution under the California manslaughter statute. The mother argued that "the statutory scheme violate[d] her right to fair notice by allowing punishment under sections 192(b) and 273(a)(1) for the same conduct that is assertedly accommodated under section 270." In rejecting this claim, the California Supreme Court explained that the statutes were clearly distinguishable and, in light of their differing objectives, the statutes could not be said to constitute inexplicably contradictory commands with respect to their respective requirements

In addressing the lack of notice claim, the State relies on the previously quoted statements in the Walker decision, particularly the conclusion that "persons relying on prayer treatment must estimate rightly" to avoid criminal prosecution because "due process requires no more." Walker, 253 Cal.Rptr. at 20–21, 763 P.2d at 871–72. Pennsylvania and Indiana have taken a similar view and rejected similar due process arguments. See Commonwealth v. Barnhart, 345 Pa.Super. 10, 497 A.2d 616 (1985), cert. denied, 488 U.S. 817 (1988); Hall v. State, 493 N.E.2d 433 (Ind.1986). The State asserts that we should also reject the Minnesota court's reasoning in McKown in part because the spiritual treatment exception in that case was contained in a criminal child abuse statute, while the provision in the Florida statute is contained in the child dependency statute.

The United States Supreme Court has stated that one of the purposes of due process is "to insure that no individual is convicted unless 'a fair warning [has first been] given to the world in language that the common world will understand, of what the law intends to do if a certain line is passed.'" Mourning v. Family Publications Serv., Inc., 411 U.S. 356 (1973) (quoting McBoyle v. United States, 283 U.S. 25, 27 (1931)). In Linville, this Court explained that a person of common intelligence must be able to determine what type of activity the statute is seeking to proscribe.

We disagree with the view of the Supreme Court of California in Walker that, in considering the application of this type of religious accommodation statute, persons relying on the statute and its allowance for prayer as treatment are granted only the opportunity to guess rightly with regard to their utilization of spiritual treatment. In commenting on this type of situation, one author has stated: "By authorizing conduct in one statute, but declaring that same conduct criminal under another statute, the State trapped the Hermansons, who had no fair warning that the State would consider their conduct criminal." Christine A. Clark, Religious Accommodation and Criminal Liability, 17 Fla.St.U.L.Rev. 559, 585 (1990) (footnotes omitted). We agree.

To say that the statutes in question establish a line of demarcation at which a person of common intelligence would know his or her conduct is or is not criminal ignores the fact that, not only did the judges of both the circuit court and the district court of appeal have difficulty understanding the interrelationship of the statutes in question, but, as indicated by their questions, the jurors also had problems understanding what was required.

In this instance, we conclude that the legislature has failed to clearly indicate the point at which a parent's reliance on his or her religious beliefs in the treatment of his or her children becomes criminal conduct. If the legislature desires to provide for religious accommodation while protecting the children of the state, the legislature must clearly indicate when a parent's conduct becomes criminal. As stated by another commentator: "Whatever choices are made . . . both the policy and the letter of the law should be clear and clearly stated, so that those who believe in healing by prayer rather than medical treatment are aware of the potential liabilities they may incur." Catherine W. Laughran, Comment, Religious Beliefs and the Criminal Justice System: Some Problems of the Faith Healer, 8 Loy.L.A.L.Rev. 396, 431 (1975).

Accordingly, for the reasons expressed, we quash the decision of the district court of appeal and remand this case with directions that the trial court's adjudication of guilt and sentence be vacated and the petitioners discharged.

NOTES

Walker v. Superior Court. The *Walker* case, 47 Cal.3d 112, 253 Cal.Rptr. 1, 763 P.2d 852 (1988), *cert. denied,* 491 U.S. 905, 109 S.Ct. 3186, 105 L.Ed.2d 695 (1989), discussed but not followed by the Florida Supreme Court in *Hermanson*, carefully detailed the legislative provisions of California law that contained a religious exception in some statutes but not in those for involuntary manslaughter and felony child endangerment. After explaining that imposing felony liability for failure to seek medical care for a seriously ill child is justified by a compelling state interest, the court added that even so, to survive a First Amendment challenge, the policy also must represent "the least restrictive alternative available to the state." They pointed out that:

> Defendant and the Church argue that civil dependency proceedings advance the governmental interest in a far less intrusive manner. This is not evident. First, we have already observed the profoundly intrusive nature of such proceedings; it is not clear that parents would prefer to lose custody of their children pursuant to a

> disruptive and invasive judicial inquiry than to face privately the prospect of criminal liability. Second, child dependency proceedings advance the governmental interest only when the state learns of a child's illness in time to take protective measures, which quite likely will be the exception rather than the rule. . . . Finally, the imposition of criminal liability is reserved for the actual loss or endangerment of a child's life and thus is narrowly tailored to those instances when governmental intrusion is absolutely compelled.
>
> We conclude that an adequately effective and less restrictive alternative is not available to further the state's compelling interest in assuring the provision of medical care to gravely ill children whose parents refuse such treatment on religious grounds. Accordingly, the First Amendment and its California equivalent do not bar defendant's criminal prosecution.

Accordingly, the court held that prosecution of the defendant for involuntary manslaughter and felony child endangerment did not violate statutory law or either the California or federal Constitution. In a separate concurring opinion, Justice Mosk notes that the majority chose not to reach the Attorney General's contention that extending the religious exemption of § 270 to the felony prosecution "would import into the proceeding a defense that offends the establishment clauses of the state and federal Constitutions." 47 Cal.3d 112, 253 Cal.Rptr. 1, 763 P.2d 852, at 873. Noting that the issue had been "timely raised and thoroughly briefed, and its importance is manifest", he expresses the view that "the statutory exemption as it now reads plainly violates the establishment clauses." Justice Broussard, in a separate dissenting and concurring opinion, states that he would direct the Court of Appeal to grant the writ of prohibition insofar as it seeks dismissal of the § 723a charge and deny it as to dismissal of the manslaughter charge.

If a state chooses to have no religious exemptions in any of its neglect, dependency or felony child endangerment statutes, would this make a difference with regard to a defense of vagueness? For charitable immunity and First Amendment defenses, *see* MICHAEL T. FLANNERY & RAYMOND C. O'BRIEN, THE SEXUAL EXPLOITATION OF CHILDREN 854–903 (2016).

The State as Monitor. In Matter of Appeal in Cochise County, 133 Ariz. 157, 650 P.2d 459 (1982), the Supreme Court of Arizona was called on to determine whether there was sufficient evidence to justify "state interference with the fundamental right of a parent to the custody and control of his or her child, particularly to 'monitor' the health of the child when there is known medical danger and when providing medical care is contrary to the parent's religious beliefs." After the death of one of her children through septicemia and peritonitis secondary to a strangulated inguinal hernia, the mother explained to Department of Economic Security (DES) case workers that "she had faith that miracles would safeguard her children" and that she would not seek medical help if any of her other seven children became ill. A juvenile court judge declined to find the children "dependent" in light of their otherwise seemingly satisfactory home life, but that decision was reversed by the Court of Appeals. The latter based its finding of present abuse on the threatened passive conduct of the mother in possibly failing to provide medical care in the future. The Supreme Court, reversing the intermediate appellate court, noted that the cases cited in justification of their decision were distinguishable because they upheld state intervention in cases in which there was present rather than future need of medical attention. However, the Supreme Court emphasized that the state continued to maintain broad supervisory powers and that the DES could "keep a close eye" on the children's progress. Also, it might be prompted to investigate further based on something less than would be required in a more typical situation.

Newmark v. Williams

Supreme Court of Delaware, 1991
588 A.2d 1108

■ MOORE, JUSTICE.

Colin Newmark,[1] a three year old child, faced death from a deadly aggressive and advanced form of pediatric cancer known as Burkitt's Lymphoma. We were presented with a clash of interests between medical science, Colin's tragic plight, the unquestioned sincerity of his parents' religious beliefs as Christian Scientists, and the legal right of the State to protect dependent children from perceived neglect when medical treatment is withheld on religious grounds. The Delaware Division of Child Protective Services ("DCPS") petitioned the Family Court for temporary custody of Colin to authorize the Alfred I. duPont Institute ("duPont Institute"), a nationally recognized children's hospital, to treat Colin's condition with chemotherapy. His parents, Morris and Kara Newmark, are well educated and economically prosperous. As members of the First Church of Christ, Scientist ("Christian Science") they rejected medical treatment proposed for Colin, preferring instead a course of spiritual aid and prayer.[2] The parents rely upon provisions of Delaware law, which exempt those who treat their children's illnesses "solely by spiritual means" from the abuse and neglect statutes. Thus, they opposed the State's petition. See 10 Del.C. § 901(11) & 16 Del.C. § 907 (emphasis added). The Newmarks also claimed that removing Colin from their custody would violate their First Amendment right, guaranteed under the United States Constitution, to freely exercise their religion. The

---

[1] We have used pseudonyms to protect the privacy of Colin and his family.

[2] Mary Baker Eddy, the founder of the Christian Science Church, professed a deep belief in spirituality. She preached that sickness was a manifestation of a diseased mind. See Eddy, Sermon Subject Christian Science Healing 7–8 (Pamphlet 1886). Eddy therefore claimed that "[m]edicine will not arrive at the Science of treating disease until disease is treated mentally and man is healed morally and physically." Id. at 17. Accordingly, Christian Scientists do not treat most sicknesses with medical care. Rather, they rely on practitioners who administer spiritual aid. See Schneider, Christian Science and the Law: Room for Compromise? 1 Colum.J.L. & Soc.Probs. 81, 81 (1965). Eddy also believed that childhood illnesses were more manifestations of their parents' own spiritual infirmities. She reasoned that "[t]he law of mortal mind and [parents'] own fears govern [their] own child more than the child's mind governs itself and they produce the very results which might have been prevented through the opposite." M. EDDY, SCIENCE AND HEALTH WITH KEY TO THE SCRIPTURES 154 (1934).

Family Court rejected both of these arguments and awarded custody of Colin to DCPS. The trial court, however, issued a stay permitting the Newmarks to file an immediate appeal to this Court.

We heard this appeal on an emergency basis. After argument on September 14, 1990, we issued an order reversing the Family Court and returned custody of Colin to his parents. At that time we noted that this more detailed opinion would follow in due course. We have concluded that Colin was not an abused or neglected child under Delaware law. Parents enjoy a well established legal right to make important decisions for their children. Although this right is not absolute, the State has the burden of proving by clear and convincing evidence that intervening in the parent-child relationship is necessary to ensure the safety or health of the child, or to protect the public at large. DCPS did not meet this heavy burden. This is especially true where the purpose of the custody petition was to administer, over the objections of Colin's parents, an extremely risky, toxic and dangerously life threatening medical treatment offering less than a 40% chance for "success".

Colin was the youngest of the three Newmark children. In late August, 1990, the Newmarks noticed that he had lost most of his appetite and was experiencing frequent vomiting. The symptoms at first appeared occasionally but soon worsened. The Newmarks reluctantly took Colin to the duPont Institute for examination. The parties stipulated that this violated the Newmarks' Christian Science beliefs in the effectiveness of spiritual healing. The parties further stipulated that the Newmarks acted out of concern for their potential criminal liability, citing a Massachusetts case which held parents liable for manslaughter for foregoing medical treatment and treating their minor child only in accordance with Christian Science tenets.

Dr. Charles L. Minor, a duPont Institute staff pediatric surgeon, examined Colin and ordered X-rays of his stomach. Dr. Minor found the X-rays inconclusive and suggested that Colin remain at the hospital for further testing. The Newmarks refused and took Colin home. Colin remained at home for approximately one week while receiving treatments under the care of a Christian Science practitioner. Colin's symptoms nonetheless quickly reappeared and the Newmarks returned him to the hospital. Dr. Minor ordered a second set of X-rays and this time discovered an obstruction in Colin's intestines. The doctor suggested immediate surgery and, again, the Newmarks consented. The Newmarks considered the procedure "mechanical" and therefore believed that it did not violate their religious beliefs.

During the operation, Dr. Minor discovered a large mass 10 to 15 centimeters wide connecting Colin's large and small bowels. He also noticed that some of Colin's lymph nodes were unusually large. Dr. Minor removed the mass and submitted tissue samples for a pathological report. There were no complications from the surgery and Colin was recovering "well."

The pathology report confirmed that Colin was suffering from a non-Hodgkins Lymphoma. Five pathologists from Children's Hospital, Philadelphia, Pennsylvania, confirmed the diagnosis. Dr. Minor, after receiving the pathology report, contacted Dr. Rita Meek, a board certified pediatric hematologist-oncologist and an attending physician at the duPont Institute.

Dr. Meek ordered two blood tests which indicated the presence of elevated levels of uric acid and LHD in Colin's system. The presence of these chemicals indicated that the disease had spread. Dr. Meek then conducted an external examination and detected a firm mass growing above Colin's right testicle. She diagnosed Colin's condition as Burkitt's Lymphoma, an aggressive pediatric cancer.[3] The doctor recommended that the hospital treat Colin with a heavy regimen of chemotherapy. Dr. Meek opined that the chemotherapy offered a 40% chance of "curing" Colin's illness. She concluded that he would die within six to eight months without treatment. The Newmarks, learning of Colin's condition only after the surgery, advised Dr. Meek that they would place him under the care of a Christian Science practitioner and reject all medical treatment for their son. Accordingly, they refused to authorize the chemotherapy. There was no doubt that the Newmarks sincerely believed, as part of their religious beliefs, that the tenets of their faith provided an effective treatment.

We start with an overview of the relevant Delaware statutory provisions. Delaware law defines a neglected child as: [A] child whose physical, mental or emotional health and well-being is threatened or impaired because of inadequate care and protection by the child's custodian, who has the ability and financial means to provide for the care but does not or will not provide adequate care; or a child who has been abused or neglected as defined by § 902 of Title 16. 10 Del.C. § 901(11). Section 902 further defines abuse and neglect as: [P]hysical injury by other than accidental means, injury resulting in a mental or emotional condition which is a result of abuse or neglect, negligent treatment, sexual abuse, maltreatment, mistreatment, nontreatment, exploitation or abandonment, of a child under the age of 18. Sections of the Delaware Code, however, contain spiritual treatment exemptions which directly affect Christian Scientists. Specifically, the exemptions state: No child who in good faith is under treatment solely by spiritual means through prayer in accordance with the tenets and practices of a recognized church or religious denomination by a duly accredited practitioner thereof shall for that reason alone be considered a neglected child for purposes of this chapter. 10 Del.C. § 901(11) & 16 Del.C. § 907. These exceptions reflect the intention of the Delaware General Assembly to provide a "safe harbor" for parents, like the Newmarks, to pursue their own religious

[3] Dr. Meek testified that Burkitt's Lymphoma cancer cells double more rapidly than any other form of pediatric cancer which inevitably results in a fast growing tumor.

beliefs. This is evident from the limited legislative history available on the subject.

As originally enacted in 1972, one of the spiritual healing exemptions appeared in the child abuse reporting section of the Code, under the general heading of "Immunity from liability." The statute included both the spiritual treatment exemption and an immunity provision applicable to reporting child abuse. See 58 Del. Laws 154 (1972). The General Assembly later amended this section of the Code in 1976 and placed the spiritual treatment exemption under a separate heading entitled "Child Under Treatment By Spiritual Means Not Neglected." See 60 Del. Laws 494 (1976); 16 Del.C. § 907. The amendment reflects the legislature's apparent intent to clarify the meaning of the exemption and to magnify its importance. The accuracy of this conclusion is less in doubt after considering the legislative history of the other identical exemption.

The General Assembly also amended the meaning of a "neglected child" in the section of the Code dealing with the Family Court. See 10 Del.C. § 901(11). The statute originally defined a neglected child as one "whose custodian refuses to provide him with adequate care." 58 Del. Laws 114 (1971). In 1978, the legislature changed the definition of a "neglected child" to include the spiritual treatment exemption found in 16 Del.C. § 907. See 61 Del. Laws 334 (1978). The amendment clearly reflects the General Assembly's intent to provide protection for parents who treat their children through statutorily defined spiritual means. Accordingly, our ruling from the bench noted that the spiritual treatment exemptions reflect, in part, "[t]he policy of this State with respect to the quality of life" a desperately ill child might have in the caring and loving atmosphere of his or her family, versus the sterile hospital environment demanded by physicians seeking to prescribe excruciating, and life threatening, treatments of doubtful efficacy.

With the considerable reflection that time has now permitted us in examining these issues, we recognize the possibility that the spiritual treatment exemptions[4] may violate the ban against the establishment of an official State religion guaranteed under both the Federal and Delaware Constitutions. Clearly, in both reality and practical effect, the language providing an exemption only to those individuals practicing "in accordance" with the "practices of a recognized church or religious denomination by a duly accredited practitioner thereof" is intended for the principal benefit of Christian Scientists.[7] Our concern is that it

[4] We express no view, and indeed, this case does not concern the good faith healing defense contained in the Delaware Criminal Code. See 11 Del.C. § 1104.

[7] The terminology used in the spiritual treatment exemption indicates that the statute was enacted as a result of a Christian Science lobbying effort. See In Child Deaths, a Test for Christian Science, N.Y. Times, Aug. 6, 1990, at 1, col. 2 (exemptions to neglect statutes passed at behest of Christian Science Church in forty state legislatures). Specifically, the requirement that a person must be a "duly accredited practitioner" mirrors the Christian Science belief that only "practitioners" receiving approval from the Christian Science Mother Church can conduct spiritual healing. See Schneider, Christian Science and the Law: Room for Compromise?, 1

possibly forces us to impermissibly determine the validity of an individual's own religious beliefs.[8] Neither party challenged the constitutionality of the spiritual treatment exemptions in either the Family Court or on appeal. Thus, except to recognize that the issue is far more complicated than was originally presented to us, we must leave such questions for another day.

Addressing the facts of this case, we turn to the novel legal question whether, under any circumstances, Colin was a neglected child when his parents refused to accede to medical demands that he receive a radical form of chemotherapy having only a forty percent chance of success. Other jurisdictions differ in their approaches to this important and intensely personal issue. Some courts resolved the question on an ad hoc basis, without a formal test, concluding that a child was neglected if the parents refused to administer chemotherapy in a life threatening situation. See In re Willmann, 24 Ohio App.3d 191, 199, 493 N.E.2d 1380, 1389 (1986); In re Hamilton, 657 S.W.2d 425, 429 (Tenn.Ct.App.1983). The California Court of Appeals in In re Ted B., 189 Cal.App.3d 996, 235 Cal.Rptr. 22 (1987), employed the best interests test to determine if a child was neglected when his parents refused to permit treatment of his cancer with "mild" chemotherapy following more intense treatment. Id. at 1006, 235 Cal.Rptr. at 27. Ted B. weighed the gravity, or potential gravity of the child's illness, the treating physician's medical evaluation of the course of care, the riskiness of the treatment and the child's "expressed preferences" to ultimately judge whether his parents' decision to withhold chemotherapy served his "best interests." Finally, the

---

Colum.J.L. & Soc.Probs. 81, 81 (1965); see also Walker v. Super. Ct. Sacramento Co., 47 Cal.3d 112, 147–48, 763 P.2d 852, 875, 253 Cal.Rptr. 1, 24 (1988) (Mosk, J., concurring), cert. denied, 491 U.S. 905, 109 S.Ct. 3186, 105 L.Ed.2d 695 (1989) (Christian Scientists sponsored spiritual treatment exception to abuse and neglect law in California and therefore it is "more than a fortuity that the word 'practitioner' " appears in California spiritual healing statute). The influence of the Church of Christ Scientist on the Delaware exemptions is also apparent when those statutes are compared with the federal spiritual healing exemption, which the Department of Health, Education and Welfare ("HEW") adopted in response to the Child Abuse Prevention and Treatment Act of 1974. See 45 C.F.R. s' 1340.1 (1990). The federal regulation provides that "[n]othing in this part should be construed as requiring or prohibiting a finding of negligent treatment or maltreatment when a parent practicing his or her religious beliefs does not, for that reason alone, provide medical treatment for a child. . . ." 45 C.F.R. § 1340.2(d)(2)(ii) (1990). (Emphasis added). The states were required to enact statutes similar to the HEW regulations to qualify for federal funds. See Comment, Faith Healing and Religious Treatment Exemptions To Child Endangerment Laws: Should Parental Religious Practices Excuse The Failure To Provide Necessary Medical Care To Children?, 13 U.Dayton L.Rev. 79, 96 (1987) (written by LeClair). Tellingly, the statute the General Assembly enacted to adopt the Child Abuse Prevention and Treatment Act of 1974 in Delaware merely incorporated the prior version of the Delaware exemption including the language "duly accredited practitioner" and "recognized religion." See 16 Del.C. § 907; 60 Del.Laws 494 (1976) (synopsis). It is perhaps more than coincidental that the legislature merely carried over the exemption without amending it to conform with the new federal regulations. Certainly, any statute passed as the result of the efforts of one religious group to benefit that one particular group to the exclusion of others bears a strong presumption against its validity as a direct violation of the Establishment Clause.

[8] At least one state has ruled that a statutory exemption to a criminal abuse and neglect statute, containing identical language as the Delaware statutes, violated both the Establishment Clause and the Equal Protection Clause of the Fourteenth Amendment. See State v. Miskimens, 22 Ohio Misc.2d 43, 43–46, 490 N.E.2d 931, 933–936 (Ohio Ct.Com.Pl.1984). . . .

Supreme Judicial Court of Massachusetts, in Custody of A Minor, 375 Mass. 733, 379 N.E.2d 1053 (1978), utilized a tripartite balancing test which weighed the interests of the parents, their child and the State to determine whether a child was neglected when his parents refused to treat his leukemia with non-invasive chemotherapy.

In the present case, the Family Court did not undertake any formal interest analysis in deciding that Colin was a neglected child under Delaware law. Instead, the trial court used the same ad hoc approach as the Ohio and Tennessee courts respectively employed in Willmann and Hamilton. Specifically, the Family Court rejected the Newmarks' proposal to treat Colin by spiritual means under the care of a Christian Science practitioner. The trial judge considered spiritual treatment an inadequate alternative to chemotherapy. The court therefore concluded that "[w]ithout any other factually supported alternative" the Newmarks' decision to refuse chemotherapy "constitute[d] inadequate parental care for their son who is in a life threatening situation and constitute[d] neglect as defined in the Delaware statute."

This Court reviews the trial court's application of legal precepts involving issues of law de novo. While we do not recognize the primacy of any one of the tests employed in other jurisdictions, we find that the trial court erred in not explicitly considering the competing interests at stake. The Family Court failed to consider the special importance and primacy of the familial relationship, including the autonomy of parental decision making authority over minor children. The trial court also did not consider the gravity of Colin's illness in conjunction with the invasiveness of the proposed chemotherapy and the considerable likelihood of failure. These factors, when applied to the facts of this case, strongly militate against governmental intrusion.

Any balancing test must begin with the parental interest. The primacy of the familial unit is a bedrock principle of law. See Stanley v. Illinois, 405 U.S. 645, 651 (1972) (citing cases); . . . ("State and society in general have a fundamental interest in preserving and protecting the family unit."); . . . We have repeatedly emphasized that the parental right is sacred which can be invaded for only the most compelling reasons. Indeed, the Delaware General Assembly has stated that the preservation of the family is "fundamental to the maintenance of a stable, democratic society. . . ." 10 Del.C. § 902(a); see 16 Del.C. § 901 (abuse, neglect reporting statute designed to ensure strength of "parental care.") Courts have also recognized that the essential element of preserving the integrity of the family is maintaining the autonomy of the parent-child relationship. In Prince v. Commonwealth of Massachusetts, 321 U.S. 158, 166 *reh'g denied*, 321 U.S. 804 (1944), the United States Supreme Court announced: It is cardinal with us that the custody, care and nurture of the child reside first in the parents, whose primary function and freedom include preparation for obligations the state can neither supply nor hinder. Parental autonomy to care for children free from government interference therefore satisfies a child's need for continuity and thus ensures his or her psychological and physical well-being.

Parental authority to make fundamental decisions for minor children is also a recognized common law principle. A doctor commits the tort of battery if he or she performs an operation under normal circumstances without the informed consent of the patient. Tort law also assumes that a child does not have the capacity to consent to an operation in most situations. Thus, the common law recognizes that the only party capable of authorizing medical treatment for a minor in "normal" circumstances is usually his parent or guardian.

Courts, therefore, give great deference to parental decisions involving minor children. In many circumstances the State simply is not an adequate surrogate for the judgment of a loving, nurturing parent. See Baskin, supra, at 1386. As one commentator aptly recognized, the "law does not have the capacity to supervise the delicately complex interpersonal bonds between parent and child."

We also recognize that parental autonomy over minor children is not an absolute right. Clearly, the State can intervene in the parent-child relationship where the health and safety of the child and the public at large are in jeopardy. Accordingly, the State, under the doctrine of parens patriae, has a special duty to protect its youngest and most helpless citizens.

The parens patriae doctrine is a derivation of the common law giving the State the right to act on behalf of minor children in certain property and marital disputes. See In re Hudson, 13 Wash.2d 673, 126 P.2d 765, 777 (1942). More recently, courts have accepted the doctrine of parens patriae to justify State intervention in cases of parental religious objections to medical treatment of minor children's life threatening conditions. The Supreme Court of the United States succinctly described the parens patriae concept in Prince, 321 U.S. at 170, 64 S.Ct. at 444. The Court found that parental autonomy, under the guise of the parents' religious freedom, was not unlimited. Rather, the Court held: Parents may be free to become martyrs themselves. But it does not follow they are free, in identical circumstances, to make martyrs of their children before they have reached the age of full and legal discretion when they can make that choice for themselves.

The basic principle underlying the parens patriae doctrine is the State's interest in preserving human life. See Cruzan v. Director, Missouri Dept. of Health, 497 U.S. 261, 110 S.Ct. 2841, 2853, 111 L.Ed.2d 224 (1990) (State may "assert an unqualified interest in the preservation of human life. . . ."); Custody Of A Minor, 375 Mass at 755, 379 N.E.2d at 1066. Yet this interest and the parens patriae doctrine are not unlimited. In its recent Cruzan opinion, the Supreme Court of the United States announced that the state's interest in preserving life must "be weighed against the constitutionally protected interests of the individual." 497 U.S. 261, 110 S.Ct. 2841, 2853 (1990).The individual interests at stake here include both the Newmarks' right to decide what is best for Colin and Colin's own right to life. We have already considered the Newmarks' stake in this case and its relationship to the parens patriae doctrine. The resolution of the issues here, however, is incomplete without a discussion of Colin's interests.

All children indisputably have the right to enjoy a full and healthy life. Colin, a three year old boy, unfortunately lacked the ability to reach a detached, informed decision regarding his own medical care.[9] This Court must therefore substitute its own objective judgment to determine what is in Colin's "best interests."

There are two basic inquiries when a dispute involves chemotherapy treatment over parents' religious objections. The court must first consider the effectiveness of the treatment and determine the child's chances of survival with and without medical care. The court must then consider the nature of the treatments and their effect on the child.

The "best interests" analysis is hardly unique or novel. Federal and State courts have unhesitatingly authorized medical treatment over a parent's religious objection when the treatment is relatively innocuous in comparison to the dangers of withholding medical care. . . . [C]ourts are reluctant to authorize medical care over parental objection when the child is not suffering a life threatening or potential life threatening illness. See In re Green, 448 Pa. 338, 348–49, 292 A.2d 387, 392 (1972) (court refused to authorize corrective spine surgery on minor); In re Seiferth, 309 N.Y. 80, 85–86, 127 N.E.2d 820, 823 (1955) (no authorization to correct cleft palate and harelip on fourteen year old minor); but cf. In re Sampson, 65 Misc.2d 658, 675–76, 317 N.Y.S.2d 641, 657–58 (N.Y.Fam.Ct.1970), aff'd, 29 N.Y.2d 900, 328 N.Y.S.2d 686, 278 N.E.2d 918 (1972) (authorizing corrective surgery on minor where parents' only objection was blood transfusion).

The linchpin in all cases discussing the "best interests of a child", when a parent refuses to authorize medical care, is an evaluation of the risk of the procedure compared to its potential success. This analysis is consistent with the principle that State intervention in the parent-child relationship is only justifiable under compelling conditions. The State's interest in forcing a minor to undergo medical care diminishes as the risks of treatment increase and its benefits decrease.

---

[9] Other jurisdictions have respected and upheld a minor's decision regarding his own medical care only when the child presented clear and convincing evidence that he was mature enough to exercise an adult's judgment and understood the consequences of his decision. See, e.g., In re E.G., 133 Ill.2d 98, 103, 139 Ill.Dec. 810, 815–16, 549 N.E.2d 322, 327–28 (1989); cf. In re Application of L.I. Jewish Med. Ctr., 147 Misc.2d at 730, 557 N.Y.S.2d at 243. Although we decline to comment on the applicability of the "mature minor doctrine" under Delaware law, it is doubtful that even the most precocious three year old could meet the standard. Yet, while not dispositive, there was evidence that Colin overheard some hospital discussion about treating him with chemotherapy. His reaction was one of fright that the proposed treatment would "kill" him. Thus, even at his young age, Colin was able to perceive the very real dangers of the treatment. Given the admittedly poor odds of its success, Colin's fear of chemotherapy was not unjustified.

The New Jersey Supreme Court implicitly recognized this principle in the seminal Quinlan case decided over a decade ago. See In re Quinlan, 70 N.J. 10, 355 A.2d 647, cert. denied, 429 U.S. 922 (1976). In deciding that a legal custodian could authorize the termination of artificial life support in certain circumstances, Quinlan noted that:

> [T]he State's interest contra weakens and the individual's right to privacy grows as the degree of bodily invasion increases and the prognosis dims. Ultimately there comes a point at which the individual's rights overcome the State interest. It is for that reason that we believe Karen's choice, if she were competent to make it, would be vindicated by the law. Her prognosis is extremely poor,—she will never resume cognitive life. And the bodily invasion is very great,—she requires 24 hour intensive nursing care, antibiotics, the assistance of a respirator, a catheter and feeding tube.

Similarly, most courts which have authorized medical treatment on a minor over parental objection have also noted that a different situation exists when the treatment is inherently dangerous and invasive. See, e.g., In re Cabrera, 381 Pa.Super. at 111, 552 A.2d at 1119; Muhlenberg Hospital, 128 N.J.Super. at 503, 320 A.2d at 521 ("if the disputed procedure involved a significant danger to the infant, the parents' wishes would be respected."); Perricone, 37 N.J. at 479–80, 181 A.2d at 760 (strong argument for parents if "there were substantial evidence that the treatment itself posed a significant danger to the infant's life"); Labrenz, 411 Ill. at 624–25, 104 N.E.2d at 773 (same); In re Hudson, 126 P.2d at 777 (court not permitted to authorize treatment "which would probably result in merciful release by death from [minor's] physical . . . handicap.").

Applying the foregoing considerations to the "best interests standard" here, the State's petition must be denied. The egregious facts of this case indicate that Colin's proposed medical treatment was highly invasive, painful, involved terrible temporary and potentially permanent side effects, posed an unacceptably low chance of success, and a high risk that the treatment itself would cause his death. The State's authority to intervene in this case, therefore, cannot outweigh the Newmarks' parental prerogative and Colin's inherent right to enjoy at least a modicum of human dignity in the short time that was left to him.

Dr. Meek originally diagnosed Colin's condition as Burkitt's Lymphoma. She testified that the cancer was "a very bad tumor" in an advanced disseminated state and not localized to only one section of the body. She accordingly recommended that the hospital begin an "extremely intensive" chemotherapy program scheduled to extend for at least six months.

The first step necessary to prepare Colin for chemotherapy involved an intravenous hydration treatment. This process, alone, posed a significant risk that Colin's kidneys would fail. Indeed, these intravenous treatments had already begun and were threatening Colin's life while the parties were arguing the case to us on September 14, 1990. Thus, if Colin's kidneys failed he also would have to undergo dialysis treatments. There also was a possibility that renal failure could occur during the chemotherapy treatments themselves. In addition, Dr. Meek recommended further pretreatment diagnostic tests including a spinal tap and a CAT scan. Dr. Meek prescribed "maximum" doses of at least six different types of cancer-fighting drugs during Colin's chemotherapy. This proposed "maximum" treatment represented the most aggressive form of cancer therapy short of a bone marrow transplant. The side effects would include hair loss, reduced immunological function creating a high risk of infection in the patient, and certain neurological problems. The drugs also are toxic to bone marrow.

The record demonstrates that this form of chemotherapy also would adversely affect other parts of Colin's body. Dr. Meek stated that the doctors would have to administer the treatments through injections in the veins and spinal fluid. The chemotherapy would reduce Colin's white blood count, and it would be extremely likely that he would suffer numerous infections. Colin would require multiple blood transfusions with a resultant additional risk of infection. The treating physicians also would have to install a catheter in Colin's chest to facilitate a constant barrage of tests and treatments. Colin also would receive food through the catheter because the chemotherapy would depress his appetite. The operation to set the catheter in place would take approximately one hour. The doctors proposed to perform biopsies on both Colin's bone marrow and the lump in his groin during the procedure.

The physicians planned to administer the chemotherapy in cycles, each of which would bring Colin near death. Then they would wait until Colin's body recovered sufficiently before introducing more drugs. Dr. Meek opined that there was no guarantee that drugs alone would "cure" Colin's illness. The doctor noted that it would then be necessary to radiate Colin's testicles if drugs alone were unsuccessful. Presumably, this would have rendered him sterile.

Dr. Meek also wanted the State to place Colin in a foster home after the initial phases of hospital treatment. Children require intensive home monitoring during chemotherapy. For example, Dr. Meek testified that a usually low grade fever for a healthy child could indicate the presence of a potentially deadly infection in a child cancer patient. She believed that the Newmarks, although well educated and financially responsible, were incapable of providing this intensive care because of their firm religious objections to medical treatment.[10]

---

[10] A doctor in a recent related case in Connecticut involving state intervention over a mother's decision to treat her minor child with traditional Chinese remedies rather than "conventional surgery" remarked that " '[i]f you do something where you need the cooperation of the entire family for the child to get better, when it's against the family's wishes your probability of success is vastly reduced.' " N.Y. Times, Dec. 13, 1990, at –5, col. 1.

Dr. Meek ultimately admitted that there was a real possibility that the chemotherapy could kill Colin. In fact, assuming the treatment did not itself prove fatal, she offered Colin at "best" a 40% chance[11] that he would "survive."[12] Dr. Meek additionally could not accurately predict whether, if Colin completed the therapy, he would subsequently suffer additional tumors.

No American court, even in the most egregious case, has ever authorized the State to remove a child from the loving, nurturing care of his parents and subject him, over parental objection, to an invasive regimen of treatment which offered, as Dr. Meek defined the term, only a forty percent chance of "survival." For example, the California Court of Appeals ruled in Eric B., that the State could conduct various procedures as part of an "observation phase" of chemotherapy over the objection of his parents. 189 Cal.App.3d at 1008–1009, 235 Cal.Rptr. at 29. The treatment included bone scans, CT scans, spinal taps and biopsies. The court specifically found that "[t]he risks entailed by the monitoring are minimal." The court also noted that the child would enjoy a 60% chance of survival with the treatments.

The Tennessee Court of Appeals awarded custody of a minor suffering from Ewing's Sarcoma to the State after her parents refused to treat the cancer with medical care. See In re Hamilton, 657 S.W.2d at 429. The child in that case enjoyed an at least 80% chance of temporary remission and a 25%–50% opportunity for long-term "cure". The court specifically noted that various hospitals had successfully treated Ewing's Sarcoma in "a significant number of patients." There was no testimony in Hamilton, however, concerning the magnitude of the proposed chemotherapy.

The Supreme Judicial Court of Massachusetts took custody away from parents who refused to administer "mild" cancer fighting drugs after the child had already undergone more "vigorous" treatment. See Custody of a Minor, 375 Mass. at 755–56, 379 N.E.2d at 1058, 1067. The trial judge, in that case, specifically found that aside from some minor side effects, including stomach cramps and constipation, the chemotherapy "bore no chance of leaving the child physically incapacitated in any way." The trial court also ruled that the chemotherapy gave the child not only a chance to enjoy a long life "but also a 'substantial' chance for cure."

The Ohio Court of Appeals awarded custody of a minor suffering from Osteogenic Sarcoma to the state when his parents consented to chemotherapy, but later refused to authorize an operation to partially

[11] Dr. Meek based her estimate on "historical" data compiled from children who have suffered from Burkitt's Lymphoma.

[12] Dr. Meek testified that there was no available medical data to conclude that Colin could survive to adulthood. Rather, she stated that the term "survival", as applied to victims of leukemia or lymphoma, refers only to the probability that the patient will live two years after chemotherapy without a recurrence of cancer.

remove his shoulder and entire left arm. In re Willmann, 24 Ohio App.3d at 193, 199, 493 N.E.2d at 1383, 1390. Although amputation is ultimately the most invasive type of surgery, there was at least a 60% chance in Willmann that the child would survive with the operation. The court also significantly noted that the child remained at home while receiving the lower court's mandated chemotherapy treatments.

Finally, the New York Supreme Court most recently ruled that the State could intervene and order chemotherapy treatments over a parent's religious objections when the medical care presented a 75% chance of short-term remission but only a 25–30% chance for "cure." See In re Application of L.I. Jewish Med. Ctr., 147 Misc.2d at 725, 557 N.Y.S.2d at 241. The seventeen year old minor in that case suffered from an advanced case of Rhabdomyosarcoma, a type of pediatric cancer affecting potential muscle tissue. This case, however, is not dispositive given the fact that the parents were not wholly opposed to chemotherapy.

The minor and his parents in L.I. Jewish Med. Ctr., were both members of the Jehovah's Witnesses religion and only objected to blood transfusions which were an incidental part of the prescribed medical treatment. There was no evidence that either party objected to the chemotherapy, which included radiation treatments. The treatments were also probably "radical" in nature given the fact that the disease had spread throughout the child's body. This New York decision is therefore in perfect accord with other well-established precedent. Courts have consistently authorized state intervention when parents object to only minimally intrusive treatment which poses little or no risk to a child's health. . . .

The aggressive form of chemotherapy that Dr. Meek prescribed for Colin was more likely to fail than succeed. The proposed treatment was also highly invasive and could have independently caused Colin's death. Dr. Meek also wanted to take Colin away from his parents and family during the treatment phase and place the boy in a foster home. This certainly would have caused Colin severe emotional difficulties given his medical condition, tender age, and the unquestioned close bond between Colin and his family.

In sum, Colin's best interests were served by permitting the Newmarks to retain custody of their child. Parents must have the right at some point to reject medical treatment for their child. Under all of the circumstances here, this clearly is such a case. The State's important and legitimate role in safeguarding the interests of minor children diminishes in the face of this egregious record. Parents undertake an awesome responsibility in raising and caring for their children. No doubt a parent's decision to withhold medical care is both deeply personal and soul wrenching. It need not be made worse by the invasions which both the

State and medical profession sought on this record. Colin's ultimate fate therefore rested with his parents and their faith.[13]

The judgment of the Family Court is, REVERSED.

NOTES

Treatment for Children in Life Threatening Circumstances: The Blood Transfusion Cases. The cases usually involve disputes between parent and state about whether medical treatment should be given to a child. The "life threatening" exception developed largely through cases involving parental opposition to blood transfusions. Despite the religious basis for such objections, courts asserted their authority and willingness to intervene to protect the life of a child. *See, e.g.*, People ex rel. Wallace v. Labrenz, 104 N.E.2d 769 (Ill.1952); State v. Perricone, 181 A.2d 751 (N.J.1962). In Raleigh Fitkin-Paul Morgan Memorial Hospital v. Anderson, 201 A.2d 537 (N.J.1964), the New Jersey Supreme Court held that blood transfusions might be administered to a pregnant mother against her wishes for the purpose of saving the life of the unborn child. The Nebraska Supreme Court upheld a state law that required a blood test for newborns, holding that such a law does not violate a parent's right of free exercise when the parent opposes the test on religious grounds. The court held that the blood test was rationally related to the state's interest in preventing the spread of disease and is a neutral requirement of general applicability. Douglas County v. Anaya, 694 N.W. 2d 601 (Neb. 2005).

The Choice of Therapy Cases. One of the more widely publicized cases involving the clash between the state and a child's parents over choice of medical care involved Chad Green, a minor afflicted with acute lymphocytic leukemia. In *Custody of a Minor*, 379 N.E.2d 1053 (Mass. 1978) The Supreme Judicial Court of Massachusetts, after a fairly elaborate explanation of the interests of the child, parent and state which must be balanced in making such a decision, determined that an order removing legal (but not physical) custody of the child from the parents was warranted under the circumstances. Key to the decision were findings that leukemia is fatal in children if untreated and that the risk of chemotherapy (the only medical treatment considered to offer a hope for cure) were minimal in comparison with the consequences of not treating the disease. The parents had been unwilling to continue chemotherapy for their child. The case again came before the court in Custody of a Minor, 393 N.E.2d 836 (Mass. 1979) in an appeal from denial of the parent's petition that an alternative treatment, "metabolic therapy" (consisting of administration of laetrile, vitamins A and C, enzyme enemas, and folic acid), be substituted for chemotherapy. Finding that such a regimen was contrary to the best interests of the child, the court continued the restrictions on the parents, who by this time had left the jurisdiction. The child later died. When the parents returned to Massachusetts afterward, a judge held them in contempt but did not impose a fine or sentence on them on the theory that they already had suffered enough.

---

[13] Tragically, Colin died shortly after we announced our oral decision.

A different tack was taken by the Court of Appeals of New York in Matter of Hofbauer, 393 N.E.2d 1009 (N.Y. 1979). A County Commissioner of Social Services sought to have a child with Hodgkins disease adjudged to be neglected because his parents failed to follow the advice of one attending physician, which would have led to conventional methods of treatment (including radiation and possibly chemotherapy) and instead elected to follow the advice of another physician to treat the child with a form of nutritional therapy and laetrile. The Court of Appeals (and the two courts below) did not find the child neglected. It noted that the child was receiving treatment by a physician licensed to practice in New York, and explained that a court cannot "assume the role of a surrogate parent and establish as the objective criteria with which to evaluate a parent's decision its own judgment as to the exact method or degree of medical treatment which should be provided, for such standard is fraught with subjectivity. Rather, in our view, the court's inquiry should be whether the parents, once having sought accredited medical assistance, and having been made aware of the seriousness of their child's affliction and the possibility of cure if a certain mode of treatment is undertaken, have provided for their child a treatment which is recommended by their physician and which has not been totally rejected by all responsible medical authority."

Inoculations. States often provide parents with a statutory religious exemption to mandatory health immunizations for their children. *See, e.g.,* N.Y. PUB. HEALTH LAW § 2164(9) (2016). Any parent seeking to excuse his or child from the immunization requirement, however, must demonstrate that opposition to immunization is genuine, sincere and rooted in religious belief. *See* Nassau County Department of Social Services v. R.B., 870 N.Y.S.2d 874 (N.Y. Fam. Ct. 2008). When parents disagree over whether the child should be vaccinated, as when one parent objects because of religious beliefs, and the other wishes the child vaccinated, courts have held that a trial court may make a determination based on the best interests of the child. Courts have held that when there is a dispute, the issue is not about religious beliefs, but about what is in the best interest of the child. Furthermore, best interest should be determined by competent, substantial evidence. Winters v. Brown, 51 So.3d 656 (Fla. Ct. App. 2011). *See also* Dorit Rubinstein Reiss & Lois A. Weithorn, *Responding to the Childhood Vaccination Crisis: Legal Framework and Tools in the Context of Parental Vaccine Refusal,* 63 BUFF. L. REV. 881 (2015); B. Jessie Hill, *Whose Body? Whose Soul? Medical Decision-Making on Behalf of Children and the Free Exercise Clause Before and After Employment Division v. Smith,* 32 CARDOZO L. REV. 1857 (2011).

2. MENTAL HEALTH CARE OF CHILD

Parham v. J.R.

Supreme Court of the United States, 1979
442 U.S. 584

■ BURGER, CHIEF JUSTICE delivered the opinion of the Court.

The question presented in this appeal is what process is constitutionally due a minor child whose parents or guardian seek state administered institutional mental health care for the child and specifically whether an adversary proceeding is required prior to or after the commitment.

Appellee, J.R., a child being treated in a Georgia state mental hospital, was a plaintiff in this class-action suit based on 42 U.S.C. § 1983, in the District Court for the Middle District of Georgia. Appellants are the State's Commissioner of the Department of Human Resources, the Director of the Mental Health Division of the Department of Human Resources and the Chief Medical Officer at the hospital where appellee was being treated. Appellee sought a declaratory judgment that Georgia's voluntary commitment procedures for children under the age of 18, Ga.Code, §§ 88–503.1, 88–503.2,[3] violated the Due Process Clause of the Fourteenth Amendment and requested an injunction against its future enforcement. . . . [A three-judge District Court] held that Georgia's statutory scheme was unconstitutional because it failed to protect adequately the appellees' due process rights. J.L. v. Parham, 412 F. Supp. 112, 139 (M.D.Ga.1976).

To remedy this violation the court enjoined future commitments based on the procedures in the Georgia statute. It also commanded Georgia to appropriate and expend whatever amount was "reasonably necessary" to provide nonhospital facilities deemed by the appellant state officials to be the most appropriate for the treatment of those members of plaintiffs' class, who could be treated in a less drastic, nonhospital environment.

Appellants challenged all aspects of the District Court's judgment. . . . J.L., a plaintiff before the District Court who is now deceased, was admitted in 1970 at the age of six years to Central State Regional Hospital in Milledgeville, Ga. Prior to his admission, J.L. had received outpatient treatment at the hospital for over two months. J.L.'s mother then requested the hospital to admit him indefinitely. The admitting physician interviewed J.L. and his parents. He learned that

---

[3] Section 88–503.1 provides:

"The superintendent of any facility may receive for observation and diagnosis . . . any individual under 18 years of age for whom such application is made by his parent or guardian. . . . If found to show evidence of mental illness and to be suitable for treatment, such person may be given care and treatment at such facility and such person may be detained by such facility for such period and under such conditions as may be authorized by law."

J.L.'s natural parents had divorced and his mother had remarried. He also learned that J.L. had been expelled from school because he was uncontrollable. He accepted the parents' representation that the boy had been extremely aggressive and diagnosed the child as having a "hyperkinetic reaction to childhood."

J.L.'s mother and stepfather agreed to participate in family therapy during the time their son was hospitalized. Under this program J.L. was permitted to go home for short stays. Apparently his behavior during these visits was erratic. After several months the parents requested discontinuance of the program. In 1972, the child was returned to his mother and stepfather on a furlough basis, i.e., he would live at home but go to school at the hospital. The parents found they were unable to control J.L. to their satisfaction which created family stress. Within two months they requested his readmission to Central State. J.L.'s parents relinquished their parental rights to the county in 1974. Although several hospital employees recommended that J.L. should be placed in a special foster home with "a warm, supported, truly involved couple," the Department of Family and Children Services was unable to place him in such a setting. On October 24, 1975, J.L. filed this suit requesting an order of the court placing him in a less drastic environment suitable to his needs.

Appellee, J.R., was declared a neglected child by the county and removed from his natural parents when he was three months old. He was placed in seven different foster homes in succession prior to his admission to Central State Hospital at the age of seven.

Immediately preceding his hospitalization, J.R. received out-patient treatment at a county mental health center for several months. He then began attending school where he was so disruptive and incorrigible that he could not conform to normal behavior patterns. Because of his abnormal behavior J.R.'s seventh set of foster parents requested his removal from their home. The Department of Family and Children Services then sought his admission at Central State. The agency provided the hospital with a complete sociomedical history at the time of his admission. In addition, three separate interviews were conducted with J.R. by the admission team of the hospital. It was determined that he was borderline retarded, and suffered an "unsocialized, aggressive reaction to childhood." It was recommended unanimously that he would "benefit from the structured environment" of the hospital and would "enjoy living and playing with boys of the same age."

J.R.'s progress was re-examined periodically. In addition, unsuccessful efforts were made by the Department of Family and Children Services during his stay at the hospital to place J.R. in various foster homes. On October 24, 1975, J.R. filed this suit requesting an order of the court placing him in a less drastic environment suitable to his needs.

Ga.Code Ann. § 19–7–5(g) (Supp.2006) provides for the voluntary admission to a state regional hospital of children such as J.L. and J.R. Under that provision admission begins with an application for hospitalization signed by a "parent or guardian." Upon application the superintendent of each hospital is given the power to admit temporarily any child for "observation and diagnosis." If, after observation, the superintendent finds "evidence of mental illness" and that the child is "suitable for treatment" in the hospital, then the child may be admitted "for such period and under such conditions as may be authorized by law." Georgia's mental health statute also provides for the discharge of voluntary patients. Any child who has been hospitalized for more than five days may be discharged at the request of a parent or guardian. § 88–503.3(a). Even without a request for discharge, however, the superintendent of each regional hospital has an affirmative duty to release any child "who has recovered from his mental illness or who has sufficiently improved that the superintendent determines that hospitalization of the patient is no longer desirable." § 88–503.2.

Georgia's Mental Health Director has not published any statewide regulations defining what specific procedures each superintendent must employ when admitting a child under 18. Instead, each regional hospital's superintendent is responsible for the procedures in his or her facility. [Noting that "substantial variation" exists between them, the Court reviews and details procedures of the different hospitals.]

Although most of the focus of the District Court was on the State's mental hospitals, it is relevant to note that Georgia presently funds over 50 community mental health clinics and 13 specialized foster care homes. The State has built seven new regional hospitals within the past 15 years and it has added a new children's unit to its oldest hospital. The State budget in fiscal year 1976 was almost $150 million for mental health care. Georgia ranks 22d among the States in per capita expenditures for mental health and 15th in total expenditures.

The District Court nonetheless rejected the State's entire system of providing mental health care on both procedural and substantive grounds. The District Court found that 46 children could be "optimally cared for in another, less restrictive, non-hospital setting if it were available." These "optimal" settings included group homes, therapeutic camps and home care services. The Governor of Georgia and the Chairmen of the two Appropriations Committees of its legislature, testifying in the District Court, expressed confidence in the Georgia program and informed the court that the State could not justify enlarging its budget during fiscal year 1977 to provide the specialized treatment settings urged by appellees in addition to those then available.

In holding unconstitutional Georgia's statutory procedure for voluntary commitment of juveniles the District Court first determined that commitment to any of the eight regional hospitals constitutes a severe deprivation of a child's liberty. The court defined this liberty interest both in terms of a freedom from bodily restraint and freedom from the "emotional and psychic harm" caused by the institutionalization. Having determined that a liberty interest is implicated by a child's admission to a mental hospital, the court considered what process is required to protect that interest. It held that the process due "includes at least the right after notice to be heard before an impartial tribunal." 412 F. Supp., at 137.

In requiring the prescribed hearing, the court rejected Georgia's argument that no adversary-type hearing was required since the State was merely assisting parents who could not afford private care by making available treatment similar to that offered in private hospitals and by private physicians. The court acknowledged that most parents who seek to have their children admitted to a state mental hospital do so in good faith. It, however, relied on one of appellees' witnesses who expressed an opinion that "some still look upon mental hospitals as a 'dumping ground.'" Id., at 138.[8] No specific evidence of such "dumping," however, can be found in the record. The District Court also rejected the argument that review by the superintendents of the hospitals and their staffs was sufficient to protect the child's liberty interest. The court held that the inexactness of psychiatry, coupled with the possibility that the sources of information used to make the commitment decision may not always be reliable, made the superintendent's decision too arbitrary to satisfy due process.

In an earlier day, the problems inherent in coping with children afflicted with mental or emotional abnormalities were dealt with largely within the family. Sometimes parents were aided by teachers or a family doctor. While some parents no doubt were able to deal with their disturbed children without specialized assistance, others, especially those of limited means and education, were not. Increasingly, they turned for assistance to local, public sources or private charities. Until recently, most of the states did little more than provide custodial institutions for the confinement of persons who were considered dangerous.

As medical knowledge about the mentally ill and public concern for their condition expanded, the states, aided substantially by federal grants, have sought to ameliorate the human tragedies of seriously disturbed children. Ironically, as most states have expanded their efforts to assist the mentally ill, their actions have been subjected to increasing litigation and heightened constitutional scrutiny. Courts have been required to resolve the thorny constitutional attacks on state programs

---

[8] In light of the District Court's holding that a judicial or quasi-judicial body should review voluntary commitment decisions, it is at least interesting to note that the witness who made the statement quoted in the text was not referring to parents as the people who "dump" children into hospitals. This witness opined that some juvenile court judges and child welfare agencies misused the hospitals. See also Rolfe & MacClintock, The Due Process Rights of Minors "Voluntarily Admitted" to Mental Institutions, 4 J. Psych. & L. 333, 351 (1976), (hereinafter Rolfe & MacClintock).

and procedures with limited precedential guidance. In this case appellees have challenged Georgia's procedural and substantive balance of the individual, family and social interests at stake in the voluntary commitment of a child to one of its regional mental hospitals.

The parties agree that our prior holdings have set out a general approach for testing challenged state procedures under a due process claim. Assuming the existence of a protectible property or liberty interest, the Court has required a balancing of a number of factors:

> "First, the private interest that will be affected by the official action; second, the risk of an erroneous deprivation of such interest through the procedures used, and the probable value, if any, of additional or substitute procedural safeguards; and finally, the Government's interest, including the function involved and the fiscal and administrative burdens that the additional or substitute procedural requirement would entail." Mathews v. Eldridge, 424 U.S. 319, 335, 96 S.Ct. 893, 903, 47 L.Ed.2d 18 (1976); Smith v. OFFER, 431 U.S. 816, 847–848, 97 S.Ct. 2094, 2111–2112, 53 L.Ed.2d 14 (1977).

In applying these criteria, we must consider first the child's interest in not being committed. Normally, however, since this interest is inextricably linked with the parents' interest in and obligation for the welfare and health of the child, the private interest at stake is a combination of the child's and parents' concerns. Next we must examine the State's interest in the procedures it has adopted for commitment and treatment of children. Finally, we must consider how well Georgia's procedures protect against arbitrariness in the decision to commit a child to a state mental hospital.

It is not disputed that a child, in common with adults has a substantial liberty interest in not being confined unnecessarily for medical treatment and that the State's involvement in the commitment decision constitutes state action under the Fourteenth Amendment. See Addington v. Texas, 441 U.S. 418, at 425–426, 99 S.Ct. 1804, at 1809, 60 L.Ed.2d 323 (1979); In re Gault, 387 U.S. 1, 27, 87 S.Ct. 1428, 1443, 18 L.Ed.2d 527 (1967). We also recognize that commitment sometimes produces adverse social consequences for the child because of the reaction of some to the discovery that the child has received psychiatric care.

This reaction, however, need not be equated with the community response resulting from being labeled by the state as delinquent, criminal, or mentally ill and possibly dangerous. The state through its voluntary commitment procedures does not "label" the child; it provides a diagnosis and treatment that medical specialists conclude the child requires. In terms of public reaction, the child who exhibits abnormal behavior may be seriously injured by an erroneous decision not to commit. Appellees overlook a significant source of the public reaction to the mentally ill, for what is truly "stigmatizing" is the symptomatology of a mental or emotional illness. The pattern of untreated, abnormal behavior—even if nondangerous—arouses at least as much negative reaction as treatment that becomes public knowledge. A person needing, but not receiving, appropriate medical care may well face even greater social ostracism resulting from the observable symptoms of an untreated disorder.

However, we need not decide what effect these factors might have in a different case. For purposes of this decision, we assume that a child has a protectible interest not only in being free of unnecessary bodily restraints but also in not being labeled erroneously by some because of an improper decision by the state hospital superintendent.

We next deal with the interests of the parents who have decided, on the basis of their observations and independent professional recommendations, that their child needs institutional care. Appellees argue that the constitutional rights of the child are of such magnitude and the likelihood of parental abuse is so great that the parents' traditional interests in and responsibility for the upbringing of their child must be subordinated at least to the extent of providing a formal adversary hearing prior to a voluntary commitment.

Our jurisprudence historically has reflected Western Civilization concepts of the family as a unit with broad parental authority over minor children. Our cases have consistently followed that course; our constitutional system long ago rejected any notion that a child is "the mere creature of the State" and, on the contrary, asserted that parents generally "have the right, coupled with the high duty, to recognize and prepare [their children] for additional obligations." Pierce v. Society of Sisters, 268 U.S. 510, 535, 45 S.Ct. 571, 573, 69 L.Ed. 1070 (1924). See also Wisconsin v. Yoder, 406 U.S. 205, 213, 92 S.Ct. 1526, 1532, 32 L.Ed.2d 15 (1972); Prince v. Massachusetts, 321 U.S. 158, 166, 64 S.Ct. 438, 442, 88 L.Ed. 645 (1944); Meyer v. Nebraska, 262 U.S. 390, 400, 43 S.Ct. 625, 627, 67 L.Ed. 1042 (1923). Surely, this includes a "high duty" to recognize symptoms of illness and to seek and follow medical advice. The law's concept of the family rests on a presumption that parents possess what a child lacks in maturity, experience, and capacity for judgment required for making life's difficult decisions. More important, historically it has recognized that natural bonds of affection lead parents to act in the best interests of their children. 1 W. Blackstone, Commentaries; 2 Kent, Commentaries on American Law.

As with so many other legal presumptions, experience and reality may rebut what the law accepts as a starting point; the incidence of child neglect and abuse cases attests to this. That some parents "may at times be acting against the interests of their child" as was stated in Bartley v. Kremens, 402 F. Supp. 1039, 1047–1048 (E.D.Pa.1975), vacated, 431 U.S. 119, 97 S.Ct. 1709, 52 L.Ed.2d 184 (1977), creates a basis for caution, but is hardly a reason to discard wholesale those pages of human experience that teach that parents generally do act in the child's best interests. The statist notion that governmental power should supersede parental authority in *all* cases because *some* parents abuse and neglect children is repugnant to American tradition.

Nonetheless, we have recognized that a state is not without constitutional control over parental discretion in dealing with children when their physical or mental health is jeopardized. See Wisconsin v. Yoder, supra, 406 U.S., at 230, 92 S.Ct., at 1540; Prince v. Massachusetts, supra, 321 U.S., at 166, 64 S.Ct., at 442. Moreover, the Court recently declared unconstitutional a state statute that granted parents an absolute veto over a minor child's decision to have an abortion. Planned Parenthood of Missouri v. Danforth, 428 U.S. 52, 96 S.Ct. 2831, 49 L.Ed.2d 788 (1976). Appellees urge that these precedents limiting the traditional rights of parents, if viewed in the context of the liberty interest of the child and the likelihood of parental abuse, require us to hold that the parents' decision to have a child admitted to a mental hospital must be subjected to an exacting constitutional scrutiny, including a formal, adversary, preadmission hearing.

Appellees' argument, however, sweeps too broadly. Simply because the decision of a parent is not agreeable to a child or because it involves risks does not automatically transfer the power to make that decision from the parents to some agency or officer of the state. The same characterizations can be made for a tonsillectomy, appendectomy or other medical procedure. Most children, even in adolescence, simply are not able to make sound judgments concerning many decisions, including their need for medical care or treatment. Parents can and must make those judgments. Here there is no finding by the District Court of even a single instance of bad faith by any parent of any member of appellees' class. We cannot assume that the result in Meyer v. Nebraska, supra, and Pierce v. Society of Sisters, supra, would have been different if the children there had announced a preference to learn only English or a preference to go to a public, rather than a church, school. The fact that a child may balk at hospitalization or complain about a parental refusal to provide cosmetic surgery does not diminish the parents' authority to decide what is best for the child. Neither state officials nor federal courts are equipped to review such parental decisions. . . .

In defining the respective rights and prerogatives of the child and parent in the voluntary commitment setting, we conclude that our precedents permit the parents to retain a substantial, if not the dominant, role in the decision, absent a finding of neglect or abuse, and that the traditional presumption that the parents act in the best interests of their child should apply. We also conclude, however, that the child's rights and the nature of the commitment decision are such that parents cannot always have absolute and unreviewable discretion to decide whether to have a child institutionalized. They, of course, retain plenary authority to seek such care for their children, subject to a physician's independent examination and medical judgment.

The State obviously has a significant interest in confining the use of its costly mental health facilities to cases of genuine need. The Georgia program seeks first to determine whether the patient seeking admission has an illness that calls for in-patient treatment. To accomplish this purpose, the State has charged the superintendents of each regional hospital with the responsibility for determining, before authorizing an admission, whether a prospective patient is mentally ill and whether the patient will likely benefit from hospital care. In addition, the State has imposed a continuing duty on hospital superintendents to release any patient who has recovered to the point where hospitalization is no longer needed. . . .

We now turn to consideration of what process protects adequately the child's constitutional rights by reducing risks of error without unduly trenching on traditional parental authority and with out undercutting "efforts to further the legitimate interests of both the state and the patient that are served by" voluntary commitments. Addington v. Texas, 441 U.S., at 419–420, 99 S.Ct., at 1806. We conclude that the risk of error inherent in the parental decision to have a child institutionalized for mental health care is sufficiently great that some kind of inquiry should be made by a "neutral factfinder" to determine whether the statutory requirements for admission are satisfied. That inquiry must carefully probe the child's background using all available sources, including, but not limited to, parents, schools and other social agencies. Of course, the review must also include an interview with the child. It is necessary that the decisionmaker have the authority to refuse to admit any child who does not satisfy the medical standards for admission. Finally, it is necessary that the child's continuing need for commitment be reviewed periodically by a similarly independent procedure. We are satisfied that such procedures will protect the child from an erroneous admission decision in a way that neither unduly burdens the state nor inhibits parental decisions to seek state help.

Due process has never been thought to require that the neutral and detached trier of fact be law-trained or a judicial or administrative officer. Surely, this is the case as to medical decisions for "neither judges nor administrative hearing officers are better qualified than psychiatrists to render psychiatric judgments." In re Roger S., 19 Cal.3d 921, 941, 141 Cal.Rptr. 298, 569 P.2d 1286, 1299 (1977) (Clark, J., dissenting). Thus, a staff physician will suffice, so long as he or she is free to evaluate independently the child's mental and emotional condition and need for treatment.

It is not necessary that the deciding physician conduct a formal or quasi-formal hearing. A state is free to require such a hearing, but due process is not violated by use of informal traditional medical investigative techniques. Since well-established medical procedures already exist, we do not undertake to outline with specificity precisely what this investigation must involve. The mode and procedure of medical diagnostic procedures is not the business of judges. What is best for a child is an individual medical decision that must be left to the judgment of physicians in each case. We do no more than emphasize that the decision should represent an independent judgment of what the child requires and that all sources of information that are traditionally relied on by physicians and behavioral specialists should be consulted.

What process is constitutionally due cannot be divorced from the nature of the ultimate decision that is being made. Not every determination by state officers can be made most effectively by use of "the procedural tools of judicial or administrative decisionmaking." Board of Curators of U. of Missouri v. Horowitz, 435 U.S. 78, 90, 98 S.Ct. 948, 955, 55 L.Ed.2d 124 (1978).

Here the questions are essentially medical in character: whether the child is mentally or emotionally ill and whether he can benefit from the treatment that is provided by the state. While facts are plainly necessary for a proper resolution of those questions, they are only a first step in the process. In an opinion for a unanimous Court, we recently stated in Addington v. Texas, supra, 441 U.S., at 429–430, 99 S.Ct., at 1811, "whether [a person] is mentally ill . . . turns on the *meaning* of the facts which must be interpreted by expert psychiatrists and psychologists."

Although we acknowledge the fallibility of medical and psychiatric diagnosis, we do not accept the notion that the shortcomings of specialists can always be avoided by shifting the decision from a trained specialist using the traditional tools of medical science to an untrained judge or administrative hearing officer after a judicial-type hearing. Even after a hearing, the nonspecialist decision-maker must make a medical-psychiatric decision. Common human experience and scholarly opinions suggest that the supposed protections of an adversary proceeding to determine the appropriateness of medical decisions for the commitment and, treatment of mental and emotional illness may well be more illusory than real.

Another problem with requiring a formalized, factfinding hearing lies in the danger it poses for significant intrusion into the parent-child relationship. Pitting the parents and child as adversaries often will be at odds with the presumption that parents act in the best interests of their child. It is one thing to require a neutral physician to make a careful review of the parents' decision in order to make sure it is proper from a medical standpoint; it is a wholly different matter to employ an adversary contest to ascertain whether the parents' motivation is consistent with the child's interests.

Moreover, it is appropriate to inquire into how such a hearing would contribute to the long range successful treatment of the patient. Surely, there is a risk that it would exacerbate whatever tensions already existed between the child and the parents. Since the parents can and usually do play a significant role in the treatment while the child is hospitalized and even more so after release, there is a serious risk that an adversary confrontation will adversely affect the ability of the parents to assist the child while in the hospital. Moreover, it will make his subsequent return home more difficult. These unfortunate results are especially critical with an emotionally disturbed child; they seem likely to occur in the context of an adversary hearing in which the parents testify. A confrontation over such intimate family relationships would distress the normal adult parents and the impact on a disturbed child almost certainly would be significantly greater.[18]

It has been suggested that a hearing conducted by someone other than the admitting physician is necessary in order to detect instances where parents are "guilty of railroading their children into asylums" or are using "voluntary commitment procedures in order to sanction behavior of which they disapprove." Ellis, Volunteering Children: Parental Commitment of Minors to Mental Institutions, 62 Calif.L.Rev. 840, 850–851 (1974). Curiously it seems to be taken for granted that parents who seek to "dump" their children on the state will inevitably be able to conceal their motives and thus deceive the admitting psychiatrists and the other mental health professionals who make and review the admission decision. It is elementary that one early diagnostic inquiry into the cause of an emotional disturbance of a child is an examination into the environment of the child. It is unlikely if not inconceivable that a decision to abandon an emotionally normal, healthy child and thrust him into an institution will be a discrete act leaving no trail of circumstances. Evidence of such conflicts will emerge either in the interviews or from secondary sources. It is unrealistic to believe that trained psychiatrists, skilled in eliciting responses, sorting medically relevant facts and sensitive to motivational nuances will often be deceived about the family situation surrounding a child's emotional disturbance.[19] Surely a lay, or even law-trained factfinder, would be no more skilled in this process than the professional.

---

[18] While not altogether clear, the District Court opinion apparently contemplated a hearing preceded by a written notice of the proposed commitment. At the hearing the child presumably would be given an opportunity to be heard and present evidence, and the right to cross-examine witnesses, including, of course, the parents. The court also required an impartial trier of fact who would render a written decision reciting the reasons for accepting or rejecting the parental application.

Since the parents in this situation are seeking the child's admission to the state institution, the procedure contemplated by the District Court presumably would call for some other person to be designated as a guardian *ad litem* to act for the child. The guardian, in turn, if not a lawyer, would be empowered to retain counsel to act as an advocate of the child's interest.

Of course, a state may elect to provide such adversary hearings in situations where it perceives that parents and a child may be at odds, but nothing in the Constitution compels such procedures.

[19] In evaluating the problem of detecting "dumping" by parents, it is important to keep in mind that each of the regional hospitals has a continuing relationship with the Department of Family and Children Services. The staffs at those hospitals refer cases to the Department when they suspect a child is being mistreated and thus are sensitive to this problem. In fact, J.L.'s situation is in point. The family conflicts and problems were well documented in the hospital records. Equally well documented, however, were the child's severe emotional disturbances and his need for treatment.

By expressing some confidence in the medical decisionmaking process, we are by no means suggesting it is error free. On occasion parents may initially mislead an admitting physician or a physician may erroneously diagnose the child as needing institutional care either because of negligence or an overabundance of caution. That there may be risks of error in the process affords no rational predicate for holding unconstitutional an entire statutory and administrative scheme that is generally followed in more than 30 states. "[P]rocedural due process rules are shaped by the risk of error inherent in the truthfinding process as applied to the generality of cases, not the rare exceptions." Mathews v. Eldridge, 424 U.S. 319, 344, 96 S.Ct. 893, 907, 47 L.Ed.2d 18 (1976). In general, we are satisfied that an independent medical decisionmaking process, which includes the thorough psychiatric investigation described earlier followed by additional periodic review of a child's condition, will protect children who should not be admitted; we do not believe the risks of error in that process would be significantly reduced by a more formal, judicial-type hearing. The issue remains whether the Georgia practices, as described in the record before us, comport with these minimum due process requirements.

Georgia's statute envisions a careful diagnostic medical inquiry to be conducted by the admitting physician at each regional hospital. The *amicus* brief of the Solicitor General explains, at pp. 7–8:

> "[I]n every instance the decision whether or not to accept the child for treatment is made by a physician employed by the State. . . .
>
> "That decision is based on interviews and recommendations by hospital or community health center staff. The staff interviews the child and the parent or guardian who brings the child to the facility . . . [and] attempts are made to communicate with other possible sources of information about the child. . . ."

Focusing primarily on what it saw as the absence of any formal mechanism for review of the physician's initial decision, the District Court unaccountably saw the medical decision as an exercise of "unbridled discretion." 412 F. Supp., at 136. But extravagant characterizations are no substitute for careful analysis and we must examine the Georgia process in its setting to determine if, indeed, any one person exercises such discretion.

In the typical case the parents of a child initially conclude from the child's behavior that there is some emotional problemCin short, that "something is wrong." They may respond to the problem in various ways, but generally the first contact with the State occurs when they bring the child to be examined by a psychologist or psychiatrist at a community mental health clinic. Most often, the examination is followed by outpatient treatment at the community clinic. In addition, the child's parents are encouraged, and sometimes required, to participate in a family therapy program to obtain a better insight into the problem. In most instances, this is all the care a child requires. However, if, after a period of outpatient care, the child's abnormal emotional condition persists, he may be referred by the local clinic staff to an affiliated regional mental hospital.

At the regional hospital an admissions team composed of a psychiatrist and at least one other mental health professional examines and interviews the child—privately in most instances. This team then examines the medical records provided by the clinic staff and interviews the parents. Based on this information, and any additional background that can be obtained, the admissions team makes a diagnosis and determines whether the child will likely benefit from institutionalized care. If the team finds either condition not met, admission is refused.

If the team admits a child as suited for hospitalization, the child's condition and continuing need for hospital care are reviewed periodically by at least one independent, medical review group. For the most part, the reviews are as frequent as weekly, but none are less often than once every two months. Moreover, as we noted earlier the superintendent of each hospital is charged with an affirmative statutory duty to discharge any child who is no longer mentally ill or in need of therapy.[21]

As with most medical procedures, Georgia's are not totally free from risk of error in the sense that they give total or absolute assurance that every child admitted to a hospital has a mental illness optimally suitable for institutionalized treatment. But it bears repeating that "procedural due process rules are shaped by the risk of error inherent in the truth-finding process as applied to the generality of cases, not the rare exceptions." Mathews v. Eldridge, supra, 424 U.S., at 344, 96 S.Ct., at 907. Georgia's procedures are not "arbitrary" in the sense that a single physician or other professional has the "unbridled discretion" the District Court saw to commit a child to a regional hospital. To so find on this record would require us to assume that the physicians, psychologists and mental health professionals who participate in the admission decision and who review each others' conclusions as to the continuing validity of the initial decision are either oblivious or indifferent to the child's welfare—or that they are incompetent. We note, however, the District Court found to the contrary; it was "impressed by the conscientious, dedicated state employed psychiatrists who, with the help of equally conscientious dedicated state employed psychologists and social workers, faithfully care for the plaintiff children. . . ." 412 F. Supp., at 138.

This finding of the District Court also effectively rebuts the suggestion made in some of the briefs *amici* that hospital administrators may not actually be "neutral and detached" because of institutional pressure to admit a child who has no need for hospital care. That such a

[21] While the record does demonstrate that the procedures may vary from case to case, it also reflects that no child in Georgia was admitted for indefinite hospitalization without being interviewed personally and without the admitting physician checking with secondary sources, such as school or work records.

practice may take place in some institutions in some places affords no basis for a finding as to Georgia's program; the evidence in the record provides no support whatever for that charge against the staffs at any of the State's eight regional hospitals. Such cases, if they are found, can be dealt with individually;[22] they do not lend themselves to class-action remedies.

We are satisfied that the voluminous record as a whole supports the conclusion that the admissions' staffs of the hospitals have acted in a neutral and detached fashion in making medical judgments in the best interests of the children. . . .

Although our review of the record in this case satisfies us that Georgia's general administrative and statutory scheme for the voluntary commitment of children is not *per se* unconstitutional, we cannot decide on this record, whether every child in appellees' class received an adequate, independent diagnosis of his emotional condition and need for confinement under the standards announced earlier in this opinion. On remand, the District Court is free to and should consider any individual claims that initial admissions did not meet the standards we have described in this opinion. . . .

On this record we are satisfied that Georgia's medical factfinding processes are reasonable and consistent with constitutional guarantees. Accordingly, it was error to hold unconstitutional the State's procedures for admitting a child for treatment to a state mental hospital. . . .

Reversed and remanded.

■ [The concurring opinion of MR. JUSTICE STEWART is omitted.]

■ [In a separate opinion MR. JUSTICE BRENNAN, joined by MR. JUSTICE MARSHALL and MR. JUSTICE STEVENS concurred in part and dissented in part.

While finding the present Georgia admission procedures "reasonably consistent" with the constitutional principles they outlined, they regard the postadmission procedures as "simply not enough to qualify as hearings—let alone reasonably prompt hearings. The procedures lack all the traditional due process safeguards." As to juvenile wards of the State, the Justices find that "the special considerations that justify postponement of formal commitment proceedings whenever parents seek to hospitalize their children are absent when the children are wards of the State and are being committed upon recommendations of their social workers." In the absence of "exigent circumstances" they would require preadmission commitment hearings for such juveniles.]

[22] One important means of obtaining individual relief for these children is the availability of habeas corpus. As the appellants' brief explains, "Ga.Code § 88–502.11 provides that at any time and without notice a person detained in a facility, or a relative or friend of such person, may petition for a writ of habeas corpus to question the cause and legality of the detention of the person." Brief for Appellants 36–37.

NOTES

The prerogative of a parent to make medical decisions concerning his or her minor child arises in the context of physical illness, mental illness, pregnancy and childbirth, and end-of-life procedures. Often, state statutes will specifically address issues arising pertaining to sexual activity, emergency situations, and when a minor may consent to treatment himself or herself. The Arkansas statute that follows offers an illustration. For commentary on medical decision-making within the context of the parent-child relationship, *see* Robin Fretwell Wilson, *The Perils of Privatized Marriage, in* MARRIAGE AND DIVORCE IN A MULTI-CULTURAL CONTEXT: RECONSIDERING THE BOUNDARIES OF CIVIL LAW AND RELIGION (Joel A. Nichols, ed., Cambridge University Press, 2011); Karen Syma Czapanskiy, *Chalimony: Seeking Equity Between Parents of Children With Disabilities and Chronic Illnesses*, 34 N.Y.U. REV. L. & SOC. CHANGE 253 (2010); Dean J. Haas, *"Doctor, I'm Pregnant and Fifteen—I Can't Tell My Parents, Please Help Me": Minor Consent, Reproductive Rights, and Ethical Principles for Physicians*, 86 N.D. L. REV. 63 (2010). In J.R. v. Hansen, 803 F.3d 1315, 1326 (11th Cir. 2015), the court considered the holding from the *Parham* decision and held that Florida's involuntary commitment scheme violated the Due Process Clause of the Fourteenth Amendment by failing to require periodic review of continued involuntary commitments by a decision-maker with the duty to consider and the authority to order release.

ARKANSAS CODE ANNOTATED (2016)

§ 20–9–601. Definition

(a) As used in this subchapter, "of unsound mind" means the inability to perceive all relevant facts related to one's condition and proposed treatment so as to make an intelligent decision based thereon, whether or not the inability is:

(1) Only temporary, has existed for an extended period of time, or occurs or has occurred only intermittently; or

(2) Due to natural state, age, shock or anxiety, illness, injury, drugs or sedation, intoxication, or other cause of whatever nature.

(b) An individual shall not be considered to be of unsound mind based solely upon his or her refusal of medical care or treatment.

§ 20–9–602. Consent Generally

It is recognized and established that, in addition to other authorized persons, any one (1) of the following persons may consent, either orally or otherwise, to any surgical or medical treatment or procedure not prohibited by law that is suggested, recommended, prescribed, or directed by a licensed physician:

(1) Any adult, for himself or herself;

(2) (A) Any parent, whether an adult or a minor, for his or her minor child or for his or her adult child of unsound mind

whether the child is of the parent's blood, an adopted child, a stepchild, a foster child not in custody of the Department of Human Services, or a preadoptive child not in custody of the Department of Human Services.

(B) However, the father of an illegitimate child cannot consent for the child solely on the basis of parenthood;

(3) Any married person, whether an adult or a minor, for himself or herself;

(4) Any female, regardless of age or marital status, for herself when given in connection with pregnancy or childbirth, except the unnatural interruption of a pregnancy;

(5) Any person standing in loco parentis, whether formally serving or not, and any guardian, conservator, or custodian, for his or her ward or other charge under disability;

(6) Any emancipated minor, for himself or herself;

(7) Any unemancipated minor of sufficient intelligence to understand and appreciate the consequences of the proposed surgical or medical treatment or procedures, for himself or herself;

(8) Any adult, for his or her minor sibling or his or her adult sibling of unsound mind;

(9) During the absence of a parent so authorized and empowered, any maternal grandparent and, if the father is so authorized and empowered, any paternal grandparent, for his or her minor grandchild or for his or her adult grandchild of unsound mind;

(10) Any married person, for a spouse of unsound mind;

(11) Any adult child, for his or her mother or father of unsound mind;

(12) Any minor incarcerated in the Department of Correction or the Department of Community Correction, for himself or herself; and

(13) (A) Any foster parent or preadoptive parent for a child in custody of the Department of Human Services in:

(i) (a) Emergency situations.

(b) As used in this subdivision, "emergency situation" means a situation in which, in competent medical judgment, the proposed surgical or medical treatment or procedures are immediately or imminently necessary and any delay occasioned by an attempt to obtain a consent would reasonably be expected to jeopardize the life, health, or safety of the person affected or would reasonably be expected to result in disfigurement or impaired faculties;

(ii) Routine medical treatment;

(iii) Ongoing medical treatment;

(iv) Nonsurgical procedures by a primary care provider; and

(v) Nonsurgical procedures by a specialty care provider.

(B) The Department of Human Services shall be given timely notice of all admissions and discharges consented to by a foster parent or preadoptive parent for a child in custody of the Department of Human Services.

(C) The consent of a representative of the Department of Human Services is required for:

(i) Nonemergency surgical procedures;

(ii) Nonemergency invasive procedures;

(iii) "End of life" nonemergency procedures such as do-not-resuscitate orders, withdrawal of life support, and organ donation; and

(iv) Nonemergency medical procedures relating to a criminal investigation or judicial proceeding that involves gathering forensic evidence.

§ 20–9–603. Implied Consent; Circumstances

In addition to any other instances in which consent is excused or implied at law, consent to surgical or medical treatment or procedures suggested, recommended, prescribed, or directed by a licensed physician will be implied in the following circumstances:

(1) (A) When an emergency exists and there is no one immediately available who is authorized, empowered to, or capable of consent.

(B) An emergency is defined as a situation in which, in competent medical judgment, the proposed surgical or medical treatment or procedures are immediately or imminently necessary and any delay occasioned by an attempt to obtain a consent would reasonably be expected to jeopardize the life, health, or safety of the person affected or would reasonably be expected to result in disfigurement or impaired faculties; and

(2) When any emergency exists, there has been a protest or refusal of consent by a person authorized and empowered to do so, and there is no other person immediately available who is authorized, empowered, or capable of consenting but there has been a subsequent material and morbid change in the condition of the affected person.

§ 20–9–604. Emergency Consent by Courts

(a) (1) Except as provided in subsection (e) of this section, consent may be given by a court when:

(A) An emergency exists;

(B) There has been a protest or refusal of consent by a person authorized and empowered to do so; and

(C) There is no other person immediately available who is authorized, empowered, or capable of consent.

(2) The consent shall be given upon the presentation of a petition accompanied by the written advice or certification of one (1) or more licensed physicians that in their professional opinion there is an immediate or imminent necessity for medical or surgical treatment or procedures.

(3) Any circuit judge may summarily grant injunctive and declaratory relief ordering and directing that the necessary surgical or medical treatment or procedures be rendered, provided that the affected person is:

(A) A pregnant female in the last trimester of pregnancy;

(B) A person of insufficient age or mental capacity to understand and appreciate the nature of the proposed surgical or medical treatment and the probable consequences of refusal of the treatment; or

(C) A parent of a minor child, provided that the court in its discretion finds that the life or health of the parent is essential to the child's financial support or physical or emotional well-being.

(b) Any circuit judge granting the declaratory and injunctive relief directing the provision of surgical or medical treatment or procedures pursuant to this section shall be immune from liability based on any claim that the surgical or medical treatment or procedures for the affected person should not have been administered.

(c) The reasonable expense incurred for emergency surgical or medical treatment or procedures administered pursuant to this section shall be borne by:

(1) The estate of the person affected;

(2) Any person liable at law for the necessities of the person affected; or

(3) If the estate or person is unable to pay, the county of residence of the person receiving the surgical or medical care.

(d) Upon request of an attending physician, any other licensed physician, or a representative of a hospital to which a patient has been admitted or presented for treatment, it shall be the duty of the prosecuting attorney, or his or her designee, of the county in which the surgical or medical care is proposed to be rendered to give his or her assistance in the presentation of the petition, with medical advice or certificate, and in obtaining an order from the court of proper jurisdiction.

(e) (1) Consent may be given by a court when an emergency exists and there is no one immediately available who is authorized, empowered to, or capable of consent for a person of unsound mind or there has been a subsequent material and morbid change in the condition of the affected person who is in the custody of the Department of Correction or the Department of Community Correction.

(2) The consent shall be given upon the presentation of a petition accompanied by the written advice or certificate of one (1) or more licensed physicians that in their professional opinion there is an immediate or imminent necessity for medical or surgical treatment or procedures.

(3) Any circuit judge may summarily grant injunctive and declaratory relief ordering and directing that the necessary surgical or medical treatment or procedures be rendered.

3. STERILIZATION OF CHILD

Stump v. Sparkman

Supreme Court of the United States, 1978
435 U.S. 349

■ WHITE, JUSTICE delivered the opinion of the Court.

. . .

The relevant facts underlying respondent's suit are not in dispute. On July 9, 1971, Ora Spitler McFarlin, the mother of respondent Linda Kay Spitler Sparkman, presented to Judge Harold D. Stump of the Circuit Court of DeKalb County, Ind., a document captioned "Petition To Have Tubal Ligation Performed On Minor and Indemnity Agreement." The document had been drafted by her attorney, a petitioner here. In this petition Mrs. McFarlin stated under oath that her daughter was 15 years of age and was "somewhat retarded," although she attended public school and had been promoted each year with her class. The petition further stated that Linda had been associating with "older youth or young men" and had stayed out overnight with them on several occasions. As a result of this behavior and Linda's mental capabilities, it was stated that it would be in the daughter's best interest if she underwent a tubal ligation in order "to prevent unfortunate circumstances. . . ." In the same document Mrs. McFarlin also undertook to indemnify and hold harmless Dr. John Hines, who was to perform the operation, and the DeKalb Memorial Hospital, where the operation was to take place, against all causes of action that might arise as a result of the performance of the tubal ligation.

The petition was approved by Judge Stump on the same day. He affixed his signature as "Judge, DeKalb Circuit Court," to the statement that he did "hereby approve the above Petition by affidavit form on behalf of Ora Spitler McFarlin, to have Tubal Ligation performed upon her minor daughter, Linda Spitler, subject to said Ora Spitler McFarlin covenanting and agreeing to indemnify and keep indemnified Dr. John Hines and the DeKalb Memorial Hospital from any matters or causes of action arising therefrom."

On July 15, 1971, Linda Spitler entered the DeKalb Memorial Hospital, having been told that she was to have her appendix removed. The following day a tubal ligation was performed upon her. She was released several days later, unaware of the true nature of her surgery. Approximately two years after the operation, Linda Spitler was married to respondent Leo Sparkman. Her inability to become pregnant led her to discover that she had been sterilized during the 1971 operation. As a result of this revelation, the Sparkmans filed suit in the United States District Court for the Northern District of Indiana against Mrs. McFarlin, her attorney, Judge Stump, the doctors who had performed and assisted in the tubal ligation, and the DeKalb Memorial Hospital. Respondents sought damages for the alleged violation of Linda Sparkman's constitutional rights; also asserted were pendent state claims for assault and battery, medical malpractice, and loss of potential fatherhood.

Ruling upon the defendants' various motions to dismiss the complaint, the District Court concluded that each of the constitutional claims asserted by respondents required a showing of state action and that the only state action alleged in the complaint was the approval by Judge Stump, acting as Circuit Court Judge, of the petition presented to him by Mrs. McFarlin. The Sparkmans sought to hold the private defendants liable on a theory that they had conspired with Judge Stump to bring about the allegedly unconstitutional acts. The District Court, however, held that no federal action would lie against any of the defendants because Judge Stump, the only state agent, was absolutely immune from suit under the doctrine of judicial immunity. . . .

The governing principle of law is well established and is not questioned by the parties. As early as 1872, the Court recognized that it was "a general principle of the highest importance to the proper administration of justice that a judicial officer, in exercising the authority vested in him, [should] be free to act upon his own convictions, without apprehension of personal consequences to himself." Bradley v. Fisher [13 Wall. 335, 347 (1872)]. For that reason the Court held that "judges of courts of superior or general jurisdiction are not liable to civil actions for their judicial acts, even when such acts are in excess of their jurisdiction, and are alleged to have been done maliciously or corruptly." Later we held that this doctrine of judicial immunity was applicable in suits under § 1 of the Civil Rights Act of 1871, 42 U.S.C. § 1983, for the legislative record gave no indication that Congress intended to abolish this long-established principle. Pierson v. Ray, 386 U.S. 547, 87 S.Ct. 1213, 18 L.Ed.2d 288 (1967).

The Court of Appeals correctly recognized that the necessary inquiry in determining whether a defendant judge is immune from suit is whether at the time he took the challenged action he had jurisdiction over the subject matter before him. Because "some of the most difficult and embarrassing questions which a judicial officer is called upon to consider and determine relate to his jurisdiction . . . " *Bradley,* supra, at 352, the scope of the judge's jurisdiction must be construed broadly where the issue is the immunity of the judge. A judge will not be deprived of immunity because the action he took was in error, was done maliciously, or was in excess of his authority; rather, he will be subject to liability only when he has acted in the "clear absence of all jurisdiction."[7] 13 Wall., at 351.

We cannot agree that there was a "clear absence of all jurisdiction" in the DeKalb County Circuit Court to consider the petition presented by Mrs. McFarlin. As an Indiana Circuit Court Judge, Judge Stump had "original exclusive jurisdiction in all cases at law and in equity whatsoever . . . " jurisdiction over the settlement of estates and over guardianships, appellate jurisdiction as conferred by law, and jurisdiction over "all other causes, matters and proceedings where exclusive jurisdiction thereof is not conferred by law upon some other court, board or officer." Ind.Code § 33–4–4–3 (1975). This is indeed a broad jurisdictional grant; yet the Court of Appeals concluded that Judge Stump did not have jurisdiction over the petition authorizing Linda Sparkman's sterilization.

In so doing, the Court of Appeals noted that the Indiana statutes provided for the sterilization of institutionalized persons under certain circumstances, see Ind.Code §§ 16–13–13–1 through 16–13–13–4 (1973), but otherwise contained no express authority for judicial approval of tubal ligations. It is true that the statutory grant of general jurisdiction to the Indiana circuit courts does not itemize types of cases those courts may hear and hence does not expressly mention sterilization petitions presented by the parents of a minor. But in our view, it is more significant that there was no Indiana statute and no case law in 1971 prohibiting a circuit court, a court of general jurisdiction, from considering a petition of the type presented to Judge Stump. The statutory authority for the sterilization of institutionalized persons in the custody of the State does

[7] In *Bradley,* the Court illustrated the distinction between lack of jurisdiction and excess of jurisdiction with the following examples: if a probate judge, with jurisdiction over only wills and estates, should try a criminal case, he would be acting in the clear absence of jurisdiction and would not be immune from liability for his action; on the other hand, if a judge of a criminal court should convict a defendant of a nonexistent crime, he would merely be acting in excess of his jurisdiction and would be immune. Id., at 352.

not warrant the inference that a court of general jurisdiction has no power to act on a petition for sterilization of a minor in the custody of her parents, particularly where the parents have authority under the Indiana statutes to "consent to and contract for medical or hospital care or treatment of [the minor] including surgery." Ind.Code § 16–8–4–2 (1973). The District Court concluded that Judge Stump had jurisdiction under § 33–4–4–3 to entertain and act upon Mrs. McFarlin's petition. We agree with the District Court, it appearing that neither by statute nor by case law has the broad jurisdiction granted to the circuit courts of Indiana been circumscribed to foreclose consideration of a petition for authorization of a minor's sterilization.

The Court of Appeals also concluded that support for Judge Stump's actions could not be found in the common law of Indiana, relying in particular on the Indiana Court of Appeals' intervening decision in A.L. v. G.R.H., 163 Ind.App. 636, 325 N.E.2d 501 (1975). In that case the Indiana court held that a parent does not have a common-law right to have a minor child sterilized, even though the parent might "sincerely believe the child's adulthood would benefit therefrom." Id., at 638, 325 N.E.2d, at 502. The opinion, however, speaks only of the rights of the parents to consent to the sterilization of their child and does not question the *jurisdiction* of a circuit judge who is presented with such a petition from a parent. Although under that case a circuit judge would err as a matter of law if he were to approve a parent's petition seeking the sterilization of a child, the opinion in A.L. v. G.R.H. does not indicate that a circuit judge is without jurisdiction to entertain the petition. Indeed, the clear implication of the opinion is that, when presented with such a petition, the circuit judge should deny it on its merits rather than dismiss it for lack of jurisdiction.

Perhaps realizing the broad scope of Judge Stump's jurisdiction, the Court of Appeals stated that, even if the action taken by him was not foreclosed under the Indiana statutory scheme, it would still be "an illegitimate exercise of his common law power because of his failure to comply with elementary principles of procedural due process." This misconceives the doctrine of judicial immunity. A judge is absolutely immune from liability for his judicial acts even if his exercise of authority is flawed by the commission of grave procedural errors. . . .

Because the court over which Judge Stump presides is one of general jurisdiction, neither the procedural errors he may have committed nor the lack of a specific statute authorizing his approval of the petition in question rendered him liable in damages for the consequences of his actions.

The respondents argue that even if Judge Stump had jurisdiction to consider the petition presented to him by Mrs. McFarlin, he is still not entitled to judicial immunity because his approval of the petition did not constitute a "judicial" act. It is only for acts performed in his "judicial" capacity that a judge is absolutely immune, they say. We do not disagree with this statement of the law, but we cannot characterize the approval of the petition as a nonjudicial act. . . . [Respondents] argue that Judge Stump's approval of the petition was not a judicial act because the petition was not given a docket number, was not placed on file with the clerk's office, and was approved in an *ex parte* proceeding without notice to the minor, without a hearing, and without the appointment of a guardian *ad litem*. . . .

The relevant cases demonstrate that the factors determining whether an act by a judge is a "judicial" one relate to the nature of the act itself, i.e., whether it is a function normally performed by a judge, and to the expectations of the parties, i.e., whether they dealt with the judge in his judicial capacity. Here, both factors indicate that Judge Stump's approval of the sterilization petition was a judicial act. State judges with general jurisdiction not infrequently are called upon in their official capacity to approve petitions relating to the affairs of minors, as for example, a petition to settle a minor's claim. Furthermore, as even respondents have admitted, at the time he approved the petition presented to him by Mrs. McFarlin, Judge Stump was "acting as a county circuit court judge." See supra, at 1106. We may infer from the record that it was only because Judge Stump served in that position that Mrs. McFarlin, on the advice of counsel, submitted the petition to him for his approval. Because Judge Stump performed the type of act normally performed only by judges and because he did so in his capacity as a Circuit Court Judge, we find no merit to respondents' argument that the informality with which he proceeded rendered his action nonjudicial and deprived him of his absolute immunity. . . .

The Indiana law vested in Judge Stump the power to entertain and act upon the petition for sterilization. He is, therefore, under the controlling cases, immune from damages liability even if his approval of the petition was in error. Accordingly, the judgment of the Court of Appeals is reversed, and the case is remanded for further proceedings consistent with this opinion.

■ MR. JUSTICE BRENNAN took no part in the consideration or decision of this case.

■ [The dissenting opinion of MR. JUSTICE STEWART, with whom MR. JUSTICE MARSHALL and MR. JUSTICE POWELL join, is omitted.]

VIRGINIA CODE ANNOTATED (2016)

§ 54.1–2975. Sterilization operations for certain children incapable of informed consent

It shall be lawful for any physician licensed by the Board of Medicine to perform a vasectomy, salpingectomy, or other surgical sexual sterilization procedure on a pers on fourteen years of age or older and less than eighteen years of age when:

1. A petition has been filed in the circuit court of the county or city wherein the child resides by the parent or parents having custody of the child or by the child's guardian, spouse, or next friend requesting that the operation be performed;

2. The court has made the child a party defendant, served the child, the child's guardian, if any, the child's spouse, if any, and the child's parent who has custody of the child with notice of the proceedings and appointed for the child an attorney-at-law to represent and protect the child's interests;

3. The court has determined that a full, reasonable, and comprehensible medical explanation as to the meaning, consequences, and risks of the sterilization operation to be performed and as to alternative methods of contraception has been given by the physician to the child upon whom the operation is to be performed, to the child's guardian, if any, to the child's spouse, if any, and, if there is no spouse, to the parent who has custody of the child;

4. The court has determined by clear and convincing evidence that the child's mental abilities are so impaired that the child is incapable of making his or her own decision about sterilization and is unlikely to develop mentally to a sufficient degree to make an informed judgment about sterilization in the foreseeable future;

5. The court, to the greatest extent possible, has elicited and taken into account the views of the child concerning the sterilization, giving the views of the child such weight in its decision as the court deems appropriate;

6. The court has complied with the requirements of § 54.1–2977; and

7. The court has entered an order authorizing a qualified physician to perform the operation not earlier than thirty days after the date of the entry of the order, and thirty days have elapsed. The court order shall state the date on and after which the sterilization operation may be performed.

§ 54.1–2969

. . .

D. A minor shall be deemed an adult for the purpose of consenting to:

1. Medical or health services needed to determine the presence of or to treat venereal disease or any infectious or contagious disease which the State Board of Health requires to be reported;

2. Medical or health services required in case of birth control, pregnancy or family planning except for the purposes of sexual sterilization;

3. Medical or health services needed in the case of outpatient care, treatment or rehabilitation for substance abuse. . .

4. Medical or health services needed in the case of outpatient care, treatment or rehabilitation for mental illness or emotional disturbance.

E. Except for the purposes of sexual sterilization, any minor who is or has been married shall be deemed an adult for the purpose of giving consent to surgical and medical treatment.

4. PREFERENCES OF THE CHILD

In re Green

Supreme Court of Pennsylvania, 1972
292 A.2d 387

■ JONES, CHIEF JUSTICE.

[Ricky Green, age fifteen, was the subject of a neglect petition seeking the appointment of a guardian who would consent to corrective surgery. The petition was dismissed but that decision was reversed by the Superior Court.]

Ricky suffers from paralytic scoliosis (94% curvature of the spine).

Due to this curvature of the spine, Ricky is presently a "sitter," unable to stand or ambulate due to the collapse of his spine; if nothing is done, Ricky could become a bed patient. Doctors have recommended a "spinal fusion" to relieve Ricky's bent position, which would involve moving bone from Ricky's pelvis to his spine. Although an orthopedic specialist testified, "there is no question that there is danger in this type of operation," the mother did consent conditionally to the surgery. The condition is that, since the mother is a Jehovah's Witness who believes that the Bible proscribes any blood transfusions which would be necessary for this surgery, she would not consent to any blood transfusions. Initially, we must recognize that, while the operation would be beneficial, there is no evidence that Ricky's life is in danger or that the operation must be performed immediately. Accordingly, we are faced with the situation of a parent who will not consent to a dangerous operation on her minor son requiring blood transfusions solely because of her religious beliefs. . . .

Almost a century ago, the United States Supreme Court enunciated the twofold concept of the Free Exercise clause: "Laws are made for the government of actions, and while they cannot interfere with mere religious belief and opinions, they may with practices." Reynolds v. United States, 98 U.S. 145, 166 (1878). Thus, it was stated in Prince v. Massachusetts, 321 U.S. 158, 166–167, 64 S.Ct. 438, 442, 88 L.Ed. 645 (1944):

> "But the family itself is not beyond regulation in the public interest, as against a claim of religious liberty. Reynolds v. United States, 98 U.S. 145, 25 L.Ed. 244; Davis v. Beason, 133 U.S. 333, 10 S.Ct. 299. And neither rights of religion nor rights

> of parenthood are beyond limitation. Acting to guard the general interest in youth's well being the state as *parens patriae* may restrict the parent's control by requiring school attendance [footnote omitted], regulating or prohibiting the child's labor [footnote omitted] and in many other ways [footnote omitted]. Its authority is not nullified merely because the parent grounds his claim to control the child's course of conduct on religion or conscience. Thus, he cannot claim freedom from compulsory vaccination for the child more than for himself on religious grounds [footnote omitted]. The right to practice religion freely does not include liberty to expose the community or the child to communicable disease or the latter to ill health or death. People v. Pierson, 176 N.Y. 201, 68 N.E. 243 [footnote omitted]. The catalogue need not be lengthened. It is sufficient to show what indeed appellant hardly disputes, that the state has a wide range of power for limiting parental freedom and authority in things affecting the child's welfare; and that this includes, to some extent, matters of conscience and religious conviction."

On the other hand, the United States Supreme Court recently stated, "to agree that religiously grounded conduct must often be subject to the broad police power of the State is not to deny that there are areas of conduct protected by the Free Exercise Clause of the First Amendment and thus beyond the power of the State to control, even under regulations of general applicability." Wisconsin v. Yoder, 406 U.S. 205, 92 S.Ct. 1526 (1972). "The conduct or actions so regulated have invariably posed some substantial threat to public safety, peace or order." Sherbert v. Verner, 374 U.S. 398, 403, 83 S.Ct. 1790, 1793 (1963). Without appearing callous, Ricky's unfortunate condition, unlike polygamy, vaccination, child labor and the like, does not pose a substantial threat to society; in this fashion, [the earlier cases] are readily distinguishable. . . .

Turning to the situation where an adult refuses to consent to blood transfusions necessary to save the life of his infant son or daughter, other jurisdictions have uniformly held that the state can order such blood transfusions over the parents' religious objections.

In our view, the penultimate question presented by this appeal is whether the state may interfere with a parent's control over his or her child in order to enhance the child's physical well-being when the child's life is in no immediate danger and when the state's intrusion conflicts with the parent's religious beliefs. Stated differently, does the State have an interest of sufficient magnitude to warrant the abridgment of a parent's right to freely practice his or her religion when those beliefs preclude medical treatment of a son or daughter whose life is not in immediate danger? We are not confronted with a life or death situation as in the cases cited earlier in this opinion. Nor is there any question in the case at bar of a parent's omission or neglect for non-religious reasons. . . .

[The Court discusses In re Sampson, 29 N.Y.2d 900, 328 N.Y.S.2d 686, 278 N.E.2d 918 (1972). The court states that the New York Court of Appeals opinion made the observation that "religious objections to blood transfusions do not 'present a bar at least where the transfusion is necessary to the success of the required surgery.' " It then adds:]

[W]e disagree with [this] observation in a non-fatal situation and express no view of the propriety of that statement in a life or death situation. If we were to describe this surgery as "required," like the Court of Appeals, our decision would conflict with the mother's religious beliefs. Aside from religious considerations, one can also question the use of that adjective on medical grounds since an orthopedic specialist testified that the operation itself was dangerous. Indeed, one can question who, other than the Creator, has the right to term certain surgery as "required." This fatal/nonfatal distinction also steers the courts of this Commonwealth away from a medical and philosophical morass: if spinal surgery can be ordered, what about a hernia or gall bladder operation or a hysterectomy? The problems created by *Sampson* are endless. We are of the opinion that as between a parent and the state, the state does not have an interest of sufficient magnitude outweighing a parent's religious beliefs when the child's life is *not immediately imperiled* by his physical condition.

Unlike *Yoder* and *Sampson*, our inquiry does not end at this point since we believe the wishes of this sixteen-year-old boy should be ascertained; the ultimate question, in our view, is whether a parent's religious beliefs are paramount to the possibly adverse decision of the child. In *Yoder*, Mr. Justice Douglas, dissenting in part, wanted to remand the matter in order to determine whether the Amish children wished to continue their education in spite of their parents' beliefs: "if an Amish child desires to attend high school, and is mature enough to have that desire respected, the State may well be able to override the parents' religiously motivated objections," 406 U.S. at 242, 92 S.Ct. at 1546. The majority opinion as well as the concurring opinion of Mr. Justice Stewart did not think it wise to reach this point for two principal reasons: (1) it was the parents, not the children, who were criminally prosecuted for their religious beliefs; and (2) the record did not indicate a parent-child conflict as the testimony of the lone child witness coincided with her parents' religious beliefs. While the record before us gives no indication of Ricky's thinking, it is the child rather than the parent in this appeal who is directly involved which thereby distinguishes *Yoder's* decision not to discuss the beliefs of the parents vis-a-vis the children. In *Sampson,* the Family Court judge decided not to "evade the responsibility for a decision now by the simple expedient of foisting upon this boy the responsibility for making a decision at some later day. . . ." 65 Misc.2d 658, 317 N.Y.S.2d at 655. While we are cognizant of the realistic problems of this approach enunciated by Judge (now Chief Judge) Fuld in his *Seaforth** dissent, we believe that Ricky should be heard.

It would be most anomalous to ignore Ricky in this situation when we consider the preference of an intelligent child of sufficient maturity in determining custody. . . . Moreover, we have held that a child of the same age can waive constitutional rights and receive a life sentence. . . . Indeed, minors can now bring a personal injury action in Pennsylvania against their parents. We need not extend this litany of the rights of children any further to support the proposition that Ricky should be heard. The record before us does not even note whether Ricky is a Jehovah's Witness or plans to become one. We shall, therefore, reserve any decision regarding a possible parent-child conflict and remand the matter for an evidentiary hearing similar to the one conducted in *Seaforth* in order to determine Ricky's wishes.

The order of the Superior Court is reversed and the matter remanded to the Court of Common Pleas of Philadelphia, Family Division, Juvenile Branch, for proceedings consistent with the views expressed in this opinion. . . .

■ EAGAN, JUSTICE (dissenting). With all due deference to the majority of this Court, I am compelled to dissent. I would affirm the order of the Superior Court.

The Court's analysis presumes there are two primary interests at stake, that of the state to protect its citizens, and that of the mother to follow her religious convictions. The difficulty, and what I believe to be the fatal flaw in this reasoning, is that too little consideration and attention is given to the interests of the health and well-being of this young boy. Although the mother's religious beliefs must be given the fullest protection and respect, I do not believe the mother's religious convictions should be our primary consideration. As Mr. Justice Rutledge aptly stated:

> "Parents may be free to become martyrs themselves. But it does not follow they are free, in identical circumstances, to make martyrs of their children before they have reached the age of full

* [In In re Seiferth, 309 N.Y. 80, 127 N.E.2d 820 (1955), the father of a fourteen year old boy with a cleft palate and harelip refused to permit corrective surgery, instead preferring to "let the natural forces of the universe work on the body". The court refused to declare the child neglected and appoint someone to consent to the surgery, saying that there was no serious threat to his health or life and, in effect, that the boy would be able to make his own decision after a few more years. Fuld, J., dissenting, stated:

> "Every child has a right, so far as is possible, to lead a normal life and, if his parents, through viciousness or ignorance, act in such a way as to endanger that right, the courts should, as the legislature has provided, act in his behalf. Such is the case before us."
>
> . . .
>
> "The welfare and interests of a child are at stake. A court should not place upon his shoulders one of the most momentous and far-reaching decisions of his life. The court should make the decision, as the statute contemplates, and leave to the good sense and sound judgment of the public authorities the job of preparing the boy for the operation and of getting him as adjusted to it as possible. We should not put off the decision on the chance that the child may change his mind and submit at some future time to the operation."—*EDS.*]

> and legal discretion when they can make that choice for themselves."

Prince v. Commonwealth, 321 U.S. 158, 170, 64 S.Ct. 438, 444 (1944).... The court below determined that the mother's exercise of control here would undoubtedly expose the child to progressively worsening ill health, but it still refused to assert the State's power by finding the child neglected....

The statute only speaks in terms of "health" not life or death. If there is a substantial threat to health, then I believe the courts can and should intervene to protect Ricky. By the decision of this Court today, this boy may never enjoy any semblance of a normal life which the vast majority of our society has come to enjoy and cherish.

Lastly, I must take issue with the manner in which the majority finally disposes of the case. I do not believe that sending the case back to allow Ricky to be heard is an adequate solution. We are herein dealing with a young boy who has been crippled most of his life, consequently, he has been under the direct control and guidance of his parents for that time. To now presume that he could make an independent decision as to what is best for his welfare and health is not reasonable. See In Matter of Seiferth, 309 N.Y. 80, 85, 127 N.E. 820, 823 (1955) (dissenting opinion, Fuld, J.). Moreover, the mandate of the Court presents this youth with a most painful choice between the wishes of his parents and their religious convictions on the one hand, and his chance for a normal, healthy life on the other hand. We should not confront him with this dilemma.

NOTES

On Remand. The lower court held an evidentiary hearing to determine Ricky's wishes respecting the proposed surgery. He indicated that he did not wish to submit to surgery. His decision was not based solely on religious grounds. He also stated that he had been in the hospital a long time already and that no one said "it is going to come out right." *In re* Green, 452 Pa. 373, 307 A.2d 279 (1973).

In *In re* Sampson, 65 Misc.2d 658, 317 N.Y.S.2d 641 (1970), with which the majority decision in *Green* expressed disagreement, Kevin Sampson, fifteen-years-old at the time his case came before a New York family court, had suffered since childhood from neurofibromatosis. A large, bag-like growth enveloped one side of his face. It caused one ear, cheek, and eyelid to droop and one side of his face to be roughly twice as large as the other. Because of his deformity, he had not attended school for several years. A lengthy and dangerous operation, followed by prolonged treatment, might alleviate his condition cosmetically but would not effect a cure. The surgery required transfusions of whole blood, but because of her beliefs as a Jehovah's Witness, Kevin's mother would allow only the use of plasma. In a proceeding instituted by the County Health Commissioner, the Family Court declared Kevin a "neglected" child and ordered his mother to permit such surgery as the Commissioner deemed necessary. The Appellate Division upheld the order, carefully pointing out that Kevin was "neglected" only in a technical sense, for his mother was not shown to have failed her son except in this one decision. The Court of Appeals affirmed per curiam. Not one judge dissented as the case passed through the state's entire judicial process.

The *Sampson* facts did not present a general pattern of abuse or culpable neglect but only a single, controversial parental decision, albeit a major one. Both the Family Court and the Appellate Division explicitly recognized that inaction did not mean probable death and that the operation would remove only some of the unsightly growth. Plastic surgery and several years of continuing treatment would be necessary. One surgeon described the initial operation as "a risky surgical procedure" of six to eight hours duration and occasioning great loss of blood. And far from demanding immediate action, according to the witness, the operation would be less hazardous if postponed until the boy reached maturity. Then the potential blood loss would be less in relation to his body's total supply. In short, it might be said that it was not the mother's refusal to consent but the operation itself that was life-threatening.

The trial court justified overriding the objections lodged both by the child's mother and his guardian ad litem by a humane desire to salvage some semblance of a normal life for Kevin Sampson:

> I am persuaded that if this court is to meet its responsibilities to this boy it can neither shift the responsibility onto his shoulders nor can it permit his mother's religious beliefs to stand in the way of obtaining through corrective surgery whatever chance he may have for a normal, happy existence, which . . . is difficult of attainment under the most propitious circumstances, but will unquestionably be impossible if the disfigurement is not corrected.

In re Sampson, 65 Misc.2d 658, 317 N.Y.S.2d 641, 657 (1970), affirmed per curiam 29 N.Y.2d 900, 328 N.Y.S.2d 686, 278 N.E.2d 918 (1972). *See also*, Lynn D. Wardle, *Controversial Medical Treatments for Children: The Roles of Parents and of the State*, 49 FAM. L. Q. 509 (2015) (discussing sexual orientation change efforts by parents); and B. Jessie Hill, *Medical Decision Making By and on Behalf of Adolescents: Reconsidering First Principles,* 15 J. HEALTH CARE & POL'Y 37 (2012).

5. ORGAN TRANSPLANTATIONS

Hart v. Brown

Superior Court of Connecticut, Fairfield County, 1972
29 Conn.Sup. 368

■ TESTO, JUDGE.

This matter is before this court by way of an action for a declaratory judgment. General Statutes § 52–29; Practice Book § 307.

The plaintiffs are Peter Hart and Eleanor Hart, the parents and natural guardians of Katheleen A. Hart and Margaret H. Hart, minors, identical twins, age seven years and ten months. The minor twins appear herein by court-appointed guardians ad litem: Attorney Thomas Dolan for the minor, Margaret, and Mrs. Sylvia Chandler for the minor Katheleen. The defendants are practicing physicians licensed in this state and the Yale-New Haven Hospital, Inc., a duly organized Connecticut corporation located in the city and county of New Haven.

The plaintiff minor Katheleen A. Hart is presently a patient in the Yale-New Haven Hospital awaiting a kidney transplant. It is reasonably probable that if such procedure does not occur soon she will die. The defendant physicians have in the past performed successful kidney transplantation operations, and they are of the opinion that a successful transplantation operation can be performed on the plaintiff minors, Katheleen A. Hart as donee and Margaret H. Hart as donor.

The plaintiffs Peter Hart and Eleanor Hart, each of whom had originally offered a kidney, have requested as parents and natural guardians of the identical twins the transplantation operation of the kidney, but the defendant physicians are unwilling to perform this operation and the defendant hospital refuses the use of its facilities unless this court declares that the parents and/or guardians ad litem of the minors have the right to give their consent to the operation upon the minor twins.

The equity powers of a court must be cautiously and sparingly exercised and only in rare instances should they be exercised. The need must be urgent, the probabilities of success should be most favorable, and the duty must be clear. If it were otherwise, a court of equity, in a case such as this might assume omnipotent powers; to do so is not the function of the court and must be avoided.

The inherent power of a court of equity to grant the relief sought herein has been decided previously in our American courts. In earlier decisions, the English courts took a broader view of this power, with respect to incompetents. Ex parte Whitbread, 2 Mer. 99, 35 Eng.Rep. 878 (Ch.1816). That case held that a court of equity has the power to make provisions for a needy brother from the estate of an incompetent. This inherent rule was followed in this country in New York; Re Willoughby, 11 Paige 257 (N.Y.Ch.1844); where the court stated that a chancellor has the power to deal with the estate of an incompetent in the same manner as the incompetent if he had his faculties. This rule has been extended to cover not only property matters but also the personal affairs of an incompetent. 27 Am.Jur.2d 592, Equity, § 69. "[A] court of equity has full and complete jurisdiction over the persons of those who labor under any legal disability. . . . The court's action . . . is not limited by any narrow bounds, but it is empowered to stretch forth its arm in whatever direction its aid . . . may be needed. While this indeed is a special exercise of equity jurisdiction, it is beyond question that by virtue thereof the court may pass upon purely personal rights." Ibid. The right to act for an incompetent has been recognized as the "doctrine of substituted judgment" and is broad enough to cover all matters touching on the well-being of legally incapacitated persons. The doctrine has been recognized in American courts since 1844.

This court is not being asked to act where a person is legally incompetent. The matter, however, does involve two minors who do not have the legal capacity to consent. This situation was dealt with in three earlier unreported cases decided in our sister state of Massachusetts. The commonwealth of Massachusetts ruled that a court of equity does have the power to permit the natural parents of minor twins to give their consent to a procedure such as is being contemplated by this court. Those cases involved minors of the ages of nineteen, fourteen and fourteen. In a similar case, Strunk v. Strunk, 445 S.W.2d 145 (Ky.1969), a court of equity was confronted with whether or not it had the power to permit the natural parent of a twenty-seven-year-old mental incompetent with a mentality of a six-year-old to give her consent to a kidney transplantation operation. The Kentucky case dealt with a transplant from the mental incompetent to his twenty-eight-year-old brother. The court held that a court of equity does have such power, applying also the "doctrine of substituted judgment." Therefore, this court is of the opinion that it has the power to act in this matter.

The facts of the case as testified to by competent medical witnesses are as follows: Katheleen Hart is a minor of the age of seven years and ten months and is suffering from a hemolytic uremic syndrome. This is a disorder of the kidneys with clots within the small blood vessels. This disease has no known etiology and is prevalent primarily in young children. The diagnosis was confirmed on November 29, 1971, after a kidney biopsy was performed. Hemodialysis treatments were commenced on December 8, 1971, along with other treatment to correct this disorder. On February 1, 1972, her kidney was biopsied for the second time because of the onset of a malignant type of blood pressure elevation, and this biopsy disclosed a new and more disastrous lesion—malignant hypertension—which could prove fatal. On February 17, 1972, a bilateral nephrectomy was performed with removal of both kidneys to control the situation. As of that date, Katheleen became a patient with fixed uremia with no potential kidney function and required dialysis treatments twice weekly. The prospect of survival is, because of her age, at best questionable. It was medically advised that she not continue this dialysis therapy but rather that a kidney transplantation take place.

The types of kidney transplantations discussed in this matter were a parental homograft—transfer of tissue from one human being to another—and an isograft, that is, a one-egg twin graft from one to another. The parental homograft always presents a serious problem of rejection by the donee. Because the human body rejects any foreign organs, the donee must be placed upon a program of immunosuppressive drugs to combat such rejection. An isograft transplantation, on the other hand, is not presented with the problem of rejection. A one-egg twin carries the same genetic material, and, because of this, rejection is not a factor in the success rate of the graft.

The chance of Katheleen's surviving dialysis therapy for a period of five years was estimated at fifty-fifty, with the possibility of many other complications setting in. The ultimate purpose of dialysis treatment in a child this age is to keep the patient alive until a kidney transplant is found. Because of the many complications involved in a transplantation procedure other than with the minor identical twin as donor, it has been medically advised that an isograft transplantation be recommended.

Since 1966, it is reported in the Ninth Report of the Human Renal Transplant Registry, twelve twin grafts have been performed. All twelve have been successful, as reported by the Registry, at one-and two-year follow-ups. In the identical-twin donations since 1966, grafts are functioning at 100 percent. Before 1966, because of technical matters, the survival rate was about 90 percent. Of all isografts followed since 1966, all are successful. In this type of a graft there is substantially a 100 percent chance that the twins will live out a normal life span—emotionally and physically.

If a parent donates the kidney, the statistics show less success. The average percent of success in that type of transplant has been 70 percent at one year and 65 percent or so over a two-year period. The falloff thereafter runs another 5 to 10 or more percent per year. The long-range survival of a parent transplant runs around 50 to 55 percent over a period of five years and appears to fall off to about 37 percent over a period of seven years.

The side effects of the immunosuppressive drugs in a parental homograft are numerous and include the possibility of bone marrow toxicity, liver damage, and a syndrome called Cushing syndrome—a roundish face, a "buffalo hump" on the back of the neck, and growth retardation. Some less common side effects are a demineralization of the bone mass which will result in the collapsing of bones of the spine; aseptic necrosis of the femoral head of the hip, making a person unable to walk; peptic ulcer disease with bleeding; hairiness; sexual immaturity; and cataracts of the eyes. It has also been reported that two suicides have occurred because of the psychological effect upon young girls resulting from immunosuppressive drugs. An overall percentage of around 70 to 77 percent would be expected to survive two years from a parental graft. It is also possible that 40 to 50 percent of the patients might still be surviving at near ten years with a parental graft.

Of 3000 recorded kidney operations of live donors, there is reported only one death of a donor, and even this death may have been from causes unrelated to the procedure. The short-range risk to a donor is negligible. The operating surgeon testified that the surgical risk is no more than the risk of the anesthesia. The operative procedure would last about two and one-half hours. There would be some minor post-operative pain but no more than in any other surgical procedure. The donor would be hospitalized for about eight days and would be able to resume normal activities in thirty days. Assuming an uneventful recovery, the donor would thereafter be restricted only from violent contact sports. She would be able to engage in all of the normal life activities of an active young girl. Medical testimony indicated that the risk to the donor is such that life insurance actuaries do not rate such individuals higher than those with two kidneys. The only real risk would be trauma to the one remaining kidney, but testimony indicated that such trauma is extremely rare in civilian life.

The tests to be performed on the donor are an intravenous pyelogram and an aortagram. The former would permit the examiner to visualize the structure and anatomy of the kidneys, while the latter would outline the blood vessels that supply the blood to the kidneys. Both tests involve a single needle puncture—one into a vein and one into an artery. There might be a skin graft test performed if necessary to confirm the fact that donor and donee are identical twins. The operation would not be performed if the medical team was not fully satisfied that the donor and the donee are identical twins.

A psychiatrist who examined the donor gave testimony that the donor has a strong identification with her twin sister. He also testified that if the expected successful results are achieved they would be of immense benefit to the donor in that the donor would be better off in a family that was happy than in a family that was distressed and in that it would be a very great loss to the donor if the donee were to die from her illness.

The donor has been informed of the operation and insofar as she may be capable of understanding she desires to donate her kidney so that her sister may return to her. A clergyman was also a witness and his testimony was that the decision by the parents of the donor and donee was morally and ethically sound. The court-appointed guardian ad litem for the donor gave testimony that he conferred with the parents, the physicians, the donor, and other men in the religious profession, and he has consented to the performance of the operation. The medical testimony given at this hearing clearly indicates that scientifically this type of procedure is a "perfect" transplant.

The court has weighed the testimony of the clergyman who stated that the natural parents are making a morally sound decision. Also, the testimony of the court-appointed guardians ad litem was that they are giving their consent to the procedure. The psychiatric testimony is of limited value only because of the ages of the minors. The testimony of the natural parents was reviewed by this court, and it is apparent that they came to their decision only after many hours of agonizing consideration.

One of the legal problems in this matter presents a balancing of the rights of the natural parents and the rights of minor children—more directly the rights of the donor child. Because of the unusual circumstances of this case and the fact of great medical progress in this field, it would appear that the natural parents would be able to substitute their consent for that of the minor children after a close, independent and objective investigation of their motivation and reasoning. This has been accomplished in this matter by the participation of a clergyman, the defendant physicians, an attorney guardian ad litem for the donor, the guardian ad litem for the donee, and, indeed, this court itself.

A further question before this court is whether it should abandon the donee to a brief medically complicated life and eventual death or permit the natural parents to take some action based on reason and medical probability in order to keep both children alive. The court will choose the latter course, being of the opinion that the kidney transplant procedure contemplated herein—an isograft—has progressed at this time to the point of being a medically proven fact of life. Testimony was offered that this type of procedure is not clinical experimentation but rather medically accepted therapy.

There is authority in our American jurisdiction that nontherapeutic operations can be legally permitted on a minor as long as the parents or other guardians consent to the procedure. Bonner v. Moran, 75 U.S.App.D.C. 156, 126 F.2d 121 (1941). That case involved skin grafting from a fifteen-year-old boy to his cousin, who was severely burned. The year of the case was 1941, when such skin homografting—transferring tissue from one human being to another—was relatively novel. "[H]ere we have a case of a surgical operation not for the benefit of the person operated on but for another, and also so involved in its technique as to require a mature mind to understand precisely what the donor was offering to give." Id., 123. The court held that the consent of the parent was necessary.

In Strunk v. Strunk, 445 S.W.2d 145 (Ky.1969), the adult donor was a legal incompetent. The court in the commonwealth of Kentucky authorized the parent to give her consent. The incompetent had the mental capacity of a six-year-old. The court further held that the saving of the life of the incompetent's brother would be of benefit to the donor. In the instant case, it has been stated that the donor would enjoy a better future life if her ailing twin sister were kept alive. The difference between the cases is subtle. The donor here is almost eight years old. In the *Strunk* case, the donor was an adult with the mentality of a six-year-old. The risks to the donee in the *Strunk* case were more than what are presented here, the procedure there being a related homograft as compared to an isograft in this case, as discussed earlier in this opinion. The accomplished results in that matter and in this matter are identical.

Thus, also, in the Massachusetts cases discussed above, where the doctrine of "grave emotional impact" to the donors was first used, the courts of that state permitted the procedures.

This court is confronted with a combination of the *Strunk* case and the Massachusetts cases in that the procedures in the latter involved minor identical twins and in the former a legally incompetent adult with the mental capacity of an infant. In the case at bar we have an identical twin donor almost eight years old. Justice was accomplished in all of the aforementioned cases. Justice will be accomplished in this case. This court can and will make a determination of this matter, using the doctrines of law as stated in the *Strunk* case, in the *Bonner* case, and in the Massachusetts cases.

The court understands that the operation on the donee is a necessity for her continued life; that there are negligible risks involved to both donor and donee; that to subject the donee to a parental homograft may be cruel and inhuman because of the possible side effects of the immunosuppressive drugs; that the prognosis for good health and long life to both children is excellent; that there is no known opposition to having the operations performed; that it will be most beneficial to the donee; and that it will be of some benefit to the donor. To prohibit the natural parents and the guardians ad litem of the minor children the right to give their consent under these circumstances, where there is supervision by this court and other persons in examining their judgment, would be most unjust, inequitable and injudicious. Therefore, natural parents of a minor should have the right to give their consent to an isograft kidney transplantation procedure when their motivation and reasoning are favorably reviewed by a community representation which includes a court of equity.

It is the judgment of this court that Eleanor Hart and Peter Hart have the right, under the particular facts and circumstances of this matter, to give their consent to the operations on both minor children and to give their consent to the defendant physicians to conduct the further medical tests that the defendants deem necessary prior to the performing of the operations, provided the defendant physicians medically establish the children to be identical twins and a report of their findings is filed with this court.

Judgment accordingly.

NOTES

In Strunk v. Strunk, 445 S.W.2d 145 (Ky.1969), the court authorized the transplant of a kidney from a mentally handicapped adult to his brother who was facing end stage renal disease and needed a transplant. The court justified the decision as a benefit to the donor by explaining that the donor's well being "would be jeopardized more severely by the loss of his brother than by removal of a kidney." In Curran v. Bosze, 141 Ill.2d 473, 153 Ill.Dec. 213, 566 N.E.2d 1319 (1990), the Supreme Court of Illinois confronted a situation in which an eight year old with undifferentiated leukemia needed a bone transplant. The father of the child and his stepbrother were not HLA identical. Several years earlier Mr. Bosze had fathered identical twins from an affair with Ms. Curran. The father filed suit seeking to have the twins submit for bone marrow harvesting over the objection of their mother. The court held that the substituted judgment doctrine was not applicable and that the best interests of the twins was not served by having them tested for compatibility when they would not benefit medically and there was some risk of harm to them in the procedure.

With advances in immunosuppression drugs and surgical and medical techniques, and programs to encourage organ donation, organ transplantation has increased. No longer is the sibling relationship so critical, and thus the primary problem faced in *Hart* and *Strunk* is much less important in most cases. A new issue that has risen concerns the decision of parents to bear another child in order to assist their existing child through tissue transplantation. For discussion of the ethical issues involved, *see* Mark P. Aulisio, Thomas May, and Geoffrey D. Block, *Procreation for Donation: The Moral and Political Permissibility of "Having a Child to Save a Child"*, 110 CAMBRIDGE QUARTERLY OF HEALTHCARE ETHICS 408 (2001). For additional commentary on organ donations taken from minors, see Doriane Lambelet Coleman, *Testing the Boundaries of Family Privacy: The Special Case of Pediatric Sibling Transplants*, 35 CARDOZO L. REV. 1289 (2014); Doriane Lambelet Coleman, *The Legal Ethics of Pediatric Research,* 57 DUKE L.J. 517 (2007); Samuel J. Tilden, *Ethical and Legal Aspects of Using an Identical Twin as a Skin Transplant Donor for a Severely Burned Minor*, 31 AM. J.L. & MED. 87 (2005).

CALIFORNIA FAMILY CODE (2016)

§ 6910. Medical treatment of minor; adult entrusted with consensual power

The parent, guardian, or caregiver of a minor who is a relative of the minor and who may authorize medical care and dental care under Section 6550, may authorize in writing an adult into whose care a minor has been entrusted to consent to medical care or dental care, or both, for the minor.

6. WITHHOLDING LIFE SUPPORT

In re Doe

Supreme Court of Georgia, 1992
418 S.E.2d 3

■ CLARKE, JUSTICE.

In this appeal from a final order in a declaratory judgment action, we face several difficult issues relating to medical decision-making for a terminally ill child. Jane Doe, a 13-year-old child, had experienced medical problems since birth. In May, 1991, she was admitted to Scottish Rite Hospital following a mild choking episode. Initially her attending physicians expected she would recover. Over the next weeks, however, her condition degenerated and she became limp and unresponsive. The doctors described her condition as "stuporous" or varying between stupor and coma states, and noted her brain stem was shrinking or degenerating. She also suffered from various systemic illnesses. The doctors agreed that she suffered from a degenerative neurological disease, but none could make a certain diagnosis.

In late May her doctors placed Jane on a respirator. By mid-July she had suffered recurrent infections and mental decline. At that time the doctors decided it was necessary to insert tracheostomy and gastronomy (feeding and breathing) tubes surgically. They discussed the possibility of a "Do Not Resuscitate" (DNR) order with her parents in case Jane suffered cardiac arrest during the procedure. Jane's mother, Susan Doe, agreed to a DNR order; her father, John Doe, did not. In August, Jane Doe's condition continued to decline. The doctors began to discuss whether deescalation of life support[1] and a DNR order might be appropriate. In early September, Susan Doe supported deescalation of life support and a DNR order. John Doe did not. At Susan Doe's request, Jane's medical situation was presented to Scottish Rite's Bioethics Committee. The Committee considered and evaluated Jane's condition and recommended the hospital back Jane's mother's desire to enter a DNR order and deescalate medical treatment.

At the time of the hearing, she favored a DNR order, but not deescalation of treatment. After an evidentiary hearing, the trial judge entered an order enjoining the hospital from deescalating treatment or from enforcing a DNR order unless both parents agreed to such a course of treatment. The state filed this appeal.[2]

We find no merit to the state's contention that the hospital had no standing to bring this declaratory judgment action. We must construe the declaratory judgment statute liberally. The statute is available in situations presenting an " 'actual controversy' . . . where interested parties are asserting adverse claims upon a state of facts wherein a legal judgment is sought that would control or direct future action." Darnell v. Tate, 206 Ga. 576, 580, 58 S.E.2d 160 (1950).

Here, the hospital was charged with a duty of care to an incompetent patient whose parents disagreed as to the appropriate course of medical treatment. Neither precedent nor statute provided a clear answer to the hospital's dilemma. Meanwhile, Jane Doe's condition continued to deteriorate and the likelihood that she would experience cardiac arrest increased daily. Without guidance as to which parent's instructions to follow, the hospital could not determine its legal obligation to its patient. On these facts, we conclude that the hospital adequately demonstrated a

---

[1] Deescalation is the discontinuation of medical measures, such as a ventilator. A DNR order means that extreme lifesaving procedures like countershock, chest compression and administration of medication to support heart rate and blood pressure will not be instituted in the event of cardiac or respiratory failure.

[2] Although Jane Doe died several weeks after the final order was entered in the declaratory judgment action below, this appeal is not moot because it is among those cases which are "capable of repetition yet evading review." In re L.H.R., 253 Ga. 439, 321 S.E.2d 716 (1984) (quoting Gerstein v. Pugh 420 U.S. 103, 95 S.Ct. 854, 43 L.Ed.2d 54 (1975)).

need for a legal judgment that would control its future action. A declaratory judgment action was appropriate.[3]

The state next contends the trial court erred in considering the hospital's petition because Jane Doe did not meet the criteria for withdrawal of life support established in In re L.H.R., 253 Ga. 439, 321 S.E.2d 716 (1984). In In re: L.H.R. we held that, in the absence of any conflicting state interest, a patient has a right to refuse medical treatment which right is not lost because of the youth or incompetence of the patient. We went on to say: We conclude that the right to refuse treatment may be exercised by the parents or legal guardian of the infant after diagnosis that the infant is terminally ill with no hope of recovery and that the infant exists in a chronic vegetative state with no reasonable possibility of attaining cognitive function. The above diagnosis must be made by the attending physician. Two physicians with no interest in the outcome of the case must concur in the diagnosis and prognosis. Although prior judicial approval is not required, the courts remain available in the event of disagreement between the parties, any case of suspected abuse, or other appropriate instances. In this case the state emphasizes Jane Doe's doctors could not diagnose with certainty the disease causing her neurological degeneration. The state also points out Jane Doe was not in a chronic vegetative state and death was not imminent.[4] Therefore, the state asserts, the hospital could not raise the issue of deescalation of medical treatment and the trial court should have dismissed the case.

First, we reject the state's argument that the trial court should have dismissed this case because Jane Doe did not meet the criteria expressed in In re L.H.R. In In re L.H.R. we addressed a specific set of circumstances and decided that the parents and physicians caring for the infant could decide whether to proceed with deescalation of medical treatment without seeking judicial approval. The opinion set up guidelines to protect the rights of incompetent patients without involving the court in the medical decision-making process for every incompetent patient. The opinion did not preclude considering the propriety of deescalation under other circumstances. During the years since we considered In re L.H.R., the legislature has enacted or amended several statutes governing the legal propriety of proxy health care decisions. See, OCGA § 31–32–1, et seq. (Living Wills); OCGA § 31–36–1, et seq. (Durable Power of Attorney for Health Care); and OCGA § 31–39–1, et

[3] Contrary to the state's suggestion, this action does not fall within the exclusive jurisdiction of Juvenile Court. See OCGA § 15–11–5. The action did not seek to terminate the legal parent-child relationship or to wrest custody or control from Jane Doe's parents. Further, Jane Doe was not a "deprived child," because both parents actively sought the best available care and treatment for her.

[4] Imminence of death is not a criterion for deescalation of medical treatment under In re L.H.R. or under the current provisions of the Living Will statute. See OCGA § 31–32–1 (1992). See also State v. McAfee, 259 Ga. 579, 385 S.E.2d 651 (1989). This court and the Georgia legislature have recognized, as have numerous other courts, scholars, and ethicists, that medical technology can extend the dying process almost indefinitely, so that technical death might not occur for many years if artificial support systems are continued.

seq. (Cardiopulmonary Resuscitation). Also, other courts have recognized that incompetent patients have the right to refuse life sustaining treatment even though they are not in a chronic vegetative state.[5] Thus, while medical technology and society's understanding of death and dying continue to evolve and change, we cannot mandate a single, static formula for deciding when deescalation of medical treatment may be appropriate. Rather, we endorse the view that medical decision-making for incompetent patients is most often best left to the patient's family (or other designated proxy) and the medical community . . . and the courts remain available to decide controversial cases.

We further reject the state's argument that Jane Doe's parents could not legally have decided to deescalate her medical treatment. The medical staff attending to Jane Doe agreed that she was in the final stages of some degenerative neurological disease, and that she vacillated between coma and stupor, responding only to deep pain stimulus. She required artificial means to support all her bodily functions. The doctors agreed she lacked the ability for any cognitive function or interactive activity, and did not have any reasonable hope for her recovery. They also agreed there was no known medical treatment that could improve her condition or halt the neurological deterioration. It was apparent that the life support system was prolonging her death, rather than her life. There was no state interest in maintaining life support systems. Thus, we conclude that those legally responsible for Jane Doe could have refused treatment on her behalf without seeking prior judicial approval.

A corollary to the above statement is that Jane Doe's parents also could have consented to treatment on her behalf. See OCGA § 31–9–2 (Persons authorized to consent to medical or surgical treatment). At the time of the hearing, both parents opposed deescalation of treatment. No party in this case argues that the parents' mutual decision to continue life support measures should have been overridden under the facts of this case.[46] This appeal does not present and we do not reach any issue

---

[5] See, e.g., Superintendent of Belchertown State Sch. v. Saikewicz, 373 Mass. 728, 370 N.E.2d 417 (1977) (chemotherapy treatment could be withheld from a profoundly retarded and disoriented man suffering from leukemia, where the chemotherapy would not cure his disease but merely prolong his suffering); In re Spring, 380 Mass. 629, 405 N.E.2d 115 (1980) (life-prolonging but noncurative hemodialysis treatment could be withheld from conscious but profoundly senile patient suffering from kidney disease); In re Hier, 18 Mass.App. 200, 464 N.E.2d 959 (1984) (surgery necessary for insertion of a stomach feeding tube could be withheld from incompetent person suffering from delusions and severe mental illness); In re Conroy, 98 N.J. 321, 486 A.2d 1209 (1985) (right to terminate life-sustaining treatment could be exercised on behalf of an incompetent person with serious and permanent mental and physical impairments and a life expectancy less than 1 year); Foody v. Manchester Mem. Hosp., 40 Conn.Sup. 127, 482 A.2d 713 (1984) (life-sustaining treatment could be withheld from semicomatose patient described as "awake but unaware").

[6] The law recognizes that parents "possess what a child lacks in maturity, experience and capacity for judgment required for making life's difficult decisions. More importantly . . . natural bonds of affection lead parents to act in the best interests of their children." In re L.H.R., 253 Ga. 439, 321 S.E.2d 716 (1984) (quoting Parham v. J.R., 442 U.S. 584, 602, 99 S.Ct. 2493, 2504, 61 L.Ed.2d 101 (1979)). Therefore, the law presumes that the parents are the appropriate parties to make their children's medical decisions. For this reason in In re L.H.R., supra, we held that, under certain circumstances, the parents of an incompetent child may exercise the

regarding "medical abuse." Therefore, the trial court correctly enjoined the hospital from deescalating treatment over both parents' objection.[7]

The state next asserts the trial court erred in holding that a DNR order requires the concurrence of both parents of the child. The statute requires the agreement of both parents, if both parents are present and actively participating in the medical decision-making process for the child. OCGA § 31–39–1 allows "any parent"[8] to consent to a DNR order for a minor child. OCGA § 31–39–6 allows "any parent" to revoke consent to an order not to resuscitate. The result is as follows: One parent may consent. If there is no second parent, if the other parent is not present, or if the other parent simply prefers not to participate in the decision, the consent of one parent to a DNR order is legally sufficient under the statute. However, if there is a second custodial parent who disagrees with the decision to forego cardiopulmonary resuscitation, the second parent may revoke consent under the terms of OCGA § 31–39–6(b). We reject the argument that only the parent who has given consent may effectively revoke consent. Where two parents have legal custody of a child, each parent shares equal decision-making responsibility for that child. If consent to a DNR order is revoked under the provision of OCGA § 31–39–6(b), the hospital must follow the statutory presumption that every patient is presumed to consent to resuscitation.[9] See OCGA § 31–39–3(a). Thus, because the father revoked consent, the trial court correctly determined the hospital could not enter a DNR order.

■ HUNT, JUSTICE, concurring.

I write in response to the state's motion for reconsideration.

The state urges that we further delineate the limits of a hospital's standing in cases like this one. In particular, the state asks us to hold, as did the trial court, that a hospital would not have standing to advocate an alternative course of treatment where the parents or legal guardians agree about the course of treatment for their child. We make no such holding, and our opinion should not be read to confer standing for a hospital under circumstances other than those presented here; that is, where the parents disagree about the course of such medical treatment. This is not to imply that, when a case presents the issue, we would interpret a hospital's standing either more broadly or more narrowly

child's right to refuse medical treatment without prior judicial approval. We have never held, however, that parents have an absolute right to make medical decisions for their children. See, e.g., Jefferson v. Griffin Spalding County Hospital Authority, 247 Ga. 86, 274 S.E.2d 457 (1981); In the Interest of C.R., 160 Ga.App. 873, 288 S.E.2d 589 (1982). The United States Supreme Court similarly does not recognize an absolute right of a parent to make medical decisions for a child. See Parham v. J.R., supra.

[7] This appeal does not present any issue regarding what should have been done if Jane Doe's parents had disagreed at trial or thereafter about the propriety of deescalating treatment.

[8] Note that the statute defines "parent" as a parent who has custody of a minor. OCGA § 31–39–2(10).

[9] The statutory presumption governs only consent to emergency cardio-pulmonary resuscitation. No statutory or other presumption governs the issue of consent to other, non-emergency medical procedures.

than we have done here. Compare Jefferson v. Griffin Spalding County Hospital Authority, 247 Ga. 86, 274 S.E.2d 457 (1981).

Montalvo v. Borkovec

Court of Appeals of Wisconsin, 2002
647 N.W.2d 413, appeal denied, 257 Wis 2d 118, *cert. denied*, 123 S.Ct. 1485 (2003)

■ WEDEMEYER, P.J.

Nancy Montalvo, Brian Vila and Emanuel L. Vila (by his guardian ad litem, Timothy J. Aiken) appeal from judgments entered after the trial court dismissed their complaint against Dr. Brent W. Arnold, Dr. Jonathan H. Berkoff, St. Mary's Hospital of Milwaukee, the Wisconsin Patients Compensation Fund and Physicians Insurance Co. of Wisconsin. The complaint alleged that the defendants were negligent for failing to sufficiently inform Montalvo and Vila of the risk of disability to Emanuel following his premature birth by cesarean section.

Montalvo, Vila, and Emanuel raise ten arguments[1] We address only those arguments necessary to the resolution of this case. Because under our current rules of pleading and procedure, substantive law, and public policy the plaintiffs' claims cannot be pursued, we affirm.

On November 21, 1996, Montalvo entered St. Mary's Hospital in Milwaukee, Wisconsin, with pre-term labor symptoms. An ultrasound revealed that the baby was 23 and 3/7 weeks old, and weighed 679 grams. Attempts to interrupt her labor and delay the birth were unsuccessful. Prior to delivery of the child, the parents executed an informed consent agreement for a cesarean procedure. Dr. Terre Borkovec performed the cesarean section. At birth, Emanuel was "handed off" to Dr. Arnold, a neonatologist, who successfully performed life-saving resuscitation measures.

On November 19, 1999, Montalvo filed a complaint against Borkovec and Arnold alleging that both physicians violated the informed consent statute, Wis. Stat. § 448.30, in performing the cesarean section. The complaint also alleged that Arnold, Berkoff, and St. Mary's Hospital were negligent for violating the same informed consent statute when they performed "life-saving measures" for Emanuel. The complaint alleged that because the physicians failed to advise the parents of "the risks or

---

[1] They argue: (1) Montalvo had a right to informed consent prior to the cesarean procedure; (2) the decision to use potentially harmful therapy is subject to informed consent; (3) Wisconsin abortion law does not apply to this situation; (4) with the exception of the drug/alcohol abuse provisions of ch. 48, expectant mothers have the absolute right to control the manner of delivery; (5) the concept of "viability" cannot mean preservation of life at any cost; (6) the lifelong ramifications of perinatal treatment decisions mandate that such decisions be made by the parents only after being fully informed of all the risks and alternatives; (7) federal funding statutes do not control Wisconsin informed consent law; (8) the Americans with Disabilities Act does not control this case; (9) there is no constitutional basis for federal or state government interference in the medical decision-making process; and (10) compelling parents to agree to surgeries or therapies whose benefit versus risk analysis is unclear puts an unfair burden on parents.

potential consequences of a child born at 23 or 24 weeks gestation and/or with a birth weight of less than 750 grams," consent was not informed and a variety of damages resulted.

Berkoff, Arnold, and St. Mary's Hospital moved to dismiss the claims contending that the complaint failed to state a claim upon which relief could be granted pursuant to Wis. Stat. § 802.06(2)(a)6. During a hearing on the motions, and prior to rendering a decision, the trial court ascertained that the plaintiffs were not alleging harm to Emanuel as the result of "extraordinary care measures" but were claiming that the decision to use "extraordinary care measures" should have been relegated to them as parents rather than left to the physicians. Lastly, the plaintiffs were not alleging that Emanuel was disabled by any actions taken by the physicians or St. Mary's Hospital.

The trial court dismissed the complaint ruling first that the only claim pled for a violation of the informed consent statute in performing the cesarean section was against Arnold.[2] Because, however, he was only a bystander to the delivery, he was not required under the statute to provide informed consent because he did not perform the procedure. Second, the trial court ruled that Wisconsin law does not leave the resuscitation decision upon the birth of a child solely to the parents because of the community's interest in protecting children, and the physicians' commitment to preserving life. Montalvo now appeals.

A motion to dismiss a complaint for failure to state a claim upon which relief may be granted tests the legal sufficiency of the pleading. Evans v. Cameron, 121 Wis.2d 421, 426, 360 N.W.2d 25 (1985). As a question of law, we review the trial court's decision independently, keeping in mind the value we accord the trial court's analysis. We must affirm a judgment dismissing a complaint for failure to state a claim if, upon review of the complaint, as liberally construed, it is quite clear that under no conditions can the plaintiff recover based upon the facts alleged and inferences reasonably drawn. Bartley v. Thompson, 198 Wis.2d 323, 332, 542 N.W.2d 227 (Ct.App.1995). With these rubrics of review in mind, we now examine the issues dispositive of this appeal.

The original defendants in this case were Drs. Borkovec, Arnold, Berkoff and St. Mary's Hospital. Borkovec, who performed the cesarean section, was voluntarily dismissed from the case. That left Arnold as the only target allegedly negligent for failure to obtain a properly informed consent for the performance of the cesarean section. Yet, it was undisputed that Arnold, although present when the cesarean section occurred, did not participate in the procedure. The trial court construed Wis. Stat. § 448.30 to provide that only the treating physician, here Borkovec, owed the responsibility of informed consent to the parents. Borkovec, however, was no longer a party to the action. The statute does

[2] For reasons undisclosed in the record, Dr. Terre Borkovec was voluntarily dismissed from the action.

not impose the duty of informed consent on non-treating physicians. Because Arnold neither participated nor assisted, he was not a treating physician with respect to the cesarean procedure, and did not have a duty to comply with the informed consent statute.

Thus, the trial court concluded that with respect to the cesarean procedure, no claim had been properly pleaded upon which relief could be granted. We know of no authority to the contrary. In this respect, the trial court did not err. On appeal, Montalvo has not contested this ruling. Consequently, the only claims remaining to be addressed by the trial court were the failure to properly obtain informed consent relating to resuscitation efforts by Arnold, Berkoff, and St. Mary's Hospital.

On the remaining informed consent issue relating to the resuscitation efforts, the essential question is whether the complaint states a legally cognizable claim against the remaining defendants. The trial court ruled it did not. Our informed consent law requires a physician to disclose information necessary for a reasonable person to make an intelligent decision with respect to the choices of treatment or diagnosis. Kuklinski v. Rodriguez, 203 Wis.2d 324, 329, 552 N.W.2d 869 (Ct.App.1996). It is a right found in both the common law of this state and in statutory provisions. Wisconsin Stat. § 448.30 codified the duty-to-disclose law recognized by Scaria v. St. Paul Fire & Marine Ins. Co., 68 Wis.2d 1, 13, 227 N.W.2d 647 (1975), and reads:

> Information on alternate modes of treatment. Any physician who treats a patient shall inform the patient about the availability of all alternate, viable medical modes of treatment and about the benefits and risks of these treatments. The physician's duty to inform the patient under this section does not require disclosure of:
>
> (1) Information beyond what a reasonably well-qualified physician in a similar medical classification would know.
>
> (2) Detailed technical information that in all probability a patient would not understand.
>
> (3) Risks apparent or known to the patient.
>
> (4) Extremely remote possibilities that might falsely or detrimentally alarm the patient.
>
> (5) Information in emergencies where failure to provide treatment would be more harmful to the patient than treatment.
>
> (6) Information in cases where the patient is incapable of consenting.

The statute is basically divided into two parts: what information a treating physician is obligated to convey to a patient and what information he/she need not convey. The plain language of the statute places an obligation on a physician to provide information only about available and viable options of treatment.

In addressing the obligatory first part of the statute, our supreme court has declared: "[W]hat a physician must disclose is contingent upon what, under the circumstances of a given case, a reasonable person in the patient's position would need to know in order to make an intelligent and informed decision." Johnson v. Kokemoor, 199 Wis.2d 615, 639, 545 N.W.2d 495 (1996). Restricting the application of the obligation, we declared in Mathias v. St. Catherine's Hospital, Inc., 212 Wis.2d 540, 569 N.W.2d 330 (Ct.App.1997): "The law in Wisconsin on informed consent is well settled . . . the duty to advise a patient of the risks of treatment lies with the doctor. . . . The court was explicit in pointing out that the duty to obtain informed consent lay with the doctor, not the hospital." *Id.* at 548, 569 N.W.2d 330 (citations omitted).[3] Thus, St. Mary's Hospital was not a proper defendant. We continue the analysis then only as the second claim applies to Arnold and Berkoff. . . .

Doubtless, the doctrine of informed consent comes into play only when there is a need to make a choice of available, viable alternatives. In other words, there must be a choice that can be made. The process of decision-making necessarily implies assessing and selecting an available alternative. In the context of treatment required after the cesarean procedure was performed on Emanuel, there are two reasons why no available, viable alternative existed to give rise to the obligation to engage in the informed consent process. First, requiring the informed consent process here presumes that a right to decide not to resuscitate the newly born child or to withhold life-sustaining medical care actually existed. This premise is faulty. In Edna M.F. v. Eisenberg, 210 Wis.2d 557, 568, 563 N.W.2d 485 (1997), our supreme court set forth the preconditions required for permitting the withholding or withdrawal of life-sustaining medical treatment. There, the appointed guardian of her incompetent sister, Edna, sought permission to direct the withholding of medical care from Edna even though she was not in a persistent vegetative state. *Id.* at 559–60, 563 N.W.2d 485. She claimed that Edna would not want to live in her condition, completely dependent on others for her care and existence, non-responsive and immobile. *Id.* at 560–61, 563 N.W.2d 485. The court, in refusing to extend the right to refuse life-sustaining medical treatment beyond individuals in a persistent vegetative state, relied on the analysis of the United States Supreme Court in Cruzan v. Director, Missouri Department of Health, 497 U.S. 261, 110 S.Ct. 2841, 111 L.Ed.2d 224 (1990): "[W]e think a State may properly decline to make judgments about the 'quality' of life that a particular individual may enjoy, and simply assert an unqualified interest in the preservation of human life to be weighed against the

---

[3] The dismissal of St. Mary's Hospital at the complaint stage has not been addressed by the plaintiffs. We therefore deem the issue abandoned. *See Reiman Assocs. v. R/A Adver. Inc.*, 102 Wis.2d 305, 306 n. 1, 306 N.W.2d 292 (Ct.App.1981).

constitutionally protected interests of the individual." Edna M.F., 210 Wis.2d at 563, 563 N.W.2d 485 (quoting Cruzan, 497 U.S. at 282, 110 S.Ct. 2841, 111 L.Ed.2d 224).

The *Edna* court, in examining the sensitive issues before it and the need to balance the interests of the individual versus those of the state, was quick to appreciate the consequences of ultimate decisions made by third-party surrogates for those who cannot speak for themselves. It thus concluded that either withholding or withdrawing life-sustaining medical treatment is not in the best interests of any patient who is not in a persistent vegetative state. Edna M.F., 210 Wis.2d at 566–68, 563 N.W.2d 485. Thus, in Wisconsin, in the absence of a persistent vegetative state, the right of a parent to withhold life-sustaining treatment from a child does not exist. It is not disputed here that there was no evidence that Emanuel was in "a persistent vegetative state." Accordingly, the alternative of withholding life-sustaining treatment did not exist.

The second reason why a viable alternative did not exist to trigger informed consent is the existence of the United States Child Abuse Protection and Treatment Act (CAPTA) of 1984, Pub.L. No. 98–457, 98 Stat. 1749 (codified at 42 U.S.C. § 5101 et seq.). Because Wisconsin has fulfilled the necessary obligations to receive federal funds under CAPTA, CAPTA and its regulations are fully applicable in this state. Jeanine B. v. Thompson, 967 F. Supp. 1104, 1111–12, 1118 (E.D.Wis.1997).

CAPTA was enacted to establish eligibility for states to obtain federal funding for the prevention of child abuse and to develop and implement a successful and comprehensive child and family protection strategy. Under CAPTA, states must have in place procedures for responding to child neglect. 42 U.S.C. § 5106(b)(4)(C). The Act includes a provision preventing "the withholding of medically indicated treatment from a disabled infant with a life-threatening condition." 45 C.F.R. § 1340.15(b)(1). In the regulations enacted under the statute, "withholding of medically indicated treatment" is defined as "the failure to respond to the infant's life-threatening conditions by providing treatment . . . which, in the treating physician's . . . reasonable medical judgment, will be most likely to be effective in . . . correcting all such conditions. . . ." 45 C.F.R. § 1340.15(b)(2). The regulations further include the "authority to initiate legal proceedings . . . to prevent the withholding of medically indicated treatment from disabled infants with life-threatening conditions." 45 C.F.R. § 1340.15(c)(2)(iii). The implied choice of withholding treatment, proposed by the plaintiffs, is exactly what CAPTA prohibits.

It is noteworthy that in the complaint, plaintiffs did not allege that Emanuel was born with a known disability or that they would have chosen to withhold life-sustaining treatment. Instead, they allege that they were not given the statistics about the possible risks that he could develop a disability if he lived, and they should have been given the opportunity to withhold life-saving measures immediately after

Emanuel's birth. Under the common law of Wisconsin and federal statutory law, however, Emanuel's parents did not have the right to withhold or withdraw immediate post-natal care from him. Thus, no viable alternative health treatment existed to trigger the informed consent process.[4]

We now examine the applicability of the second part of the informed consent statute; i.e., the six exception sections, providing conditions under which the treating physician is not obligated to inform the patient. Germane to our analysis is subsection (5) which renders unnecessary the disclosure of "information in emergencies where failure to provide treatment would be more harmful to the patient than treatment."

The complaint alleges that "attempts . . . to interrupt the preterm labor . . . [were] unsuccessful" resulting in Emanuel's premature birth by cesarean section, and that "upon Emanuel Vila's delivery, he was immediately handed off to defendant Brent Arnold, M.D. who initiated heroic and extraordinary life saving measures" on him. The allegations suggest that an emergency arose requiring an immediate response, which occurred. Montalvo does not suggest that all emergency actions should have ceased while Arnold explained possible options. Such an argument would be frivolous. Given the allegations of the complaint, it cannot be gainsaid that failure to provide treatment would have been more harmful than treatment.

Although Montalvo concedes that as parents they have "no right to terminate the child's life," they assert that if "there is a balance between giving therapies that help, but which may also seriously harm, the parents should be the final arbiters of that choice." In the exigent circumstances confronting the treating physician here, no "balance" existed as proposed by the parents. Failure to treat was tantamount to a death sentence. Under the pleaded circumstances, informed consent was not required.

The trial court, in rendering its oral decision reasoned:

> That as far as I can read from reading the materials in the complaint that presumes that the parents had a legally enforceable right to reject or withhold treatment. From what is alleged in the complaint there was no gap, space in time for which they could sit down and discuss statistics or any other manners of dealing with the situation. It was a life or death situation. When a child is not breathing there is no time—there

[4] In *Iafelice v. Zarafu,* 221 N.J.Super. 278, 534 A.2d 417 (1987), the New Jersey Appellate Division examined the exact same issue presented by this appeal and exclaimed:

> The mistaken premise of this appeal is that allowing the child to die untreated was a legally viable alternative . . . we find no support for the belief that a newborn child may be put to death through [allowing a natural delivery with no resuscitation efforts upon birth] on the mere expectation that she will, in some unquantified way, be a defective person. As the Supreme Court wrote in *Berman v. Allan,* 80 N.J. 421, 430, 404 A.2d 8 (1979), "It is life itself, that is jealously safeguarded, not life in a perfect state."

> is no time. Any—any amount of loss of oxygen could be devastating to the child certainly. . . .
>
> What the doctors did was save this child's life, and I understand the legal position of the parents is that was a decision they should make, but I don't believe that's one that we as a community in our public policy that's been adopted by our state and our court can place wholly in the hands of the parents.
>
> Protection of children is something that the community has an interest, in and a parent does not have the right to withhold necessary emergency treatment, and I agree entirely that had the doctors acted in any other way they would face not only civil—civil cases against them but possibly criminal cases. We simply can't say that the possibility that this child could be disabled or even the probability if it is that strong is sufficient to withhold li[f]e-saving measures and decide this child does not deserve to live.

Without a doubt, a major underpinning of the court's decision was public policy. In Wisconsin, the interest in preserving life is of paramount significance. In re L.W., 167 Wis.2d 53, 90, 482 N.W.2d 60 (1992). As a result, there is a presumption that continued life is in the best interests of a patient. *Id.* at 86, 482 N.W.2d 60. In the absence of proof of a persistent vegetative state, our courts have never decided it is in the best interests of a patient to withhold or withdraw life-sustaining medical care. When appropriate circumstances are present, Wisconsin courts have not hesitated to dismiss complaints on public policy grounds, particularly where allowing recovery would place an unreasonable burden on physicians or where allowing recovery would provoke an exercise that has no sensible or just terminal point. Rieck v. Medical Protective Co., 64 Wis.2d 514, 518–19, 219 N.W.2d 242 (1974).

The physicians involved in the resuscitation measures could be faced with a "damned if you do, damned if you don't" dilemma as demonstrated by the result of Burks v. St. Joseph's Hospital, 227 Wis.2d 811, 596 N.W.2d 391 (1999). In *Burks,* the physicians made a decision not to resuscitate based upon a judgment that a premature baby was not viable. *Id.* at 813, 596 N.W.2d 391. The baby died. *Id.* The parents brought a claim under the Emergency Medical Treatment and Active Labor Act (EMTALA) against the physician who determined that the infant was not viable and who did not resuscitate the child. *Id.* at 814, 596 N.W.2d 391. The claim was allowed because a hospital is required to provide emergency room patients with a medical screening examination including care to stabilize them. *Id.* at 817–18, 596 N.W.2d 391. If treating physicians can be sued for failing to resuscitate a baby they feel is not viable, and for resuscitating a viable baby such as Emanuel, they are placed in a continuing "damned" status. The public policy of Wisconsin does not tolerate such a "lose-lose" enigma.

If the parents' claim is allowed to proceed, courts will be required to decide which potential imperfections or disabilities are, as characterized in appellant's brief, "worse than death." They will have to determine which disability entitles a child to live and which disability allows a third-party surrogate to withhold or withdraw life-sustaining treatment with the intent to allow a disabled person to die. This determination could vary greatly based on the parents' beliefs. One set of parents may view a particular disability as "worse than death," while another set of parents would not. Such a process, not unreasonably, has kaleidoscopic, unending implications. The trial court did not err in reaching its conclusion based upon public policy reasons.

Judgments affirmed.

NOTES

In *In re* E.G., 133 Ill.2d 98, 139 Ill.Dec. 810, 549 N.E.2d 322 (1989), the Supreme Court of Illinois held that a 17-year-old minor with leukemia could reject blood transfusions that both she and her mother opposed on religious grounds, even though the choice could be fatal. Although she had not reached the age of legal majority, it was determined that she was mature enough to make health care choices of her own, with the court noting that minors could make decisions in many other contexts ranging from freedom of expression to abortion. The court explained that:

> The State's persons patriae authority fades . . . as the minor gets older and disappears upon her reaching adulthood.

Modern Natural Death Acts, which provide a means through which a person can make an advance election about what treatment will be rendered during a terminal illness, generally do not permit minors to execute a declaration. The Virginia Health Care Decisions Act, which applies to "competent adults", provides in VA. CODE ANN. § 54.1–2992 (2016) that:

> The provisions of this article are cumulative with existing law regarding an individual's right to consent or refuse to consent to medical treatment and shall not impair any existing rights or responsibilities which a health care provider, a patient, including a minor or incapacitated patient, or a patient's family may have in regard to the providing, withholding or withdrawal of life-prolonging medical procedures under the common law or statutes of the Commonwealth; however, this section shall not be construed to authorize violations of § 54.1–2990.

In response to publicity concerning a young man's wish to avoid a particular repeat treatment in connection with a major illness, "Abraham's law" was enacted by the Virginia General Assembly in 2007 as an amendment to VA. CODE ANN. § 63.2–100, the State's child abuse law. Subsection 2 of the statute, (the amended part) is reproduced below. The italicized portion includes the new text.

> "Abused or neglected child means any child less than 18 years of age . . .
>
> 2. Whose parents or other person responsible for his care neglects or refuse to provide care necessary for his health. However, no child who in good faith is under treatment solely by spiritual means through prayer in accordance with the tenets and practices of a recognized church or religious denomination shall for that reason alone be considered to be an abused or neglected child. *Further, a decision by parents who have legal authority for the child or, in the absence of parents with legal authority for the child, any person with legal authority for the child, who refuses a particular medical treatment for a child with a life-threatening condition shall not be deemed a refusal to provide necessary care if (i) such decision is made jointly by the parents or other person with legal authority and the child; (ii) the child has reached 14 years of age and is sufficiently mature to have an informed opinion on the subject of his medical treatment; (iii) the parents or other person with legal authority and the child have considered alternative treatment options; and (iv) the parents or other person with legal authority, and the child believe in good faith that such decision is in the child's best interest. Nothing in this subdivision shall be construed to limit the provisions of § 16.1–278.4.*

VA. CODE ANN. § 63.2–100 (2016).

PROBLEM ONE

Kevin, a 21-year-old new father, became frustrated when Aleah, his six-months-old daughter, cried while he was playing video games. He violently shook her, causing catastrophic brain injuries. Officers arrested Kevin. Aleah's mother, Virginia, initially agreed to a Do Not Resuscitate (DNR) order for Aleah, at the urging of doctors who said the child would die within minutes. That prediction proved wrong. Later, Aleah's mother rescinded consent to the DNR order. The doctors disagreed, they thought the DNR should be reinstated so they could give Aleah medications to ease her pain although the medications might hasten the child's death. Maine's Department of Health and Human Services (DHHS) then moved to deprive Aleah's mother of the power to make decisions that would keep Aleah alive. They thought the doctors were right and Aleah's mother was not involved enough to make good decisions for the child. DHHS took custody of Aleah through a child protective order pursuant to 22 Maine Revised Statute § 4037 (2015). A trial judge authorized DHHS to consent to a DNR over Virginia's objection, and to authorize doctors to give the child pain medications that might end Aleah's life—saying it was in Aleah's best interest. The judge accepted DHHS' claims and further found that Virginia had a conflict of interest in desiring to keep Aleah alive since Aleah's death could result in a murder or manslaughter charge against Kevin. The judge also faulted Virginia for not visiting the child more while she was in foster care, saying this meant Virginia did not understand the seriousness of Aleah's trauma. But the judge stopped short of terminating Virginia's parental rights. After publicity over the case, state officials disavowed

DHHS' action and the DHHS Commissioner refused to allow the agency to change Aleah's status to DNR without Virginia's consent since Virginia's parental rights were not terminated. What should the judge have done in response to the DHHS' request to override the mother's wishes?

F. A TORT ACTION BETWEEN PARENT AND CHILD?

Newman v. Cole

Supreme Court of Alabama, 2003
872 So.2d 138

■ PER CURIAM.

In this wrongful-death action, Anna Belle Newman, the personal representative of the estate of the decedent, Clinton Patterson Cole ("Clinton"), sued Clinton's father, John Cole, and his stepmother, Tara Cole (sometimes referred to hereinafter collectively as "the Coles"), for allegedly causing Clinton's death. Newman's complaint asserted claims of negligence, wantonness, and willful and intentional conduct.

The Coles moved to dismiss the complaint based on the doctrine of parental immunity. That doctrine was judicially created in the case of Hewellette v. George, 68 Miss. 703, 9 So. 885 (Miss.1891), abrogated by Glaskox v. Glaskox, 614 So.2d 906 (Miss.1992), and was adopted by the this Court in Owens v. Auto Mutual Indemnity Co., 235 Ala. 9, 177 So. 133 (Ala.1937). The present form of the doctrine in this State was most recently discussed by the Court of Civil Appeals:

> "Under Alabama law, '[t]he parental immunity doctrine prohibits all civil suits brought by unemancipated minor children against their parents for the torts of their parents.' Mitchell v. Davis, 598 So.2d 801, 803 (Ala.1992). Only one exception to this rule has emerged-when a child alleges sexual abuse by a parent, the parental immunity doctrine will not bar an action against the parent, although proof of the alleged conduct must be tested under a 'clear and convincing' standard. Hurst v. Capitell, 539 So.2d 264, 266 (Ala.1989)."

Hinson v. Holt, 776 So.2d 804, 811 (Ala.Civ.App.1998).

On July 3, 2002, the trial court granted the Coles' motion to dismiss the complaint. Newman appealed, arguing that this Court should abolish the doctrine, or, in the alternative, craft an exception to the doctrine that encompasses the facts alleged in this case.

Clinton was 16 years old at the time of his death, which occurred during an altercation with his father over Clinton's failure to perform household chores; Newman asserts that the altercation ended with the father's striking Clinton repeatedly in the chest and then holding him on the ground in a "choke hold" while Tara Cole sprayed him in the face with water from a garden hose. The father held Clinton on the ground for approximately 20 minutes; he let go of Clinton when a police officer arrived. Clinton was unconscious, and he was taken to a local hospital; he died the next day.

Although the facts in this case are tragic and compelling, the legal issue is clear-cut: Whether this Court should abolish the doctrine of parental immunity, or to what extent, if any, it should modify the application of the doctrine in light of the circumstances of this case. We hold that a further exception to the doctrine should be recognized where it is shown by clear and convincing evidence that a parent's willful and intentional injury caused the death of his or her child.

Newman asserts that Alabama is the last state not to have entirely abrogated or significantly modified the doctrine. Newman's argument, supported by the briefs of amici curiae National Crime Victims Bar Association and Alabama Trial Lawyers Association, asserts that to apply the parental-immunity doctrine in the circumstances of this case is fundamentally unjust and contrary to long-settled principles of tort law. Newman and the amici support their argument by noting the large number of other states that have abrogated, or significantly modified, the doctrine.[1] Newman argues that this Court should abrogate the doctrine entirely, or, alternatively, either craft an exception to the doctrine in the case of a parent who intentionally or willfully and wantonly injures his or her child, or craft an exception for a wrongful-death action in which a parent is accused of causing a child's death. Newman and the amici assert, without significant rebuttal from the Coles, that Alabama's application of the doctrine is the strictest imposition of parental immunity against minors in the United States. . . .

The Coles, on the other hand, argue that the Legislature is the entity that should make any changes to the settled doctrine of parental immunity, and that abrogation of the doctrine would adversely impact families and give rise to unwarranted lawsuits by unemancipated minors against their parents.

Thus, the parties' arguments offer the Court three options: (1) we might simply decline to interfere with the doctrine, (2) we might abrogate the doctrine entirely, or (3) we might craft an exception to the doctrine, as we did in Hurst v. Capitell, 539 So.2d 264 (Ala.1989), to fit the circumstances of this case.

We discussed the history of the doctrine in this State, and the rationale for crafting an exception, in *Hurst* . . .

> " 'If . . . the relation of parent and child had been finally dissolved, insofar as that relationship imposed the duty upon the parent to protect and care for and control, and the child to

[1] Six states—Hawaii, Nevada, North Dakota, South Dakota, Utah, and Vermont, and the District of Columbia—have declined to adopt the doctrine. . . . Eleven states . . . adopted the doctrine at some point but subsequently abolished it. . . . The remaining 33 states all retain the doctrine in some form, usually with one or more significant exceptions.

aid and comfort and obey, *then it may be the child could successfully maintain an action against the parent for personal injuries.* But so long as the parent is under obligation to care for, guide, and control, and the child is under reciprocal obligation to aid and comfort and obey, no such action as this can be maintained.'

"*Id.,* 68 Miss. at 711, 9 So. at 887. (Emphasis added [in *Hurst*].)

"The first Alabama case addressing the issue of parental immunity, Owens v. Auto Mut. Indemnity Co., 235 Ala. 9, 177 So. 133 (1937), quoted from a New Hampshire case that states a similar reason for the rule:

" 'It is declared in *Lloyd* Dunlap v. Dunlap, 84 N.H. 352, 150 A. 905, 71 A.L.R. 1055 [1930] that the' disability of a child to sue the parent for an injury negligently inflicted by the latter upon the former while a minor *is not absolute, but is imposed for the protection of family control and harmony, and exists only where the suit, or the prospect of a suit, might disturb the family relations. . . .*"

"*Because the doctrine was judicially created, it is not exclusively a legislative issue and it may be judicially qualified.* Since our decision in *Hill* to defer to the Legislature on this issue, the Legislature has declined to act in regard to the doctrine, while the incidents of sexual abuse involving children have continued to occur. To leave children who are victims of such wrongful, intentional, heinous acts without a right to redress those wrongs in a civil action is unconscionable, especially where the harm to the family fabric has already occurred through that abuse. Because we see no reason to adhere to the doctrine of parental immunity when the purpose for that immunity is no longer served, as in Melissa's case, we are today creating an exception to the doctrine, limited to sexual abuse cases only.

"In creating this exception for sexual abuse cases, we believe it is unnecessary to spell out a separate body of procedural and substantive rules to govern such cases. Traditional rules of tort law relating to intentional infliction of personal injury are generally sufficient for the governance of such claims and the defenses asserted thereto.

"In the interest of preserving the unqualified right of parents to reasonably discipline their children, we do deem it appropriate, however, to require that the proof of alleged sexually abusive conduct be tested under a 'clear and convincing' standard, as opposed to a mere 'substantial evidence' standard. Because we are restricting this exception to the general rule to cases involving 'sexual abuse,' and requiring a 'clear and convincing' standard of proof, we do not perceive of our recognition of this

> narrow exception as posing an undue risk of limiting the parents' legitimate role in the disciplining of their children."

539 So.2d at 265–66 (last emphasis added).

At this time, some 14 years after *Hurst* was decided, the Legislature has made no other modification to the doctrine. During that same time, we considered the doctrine once more in Mitchell v. Davis, 598 So.2d 801 (Ala.1992), holding that the doctrine of parental immunity applied to foster parents and recognizing the exception crafted in *Hurst.* As stated in *Hurst,* the doctrine was judicially created, and it is therefore subject to judicial modification. But this Court still attaches great importance to the underlying reason for the doctrine-to avoid unduly limiting the legitimate interest of parents in rearing and disciplining their children. In Broadwell v. Holmes, 871 S.W.2d 471 (Tenn.1994), the Supreme Court of Tennessee articulated well the importance of this interest:

> "The parental right to govern the rearing of a child has been afforded protection under both the federal and state constitutions. This Court has stated, 'Tennessee's historically strong protection of parental rights and the reasoning of federal constitutional cases convince us that parental rights constitute a fundamental liberty interest under Article I, Section 8 of the Tennessee Constitution.' Hawk v. Hawk, 855 S.W.2d 573, 579 (Tenn.[1993]); see also Davis v. Davis, 842 S.W.2d 588, 601 (Tenn.1992)[,] *cert. denied,* 507 U.S. 911, 113 S.Ct. 1259, 122 L.Ed.2d 657 (1993); Bellotti v. Baird, 443 U.S. 622, 638, 99 S.Ct. 3035, 3045, 61 L.Ed.2d 797 (1979) (recognition of parents' right to be free of undue, adverse interference by state); Quilloin v. Walcott, 434 U.S. 246, 255, 98 S.Ct. 549, 554, 54 L.Ed.2d 511 (1978) (recognition that parent-child relationship is constitutionally protected); Wisconsin v. Yoder, 406 U.S. 205, 232, 92 S.Ct. 1526, 1541, 32 L.Ed.2d 15 (1972) (recognition of parents' primary role in child rearing as a 'fundamental interest' and 'an enduring American tradition'); Prince v. Massachusetts, 321 U.S. 158, 166, 64 S.Ct. 438, 442, 88 L.Ed. 645 (1944) (recognition that the custody, care and nurture of the child 'reside first in the parents, whose primary function and freedom include preparation for obligations the state can neither supply nor hinder'). The integrity of the family unit has found protection against arbitrary state interference in the Due Process Clause of the Fourteenth Amendment, Cleveland Board of Education v. LaFleur, 414 U.S. 632, 639–40, 94 S.Ct. 791, 796–97, 39 L.Ed.2d 52 (1974); Roe v. Wade, 410 U.S. 113, 152–53, 93 S.Ct. 705, 726–27, 35 L.Ed.2d 147 (1973); Meyer v. Nebraska, 262 U.S. 390, 399, 43 S.Ct. 625, 626, 67 L.Ed. 1042 (1923); the equal protection clause of the Fourteenth Amendment, Skinner v. Oklahoma, 316 U.S. 535, 541, 62 S.Ct. 1110, 1113, 86 L.Ed. 1655 (1942); and the Ninth Amendment.

> [Griswold] v. Connecticut, 381 U.S. 479, 496, 85 S.Ct. 1678, 1688, 14 L.Ed.2d 510 (1965) (Goldberg, J., concurring).
>
> "Courts have expressed a concern that without the imposition of parent-child immunity, juries would feel free to express their disapproval of what they consider to be unusual or inappropriate child rearing practices by awarding damages to children whose parents' conduct was only unconventional. See, e.g., Pedigo v. Rowley, 101 Idaho 201, 205, 610 P.2d 560, 564 (1980); Holodook v. Spencer, [36 N.Y.2d 35,] 364 N.Y.S.2d [859] at 869–71, 324 N.E.2d [338] at 345–46 (N.Y.1974). Courts also properly have found that parents whose '[p]hysical, mental or financial weakness [causes them] to provide what many a reasonable man would consider substandard maintenance, guidance, education and recreation for their children, and in many instances to provide a family home which is not reasonably safe as a place of abode,' should not be liable to the child for these 'unintended injuries.' Chaffin v. Chaffin, 239 Or. 374, 397 P.2d 771, 774 (1964) (en banc), *overruled by* Heino v. Harper, 306 Or. 347, 759 P.2d 253 (1988) (abolishing interspousal immunity); *accord* Cannon v. Cannon, 287 N.Y. 425, 40 N.E.2d 236, 237–38 (1942), *overruled by* Gelbman v. Gelbman, 23 N.Y.2d 434, 297 N.Y.S.2d 529, 245 N.E.2d 192, 193 (1969) (abolishing bar to intrafamily lawsuits), *but see Holodook v. Spencer,* 364 N.Y.S.2d at 865, 324 N.E.2d at 342 (negligent failure to supervise child not recognized as a tort). Such imposition of liability could effectively curtail the exercise of constitutionally guaranteed parental discretion in matters of child rearing. Consequently, it reasonably can be argued that parental immunity that relates to the right and duty to rear children implements a constitutional right. *See* Hawk v. Hawk, 855 S.W.2d at 579 (recognizing a fundamental constitutional right of parents to care for their children without unwarranted state intervention)."

871 S.W.2d at 475–76.

This Court has been equally loathe to interfere with the parent-child relationship:

> " '. . . So strong is the presumption, that "the care which is prompted by the parental instinct, and responded to by filial affection, is most valuable of all"; and so great is the reluctance of the court to separate a child of tender years from those who according to the ordinary laws of human nature, must feel the greatest affection for it, and take the deepest interest in its welfare-that the parental authority will not be interfered with, except in case of gross misconduct or where, from some other cause, the parent wants either the capacity or the means for the proper nurture and training of the child.' "

Ex parte Sullivan, 407 So.2d 559, 563 (Ala.1981) (quoting Striplin v. Ware, 36 Ala. 87, 89–90 (1860)). See also R.J.D. v. Vaughan Clinic, P.C., 572 So.2d 1225, 1228 (Ala.1990).

Given the weight we assign to the sanctity of the parent-child relationship, we decline to follow the example of many of our sister states and wholly abrogate the doctrine of parental immunity. Further, we decline to consider any exception to the doctrine that would permit a claim by an injured child against a parent where the injury was not willful and intentional. In *Hurst* we held that the exception to the parental-immunity doctrine giving the injured child a right to redress was in response to "wrongful, intentional, heinous acts," 539 So.2d at 266, committed by the parent. Most recently, in *Mitchell,* supra, we held that the parental-immunity doctrine also protected foster parents as to any claim by a foster child based upon the foster parents' alleged negligence. As the court stated in *Broadwell:*

> "[T]he rights, responsibilities, and privileges of parents in relation to their children are so unique that the ordinary standards of care which regulate conduct between others are not applicable to conduct incident to the particular relationship of parent and child. That relationship includes responsibilities not owed by parents to any persons other than their children; these responsibilities are inseparable from the privileges that parents have in rearing their children which are not recognized in any other relationship."

871 S.W.2d at 475. . . .

In assessing the balance between the unique nature and critical importance of the parent-child relationship and the right of any victim for redress for a willful or intentional injury, we find the analysis of the Supreme Court of West Virginia instructive. In Courtney v. Courtney, 186 W.Va. 597, 413 S.E.2d 418 (1991), that court considered claims by a mother and her son against her ex-husband and the son's father for a number of intentional assaults. The court stated:

> "Courts have recognized that not every physical touching of a child will result in liability. Parents are able to discipline their children by administering reasonable physical punishment. However, when such punishment becomes excessive and results in substantial traumatic injury to the child, liability arises. Several courts have quoted this language from the California Supreme Court in Emery v. Emery, 45 Cal.2d 421, 429–30, 289 P.2d 218, 224 (1955):
>
> > " 'Since the law imposes on the parent a duty to rear and discipline his child and confers the right to prescribe a course of reasonable conduct for its development, the parent has a wide discretion in the performance of his parental functions, but that discretion does not include the right

> wilfully to inflict personal injuries beyond the limits of reasonable parental discipline. No sound public policy would be subserved by extending it beyond those limits. While it may seem repugnant to allow a minor to sue his parent, we think it more repugnant to leave a minor child without redress for the damage he has suffered by reason of his parent's wilful or malicious misconduct. A child, like every other individual, has a right to freedom from such injury.'

"See Attwood v. Attwood's Estate, 276 Ark. 230, 633 S.W.2d 366 (1982); Rodebaugh v. Grand Trunk W.R.R. Co., 4 Mich.App. 559, 145 N.W.2d 401 (1966).

"Thus, the general rule is that parental immunity is abrogated where the parent causes injury or death to his or her child from intentional or wilful conduct, but liability does not arise from reasonable corporal punishment for disciplinary purposes."

186 W.Va. at 607, 413 S.E.2d at 428.

Similarly, we recognize an exception to the doctrine of parental immunity in this State for a civil wrongful-death action by the personal representative of a decedent child against the child's parent where the parent willfully and intentionally inflicted the injury that caused the child's death. As in *Hurst,* supra, "in the interest of preserving the unqualified right of parents to reasonably discipline their children," 539 So.2d at 266, we require that the proof of the alleged willful and intentional nature of the injury that caused the child's death be tested under the clear-and-convincing-evidence standard rather than the substantial-evidence standard.

Accordingly, the judgment of the trial court is affirmed with respect to Newman's wrongful-death claims based on negligence and wantonness; the judgment is reversed with respect to Newman's wrongful-death claim based upon willful and intentional conduct, to the extent that claim implicates a willful and intentional injury, and the cause is remanded for further proceedings consistent with this opinion.

AFFIRMED IN PART; REVERSED IN PART; AND REMANDED.

■ JOHNSTONE and WOODALL, JJ., concur; HOUSTON and HARWOOD, JJ., concur in the result.

■ LYONS, J., concurs in the result in part and dissents in part; MOORE, C.J., and SEE, BROWN, and STUART, JJ., dissent, [all of which are omitted].

G. EMANCIPATION: "DIVORCE" BETWEEN PARENT AND CHILD?

CALIFORNIA FAMILY CODE (2016)

§ 7001. Purpose of Part

It is the purpose of this part to provide a clear statement defining emancipation and its consequences and to permit an emancipated minor to obtain a court declaration of the minor's status. This part is not intended to affect the status of minors who may become emancipated under decisional case law that was in effect before the enactment of Chapter 1059 of the Statutes of 1978.

§ 7002. Emancipated minor; description

A person under the age of 18 years is an emancipated minor if any of the following conditions is satisfied:

(a) The person has entered into a valid marriage, whether or not the marriage has been dissolved.

(b) The person is on active duty with the armed forces of the United States.

(c) The person has received a declaration of emancipation pursuant to Section 7122.

§ 7120. Petitions for declaration of emancipation; contents

(a) A minor may petition the superior court of the county in which the minor resides or is temporarily domiciled for a declaration of emancipation.

(b) The petition shall set forth with specificity all of the following facts:

(1) The minor is at least 14 years of age.

(2) The minor willingly lives separate and apart from the minor's parents or guardian with the consent or acquiescence of the minor's parents or guardian.

(3) The minor is managing his or her own financial affairs. As evidence of this, the minor shall complete and attach a declaration of income and expenses as provided in Judicial Council form FL–150.

(4) The source of the minor's income is not derived from any activity declared to be a crime by the laws of this state or the laws of the United States.

§ 7122. Findings of court; issuance of declaration of emancipation

(a) The court shall sustain the petition if it finds that the minor is a person described by Section 7120 and that emancipation would not be contrary to the minor's best interest.

(b) If the petition is sustained, the court shall forthwith issue a declaration of emancipation, which shall be filed by the clerk of the court.

(c) A declaration is conclusive evidence that the minor is emancipated.

NOTES

A 1979 Connecticut statute did permit a minor when 16 or older to petition for emancipation in circumstances that were comparable to divorce under the ground of irretrievable breakdown. It stayed in effect only a short time. The law as originally adopted is shown below, with amendments and additions to the text made by the legislature in 1980. Additions are shown by capital letters and deletions are indicated by ~~strikeouts~~. The former section of the code provided:

§ 46b–150b

If the court, after hearing, finds that: (1) The minor has entered into a valid marriage, whether or not that marriage has been terminated by dissolution; or (2) the minor is on active duty with any of the armed forces of the United States of America; or (3) the minor willingly lives separate and apart from his parents or guardian, with or without the consent of the parents or guardian, and that the minor is managing his own financial affairs, regardless of the source of any lawful income; or (4) [~~other facts exist which demonstrate that the parent child relationship has irretrievably broken down~~] FOR GOOD CAUSE SHOWN, IT IS IN THE BEST INTEREST OF EITHER OR BOTH PARTIES, the court [~~shall~~] MAY enter an order declaring that the minor is emancipated.

It was replaced by amended CONN. GEN. STAT ANN. § 46b–150d (2016):

§ 46b–150d. Effect of emancipation

An order that a minor is emancipated shall have the following effects: (1) The minor may consent to medical, dental or psychiatric care, without parental consent, knowledge or liability; (2) the minor may enter into a binding contract; (3) the minor may sue and be sued in such minor's own name; (4) the minor shall be entitled to such minor's own earnings and shall be free of control by such minor's parents or guardian; (5) the minor may establish such minor's own residence; (6) the minor may buy and sell real and personal property; (7) the minor may not thereafter be the subject of (A) a petition under section 46b–129 as an abused, neglected or uncared for child or youth, (B) a petition under section 46b–128 or 46b–133 as a delinquent child for any act committed before the date of the order, or (C) a petition under section 46b–149 alleging that the minor is a child from a family with service needs; (8) the minor may enroll in any school or college, without parental consent; (9) the minor shall be deemed to be over eighteen years of age for purposes of securing an operator's license under section 14–36 and a marriage license under subsection (b) of section 46b–30; (10) the minor shall be deemed to be over eighteen years of age for purposes of registering a motor vehicle under section 14–12; (11) the parents of the minor shall no longer be the guardians of the minor under section 45a–606; (12) the parents of a minor shall be relieved of any obligations respecting such minor's school attendance under section 10–184; (13) the parents shall be relieved of all obligation to support the minor; (14) the minor shall be emancipated for the purposes of parental liability for such minor's acts under section 52–572; (15) the minor may execute releases in such minor's own name under section 14–118; and (16) the minor may enlist in the armed forces of the United States without parental consent.

§ 46b–150e. Emancipation under common law

Nothing in sections 46b–150 to 46b–150e, inclusive, shall affect the status of minors who are or may become emancipated under the common law of this state.

CHAPTER VIII

VYING FOR CUSTODY

Custody determinations are the most difficult decisions for courts, for attorneys, for parents, and most of all for children. Any decision illustrates the axiom of Oliver Wendell Holmes, Jr., writing in THE COMMON LAW, that "The life of the law has not been logic; it has been experience." Experience dictates that custody decisions, involving a minor unable to enter into the contractual arrangements available to parents and remaining within the *parens patriae* authority of the state, are the most modifiable and least settled decisions within family law litigation.

Custody decisions involve three constructs, each with appropriate presumptions. First, most of the cases involve a parent versus parent construct. Second, in a parent versus third party construct, such as a psychological parent, courts have been all too willing to apply a presumption in favor of the natural parent. And third, in increasing numbers of cases involving abuse and neglect, there is a parent versus state construct, in which the child is removed from the parent's custody by the state, but the courts are again usually willing to apply a presumption in favor of the parent. Sometimes the constructs overlap; for example, increasing recognition of psychological parentage in some jurisdictions may largely merge the first two constructs as to the applicable rules or guidelines. And often the child is shifted from one construct to another in the course of changing tensions and problems.

Difficult questions arise throughout the materials: Is an adversary style judicial proceeding truly in the best interest of the child? What is the influence of individual values or beliefs in judicial determinations? Would non-judicial mediation be a better process for determination? What is the appropriate role of an attorney for a parent or child? Is it wise to make distinctions between legal and physical custody, or to create presumptions or preferences for newer approaches such as joint custody? Would federal control be preferable to the historic state approach? Do statutes unduly deprive courts of flexibility and can they be updated as needed within a reasonable time frame?

A. PARENT VERSUS PARENT

CALIFORNIA FAMILY CODE (2016)

§ 3002. Joint custody

"Joint custody" means joint physical custody and joint legal custody.

§ 3003. Joint legal custody

"Joint legal custody" means that both parents shall share the right and the responsibility to make the decisions relating to the health, education, and welfare of a child.

§ 3004. Joint physical custody

"Joint physical custody" means that each of the parents shall have significant periods of physical custody. Joint physical custody shall be shared by the parents in such a way so as to assure a child of frequent and continuing contact with both parents, subject to Sections 3011 and 3020. . . .

§ 3006. Sole legal custody

"Sole legal custody" means that one parent shall have the right and the responsibility to make the decisions relating to the health, education, and welfare of a child.

§ 3007. Sole physical custody

"Sole physical custody" means that a child shall reside with and be under the supervision of one parent, subject to the power of the court to order visitation.

1. THE BEST INTEREST OF THE CHILD

UNIFORM MARRIAGE AND DIVORCE ACT (1973)

§ 402. Best Interest of the Child

The court shall determine custody in accordance with the best interest of the child. The court shall consider all relevant factors including:

(1) the wishes of the child's parent or parents as to his custody;

(2) the wishes of the child as to his custodian;

(3) the interaction and interrelationship of the child with his parent or parents, his siblings, and any other person who may significantly affect the child's best interest;

(4) the child's adjustment to his home, school, and community; and

(5) the mental and physical health of all individuals involved.

The court shall not consider conduct of a proposed custodian that does not affect his relationship to the child.

CALIFORNIA FAMILY CODE (2016)

§ 3011. Best interest of the child: Considerations

In making a determination of the best interest of the child in a proceeding described in Section 3021, the court shall, among any other factors it finds relevant, consider all of the following:

(a) The health, safety, and welfare of the child.

(b) Any history of abuse by one parent or any other person seeking custody against any of the following:

(1) Any child to whom he or she is related by blood or affinity or with whom he or she has had a caretaking relationship, no matter how temporary.

(2) The other parent.

(3) A parent, current spouse, or cohabitant, of the parent or person seeking custody, or a person with whom the parent or person seeking custody has a dating or engagement relationship.

As a prerequisite to the consideration of allegations of abuse, the court may require substantial independent corroboration, including, but not limited to, written reports by law enforcement agencies, child protective services or other social welfare agencies, courts, medical facilities, or other public agencies or private nonprofit organizations providing services to victims of sexual assault or domestic violence. As used in this subdivision, "abuse against a child" means "child abuse" as defined in Section 11165.6 of the Penal Code and abuse against any of the other persons described in paragraph (2) or (3) means "abuse" as defined in Section 6203 of this code.

(c) The nature and amount of contact with both parents, except as provided in Section 3046.

(d) The habitual or continual illegal use of controlled substances or habitual or continual abuse of alcohol by either parent. Before considering these allegations, the court may first require independent corroboration, including, but not limited to, written reports from law enforcement agencies, courts, probation departments, social welfare agencies, medical facilities, rehabilitation facilities, or other public agencies or nonprofit organizations providing drug and alcohol abuse services. As used in this subdivision, "controlled substances" has the same meaning as defined in the California Uniform Controlled Substances Act, Division 10 (commencing with Section 11000) of the Health and Safety Code.

(e) (1) Where allegations about a parent pursuant to subdivision (b) or (d) have been brought to the attention of the court in the current proceeding, and the court makes an order for sole or joint custody to that parent, the court shall state its reasons in writing or on the record. In these circumstances, the court shall ensure that any order regarding custody or visitation is specific as to time, day, place, and manner of transfer of the child as set forth in subdivision (b) of Section 6323.

(2) The provisions of this subdivision shall not apply if the parties stipulate in writing or on the record regarding custody or visitation.

§ 3020. Legislative findings and declarations; health, safety, and welfare of children; continuing contact with parents

(a) The Legislature finds and declares that it is the public policy of this state to assure that the health, safety, and welfare of children shall be the court's primary concern in determining the best interest of children when making any orders regarding the physical or legal custody or visitation of children. The Legislature further finds and declares that the perpetration of child abuse or domestic violence in a household where a child resides is detrimental to the child.

(b) The Legislature finds and declares that it is the public policy of this state to assure that children have frequent and continuing contact with both parents after the parents have separated or dissolved their marriage, or ended their relationship, and to encourage parents to share the rights and responsibilities of child rearing in order to effect this policy, except where the contact would not be in the best interest of the child, as provided in Section 3011.

(c) Where the policies set forth in subdivisions (a) and (b) of this section are in conflict, any court's order regarding physical or legal custody or visitation shall be made in a manner that ensures the health, safety, and welfare of the child and the safety of all family members.

AMERICAN LAW INSTITUTE, PRINCIPLES OF THE LAW OF FAMILY DISSOLUTION (2002)

§ 2.08. Allocation of Custodial Responsibility

(1) Unless otherwise resolved by agreement of the parents . . . , the court should allocate custodial responsibility so that the proportion of custodial time the child's spends with each parent approximates the proportion of time each parent spent performing caretaking functions for the child prior to the parents' separation or, if the parents never lived together, before the filing of the action, except to the extent

. . . necessary to achieve one or more of the following objectives:

(a) to permit the child to have a relationship with each parent which, in the case of a legal parent or a parent by estoppel who has performed a reasonable share of parenting functions, should be not less than a presumptive amount of custodial time set by a uniform rule of statewide application;

(b) to accommodate the firm and reasonable preferences of a child who has reached a specific age, set by a uniform rule of statewide application;

(c) to keep siblings together when the court finds that doing so is necessary to their welfare;

(d) to protect the child's welfare when the presumptive allocation under this section would harm the child because of the gross disparity in the quality of the emotional attachment between each parent and the child or in each parent's demonstrated ability or availability to meet the child's needs;

(e) to take into account any prior agreement . . . ;

(f) to avoid an allocation of custodial responsibility that would be extremely impractical or that would interfere substantially with the child's need for stability in light of economic, physical, or other circumstances, including the distance between the parents' residences, the cost and difficulty of transporting the child, each parent's and the child's daily schedules, and the ability of the parents to cooperate in the arrangement . . .

(h) to avoid substantial and almost certain harm to the child. . . .

§ 2.05. Parenting Plan

(1) An individual seeking a judicial allocation of custodial responsibility or decision-making responsibility under this Chapter should be required to file with the court a proposed parenting plan containing proposals for each of the provisions specified in Paragraph (5). Individuals should be allowed to file a joint plan. . . .

(5) After consideration of any proposed parenting plans submitted in the case and any evidence presented in support thereof, the court should order a parenting plan that is consistent with the provisions of §§ 2.08–2.12 and contains the following provisions:

(a) a provision for the child's living arrangements and for each parent's custodial responsibility, which should include either

(i) a custodial schedule that designates in which parent's home each minor child will reside on given days of the year; or

(ii) a formula or method for determining such a schedule in sufficient detail that, if necessary, the schedule can be enforced in a subsequent proceeding.

(b) an allocation of decision-making responsibility as to significant matters reasonably likely to arise with respect to the child; and

(c) a provision consistent with § 207 for resolution of disputes that arise under the plan, and a provision establishing remedies for violation of the plan.

NOTES

When fit parents vie for custody of their children they do so without the benefit of a presumption in favor of a fit parent; both parents are presumptive equals, and the court is tasked with deciding who should be given primary physical custody. Thus, as both the Uniform Marriage and Divorce Act (1973) and the California Family Code illustrate, many state courts begin by looking at the best interests of the child. Formerly, courts most often awarded physical custody to the mother through what was termed a "Tender Years Presumption," but the practice has been rejected under gender discrimination. *See, e.g.,* State ex rel. Watts v. Watts, 350 N.Y.S.2d 285 (1973). As a substitute, a few states enacted a primary caretaker presumption, but this was criticized as discriminating against people who work outside the home and thus some states expressly rejected it by statute. *See, e.g.,* MINN. STAT. ANN. § 518.17(a) (West 2012). In rare circumstances joint physical custody, discussed *infra,* is an option, but it is premised upon the ability of the parents' mutual cooperation. For an analysis of joint physical custody, *see* Michael T. Flannery, *Is "Bird Nesting" In the Best Interest of Children?*, 57 SMU L. REV. 295 (2004).

Another approach submitted by the American Law Institute ("ALI"), provided here via statute, is premised upon parents cooperating in submitting a "parenting plan" that they can arrive at together and that can then be enforced by courts. Under § 2.06 of the ALI proposal, the parenting plan provides a presumptive custody and visitation arrangement and states "the court should order provisions of a parenting plan agreed to by the parents, unless the agreement (a) is not knowing or voluntary, or (b) would be harmful to the child." West Virginia, as did other states, enacted the ALI approach after abolishing the primary caretaker presumption. *See* W. VA. CODE ANN. § 48–9–206 (West 2012). The ALI approach has been lauded by some commentators. *See, e.g.*, Richard A. Warshak, *Punching the Parenting*

Time Clock: The Approximation Rule, Social Science, and the Baseball Bat Kids, 45 FAM. CT. REV. 600 (2007) (suggesting that the ALI approach does not always correctly measure a parent's contribution); Katharine T. Bartlett, *Preference, Presumption, Predisposition, and Common Sense: From Traditional Custody Doctrines to the American Law Institute's Family Dissolution Project*, 36 FAM. L.Q. 11 (2002). Other commentators have criticized the ALI approach. *See, e.g.*, Margaret F. Brinig, *Feminism and Child Custody Under Chapter Two of the American Law Institute's Principles of The Law of Family Dissolution*, 8 DUKE J. GENDER L. & POL'Y 301 (2001) (arguing that the approach fosters traditional gender roles). For further analysis, *see* Stacy Platt, *Set Another Place at the Table: Child Participation in Family Separation* Cases, 17 CARDOZO J. CONFLICT RESOL. 749 (2016) (arguing that children who are able should have a voice in custody determination); Rebecca Aviel, *A New Formalism for Family Law*, 55 WM. & MARY L. REV. 2003 (2014) (arguing for a return to more formal decision making for child custody determinations); Matthew B. Firing, *In Whose Best Interests? Courts' Failure to Apply State Custodial Laws Equally Amongst Spouses and Its Constitutional Implications*, 20 QUINNIPIAC PROB. L. J. 223 (2007); Robert J. Levy, *Custody Law and the ALI's Principles: A Little History, a Little Policy, and Some Very Tentative Judgments*, in RECONCEIVING THE FAMILY 67–89 (Robin Fretwell Wilson ed., 2006).

2. CUSTODY CONSIDERATIONS

A. RELIGION

Johnson v. Johnson

Supreme Court of Alaska, 1977
564 P.2d 71, *cert. denied*, 434 U.S. 1048 (1978)

■ BURKE, JUSTICE.

In this case, appellant Rudy Johnson challenges the superior court's reliance on the tender years presumption in awarding custody of his young children to their mother, Linda Johnson.

Rudy and Linda Johnson were married in 1966. Their daughter, April, was born in 1968 and their son, Darrin, in 1970. Several years after their marriage, Rudy and Linda became involved with the Jehovah's Witnesses, and both were baptized into the congregation. However, in 1974, Rudy Johnson became disenchanted with the religion and was excommunicated or "disfellowshipped" from the congregation for willfully smoking cigarettes. Although Rudy attempted to persuade Linda to abandon the religious principles which he had rejected, Linda remained with the church, and a severe strain was placed upon the marriage. Rudy filed for divorce on April 8, 1975, and the children were temporarily placed in his custody, pending trial.

Judge Carlson presided over the five day trial in this divorce action, the only issue at trial being the custody of the two Johnson children. At the time of trial April was seven and Darrin five. The heart of Rudy Johnson's case was that if he were denied custody of the children, he would have virtually no input into their lives because of his disfellowshipped status. Testimony was adduced at trial that since a disfellowshipped member of the Jehovah's Witnesses is believed to be under, or in danger of coming under, satanic control, members of the congregation will not associate with him.

Rudy Johnson also introduced evidence that his children's development would be better served by an award of their custody to him. Dr. LaVere Edwin Clawson, a psychologist, and his wife Darleen Morel, a family counselor, concluded that the children should be awarded to their father since he appeared more willing to offer them "increased exposure to the usual experiences of children their age." Rudy testified to the same effect, stating that Linda had not taught the children such simple tasks as counting money, washing themselves, and helping to clean around the house. He also emphasized the fact that Linda would not allow the children to celebrate holidays, birthdays or allow them to join such organizations as the Brownies. She also does not believe in college for the children. In short, Rudy's case centered around the fact that Linda's plan to raise the children in strict accordance with the church's rules and decrees would not serve the children's best interest.

Aside from rebutting Rudy's testimony and that of Dr. Clawson and Ms. Morel, Linda's evidence focused on Rudy's instability, as evidenced by threats of suicide and an unsuccessful suicide attempt, and his capacity for violence when frustrated. Linda offered proof that Rudy was unreasonable about Linda's visitation during the period in which he had temporary custody and introduced into evidence the deposition of Marilyn Kerr, a court-appointed social worker, who recommended that Linda have custody of April and Darrin.

The trial court, in extensive findings of fact, concluded that both parents were fit to have custody of the children and based its award of physical custody of the children to Linda on the tender years presumption. After citing AS 09.55.205[1] for the proposition that his award of custody should be guided by the best interests of the children, the trial judge stated:

The statute has been interpreted in several cases and the following principles have emerged: . . .

2. a mother of young children will generally be given preference for custody if the other factors are evenly balanced. Harding v. Harding, 477

---

[1] AS 09.55.205 provides in part:

[I]n awarding custody the court is to be guided by the following considerations:

(1) by what appears to be for the best interests of the child and if the child is of a sufficient age and intelligence to form a preference, the court may consider that preference in determining the question;

(2) as between parents adversely claiming the custody neither parent is entitled to it as of right.

[377] P.2d 378 (Alaska 1962); Sheridan v. Sheridan, 466 P.2d 821, 824 (Alaska 1970).

The trial court further reasoned:

> The reasons for my conclusion that the best interests of the children are served by awarding their primary physical custody to Mrs. Johnson are the ages of April and Darrin and the fact that until their interim custody was awarded to Mr. Johnson in April, 1975, Mrs. Johnson had attended to nearly all of the physical needs of the children.

Judge Carlson awarded legal custody of the children to both parents so that Rudy could consent to medical care for them.

Appellant Rudy Johnson appeals the trial court's decision on two grounds. First, he contends that the trial court erred in applying the tender years presumption to the facts since that presumption is inconsistent with the statute's requirement that the best interests of the child be considered. He also argues that the tender years doctrine constitutes a denial of equal protection. Rudy's second argument is that the trial court abused its discretion in failing to award the children to him. Appellee Linda Johnson cross appeals, contending that the trial court erred in failing to award her costs and attorney's fees.

Trial courts have wide discretion in determining custody issues, but that discretion is not unlimited. This court must determine on review "whether that discretion has been abused, perhaps by assigning too great a weight to some factors while ignoring others. . . ." Horton v. Horton, 519 P.2d 1131, 1132 (Alaska 1974). Furthermore, if we find that the trial court has used an impermissible criterion in its determination, we will remand the case for a decision in which proper factors are considered. In the instant case, we must determine whether the trial court assigned too great a weight to the age of the Johnson children and whether the tender years doctrine is now an impermissible criterion for the trial courts in Alaska to use.

Appellant challenges the trial court's reliance on the doctrine of tender years on two grounds. He first argues that the doctrine is no longer the law in Alaska and is inconsistent with AS 09.55.205, which provides that the courts should consider the best interests of the child in determining custody matters. The trial court viewed the tender years doctrine as a judicial interpretation of AS 09.55.205. However, Sheridan v. Sheridan, 466 P.2d 821 (Alaska 1970), and other cases decided since the enactment of AS 09.55.205 in 1968 reflect a growing trend away from use of the tender years doctrine or any other mechanical formula in determining custody issues.

In *Sheridan,* we noted our disapproval of the "mechanistic application" of custody rules and reversed the trial court's award of the children to their mother on the ground that:

> It appears that the basis for resolution of the custody issue was the tender years' doctrine to the exclusion of any other legal criteria or relevant factual considerations. Seemingly ignored in the decisional process was the paramount criterion of the welfare and best interests of the children which should be determinative. (footnote omitted) 466 P.2d at 825.

Clearly we did not, in *Sheridan,* equate the tender years doctrine with the best interests of the child as the trial court appeared to do. . . .

Although the age of the children in a custody dispute is one factor which may be considered by the trial court in its determination of the best interests of the child, it is only one factor, to be weighed with many others. In Turner v. Pannick, 540 P.2d 1051 (Alaska 1975), we suggested factors which a trial court might wish to consider in its deliberations.

> [U]nder the "best interests' test, the court is free to consider a number of factors including the moral fitness of the two parties; the home environment offered by the parties; the emotional ties to the parties by the child; the emotional ties to the child by the parties; the age, sex or health of the child; the desirability of continuing an existing child-third party relationship; and the preference of the child." 540 P.2d at 1054.

Certainly the trial court's use of the tender years presumption is inconsistent with the delicate weighing and balancing process suggested in *Pannick* as a method of determining the child's best interests.

Courts in other jurisdictions have also held the tender years doctrine to be inconsistent with a "best interests" statute. In State ex rel. Watts v. Watts, 77 Misc.2d 178, 350 N.Y.S.2d 285 (1973), the court reversed a custody decision which was based on the tender years presumption. New York's domestic relations statute is similar to Alaska's in that it affords no prima facie right to custody to either party, the controlling consideration being the best interest of the child. The *Watts* court reasoned that the statute was designed to eliminate such sex-based presumptions in favor of the best interests of the child.

The *Watts* court . . . concluded that the tender years doctrine should be discarded since it is based on "outdated social stereotypes."

> Studies of maternal deprivation have shown that the essential experience for the child is that of mothering-the warmth, consistency and continuity of the relationship rather than the sex of the individual who is performing the mothering function. (citations omitted) 350 N.Y.S.2d at 290.

As the court in In re Marriage of Bowen, 219 N.W.2d 683 (Iowa 1974), remarked in abandoning the tender years doctrine:

> The real issue is not the sex of the parent but which parent will do better in raising the children. Resolution of that issue

> depends upon what the evidence actually reveals in each case, not upon what someone predicts it will show in many cases . . . ,
>
> We do not think either parent should have a greater burden than the other in attempting to obtain custody in a dissolution proceeding. It is neither necessary or useful to infer in advance that the best interests of young children will be better served if their custody is awarded to their mothers instead of their fathers. 219 N.W.2d at 688.

We conclude that the doctrine of tender years is not an appropriate criterion for determination of the best interests of the child under AS 09.55.205. Due to our disposition of this issue, we need not reach appellant's contention that use of the tender years doctrine violated his right to equal protection of the laws.

Appellant next argues that in light of all the evidence presented at trial, the trial court abused its discretion in not awarding the children to him. Appellant cites three main areas in support of this contention. First, he argues that he will be allowed little, if any, access to his children by virtue of his disfellowshipped status. Second, he argues that Linda will restrict his children's educational and cultural environment. He states that he plans to send the children to college, while Linda does not. Third, he cites the psychologists' reports in support of the contention that he will provide the expansive atmosphere necessary for the children's emotional development, while Linda would restrict them in their development. All of these factors center around Linda's plans to raise the children as Jehovah's Witnesses, and this court cannot deem the trial court's decision to award the children to Linda an abuse of discretion simply because of these plans. In Carle v. Carle, 503 P.2d 1050, 1055 (Alaska 1972), we found that the trial court erred in deciding the issue of custody on the premise that the child's best interest would be served by assimilation into the dominant culture and stated:

> It is not the function of our courts to homogenize Alaskan society. Recently, we had occasion to observe that "The United States of America, and Alaska in particular, reflect a pluralistic society, grounded upon such basic values as the preservation of maximum individual choice, protection of minority sentiments, and appreciation for divergent lifestyles." citing Breese v. Smith, 501 P.2d 159, 169 (Alaska 1972).

Certainly, we cannot use Linda's continued membership in the Jehovah's Witnesses as a basis for directing the trial court to award the children to Rudy. To do so would be violative of her right to freedom of religion under the First Amendment to the United States Constitution and of the principles articulated by this court in *Carle*. Furthermore, liberal and specific visitation rights with the children, such as those directed by the trial court, would give Rudy the access which he desires. . . .

In view of the fact that the trial court based its award of physical custody of the children to Linda on the tender years presumption, it is necessary to remand the case to the trial court for further consideration of the custody issue in accordance with the criteria set forth in this opinion.

NOTES

As *Johnson* illustrates, a parent has a constitutionally protected right to the free exercise of religion, but courts are often tasked with determining when that right adversely impacts the judicial system's responsibility to further the best interests of the child. When analyzing the issue, the Kansas Supreme Court has ruled that its courts may not: (1) speculate about behavior that religious beliefs may motivate in the future; (2) weigh the merit of one parent's religious beliefs or lack of belief against the other's; and (3) meditate on theological disputes. In affirming the state trial court, the Kansas state's highest court held that, in making child custody decisions, courts may consider the ways in which current religiously motivated conduct affected a child's best interest. *See* Harrison v. Tauheed, 256 P.3d 851 (Kan. 2011).

In addition to an initial award of custody, the religious beliefs of a custodial parent may be a basis for modification of a custody decree. In *In re* Marriage of Boldt, 344 Or. 1 (Or. 2008), the Oregon Supreme Court held that even though a custodial parent has the presumptive right to make medical decisions regarding elective surgery for a child, forcing a twelve-year-old boy to undergo circumcision against his will could adversely affect his relationship with his custodial father and may be the basis for a modification of the custody award. The father was converting to Judaism and sought to circumcise his son so that the son could convert as well.

Courts have been willing to modify visitation schedules so as to accommodate a parent's desire to continue the religious observance of a child. *See, e.g.,* Gerson v. Gerson, 57 A.D.3d 606 (N.Y. Ct. App. 2008). Courts have refused to enforce religion-based custody decrees issued in foreign countries when the decree was not based on the best interest of the child. *See, e.g.,* Charara v. Yatim, 937 N.E.2d 490 (Mass. Ct. App. 2010) (refusing to enforce an Islamic tribunal's custody determination made in Lebanon). For commentary on the role of religion in custody and visitation, *see* Ann Laquer Estin, *Foreign and Religious Family Law: Comity, Contract, and the Constitution,* 41 PEPP. L. REV. 1029 (2014); Carl P. Funderburk, *Best Interest of the Child Should Not Be An Ambiguous Term*, 33 CHILD. LEGAL RTS. J. 229 (2013); Keith W. Barlow, Comment, *"Can They Do That?": Why Religious Parents and Communities May Fear the Future Regarding State Interests and Custodial Law*, 2012 BYU L. REV. 281 (2012).

B. DISABILITY

In re Marriage of Carney

Supreme Court of California, 1979
598 P.2d 36

■ MOSK, JUSTICE.

Appellant father (William) appeals from that portion of an interlocutory decree of dissolution which transfers custody of the two minor children of the marriage from himself to respondent mother (Ellen).

In this case of first impression we are called upon to resolve an apparent conflict between two strong public policies: the requirement that a custody award serve the best interests of the child, and the moral and legal obligation of society to respect the civil rights of its physically handicapped members, including their right not to be deprived of their children because of their disability. As will appear, we hold that upon a realistic appraisal of the present-day capabilities of the physically handicapped, these policies can both be accommodated. The trial court herein failed to make such an appraisal, and instead premised its ruling on outdated stereotypes of both the parental role and the ability of the handicapped to fill that role. Such stereotypes have no place in our law. Accordingly, the order changing custody on this ground must be set aside as an abuse of discretion.

William and Ellen were married in New York in December 1968. Both were teenagers. Two sons were soon born of the union, the first in November 1969 and the second in January 1971. The parties separated shortly afterwards, and by written agreement executed in November 1972 Ellen relinquished custody of the boys to William. For reasons of employment he eventually moved to the West Coast. In September 1973 he began living with a young woman named Lori Rivera, and she acted as stepmother to the boys. In the following year William had a daughter by Lori, and she proceeded to raise all three children as their own.

In August 1976, while serving in the military reserve, William was injured in a jeep accident. The accident left him a quadriplegic, i.e., with paralyzed legs and impaired use of his arms and hands. He spent the next year recuperating in a veterans' hospital; his children visited him several times each week, and he came home nearly every weekend.[1] He also bought a van, and it was being fitted with a wheelchair lift and hand controls to permit him to drive.

In May 1977 William filed the present action for dissolution of his marriage. Ellen moved for an order awarding her immediate custody of both boys. It was undisputed that from the date of separation (Nov. 1972) until a few days before the hearing (Aug. 1977) Ellen did not once visit

---

1 He was scheduled to be discharged shortly after the trial proceedings herein.

her young sons or make any contribution to their support. Throughout this period of almost five years her sole contact with the boys consisted of some telephone calls and a few letters and packages. Nevertheless the court ordered that the boys be taken from the custody of their father, and that Ellen be allowed to remove them forthwith to New York State.[2] Pursuant to stipulation of the parties, an interlocutory judgment of dissolution was entered at the same time. William appeals from that portion of the decree transferring custody of the children to Ellen.

William contends the trial court abused its discretion in making the award of custody.[3] Several principles are here applicable. First, since it was amended in 1972 the code no longer requires or permits the trial courts to favor the mother in determining proper custody of a child "of tender years." (E. g., White v. White (1952) 109 Cal.App.2d 522, 523, 240 P.2d 1015.) Civil Code section 4600 now declares that custody should be awarded "To either parent according to the best interests of the child." (Id., subd. (a).) Regardless of the age of the minor, therefore, fathers now have equal custody rights with mothers; the sole concern, as it should be, is "the best interests of the child." (See Taber v. Taber (1930) 209 Cal. 755, 756–757, 290 P. 36, 37.)

Next, those "best interests" are at issue here in a special way: this is not the usual case in which the parents have just separated and the choice of custody is being made for the first time. In such instances the trial court rightly has a broad discretion. (Gudelj v. Gudelj (1953) 41 Cal.2d 202, 208–209, 259 P.2d 656.) Here, although this is the first actual court order on the issue, we deal in effect with a complete change in custody: after the children had lived with William for almost five years virtually all their lives up to that point Ellen sought to remove them abruptly from the only home they could remember to a wholly new environment some 3,000 miles away.

It is settled that to justify ordering a change in custody there must generally be a persuasive showing of changed circumstances affecting the

---

[2] The court also imposed substantial financial obligations on William. He was ordered to pay all future costs of transporting his sons back to California to visit him, plus $400 a month for child support, $1,000 for Ellen's attorney's fees, $800 for her travel and hotel expenses, and $750 for her court costs.

[3] He also contends the ruling violated his right to equal protection and due process of law. (*Adoption of Richardson* (1967) 251 Cal.App.2d 222, 239–240, 59 Cal.Rptr. 323, see generally Achtenberg, Law and the Physically Disabled: An Update with Constitutional Implications (1976) 8 Sw.U.L.Rev. 847; Burgdorf & Burgdorf, A History of Unequal Treatment: The Qualifications of Handicapped Persons as a "Suspect Class" Under the Equal Protection Clause (1975) 15 Santa Clara Law. 855; Comment, The Equal Protection and Due Process Clauses: Two Means of Implementing "Integrationism" for Handicapped Applicants for Public Employment (1978) 27 DePaul L.Rev. 1169; Note, Abroad in the Land: Legal Strategies to Effectuate the Rights of the Physically Disabled (1973) 61 Geo.L.J. 1501.) In the view we take of the case we need not reach the constitutional issues at this time. William further complains that the trial court erred in declining several offers of evidence of alleged misconduct of Ellen occurring at various times prior to the hearing. We have reviewed the relevant portions of the record and conclude that certain of the offers were properly refused because the evidence in question was too remote (*Prouty v. Prouty* (1940) 16 Cal.2d 190, 194), while others should probably have been accepted but failure to do so could not have resulted in prejudice (*People v. Watson* (1956) 46 Cal.2d 818, 836, 299 P.2d 243).

child. (Goto v. Goto (1959) 52 Cal.2d 118, 122–123, 338 P.2d 450.) And that change must be substantial: a child will not be removed from the prior custody of one parent and given to the other "unless the material facts and circumstances occurring subsequently are of a kind to render it essential or expedient for the welfare of the child that there be a change." (Washburn v. Washburn (1942) 49 Cal.App.2d 581, 588, 122 P.2d 96, 100.1) The reasons for the rule are clear: "It is well established that the courts are reluctant to order a change of custody and will not do so except for imperative reasons; that it is desirable that there be an end of litigation and undesirable to change the child's established mode of living." (Connolly v. Connolly (1963) 214 Cal.App.2d 433, 436, 29 Cal.Rptr. 616, 618, and cases cited.)[4]

Moreover, although a request for a change of custody is also addressed in the first instance to the sound discretion of the trial judge, he must exercise that discretion in light of the important policy considerations just mentioned. For this reason appellate courts have been less reluctant to find an abuse of discretion when custody is changed than when it is originally awarded, and reversals of such orders have not been uncommon. (E. g., In re Marriage of Kern (1978) 87 Cal.App.3d 402, 410–411, 150 Cal.Rptr. 860; In re Marriage of Russo (1971) 21 Cal.App.3d 72, 98 Cal.Rptr. 501; Denham v. Martina (1963) 214 Cal.App.2d 312, 29 Cal.Rptr. 377; Ashwell v. Ashwell (1955) 135 Cal.App.2d 211, 286 P.2d 983; Sorrels v. Sorrels (1951) 105 Cal.App.2d 465, 234 P.2d 103; Bemis v. Bemis (1948) 89 Cal.App.2d 80, 200 P.2d 84; Juri v. Juri (1945) 69 Cal.App.2d 773, 160 P.2d 73; Washburn v. Washburn (1942) supra, 49 Cal.App.2d 581, 122 P.2d 96.)

Finally, the burden of showing a sufficient change in circumstances is on the party seeking the change of custody. (Prouty v. Prouty (1940) supra, 16 Cal.2d 190, 193, 105 P.2d 295; In re Marriage of Kern (1978) supra, 87 Cal.App.3d 402, 410–411, 150 Cal.Rptr. 860; In re Marriage of Mehlmauer (1976) 60 Cal.App.3d 104, 108–109, 131 Cal.Rptr. 325.) In attempting to carry that burden Ellen relied on several items of testimony given at the hearing; even when these circumstances are viewed in their totality, however, they are insufficient for the purpose.

First, Ellen showed that although she had been unemployed when William was given custody in 1972, at the time of trial she had a job as a medical records clerk in a New York hospital. But her gross income from that job was barely $500 per month, and she admitted she would not be able to support the boys without substantial financial assistance from

[4] Ellen relies on *Loudermilk v. Loudermilk* (1962) 208 Cal.App.2d 705, 707–708, 25 Cal.Rptr. 434, which held that the foregoing rule is "not applicable" when custody was originally awarded pursuant to an agreement between the parties rather than a judicial decree. But the opinion gave scant authority for this asserted exception, and it has since been cited only once in dictum. It is also wrong in principle: regardless of how custody was originally decided upon, after the child has lived in one parent's home for a significant period it surely remains "undesirable" to uproot him from his "established mode of living," and a substantial change in his circumstances should ordinarily be required to justify that result. To the extent it declares a contrary rule, Loudermilk is disapproved.

William. (See fn. 2, Ante.) By contrast, at the time of the hearing William's monthly income from a combination of veteran's disability compensation payments and social security benefits had risen to more than $1,750 per month, all tax-free.

Ellen next pointed to the fact that William's relationship with Lori might be in the process of terminating.[5] From this evidence Ellen argued that if Lori were to leave, William would have to hire a baby-sitter to take care of the children. On cross-examination, however, Ellen admitted that if custody were transferred to her she would likewise be compelled because of her job to place the children "in a child care center under a baby-sitter nine hours a day," and she intended to do so. During that period, of course, the children would not be under her supervision; by contrast, William explained that because he is not employed he is able to remain at home "to see to their upbringing during the day as well as the night."

Additional claims lacked support in the record. Thus Ellen impliedly criticized William's living arrangements for the boys, and testified that if she were given custody she intended to move out of her one-bedroom apartment into an apartment with "at least" two bedrooms. Yet it was undisputed that the boys were presently residing in a private house containing in effect four bedrooms, with a large living room and a spacious enclosed back yard; despite additional residents, there was no showing that the accommodations were inadequate for the family's needs. Ellen further stated that in her opinion the older boy should be seen by a dentist; there was no expert testimony to this effect, however, and no evidence that the child was not receiving normal dental care. She also remarked that the younger boy seemed to have a problem with wetting his bed but had not been taken to a doctor about it; again there was no evidence that medical intervention in this matter was either necessary or desirable. We obviously cannot take judicial notice of the cause of, or currently recommended cure for, childhood enuresis.[6]

In short, if the trial court had based its change of custody order on the foregoing circumstances alone, it would in effect have revived the "mother's preference" rule abrogated by the Legislature in 1972. The record discloses, however, that the court gave great weight to another

[5] Lori candidly testified she had been "thinking about" leaving. She added, however, that "Bill and I have had some problems, just like anyone else in our situation would have, and we are going to get counseling, and hopefully that will settle the matters." And she declared that she loved both of the boys and wanted to continue being their "substitute mother."

[6] In the only testimony on the point Ellen reported that William's cousin, who had been living with the family explained to her the reason the boy wet the bed is "because he wears himself out so much playing that he just doesn't get up at night." Ellen advanced other grounds for a change of custody that are even more insubstantial. Thus she claimed she wanted to enroll the boys in "some kind of church" a choice of words scarcely indicative of a deep religious commitment on her part. And she complained that because William had moved several times in the past five years the boys had not had a chance to "get established" in a school or neighborhood a strange objection coming from one who proposed to move them 3,000 miles. In any event, the record indicated that most of William's moves were job-related and took place prior to the date of his injury, and hence were irrelevant to the family's present situation.

factor William's physical handicap and its presumed adverse effect on his capacity to be a good father to the boys. Whether that factor will support the reliance placed upon it is a difficult question to which we now turn.

Ellen first raised the issue in her declaration accompanying her request for a change of custody, asserting that because of William's handicap "it is almost impossible for (him) to actually care for the minor children," and "since (he) is confined to a hospital bed, he is never with the minor children and thus can no longer effectively care for the minor children or see to their physical and emotional needs." When asked at the hearing why she believed she should be given custody, she replied inter alia, "Bill's physical condition." Thereafter she testified that according to her observations William is not capable of feeding himself or helping the boys prepare meals or get dressed; and she summed up by agreeing that he is not able to do "anything" for himself.

The trial judge echoed this line of reasoning throughout the proceedings. Virtually the only questions he asked of any witness revolved around William's handicap and its physical consequences, real or imagined. Thus although William testified at length about his present family life and his future plans, the judge inquired only where he sat when he got out of his wheelchair, whether he had lost the use of his arms, and what his medical prognosis was. Again, when Lori took the stand and testified to William's good relationship with his boys and their various activities together, the judge interrupted to ask her in detail whether it was true that she had to bathe, dress, undress, cook for and feed William. Indeed, he seemed interested in little else.

The final witness was Dr. Jack Share, a licensed clinical psychologist specializing in child development, who had visited William's home and studied his family.[7] Dr. Share testified that William had an IQ of 127, was a man of superior intelligence, excellent judgment and ability to plan, and had adapted well to his handicap. He observed good interaction between William and his boys, and described the latter as self-disciplined, sociable, and outgoing. On the basis of his tests and observations, Dr. Share gave as his professional opinion that neither of the children appeared threatened by William's physical condition; the condition did not in any way hinder William's ability to be a father to them, and would not be a detriment to them if they remained in his home; the present family situation in his home was a healthy environment for the children; and even if Lori were to leave, William could still fulfill his functions as father with appropriate domestic help.

Ellen made no effort on cross-examination to dispute any of the foregoing observations or conclusions, and offered no expert testimony to the contrary. The judge then took up the questioning, however, and focused on what appears to have been one of his main concerns in the case i.e., that because of the handicap William would not be able to

---

[7] Dr. Share is also a credentialed schoolteacher and a licensed marriage counselor.

participate with his sons in sports and other physical activities. Thus the court asked Dr. Share, "It's very unfortunate that he's in this condition, but when these boys get another two, three years older, would it be better, in your opinion, if they had a parent that was able to actively go places with them, take them places, play Little League baseball, go fishing? Wouldn't that be advantageous to two young boys?" Dr. Share replied that "the commitment, the long-range planning, the dedication" of William to his sons were more important, and stated that from his observations William was "the more consistent, stable part of this family regardless of his physical condition at this point." The judge nevertheless persisted in stressing that William "is limited in what he can do for the boys," and demanded an answer to his question as to "the other activities that two growing boys should have with a natural parent." Dr. Share acknowledged William's obvious physical limitations, but once more asserted that "on the side dealing with what I have called the stability of the youngsters, which I put personally higher value on, I would say the father is very strong in this area." Finally, when asked on redirect examination what effect William's ability to drive will have, Dr. Share explained, "this opens up more vistas, greater alternatives when he's more mobile such as having his own van to take them places. . . ."

We need not speculate on the reasons for the judge's ensuing decision to order the change of custody, as he candidly stated them for the record. First he distinguished a case cited by William, emphasizing "There was no father there or mother that was unable to care for the children because of physical disabilities. . . ." Next he found William and Ellen to be "both good, loving parents," although he strongly chided the latter for failing to visit her sons for five years, saying "She should have crawled on her hands and knees out here if she had to get the children. . . ." The judge then returned to the theme of William's physical inability to personally take care of the children: speculating on Lori's departure, the judge stressed that in such event "a housekeeper or a nursery" would have to be hired overlooking the admitted fact that Ellen would be compelled to do exactly the same herself for nine hours a day. And he further assumed "There would have to be pick up and probably delivery of the children even though (William) drives his van" a non sequitur revealing his misunderstanding of the purpose and capabilities of that vehicle.

More importantly, the judge conceded that Dr. Share "saw a nice, loving relationship, and that's absolutely true. There's a great relationship between (William) and the boys. . . ." Yet despite this relationship the judge concluded "I think it would be detrimental to the boys to grow up until age 18 in the custody of their father. It wouldn't be a normal relationship between father and boys." And what he meant by "normal" was quickly revealed: "It's unfortunate (William) has to have help bathing and dressing and undressing. He can't do anything for the boys himself except maybe talk to them and teach them, be a tutor, which is good, but it's not enough. I feel that it's in the best interests of the two boys to be with the mother even though she hasn't had them for five years." (Italics added.)

Such a record approaches perilously close to the showing in Adoption of Richardson (1967) supra, 251 Cal.App.2d 222, 59 Cal.Rptr. 323. There the trial court denied a petition to adopt an infant boy because of the physical handicap of the proposed adoptive parents, who were deaf-mutes. As here, professional opinions were introduced and remained uncontradicted stating that the petitioners had adjusted well to their handicap and had a good relationship with the child, and that their disability would have no adverse effects on his physical or emotional development. Nevertheless, in language strangely similar to that of the judge herein, the trial court reasoned: "Is this a normally happy home? There is no question about it, it is a happy home, but is it a normal home? I don't think the Court could make a finding that it is a normal home when these poor unfortunate people, they are handicapped, and what can they do in the way of bringing this child up to be the type of citizen we all want him to be." (*Id.* at p. 228, 59 Cal.Rptr. at p. 327.) The Court of Appeal there concluded from this and other evidence that the trial judge was prejudiced by a belief that no deaf-mute could ever be a good parent to a "normal" child. While recognizing the rule that the granting or denial of a petition for adoption rests in the discretion of the judge, the appellate court held that such discretion had been abused and accordingly reversed the judgment. (*Id.* at p. 237, 59 Cal.Rptr. 323.)

While it is clear the judge herein did not have the totally closed mind exhibited in Richardson, it is equally plain that his judgment was affected by serious misconceptions as to the importance of the involvement of parents in the purely physical aspects of their children's lives. We do not mean, of course, that the health or physical condition of the parents may not be taken into account in determining whose custody would best serve the child's interests. In relation to the issues at stake, however, this factor is ordinarily of minor importance; and whenever it is raised whether in awarding custody originally or changing it later it is essential that the court weigh the matter with an informed and open mind.

In particular, if a person has a physical handicap it is impermissible for the court simply to rely on that condition as prima facie evidence of the person's unfitness as a parent or of probable detriment to the child; rather, in all cases the court must view the handicapped person as an individual and the family as a whole. To achieve this, the court should inquire into the persons's actual and potential physical capabilities, learn how he or she has adapted to the disability and manages its problems, consider how the other members of the household have adjusted thereto, and take into account the special contributions the person may make to the family despite or even because of the handicap. Weighing these and all other relevant factors together, the court should then carefully determine whether the parent's condition will in fact have a substantial and lasting adverse effect on the best interests of the child.[8]

The record shows the contrary occurred in the case at bar. To begin with, the court's belief that there could be no "normal relationship between father and boys" unless William engaged in vigorous sporting activities with his sons is a further example of the conventional sex-stereotypical thinking that we condemned in another context in Sail'er Inn v. Kirby (1971) 5 Cal.3d 1, 95 Cal.Rptr. 329, 485 P.2d 529. For some, the court's emphasis on the importance of a father's "playing baseball" or "going fishing" with his sons may evoke nostalgic memories of a Norman Rockwell cover on the old Saturday Evening Post. But it has at least been understood that a boy need not prove his masculinity on the playing fields of Eton, nor must a man compete with his son in athletics in order to be a good father: their relationship is no less "normal" if it is built on shared experiences in such fields of interest as science, music, arts and crafts, history or travel, or in pursuing such classic hobbies as stamp or coin collecting. In short, an afternoon that a father and son spend together at a museum or the zoo is surely no less enriching than an equivalent amount of time spent catching either balls or fish.[9]

Even more damaging is the fact that the court's preconception herein, wholly apart from its outdated presumption of proper gender roles, also stereotypes William as a person deemed forever unable to be a good parent simply because he is physically handicapped. Like most stereotypes, this is both false and demeaning. On one level it is false because it assumes that William will never make any significant recovery from his disability. There was no evidence whatever to this effect. On the contrary, it did appear that the hearing was being held only one year after the accident, that William had not yet begun the process of rehabilitation in a home environment, and that he was still a young man in his twenties. In these circumstances the court could not presume that modern medicine, helped by time, patience, and determination, would be powerless to restore at least some of William's former capabilities for active life.

Even if William's prognosis were poor, however, the stereotype indulged in by the court is false for an additional reason: it mistakenly assumes that the parent's handicap inevitably handicaps the child. But children are more adaptable than the court gives them credit for; if one path to their enjoyment of physical activities is closed, they will soon find

---

[8] A recent statute makes the point in a closely related context: a child may be made a ward of the court because of lack of parental care and control, but "No parent shall be found to be incapable of exercising proper and effective parental care or control solely because of a physical disability. . . ." (Welf. & Inst. Code, s 300, subd. (a); see, e. g., *In re W. O.* (1979) 88 Cal.App.3d 906, 910, 152 Cal.Rptr. 130 (mother's epilepsy no ground for removing children from her custody).)

[9] The sex stereotype, of course, cuts both ways. If the trial court's approach herein were to prevail, in the next case a divorced mother who became physically handicapped could be deprived of her young daughters because she is unable to participate with them in embroidery, Haute cuisine, or the fine arts of washing and ironing. To state the proposition is to refute it.

another. Indeed, having a handicapped parent often stimulates the growth of a child's imagination, independence, and self-reliance. Today's urban youngster, moreover, has many more opportunities for formal and informal instruction than his isolated rural predecessor. It is true that William may not be able to play tennis or swim, ride a bicycle or do gymnastics; but it does not follow that his children cannot learn and enjoy such skills, with the guidance not only of family and friends but also the professional instructors available through schools, church groups, playgrounds, camps, the Red Cross, the YMCA, the Boy Scouts, and numerous service organizations. As Dr. Share pointed out in his testimony, ample community resources now supplement the home in these circumstances.

In addition, it is erroneous to presume that a parent in a wheelchair cannot share to a meaningful decree in the physical activities of his child, should both desire it. On the one hand, modern technology has made the handicapped increasingly mobile, as demonstrated by William's purchase of a van and his plans to drive it by means of hand controls. In the past decade the widespread availability of such vans, together with sophisticated and reliable wheelchair lifts and driving control systems, have brought about a quiet revolution in the mobility of the severely handicapped. No longer are they confined to home or institution, unable to travel except by special vehicle or with the assistance of others; today such persons use the streets and highways in ever-growing numbers for both business and pleasure. Again as Dr. Share explained, the capacity to drive such a vehicle "opens more vistas, greater alternatives" for the handicapped person.

At the same time the physically handicapped have made the public more aware of the many unnecessary obstacles to their participation in community life. Among the evidence of the public's change in attitude is a growing body of legislation intended to reduce or eliminate the physical impediments to that participation, i. e., the "architectural barriers" against access by the handicapped to buildings, facilities, and transportation systems used by the public at large. . . .

While there is obviously much room for continued progress in removing these barriers, the handicapped person today need not remain a shut-in. Although William cannot actually play on his children's baseball team, he may nevertheless be able to take them to the game, participate as a fan, a coach, or even an umpire and treat them to ice cream on the way home. Nor is this companionship limited to athletic events: such a parent is no less capable of accompanying his children to theaters or libraries, shops or restaurants, schools or churches, afternoon picnics or long vacation trips. Thus it is not true that, as the court herein assumed, William will be unable "to actively go places with (his children), take them places. . . ."

On a deeper level, finally, the stereotype is false because it fails to reach the heart of the parent-child relationship. Contemporary psychology confirms what wise families have perhaps always known that the essence of parenting is not to be found in the harried rounds of daily carpooling endemic to modern suburban life, or even in the doggedly dutiful acts of "togetherness" committed every weekend by well-meaning fathers and mothers across America. Rather, its essence lies in the ethical, emotional, and intellectual guidance the parent gives to the child throughout his formative years, and often beyond. The source of this guidance is the adult's own experience of life; its motive power is parental love and concern for the child's well-being; and its teachings deal with such fundamental matters as the child's feelings about himself, his relationships with others, his system of values, his standards of conduct, and his goals and priorities in life. Even if it were true, as the court herein asserted, that William cannot do "anything" for his sons except "talk to them and teach them, be a tutor," that would not only be "enough" contrary to the court's conclusion it would be the most valuable service a parent can render. Yet his capacity to do so is entirely unrelated to his physical prowess: however limited his bodily strength may be, a handicapped parent is a whole person to the child who needs his affection, sympathy, and wisdom to deal with the problems of growing up. Indeed, in such matters his handicap may well be an asset: few can pass through the crucible of a severe physical disability without learning enduring lessons in patience and tolerance.

No expert testimony was necessary to establish these facts. As the Court of Appeal correctly observed in a somewhat different context, "It requires no detailed discussion to demonstrate that the support and, even more, the control of the child is primarily a mental function to which soundness of mind is a crucial prerequisite. It is also well known that physical handicaps generally have no adverse effect upon mental functions. . . . It is also a matter of common knowledge that many persons with physical handicaps have demonstrated their ability to adequately support and control their children and to give them the benefits of stability and security through love and attention." (In re Eugene W. (1972) 29 Cal.App.3d 623, 629–630, 105 Cal.Rptr. 736, 741, 742.)

We agree, and conclude that a physical handicap that affects a parent's ability to participate with his children in purely physical activities is not a changed circumstance of sufficient relevance and materiality to render it either "essential or expedient" for their welfare that they be taken from his custody. This conclusion would be obvious if the handicap were heart dysfunction, emphysema, arthritis, hernia, or slipped disc; it should be no less obvious when it is the natural consequence of an impaired nervous system. Accordingly, pursuant to the authorities cited above the order changing the custody of the minor children herein from William to Ellen must be set aside as an abuse of discretion.

Both the state and federal governments now pursue the commendable goal of total integration of handicapped persons into the mainstream of society: the Legislature declares that "It is the policy of this state to encourage and enable disabled persons to participate fully in the social and economic life of the state. . . ." (Gov. Code, § 19230, subd. (a).) Thus far these efforts have focused primarily on such critical areas as employment, housing, education, transportation, and public access. . . . No less important to this policy is the integration of the handicapped into the responsibilities and satisfactions of family life, cornerstone of our social system. Yet as more and more physically disabled persons marry and bear or adopt children or, as in the case at bar, previously nonhandicapped parents become disabled through accident or illness custody disputes similar to that now before us may well recur. In discharging their admittedly difficult duty in such proceedings, the trial courts must avoid impairing or defeating the foregoing public policy. With the assistance of the considerations discussed herein, we are confident of their ability to do so.

Lastly, we recognize that during the pendency of this appeal, additional circumstances bearing on the best interests of the children herein may have developed. Any such circumstances may, of course, be considered by the trial court on remand. (See In re Marriage of Russo (1971) supra, 21 Cal.App.3d 72, 93–94, 98 Cal.Rptr. 501.)

The portion of the interlocutory decree of dissolution transferring custody of appellant's minor children to respondent is reversed.

NOTES

Among the factors listed for determining custody in The Uniform Marriage and Divorce Act, which promote the best interest of the child, is the "mental and physical health of all individuals involved." *See* Section 402(5). Accommodation of all aspects of disabilities has resulted from court emphasis upon actual harm to the best interests of the child, rather than conjecture. This is illustrated in *Carney*. Legislation supports this accommodation too. *See, e.g.*, AMERICANS WITH DISABILITIES ACT, 42 U.S.C. § 12101 *et seq.*

For further commentary on alleged discrimination based on physical or mental disabilities, *see, e.g.*, Jamie A. Rosen, *View from the Bench: Parental Mental Health and Child Custody,* 54 FAM. CT. REV. 10 (2016); Emily A. Benfer, *Health Justice: A Framework (And Call to Action) For the Elimination of Health Inequity and Social Justice*, 65 AM. U. L. REV. 275, 320–324 (2015); Claire Chiamulera, *Representing Parents With Disabilities: Best Practices*, 34 NO. 2 CHILD L. PRAC. 17 (2015) (providing statistical data on removal of children from parents with disabilities).

C. RACE

Palmore v. Sidoti

Supreme Court of the United States, 1984
466 U.S. 429

■ BURGER, CHIEF JUSTICE delivered the opinion of the Court.

We granted certiorari to review a judgment of a state court divesting a natural mother of the custody of her infant child because of her remarriage to a person of a different race.

When petitioner Linda Sidoti Palmore and respondent Anthony J. Sidoti, both Caucasians, were divorced in May 1980 in Florida, the mother was awarded custody of their three-year-old daughter. In September 1981 the father sought custody of the child by filing a petition to modify the prior judgment because of changed conditions. The change was that the child's mother was then cohabiting with a Negro, Clarence Palmore, Jr., whom she married two months later. Additionally, the father made several allegations of instances in which the mother had not properly cared for the child.

After hearing testimony from both parties and considering a court counselor's investigative report, the court noted that the father had made allegations about the child's care, but the court made no findings with respect to these allegations. On the contrary, the court made a finding that "there is no issue as to either party's devotion to the child, adequacy of housing facilities, or respect[a]bility of the new spouse of either parent."

The court then addressed the recommendations of the court counselor, who had made an earlier report "in [another] case coming out of this circuit also involving the social consequences of an interracial marriage. Niles v. Niles, 299 So.2d 162." From this vague reference to that earlier case, the court turned to the present case and noted the counselor's recommendation for a change in custody because "[t]he wife [petitioner] has chosen for herself and for her child, a life-style unacceptable to her father *and to society*. . . . The child . . . is, or at school age will be, subject to environmental pressures not of choice." The court then concluded that the best interests of the child would be served by awarding custody to the father. The court's rationale is contained in the following:

> "The father's evident resentment of the mother's choice of a black partner is not sufficient to wrest custody from the mother. It is of some significance, however, that the mother did see fit to bring a man into her home and carry on a sexual relationship with him without being married to him. Such action tended to place gratification of her own desires ahead of her concern for the child's future welfare. *This Court feels that despite the strides that have been made in bettering relations between the*

races in this country, it is inevitable that Melanie will, if allowed to remain in her present situation and attains school age and thus more vulnerable to peer pressures, suffer from the social stigmatization that is sure to come." App. to Pet. for Cert. 26–27 (emphasis added).

The Second District Court of Appeal affirmed without opinion, thus denying the Florida Supreme Court jurisdiction to review the case. We granted certiorari, and we reverse.

The judgment of a state court determining or reviewing a child custody decision is not ordinarily a likely candidate for review by this Court. However, the court's opinion, after stating that the "father's evident resentment of the mother's choice of a black partner is not sufficient" to deprive her of custody, then turns to what it regarded as the damaging impact on the child from remaining in a racially-mixed household. This raises important federal concerns arising from the Constitution's commitment to eradicating discrimination based on race.

The Florida court did not focus directly on the parental qualifications of the natural mother or her present husband, or indeed on the father's qualifications to have custody of the child. The court found that "there is no issue as to either party's devotion to the child, adequacy of housing facilities, or respect[a]bility of the new spouse of either parent." This, taken with the absence of any negative finding as to the quality of the care provided by the mother, constitutes a rejection of any claim of petitioner's unfitness to continue the custody of her child. The court correctly stated that the child's welfare was the controlling factor. But that court was entirely candid and made no effort to place its holding on any ground other than race. Taking the court's findings and rationale at face value, it is clear that the outcome would have been different had petitioner married a Caucasian male of similar respectability.

A core purpose of the Fourteenth Amendment was to do away with all governmentally-imposed discrimination based on race. Classifying persons according to their race is more likely to reflect racial prejudice than legitimate public concerns; the race, not the person, dictates the category. Such classifications are subject to the most exacting scrutiny; to pass constitutional muster, they must be justified by a compelling governmental interest and must be "necessary . . . to the accomplishment" of its legitimate purpose, McLaughlin v. Florida, 379 U.S. 184, 196, 85 S.Ct. 283, 290, 13 L.Ed.2d 222 (1964). See Loving v. Virginia, 388 U.S. 1, 11, 87 S.Ct. 1817, 1823, 18 L.Ed.2d 1010 (1967).

The State, of course, has a duty of the highest order to protect the interests of minor children, particularly those of tender years. In common with most states, Florida law mandates that custody determinations be made in the best interests of the children involved. Fla. Stat. § 61.13(2)(b)(1) (1983). The goal of granting custody based on the best interests of the child is indisputably a substantial governmental interest for purposes of the Equal Protection Clause.

It would ignore reality to suggest that racial and ethnic prejudices do not exist or that all manifestations of those prejudices have been eliminated. There is a risk that a child living with a step-parent of a different race may be subject to a variety of pressures and stresses not present if the child were living with parents of the same racial or ethnic origin.

The question, however, is whether the reality of private biases and the possible injury they might inflict are permissible considerations for removal of an infant child from the custody of its natural mother. We have little difficulty concluding that they are not.[2] The Constitution cannot control such prejudices but neither can it tolerate them. Private biases may be outside the reach of the law, but the law cannot, directly or indirectly, give them effect. "Public officials sworn to uphold the Constitution may not avoid a constitutional duty by bowing to the hypothetical effects of private racial prejudice that they assume to be both widely and deeply held." Palmer v. Thompson, 403 U.S. 217, 260–261, 91 S.Ct. 1940, 1962, 29 L.Ed.2d 438 (1971) (WHITE, J., dissenting). . . .

Whatever problems racially-mixed households may pose for children in 1984 can no more support a denial of constitutional rights than could the stresses that residential integration was thought to entail in 1971. The effects of racial prejudice, however real, cannot justify a racial classification removing an infant child from the custody of its natural mother found to be an appropriate person to have such custody.

NOTES

While it would appear from *Palmore* that the mother won, the decision did not result in the child's return to her mother in Florida. The Supreme Court decision did not reinstate the original custody decree, and when the 1984 decision was announced the father immediately petitioned the state court for custody of his daughter. By then, he and the eight-year-old girl were living in Texas, and the Florida trial court declined jurisdiction because of the child's absence. The Florida appellate court affirmed, holding that the girl resided permanently in Texas, and her best interest would not be served by a new placement. *See* Palmore v. Sidoti, 472 So.2d 843 (Fla. Ct. App. 1985); *see also* RANDALL KENNEDY, INTERRACIAL INTIMACIES: SEX, MARRIAGE, IDENTITY AND ADOPTION 384–385 (2003).

The Indian Child Welfare Act of 1978 (ICWA) is an exception to racial consideration. The Act is an attempt to preserve tribal identity by giving the Indian tribe exclusive jurisdiction over any child custody proceeding involving an Indian child who resides, or is domiciled with, the reservation of such tribe. *See* 25 U.S.C. § 1911(a). Normally, as *Palmore* holds, race cannot be a consideration. *See, e.g.*, MULTIETHNIC PLACEMENT ACT OF 1994 (MEPA), Pub. L. No. 103–382, 553(a)(1), 108 Stat. 3518, 4056 (amended

[2] In light of our holding based on the Equal Protection Clause, we need not reach or resolve petitioner's claim based on the Fourteenth Amendment's Due Process Clause.

1996); ALI, *Principles of the Law of Family Dissolution: Analysis and Recommendations* § 2.12(1)(a) (2002). It is arguable, however, that race continues to be a subtle factor in some cases. *See, e.g.*, Parker v. Parker, 986 S.W.2d 557 (Tenn. 1999) (finding that an interracial relationship may have been a subtle factor in the denial of custody to the child's primary caretaker). For commentary on custody and race, *see* Justin Desautels-Stein, *Race as a Legal* Concept, 2 COLUM. J. RACE & L. 1 (2012); James G. Dwyer, *Parents' Self-Determination and Children's Custody: A New Analytical Framework for State Structuring of Children's Family Life*, 54 ARIZ. L. REV. 79 (2012); Rose Cuison Villazor, *The Other* Loving*: Uncovering the Federal Government's Racial Regulation of Marriage*, 86 N.Y.U. L. REV. 1361 (2011).

3. JOINT PHYSICAL AND/OR LEGAL CUSTODY

CALIFORNIA FAMILY CODE (2016)

§ 3040. Order of preference

(a) Custody should be granted in the following order of preference according to the best interest of the child as provided in Sections 3011 and 3020:

  (1) To both parents jointly pursuant to Chapter 4 (commencing with Section 3080) or to either parent. In making an order granting custody to either parent, the court shall consider, among other factors, which parent is more likely to allow the child frequent and continuing contact with the noncustodial parent, consistent with Section 3011 and 3020, and shall not prefer a parent as custodian because of that parent's sex. The court, in its discretion, may require the parents to submit to the court a plan for the implementation of the custody order. . . .

(b) This section establishes neither a preference nor a presumption for or against joint legal custody, joint physical custody, or sole custody, but allows the court and the family the widest discretion to choose a parenting plan that is in the best interest of the child.

§ 3080. Presumption of joint custody

There is a presumption, affecting the burden of proof that joint custody is in the best interest of the minor child. Subject to Section 3011, where the parents have agreed to joint custody or so agree in open court at a hearing for the purpose of determining the custody of the minor child.

§ 3081. Grant of joint custody absent agreement of parents

On the application of either parent, joint custody may be ordered in the discretion of the court. . . .

WISCONSIN STATUTES ANN. (2015–2016)

767.41(b)(2) Custody to party; joint or sole

(a) Subject to pars. (am) to (e) based on the best interest of the child and after considering the factors under sub. (5)(am), subject to sub. (5)(bm), the court may give joint legal custody or sole legal custody of a minor child.

(am) Except as provided in par. (d), the court shall presume that joint legal custody is in the best interest of the child.

(b) The court may give sole legal custody only if it finds that doing so is in the child's best interest and that either of the following applies:

1. Both parties agree to sole legal custody with the same party.

2. The parties do not agree to sole legal custody with the same party, but at least one party requests sole legal custody and the court specifically finds any of the following:

   a. One party is not capable of performing parental duties and responsibilities or does not wish to have an active role in raising the child.

   b. One or more conditions exist at that time that would substantially interfere with the exercise of joint legal custody.

   c. The parties will not be able to cooperate in the future decision making required under an award of joint legal custody. In making this finding the court shall consider, along with any other pertinent items, any reasons offered by a party objecting to joint legal custody. Evidence that either party engaged in abuse . . . of the child . . . or evidence of interspousal battery . . . or domestic abuse . . . creates a rebuttable presumption that the parties will not be able to cooperate in the future decision making required.

(c) Except as provided in par. (d), the court may not give sole legal custody to a parent who refuses to cooperate with the other parent if the court finds that the refusal to cooperate is unreasonable . . .

In re Marriage of Weidner

Supreme Court of Iowa, 1983
338 N.W.2d 351

■ WOLLE, JUSTICE.

Appellant Marvin Weidner (Marvin) appeals from several provisions of a dissolution decree under which appellee Betsy Weidner (Betsy) was granted sole custody of the parties' two children. The principal issue is whether the court should have provided for joint custody as requested by Marvin. Marvin also contends that if joint custody was not appropriate then he, rather than Betsy, should have received custody of the children. We first address the issue of child custody, then the economic and other issues raised by the parties.

Marvin and Betsy Weidner were married on August 29, 1970, and two children were born of the marriage, Elizabeth (Libby) born on December 18, 1971 and Seth born on December 27, 1974. After Marvin and Betsy graduated from Iowa Wesleyan College in 1972, Marvin received his degree in theology from Garrett Theological Seminary in Evanston, Illinois. Marvin then served Methodist churches in Humboldt, Iowa until 1975 and Burlington, Iowa until 1977, when the parties moved to Des Moines. Marvin is now Director of the Iowa Refugee Service Center. Betsy obtained a teaching certificate in college, but she did not work outside the home on a full time basis until the parties moved to Des Moines. She has had several part time jobs and now is employed full time as an office receptionist in a Des Moines department store.

As early as 1975, disagreements between Marvin and Betsy caused them to live apart for one week. More serious difficulties later arose. Marvin moved out of the family home between June and November of 1980, and after living together for nine more months the parties separated permanently in August of 1981. During the sixteen months between the final separation and the entry of the court's decree Betsy was the primary physical custodian of the children, but Marvin was with them almost half the time. In general Betsy was the person who took care of the children's day-to-day activities, such as getting them ready for school, packing lunches, doing laundry and taking care of them while they were ill. Marvin was with the children every weekend and one other day each week; he also maintained daily contact with the children both by personal visits to the home and through phone calls. Even though both parties spent equivalent amounts of time with the children, by the time of their final separation the parties neither trusted each other nor enjoyed being in each other's company. The friction which this lack of trust and frequent contact created was exacerbated by Marvin's friendship with a woman friend with whom he often spent considerable time while he had physical custody of the children.

Considering these and other circumstances hereafter discussed we must decide if the trial court properly placed Libby and Seth in the custody of Betsy subject to specified periods of visitation for Marvin rather than providing in the decree for joint custody or sole custody in Marvin.

The primary issue in this case is whether the trial court should have provided for joint custody rather than awarding custody to Betsy. Until recently, the principles governing joint custody awards were those set forth in In re Marriage of Burham, 283 N.W.2d 269 (Iowa 1979).... Effective July 1, 1982, section 598.21(6) was changed to make joint custody awards subject to the more explicit statutory guidelines which are now codified in section 598.41.... Iowa Code section 598.41 (1983) provides in pertinent part as follows:

Custody of children.

1. The court, insofar as is reasonable and in the best interest of the child, shall order the custody award, including liberal visitation rights where appropriate, which will assure a minor child frequent and continuing contact with both parents after the parents have separated or dissolved the marriage, and which will encourage parents to share the rights and responsibilities of raising the child. Unless otherwise ordered by the court in the custody decree, both parents shall have legal access to information concerning the child, including but not limited to medical, educational and law enforcement records.

2. On the application of either parent, the court shall consider granting joint custody in cases where the parents do not agree to joint custody. If the court does not grant joint custody under this subsection, the court shall state in its decision the reasons for denying joint custody. Before ruling upon the joint custody petition in these cases, the court may require the parties to participate in custody mediation counseling to determine whether joint custody is in the best interest of the child. The court may require the child's participation in the mediation counseling insofar as the court determines the child's participation is advisable.

The costs of custody mediation counseling shall be paid in full or in part by the parties and taxed as court costs.

3. In considering what custody arrangement under either subsection 1 or 2 is in the best interests of the minor child, the court shall consider the following factors:

a. Whether each parent would be a suitable custodian for the child.

b. Whether the psychological and emotional needs and development of the child will suffer due to lack of active contact with and attention from both parties.

c. Whether the parents can communicate with each other regarding the child's needs.

d. Whether both parents have actively cared for the child before and since the separation.

e. Whether each parent can support the other parent's relationship with the child.

f. Whether the custody arrangement is in accord with the child's wishes or whether the child has strong opposition, taking into consideration the child's age and maturity.

g. Whether one or both the parents agree or are opposed to joint custody.

h. The geographic proximity of the parents.

4. Joint legal custody does not require joint physical care. When the court determines such action would be in the child's best interest, physical care may be given to one joint custodial parent and not to the other. However, physical care given to one parent does not affect the other parent's rights and responsibilities as a legal custodian of the child.

It may be instructive to note that this statutory language which encourages courts to consider and grant joint custody was enacted within a few months after publication of In re Marriage of Castle, 312 N.W.2d 147 (Iowa App.1981). There the Iowa Court of Appeals in a three to two decision denied a request for joint custody primarily on the ground that our *Burham* decision seemed to allow one party to veto joint custody by expressing disapproval of such arrangements. The specially concurring judges in *Castle* suggested that the law should presume joint custody to be in the best interests of children. In enacting section 598.41 the legislature did not use the word presumption and we find no such presumption in Iowa law. Clearly, however, our statutes now express a preference for joint custody over other custodial arrangements and do not allow one-party vetoes. One parent's opposition to joint custody is only one of the several factors which the court must consider when the other parent has requested joint custody.

These new principles governing joint custody, and the specific listed factors which are to be considered when a parent requests joint custody, are the bench marks by which our courts are to determine whether joint custody is in the best interest of children of dissolved marriages. Applying them we now must determine whether under the evidence here joint custody should have been granted as being in the best interests of the Weidner children Libby and Seth . . . ,

The trial court's findings of fact demonstrate that before awarding Betsy sole custody of the children, the court carefully considered Marvin's request for joint custody. The court said:

> While this case was awaiting trial, the parties attempted to have the children with each parent approximately one-half of the time. Originally the children, even during the school year, were with the petitioner from Tuesday morning until Wednesday morning of each week and from Friday morning until Sunday night of each week. When the children returned to the custody of the respondent, they were tired, somewhat crabby

> and did not want the fun they had been having (while with petitioner) to stop. It was difficult for the respondent and for the children, for the children to get back into the routine of going to school.
>
> On a number of occasions an argument arose over who was going to have the children at a particular time. On one of these occasions when the respondent had the children with her in her car, the petitioner came upon them while he was in his car. The respondent drove into a driveway at a fire station and petitioner did, too. The police were called and arrived upon the scene. No court order was in effect at the time as to who was to have the children, and the officer would not intercede except to keep the peace. Following this incident a court order was entered giving respondent temporary custody and the petitioner visitation for the times he previously had the children with him, except that the weekend visitation ended on Sunday morning.
>
> The court after a consideration of all the evidence finds that joint custody should not be granted in this case. While the parties are both fit and suitable to act as a custodial parent, they have not demonstrated that they are able to communicate and give priority to the welfare of the children by reaching shared decisions that are in the best interests of the children.

The trial court also highlighted certain other matters in its findings of fact, providing us further insight into why it decided against joint custody. The findings of fact emphasize the complication in the lives of Marvin and the children caused by the presence of his woman friend. According to the trial court's findings, Marvin and she "had had an open, ongoing, intimate relationship for about a year." The trial court indicated this relationship had been a serious concern of the court-appointed family therapist who had based his recommendation of joint custody in part upon recommending minimal involvement of other adults in the relationship between the parents and their children. The trial court found that Marvin used poor judgment in discussing frightening ideas, such as a nuclear holocaust, with the children shortly before returning them to Betsy. It expressed concern about the petitioner's discussions with the children concerning his relationship with his woman friend and other matters pertaining to the dissolution case which caused them anxiety.

There is solid support in the record for each and all of the trial court's findings of fact and expressions of concern about the feasibility of joint custody for these particular parents. The court not only commented on the parties' general inability to communicate and reach shared child-raising decisions, but also focused upon specific unpleasant scenes from the failing marriage when the parties' dislike and mistrust of each other was made painfully clear to the children. Such incidents seem truly to have wreaked havoc in the lives of the parents and, more importantly, the day-to-day lives of their children. We need not further encumber these printed pages with the details of each unpleasant event which followed the final separation of Marvin and Betsy. Suffice it to say that neither party seems now to respect the other. Neither parent has been able to function well except when completely separated from the other. For example, Marvin's repeated efforts to speak with and visit the children on occasions when they have been in the physical care of Betsy have been stressful for Betsy and the children. Marvin's tape recording of some of his phone conversations with Betsy is symptomatic of the extent to which the parents dislike each other. This attempt by Marvin to obtain evidence for trial led Betsy to communicate with him exclusively through written notes.

We are here primarily concerned not with the effect upon Marvin and Betsy of this regular pattern of highly unpleasant episodes, but rather with the adverse effect upon Libby and Seth, their children. This is reflected not only in the parties' testimony but also in the written report and testimony of the court-appointed therapist who performed testing, interviewed the family members on several occasions, and then provided recommendations to the court. Marvin relied heavily on the therapist's recommendation of joint custody, but we find much in the report which seems inconsistent with that recommendation. His first recommendation was

> That joint custody be reconsidered for the children's sake, if both Betsy and Marvin are willing to work toward its success . . . and if Marvin and Betsy each follow recommendations listed below for extensive therapy. Without compliance joint custody does not appear a promising alternative.

The recommendation included 10 to 12 months of post-decree therapeutic work. He indicated this was needed for several reasons; these reasons themselves reflect how serious had been the strife created by the parents and thrust upon the children. He reported that neither child had truly accepted or understood the parent's bitterness and sense of failure. It appears the post-separation period of living first with one parent and then the other was confusing to both children. The older child Libby (then "an intelligent, sensitive young girl of 10") was reported by the therapist as "trapped in a loyalty conflict", feeling herself to be a comforter for both parents and responsible for the hurt that might result from either parent's loss of custody. The family therapist was also "concerned about Seth's adjustment" during the period of parental separation. He reported that the children both "have already endured a sense of rootlessness in their development, with the family moves and continued uncertainty of their parents' marriage." He opined also that the children "need frequent time alone with each parent, without the regular involvement of other adults being present with the parent-even other relatives." On cross examination he explained that the "grieving process" needed for repairing and understanding emotional scars of the bad marriage was still in process for the parents and had not even started for these two young children-"they're denying how much disruption is going on." He attributed this in part to the entry of Marvin's woman friend into this situation. In this regard he stated:

> But again, in light of the whole thing of restructuring their primary contacts and their emotional bonds with each individual parent, it's going to be imperative that they have as much time as they want, not as much time as the individual parent wants, to have alone with that natural parent, be that their father or their mother.

It is reasonable to conclude from his testimony that a joint custody arrangement probably would not work unless the parties both would change their recent pattern of behavior, believe in the positive effects of such an arrangement, and respond satisfactorily to about a year of active post-marital counseling and therapy. We agree with the trial court in concluding that those pre-conditions to successful joint custody arrangements are unlikely to be satisfactorily met, based on the parties' demonstrated antagonism toward each other since the marriage failed.

We would be remiss if we did not mention and correct certain misconceptions counsel and trial courts may have concerning joint custody. None of the eight factors which judges must weigh in the balance are conditions precedent to a joint custody determination. The trial court should consider and express itself in writing on those factors among the eight listed which are pertinent in disputed cases, but there is no magic number of the factors which, when satisfied, will mandate a decision for or against joint custody. The quality of the total family custodial setting rather than a given quantity of the listed factors should be determinative on the issue of joint custody. Here, no factor alone has dissuaded us from putting in place a joint custody arrangement. We have concluded, however, that on the record in this case Marvin and Betsy would be unable adequately to communicate with each other regarding their children's needs, neither parent would be adequately supportive of the other parent's relationship with the children, and Betsy is opposed to joint custody for reasons reasonably attributable in substantial part to the actions and attitude of Marvin.

Furthermore, no parent and no attorney representing a party should be concerned that a request for joint custody is a sign of weakness, a suggestion to the court that if joint custody is not decreed the party opposing joint custody may have an edge in obtaining sole custody. Conversely, and as was noted in our recent *Bolin* decision, a court may properly consider that a parent's unreasonable or obdurate resistance to joint custody is a factor which can weigh in favor of awarding sole custody to the other parent. In re Marriage of Bolin, 336 N.W.2d [441], at 446 [Iowa 1983].

In the last analysis, the custodial determination must reflect and accomplish whatever is in the best interest of the affected children. Joint custody is preferred because, properly tailored to the parties' circumstances, joint custodial arrangements will often go a long way toward encouraging both parents to share the rights, responsibilities, and frequently joyful and meaningful experiences of raising their children.

We reluctantly but firmly conclude, as did the trial court, that the circumstances here are not conducive to a workable joint custody arrangement which would be in the best interests of the parties' children Libby and Seth. . . .

We therefore affirm the trial court's decree. . . .

NOTES

Confusion often arises over the legal distinction between joint physical custody and joint legal custody. The statutory provisions in *Weidner* and the California and Wisconsin code provisions are provided to illustrate the distinction between the two custody arrangements. As the statutes indicate, joint legal custody is easier for the courts to award than joint physical custody. For confirmation, *see* E. MACCOBY AND R. MNOOKIN, DIVIDING THE CHILD: SOCIAL AND LEGAL DILEMMAS OF CUSTODY (1992). Agreement between the parents seems to be a necessary element prior to an award of joint physical custody. For commentary on joint custody arrangements, *see, e.g.*, Katharine T. Bartlett and Elizabeth S. Scott, *Prioritizing Past Caretaking in Child-Custody Decisionmaking*, 77 LAW & CONTEMP. PROBS. 29 (2014); Mary Jean Dolan and Daniel J. Hyman, *Fighting Over Bedtime Stories: An Empirical Study of the Risks of Valuing Quantity Over Quality in Child Custody Decisions*, 38 LAW & PSYCHOL. REV. 45 (2013–2014); Cynthia Lee Starnes, *Lovers, Parents, and Partners: Disentangling Spousal and Co-Parenting Commitments*, 54 ARIZ. L. REV. 197 (2012).

4. VISITATION RIGHTS

Schutz v. Schutz

Supreme Court of Florida, 1991
581 So.2d 1290

■ KOGAN, JUSTICE.

. . .

A final judgment dissolving the six-year marriage of petitioner, Laurel Schutz (mother) and respondent, Richard R. Schutz (father) was entered by the trial court on November 13, 1978. Although custody of the parties' minor children was originally granted to the father, the final judgment was later modified in 1979. Under the modified judgment, the mother was awarded sole custody of the children, and the father was both granted visitation rights and ordered to pay child support.

As noted by the trial court, the ongoing "acrimony and animosity between the adult parties" is clear from the record. The trial court found that in February 1981 the mother moved with the children from Miami to Georgia without notifying the father. After moving, the mother advised the father of their new address and phone number. Although the father and children corresponded after the move, he found an empty house on the three occasions when he traveled to Georgia to visit the children. The father was not notified that after only seven months in Georgia the mother and children had returned to Miami. Four years later in 1985, upon discovering the children's whereabouts, the father visited the children only to find that they "hated, despised, and feared" him due to his failure to support or visit them. After this visit, numerous motions concerning visitation, custody and support were filed by the parties.

After a final hearing on the motions, the trial court found that "the cause of the blind, brainwashed, bigoted belligerence of the children toward the father grew from the soil nurtured, watered and tilled by the mother." The court further found that "the mother breached every duty she owed as the custodial parent to the noncustodial parent of instilling love, respect and feeling in the children for their father." The trial court's findings are supported by substantial competent evidence.

Based on these findings, the trial court ordered the mother "to do everything in her power to create in the minds of [the children] a loving, caring feeling toward the father . . . [and] to convince the children that it is the mother's desire that they see their father and love their father." The court further ordered that breach of the obligation imposed "either in words, actions, demeanor, implication or otherwise" would result in the "severest penalties . . . including contempt, imprisonment, loss of residential custody or any combination thereof."

Although the district court construed the above quoted portions of the order to require the mother to "instruct the children to love and respect their father," 522 So.2d at 875, it concluded that she was not " 'protected' by the first amendment from a requirement that she fulfill her legal obligation to undo the harm she had already caused." *Id.*

We begin our analysis by noting our agreement with the district courts of appeal that have found a custodial parent has an affirmative obligation to encourage and nurture the relationship between the child and the noncustodial parent. This duty is owed to both the noncustodial parent and the child. This obligation may be met by encouraging the child to interact with the noncustodial parent, taking good faith measures to ensure that the child visit and otherwise have frequent and continuing contact with the noncustodial parent and refraining from doing anything likely to undermine the relationship naturally fostered by such interaction.

Consistent with this obligation, we read the challenged portion of the order at issue to require nothing more of the mother than a good faith effort to take those measures necessary to restore and promote the frequent and continuing positive interaction (e.g., visitation, phone calls, letters) between the children and their father and to refrain from doing or saying anything likely to defeat that end. There is no requirement that petitioner express opinions that she does not hold, a practice disallowed by the first amendment. . . .

Under this construction of the order, any burden on the mother's first amendment rights is merely "incidental."[2] Therefore, the order may be sustained against a first amendment challenge if "it furthers an important or substantial governmental interest . . . and if the incidental restriction on alleged First Amendment freedoms is no greater than is essential to the furtherance of that interest." United States v. O'Brien, 391 U.S. 367, 377, 88 S.Ct. 1673, 1679, 20 L.Ed.2d 672 (1968). Accordingly, we must balance the mother's right of free expression against the state's parens patriae interest in assuring the well-being of the parties' minor children. However, as with all matters involving custody of minor children, the interests of the father and of the children, which here happen to parallel those of the state, must also factor into the equation.

In this case, the court, acting on behalf of the state as parens patriae, sought to resolve the dispute between the parties in accordance with the best interests of their children by attempting to restore a meaningful relationship between the children and their father by assuring them unhampered, frequent and continuing contact with him. . . . In resolving the matter, the court also properly considered the father's constitutionally protected "inherent right" to a meaningful relationship with his children,[3] a personal interest which in this case is consistent with the state's interest in promoting meaningful family relationships.

There is no question that the state's interest in restoring a meaningful relationship between the parties' children and their father, thereby promoting the best interests of the children, is at the very least substantial. Likewise, any restriction placed on the mother's freedom of expression is essential to the furtherance of the state's interests because affirmative measures taken by the mother to encourage meaningful interaction between the children and their father would be for naught if she were allowed to contradict those measures by word or deed. Moreover, as evinced by this record, the mother as custodial parent has the ability to undermine the association to which both the father and the parties' children are entitled. . . . Therefore, not only is the incidental burden placed on her right of free expression essential to the furtherance of the state's interests as expressed in chapter 61, but also it is necessary to protect the rights of the children and their father to the meaningful relationship that the order seeks to restore.

---

[2] The burden is "incidental" because the state interests which are furthered by the order are "unrelated to the suppression of free expression." *United States v. O'Brien*, 391 U.S. 367, 377, 88 S.Ct. 1673, 1679, 20 L.Ed.2d 672 (1968).

[3] *Frazier v. Frazier*, 109 Fla. 164, 172, 147 So. 464, 467 (1933) (noncustodial father is "entitled to have and enjoy [child's] society for a reasonably sufficient length of time each year to enable him to inculcate in her mind a spirit of love, affection and respect for her father," if such is not contrary to best interest of child). . . .

Accordingly, construing the order as we do, we find no abuse of discretion by the trial court, nor impermissible burden on the petitioner's first amendment rights. Although we do not approve the district court's construction of that portion of the order under review, nor the analysis employed below, the result reached is approved. . . .

NOTES

Courts have not been shy in ordering innovative approaches to allow communications between parents and children. *See, e.g.*, Burke v. Burke, 2001 WL 921770 (Tenn. Ct. App. 2001), where the court ordered the mother to install a point-to-point video telecommunications device on her home computer so that a couple's two children may communicate with their father when in her physical custody. The father was ordered to pay for the device and the installation. The North Carolina Court of Appeals cautioned that any use of electronic devices in conjunction with parental visitation must comply with state statutes, specifically whether the device would be in the best interest of the child and whether it is affordable to the parents. *See In re* T.R.T., 737 S.E.2d 823 (N.C. Ct. App. 2013). But the attitude of the courts towards electronic visitation appears to be positive if utilization meets the best interest of the children. *See, e.g., In re* Marriage of Rohdy, 838 N.W.2d 870 (Iowa Ct. App. 2013) ("The weekly time the children spend at their maternal grandmother's home to Skype with Michelle [mother] seems to us to be a creative approach by the court to provide for regular, ongoing, emotional contact between the children and Michelle when physical contact is not feasible.")

And courts have protected a person's right to make threatening speech against the other parent as long as there is no history of domestic violence and the other parent was at no time in fear of immediate or soon-to-be-inflicted harm. Lawrence v. Delkamp, 620 N.W.2d 151 (N.D. 2000).

MICHIGAN COMPILED LAWS ANN. (2016)

552.642. Makeup parenting time policy for wrongful denial of parenting time

Sec. 42. (1) Each circuit shall establish a makeup parenting time policy under which a parent who has been wrongfully denied parenting time is able to make up the parenting time at a later date. The policy does not apply until it is approved by the chief circuit judge. A makeup parenting time policy established under this section shall provide all of the following:

(a) That makeup parenting time shall be at least the same type and duration of parenting time as the parenting time that was denied, including, but not limited to, weekend parenting time for weekend parenting time, holiday parenting time for holiday parenting time, weekday parenting time for weekday parenting time, and summer parenting time for summer parenting time.

(b) That makeup parenting time shall be taken within 1 year after the wrongfully denied parenting time was to have occurred.

(c) That the wrongfully denied parent shall choose the time of the makeup parenting time.

(d) That the wrongfully denied parent shall notify both the office of the friend of the court and the other parent in writing not less than 1 week before making use of makeup weekend or weekday parenting time or not less than 28 days before making use of makeup holiday or summer parenting time.

(2) If wrongfully denied parenting time is alleged and the friend of the court determines that action should be taken, the office of the friend of the court shall send each party a notice containing the following statement in boldfaced type of not less than 12 points:

"FAILURE TO RESPOND IN WRITING TO THE OFFICE OF THE FRIEND OF THE COURT WITHIN 21 DAYS AFTER THIS NOTICE WAS SENT SHALL BE CONSIDERED AS AN AGREEMENT THAT PARENTING TIME WAS WRONGFULLY DENIED AND THAT THE MAKEUP PARENTING TIME POLICY ESTABLISHED BY THE COURT WILL BE APPLIED."

(3) If a party to the parenting time order does not respond in writing to the office of the friend of the court, within 21 days after the office sends the notice required under subsection (2), to contest the application of the makeup parenting time policy, the office of the friend of the court shall notify each party that the makeup parenting time policy applies. If a party makes a timely response to contest the application of the makeup parenting time policy, the office of the friend of the court shall utilize a procedure authorized under section 41 other than the application of the makeup parenting time policy.

Harrington v. Harrington

Supreme Court of Mississippi, 1994
648 So.2d 543

■ SULLIVAN, JUSTICE, for the Court:

These parties were divorced on November 8, 1991. The Judgment of Divorce included a Child Custody, Child Support and Property Settlement agreement, in which Mark Harrington was granted overnight visitation on the first and third weekends of every month with his two daughters; Britanny, born on April 24, 1982, and Courtney, born May 22, 1983. He was also granted holiday visitation and summer visitation.

Donnett Harrington filed a Motion to Modify Judgment of Divorce in the Jasper County Chancery Court on August 26, 1992. Donnett alleged a material change in circumstances adversely affecting the children; namely that Mark Harrington was living with a female, Stephanie Milam, without the benefit of marriage.

The case was heard on January 26, 1993, before Chancellor H. David Clark, II. The chancellor found that a modification of Mark's visitation with his two minor daughters was warranted based on the fact that Mark was living with Stephanie without the benefit of marriage while simultaneously teaching his children Christian principles.

On March 11, 1993, Chancellor Clark ruled that Mark would no longer enjoy overnight visitation with his children. Mark was granted physical custody of the children every other weekend from 9:00 a.m. to 3:00 p.m. on Saturdays, and from 1:00 p.m. until 5:00 p.m. on Sundays. The chancellor ordered that at no time during the visitation would the children be allowed to be in the presence of Stephanie, nor would Mark be permitted to discuss his relationship with Stephanie-past, present or future.

Mark assigns one error on appeal:

That the new visitation rights granted unto him by the chancellor constitutes unreasonable visitation.

Donnett admitted that Mark has complied with the terms of the child custody, child support and property settlement agreement. At the hearing, Mark admitted living with Stephanie without being married to her, and that she stays in the house with him when the girls spend the night.

Mark stated that he is a Catholic and that he attempts to raise his children in a Christian environment. He admitted that he did not lead a perfect life and that in fact he did not believe in divorce but had to accept his situation. While admitting that he lived with Stephanie without the benefit of marriage, Mark stated that he did not believe that this confused or had any detrimental effect on the children. Mark denied that he has any knowledge of Stephanie ever cursing his children. Mark did admit, however, that Stephanie occasionally used foul language around adults. He added that his ex-wife, Donnett, had a whole vocabulary of foul language ready for use when her temper flared up.

Donnett testified that she believed Mark's living arrangement was detrimental to the children. She stated that the oldest daughter, Britanny, came home crying once because of something Stephanie said to her; specifically, "Britanny get off your f. . . ass;" and on another occasion, "get off your lazy ass." Donnett claims that she contacted Mark after the first incident and that Mark defended Stephanie. Mark's testimony on this point was that he remembered being contacted by Donnett, but recalled telling her that he would find out what had happened. Mark further testified that he spoke to both Britanny, and the younger child, Courtney, and they told him that Donnett, not Britanny, was upset.

Donnett was concerned that the youngest child, Courtney, thinks it's okay for Mark to have somebody there with him like that and the ten-year-old does not like it. She knows it's wrong. Mark testified that the children asked him on at least three occasions when he would be marrying Stephanie.

The chancellor found there to be a conflict in Mark's life (living with a woman to which he was not married while advocating Christian principles) which was detrimental and not in the best interest of the children. The chancellor cited evidence in the record to support his conclusion-namely, that the oldest daughter was upset. . . .

The chancellor has broad discretion when determining appropriate visitation and the limitations thereon. White v. Thompson, 569 So.2d 1181 (Miss.1990); citing Newsom v. Newsom, 557 So.2d 511, 517 (Miss.1990); Clark v. Myrick, 523 So.2d 79, 83 (Miss.1988); Cheek v. Ricker, 431 So.2d 1139, 1146 (Miss.1983). When the chancellor determines visitation, he must keep the best interest of the child as his paramount concern while always being attentive to the rights of the non-custodial parent, recognizing the need to maintain a healthy, loving relationship between the non-custodial parent and his child. *Id.*

This Court will not reverse a chancellor's findings of fact so long as they are supported by substantial evidence in the record. Tedford v. Dempsey, 437 So.2d 410, 417 (Miss.1983). However, this Court "will reverse when he is manifestly in error in his finding of fact or has abused his discretion." Hammett v. Woods, 602 So.2d 825, 828 (Miss.1992).

In Dunn v. Dunn, 609 So.2d 1277, 1286 (Miss.1992), this Court stated that there must be evidence presented that a particular restriction on visitation is necessary to avoid harm to the child before a chancellor may properly impose the restriction. Otherwise, the chancellor's imposition of a restriction on a non-custodial parent's visitation is manifest error and an abuse of discretion. *Id. See also* Wood v. Wood, 579 So.2d 1271 (Miss.1991). This Court, in Cox v. Moulds, 490 So.2d 866, 870 (Miss.1986), stated that

> the chancellor should approach the fixing of visitation rights with the thought in mind that, absent extraordinary circumstances militating to the contrary, the non-custodial parent will during the periods of visitation have broad authority and discretion with respect to the place and manner of the exercise of same, subject only to the time constrictions found reasonable and placed in the decree. Overnight visitation with the non-custodial parent is the rule, not the exception; indeed, a non-custodial parent is presumptively entitled during reasonable times to overnight visitation with the children.

The *Dunn* opinion held that the chancellor erred and abused his discretion by restricting visitation where there was no evidence presented that the child was being harmed or in any danger because of contact with the non-custodial parent's lover. *Dunn* at 1286. Furthermore, in Morrow v. Morrow, 591 So.2d 829, 833 (Miss.1991), this Court stated that "[a]n extramarital relationship is not, *per se,* an adverse circumstance."

In the instant case, the chancellor lamented our present law in this area, stating:

> Beginning not too many years ago, as our Supreme Court began to change, so did the law in this area. The law now, as this Court understands it, is that there must be some detrimental effect exhibited in order to modify the visitation as requested in this particular case. In other words, our present Supreme Court or the Supreme Court which has ruled on most recent cases in this arena has held that a Court-a trial court, hearing a case of this nature, cannot assume or presume detrimental effect, that it must be shown by testimony. There were times in the past when, in all honesty, a case of this nature probably would never have come to trial. There was a time when courts, such as this Court, relied upon what we shall loosely refer to as morals to make decisions of this nature. Was it or was it not morally correct? Then our society began to change, and there are those who have said that, in our society, morals are going to hell in a handbag. That has been said millions of times; and, obviously, that's true. Unfortunately, our Supreme Court, on occasion, appears to be carrying that handbag. Instead of defending Judeo-Christian principles, upon which this nation was founded, the Supreme Court has dictated that courts of equity must go along with society; and, if society goes down the toilet, I assume we shall follow it. Society has definitely changed. It is not fashionable in certain circles to discuss things, such as morals or ethics. And, ultimately, in applying the law, as given to us by the Supreme Court, this Court cannot make the decision before it based upon morals or ethics, even though it is a court of equity. What is right, just and proper, according to current law, may not necessarily be moral or ethical.

So, as required by the most recent decisions from our Supreme Court, the Court will set aside its own notions of morality and ethics and set aside its own understanding of Christian principles and must make the decision before it, based upon whether or not it is in the best interest of the minor children to continue the visitation schedule as it currently exists in the November 8, 1991, Judgment of Divorce.

The chancellor went on to find that the visitation granted in the previous decree was not in the best interests of the children, citing the following evidence: (1) Mark teaches his children Christian principles while living with someone to whom he is not married; (2) the confusion that is caused by Mark's teaching one thing and living another; (3) the children are aware of this living arrangement and have inquired as to when Mark and Stephanie would marry; (4) Donnett's testimony stating that the daughters were upset because Mark lived with Stephanie out of wedlock; (5) the children were upset because of things said to them while exercising visitation with Mark.

The chancellor accorded great weight to the fact that Mark was professing one lifestyle while living another. There is substantial evidence in the record that Mark lives with Stephanie and that they are not married. There is also evidence that Mark is Christian and admittedly raises his children in a Christian environment. With regard to this issue, the chancellor stated:

> All parents are called upon, morally, ethically, and legally, to teach their children certain things. One of the major problems that the Court sees in the case before it at this time is that you're trying to teach your children, or you are, in fact, teaching your children two different things; and, in the opinion of the Court, *you've got to choose one or the other.* It is not in the best interest of your children to be put in that situation. Whichever you choose is totally within your discretion. That's not a decision to be made by the Court. (Emphasis added).

One could conclude from the chancellor's analysis that if Mark were agnostic or atheist, there would be no problem with overnight visitation because the hypocrisy would be removed.

That notwithstanding, there is no indication from the record that Mark has, from a Christian standpoint, emphasized that living with a person of the opposite sex without being married to them is wrong. He is a Christian and arguably by his actions has condoned his living arrangement as an acceptable one. However, the chancellor maintains that Mark's living arrangement is detrimental to the children because (1) it is in conflict with his religion; and, (2) this conflict leads to his children being confused. Mark is Catholic. The divorce itself is in conflict with his religion.

There simply is not substantial evidence in the record supporting the chancellor's finding that the children are confused. Although Donnett testified that Britanny came home crying because Stephanie spoke to her in a harsh manner, there is no indication from the record that she was suffering harm because of confusion resulting from her father's alleged hypocrisy. Furthermore, it is admitted by Donnett that the younger daughter thinks it is fine that her father lives with Stephanie. Moreover, even if Britanny is confused, or does not like her father living with Stephanie, this is not the type of harm that rises to the level necessary to overcome the presumption that a non-custodial parent is entitled to overnight visitation.

The chancellor also gave weight to the fact that the children were aware of Mark's living arrangement, and were concerned to the point of asking him when he would marry Stephanie. These facts are contained in the record. However, this does not constitute substantial evidence of harm or detriment to the children. Nothing in the record points to their alleged confusion being the source of their inquiry as to when their father would marry. The children may well have inquired about their father marrying Stephanie because they look forward to the marriage-because they like her and want them to be married.

In further support of his ruling, the chancellor relied on Donnett's testimony that Stephanie had spoken harshly to Britanny on two occasions. While we cannot condone that type of behavior, two instances of harsh language directed at a young girl by a non-custodial parent's lover, in order to discipline the child, is not substantial enough evidence of harm to restrict the visitation of the non-custodial parent in the manner done by the chancellor here. If that sort of verbal attack were an ongoing problem, or coupled with some other evidence of detrimental effect, like the children being unwilling to go visit with their father, restricted visitation might be warranted. Here, there is only evidence that this has taken place on two occasions, and both parties stated that there had been no difficulty in Mark exercising his visitation. Donnett furthermore stated that the children would be upset if they did not get to go visit with their father.

In response to a question from the chancellor Mark said that if his visitation were continued as it was, that perhaps he should not allow Stephanie to be at his home while the children were enjoying visitation.

This goes further than the law requires. While it is difficult for a mere human to live up to the tenets of Christianity, it is rare that the courts of this State punish such a failure. There are numerous Mississippi cases that would allow Mark to have visitation with his children without any restriction on his relationship with Stephanie. The better course of action would be that Stephanie did not stay overnight in the home with the children during that visitation. Morrow v. Morrow, 591 So.2d 829 (Miss.1991); Kavanaugh v. Carraway, 435 So.2d 697 (Miss.1983); Ballard v. Ballard, 434 So.2d 1357 (Miss.1983); and Cheek v. Ricker, 431 So.2d 1139 (Miss.1983).

The cases cited above primarily deal with actual custody and did not result in a change thereof. A change in custody is a far more drastic remedy than a change in visitation. The chancellor was absolutely without authority to prohibit Mark from discussing Stephanie with his children or his past, present or future plans concerning Stephanie. It is our opinion that the chancellor was manifestly wrong on the record in this case to restrict visitation and amend the prior visitation order. We therefore reverse the chancellor and reinstate the visitation under the prior order.

REVERSED AND RENDERED.

■ HAWKINS, C.J., PRATHER, P.J., and BANKS, MCRAE and SMITH, JJ., concur.

■ JAMES L. ROBERTS, JR., J., concurs in results only.

■ DAN M. LEE, P.J., concurs in part and dissents in part with separate written opinion joined by PITTMAN and JAMES L. ROBERTS, JR., JJ.

■ DAN M. LEE, Presiding JUSTICE, concurring in part; dissenting in part.

I concur with the majority's decision that the chancellor abused his discretion when he ordered that Herman Harrington not discuss his relationship with Stephanie Milam while in the presence of his two daughters. However, I respectfully dissent from the majority's opinion in that I do not believe that the chancellor abused his discretion when he restricted Herman Harrington's overnight visitation rights with his two minor daughters.

Visitation and restrictions placed upon it are within the sound discretion of the chancellor. White v. Thompson, 569 So.2d 1181, 1185 (Miss.1990), *citing* Newsom v. Newsom, 557 So.2d 511, 517 (Miss.1990). Visitation should be established with the best interests of the children as the paramount consideration, keeping in mind the rights of the non-custodial parent and the objective that parent and child should have as normal a relationship as possible despite the fact that they do not live together. White, 569 So.2d at 1185, *citing* Clark v. Myrick, 523 So.2d 79, 83 (Miss.1988). This Court will not reverse the chancellor's decision to restrict or limit visitation unless the chancellor abused his discretion. White, 569 So.2d at 1185.

In this case, the chancellor, after hearing all of the testimony, found that Herman Harrington should not have overnight visitation with his two minor daughters. The chancellor held that as long as Herman cohabited with Miss Milam without the benefit of marriage, he could not have overnight visitation with his two young daughters. It certainly appears to this Justice that the chancellor's decision to restrict Harrington's overnight visitation rights was not an abuse of discretion nor was it manifest error to restrict the girls' overnight visits. Hammett v. Woods, 602 So.2d 825, 828 (Miss.1992), *citing* Lawrence v. Lawrence, 574 So.2d 1376, 1382 (Miss.1991).

The issue in this case is quite simple. Shall this Court condone Herman's violation of Mississippi statutory law by reversing the chancellor's ruling, or shall this Court uphold the chancellor's decision and require that Herman follow the law of this State?

The chancellor in his Bench Opinion of January 26, 1993, found:

> The Court has previously determined that, based upon the evidence presented before it, the visitation schedule, as set forth in the November '91 Judgment of Divorce, is not in the best interest of the minor children. That determination is based upon the opinion of the Court that Mr. Harrington, although he chooses to teach his children Christian principles, is, also, and, at the same time, living in the home with a person to whom he is not married in the presence of his children, who are well aware of that situation and have discussed it with him, to the extent of inquiring as to when he would marry. In the opinion of

> the Court, certainly that would be detrimental and not in the best interest of the children.

In the case at bar, the chancellor's concern was whether it was in the Harrington girls' best interest to have overnight visitation with their father interrupted while their father lived openly with Stephanie Milam in violation of the laws of the State of Mississippi. The majority goes into an unnecessary discourse as to whether Herman's attempts to raise his daughters in a moral atmosphere conflicts with his living with Miss Milam. While Herman's self-professed attempt to raise his children in a morally proper way appears to conflict with his current living arrangements, under the particular facts of this case, all that matters is that the chancellor, through the exercise of his discretion, after hearing all of the testimony, found that it was detrimental to the Harrington girls to have overnight visits with their father and his admitted live-in lover.

In Harris v. Harris, 343 So.2d 762, 764 (Miss.1977), this Court reversed the chancellor's decision to modify a mother's right to custody of her young son because the mother belonged to a religion that practiced snake handling as part of their religious beliefs. This Court held that there was no evidence to indicate that the mother's attendance of this church had increased the child's risk of being bitten by a snake. This Court held that the chancellor had no authority to dictate what religion she should teach her child so long as it did not involve exposing him to physical danger or to what society in general deems immoral.

Likewise, should it not be said that the chancellor should not dictate Herman's personal behavior and how it affects his children *unless* his actions expose his children to physical danger or to what society deems as immoral practices.

In the case *sub judice,* Herman Harrington admitted that he lived with Stephanie Milam and that they were not married. Harrington's and Milam's actions violate Miss.Code Ann. § 97–29–1 (1972). This section provides:

> If any man and woman shall unlawfully cohabit, whether in adultery or fornication, they shall be fined in any sum not more than five hundred dollars each, and imprisoned in the county jail not more than six months; and it shall not be necessary, to constitute the offense, that the parties shall dwell together as husband and wife, but it may be proved by circumstances which show habitual sexual intercourse.

Whether Herman Harrington professed to be a Catholic, Baptist, Methodist, Jew, Muslim, Buddhist, Agnostic, or Atheist, the law of this state deems it immoral for two persons of the opposite sex who are not married to cohabit. Miss.Code Ann. § 97–29–1 (1972). In fact, Section 97 Chapter 29 is entitled *Crimes Against Public Morals and Decency.* It is quite clear that the legislature proscribed this behavior as immoral for all citizens, be they religious or not. Therefore, it is quite clear to this

Justice that the chancellor below found that Herman's living arrangements violated the laws of this state and that this violation of the law was detrimental to the Harrington girls. Accordingly, I would suggest that the chancellor did not abuse his discretion when he restricted Herman's overnight visits with his daughter. For the reasons stated above, I concur in part and dissent in part.

■ PITTMAN and JAMES L. ROBERTS, JR., JJ., join this opinion.

NOTES

Recent cases evidence *Harrington's* finding that trial courts may not restrict or modify visitation schedules based on speculation. Rather, visitation with a child may be restricted based on what may be actually shown to be in the child's best interest. *See, e.g.*, Ward v. Ward, 710 S.E.2d 555 (Ga. 2011) (holding that the trial court erred in banning overnight visits by the mother's male friends after the court inferred an adverse reaction by the children who were present in the home at the same time); Barker v. Chandler, 2010 WL 2593810 (Tenn. Ct. App. 2010) (holding that trial court erred when it banned overnight visits by the mother's same-sex paramour when her children were present in the home).

Courts are willing to restrict parent-child visitation when there is an actual threat. For example, in Martin v. Martin, 455 S.W.2d 360 (Ark. Ct. App. 2015) the court held that the husband's text messages to wife describing her inability to satisfy him sexually, describing incestuous relationships he had with members of his family, and his desire to engage in sexually deviant conduct, together with statement to wife that he wanted to "train [child] on sexual matters" when she was old enough, presented extraordinary circumstances that justified limiting his visitation with child to supervised visitation for 16 hours per month.

Troxel v. Granville

Supreme Court of the United States, 2000
530 U.S. 57

■ JUSTICE O'CONNOR announced the judgment of the Court and delivered an opinion, in which THE CHIEF JUSTICE, JUSTICE GINSBURG, and JUSTICE BREYER join.

Section 26.10.160(3) of the Revised Code of Washington permits "[a]ny person" to petition a superior court for visitation rights "at any time," and authorizes that court to grant such visitation rights whenever "visitation may serve the best interest of the child." Petitioners Jenifer and Gary Troxel petitioned a Washington Superior Court for the right to visit their grandchildren, Isabelle and Natalie Troxel. Respondent Tommie Granville, the mother of Isabelle and Natalie, opposed the petition. The case ultimately reached the Washington Supreme Court, which held that § 26.10.160(3) unconstitutionally interferes with the fundamental right of parents to rear their children.

Tommie Granville and Brad Troxel shared a relationship that ended in June 1991. The two never married, but they had two daughters, Isabelle and Natalie. Jenifer and Gary Troxel are Brad's parents, and thus the paternal grandparents of Isabelle and Natalie. After Tommie and Brad separated in 1991, Brad lived with his parents and regularly brought his daughters to his parents' home for weekend visitation. Brad committed suicide in May 1993. Although the Troxels at first continued to see Isabelle and Natalie on a regular basis after their son's death, Tommie Granville informed the Troxels in October 1993 that she wished to limit their visitation with her daughters to one short visit per month.

In December 1993, the Troxels commenced the present action by filing, in the Washington Superior Court for Skagit County, a petition to obtain visitation rights with Isabelle and Natalie. The Troxels filed their petition under two Washington statutes, Wash. Rev.Code §§ 26.09.240 and 26.10.160(3) (1994). Only the latter statute is at issue in this case. Section 26.10.160(3) provides: "Any person may petition the court for visitation rights at any time including, but not limited to, custody proceedings. The court may order visitation rights for any person when visitation may serve the best interest of the child whether or not there has been any change of circumstances." At trial, the Troxels requested two weekends of overnight visitation per month and two weeks of visitation each summer. Granville did not oppose visitation altogether, but instead asked the court to order one day of visitation per month with no overnight stay. In 1995, the Superior Court issued an oral ruling and entered a visitation decree ordering visitation one weekend per month, one week during the summer, and four hours on both of the petitioning grandparents' birthdays.

Granville appealed, during which time she married Kelly Wynn. Before addressing the merits of Granville's appeal, the Washington Court of Appeals remanded the case to the Superior Court for entry of written findings of fact and conclusions of law. On remand, the Superior Court found that visitation was in Isabelle and Natalie's best interests:

> The Petitioners [the Troxels] are part of a large, central, loving family, all located in this area, and the Petitioners can provide opportunities for the children in the areas of cousins and music.

". . . The court took into consideration all factors regarding the best interest of the children and considered all the testimony before it. The children would be benefitted from spending quality time with the Petitioners, provided that that time is balanced with time with the childrens' *[sic]* nuclear family. The court finds that the childrens' *[sic]* best interests are served by spending time with their mother and stepfather's other six children." App. 70a.

Approximately nine months after the Superior Court entered its order on remand, Granville's husband formally adopted Isabelle and Natalie. The Washington Court of Appeals reversed the lower court's visitation order and dismissed the Troxels' petition for visitation, holding that nonparents lack standing to seek visitation under § 26.10.160(3) unless a custody action is pending. In the Court of Appeals' view, that limitation on nonparental visitation actions was "consistent with the constitutional restrictions on state interference with parents' fundamental liberty interest in the care, custody, and management of their children." 87 Wash.App., at 135, 940 P.2d, at 700 (internal quotation marks omitted). Having resolved the case on the statutory ground, however, the Court of Appeals did not expressly pass on Granville's constitutional challenge to the visitation statute.

The Washington Supreme Court granted the Troxels' petition for review and, after consolidating their case with two other visitation cases, affirmed. The court disagreed with the Court of Appeals' decision on the statutory issue and found that the plain language of § 26.10.160(3) gave the Troxels standing to seek visitation, irrespective of whether a custody action was pending. The Washington Supreme Court nevertheless agreed with the Court of Appeals' ultimate conclusion that the Troxels could not obtain visitation of Isabelle and Natalie pursuant to § 26.10.160(3). The court rested its decision on the Federal Constitution, holding that § 26.10.160(3) unconstitutionally infringes on the fundamental right of parents to rear their children. In the court's view, there were at least two problems with the nonparental visitation statute. First, according to the Washington Supreme Court, the Constitution permits a State to interfere with the right of parents to rear their children only to prevent harm or potential harm to a child. Section 26.10.160(3) fails that standard because it requires no threshold showing of harm. Id., at 15–20, 969 P.2d, at 28–30. Second, by allowing " 'any person' to petition for forced visitation of a child at 'any time' with the only requirement being that the visitation serve the best interest of the child," the Washington visitation statute sweeps too broadly. "It is not within the province of the state to make significant decisions concerning the custody of children merely because it could make a 'better' decision." Ibid., 969 P.2d, at 31. The Washington Supreme Court held that "[p]arents have a right to limit visitation of their children with third persons," and that between parents and judges, "the parents should be the ones to choose whether to expose their children to certain people or ideas." Four justices dissented from the Washington Supreme Court's holding on the constitutionality of the statute. We granted certiorari, 527 U.S. 1069, 120 S.Ct. 11, 144 L.Ed.2d 842 (1999), and now affirm the judgment.

The demographic changes of the past century make it difficult to speak of an average American family. The composition of families varies greatly from household to household. While many children may have two married parents and grandparents who visit regularly, many other children are raised in single-parent households. In 1996, children living with only one parent accounted for 28 percent of all children under age 18 in the United States. U.S. Dept. of Commerce, Bureau of Census, Current Population Reports, 1997 Population Profile of the United States

27 (1998). Understandably, in these single-parent households, persons outside the nuclear family are called upon with increasing frequency to assist in the everyday tasks of child rearing. In many cases, grandparents play an important role. For example, in 1998, approximately 4 million children—or 5.6 percent of all children under age 18—lived in the household of their grandparents. U.S. Dept. of Commerce, Bureau of Census, Current Population Reports, Marital Status and Living Arrangements: March 1998 (Update), p. *i* (1998).

The nationwide enactment of nonparental visitation statutes is assuredly due, in some part, to the States' recognition of these changing realities of the American family. Because grandparents and other relatives undertake duties of a parental nature in many households, States have sought to ensure the welfare of the children therein by protecting the relationships those children form with such third parties. The States' nonparental visitation statutes are further supported by a recognition, which varies from State to State, that children should have the opportunity to benefit from relationships with statutorily specified persons-for example, their grandparents. The extension of statutory rights in this area to persons other than a child's parents, however, comes with an obvious cost. For example, the State's recognition of an independent third-party interest in a child can place a substantial burden on the traditional parent-child relationship. Contrary to Justice STEVENS' accusation, our description of state nonparental visitation statutes in these terms, of course, is not meant to suggest that "children are so much chattel." *Post,* at 2072 (dissenting opinion). Rather, our terminology is intended to highlight the fact that these statutes can present questions of constitutional import. In this case, we are presented with just such a question. Specifically, we are asked to decide whether § 26.10.160(3), as applied to Tommie Granville and her family, violates the Federal Constitution.

The Fourteenth Amendment provides that no State shall "deprive any person of life, liberty, or property, without due process of law." We have long recognized that the Amendment's Due Process Clause, like its Fifth Amendment counterpart, "guarantees more than fair process." The Clause also includes a substantive component that "provides heightened protection against government interference with certain fundamental rights and liberty interests. . . ."

The liberty interest at issue in this case—the interest of parents in the care, custody, and control of their children—is perhaps the oldest of the fundamental liberty interests recognized by this Court. More than 75 years ago, in Meyer v. Nebraska, 262 U.S. 390, 399, 401, 43 S.Ct. 625, 67 L.Ed. 1042 (1923), we held that the "liberty" protected by the Due Process Clause includes the right of parents to "establish a home and bring up children" and "to control the education of their own." Two years later, in Pierce v. Society of Sisters, 268 U.S. 510, 534–535, 45 S.Ct. 571, 69 L.Ed. 1070 (1925), we again held that the "liberty of parents and guardians" includes the right "to direct the upbringing and education of children under their control." We explained in Pierce that "[t]he child is not the mere creature of the State; those who nurture him and direct his destiny have the right, coupled with the high duty, to recognize and prepare him for additional obligations." *Id.*, at 535, 45 S.Ct. 571. We returned to the subject in Prince v. Massachusetts, 321 U.S. 158, 64 S.Ct. 438, 88 L.Ed. 645 (1944), and again confirmed that there is a constitutional dimension to the right of parents to direct the upbringing of their children. "It is cardinal with us that the custody, care and nurture of the child reside first in the parents, whose primary function and freedom include preparation for obligations the state can neither supply nor hinder." *Id.*, at 166, 64 S.Ct. 438.

In subsequent cases also, we have recognized the fundamental right of parents to make decisions concerning the care, custody, and control of their children. See, *e.g.*, Stanley v. Illinois, 405 U.S. 645, 651, 92 S.Ct. 1208, 31 L.Ed.2d 551 (1972) ("It is plain that the interest of a parent in the companionship, care, custody, and management of his or her children 'come[s] to this Court with a momentum for respect lacking when appeal is made to liberties which derive merely from shifting economic arrangements'" (citation omitted)); Wisconsin v. Yoder, 406 U.S. 205, 232, 92 S.Ct. 1526, 32 L.Ed.2d 15 (1972) ("The history and culture of Western civilization reflect a strong tradition of parental concern for the nurture and upbringing of their children. This primary role of the parents in the upbringing of their children is now established beyond debate as an enduring American tradition"); Quilloin v. Walcott, 434 U.S. 246, 255, 98 S.Ct. 549, 54 L.Ed.2d 511 (1978) ("We have recognized on numerous occasions that the relationship between parent and child is constitutionally protected"); Parham v. J. R., 442 U.S. 584, 602, 99 S.Ct. 2493, 61 L.Ed.2d 101 (1979) ("Our jurisprudence historically has reflected Western civilization concepts of the family as a unit with broad parental authority over minor children. Our cases have consistently followed that course"); Santosky v. Kramer, 455 U.S. 745, 753, 102 S.Ct. 1388, 71 L.Ed.2d 599 (1982) (discussing "[t]he fundamental liberty interest of natural parents in the care, custody, and management of their child"); Glucksberg, supra, at 720, 117 S.Ct. 2258 ("In a long line of cases, we have held that, in addition to the specific freedoms protected by the Bill of Rights, the 'liberty' specially protected by the Due Process Clause includes the righ[t] . . . to direct the education and upbringing of one's children" (citing *Meyer* and *Pierce*)). In light of this extensive precedent, it cannot now be doubted that the Due Process Clause of the Fourteenth Amendment protects the fundamental right of parents to make decisions concerning the care, custody, and control of their children.

Section 26.10.160(3), as applied to Granville and her family in this case, unconstitutionally infringes on that fundamental parental right. The Washington nonparental visitation statute is breathtakingly broad. According to the statute's text, "*[a]ny person* may petition the court for visitation rights *at any time*," and the court may grant such visitation rights whenever "visitation may serve *the best interest of the child*." § 26.10.160(3) (emphases added). That language effectively permits any third party seeking visitation to subject any decision by a parent concerning visitation of the parent's children to state-court review. Once the visitation petition has been filed in court and the matter is placed before a judge, a parent's decision that visitation would not be in the child's best interest is accorded no deference. Section 26.10.160(3) contains no requirement that a court accord the parent's decision any presumption of validity or any weight whatsoever. Instead, the Washington statute places the best-interest determination solely in the hands of the judge. Should the judge disagree with the parent's estimation of the child's best interests, the judge's view necessarily prevails. Thus, in practical effect, in the State of Washington a court can disregard and overturn *any* decision by a fit custodial parent concerning visitation whenever a third party affected by the decision files a visitation petition, based solely on the judge's determination of the child's best interests. The Washington Supreme Court had the opportunity to give § 26.10.160(3)a narrower reading, but it declined to do so. See, *e.g.*, 137 Wash.2d, at 5, 969 P.2d, at 23 ("[The statute] allow[s] any person, at any time, to petition for visitation without regard to relationship to the child, without regard to changed circumstances, and without regard to harm"); id., at 20, 969 P.2d, at 30 ("[The statute] allow[s] 'any person' to petition for forced visitation of a child at 'any time' with the only requirement being that the visitation serve the best interest of the child").

Turning to the facts of this case, the record reveals that the Superior Court's order was based on precisely the type of mere disagreement we have just described and nothing more. The Superior Court's order was not founded on any special factors that might justify the State's interference with Granville's fundamental right to make decisions concerning the rearing of her two daughters. To be sure, this case involves a visitation petition filed by grandparents soon after the death of their son—the father of Isabelle and Natalie-but the combination of several factors here compels our conclusion that § 26.10.160(3), as applied, exceeded the bounds of the Due Process Clause.

First, the Troxels did not allege, and no court has found, that Granville was an unfit parent. That aspect of the case is important, for there is a presumption that fit parents act in the best interests of their children. As this Court explained in Parham:

> "[O]ur constitutional system long ago rejected any notion that a child is the mere creature of the State and, on the contrary, asserted that parents generally have the right, coupled with the high duty, to recognize and prepare [their children] for additional obligations. . . . The law's concept of the family rests on a presumption that parents possess what a child lacks in maturity, experience, and capacity for judgment required for

> making life's difficult decisions. More important, historically it has recognized that natural bonds of affection lead parents to act in the best interests of their children." 442 U.S., at 602, 99 S.Ct. 2493 (alteration in original) (internal quotation marks and citations omitted).

Accordingly, so long as a parent adequately cares for his or her children (*i.e.,* is fit), there will normally be no reason for the State to inject itself into the private realm of the family to further question the ability of that parent to make the best decisions concerning the rearing of that parent's children.

The problem here is not that the Washington Superior Court intervened, but that when it did so, it gave no special weight at all to Granville's determination of her daughters' best interests. More importantly, it appears that the Superior Court applied exactly the opposite presumption. In reciting its oral ruling after the conclusion of closing arguments, the Superior Court judge explained:

> "The burden is to show that it is in the best interest of the children to have some visitation and some quality time with their grandparents. I think in most situations a commonsensical approach [is that] it is normally in the best interest of the children to spend quality time with the grandparent, unless the grandparent, *[sic]* there are some issues or problems involved wherein the grandparents, their lifestyles are going to impact adversely upon the children. That certainly isn't the case here from what I can tell." Verbatim Report of Proceedings in *In re Troxel,* No. 93–3–00650–7 (Wash.Super.Ct., Dec. 14, 19, 1994), p. 213 (hereinafter Verbatim Report).

The judge's comments suggest that he presumed the grandparents' request should be granted unless the children would be "impact[ed] adversely." In effect, the judge placed on Granville, the fit custodial parent, the burden of *disproving* that visitation would be in the best interest of her daughters. The judge reiterated moments later: "I think [visitation with the Troxels] would be in the best interest of the children and I haven't been shown it is not in [the] best interest of the children." *Id.*, at 214, 113 S.Ct. 1439.

The decisional framework employed by the Superior Court directly contravened the traditional presumption that a fit parent will act in the best interest of his or her child. In that respect, the court's presumption failed to provide any protection for Granville's fundamental constitutional right to make decisions concerning the rearing of her own daughters. Cf., *e.g.,* Cal. Fam.Code Ann. § 3104(e) (West 1994) (rebuttable presumption that grandparent visitation is not in child's best interest if parents agree that visitation rights should not be granted); Me.Rev.Stat. Ann., Tit. 19A, § 1803(3) (1998) (court may award grandparent visitation if in best interest of child and "would not significantly interfere with any parent-child relationship or with the parent's rightful authority over the child"); Minn.Stat. § 257.022(2)(a)(2) (1998) (court may award grandparent visitation if in best interest of child and "such visitation would not interfere with the parent-child relationship"); Neb.Rev.Stat. § 43–1802(2) (1998) (court must find "by clear and convincing evidence" that grandparent visitation "will not adversely interfere with the parent-child relationship"); R.I. Gen. Laws § 15–5–24.3(a)(2)(v) (Supp.1999) (grandparent must rebut, by clear and convincing evidence, presumption that parent's decision to refuse grandparent visitation was reasonable); Utah Code Ann. § 30–5–2(2)(e) (1998) (same); Hoff v. Berg, 595 N.W.2d 285, 291–292 (N.D.1999) (holding North Dakota grandparent visitation statute unconstitutional because State has no "compelling interest in presuming visitation rights of grandparents to an unmarried minor are in the child's best interests and forcing parents to accede to court-ordered grandparental visitation unless the parents are first able to prove such visitation is not in the best interests of their minor child"). In an ideal world, parents might always seek to cultivate the bonds between grandparents and their grandchildren. Needless to say, however, our world is far from perfect, and in it the decision whether such an intergenerational relationship would be beneficial in any specific case is for the parent to make in the first instance. And, if a fit parent's decision of the kind at issue here becomes subject to judicial review, the court must accord at least some special weight to the parent's own determination.

Finally, we note that there is no allegation that Granville ever sought to cut off visitation entirely. Rather, the present dispute originated when Granville informed the Troxels that she would prefer to restrict their visitation with Isabelle and Natalie to one short visit per month and special holidays. See 87 Wash.App., at 133, 940 P.2d, at 699; Verbatim Report 12. In the Superior Court proceedings Granville did not oppose visitation but instead asked that the duration of any visitation order be shorter than that requested by the Troxels. While the Troxels requested two weekends per month and two full weeks in the summer, Granville asked the Superior Court to order only one day of visitation per month (with no overnight stay) and participation in the Granville family's holiday celebrations. See 87 Wash.App., at 133, 940 P.2d, at 699; Verbatim Report 9 ("Right off the bat we'd like to say that our position is that grandparent visitation is in the best interest of the children. It is a matter of how much and how it is going to be structured") (opening statement by Granville's attorney). The Superior Court gave no weight to Granville's having assented to visitation even before the filing of any visitation petition or subsequent court intervention. The court instead rejected Granville's proposal and settled on a middle ground, ordering one weekend of visitation per month, one week in the summer, and time on both of the petitioning grandparents' birthdays. See 87 Wash.App., at 133–134, 940 P.2d, at 699; Verbatim Report 216–221. Significantly, many other States expressly provide by statute that courts may not award visitation unless a parent has denied (or unreasonably denied) visitation to the concerned third party. See, *e.g.,* Miss.Code Ann. § 93–16–3(2)(a) (1994) (court must find that "the parent or custodian of the child unreasonably denied the grandparent visitation rights with the child"); Ore.Rev.Stat. § 109.121(1)(a)(B) (1997) (court may award visitation if the "custodian of the child has denied the grandparent reasonable opportunity to visit the child"); R.I. Gen. Laws § 15–5–24.3(a)(2)(iii)-(iv) (Supp.1999) (court must find that parents prevented grandparent from visiting grandchild and that "there is no other way the petitioner is able to visit his or her grandchild without court intervention").

Considered together with the Superior Court's reasons for awarding visitation to the Troxels, the combination of these factors demonstrates that the visitation order in this case was an unconstitutional infringement on Granville's fundamental right to make decisions concerning the care, custody, and control of her two daughters. The Washington Superior Court failed to accord the determination of Granville, a fit custodial parent, any material weight. In fact, the Superior Court made only two formal findings in support of its visitation order. First, the Troxels "are part of a large, central, loving family, all located in this area, and the [Troxels] can provide opportunities for the children in the areas of cousins and music." App. 70a. Second, "[t]he children would be benefitted from spending quality time with the [Troxels], provided that that time is balanced with time with the childrens' *[sic]* nuclear family." *Ibid.* These slender findings, in combination with the court's announced presumption in favor of grandparent visitation and its failure to accord significant weight to Granville's already having offered meaningful visitation to the Troxels, show that this case involves nothing more than a simple disagreement between the Washington Superior Court and Granville concerning her children's best interests. The Superior Court's announced reason for ordering one week of visitation in the summer demonstrates our conclusion well: "I look back on some personal experiences. . . . We always spen[t] as kids a week with one set of grandparents and another set of grandparents, [and] it happened to work out in our family that [it] turned out to be an enjoyable experience. Maybe that can, in this family, if that is how it works out." Verbatim Report 220–221. As we have explained, the Due Process Clause does not permit a State to infringe on the fundamental right of parents to make childrearing decisions simply because a state judge believes a "better" decision could be made. Neither the Washington nonparental visitation statute generally—which places no limits on either the persons who may petition for visitation or the circumstances in which such a petition may be granted—nor the Superior Court in this specific case required anything more. Accordingly, we hold that § 26.10.160(3), as applied in this case, is unconstitutional.

Because we rest our decision on the sweeping breadth of § 26.10.160(3) and the application of that broad, unlimited power in this case, we do not consider the primary constitutional question passed on by the Washington Supreme Court—whether the Due Process Clause requires all nonparental visitation statutes to include a showing of harm or potential harm to the child as a condition precedent to granting visitation. We do not, and need not, define today the precise scope of the parental due process right in the visitation context.... Because much state-court adjudication in this context occurs on a case-by-case basis, we would be hesitant to hold that specific nonparental visitation statutes violate the Due Process Clause as a *per se* matter....

Accordingly, the judgment of the Washington Supreme Court is affirmed.

■ JUSTICE STEVENS, dissenting.

The Court today wisely declines to endorse either the holding or the reasoning of the Supreme Court of Washington. In my opinion, the Court would have been even wiser to deny certiorari. Given the problematic character of the trial court's decision and the uniqueness of the Washington statute, there was no pressing need to review a State Supreme Court decision that merely requires the state legislature to draft a better statute.

Having decided to address the merits, however, the Court should begin by recognizing that the State Supreme Court rendered a federal constitutional judgment holding a state law invalid on its face. In light of that judgment, I believe that we should confront the federal questions presented directly. For the Washington statute is not made facially invalid either because it may be invoked by too many hypothetical plaintiffs, or because it leaves open the possibility that someone may be permitted to sustain a relationship with a child without having to prove that serious harm to the child would otherwise result....

The task of reviewing a trial court's application of a state statute to the particular facts of a case is one that should be performed in the first instance by the state appellate courts. In this case, because of their views of the Federal Constitution, the Washington state appeals courts have yet to decide whether the trial court's findings were adequate under the statute.... Any as-applied critique of the trial court's judgment that this Court might offer could only be based upon a guess about the state courts' application of that State's statute, and an independent assessment of the facts in this case—both judgments that we are ill-suited and ill-advised to make....

As I read the State Supreme Court's opinion, In re Smith, 137 Wash.2d 1, 19–20, 969 P.2d 21, 30–31 (1998), its interpretation of the Federal Constitution made it unnecessary to adopt a definitive construction of the statutory text, or, critically, to decide whether the statute had been correctly applied in this case. In particular, the state court gave no content to the phrase, "best interest of the child," Wash. Rev.Code § 26.10.160(3) (Supp.1996)—content that might well be gleaned from that State's own statutes or decisional law employing the same phrase in different contexts, and from the myriad other state statutes and court decisions at least nominally applying the same standard. . . .

We are thus presented with the unconstrued terms of a state statute and a State Supreme Court opinion that, in my view, significantly misstates the effect of the Federal Constitution upon any construction of that statute. Given that posture, I believe the Court should identify and correct the two flaws in the reasoning of the state court's majority opinion, and remand for further review of the trial court's disposition of this specific case.

In my view, the State Supreme Court erred in its federal constitutional analysis because neither the provision granting "any person" the right to petition the court for visitation, 137 Wash.2d, at 20, 969 P.2d, at 30, nor the absence of a provision requiring a "threshold . . . finding of harm to the child," ibid., provides a sufficient basis for holding that the statute is invalid in all its applications. I believe that a facial challenge should fail whenever a statute has "a 'plainly legitimate sweep,'" Washington v. Glucksberg, 521 U.S. 702, 739–740 and n. 7, 117 S.Ct. 2258 (1997) (STEVENS, J., concurring in judgment). . . . Under the Washington statute, there are plainly any number of cases—indeed, one suspects, the most common to arise-in which the "person" among "any" seeking visitation is a once-custodial caregiver, an intimate relation, or even a genetic parent. Even the Court would seem to agree that in many circumstances, it would be constitutionally permissible for a court to award some visitation of a child to a parent or previous caregiver in cases of parental separation or divorce, cases of disputed custody, cases involving temporary foster care or guardianship, and so forth. As the statute plainly sweeps in a great deal of the permissible, the State Supreme Court majority incorrectly concluded that a statute authorizing "any person" to file a petition seeking visitation privileges would invariably run afoul of the Fourteenth Amendment.

The second key aspect of the Washington Supreme Court's holding-that the Federal Constitution requires a showing of actual or potential "harm" to the child before a court may order visitation continued over a parent's objections—finds no support in this Court's case law. While, as the Court recognizes, the Federal Constitution certainly protects the parent-child relationship from arbitrary impairment by the State, see *infra,* at 2071–2072 we have never held that the parent's liberty interest in this relationship is so inflexible as to establish a rigid constitutional shield, protecting every arbitrary parental decision from any challenge absent a threshold finding of harm. . . . The presumption that parental decisions generally serve the best interests of their children is sound, and clearly in the normal case the parent's interest is paramount. But even a fit parent is capable of treating a child like a mere possession. . . .

Cases like this do not present a bipolar struggle between the parents and the State over who has final authority to determine what is in a child's best interests. There is at a minimum a third individual, whose interests are implicated in every case to which the statute applies-the child. . . .

Despite this Court's repeated recognition of . . . significant parental liberty interests, these interests have never been seen to be without limits. In Lehr v. Robertson, 463 U.S. 248, 103 S.Ct. 2985, 77 L.Ed.2d 614 (1983), for example, this Court held that a putative biological father who had never established an actual relationship with his child did not have a constitutional right to notice of his child's adoption by the man who had married the child's mother. As this Court had recognized in an earlier case, a parent's liberty interests " 'do not spring full-blown from the biological connection between parent and child. They require relationships more enduring.' " Id., at 260, 103 S.Ct. 2985 (quoting Caban v. Mohammed, 441 U.S. 380, 397, 99 S.Ct. 1760, 60 L.Ed.2d 297 (1979)).

Conversely, in Michael H. v. Gerald D., 491 U.S. 110, 109 S.Ct. 2333, 105 L.Ed.2d 91 (1989), this Court concluded that despite both biological parenthood and an established relationship with a young child, a father's due process liberty interest in maintaining some connection with that child was not sufficiently powerful to overcome a state statutory presumption that the husband of the child's mother was the child's parent. As a result of the presumption, the biological father could be denied even visitation with the child because, as a matter of state law, he was not a "parent." A plurality of this Court there recognized that the parental liberty interest was a function, not simply of "isolated factors" such as biology and intimate connection, but of the broader and apparently independent interest in family. See, *e.g.*, *id.*, at 123, 109 S.Ct. 2333; see also Lehr, 463 U.S., at 261, 103 S.Ct. 2985; Smith v. Organization of Foster Families For Equality & Reform, 431 U.S. 816, 842–847, 97 S.Ct. 2094, 53 L.Ed.2d 14 (1977); Moore v. East Cleveland, 431 U.S. 494, 498–504, 97 S.Ct. 1932, 52 L.Ed.2d 531 (1977). . . .

While this Court has not yet had occasion to elucidate the nature of a child's liberty interests in preserving established familial or family-like bonds, 491 U.S., at 130, 109 S.Ct. 2333 (reserving the question), it seems to me extremely likely that, to the extent parents and families have fundamental liberty interests in preserving such intimate relationships, so, too, do children have these interests, and so, too, must their interests be balanced in the equation. At a minimum, our prior cases recognizing that children are, generally speaking, constitutionally protected actors require that this Court reject any suggestion that when it comes to parental rights, children are so much chattel . . . The constitutional protection against arbitrary state interference with parental rights should not be extended to prevent the States from protecting children against the arbitrary exercise of parental authority that is not in fact motivated by an interest in the welfare of the child. . . .

This is not, of course, to suggest that a child's liberty interest in maintaining contact with a particular individual is to be treated invariably as on a par with that child's parents' contrary interests. Because our substantive due process case law includes a strong presumption that a parent will act in the best interest of her child, it would be necessary, were the state appellate courts actually to confront a challenge to the statute as applied, to consider whether the trial court's assessment of the "best interest of the child" incorporated that presumption. . . .

But presumptions notwithstanding, we should recognize that there may be circumstances in which a child has a stronger interest at stake than mere protection from serious harm caused by the termination of visitation by a "person" other than a parent. The almost infinite variety of family relationships that pervade our ever-changing society strongly counsel against the creation by this Court of a constitutional rule that treats a biological parent's liberty interest in the care and supervision of her child as an isolated right that may be exercised arbitrarily. It is indisputably the business of the States, rather than a federal court employing a national standard, to assess in the first instance the relative importance of the conflicting interests that give rise to disputes such as this. Far from guaranteeing that parents' interests will be trammeled in the sweep of cases arising under the statute, the Washington law merely gives an individual—with whom a child may have an established relationship—the procedural right to ask the State to act as arbiter, through the entirely well-known best-interests standard, between the parent's protected interests and the child's. It seems clear to me that the Due Process Clause of the Fourteenth Amendment leaves room for States to consider the impact on a child of possibly arbitrary parental decisions that neither serve nor are motivated by the best interests of the child.

Accordingly, I respectfully dissent.

[The concurring opinions of JUSTICES SOUTER and THOMAS, and the dissenting opinions of JUSTICES KENNEDY and SCALIA are omitted.]

CALIFORNIA FAMILY CODE (2016)

§ 3101. Stepparent's visitation rights

(a) Notwithstanding any other provision of law, the court may grant reasonable visitation to a stepparent, if visitation by the stepparent is determined to be in the best interest of the minor child.

(b) If a protective order, as defined in Section 6218, has been directed to a stepparent to whom visitation may be granted pursuant to this section, the court shall consider whether the best interest of the child requires that any visitation by the stepparent be denied.

(c) Visitation rights may not be ordered under this section that would conflict with a right of custody or visitation of a birth parent who is not a party to the proceeding.

(d) As used in this section:

(1) "Birth parent" means "birth parent" as defined in Section 8512.

(2) "Stepparent" means a person who is a party to the marriage that is the subject of the proceeding, with respect to a minor child of the other party to the marriage.

§ 3102. Deceased parent; visitation rights of close relatives; adoption of child

(a) If either parent of an unemancipated minor child is deceased, the children, siblings, parents, and grandparents of the deceased parent may be granted reasonable visitation with the child during the child's minority upon a finding that the visitation would be in the best interest of the minor child.

(b) In granting visitation pursuant to this section to a person other than a grandparent of the child, the court shall consider the amount of personal contact between the person and the child before the application for the visitation order.

(c) This section does not apply if the child has been adopted by a person other than a stepparent or grandparent of the child. Any visitation rights granted pursuant to this section before the adoption of the child automatically terminate if the child is adopted by a person other than a stepparent or grandparent of the child.

§ 3104. Grandparent's rights; petition by grandparent

(a) On petition to the court by a grandparent of a minor child, the court may grant reasonable visitation rights to the grandparent if the court does both of the following:

(1) Finds that there is a preexisting relationship between the grandparent and the grandchild that has engendered a bond such that visitation is in the best interest of the child.

(2) Balances the interest of the child in having visitation with the grandparent against the right of the parents to exercise their parental authority.

(b) A petition for visitation under this section may not be filed while the natural or adoptive parents are married, unless one or more of the following circumstances exist:

(1) The parents are currently living separately and apart on a permanent or indefinite basis.

(2) One of the parents has been absent for more than one month without the other spouse knowing the whereabouts of the absent spouse.

(3) One of the parents joins in the petition with the grandparents.

(4) The child is not residing with either parent.

At any time that a change of circumstances occurs such that none of these circumstances exist, the parent or parents may move the court to terminate grandparental visitation and the court shall grant the termination.

(c) The petitioner shall give notice of the petition to each of the parents of the child, any stepparent, and any person who has physical custody of the child, by personal service pursuant to Section 415.10 of the Code of Civil Procedure.

(d) If a protective order as defined in Section 6218 has been directed to the grandparent during the pendency of the proceeding, the court shall consider whether the best interest of the child requires that any visitation by that grandparent should be denied.

(e) There is a rebuttable presumption that the visitation of a grandparent is not in the best interest of a minor child if the natural or adoptive parents agree that the grandparent should not be granted visitation rights.

(f) There is a rebuttable presumption affecting the burden of proof that the visitation of a grandparent is not in the best interest of a minor child if the parent who has been awarded sole legal and physical custody of the child in another proceeding or with whom the child resides if there is currently no operative custody order objects to visitation by the grandparent.

(g) Visitation rights may not be ordered under this section if that would conflict with a right of custody or visitation of a birth parent who is not a party to the proceeding.

(h) Visitation ordered pursuant to this section shall not create a basis for or against a change of residence of the child, but shall be one of the factors for the court to consider in ordering a change of residence.

(i) When a court orders grandparental visitation pursuant to this section, the court in its discretion may, based upon the relevant circumstances of the case:

(1) Allocate the percentage of grandparental visitation between the parents for purposes of the calculation of child support pursuant to the statewide uniform guideline (Article 2 (commencing with Section 4050) of Chapter 2 of Part 2 of Division 9).

(2) Notwithstanding Sections 3930 and 3951, order a parent or grandparent to pay to the other, an amount for the support of the child or grandchild. For purposes of this paragraph, "support" means costs related to visitation such as any of the following:

(A) Transportation.

(B) Provision of basic expenses for the child or grandchild, such as medical expenses, day care costs, and other necessities.

(j) As used in this section, "birth parent" means "birth parent" as defined in Section 8512.

NOTES

Litigation over the effect of the *Troxel* decision continues unabated. The issue involves establishing what factors will overcome a parent's fundamental Due Process right to decide what is in the child's best interest. A California appellate decision recently construed Section 3104 of the California Family Code, *see supra*, and held that the statute did not violate the Due Process rights of parents when a parent sought to prohibit the paternal grandparents from visiting with his daughter. After reviewing the facts, the court held that the California statute upon which the grandparents relied, Section 3104, met constitutional safeguards and the court granted grandparents continuous visitation time with their granddaughter. *See* Stuard v. Stuard, 244 Cal.App.4th 768 (2016). The parents had allowed the grandparents to be a part of the child's life from birth, providing daycare for at least 25 days a month, constant access, and continuous interaction with the child. When the parents divorced and, after being awarded custody of his daughter, the father moved into his parent's home with his daughter. But the relationship soured and when the child was nine years-old her father left the home and sought to prohibit his parents from any contact with their granddaughter. The grandparents filed a visitation petition under Section 3104, arguing that they had a preexisting relationship with their grandchild and this engendered a bond that must be considered when evaluating the best interest of the child. The court granted their visitation petition over the objection of the parent, holding that: "The decision of father and his wife about whether and under what conditions grandparents should have visitation with their grandchildren is entitled to 'special weight' under *Troxel*—assuming both are fit parents—but no more." *Id.* at 784. The court considered the lengthy interaction the parent had allowed to occur between the child and the grandparents and held that this was sufficient to rebut the parental Due Process rights. The court held that, "The extent to which parents encourage a grandparent-grandchild relationship is relevant to overcoming the presumption against granting a grandparent visitation petition. Matthew's [father] change of heart regarding Jeff and Cindy's [grandparents] role in Riley's [child] life does not render unconstitutional the trial court's consideration of his earlier conduct in fostering the grandparent-grandchild relationship." *Id.* at 787.

Establishing parentage has long been an issue in same sex relationships. When the United States Supreme Court ruled that the Fourteenth Amendment required states to license same sex marriages and to recognize same sex marriages valid in other states, *see* Obergefell v. Hodges, 135 S.Ct. 2584 (2015), marriage became an option for same sex couples, which could result in easier establishment of parentage. However, prior to that time many same sex couples often found themselves embroiled in the controversy addressed in *Troxel*. The facts often involve two same sex domestic partners and one would become a biological parent to a child, most likely with the understanding that both partners would raise the child as parents. But then the partners separate and the biological parent restricts visitation by the non-biological former partner, relying upon the *Troxel* holding that a parent has a fundamental right to make decisions pertaining to the child. Case results varied. *See, e.g.*, Truman v. Lillard, 404 S.W.3d 863 (Ky. Ct. App. 2013) (holding that same sex partner had no right to visitation over the objection of child's parent); *but see* A.H. v. M.P., 857 N.E.2d 1061 (Mass. 2006) (holding that partner was not entitled to custody and visitation under theory of parent by estoppel based on a private agreement with mother to raise the child); *In re* Custody of H.S.H.-K., 533 N.W.2d 419 (Wis. 1995) (holding that a parent-like relationship with child may justify an award of visitation over a parent's objection). Same sex marriage may have an impact on this issue. *See* Kenji Yoshino, *A New Birth of Freedom?: Obergefell v. Hodges*, 129 HARV. L. REV. 147 (2015). For further commentary on *Troxel* and its impact on unmarried partners, *see* Jeffrey A. Parness, *Troxel Revisited: A New Approach to Third-Party Childcare*, 18 RICH. J. L. & PUB. INT. 227 (2015); Deborah A. Widiss, *Non-Marital Families and (Or After?) Marriage Equality*, 42 FLA. ST. U. L. REV. 547 (2015); Nancy D. Polikoff, *From Third Parties to Parents: The Case of Lesbian Couples and Their Children*, 77 LAW & CONTEMP. PROBS. 195 (2014); Joanna L. Grossman, *The New Illegitimacy: Tying Parentage to Marital Status for Lesbian Co-Parents*, 20 AM. U. J. GENDER SOC. POL'Y & L. 671 (2012); Nancy D. Polikoff, *The Impact of Troxel v. Granville on Lesbian and Gay Parents*, 32 RUTGERS L. J. 825 (2001).

Parental rights vis-à-vis third parties, nonparents, will be discussed further in the next section.

B. PARENT VERSUS THIRD PARTY

Painter v. Bannister

Supreme Court of Iowa, 1966
140 N.W.2d 152, *cert denied*, 385 U.S. 949

■ STUART, JUSTICE.

We are here setting the course for Mark Wendell Painter's future. Our decision on the custody of this 7 year old boy will have a marked influence on his whole life. The fact that we are called upon many times a year to determine custody matters does not make the exercising of this awesome responsibility any less difficult. Legal training and experience are of little practical help in solving the complex problems of human relations. However, these problems do arise and under our system of government, the burden of rendering a final decision rests upon us. It is frustrating to know we can only resolve, not solve, these unfortunate situations.

The custody dispute before us in this habeas corpus action is between the father, Harold Painter, and the maternal grandparents, Dwight and Margaret Bannister. Mark's mother and younger sister were killed in an automobile accident on December 6, 1962 near Pullman, Washington. The father, after other arrangements for Mark's care had proved unsatisfactory, asked the Bannisters to take care of Mark. They went to California and brought Mark to their farm home near Ames in July, 1963. Mr. Painter remarried in November, 1964 and about that time indicated he wanted to take Mark back. The Bannisters refused to let him leave and this action was filed in June, 1965. Since July, 1965 he has continued to remain in the Bannister home under an order of this court staying execution of the judgment of the trial court awarding custody to the father until the matter could be determined on appeal. For reasons hereinafter stated, we conclude Mark's better interests will be served if he remains with the Bannisters.

Mark's parents came from highly contrasting backgrounds. His mother was born, raised and educated in rural Iowa. Her parents are college graduates. Her father is agricultural information editor for the Iowa State University Extension Service. The Bannister home is in the Gilbert Community and is well kept, roomy and comfortable. The Bannisters are highly respected members of the community. Mr. Bannister has served on the school board and regularly teaches a Sunday school class at the Gilbert Congregational Church. Mark's mother graduated from Grinnell College. She then went to work for a newspaper in Anchorage, Alaska, where she met Harold Painter.

Mark's father was born in California. When he was 2 1/2 years old, his parents were divorced and he was placed in a foster home. Although he has kept in contact with his natural parents, he considers his foster parents, the McNelly's as his family. He flunked out of a high school and a trade school because of a lack of interest in academic subjects, rather than any lack of ability. He joined the navy at 17. He did not like it. After receiving an honorable discharge, he took examinations and obtained his high school diploma. He lived with the McNelly's and went to college for 2 1/2 years under the G.I. bill. He quit college to take a job on a small newspaper in Ephrata, Washington in November 1955. In May 1956, he went to work for the newspaper in Anchorage which employed Jeanne Bannister. Harold and Jeanne were married in April, 1957. Although there is a conflict in the evidence on the point, we are convinced the marriage, overall, was a happy one with many ups and downs as could be expected in the uniting of two such opposites.

We are not confronted with a situation where one of the contesting parties is not a fit or proper person. There is no criticism of either the Bannisters or their home. There is no suggestion in the record that Mr. Painter is morally unfit. It is obvious the Bannisters did not approve of their daughter's marriage to Harold Painter and do not want their grandchild raised under his guidance. The philosophies of life are entirely different. As stated by the psychiatrist who examined Mr. Painter at the request of Bannisters' attorneys: "It is evident that there exists a large difference in ways of life and value systems between the Bannisters and Mr. Painter, but in this case, there is no evidence that psychiatric instability is involved. Rather, these divergent life patterns seem to represent alternative normal adaptations."

It is not our prerogative to determine custody upon our choice of one of two ways of life within normal and proper limits and we will not do so. However, the philosophies are important as they relate to Mark and his particular needs. The Bannister home provides Mark with a stable, dependable, conventional, middleclass, middlewest background and an opportunity for a college education and profession, if he desires it. It provides a solid foundation and secure atmosphere. In the Painter home, Mark would have more freedom of conduct and thought with an opportunity to develop his individual talents. It would be more exciting and challenging in many respects, but romantic, impractical and unstable . . .

Our conclusion as to the type of home Mr. Painter would offer is based upon his Bohemian approach to finances and life in general. We feel there is much evidence which supports this conclusion. His main ambition is to be a free lance writer and photographer. He has had some articles and picture stories published, but the income from these efforts has been negligible. At the time of the accident, Jeanne was willingly working to support the family so Harold could devote more time to his writing and photography. In the 10 years since he left college, he has changed jobs seven times. He was asked to leave two of them; two he quit because he didn't like the work; two because he wanted to devote more time to writing and the rest for better pay. He was contemplating a move to Berkeley at the time of trial. His attitude toward his career is typified by his own comments concerning a job offer:

> "About the Portland news job, I hope you understand when I say it took guts not to take it; I had to get behind myself and push. It was very, very tempting to accept a good salary and settle down to a steady, easy routine. As I approached Portland, with the intention of taking the job, I began to ask what, in the long run, would be the good of this job: 1, it was not *really* what I wanted; 2, Portland is just another big farm town, with none of the stimulation it takes to get my mind sparking. Anyway, I decided Mark and myself would be better off if I went ahead with what I've started and the hell with the rest, sink, swim or starve."

There is general agreement that Mr. Painter needs help with his finances. Both Jeanne and Marilyn, his present wife, handled most of them. Purchases and sales of books, boats, photographic equipment and houses indicate poor financial judgment and an easy come easy go attitude. He dissipated his wife's estate of about $4300, most of which was a gift from her parents and which she had hoped would be used for the children's education. The psychiatrist classifies him as "a romantic and somewhat of a dreamer". An apt example are the plans he related for himself and Mark in February 1963: "My thought now is to settle Mark and myself in Sausalito, near San Francisco; this is a retreat for wealthy artists, writers, and such aspiring artists and writers as can fork up the rent money. My plan is to do expensive portraits ($150 and up), sell prints ($15 and up) to the tourists who flock in from all over the world. . . ."

The house in which Mr. Painter and his present wife live, compared with the well kept Bannister home, exemplifies the contrasting ways of life. In his words "it is a very old and beat up and lovely home. . . ." They live in the rear part. The interior is inexpensively but tastefully decorated. The large yard on a hill in the business district of Walnut Creek, California, is of uncut weeds and wild oats. The house "is not painted on the outside because I do not want it painted. I am very fond of the wood on the outside of the house."

The present Mrs. Painter has her master's degree in cinema design and apparently likes and has had considerable contact with children. She is anxious to have Mark in her home. Everything indicates she would provide a leveling influence on Mr. Painter and could ably care for Mark. Mr. Painter is either an agnostic or atheist and has no concern for formal religious training. He has read a lot of Zen Buddhism and "has been very much influenced by it". Mrs. Painter is Roman Catholic. They plan to send Mark to a Congregational Church near the Catholic Church, on an irregular schedule. He is a political liberal and got into difficulty in a job at the University of Washington for his support of the activities of the American Civil Liberties Union in the university news bulletin. There were "two funerals" for his wife. One in the basement of his home in which he alone was present. He conducted the service and wrote her a long letter. The second at a church in Pullman was for the gratification of her friends. He attended in a sport shirt and sweater.

These matters are not related as a criticism of Mr. Painter's conduct, way of life or sense of values. An individual is free to choose his own values, within bounds, which are not exceeded here. They do serve however to support our conclusion as to the kind of life Mark would be exposed to in the Painter household. We believe it would be unstable, unconventional, arty, Bohemian, and probably intellectually stimulating.

Were the question simply which household would be the most suitable in which to raise a child, we would have unhesitatingly chosen the Bannister home. We believe security and stability in the home are more important than intellectual stimulation in the proper development of a child. There are, however, several factors which have made us pause.

First, there is the presumption of parental preference, which though weakened in the past several years, exists by statute. . . . We have a great deal of sympathy for a father, who in the difficult period of adjustment following his wife's death, turns to the maternal grandparents for their help and then finds them unwilling to return the child. There is no merit in the Bannister claim that Mr. Painter permanently relinquished custody. It was intended to be a temporary arrangement. A father should be encouraged to look for help with the children, from those who love them without the risk of thereby losing the custody of the children permanently. This fact must receive consideration in cases of this kind. However, as always, the primary consideration is the best interest of the child and if the return of custody to the father is likely to have a seriously disrupting and disturbing effect upon the child's development, this fact must prevail. . . .

Second, Jeanne's will named her husband guardian of her children and if he failed to qualify or ceased to act, named her mother. The parent's wishes are entitled to consideration. . . .

Third, the Bannisters are 60 years old. By the time Mark graduates from high school they will be over 70 years old. Care of young children is a strain on grandparents and Mrs. Bannister's letters indicate as much.

We have considered all of these factors and have concluded that Mark's best interest demands that his custody remain with the Bannisters. Mark was five when he came to their home. The evidence clearly shows he was not well adjusted at that time. He did not distinguish fact from fiction and was inclined to tell "tall tales" emphasizing the big "I". He was very aggressive toward smaller children, cruel to animals, not liked by his classmates and did not seem to know what was acceptable conduct. As stated by one witness: "Mark knew where his freedom was and he didn't know where his boundaries were." In two years he made a great deal of improvement. He now appears to be well disciplined, happy, relatively secure and popular with his classmates, although still subject to more than normal anxiety.

We place a great deal of reliance on the testimony of Dr. Glenn R. Hawks, a child psychologist. The trial court, in effect, disregarded Dr. Hawks' opinions stating: "The court has given full consideration to the good doctor's testimony, but cannot accept it at full face value because of exaggerated statements and the witness' attitude on the stand." We, of course, do not have the advantage of viewing the witness' conduct on the stand, but we have carefully reviewed his testimony and find nothing in the written record to justify such a summary dismissal of the opinions of this eminent child psychologist.

Dr. Hawks is head of the Department of Child Development at Iowa State University. However, there is nothing in the record which suggests that his relationship with the Bannisters is such that his professional opinion would be influenced thereby. Child development is his specialty and he has written many articles and a textbook on the subject. He is recognized nationally, having served on the staff of the 1960 White House Conference on Children and Youth and as consultant on a Ford Foundation program concerning youth in India. . . .

Between June 15th and the time of trial, he spent approximately 25 hours acquiring information about Mark and the Bannisters, including appropriate testing of and "depth interviews" with Mark. Dr. Hawks' testimony covers 70 pages of the record and it is difficult to pinpoint any bit of testimony which precisely summarizes his opinion. He places great emphasis on the "father figure" and discounts the importance of the "biological father". "The father figure is a figure that the child sees as an authority figure, as a helper, he is a nutrient figure, and one who typifies maleness and stands as maleness as far as the child is concerned." His investigation revealed: " . . . the strength of the father figure before Mark came to the Bannisters is very unclear. Mark is confused about the father figure prior to his contact with Mr. Bannister." Now, "Mark used Mr. Bannister as his father figure. This is very evident. It shows up in the depth interview, and it shows up in the description of Mark's life given by Mark. He has a very warm feeling for Mr. Bannister."

Dr. Hawks concluded that it was not for Mark's best interest to be removed from the Bannister home. He is criticized for reaching this conclusion without investigating the Painter home or finding out more about Mr. Painter's character. He answered:

> "I was most concerned about the welfare of the child, not the welfare of Mr. Painter, not about the welfare of the Bannisters. In as much as Mark has already made an adjustment and sees the Bannisters as his parental figures in his psychological make-up, to me this is the most critical factor. Disruption at this point, I think, would be detrimental to the child even tho Mr. Painter might well be a paragon of virtue. I think this would be a kind of thing which would not be in the best interest of the

> child. I think knowing something about where the child is at the present time is vital. I think something about where he might go, in my way of thinking is essentially untenable to me, and relatively unimportant. It isn't even helpful. The thing I was most concerned about was Mark's view of his own reality in which he presently lives. If this is destroyed I think it will have rather bad effects on Mark. I think then if one were to make a determination whether it would be the parents' household, or the McNelly household, or X-household, then I think the further study would be appropriate."

Dr. Hawks stated: "I am appalled at the tremendous task Mr. Painter would have if Mark were to return to him because he has got to build the relationship from scratch. There is essentially nothing on which to build at the present time. Mark is aware Mr. Painter is his father, but he is not very clear about what this means. In his own mind the father figure is Mr. Bannister. I think it would take a very strong person with everything in his favor in order to build a relationship as Mr. Painter would have to build at this point with Mark."

It was Dr. Hawks' opinion "the chances are very high (Mark) will go wrong if he is returned to his father". This is based on adoption studies which "establish that the majority of adoptions in children who are changed, from ages six to eight, will go bad, if they have had a prior history of instability, some history of prior movement. When I refer to instability I am referring to where there has been no attempt to establish a strong relationship." Although this is not an adoption, the analogy seems appropriate, for Mark who had a history of instability would be removed from the only home in which he has a clearly established "father figure" and placed with his natural father about whom his feelings are unclear.

We know more of Mr. Painter's way of life than Dr. Hawks. We have concluded that it does not offer as great a stability or security as the Bannister home. Throughout his testimony he emphasized Mark's need at this critical time is stability. He has it in the Bannister home. Other items of Dr. Hawks' testimony which have a bearing on our decision follow. He did not consider the Bannisters' age anyway disqualifying. He was of the opinion that Mark could adjust to a change more easily later on, if one became necessary, when he would have better control over his environment. He believes the presence of other children in the home would have a detrimental effect upon Mark's adjustment whether this occurred in the Bannister home or the Painter home.

The trial court does not say which of Dr. Hawks' statements he felt were exaggerated. We were most surprised at the inconsequential position to which he relegated the "biological father". He concedes "child psychologists are less concerned about natural parents than probably other professional groups are." We are not inclined to so lightly value the role of the natural father, but find much reason for his evaluation of this particular case.

Mark has established a father-son relationship with Mr. Bannister, which he apparently had never had with his natural father. He is happy, well adjusted and progressing nicely in his development. We do not believe it is for Mark's best interest to take him out of this stable atmosphere in the face of warnings of dire consequences from an eminent child psychologist and send him to an uncertain future in his father's home. Regardless of our appreciation of the father's love for his child and his desire to have him with him, we do not believe we have the moral right to gamble with this child's future. He should be encouraged in every way possible to know his father. We are sure there are many ways in which Mr. Painter can enrich Mark's life.

For the reasons stated, we reverse the trial court and remand the case for judgment in accordance herewith.

NOTES

In its 1966 *Painter* decision the Iowa Supreme Court had not discovered the lesson of *Troxel*, that a parent has a fundamental Due Process right to the care, custody and control of his child, which may only be overcome with clear and convincing evidence. There is no evidence in *Painter* that the father's conduct provided such clear and convincing evidence so as to rebut his parental presumption. But the case illustrates the tendencies of jurists and legislatures to place parents and third parties on a level playing field and only inquire as to what would be in the best interest of a child. The Constitution forbids this and *Troxe*l holds to this proposition. Nonetheless, there are instances when clear and convincing evidence will rebut the parent's presumption of custody and illustrations are provided in the cases that follow. Please note however, that following the *Painter* decision, Mark was eventually reunited with his father after a couple of visits to his father's home. Mr. Painter was given temporary custody by a California court on August 8, 1968 and the father then published a book describing the facts of the case, MARK, I LOVE YOU, in 1969.

Bennett v. Jeffreys

Court of Appeals of New York, 1976
356 N.E.2d 277

■ BREITEL, CHIEF JUDGE.

Petitioner is the natural mother of Gina Marie Bennett, now an eight-year-old girl. The mother in this proceeding seeks custody of her daughter from respondent, to whom the child had been entrusted since just after birth. Family Court ruled that, although the mother had not surrendered or abandoned the child and was not unfit, the child should remain with the present custodian, a former schoolmate of the child's grandmother. The Appellate Division reversed, one Justice dissenting, and awarded custody to the mother. Respondent custodian appeals.[1] The issue is whether the natural mother, who has not surrendered, abandoned, or persistently neglected her child, may, nevertheless, be deprived of the custody of her child because of a prolonged separation from the child for most of its life.

There should be a reversal and a new hearing before the Family Court. The State may not deprive a parent of the custody of a child absent surrender, abandonment, persisting neglect, unfitness or other like extraordinary circumstances. If any such extraordinary circumstances are present, the disposition of custody is influenced or controlled by what is in the best interest of the child. In the instant case extraordinary circumstances, namely, the prolonged separation of mother and child for most of the child's life, require inquiry into the best interest of the child. . . .

Some eight years ago, the mother, then 15 years old, unwed, and living with her parents, gave birth to the child. Under pressure from her mother, she reluctantly acquiesced in the transfer of the newborn infant to an older woman, Mrs. Jeffreys, a former classmate of the child's grandmother. The quality and quantity of the mother's later contacts with the child were disputed. The Family Court found, however, that there was no statutory surrender or abandonment. Pointedly, the Family Court found that the mother was not unfit. The Appellate Division agreed with this finding.

There was evidence that Mrs. Jeffreys intended to adopt the child at an early date. She testified, however, that she could not afford to do so and admitted that she never took formal steps to adopt. The natural mother is now 23 and will soon graduate from college. She still lives with her family, in a private home with quarters available for herself and the child. The attitude of the mother's parents, however, is changed and they are now anxious that their daughter keep her child. Mrs. Jeffreys, on the other hand, is now separated from her husband, is employed as a domestic and, on occasion, has kept the child in a motel. It is significant that Mrs. Jeffreys once said that she was willing to surrender the child to the parent upon demand when the child reached the age of 12 or 13 years.

At the outset, it is emphasized that not involved is an attempted revocation of a voluntary surrender to an agency or private individual for adoption (see Social Services Law, § 383, subd. 5; People ex rel. Scarpetta v. Spence-Chapin Adoption Serv., 28 N.Y.2d 185, 321 N.Y.S.2d 65, 269 N.E.2d 787, cert. denied, 404 U.S. 805) . . . Nor is abandonment involved. Nor does the proceeding involve an attempted permanent termination of custody (Family Ct. Act, § 614, subd. 1; § 631) . . . Nor is there involved the temporary placement into foster care by an authorized agency which

[1] The child is currently with her mother and will remain there pending final determination of this litigation, a stay of the Appellate Division order having been denied by that court.

is obliged to conduct an investigation and to determine the qualification of foster parents before placement of a child in need of such care (see Social Services Law, § 383, subds. 1–3; Matter of Jewish Child Care Assn. of N.Y. [Sanders], 5 N.Y.2d 222, 224–225, 183 N.Y.S.2d 65, 66, 156 N.E.2d 700, 701. . . . Instead, this proceeding was brought by an unwed mother to obtain custody of her daughter from a custodian to whom the child had been voluntarily, although not formally, entrusted by the mother's parents when the mother was only 15 years old. Thus, as an unsupervised private placement, no statute is directly applicable, and the analysis must proceed from common-law principles.

Absent extraordinary circumstances, narrowly categorized, it is not within the power of a court, or, by delegation of the Legislature or court, a social agency, to make significant decisions concerning the custody of children, merely because it could make a better decision or disposition. The State is *parens patriae* and always has been, but it has not displaced the parent in right or responsibility. Indeed, the courts and the law would, under existing constitutional principles, be powerless to supplant parents except for grievous cause or necessity. Examples of cause or necessity permitting displacement of or intrusion on parental control would be fault or omission by the parent seriously affecting the welfare of a child, the preservation of the child's freedom from serious physical harm, illness or death, or the child's right to an education, and the like. . . .

The parent has a "right" to rear its child, and the child has a "right" to be reared by its parent. However, there are exceptions created by extraordinary circumstances, illustratively, surrender, abandonment, persisting neglect, unfitness, and unfortunate or involuntary disruption of custody over an extended period of time. It is these exceptions which have engendered confusion, sometimes in thought but most often only in language.

The day is long past in this State, if it had ever been, when the right of a parent to the custody of his or her child, where the extraordinary circumstances are present, would be enforced inexorably, contrary to the best interest of the child, on the theory solely of an absolute legal right. Instead, in the extraordinary circumstance, when there is a conflict, the best interest of the child has always been regarded as superior to the right of parental custody. Indeed, analysis of the cases reveals a shifting of emphasis rather than a remaking of substance. This shifting reflects more the modern principle that a child is a person, and not a subperson over whom the parent has an absolute possessory interest. A child has rights too, some of which are of a constitutional magnitude.

Earlier cases emphasized the right of the parent, superior to all others, to the care and custody of the child. This right could be dissolved only by abandonment, surrender, or unfitness. Of course, even in these earlier cases, it was recognized that parental custody is lost or denied not as a moral sanction for parental failure, but because "the child's welfare compels awarding its custody to the nonparent". Although always recognizing the parent's custodial rights, the concern in the later cases, given the extraordinary circumstances, was consciously with the best interest of the child. . . . [I]n People ex rel. Scarpetta v. Spence-Chapin Adoption Serv., 28 N.Y.2d 185, 321 N.Y.S.2d 65, 269 N.E.2d 787, . . . the court held "that the record before us supports the finding by the courts below that the surrender was improvident and that the child's best interestsCmoral and temporalCwill be best served by its return to the natural mother", p. 194, 321 N.Y.S.2d p. 72, 269 N.E.2d p. 792.

Finally in Matter of Spence-Chapin Adoption Serv. v. Polk, 29 N.Y.2d 196, 204, 324 N.Y.S.2d 937, 944, 274 N.E.2d 431, 436, the court rejected any notion of absolute parental rights. The court restated the abiding principle that the child's rights and interests are "paramount" and are not subordinated to the right of parental custody, as important as that right is, p. 204, 324 N.Y.S.2d p. 944, 274 N.E.2d p. 436. Indeed, and this is key, the rights of the parent and the child are ordinarily compatible, for "the generally accepted view [is] that a child's best interest is that it be raised by its parent unless the parent is disqualified by gross misconduct" p. 204, 324 N.Y.S.2d p. 944, 274 N.E.2d 436.

Recently enacted statute law, applicable to related areas of child custody such as adoption and permanent neglect proceedings, has explicitly required the courts to base custody decisions solely upon the best interest of the child (*Social Services Law*, § 383, subd. 5; *Domestic Relations Law*, § 115–b, subd. 3, par. [d], cl. [v]; Family Ct. Act, § 614, subd. 1, par. [e]; § 631) . . . Under these statutes, there is no presumption that the best interest of the child will be promoted by any particular custodial disposition. Only to this limited extent is there a departure from the pre-existing decisional rule, which never gave more than rebuttable presumptive status, however strongly, to the parent's "right. . . ." But neither decisional rule nor statute can displace a fit parent because someone else could do a "better job" of raising the child in the view of the court (or the Legislature), so long as the parent or parents have not forfeited their "rights" by surrender, abandonment, unfitness, persisting neglect or other extraordinary circumstance. These "rights" are not so much "rights", but responsibilities which reflect the view, noted earlier, that, except when disqualified or displaced by extraordinary circumstances, parents are generally best qualified to care for their own children and therefore entitled to do so.

Indeed, as said earlier, the courts and the law would, under existing constitutional principles, be powerless to supplant parents except for grievous cause or necessity. . . . But where there is warrant to consider displacement of the parent, a determination that extraordinary circumstances exist is only the beginning, not the end, of judicial inquiry. Extraordinary circumstances alone do not justify depriving a natural parent of the custody of a child. Instead, once extraordinary circumstances are found, the court must then make the disposition that is in the best interest of the child.

Although the extraordinary circumstances trigger the "best interests of the child" test, this must not mean that parental rights or responsibilities may be relegated to a parity with all the other surrounding circumstances in the analysis of what is best for the child. So for one example only, while it is true that disruption of custody over an extended period of time is the touchstone in many custody cases, where it is voluntary the test is met more easily but where it is involuntary the test is met only with great difficulty, for evident reasons of humanity and policy.

The child's "best interest" is not controlled by whether the natural parent or the nonparent would make a "better" parent, or by whether the parent or the nonparent would afford the child a "better" background or superior creature comforts. Nor is the child's best interest controlled alone by comparing the depth of love and affection between the child and those who vie for its custody. Instead, in ascertaining the child's best interest, the court is guided by principles which reflect "considered social judgments in this society respecting the family and parenthood" (Matter of Spence-Chapin Adoption Serv. v. Polk, 29 N.Y.2d 196, 204, 324 N.Y.S.2d 937, 944, 274 N.E.2d 431, 436). These principles do not, however, dictate that the child's custody be routinely awarded to the natural parent. . . .

To recapitulate: intervention by the State in the right and responsibility of a natural parent to custody of her or his child is warranted if there is first a judicial finding of surrender, abandonment, unfitness, persistent neglect, unfortunate or involuntary extended disruption of custody, or other equivalent but rare extraordinary circumstance which would drastically affect the welfare of the child. It is only on such a premise that the courts may then proceed to inquire into the best interest of the child and to order a custodial disposition on that ground.

In custody matters parties and courts may be very dependent on the auxiliary services of psychiatrists, psychologists, and trained social workers. This is good. But it may be an evil when the dependence is too obsequious or routine or the experts too casual. Particularly important is this caution where one or both parties may not have the means to retain their own experts and where publicly compensated experts or experts compensated by only one side have uncurbed leave to express opinions which may be subjective or are not narrowly controlled by the underlying facts.

The court's determination may be influenced by whether the child is in the present custody of the parent or the nonparent. Changes in conditions which affect the relative desirability of custodians, even when the contest is between two natural parents, are not to be accorded significance unless the advantages of changing custody outweigh the essential principle of continued and stable custody of children. . . . Moreover, the child may be so long in the custody of the nonparent that, even though there has been no abandonment or persisting neglect by the parent, the psychological trauma of removal is grave enough to threaten destruction of the child. Of course, such a situation would offer no opportunity for the court, under the guise of determining the best interest of the child, to weigh the material advantages offered by the adverse parties. . . .

Before applying these principles to this case, a factor should be mentioned which, although not here present, often complicates custody dispositions. The resolution of cases must not provide incentives for those likely to take the law into their own hands. Thus, those who obtain custody of children unlawfully, particularly by kidnapping, violence, or flight from the jurisdiction of the courts, must be deterred. Society may not reward, except at its peril, the lawless because the passage of time has made correction inexpedient. Yet, even then, circumstances may require that, in the best interest of the child, the unlawful acts be blinked.

In this case, there were extraordinary circumstances present, namely, the protracted separation of mother from child, combined with the mother's lack of an established household of her own, her unwed state, and the attachment of the child to the custodian. Thus, application of the principles discussed required an examination by the court into the best interest of the child.

In reaching its conclusion that the child should remain with the nonparent custodian, the Family Court relied primarily upon the seven-year period of custody by the nonparent and evidently on the related testimony of a psychologist. The court did not, however, adequately examine into the nonparent custodian's qualifications and background. Also, the court apparently failed to consider the fact that, absent a finding of abandonment or neglect by the mother, or her consent, the nonparent cannot adopt the child. Family Court's disposition, if sustained, would therefore have left the child in legal limbo, her status indefinite until the attainment of her majority. For a single example, a question could arise as to whose consent, the parent's or the nonparent custodian's, would be necessary for the child to marry while underage (see *Domestic Relations Law*, § 15, subd. 2 [consent of "parent" or "guardian" required]). A similar question could arise with respect to many situations affecting employment and entry into occupations, an adoption, and any other matters requiring the consent of a parent or legal guardian.

On the other hand, the Appellate Division, in awarding custody to the mother, too automatically applied the primary principle that a parent is entitled to the custody of the child. This was not enough if there were extraordinary circumstances, as indeed there were. Other than to agree with Family Court that she was not "unfit", the court did not pursue a further analysis. Most important, no psychological or other background examination of the mother had ever been obtained. There was, therefore, no consideration of whether the mother is an adequate parent, in capacity, motivation, and efficacious planning. Nevertheless, the Appellate Division determination may well be right.

Thus, a new hearing is required because the Family Court did not examine enough into the qualifications and background of the long-time custodian, and the Appellate Division did not require further examination into the qualifications and background of the mother. Each court was excessive in applying abstract principles, a failing, however important those principles are.

At the cost of some repetition, perhaps unnecessary, it should be said, given the extraordinary circumstances present in this case, in determining the best interest of the child, the age of the child, and the fact and length of custody by the nonparent custodian are significant. Standing alone, these factors may not be sufficient to outweigh the mother's "right" to custody. However, taken together with the testimony of the psychologist that return to her mother would be "very traumatic for the child", the relatively lengthy period of nonparent custody casts the matter in sufficient doubt with respect to the best interest of the child to require a new hearing. At this hearing, the mother's adequacy may be explored and positively established, and if so, in connection with the parent's past visiting it might well weight the balance in her favor. Then too, the circumstances and environment of the custodian, the stability of her household, her inability to adopt, her age, and any other circumstances bearing upon the fitness or adequacy of a child's custodian over the whole period of childhood, are all relevant.

In all of this troublesome and troubled area there is a fundamental principle. Neither law, nor policy, nor the tenets of our society would allow a child to be separated by officials of the State from its parent unless the circumstances are compelling. Neither the lawyers nor Judges in the judicial system nor the experts in psychology or social welfare may displace the primary responsibility of child-raising that naturally and legally falls to those who conceive and bear children. Again, this is not so much because it is their "right", but because it is their responsibility. The nature of human relationships suggests over-all the natural workings of the child-rearing process as the most desirable alternative. But absolute generalizations do not fulfill themselves and multifold exceptions give rise to cases where the natural workings of the process fail, not so much because a legal right has been lost, but because the best interest of the child dictates a finding of failure.

Accordingly, the order of the Appellate Division should be reversed, without costs, and the proceeding remitted to Family Court for a new hearing.

■ FUCHSBERG, JUDGE (concurring).

I welcome the express recognition the court today gives to the concept that, under evolving child custody law in New York, circumstances other than the statutory and traditional ones of abandonment, surrender, permanent neglect and unfitness may form the basis for termination of a biological parent-child relationship, and I agree with the result it reaches. However, in concurring, the strength of my conviction that even greater movement in this area of the law is long overdue requires me to indicate the nature of some of my reservations.

Security, continuity and "long-term stability" in an on-going custodial relationship, whether maintained with a natural parent or a third party, are vital to the successful personality development of a child, and authorities (cited therein). Indeed, that is one of the soundest justifications for the priority which our society accords natural parents when the continuance of their status as parents is under legal attack.

The same considerations, however, it seems to me, dictate that, where a natural parent has affirmatively brought about or acquiesced in the creation of a secure, stable and continuing parent-child relationship with a third party who has become the psychological parent,[1] there comes a point where the "rebuttable presumption" which, absent such a change, is employed to favor the natural parent, disappears, as evidentiary presumptions usually do in the face of facts. Accordingly, when that point is reached, the determination of whether the original parental relationship has terminated should proceed without such bolstering of the natural parent's position vis-à-vis that of the child, the custodial parent or any other proper parties in interest. Generally speaking, when displaced by a state of facts contraindicating their further utility in a fact-finding setting, presumptions can only get in the way of substance, and, as a practical matter, when that happens, the less they are relied upon the better. I would, therefore, that we had spelled out an evidentiary balance consistent with these principles for application in custody litigation, always bearing in mind that each custody case, dealing as it does with emotion-laden and highly sensitive human relationships, is unique.[2]

---

1 Goldstein, Freud and Solnit, Beyond the Best Interests of the Child [1973]; Erikson, Growth and Crisis of the "Healthy Personality" in Personality, in Nature, Society and Culture [1955], 185–225; Bowley, Child Care and Growth of Love [1953]; Freud, Some Remarks on Infant Observation, 8 Psychoanalytic Study of the Child.)

2 Commentators point out that presumptions and the burden to rebut them should be allocated "on the basis of pragmatic considerations of fairness, convenience, and policy" (James, Burdens of Proof, 47 Va.L.Rev. 51, 60). Thus, where the burden of proof is allocated on policy grounds, it is most often done in order to "handicap" a party whose cause is disfavored (at p. 61). That was the historical basis for casting the entire burden of rebutting the presumption in favor of natural parents on third parties in custody proceedings, the resulting substantive effect varying with the extent to which the "handicap", combined with other evidentiary strictures, rendered the nonparent's case difficult to maintain. In those jurisdictions where that policy was fully developed, it produced essentially the same results as were obtained under the old theory that children were the chattels of their parents (see Note, *Alternatives to "Parental Right" in*

Further, I do not agree that inquiry into the best interests of a child must await a determination that, because of surrender, abandonment, neglect or "extraordinary" circumstances, a natural parent's "rights" to a child are at an end. Willy-nilly, concern for the best interests of the child must play a central and unavoidable role in the resolution of such questions.

Moreover, even under prior law, when only a finding of abandonment, surrender or neglect could defeat the presumption in favor of natural parents, the best interests of the child were involved from the very outset. Unfitness, for instance, cannot be determined abstractly or in isolation, but only relative to the psychological needs of a particular child, given its age, its mental health, its physical well-being and the like. And the very same conduct which constitutes clear neglect towards one child might not be so at all with regard to another child whose level of independence and emotional requirements are different. It follows that evidence offered to show that the State must intervene in a natural parent-child relationship is, by its very nature, evidence as to the best interests of the child. In short, termination or intervention, on the one hand, and best interests, on the other, are not discrete matters. Pragmatically, they are closely interrelated. Proof of one overlaps the other and I do not believe they should be considered separately.

I would add too that I am not completely convinced that there was not a sufficient basis for the decision of the Trial Judge, despite the unfortunate limitation on resources available to the Family Court and, often, the parties who appear before it (see Gordon, Terminal Placements of Children and Permanent Termination of Parental Rights: The New York Permanent Neglect Statute, 46 St. John's L. Rev. 215, 256, n. 204, and citations therein). Among other things, the trial court here fully heard out both Mrs. Jeffreys and Ms. Bennett, conducted an *in camera* interview with the child following which he concluded that she was a "happy, well-adjusted young girl" who "was most adamant about the fact that she wished to continue residing with Mrs. Jeffreys", and, in aid of his determination, sought and had the benefit of a formal psychological study. Nevertheless, since painstaking fact finding is so far superior to presumptions and assumptions, and, therefore, should be encouraged, I join in the decision to remit this case for further information-gathering, noting, in doing so, that it is clear that it should not be controlling that Ms. Bennett, the natural mother, because she is now pursuing collegiate studies may at some time in the future be more likely to afford greater creature comforts for the child than is Mrs. Jeffreys, whose modest position on the vocational social scale did not prevent her from undertaking to act as surrogate mother and thus to form psychological bonds between the child and herself. And, needless to say, any profession by Mrs. Jeffreys that she would have been willing to return the child to

---

Child Custody Disputes Involving Third Parties, 73 Yale L.J. 151, 154, n. 18, and accompanying text).

her biological mother when she was older *if* it were in the best interests of the child for her to do so would be an evidence of altruistic maternal concern that would win the approval of every sound practitioner of child psychiatry from King Solomon on.

Bennett v. Marrow

New York Supreme Court, Appellate Division, Second Department, 1977
59 A.D.2d 492

■ O'CONNOR, JUSTICE.

There is here presented one of the most difficult and disturbing problems known to the law—the custody of a child. The problem is, of course, compounded when, as here, the conflict rages between the natural mother and a foster mother. The Family Court awarded custody of the child to the foster mother and, after carefully studying this meticulously compiled record, we conclude that the order should be affirmed.

[The court reviews the custody determination principles from the opinion in *Bennett v. Jeffreys*, which remitted this case to Family Court for a hearing.]

The new hearing extended over a four-week period and contains the testimony of some 26 witnesses; that record and the order entered thereon are now before us for review.

We are here concerned with an unsupervised, private placement and, hence, any analysis of the decision of the Family Court must be predicated not upon statute, but upon common law principles. Fortunately, the hearing was held before the same Judge who had presided at the first hearing some two years before. Predicated upon his observations and findings at the 1975 hearing, the court was in a rather unique position to completely re-examine and re-evaluate the testimony of those witnesses who had testified at both hearings. In the light of his intimate knowledge of the background and history of the case, he was able to conduct a more in-depth examination of the psychiatrists, psychologists, social workers, teachers and other witnesses called by the parties. Most importantly, the court was enabled to clearly and closely observe for a second time the conduct and deportment of the principals, namely the petitioner-appellant (the natural parent), the respondent (the foster parent) and Gina Marie (the infant involved). His comments therefore concerning the changes he found in the personality and demeanor of Gina Marie become all the more significant and persuasive in view of the fact that the child, in the intervening 15 months, had been living in the home of the petitioner, her natural mother.

The trial court, after noting that during the first hearing Gina Marie appeared to be a well-adjusted, happy child, went on to say that "the fact is that notwithstanding a period of some 15 months spent in the home of her mother, Gina Marie has not settled into the household. She does not feel comfortable there, she is not happy there. She continues unswerving in her request to be restored to the custody of Mrs. Marrow."

These surface observations, while bearing some significance, are certainly not controlling; but the court's conclusions concerning the natural mother are perhaps more revealing. The court said: "To the extent that the petitioner has responded to Gina Marie's needs to be housed, to be clothed, to be fed, she could be considered to have performed adequately as a parent. But she has not begun to respond to Gina Marie's emotional needs." At another point the court observed: "I am constrained to consider that Miss Bennett's motivation in seeking custody of Gina Marie stems from a feeling that she is her child and should reside with her. That she has feeling for Gina Marie I am certainly prepared to believe, but in view of the testimony presented during the course of these proceedings, I have serious reservations that she is capable of giving Gina Marie the emotional support so vital to her well-being."

The court then concluded: "This Court was asked to determine whether the mother is an adequate parent. As stated previously, she has provided materially for Gina Marie. That is to say, she has made available to Gina Marie what Welfare has provided in the first instance. But that is virtually all she has given Gina Marie. She had not given significantly of herself. I find that an emotional void exists between mother and daughter that shows no signs of being bridged despite the time they have resided together. This child continues to mourn the loss of her 'mother.' "

Addressing itself then to the relationship between the respondent and Gina Marie, the court gave credence to the testimony of a witness called by the Law Guardian, Dr. Sally Provence, a child psychiatrist from Yale University. Finding her to be "certainly the most impressive expert witness who appeared in this proceeding", the hearing court accepted Dr. Provence's testimony that a psychological parent-child relationship had developed between respondent and the child and the court noted that such bond "appears as strong today as when this case was first heard."

It was Dr. Provence's further testimony, in substance, that to remove the child from such a relationship would endanger the development of the child in many ways and could affect her academic success and her motivation to learn.

This testimony is all the more significant in view of the record, which discloses that in January, 1977 an intelligence test was administered to Gina Marie resulting in a score of 84, in the low-normal range, whereas in April, 1975 she had scored 113. Despite efforts to explain away this rather disturbing pattern, it seems to be, at least to some extent, buttressed by the obvious and drastic decline in the physical, mental and emotional make-up of Gina Marie.

Reflection upon the totality of the testimony and careful consideration of all of the factors involved leads but to one conclusion, the order of the Family Court should be affirmed.

We note in closing that that order properly and fully protects petitioner's rights of visitation but, under the extraordinary circumstances here presented, the best interests of the child require that custody of Gina Marie be awarded to respondent.

NOTES

The extraordinary circumstances illustrated in *Bennett* offer a means by which to rebut the parent's fundamental presumption to best provide for the care and custody of his or her child. The presumption retains constitutional importance, and some states have codified it. *See, e.g.*, CAL. FAM. CODE § 3041 (2012) (custody of a child may be awarded to a non-parent only if "granting custody to a parent would be detrimental to the child and that granting custody to the nonparent is required to serve the best interest of the child."); WIS. STAT. ANN. § 767.41(3)(a) (2012) (custody of a child may be awarded to a relative if "neither parent is able to care for the child adequately or . . . neither parent is fit and proper to have the care and custody of the child."). The New York decision in *Bennett* permits an award of custody to a non-parent with rebuttal of the parental presumption by the extraordinary circumstances. A second rebuttal factor occurs whenever there is emotional abandonment and resulting psychological parenthood, illustrated in the California decision of *Guardianship of Phillip B.*, *infra*. Under this approach, the biological parent's presumption may be successfully rebutted by an adult who has actually functioned as the child's primary caretaker and with whom the child psychologically identifies as a parent. *See also* C.R.S. v. T.A.M., 892 P.2d 246 (Colo. 1995). A third approach rebuts the parental presumption by classifying the non-parent as a de facto parent. The American Law Institute defines a de facto parent as "an individual other than a legal parent or a parent by estoppel who, for a significant period of time not less than two years, (i) lived with the child, and (ii) for reasons primarily other than financial compensation, and with the agreement of a legal parent to form a parent-child relationship, or as a result of a complete failure or inability of any legal parent to perform caretaking functions, (A) regularly performed a majority of the caretaking functions for the child, or (B) regularly performed a share of caretaking functions at least as great as that of the parent with whom the child primarily lived." ALI, Principles of the Law of Family Dissolution § 2.03(c) (2002). *See, e.g.*, Youmans v. Ramos, 711 N.E.2d 165 (Mass. 1998). For an analysis, *see* Robin Fretwell Wilson, *Trusting Mothers: A Critique of the American Law Institute's Treatment of De Facto Parents*, 38 HOFSTRA L. REV. 1103 (2010).

In 2015 the highest court in New York had occasion to reexamine its holding in its 1976 decision of *Bennett v. Jeffreys*. *See* Matter of Suarez v. Williams, 44 N.E.3d 915 (N.Y. 2015). The facts of the 2015 decision involved a boy born in 2002 who lived with his paternal grandparents beginning when he was less than 10 days-old and continued until he was almost 10 years-old.

The boy's father moved out of the state, but the mother lived with her children from a prior relationship near her son and his grandparents. She had daily updates on the boy and, at times, weekly overnight visits and vacations with the boy. In 2006 the mother and father went to court to establish custody over their son and they were awarded joint legal custody but physical custody was awarded to mother. The grandparents did not participate in the legal proceedings. Then, in 2012, the mother began a relationship with a new boyfriend and they planned on living together, prompting the mother to seek the return of her son. Following this, after the boy spent the night with his mother she refused to return him to his grandparents, relying upon the 2006 custody award made by the court involving the mother and the father. Seeking the return of their grandchild the grandparents petitioned the court asking for primary physical custody of the boy. The lower court granted their petition based on the voluntary extraordinary circumstances brought about by the mother. But the appellate court reversed, holding that the mother's constant presence in the boy's life while he was living with the grandparents mitigated against extraordinary circumstances necessary to rebut the parental presumption.

In addressing the appellate court's decision, the New York Court of Appeals reflected on its holding in *Bennett v. Jeffreys*, stating that the *Bennett* decision, a product of common law, demanded extraordinary circumstances lasting over an extended period of time and, if this is found, then the court may rebut the parent's right to the child and make a child custody award based on what would be in the best interest of the child. The court then considered a more recent factor, a state statute enacted in 2003, long after the *Bennett* decision, which defined extraordinary circumstances to include, among other things, a parent voluntarily relinquishing control of a child and the child living in the same household of a grandparent for at least 24 months. *See* DOMESTIC RELATIONS LAW § 72 (2)(b). The 2003 statute defines extraordinary circumstances specifically in reference to grandparents and in the context of an extended disruption of custody by a parent. It sets forth three elements necessary to demonstrate extraordinary circumstances: (1) a 24-month separation of parent and child, (2) the parent's voluntary relinquishment of care and control of the child during this period, and (3) the residence of the child is in the grandparent's household. Based on what the statute brings to *Bennett v. Jeffreys*, the court holds that the parent does not have to surrender *all* care and control of the child, but rather whether the parent has surrendered making the *important decisions* affecting the child's life. Even though the mother visited with her child, she effectively transferred custody of the child to the paternal grandparents for more than 24 months. She permitted the grandparents to make all medical and education decisions pertaining to the child. This relinquishment of substantial control created the extraordinary circumstances necessitated by the state statute and permits the court to remand the case to the lower court to make a determination of what would now be in the best interest of the child.

Guardianship of Phillip B.

Court of Appeals, First District, Division 1, 1983
139 Cal.App.3d 407

■ RACANELLI, PRESIDING JUSTICE.

Few human experiences evoke the poignancy of a filial relationship and the pathos attendant upon its disruption in society's effort to afford every child a meaningful chance to live life to its fullest promise. This appeal, posing a sensitive confrontation between the fundamental right of parental custody and the well being of a retarded child, reflects the deeply ingrained concern that the needs of the child remain paramount in the judicial monitoring of custody. In reaching our decision to affirm, we neither suggest nor imply that appellants' subjectively motivated custodial objectives affront conventional norms of parental fitness; rather, we determine only that on the unusual factual record before us, the challenged order of guardianship must be upheld in order to avert potential harm to the minor ward likely to result from appellants' continuing custody and to subserve his best interests. . . .

On February 23, 1981, respondents Herbert and Patsy H. filed a petition for appointment as guardians of the person and estate of Phillip B., then 14 years of age. Phillip's parents, appellants Warren and Patricia B., appeared in opposition to the petition. On August 7, 1981, following a 12-day trial, the trial court filed a lengthy memorandum of decision ordering—inter alia—1) the issuance of letters of guardianship to respondents with authority to permit a heart catheterization to be performed on Phillip, and 2) the immediate delivery (by appellants) of Phillip to the Sheriff and Juvenile Authority of Santa Clara County. That same day appellants filed a notice of appeal from both orders followed by a petition to this court for a writ of supersedeas which we summarily denied.

On August 20, 1981, the California Supreme Court granted appellants' petition for hearing, stayed the trial court's order authorizing heart catheterization and retransferred the cause to this court with directions to issue an order to show cause why a writ of supersedeas should not issue.

Meanwhile, on September 24, the trial court filed formal findings of fact and conclusions of law and entered a "final order" confirming issuance of letters of guardianship and authorizing a heart catheterization. A second notice of appeal specifying both orders was thereafter filed by appellants.

On October 19, 1981, we again denied supersedeas in an unpublished opinion.

On November 18, 1981, the California Supreme Court granted a second petition for hearing, issued its writ of supersedeas limited to the trial court's orders of August 7 and September 24 "insofar as they give authority for a heart catheterization upon Phillip B.," and retransferred the cause to this court for determination of the merits of the appeal upon the completed record and full briefing. Thereafter, the matter was duly argued and submitted for decision.

Appellants raise several claims of reversible error relating to the sufficiency of evidence to support the findings, the admissibility of certain evidence and procedural due process. For the reasons which we explain, we find no error as claimed and affirm the order or judgment appealed. . . .

Phillip B. was born on October 16, 1966, with Down's Syndrome, a chromosomal anomaly-usually the presence of an extra chromosome attached to the number 21 pair-resulting in varying degrees of mental retardation and a number of abnormal physical characteristics. Down's Syndrome reportedly occurs in approximately 1/10 of 1 percent of live births. Appellants, deeply distraught over Phillip's disability, decided upon institutionalization, a course of action recommended by a state social worker and approved by appellants' pediatrician. A few days later, Phillip was transferred from the hospital to a licensed board and care facility for disabled youngsters. Although the facility was clean, it offered no structured educational or developmental programs and required that all the children (up to 8 years of age) sleep in cribs. Appellants initially visited Phillip frequently; but soon their visits became less frequent and they became more detached from him.

When Phillip was three years old a pediatrician informed appellants that Phillip had a congenital heart defect, a condition afflicting half of Down's Syndrome children. Open heart surgery was suggested when Phillip attained age six. However appellants took no action to investigate or remedy the suspected medical problem.

After the board and care facility had been sold during the summer of 1971, appellants discovered that the condition of the facility had seriously deteriorated under the new management; it had become dirty and cluttered with soiled clothing, and smelled strongly of urine. Phillip was very thin and listless and was being fed watery oatmeal from a bottle. At appellants' request, a state social worker arranged for Phillip's transfer in January, 1972, to We Care, a licensed residential facility for developmentally disabled children located in San Jose, where he remained up to the time of trial. At that time, the facility-which cared for about 20 children more severely handicapped than Phillip-operated under very limited conditions: it had no programs of education or therapy; the children were not enrolled in outside programs; the facility lacked an outdoor play area; the building was in poor repair; and the kitchen had only a two-burner hot plate used to cook pureed food.

In April 1972, We Care employed Jeanne Haight (later to become program director and assistant administrator of the facility) to organize a volunteer program. Mrs. Haight quickly noticed Phillip's debilitated condition. She found him unusually small and thin for his age (five); he was not toilet trained and wore diapers, still slept in a crib, walked like a toddler, and crawled down stairs only inches high. His speech was limited and mostly unintelligible; his teeth were in poor condition. Mrs. Haight, who undertook a recruitment program for volunteers, soon recruited respondent Patsy H., who had helped to found a school for children with learning disabilities where Mrs. Haight had once been vice-principal. Mrs. H. began working at We Care on a daily basis. Her husband, respondent Herbert H., and their children, soon joined in the volunteer activities.

Mrs. H., initially assigned to work with Phillip and another child, assisted Phillip in experimenting with basic sensory experiences, improving body coordination, and in overcoming his fear of steps. Mr. H. and one of the H. children helped fence the yard area, put in a lawn, a sandbox, and install some climbing equipment.

Mrs. Haight promptly initiated efforts to enroll Phillip in a preschool program for the fall of 1972, which required parental consent.[4] She contacted Mr. B. who agreed to permit Phillip to participate provided learning aptitude could be demonstrated. Mrs. H. used vocabulary cards to teach Phillip 25 to 50 new words and to comprehend word association. Although Mr. B. failed to appear at the appointed time in order to observe what Phillip had learned, he eventually gave his parental consent enabling Phillip to attend Hope Preschool in October, 1972. Respondents continued working with Phillip coordinating their efforts with his classroom lessons. Among other things, they concentrated on development of feeding skills and toilet training and Mr. H. and the two eldest children gradually became more involved in the volunteer program.

Phillip subsequently attended a school for the trainable mentally retarded (TMR) where the children are taught basic survival words. They are capable of learning to feed and dress themselves appropriately, doing basic community activities such as shopping, and engaging in recreational activities. There is no attempt to teach them academics, and they are expected to live in sheltered settings as adults. In contrast, children capable of attending classes for the educable mentally retarded (EMR) are taught reading, writing, and simple computation, with the objective of developing independent living skills as adults.

A pattern of physical and emotional detachment from their son was developed by appellants over the next several years. In contrast, during the same period, respondents established a close and caring relationship with Phillip. Beginning in December, 1972, Phillip became a frequent visitor at respondents' home; with appellants' consent, Phillip was permitted to spend weekends with respondents, a practice which continued regularly and often included weekday evenings. At the same

[4] Apparently, Phillip had received no formal preschool education for the retarded even though such training programs were available in the community. Expert testimony established that early introduction to preschool training is of vital importance in preparing a retarded child for entry level public education.

time respondents maintained frequent contact with Phillip at We Care as regular volunteer visitors. Meanwhile, appellants visited Phillip at the facility only a few times a year; however, no overnight home visits occurred until after the underlying litigation ensued.

Respondents played an active role in Phillip's behavioral development and educational training. They consistently supplemented basic skills training given Phillip at We Care.[5] Phillip was openly accepted as a member of the H. family whom he came to love and trust. He eventually had his own bedroom; he was included in sharing household chores. Mr. H. set up a workbench for Phillip and helped him make simple wooden toys; they attended special Boy Scout meetings together. And Philip regularly participated in family outings. Phillip referred to the H. residence as "my house." When Phillip began to refer to the H. as "Mom" and "Dad," they initially discouraged the familiar reference, eventually succeeding in persuading Phillip to use the discriminate references "Mama Pat" and "Dada Bert" and "Mama B." and "Daddy B."[6] Both Mrs. Haight and Phillip's teacher observed significant improvements in Phillip's development and behavior. Phillip had developed, in Mrs. Haight's opinion, "true love and strong [emotional] feelings" for respondents.

Meanwhile, appellants continued to remain physically and emotionally detached from Phillip. The natural parents intellectualized their decision to treat Phillip differently from their other children. Appellants testified that Phillip, whom they felt would always require institutionalization, should not be permitted to form close emotional attachments which—upon inevitable disruption—would traumatize the youngster.

In matters of Phillip's health care needs, appellants manifested a reluctant—if not neglectful—concern. When Dr. Gathman, a pediatric cardiologist, diagnosed a ventricular septal defect[7] in Phillip's heart in early 1973 and recommended catheterization (a medically accepted pre-surgery procedure to measure pressure and to examine the interior of the heart), appellants refused their consent. In the spring of 1977, Dr. Gathman again recommended heart catheterization in connection with the anticipated use of general anesthesia during Phillip's major dental surgery. Appellants consented to the preoperative procedure which revealed that the heart defect was surgically correctable with a maximum risk factor of 5 percent. At a conference attended by appellants

[5] In addition to their efforts to improve Phillip's communication and reading skills through basic sign language and word association exercises, respondents toilet-trained Phillip and taught him to use eating utensils and to sleep in a regular bed (the latter frequently monitored during the night).

[6] At respondents' suggestion, Mrs. Haight requested a photograph of appellants to show Phillip who his parents were; but appellants failed to provide one.

[7] The disease, found in a large number of Down's Syndrome children, consists of an opening or "hole" between the heart chambers resulting in elevated blood pressure and impairment of vascular functions. The disease can become a progressive, and ultimately fatal, disorder.

and Mrs. Haight in June, 1977, Dr. Gathman recommended corrective surgery in order to avoid a progressively deteriorating condition resulting in a "bed-to-chair existence" and the probability of death before the age of 30.[8] Although Dr. Gathman—as requested by Mrs. B.—supplied the name of a parent of Down's Syndrome children with similar heart disease, no contact was ever made. Later that summer, appellants decided—without obtaining an independent medical consultation—against surgery. Appellants' stated reason was that Dr. Gathman had "painted" an inaccurate picture of the situation. They felt that surgery would be merely life-prolonging rather than life-saving, presenting the possibility that they would be unable to care for Phillip during his later years.[9] A few months later, in early 1978, appellants' decision was challenged in a juvenile dependency proceeding initiated by the district attorney on the ground that the withholding of surgery constituted neglect within the meaning of Welfare and Institutions Code section 300 subdivision (b); the juvenile court's dismissal of the action on the basis of inconclusive evidence was ultimately sustained on appeal (In re Phillip B. (1979) 92 Cal.App.3d 796, 156 Cal.Rptr. 48, cert. denied sub nom. Bothman v. Warren B. (1980) 445 U.S. 949, 100 S.Ct.1597, 63 L.Ed.2d 784).

In September, 1978, upon hearing from a staff member of We Care that Phillip had been regularly spending weekends at respondents' home, Mr. B. promptly forbade Phillip's removal from the facility (except for medical purposes and school attendance) and requested that respondents be denied personal visits with Phillip at We Care. Although respondents continued to visit Phillip daily at the facility, the abrupt cessation of home visits produced regressive changes in Phillip's behavior: he began acting out violently when respondents prepared to leave, begging to be taken "home"; he resorted to profanity; he became sullen and withdrawn when respondents were gone; bed-wetting regularly occurred, a recognized symptom of emotional disturbance in children. He began to blame himself for the apparent rejection by respondents; he began playing with matches and on one occasion he set his clothes afire; on another, he rode his tricycle to respondents' residence a few blocks away proclaiming on arrival that he was "home." He continuously pleaded to return home with respondents. Many of the behavioral changes continued to the time of trial.

Appellants unsuccessfully pressed to remove Phillip from We Care notwithstanding the excellent care he was receiving. However, in January, 1981, the regional center monitoring public assistance for residential care and training of the handicapped, consented to Phillip's

---

[8] Dr. Gathman's explicit description of the likely ravages of the disease created anger and distrust on the part of appellants and motivated them to seek other opinions and to independently assess the need for surgery.

[9] Oddly, Mr. B. expressed no reluctance in the hypothetical case of surgery for his other two sons if they had the "same problem," justifying the distinction on the basis of Phillip's retardation.

removal to a suitable alternate facility. Despite an extended search, none could be found which met Phillip's individualized needs. Meanwhile, Phillip continued living at We Care, periodically visiting at appellants' home. But throughout, the strong emotional attachment between Phillip and respondents remained intact.

Evidence established that Phillip, with a recently tested I.Q. score of 57,[11] is a highly functioning Down's Syndrome child capable of learning sufficient basic and employable skills to live independently or semi-independently in a non-institutional setting.

Courts generally may appoint a guardian over the person or estate of a minor "if it appears necessary or convenient." (Prob.Code, § 1514, subd. (a).) But the right of parents to retain custody of a child is fundamental and may be disturbed " . . . only in extreme cases of persons acting in a fashion incompatible with parenthood.' " (In re Angelia P. (1981) 28 Cal.3d 908, 916, 171 Cal.Rptr. 637, 623 P.2d 198, quoting In re Carmaleta B. (1978) 21 Cal.3d 482, 489, 146 Cal.Rptr. 623, 579 P.2d 514.) Accordingly, the Legislature has imposed the stringent requirement that before a court may make an order awarding custody of a child to a nonparent without consent of the parents, "it shall make a finding that an award of custody to a parent would be detrimental to the child and the award to a nonparent is required to serve the best interests of the child." (Civ.Code, § 4600, subd. (c); see In re B.G. (1974) 11 Cal.3d 679, 695–699, 114 Cal.Rptr. 444, 523 P.2d 244.)[12] That requirement is equally applicable to guardianship proceedings under Probate Code section 1514, subdivision (b). The legislative shift in emphasis from parental unfitness to detriment to the child did not, however, signal a retreat from the judicial practice granting custodial preference to nonparents "only in unusual or extreme cases." (In re B.G., supra, 11 Cal.3d 679, 698, 114 Cal.Rptr. 444, 523 P.2d 244, see Guardianship of Marino (1973) 30 Cal.App.3d 952, 958, 106 Cal.Rptr. 655.)

The trial court expressly found that an award of custody to appellants would be harmful to Phillip in light of the psychological or "de facto" parental relationship established between him and respondents. Such relationships have long been recognized in the fields of law and psychology. As Justice Tobriner has cogently observed, "The fact of biological parenthood may incline an adult to feel a strong concern for the welfare of his child, but it is not an essential condition; a person who assumes the role of parent, raising the child in his own home, may in time acquire an interest in the 'companionship, care, custody and

---

[11] A retarded child within an I.Q. range of 55–70 is generally considered as mildly retarded and classified as educable under California school standards.

[12] Civil Code section 4600 was enacted in response to the celebrated case of *Painter v. Bannister* (1966) 258 Iowa 1390, 140 N.W.2d 152, cert. den. 385 U.S. 949, 87 S.Ct. 322, 17 L.Ed.2d 227 in which the state court awarded custody of a young boy to his grandparents because it disapproved of the father's "Bohemian" lifestyle in California (see *In re B.G.*, supra, 11 Cal.3d at pp. 697–698, 114 Cal.Rptr. 444, 523 P.2d 244, citing Report of Assembly Judiciary Committee, 4 Assem.J. (1969 Reg.Sess. pp. 8060–8061)).

management' of that child. The interest of the 'de facto parent' is a substantial one, recognized by the decision of this court in Guardianship of Shannon (1933) 218 Cal. 490 [23 P.2d 1020] and by courts of other jurisdictions and deserving of legal protection." (*In re B.G.*, supra, 11 Cal.3d 679, 692–693, 114 Cal.Rptr. 444, 523 P.2d 244 [fns. omitted], citing the seminal study of Goldstein, Freud & Solnit, Beyond the Best Interests of the Child (1973) pp. 17–20, hereafter Goldstein.) Persons who assume such responsibility have been characterized by some interested professional observers as "psychological parents": "Whether any adult becomes the psychological parent of a child is based . . . on day-to-day interaction, companionship, and shared experiences. The role can be fulfilled either by a biological parent or by an adoptive parent or by any other caring adult—but never by an absent, inactive adult, whatever his biological or legal relationship to the child may be." (Goldstein, supra, p. 19.)

Appellants vigorously challenge the evidence and finding that respondents have become Phillip's de facto or psychological parents since he did not reside with them full-time, as underscored in previous California decisions which have recognized de facto parenthood. They argue that the subjective concept of psychological parenthood, relying on such nebulous factors as "love and affection" is susceptible to abuse and requires the countervailing element of objectivity provided by a showing of the child's long-term residency in the home of the claimed psychological parent.

We disagree. Adoption of the proposed standard would require this court to endorse a novel doctrine of child psychology unsupported either by a demonstrated general acceptance in the field of psychology or by the record before us. Although psychological parenthood is said to result from "day-to-day attention to [the child's] needs for physical care, nourishment, comfort, affection, and stimulation" (Goldstein, supra, p. 17), appellants fail to point to any authority or body of professional opinion that equates daily attention with full-time residency. To the contrary, the record contains uncontradicted expert testimony that while psychological parenthood usually will require residency on a "24-hour basis," it is not an absolute requirement; further, that the frequency and quality of Phillip's weekend visits with respondents, together with the regular weekday visits at We Care, provided an adequate foundation to establish the crucial parent-child relationship.

Nor are we persuaded by appellants' suggested policy considerations concerning the arguably subjective inquiry involved in determining psychological parenthood. Trial fact-finders commonly grapple with elusive subjective legal concepts without aid of "countervailing" objective criteria. . . . Moreover, the suggested standard is itself vulnerable to a claim of undue subjectivity in its vague requirement of residency for a "considerable period of time."[15]

Appellants also challenge the sufficiency of the evidence to support the finding that their retention of custody would have been detrimental to Phillip. In making the critical finding, the trial court correctly applied the "clear and convincing" standard of proof necessary to protect the fundamental rights of parents in all cases involving a nonparent's bid for custody. . . .

The record contains abundant evidence that appellants' retention of custody would cause Phillip profound emotional harm. Notwithstanding Phillip's strong emotional ties with respondents, appellants abruptly foreclosed home visits and set out to end all contact between them. When Phillip's home visits terminated in 1978, he displayed many signs of severe emotional trauma: he appeared depressed and withdrawn and became visibly distressed at being unable to return to "my house," a request he steadily voiced up until trial. He became enuretic, which a psychologist, Dr. Edward Becking, testified indicates emotional stress in children. . . . Dr. Becking testified to other signs of emotional disturbance which were present nearly three years after the termination of home visits.

Our law recognizes that children generally will sustain serious emotional harm when deprived of the emotional benefits flowing from a true parent-child relationship. There was uncontroverted expert testimony that Phillip would sustain further emotional trauma in the event of total separation from respondents: that testimony indicated that, as with all children, Phillip needs love and affection, and he would be profoundly hurt if he were deprived of the existing psychological parental relationship with respondents in favor of maintaining unity with his biological parents.

Phillip's conduct unmistakably demonstrated that he derived none of the emotional benefits attending a close parental relationship largely as a result of appellants' individualized decision to abandon that traditional supporting role. Dr. Becking testified that no "bonding or attachment" has occurred between Phillip and his biological parents, a result palpably consistent with appellants' view that Phillip had none of the emotional needs uniquely filled by natural parents. We conclude that such substantial evidence adequately supports the finding that parental

---

[15] Appellants also fear that, absent a full-time residency requirement, anyone who visits an institutionalized child can lay claim to psychological parenthood. As earlier discussed, development of a parent-child relationship requires long-term nurturing and fulfillment of the child's total needs which can rarely occur without full-time residency. But it was manifested here only as a direct result of respondents' unique relationship with Phillip as We Care volunteers, their previously uninterrupted weekend close contacts and appellants' physical and emotional detachment from the child. All of such important factors contributed to respondents' ability to devote the enormous amount of time and loving care essential to fill the tangible and emotional needs in Phillip's life.

custody would have resulted in harmful deprivation of these human needs contrary to Phillip's best interests.

Finally, there was also evidence that Phillip would experience educational and developmental injury if parental custody remains unchanged. At Phillip's functioning level of disability, he can normally be expected to live at least semi-independently as an adult in a supervised residential setting and be suitably trained to work in a sheltered workshop or even a competitive environment (e.g., performing assembly duties or custodial tasks in a fast-food restaurant). Active involvement of a parent figure during the formative stages of education and habilitation is of immeasurable aid in reaching his full potential. Unfortunately, appellants' deliberate abdication of that central role would effectively deny Phillip any meaningful opportunity to develop whatever skills he may be capable of achieving. Indeed, Dr. Becking testified that further separation from respondents would not only impair Phillip's ability to form new relationships but would "for a long while" seriously impair Phillip's development of necessary prevocational and independent-living skills for his future life.

Nor can we overlook evidence of potential physical harm to Phillip due to appellants' passive neglect in response to Phillip's medical condition. Although it appears probable that the congenital heart defect is no longer correctible by surgery,[18] the trial court could have reasonably concluded that appellants' past conduct reflected a dangerously passive approach to Phillip's future medical needs.[19]

It is a clearly stated legislative policy that persons with developmental disabilities shall enjoy—inter alia—the right to treatment and rehabilitation services, the right to publicly supported education, the right to social interaction, and the right to prompt medical care and treatment. (Welf. & Inst. Code, § 4502.) Moreover, the legislative purpose underlying Civil Code section 4600 is to protect the needs of children generally " . . . to be raised with love, emotional security and physical safety.' " (In re D.L.C., supra, 54 Cal.App.3d 840, 851, 126 Cal.Rptr. 863.) When a trial court is called upon to determine the custody of a developmentally disabled or handicapped child, as here, it must be guided by such overriding policies rather than by the personal beliefs or attitudes of the contesting parties, since it is the child's interest which remains paramount. . . . Clearly, the trial court faithfully complied with

[18] A pediatric cardiologist estimated that the surgery now might have a one-third chance of harming him, a one-third chance of helping him and a one-third chance of causing no appreciable change in his condition. Dr. Gathman testified that it is "highly probable" that Phillip's condition is no longer correctible by surgery, but that a heart catheterization is required to be certain.

[19] Notably, the failure to obtain competent medical advice concerning the heart disease and the admitted willingness to forego medical treatment solely by reason of Phillip's retarded condition. The gravity of such dangerous inaction was dramatically illustrated by Mr. B.'s reaction to Phillip's recent undiagnosed episodes of apparent semi-consciousnessCdiscounting their existence without even the benefit of a medical consultation.

such legislative mandate in exercising its sound discretion based upon the evidence presented. We find no abuse as contended by appellants.

We strongly emphasize, as the trial court correctly concluded, that the fact of detriment *cannot* be proved solely by evidence that the biological parent has elected to institutionalize a handicapped child, or that nonparents are able and willing to offer the child the advantages of their home in lieu of institutional placement. Sound reasons may exist justifying institutionalization of a handicapped child. But the totality of the evidence under review permits of no rational conclusion other than that the detriment caused Phillip, and its possible recurrence, was due not to appellants' choice to institutionalize but their calculated decision to remain emotionally and physically detached—abdicating the conventional role of competent decisionmaker in times of demonstrated need—thus effectively depriving him of *any* of the substantial benefits of a true parental relationship. *It is the emotional abandonment of Phillip, not his institutionalization,* which inevitably has created the unusual circumstances which led to the award of limited custody to respondents. We do not question the sincerity of appellants' belief that their approach to Phillip's welfare was in their combined best interests. But the record is replete with substantial and credible evidence supporting the trial court's determination, tested by the standard of clear and convincing proof, that appellants' retention of custody has caused and will continue to cause serious detriment to Phillip and that his best interests will be served through the guardianship award of custody to respondents. In light of such compelling circumstances, no legal basis is shown to disturb that carefully considered determination. . . .

NOTES

In *The Guardianship of Phillip B.: Jay Spears' Achievement*, 40 STAN. L. REV. 841 (1988), author Robert H. Mnookin provides a follow-up on Phillip Becker-Heath, who turned twenty-one years old in late 1987. Phillip eventually was adopted by the Heaths and underwent successful open heart surgery. He enrolled in school, obtained a part-time job, and became a Joe Montana fan. Professor Mnookin's account of the poignant case is especially sensitive and it carries a sorrowful message. While the outcome for Phillip B. was far more favorable than most observers expected, the article appears as one of a series of memorial tributes to Jay Spears, the young lawyer whose enormous efforts and commitment were key to the case and who died in December 1986. For additional commentary, *see, e.g.,* Margaret F. Brinig, *Explaining Abuse of the Disabled Child*, 46 FAM. L. Q. 269 (2012); Rebecca L. Scharf, *Psychological Parentage, Troxel, and the Best Interests of the Child*, 13 GEO. J. GENDER & L. 615 (2012).

C. PARENT VERSUS STATE: FOSTER CARE PLACEMENT

Smith v. Organization of Foster Families for Equality & Reform

Supreme Court of the United States, 1977
431 U.S. 816

[Justice Brennan delivered the opinion, which addressed the rights of an organization of foster parents who sought declaratory and injunctive relief against New York officials based on asserted rights under the Due Process and Equal Protection Clauses of the Fourteenth Amendment. Specifically, the organization argued that the removal of children placed in foster care without a hearing at which the foster parents may object violated their liberty interests under the Due Process Clause. The New York statutory and regulatory scheme did provide for the following: (1) removal of the children at the discretion of the authorizing agency; (2) a ten day notice to the foster parents prior to the removal; (3) the foster parents may request a conference with the agency, which must be held within ten days; (4) foster parents may appear with counsel and reasons provided for the removal, as well as an opportunity for the foster parent to argue as to why removal is not in the best interest of the children; (5) the agency must render a decision in writing and notify all of the parties; and (6) the foster parents may appeal to the state's Department of Social Services for a full adversary administrative hearing, the determination of which is subject to judicial review. Furthermore, if the child is being transferred to another foster home, as compared to being returned to the child's family, the foster parents may request a full trial-type hearing before the child is removed. Also, if a child has been in foster care for more than eighteen months the state family court has the ability to order the agency to leave the child with the present foster parents.]

■ BRENNAN, JUSTICE delivered the opinion of the Court.

. . .

But there are also important distinctions between the foster family and the natural family. First, unlike the earlier cases recognizing a right to family privacy, the State here seeks to interfere, not with a relationship having its origins entirely apart from the power of the State, but rather with a foster family which has its source in state law and contractual arrangements. . . . Here, however, whatever emotional ties may develop between foster parent and foster child have their origin in an arrangement in which the State has been a partner from the outset. While the Court has recognized that liberty interests may in some cases arise from positive law sources [citations omitted], in such a case, and particularly where, as here, the claimed interest derives from a knowingly assumed contractual relationship with the State, it is appropriate to ascertain from state law the expectations and entitlements of the parties. In this case, the limited recognition accorded to the foster family by the New York statutes and the contracts executed by the foster parents argue against any but the most limited constitutional "liberty" in the foster family.

A second consideration related to this is that ordinarily procedural protection may be afforded to a liberty interest of one person without derogating from the substantive liberty of another. Here, however, such a tension is virtually unavoidable. Under New York law, the natural parent of a foster child in voluntary placement has an absolute right to the return of his child in the absence of a court order obtainable only upon compliance with rigorous substantive and procedural standards, which reflect the constitutional protection accorded the natural family. [Citations omitted] Moreover, the natural parent initially gave up his child to the State only on the express understanding that the child would be returned in those circumstances. These rights are difficult to reconcile with the liberty interest in the foster family relationship claimed by appellees. It is one thing to say that individuals may acquire a liberty interest against arbitrary governmental interference in the family-like associations into which they have freely entered, even in the absence of biological connection or state-law recognition of the relationship. It is quite another to say that one may acquire such an interest in the face of another's constitutionally recognized liberty interest that derives from blood relationship, state-law sanctioned, and basic human right—an interest the foster parent has recognized by contract from the outset. [Citations omitted] Whatever liberty interest might otherwise exist in the foster family as an institution, that interest must be substantially attenuated where the proposed removal from the foster family is to return the child to his natural parents.

As this discussion suggests, appellees' claim to a constitutionally protected liberty interest raises complex and novel questions. It is unnecessary for us to resolve those questions definitively in this case, however, for like the District Court, we conclude that "narrower grounds exist to support" our reversal [of the decision in support of the claims of the foster parents in the United States District Court for the Southern District of New York]. We are persuaded that, even on the assumption that appellees have a protected "liberty interest," the District Court erred in holding that the preremoval procedures presently employed by the State are constitutionally defective. . . .

ADOPTION AND SAFE FAMILIES ACT OF 1997

42 U.S.C. § 675. States Required to Initiate or Join Proceedings to Terminate Parental Rights for Certain Children in Foster Care

. . .

(E) in the case of a child who has been in foster care under the responsibility of the State for 15 of the most recent 22 months, or, if a court of competent jurisdiction has determined a child to be an abandoned infant (as defined under State law) or has made a determination that the parent has committed murder of another child of the parent, committed voluntary manslaughter of another child of the parent, aided or abetted, attempted, conspired, or solicited to commit such a murder or such a voluntary manslaughter, or committed a felony assault that has resulted in serious bodily injury to the child or to another child of the parent, the State shall file a petition to terminate the parental rights of the child's parents (or, if such a petition has been filed by another party, seek to be joined as a party to the petition), and, concurrently, to identify, recruit, process, and approve a qualified family for an adoption, unless—

(i) at the option of the State, the child is being care for by a relative;

(ii) the State agency has documented in the case plan (which shall be available for court review) a compelling reason for determining that filing such a petition would not be in the best interest of the child; or

(iii) the State has not provided to the family of the child, consistent with the time period in the State case plan, such services as the State deems necessary for the safe return of the child to the child's home, if reasonable efforts of the type described in section 471(a)(15)(B)(ii) are required to be made with respect to the child[.] . . .

NOTES

The holding in *Smith*, affirmed in subsequent decisions, reiterates the fundamental right of legal parents to the custody of their children when confronted by foster parents' claims of a protected Fourteenth Amendment liberty interest. *See, e.g.*, Rodriguez v. McLoughlin, 214 F.3d 328 (2d Cir. 2000), *cert. denied*, 532 U.S. 1051 (2001); *In re* Dependency of J.H., 815 P.2d 1380 (Wash. 1991). As the federal Adoption and Safe Families Act of 1997 suggests, however, parents no longer have an unlimited time to rectify behavior that precipitated removal of a dependent child. In addition, to provide the child with permanence many states have permitted foster parents to adopt children placed in their care when parental rights are terminated. This is a shift from previous policy which emphasized the temporary nature of foster care and disfavored foster parent adoption. For commentary, *see* Cassie Statuto Bevan, *The Impact of Liberal Ideology on Child Protection Reform*, 24 WM. & MARY BILL RTS. J. 709 (2016); Richard J. Gelles, *Why the American Child Welfare System is Not Child Centered*, 24 WM. & MARY BILL RTS. J. 733 (2016); Brent Pattison, *When Children Object: Amplifying an Older Child's Objection to Termination of Parental Rights*, 49

U. MICH. J.L. Reform 689 (2016); Steven W. Fitschen & Eric A. DeGroff, *Is It Time to Accept the O.F.F.E.R.? Applying* Smith v. Organization of Foster Families for Equality and Reform *to Promote Clarity, Consistency, and Federalism in the World of De Facto Parenthood*, 24 CAL. INTERDISC. L. J. 415 (2015); Raymond C. O'Brien, *Reasonable Efforts and Parent-Child Reunification*, 2013 MICH. ST. L. REV. 1029; Lashanda Taylor, *Resurrecting Parents of Legal Orphans: Un-Terminating Parental Rights*, 17 VA. J. SOC. POL'Y & L. 318 (2010); Richard Wexler, *Take the Child and Run: How ASFA and the Mentality Behind It Harm Children*, 13 U.D.C. L. REV. 435 (2010). Some states have enacted legislation providing for long-term or permanent foster care for children. *See, e.g.*, VA. CODE ANN. § 63.2–908 (2008).

D. CONTENDING WITH THE ADVERSARY PROCESS

1. JURISDICTION

In re Amberley D.

Supreme Judicial Court of Maine, 2001
775 A.2d 1158

■ ALEXANDER, JUSTICE.

Joann R., mother of Amberley D., appeals the judgment of the Waldo County Probate Court appointing Diana and Richard B. coguardians of Amberley pursuant to 18–A M.R.S.A. § 5–204 (1998 & Supp.2000). On appeal, Joann contends that: (1) the court erred by appointing temporary guardians without notice to her; (2) the court lacked jurisdiction and venue over the guardianship petition; (3) no clear and convincing evidence supported the petition; and (4) the guardianship statute is unconstitutional as applied. We affirm the judgment.

Amberley D. was born on January 19, 1985, and grew up with her mother, Joann R., her stepfather, Charles R., and her two siblings, moving many times and living in Maine, Vermont and several other states.[1] Joann and Charles separated several times, during which Joann and the children utilized various temporary living arrangements, including friends' homes, motels, and a shelter.

In the spring of 1999, Joann and Charles separated and filed for divorce in Vermont. Joann and the children then moved to New Hampshire, staying in motels and with friends. Amberley, who was in the eighth grade, stopped going to school. By this time, she had been enrolled in approximately twenty-seven different schools. Amberley testified that Joann was abusing drugs and alcohol, providing them to her, staying out all night drinking, and engaging in sexual activity in front of her. Amberley also testified that she had been sexually molested several times, and that she reported this to Joann, who had done nothing.

---

[1] Amberley's biological father, Mark M., never developed a relationship with her and did not participate in the proceedings.

In late 1999, Amberley ran away on two occasions. She was found at her boyfriend's home and then at Charles' home, and returned to Joann. In January 2000, Amberley ran away again to Charles' home in Vermont. Charles drove her to a friend's place in Massachusetts. From there, Amberley took a bus to Augusta to meet Charles' parents, Diana and Richard B., who reside in Stockton Springs. Joann notified law enforcement agencies that Amberley was missing, then departed for a California vacation. Upon her return, she was informed by the Waldo County Sheriff's Office that Amberley was with Diana and Richard B.

Shortly after Amberley's arrival, Diana and Richard B. filed a petition requesting appointment as temporary coguardians of a minor pursuant to 18–A M.R.S.A. § 5–207(c) (Supp.2000).[2] After a hearing, the court granted a temporary, six-month guardianship, finding that Amberley was in an intolerable living situation at her mother's, inadequately cared for, and subject to abuse by others. Joann was served with notice of the appointment and, representing herself, filed a motion to dismiss the temporary guardianship. Subsequently, through counsel, she filed another motion to dismiss the guardianship and an answer to the petition. After a hearing, the court denied the motion.

A hearing on full guardianship was held, which Joann had notice of and participated in. The court found by clear and convincing evidence a history of abuse, neglect, and mistreatment, and a living situation that was at least temporarily intolerable for Amberley, and that the guardians would provide a living situation in her best interest. *See* 18–A M.R.S.A. § 5–204(c). The court then entered an order appointing Diana and Richard B. full coguardians of Amberley pursuant to 18–A M.R.S.A. § 5–204.**3** The record does not indicate that there was any other prior or pending order from any other court in any state addressing custody or parental rights for Amberley during this time. Joann brought this appeal from the Probate Court's order.

---

[2] Section 5–207(c) states that "[i]f necessary, the court may appoint a temporary guardian, with the status of an ordinary guardian of a minor, but the authority of a temporary guardian may not last longer than 6 months."

[3] Section 5–204 states in relevant part:

The court may appoint a guardian or coguardians for an unmarried minor if:

(a) All parental rights of custody have been terminated or suspended by circumstance or prior court order;

(b) Each living parent whose parental rights and responsibilities have not been terminated or the person who is the legal custodian of the unmarried minor consents to the guardianship and the court finds that the consent creates a condition that is in the best interest of the child; or

(c) The person or persons whose consent is required under subsection (b) do not consent, but the court finds by clear and convincing evidence that the person or persons have failed to respond to proper notice or a living situation has been created that is at least temporarily intolerable for the child even though the living situation does not rise to the level of jeopardy required for the final termination of parental rights, and that the proposed guardian will provide a living situation that is in the best interest of the child.

The Probate Court, in appointing Diana and Richard B. temporary guardians of Amberley, waived notice of hearing to Amberley's parents pursuant to 18–A M.R.S.A. § 5–207, which states that "[u]pon a showing of good cause, the court may waive service of the notice of hearing on any person, other than the minor, if the minor is at least 14 years of age." Joann contends that the Uniform Child Custody Jurisdiction, and Enforcement Act (UCCJEA), 19–A M.R.S.A. §§ 1731–1783 (Supp.2000), which defers to state notice provisions for child custody determinations, is preempted by the Parental Kidnapping Prevention Act (PKPA), 28 U.S.C. § 1738A (1994 & Supp.2000), and that she was entitled to notice of the emergency guardianship hearing under the PKPA.

The UCCJEA provides that notice to persons outside the state "may be given in a manner prescribed by the law of this State for service of process or by the law of the state in which the service is made." 19–A M.R.S.A. § 1738(1). In the event of a conflict, the PKPA preempts the UCCJEA. However, the PKPA addresses jurisdictional issues only when existing orders have been entered by courts of other states concerning the custody or visitation of a child. *See* Thompson v. Thompson, 484 U.S. 174, 177, 108 S.Ct. 513, 98 L.Ed.2d 512 (1988) ("[a]s the legislative scheme suggests, and as Congress explicitly specified, one of the chief purposes of the PKPA is to avoid jurisdictional competition and conflict between State courts") (citation omitted). The PKPA is not applicable in this case because no competing custody order regarding Amberley was pending or entered in another state.[4]

Joann also contends that 18–A M.R.S.A. § 5–207, as applied, violates due process by depriving her of fundamental parental rights. In assessing what process is due, we apply the *Mathews* factors:

> First, the private interest that will be affected by the official action; second, the risk of an erroneous deprivation of such interest through the procedures used, and the probable value, if any, of additional or substitute procedural safeguards; and finally, the Government's interest, including the function involved and the fiscal and administrative burdens that the additional or substitute procedural requirement would entail.

In re Heather C., 2000 ME 99, § 22, 751 A.2d 448, 454 (citing Mathews v. Eldridge, 424 U.S. 319, 335, 96 S.Ct. 893, 47 L.Ed.2d 18 (1976)). *See also* Rideout v. Riendeau, 2000 ME 198, § 14, 761 A.2d 291, 297–98 ("[i]f we can reasonably interpret a statute as satisfying those constitutional requirements, we must read it in such a way, notwithstanding other possible unconstitutional interpretations of the same statute").

Joann has a fundamental parental right, and the government has a significant interest in protecting children. *See Heather C.,* 2000 ME 99, §§ 23–28, 751 A.2d at 454–56. The risk of a due process violation occurs

---

[4] However, the PKPA is relevant to initial custody determinations by providing guidelines to prevent jurisdictional disputes. *See Wambold v. Wambold,* 651 A.2d 330, 332 (Me.1994).

when an emergency guardian may be appointed without notice to parents, temporarily depriving them of parental rights, before a hearing takes place. However, section 5–207(c) limits the emergency guardianship to six months. Further, upon notice that a guardian has been appointed, a parent can petition for removal of the guardian pursuant to 18–A M.R.S.A. § 5–212 (1998),[5] entitling them to a hearing. At the hearing, the guardian has the burden of demonstrating that continuation of the guardianship is in the child's best interest. 18–A M.R.S.A. § 5–212(d). Joann received notice of the six-month guardianship appointment, filed a motion to dismiss, and a prompt hearing was held on her motion, at which her attorneys were present. She also received notice of and participated in the hearing on full guardianship. Thus, the guardianship statute, providing for waiver of notice in limited circumstances, but with subsequent opportunity to be heard, did not violate Joann's due process rights.

Joann contends that New Hampshire has jurisdiction over the guardianship petition pursuant to the PKPA and the UCCJEA. As set forth above, the PKPA is not directly at issue where no competing court order is involved. However, the jurisdictional requirements of the PKPA, which are similar but not identical to the UCCJEA, must be met, or the decree risks being denied full faith and credit by courts of other states. *See* Wambold v. Wambold, 651 A.2d 330, 333 (Me.1994).

Both the PKPA and the UCCJEA provide that a state has jurisdiction over a child custody proceeding if the state is the "home state" of the child on the date the proceeding is commenced, or was the home state within six months before the date the proceeding is commenced.[6] *See* 28 U.S.C. § 1738A(c); 19–A M.R.S.A. § 1745. The PKPA and the UCCJEA define the home state as the state in which the child lived with a parent, or a person acting as a parent, for at least six consecutive months immediately before the commencement of a child custody proceeding, and include periods of temporary absence as part of the period. 28 U.S.C. § 1738A(b)(4); 19–A M.R.S.A. § 1732(7).

Immediately prior to the filing of the temporary guardianship petition, Amberley lived in New Hampshire, but for less than six months. Nevertheless, Joann contends that New Hampshire is Amberley's home state because she lived there for almost six months, last attended school

---

[5] Section 5–212 reads in relevant part:

(a) Any person interested in the welfare of a ward, or the ward, if 14 or more years of age, may petition for removal of a guardian on the ground that removal would be in the best interest of the ward. A guardian may petition for permission to resign. A petition for removal or for permission to resign may, but need not, include a request for appointment of a successor guardian.

(b) After notice and hearing on a petition for removal or for permission to resign, the court may terminate the guardianship and make any further order that may be appropriate

[6] The UCCJEA's child custody jurisdiction provisions generally track the PKPA's, although they differ slightly in some respects. *See* Wambold, 651 A.2d at 332–33; 19–A M.R.S.A. § 1745 comment (2000); 19–A M.R.S.A. § 1748 comment (2000).

there, and had contacts with individuals providing services in the state, such as her physician and the New Hampshire Department of Health and Human Services' workers concerning her truancy. However, this evidence is inadequate because the six-month requirement was not met, due to Joann and Amberley's transitory living situation. New Hampshire cannot be considered Amberley's home state.

When the child has no home state, the PKPA and the UCCJEA require the court to examine whether a sufficiently significant connection and substantial evidence exists to exercise jurisdiction. Pursuant to the PKPA, in the absence of a home state, a state can exercise jurisdiction when it is in the child's best interest because "the child and his parents, or the child and at least one contestant, have a significant connection with such State other than mere physical presence," and "substantial evidence" is available in the state concerning the child's care. 28 U.S.C. § 1738A(c)(2)(B). The corresponding UCCJEA provision, which does not include the "best interest" language, states that jurisdiction is proper when "the child and at least one parent or a person acting as a parent" has a significant connection with the state. 19–A M.R.S.A. § 1745(1)(B)(1).

Diana and Richard B. are residents of Maine. They have had physical custody and care of Amberley since her arrival in this state, and they are the parents of her stepfather. The record indicates that Amberley has visited them on a regular basis in the past, and that she lived and attended school in Maine for periods during 1991–97. Consequently, the significant connection and substantial evidence requirements were satisfied under the UCCJEA and the PKPA, and the Probate Court has jurisdiction over the guardianship petition. *See* Gabriel W., 666 A.2d at 509–10.

Regarding Joann's claim that venue did not exist, under 18–A M.R.S.A. § 5–205 (1998), venue for guardianship proceedings for minors is "in the place where the minor resides or is present." Amberley's presence within Maine was determinative in establishing venue. *See* Guardianship of Zachary Z., 677 A.2d 550, 552–53 (Me.1996).

Pursuant to 18–A M.R.S.A. § 5–204(c), absent the consent of a parent or legal custodian to the guardianship appointment, the Probate Court must find by clear and convincing evidence that "a living situation has been created that is at least temporarily intolerable for the child even though the living situation does not rise to the level of jeopardy required for the final termination of parental rights, and that the proposed guardian will provide a living situation that is in the best interest of the child." Neither the child protective statute, 22 M.R.S.A. §§ 4001–4091 (1992 & Supp.2000), nor the protection from abuse statute, 19–A M.R.S.A. §§ 4001–4014 (1998 & Supp.2000), prohibits the Probate Court from appointing emergency guardians for minors, absent parental consent, when the requisite findings are made.

On a direct appeal from the Probate Court, we review the court's findings for clear error. *See* Conservatorship of Justin R., 662 A.2d 232, 234 (Me.1995) (citing Estate of Paine, 609 A.2d 1150, 1152 (Me.1992)). In its guardianship order, the court found that the testimony established a history of abuse, neglect and mistreatment of Amberley by her mother. Among the evidence cited by the court was the unstable living arrangement involving multiple moves, and Amberley's fear for her own safety. The court further cited the testimony that Joann used alcohol and marijuana and provided them to Amberley, and that she engaged in sexual activity in Amberley's presence. In addition, the court cited Joann's apparent disregard for Amberley's well-being in taking a vacation when she was missing. The court determined that Diana and Richard B., with whom Amberley had spent considerable time during her life, offer her a stable, loving home and have met her physical, educational, emotional, and social needs.

The evidence is sufficient to support the court's findings that a living situation was created that was at least temporarily intolerable for Amberley and that Diana and Richard B. provide a living situation in her best interests. Joann claims that the testimony presented at the hearing was self-interested and conflicting. However, it is the factfinder's responsibility to assess the credibility of witnesses and the weight and significance of the evidence. Guardianship of Boyle, 674 A.2d 912, 913 (Me.1996) (citation omitted). Absent clear error, we defer to that assessment. *Id.*

Amberley's age and her participation in the proceedings further supports the court's best interest determination. Amberley was fifteen at the time the petition was filed and granted, and the record indicates she nominated Diana and Richard B. to be her guardians pursuant to 18–A M.R.S.A. § 5–206 (1998).[7] Minors who are older are permitted, under certain circumstances, to exercise a greater degree of choice. *See, e.g.,* 15 M.R.S.A. § 3506–A (Supp.2000) (allowing sixteen-year-olds to seek emancipation). The court did not err in appointing guardians based on this evidence.

Apart from her notice claim, Joann challenges the constitutionality of the guardianship statute by contending her parental rights have effectively been terminated, but that unlike a child protective termination proceeding, no home study was made, and no agency or individual will work with Joann towards reunification. However, guardianship determinations are not final. Under 18–A M.R.S.A. § 5–212(a), any person who is interested in the welfare of the ward, or the ward if over fourteen years old, may petition for removal of the guardian. When the guardian does not consent to removal, the guardian has the burden of showing, by a preponderance of the evidence, that continuation

---

7 Section 5–206 states in relevant part that "[t]he court shall appoint a person nominated by the minor, if the minor is 14 years of age or older, unless the court finds the appointment contrary to the best interests of the minor."

of the guardianship is in the best interest of the ward pursuant to 18–A M.R.S.A. § 5–212(d).[8] Because the parent retains the right to regain custody, the same degree of procedural safeguards as in termination proceedings is not constitutionally required. *See, e.g.,* In re Sabrina M., 460 A.2d 1009, 1015–16 (Me.1983) ("the nature of the interests concerned in a child protection proceeding significantly differs from that in a proceeding to terminate parental rights").

Finally, we do not address the question of visitation. The record does not indicate that Joann has made an effort to obtain contact with Amberley, or that Diana and Richard B. attempted to restrict visitation between them. As a result, this issue is not reached.

The entry is: Judgment affirmed.

NOTES

Child custody and visitation orders are not subject to interstate enforcement through the Full Faith and Credit Clause, hence the necessity of the UCCJEA and the PKPA. In its Prefatory Note, the objectives of the UCCJEA are listed: (1) to effectively prioritize home-state jurisdiction; (2) clarify emergency jurisdictional issues; (3) establish the basis for continuing exclusive jurisdictional issues; and (4) to specify the types of custody proceedings subject to the UCCJEA. Once jurisdiction is established and a custody decision made, that state retains jurisdiction until the child, the child's parents, or any other person acting as a parent no longer resides in that state. Internationally, a valid custody order may be enforced through the Hague Convention on the Civil Aspects of International Child Abduction, *see infra*.

For commentary on jurisdictional issues, *see* Jeffrey A. Parness, *Choosing Among Imprecise American State Parentage Laws*, 76 LA. L. REV. 481 (2015); Andrea Charlow, *There's No Place Like Home: Temporary Absences in the UCCJEA Home State*, 28 AM. ACAD. MATRIM. LAW 25 (2015); Linda D. Elrod, *A Review of the Year in Family Law: Looking at Interjurisdictional Recognition*, 43 FAM. L. Q. 923 (2010); Kelly Gaines Stoner, *The Uniform Child Custody Jurisdiction & Enforcement Act (UCCJEA)—A Metamorphosis of the Uniform Child Custody Jurisdiction Act (UCCJA)*, 75 N. DAKOTA L. REV. 301 (1999).

[8] Because Joann has not yet petitioned for removal of the guardian, we do not reach her claims that the process for such a petition would violate her due process rights.

2. APPOINTMENT OF COUNSEL TO REPRESENT THE CHILD

In re Interest of D.B.

Supreme Court of Florida, 1980
385 So.2d 83

■ OVERTON, JUSTICE.

This appeal by the State of Florida is from circuit court orders directing the state to pay attorney's fees for representation of both indigent children and parents in all juvenile dependency proceedings. The orders by the circuit court held that the state must provide this legal representation as a fundamental constitutional right under the due process clause of the Florida Constitution and the United States Constitution. This finding was based on the decision of the United States District Court for the Southern District of Florida in Davis v. Page, 442 F. Supp. 258 (S.D.Fla.1977). The holding of the circuit court in the instant cases directly construed the Florida and the United States Constitutions. The circuit court order, which was precipitated by the federal district court decision, affects all juvenile dependency proceedings in Dade County, which total approximately 2,000 annually, and could affect the 20,000 annual dependency proceedings statewide. We have jurisdiction. Art. V, s 3(b)(1), Fla.Const.

We reject the holdings of both the state circuit court and the United States District Court that all indigent participants in juvenile dependency proceedings are entitled, as a fundamental right, to have counsel supplied to them by the state. We find that a constitutional right to counsel necessarily arises where the proceedings can result in permanent loss of parental custody. In all other circumstances the constitutional right to counsel is not conclusive; rather, the right to counsel will depend upon a case-by-case application of the test adopted in Potvin v. Keller, 313 So.2d 703 (Fla.1975). We recognize that in all instances the trial court must ensure that proper notice and an opportunity to be heard be provided to the participants. We find that when counsel is constitutionally required, the county, rather than the state, must compensate appointed counsel under a formula which recognizes both the obligation of the government to provide counsel and the obligation of the legal profession to represent the poor. As a result of these findings, we direct the judiciary of this state to follow the views expressed in this opinion rather than the views expressed by the United States District Court in Davis v. Page. We find that the federal district court should have refrained from passing on this new constitutional right and allowed the claim to be presented in the state system.

To fully explain these conclusions, it is necessary to set forth the specific facts of each of these two separate dependency causes. At age five D. B. was surrendered by her mother to Catholic Services Bureau, Inc., for permanent commitment and adoption. The mother had been a prostitute and a heroin addict, and the child was born with a heroin addiction. The natural father was never married to the mother. At the time of the commitment proceedings, the father was incarcerated in the Florida state prison system for burglary, and was wanted in New Jersey for violation of parole. Approximately four months after surrender of the child, the mother sought to set aside her surrender of the child. In the trial court proceedings she was represented by Legal Services of Greater Miami, Inc. That representation is not in issue in these proceedings. Both the natural mother and the natural father sought custody of the child. The trial court appointed private counsel to represent the imprisoned father of this child, and appointed another private counsel as guardian ad litem for the child. The trial court found both natural parents to be unfit, stating:

> (T)he Court finds that the said (mother) and (father) are unfit by reason of conduct, lifestyles and circumstances which have resulted in actual and constructive abandonment, abuse and neglect of the child, and it is manifestly in the best interest of the child that the parental rights of the natural parents . . . be terminated.

Following the entry of this judgment, the trial court entered an order directing the State of Florida to pay $1,090 to the attorney representing the father of the child and $1,000 to counsel acting as guardian ad litem for the child.

The second dependency action, for D. S., commenced when the child was nine months old because the child's mother, age 16, had abandoned him at his grandmother's home and was threatening to burn down the grandmother's house. The sixteen-year-old mother was taken into custody and detained in the juvenile detention center. Temporary custody of the child was sought by the Department of Health and Rehabilitative Services (HRS). Private counsel was appointed to represent the indigent mother in these temporary custody dependency proceedings. In addition, separate private counsel was appointed guardian ad litem for the child. The trial court found the child dependent and committed him to the temporary custody of HRS, with the understanding that the child eventually would reside with the teenage mother. This custody was subject to the continuing supervision of HRS to ensure proper care of the child. Subsequent to the entry of this temporary order and upon motion of appointed counsel, the trial court directed the State of Florida to pay $400 to counsel for the teenage mother and $285 to the guardian ad litem for the nine-month-old child.

In his order directing payment of attorney's fees in the instant cases, the trial court held:

> The Judges of the Juvenile and Family Division of the Eleventh Judicial Circuit were named as defendants in a federal class action styled Davis v. Page, 442 F. Supp. 258 (S.D.Fla.1977). The plaintiffs in that suit were Hilary Davis and all indigent

> parents who have been, or may be, defendants in child dependency proceedings in the Juvenile and Family Division of the Circuit Court of Dade County, Florida and who have not been advised of their right to counsel or afforded counsel at state's expense. The United States District Court entered judgment in favor of the plaintiffs and against the judges of this Court, and held that indigent parents have a constitutional right to appointed counsel in dependency proceedings. . . . (T)his Court must comply with the judgment of the federal court until and unless the decision is reversed or vacated, nothwithstanding (sic) the fact that the Florida Supreme Court has reached a contrary conclusion in Potvin v. Kelley (sic), 313 So.2d 703 (Fla.1975). See U.S. Constitution, Art. VII, Cl. 2. This Court, therefore, holds that unless Davis v. Page is reversed on appeal, all indigent parents in dependency proceedings brought in this Court pursuant to Chapter 39, Florida Statutes, have a right to appointed counsel.
>
> As a result of Davis v. Page, this Court also appoints attorneys as guardians ad litem to represent children of indigent parents in dependency proceedings when the Court determines that the appointment of a guardian ad litem is necessary to protect the child's interests. The Court is mindful that the Florida Supreme Court has held that the constitutional right to counsel is mandatory only in juvenile proceedings which concern a possible adjudication of delinquency. In the Interest of Hutchins, 345 So.2d 703 (Fla.1977). Hutchins, however, cannot be controlling since this Court is now required by Davis to provide counsel to indigent parents in dependency proceedings. It is inconceivable to this Court that while it is required to appoint counsel for indigent parents in dependency proceedings, that an indigent child, whose interests may be adverse to the desires of his parents and the State, would not have an attendant right to appointed counsel. Since the Court is required to provide counsel for parents, the Court therefore holds that unless Davis is reversed on appeal, the due process and equal protection clauses of the Fourteenth Amendment to the United States Constitution as well as the due process provisions contained within Article I, Section 9 of the Florida Constitution, require the Court to appoint counsel to serve as guardians ad litem for children in dependency proceedings when the Court finds that such an appointment is necessary in order to protect the intersts (sic) of the child. . . . (Emphasis supplied.)

No better hypothetical script could have been written to set forth the problems of dependent children than is illustrated by these two factual situations. The principal issues are what legal representation is constitutionally required, and in what manner attorneys should be compensated when appointed to represent indigent parties in dependency matters.

The right of an indigent party to have counsel furnished in a legal proceeding is dependent upon the nature of the proceeding. This is an evolving constitutional issue which concerns the application of the sixth and fourteenth amendments of the United States Constitution. In a series of well-publicized cases, the United States Supreme Court has found that a constitutional right to government-furnished counsel is mandated whenever imprisonment can be imposed. Powell v. Alabama, 287 U.S. 45, 53 S.Ct. 55, 77 L.Ed. 158 (1932)(right to counsel in a death case); Gideon v. Wainwright, 372 U.S. 335, 83 S.Ct. 792, 9 L.Ed.2d 799 (1963) (right to counsel for noncapital serious offenses); In re Gault, 387 U.S. 1, 87 S.Ct. 1428, 18 L.Ed.2d 527 (1967) (right to counsel in juvenile delinquency proceedings where the issue concerned the commitment of a juvenile for criminal conduct); and Argersinger v. Hamlin, 407 U.S. 25, 92 S.Ct. 2006, 32 L.Ed.2d 530 (1972) (right to counsel for petit offenses whenever imprisonment could be imposed). On the other hand, the United States Supreme Court has rejected the absolute constitutional right to counsel in other civil and criminal matters. It rejected a right to counsel for parole revocation proceedings in Gagnon v. Scarpelli, 411 U.S. 778, 93 S.Ct. 1756, 36 L.Ed.2d 656 (1973), and similarly rejected such a right for the purpose of seeking discretionary appellate review of criminal cases in Ross v. Moffitt, 417 U.S. 600, 94 S.Ct. 2437, 41 L.Ed.2d 341 (1974). In Goldberg v. Kelly, 397 U.S. 254, 90 S.Ct. 1011, 25 L.Ed.2d 287 (1970), in a proceeding terminating welfare payments, Justice Brennan rejected a procedural due process right to counsel, saying: "We do not say that counsel must be provided at the pre-termination hearing, but only that the recipient must be allowed to retain an attorney if he so desires." 397 U.S. at 270, 90 S.Ct. at 1022.

We believe it is important to note that the right to counsel, as it has been presently established by the United States Supreme Court, applies only in criminal cases and flows principally from the sixth amendment right to counsel, applied to the states through the fourteenth amendment, rather than from the fourteenth amendment due process guarantee. Right to counsel in dependency proceedings, on the other hand, is governed by due process considerations, rather than the sixth amendment. The extent of procedural due process protections varies with the character of the interest and nature of the proceeding involved. Morrissey v. Brewer, 408 U.S. 471, 92 S.Ct. 2593, 33 L.Ed.2d 484 (1972).

The decision of the United States District Court in Davis directs circuit judges sitting on juvenile delinquency matters in Dade County, Florida, to provide counsel at government expense for indigent parents in all child dependency proceedings irrespective of the nature of the commitment, be it temporary or permanent. The Davis decision clearly concerned only temporary custody of the child. At the time of the action Ms. Davis had obtained weekend home visits with her son, and prior to the United States District Court's decision had secured the return of her son subject to continuing supervision under the jurisdiction of the circuit court. The Davis court, based on these facts, held there were fundamental due process and equal protection rights at stake that could be adequately safeguarded only by providing counsel to indigent parents in all dependency proceedings. In so holding, the United States District Court rejected the view of the Ninth Circuit Court of Appeals in Cleaver v. Wilcox, 499 F.2d 940 (9th Cir. 1974), which this Court expressly adopted in Potvin v. Keller, 313 So.2d 703 (Fla.1975).

To accurately characterize the proceeding involved, it should be recognized that juvenile dependency proceedings and juvenile delinquency proceedings have distinct and separate purposes. Dependency proceedings exist to protect and care for the child that has been neglected, abused, or abandoned. Delinquency proceedings, on the other hand, exist to remove children from the adult criminal justice system and punish them in a manner more suitable and appropriate for children. We reject the contention that In re Gault, which the Davis court found applicable, requires the appointment of counsel in a juvenile dependency proceeding. The holding in Gault, in our opinion, only requires the appointment of counsel for an indigent child in delinquency proceedings which might result in detention as a punishment. Further, there are numerous types of juvenile dependency proceedings, but all concern the care, not the punishment, of the child. Some provide very temporary types of relief and custody, while other dependency proceedings permanently terminate the custody and care of a child. See s 39, Fla.Stat. (1979); Bell, Dependency Law in Florida, 53 Fla.Bar J. 652 (1979).

We recognize that there is a constitutionally protected interest in preserving the family unit and raising one's children. Moore v. East Cleveland, 431 U.S. 494, 97 S.Ct. 1932, 52 L.Ed.2d 531 (1976); Stanley v. Illinois, 405 U.S. 645, 92 S.Ct. 1208, 31 L.Ed.2d 551 (1972); May v. Anderson, 345 U.S. 528, 73 S.Ct. 840, 97 L.Ed. 1221 (1953); Meyer v. Nebraska, 262 U.S. 390, 43 S.Ct. 625, 67 L.Ed. 1042 (1923). Because the interest at stake is so important and fundamental in nature, we recognize, consistent with our holding in Potvin, that a right to counsel may be required in certain circumstances. We agree in part with the Davis court and the trial judge that counsel is necessarily required under the due process clause of the United States and Florida Constitutions, in proceedings involving the permanent termination of parental rights to a child, or when the proceedings, because of their nature, may lead to criminal child abuse charges.[1] It is our view that under the Cleaver test,

[1] This position aligns us with other state courts, all of which have recognized a fundamental right to counsel where indigent parents face a permanent loss of custody. *Chambers v. District Court of Dubuque County*, 261 Iowa 31, 152 N.W.2d 818 (1967); *Danforth v. State Dept. of Health and Welfare*, 303 A.2d 794 (Me.1973); *Reist v. Bay County Circuit Judge*, 396 Mich. 326, 241 N.W.2d 55 (1976); *In Interest of Friesz*, 190 Neb. 347, 208 N.W.2d 259 (1973); *Crist v. Division of Youth and Family Services*, 128 N.J.Super. 402, 320 A.2d 203 (1974); *In Re B*, 30 N.Y.2d 352, 334 N.Y.S.2d 133, 285 N.E.2d 288 (C.A.N.Y. 1972); *State v. Jamison*, 444 P.2d

counsel will always be required where permanent termination of custody might result, but where there is no threat of permanent termination of parental custody, the test should be applied on a case-by-case basis.[2]

We conclude that where permanent termination or child abuse charges might result, counsel must be appointed for (1) the natural married or divorced indigent parents of the child, (2) the natural indigent mother of an illegitimate child, and (3) the natural indigent father of an illegitimate child when he legally has recognized or is in fact maintaining the child. We reject, however, any requirement for the mandatory appointment of counsel for the father of an illegitimate child who has not legally acknowledged or in fact supported the child. It should be realized that the possible temporary loss of custody in a dependency matter is no different than what regularly occurs in domestic relation proceedings when custody is an issue. Where the trial judge finds no constitutional right to counsel under Cleaver, he may nonetheless use his historical authority to provide legal assistance. Further, certain due process requirements must be observed even though counsel is not constitutionally required. All parents must be given notice of a dependency hearing, advised that they have a right to be represented by counsel of their choice, and afforded a period of time to obtain counsel which is reasonable under the circumstances.

Finally, we find there is no constitutional right to counsel for the subject child in a juvenile dependency proceeding. By statute, counsel as guardian ad litem must be appointed in any child abuse judicial proceeding under section 827.07(16), Florida Statutes (1979). In all other instances, the appointment of counsel as guardian ad litem for the child is left to the traditional discretion of the trial court, and should be made only where warranted under Florida Rule of Juvenile Procedure 8.300.

In the instant case concerning D. B., the representation of the mother is not in question. The issues concern the appropriateness of the mandatory appointment of counsel for both the father and the child. In our opinion, the indigent father of D. B. has no constitutional right to counsel. He was never married to the mother, and has neither legally recognized nor supported the child. We do not read Stanley v. Illinois, 405 U.S. 645, 92 S.Ct. 1208, 31 L.Ed.2d 551 (1972), as requiring counsel to be appointed in such a circumstance. We recognize that the father is entitled to notice that the child is being permanently committed under

---

15 (1968); *In Re Adoption of R.I.*, 455 Pa. 29, 312 A.2d 601 (1973); *In Re Myricks*, 85 Wash.2d 252, 251 Or. 114, 533 P.2d 841 (1975); *State ex rel. Lemaster v. Oakley*, 203 S.E.2d 140 (W.Va. 1974). *See* Annot., 80 A.L.R.3d 1141 (1977).

[2] In so holding, we realize that there are some jurisdictions and commentators who would require appointment of counsel for indigent participants in *all* dependency proceedings. *Chambers v. District Court of Dubuque, County*, 261 Iowa 31, 152 N.W.2d 818 (1967); *Danforth v. State Dept. of Health and Welfare*, 303 A.2d 794 (Me. 1973); *Crist v. Division of Youth and Family Services*, 128 N.J.Super. 402, 320 A.2d 203 (1974); *In Re Myricks*, 85 Wash.2d 252, 533 P.2d 841 (1975); Note, *Child Neglect: Due Process for the Parent*, 70 Colum.L.Rev. 415 (1970); Comment, *The Indigent Parent's Right to Appointed Counsel in Actions to Terminate Parental Rights*, 43 U.Cinn.L.Rev. 635 (1974).

section 39.413, Florida Statutes, and is allowed an opportunity to contest the commitment and be represented by private counsel under section 39.406, Florida Statutes. However, we find no statutory authority and no constitutional requirement to provide counsel for this father at public expense. While we hold that the appointment of counsel to serve as guardian ad litem for a child is never constitutionally required in a dependency proceeding, it was an appropriate appointment under the facts of this case which include the mother's contest of a prior surrender of the child, the mother's history as a prostitute and heroin addict, and a father in prison seeking custody.

In the case relating to D. S., the sixteen-year-old mother was entitled to the appointment of counsel for the juvenile delinquency offense associated with the abandonment of her child. Absent the delinquency offense, we find there was no constitutional requirement that counsel be provided at state expense for this indigent mother when only temporary custody and supervision was sought. Similarly, the appointment of counsel as guardian ad litem for the nine-month-old child was not constitutionally required. Further, we find the appointment was not appropriate since the proceedings were instituted by HRS to protect the interests of the child and there were no factors here which would justify the appointment of a guardian ad litem in addition to HRS to safeguard the interests of the child. Although we find the appointment of counsel for the father of D. B. and the appointment of a guardian ad litem for D. S. to be neither constitutionally required nor appropriate under the circumstances of these cases, we recognize counsel did in fact represent their designated clients at the trial court's direction with the understanding that they would be paid for their services. Therefore, we find that these causes should be remanded and counsel should be compensated in accordance with the Rush fee formula set forth in this opinion.

The instant trial court orders require the state to pay five separate attorneys, in addition to payment of counsel necessary to represent the state. In sum, seven lawyers would be necessary to resolve the issues in these two dependency matters. These factual circumstances illustrate the substantial legal and fiscal impact this trial court decision would have on the 20,000 annual juvenile dependency proceedings in this state. We could foresee that this relatively new civil process of juvenile dependency proceedings, intended to protect abandoned, neglected, or abused children, could be crushed by the combined weight of taxpayer expense for multiple legal representation and the expansion of the process into more formalized adversary legal proceedings. The state might choose not to supply this protection for children unless or until a criminal abuse had occurred.

We have chosen the middle road in this opinion by requiring counsel to be appointed when parents are threatened with permanent loss of custody or when criminal charges may arise from the proceeding, and by applying the Cleaver test on a case-by-case basis in all other circumstances. In our view, this is clearly sufficient to protect both the safety of the children of this state and the constitutional rights of their parents. We direct Florida's judiciary to follow the dictates of this opinion as it concerns the right to counsel in juvenile dependency matters, until further modification or reversal by this Court or the United States Supreme Court. This directive, however, shall not apply to any Eleventh Circuit judges of the Juvenile and Family Division who might be under a direct, valid order of the federal district court in Davis v. Page until that order is reversed or vacated. This cause is remanded to the trial court to reconsider the attorney's fees in accordance with the formula expressed in this opinion and to enter the appropriate orders directing the county to pay such fees when they are established.

It is so ordered.

■ ENGLAND, C. J., ADKINS, BOYD, SUNDBERG and ALDERMAN, JJ., and VANN, Associate Justice, concur.

CALIFORNIA FAMILY CODE (2016)

§ 3150. Appointment of private counsel

(a) If the court determines that it would be in the best interest of the minor child, the court may appoint private counsel to represent the interests of the child in a custody or visitation proceeding.

(b) Upon entering an appearance on behalf of a child pursuant to this chapter, counsel shall continue to represent that child unless relieved by the court upon the substitution of other counsel by the court or for cause.

§ 3151.5. Judicial determinations of custody or visitation; consideration of statements by child's counsel

If a child is represented by court appointed counsel, at every hearing in which the court makes a judicial determination regarding custody or visitation the court shall consider any statement of issues and contentions of the child's counsel. Any party may subpoena as a witness any person listed in the statement of issues and contentions as having provided information to the attorney, but the attorney shall not be called as a witness.

§ 3151. Duties and rights of private counsel

(a) The child's counsel appointed under this chapter is charged with the representation of the child's best interests. The role of the child's counsel is to gather facts that bear on the best interests of the child, and present those facts to the court, including the child's wishes when counsel deems it appropriate for consideration by the court pursuant to

Section 3042. The counsel's duties, unless under the circumstances it is inappropriate to exercise the duty, include interviewing the child, reviewing the court files and all accessible relevant records available to both parties, and making any further investigations as the counsel considers necessary to ascertain facts relevant to the custody or visitation hearings.

(b) At the court's request, counsel shall prepare a written statement of issues and contentions setting forth the facts that bear on the best interests of the child. The statement shall set forth a summary of information received by counsel, a list of the sources of information, the results of the counsel's investigation, and such other matters as the court may direct. The statement of issues and contentions shall not contain any communication subject to Section 954 of the Evidence Code. The statement of issues and contentions shall be filed with the court and submitted to the parties or their attorneys of record at least 10 days before the hearing, unless the court orders otherwise. At the court's request, counsel may orally state the wishes of the child if that information is not a privileged communication subject to Section 954 of the Evidence Code, for consideration by the court pursuant to Section 3042. Counsel shall not be called as a witness in the proceeding. Counsel may introduce and examine counsel's own witnesses, present arguments to the court concerning the child's welfare, and participate further in the proceeding to the degree necessary to represent the child adequately. In consultation with representatives of the Family Law Section of the State Bar and the Senate and Assembly Judiciary Committees, the Judicial Council may specify standards for the preparation of the statement of issues and contentions and may promulgate a model statement of issues and contentions, which shall include simple instructions regarding how to subpoena a witness, and a blank subpoena form.

(c) The child's counsel shall have the following rights:

(1) Reasonable access to the child.

(2) Standing to seek affirmative relief on behalf of the child.

(3) Notice of any proceeding, and all phases of that proceeding, including a request for examination affecting the child.

(4) The right to take any action that is available to a party to the proceeding, including, but not limited to, the

following: filing pleadings, making evidentiary objections, and presenting evidence and being heard in the proceeding, which may include, but shall not be limited to, presenting motions and orders to show cause, and participating in settlement conferences, trials, seeking writs, appeals, and arbitrations.

(5) Access to the child's medical, dental, mental health, and other health care records, school and educational records, and the right to interview school personnel, caretakers, health care providers, mental health professionals, and others who have assessed the child or provided care to the child. The release of this information to counsel shall not constitute a waiver of the confidentiality of the reports, files, and any disclosed communications. Counsel may interview mediators; however, the provisions of Sections 3177 and 3182 shall apply.

(6) The right to reasonable advance notice of and the right to refuse any physical or psychological examination or evaluation, for purposes of the proceeding, which has not been ordered by the court.

(7) The right to assert or waive any privilege on behalf of the child.

(8) The right to seek independent psychological or physical examination or evaluation of the child for purposes of the pending proceeding, upon approval by the court.

§ 3153. Compensation and expenses of private counsel

(a) If the court appoints counsel under this chapter to represent the child, counsel shall receive a reasonable sum for compensation and expenses, the amount of which shall be determined by the court. Except as provided in subdivision (b), this amount shall be paid by the parties in the proportions the court deems just.

(b) Upon its own motion or that of a party, the court shall determine whether both parties together are financially unable to pay all or a portion of the cost of counsel appointed pursuant to this chapter, and the portion of the cost of that counsel which the court finds the parties are unable to pay shall be paid by the county. The Judicial Council shall adopt guidelines to assist in determining financial eligibility for county payment of counsel appointed by the court pursuant to this chapter.

NOTES

The Florida Supreme Court's decision illustrates that there is no specific constitutional requirement that children be provided with an attorney in any dependency or termination proceeding. The issue then becomes whether the Due Process Clause, or a specific state statute such as the California Family Code, *supra*, provides a right to appointment of an attorney. The Florida court presciently points out that if attorneys were appointed and paid reasonable compensation the state coffers could be "crushed by the combined weight of taxpayer expense." *In re* Interest of D.B., 385 So.2d 83, 94 (Fla. 1980). But in a deleted portion of the decision, the court recommends that judges "use all available legal aid services, and when these services are unavailable, [the judge] should request private counsel to provide the necessary services. Under these circumstances, no compensation is available, and the services are part of the lawyer's historical professional responsibility to represent the poor." *Id.* at 92.

In another state, the Washington Supreme Court employed the balancing factors utilized in Mathews v. Eldridge, 424 U.S. 319 (1976), when it ruled that a state law that authorizes, but does not require, trial courts to appoint counsel for children who are the subject of dependency or termination proceedings is sufficient to meet the requirements of the due process clause. *See In re* MSR, 271 P.2d 234 (Wash. 2012). The Washington court also noted that the United States Constitution does not require states to appoint counsel to parents involved in termination proceedings, a decision that followed the 1980 Florida Supreme Court case, *supra*. *See* Lassiter v. Dep't of Soc. Servs. Of Durham City, N.C., 452 U.S. 18 (1981), *infra*, at Severing Parental Rights Involuntarily. For additional commentary on the obligation to appoint attorneys to assist children, *see, e.g.*, Noah Dennison, *State Constitutional Law—Due Process—Protecting the People and the State Beyond Constitutional Minimums. In re C.M., 48 A.3d 942 (N.H. 2012)*, 44 RUTGERS L. J. 661 (2014); Raymond C. O'Brien, *Reasonable Efforts and Parent-Child Reunification*, 2013 MICH. ST. L. REV. 1029 (supporting efforts of Court Appointed Special Volunteers (CASA) to promote the interests of children in dependency proceedings); Shireen Y. Husain, *A Voice for the Voiceless: A Child's Right to Legal Representation in Dependency Proceedings,* 79 GEO. WASH. L. REV. 232 (2010).

3. COUNSELING THE PARENTS

FLORIDA STATUTES ANN. (2016)

§ 61.21. Parenting course authorized; fees; required attendance authorized; contempt

(1) Legislative findings; purpose. It is the finding of the Legislature that:

(a) A large number of children experience the separation or divorce of their parents each year. Parental conflict related to divorce is a societal concern because children suffer potential short-term and long-term detrimental economic, emotional, and educational effects during this difficult period of family transition. This is particularly true when parents engage in lengthy legal conflict.

(b) Parents are more likely to consider the best interests of their children when determining parental arrangements if courts provide families with information regarding the process by which courts make decisions on issues affecting their children and suggestions as to how parents may ease the coming adjustments in family structure for their children.

(c) It has been found to be beneficial to parents who are separating or divorcing to have available an educational program that will provide general information regarding:

1. The issues and legal procedures for resolving custody and child support disputes.
2. The emotional experiences and problems of divorcing adults.
3. The family problems and the emotional concerns and needs of the children.
4. The availability of community services and resources.

(d) Parents who are separating or divorcing are more likely to receive maximum benefit from a program if they attend such program at the earliest stages of their dispute, before extensive litigation occurs and adversarial positions are assumed or intensified.

(2) The Department of Children and Family Services shall approve a parenting course which shall be a course of a minimum of 4 hours designed to educate, train, and assist divorcing parents in regard to the consequences of divorce on parents and children.

(a) The parenting course referred to in this section shall be named the Parent Education and Family Stabilization Course and may include, but need not be limited to, the following topics as they relate to court actions between parents involving custody, care, visitation, and support of a child or children:

1. Legal aspects of deciding child-related issues between parents.
2. Emotional aspects of separation and divorce on adults.

3. Emotional aspects of separation and divorce on children.
4. Family relationships and family dynamics.
5. Financial responsibilities to a child or children.
6. Issues regarding spousal or child abuse and neglect.
7. Skill-based relationship education that may be generalized to parenting, workplace, school, neighborhood, and civic relationships.

(b) Information regarding spousal and child abuse and neglect shall be included in every parent education and family stabilization course. A list of local agencies that provide assistance with such issues shall also be provided.

(c) The parent education and family stabilization course shall be educational in nature and shall not be designed to provide individual mental health therapy for parents or children, or individual legal advice to parents or children.

(d) Course providers shall not solicit participants from the sessions they conduct to become private clients or patients.

(e) Course providers shall not give individual legal advice or mental health therapy.

(3) Each course provider offering a parenting course pursuant to this section must be approved by the Department of Children and Family Services.

(a) The Department of Children and Family Services shall provide each judicial circuit with a list of approved course providers and sites at which the parent education and family stabilization course may be completed. Each judicial circuit must make information regarding all course providers approved for their circuit available to all parents.

(b) The Department of Children and Family Services shall include on the list of approved course providers and sites for each circuit at least one site in that circuit where the parent education and family stabilization course may be completed on a sliding fee scale, if available.

(c) The Department of Children and Family Services shall include on the list of approved course providers, without limitation as to the area of the state for which the course is approved, a minimum of one statewide approved course to be provided through the Internet and one statewide approved course to be provided through correspondence. The purpose of the Internet and correspondence courses is to ensure that the parent education and stabilization course is available in the home county of each state resident and to those out-of-state persons subject to this section.

(d) The Department of Children and Family Services may remove a provider who violates this section, or its implementing rules, from the list of approved court providers.

(e) The Department of Children and Family Services shall adopt rules to administer subsection (2) and this subsection.

(4) All parties to a dissolution of marriage proceeding with minor children or a paternity action that involves issues of parental responsibility shall be required to complete the Parent Education and Family Stabilization Course prior to the entry by the court of a final judgment. The court may excuse a party from attending the parenting course, or from completing the course within the required time, for good cause.

(5) All parties required to complete a parenting course under this section shall begin the course as expeditiously as possible. For dissolution of marriage actions, unless excused by the court pursuant to subsection (4), the petitioner must complete the course within 45 days after the filing of the petition, and all other parties must complete the course within 45 days after service of the petition. For paternity actions, unless excused by the court pursuant to subsection (4), the petitioner must complete the course within 45 days after filing the petition, and any other party must complete the course within 45 days after an acknowledgment of paternity by that party, an adjudication of paternity of that party, or an order granting visitation to or support from that party. Each party to a dissolution or paternity action shall file proof of compliance with this subsection with the court prior to the entry of the final judgment.

(6) All parties to a modification of a final judgment involving shared parental responsibilities, custody, or visitation may be required to complete a court-approved parenting course prior to the entry of an order modifying the final judgment.

(7) A reasonable fee may be charged to each parent attending the course.

(8) Information obtained or statements made by the parties at any educational session required under this statute shall not be considered in the adjudication of a pending or subsequent action, nor shall any report resulting from such educational session become part of the record of the case unless the parties have stipulated in writing to the contrary.

(9) The court may hold any parent who fails to attend a required parenting course in contempt, or that parent may be denied shared parental responsibility or visitation or otherwise sanctioned as the court deems appropriate.

(10) Nothing in this section shall be construed to require the parties to a dissolution of marriage to attend a court-approved parenting course together.

(11) The court may, without motion of either party, prohibit the parenting course

4. RELOCATION

In re Heinrich and Curotto

Supreme Court of New Hampshire, 2010
7 A.3d 1158

■ HICKS, JUSTICE.

The respondent, Mary Ellen Curotto (wife), appeals the final divorce decree issued by the Derry Family Division (*Moore*, J.), which denied her request to relocate to Florida with the three minor children from her marriage to the petitioner, Eric W. Heinrich (husband). She also contends that the court erred in ruling that the husband was entitled to reimbursement for an overpayment of child support and by requiring that the children be in the care of a third-party caretaker for more than forty-eight hours before the other parent is offered the right to care for them. We affirm in part, vacate in part, and remand.

The record supports the following facts. The parties married in Florida in December 1996 and have three minor sons born in 2000, 2002 and 2004. During their twelve-year marriage, the parties moved from Florida to New Hampshire, following employment opportunities for the husband, who works as a professional chef. The wife worked part-time in the hospitality industry as a waitress and bartender. In 2002, the parties relocated to Derry where two of their three sons were born. According to the wife, the parties' stay in New Hampshire was to be temporary, no longer than five years, after which they intended to return to Florida. The husband disputes this.

On November 10, 2006, the husband filed for divorce, alleging that irreconcilable differences between the parties caused an irremediable breakdown of the marriage. The wife filed an answer and cross-motion to petition for divorce on March 11, 2007. In this petition, the wife asked the court to award her primary residential responsibility for the children so that she could "relocate the children to the State of Florida." The wife's extended family lives in the St. Petersburg, Florida area and owns and operates the Bon-Aire Motel on St. Petersburg Beach. Her family offered her a position as assistant general manager of the hotel with a number of benefits, including health insurance and a flexible work schedule to take care of the children. The husband opposed this move, primarily because he did not believe it was in the children's best interests. The children would not be able to see him weekly and would have to move from the only home they have known.

On April 5, 2007, a Marital Master (*Cross,* M.) held a hearing and issued a temporary parenting plan that gave primary residential responsibility to the wife but awarded the husband regular parenting time. The parenting plan provided that RSA 461–A:12 (Supp. 2009), entitled "Relocation of a Residence of a Child," would govern any proposed relocation. "Pending agreement or further order," the court also barred relocation outside of New Hampshire and appointed a guardian ad litem (GAL) to study, among other issues, whether relocation would be in the children's best interests. In August 2007, the GAL submitted a detailed preliminary report in which she reported that "the children are strongly bonded to both parents," that both "are good parents," and that the children would "suffer a loss" if they were separated from either parent. Based upon this report, the trial court partially modified the existing temporary parenting plan giving the father greater parenting time and denied the wife's request to relocate temporarily to Florida with the children.

At the final hearing, the parties presented the court with two separately negotiated and agreed to parenting plans, one based upon the children's residence in New Hampshire and the other based upon their residence in Florida. The parties disagreed as to whether the wife should relocate with the children to Florida and as to which legal standard governed this proposed relocation—the best interests of the child standard set forth in RSA 461–A:4 (Supp. 2009) and RSA 461–A:6 (Supp. 2009) or the burden-shifting standard set forth in RSA 461–A:12. To decide these issues, the trial court heard testimony from the parties and witnesses and considered the GAL's final report. In her final report, the GAL analyzed the proposed relocation request and recommended that it be denied and "that the children remain in New Hampshire with both parents." The trial court agreed.

In March 2009, the trial court issued a final order, denying the wife's request to relocate to Florida based upon the burden-shifting standard set forth in RSA 461–A:12. The trial court found that the wife had demonstrated a legitimate reason for the proposed relocation to Florida—she had a unique job opportunity in her family's business as well as an extended family network that would help her raise the children in Florida. The trial court then applied the factors set forth in Tomasko v. DuBuc, 145 N.H. 169, 761 A.2d 407 (2000), to determine whether the proposed relocation was in the sons' best interests. The court found that: the [wife] has not resided in the State of Florida for quite some time, that the parties have resided in the State of New Hampshire for over six years, two of their children have been born in this State, all three children have known no other home other than their home in Derry, New Hampshire, the children are well acclimated to the Derry area, the local schools and the community, and the [better] quality of life argument raised by the [wife] does not overcome the negative impact to the quality of the [husband's] relationship with the parties' minor children if the [wife were] to relocate to Florida.

The court noted that the husband was "an involved father" and that his family "has bonded" with the children. If the children relocated to Florida, the court observed that the husband's parenting time with the children would "noticeab[ly] decrease" and that the children "will suffer a loss." (Quotation omitted.) Therefore, the trial court denied the wife's request to relocate and found that the New Hampshire parenting plan should apply. The wife filed a motion for reconsideration, which the court denied. This appeal followed.

The wife first argues that the trial court erred when it applied RSA 461–A:12 in denying her petition to relocate with the children to Florida. She contends that RSA 461–A:12 applies only to a post-divorce relocation request to modify an existing permanent parenting decree. Here, she asserts, there was no permanent parenting decree in place, and, therefore, the court should have applied the best interests of the child standard set forth in RSA 461–A:4 and RSA 461–A:6. The wife's argument requires us to construe the pertinent statutes. The interpretation of a statute is a question of law, which we review *de novo*. Kenison v. Dubois, 152 N.H. 448, 451, 879 A.2d 1161 (2005). We are the final arbiter of the intent of the legislature as expressed in the words of the statute considered as a whole. *Id.* We first examine the language of the statute, and, where possible, we ascribe the plain and ordinary meanings to the words used. *Id.* When the language of a statute is clear on its face, its meaning is not subject to modification. Dalton Hydro v. Town of Dalton, 153 N.H. 75, 78, 889 A.2d 24 (2005). We will neither consider what the legislature might have said nor add words that it did not see fit to include. *Id.*

RSA 461–A:4 governs parenting plans and the determination of parental rights and responsibilities. It directs that "[i]n developing a parenting plan under this section, the court shall consider only the best interests of the child as provided under RSA 461–A:6 and the safety of the parties." RSA 461–A:4, I. RSA 461–A:4, II states that a parenting plan may include provisions relative to "[d]ecision-making responsibility and residential responsibility" for the children, "[p]arenting schedule," as well as the "[r]elocation of parents" among other matters. RSA 461–A:4, II. RSA 461–A:4, in conjunction with RSA 461–A:6, does not specifically address the relocation of a residence of a child. RSA 461–A:12, however, does. RSA 461–A:12, V–VI, lays out a two-part test, known as the burden-shifting test, for a court to apply if a parent seeks to relocate the residence of a child. Under this test, the parent petitioning for relocation must demonstrate that the relocation is for a legitimate purpose and is reasonable in light of that purpose. RSA 461–A:12, V. If the petitioning parent meets this burden, the opposing party then has the burden of proving that the relocation is not in the best interests of the child. RSA 461–A:12, VI. RSA 461–A:12 states:

> I. This section shall apply if the existing parenting plan, order on parental rights and responsibilities, or other enforceable agreement between the parties does not expressly govern the relocation issue. This section shall not apply if the relocation results in the residence being closer to the other parent or to any location within the child's current school district.
>
> II. This section shall apply to the relocation of any residence in which the child resides at least 150 days a year.

RSA 461–A:12, I, II. Nothing in RSA 461–A:12 purports to limit its applicability to relocations proposed after a final divorce decree has been entered, and we decline to read in such a limitation. It is a well settled rule that to the extent that two statutes conflict, the more specific statute, here RSA 461–A:12, controls over the general statute, RSA 461–A:4. Favazza v. Braley, 160 N.H. 349, ___, 999 A.2d 1088 (2010). RSA 461–A:4, the general parenting plan statute, lists as one possible provision the "[r]elocation of parents." RSA 461–A:4, 11(f). It does not provide any detail as to relocation of the children as RSA 461–A:12 does.

The wife next argues that the trial court unsustainably exercised its discretion in denying her request to relocate to Florida with the children under RSA 461–A:12. Specifically, she contends that the trial court "failed to give proper weight to evidence and testimony proffered by [her] relative to the opportunities" available to the children in Florida. These opportunities include the ability of the children to attend private school, participate in their family's hotel legacy, and attend monthly scheduled parenting time with their father. The wife further asserts that she would be able to provide a better lifestyle for the children in Florida than in New Hampshire and that the parties had agreed to move from New Hampshire to Florida after five years. By ignoring these factors, the trial court placed too much emphasis on how the relocation would negatively affect the husband's relationship and parenting time with the children. She asserts there would be no negative effect; the husband would have the same quality of parenting time whether the children live in New Hampshire or Florida.

As previously stated, RSA 461–A:12 provides the analytical framework to determine whether relocation is warranted. Under RSA 461–A:12, the parent seeking to relocate has the initial burden of demonstrating, by a preponderance of the evidence, that the relocation is for a legitimate purpose and is reasonable in light of that purpose. RSA 461–A:12, V. Once the parent has met this *prima facie* burden, the burden shifts to the other parent to prove, by a preponderance of the evidence, that relocating is not in the child's best interests. RSA 461–A:12, VI.

Whether the wife met her *prima facie* burden is not at issue here. This appeal concerns only whether the trial court properly concluded that the father met his burden of showing the relocation was not in the children's best interests. We review the trial court's analysis under our unsustainable exercise of discretion standard. *See* Tomasko, 145 N.H. at 172, 761 A.2d 407; *see also* State v. Lambert, 147 N.H. 295, 296, 787 A.2d 175 (2001) (explaining unsustainable exercise of discretion standard). "This means that we review only whether the record establishes an objective basis sufficient to sustain the discretionary judgment made." In the Matter of Lockaby & Smith, 148 N.H. 462, 465, 808 A.2d 832 (2002) (quotation omitted). Here, the trial court, after reviewing the GAL's final report, hearing testimony from witnesses, and listening to the parties and reading their written submissions, found that the father had established that a relocation to Florida was not in the children's best interests. In reaching this conclusion, the trial court carefully analyzed each of the factors listed in *Tomasko.* These factors include:

> (1) each parent's reasons for seeking or opposing the move; (2) the quality of the relationships between the child and the custodial and noncustodial parents; (3) the impact of the move on the quantity and quality of the child's future contact with the noncustodial parent; (4) the degree to which the custodial parent's and child's life may be enhanced economically, emotionally, and educationally by the move; (5) the feasibility of preserving the relationship between the noncustodial parent and child through suitable visitation arrangements; (6) any negative impact from continued or exacerbated hostility between the custodial and noncustodial parents; and (7) the effect that the move may have on any extended family relations.
>
> Tomasko, 145 N.H. at 172, 761 A.2d 407.

The trial court focused upon how the relocation would affect the quality of the relationship of the husband, "an involved father," with his children. The court found that this relationship would suffer because the husband's "day to day contact with the parties' minor children will be eliminated." Under the proposed Florida plan, the husband's contact would be limited to three-day weekends, major holidays and the summer, a time period the court noted that the husband "will not be able to take advantage of given[ ] his employment" as a chef. The court also worried that the Florida parenting plan "would require significant air travel, which involves a cost factor that the parties may or may not be able to realistically afford, as well as requiring the parties to effectively communicate, which they have been unable to do so to date." Finally, the court noted that the children are "well acclimated to the Derry area, the local schools and the community."

The wife asserts that these factors are far outweighed by the economic, emotional, and educational benefits of the move. She would have a flexible lucrative career with family support and the children could attend private school in Florida. The trial court addressed this argument, stating at the hearing, "I fully understand. Your client wants to relocate to Florida because she is offered a job that she could not obtain in New Hampshire. She could not get a job with the same benefits . . . and she feels that being with her family and having her family support is in her children's best interest." But the trial court found that the "quality of life argument raised by the [wife] does not overcome the negative impact to the quality of the [husband's] relationship with the parties' minor children if the [wife were] to relocate to Florida."

The record supports the trial court's findings. There is evidence that the husband was an involved, caring father. His family gathers together regularly at his parents' house on Sundays to relax, play games, and swim. He is involved in extra-curricular activities as an assistant coach, helps the children with their homework, and attends school activities. The GAL noted that there are times when the husband could not exercise his parenting time because of his work schedule and relies upon a third party for day care. Nevertheless, the GAL opined that she believed it was important for the children "to have . . . access to their dad" regularly. The GAL noted in her report that while the Florida parenting plan would allow the husband and children "to maintain *a* relationship, . . . it will not be the same type of relationship, which exists now. The reality is that the ability to have day to day contact with the boys will be eliminated." She concluded that the boys "will suffer a loss."

We are unpersuaded by the wife's attempts to liken this case to Zaleski v. Zaleski, 128 A.D.2d 865, 513 N.Y.S.2d 784, *appeal denied* 70 N.Y.2d 603, 518 N.Y.S.2d 1026, 512 N.E.2d 552 (1987). In *Zaleski,* an appellate court upheld the trial court's grant of a mother's petition to relocate intrastate from Long Island to Syracuse, New York, in order for her new husband to pursue a unique employment opportunity in "an ongoing family concern." Zaleski, 513 N.Y.S.2d at 786. Because the wife had proposed a liberal visitation schedule and the parties had communicated well, the court concluded that the intrastate relocation "will not . . . effectively curtail the visitation rights of the father or deprive him of regular access to the children." *Id.* In comparison, here the wife has proposed an interstate move of great distance, the parties have had difficulty communicating, and the proposed visitation schedule would greatly limit the father's parenting time with the children.

The wife also asserts that the trial court should not have relied upon the GAL's report and testimony because the GAL's "[p]ersonal '[p]hilosophy' [i]nterfered with her [r]ecommendations." Specifically, the wife contends that the GAL's support of third-party care and working mothers unacceptably influenced her report. "[T]he recommendations of a GAL do not, and should not, carry any greater presumptive weight than the other evidence in a case." In the Matter of Choy & Choy, 154 N.H. 707, 714, 919 A.2d 801 (2007). The trial court here did not rely solely upon the GAL's report. The court considered the testimony of both parties and their witnesses, and the submitted documents. Further, the trial court did not commit an unsustainable exercise of discretion by relying upon the GAL's report. At the hearing, the GAL acknowledged her difference of opinion as to third-party care, stating:

> I think of [third-party care] as . . . a necessary evil, and you know, so many people have to, and you do the best you can to keep your children safe when you have to utilize [it].
>
> [The wife] doesn't want to utilize it at all. . . . I respect [that]; I just don't agree with it.
>
> The trial court, therefore, was able to consider these differences in philosophy and to weigh the GAL's report accordingly. We defer to the judgment of the trial court in these matters because a trial court is in the best position to assign weight to evidence and to assess the credibility of witnesses. In re Guardianship of E.L., 154 N.H. 292, 296, 911 A.2d 35 (2006).

Based upon our review of the record, we cannot say that the trial court unsustainably exercised its discretion in finding that it would not be in the children's best interests to relocate to Florida. *See* In the Matter of Pfeuffer & Pfeuffer, 150 N.H. 257, 260–62, 837 A.2d 311 (2003); Tomasko, 145 N.H. at 173–75, 761 A.2d 407. We, therefore, affirm the trial court's ruling.

Next, the wife contends that the trial court erred in ruling that the husband was entitled to reimbursement of $2,472 spread over twelve months. The parties do not dispute that the husband overpaid child support from January 2008. Prior to the final hearing, the parties submitted that all overpayments had been settled by their partial permanent stipulation through November 1, 2008. The court needed to calculate only overpayments after November 2, 2008. The court, however, incorrectly calculated overpayments for the entire period. We vacate and remand for recalculation of the overpayments.

Finally, the wife asserts that the trial court unsustainably exercised its discretion in requiring the children to be in the care of a third-party caretaker for greater than forty-eight hours before the other parent is offered the right to care for the children. She proposes that a six-hour or shorter time period is more acceptable. Based upon our review of the record, we cannot say that the trial court unsustainably exercised its discretion in imposing a forty-eight hour period.

Affirmed in part; vacated in part; and remanded.

■ BRODERICK, C.J., and DUGGAN and CONBOY, JJ, concurred; DALIANIS, J., concurred specially.

NOTES

In 1988, the New Jersey Supreme Court held that a custodial parent may move with the children of the marriage to another state as long as the move does not interfere with the best interests of the children or the visitation rights of the non-custodial parent. *See* Holder v. Polanski, 544 A.2d 852 (N.J. 1988). The decision modified previous court rulings, which held that prior to relocating to another state, the custodial parent had to demonstrate that there was a real advantage to the parent from the move. Usually, this was an effective bar to relocation. In 1996, the California Supreme Court ruled that relocation is similar to any other modification of custody or visitation. The custodial parent has a presumptive right to relocate with the children, and the parent whose visitation rights would be adversely affected has the burden of proving that the relocation would be a significant change of circumstance that would not be in the best interest of the children. *See* Burgess v. Burgess, 913 P.2d 473 (Cal. 1996). *See also* CAL. FAM. CODE § 7501 (specifying that a parent with custody of a child has a right to relocate with the child unless the relocation would prejudice the rights or welfare of the child). New York adopted a balancing test that permits a court to look at factors such as impact of the move on the child, the good faith of both parents, and the existence of a schedule that will allow the child to continue a relationship with the non-custodial parent. *See* Tropea v. Tropea, 642 N.Y.S.2d 575 (1996). While the New York approach fails to create a presumption in favor of the custodial parent to act in the best interest of the child, it has adopted a best interest approach that does favor relocation. The American Law Institute takes the position that relocation by the custodial parent should be permitted as part of the modern trend to permit each party to bid each other farewell. But some states continue to disfavor relocation by the custodial parent. *See, e.g.,* Brown v. Brown, 621 N.W.2d 70 (Neb. 2000) (finding that the custodial parent has the burden of proving that the relocation is in the best interest of the child).

There is extensive commentary on the various state approaches toward relocation. *See, e.g.*, Stanley W. Abraham, Note, *Keeping Kids First: Trial Court Discretion and the Best Interest of the Child in Light of* D'Amato, 68 ME. L. REV. 347 (2016); Patrick Parkinson & Judy Cashmore, *When Mothers Stay: Adjusting to Loss After Relocation Disputes*, 43 FAM. L. Q. 65 (2013); Philip M. Stahl, *Emerging Issues in Relocation* Cases, 25 J. AM. ACAD. MATRIM. LAW. 425 (2013); Brian S. Kennedy, *Moving Away From Certainty: Using Mediation to Avoid Unpredictable Outcomes in Relocation Disputes Involving Joint Physical Custody*, 53 B.C. L. REV. 265 (2012); Ruth Savronsky, *The Relocation Dilemma: In Search of "Best Interests"*, 75 ALB. L. REV. 1075 (2012); Maryl Sattler, *The Problem of Parental Relocation: Closing the Loophole in the Law of International Child Abduction*, 67 WASH. & LEE L. REV. 1709 (2010).

E. ABDUCTION OF CHILDREN

UNIFORM CHILD ABDUCTION PREVENTION ACT

9 U.L.A. Pt. IA 41 et seq. (Supp. 2010)

§ 4. Actions for Abduction Prevention Measures

(a) A court on its own motion may order abduction prevention measures in a child custody proceeding if the court finds that the evidence establishes a credible risk of abduction of the child.

(b) A party to a child-custody determination or another individual or entity having a right under the law of this state or any other state to seek a child-custody determination for the child may file a petition seeking abduction prevention measures to protect the child under this [act].

(c) A prosecutor or public authority designated under [insert citation to Section 315 of the Uniform Child Custody Jurisdiction and Enforcement Act or applicable law of this state] may seek a warrant to take physical custody of a child under Section 9 or other appropriate prevention measures.

UNIFORM CHILD CUSTODY JURISDICTION AND ENFORCEMENT ACT

9 U.L.A. Pt. IA et seq. (1999)

§ 311. Warrant to Take Physical Custody of Child

(a) Upon the filing of a petition seeking enforcement of a child-custody determination, the petitioner may file a verified application for the issuance of a warrant to take physical custody of the child if the child is immediately likely to suffer serious physical harm or to be removed from this State.

(b) If the court, upon the testimony of the petitioner or other witness finds that the child is imminently likely to suffer serious physical harm or be removed from this State, it may issue a warrant to take physical custody of the child. The petition must be heard on the next judicial day after the warrant is executed unless that date is impossible. In that event, the court shall hold the hearing on the first judicial day possible. The application for the warrant must include the statements required by Section 308(b).

(c) A warrant to take physical custody of a child must:

(1) recite the facts upon which a conclusion of imminent serious physical harm or removal from the jurisdiction is based;

(2) direct law enforcement officers to take physical custody of the child immediately; and

(3) provide for the placement of the child pending final relief.

(d) The respondent must be served with the petition, warrant, and order immediately after the child is taken into physical custody.

(e) A warrant to take physical custody of a child is enforceable throughout this State. If the court finds on the basis of the testimony of the petitioner or other witness that a less intrusive remedy is not effective, it may authorize law enforcement officers to enter private property to take physical custody of the child. If required by exigent circumstances of the case, the court may authorize law enforcement officers to make a forcible entry at any hour.

(f) The court may impose conditions upon placement of a child to ensure the appearance of the child and the child's custodian.

INTERNATIONAL PARENTAL KIDNAPPING CRIME ACT OF 1993

Pub. L. No. 103–173, 107 Stat. (1998)

18 U.S.C. § 1204

(a) Whoever removes a child from the United States, or attempts to do so, or retains a child (who has been in the United States) outside the United States with intent to obstruct the lawful exercise of parental rights shall be fined under this title or imprisoned not more than 3 years, or both.

(b) As used in this section—

(1) the term "child" means a person who has not attained the age of 16 years; and

(2) the term "parental rights", with respect to a child, means the right to physical custody of the child—

(A) whether joint or sole (and includes visiting rights); and

(B) whether arising by operation of law, court order, or legally binding agreements of the parties.

(c) It shall be an affirmative defense under this section that—

(1) he defendant acted within the provisions of a valid court order granting the defendant legal custody or visitation rights and that the order was obtained pursuant to the Uniform Child Custody Jurisdiction Act or the Uniform Child Custody Jurisdiction and Enforcement Act and was in effect at the time of the offense;

(2) the defendant was fleeing an incidence or pattern of domestic violence; or

(3) the defendant had physical custody of the child pursuant to a court order granting legal custody or visitation rights and failed to return the child as a result of circumstances beyond the defendant's control, and the defendant notified or made reasonable attempts to notify the other parent or lawful custodian of the child of such circumstances within 24 hours after the visitation period had expired and returned the child as soon as possible.

(d) This section does not detract from the Hague Convention on the Civil Aspects of International Parental Child Abduction, done at the Hague on October 25, 1980.

Delvoye v. Lee

United States Court of Appeals, Third Circuit, 2003
329 F.3d 330

■ SCHWARZER, SENIOR DISTRICT JUDGE.

This is an appeal from an order of the district court denying Wim Delvoye's petition to return Baby S to Belgium under the *Hague Convention on the Civil Aspects of International Child Abduction,* Oct. 25, 1980; T.I.A.S. No. 11670, 19 I.L.M. 1501 (the "Convention"). The district court found and concluded that petitioner had failed to meet his burden of proving that Baby S was an habitual resident of Belgium and thus was wrongfully removed from that country. We affirm.

Petitioner and respondent met in New York early in 2000. Petitioner resided in Belgium but made several trips to visit respondent. On his visits to New York, a romantic relationship developed between them. In August 2000, respondent moved into petitioner's New York apartment. While continuing to live in Belgium, petitioner spent about a quarter of his time in New York. In September 2000, respondent learned that she was pregnant with petitioner's child. Respondent began prenatal care in New York, but because petitioner refused to pay the cost of delivery of the baby in the United States and Belgium offered free medical services, respondent agreed to have the baby in Belgium. In November 2000, she traveled to Belgium on a three-month tourist visa, bringing along only one or two suitcases. She left the rest of her belongings, including her non-maternity clothes, in the New York apartment. While in Belgium respondent lived out of her suitcases. When her visa expired she did not extend it. The baby was born on May 14, 2001. By then the relationship between the parties had deteriorated. After initially resisting, petitioner signed the consent form that enabled respondent to get an American passport for Baby S and agreed to respondent's return to the United States with Baby S in July 2001. Over the next two months, petitioner made several trips to the United States and the parties made several attempts to reconcile. When those efforts failed, petitioner filed this petition. Following an evidentiary hearing, the district court denied the petition. This appeal followed. Because the order is a final disposition of the petition, we have jurisdiction under 28 U.S.C. § 1291.

Article 3 of the Convention provides in relevant part:

> The removal . . . of a child is to be considered wrongful where— a) it is in breach of rights of custody attributed to a person . . . either jointly or alone, under the law of the State in which the child was *habitually resident* immediately before the removal. . . . (Emphasis added.)

The determination of a person's habitual residence is a mixed question of fact and law. We review the district court's findings of historical and narrative facts for clear error, but exercise plenary review over the court's application of legal precepts to the facts. Feder v. Evans-Feder, 63 F.3d 217, 222 n. 9 (3d Cir.1995); *see also* Mozes v. Mozes, 239 F.3d 1067, 1073 (9th Cir.2001).

The issue before us is whether Baby S was "habitually resident" in Belgium at the time of his removal to the United States. In *Feder,* we defined the relevant concept:

> [A] child's habitual residence is the place where he . . . has been physically present for an amount of time sufficient for acclimatization and which has a "degree of settled purpose" from the child's perspective. . . . [A] determination of whether any particular place satisfies this standard must focus on the child and consists of an analysis of the child's circumstances in that place and the parents' present, shared intentions regarding their child's presence there.

63 F.3d at 224.

The district court held that petitioner had failed to meet his burden of proving that Baby S was an habitual resident of Belgium. It reasoned that a two-month-old infant, who is still nursing, has not been present long enough to have an acclimatization apart from his parents. This case then presents the unique question of whether and when a very young infant acquires an habitual residence. It differs from the run of decisions under the Convention where the child is assumed to have an habitual residence initially and the controversy is over a change of that residence. No decisions have squarely addressed the issue before us. The leading treatise on the Convention provides some general guidance:

> There is general agreement on a theoretical level that because of the factual basis of the concept there is no place for habitual residence of dependence. However, in practice it is often not possible to make a distinction between the habitual residence of a child and that of its custodian. Where a child is very young it would, under ordinary circumstances, be very difficult for him . . . to have the capability or intention to acquire a separate habitual residence.

Paul Beaumont & Peter McEleavy, *The Hague Convention on International Child Abduction* 91 (1999). An English court has said: "The habitual residence of the child is where it last had a settled home which was in essence where the matrimonial home was." Dickson v. Dickson, 1990 SCLR 692. And an Australian court has stated: "A young child cannot acquire habitual residence in isolation from those who care for him. While 'A' lived with both parents, he shared their common habitual residence or lack of it." Re F (1991) 1 F.L.R. 548, 551.[2]

Where a matrimonial home exists, i.e., where both parents share a settled intent to reside, determining the habitual residence of an infant presents no particular problem, it simply calls for application of the analysis under the Convention with which courts have become familiar. Where the parents' relationship has broken down, however, as in this case, the character of the problem changes. Of course, the mere fact that conflict has developed between the parents does not *ipso facto* disestablish a child's habitual residence, once it has come into existence. But where the conflict is contemporaneous with the birth of the child, no habitual residence may ever come into existence.

That is not to say that the infant's habitual residence automatically becomes that of his mother. In Nunez-Escudero v. Tice-Menley, 58 F.3d 374 (8th Cir.1995), Nunez-Escudero and Tice-Menley married in Mexico in August 1992. A child was born there in July 1993. In September, Tice-Menley left Mexico with her two-month-old infant and returned to the United States. Nunez-Escudero filed a petition under the Convention alleging that his son had been wrongfully removed. The district court denied the petition on the ground that return of the child would subject him to a grave risk of harm. The court of appeals reversed and remanded. The mother contended that the court should affirm, notwithstanding the erroneous grave risk of harm determination, on the ground that the infant was not an habitual resident of Mexico. The court rejected the

---

2 These cases assume that the parents had joint custody. This is true under Belgian law regardless of whether the parents are married. *See* H. Bocken and W. DeBondt, *Introduction to Belgian Law* 150 (cohabiting parents) (2001). But the situation is different where only one parent has custody rights. Thus, "where a child of [two years of age] [was] in the sole lawful custody of the mother, his situation with regard to habitual residence will necessarily be the same as hers." *In re J (C v. S)* [1990] 2 AC 562, 579.

argument and remanded for a determination of the child's habitual residence, stating.

> To say that the child's habitual residence derived from his mother would be inconsistent with the Convention, for it would reward an abducting parent and create an impermissible presumption that the child's habitual residence is where the mother happens to be.

58 F.3d at 379.

The instant case differs from *Nunez-Escudero.* Because the petitioner and respondent had married in Mexico and lived there together for nearly a year before the child was born, a basis existed for finding the child's habitual residence to be in Mexico. Here, in contrast, the district court found that respondent, at petitioner's urging, had traveled to Belgium to avoid the cost of the birth of the child and intended to live there only temporarily. She retained her ties to New York, not having taken her non-maternity clothes, holding only a three-month visa and living out of the two suitcases she brought with her. Thus, there is lacking the requisite "degree of common purpose" to habitually reside in Belgium. As explained in *Re Bates,*

> There must be a degree of settled purpose. . . . All that is necessary is that the purpose of living where one does has a sufficient degree of continuity to be properly described as settled.

No. CA 122–89, High Court of Justice, Family Div'l Ct. Royal Courts of Justice, United Kingdom (1989), quoted in Feder, 63 F.3d at 223.

Because petitioner and respondent lacked the "shared intentions regarding their child's presence [in Belgium]," Feder, 63 F.3d at 224, Baby S did not become an habitual resident there. Even if petitioner intended that he become an habitual resident, respondent evidenced no such intention. Addressing the status of a newborn child, one Scottish commentator said:

> [A] newborn child born in the country where his . . . parents have their habitual residence could normally be regarded as habitually resident in that country. Where a child is born while his . . . mother is temporarily present in a country other than that of her habitual residence it does seem, however, that the child will normally have no habitual residence until living in a country on a footing of some stability.

Dr. E.M. Clive, "The Concept of Habitual Residence," *The Juridical Review part 3,* 138, 146 (1997).

Based on the district court's factual findings, which have not been challenged, we conclude that petitioner failed to prove that Baby S was habitually resident in Belgium.

We affirm the district court's order.

NOTES

The United States ratified the Convention on April 29, 1988. On the same day, Congress enacted the International Child Abduction Remedies Act. By so doing, the United States sought to deter the international abduction of children aged sixteen or younger. In 2014 Professor Estin provided statistical data on international child abduction. She wrote:

> The Abduction Convention came into effect in the United States on July 1, 1988, following Congress's enactment of the International Child Abduction Remedies Act (ICARA). At that time, there were a total of ten Contracting States; there are now more than ninety. Under ICARA and the Convention, a party claiming that a child has been wrongfully removed to or retained in the United States from another Convention country may file an action in state or federal court seeking return of the child. Data from the Office of Children's Issues in the State Department (OCI) show 364 new reports of incoming parental child abductions involving 518 children were made in the United States in 2013, in addition to 702 reports of out-going abductions involving 1,004 children. Case closing statistics from OCI for 2013 show that, of the reported incoming child abduction cases resolved by judicial decision under the Convention, courts ordered the child's return in 104 cases, and denied return orders in fifty-seven cases.

Ann Laquer Estin, *The Hague Convention and the United States Supreme Court*, 48 FAM. L. Q. 235, 236 (2014). For additional commentary please *see* Erin M. Gallagher, Note, *A House is Not (Necessarily) a Home: A Discussion of the Common Law Approach to Habitual Residence*, 47 N.Y.U. J. INT'L L. & POL. 463 (2015); Tracy Jones, Recent Decision, *A Ne Exeat Right is a "Right of Custody" for the Purposes of the Hague Convention:* Abbott v. Abbott, 49 DUQ. L. REV. 523 (2011); Jennifer Costa, *If Japan Signs the Hague Convention on the Civil Aspects of International Child Abduction: Real Change or Political Maneuvering?*, 12 OR. REV. INT'L L. 369 (2010); Kevin O'Gorman and Efren C. Olivares, *The Hague Convention on the Civil Aspects of Child Abduction: An Update after Abbott*, 33 HOUS. J. INT'L L. 39 (2010).

Friedrich v. Friedrich

United States Court of Appeals, Sixth Circuit, 1996
78 F.3d 1060

■ BOGGS, CIRCUIT JUDGE.

For the second time, we address the application of the Hague Convention on the Civil Aspects of International Child Abduction ("the Convention") and its implementing legislation, the International Child Abduction Remedies Act ("the Act"), 42 U.S.C. §§ 11601–11610, to the life of Thomas Friedrich, now age six. We affirm the district court's order that Thomas was wrongfully removed from Germany and should be returned.

Thomas was born in Bad Aibling, Germany, to Jeana Friedrich, an American servicewoman stationed there, and her husband, Emanuel

Friedrich, a German citizen. When Thomas was two years old, his parents separated after an argument on July 27, 1991. Less than a week later, in the early morning of August 2, 1991, Mrs. Friedrich took Thomas from Germany to her family home in Ironton, Ohio, without informing Mr. Friedrich. Mr. Friedrich sought return of the child in German Family Court, obtaining an order awarding him custody on August 22. He then filed this action for the return of his son in the United States District Court for the Southern District of Ohio on September 23.

We first heard this case three years ago. Friedrich v. Friedrich, 983 F.2d 1396 (6th Cir.1993) ("*Friedrich I*"). At that time, we reversed the district court's denial of Mr. Friedrich's claim for the return of his son to Germany pursuant to the Convention. We outlined the relevant law on what was then an issue of first impression in the federal appellate courts, and remanded with instructions that the district court determine whether, as a matter of German law, Mr. Friedrich was exercising custody rights to Thomas at the time of removal. We also asked the district court to decide if Mrs. Friedrich could prove any of the four affirmative defenses provided by the Convention and the Act. Thomas, meanwhile, remained with his mother and his mother's parents in Ohio.

On remand, the district court allowed additional discovery and held a new hearing. The court eventually determined that, at the time of Thomas's removal on August 1, 1991, Mr. Friedrich was exercising custody rights to Thomas under German law, or would have been exercising such rights but for the removal. The court then held that Mrs. Friedrich had not established any of the affirmative defenses available to her under the Convention. The court ordered Mrs. Friedrich to return Thomas to Germany "forthwith," but later stayed the order, upon the posting of a bond by Mrs. Friedrich, pending the resolution of this appeal.[1]

Mrs. Friedrich's appeal raises two issues that are central to the young jurisprudence of the Hague Convention. First, what does it mean to "exercise" custody rights? Second, when can a court refuse to return a child who has been wrongfully removed from a country because return of the abducted child would result in a "grave" risk of harm?

In answering both these questions, we keep in mind two general principles inherent in the Convention and the Act, expressed in Friedrich I, and subsequently embraced by unanimous federal authority. First, a court in the abducted-to nation has jurisdiction to decide the merits of an abduction claim, but not the merits of the underlying custody dispute. Hague Convention, Article 19; 42 U.S.C.§ 11601(b)(4); Friedrich I, 983 F.2d at 1400; Rydder v. Rydder, 49 F.3d 369, 372 (8th Cir.1995); Feder v.

[1] The stay of the judge's order pending appeal, hotly contested below, is not now challenged by Mr. Friedrich. It may have been improvident. Staying the return of a child in an action under the Convention should hardly be a matter of course. The aim of the Convention is to secure prompt return of the child to the correct jurisdiction, and any unnecessary delay renders the subsequent return more difficult for the child, and subsequent adjudication more difficult for the foreign court.

Evans-Feder, 63 F.3d 217, 221 (3d Cir.1995); Journe v. Journe, 911 F. Supp. 43 (D.P.R.1995). Second, the Hague Convention is generally intended to restore the pre-abduction status quo and to deter parents from crossing borders in search of a more sympathetic court. Pub. Notice 957, 51 Fed.Reg. 10494, 10505 (1986); Friedrich I, 983 F.2d at 1400; Rydder, 49 F.3d at 372; Feder, 63 F.3d at 221; Wanninger v. Wanninger, 850 F. Supp. 78, 80 (D.Mass.1994).

The removal of a child from the country of its habitual residence is "wrongful" under the Hague Convention if a person in that country is, or would otherwise be, exercising custody rights to the child under that country's law at the moment of removal. Hague Convention, Article 3. The plaintiff in an action for return of the child has the burden of proving the exercise of custody rights by a preponderance of the evidence. 42 U.S.C. § 11603(e)(1)(A). We review the district court's findings of fact for clear error and review its conclusions about American, foreign, and international law de novo. See Fed.R.Civ.P. 44.1 (a district court's determination of foreign law should be reviewed as a ruling on a question of law)....

The district court held that a preponderance of the evidence in the record established that Mr. Friedrich was exercising custody rights over Thomas at the time of Thomas's removal. Mrs. Friedrich alleges that the district court improperly applied German law. Reviewing de novo, we find no error in the court's legal analysis. Custody rights "may arise in particular by operation of law or by reason of a judicial or administrative decision, or by reason of an agreement having legal effect under the law of the State." Hague Convention, Article 3. German law gives both parents equal de jure custody of the child, German Civil Code 1626(1), and, with a few exceptions, this de jure custody continues until a competent court says otherwise. See Currier v. Currier, 845 F. Supp. 916, 920 (D.N.H.1994) ("under German law both parents retain joint rights of custody until a decree has been entered limiting one parent's rights"); Wanninger, 850 F. Supp. at 78 (D.Mass.1994).

Mrs. Friedrich argues that Mr. Friedrich "terminated" his custody rights under German law because, during the argument on the evening of July 27, 1991, he placed Thomas's belongings and hers in the hallway outside of their apartment. The district court properly rejected the claim that these actions could end parental rights as a matter of German law. We agree. After examining the record, we are uncertain as to exactly what happened on the evening of July 27, but we do know that the events of that night were not a judicial abrogation of custody rights. Nor are we persuaded by Mrs. Friedrich's attempts to read the German Civil Code provisions stipulated to by the parties in such a way as to create the ability of one parent to terminate his or her custody rights extrajudicially.[2]

[2] Mrs. Friedrich cites German Civil Code § 1629, which says that a parent who exercises parental care alone can also represent the child in legal matters alone. Obviously, the ability of

Mrs. Friedrich also argues that, even if Mr. Friedrich had custody rights under German law, he was not exercising those custody rights as contemplated by the Hague Convention. She argues that, since custody rights include the care for the person and property of the child, Mr. Friedrich was not exercising custody rights because he was not paying for or taking care of the child during the brief period of separation in Germany.

The Hague Convention does not define "exercise." As judges in a common law country, we can easily imagine doing so ourselves. One might look to the law of the foreign country to determine if custody rights existed de jure, and then develop a test under the general principles of the Hague Convention to determine what activities—financial support, visitation—constitute sufficient exercise of de jure rights. The question in our immediate case would then be: "was Mr. Friedrich's single visit with Thomas and plans for future visits with Thomas sufficient exercise of custodial rights for us to justify calling the removal of Thomas wrongful?" One might even approach a distinction between the exercise of "custody" rights and the exercise of "access" or "visitation" rights.[3] If Mr. Friedrich, who has de jure custody, was not exercising sufficient de facto custody, Thomas's removal would not be wrongful.

We think it unwise to attempt any such project. Enforcement of the Convention should not to be made dependent on the creation of a common law definition of "exercise." The only acceptable solution, in the absence of a ruling from a court in the country of habitual residence, is to liberally find "exercise" whenever a parent with de jure custody rights keeps, or seeks to keep, any sort of regular contact with his or her child.

We see three reasons for this broad definition of "exercise." First, American courts are not well suited to determine the consequences of parental behavior under the law of a foreign country. It is fairly easy for the courts of one country to determine whether a person has custody rights under the law of another country. It is also quite possible for a court to determine if an order by a foreign court awards someone "custody" rights, as opposed to rights of "access."[4] Far more difficult is

---

one parent to "represent" the child does not imply that the other parent has no custody rights. Mrs. Friedrich also cites German Civil Code § 1631, which says that the Family Court, if petitioned, can assist the parents in providing parental care. We have no idea how this provision, which is essentially no more than a grant of jurisdiction to appoint and direct a family services officer, can support Mrs. Friedrich's claim that "a German parent can certainly relinquish custody or parental rights absent a judicial determination." Defendants-Appellants' Brief at 15.

[3] Article 21 of the Hague Convention instructs signatory countries to protect the "rights of access" of non-custodial parents to their children. Courts have yet to address the question whether Article 21 implies that a custodial parent can remove a child from its country of habitual residence without the permission of a parent whose rights that country's courts have expressly limited to "visitation." See infra n.

[4] For a particularly difficult situation, ably resolved, see David S. v. Zamira, 151 Misc.2d 630, 574 N.Y.S.2d 429 (Fam.Ct.1991), aff'd In re Schneir, 17 F.L.R. 1237 (N.Y.App.Div.2d Dep't). The court here held that an order giving the non-custodial parent visitation rights and restricting the custodial parent from leaving the country constitutes an order granting "custodial" rights to both parents under the Hague Convention.

the task of deciding, prior to a ruling by a court in the abducted-from country, if a parent's custody rights should be ignored because he or she was not acting sufficiently like a custodial parent. A foreign court, if at all possible, should refrain from making such policy-oriented decisions concerning the application of German law to a child whose habitual residence is, or was, Germany.

Second, an American decision about the adequacy of one parent's exercise of custody rights is dangerously close to forbidden territory: the merits of the custody dispute. The German court in this case is perfectly capable of taking into account Mr. Friedrich's behavior during the August 1991 separation, and the German court presumably will tailor its custody order accordingly. A decision by an American court to deny return to Germany because Mr. Friedrich did not show sufficient attention or concern for Thomas's welfare would preclude the German court from addressing these issuesCand the German court may well resolve them differently.

Third, the confusing dynamics of quarrels and informal separations make it difficult to assess adequately the acts and motivations of a parent. An occasional visit may be all that is available to someone left, by the vagaries of marital discord, temporarily without the child. Often the child may be avoided, not out of a desire to relinquish custody, but out of anger, pride, embarrassment, or fear, vis a vis the other parent.[5] Reading too much into a parent's behavior during these difficult times could be inaccurate and unfair. Although there may be situations when a long period of unexplainable neglect of the child could constitute non-exercise of otherwise valid custody rights under the Convention, as a general rule, any attempt to maintain a somewhat regular relationship with the child should constitute "exercise." This rule leaves the full resolution of custody issues, as the Convention and common sense indicate, to the courts of the country of habitual residence.

We are well aware that our approach requires a parent, in the event of a separation or custody dispute, to seek permission from the other parent or from the courts before taking a child out of the country of its habitual residence. Any other approach allows a parent to pick a "home court" for the custody dispute ex parte, defeating a primary purpose of the Convention. We believe that, where the reason for removal is legitimate, it will not usually be difficult to obtain approval from either the other parent or a foreign court. Furthermore, as the case for removal of the child in the custody of one parent becomes more compelling, approval (at least the approval of a foreign court) should become easier to secure.

---

[5] When Mrs. Friedrich took Thomas and her belongings from the family apartment on the morning of July 28, she was accompanied by some friends from work: soldiers of the United States Army. Mr. Friedrich testified that he was "intimidated" by the presence of the soldiers, and discouraged from making a stronger objection to the removal of his child.

Mrs. Friedrich argues that our approach cannot adequately cope with emergency situations that require the child and parent to leave the country. In her case, for example, Mrs. Friedrich claims that removal of Thomas to Ohio was necessary because she could no longer afford to have the child stay at the army base, and Mr. Friedrich refused to provide shelter. Examining the record, we seriously doubt that Mr. Friedrich would have refused to lodge Thomas at his expense in Germany. In any event, even if an emergency forces a parent to take a child to a foreign country, any such emergency cannot excuse the parent from returning the child to the jurisdiction once return of the child becomes safe. Nor can an emergency justify a parent's refusal to submit the child to the authority of the foreign court for resolution of custody matters, including the question of the appropriate temporary residence of the child. See Viragh v. Foldes, 415 Mass. 96, 612 N.E.2d 241 (1993) (child removed to America by one parent without notification to other parent may remain in America in light of decision by Hungarian court in parallel proceeding that best interests of the child require exercise of sole custody by parent in America).

We therefore hold that, if a person has valid custody rights to a child under the law of the country of the child's habitual residence, that person cannot fail to "exercise" those custody rights under the Hague Convention short of acts that constitute clear and unequivocal abandonment of the child.[6] Once it determines that the parent exercised custody rights in any manner, the court should stop—completely avoiding the question whether the parent exercised the custody rights well or badly. These matters go to the merits of the custody dispute and are, therefore, beyond the subject matter jurisdiction of the federal courts. 42 U.S.C. § 11601(b)(4).

In this case, German law gave Mr. Friedrich custody rights to Thomas. The facts before us clearly indicate that he attempted to exercise these rights during the separation from his wife. Mr. and Mrs. Friedrich argued during the evening of July 27, 1991, and separated on the morning of July 28. Mrs. Friedrich left with her belongings and Thomas. She stayed on the army base with the child for four days. Mr. Friedrich telephoned Mrs. Friedrich on July 29 to arrange a visit with Thomas, and spent the afternoon of that day with his son. Mr. and Mrs. Friedrich met on August 1 to talk about Thomas and their separation. The parties dispute the upshot of this conversation. Mrs. Friedrich says that Mr. Friedrich expressed a general willingness that Thomas move to America with his mother. Mr. Friedrich denies this. It is clear, however, that the parties did agree to immediate visitations of Thomas by Mr. Friedrich,

[6] The situation would be different if the country of habitual residence had a legal rule regarding the exercise of custody rights clearly tied to the Hague concept of international removal. If, for example, Germany had a law stating that, for the purposes of the Convention, mere visitation without financial support during a period of informal separation does not constitute the "exercise" of custody rights, we would, of course, be bound to apply that law in this case.

scheduling the first such visit for August 3. Shortly after midnight on August 2, Mrs. Friedrich took her son and, without informing her husband,[7] left for America by airplane.

Because Mr. Friedrich had custody rights to Thomas as a matter of German law, and did not clearly abandon those rights prior to August 1, the removal of Thomas without his consent was wrongful under the Convention, regardless of any other considerations about Mr. Friedrich's behavior during the family's separation in Germany.

Once a plaintiff establishes that removal was wrongful, the child must be returned unless the defendant can establish one of four defenses. Two of these defenses can be established by a preponderance of the evidence, 42 U.S.C. § 11603(e)(2)(B): the proceeding was commenced more than one year after the removal of the child and the child has become settled in his or her new environment, Hague Convention, Article 12; or, the person seeking return of the child consented to or subsequently acquiesced in the removal or retention, Hague Convention, Article 13a. The other two defenses must be shown by clear and convincing evidence, 42 U.S.C. § 11603(e)(2)(A): there is a grave risk that the return of the child would expose it to physical or psychological harm, Hague Convention, Article 13b; or, the return of the child "would not be permitted by the fundamental principles of the requested State relating to the protection of human rights and fundamental freedoms," Hague Convention, Article 20.[8]

All four of these exceptions are "narrow," 42 U.S.C. § 11601(a)(4). They are not a basis for avoiding return of a child merely because an American court believes it can better or more quickly resolve a dispute. See Rydder, 49 F.3d at 372 (citing Friedrich I, 983 F.2d at 1400). In fact, a federal court retains, and should use when appropriate, the discretion to return a child, despite the existence of a defense, if return would further the aims of the Convention. Feder, 63 F.3d at 226 (citing Pub. Notice 957, 51 Fed.Reg. 10494, 10509 (1986)).

Mrs. Friedrich alleges that she proved by clear and convincing evidence in the proceedings below that the return of Thomas to Germany would cause him grave psychological harm. Mrs. Friedrich testified that Thomas has grown attached to family and friends in Ohio. She also hired an expert psychologist who testified that returning Thomas to Germany would be traumatic and difficult for the child, who was currently happy and healthy in America with his mother. [Thomas] definitely would experience the loss of his mother . . . if he were to be removed to Germany. Than that would be a considerable loss. And there then would be the

---

[7] Q. You didn't call your husband, Mrs. Friedrich, because you didn't want him to know you were leaving; isn't that the reason? A. Yes it is. Transcript of October 16, 1991, Proceedings at 36.

[8] The situation changes somewhat when the child is older. The Hague Convention allows a court in the abducted-to country to "refuse to order the return of the child if it finds that the child objects to being returned and has attained an age and degree of maturity at which it is appropriate to take account of its views." Hague Convention, Article 13.

probabilities of anger both towards his mother, who it might appear that she has abandoned him [sic], and towards the father for creating that abandonment. [These feelings] could be plenty enough springboard for other developmental or emotional restrictions which could include nightmares, antisocial behavior, a whole host of anxious-type behavior. Blaske Deposition at 28–29.

If we are to take the international obligations of American courts with any degree of seriousness, the exception to the Hague Convention for grave harm to the child requires far more than the evidence that Mrs. Friedrich provides. Mrs. Friedrich alleges nothing more than adjustment problems that would attend the relocation of most children. There is no allegation that Mr. Friedrich has ever abused Thomas. The district court found that the home that Mr. Friedrich has prepared for Thomas in Germany appears adequate to the needs of any young child. The father does not work long hours, and the child's German grandmother is ready to care for the child when the father cannot. There is nothing in the record to indicate that life in Germany would result in any permanent harm or unhappiness.

Furthermore, even if the home of Mr. Friedrich were a grim place to raise a child in comparison to the pretty, peaceful streets of Ironton, Ohio, that fact would be irrelevant to a federal court's obligation under the Convention. We are not to debate the relevant virtues of Batman and Max und Moritz, Wheaties and Milchreis. The exception for grave harm to the child is not license for a court in the abducted-to country to speculate on where the child would be happiest. That decision is a custody matter, and reserved to the court in the country of habitual residence.

Mrs. Friedrich advocates a wide interpretation of the grave risk of harm exception that would reward her for violating the Convention. A removing parent must not be allowed to abduct a child and then—when brought to court—complain that the child has grown used to the surroundings to which they were abducted.[9] Under the logic of the Convention, it is the abduction that causes the pangs of subsequent return. The disruption of the usual sense of attachment that arises during most long stays in a single place with a single parent should not be a "grave" risk of harm for the purposes of the Convention.

In thinking about these problems, we acknowledge that courts in the abducted-from country are as ready and able as we are to protect children. If return to a country, or to the custody of a parent in that country, is dangerous, we can expect that country's courts to respond accordingly. Cf. Nunez-Escudero v. Tice-Menley, 58 F.3d 374, 377 (8th Cir.1995) (if parent in Mexico is abusive, infant returned to Mexico for custody determination can be institutionalized during pendency of

[9] We forgo the temptation to compare this behavior to the standard definition of "chutzpah." See A. Kozinski & E. Volokh, Lawsuit, Shmawsuit, 103 Yale L.J. 463, 467 (1993).

custody proceedings). And if Germany really is a poor place for young Thomas to grow up, as Mrs. Friedrich contends, we can expect the German courts to recognize that and award her custody in America. When we trust the court system in the abducted-from country, the vast majority of claims of harm-those that do not rise to the level of gravity required by the Convention-evaporate.

The international precedent available supports our restrictive reading of the grave harm exception. In *Thomson v. Thomson*, 119 D.L.R.4th 253 (Can.1994), the Supreme Court of Canada held that the exception applies only to harm "that also amounts to an intolerable situation." *Id.* at 286. The Court of Appeal of the United Kingdom has held that the harm required is "something greater than would normally be expected on taking a child away from one parent and passing him to another." *In re A.,* 1 F.L.R. 365, 372 (Eng.C.A.1988). And other circuit courts in America have followed this reasoning in cases decided since Friedrich I. See Nunez-Escudero, 58 F.3d at 377 (citing *Thomson,* 119 D.L.R.4th at 286, and *In re A.*, 1 F.L.R. at 372); Rydder, 49 F.3d at 373 (affirming district court order for return of child over abducting parent's objection that return would cause grave harm). Finally, we are instructed by the following observation by the United States Department of State concerning the grave risk of harm exception. This provision was not intended to be used by defendants as a vehicle to litigate (or relitigate) the child's best interests. Only evidence directly establishing the existence of a grave risk that would expose the child to physical or emotional harm or otherwise place the child in an intolerable situation is material to the court's determination. The person opposing the child's return must show that the risk to the child is grave, not merely serious. A review of deliberations on the Convention reveals that "intolerable situation" was not intended to encompass return to a home where money is in short supply, or where educational or other opportunities are more limited than in the requested State. An example of an "intolerable situation" is one in which a custodial parent sexually abuses the child. If the other parent removes or retains the child to safeguard it against further victimization, and the abusive parent then petitions for the child's return under the Convention, the court may deny the petition. Such action would protect the child from being returned to an "intolerable situation" and subjected to a grave risk of psychological harm. Public Notice 957, 51 FR 10494, 10510 (March 26, 1986) (emphasis added).

For all of these reasons, we hold that the district court did not err by holding that "[t]he record in the instant case does not demonstrate by clear and convincing evidence that Thomas will be exposed to a grave risk of harm." Although it is not necessary to resolve the present appeal, we believe that a grave risk of harm for the purposes of the Convention can exist in only two situations. First, there is a grave risk of harm when return of the child puts the child in imminent danger prior to the resolution of the custody dispute-e.g., returning the child to a zone of war, famine, or disease. Second, there is a grave risk of harm in cases of serious abuse or neglect, or extraordinary emotional dependence, when the court in the country of habitual residence, for whatever reason, may be incapable or unwilling to give the child adequate protection. Psychological evidence of the sort Mrs. Friedrich introduced in the proceeding below is only relevant if it helps prove the existence of one of these two situations.[10]

Mrs. Friedrich also claims that the district court erred in ordering Thomas's return because Mrs. Friedrich proved by a preponderance of the evidence that Mr. Friedrich (i) consented to, and (ii) subsequently acquiesced in, the removal of Thomas to America.[11]

Mrs. Friedrich bases her claim of consent to removal on statements that she claims Mr. Friedrich made to her during their separation. Mr. Friedrich flatly denies that he made these statements. The district court was faced with a choice as to whom it found more believable in a factual dispute. There is nothing in the record to suggest that the court's decision to believe Mr. Friedrich, and hold that he "did not exhibit an intention or a willingness to terminate his parental rights," was clearly erroneous. In fact, Mr. Friedrich's testimony is strongly supported by the circumstances of the removal of Thomas-most notably the fact that Mrs. Friedrich did not inform Mr. Friedrich that she was departing. *Supra* n. 7. The deliberately secretive nature of her actions is extremely strong evidence that Mr. Friedrich would not have consented to the removal of Thomas. For these reasons, we hold that the district court did not abuse its discretion in finding that Mrs. Friedrich took Thomas to America without Mr. Friedrich's consent.

Mrs. Friedrich bases her claim of subsequent acquiescence on a statement made by Mr. Friedrich to one of her commanding officers, Captain Michael Farley, at a cocktail party on the military base after Mrs. Friedrich had left with Thomas. Captain Farley, who cannot date the conversation exactly, testified that: During the conversation, Mr. Friedrich indicated that he was not seeking custody of the child, because he didn't have the means to take care of the child. Farley Deposition at 13. Mr. Friedrich denies that he made this statement. The district court made no specific finding regarding this fact.

We believe that the statement to Captain Farley, even if it was made, is insufficient evidence of subsequent acquiescence. Subsequent acquiescence requires more than an isolated statement to a third-party. Each of the words and actions of a parent during the separation are not

---

[10] The only other circuit addressing the issue had its own doubts about whether a psychological report concerning the difficulty that a child would face when separated from the abducting parent is ever relevant to a Hague Convention action. Nunez-Escudero, 58 F.3d at 378 (such reports are not per se irrelevant, but they are rarely dispositive).

[11] Article 13a provides a defense to an action for return if the petitioner "consented to or subsequently acquiesced in the removal or retention" of the child. The Convention does not define consent or acquiescence in any more definite manner, and there is no statement to guide us in the text or legislative history of the Act.

to be scrutinized for a possible waiver of custody rights. See Wanninger, 850 F. Supp. at 81–82 (refusing to construe father's personal letters to wife and priest as sufficient evidence of acquiescence where father consistently attempted to keep in contact with child). Although we must decide the matter without guidance from previous appellate court decisions, we believe that acquiescence under the Convention requires either: an act or statement with the requisite formality, such as testimony in a judicial proceeding;[12] a convincing written renunciation of rights;[13] or a consistent attitude of acquiescence over a significant period of time.

By August 22, 1991, twenty-one days after the abduction, Mr. Friedrich had secured a German court order awarding him custody of Thomas. He has resolutely sought custody of his son since that time. It is by these acts, not his casual statements to third parties, that we will determine whether or not he acquiesced to the retention of his son in America. Since Mrs. Friedrich has not introduced evidence of a formal renunciation or a consistent attitude of acquiescence over a significant period of time, the judgment of the district court on this matter was not erroneous.

The district court's order that Thomas be immediately returned to Germany is AFFIRMED, and the district court's stay of that order pending appeal is VACATED. Because Thomas's return to Germany is already long-overdue, we order, pursuant to Fed.R.App.P. 41(a), that our mandate issue forthwith.

---

[12] In Journe v. Journe, 911 F. Supp. 43 (D.P.R.1995), a French father instituted custody proceedings in France after the mother took the children to Puerto Rico. The mother returned to France, presumably without the children, to participate in the proceedings. The father voluntarily dismissed the French custody proceedings, but continued to pursue Hague Convention remedies The district court held that the father had waived his rights to have a French court determine custody issues by virtue of the voluntary dismissal of his French case. Id. at 48. The court reached that decision because of "its equitable powers," not because the dismissal constituted "acquiescence" for the purposes of the Convention.

[13] A hastily-drafted and soon-rued written agreement was found insufficient indication of consent in Currier v. Currier, 845 F. Supp. 916 (D.N.H.1994).

CHAPTER IX

PARENTAL RIGHTS TERMINATION AND ADOPTION

A. SEVERING PARENTAL RIGHTS INVOLUNTARILY

The United States Supreme Court has consistently upheld the fundamental right of a parent to the care, custody, and control of his or her child. *See, e.g.*, Troxel v. Granville, 530 U.S. 57, 65–66 (2000); Pierce v. Society of the Sisters of the Holy Names of Jesus and Mary, 268 U.S. 534–535 (1925); Meyer v. Nebraska, 262 U.S. 390, 400 (1923). In the *Santosky* decision the Court holds that procedural due process requires states to apply a standard of proof equal or greater than clear and convincing evidence when involuntarily terminating parental rights. Santosky v. Kramer, 455 U.S. 745, 747–748 (1982). In previous chapters of this casebook we have read cases when courts were willing to overcome the fundamental rights of parents, such as when there are extraordinary circumstances, Bennett v. Jeffreys, 356 N.E.2d 277 (N.Y. 1976), or emotional abandonment, Guardianship of Phillip B., 139 Cal.App.3d 407 (1983). References have been made to de facto parenthood as a means of rebutting the parental presumption, *see, e.g., In re* Matter of the Custody of B. M.H., 315 P.3d 470 (Wash. 2013). So too, there are instances when a parent voluntarily surrenders a child, often prompted to do so because of poverty, youth, or illness. And then there are instances when a child is involuntarily removed from a parent because of parental neglect, abuse or abandonment. There are illustrations of these in this chapter.

But the dissent in *Santosky* describes the compelling interests of the children involved in termination of parental rights: "On the other side of the termination proceeding are the often countervailing interests of the child." Santosky v. Kramer, 455 U.S. 745, 788 (1982). Similar concern for the due process rights of children during custody proceedings was raised by Justice Stevens in *Troxel.* He wrote that parents' rights are not "absolute, but rather are limited by the existence of an actual, developed relationship with a child, and are tied to the presence or absence of some embodiment of family." Troxel v. Granville, 120 S.Ct. 2054, 2072 (2000). Moreover, Justice Stevens believed that children's liberty interests in "preserving established familial or family-like bonds" should be recognized and considered alongside the interests of the parents. *Id.* Likewise, Justice Stevens would surely wish a child to have a permanent home, be free of physical and emotional abuse, and be supported by a community, a family. Admittedly, there are instances in which the due process rights of minors have been recognized by the Court, the most notable of which is *In re* Gault, 387 U.S. 1 (1967) (due process in criminal proceedings). But, at present, the majority in *Santosky* weighs the rights of the parent as presumptively inclusive of any rights possessed by the child, the effect of which has an impact on the child.

And there is a third party in termination proceedings, the state acting as parent patriae, or parent of the country. In this context the state is tasked with safeguarding the parents' fundamental right to raise a child but mindful of what is in the best interest of the child. Government has increasingly become more aggressive in defining abuse, neglect, sexual exploitation and corresponding defenses such as parental discipline or religion-based faith healing. Internet and ease of national and international travel have challenged states to define, prosecute, and often terminate the rights of parents in the context of harm done to children. *See generally* MICHAEL T. FLANNERY AND RAYMOND C. O'BRIEN, THE SEXUAL EXPLOITATION OF CHILDREN (2016).

The following decisions, statutes, and materials should be considered in the context of these due process rights of parents and children, and the overall responsibility of the state to protect the interests of both.

1. CONSTITUTIONAL DIMENSIONS

A. BURDEN OF PROOF FOR TERMINATION OF PARENTAL RIGHTS

Santosky v. Kramer

Supreme Court of the United States, 1982
455 U.S. 745

■ JUSTICE BLACKMUN delivered the opinion of the Court.

Under New York law, the State may terminate, over parental objection, the rights of parents in their natural child upon a finding that the child is "permanently neglected." N.Y. Soc. Serv. Law §§ 384–b.4.(d), 384–b.7.(a). The New York Family Court Act § 622 requires that only a "fair preponderance of the evidence" support that finding. Thus, in New York, the factual certainty required to extinguish the parent-child relationship is no greater than that necessary to award money damages in an ordinary civil action. Today we hold that the Due Process Clause of the Fourteenth Amendment demands more than this. Before a State may sever completely and irrevocably the rights of parents in their natural child, due process requires that the State support its allegations by at least clear and convincing evidence.

New York authorizes its officials to remove a child temporarily from his or her home if the child appears "neglected," within the meaning of Art. 10 of the Family Court Act. Once removed, a child under the age of 18 customarily is placed "in the care of an authorized agency," usually a state institution or a foster home. At that point, "the state's first obligation is to help the family with services to . . . reunite it. . . ." But if convinced that "positive, nurturing parent-child relationships no longer exist," the State may initiate "permanent neglect" proceedings to free the child for adoption.

The State bifurcates its permanent neglect proceeding into "factfinding" and "dispositional" hearings. Fam.Ct.Act §§ 622, 623. At the factfinding stage, the State must prove that the child has been "permanently neglected," as defined by Fam.Ct.Act §§ 614.1.(a)–(d) and Soc.Serv.Law § 384–b.7.(a). The Family Court judge then determines at a subsequent dispositional hearing what placement would serve the child's best interests. At the factfinding hearing, the State must establish, among other things, that for more than a year after the child entered state custody, the agency "made diligent efforts to encourage and strengthen the parental relationship." Fam.Ct.Act §§ 614.1.(c), 611. The State must further prove that during that same period, the child's natural parents failed "substantially and continuously or repeatedly to maintain contact with or plan for the future of the child although physically and financially able to do so." § 614.1.(d). Should the State support its allegations by "a fair preponderance of the evidence," § 622, the child may be declared permanently neglected. § 611. That declaration empowers the Family Court judge to terminate permanently the natural parents' rights in the child. §§ 631(c), 634. Termination denies the natural parents physical custody, as well as the rights ever to visit, communicate with, or regain custody of the child.

New York's permanent neglect statute provides natural parents with certain procedural protections.[2] But New York permits its officials to establish "permanent neglect" with less proof than most States require. Thirty-three States, the District of Columbia, and the Virgin Islands currently specify a higher standard of proof, in parental rights termination proceedings, than a "fair preponderance of the evidence." . . . The question here is whether New York's "fair preponderance of the evidence" standard is constitutionally sufficient.

> Petitioners John Santosky II and Annie Santosky are the natural parents of Tina and John III. In November 1973, after incidents reflecting parental neglect, respondent Kramer, Commissioner of the Ulster County Department of Social Services, initiated a neglect proceeding under Fam.Ct.Act § 1022 and removed Tina from her natural home. About 10 months later, he removed John III and placed him with foster parents. On the day John was taken, Annie Santosky gave birth to a third child, Jed. When Jed was only three days old, respondent transferred him to a foster home on the ground that immediate removal was necessary to avoid imminent danger to his life or health.

[2] Most notably, natural parents have a statutory right to the assistance of counsel and of court-appointed counsel if they are indigent. Fam.Ct.Act § 262(a)(iii).

In October 1978, respondent petitioned the Ulster County Family Court to terminate petitioners' parental rights in the three children. Petitioners challenged the constitutionality of the "fair preponderance of the evidence" standard specified in Fam.Ct.Act § 622. The Family Court judge rejected this constitutional challenge, and weighed the evidence under the statutory standard. While acknowledging that the Santoskys had maintained contact with their children, the judge found those visits "at best superficial and devoid of any real emotional content." After deciding that the agency had made " 'diligent efforts' to encourage and strengthen the parental relationship," he concluded that the Santoskys were incapable, even with public assistance, of planning for the future of their children. The judge later held a dispositional hearing and ruled that the best interests of the three children required permanent termination of the Santoskys' custody.[5]

Petitioners appealed, again contesting the constitutionality of § 622's standard of proof. The New York Supreme Court, Appellate Division, affirmed, holding application of the preponderance of the evidence standard "proper and constitutional." In re John AA, 75 App.Div.2d 910, 427 N.Y.S.2d 319, 320 (1980). That standard, the court reasoned, "recognizes and seeks to balance rights possessed by the child . . . with those of the natural parents. . . ." Ibid. The New York Court of Appeals then dismissed petitioners' appeal to that court "upon the ground that no substantial constitutional question is directly involved." . . .

Last term, in Lassiter v. Department of Social Services, 452 U.S. 18, 101 S.Ct. 2153, 68 L.Ed.2d 640 (1981), this Court, by a 5–4 vote, held that the Fourteenth Amendment's Due Process Clause does not require the appointment of counsel for indigent parents in every parental status termination proceeding. The case casts light, however, on the two central questions hereCwhether process is constitutionally due a natural parent at a State's parental rights termination proceeding, and, if so, what process is due. In *Lassiter,* it was "not disputed that state intervention to terminate the relationship between [a parent] and [the] child must be accomplished by procedures meeting the requisites of the Due Process Clause." The absence of dispute reflected this Court's historical recognition that freedom of personal choice in matters of family life is a fundamental liberty interest protected by the Fourteenth Amendment.

The fundamental liberty interest of natural parents in the care, custody, and management of their child does not evaporate simply because they have not been model parents or have lost temporary custody of their child to the State. Even when blood relationships are strained, parents retain a vital interest in preventing the irretrievable destruction

[5] Since respondent took custody of Tina, John III, and Jed, the Santoskys have had two other children, James and Jeremy. The State has taken no action to remove these younger children. At oral argument, counsel for respondent replied affirmatively when asked whether he was asserting that petitioners were "unfit to handle the three older ones but not unfit to handle the two younger ones."

of their family life. If anything, persons faced with forced dissolution of their parental rights have a more critical need for procedural protections than do those resisting state intervention into ongoing family affairs. When the State moves to destroy weakened familial bonds, it must provide the parents with fundamentally fair procedures.

In *Lassiter,* the Court and three dissenters agreed that the nature of the process due in parental rights termination proceedings turns on a balancing of the "three distinct factors" specified in Mathews v. Eldridge, 424 U.S. 319, 335, 96 S.Ct. 893, 903, 47 L.Ed.2d 18 (1976): the private interests affected by the proceeding; the risk of error created by the State's chosen procedure; and the countervailing governmental interest supporting use of the challenged procedure. . . .

In *Lassiter,* to be sure, the Court held that fundamental fairness may be maintained in parental rights termination proceedings even when some procedures are mandated only on a case-by-case basis, rather than through rules of general application. 452 U.S., at 31–32, 101 S.Ct., at 2161–2162 (natural parent's right to court-appointed counsel should be determined by the trial court, subject to appellate review). But this Court never has approved case-by-case determination of the proper *standard of proof* for a given proceeding. Standards of proof, like other "procedural due process rules[,] are shaped by the risk of error inherent in the truth-finding process as applied to the *generality of cases,* not the rare exceptions." Mathews v. Eldridge, 424 U.S., at 344, 96 S.Ct., at 907 (emphasis added). Since the litigants and the factfinder must know at the outset of a given proceeding how the risk of error will be allocated, the standard of proof necessarily must be calibrated in advance. Retrospective case-by-case review cannot preserve fundamental fairness when a class of proceedings is governed by a constitutionally defective evidentiary standard.

In parental rights termination proceedings, the private interest affected is commanding; the risk of error from using a preponderance standard is substantial; and the countervailing governmental interest favoring that standard is comparatively slight. Evaluation of the three *Eldridge* factors compels the conclusion that use of a "fair preponderance of the evidence" standard in such proceedings is inconsistent with due process. "The extent to which procedural due process must be afforded the recipient is influenced by the extent to which he may be 'condemned to suffer grievous loss.' " Whether the loss threatened by a particular type of proceeding is sufficiently grave to warrant more than average certainty on the part of the factfinder turns on both the nature of the private interest threatened and the permanency of the threatened loss.

Lassiter declared it "plain beyond the need for multiple citation" that a natural parent's "desire for and right to 'the companionship, care, custody, and management of his or her children' " is an interest far more precious than any property right. 452 U.S, at 27, 101 S.Ct., at 2160, quoting Stanley v. Illinois, 405 U.S., at 651, 92 S.Ct., at 1212. When the

State initiates a parental rights termination proceeding, it seeks not merely to infringe that fundamental liberty interest, but to end it. "If the State prevails, it will have worked a unique kind of deprivation. . . . A parent's interest in the accuracy and justice of the decision to terminate his or her parental status is, therefore, a commanding one." 452 U.S., at 27, 101 S.Ct., at 2160.

In government-initiated proceedings to determine juvenile delinquency, this Court has identified losses of individual liberty sufficiently serious to warrant imposition of an elevated burden of proof. Yet juvenile delinquency adjudications, civil commitment, deportation, and denaturalization, at least to a degree, are all *reversible* official actions. Once affirmed on appeal, a New York decision terminating parental rights is *final* and irrevocable. Few forms of state action are both so severe and so irreversible. Thus, the first *Eldridge* factor—the private interest affected—weighs heavily against use of the preponderance standard at a State-initiated permanent neglect proceeding. We do not deny that the child and his foster parents are also deeply interested in the outcome of that contest. But at the factfinding stage of the New York proceeding, the focus emphatically is not on them.

The factfinding does not purport—and is not intended—to balance the child's interest in a normal family home against the parents' interest in raising the child. Nor does it purport to determine whether the natural parents or the foster parents would provide the better home. Rather, the factfinding hearing pits the State directly against the parents. The State alleges that the natural parents are at fault. The questions disputed and decided are what the State did—"made diligent efforts," § 614.1.(c)—and what the natural parents did not do—"maintain contact with or plan for the future of the child." § 614.1.(d). The State marshals an array of public resources to prove its case and disprove the parents' case. Victory by the State not only makes termination of parental rights possible; it entails a judicial determination that the parents are unfit to raise their own children.[10]

At the factfinding, the State cannot presume that a child and his parents are adversaries. After the State has established parental unfitness at that initial proceeding, the court may assume at the *dispositional* stage that the interests of the child and the natural parents do diverge. But until the State proves parental unfitness, the child and his parents share a vital interest in preventing erroneous termination of

---

[10] The Family Court judge in the present case expressly refused to terminate petitioners' parental rights on a "non-statutory, no-fault basis." Nor is it clear that the State constitutionally could terminate a parent's rights *without* showing parental unfitness. See Quilloin v. Walcott, 434 U.S. 246, 255, 98 S.Ct. 549, 554, 54 L.Ed.2d 511 (1978) ("We have little doubt that the Due Process Clause would be offended '[i]f a State were to attempt to force the breakup of a natural family, over the objections of the parents and their children, without some showing of unfitness and for the sole reason that to do so was thought to be in the children's best interest,' " quoting Smith v. Organization of Foster Families, 431 U.S. 816, 862–863, 97 S.Ct. 2094, 2119, 53 L.Ed.2d 14 (1977) (Stewart, J., concurring in the judgment)).

their natural relationship.[11] Thus, at the factfinding, the interests of the child and his natural parents coincide to favor use of error-reducing procedures.

However substantial the foster parents' interests may be, they are not implicated directly in the factfinding stage of a State-initiated permanent neglect proceeding against the natural parents. If authorized, the foster parents may pit their interests directly against those of the natural parents by initiating their own permanent neglect proceeding. Fam.Ct.Act § 615, 1055(d); Soc.Serv.Law § 392.7.(c). Alternatively, the foster parents can make their case for custody at the dispositional stage of a State-initiated proceeding, where the judge already has decided the issue of permanent neglect and is focusing on the placement that would serve the child's best interests. Fam.Ct.Act §§ 623, 631. For the foster parents, the State's failure to prove permanent neglect may prolong the delay and uncertainty until their foster child is freed for adoption. But for the natural parents, a finding of permanent neglect can cut off forever their rights in their child. Given this disparity of consequence, we have no difficulty finding that the balance of private interests strongly favors heightened procedural protections.

Under Mathews v. Eldridge, we next must consider both the risk of erroneous deprivation of private interests resulting from use of a "fair preponderance" standard and the likelihood that a higher evidentiary standard would reduce that risk . . . In New York, the factfinding stage of a State-initiated permanent neglect proceeding bears many of the indicia of a criminal trial. The Commissioner of Social Services charges the parents with permanent neglect. They are served by summons. The factfinding hearing is conducted pursuant to formal rules of evidence. The State, the parents, and the child are all represented by counsel. The State seeks to establish a series of historical facts about the intensity of its agency's efforts to reunite the family, the infrequency and insubstantiality of the parents' contacts with their child, and the parents' inability or unwillingness to formulate a plan for the child's future. The attorneys submit documentary evidence, and call witnesses who are subject to cross-examination. Based on all the evidence, the judge then determines whether the State has proved the statutory elements of permanent neglect by a fair preponderance of the evidence.

At such a proceeding, numerous factors combine to magnify the risk of erroneous factfinding. Permanent neglect proceedings employ imprecise substantive standards that leave determinations unusually

[11] For a child, the consequences of termination of his natural parents' rights may well be far-reaching. In Colorado, for example, it has been noted: "The child loses the right of support and maintenance, for which he may thereafter be dependent upon society; the right to inherit; and all other rights inherent in the legal parent-child relationship not just for [a limited] period . . . , but forever." In re K.S., 33 Colo.App. 72, 76, 515 P.2d 130, 133 (1973). Some losses cannot be measured. In this case, for example, Jed Santosky was removed from his natural parents' custody when he was only three days old; the judge's finding of permanent neglect effectively foreclosed the possibility that Jed would ever know his natural parents.

open to the subjective values of the judge. In appraising the nature and quality of a complex series of encounters among the agency, the parents, and the child, the court possesses unusual discretion to underweigh probative facts that might favor the parent.[12] Because parents subject to termination proceedings are often poor, uneducated, or members of minority groups, such proceedings are often vulnerable to judgments based on cultural or class bias.

The State's ability to assemble its case almost inevitably dwarfs the parents' ability to mount a defense. No predetermined limits restrict the sums an agency may spend in prosecuting a given termination proceeding. The State's attorney usually will be expert on the issues contested and the procedures employed at the factfinding hearing, and enjoys full access to all public records concerning the family. The State may call on experts in family relations, psychology, and medicine to bolster its case. Furthermore, the primary witnesses at the hearing will be the agency's own professional caseworkers whom the State has empowered both to investigate the family situation and to testify against the parents. Indeed, because the child is already in agency custody, the State even has the power to shape the historical events that form the basis for termination.[13]

The disparity between the adversaries' litigation resources is matched by a striking asymmetry in their litigation options. Unlike criminal defendants, natural parents have no "double jeopardy" defense against repeated state termination efforts. If the State initially fails to win termination, as New York did here, it always can try once again to cut off the parents' rights after gathering more or better evidence. Yet even when the parents have attained the level of fitness required by the State, they have no similar means by which they can forestall future termination efforts.

Coupled with a "preponderance of the evidence" standard, these factors create a significant prospect of erroneous termination. A standard of proof that by its very terms demands consideration of the quantity,

---

[12] For example, a New York court appraising an agency's "diligent efforts" to provide the parents with social services can excuse efforts *not* made on the grounds that they would have been "detrimental to the moral and temporal welfare of the child." Fam.Ct.Act § 614.1.(c). In determining whether the parent "substantially and continuously or repeatedly" failed to "maintain contact with . . . the child." § 614.1.(d), the judge can discount actual visits or communications on the grounds that they were insubstantial or "overtly demonstrat[ed] a lack of affection and concerned parenthood." Soc.Serv.Law § 384–b.7.(b). When determining whether the parent planned for the child's future, the judge can reject as unrealistic plans based on overly optimistic estimates of physical or financial ability. § 384.b.7.(c). . . .

[13] In this case, for example, the parents claim that the State sought court orders denying them the right to visit their children, which would have prevented them from maintaining the contact required by Fam.Ct.Act § 614.1.(d). The parents further claim that the State cited their rejection of social services they found offensive or superfluous as proof of the agency's "diligent efforts" and their own "failure to plan" for the children's future.

We need not accept these statements as true to recognize that the State's unusual ability to structure the evidence increases the risk of an erroneous factfinding. Of course, the disparity between the litigants' resources will be vastly greater in States where there is no statutory right to court-appointed counsel. . . .

rather than the quality, of the evidence may misdirect the factfinder in the marginal case. Given the weight of the private interests at stake, the social cost of even occasional error is sizable. . . .

The Appellate Division approved New York's preponderance standard on the ground that it properly "balanced rights possessed by the child . . . with those of the natural parents. . . ." 75 App.Div.2d, at 910, 427 N.Y.S.2d, at 320. By so saying, the court suggested that a preponderance standard properly allocates the risk of error *between* the parents and the child. That view is fundamentally mistaken.

The court's theory assumes that termination of the natural parents' rights invariably will benefit the child.[15] Yet we have noted above that the parents and the child share an interest in avoiding erroneous termination. Even accepting the court's assumption, we cannot agree with its conclusion that a preponderance standard fairly distributes the risk of error between parent and child. Use of that standard reflects the judgment that society is nearly neutral between erroneous termination of parental rights and erroneous failure to terminate those rights. Cf. In re Winship, 397 U.S., at 371, 90 S.Ct., at 1076 (Harland, J., concurring). For the child, the likely consequence of an erroneous failure to terminate is preservation of an uneasy status quo.[16] For the natural parents, however, the consequence of an erroneous termination is the unnecessary destruction of their natural family. A standard that allocates the risk of error nearly equally between those two outcomes does not reflect properly their relative severity.

Two state interests are at stake in parental rights termination proceedings—a *parens patriae* interest in preserving and promoting the

---

[15] This is a hazardous assumption at best. Even when a child's natural home is imperfect, permanent removal from that home will not necessarily improve his welfare. See, e.g., Wald, State Intervention on Behalf of "Neglected" Children: A Search for Realistic Standards, 27 Stan.L.Rev. 985, 993 (1975) ("In fact, under current practice, coercive intervention frequently results in placing a child in a more detrimental situation than he would be in without intervention.").

Nor does termination of parental rights necessarily ensure adoption. See Brief for Community Action for Legal Services, Inc., et al., as *Amicus Curiae* 22–23 (in 1979; only 12% of the adoptable children in foster care in New York City were actually adopted, although some had been waiting for years, citing Redirecting Foster Care, A Report to the Mayor of the City of New York 69, 43 (1980)). Even when a child eventually finds an adoptive family, he may spend years moving between state institutions and "temporary" foster placements after his ties to his natural parents have been severed. See Smith v. Organization of Foster Families, 431 U.S., at 833–838, 97 S.Ct., at 2103–06 (describing the "limbo" of the New York foster care system).

[16] When the termination proceeding occurs, the child is not living at his natural home. A child cannot be adjudicated "permanently neglected" until, "for a period of more than a year," he has been in "the care of an authorized agency." Soc.Serv.Law § 384–b.7.(a); Fam.Ct.Act § 614.1.(d). See also dissenting opinion, at 20–21.

Under New York law, a judge has ample discretion to ensure that, once removed from his natural parents on grounds of neglect, a child will not return to a hostile environment. In this case, when the State's initial termination effort failed for lack of proof, see n. 4, supra, the court simply issued orders under Fam.Ct.Act § 1055(b) extending the period of the child's foster home placement. See App. 19–20. See also Fam.Ct.Act § 632(b) (when State's permanent neglect petition is dismissed for insufficient evidence, judge retains jurisdiction to reconsider underlying orders of placement); § 633 (judge may suspend judgment at dispositional hearing for an additional year).

welfare of the child and a fiscal and administrative interest in reducing the cost and burden of such proceedings. A standard of proof more strict than preponderance of the evidence is consistent with both interests.

"Since the State has an urgent interest in the welfare of the child, it shares the parent's interest in an accurate and just decision" at the *factfinding* proceeding. As *parens patriae,* the State's goal is to provide the child with a permanent home. Yet while there is still reason to believe that positive, nurturing parent-child relationships exist, the *parens patriae* interest favors preservation, not severance, of natural familial bonds.[17] § 384–b.1.(a)(ii). "[T]he State registers no gain towards its declared goals when it separates children from the custody of fit parents." Stanley v. Illinois, 405 U.S., at 652, 92 S.Ct., at 1213.

The State's interest in finding the child an alternative permanent home arises only "when it is *clear* that the natural parent cannot or will not provide a normal family home for the child." Soc.Serv.Law § 384–b.1.(a)(iv) (emphasis added). At the factfinding, that goal is served by procedures that promote an accurate determination of whether the natural parents can and will provide a normal home. Unlike a constitutional requirement of hearings, or court-appointed counsel, a stricter standard of proof would reduce factual error without imposing substantial fiscal burdens upon the State. . . . Nor would an elevated standard of proof create any real administrative burdens for the State's factfinders. New York Family Court judges already are familiar with a higher evidentiary standard in other parental rights termination proceedings not involving permanent neglect. . . . New York also demands at least clear and convincing evidence in proceedings of far less moment than parental rights termination proceedings. . . .

We . . . express no view on the merits of petitioners' claims. At a hearing conducted under a constitutionally proper standard, they may or may not prevail. Without deciding the outcome under any of the standards we have approved, we vacate the judgment of the Appellate Division and remand the case for further proceedings not inconsistent with this opinion.

■ JUSTICE REHNQUIST, with whom THE CHIEF JUSTICE, JUSTICE WHITE, and JUSTICE O'CONNOR join, dissenting.

. . .

New York has created an exhaustive program to assist parents in regaining the custody of their children and to protect parents from the unfair deprivation of their parental rights. And yet the majority's myopic scrutiny of the standard of proof blinds it to the very considerations and procedures which make the New York scheme "fundamentally fair."

---

[17] Any *parens patriae* interest in terminating the natural parents' rights arises only at the dispositional phase, *after* the parents have been found unfit.

[The opinion reviews the procedures of the New York statute both with regard to temporary removal of children from the home and termination of parental rights.]

The three children to which this case relates were removed from petitioners' custody in 1973 and 1974, before petitioners' other two children were born. The removals were made pursuant to the procedures detailed above and in response to what can only be described as shockingly abusive treatment.[10] At the temporary removal hearing held before the Family Court on September 30, 1974, petitioners were represented by counsel, and allowed the Ulster County Department of Social Services ("Department") to take custody of the three children.

Temporary removal of the children was continued at an evidentiary hearing held before the Family Court in December 1975, after which the court issued a written opinion concluding that petitioners were unable to resume their parental responsibilities due to personality disorders. Unsatisfied with the progress petitioners were making, the court also directed the Department to reduce to writing the plan which it had designed to solve the problems at petitioners' home and reunite the family. A plan for providing petitioners with extensive counseling and training services was submitted to the court and approved in February 1976. Under the plan, petitioners received training by a mother's aide, a nutritional aide, and a public health nurse, and counseling at a family planning clinic. In addition, the plan provided psychiatric treatment and vocational training for the father, and counseling at a family service center for the mother. Between early 1976 and the final termination decision in April 1979, the State spent more than $15,000 in these efforts to rehabilitate petitioners as parents.

Petitioners' response to the State's effort was marginal at best. They wholly disregarded some of the available services and participated only sporadically in the others. As a result, and out of growing concern over the length of the childrens' stay in foster care, the Department petitioned in September 1976 for permanent termination of petitioners' parental rights so that the children could be adopted by other families. Although the Family Court recognized that petitioners' reaction to the State's efforts was generally "non-responsive, even resentful," the fact that they were "at least superficially cooperative" led it to conclude that there was

[10] Tina Apel, the oldest of petitioners' five children, was removed from their custody by court order in November 1973 when she was two years old. Removal proceedings were commenced in response to complaints by neighbors and reports from a local hospital that Tina had suffered injuries in petitioners' home including a fractured left femur, treated with a homemade splint; bruises on the upper arms, forehead, flank, and spine; and abrasions of the upper leg. The following summer John Santosky III, petitioners' second oldest child, was also removed from petitioners' custody. John, who was less than one year old at the time, was admitted to the hospital suffering malnutrition, bruises on the eye and forehead, cuts on the foot, blisters on the hand, and multiple pin pricks on the back. Jed Santosky, the third oldest of petitioners' children, was removed from his parents' custody when only three days old as a result of the abusive treatment of the two older children.

yet hope of further improvement and an eventual reuniting of the family. Accordingly, the petition for permanent termination was dismissed.

Whatever progress petitioners were making prior to the 1976 termination hearing, they made little or no progress thereafter. In October 1978, the Department again filed a termination petition alleging that petitioners had completely failed to plan for the childrens' future despite the considerable efforts rendered in their behalf. This time, the Family Court agreed. The court found that petitioners had "failed in any meaningful way to take advantage of the many social and rehabilitative services that have not only been made available to them but have been diligently urged upon them." In addition, the court found that the "infrequent" visits "between the parents and their children were at best superficial and devoid of any real emotional content." The court thus found "nothing in the situation which holds out any hope that [petitioners] may ever become financially self sufficient or emotionally mature enough to be independent of the services of social agencies. More than a reasonable amount of time has passed and still, in the words of the case workers, there has been no discernible forward movement. At some point in time, it must be said 'enough is enough.' " In accordance with the statutory requirements set forth above, the court found that petitioners' failure to plan for the future of their children, who were then seven, five, and four years old and had been out of petitioners' custody for at least four years, rose to the level of permanent neglect. At a subsequent dispositional hearing, the court terminated petitioners' parental rights, thereby freeing the three children for adoption.

As this account demonstrates, the State's extraordinary four-year effort to reunite petitioners' family was not just unsuccessful, it was altogether rebuffed by parents unwilling to improve their circumstances sufficiently to permit a return of their children. At every step of this protracted process petitioners were accorded those procedures and protections which traditionally have been required by due process of law. Moreover, from the beginning to the end of this sad story all judicial determinations were made by one family court judge. After four and one-half years of involvement with petitioners, more than seven complete hearings, and additional periodic supervision of the State's rehabilitative efforts, the judge no doubt was intimately familiar with this case and the prospects for petitioners' rehabilitation.

It is inconceivable to me that these procedures were "fundamentally unfair" to petitioners. Only by its obsessive focus on the standard of proof and its almost complete disregard of the facts of this case does the majority find otherwise[11]. . . . [S]uch a focus does not comport with the

[11] The majority finds, without any reference to the facts of this case, that "numerous factors [in New York termination proceedings] combine to magnify the risk of erroneous factfinding." Among the factors identified by the majority are the "unusual discretion" of the family court judge "to underweigh probative facts that might favor the parent"; the often uneducated, minority status of the parents and their consequent "vulnerab[ility] to judgments based on cultural or class bias"; the "State's ability to assemble its case," which "dwarfs the

flexible standard of fundamental fairness embodied in the Due Process Clause of the Fourteenth Amendment.

In addition to the basic fairness of the process afforded petitioners, the standard of proof chosen by New York clearly reflects a constitutionally permissible balance of the interests at stake in this case. The standard of proof "represents an attempt to instruct the factfinder concerning the degree of confidence our society thinks he should have in the correctness of factual conclusions for a particular type of adjudication." In re Winship, 397 U.S. 358, 370, 90 S.Ct. 1068, 1076, 25 L.Ed.2d 368 (1970) (Harlan, J. concurring); Addington v. Texas, 441 U.S. 418, 423, 99 S.Ct. 1804, 1807, 60 L.Ed.2d 323 (1979). In this respect, the standard of proof is a crucial component of legal process, the primary function of which is "to minimize the risk of erroneous decisions."[12]

---

parents' ability to mount a defense" by including an unlimited budget, expert attorneys, and "full access to all public records concerning the family"; and the fact that "natural parents have no 'double jeopardy' defense against repeated state" efforts, "with more or better evidence," to terminate parental rights "even when the parents have attained the level of fitness required by the State." In short, the majority characterizes the State as a wealthy and powerful bully bent on taking children away from defenseless parents. Such characterization finds no support in the record.

The intent of New York has been stated with eminent clarity: "the [S]tate's *first obligation* is to *help* the family with services to *prevent* its break-up or to *reunite* it if the child has already left home." SSL § 384–b(1)(a)(iii) (emphasis added). There is simply no basis in fact for believing, as the majority does, that the State does not mean what it says; indeed, the facts of this case demonstrate that New York has gone the extra mile in seeking to effectuate its declared purpose. More importantly, there should be no room in the jurisprudence of this Court for decisions based on unsupported inaccurate assumptions.

A brief examination of the "factors" relied upon by the majority demonstrates its error. The "unusual" discretion of the family court judge to consider the "affectio[n] and concer[n]" displayed by parents during visits with their children, is nothing more than discretion to consider reality; there is not one shred of evidence in this case suggesting that the determination of the family court was "based on cultural or class bias"; if parents lack the "ability to mount a defense," the State provides them with the full services of an attorney, FCA § 262, and they, like the State, have "full access to all *public* records concerning the family" (emphasis added); and the absence of "double jeopardy" protection simply recognizes the fact that family problems are often ongoing and may in the future warrant action that currently is unnecessary. In this case the family court dismissed the first termination petition because it desired to give petitioners "the benefit of the doubt," and a second opportunity to raise themselves to "an acceptable minimal level of competency as parents." It was their complete failure to do so that prompted the second, successful termination petition.

[12] It is worth noting that the significance of the standard of proof in New York parental termination proceedings differs from the significance of the standard in other forms of litigation. In the usual adjudicatory setting, the factfinder has had little or no prior exposure to the facts of the case. His only knowledge of those facts comes from the evidence adduced at trial, and he renders his findings solely upon the basis of that evidence. Thus, normally, the standard of proof is a crucial factor in the final outcome of the case, for it is the scale upon which the factfinder weighs his knowledge and makes his decision.

Although the standard serves the same function in New York parental termination proceedings, additional assurances of accuracy are present in its application. As was adduced at oral argument, the practice in New York is to assign one judge to supervise a case from the initial temporary removal of the child to the final termination of parental rights. Therefore, as discussed above, the factfinder is intimately familiar with the case before the termination proceedings ever begin. Indeed, as in this case, he often will have been closely involved in protracted efforts to rehabilitate the parents. Even if a change in judges occurs, the Family Court retains jurisdiction of the case and the newly assigned judge may take judicial notice of all prior proceedings. Given this familiarity with the case, and the necessarily lengthy efforts which must precede a termination action in New York, decisions in termination cases are made by judges steeped in the background of the case and peculiarly able to judge the accuracy of

In determining the propriety of a particular standard of proof in a given case, however, it is not enough simply to say that we are trying to minimize the risk of error. Because errors in factfinding affect more than one interest, we try to minimize error as to those interests which we consider to be most important. As Justice Harlan explained in his well-known concurrence to In re Winship:

> "In a lawsuit between two parties, a factual error can make a difference in one of two ways. First, it can result in a judgment in favor of the plaintiff when the true facts warrant a judgment for the defendant. The analogue in a criminal case would be the conviction of an innocent man. On the other hand, an erroneous factual determination can result in a judgment for the defendant when the true facts justify a judgment in plaintiff's favor. The criminal analogue would be the acquittal of a guilty man.
>
> The standard of proof influences the relative frequency of these two types of erroneous outcomes. If, for example, the standard of proof for a criminal trial were a preponderance of the evidence rather than proof beyond a reasonable doubt, there would be a smaller risk of factual errors that result in freeing guilty persons, but a far greater risk of factual errors that result in convicting the innocent. Because the standard of proof affects the comparative frequency of these two types of erroneous outcomes, the choice of the standard to be applied in a particular kind of litigation should, in a rational world, reflect an assessment of the comparative social disutility of each." 397 U.S., at 370–372, 90 S.Ct., at 1076.

When the standard of proof is understood as reflecting such an assessment, an examination of the interests at stake in a particular case becomes essential to determining the propriety of the specified standard of proof. Because proof by a preponderance of the evidence requires that "[t]he litigants . . . share the risk of error in a roughly equal fashion," Addington v. Texas, supra, 441 U.S., at 423, 99 S.Ct. at 1808, it rationally should be applied only when the interests at stake are of roughly equal societal importance. The interests at stake in this case demonstrate that New York has selected a constitutionally permissible standard of proof.

On one side is the interest of parents in a continuation of the family unit and the raising of their own children. The importance of this interest cannot easily be overstated. Few consequences of judicial action are so grave as the severance of natural family ties. Even the convict committed to prison and thereby deprived of his physical liberty often retains the love and support of family members. "This Court's decisions have by now made plain beyond the need for multiple citation that a parent's desire

---

evidence placed before them. This does not mean that the standard of proof in these cases can escape due process scrutiny, only that additional assurances of accuracy attend the application of the standard in New York termination proceedings.

for and right to 'the companionship, care, custody and management of his or her children' is an important interest that 'undeniably warrants deference and, absent a powerful countervailing interest, protection.' Stanley v. Illinois, 405 U.S. 645, 651 [92 S.Ct. 1208, 1212, 31 L.Ed.2d 551]." Lassiter v. Department of Social Services, 452 U.S. 18, 27, 101 S.Ct. 2153, 2161, 68 L.Ed.2d 640 (1981). In creating the scheme at issue in this case, the New York legislature was expressly aware of this right of parents "to bring up their own children." SSL § 384–b(1)(a)(ii).

On the other side of the termination proceeding are the often countervailing interests of the child.[13] A stable, loving homelife is essential to a child's physical, emotional, and spiritual well-being. It requires no citation of authority to assert that children who are abused in their youth generally face extraordinary problems developing into responsible, productive citizens. The same can be said of children who, though not physically or emotionally abused, are passed from one foster home to another with no constancy of love, trust, or discipline. If the Family Court makes an incorrect factual determination resulting in a failure to terminate a parent-child relationship which rightfully should be ended, the child involved must return either to an abusive home or to the often unstable world of foster care. The reality of these risks is magnified by the fact that the only families faced with termination actions are those which have voluntarily surrendered custody of their child to the State, or, as in this case, those from which the child has been removed by judicial action because of threatened irreparable injury

[13] The majority dismisses the child's interest in the accuracy of determinations made at the factfinding hearing because "[t]he factfinding does not purport . . . to balance the child's interest in a normal family life against the parents' interest in raising the child," but instead "pits the State directly against the parents." Only "[a]fter the State has established parental unfitness," the majority reasons, may the court "assume . . . that the interests of the child and the natural parents do diverge."

This reasoning misses the mark. The child has an interest in the outcome of the factfinding hearing independent of that of the parent. To be sure, "the child and his parents share a vital interest in preventing *erroneous* termination of their natural relationship." (emphasis added). But the child's interest in a continuation of the family unit exists only to the extent that such a continuation would not be harmful to him. An error *in the factfinding hearing* that results in a failure to terminate a parent-child relationship which rightfully should be terminated may well detrimentally affect the child.

The preponderance of the evidence standard, which allocates the risk of error more or less evenly, is employed when the social disutility of error *in either direction* is roughly equalCthat is, when an incorrect finding of fault would produce consequences as undesirable as the consequences that would be produced by an incorrect finding of *no* fault. Only when the disutility of error in one direction discernibly outweighs the disutility of error in the other direction do we choose, by means of the standard of proof, to reduce the likelihood of the more onerous outcome. See In re Winship, 397 U.S. 358, 370–372, 90 S.Ct. 1068, 1075–1077, 25 L.Ed.2d 368 (1970), (Harlan, J., concurring).

New York's adoption of the preponderance of the evidence standard reflects its conclusion that the undesirable consequence of an erroneous finding of parental unfitness—the unwarranted termination of the family relationship—is roughly equal to the undesirable consequence of an erroneous finding of parental fitness—the risk of permanent injury to the child either by return of the child to an abusive home or by the child's continued lack of a permanent home. Such a conclusion is well within the province of state legislatures. It cannot be said that the New York procedures are unconstitutional simply because a majority of the members of this Court disagree with the New York legislature's weighing of the interests of the parents and the child in an error-free factfinding hearing.

through abuse or neglect. Permanent neglect findings also occur only in families where the child has been in foster care for at least one year.

In addition to the child's interest in a normal homelife, "the State has an urgent interest in the welfare of the child." Lassiter v. Department of Social Services, supra, at 27, 101 S.Ct., at 2160.[16] Few could doubt that the most valuable resource of a self-governing society is its population of children who will one day become adults and themselves assume the responsibility of self-governance. "A democratic society rests, for its continuance, upon the healthy, well-rounded growth of young people into full maturity as citizens, with all that implies." Prince v. Massachusetts, 321 U.S. 158, 168, 64 S.Ct. 438, 443, 88 L.Ed. 645 (1944). Thus, "the whole community" has an interest "that children be both safeguarded from abuses and given opportunities for growth into free and independent well-developed . . . citizens." *Id.*, at 165.

When, in the context of a permanent neglect termination proceeding, the interests of the child and the State in a stable, nurturing homelife are balanced against the interests of the parents in the rearing of their child, it cannot be said that either set of interests is so clearly paramount as to require that the risk of error be allocated to one side or the other. Accordingly, a State constitutionally may conclude that the risk of error should be borne in roughly equal fashion by use of the preponderance of the evidence standard of proof. . . .

For the reasons heretofore stated, I believe that the Court today errs in concluding that the New York standard of proof in parental-rights termination proceedings violates due process of law. The decision disregards New York's earnest efforts to *aid* parents in regaining the custody of their children and a host of procedural protections placed around parental rights and interests. The Court finds a constitutional violation only by a tunnel-vision application of due process principles that altogether loses sight of the unmistakable fairness of the New York procedure.

Even more worrisome, today's decision cavalierly rejects the considered judgment of the New York legislature in an area traditionally entrusted to state care. The Court thereby begins, I fear, a trend of federal intervention in state family law matters which surely will stifle creative responses to vexing problems. Accordingly, I dissent.

NOTES

The *Santosky* decision remains a crucial decision when a state seeks to terminate a parent's right to his or her child. To cite a recent example, the Tennessee Appellate Court was petitioned to review a lower court's termination of the parental rights of a mother over her four children. *In re*

[16] The majority's conclusion that a state interest in the child's well-being arises only after a determination of parental unfitness suffers from the same error as its assertion that the child has no interest, separate from that of its parents, in the accuracy of the factfinding hearing.

Bailey W., 2016 WL 3394245 (Tenn. Ct. App. 2016). The mother exposed the children to domestic violence, marijuana, and pain killers and the children were removed from her custody, placed in foster care, and a permanency plan was established to assist the mother reunify with her children. The mother failed to cooperate with the elements of the plan, resulting in the children remaining in foster care. When petitioned to terminate the mother's parental rights, the court determined that there was "substantial noncompliance with the permanency plan" and this constituted sufficient clear and convincing evidence to terminate parental rights. In commenting on the interaction between the parent and her children, plus the obligation of the state to safeguard the children, the court wrote: "[W]e conclude prolonging this case will greatly diminish the chances the children will have a safe and stable home at an early date. These children have been in foster care [for thirteen months], and they are tiring of the meetings and appointments associated with being in foster care. Given the unlikelihood Mother will remedy her issues in the near future, we conclude DCS met its burden of proving all three elements of this ground for termination."

The court relied extensively on the due process analysis of *Santosky*, writing that "[f]ew consequences of judicial action are so grave as the severance of natural family ties." Santosky v. Kramer, 455 U.S. 745, 787 (1982). "While fundamental, parental rights are not absolute. The State may interfere with parental rights, through judicial action, in some limited circumstances." *Id.* at 747. And the court also references the *Lassiter* decision, which preceded *Santosky* by one year and is described in the next section of this casebook. The two decisions are inextricably intertwined. The *In re* Bailey Tennessee court illustrates this when it discusses the nature of due process. While "due process" has never been precisely defined, inherent in the phrase is a requirement of "fundamental fairness." Delineating what "fundamental fairness" encompasses in a given situation requires a consideration of relevant case law and an assessment of the interests at stake. Lassiter v. Dep't of Soc. Servs., 452 U.S. 18, 24–25 (1981).

B. APPOINTMENT OF LEGAL COUNSEL FOR INDIGENT PARENTS

In Lassiter v. Department of Social Services, 452 U.S. 18, 101 S.Ct. 2153, 68 L.Ed.2d 640 (1981), discussed in *Santosky*, the petitioner-mother's infant son had been declared a neglected child and placed in custody of a state agency in 1975. The mother was convicted of second-degree murder a year afterward and began serving a 25–40 year prison term. A termination proceeding was commenced in 1978 and petitioner was brought from prison to the hearing. Finding that she had been given ample time to obtain counsel and that her failure to do so was without just cause, the court declined to postpone the proceeding. Counsel was not appointed for petitioner because she did not aver that she was indigent. During the hearing, petitioner and her mother responded to questions by the court, and petitioner cross-examined a social worker. Determining that she had "willfully failed to maintain concern or responsibility for the welfare of the minor," the court terminated petitioner's parental rights, on appeal the issue was whether failure to appoint counsel for petitioner was a denial of due process.

Explaining how to determine whether counsel need be appointed in a particular case, the opinion of the *Lassiter* Court stated:

> The case of Mathews v. Eldridge, 424 U.S. 319, 335, 96 S.Ct. 893, 47 L.Ed.2d 18, propounds three elements to be evaluated in deciding what due process requires, viz., the private interests at stake, the government's interest, and the risk that the procedures used will lead to erroneous decisions. We must balance these elements against each other, and then set their net weight in the scales against the presumption that there is a right to appointed counsel only where the indigent, if he is unsuccessful, may lose his personal freedom.
>
> This Court's decisions have by now made plain beyond the need for multiple citation that a parent's desire for and right to "the companionship, care, custody and management of his or her children" is an important interest that "undeniably warrants deference and, absent a powerful countervailing interest, protection." Stanley v. Illinois, 405 U.S. 645, 651. Here the State has sought not simply to infringe upon that interest but to end it. If the State prevails, it will have worked a unique kind of deprivation. *Cf.* May v. Anderson, 345 U.S. 528, 533; Armstrong v. Manzo, 380 U.S. A parent's interest in the accuracy and justice of the decision to terminate his or her parental status is, therefore a commanding one.[3]
>
> Since the State has an urgent interest in the welfare of the child, it shares the parent's interest in an accurate and just decision. For this reason, the State may share the indigent parent's interest in the availability of appointed counsel. If, as our adversary system presupposes, accurate and just results are most likely to be obtained through the equal contest of opposed interests, the State's interest in the child's welfare may perhaps best be served by a hearing in which both the parent and the State acting for the child are represented by counsel, without whom the contest of interests may become unwholesomely unequal. North Carolina itself acknowledges as much by providing that where a parent files a written answer to a termination petition, the State must supply a lawyer to represent the child. N.C. Gen. Stat. § 7A–289.29.
>
> The State's interests, however, clearly diverge from the parent's insofar as the State wishes the termination decision to be made as economically as possible and thus wants to avoid

---

[3] Some parents will have an additional interest to protect. Petitions to terminate parental rights are not uncommonly based on alleged criminal activity. Parents so accused may need legal counsel to guide them in understanding the problems such petitions may create.

both the expense of appointed counsel and the cost of the lengthened proceedings his presence may cause. But though the State's pecuniary interest is legitimate, it is hardly significant enough to overcome private interests as important as those here, particularly in light of the concession in the respondent's brief that the "potential costs of appointed counsel in termination proceedings . . . is [*sic*] admittedly *de minimis* compared to the costs in all criminal actions."

Finally, consideration must be given to the risk that a parent will be erroneously deprived of his or her child because the parent is not represented by counsel. . . .

The respondent argues that the subject of a termination hearing—the parent's relationship with her child—far from being abstruse, technical, or unfamiliar, is one as to which the parent must be uniquely well informed and to which the parent must have given prolonged thought. The respondent also contends that a termination hearing is not likely to produce difficult points of evidentiary law, or even of substantive law, since the evidentiary problems peculiar to criminal trials are not present and since the standards for termination are not complicated. In fact, the respondent reports, the North Carolina Departments of Social Services are themselves sometimes represented at termination hearings by social workers instead of by lawyers.

Yet the ultimate issues with which a termination hearing deals are not always simple, however commonplace they may be. Expert medical and psychiatric testimony, which few parents are equipped to understand and fewer still to confute, is sometimes presented. The parents are likely to be people with little education, who have had uncommon difficulty in dealing with life, and who are, at the hearing, thrust into a distressing and disorienting situation. That these factors may combine to overwhelm an uncounseled parent is evident from the findings some courts have made. Thus, courts have generally held that the State must appoint counsel for indigent parents at termination proceedings. The respondent is able to point to no presently authoritative case, except for the North Carolina judgment now before us, holding that an indigent parent has no due process right to appointed counsel in termination proceedings.

The dispositive question . . . is whether the three *Eldridge* factors, when weighed against the presumption that there is no right to appointed counsel in the absence of at least a potential deprivation of physical liberty, suffice to rebut that presumption and thus to lead to the conclusion that the Due Process Clause requires the appointment of counsel when a State seeks to terminate an indigent's parental status. To summarize the above discussion of the *Eldridge* factors: the parent's interest is an extremely important one (and may be supplemented by the dangers of criminal liability inherent in some termination proceedings); the State shares with the parent an interest in a correct decision, has a relatively weak pecuniary interest, and, in some but not all cases, has a possibly stronger interest in informal procedures; and the complexity of the proceeding and the incapacity of the uncounseled parent could be, but would not always be, great enough to make the risk of an erroneous deprivation of the parent's rights insupportably high.

If, in a given case, the parent's interests were at their strongest, the State's interests were at their weakest, and the risks of error were at their peak, it could not be said that the *Eldridge* factors did not overcome the presumption against the right to appointed counsel, and that due process did not therefore require the appointment of counsel. But since the *Eldridge* factors will not always be so distributed, and since "due process is not so rigid as to require that the significant interests in informality, flexibility and economy must always be sacrificed," Gagnon v. Scarpelli, supra, 411 U.S., at 788, 93 S.Ct., at 1762, neither can we say that the Constitution requires the appointment of counsel in every parental termination proceeding. We therefore adopt the standard found appropriate in *Gagnon v. Scarpelli*, and leave the decision whether due process calls for the appointment of counsel for indigent parents in termination proceedings to be answered in the first instance by the trial court, subject, of course, to appellate review. . . .

In its Fourteenth Amendment, our Constitution imposes on the States the standards necessary to ensure that judicial proceedings are fundamentally fair. A wise public policy, however, may require that higher standards be adopted than those minimally tolerable under the Constitution. Informed opinion has clearly come to hold that an indigent parent is entitled to the assistance of appointed counsel not only in parental termination proceedings, but in dependency and neglect proceedings as well. Most significantly, 33 States and the District of Columbia provide statutorily for the appointment of counsel in termination cases. The Court's opinion today in no way implies that the standards increasingly urged by informed public opinion and now widely followed by the States are other than enlightened and wise.

NOTES

Providing legal counsel for indigent parents who are parties in civil termination actions has produced a considerable variation of responses.

Some states have mandated the appointment of counsel and related services, thus exceeding the minimum requirements set forth in *Lassiter*. Often, if the state brings the termination action then it must provide counsel for the indigent parent, but there is no such federal constitutional requirement if the action is brought by an individual seeking to terminate parental rights, such as a foster parent. An example of such seeming inconsistency is seen in the case of *In re* J.C., 250 S.W.3d 436 (2008) (cert. denied by Supreme Court, Rhine v. Deaton, 130 S.Ct. 1281 (2010). After Texas Child Protective Services brought a termination action against an indigent mother, counsel was appointed and the case was nonsuited. The foster parents then brought a termination action within weeks and that action was a private action. Under these circumstances the judge refused to appoint counsel and the mother was forced to appear at the action pro se. The author of a law review comment has reviewed this decision and made a very cogent argument for a clearer and broader approach to representation for indigents in similar cases. *See* Elizabeth Mills Vineyal, Comment, *The Right to Counsel in Parental Rights Termination Cases: How a Clear and Consistent Legal Standard Would Better Protect Indigent Families*, 63 S.M.U. L. REV. 1403 (2010). For additional commentary, *see, e.g.*, Janet L. Wallace and Lisa R. Pruitt, *Judging Parents, Judging Place: Poverty, Rurality, and Termination of Parental Rights*, 77 MO. L. REV. 95 (2012). And strained state budgets may result in even fewer services being offered to indigent parents in termination proceedings. *See, e.g.*, *In re* Shirley B., 18 A.3d 40 (Md. 2011).

C. NOTICE RIGHTS OF THE FATHER TO A BORN OUT-OF-WEDLOCK CHILD

Our laws once were seemingly more protective of the rights of mothers of children born out of wedlock than those of fathers or possible (putative) fathers. Perhaps reflecting in part mounting concern about sexual discrimination and increasing prevalence of nonmarital relations, the Supreme Court of the United States in 1972 decided Stanley v. Illinois, 405 U.S. 645 (1972). The Court held that a father had a constitutional right to a fitness hearing before losing custody or parental rights over the child. This loss might arise in a number of possible instances, including that of a mother's consent to or relinquishment of the child for adoption. Providing notice to putative and absent fathers became a major concern prior to the child's adoption. One technique providing for notice was establishment of putative father registries, which listed a group of relationships that could trigger the need for notice to certain fathers or putative fathers. A putative father included within any of the categories might notify the registry that he wishes to receive notice of an adoption proceeding. *See, e.g.*, UNIFORM PARENTAGE ACT § 402. A question still remaining is whether such a registry provides reasonable notice to all putative fathers who might be entitled to it. In an action by the putative father of a three year old girl not in one of the designated register categories who neither received nor requested notice, the Supreme Court held that making the registry available had been adequate to protect the putative father. *See* Lehr v. Robertson, 463 U.S.

248 (1983). The sheer variety of potential scenarios makes it difficult to arrive at a consensus as to when, whether and how notice must be given to possible nonmarital fathers. *See also* Ivy Waisbor, Note, *Amending State Putative Father Registries: Affording More Rights and Protections to America's Unwed Fathers*, 44 HOFSTRA L. REV. 565 (2015).

2. SAFE HAVEN STATUTES

FLORIDA STATUTE ANN. (2016)

§ 383.50. Treatment of surrendered newborn infant

(1) As used in this section, the term "newborn infant" means a child who a licensed physician reasonably believes is approximately 7 days old or younger at the time the child is left at a hospital, emergency medical services station, or fire station.

(2) There is a presumption that the parent who leaves the newborn infant in accordance with this section intended to leave the newborn infant and consented to termination of parental rights.

(3) Each emergency medical services station or fire station staffed with full-time firefighters, emergency medical technicians, or paramedics shall accept any newborn infant left with a firefighter, emergency medical technician, or paramedic. The firefighter, emergency medical technician, or paramedic shall consider these actions as implied consent to and shall:

   (a) Provide emergency medical services to the newborn infant to the extent he or she is trained to provide those services, and

   (b) Arrange for the immediate transportation of the newborn infant to the nearest hospital having emergency services . . .

(5) Except when there is actual or suspected child abuse or neglect, any parent who leaves a newborn infant with a firefighter, emergency medical technician, or paramedic at a fire station or emergency room of a hospital and expresses an intent to leave the newborn infant and not return, has the absolute right to remain anonymous and to leave at any time and may not be pursued or followed unless the parent seeks to reclaim the newborn infant. When the infant is born in a hospital and the mother expresses intent to leave the infant and not return, upon the mother's request, the hospital or registrar shall complete the infant's birth certificate without naming the mother thereon.

(6) A parent of a newborn infant left at a hospital, emergency medical services station, or fire station under this section may claim his or her newborn infant up until the court enters a judgement terminating his or her parental rights. A claim to the newborn infant must be made to the entity having physical or legal custody of the newborn infant or to the circuit court before whom proceedings involving the newborn infant are pending.

(7) Upon admitting a newborn infant under this section, the hospital shall immediately contact a local licensed child-placing agency or alternatively contact the statewide central abuse hotline for the name of a licensed child-placing agency for purposes of transferring physical custody of the newborn infant. The hospital shall notify the licensed child-placing agency that a newborn infant has been left with the hospital and approximately when the licensed child-placing agency can take physical custody of the child. In cases where there is actual or suspected child abuse or neglect, the hospital or any of its licensed health care professionals shall report the actual or suspected child abuse or neglect in accordance with §§ 39.201 and 395.1023 in lieu of contacting a licensed child-placing agency.

(8) Any newborn infant admitted to a hospital in accordance with this section is presumed eligible for coverage under Medicaid, subject to federal rules.

(9) A newborn infant left at a hospital, emergency medical services station, or fire station in accordance with this section shall not be deemed abandoned and subject to reporting and investigation requirements under § 39.201 unless there is actual or suspected child abuse or until the department takes physical custody of the child.

(10) A criminal investigation shall not be initiated solely because a newborn infant is left at a hospital under this section unless there is actual or suspected child abuse or neglect.

§ 383.51. Confidentiality; identification of parent leaving newborn infant at hospital, emergency medical services station, or fire station

The identity of a parent who leaves a newborn infant at a hospital, emergency medical services station, or fire station in accordance with s. 383.50 is confidential and exempt from s. 119.07(1) and s. 24(a), Art. I of the State Constitution. The identity of a parent leaving a child shall be disclosed to a person claiming to be a parent of the newborn infant.

NOTES

In recent years many states have enacted what are known as "safe haven" statutes. In order to provide an alternative to a parent's abandonment of a newborn infant, the statute permits a parent to anonymously leave a child under a specified age (Florida specifies less than seven days) at a specified location (Florida specifies a hospital, emergency medical facility, or fire station). By leaving the infant at such a location a presumption is created that the parents are consenting to termination of their parental rights. Then, once the parental rights have been terminated, an adoption or other placement may occur. Legal discussion in the future will focus on the adequacy of notice for a biological parent unaware of the relinquishment of the infant at a safe haven center. For commentary on safe havens, *see, e.g.*, Arielle Bardzell and Nicholas Bernard, *Adoption and Foster Care,* 16 GEO. J. GENDER & LAW 3 (2015); Diane S. Kaplan, *Who Are the Mothers Who Need Save Haven Laws? An Empirical Investigation of Mothers Who Kill, Abandon, or Safely Surrender Their Newborns*, 29 WIS. J.L. GENDER & SOC'Y 447 (2014); Steven Stewart, Comment, *Surrendered & Abused: An Inquiry Into the Inclusiveness of California's Safe Surrender Law*, 10 WHITTIER J. CHILD & FAM. ADVOC. 291 (2011); Susan Ayres, *Kairos and Safe Havens: The Timing and Calamity of Unwanted Birth*, 15 WM. & MARY J. WOMEN & L. 227 (2009); Jeffrey A. Parness, *Lost Paternity in the Culture of Motherhood: A Different View of Safe Haven Laws*, 42 VAL. U. L. REV. 221 (2007); Carol Sanger, *Infant Safe Haven Laws: Legislating in the Culture of Life*, 106 COLUM. L. REV. 753 (2006).

3. FACTORS JUSTIFYING INTERVENTION IN PARENT-CHILD FAMILY

A. ENVIRONMENTAL FACTORS: POVERTY

In re K.A.W.

Supreme Court of Missouri, En Banc, 2004
133 S.W.3d 1

■ TEITELMAN, JUDGE.

K.A.W. and K.A.W. (twins) are minor children born to T.W. ("Mother"). Mother's parental rights were terminated on December 11, 2002, pursuant to section 211.447,[1] and she appeals.[2] Mother argues that the trial court's findings with respect to sections 211.447.4(2), (3) and (6) and 211.447.6 were insufficient. She also contends that the trial court erred because it failed to make required findings. This case was transferred to this Court prior to disposition by the court of appeals because of this Court's desire to resolve this case forthwith in accordance

[1] All statutory references are to RSMo 2000.

[2] A.W., the twins' father, consented to termination of his parental rights in October 2002. He did not appeal the termination of his parental rights.

with the admonition of section 453.011.1 that cases involving termination of parental rights and adoption be given priority.[3]

The judgment is reversed, and the cause is remanded. If further proceedings include the termination of Mother's parental rights, the trial court is directed to consider and make findings on each of the statutorily required subdivisions or factors for all grounds for termination of parental rights on which the trial court bases its decision.

When Mother was pregnant with the twins she was already raising three other young children on her own while trying to hold a job. Overwhelmed, she struggled with the question of whether it was best to place her twins up for adoption. Eventually, Mother decided that she should place them up for adoption because, as she later testified, she wanted them "to have a better life." The twin girls were born in June 2000, approximately three months premature. They required a two-month hospital stay. Although Mother had decided to place her twins for adoption, she did not abandon them. Rather, she visited the twins in the hospital daily and continued caring for them, holding, feeding and talking to them. Mother expressed breastmilk for their best care rather than allowing them to be fed formula. She took a special class to learn more about how to care for her premature twins. When the twins were released from the hospital, Mother woke hourly to feed and administer medicine to them, while still maintaining her obligations to her other children and her job.

While caring for her children, Mother carefully tried to investigate prospective families that might be suitable for the twins. She obtained the help of adoption professionals and attorneys. She expressed interest in an "open adoption" so that she could maintain contact with the twins and continue to support them. Mother was told she would need to look beyond Missouri, which does not allow "open adoption."[4]

An adoption facilitator presented a prospective family from California. Mother visited the couple for 10 days to be sure they were fit. Later, Mother became convinced that the California couple was not as good a placement as she originally believed (among other things, they were becoming reluctant to maintain contact), so when she was in

---

[3] Transfer is pursuant to Mo. Const. art. V, section 10. Rule 83.01 allows for transfer upon application prior to disposition by the appellate court:

> This Court on its own motion or on application of a party may transfer to this Court from the court of appeals a case in which there has been no disposition. The transfer shall be for any of the reasons stated in Rule 83.02 or for the purpose of equalizing the workload of the appellate courts.

Rule 83.02 authorizes transfer to this Court "because of the general interest or importance of a question involved in the case or for the purpose of reexamining existing law." This Court's transfer ameliorates the effect of repeated delays in the preparation of the transcript, that in turn caused a nearly one-year delay in consideration of the case by the appellate court.

[4] Subsequent media reports that Mother sold her twins on the internet were investigated by the state and revealed to be completely false. There was some evidence that Mother accepted small gifts, including earrings, but no gift was worth more than $100 and nothing in the record supports the media suggestions that Mother was attempting to sell the twins.

California for a visit, she retained the twins in her custody and began to seek another placement. Mother was advised that a British couple was still interested in adopting her babies. Mother had previously investigated the couple and believed them to be excellent candidates. The husband was an attorney, and the couple supported doing an open adoption. The British couple came to California, and the twins, Mother and the couple traveled a circuitous route from California to Arkansas by car. Mother was counseled by a British social worker and three attorneys that she should complete the adoption there because open adoption was not permitted in Missouri. Mother was advised to claim that she was an Arkansas resident. She refused, but she did provide an Arkansas address that belonged to a relative. An Arkansas judge approved the adoption.

Eventually, British officials determined that the British couple was unfit. The twins were taken into the custody of a British children's services agency. The Arkansas court entered an order setting aside the adoption decree for lack of jurisdiction because none of the parties were Arkansas residents. The twins were returned to Missouri, where they were placed in the custody of the Missouri division of family services (DFS). When Mother learned that the second adoption effort had failed, she decided that adoption was not the appropriate option, and she resolved to rear the babies herself and rally the support of her family so that she could do it well.[5]

The record indicates that, once DFS gained jurisdiction of the twins, Mother's equivocation ceased other than a few week period shortly after DFS took jurisdiction, when she considered allowing the foster parents to adopt the children but ultimately rejected that alternative and strove to gain back custody of the twins instead. After DFS gained jurisdiction of the twins, there is no evidence that any of Mother's conduct would indicate a likelihood of future problems. Instead, all of the evidence indicates that Mother remedied every potential problem noted by DFS. She complied fully with DFS's entire parenting plan, which had as its ostensible goal reunification:

- The plan required Mother to take parenting classes. Mother took parenting classes, and her instructor testified that Mother was the most involved and participatory member of the class.
- The plan required Mother to visit the twins regularly. Mother visited the twins as often as the court would allow and fought for the right to visit more frequently.
- The plan required Mother to provide financial support for the twins. Mother did so and frequently paid in advance.

[5] Mother twice failed in her efforts to find a suitable placement for her twins, yet this is not uncommon. The difficulty in finding safe permanent homes for children is illustrated by data that children in the custody of Missouri DFS are moved from placement to placement an average of over three times per child. Citizens for Missouri's Children, Children's Trust Fund, KIDS COUNT in Missouri 2002 Data Book, 36 (2003).

- Mother was required to undergo a psychological examination, and she did so willingly. On her own initiative, she also obtained counseling.
- She submitted to drug screenings (which she passed) although there was no allegation of drug use.

A DFS worker later testified that Mother complied with everything that had been asked of her including every element of the plan. Nevertheless, the juvenile officer filed a petition to terminate Mother's parental rights. The petition alleged that termination was warranted according to sections 211.447.4(2), (3) and (6) and that termination was in the twins' best interests.

The trial court conducted a hearing and issued "Findings, Conclusions and Judgment Terminating Parental Rights." The trial court's findings incorporated its earlier "Findings and Judgment of Disposition" and "Permanency Planning Order." The trial court terminated Mother's parental rights under subdivisions (2), (3) and (6) of section 211.447.4, ruling:

> 15. . . . "Mother" has abused and neglected "The Twins". Section 211.447.4(2), RSMo.
>
> (a) "Mother" has committed severe and recurrent acts of emotional abuse toward "The Twins." Section 211.447.4(2)(c), RSMo. These acts include the multiple, unstable, inappropriate, temporary placements including, but not limited to, placements in California, Arkansas, and Great Britain within a span of a few months during the first months of "The Twins" lives. . . .
>
> 16. . . . [T]he conditions which caused this Court to assume jurisdiction over "The Twins" or conditions of a potentially harmful nature continue to exist and will not be remedied at an early date to permit return of "The Twins" in the near future to the custody of "Mother", and under all the circumstances, continuation of any relationship between the "Mother" and "The Twins" greatly diminishes the prospects of "The Twins" for early integration into a stable and permanent home. Section 211.447.4(3), RSMo. These conditions include, but are not limited to, the multiple placements of "The Twins" during the first months of their lives and the resulting instability; "Mother's" continued stress and being overwhelmed with the reality of The Twins; the continued indecisiveness of "Mother" in dealing with "The Twins"; and the lack of family support for "Mother" in caring for the needs of "The Twins." Additionally, further movement of "The Twins" from the stability of their environment since April 18, 2001, would be harmful to "The Twins" in light of the Reactive Detachment [sic] Disorder in Partial Remission, a major mental disorder, suffered by "The

> Twins" as a result of the multiple placements and resulting instability. . . .
>
> 17. . . . "Mother" is unfit to be a party to the parent-child relationship with "The Twins" because of her consistent pattern of emotional abuse and, additionally, because of specific conditions directly relating to her relationship with "The Twins", all of which are of a duration and nature rendering "Mother" unable for the reasonably foreseeable future to care appropriately for the ongoing physical, mental and emotional needs of "The Twins". Section 211.447.4(6), RSMo. These considerations include, but are not limited to, "Mother's" continued indecisiveness in dealing with the lives of "The Twins" and their welfare; and the lack of family support for "Mother" in caring for health and welfare of "The Twins." . . .
>
> 19. . . . [T]here are no emotional ties between "The Twins" and "Mother". This is a direct result of the actions of "Mother" in her multiple placements of "The Twins" and resulting instability and emotional harm suffered by "The Twins". Section 211.447.6(1), RSMo.
>
> 20. . . . "The Twins" are not bonded with "Mother". This is a direct result of the deliberate acts of "Mother", who knew or should have known said acts would subject "The Twins" to a substantial and real risk of physical and mental harm. Section 211.447.6(7), RSMo. . . .
>
> 22. The multiple placements and instability of "Mother" have caused emotional harm to "The Twins", and these actions by "Mother" continue to affect "The Twins" to this day, and "Mother" is unwilling or unable to provide "The Twins" with the stability necessary for their overall welfare.
>
> 23. Termination of the parental rights of "Mother" is necessary to serve the best interests of "The Twins", in light of all the evidence, and . . . the evidence supporting termination of the parental rights of "Mother" is clear, cogent and convincing. Section 211.447.5, RSMo. . . .
>
> 25. This Court has considered all subsections of Section 211.447.4 and Section 211.447.6, RSMo, and except as expressly provided herein, finds the subsections irrelevant because there was inadequate evidence of their applicability presented during the evidentiary hearing. . . .
>
> 27. The parental rights of "Mother" . . . with "The Twins" . . . shall be, and hereby are, terminated.

Mother appeals, arguing that the trial court's findings with respect to sections 211.447.4(2), (3) and (6) and 211.447.6 were insufficient. She also contends that the trial court erred because it failed to make required findings. . . .

An essential part of any determination whether to terminate parental rights is whether, considered at the time of the termination and looking to the future, the child would be harmed by a continued relationship with the parent. A prospective analysis is required to determine whether grounds exist and what is in the best interests of the child for the reasonably foreseeable future. Obviously, it is difficult to predict the future. Section 211.447 provides for detailed consideration of the parent's past conduct as well as the parent's conduct following the trial court's assumption of jurisdiction as good evidence of future behavior. *In the Interest of M.E.W.*, 729 S.W.2d 194, 196 (Mo. banc 1987) (court needs to consider existing conditions, which may have arisen or were discovered after it assumed jurisdiction); *In the Interest of C.L.W.*, 115 S.W.3d 354, 356 (Mo.App.2003) (court must look at totality of parent's conduct both prior to and after filing of termination petition); *In the Interest of S.H.*, 915 S.W.2d 399, 404–5 (Mo.App.1996) (past patterns provide vital clues to present and future conduct).

However, it is insufficient merely to point to past acts, note that they resulted in abuse or neglect and then terminate parental rights. *In the Interest of C.L.W.*, 115 S.W.3d at 356. Past behavior can support grounds for termination, but only if it is convincingly linked to predicted future behavior.[6] There must be some explicit consideration of whether the past acts provide an indication of the likelihood of future harm. *In the Interest of L.G.*, 764 S.W.2d 89, 95 (Mo. banc 1989) (state met its burden by proving likely harm to child would occur in future). "A judge may properly be guided by evidence demonstrating reason to believe that a parent will correct a condition or weakness that currently disables the parent from serving his or her child's best interests." 2 Am Jur 2d Adoption sec. 135 (2003).

Courts have required that abuse or neglect sufficient to support termination under section 211.447.4(2) be based on conduct at the time of termination, not just at the time jurisdiction was initially taken. *In the Interest of B.C.K. and K.S.P.*, 103 S.W.3d at 328; *In the Interest of T.A.S.*, 32 S.W.3d 804, 812 (Mo.App.2000) (*T.A.S. I*). Similarly, courts have required that a failure to rectify sufficient to support termination under section 211.447.4(3) be based on a determination that conditions of a potentially harmful nature continued to exist as of the termination, rather than a mere finding that conditions that led to the assumption of jurisdiction still persisted. *In the Interest of T.A.S.*, 62 S.W.3d 650, 656–7 (Mo.App.2001) (*T.A.S. II*). Section 211.447.4(6) explicitly requires analysis of the "reasonably foreseeable future." *In the Interest of C.W. and*

---

6 "[I]t is inappropriate to use prior determinations of neglect as dispositive on the neglect issue at the time of the termination hearing. Courts are generally required to make new findings of fact based on the changed conditions in light of the parents' history of neglect and likely future neglect. . . . Most courts will agree that neglect must exist at the time of the termination hearing, and that it is inappropriate to terminate a parent's rights on the basis of neglect that happened in the remote past and no longer exists." 32 Am Jur Proof of Facts 3d Parental Rights sec. 6 (2003).

S.J.W., 64 S.W.3d 321, 325 (Mo.App.2001). Findings supporting earlier determinations are not irrelevant, but they must be updated to address the extent to which they describe the time of the termination and the potential for future harm. *T.A.S. I* at 812; *T.A.S. II* at 656–7. To that end, a trial court cannot support a termination by merely incorporating earlier findings supporting its assumption of jurisdiction or some other earlier disposition.

Whether it has been created following a court order or on the independent initiative of DFS, a parenting, social services, reunification or treatment plan can provide a trial court with highly relevant evidence. A parent's efforts to comply with such a plan will provide the court with an indication of the parent's likely efforts in the future to care for the child. *In the Interest of B.C.K. and K.S.P.*, 103 S.W.3d at 328–9. A lack of effort to comply with a plan, or a lack of success despite effort, can predict future problems. *In the Interest of C.L.W.*, 115 S.W.3d at 360. Such evidence cannot be irrelevant. While a plan is no longer mandatory, if one exists, it is error for a trial court to ignore it when considering termination of parental rights. *In the Interest of A.S.O.*, 52 S.W.3d 59, 66 (Mo.App.2001) (purpose is to ensure that all reasonable means to help the parent remedy the adverse conditions were utilized to no avail); T.A.S. I at 813.

Another essential part of any determination whether to terminate parental rights is whether the cited conduct of the parent has had or will have a detrimental impact upon the child. *In the Interest of P.C., B.M., and C.M.*, 62 S.W.3d 600, 604 (Mo.App.2001) (the trial court must hear some evidence describing what impact the questioned conduct has had on the children). Poor conduct or character flaws are not relevant unless they could actually result in future harm to the child. For example, sections 211.447.4(2)(a) and 211.447.4(3)(c) provide that the parent's mental condition is a factor supporting termination only if it "renders the parent unable to knowingly provide the child the necessary care, custody and control."

Another essential part of any determination whether to terminate parental rights is whether the cited acts or conditions of the parent, and their accompanying impact upon the child, are severe enough to constitute abuse or neglect. *In the Interest of P.C., B.M., and C.M.*, 62 S.W.3d at 604 (parent's acts may have been inappropriate but were not severe enough to support termination). Some parental conduct will harm a child without constituting abuse or neglect. *In the Interest of B.C.K. and K.S.P.*, 103 S.W.3d at 328. It is essential that the trial court determine whether the parent's acts are of sufficient severity.

For some types of parenting problems, the required level of severity the court must find is specified by the statute. For example, sections 211.447.4(2)(b) and 211.447.4(3)(d) provide that chemical dependency is of sufficient severity to support termination if it "prevents the parent from consistently providing the necessary care, custody and control over the child and which cannot be treated so as to enable the parent to consistently provide such care, custody and control." For another example, not every criminal act committed by the parent is severe enough to be abuse or neglect. Section 211.447.4(4) provides that it will be a grounds for termination of parental rights if the "parent has been found guilty or pled guilty to a felony violation of chapter 566, RSMo [sexual offenses], when the child or any child in the family was a victim, or a violation of section 568.020, RSMo [incest], when the child or any child in the family was a victim." Section 211.447.6(6) provides for consideration of the "conviction of the parent of a felony offense that the court finds is of such a nature that the child will be deprived of a stable home for a period of years. . . ." These sections provide guidance as to how severe a parent's criminal conduct must be to constitute abuse.[7]

Isolated abusive acts or conditions may not support termination when considered individually, but if they form a consistent pattern, are recurrent or are repeated, they can, when considered in combination, rise to the level of abuse and support termination. Sec. 211.447.4(2)(c), (2)(d), (3), (6). . . .

The trial court relied upon several specific acts and conditions of Mother in support of the grounds for termination. Each one must be supported by clear, cogent and convincing evidence and will be analyzed for: whether there was sufficient reason to believe that it had an impact upon the twins, whether it was severe enough to constitute abuse or neglect and whether it provides an indication of the likelihood of future harm to the twins. The trial court found that Mother's acts included "multiple, unstable, inappropriate, temporary placements including, but not limited to, placements in California, Arkansas, and Great Britain within a span of a few months during the first months of 'The Twins' lives."

There is no dispute that Mother twice attempted to place her twins for adoption. However, the record does not contain evidence that the first placement in California was unstable or inappropriate. The "placements in . . . Arkansas and Great Britain" refer to the single attempted adoption of the twins in Arkansas by the couple from Great Britain and, thus, constitute but one placement.

The two attempts at placement of the twins for adoption may have been mistakes, and may even have harmed the twins, but no reported Missouri case has ever held that placing a child up for adoption more than once rises to the level of abuse, and there is no reason to consider it abuse in this case. Mother's two attempts at placing her twins for adoption are not an indication of potential future harm to the twins,

[7] Although it was not explicitly relied upon by the trial court in the termination of parental rights, Mother pleaded guilty to welfare fraud because she provided false information and failed to provide required information to the state. Considering the severity of the crimes described in subdivisions 211.447.4(4) and 211.447.6(6), welfare fraud of this nature is not abuse, and the trial court correctly declined to include it as supporting termination.

especially without evidence that she would try to again place the twins for adoption if she regains custody of them. There is no evidence in the record that Mother intends to do anything other than regain permanent custody of her twins.

The trial court erred in concluding that these placements support findings that Mother committed "severe and recurrent acts of emotional abuse" and that Mother created "conditions of a potentially harmful nature [that] continue to exist and will not be remedied at an early date." There is no evidence that the placements were abusive or that they indicate a likelihood of future harm. Therefore, they do not constitute evidence that "instantly tilts the scales in favor of termination." *T.A.S. II* at 655. The trial court found that Mother suffered from "continued stress and being overwhelmed with the reality of The Twins," and "continued indecisiveness . . . in dealing with 'The Twins.' "

Mother's mental state cannot constitute abuse unless it rises to the level described by sections 211.447.4(2)(a) and (3)(c): "[a] mental condition which is shown by competent evidence either to be permanent or such that there is no reasonable likelihood that the condition can be reversed and which renders the parent unable to knowingly provide the child the necessary care, custody and control."[8] *In the Interest of C.L.W.*, 115 S.W.3d at 360–1 (Prewitt, J., dissenting); Mark Hardin and Robert Lancour, *Early Termination of Parental Rights: Developing Appropriate Statutory Grounds*, 14 (1996) (more required than just presence of mental or emotional disability—incapacity must be so severe that parent is incapable of providing minimally acceptable care).

It is hard to imagine a single working mother of five children living in poverty without enormous stress. Feeling overwhelmed in this context is not an indication of emotional instability, nor is it child abuse; rather, it is normal. DFS hired an expert to evaluate Mother's mental ability to care for her children. The expert found that Mother's "difficulties in parenting are not substantially different from those of many other single parents caring for large families . . . she appears to be an adequate parent, and there is no evidence that her parental rights should be terminated."

Sections 211.447.4(2)(a) and 211.447.4(3)(c) provide that a mental or emotional condition must be analyzed in three prongs to make an adequate finding: (1) documentation—whether the condition is supported by competent evidence; (2) duration—whether the condition is

[8] "Before the court can use mental incapacity as the basis for terminating a parent's rights, it must find that the mental defect or disability renders the parent unable to provide for the needs and well-being of his or her children. . . . It is sufficient to show that the parent's emotional problems are so severe as to prevent the maintenance of any meaningful relationship with his or her children. In such cases, it is often necessary to provide expert testimony that the parent's emotional instability is not likely to improve in the future. . . . In order to prevail in a termination proceeding based on mental incapacity, the petition should present sufficient evidence of the adverse effects which the parent's incapacity has on the well-being of the child. Absent such a showing, most courts will be reluctant to order termination on this ground alone." 32 Am Jur Proof of Facts 3d Parental Rights sec. 5 (2003).

permanent or such that there is no reasonable likelihood that it can be reversed; and (3) severity of effect—whether the condition is so severe as to render the parent unable to knowingly provide the child necessary care, custody and control.

Considering each of these three prongs, the problems cited by the trial court (stress, feeling overwhelmed and indecisiveness) do not support termination of parental rights. The expert evidence as to Mother's mental state did not constitute competent evidence that these problems were abnormal. These problems were situational and not necessarily permanent; therefore, the importance of the parenting or reunification plan and the services provided by DFS to Mother. There is evidence that Mother complied with the plan and that the services helped. The trial court's use of the word "continued" is without any support in the record. Even if there was reason to believe that these problems "continued," there is no evidence in the record that such a combination of problems ever caused abuse or would cause future harm. The only evidence on this question was provided by the DFS expert who concluded that these reactions were expectable and not a potential cause of future harm. Therefore, these findings do not support the termination of Mother's parental rights. . . .

There is evidence that, with substantial help from her extended family, Mother has reared her other children in a loving, supportive environment, free from abuse or neglect. For example, despite financial hardship and inconvenience, Mother placed one of her children in a private school more than 25 miles away from her home because she thought it best for that child. A school official there described Mother as a very engaged and interested parent who gave more to the school than many of the school's two parent families. For her other children, Mother received help from family to register the other children for school in Ladue, Missouri, because it is reputed to be an excellent district. Mother and her family also tend to the children's extra-curricular interests by arranging for them to participate in soccer, swimming, gymnastics, cub scouts, fishing and camping.

The trial court's finding of a lack of family support is not supported by clear, cogent and convincing evidence. Even if it were, a lack of family support is not evidence that instantly tilts the scales in favor of termination without additional evidence as to the necessity of the family support. Therefore, this finding does not support termination of Mother's parental rights. . . .

■ WHITE, C.J., WOLFF and STITH, JJ., concur. PRICE, J., dissents in separate opinion filed.

■ BENTON and LIMBAUGH, JJ., concur in opinion of PRICE, J.

■ WILLIAM RAY PRICE, JR., JUDGE, dissenting.

. . .

Mother testified she first considered adoption because the twins' father told her no man would want her with three children, much less five of them. A disturbing statement in its own right, it prefaced Mother's chain of decisions predicated on her own desires that demonstrated her "unfit to be a party to the parent and child relationship." Sec. 211.447.4(6).

Mother first attempted to place the twins with R.A. and V.A., a married couple residing in California. She admitted placing the twins with them "because they were well off financially." Mother acknowledged that she was aware of V.A.'s criminal record before placing the twins with them. After leaving the twins in the custody of R.A. and V.A., Mother surreptitiously removed the twins from their home a month and a half later because she heard a rumor "they were strapped for money or they were filing for bankruptcy" and because when Mother called them, V.A. "acted nonchalant."[6] She told R.A. and V.A. she was taking them out for a visit, when in fact she took them to a hotel where A.K. and J.K., a married couple residing in the United Kingdom, met her two days later.

After driving from California to Arkansas with A.K. and J.K., Mother transferred custody of the twins to them. A child abuse investigator from DFS testified that Mother said she had placed her children with A.K. and J.K. because they were going to allow her to come to the United Kingdom every year on the twins' birthday, which would be a good experience for her, and that she thought they would pay her airfare for those annual visits.

Mother's first objection to A.K. and J.K. having custody of the twins occurred approximately on January 16, 2001, as a response to media reports that she had sold the twins over the Internet.[7] British authorities rendered the placement with A.K. and J.K. short-term by taking custody of the twins on January 18, 2001, approximately two and a half weeks after their arrival in the United Kingdom, based on allegations of A.K.'s and J.K.'s unfitness.[8] Both placements of the twins, with R.A. and V.A.

[6] Mother testified that she called or talked to V.A. "practically every day" when the twins were in R.A. and V.A.'s custody, which was from approximately October 19 through November 29, 2001. Mother stated V.A. made her feel like she "was being a pest" and V.A. "act[ed] nonchalant, like why was [Mother] calling her" one day when Mother called. Mother cited this conversation and reports of their financial problems as the only reasons she withdrew the children from R.A. and V.A.'s custody.

[7] As Mother put it, "January 16th is when my life was on the news." She expressed no concern as to any effect this media exposure may have had on the twins.

[8] During the summer of 2001, Mother resumed her attempts to place the twins for adoption. She requested a meeting with the twins' foster parents in July to speak with them about adopting the twins. By the end of August, however, she had changed her mind again and withdrawn her offer to consent to adoption.

Even though she had previously declined to attempt to place the twins with her family and her mother had indicated earlier she did not want the twins, in April 2002 Mother testified that she would be amenable to letting her mother adopt the twins because then she could stay with them at her mother's.

and with A.K. and J.K., were illegal under Missouri law. The transfer of custody from Mother to both couples violated section 453.110,[9] the purpose of which is "to prohibit the indiscriminate transfer of children" and to prevent parents from passing them on "like chattel to a new owner." *In re Baby Girl* 64, 850 S.W.2d 64, 68 (Mo. banc 1993).

Mother also admitted that she gave a false address to the Arkansas court to effect the twins' placement with A.K. and J.K. Mother told a psychologist that she knew she was required to be an Arkansas resident to ensure the twins' adoption there, so she used an aunt's Arkansas address instead of her own. Relying on her falsified information, the probate court of Pulaski County, Arkansas, entered an adoption decree for the twins on December 22, 2000. After learning that none of the parties was an Arkansas resident at the time the adoption decree was entered, the Arkansas court entered an order on March 6, 2001, to set aside that decree for lack of jurisdiction.

Throughout the course of seeking an "open adoption,"[10] Mother accepted multiple gifts from the prospective parents. From R.A. and V.A., she received approximately $300 worth of clothes for her other children. They paid approximately $50 to have her hair braided and gave Mother a pair of diamond earrings. A.K. and J.K. brought some small gifts for N.W. when they met Mother in California and mailed N.W. more gifts

[9] Section 453.110 provides:

> 1. No person, agency, organization or institution shall surrender custody of a minor child, or transfer the custody of such a child to another, and no person, agency, organization or institution shall take possession or charge of a minor child so transferred, without first having filed a petition before the circuit court . . . and having obtained such an order form such court approving or ordering transfer of custody.
>
> . . .
>
> 3. Any person violating the terms of this section shall be guilty of a class D felony.

[10] "Open adoption" permits a continuing relationship between the biological parents and the adoptee. Naomi Cahn, *Perfect Substitutes or the Real Thing?*, 52 Duke L.J. 1077, 1151 (2003). Traditionally, adoption law required the severance of all legal ties between the child and the biological parents, thereby precluding even informal ties by denying both sets of parents information about the other. Carol Sanger, *Separating From Children*, 96 Colum. L.Rev. 375, 489 (1996).

During the last two decades, organizations of adult adoptees have "argued that secrecy was not at all in their best interests and demanded information about their biological origins." *Id.* Forty-one states have responded to these demands and now allow adult adoptees to receive "nonidentifying information" about their biological parents. Id. at 489–90.

The release of this information ideally benefits the child by providing adoptees and their parents with medical or genetic histories and satisfying—at least to some extent—the psychological needs of the children. *Id.* at 490. "In contrast, demands by birth mothers themselves to discover what became of their children have rarely been considered sufficient to breach the confidentiality of the closed records." Id. Missouri law allows for post-adoption contact only "at the discretion of the adoptive parents." Sec. 453.080.4.

In this case, Mother did not seek an open adoption because it would benefit the twins psychologically or provide them a complete medical history. Instead, she testified that she desired an open adoption because: "I wanted to see my girls. I wanted my girls to know who I was. I wanted my kids to be able to see their siblings. I wanted pictures, letters." These reasons, which only benefit the birth parent, typically provide inadequate justification for infringing upon the privacy of closed adoption records. *See* Carol Sanger, *Separating From Children*, 96 Colum. L.Rev. 375, 490 (1996).

later that year. During the drive from California to St. Louis, they purchased additional items for Mother's children.

The placements in California and the United Kingdom permitted Mother to receive free travel, lodging, meals, and airfare. She, N.W., and the twins stayed at R.A. and V.A.'s house in California for nine days without Mother contributing to any of the expenses. A.K. and J.K. paid the remainder of Mother's and N.W.'s expenses for that trip. Mother also did not pay for the airfare to visit the twins in the United Kingdom.

Mother further used her children as a means to receive more welfare benefits than she was entitled. In an application dated January 2001, Mother listed her household as including all five of her children. She later admitted that her two sons had been living with her mother since August 2000, and the twins had been residing in adoptive homes since October 2000. As a result of this false statement, Mother received approximately $3,000 in temporary aid and food stamp benefits to which she was not entitled. Mother pleaded guilty to welfare fraud and was ordered to pay restitution for this crime. When Mother, N.W., the twins, A.K. and J.K. were driving cross-country, they were stopped by police in Kansas for speeding. In an effort to avoid the consequences, A.K., J.K., and Mother conspired to tell the police they were speeding because the twins were sick. Even though the twins were not sick at the time, one of them was then taken to the hospital and examined as a result of this ruse.

In her attempts to justify why she vacillated regarding adoption of the twins, why she placed them with the couples she chose, or why she withdrew them from custody, Mother never explained her actions in the context of what was best for the twins. In every situation, as she explained it, her decisions rested on what was better for her: whether she could obtain a boyfriend with five children, whether the twins would know her and she would receive letters and photos of them, whether the couple she selected was financially sound, and whether she could visit another country. . . .

The majority cites, in its conclusion, studies showing that children needlessly separated from their parents suffer resulting deficits in their emotional and intellectual development. This point is undisputed. Even Mother, despite her initial testimony that she had never considered the emotional impact on the twins of her consistent pattern of placing and removing them and that she was the victim in this case, admitted subsequently that the twins were harmed by the multiple placements.

The majority also relies on authority that a child's developmental progress can be hampered by state intrusion. The majority ignores, however, that since the twins were released from the hospital in August 2000, they have been in Mother's sole care, custody, and control for 52 days.[15] The absence of the twins from her custody was not her choice after

[15] This total of 52 days includes the nine days Mother was staying in the house of R.A. and V.A.

DFS removed them upon their return from the United Kingdom, but the failed placements were direct consequences of her decisions and actions accomplished without mention of concern for the twins' well-being. The majority ignores that Mother voluntarily succumbed the custody of the twins to others—both times purportedly permanently—and that the state intervened only after the second placement was deemed unfit by foreign authorities acting on behalf of the twins' welfare. Any compromise in her family's integrity was accomplished directly as a result of Mother's decisions made without consideration of the twins' well-being.

The reality of this case is that the twins were born on June 26, 2000, and have been in the custody of foster parents since April 18, 2001, where they also have an adopted sibling. The testimony revealed that the twins need a stable environment and special attention to their emotional and physical needs, and Mother has never exhibited any ability to provide that for them.

When the trial court has received conflicting evidence, as in the instant case, the role of this Court is to "review the facts in the light most favorable to the trial court's judgment." M.E.W., 729 S.W.2d at 196. In its review, the Court should "give due regard to the trial court's opportunity to judge the credibility of witnesses and sustain the decree unless there is no substantial evidence to support it, it is contrary to the evidence or it erroneously declares or applies the law." *Id.* at 195–96. "As long as the record contains credible evidence upon which the trial court could have formulated its beliefs," an appellate court should not "substitute its judgment for that of the trial court." *Patton v. Patton*, 973 S.W.2d 139, 145 (Mo.App.1998).

The standard of review precludes this Court from searching the record for facts that could have supported a contrary judgment from the trial court. Unfortunately, that is exactly what the majority has chosen to do. Perhaps more unfortunately, the majority has chosen to sacrifice the best interests and welfare of two innocent children in favor of a parent who has demonstrated, time and again, her inability to make appropriate decisions concerning their care. In doing so, the majority deviates from the dictate of section 211.443, which requires courts to interpret the termination of parental rights statutes "so as to promote the best interests and welfare of the child."

Substantial clear, cogent, and convincing evidence supports the trial court's finding that termination of Mother's parental rights was justified pursuant to section 211.447.4(6) and that termination was in the twins' best interests. I would affirm the judgment.

NOTES

For commentary on poverty and parenting, *see e.g.*, Michele Estrin Gilman, *The Poverty Defense,* 47 U. RICH. L. REV. 495 (2013); Susan Frelich

Appleton, *Reproduction and Regret,* 23 YALE J.L. & FEMINISM 255 (2011); Stephanie Bornstein, *Work, Family, and Discrimination at the Bottom of the Ladder*, 19 GEO. J. ON POVERTY L. & POL'Y, 1 (2012); Pamela Gershuny, *The Combined Impact of PRWORA, FMLA, IRC, FRD, DPPA, and BAPCPA on Single Mothers and Their Children*, 18 WM. & MARY J. WOMEN & L. 475 (2012); and Janet L. Wallace and Lisa R. Pruitt, *Judging Parents, Judging Place: Poverty, Rurality, and Termination of Parental Rights*, 77 MO. L. REV. 95 (2012).

B. ADDICTIONS

New Jersey Division of Youth and Family Services v. B.G.S.

Superior Court of New Jersey, Appellate Division, 1996
677 A.2d 1170

■ PETRELLA, P.J.A.D.

B.G.S. challenges an order of the Chancery Division, Family Part, which terminated her parental rights as natural mother to her son, M.A.S. The order, prompted by an application made by the Division of Youth and Family Services (DYFS), conditioned the termination upon visitation between B.G.S. and M.A.S. until the initiation of adoption proceedings, at which time B.G.S. was to be given notification to permit her to pursue post-adoption visitation.[1] Although B.G.S. concedes her inability to care for M.A.S. and seeks neither removal of her son from his legal guardian nor interference with his custody, she asserts that the statutory criteria for termination were not satisfied by clear and convincing evidence. DYFS cross-appeals nunc pro tunc to strike from the orders any mandated post-termination visitation or notification provisions.[2] Our review of the record in light of the arguments presented satisfies us that there is overwhelming evidence supporting the propriety of the termination order. The conditions imposed in that order relating to post-termination visitation and notification of adoption are, however, in contravention of applicable law and are thus stricken.

B.G.S. was forty-two years old in 1994 when the DYFS complaint for termination of her parental rights proceeded to trial. She had abused drugs and alcohol since she was thirteen; her longest period of sobriety had been one year. Her first hospitalization for mental illness occurred at seventeen. She now suffers from bipolar disorder and polysubstance

---

[1] At oral argument, we were informed that B.G.S. paid a "final visit" to her son in June 1995. She has not sought to exercise her right to visitation during the pendency of this appeal.

[2] Although originally acquiescing, DYFS has objected to the visitation and notification provisions being included in the Family Part's termination order. During the pendency of this appeal, DYFS moved for summary disposition to strike those provisions from the order. That motion was only considered recently and was denied in the face of the imminent consideration of this calendared appeal. . . . After oral argument DYFS moved for leave to file the cross-appeal nunc pro tunc. We have granted that motion as well as its motions for stay of the visitation and notification provisions of the order.

dependence. M.A.S.'s father, A.R., has apparently shared a history of substance abuse as well.

DYFS first became aware of M.A.S. when his paternal grandfather reported on December 19, 1988, that B.G.S. had left M.A.S., her one-month-old infant son,[3] alone in her Irvington apartment and had travelled to the grandfather's South Orange home without either a coat or shoes. As there was no family member able to care for M.A.S., B.G.S. voluntarily placed him into foster care and sought hospitalization for herself. B.G.S. regained custody of M.A.S. on October 17, 1989, when he was eleven months old.

On April 17, 1990, B.G.S. contacted DYFS to report that A.R. had physically abused her and her son. In addition, B.G.S. stated that M.A.S. may have been sexually abused, either by his baby-sitter or A.R. During a DYFS investigation, the baby-sitter reported that B.G.S. had been abusing drugs and that M.A.S. had been poorly clothed, dirty, and smelly. B.G.S. was later apprehended by Summit police while she was driving eastbound in the westbound lanes of Route 24 with M.A.S. in the back seat. She had apparently suffered an acute incidence of substance abuse. When A.R. declined to care for M.A.S., DYFS again took custody of the child on July 29, 1990.

B.G.S. was initially permitted supervised overnight visitations with M.A.S. in his paternal grandmother's home. At first, he had difficulty during and in concluding these visits, throwing tantrums and pulling out his own hair. On one occasion, he had returned with bruises that appeared not to have been accidental but were nonetheless possibly attributable to his grandmother's attempts to restrain him during those tantrums. These home visits eventually ceased after M.A.S.'s grandmother declined further supervision following A.R.'s attempt to break into her home while intoxicated. In any event, DYFS had already discovered that B.G.S. had circumvented supervision by taking M.A.S. to her apartment, where he was allowed unauthorized contact with A.R.

M.A.S. was psychologically evaluated in foster care for tantrums, self-abusive behavior, and unprovoked aggression towards other children, the results of which indicated that he was developmentally delayed. His aggression towards other children in his first foster home caused M.A.S. to be moved to another foster home and then to an interim foster home on August 23, 1991. The record indicates that M.A.S. was placed in his current foster home on August 27, 1991, where he has since remained.

By the spring of 1991, M.A.S. had begun to flourish in foster care and to approximate normal levels for his age despite his developmental delay. In accordance with his observations of April 12, 1991, psychologist David Sard had recommended that M.A.S. could be returned to B.G.S. if she continued to progress in her treatment. In a progress report covering

[3] M.A.S. was born on November 15, 1988.

the period from May through August 1991, a therapist had cautiously reported progress, but had emphasized that reunification should occur only when mother and child were likely to remain together.

While M.A.S. was in foster care, B.G.S. regularly visited with him, demonstrating interest and concern for him as well as showing some improvement in her parenting skills. B.G.S. periodically participated in therapy but soon relapsed into bouts of mental illness and substance abuse. She also separated from A.R. but later resumed cohabitation with him. The record indicates that domestic violence was commonplace in their relationship. A.R. infrequently visited with M.A.S., occasionally while under the influence of an intoxicating substance. A.R. was generally uncooperative with DYFS.

Although scheduled to return to B.G.S. on December 15, 1991, M.A.S. remained in foster care because B.G.S. had relapsed into substance abuse and mental illness following her reconciliation with A.R. Indeed, M.A.S.'s therapist reported in February 1992 that he was progressing, but that B.G.S. was experiencing difficulty. DYFS then shifted its objective from reconciliation to adoption.

DYFS's expert psychologist, Frank Dyer, concluded that M.A.S. had bonded to his foster mother, that it was in his best interest not to be moved again, and that visitation with B.G.S. should therefore cease. The psychologist characterized an attempt to relocate M.A.S. as likely to be a "devastating psychological blow" of potentially permanent impact. In a June 1993 report, Dyer reiterated that it would be catastrophic to remove M.A.S. from his foster family. Dyer opined at trial that removal of M.A.S. from his foster home would likely cause "extreme psychological harm" that would be a "disaster" likely to affect his self-esteem, basic trust, and capacity to have relationships with new caretakers. The expert considered M.A.S.'s foster parents to be his "only hope for developing into a psychologically well-functioning adult." Dyer also opined that any short-term problem posed by ending visitation with B.G.S. would not constitute a significant loss to M.A.S. According to the psychologist, it would be harmful to M.A.S. if he remained in foster care indefinitely because it promised no stability and was likely to create anxiety and uncertainty. In fact, M.A.S. had told Dyer that he wished to remain with his foster family. Although he said he would feel sad if he no longer visited with B.G.S., M.A.S. responded "maybe not" when asked whether he would like to live with B.G.S.

B.G.S.'s expert psychologist, Donald Skinner, agreed that M.A.S. had bonded to his foster family and that separation was likely to cause M.A.S. serious, long-term psychological harm. He added that separating M.A.S. from B.G.S. would similarly represent a loss, albeit not to the degree that separation from the foster family would jeopardize his mental health. In a March 1993 psychiatric evaluation of B.G.S., Dr. Stephen Simring, a psychiatrist, concluded that B.G.S. was unable to function as a parent, but not solely because of her mental health. He determined that she was mentally capable to surrender her parental rights. An April 1994 psychiatric evaluation prepared by Dr. Ellen Platt indicated that B.G.S. was then psychiatrically stable, but involved in a highly dysfunctional relationship with A.R., with whom she still cohabitated. Platt confirmed that B.G.S. could not parent M.A.S. and that her maximal relationship with him could only be supervised visitation.

According to Platt, B.G.S. was afflicted with a bipolar disorder, manic depression, the nature of which is the unpredictability of its cycles. A person with the disorder may suddenly become psychologically unstable for no apparent reason, even if faithfully taking medication. The inherent instability of the disease is exacerbated by drug abuse. Because B.G.S. lacked a support system, Platt concluded that B.G.S. was not capable of caring for M.A.S. on a sustained basis. Moreover, she testified that B.G.S. had impaired judgment and limited ability to cope with stress.

By May 1994, A.R. was HIV-positive and had continued to abuse drugs and alcohol. B.G.S. nevertheless justified her continued cohabitation with A.R. on the ground that she could not abandon him because he was sick and his family had rejected him. B.G.S. claimed that she would discontinue her relationship with A.R. if necessary to continue seeing M.A.S. B.G.S. admitted, however, that DYFS had always made it clear to her that she could not regain custody of M.A.S. so long as she cohabitated with A.R. Furthermore, B.G.S. conceded that she could not parent M.A.S. and offered no plan for M.A.S. other than indefinite foster care until such time as she overcame her mental illness and drug abuse. As of the time of trial, B.G.S. had purportedly abstained from illicit drugs and alcohol for five and one-half months. Even so, M.A.S.'s foster parents wish to adopt him and object strenuously to any post-termination visitation or notice to B.G.S. of the adoption proceeding.

B.G.S.'s contention that DYFS has failed to prove the statutory criteria by clear and convincing evidence is without merit. R. 2:11–3(e)(1)(A) and (E). The Family Part Judge's finding that B.G.S. was not able to care for M.A.S. and that he had so bonded to his foster parents that removal would cause him irreparable harm are fully supported in the record. Indeed, the judge emphasized that clear and compelling evidence had persuasively established the need to terminate B.G.S.'s parental rights despite the fact that he also authorized post-termination visitation.

Notwithstanding their profound nature, parental rights are not inviolate when a child's physical or mental health is jeopardized. New Jersey Division of Youth & Family Services v. A.W., 103 N.J. 591, 599, 512 A.2d 438 (1986). N.J.S.A. 30:4C–15.1 codifies the four-prong test set forth in A.W. and provides that DYFS shall initiate an action to terminate parental rights in the child's best interest if a. [t]he child's health and development have been or will continue to be endangered by the parental relationship; b. [t]he parent is unwilling or unable to eliminate the harm facing the child or is unable or unwilling to provide a safe and stable home for the child and the delay of permanent placement will add to the harm. Such harm may include evidence that separating the child from his foster parents would cause serious and enduring emotional or psychological harm to the child; c. [t]he division has made diligent efforts to provide services to help the parent correct the circumstances which led to the child's placement outside the home and the court has considered alternatives to termination of parental rights; and d. [t]ermination of parental rights will not do more harm than good. Each of these statutory elements must be established by clear and convincing evidence. In re Guardianship of J.C., 129 N.J. 1, 10, 608 A.2d 1312 (1992). These standards are "fully consistent with constitutional doctrine." Id. at 9, 608 A.2d 1312.

The judge found that B.G.S.'s ability to adequately care for M.A.S. has endangered his health and development. We reject B.G.S.'s contention that the first prong of the statute could not have been satisfied because M.A.S.'s mental and emotional well-being improved in foster care despite her visits. Overwhelming evidence clearly and convincingly established that M.A.S. was initially harmed by B.G.S.'s inability adequately to care for him and to protect him from A.R. and that M.A.S. is subject to continued psychological damage because of his need for a permanent home and identity. Evidence of serious emotional injury or developmental delay satisfies this prong. In re Guardianship of K.L.F., 129 N.J. 32, 44, 608 A.2d 1327 (1992).

Moreover, harms attributable to a biological parent include the prolonged inattention to a child's needs, which encourages the development of a stronger, "bonding relationship" to foster parents, "the severing of which would cause profound harm. . . ." In re Guardianship of J.C., supra, 129 N.J. at 18, 608 A.2d 1312. The experts agreed that M.A.S. had bonded with his foster family and would suffer serious, long-term psychological harm if removed from the foster home.

The record clearly evinces B.G.S.'s inability or unwillingness to resolve the problems with respect to her mental health and substance abuse, thus satisfying the second prong of the A.W. test. M.A.S.'s long participation in foster care distinguishes this case from In re A., 277 N.J.Super. 454, 471–472, 649 A.2d 1310 (App.Div.1994), where there was disagreement with the permanency of the harm to the child resulting from separation from the foster parents. Unlike the situation in In re A., B.G.S. conceded her inability to parent or care for M.A.S. Her drug and alcohol addiction was complicated by chronic mental illness as well as by her continued cohabitation with A.R. in direct contravention of DYFS's clear admonition that M.A.S. could not be returned to her under such circumstances. We are convinced, therefore, that it would not be in the best interest of M.A.S. to prolong the resolution of his status by indefinitely extending his current foster care placement.[4] N.J.S.A. 30:4C–53.4 and 30:4C–60(d) effectuate the legislative policy that children be placed in "stable and permanent homes" instead of indefinite long-term foster care. See N.J.S.A. 30:4C–53.1d. The record amply demonstrates that M.A.S. needs stability and relief from the anxiety associated with his lack of permanency. The Family Part Judge appropriately concluded that further delay would harm M.A.S.

As to the third prong, there is little dispute that DYFS was diligent in its efforts to assist B.G.S. When DYFS's efforts to remedy the underlying family problems indicated that there was no prospect of rehabilitation and no available family member to provide care for M.A.S., the lack of any alternative to foster care became readily apparent. The child's need for stability and attachment had become paramount. See DYFS v. A.W., supra, 103 N.J. at 609–610, 512 A.2d 438.

The fourth prong of the A.W. test addresses the effect of termination. A court should hesitate to terminate parental rights in the absence of a permanent plan that will satisfy the child's needs. See id. at 610–611, 512 A.2d 438. The Family Part Judge appropriately concluded that termination here would not do more harm than good as DYFS had a permanent plan in the form of adoption.

B.G.S. nonetheless contends that this prong could not have been satisfied in light of expert testimony that M.A.S. would be saddened if visitation with B.G.S. ceased, even though he wished to remain with his foster parents and was better off doing so. In determining whether the child's bonding with the foster parent in itself justifies termination of parental rights, "[t]he standard is not that the end result cause no pain or trauma but that the child be kept from its parents only to avoid serious and lasting harm." In re Guardianship of K.L.F., supra, 129 N.J. at 45, 608 A.2d 1327. Thus, the child's separation from the foster parents must be shown to threaten "serious and enduring emotional or psychological harm." In re Guardianship of J.C., supra, 129 N.J. at 19, 608 A.2d 1312. Such was the case here. In any event, the present termination action was not predicated upon bonding, but rather reflected M.A.S.'s need for permanency and B.G.S.'s inability to care for him in the foreseeable future. The record supports the conclusion that greater harm is likely to befall M.A.S. by perpetuating any relationship with his natural mother. DYFS satisfied the four-prong test in A.W., and the Family Part Judge accomplished the goal of securing a permanent resolution of M.A.S.'s status through his decision. DYFS v. A.W., supra, 103 N.J. at 610, 512 A.2d 438.

We turn next to DYFS's objection to the termination order inasmuch as it authorized B.G.S. to continue visitation with M.A.S. pending adoption proceedings, of which she was to be notified presumably to allow

[4] We note that M.A.S. had been in foster care for most of his five and one-half years by the time of the trial.

her the opportunity to seek continued visitation rights or to object to the adoption. In imposing the visitation and notice conditions on termination, the Family Part Judge acknowledged that his authority to order post-termination visitation between the child and the biological parent was by no means clear under present law. His stated intention was to provide visitation in M.A.S.'s best interest "until some Appellate Court . . . tells me I . . . can't do that."

At the outset, we distinguish between visitation acquiesced in by foster or adoptive parents and visitation ordered by a court notwithstanding termination of parental rights. Although some of our cases have discussed potential continued visitation by natural parents after termination of parental rights or adoption,[5] we hold that the definition of best interest does not include post-termination visitation where an objection is raised. Our Supreme Court explained in In re Adoption of a Child by D.M.H., 135 N.J. 473, 491, 641 A.2d 235, cert. denied sub nom., Hollingshead v. Hoxworth, 513 U.S. 967, 115 S.Ct. 433, 130 L.Ed.2d 345 (1994), that New Jersey courts, like those of most jurisdictions, do not recognize the parental right of visitation following a final order of adoption by non-relative, adoptive parents.

In New Jersey Division of Youth & Family Services v. D.C., 118 N.J. 388, 395, 571 A.2d 1295 (1990), termination under N.J.S.A. 30:4C–11 to –24 was held to have ended a child's visitation with its biological parents. "Termination of parental rights permanently cuts off the relationship between children and their biological parents." In re Guardianship of J.C., supra, 129 N.J. at 10, 608 A.2d 1312. The potential harm in cutting off access to a biological parent is an inherent feature of termination, necessary to achieve the greater good of securing for the child a permanent home. Id. at 26, 608 A.2d 1312.

---

[5] Our Supreme Court has declined to reach the question of when post-termination visitation may be appropriate. See In re Adoption of a Child by D.M.H., 135 N.J. 473, 494, 641 A.2d 235, cert. denied sub nom., Hollingshead v. Hoxworth, 513 U.S. 967, 115 S.Ct. 433, 130 L.Ed.2d 345 (1994); In re Guardianship of J.C., supra, 129 N.J. at 26, 608 A.2d 1312. N.J.S.A. 9:3–37 does advocate liberal construction of the adoption act to promote the child's best interest. Relying upon Kattermann v. DiPiazza, 151 N.J.Super. 209, 376 A.2d 955 (App.Div.1977), and In re Adoption of Children by F., 170 N.J.Super. 419, 406 A.2d 986 (Ch.Div.1979), one commentator has suggested that New Jersey law thus permits post-termination visitation to promote the child's best interest. See Annotation, Postadoption Visitation by Natural Parent, 78 A.L.R. 4th 218, 239–242 (1990). In Kattermann v. DiPiazza, supra, 151 N.J.Super. at 213, 376 A.2d 955, we considered a situation in which the adoptive grandparents of a fifteen-year-old child had consented to extensive informal visitation, including long periods of child care while they worked, between the biological mother and child until shortly before the court action. We did not order visitation there, however, but rather remanded for a plenary hearing to determine whether visitation was in the child's best interest, noting under the "highly unusual" facts presented that the policy of protecting adoptive parents from disruption within the context of intra-family adoptions was "outside the zone of primary concern of the Legislature in enacting N.J.S.A. 9:3–17 et seq." Id. at 212–214, 376 A.2d 955. The intra-family context presented by Kattermann thus distinguishes that case from the instant appeal. Nor does In re Adoption of Children by F., supra, 170 N.J.Super. 419, 406 A.2d 986 support post-termination visitation here. The applicable statute there was the former version of N.J.S.A. 9:3–50a, amended by P.L. 1993, c. 345, which had provided that adoption would not alter the relationship between the child and the biological parent consenting to the adoption by a step-parent. 170 N.J.Super. at 422, 406 A.2d 986.

We have acknowledged the absolute nature of the language in N.J.S.A. 30:4C–20 to –22 as to the post-termination guardianship authority of DYFS. See In re Guardianship of R.O.M.C., 243 N.J.Super. 631, 633–634, 581 A.2d 113 (App.Div.1990). The natural parent in R.O.M.C. had intended the "open adoption"[6] of her children by foster parents. Even though intervening events could have disturbed that plan, we upheld the absolute authority of DYFS to allow visitation there on an informal basis. We nonetheless reversed and remanded a portion of the termination order, however, on the ground that the judge could not order continued visitation, especially given the unconditional authority of DYFS over the child following termination. 243 N.J.Super. at 634, 581 A.2d 113; see New Jersey Division of Youth & Family Services v. Torres, 185 N.J.Super. 234, 242, 447 A.2d 1372 (J. & D.R. Ct.1980), aff'd. o.b., 185 N.J.Super. 182, 447 A.2d 1343 (App.Div.1982).

The New York Court of Appeals has similarly concluded that post-adoptive visitation between a child and the biological family, regardless of the desirability of such "open adoptions," could not be incorporated into a termination order where a New York statute spoke unequivocally of termination of all parental duties and responsibilities. See In re Gregory B., 74 N.Y.2d 77, 544 N.Y.S.2d 535, 542, 542 N.E.2d 1052, 1059, reargument denied sub nom., In re Willie John B., 74 N.Y.2d 880, 547 N.Y.S.2d 841, 547 N.E.2d 96 (1989). The same result would appear inevitable under New Jersey's recently amended private adoption statute, N.J.S.A. 9:3–50a, which likewise provides for the complete termination of parental rights upon the entry of an adoption judgment.[7] See In re Adoption of Child by D.M.H., supra, 135 N.J. at 491, 641 A.2d 235 (articulating New Jersey's policy of protecting adoptive parents from interference in relationship with child by natural parents whose parental rights had been voluntarily surrendered or judicially severed); see also N.J.S.A. 9:3–45(b)(2) (expressly precluding notice of adoption proceeding to parent whose rights have been previously terminated).

We view the legislative policy of protecting adoptive families from disruption as strongest in cases where DYFS must take legal action to terminate parental rights. As DYFS argued in In re Guardianship of

---

6 An "open adoption" is one in which the final judgment incorporates the parties' pre-adoption written agreement "that the child will have continuing contact with one or more members of his or her biological family after the adoption is completed." Amadio and Deutsch, Open Adoption: Allowing Adopted Children To "Stay In Touch" With Blood Relatives, 22 J.Fam.L., 59, 60 (1983–1984). Insofar as the record and our research discloses, theories of the advocates of non-consensual open adoptions have not been shown to be workable.

7 D.M.H. also analyzed the legislative history of recent amendments to the private adoption statute and noted the Senate Judiciary Committee's express omission of provisions relating to "open adoptions," described by the committee as a "significant policy issue which should be addressed in separate legislation." In re Adoption of Child by D.M.H., supra, 135 N.J. at 494, 641 A.2d 235 (quoting Senate Judiciary Committee, Statement to Senate Bill No. 685 (1993)). In the absence of express provisions for "open adoption" in the private-adoption statute, D.M.H. thus concluded that post-termination visitation may not be judicially mandated without regard to the validity of a visitation provision in a voluntary and consensual pre-adoption agreement between the biological and adoptive parents. Ibid.

R.O.M.C., supra, 243 N.J.Super. at 633, 581 A.2d 113, the adoption prospects of all of its wards would be diminished if prospective adoptive parents learned that orders terminating the biological parents' rights could be conditional. The biological mother in R.O.M.C. opposed termination but favored the adoption. Although the parties in that case had agreed to continue visitation voluntarily, DYFS and the adoptive parents had opposed the mandatory order because they feared that it would have required continued visitation even if the biological mother's mental illness worsened to such a degree as to make continued visitation inimical to the child's best interest. Ibid. In this case, where B.G.S. has actively sought to retain parental rights, the foster (prospective adoptive) parents have essentially invoked this State's policy of protecting adoptive families from disruption by adamantly opposing post-adoption visitation here for comparable reasons.

Where termination is based solely upon the child's bonding with its foster parents, we have suggested alternatives that have included either a gradual transition back to the custody of the biological family or continued foster care with regular visitation of the biological parents, but not termination with continued visitation by the biological parents. See New Jersey Division of Youth & Family Services v. T.C., 251 N.J.Super. 419, 440–441, 598 A.2d 899 (App.Div.1991). We find unpersuasive the reasoning of cases in other jurisdictions, which have addressed the voluntary surrendering of parental rights subject to visitation in a manner supporting notification of adoption proceedings and perhaps post-adoption visitation when found to be in the child's best interest. See, e.g., In re S.A.H., 537 N.W.2d 1, 6–7 (S.D.1995); Petition of Dep't of Social Services to Dispense with Consent to Adoption, 392 Mass. 696, 702, 467 N.E.2d 861, 866 (Mass.1984); In re Adoption of Francisco A., 116 N.M. 708, 714, 866 P.2d 1175, 1181 (App.1993).

Nor does any theory advocating such visitation and notification provisions demonstrate the propriety of compulsory post-adoption visitation here.[8] Permitting voluntary agreements for visitation where biological parents voluntarily surrender their right is not the same as authorizing courts to mandate post-adoption visitation in involuntary termination cases.[9] See, e.g., Michaud v. Wawruck, 209 Conn. 407, 414,

[8] See, e.g., Appell, Blending Families through Adoption: Implications for Collaborative Adoption Law and Practice, 75 B.U. L.Rev. 997, 1040 (1995) (observing that "[c]ourts have ordered postadoption visitation when the parties have agreed that such visitation should occur and when the courts have found such visitation is in the best interest of the child.") (footnote omitted and emphasis supplied); Amadio and Deutsch, supra (22 J. Fam. L. at 83–86) (discussing feasibility of open adoptions "where the child, the birth parents and the foster family desired the foster parents to adopt the child and where all parties to the adoption desired the biological parent or parents to maintain some contact with the child and adoptive family") (footnotes omitted and emphasis supplied). Under the circumstances of this case, we find no advantage for M.A.S. in compelling his visitation with his mother, who has been diagnosed with bipolar disorder and polysubstance dependence, based solely upon the application of a social theory that has not been tested in the crucible of the sobering reality now facing this child.

[9] Furthermore, cases that grant grandparents visitation rights are also distinguishable because such rights are often created by statute. See, e.g., N.J.S.A. 9:2–7.1; Bopp v. Lino, 110 Nev. 1246, 1251 n. 2, 885 P.2d 559, 562 n. 2 (Nev.1994); Oregon ex rel. Costello v. Cottrell, 318

551 A.2d 738, 741 (Conn.1988) (enforcing as not violative of public policy pre-adoption agreement between biological and adoptive parents providing for post-adoption visitation if in child's best interest); Weinschel v. Strople, 56 Md.App. 252, 261, 466 A.2d 1301, 1305 (1983) (biological mother's consent to step-mother's adoption of child may be conditioned upon post-adoption visitation).

In In re Adoption of Ridenour, 61 Ohio St.3d 319, 326–328, 574 N.E.2d 1055, 1062–1063 (Ohio 1991), the Ohio Supreme Court concluded that the finality of adoption and the establishment of the adoptive family is ultimately in the child's best interest and that the biological family's desire to maintain some relationship must succumb to the paramount need to cement the new family relationship. Likewise, our termination statute is expressly predicated upon termination being in the child's best interest. N.J.S.A. 30:40C–15.1; In re Guardianship of J.C., supra, 129 N.J. at 8, 608 A.2d 1312.

Even if post-termination visitation may be in the best interest of some child, the record here did not support the Family Part Judge's findings with respect to B.G.S.'s right to visitation with her son. No witness in this case contended that continued visitation was in M.A.S.'s best interest. To the contrary, Dyer characterized M.A.S.'s loss of his relationship to B.G.S. as a short-term problem, not a significant loss. Skinner also described it as a loss, but not one that would jeopardize M.A.S.'s mental health.

The order of termination of parental rights of B.G.S. is affirmed. The visitation and notification provisions of the judge's termination order are reversed.

NOTES

Open adoption is the arrangement sought by the mother in this New Jersey decision. That is, even though her parental rights may be terminated she sought continued visitation with her child in his post-termination placement. Some states specifically reject this practice. *See, e.g.,* C.S. v. Mobile Cty. Dep't of Human Res., 166 So.3d 680 (Alabama Ct. App. 2014). But not every state forbids open adoption, some will allow it if it can be demonstrated that it would be in the best interest of the child. For example, New York permits open adoption, providing for this by statute. *See* Matter of Jacob, 660 N.E.2d 397 (N.Y. 1995). For commentary on open adoption, *see* Kristina V. Foehrkolb, Comment, *When the Child's Best Interest Calls for It: Post-Adoption Contact by Court Order in Maryland*, 71 MD. L. REV. 490 (2012).

Or. 338, 345, 867 P.2d 498, 502 (Or.1994); In re Robinson, 517 So.2d 477, 479 (La.Ct.App.1987); Scranton v. Hutter, 40 A.D.2d 296, 339 N.Y.S.2d 708, 711 (1973). The same is true with respect to siblings. See, e.g., In re Adoption of Anthony, 113 Misc.2d 26, 448 N.Y.S.2d 377, 380 n. 14 (N.Y.Fam.Ct.1982).

C. INCARCERATION

Matter of Gregory B.

Court of Appeals of New York, 1989
542 N.E.2d 1052

■ ALEXANDER, JUDGE.

The common issue presented on these appeals is whether the evidence adduced in each case supported a finding that the incarcerated parent "permanently neglected" his child within the meaning of Social Services Law § 384–b(7)(a), thus justifying the termination of his parental rights and the concomitant freeing of his child for adoption. For the reasons that follow, we conclude that the termination of parental rights was, in each case, proper and supported by clear and convincing evidence.

Evidence was presented at the fact-finding hearing that respondent father has been incarcerated since August 1980 and is currently serving a prison sentence of 10 to 20 years at Green Haven Correctional Facility upon his felony conviction. His children, Gregory and Kareem, were born on December 28, 1979 and November 20, 1980 respectively. Should respondent serve the maximum term imposed, his children will be well into their majorities by the time of his release.[1] Gregory, now 9 years old, and Kareem, now 8 years old, entered foster care on October 24, 1981 pursuant to voluntary placement agreements executed by their mother placing them under the supervision of petitioner St. Dominic's Home, an authorized child care agency. Petitioner placed Gregory and Kareem, along with their older half-brother Quaron,[2] in the same foster family with whom all three boys have resided since November 1981. Although it appears that Gregory and Kareem suffer from various physical and psychological maladies, with Kareem having required periodic hospitalization for an asthmatic condition, both children continue to thrive in their original foster home and their foster parents apparently wish to adopt them.

In July 1986, petitioner filed petitions in Family Court under Social Services Law § 384–b(7) seeking to terminate the rights of both biological parents on the ground of permanent neglect and to free the children for adoption. At the fact-finding hearing petitioner presented evidence of having actively encouraged and nurtured the parent-child relationship by arranging numerous visits between respondent and his children at prison and by attempting to secure the assistance of relatives offered by respondent as possible custodians for Gregory and Kareem. Respondent's initial plan was to have the children live with his mother until his release from prison. In a foster care review proceeding held in 1985, however, it

---

[1] Respondent will not become eligible for parole until June 1990.

[2] Respondent is not the father of Quaron who already has been adopted by the foster family.

was determined that discharge of the children to their paternal grandmother was not a viable option because she was neither physically nor emotionally up to the task of raising two young children with Gregory's and Kareem's special needs. No appeal was taken from this ruling. When advised of the court's decision, respondent's only alternative plan was to have his children remain in foster care until his eventual return to society.

Based on this evidence, Family Court concluded that the children had been permanently neglected by both parents "despite the agency's efforts to nurture all available familial resources" and specifically noted that "[t]he term of imprisoned parents must be a factor in evaluating the viability of their plan for the future of their children." After holding a dispositional hearing at which it concluded that the best interests of both children would be served by the termination of parental rights, the court terminated the parental rights of both biological parents and transferred guardianship and custody of the children to petitioner and the Commissioner of Social Services for the purpose of adoption. On respondent's appeal from Family Court's order, the Appellate Division affirmed, without opinion.[3] 143 A.D.2d 548, 538 N.Y.S.2d 889.

D. INABILITY TO MEET CHILD'S SPECIAL NEEDS

In re Jeffrey E.

Supreme Judicial Court of Maine, 1989
557 A.2d 954

■ CLIFFORD, JUSTICE.

Linda and James E., the parents of Jeffrey E., appeal from an order of the District Court terminating their parental rights . . . On appeal they contend the District Court's termination order is not supported by clear and convincing evidence. We affirm the District Court.

At the hearing on a petition filed by the Department of Human Services (Department) for the termination of the parental rights of Linda and James E., the District Court would have been warranted in finding the following facts.

Jeffrey E. was born on February 1, 1984 to Linda and James E. He has three brothers who currently reside with Linda and James. Linda is the primary caretaker of the children, while James is an unusually passive parent who contributes virtually nothing toward the care of the children and does not assist in performing any household duties.

Jeffrey suffered from pneumonia and was hospitalized several times in 1984 and 1985. In the spring of 1985, Jeffrey was hospitalized and spent time in a Boston hospital with pneumonia and a collapsed lung. When he returned home, he was put on a regimented treatment program

[3] The mother has not appealed from Family Court's order terminating her parental rights.

that was essential for a healthy recovery. Linda and James, however, were unable to follow through with providing the medications and therapies ordered by Jeffrey's physician, even with the help of a nurse from Androscoggin Home Health Associates. Consequently, Jeffrey became ill and had to be hospitalized again.

In July of 1985, Jeffrey was temporarily removed from his parents' home and placed in foster care, see 22 M.R.S.A. § 4034 (Supp.1988), and in 1986, after a hearing on the Department's Petition for a Final Protection Order, the District Court found Jeffrey to be in circumstances of jeopardy to his health and welfare should he be returned to the custody of his parents and awarded custody to the Department.

When he arrived at the foster home, Jeffrey was seventeen months old; he spoke only two words; he was unable to understand simple sentences; and he was not using a cup or spoon. After a great deal of work and attention, Jeffrey's medical condition improved and he advanced developmentally. Within a few days in the foster home, he was able to close his mouth enough to drink out of a cup. He was walking within six weeks and had increased his vocabulary from two to thirty words within three months of his arrival at the foster home. His medical condition improved with his foster mother's strict attention to the complicated medical instructions.

The Department pursued three reunification plans, in the form of written service agreements, in accordance with 22 M.R.S.A. § 4041 (Supp.1988). The reunification plans addressed three areas of concern: the family's health, the discipline and structure in the home, and the formulation of ways to stimulate the learning and development of Jeffrey. Because Linda and James did not comply with the terms of the agreement and the Department's service providers did not see any improvement in Linda's or James' parenting abilities, the Department discontinued reunification efforts in October of 1987 and petitioned the court for termination of the parental rights of Jeffrey's parents. See 22 M.R.S.A. § 4052 (Supp.1988). After a hearing in June 1988, the District Court ordered that the parental rights of Linda and James be terminated. This appeal followed.

Pursuant to the requirements for the termination of parental rights set out in 22 M.R.S.A. § 4055,[1] the court found by clear and convincing

---

[1] Pursuant to 22 M.R.S.A. § 4055 (Supp.1988), parental rights may be terminated if the court finds by clear and convincing evidence that:

(a) Termination is in the best interest of the child; and

(b) Either:

  (i) The parent is unwilling or unable to protect the child from jeopardy and these circumstances are unlikely to change within a time which is reasonably calculated to meet the child's needs;

  (ii) The parent has been unwilling or unable to take responsibility for the child within a time which is reasonably calculated to meet the child's needs;

  (iii) The child has been abandoned; or

  (iv) The parent has failed to make a good faith effort to rehabilitate and reunify with the child pursuant to section 4041.

evidence that the parents were unwilling or unable to protect Jeffrey from jeopardy and that those circumstances were unlikely to change within a time which is reasonably calculated to meet the needs of Jeffrey (22 M.R.S.A. § 4055(1)(B)(2)(b)(i)), and that they were unwilling or unable to take responsibility for Jeffrey within a time which is reasonably calculated to meet his needs (22 M.R.S.A. § 4055(1)(B)(2)(b)(ii)). In addition, the court found that Linda and James had failed to make a good-faith effort to rehabilitate and reunify with Jeffrey pursuant to 22 M.R.S.A. § 4041 (22 M.R.S.A. § 4055(1)(B)(2)(b)(iv)). The court also made the requisite finding that termination of the parental rights of Linda and James was in the best interest of Jeffrey. 22 M.R.S.A. § 4055(1)(B)(2)(a).

In reviewing the District Court's findings, we examine the entire record to determine whether the court rationally could have found clear and convincing evidence in support of its factual conclusions. When clear and convincing evidence is required, we review whether the factfinder could reasonably have been persuaded that the required factual findings were proved to be highly probable.

A finding of jeopardy may be based on the parents' inability to meet a child's special needs. In re Dean A., 491 A.2d 572, 574–75 (Me.1985). These needs may be developmental, and they may include health care. 22 M.R.S.A. § 4002(6)(B).**2** Linda and James contend that it was improper for the court to consider their inability to provide medical attention to Jeffrey because Jeffrey was in good health at the time of the termination proceeding. We disagree.

In order for a court to take into account the special medical needs of a child, a present medical emergency need not exist, nor does such a medical emergency have to be imminent or even certain to recur. The evidence in this case disclosed that, because of past medical history, Jeffrey was susceptible to medical problems that parents with average skills easily would be able to treat at home, but that Linda and James clearly would be unable to cope with. According to a nurse who worked closely with the family for three years, Linda and James have not improved at all in their ability to provide medical care for themselves or their children. Indeed, Linda testified that she does not force her children to take medications, and does not even have a thermometer in her home. Moreover, in the years between Jeffrey's placement in foster care and the current termination proceeding, Linda did not properly seek medical care for herself when she had pneumonia, or for her youngest son to alleviate his numerous upper respiratory ailments.

In addition to Jeffrey's special medical needs, there was evidence as to his special developmental needs. A psychologist testified that Jeffrey

---

[2] 22 M.R.S.A. § 4002(6)(B) (1988) provides:

"Jeopardy to health or welfare" or "jeopardy" means serious abuse or neglect as evidenced by: . . .

B. Deprivation of adequate food, clothing, shelter, supervision or care, including health care when that deprivation causes a threat of serious harm.

is much more dependent on stimulation from his environment than the average child in order to develop intellectually. Without constant intensive encouragement Jeffrey would regress and fall behind his peers. According to the testimony of the service providers who worked with the family, the home of Linda and James E. would not provide such a nurturing atmosphere. The testimony established that Linda and James did not appropriately discipline their children, did not provide intellectual stimulation in their home and provided their children with a home environment that the court justifiably found to be chaotic. For example, Linda testified that "the arguing and fighting gets sickening when it happens every day." Service providers further testified that in response to kicking, screaming and hitting among the boys in the household, Linda would scream and swear at the children.

Given the special medical and developmental needs of Jeffrey, we conclude that the District Court could reasonably have been persuaded that it was highly probable that Linda and James were unable to protect Jeffrey from jeopardy and unable to take responsibility for him within a time which is reasonably calculated to meet the child's needs. Dean A., 491 A.2d at 574–75. Having found that the District Court was justified in finding that Linda and James E. were unable to protect their child from jeopardy and take responsibility within a time reasonably calculated to meet the child's needs, we need not and do not address the court's determination that the parents failed to make a good-faith effort to rehabilitate and reunify with the child, an alternative ground for terminating the parental rights of Linda and James. See In re Randy Scott B., 511 A.2d 450, 455 (Me.1986) (under 22 M.R.S.A. § 4055(1)(B)(2)(b), court's findings of inability to protect from jeopardy and to take responsibility for the child are each independently adequate to justify termination).

We further conclude that there was substantial evidence on the record, including evidence of the inability of Linda and James to protect Jeffrey from jeopardy or to take responsibility for him, to reasonably persuade the court that it was highly probable that termination of the parental rights was in the best interest of Jeffrey.

NOTES

For commentary on the status of children of mentally challenged parents, *see, e.g.*, Anat S. Geva, *Judicial Determination of Child Custody When a Parent Is Mentally Ill: A Little Bit of Law, a Little Bit of Pop Psychology, and a Little Bit of Common Sense*, 16 UC DAVIS J. JUV. L. & POL'Y 1 (2012); Jude T. Pannell, *Unaccommodated: Parents With Mental Disabilities in Iowa's Child Welfare System and the Americans With Disabilities Act*, 59 DRAKE L. REV. 1165 (2011).

B. ADOPTION OF MINORS

1. HISTORICAL BACKGROUND AND LEGISLATIVE RESPONSE

Adoption creates a legal relationship of parent and child between persons without such a previous relationship. In the United States today it is largely a creature of statute rather than common law. State laws establish or confirm the legitimate legal status of adoptive parent and adopted child and set forth the possible procedures for effecting an adoption. In some instances federal statutes may preempt state laws in reference to such matters as race, ethnicity, or international applications and they may be controlling on certain constitutional issues.

Adoption has ancient roots. Early laws in some other countries might deal with matters ranging from effecting inheritance or political succession, to assuring continuation of family religious rites. The procedures and their effects typically were confined to adults and might serve as much to gratify adopters as to benefit adoptees. In the 1800s adoption was incorporated into the French Civil Code with significant limitations. For instance, the adopter had to be at least 50 years old and without legitimate child or descendants, and the adoptee had to be an adult. Adoption was introduced into English law by statute in 1926.

The first "modern" adoption statute in the United States was enacted in Massachusetts in 1851. A proposal in the 1861 Civil Code for New York (the Field Code) was one of the earliest statutory models. The Field Code never became law in New York, but its provisions on adoption were enacted in several western states. It is appropriate to distinguish adoption acts today as "modern" because their main objective was to *benefit* children as well as to provide children for parents. That focus is widely regarded as indigenous in adoption law in the United States. In 1959, a Uniform Adoption Act was promulgated by the NCCUSL, followed by a Revised Uniform Adoption Act in 1969, and a New Uniform Adoption Act in 1999. These various acts, although never widely enacted in total, served as a significant influence on the laws of many states.

Adoption placements sometimes are categorized (or labeled) according to the method of placement (e.g., by a licensed or state agency, or privately) or whether a prior kinship relationship exists between the parties (a relative placement). Judicial action in accordance with each state's adoption statute is required in every state. In agency placements, a licensed or state agency investigates the suitableness of the prospective adoptees and their home before a final decree is issued. An agency placement can be effected by a surrender (relinquishment of parental rights) if parental rights have not been terminated previously.

Although confidentiality in adoption is eroding in a number of jurisdictions, some states still follow a fairly strict procedure for insulating adoptive parents and adopted children from information about their pre-adoption identities. Maintaining such confidentiality ordinarily can be done in agency placements where parental rights have been terminated by surrender or court order prior to placement, and when official notice of adoption to the natural parents is not needed. After the adoption a new birth certificate is issued, showing the names of the adopter or adopters as parents and the name of the child after the adoption. The original birth certificate typically becomes confidential, viewable by court permission for good cause. Such a good cause could be to provide important genetic information. Today, many jurisdictions require agencies to retain and distribute as much of the information as available or feasible. The Uniform Adoption Act would require a "person placing a minor" to furnish a written report to a prospective adopter containing

> "a current medical and psychological history, including an account of the minor's prenatalcare, medical condition at birth, any drug or medication taken by the minor's mother during pregnancy, any subsequent medical, psychological, or psychiatric examination and diagnosis, any physical, sexual or emotional abuse suffered by the minor, and a record of immunizations and healthcare received while in foster or other care."

The previous reportage requirement is contained in Section 2–106(1). The need for further information is contained in subsections (2)-(6) of the Act. The following provisions of the California Family Code illustrate current requirements.

CALIFORNIA FAMILY CODE (2016)

Section 8700. Relinquishment of child to department or a licensed adoption agency; minor parents; rescission; termination of parental rights

(a) Either birth parent may relinquish a child to the department or a licensed adoption agency for adoption by a written statement signed before two subscribing witnesses and acknowledged before an authorized official of the department or agency. The relinquishment, when reciting that the person making it is entitled to the sole custody of the child and acknowledged before the officer, is prima facie evidence of the right of the person making it to the sole custody of the child and the person's sole right to relinquish.

(b) A relinquishing parent who is a minor has the right to relinquish his or her child for adoption to the department or a licensed adoption agency, and the relinquishment is not subject to revocation by reason of the minority.

(c) If a relinquishing parent resides outside this state and the child is being cared for and is or will be placed for adoption by the department or a licensed adoption agency, the relinquishing parent may relinquish the child to the department or agency by a written statement signed by the relinquishing parent before a notary on a form prescribed by the department, and previously signed by an authorized official of the department or agency, that signifies the willingness of the department or agency to accept the relinquishment.

(d) If a relinquishing parent and child reside outside this state and the child will be cared for and will be placed for adoption by the department or a licensed adoption agency, the relinquishing parent may relinquish the child to the department or agency by a written statement signed by the relinquishing parent, after that parent has satisfied the following requirements:

(1) Prior to signing the relinquishment, the relinquishing parent shall have received, from a representative of an agency licensed or otherwise approved to provide adoption services under the laws of the relinquishing parent's state of residence, the same counseling and advisement services as if the relinquishing parent resided in this state.

(2) The relinquishment shall be signed before a representative of an agency licensed or otherwise approved to provide adoption services under the laws of the relinquishing parent's state of residence whenever possible or before a licensed social worker on a form prescribed by the department, and previously signed by an authorized official of the department or agency, that signifies the willingness of the department or agency to accept the relinquishment.

(e) (1) The relinquishment authorized by this section has no effect until a certified copy is sent to, and filed with, the department. The licensed adoption agency shall send that copy by certified mail, return receipt requested, or by overnight courier or messenger, with proof of delivery, to the department no earlier than the end of the business day following the signing thereof. The relinquishment shall be final 10 business days after receipt of the filing by the department, unless any of the following apply:

(A) The department sends written acknowledgment of receipt of the relinquishment prior to the expiration of that 10-day period, at which time the relinquishment shall be final.

(B) A longer period of time is necessary due to a pending court action or some other cause beyond control of the department.

(2) After the relinquishment is final, it may be rescinded only by the mutual consent of the department or licensed adoption agency to which the child was relinquished and the birth parent or parents relinquishing the child.

(f) The relinquishing parent may name in the relinquishment the person or persons with whom he or she intends that placement of the child for adoption be made by the department or licensed adoption agency.

(g) Notwithstanding subdivision (e), if the relinquishment names the person or persons with whom placement by the department or licensed adoption agency is intended and the child is not placed in the home of the named person or persons or the child is removed from the home prior to the granting of the adoption, the department or agency shall mail a notice by certified mail, return receipt requested, to the birth parent signing the relinquishment within 72 hours of the decision not to place the child for adoption or the decision to remove the child from the home.

(h) The relinquishing parent has 30 days from the date on which the notice described in subdivision (g) was mailed to rescind the relinquishment.

(1) If the relinquishing parent requests rescission during the 30-day period, the department or licensed adoption agency shall rescind the relinquishment.

(2) If the relinquishing parent does not request rescission during the 30-day period, the department or licensed adoption agency shall select adoptive parents for the child.

(3) If the relinquishing parent and the department or licensed adoption agency wish to identify a different person or persons during the 30-day period with whom the child is intended to be placed, the initial relinquishment shall be rescinded and a new relinquishment identifying the person or persons completed.

(i) If the parent has relinquished a child, who has been found to come within Section 300 of the Welfare and Institutions Code or is the subject of a petition for jurisdiction of the juvenile court under Section 300 of the Welfare and Institutions Code, to the department or a licensed adoption agency for the purpose of adoption, the department or agency accepting the relinquishment shall provide written notice of the relinquishment within five court days to all of the following:

(1) The juvenile court having jurisdiction of the child.

(2) The child's attorney, if any.

(3) The relinquishing parent's attorney, if any.

(j) The filing of the relinquishment with the department terminates all parental rights and responsibilities with regard to the child, except as provided in subdivisions (g) and (h).

(k) The department shall adopt regulations to administer the provisions of this section.

Section 8702. Statement presented to birth parents at time of relinquishment; content; form

(a) The department shall adopt a statement to be presented to the birth parents at the time a relinquishment is signed and to prospective adoptive parents at the time of the home study. The statement shall, in a clear and concise manner and in words calculated to ensure the confidence of the birth parents in the integrity of the adoption process, communicate to the birth parents of a child who is the subject of an adoption petition all of the following facts:

(1) It is in the child's best interest that the birth parent keep the department or licensed adoption agency to whom the child was relinquished for adoption informed of any health problems that the parent develops that could affect the child.

(2) It is extremely important that the birth parent keep an address current with the department or licensed adoption agency to whom the child was relinquished for adoption in order to permit a response to inquiries concerning medical or social history.

(3) Section 9203 of the Family Code authorizes a person who has been adopted and who attains the age of 21 years to request the department or the licensed adoption agency to disclose the name and address of the adoptee's birth parents. Consequently, it is of the utmost importance that the birth parent indicate whether to allow this disclosure by checking the appropriate box provided on the form.

(4) The birth parent may change the decision whether to permit disclosure of the birth parent's name and address, at any time, by sending a notarized letter to that effect, by certified mail, return receipt requested,

to the department or to the licensed adoption agency that joined in the adoption petition.

(5) The relinquishment will be filed in the office of the clerk of the court in which the adoption takes place. The file is not open to inspection by any persons other than the parties to the adoption proceeding, their attorneys, and the department, except upon order of a judge of the superior court.

(b) The department shall adopt a form to be signed by the birth parents at the time the relinquishment is signed, which shall provide as follows:

"Section 9203 of the Family Code authorizes a person who has been adopted and who attains the age of 21 years to make a request to the State Department of Social Services, or the licensed adoption agency that joined in the adoption petition, for the name and address of the adoptee's birth parents. Indicate by checking one of the boxes below whether or not you wish your name and address to be disclosed:

[ ] YES

[ ] NO

[ ] UNCERTAIN AT THIS TIME; WILL NOTIFY AGENCY AT LATER DATE."

Section 8706. Medical report; background of child and biological parents; contents; blood sample

(a) An agency may not place a child for adoption unless a written report on the child's medical background and, if available, the medical background of the child's biological parents so far as ascertainable, has been submitted to the prospective adoptive parents and they have acknowledged in writing the receipt of the report.

(b) The report on the child's background shall contain all known diagnostic information, including current medical reports on the child, psychological evaluations, and scholastic information, as well as all known information regarding the child's developmental history and family life.

(c) (1) The biological parents may provide a blood sample at a clinic or hospital approved by the State Department of Health Services. The biological parents' failure to provide a blood sample shall not affect the adoption of the child.

(2) The blood sample shall be stored at a laboratory under contract with the State Department of Health Services for a period of 30 years following the adoption of the child.

(3) The purpose of the stored sample of blood is to provide a blood sample from which DNA testing can be done at a later date after entry of the order of adoption at the request of the adoptive parents or the adopted child. The cost of drawing and storing the blood samples shall be paid for by a separate fee in addition to the fee required under Section 8716. The amount of this additional fee shall be based on the cost of drawing and storing the blood samples but at no time shall the additional fee be more than one hundred dollars ($100).

(d) (1) The blood sample shall be stored and released in such a manner as to not identify any party to the adoption.

(2) Any results of the DNA testing shall be stored and released in such a manner as to not identify any party to the adoption.

NOTES

The California statute is more elaborate than many, but it reflects the trend of specifying in detail what must be done in the process of relinquishment to and placement by an agency. In Tyler v. Children's Home Society of California, 35 Cal.Rptr.2d 291 (1994), *cert. denied,* 515 U.S. 1160 (1995), birth parents who had relinquished their child to a licensed private agency for adoption sought to void their relinquishments due to failure of the agency and one of its employees to comply with Department of Social Services (DSS) regulations. In addition to accusations of coercion and intimidation, the plaintiffs asserted that the agency failed to give plaintiffs full counseling, copies of the signed and filed forms, and to obtain a full medical history from the father. The agency employee admitted noncompliance in that she did not discuss the option of placement with extended family members or educational or employment resources, and did not give plaintiffs copies of the executed documents or obtain the father's medical history before the relinquishments were signed. Concluding that the plaintiffs failed to show prejudice from any of the regulatory violations, the California Court of Appeal, Third District, affirmed the judgment below refusing to void the relinquishment agreement.

At one time it was not uncommon that a relinquishing parent could legally withdraw consent as a matter of right before an interlocutory decree of adoption had been rendered. Legislative provisions generally were added to limit or bar revocation of consent upon relinquishment to an agency or at least after the child had been placed by an agency. Sometimes the easier revocation rule remained for private placement cases. Today the widely accepted approach is not only to require that revocation must take place prior to adoption, but also to limit revocation very substantially even before adoption has taken place. The latest Uniform Adoption Act (1994) provides separate, detailed requirements for revocation of consent from a private individual or guardian, (section 2–408) and revocation of a relinquishment to an agency (Section 2–409). Many states provide that consent to relinquish is not valid unless executed a certain number of days after birth of the child. *See, e.g.,* KY. REV. STAT. 199.500(5) (2016) (consent not valid if given before 72 hours after birth). This can provide a safeguard to problems of relinquishment during a period of postpartum stress.

One situation in which a placing agency might wish to remove a child before adoption has taken place is when the potential adopters are a couple whose marriage is troubled. For a decision upholding an agency's authority to remove a child in such an instance if adequate procedures to insure fairness are followed, *see* Marten v. Thies, 160 Cal.Rptr. 57 (1979), *cert. denied,* 449 U.S. 831, 101 S.Ct. 99 (1980).

2. POTENTIAL LEGAL LIABILITIES OF AGENCIES AND FACILITATORS

Wyatt v. McDermott

Supreme Court of Virginia, 2012
725 S.E.2d 555

■ MILLETTE, JUSTICE

. . .

John M. Wyatt, III, is seeking monetary damages for the unauthorized adoption of his baby, herein referred to as E.Z. E.Z. is the biological daughter of Wyatt and Colleen Fahland, who are unmarried residents of Virginia. Prior to E.Z.'s birth, Wyatt accompanied Fahland to doctors' appointments and made plans with Fahland to raise their child together. Without Wyatt's knowledge, Fahland's parents retained attorney Mark McDermott to arrange for an adoption. While Fahland informed Wyatt of her parents' desire that she see an adoption attorney, she assured Wyatt that they would raise the baby as a family. During a January 30, 2009 meeting with McDermott, Fahland signed a form identifying Wyatt as the birth father and indicating that he wanted to keep the baby. Fahland offered to provide Wyatt's address, but McDermott told her to falsely indicate on the form that the address was unknown to her, which she did. She also signed an agreement in which she requested that the adoptive parents discuss adoption plans with the birth father. Wyatt was "purposely kept in the dark" about this meeting, and Fahland continued to make false statements to Wyatt at the urging of McDermott, indicating that she planned to raise the baby with Wyatt, with the purpose that he would not take steps to secure his parental rights and prevent the adoption. To facilitate an adoption, McDermott contacted "A Act of Love" (Act of Love), a Utah adoption agency, and Utah attorney Larry Jenkins with Wood Jenkins LLP, a Utah law firm representing Act of Love.

Approximately one week prior to E.Z.'s birth, Fahland and her father met again with McDermott. At McDermott's urging, Fahland spoke to Wyatt briefly on the phone and then sent him a text message informing him that she was receiving information about a potential adoption. Later that day and throughout the week prior to E.Z.'s birth, Fahland continued to assure Wyatt that she still planned to raise the baby with him.

Fahland concealed the fact that she was in labor during conversations with Wyatt, at the direction of McDermott and on behalf of the other defendants. E.Z. was born two weeks early, on February 10, 2009, in Virginia, and Wyatt was not informed of the birth. The next day, Fahland signed an affidavit stating that she had informed Wyatt she was working with a Utah adoption agency and an affidavit of paternity identifying Wyatt as the father. Despite her full knowledge of his address, she placed question marks as to his contact information on the notarized documents at the urging of McDermott. Thomas and Chandra Zarembinski, Utah residents who retained Act of Love to assist them in adopting a child and planned to adopt E.Z., signed an agreement stating that they were aware that E.Z.'s custody status might be unclear. On February 12, Fahland signed an affidavit of relinquishment and transferred custody to the Zarembinskis, who had travelled to Virginia to pick up the child. Wyatt claims all defendants induced Fahland to waive her parental rights knowing that Fahland did not want to relinquish rights to the baby and that Wyatt believed he would have parental rights.

On February 18, Wyatt initiated proceedings in the Juvenile and Domestic Relations Court of Stafford County, Virginia, to obtain custody of E.Z. Although Wyatt was ultimately awarded custody by the juvenile and domestic relations court, the Utah courts have awarded custody of E.Z. to the Zarembinskis. Wyatt has been involved in a protracted custody battle, the facts and proceedings of which are extensive; the salient details are simply that, at the time of the certification order, adoption proceedings were still pending in Utah, and E.Z. remains with the Zarembinskis in Utah to this date.

Wyatt filed an action in the district court against McDermott, Jenkins, Wood Jenkins LLP, Act of Love, the Zarembinskis, and Lorraine Moon, the Act of Love employee who facilitated the adoption (collectively, Defendants), seeking compensatory and punitive damages for the unauthorized adoption as well as a declaratory judgment under the Parental Kidnapping Prevention Act of 1980, Pub. L. No. 96–611, 94 Stat. 3568–3573, that Virginia had jurisdiction to award custody of the child. Wyatt asserted numerous claims, including one for tortious interference with parental rights. Upon consideration of a motion to dismiss filed by Defendants, the district court denied the motion as to the claim for tortious interference with parental rights pending its request that this Court adjudicate whether Virginia recognizes such a cause of action. . . .[1]

---

[1] The district court granted Defendants' motion to dismiss as to claims for assault, battery, and kidnapping; denial of civil rights under 42 U.S.C. § 1983; and a declaratory judgment under the Parental Kidnapping Prevention Act. The district court denied the motion

A statutory basis for tortious interference with parental rights is clearly absent from the Virginia Code; we therefore focus our analysis on whether this tort exists at common law. We conclude that, although no Virginia court has had occasion to consider the cause of action, the tort in question has indeed existed at common law and continues to exist today. Furthermore, rejecting tortious interference with parental rights as a legitimate cause of action would leave a substantial gap in the legal protection afforded to the parent-child relationship.

We recognize the essential value of protecting a parent's right to form a relationship with his or her child. We have previously acknowledged that "the relationship between a parent and child is constitutionally protected by the Due Process Clause of the Fourteenth Amendment." *Copeland v. Todd*, 282 Va. 183, 198, 715 S.E.2d 11, 19 (2011) (citing *Quilloin v. Walcott*, 434 U.S. 246, 255, 98 S.Ct. 549, 54 L.Ed.2d 511 (1978)). Indeed, the Supreme Court of the United States has characterized a parent's right to raise his or her child as "perhaps the oldest of the fundamental liberty interests recognized by this Court." *Troxel v. Granville*, 530 U.S. 57, 65, 120 S.Ct. 2054, 147 L.Ed.2d 49 (2000).

It follows, then, that a parent has a cause of action against third parties who seek to interfere with this right. In the analogous case of *Chaves v. Johnson*, 230 Va. 112, 335 S.E.2d 97 (1985), we explicitly recognized the common law tort of tortious interference with contract rights for the first time, noting its historical basis in the Commonwealth. We said:

> We have not previously had occasion to consider this precise aspect of the law of torts, although in *Worrie v. Boze*, 198 Va. 533, 95 S.E.2d 192 (1956), we affirmed a judgment granting relief for a tortious conspiracy to procure a breach of contract. There, we said: "It is well settled that the right to performance of a contract and the right to reap profits therefrom are property rights which are entitled to protection in the courts. Consequently, suits for procuring breach of contract proceed on this basis." *Id.* at 536, 95 S.E.2d at 196.

Id. at 119–20, 337 S.E.2d at 102. In *Chaves*, we were not creating a new tort but rather recognizing that the common law provided a cause of action for tortious interference with contract rights. The historical happenstance that the tort in question had not previously been invoked in Virginia did not prevent us from recognizing that the common law right of contract necessarily brought with it, as a corollary, a right to seek recompense against those who interfered with a valid contract. Noting the recognition of tortious interference with contract by many of our sister states, by many English courts, and in the Restatement of Torts,

as to claims for conspiracy, fraud, and constructive fraud, finding that Wyatt had pled sufficient facts to state a claim for relief under each of those theories.

we concluded that a claim for tortious interference with contract could be brought in Virginia. *Id.* It would be remarkable indeed if the common law right to be free from interference in contract were to be deemed to be more valuable than the common law right of a parent to be free from interference in a relationship with his or her child.

In this case, following the blueprint set forth in *Chaves*, we would not be creating a new tort, but rather recognizing that the common law right to establish and maintain a relationship with one's child necessarily implies a cause of action for interference with that right. To hold otherwise in this case would be to recognize "a right without a remedy-a thing unknown to the law." *Norfolk City v. Cooke*, 68 Va. (27 Gratt.) 430, 439 (1876).

We acknowledge that the most direct and proper remedy, the return of the child and restoration of the parent-child relationship, may never be achieved through a tort action. When a parent has been unduly separated from a child by a third party for a substantial period of time without due process of law, however, other legitimate harms may be suffered that are properly recoverable in tort, including loss of companionship, mental anguish, loss of services, and expenses incurred to recover the child.

An examination of our law shows that the redress of these wrongs is in some circumstances otherwise unavailable in the Commonwealth. Wrongful custodial interference is codified in Code § 18.2–49.1 as a criminal offense, but this statute provides no civil recovery. Virginia also has well-developed custody laws to manage intra-familial disputes, but custody disputes do not implicate rights or duties of third parties, such as are at issue here.[2] The Commonwealth provides for causes of action for fraud and constructive fraud, but a third party can wrongfully interfere with parental rights without engaging in fraudulent behavior. There remain many cognizable scenarios in which intentional tortious interference with parental rights could be invoked not as a legal redundancy, but as a unique remedy.

The recognition of tortious interference with parental rights finds precedent in our common law. We have previously stated that "our adoption of English common law . . . ends in 1607 upon the establishment of the first permanent English settlement in America, Jamestown. From that time forward, the common law we recognize is that which has been developed in Virginia." *Commonwealth v. Morris*, 281 Va. 70, 82, 705

[2] Neither are we persuaded by the argument that, since an action for tortious interference with parental rights requires a threshold element of establishing parental rights, the cause of action cannot lie because this determination cannot be made in tort. Our law regularly allows for adjudications of elements in tort that lie separate from adjudications for other purposes, such as when a defendant may be held civilly liable but not criminally guilty for the same offense. The fact that parental rights are an element of the tort does not act as a per se bar to the recognition of the tort. The finding of parental rights in tort would not dictate the outcome of a custody proceeding or adoption, although a custody determination or adoption could provide evidence of parental rights in a tort proceeding.

S.E.2d 503 (2011). Prior to 1607, a comparable cause of action did lie in England, providing a father with recourse for the abduction of his heir or sons rendering services. See *Pickle v. Page*, 252 N.Y. 474, 169 N.E. 650, 651 (1930) (citing *Barham v. Dennis*, (1599) 78 Eng. Rep. 1001 (K.B.); Cro. Eliz. 770).

Clearly, there are ways in which this ancient writ is markedly different from the modern cause of action urged by Wyatt, which would permit recourse for either parent, regardless of gender, and which encompasses a recovery not merely for loss of services but also for loss of companionship. This difference reflects society's changing values as reflected in this Court's rulings over the centuries, including principles of gender equality, an inherent value in the relationship between parents and their children beyond the value of services rendered, and the modern trend in tort law to make plaintiffs whole by compensating not only pure pecuniary loss but also emotional harm.

Although the action has not heretofore been brought in Virginia, and hence has never come before this Court, its evolution elsewhere can be clearly identified. Blackstone wrote that the abduction of any child, not merely an heir, was "remediable by writ of *ravishment*, or, action of *trespass vi et armis, de filio, vel filia, rapto vel abducto*; in the same manner as the husband may have it, on account of the abduction of his wife." 3 William Blackstone, Commentaries (internal footnote omitted). By 1938, the American Law Institute's first Restatement of Torts included recovery for the abduction of a child, and the Restatement (Second) of Torts section 700 recites the more modern embodiment of the ancient writ: "One who, with knowledge that the parent does not consent, abducts or otherwise compels or induces a minor child to leave a parent legally entitled to its custody or not to return to the parent after it has been left him, is subject to liability to the parent. . . ."

The overwhelming majority of the high courts of our sister states that have considered the issue have also recognized such a tort, many of them tracing its evolution in the common law. *See, e.g., Anonymous v. Anonymous*, 672 So.2d 787, 789, (Ala.1995) (noting that the Restatement (Second) of Torts § 700 does not represent a new tort in Alabama but rather "accurately reflects the common law principle that parents have a right to the care, custody, services and companionship of their minor children, and [that] when they are wrongfully deprived thereof by another, they have an action therefor" (internal quotation marks omitted)); *Washburn v. Abram*, 122 Ky. 53, 90 S.W. 997, 998 (1906) (concluding that, although the common law right of action historically arose from the right of the father to recover for lost services of his child and such allegations are necessary for recovery, "[i]t matters not whether the child [actually] renders such services; and [the parent] is not confined in a recovery to the loss of services alone, but may recover damages for injury to his feelings and the loss of companionship of his child"); *Khalifa v. Shannon*, 404 Md. 107, 945 A.2d 1244, 1248–62 (2008) (recognizing a common law action of interference with parental-child relations against one who abducts and/or harbors a child, and, in a thorough discussion of the evolution of the common law, finding that loss of services was never a substantive element of the common law tort but rather tied to certain ancient English forms of remedy); *Plante v. Engel*, 124 N.H. 213, 469.

A.2d 1299, 1302 (1983) (holding the intentional aiding and abetting in the interference of parental rights to be an actionable tort in New Hampshire); *Silcott v. Oglesby*, 721 S.W.2d 290, 293 (Tex.1986) (recognizing that the common law had evolved to substantially track the Restatement (Second) of Torts § 700); *Kessel v. Leavitt*, 204 W.Va. 95, 511 S.E.2d 720 (1998) (upholding a finding of tortious custodial interference against maternal grandparents, uncle, and mother's attorney, but not the child's mother, due to her equal parental rights). *Kessel*, which likewise addressed an adoption dispute, provides a particularly helpful model for the elements of the tort.[3] . . .

The Court is now left to determine what elements are essential to the tort as it exists today, consistent with the original writ, but in line with equal protection and modern law. *Kessel* succinctly lays out the elements of this cause of action, consistent with Virginia law:

> (1) the complaining parent has a right to establish or maintain a parental or custodial relationship with his/her minor child; (2) a party outside of the relationship between the complaining parent and his/her child intentionally interfered with the complaining parent's parental or custodial relationship with his/her child by removing or detaining the child from returning to the complaining parent, without that parent's consent, or by otherwise preventing the complaining parent from exercising his/her parental or custodial rights; (3) the outside party's intentional interference caused harm to the complaining parent's parental or custodial relationship with his/her child; and (4) damages resulted from such interference.

511 S.E.2d at 765–66.

---

[3] Justice McClanahan asserts in her dissent that the recognition of custodial interference torts, addressed in some of the above-referenced cases, is irrelevant to the tort of parental interference in the context of an unauthorized adoption because "Comment (c) [of the Restatement (Second) of Torts § 700] states that [the cause of action] does not apply when parents are entitled to joint custody and can only be brought by the parent with sole or superior custody rights."

Comment (c) states:

> *When both parents entitled to custody and earnings.* When the parents are by law jointly entitled to the custody and earnings of the child, no action can be brought against one of the parents who abducts or induces the child to leave the other. When by law only one parent is entitled to the custody and earnings of the child, only that parent can maintain an action under the rule stated in this Section. One parent may be liable to the other parent for the abduction of his own child if by judicial decree the sole custody of the child has been awarded to the other parent.

Thus, Comment (c) indeed bars suits between parents with equal rights. It does not, however, bar proceedings against third parties, nor does it require a custodial adjudication to warrant a suit against a third party.

Given the nature of the original English common law writ, we must consider whether the harm and recoverable damages must be limited solely to tangible loss of service. We join the high court of Maryland in concluding that "a focused analysis reveals that loss of services has never been an element of the tort itself, but rather, arose from common law pleading requirements in force in England," which contained "artificial divisions" between tangible loss of services and intangible losses such as comfort and society.[4] *Khalifa*, 945 A.2d at 1256, 1262. The evolution from form- to fact-based pleading in Maryland, as in Virginia, dictates that the ancient pleading requirements of English writs "no longer serve to define the elements of the tort." *Id.* at 1262. We therefore conclude that the modern iteration of this common law tort encompasses both tangible and intangible damages, including compensatory damages for the expenses incurred in seeking the recovery of the child, lost services, lost companionship, and mental anguish. Equitable remedies such as injunctions or custody orders may not be awarded under this cause of action.

Finally, as we have previously stated, "[I]f a tortfeasor's tort was intentional rather than negligent, i.e., deliberately committed with intent to harm the victim . . . and if the evidence is sufficient to support an award of compensatory damages, the victim's right to punitive damages and the quantum thereof are jury questions." *Smith v. Litten*, 256 Va. 573, 579, 507 S.E.2d 77, 80 (1998); *see also Giant of Virginia, Inc. v. Pigg*, 207 Va. 679, 685–86, 152 S.E.2d 271, 277 (1967).

We adhere to the ordinary burden in civil actions of preponderance of the evidence. *Fudge v. Payne*, 86 Va. 303, 308, 10 S.E. 7, 8 (1889). We find no precedent to indicate that this writ required any heightened standard of proof. We require a heightened standard of clear and convincing evidence for intentional infliction of emotional distress, for instance, because it is an action not favored by this Court due to the inherent ambiguity in proving harm to one's emotions or mind. *Russo v. White*, 241 Va. 23, 26, 400 S.E.2d 160, 162 (1991). Although, as with many torts, juries may award some compensation for mental anguish in intentional interference cases, the harm lies in the physical interruption of the parent-child relationship, a concrete factor. Thus, we conclude that the ordinary burden of preponderance of the evidence is appropriate for a claim of intentional interference with parental rights.

---

[4] Under English form pleadings, interference with the parent-child relationship could be redressed by an action of trespass, and the plaintiff was required to elect between pleading trespass vi et armis, which claimed direct tangible injury, and trespass on the case, which claimed indirect intangible injury. Khalifa, 945 A.2d at 1256–57. Virginia has since rejected this distinction as "so nice and useless that both the courts and the legislatures have manifested a decided purpose to abolish the distinction." *Stonegap Colliery v. Hamilton*, 119 Va. 271, 279–80, 89 S.E. 305, 307 (1916).

The minority of states that have resisted recognition of tortious interference with parental or custodial rights have done so based on policy grounds, citing concern for the best interest of the child. In *Larson v. Dunn*, 460 N.W.2d 39 (Minn.1990), the Minnesota Supreme Court concluded that it was not in the best interest of children to permit such a tort, because "the law should not provide a means of escalating intrafamily warfare." *Id.* at 46. The court concluded that a tort possessing the potential for such significant impact on children should be properly evaluated as a matter of public policy by the legislature rather than created by the courts. *Id.* at 47. The Minnesota Supreme Court's emphasis on the best interest of the child was followed two years later by the Oklahoma Supreme Court in *Zaharias v. Gammill*, 844 P.2d 137, 140 (Okla.1992) ("We are convinced that the tort of interference with custodial relations would not enhance the scheme of family law in Oklahoma, and we expressly disapprove of it.").

We share these courts' concern for the well-being of children caught in intra-familial disputes, a concern that was not as prominent an issue in 1607, when only a male parent could bring this cause of action. The fear that this cause of action would be used as a means of escalating intra-familial warfare can be largely disposed of by barring the use of this tort between parents, as other state courts have done. The West Virginia high court put this well in *Kessel*:

> [W]e hold that a parent cannot charge his/her child's other parent with tortious interference with parental or custodial relationship if both parents have equal rights, or substantially equal rights (as in the case of a nonmarital child where the putative biological father seeks to establish a meaningful parent-child relationship with his child and, until such a relationship has been commenced, does not have rights identical to those of the child's biological mother), to establish or maintain a parental or custodial relationship with their child. In other words, when no judicial award of custody has been made to either parent, thereby causing the parents' parental and custodial rights to be equal, no cause of action for tortious interference can be maintained by one parent against the other parent. Likewise, where no judicial decree has been entered awarding custody of a nonmarital child to one or the other of the child's biological parents, the complaining biological parent cannot assert a claim of tortious interference with parental or custodial relationship against the other biological parent.

511 S.E.2d at 766. A similar bar is articulated in Comment (c) to the

Restatement (Second) of Torts § 700, excerpted in footnote 3, *supra*. Thus, we conclude that a defendant may raise an affirmative defense of "substantially equal rights," as explained above in *Kessel*, as it is to the advantage of all parties that such a determination be made early in the proceedings.

Additionally, in the interest of the child, we note with approval the affirmative defense of justification as set forth in Kessel, wherein the court held that a party should not be held liable if he or she

> possessed a reasonable, good faith belief that interference with the parent's parental or custodial relationship was necessary to protect the child from physical, mental, or emotional harm[; or] possessed a reasonable, good faith belief that the interference was proper (i.e., no notice or knowledge of an original or superseding judicial decree awarding parental or custodial rights to complaining parent); or reasonably and in good faith believed that the complaining parent did not have a right to establish or maintain a parental or custodial relationship with the minor child (i.e., mistake as to identity of child's biological parents where paternity has not yet been formally established).

511 S.E.2d at 766.

We do not cite these as an exhaustive list of available defenses, but rather note them due to their particular importance, so that our explicit recognition of this tort does not promote unnecessary intra-familial litigation or deter an individual from acting when he or she holds a good-faith belief that a child is in danger.

Often, in considering a certified question of law, the facts of a particular case serve only to define the scope of the inquiry to yield a determinative answer for the presiding court. In this instance, however, the facts as pled are illustrative of the basis and continuing need for this action in tort. It is both astonishing and profoundly disturbing that in this case, a biological mother and her parents, with the aid of two licensed attorneys and an adoption agency, could intentionally act to prevent a biological father-who is in no way alleged to be an unfit parent-from legally establishing his parental rights and gaining custody of a child whom the mother did not want to keep, and that this father would have no recourse in the law. The facts as pled indicate that the Defendants went to great lengths to disguise their agenda from the biological father, including preventing notice of his daughter's birth and hiding their intent to have an immediate out-of-state adoption, in order to prevent the legal establishment of his own parental rights. This Court has long recognized that the rights of an unwed father are deserving of protection. *Hayes v. Strauss*, 151 Va. 136, 141, 144 S.E. 432, 434 (1928). The tort of tortious interference with parental rights may provide one means of such protection. Finally, we hope that the threat of a civil action would help deter third parties such as attorneys and adoption agencies from engaging in the sort of actions alleged to have taken place.

For the aforementioned reasons, we answer the first certified question in the affirmative, and we answer the second certified question by referring the United States District Court for the Eastern District of Virginia to Part II.D. of this opinion.

■ JUSTICE MCCLANAHAN, with whom JUSTICE GOODWYN joins, dissenting.

While the facts as pled by Wyatt are unquestionably disturbing, I cannot join the majority's effort to deter such conduct by legislating public policy in Virginia through judicial pronouncement. . . .

Because I do not believe the tort of interference with parental rights currently exists in Virginia, the decision of whether to create such a cause of action should be left to the legislature in light of the competing and far-reaching public policy considerations that are involved. *Bell v. Hudgins*, 232 Va. 491, 495, 352 S.E.2d 332, 334 (1987). *See also Advanced Towing Co., LLC v. Board of Supervisors*, 280 Va. 187, 191, 694 S.E.2d 621, 623 (2010) ("[r]espect for the separation of the powers of the legislative and judicial branches of government is an essential element of our constitutional system"); *Taylor v. Worrell Enters., Inc.*, 242 Va. 219, 221, 409 S.E.2d 136, 137–38 (1991) (the principle of separation of powers "prevents one branch from engaging in the functions of another, such as the judicial branch performing a legislative function, or the legislative branch taking on powers of a judicial nature") (citations omitted). When the question of whether to recognize a new theory of liability involves a multitude of competing interests,

> which courts are ill-equipped to balance, . . . the legislative machinery is specially geared to the task. A legislative change in the law is initiated by introduction of a bill which serves as public notice to all concerned. The legislature serves as a forum for witnesses representing interests directly affected by the decision. The issue is tried and tested in the crucible of public debate. The decision reached by the chosen representatives of the people reflects the will of the body politic. And when the decision is likely to disrupt the historic balance of competing values, its effective date can be postponed to give the public time to make necessary adjustments.

Bruce Farms, Inc. v. Coupe, 219 Va. 287, 293, 247 S.E.2d 400, 404 (1978).

In creating an action for tortious interference with parental rights arising from an unauthorized adoption, there are many significant and varying interests that will be affected. The interests of the biological parents, the adoptive parents, and the child[6] are impacted as well as the legitimate interest in facilitating adoptions for those who seek to place their child for adoption and for those who wish to be adoptive parents. The recognition of this new cause of action also affects the operations and actions of adoption agencies, adoption attorneys and other professionals or governmental agencies involved in the adoption process, which may be subject to liability. Furthermore, the General Assembly has already

[6] The meaning of "the best interests of the child" is different in the context of custody disputes than it is in the context of adoptions since the biological parents' due process rights in their relationship to their child must be considered. Copeland, 282 Va. at 197, 715 S.E.2d at 19.

enacted specific provisions governing the rights of the biological and adoptive parents.[7] Moreover, the factual and legal determinations in a tort action may necessarily involve the same factual and legal questions pending or already ruled upon in the context of adoption or custody proceedings based on the statutory provisions governing such proceedings. "The sheer number of issues that can be raised in a debate of this nature demonstrates the inadequacy of the judicial process to balance these competing concerns." *Robinson v. Matt Mary Moran, Inc.*, 259 Va. 412, 418, 525 S.E.2d 559, 563 (2000). In my view, the answers to the questions raised by these competing policy interests "should come from the General Assembly and not the courts." Bell, 232 Va. at 495, 352 S.E.2d at 334.[8]

We recently reaffirmed the principle that decisions involving competing individual and societal interests fall within the scope of legislative, not judicial, authority. *Bevel v. Commonwealth*, 282 Va. 468, 479–80, 717 S.E.2d 789, 795 (2011) (if it is to be the policy in Virginia that a criminal conviction will abate upon defendant's death while appeal is pending, "the adoption of such a policy and the designation of how and in what court such a determination should be made is more appropriately decided by the legislature, not the courts"). *See also Uniwest Constr., Inc. v. Amtech Elevator Servs.*, 280 Va. 428, 440, 699 S.E.2d 223, 229 (2010) ("The public policy of the Commonwealth is determined by the General

---

[7] The Virginia General Assembly has enacted comprehensive legislation governing the issues relating to parental rights, specifically including establishment of a parental relationship, child custody, and adoption. *See, e.g.*, Code § 20–49.1 (how parent and child relationship established); Code § 20–49.2 et seq. (proceedings to determine parentage or establish paternity); Code § 20–124.1 et seq. (custody and visitation); Code § 63.2–1200 et seq. (adoption). The General Assembly has also enacted legislation criminalizing certain actions that may interfere with parental or custodial relationships. *See, e.g.*, Code § 18.2–47 (abduction and kidnapping); Code § 18.2–49.1 (violation of court orders regarding custody and visitation). The General Assembly has not, however, enacted legislation imposing civil liability or otherwise permitting the recovery of money damages for acts that interfere with parental or custodial rights.

[8] The majority has chosen to follow the decision of the Supreme Court of West Virginia in *Kessel v. Leavitt*, 204 W.Va. 95, 511 S.E.2d 720 (1998), recognizing tortious interference with parental rights in the context of an unauthorized adoption. The court in *Kessel* discussed at length the competing interests of the various parties involved in the adoption process, noting that there are several cases of national prominence involving the "trampling" of a biological father's rights resulting in the "wrenching of children from their adoptive families" and that cases involving the placement of a child in another jurisdiction are an "increasingly common . . . method by which to thwart a biological father's parental rights." *Id.* at 823–24. Recognizing that its decision was "not an appropriate forum in which to dissect and repair all of the ailments of existing adoption procedures," it nonetheless proceeded to "redress, in part, the intentional deprivation of a biological father's right to establish a relationship with his child," while simultaneously acknowledging that its legislature has already taken action in that regard. *Id.* at 824. In fact, the court conceded the scope of its decision may be limited by legislative enactments. *Id.* at 756, n. 37. In my opinion, the rationale espoused by the *Kessel* court does not support the majority's creation of this new tort in Virginia. To the contrary, it aptly illustrates the serious policy considerations involved in determining the existence and scope of such a cause of action.

In the Commonwealth of Virginia, it is not the role of the judiciary to weigh these competing interests and adopt a policy of law that will best serve these interests. It is the role of the legislature "to formulate public policy, to strike the appropriate balance between competing interests, and to devise standards for implementation." *Wood v. Board of Supervisors*, 236 Va. 104, 115, 372 S.E.2d 611, 618 (1988).

Assembly [because] it is the responsibility of the legislature, and not the judiciary, . . . to strike the appropriate balance between competing interests.") (internal quotation marks and citation omitted). Likewise, if public policy demands that parties involved in the adoption process should be held liable in tort for interference with parental rights, "this should be accomplished, [I] think, by an appropriate act of the General Assembly, and not by judicial pronouncement." *Hackley v. Robey*, 170 Va. 55, 66, 195 S.E. 689, 693 (1938).[9]

Accordingly, because I do not believe that Virginia currently recognizes a cause of action for tortious interference with parental rights arising from an unauthorized adoption, and that the decision to recognize this tort in Virginia should be made by the General Assembly, I would answer certified question one in the negative.

M. H. and J .L. H. v. Caritas Family Services

Supreme Court of Minnesota, 1992
488 N.W.2d 282

■ WAHL, JUSTICE.

We are asked to decide whether public policy precludes an action against an adoption agency for alleged negligent misrepresentations made during the placement of a child in adoption proceedings. . . .

Plaintiffs M.H. and J.L.H., who married in 1977, sought to adopt a child after learning J.L.H. was unlikely to conceive a child. Plaintiffs first contacted Caritas Family Services, a Catholic social service agency active in placing children for adoption, in early 1980. In May of that year, they filled out an application for adoption during an interview in their home by a Caritas social worker. On November 23, 1981, Caritas conducted a second home visit. The purpose of the second visit was, according to Caritas' adoption summary, "to explore with [the H.s] their feelings regarding a child with incest in the background." According to the summary, the H.s "appeared open to any child except one with a very serious mental deficiency." Two days later, in a telephone conversation,

[9] As the majority notes, a significant number of other states have recognized a cause of action for intentional interference with custodial rights based on the Restatement (Second) of Torts § 700 (1977). That section, entitled "Causing [a] Minor Child to Leave or not to Return Home [,]" provides that "one who, with knowledge that the parent does not consent, abducts or otherwise compels or induces a minor child to leave a parent legally entitled to its custody or not to return to the parent after it has been left him, is subject to liability to the parent." Comment (c) to this section states that it does not apply when parents are entitled to joint custody and can only be brought by the parent with sole or superior custody rights. Adopting or relying on this section, these courts have recognized a cause of action for interference with custodial rights in this context. But Wyatt does not seek recognition of a cause of action for the taking of a child in the context of a violation of a custody order in which he has sole or superior lawful custody. Rather, he seeks recognition of a cause of action for tortious interference with parental rights arising from an unauthorized adoption. The only decision cited by the majority recognizing a cause of action for an unauthorized adoption is *Kessel*. Instead of weighing the serious policy considerations impacted by creating a cause of action arising from an unauthorized adoption as the court did in *Kessel*, however, I would leave that task to the General Assembly, which bears the responsibility for formulating the public policy of Virginia.

Sister Cathan Culhane, a Caritas social worker, told J.L.H. that Caritas had a child the H.s might wish to adopt. According to J.L.H., Sister Culhane told her there was a "possibility of incest in the family." J.L.H. said she told sister Culhane, "Well, it's a baby. We're happy. As long as it's in the family, it didn't affect him." Sister Culhane described the baby as having a plugged tear duct and an undescended testicle, but otherwise in good health.

Two days after this telephone call, the H.s met with Sister Culhane in Caritas' office in St. Cloud. Sister Culhane again raised the question of incest and, according to M.H. and J.L.H., asked "Did it matter if there was incest in the family's background?" M.H. said he replied, "No problem, didn't matter to me in the background." According to M.H., Sister Culhane said there was a slight chance that the child might have abnormalities related to incest in his "background." The H.s asked no further questions and there was no more discussion of incest.

At this meeting, Caritas gave the H.s a document with information about the child, including his name, birth date, birth weight and length, cultural heritage, and a description of the genetic parents. The health of the genetic parents was described as follows: HEALTH Both parents of normal intelligence and in good health as are their parents, brothers and sisters. Older members of their families—(Grandparents' generation) have had coronary trouble, Muscular Dystrophy and also nervous breakdown. One cousin of the natural mother is retarded and an uncle had an ulcer. Both parents planned for the adoption of their child because they are young, still in school, and unable to assume the role of parents at this time.

The H.s took the baby, C.H., home with them that day. He was 45 days old. The H.s soon noticed that C.H. was jumpy, nervous, cried a lot, and did not sleep very much. The H.s consulted their physician who wanted information as to whether C.H.'s genetic mother had taken drugs during pregnancy. Mrs. H. contacted Sister Culhane who said that the genetic mother was not on drugs during pregnancy.

Sometime between November 1981 and when the adoption became final in September 1982, Caritas sent the H.s a document saying the birth mother was 17 years old instead of 13 as they had been previously told. The document also mentioned the "possibility of incest" but said nothing more specific on the subject. The H.s inquired about the discrepancy in the genetic mother's age and were assured by Sister Culhane that the original information given them about the genetic mother's age (that she was 13) was correct and a new document was sent to replace the mistaken one. Neither the H.s or Sister Culhane discussed incest at this time.

Throughout his childhood, C.H. has had serious behavioral and emotional problems. He has been diagnosed as having attention deficit hyperactivity disorder. He has exhibited hyperactivity, violent behavior when upset (i.e. kicking, biting, pulling hair), and has set fires indoors.

On one occasion, he struck, punched, bit, and scratched J.L.H. while she took him to an appointment with his psychiatrist. He has difficulty with small motor skills and has had social problems in school. He is not mentally retarded, however, and his adoptive parents characterize him as smart.

The H.s consulted psychologists to help C.H. regarding his behavior. In 1987, one of the psychologists asked for more information regarding C.H.'s genetic background. In response to this request, Caritas produced and gave to the H.s a 2-page document entitled "Background History of [C.H.]" in December 1987. This document revealed to the H.s, for the first time, that C.H.'s genetic parents were a 17-year old boy and his 13-year old sister. Caritas admits that it knew of this relationship from the time it first considered placing C.H. with the H.s.

Caritas subsequently also disclosed that the genetic father was considered "borderline hyperactive" which caused problems for him in school; that he had tested in the low average range of intelligence; and that he had been seen at the local mental health center at age of 11 for six weeks, but was discharged from treatment because he was not cooperating with his therapist. The H.s were also told that a physician, possibly a neurologist, had prescribed medication for the genetic father's hyperactivity. Caritas has denied knowing this information about the genetic father's mental health history until its inquiry in 1987.

After learning these facts regarding H.'s genetic parents, the H.s filed an action against Caritas in October 1989. Count I of their complaint alleged that Caritas failed to disclose the relationship of C.H.'s genetic parents and all relevant history known to Caritas concerning the birth parents with the intent to induce the H.s to adopt the child. Count II alleged that Caritas negligently failed to disclose that information as well as other relevant information it had about the child's genetic parents. The complaint also alleged that because of the misrepresentations, whether intentional or negligent, the plaintiffs had suffered mental pain and anguish and had incurred considerable expense.

During discovery Caritas refused to reveal information relating to what it knew about C.H.'s genetic parents prior to adoption, its attempts to place him with other families, and its sources of information about the genetic parents without a court order permitting it to do so, citing the state adoption statute (Minn.Stat. ch. 259), the Minnesota Government Data Practices Act (Minn.Stat. ch. 13), and unspecified federal regulations. Caritas agreed to stipulate to a court order to permit it to disclose its discussions held between the agency's employees and the adoptive parents, but not its written records. No such order was ever requested, however, or granted by the court.

On October 8, 1990, Caritas moved for summary judgment on both counts of the complaint, the intentional misrepresentation claim on the grounds of insufficient evidence and the negligent misrepresentation claim on grounds of public policy. Caritas also moved for summary judgment on a count of intentional infliction of emotional distress that it anticipated the respondents would try to add to their complaint. Plaintiffs then did move to amend their complaint to add allegations of intentional and negligent infliction of emotional distress and a prayer for punitive damages. They also moved to compel discovery of Caritas' pre-adoption records. The district court granted Caritas' motions for summary judgment, except as to negligent misrepresentation. The court certified the question we have before us. . . .

Plaintiffs in the case before us allege that the adoption agency disclosed information about the child's genetic parents but negligently failed to communicate that information fully and accurately and that such negligence caused them damages. Whether public policy precludes an action against an adoption agency for alleged negligent misrepresentation during the placement of a child in adoption proceedings is a question of law and a question of first impression in Minnesota. A review at the outset of cases from jurisdictions that have considered the issue is instructive, however. See generally Mary E. Schwartz, Note, Fraud in the Nursery: Is the Wrongful Adoption Remedy Enough?, 26 Val.U.L.Rev. 807 (1992). On the one hand, the cases seem to agree that adoption agencies may be held liable for damages caused by intentional, affirmative misrepresentations of facts regarding the child to the adopting parents. See, e.g., Michael J. v. County of Los Angeles, 201 Cal.App.3d 859, 247 Cal.Rptr. 504, 512–13 (1988) (public policy does not condone concealment or intentional misrepresentation that misleads adopting parents); Burr v. Board of County Comm'rs of Stark County, 23 Ohio St.3d 69, 491 N.E.2d 1101, 1109 (Ohio 1986) (same). On the other hand, there is agreement that an adoption agency cannot be expected to be "a guarantor of the infant's future good health" and negligence suits tending to have that effect have been rejected. Richard P. v. Vista Del Mar Child Care Serv., 106 Cal.App.3d 860, 165 Cal.Rptr. 370, 374 (1980); see also Foster v. Bass, 575 So.2d 967, 980 (Miss.1990). The question we are asked to decide falls between these two extremes: whether public policy bars actions holding adoption agencies liable for damages for negligent misrepresentation of facts concerning the child's genetic parents and medical history.

We have recognized the tort of negligent misrepresentation, Bonhiver v. Graff, 311 Minn. 111, 121–23, 248 N.W.2d 291, 298–99 (1976), but conduct actionable against one class of defendant is not automatically actionable against another class of defendants. Tort liability in the first instance always depends on whether the party accused of the tort owes a duty to the accusing party. If such a duty is owed, then one who undertakes to act must, under common law principles, act with reasonable care. No duty is owed, however, unless the plaintiff's interests are entitled to legal protection against the defendant's conduct. Whether the plaintiff's interests are entitled to legal protection against the defendant's conduct is a matter of public policy.

Which brings us to the certified question stated somewhat more precisely: Does public policy favor legal protection of the interests of adoptive parents against the negligent conduct of adoption agencies?

Caritas and amici adoption agencies emphatically answer that question in the negative. They ask this court to hold as a matter of law that public policy precludes recognition of a legal duty of care with regard to negligent representations of fact by adoption agencies to adoptive parents. They argue that recognition of such a duty would place an unreasonable burden on adoption agencies by requiring them to independently verify family histories given them by the genetic parent. Adoptions would be discouraged, they say, if agencies were required to disclose information that might render certain children more difficult to place or would unnecessarily stigmatize them once adopted. They further argue it is unreasonable to impose liability on agencies for negligently failing to discover certain aspects of a child's genetic history when the number of genetic-related conditions and the cost of tests to discover them are increasing at a rapid rate. Finally, Caritas and amici argue that requiring adoption agencies to defend negligent misrepresentation suits would conflict with confidentiality policies required by state and federal law to protect the identity of genetic parents.

We appreciate that these are legitimate policy concerns. We recognize the unique nature and mission of adoption agencies as they seek to meet both the need of adoptive parents to experience the joys and challenges of parenthood and the need of every child to have a stable, loving family. We also recognize, however, the compelling need of adoptive parents for full disclosure of medical background information that may be known to the agency on both the child they may adopt and the child's genetic parents, not only to secure timely and appropriate medical care for the child, but also to make vital personal, health and family decisions.

While under other circumstances the policy concerns of the adoption agencies may preclude a cause of action, on the facts of this case, the policy concerns are not implicated. Plaintiffs do not allege that Caritas insufficiently investigated C.H.'s background: Caritas knew from the start of these adoption proceedings that C.H.'s genetic parents were brother and sister. Neither do plaintiffs assert that Caritas had a duty to test C.H. for genetic abnormalities. There is no suggestion nor do plaintiffs allege that Caritas had an affirmative common law duty to disclose facts surrounding C.H.'s parentage beyond those required by statute or administrative rule.[5] Furthermore, confidentiality policies are necessary to protect the identity of the genetic parents, not to inhibit communication of vital health and medical information. Plaintiffs assert only that once Caritas undertook to disclose the information that incest

---

[5] See, e.g., Minn.R. 9560.0060 (1991) (adoption agencies required to provide adoptive parents with written health history of the child that is understandable and meaningful to the adoptive family).

existed in C.H.'s background, it assumed a duty to use due care that its disclosure be complete and adequate to ensure that the adoptive parents were not misled as to the true nature of their son's genetic parentage. This is the common law duty plaintiffs allege Caritas breached.

We long ago recognized that even if one has no duty to disclose a particular fact, if one chooses to speak he must say enough to prevent the words from misleading the other party. We have also held that a duty to disclose facts may exist "when disclosure would be necessary to clarify information already disclosed, which would otherwise be misleading," particularly when a confidential or fiduciary relationship exists between the parties. L & H Airco, 446 N.W.2d at 380. We are not persuaded that adoption agencies should be immune from this common law rule.[6] Recognition of this duty imposes no extraordinary or onerous burden on adoption agencies. It merely requires them to use due care to ensure that when they undertake to disclose information about a child's genetic parents and medical history, they disclose that information fully and adequately so as not to mislead prospective adoptive parents. Caritas had a legal duty to not mislead plaintiffs by only partially disclosing the truth.

The district court, in denying Caritas' motion for summary judgment on negligent misrepresentation on policy grounds, and the court of appeals in affirming that denial, relied on Meracle v. Children's Serv. Soc. of Wis., 149 Wis.2d 19, 437 N.W.2d 532 (1989). In Meracle, the Wisconsin Supreme Court recognized a cause of action where an adoption agency negligently told adoptive parents that, though the child's paternal grandmother had Huntington's Disease, the child's genetic father had tested negative for that disease, thus negating the child's chances of developing the disease. In fact no such test existed and the father could not have been tested. Id. 437 N.W.2d at 533. The court recognized that public policy requires that adoption agencies should not be exposed to unlimited liability or be made guarantors of the health of children they place in adoptive homes. Id. at 537. It held, however, that public policy did not bar a negligent misrepresentation action when the agency assumed a duty of informing adoptive parents about the child's health history but did so negligently. "To avoid liability, agencies simply must refrain from making affirmative misrepresentations about a child's health." Id. See also Roe v. Catholic Charities, 588 N.E.2d 354, 365 (Ill.App.1992).

We, like the court of appeals, find Meracle persuasive. Like the Meracle court, we reject the argument that potential liability will inhibit adoptions. "Indeed, [our decision] will give potential parents more confidence in the adoption process and in the accuracy of the information they receive. Such confidence would be eroded if we were to immunize agencies from liability for false statements made during the adoption

---

[6] If there are policy considerations that should override the agency's common law liability for misrepresentation, the legislature is the appropriate body to extend such immunity.

process." Meracle, 437 N.W.2d at 537. This is particularly true because adoption agencies are the adoptive parents' only source of information about the child's medical and genetic background.

We hold that public policy does not preclude a negligent misrepresentation action against an adoption agency where the agency, having undertaken to disclose information about the child's genetic parents and medical background to the adoptive parents, negligently withholds information in such a way that the adoptive parents were misled as to the truth. We affirm the court of appeals and answer the certified question in the negative.

The district court granted Caritas summary judgment on plaintiffs' intentional misrepresentation claim because it found that Caritas had made no affirmative misrepresentation to plaintiffs. Plaintiffs argue that Caritas made two discrete misrepresentations, one regarding the incest in C.H.'s background and the other by affirmatively stating that C.H.'s genetic father was in "good health." Plaintiffs argue that either representation was specific enough to support their claim of intentional misrepresentation. The court of appeals agreed and reinstated the claim for both representations.

An intentional misrepresentation claim requires plaintiffs to allege that defendant (1) made a representation (2) that was false (3) having to do with a past or present fact (4) that is material (5) and susceptible of knowledge (6) that the representor knows to be false or is asserted without knowing whether the fact is true or false (7) with the intent to induce the other person to act (8) and the person in fact is induced to act (9) in reliance on the representation (10) that the plaintiff suffered damages (11) attributable to the misrepresentation. A misrepresentation may be made either (1) by an affirmative statement that is itself false or (2) by concealing or not disclosing certain facts that render the facts that are disclosed misleading.

The statements Caritas made regarding incest were of the latter type. Their falsity arose, if at all, from Caritas' failure to disclose additional facts, not from the statements themselves which were true on their face. Plaintiffs, however, have not alleged any facts or produced any evidence implying that Caritas intended to mislead plaintiffs by deliberately withholding the full facts regarding incest in C.H.'s background. Indeed, the evidence suggests the opposite: if Caritas intended to mislead plaintiffs, it is unlikely it would have raised the question of incest with them at all. In the absence of evidence that the statements regarding incest were calculated to mislead plaintiffs, they were insufficient as a matter of law to establish a case of intentional misrepresentation.[7]

---

[7] Plaintiffs contend that Caritas' refusal to grant them access to its pre-adoption records should estop it from receiving summary judgment on this claim. The records might contain direct evidence of Caritas' intent to mislead plaintiffs by deliberately referring to the incest in an oblique manner calculated to obscure the actual truth. Plaintiffs did not file a motion to

Neither will Caritas' statement regarding the genetic father's "good health" support an intentional misrepresentation claim because plaintiffs have not shown it was either false on its face or deliberately misleading. Caritas' statement in 1981 that the genetic father was in good health is not made false by the fact that the genetic father had been hyperactive and had undergone psychiatric treatment several years before. Plaintiffs must, therefore, produce evidence that Caritas intentionally misled them by withholding the information. Even if Caritas knew of the genetic father's mental health history in 1981,[8] plaintiffs have not produced any facts to suggest that Caritas' failure to disclose that fact was intended to mislead them.

We reverse the court of appeals and hold that the district court properly granted defendant Caritas summary judgment on the intentional misrepresentation claim.

Plaintiffs moved the trial court to amend their complaint to add claims for intentional infliction of emotional distress, negligent infliction of emotional distress, and punitive damages. The trial court denied the motion, holding that the dismissal of the intentional misrepresentation claim left the record bare of allegations of outrageous and willful misconduct required for either claim of infliction of emotional distress and the punitive damages claim. The court of appeals, having reinstated the intentional misrepresentation claim, reversed.

Infliction of emotional distress, whether intentional or negligent, generally requires plaintiffs to suffer a physical injury as evidence of their severe emotional distress. Because plaintiffs have alleged no physical injury resulting from their alleged emotional distress, their motion to amend was properly denied unless they alleged a "direct invasion" of their rights by "willful, wanton, or malicious conduct." State Farm Mut. Auto. Ins. Co. v. Village of Isle, 265 Minn. 360, 367–68, 122 N.W.2d 36, 41 (1963). There is no evidence of such a direct invasion of plaintiffs' rights, or of willful, wanton, or malicious conduct on the part of Caritas. Plaintiffs have provided no evidence that Caritas deliberately misled them, much less wantonly did so. . . . [T]he district court did not abuse its discretion in denying plaintiffs leave to amend their complaint to add claims of intentional and negligent infliction of emotional distress.

Similarly, plaintiffs have not alleged sufficient facts to support a finding that there is "clear and convincing evidence that the acts of the defendant show a deliberate disregard for the rights or safety of others" required to recover punitive damages. The court of appeals is therefore reversed and the district court's denial of leave to add a claim for punitive damages is affirmed. . . . Case remanded for trial.

---

compel discovery of these records until more than a year and three months after the suit was filed and over three months after Caritas filed its motion for summary judgment, however. Having delayed so long, they cannot now complain that they lack the facts to support their complaint.

[8] Caritas asserts it did not learn of those problems until 1987.

NOTES

Types of adoptive placements isolated from the agency framework have significantly increased. One option is independent adoption. *See, e.g.,* CAL. FAM. CODE § 8524 (2016): " 'Independent adoption' means the adoption of a child in which neither the department, county adoption agency, nor agency licensed by the department is a party to, or joins in, the adoption petition." Then, Section 8623 of the Code provides that: "A person or organization is an adoption facilitator if the person or organization is not licensed as an adoption agency by the State of California and engages in either of the following activities:

> (a) Advertises for the purpose of soliciting parties to an adoption or locating children for an adoption or acting as an intermediary between the parties to an adoption.
>
> (b) Charges a fee or other valuable consideration for services rendered relating to an adoption."

Most states now recognize the tort action of negligent or intentional misrepresentation. Such a tort would allow for an adoptive parent to recover damages for material misrepresentation of an adoptive child's history prior to adoption. For commentary, *see e.g.*, S. Megan Testerman, Note, *A World Wide Web of Unwanted Children: The Practice, the Problem, and the Solution to Private Re-Homing,* 67 FLA. L. REV. 2103 (2015); Mehrnoosh Torbatnejad, Note, *Untold Truths: What Adoptive Parents Should Know About Their Adoptee's in Utero Drug and Alcohol Exposure,* 19 CARDOZO J.L. & GENDER 213 (2012); Amanda Trefethen, *The Emerging Tort of Wrongful Adoption*, 11 J. CONTEMP. LEGAL ISSUES 620 (2000); D. Marianne Brower Blair, *Lifting the Genealogical Veil: A Blueprint for Legislative Reform of the Disclosure of Health Related Information in Adoption*, 70 N.C. L. REV. 681 (1992). A number of state courts have permitted civil actions for recovery. *See, e.g.,* Burr v. Board of County Com'rs of Stark Cty., 23 Ohio St.3d 69, 491 N.E.2d 1101 (1986) (listing the elements of the tort); *but see*, Dahlin v. Evangelical Family Agency, 2001 WL 84037 (N.D. Ill. 2001) (disallowing an adoptive child from bringing suit against an adoption agency for wrongful adoption).

3. ABROGATION OF ADOPTION

Ann Marie N. v. City and County of San Francisco

Court of Appeal of California, First District, 2001
2001 WL 1261958

■ KAY, JUSTICE.

Plaintiff Ann Marie N. sued the City and County of San Francisco (City) when she discovered the child she had adopted through the City's Department of Social Services was infected with HIV (human immunodeficiency virus). She alleged negligence, intentional misrepresentation, and intentional concealment. The trial court granted the City's motion for summary adjudication, eliminating the negligence and the intentional misrepresentation claims. The matter proceeded to trial on the intentional concealment claim, but after plaintiff presented her evidence, the trial court granted the City's motion for nonsuit.

Ann Marie N. contends she had ample evidence of negligent and intentional conduct and that all the claims she alleged should have been submitted to a jury. We find the trial court properly eliminated the negligence and intentional misrepresentation claims, but that the intentional concealment claim should have been submitted to the jury. We reverse the judgment with respect to that claim, but affirm the judgment in all other respects.

Mathew N. was born on August 7, 1986, with alcohol and cocaine in his system. His mother stated she regularly used cocaine and drank alcohol during her pregnancy. She was known to the City's Department of Social Services "because of her substance abuse, transient and unstable lifestyle, and involvement in prostitution." Mathew was immediately removed from the custody of his mother and, on January 14, 1987, declared a dependent of the San Francisco County Juvenile Court. Later, the court terminated the parental rights of his birth parents and freed Mathew for adoption.

In October 1988, Ann Marie N. saw a television program on children waiting for adoption that featured Mathew. Ann Marie N. lived in Stockton and was a social worker for the County of San Joaquin. Ann Marie N. contacted the City's Department of Social Services, expressed interest in adopting Mathew, and began the adoption process. She filled out a questionnaire in which she indicated she did not want to adopt a child with a "blood disorder." During the adoption process, Ann Marie N. learned Mathew had been a "drug exposed" infant. She was aware his mother had used alcohol and drugs during her pregnancy and that Mathew was born addicted to alcohol and drugs. She was not aware of the mother's involvement in prostitution.

On May 14, 1989, Mathew was placed in Ann Marie N.'s home. Shortly after the placement Ann Marie N. took Mathew to see Bryant Williams, M.D., a pediatrician. Ann Marie N. told Dr. Bryant that Mathew was born " 'addicted to drugs' " and that he had a history of respiratory problems including asthma. Dr. Bryant found Mathew to be a " 'well child' " and cleared him for nursery school. He did not think it was medically necessary to test Mathew for HIV in 1990. But he would have suggested testing if he had been told the birth mother "had a lengthy history of involvement in prostitution, substance abuse, and transient lifestyle." Ann Marie N.'s adoption of Mathew became final on February 14, 1990.

In 1996, a social worker for the City called Ann Marie N. and told her that Mathew's birth mother had died of AIDS (acquired immunodeficiency syndrome). Ann Marie N. took Mathew to a medical clinic for testing, and, on September 18, 1996, learned Mathew was HIV positive. According to Ann Marie N., she would not have adopted Mathew if she knew he was HIV positive. The City had begun developing procedures for HIV testing for children in dependency proceedings in 1987, but it did not implement any procedures until 1993.

Ann Marie N. sued both the City and the County of Stanislaus, which had assisted in the adoption process by evaluating Ann Marie N.'s suitability as an adoptive parent. In her claim for intentional misrepresentation of fact, Ann Marie N. alleged defendants had represented and assured her that Mathew was in good health and suitable for adoption, when in fact he was infected with HIV. In her claim for intentional concealment, she alleged defendants knew Mathew was infected with HIV and failed to reveal that fact. In her claim for negligence, she alleged: "As revealed in and reinforced by defendants' own internal polices [sic] and procedures, defendants owed a duty to prospective adoptive parents to identify whether or not children committed to their care were 'high risk' for HIV infection, to accurately screen and test such high risk children for HIV, and to accurately convey the results of such testing to prospective adoptive parents so that said prospective parents might make informed decisions as to any prospective adoption."

The City moved for summary judgment or, in the alternative, summary adjudication. The trial court granted the motion for summary adjudication on the negligence claim, finding as a matter of law that an adoption agency cannot be liable for mere negligence. The trial court also granted summary adjudication on the intentional misrepresentation claim, finding the defendants' statement that Mathew " 'is considered to be medically, socially, and psychologically a suitable subject for adoption' " was not an actionable misrepresentation of fact.[1] The trial court denied summary adjudication on the intentional concealment claim, finding a triable issue of material fact as to whether the City fraudulently failed to disclose that Mathew's natural mother was involved in prostitution.

The trial on the intentional concealment claim added few new facts. Ann Marie N. testified that two social workers, one from the City and one from the County of Stanislaus, were involved in handling the adoption of Mathew. Ann Marie N. remembered receiving some information regarding the health of Mathew and his birth mother from the Stanislaus social worker. She generally did not remember the substance of her conversations with the City's social worker, Bill Holman. She did not think that Holman gave her any information regarding Mathew's health before the completion of the adoption. Someone told her about Mathew's exposure to drugs and alcohol, but no one told her that Mathew's birth mother was involved in prostitution.

---

1 The statement quoted by the trial court was contained in a report prepared by the Stanislaus County Department of Social Services. Ann Marie N. received a copy of the report before the adoption became final. The trial court granted summary judgment in favor of Stanislaus County and Ann Marie N. has not appealed from that judgment.

The City called Holman to testify out of order during Ann Marie N.'s case. He testified that he did not know Mathew was at risk for contracting HIV or AIDS. He knew intravenous drug use was a risk factor, though he could not pinpoint exactly when he gained that knowledge. With regard to transmission of HIV from mothers to their babies, he was certain only that if the mother was HIV positive, her baby was at risk.

Ann Marie N. called Mildred Crear, the City's director of Children's Medical Services during the relevant time period, as an adverse witness pursuant to Evidence Code section 776. She testified regarding the City's procedures for testing dependent children for HIV or AIDS. According to Crear, a committee composed of personnel from various City agencies considered HIV transmission to children. The risk factors considered by the committee included a mother who used drugs intravenously or who had sexual contact with persons with AIDS or HIV. A newborn baby testing positive for drugs abused intravenously was also considered a risk factor. Prostitution itself was not considered a risk. Because of their occupation, prostitutes "had better safe sex practices" than the general population. The testing guidelines were not completed and disseminated to the City's Department of Social Services personnel until 1993.

Finally, the parties stipulated that, if called, Lillian Johnson, the coordinator of a fragile infant special care program at St. Elizabeth's Hospital, would testify that in 1987 there were approximately 50 infants with AIDS in San Francisco. That number was expected to increase significantly. At St. Elizabeth's in 1987 and early 1988, one infant had died of AIDS, two had AIDS, and two others were HIV positive.

After Ann Marie N. presented her evidence, the City moved for nonsuit. In an order dated October 25, 2000, the trial court granted the motion, noting that Holman denied having any knowledge that Mathew was at risk for HIV, and that there was no evidence to the contrary. The trial court refused to impute the knowledge of Crear or Johnson to Holman. Ann Marie N. purports to appeal from a "judgment, encompassing, but not limited to, the order granting nonsuit entered October 25, 2000, and the order granting summary adjudication of issues entered on February 9, 2000." There is no judgment in the record before us, and apparently no judgment was entered in this matter. The order granting nonsuit is an appealable order. (Galanek v. Wismar (1999) 68 Cal.App.4th 1417, 1420, fn. 1.) An order granting summary adjudication of issues is not. (City of Oakland v. Superior Court (1996) 45 Cal.App.4th 740, 750.) To avoid multiple appeals and piecemeal dispositions, we will treat the order granting nonsuit as having the legal effect of a judgment, allowing review of the trial court's intermediate ruling on the motion for summary adjudication. (See Santa Barbara Pistachio Ranch v. Chowchilla Water Dist. (2001) 88 Cal.App.4th 439, 448, fn. 1.). . . .

Adoption agencies in this state are not liable for "mere negligence in providing information regarding the health of a prospective adoptee."

(Michael J. v. Los Angeles County Dept. of Adoptions (1988) 201 Cal.App.3d 859, 874–875 (Michael J.); Richard P. v. Vista Del Mar Child Care Service (1980) 106 Cal.App.3d 860, 866–867 (Richard P.).) In both *Michael J.* and *Richard P.* the adoptive parents alleged the adoption agency possessed material information that it failed to convey. In *Michael J.*, the defendant allegedly knew or in the exercise of reasonable care should have known a birthmark on the adopted child was a manifestation of Sturge Weber Syndrome. (Michael J., *supra*, at pp. 863–864.) In *Richard P.*, the adoptive parents alleged the defendants were negligent in representing the child was healthy when it could have been predicted the child would suffer neurological damage in the future. (Richard P., *supra*, at pp. 863–864.) For reasons of public policy, the Courts of Appeal in *Michael J.* and *Richard P.* rejected the negligence claims based on these allegations. (Michael J., *supra*, at pp. 872–875; Richard P., *supra*, at pp. 866–867.)

Ann Marie N. believes Michael J. and Richard P. are no longer good law, and that it is time for courts to impose a duty on adoption agencies to investigate a child's medical condition and to convey accurate information to adoptive parents. Ann Marie N. points to the trend in other states to recognize claims against adoption agencies for negligent misrepresentation (see Annot., Wrongful Adoption (1999) 74 A.L.R.5th 1 [collecting cases]), and the policy of this state to disclose an adoptee's background to adoptive parents (see e.g., Family Code, §§ 8706, 8817 [requiring a written report on child's medical background and, if possible, medical background of biological parents]; Health & Saf.Code, § 121020 [permitting HIV testing of dependent children pursuant to court order].)[2]

We find no basis to depart from *Michael J.* and *Richard P.* in this case. The Legislature has not overruled *Michael J.* and *Richard P.* even as it has demonstrated an intent to provide prospective adoptive parents with as much information as possible.[3] And though Ann Marie N. now

---

[2] At the time of Mathew's adoption, the medical report requirement was contained in former Civil Code section 224s (Stats.1984, ch. 1116, § 1, p. 3761). That section, in pertinent part, provided: "(a) No agency shall place a child for adoption unless a written medical report on the child's medical background, and if available, so far as ascertainable, the medical background of the child's birth parents, has been submitted to the prospective adopting parents and the prospective adoptive parents have acknowledged in writing the receipt of such report. [¶] The report on the child's background shall contain all known diagnostic information, including current medical reports on the child, psychological evaluations, and scholastic information, as well as all known information regarding the child's developmental history and family life. [¶] . . . [¶] (b) The State Department of Social Services shall adopt regulations specifying the form and content of the report required by this section. In addition to any other material that may be required by the department, the form shall include inquiries designed to elicit information on any illness, disease, or defect of a genetic or hereditary nature. All licensed adoption agencies shall cooperate with and assist the department in devising a plan that will effectuate the effective and discreet transmission to adoptees or adoptive parents of pertinent medical information reported to the department or the licensed agency, upon the request of the person reporting the medical information."

[3] Ann Marie N. requests that we take judicial notice of legislative documents relating to the enactment of statutes for medical reports and HIV testing of dependent children. We may take judicial notice of such documents and we hereby do so. (Aguilar v. Atlantic Richfield Co., *supra*, 25 Cal.4th at p. 848, fn. 6.) Ann Marie N. also requests that we take judicial notice of an excerpt from a "sociological monograph reporting a statistical study evidencing the problem

relies on the Family Code section 8706, she did not allege a violation of then existing statutory requirement for delivery of a medical report, nor has she cited any evidence showing the City failed to comply with the requirement.

Ann Marie N., the City, and amicus curiae California State Association of Counties have advanced policies for and against imposing liability on adoption agencies for negligence. Those policies deserve consideration from a legislative body so that the issue can be resolved for the greatest good of children waiting for adoption and adoptive parents. . . .

It was undisputed that Ann Marie N. had no basis for believing the City's social workers concealed the fact that Mathew was HIV positive, and we find no evidence of any misrepresentation made with an intent to deceive. Her argument on this point is devoid of any citation to evidence in the record to support her allegation that the City made assurances regarding Mathew's health. In opposing the motion for summary judgment or adjudication, she cited only the report prepared by the County of Stanislaus as evidence of representations regarding Mathew's medical suitability for adoption. But even if we assume Holman, who apparently was the only City employee to provide information to Ann Marie N., represented that Mathew was healthy, there was no evidence offered in opposition to the summary judgment motion that he believed otherwise. . . .

At trial Ann Marie N. attempted to prove the City intentionally concealed the risk that Mathew was HIV positive.[4] The only witnesses she presented on this issue were herself and Crear, who testified as an adverse witness. The stipulated offer of proof regarding the testimony of Lillian Johnson added some statistics regarding infants infected with HIV or AIDS. Other witnesses testified regarding damages. Holman testified out of order for the defense.

The trial court held Ann Marie N. had failed to present facts that were "(1) sufficient to establish the existence of a duty to disclose the material fact here at issue, or (2) sufficient to permit a jury to find an intentional concealment or suppression of that fact." The trial court noted the material fact at issue was whether Mathew was at risk for HIV infection based on his birth mother's health and lifestyle and Mathew's

[Family Code section 8706] was intended to address." The City opposes the request. We cannot determine whether the facts and propositions stated in the excerpt are reasonably subject to dispute. Therefore, we decline to take judicial notice of the excerpt. (Evid.Code, § 452, subd. (h); § 459, subd. (a).)

4 Ann Marie N. pled the City knew Mathew was infected with HIV and suppressed that fact. When it became apparent the City was not aware Mathew was HIV positive, Ann Marie N. offered to amend her complaint. The trial court ruled an amendment was not necessary because the complaint put the City on notice of a claim for intentional concealment of risk factors. We further note that though this case survived the City's summary judgment motion based on a triable issue of fact as to whether the City fraudulently failed to disclose that Mathew's birth mother was involved in prostitution, the case proceeded to trial on a more general theory of failure to disclose Mathew was at risk for HIV.

own health. The trial court relied on Holman's testimony regarding his knowledge of HIV transmission, stating in its order: "Mr. Holman, who is the person claimed to have intentionally withheld information, denied having any knowledge or information at or before the finalization of the adoption to the effect that Mathew was at risk for HIV-positive status."

Ann Marie N. argues a jury could have found Holman was lying when he disclaimed any knowledge that Mathew was at risk. She also advances a complex agency theory under which the knowledge of Crear would be imputed to Holman. Holman's testimony should have been disregarded in connection with the motion for nonsuit. It was not favorable to Ann Marie N.'s case and he was not her witness. For purposes of the nonsuit motion, the only relevant evidence was Ann Marie N.'s own testimony, the stipulated testimony of Johnson, and the testimony of Crear favorable to Ann Marie N.'s case (see *Ashcraft v. King* (1991) 228 Cal.App.3d 604, 611 [testimony favorable to plaintiff adduced from an adverse witness under Evid.Code § 776 must be taken as true and unfavorable portions disregarded]).

Ann Marie N. testified that Holman did not give her any information regarding Mathew's health. According to Ann Marie N., she was not given Mathew's medical records until after the adoption was final. Nor was she told that a child born addicted to drugs was at risk for HIV, or that prostitution was a risk factor. She was not told Mathew's mother had a history of prostitution. Crear testified that it was known by 1988 that intravenous drug use by a birth mother was a risk factor in HIV transmission to her baby. Crear also acknowledged that a baby born addicted to drugs abused intravenously by the mother was at risk. Prostitution was not a known risk factor, according to Crear, but a mother who had sexual contact with persons infected with HIV or AIDS was a risk factor.

Though there was no direct evidence Holman concealed the fact that Mathew was at risk for HIV or that Mathew's birth mother was involved in prostitution, the jury could have inferred from his silence on Mathew's health and on the birth mother's history (according to Ann Marie N.), that he was concealing important facts in order to complete the adoption of Mathew. The nondisclosure of a significant fact may suggest fraud. (Michael J., *supra*, 201 Cal. App.3d at p. 875.) However weak the evidence, it showed the existence of HIV risk factors known to City employees and not disclosed or discussed with Ann Marie N. Bearing in mind that Holman's testimony had to be disregarded in considering the motion for nonsuit, the state of the evidence was sufficient to require the City to offer evidence regarding Holman's discussions with Ann Marie N. and his knowledge of HIV risk factors, or evidence that Ann Marie N. would have adopted Mathew even if she had been told he was at risk.[5]

[5] We agree with the trial court and the City that Crear's knowledge cannot be imputed to Holman. (See *Godwin v. City of Bellflower* (1992) 5 Cal.App.4th 1625, 1631 [there is no principle of agency law imputing the knowledge of one agent to all others].) We disagree, however, with

We reverse the judgment with respect to the nonsuit on the intentional concealment claim. In all other respects the judgment is affirmed. The parties shall bear their own costs on appeal.

■ REARDON, ACTING P.J. and SEPULVEDA, J., concur.

4. INTERETHNIC ADOPTION

42 U.S.C.A. § 1996b (2016)

§ 1996b. Interethnic adoption

(1) Prohibited conduct. A Person or government that is involved in adoption or foster care placements may not-

(A) deny to any individual the opportunity to become an adoptive or a foster parent, on the basis of the race, color, or national origin of the individual, or of the child, involved; or

(B) delay or deny the placement of a child for adoption or into foster care, on the basis of the race, color, or national origin of the adoptive or foster parent, or the child, involved.

(2) Enforcement. Noncompliance with paragraph (1) is deemed a violation of title VI of the Civil Rights Act of 1964 [42 U.S.C.A. § 2000d et seq.].

(3) No effect on the Indian Child Welfare Act of 1978. This submission shall not be construed to affect the application of the Indian Child Welfare Act of 1978 [25 U.S.C.A. § 1901 et seq.].

NOTES

Critics of the policy implemented by this statute argue that often the best interest of the child will be served by being raised in a household with the same racial characteristics. *See, e.g.*, EVAN B. DONALDSON ADOPTION INSTITUTE, FINDING FAMILIES FOR AFRICAN AMERICAN CHILDREN: THE ROLE OF RACE & LAW IN ADOPTION FROM FOSTER CARE (2008); David D. Meyer, Palmore *Comes of Age: The Place of Race in the Placement of Children*, 18 U. FLA. J.L. & PUB. POL'Y 183 (2007).

---

the suggestion of amicus curiae that the City is entitled to immunity for the discretionary acts of its employees under Government Code sections 815.2 and 820.2. We fail to see how the alleged fraudulent concealment of HIV risk factors could be considered a discretionary act, and amicus curiae offers no legal argument on this point.

5. CHILD OF INDIAN PARENTS

Mississippi Band of Choctaw Indians v. Holyfield

Supreme Court of the United States, 1989
490 U.S. 30

■ JUSTICE BRENNAN delivered the opinion of the Court.

This appeal requires us to construe the provisions of the Indian Child Welfare Act that establish exclusive tribal jurisdiction over child custody proceedings involving Indian children domiciled on the tribe's reservation.

The Indian Child Welfare Act of 1978 (ICWA), 92 Stat. 3069, 25 U.S.C. §§ 1901–1963, was the product of rising concern in the mid-1970's over the consequences to Indian children, Indian families, and Indian tribes of abusive child welfare practices that resulted in the separation of large numbers of Indian children from their families and tribes through adoption or foster care placement, usually in non-Indian homes. Senate oversight hearings in 1974 yielded numerous examples, statistical data, and expert testimony documenting what one witness called "the wholesale removal of Indian children from their homes, . . . the most tragic aspect of Indian life today." Indian Child Welfare Program, Hearings before the Subcommittee on Indian Affairs of the Senate Committee on Interior and Insular Affairs, 93d Cong., 2d Sess., 3 (hereinafter 1974 Hearings) (statement of William Byler). Studies undertaken by the Association on American Indian Affairs in 1969 and 1974, and presented in the Senate hearings, showed that 25 to 35 percent of all Indian children had been separated from their families and placed in adoptive families, foster care, or institutions. Adoptive placements counted significantly in this total: in the State of Minnesota, for example, one in eight Indian children under the age of 18 was in an adoptive home, and during the year 1971–1972 nearly one in every four infants under one year of age was placed for adoption. The adoption rate of Indian children was eight times that of non-Indian children. Approximately 90% of the Indian placements were in non-Indian homes. A number of witnesses also testified to the serious adjustment problems encountered by such children during adolescence,[1] as well as the impact of the adoptions on Indian parents and the tribes themselves.

---

[1] For example, Dr. Joseph Westermeyer, a University of Minnesota social psychiatrist, testified about his research with Indian adolescents who experienced difficulty coping in white society, despite the fact that they had been raised in a purely white environment:

> "[T]hey were raised with a white cultural and social identity. They are raised in a white home. They attended, predominantly white schools, and in almost all cases, attended a church that was predominantly white, and really came to understand very little about Indian culture, Indian behavior, and had virtually no viable Indian identity. They can recall such things as seeing cowboys and Indians on TV and feeling that Indians were a historical figure but were not a viable contemporary social group. . . .Then during adolescence, they found that society was not to grant them the white identity that they had. They began to find this out in a number of ways. For

Further hearings, covering much the same ground, were held during 1977 and 1978 on the bill that became the ICWA. While much of the testimony again focused on the harm to Indian parents and their children who were involuntarily separated by decisions of local welfare authorities, there was also considerable emphasis on the impact on the tribes themselves of the massive removal of their children. For example, Mr. Calvin Isaac, Tribal Chief of the Mississippi Band of Choctaw Indians and representative of the National Tribal Chairmen's Association, testified as follows:

> "Culturally, the chances of Indian survival are significantly reduced if our children, the only real means for the transmission of the tribal heritage, are to be raised in non-Indian homes and denied exposure to the ways of their People. Furthermore, these practices seriously undercut the tribes' ability to continue as self-governing communities. Probably in no area is it more important that tribal sovereignty be respected than in an area as socially and culturally determinative as family relationships."

Chief Isaac also summarized succinctly what numerous witnesses saw as the principal reason for the high rates of removal of Indian children:

> "One of the most serious failings of the present system is that Indian children are removed from the custody of their natural parents by nontribal government authorities who have no basis for intelligently evaluating the cultural and social premises underlying Indian home life and childrearing. Many of the individuals who decide the fate of our children are at best ignorant of our cultural values, and at worst contemptful of the Indian way and convinced that removal, usually to a non-Indian household or institution, can only benefit an Indian child."[4]

---

example, a universal experience was that when they began to date white children, the parents of the white youngsters were against this, and there were pressures among white children from the parents not to date these Indian children. . . . The other experience was derogatory name calling in relation to their racial identity. . . . [T]hey were finding that society was putting on them an identity which they didn't possess and taking from them an identity that they did possess." 1974 Hearings, at 46.

4 One of the particular points of concern was the failure of non-Indian child welfare workers to understand the role of the extended family in Indian society. The House Report on the ICWA noted: "An Indian child may have scores of, perhaps more than a hundred, relatives who are counted as close, responsible members of the family. Many social workers, untutored in the ways of Indian family life or assuming them to be socially irresponsible, consider leaving the child with persons outside the nuclear family as neglect and thus as grounds for terminating parental rights." At the conclusion of the 1974 Senate hearings, Senator Abourezk noted the role that such extended families played in the care of children: "We've had testimony here that in Indian communities throughout the Nation there is no such thing as an abandoned child because when a child does have a need for parents for one reason or another, a relative or a friend will take that child in. It's the extended family concept." 1974 Hearings 473. See also Wisconsin Potowatomies of Hannahville Indian Community v. Houston, 393 F. Supp. 719 (W.D.Mich.1973) (discussing custom of extended family and tribe assuming responsibility for care of orphaned children).

The congressional findings that were incorporated into the ICWA reflect these sentiments. The Congress found:

> "(3) that there is no resource that is more vital to the continued existence and integrity of Indian tribes than their children . . . ;
>
> "(4) that an alarmingly high percentage of Indian families are broken up by the removal, often unwarranted, of their children from them by nontribal public and private agencies and that an alarmingly high percentage of such children are placed in non-Indian foster and adoptive homes and institutions; and
>
> "(5) that the States, exercising their recognized jurisdiction over Indian child custody proceedings through administrative and judicial bodies, have often failed to recognize the essential tribal relations of Indian people and the cultural and social standards prevailing in Indian communities and families." 25 U.S.C. § 1901.

At the heart of the ICWA are its provisions concerning jurisdiction over Indian child custody proceedings. Section 1911 lays out a dual jurisdictional scheme. Section 1911(a) establishes exclusive jurisdiction in the tribal courts for proceedings concerning an Indian child "who resides or is domiciled within the reservation of such tribe," as well as for wards of tribal courts regardless of domicile. Section 1911(b), on the other hand, creates concurrent but presumptively tribal jurisdiction in the case of children not domiciled on the reservation: on petition of either parent or the tribe, state-court proceedings for foster care placement or termination of parental rights are to be transferred to the tribal court, except in cases of "good cause," objection by either parent, or declination of jurisdiction by the tribal court.

Various other provisions of ICWA Title I set procedural and substantive standards for those child custody proceedings that do take place in state court. The procedural safeguards include requirements concerning notice and appointment of counsel; parental and tribal rights of intervention and petition for invalidation of illegal proceedings; procedures governing voluntary consent to termination of parental rights; and a full faith and credit obligation in respect to tribal court decisions. See §§ 1901–1914. The most important substantive requirement imposed on state courts is that of § 1915(a), which, absent "good cause" to the contrary, mandates that adoptive placements be made preferentially with (1) members of the child's extended family, (2) other members of the same tribe, or (3) other Indian families.

The ICWA thus, in the words of the House Report accompanying it, "seeks to protect the rights of the Indian child as an Indian and the rights of the Indian community and tribe in retaining its children in its society." It does so by establishing "a Federal policy that, where possible, an Indian child should remain in the Indian community," ibid., and by making sure that Indian child welfare determinations are not based on "a white, middle-class standard which, in many cases, forecloses placement with [an] Indian family."

This case involves the status of twin babies, known for our purposes as B.B. and G.B., who were born out of wedlock on December 29, 1985. Their mother, J.B., and father, W.J., were both enrolled members of appellant Mississippi Band of Choctaw Indians (Tribe), and were residents and domiciliaries of the Choctaw Reservation in Neshoba County, Mississippi. J.B. gave birth to the twins in Gulfport, Harrison County, Mississippi, some 200 miles from the reservation. On January 10, 1986, J.B. executed a consent-to-adoption form before the Chancery Court of Harrison County.[7] W.J. signed a similar form.[8] On January 16, appellees Orrey and Vivian Holyfield filed a petition for adoption in the same court, and the chancellor issued a Final Decree of Adoption on January 28. Id., at 13–14.[10] Despite the court's apparent awareness of the ICWA, the adoption decree contained no reference to it, nor to the infants' Indian background.

Two months later the Tribe moved in the Chancery Court to vacate the adoption decree on the ground that under the ICWA exclusive jurisdiction was vested in the tribal court.[12] On July 14, 1986, the court overruled the motion, holding that the Tribe "never obtained exclusive jurisdiction over the children involved herein. . . ." The court's one-page opinion relied on two facts in reaching that conclusion. The court noted first that the twins' mother "went to some efforts to see that they were born outside the confines of the Choctaw Indian Reservation" and that the parents had promptly arranged for the adoption by the Holyfields. Second, the court stated: "At no time from the birth of these children to

---

[7] Section 1913(a) of the ICWA requires that any voluntary consent to termination of parental rights be executed in writing and recorded before a judge of a "court of competent jurisdiction," who must certify that the terms and consequences of the consent were fully explained and understood. Section 1913(a) also provides that any consent given prior to birth or within 10 days thereafter is invalid. In this case the mother's consent was given 12 days after the birth.

[8] W.J.'s consent to adoption was signed before a notary public in Neshoba County on January 11, 1986. Record 11–12. Only on June 3, 1986, howeverCwell after the decree of adoption had been entered and after the Tribe had filed suit to vacate that decreeCdid the chancellor of the Chancery Court certify that W.J. had appeared before him in Harrison County to execute the consent to adoption. Id., at 12–A.

[10] Mississippi adoption law provides for a 6-month waiting period between interlocutory and final decrees of adoption, but grants the chancellor discretionary authority to waive that requirement and immediately enter a final decree of adoption. See Miss.Code Ann. § 93–17–13 (1972). The chancellor did so here, Record 14, with the result that the final decree of adoption was entered less than one month after the babies' birth.

[12] The ICWA specifically confers standing on the Indian child's tribe to participate in child custody adjudications. Section 1914 authorizes the tribe (as well as the child and its parents) to petition a court to invalidate any foster care placement or termination of parental rights under state law "upon a showing that such action violated any provision of sections 1911, 1912, and 1913" of the ICWA. See also § 1911(c) (Indian child's tribe may intervene at any point in state-court proceedings for foster care placement or termination of parental rights). "Termination of parental rights" is defined in § 1903(1)(ii) as "any action resulting in the termination of the parent-child relationship."

the present date have either of them resided on or physically been on the Choctaw Indian Reservation."

The Supreme Court of Mississippi affirmed. 511 So.2d 918 (1987). It rejected the Tribe's arguments that the state court lacked jurisdiction and that it, in any event, had not applied the standards laid out in the ICWA. The court recognized that the jurisdictional question turned on whether the twins were domiciled on the Choctaw Reservation. It answered that question as follows:

> "At no point in time can it be said the twins resided on or were domiciled within the territory set aside for the reservation. Appellant's argument that living within the womb of their mother qualifies the children's residency on the reservation may be lauded for its creativity; however, apparently it is unsupported by any law within this state, and will not be addressed at this time due to the far-reaching legal ramifications that would occur were we to follow such a complicated tangential course."

The court distinguished Mississippi cases that appeared to establish the principle that "the domicile of minor children follows that of the parents". It noted that "the Indian twins . . . were voluntarily surrendered and legally abandoned by the natural parents to the adoptive parents, and it is undisputed that the parents went to some efforts to prevent the children from being placed on the reservation as the mother arranged for their birth and adoption in Gulfport Memorial Hospital, Harrison County, Mississippi." Therefore, the court said, the twins' domicile was in Harrison County and the state court properly exercised jurisdiction over the adoption proceedings. Indeed, the court appears to have concluded that, for this reason, none of the provisions of the ICWA was applicable. . . . In any case, it rejected the Tribe's contention that the requirements of the ICWA applicable in state courts had not been followed. . . .

We now reverse.

Tribal jurisdiction over Indian child custody proceedings is not a novelty of the ICWA. Indeed, some of the ICWA's jurisdictional provisions have a strong basis in pre-ICWA case law in the federal and state courts. . . . In enacting the ICWA Congress confirmed that, in child custody proceedings involving Indian children domiciled on the reservation, tribal jurisdiction was exclusive as to the States.

The state-court proceeding at issue here was a "child custody proceeding." That term is defined to include any " 'adoptive placement' which shall mean the permanent placement of an Indian child for adoption, including any action resulting in a final decree of adoption." 25 U.S.C. § 1903(1)(iv). Moreover, the twins were "Indian children." See 25 U.S.C. § 1903(4). The sole issue in this case is, as the Supreme Court of

Mississippi recognized, whether the twins were "domiciled" on the reservation.[16]

The meaning of "domicile" in the ICWA is, of course, a matter of Congress' intent. The ICWA itself does not define it. The initial question we must confront is whether there is any reason to believe that Congress intended the ICWA definition of "domicile" to be a matter of state law. . . .

First, and most fundamentally, the purpose of the ICWA gives no reason to believe that Congress intended to rely on state law for the definition of a critical term; quite the contrary. It is clear from the very text of the ICWA, not to mention its legislative history and the hearings that led to its enactment, that Congress was concerned with the rights of Indian families and Indian communities vis-à-vis state authorities. More specifically, its purpose was, in part, to make clear that in certain situations the state courts did *not* have jurisdiction over child custody proceedings. Indeed, the congressional findings that are a part of the statute demonstrate that Congress perceived the States and their courts as partly responsible for the problem it intended to correct. . . . Under these circumstances it is most improbable that Congress would have intended to leave the scope of the statute's key jurisdictional provision subject to definition by state courts as a matter of state law.

Second, Congress could hardly have intended the lack of nationwide uniformity that would result from state-law definitions of domicile. An example will illustrate. In a case quite similar to this one, the New Mexico state courts found exclusive jurisdiction in the tribal court pursuant to § 1911(a), because the illegitimate child took the reservation domicile of its mother at birthCnotwithstanding that the child was placed in the custody of adoptive parents two days after its off-reservation birth and the mother executed a consent to adoption ten days later. In re Adoption of Baby Child, 102 N.M. 735, 737–738, 700 P.2d 198, 200–201 (App.1985). Had that mother traveled to Mississippi to give birth, rather than to Albuquerque, a different result would have obtained if state-law definitions of domicile applied. The same, presumably, would be true if the child had been transported to Mississippi for adoption after her off-reservation birth in New Mexico. While the child's custody proceeding would have been subject to exclusive tribal jurisdiction in her home State, her mother, prospective adoptive parents, or an adoption intermediary could have obtained an adoption decree in state court merely by transporting her across state lines. Even if we could conceive of a federal statute under which the rules of domicile (and thus of jurisdiction)

[16] "Reservation" is defined quite broadly for purposes of the ICWA. See 25 U.S.C. § 1903(10). There is no dispute that the Choctaw Reservation falls within that definition.

Section 1911(a) does not apply "where such jurisdiction is otherwise vested in the State by existing Federal law." This proviso would appear to refer to Pub.L. 280, 67 Stat. 588, as amended, which allows States under certain conditions to assume civil and criminal jurisdiction on the reservations. ICWA § 1918 permits a tribe in that situation to reassume jurisdiction over child custody proceedings upon petition to the Secretary of the Interior. The State of Mississippi has never asserted jurisdiction over the Choctaw Reservation under Public Law 280. See F. Cohen, Handbook of Federal Indian Law 362–363, and nn. 122–125 (1982); . . . .

applied differently to different Indian children, a statute under which different rules apply from time to time to the same child, simply as a result of her transport from one State to another, cannot be what Congress had in mind.[21]

We therefore think it beyond dispute that Congress intended a uniform federal law of domicile for the ICWA. It remains to give content to the term "domicile" in the circumstances of the present case. The holding of the Supreme Court of Mississippi that the twin babies were not domiciled on the Choctaw Reservation appears to have rested on two findings of fact by the trial court: (1) that they had never been physically present there, and (2) that they were "voluntarily surrendered" by their parents. The question before us, therefore, is whether under the ICWA definition of "domicile" such facts suffice to render the twins nondomiciliaries of the reservation. . . .

That we are dealing with a uniform federal rather than a state definition does not, of course, prevent us from drawing on general state-law principles to determine "the ordinary meaning of the words used." Well-settled state law can inform our understanding of what Congress had in mind when it employed a term it did not define. Accordingly, we find it helpful to borrow established common-law principles of domicile to the extent that they are not inconsistent with the objectives of the congressional scheme.

"Domicile" is, of course, a concept widely used in both federal and state courts for jurisdiction and conflict-of-laws purposes, and its meaning is generally uncontroverted. "Domicile" is not necessarily synonymous with "residence," and one can reside in one place but be domiciled in another. For adults, domicile is established by physical presence in a place in connection with a certain state of mind concerning one's intent to remain there. Texas v. Florida, 306 U.S. 398, 424 (1939). One acquires a "domicile or origin" at birth, and that domicile continues until a new one (a "domicile of choice") is acquired. Since most minors are legally incapable of forming the requisite intent to establish a domicile, their domicile is determined by that of their parents. In the case of an illegitimate child, that has traditionally meant the domicile of its mother. Under these principles, it is entirely logical that "[o]n occasion, a child's domicil of origin will be in a place where the child has never been." Restatement § 14, Comment *b*.

It is undisputed in this case that the domicile of the mother (as well as the father) has been, at all relevant times, on the Choctaw Reservation. Thus, it is clear that at their birth the twin babies were also domiciled on the reservation, even though they themselves had never been there. The statement of the Supreme Court of Mississippi that "[a]t no point in time can it be said the twins . . . were domiciled within the

---

[21] For this reason, the general rule that domicile is determined according to the law of the forum, see Restatement (Second) of Conflict of Laws § 13 (1971) (hereinafter Restatement), can have no application here.

territory set aside for the reservation," 511 So.2d, at 921, may be a correct statement of that State's law of domicile, but it is inconsistent with generally accepted doctrine in this country and cannot be what Congress had in mind when it used the term in the ICWA.

Nor can the result be any different simply because the twins were "voluntarily surrendered" by their mother. Tribal jurisdiction under § 1911(a) was not meant to be defeated by the actions of individual members of the tribe, for Congress was concerned not solely about the interests of Indian children and families, but also about the impact on the tribes themselves of the large numbers of Indian children adopted by non-Indians. . . .

In addition, it is clear that Congress' concern over the placement of Indian children in non-Indian homes was based in part on evidence of the detrimental impact on the children themselves of such placements outside their culture. Congress determined to subject such placements to the ICWA's jurisdictional and other provisions, even in cases where the parents consented to an adoption, because of concerns going beyond the wishes of individual parents. As the 1977 Final Report of the congressionally established American Indian Policy Review Commission stated, in summarizing these two concerns, "[r]emoval of Indian children from their cultural setting seriously impacts a long-term tribal survival and has damaging social and psychological impact on many individual Indian children."[25]

These congressional objectives make clear that a rule of domicile that would permit individual Indian parents to defeat the ICWA's jurisdictional scheme is inconsistent with what Congress intended. See In re Adoption of Child of Indian Heritage, 111 N.J. 155, 168–171, 543 A.2d 925, 931–933 (1988). The appellees in this case argue strenuously that the twins' mother went to great lengths to give birth off the reservation so that her children could be adopted by the Holyfields. But that was precisely part of Congress' concern. Permitting individual members of the tribe to avoid tribal exclusive jurisdiction by the simple expedient of giving birth off the reservation would, to a large extent, nullify the purpose the ICWA was intended to accomplish.[27] The

[25] While the statute itself makes clear that Congress intended the ICWA to reach voluntary as well as involuntary removal of Indian children, the same conclusion can also be drawn from the ICWA's legislative history. For example, the House Report contains the following expression of Congress' concern with both aspects of the problem:

> "One of the effects of our national paternalism has been to so alienate some Indian [parents] from their society that they abandon their children at hospitals or to welfare departments rather than entrust them to the care of relatives in the extended family. Another expression of it is the involuntary, arbitrary, and unwarranted separation of families."

[27] It appears, in fact, that all Choctaw women give birth off the reservation because of the lack of appropriate obstetric facilities there. In most cases, of course, the mother and child return to the reservation after the birth, and this would presumably be sufficient to make the child a reservation domiciliary even under the Mississippi court's theory. Application of the Mississippi domicile rule would, however, permit state authorities to avoid the tribal court's exclusive

Supreme Court of Utah expressed this well in its scholarly and sensitive opinion in what has become a leading case on the ICWA:

> "To the extent that [state] abandonment law operates to permit [the child's] mother to change [the child's] domicile as part of a scheme to facilitate his adoption by non-Indians while she remains a domiciliary of the reservation, it conflicts with and undermines the operative scheme established by subsections [1911(a)] and [1913(a)] to deal with children of domiciliaries of the reservation and weakens considerably the tribe's ability to assert its interest in its children. The protection of this tribal interest is at the core of the ICWA, which recognizes that the tribe has an interest in the child which is distinct from but on a parity with the interest of the parents. This relationship between Indian tribes and Indian children domiciled on the reservation finds no parallel in other ethnic cultures found in the United States. It is a relationship that many non-Indians find difficult to understand and that non-Indian courts are slow to recognize. It is precisely in recognition of this relationship, however, that the ICWA designates the tribal court as the exclusive forum for the determination of custody and adoption matters for reservation-domiciled Indian children, and the preferred forum for nondomiciliary Indian children. [State] abandonment law cannot be used to frustrate the federal legislative judgment expressed in the ICWA that the interests of the tribe in custodial decisions made with respect to Indian children are as entitled to respect as the interests of the parents." In re Adoption of Halloway, 732 P.2d 962, 969–970 (1986).

We agree with the Supreme Court of Utah that the law of domicile Congress used in the ICWA cannot be one that permits individual reservation-domiciled tribal members to defeat the tribe's exclusive jurisdiction by the simple expedient of giving birth and placing the child for adoption off the reservation. Since, for purposes of the ICWA, the twin babies in this case were domiciled on the reservation when adoption proceedings were begun, the Choctaw tribal court possessed exclusive jurisdiction pursuant to 25 U.S.C. § 1911(a). The Chancery Court of Harrison County was, accordingly, without jurisdiction to enter a decree of adoption; under ICWA § 1914 its decree of January 28, 1986, must be vacated.

We are not unaware that over three years have passed since the twin babies were born and placed in the Holyfield home, and that a court deciding their fate today is not writing on a blank slate in the same way it would have in January 1986. Three years' development of family ties

---

§ 1911(a) jurisdiction by removing a newborn from an allegedly unfit mother while in the hospital, and seeking to terminate her parental rights in state court.

cannot be undone, and a separation at this point would doubtless cause considerable pain.

Whatever feelings we might have as to where the twins should live, however, it is not for us to decide that question. We have been asked to decide the legal question of *who* should make the custody determination concerning these children—not what the outcome of that determination should be. The law places that decision in the hands of the Choctaw tribal court. Had the mandate of the ICWA been followed in 1986, of course, much potential anguish might have been avoided, and in any case the law cannot be applied so as automatically to "reward those who obtain custody, whether lawfully or otherwise, and maintain it during any ensuing (and protracted) litigation." It is not ours to say whether the trauma that might result from removing these children from their adoptive family should outweigh the interest of the Tribe—and perhaps the children themselves—in having them raised as part of the Choctaw community.[28] Rather, "we must defer to the experience, wisdom, and compassion of the [Choctaw] tribal courts to fashion an appropriate remedy."

The judgment of the Supreme Court of Mississippi is reversed and the case remanded for further proceedings not inconsistent with this opinion.

■ JUSTICE STEVENS, with whom THE CHIEF JUSTICE and JUSTICE KENNEDY join, dissenting.

The parents of these twin babies unquestionably expressed their intention to have the state court exercise jurisdiction over them. J.B. gave birth to the twins at a hospital 200 miles from the Reservation, even though a closer hospital was available. Both parents gave their written advance consent to the adoption and, when the adoption was later challenged by the Tribe, they reaffirmed their desire that the Holyfields adopt the two children. As the Mississippi Supreme Court found, "the parents went to some efforts to prevent the children from being placed on the reservation as the mother arranged for their birth and adoption in Gulfport Memorial Hospital, Harrison County, Mississippi." 511 So.2d 918, 927 (1987). Indeed, both parents appear before us today, urging that Vivian Holyfield be allowed to retain custody of B.B. and G.B.

Because J.B.'s domicile is on the reservation and the children are eligible for membership in the Tribe, the Court today closes the state courthouse door to her. I agree with the Court that Congress intended a uniform federal law of domicile for the Indian Child Welfare Act of 1978 (ICWA), and that domicile should be defined with reference to the objectives of the congressional scheme. . . . I cannot agree, however, with the cramped definition the Court gives that term. To preclude parents domiciled on a reservation from deliberately invoking the adoption

[28] We were assured at oral argument that the Choctaw court has the authority under the tribal code to permit adoption by the present adoptive family, should it see fit to do so.

procedures of state court, the Court gives "domicile" a meaning that Congress could not have intended and distorts the delicate balance between individual rights and group rights recognized by the ICWA.

The ICWA was passed in 1978 in response to congressional findings that "an alarmingly high percentage of Indian families are broken up by the *removal,* often unwarranted, of their children from them by nontribal public and private agencies" and that "the States, exercising their recognized jurisdiction over Indian child custody proceedings through administrative and judicial bodies, have often failed to recognize the essential tribal relations of Indian people and the cultural and social standards prevailing in Indian communities and families." 25 U.S.C. § 1901(4), (5). (Emphasis added.) The Act is thus primarily addressed to the unjustified removal of Indian children from their families through the application of standards that inadequately recognized the distinct Indian culture.

The most important provisions of the ICWA are those setting forth minimum standards for the placement of Indian children by state courts and providing procedural safeguards to insure that parental rights are protected. The Act provides that any party seeking to effect a foster care placement of, or involuntary termination of parental rights to, an Indian child must establish by stringent standards of proof that efforts have been made to prevent the breakup of the Indian family and that the continued custody of the child by the parent is likely to result in serious emotional or physical damage to the child. §§ 1912(d), (e), (f). Each party to the proceeding has a right to examine all reports and documents filed with the court and an indigent parent or custodian has the right to appointment of counsel. §§ 1912(b), (c). In the case of a voluntary termination, the ICWA provides that consent is valid only if given after the terms and consequences of the consent have been fully explained, may be withdrawn at any time up to the final entry of a decree of termination or adoption, and even then may be collaterally attacked on the grounds that it was obtained through fraud or duress. § 1913. Finally, because the Act protects not only the rights of the parents, but also the interests of the tribe and the Indian children, the Act sets forth criteria for adoptive, foster care, and preadoptive placements that favor the Indian child's extended family or tribe, and that can be altered by resolution of the tribe. § 1915.

The Act gives Indian tribes certain rights, not to restrict the rights of parents of Indian children, but to complement and help effect them. The Indian tribe may petition to transfer an action in state court to the tribal court, but the Indian parent may veto the transfer. § 1911(b). The Act provides for a tribal right of notice and intervention in involuntary proceedings but not in voluntary ones. §§ 1911(c), 1912(a). Finally, the tribe may petition the court to set aside a parental termination action upon a showing that the provisions of the ICWA that are designed to protect parents and Indian children have been violated. § 1914.[5]

While the Act's substantive and procedural provisions effect a major change in state child custody proceedings, its jurisdictional provision is designed primarily to preserve tribal sovereignty over the domestic relations of tribe members and to confirm a developing line of cases which held that the tribe's exclusive jurisdiction could not be defeated by the temporary presence of an Indian child off the reservation. . . .

Although parents of Indian children are shielded from the exercise of state jurisdiction when they are temporarily off the reservation, the Act also reflects a recognition that allowing the tribe to defeat the parents' deliberate choice of jurisdiction would be conducive neither to the best interests of the child nor to the stability and security of Indian tribes and families. Section 1911(b), providing for the exercise of concurrent jurisdiction by state and tribal courts when the Indian child is not domiciled on the reservation, gives the Indian parents a veto to prevent the transfer of a state court action to tribal court.[8] "By allowing the Indian parents to 'choose' the forum that will decide whether to sever the parent-child relationship, Congress promotes the security of Indian families by allowing the Indian parents to defend in the court system that most reflects the parents' familial standards." Jones, 21 Ariz.L.Rev., at 1141. As Mr. Calvin Isaac, Tribal Chief of the Mississippi Band of Choctaw Indians stated in testimony to the House Subcommittee on Indian Affairs and Public Lands with respect to a different provision:

> "The ultimate responsibility for child welfare rests with the parents and we would not support legislation which interfered with that basic relationship."

If J.B. and W.J. had established a domicile off the Reservation, the state courts would have been required to give effect to their choice of jurisdiction; there should not be a different result when the parents have

---

[5] Significantly, the tribe cannot set aside a termination of parental rights on the grounds that the adoptive placement provisions of § 1915, favoring placement with the tribe, have not been followed.

[8] The explanation of this subsection in the House Committee Report reads as follows:

> "Subsection (b) directs a State court, having jurisdiction over an Indian child custody proceeding to transfer such proceeding, absent good cause to the contrary, to the appropriate tribal court upon the petition of the parents or the Indian tribe. Either parent is given the right to veto such transfer. The subsection is intended to permit a State court to apply a modified doctrine of forum non conveniens, in appropriate cases, to insure that the rights of the child as an Indian, the Indian parents or custodian, and the tribe are fully protected." Id., at 21.

In commenting on the provision, the Department of Justice suggested that the section should be clarified to make it perfectly clear that a state court need not surrender jurisdiction of a child custody proceeding if the Indian parent objected. The Department of Justice letter stated:

> "Section 101(b) should be amended to prohibit clearly the transfer of a child placement proceeding to a tribal court when any parent or child over the age of 12 objects to the transfer." Id., at 32.

Although the specific suggestion made by the Department of Justice was not in fact implemented, it is noteworthy that there is nothing in the legislative history to suggest that the recommended change was in any way inconsistent with any of the purposes of the statute.

not changed their own domicile, but have expressed an unequivocal intent to establish a domicile for their children off the Reservation. The law of abandonment, as enunciated by the Mississippi Supreme Court in this case, does not defeat, but serves the purposes of the Act. An abandonment occurs when a parent deserts a child and places the child with another with an intent to relinquish all parental rights and obligations. Restatement (Second) of Conflict of Laws § 22, Comment e (1971) (hereinafter Restatement); In re Adoption of Halloway, 732 P.2d 962, 966 (Utah 1986). If a child is abandoned by his mother, he takes on the domicile of his father; if the child is abandoned by his father, he takes on the domicile of his mother. If the child is abandoned by both parents, he takes on the domicile of a person other than the parents who stands in loco parentis to him. To be effective, the intent to abandon or the actual physical abandonment must be shown by clear and convincing evidence.

When an Indian child is temporarily off the reservation, but has not been abandoned to a person off the reservation, the tribe has an interest in exclusive jurisdiction. The ICWA expresses the intent that exclusive tribal jurisdiction is not so frail that it should be defeated as soon as the Indian child steps off the reservation. Similarly, when the child is abandoned by one parent to a person off the reservation, the tribe and the other parent domiciled on the reservation may still have an interest in the exercise of exclusive jurisdiction. That interest is protected by the rule that a child abandoned by one parent takes on the domicile of the other. But when an Indian child is deliberately abandoned by both parents to a person off the reservation, no purpose of the ICWA is served by closing the state courthouse door to them. The interests of the parents, the Indian child, and the tribe in preventing the unwarranted removal of Indian children from their families and from the reservation are protected by the Act's substantive and procedural provisions. In addition, if both parents have intentionally invoked the jurisdiction of the state court in an action involving a non-Indian, no interest in tribal self-governance is implicated.

The interpretation of domicile adopted by the Court requires the custodian of an Indian child who is off the reservation to haul the child to a potentially distant tribal court unfamiliar with the child's present living conditions and best interests. Moreover, it renders any custody decision made by a state court forever suspect, susceptible to challenge at any time as void for having been entered in the absence of jurisdiction.[12] Finally, it forces parents of Indian children who desire to

---

[12] The facts of In re Adoption of Halloway, 732 P.2d 962 (Utah 1986), which the Court cites approvingly, vividly illustrate the problem. In that case, the mother, a member of an Indian Tribe in New Mexico, voluntarily abandoned an Indian child to the custody of the child's maternal aunt off the Reservation with the knowledge that the child would be placed for adoption in Utah. The mother learned of the adoption two weeks after the child left the Reservation and did not object and, two months later, she executed a consent to adoption. Nevertheless, some two years after the petition for adoption was filed, the Indian Tribe intervened in the proceeding and set aside the adoption. The Tribe argued successfully that regardless of whether the Indian parent consented to it, the adoption was void because she

invoke state court jurisdiction to establish a domicile off the reservation. Only if the custodial parent has the wealth and ability to establish a domicile off the reservation will the parent be able use the processes of state court. I fail to see how such a requirement serves the paramount congressional purpose of "promot[ing] the stability and security of Indian tribes and families." 25 U.S.C. § 1902.

The Court concludes its opinion with the observation that whatever anguish is suffered by the Indian children, their natural parents, and their adoptive parents because of its decision today is a result of their failure to initially follow the provisions of the ICWA. By holding that parents who are domiciled on the reservation cannot voluntarily avail themselves of the adoption procedures of state court and that all such proceedings will be void for lack of jurisdiction, however, the Court establishes a rule of law that is virtually certain to ensure that similar anguish will be suffered by other families in the future. Because that result is not mandated by the language of the ICWA and is contrary to its purposes, I respectfully dissent.

Adoption of F.H.

Supreme Court of Alaska, 1993
851 P.2d 1361

■ COMPTON, JUSTICE.

The Native Village of Noatak (Noatak) and the State of Alaska, Division of Family and Youth Services (DFYS), opposed the adoption of F.H., an Indian child, by the Hartleys, a non-Indian couple. Superior Court Judge Elaine M. Andrews determined that F.H.'s case presented good cause to deviate from the Indian Child Welfare Act (ICWA) adoptive placement preferences. Noatak and DFYS appeal this determination.

F.H. was born on February 24, 1990. Her mother, E.P.D., had a blood alcohol level of about .275 at the time of birth. F.H.'s biological father is unknown. F.H. is an Indian child as defined by ICWA. 25 U.S.C. § 1903. She and her mother are members of the Native Village of Noatak. DFYS took custody of F.H. shortly after her birth, based on her mother's homelessness and high blood alcohol level at the time of birth. DFYS filed a Child in Need of Aid (CINA) petition (3AN–90–159) and notified Noatak. DFYS filed a petition to terminate parental rights in August 1990.[1]

---

resided on the Reservation and thus the tribal court had exclusive jurisdiction. Although the decision in *Halloway,* and the Court's approving reference to it, may be colored somewhat by the fact that the mother in that case withdrew her consent (a fact which would entitle her to relief even if there were only concurrent jurisdiction, see 25 U.S.C. § 1913(c)), the rule set forth by the majority contains no such limitation. As the Tribe acknowledged at oral argument, any adoption of an Indian child effected through a state court will be susceptible of challenge by the Indian tribe no matter how old the child and how long it has lived with its adoptive parents.

[1] The CINA proceeding was briefly consolidated with the adoption proceeding. That consolidation was vacated and the adoption trial was held first. The CINA petition was dismissed when the Hartleys' petition for adoption was granted.

F.H. has experienced a number of medical problems, symptomatic of Fetal Alcohol Syndrome (FAS) or Fetal Alcohol Effects (FAE). The Alaska Area Native Health Service has determined that F.H. does not have FAS, but is at high risk for FAE, which is not as severe. Her prenatal exposure to alcohol has placed her at risk for developmental delay and learning and behavioral problems. F.H. lived in four different foster homes before she was adopted by the Hartleys in March 1992. The Hartleys were her third foster placement. F.H. lived with them from June 1990 until June 1991, when Carol Hartley was transferred to Washington State. F.H. now lives with the Hartleys in Kennewick, Washington.

While F.H. was in foster homes, E.P.D. expressed an interest in relinquishing her custody to at least five different people, including her cousin, Mary Penn, and the Hartleys. As E.P.D.'s cousin, Mary Penn is a first place adoptive placement preference under ICWA. 25 U.S.C. § 1915(a). Based upon a favorable home study, DFYS concluded that F.H. should be placed with Mary Penn, though F.H. never lived with her. Trial on the petition to terminate parental rights was set for September 18, 1991.

On September 16, E.P.D. executed three documents before Probate Master Lucinda McBurney relinquishing her parental rights to the Hartleys. Her relinquishment was conditioned upon the Hartleys' adoption of F.H., F.H.'s retention of inheritance rights from E.P.D., and E.P.D.'s and her family's retention of contact and visitation rights with F.H. The next day, the Hartleys filed a Petition for Adoption. Since signing the papers, E.P.D. has consistently supported an adoption by the Hartleys.

E.P.D. has not been to Noatak for several years and plans never to return. She abuses alcohol. Her father died of alcoholism. Her mother was murdered by her brother. None of her siblings were raised in Noatak. F.H. has never been to Noatak. E.P.D. believes she could visit F.H. more easily in Kennewick, Washington, than in Noatak.

An early interventionist, who worked with F.H. in the Hartleys' home twice a month for almost one year, believes F.H. made a lot of progress during that period and that F.H.'s bond with Nancy Hartley is the best F.H. will ever have. Both guardians ad litem assigned to F.H. testified that they believe F.H.'s best interest is to be placed with the Hartleys. The DFYS social worker assigned to F.H.'s case until June 1991 believed that F.H. should have stayed with the Hartleys.

After several hearings at which Noatak,[2] E.P.D., the Hartleys, DFYS, and F.H. were represented, Probate Master John E. Duggan

---

2 The Hartleys assert that Noatak's opposition to their adoption is barred by the doctrine of laches. Noatak was sent notices of F.H.'s CINA case in March and August 1990. In October 1991 Noatak received notice of the Hartleys' adoption petition and only then moved to intervene in both the adoption and the CINA cases. Alaska Adoption Rule 12(a) states that "[i]n any adoption or relinquishment proceeding involving an Indian child, the Indian child's tribe and an Indian custodian, if any, may intervene as a matter of right at any stage in the proceeding." (Emphasis added). In light of this rule, it is doubtful laches may be raised as a defense to

recommended that the superior court find good cause to deviate from ICWA preferences. The primary basis for his recommendation was the "strong and consistent preference of the biological mother for this open adoption by the petitioners and against placement of her daughter in the village of Noatak." Secondary considerations included 1) the bond between Nancy Hartley and F.H., 2) the uncertainty of F.H.'s future if the adoption were not allowed, and 3) the "open adoption" petition allowing E.P.D. access to F.H. and possibly giving F.H. exposure to her Native American heritage.

Judge Andrews accepted Master Duggan's recommendation. Judge Andrews stressed the importance of the mother's preference, which was based in part on the adoption of F.H. being "open." E.P.D. retained contact and visitation rights, while F.H. retained her inheritance rights from E.P.D. In contrast, "[t]here is no written evidence suggesting that the proposed Penn adoption would be 'open.' "

In support of its Motion for Reconsideration, Noatak submitted the affidavit of Mary Penn and an excerpt from a study of Northwest Alaskan Family traditions to show that E.P.D. and others in F.H.'s blood family would have access to F.H. if she lived with Mary Penn. Judge Andrews denied the motion.

Superior Court Judge Brian C. Shortell conducted a hearing on the remaining issues. He granted the Decree of Adoption on March 5, 1992. This appeal followed.

The question on appeal is whether the superior court erred in concluding that good cause existed to deviate from the adoptive placement preferences mandated under ICWA (25 U.S.C. 1901–1963). Under state law, the Hartleys have the burden of proof by a preponderance of the evidence that there is good cause for allowing a non-preferred placement. Alaska Adoption Rule 11(f). A good cause determination is within the superior court's discretion. See In re Adoption of M., 66 Wash.App. 475, 832 P.2d 518, 522–23 (1992); In re Appeal in Coconino County Juvenile Action No. J–10175, 153 Ariz. 346, 349–50, 736 P.2d 829, 832–33 (App.1987). We will reverse an adoptive placement preference determination only if convinced that the record as a whole reveals an abuse of discretion or if controlling factual findings are clearly erroneous. Farrell v. Farrell, 819 P.2d 896, 898 (Alaska 1991). Abuse of discretion is established if the superior court considered improper factors or improperly weighted certain factors in making its determination. See id. Whether there is good cause to deviate in a particular case depends on many factors including, but not necessarily limited to, the best interests of the child, the wishes of the biological parents, the suitability of persons preferred for placement and the child's ties to the tribe. In re Adoption of M., 832 P.2d at 522.

---

intervention "at any stage in the proceeding." In view of our decision on the merits, we need not address laches.

ICWA was enacted to discourage the separation of Indian children from their families and tribes through adoption or foster care placement to non-Indian homes. 25 U.S.C. § 1901; Mississippi Band of Choctaw Indians v. Holyfield, 490 U.S. 30, 36, 109 S.Ct. 1597, 1601, 104 L.Ed.2d 29 (1989). Congress found that no resource "is more vital to the continued existence and integrity of Indian tribes than their children." 25 U.S.C. § 1901(3); Holyfield, 490 U.S. at 38, 109 S.Ct. at 1603. In order "to protect the best interests of Indian children and to promote the stability and security of Indian tribes and families," Congress established minimum federal standards for the placement of Indian children in foster or adoptive homes. 25 U.S.C. § 1902.

ICWA provides preferences in placing Indian children for adoption. In any adoptive placement of an Indian child under State law, a preference shall be given, in the absence of good cause to the contrary, to a placement with (1) a member of the child's extended family; (2) other members of the Indian child's tribe; or (3) other Indian families. 25 U.S.C. § 1915(a). ICWA does not define "good cause."[3]

Master Duggan found good cause to deviate from ICWA's preferences. The factual bases upon which Master Duggan made his determination were E.P.D.'s preference for the Hartleys, the bond between Nancy Hartley and F.H., the uncertainty of F.H.'s future if the adoption were not allowed, and the "openness" of the Hartleys' adoption.

At a hearing in which the terms and consequences were fully explained to her, E.P.D. signed three documents relinquishing her parental rights on condition that the Hartleys adopt F.H. Four months later, at a hearing in front of Master Duggan, E.P.D. testified that she wanted F.H. to be adopted by the Hartleys. Noatak argues that under Holyfield, parental preference cannot defeat the interests of the tribe. In Holyfield, the United States Supreme Court held that parents can not defeat tribal jurisdiction by giving birth off a reservation. Id. at 53, 109 S.Ct. at 1610. Since jurisdiction is not an issue in this case, Holyfield is not apposite.

ICWA states, with regard to the order of the preferences, "[w]here appropriate, the preference of the Indian child or parent shall be considered." 25 U.S.C. § 1915(c). The Bureau of Indian Affairs publication "Guidelines for State Courts; Indian Child Custody Proceedings" (Guidelines) provides that good cause not to follow the order of preference may be based on parental preference. 44 Fed.Reg. 67584, § F.3 (1979). Although the Guidelines do not have binding effect, this court has looked to them for guidance. In re L.A.M., 727 P.2d 1057, 1060 n. 6 (Alaska 1986). ICWA and the Guidelines indicate that courts may consider parental preference when determining whether there is good cause to deviate from ICWA preferences. E.P.D.'s preference for the

[3] Noatak's argument that the three ICWA preferential placements must be rejected before consideration of an alternative ignores the "good cause" exception.

Hartleys was an appropriate factor for the superior court to consider in its finding of good cause.

Noatak argues that even if a mother's preference constitutes good cause to deviate from ICWA placement preferences, E.P.D.'s relinquishment should be given little weight since it was neither reasonable nor knowledgeable. E.P.D. had offered to relinquish F.H. to several different people, including Mary Penn. At least once she adamantly opposed placement with the Hartleys. She admitted that when she signed the relinquishment to the Hartleys she was so mixed up she would have signed anything. Noatak argues that E.P.D.'s decision was based in part on her belief that F.H. had serious health problems. However, Master McBurney certified that E.P.D. understood and voluntarily signed the documents. Since signing them, E.P.D. has consistently supported an adoption by the Hartleys. E.P.D. gave several reasons she would not want to return to Noatak or have her daughter raised there. The finding that E.P.D. preferred that the Hartleys adopt F.H. was not clearly erroneous.

Both guardians ad litem testified to a strong bond between Nancy Hartley and F.H. An early interventionist stated that F.H.'s bond with Nancy Hartley is the best she will ever have. Bonding between Nancy Hartley and F.H. was a proper factor for the superior court to consider. The finding of bonding was not clearly erroneous.

Master Duggan recognized that F.H.'s situation would be uncertain if the Hartleys' adoption petition were dismissed and E.P.D. withdrew her conditional relinquishment. E.P.D.'s relinquishment was conditional on the Hartleys' adoption of F.H. If the Hartleys' adoption petition were dismissed, F.H. would have continued to be in DFYS' temporary custody. DFYS' petition to terminate permanently E.P.D.'s parental rights had not been granted. No other petition to adopt F.H. had been filed. Although DFYS expressed an intent to place F.H. with Mary Penn immediately, further legal proceedings would have been necessary for a permanent adoption by Mary Penn. The superior court properly considered F.H.'s situation if the adoption petition were dismissed. It was not clearly erroneous for the superior court to find that F.H.'s uncertain situation would have continued if the Hartleys were not allowed to adopt F.H.

Master Duggan and Judge Andrews found that an adoption by the Hartleys would be open, since E.P.D. and her family would have access to F.H. Noatak argues that an adoption by Mary Penn would ensure access to F.H. by E.P.D. and other relatives. E.P.D. testified that she could visit F.H. more easily in Kennewick, Washington than in Noatak. The finding that an adoption by the Hartleys would be open was not clearly erroneous and was a proper factor for the superior court to consider.

Given the possibility of a placement with a relative in Noatak, this case presented a close question to the superior court. However, the factual findings which supported deviation from ICWA preferences are not clearly erroneous. Further, they address factors which are proper to consider in determining whether good cause exists to deviate from the preferences. The record as a whole reveals no abuse of discretion. Therefore, the order approving Master Duggan's finding of good cause is AFFIRMED and the decision to grant the Hartleys' Petition for Adoption is AFFIRMED.

NOTES

In *In re* Adoption of T.N.F., 781 P.2d 973 (Alaska 1989), *cert. denied,* 494 U.S. 1030, 110 S.Ct. 1480 (1990), the Supreme Court of Alaska held that the Indian Child Welfare Act was applicable to an action by a non-Indian wife of an Indian husband who sought as a step-parent to adopt her husband's child who had been born to her own sister (also a non-Indian) under a surrogate parentage agreement in which petitioner's husband was the sperm donor. Although such an interpretation might have served to disrupt an Indian family, the court noted that in enacting the ICWA, Congress did not simply seek to protect the interests of individual Indian parents. Rather, Congress sought to also protect the interests of Indian tribes and communities, and the interests of the Indian children themselves.

The court, however, did determine that the ICWA incorporates state statutes of limitation for actions to set aside consents that are invalid under the ICWA except when the challenges are based on fraud or duress. No allegations of the latter having been raised, the court held that an action by the natural mother to vacate the adoption by her sister that had been granted by an Alaska state court was barred by the Alaska one year statute of limitations for actions to set aside adoption decrees.

In Matter of Adoption of Riffle, 922 P.2d 510 (Mont. 1996), the Supreme Court of Montana rejected the application of the "best interests of the child" test in determining whether the good cause exception in ICWA applied.

In Matter of Adoption of a Child of Indian Heritage, 543 A.2d 925 (1988), the Supreme Court of New Jersey held that the fact that an unwed mother had voluntarily relinquished her child for a private adoptive placement without having lived with an Indian family or in an Indian environment did not preclude application of the Indian Child Welfare Act (ICWA). Because the mother was only 9/32 Rosebud Sioux, the child was ineligible for tribal membership unless the father's lineage would establish that the child had a quarter or more of Rosebud Sioux blood.

A putative father, who was 17/32 Rosebud Sioux and an enrolled member of the tribe, sought to establish his paternity and vacate the private placement adoption that had taken place with the mother's consent. At the time of the hearing, the tribe had refused to enroll the child for membership. However the putative father's ancestry seemingly would have made the child eligible for membership if his paternity were established. The ICWA, in 25 U.S.C.A. § 1903(9), refers to

> any biological parent or parents of an Indian child or any Indian person who has lawfully adopted an Indian child, including

adoptions under tribal law or custom. It does not include the unwed father where paternity has not been acknowledged or established.

The ICWA provides no standard for establishing paternity. The court therefore applied the New Jersey Parentage Act, which was patterned after the Uniform Parentage Act (1973). The court held that the putative father, who had been living with the mother within a month of the child's birth and knew of the adoptive placement but took no steps to protect his paternal rights for twenty-one months, had not satisfied the requirements of the Parentage Act before a final adoption was effected and had not made "timely acknowledgment of paternity within the contemplation of the ICWA". The trial court's refusal to vacate the adoption therefore was upheld.

In *In re* Marinna J., 109 Cal.Rptr.2d 267 (2001), the California Court of Appeal held that the requirement of notice to the tribe of a child whose parental rights were being terminated was mandatory under 25 U.S.C.A. 1912. The issue did not arise until an appeal from a termination of parental rights, but the court nevertheless held that the statutory did not provide for a waiver by the parents. A purpose of giving notice is to protect tribal interests.

Another Supreme Court decision generated controversy when, in a brief opinion, Justice Alito wrote for the majority holding that the ICWA section providing placement preferences for adoption of Indian children does not bar a non-Indian family from adopting an Indian child when no other eligible candidates have sought to adopt the child. *See* Adoptive Couple v. Baby Girl, 133 S.Ct. 2552 (2013). The case involved an adoptive couple seeking to adopt a child and the child's father objected, he was joined by the Cherokee Nation. The state family court denied the adoption petition, returning the child to the child's father, and the South Carolina Supreme Court affirmed. But the Supreme Court reversed, holding that because the father had not seen the child until the child was 27 months old, the provisions of the ICWA do not apply. These federal statute's provisions condition involuntary termination of parental rights upon a showing that remedial efforts have been made to prevent the breakup of the Indian family. These efforts did not apply under the facts of this case because the father never had custody of the child so as to create a family. Because the state had no need to provide services to the child's family the state was free to terminate parental rights and permit adoption by a non-Indian.

The Indian Child Welfare Act continues to precipitate commentary, *see, e.g.*, Bethany R. Berger, *In the Name of the Child: Race, Gender, and Economics in Adoptive Couple v. Baby Girl*, 67 FLA. L. REV. 295 (2015); Christina L. Lewis, Note, *Born Native, Raised White: The Divide Between Federal and Tribal Jurisdiction With Extra-Tribal Native American Adoption*, 7 GEO. J.L & MOD. CRITICAL RACE PERSP. 245 (2015); Shannon M. Morris, *Baby Veronica Ruling: Implications for Indian Child Welfare Act in Indian Child Removals and Adoptions by Non-Indian Custodians*, 2 NAT'L LAW. GUILD REV. 1 (2015); Allison E. Burke, *Adoptive Couple v. Baby Girl: From Strict Construction to Serious Confusion*, 43 HOFSTRA L. REV. 139 (2014); Shreya A. Fadia, Note, *Adopting "Biology Plus" In Federal Indian*

Law: Adoptive Couple v. Baby Girl's Refashioning of ICWA's Framework, 114 COLUM. L. REV. 2007 (2014).

6. SUBSIDIZED OR SPECIAL NEEDS ADOPTIONS

VIRGINIA CODE ANN. (2016)

Virginia Statute for Adoption Assistance for Children with Special Needs

§ 63.2–1300. Purpose and intent of adoption assistance; eligibility

The purpose of adoption assistance is to facilitate adoptive placements and ensure permanency for children with special needs. Adoption assistance may include Title IV-E maintenance payments, state-funded maintenance payments, state special services payments and nonrecurring expense payments made pursuant to requirements set forth in this chapter.

A child with special needs is a child who is a citizen or legal resident of the United States who is unlikely to be adopted within a reasonable period of time due to one or more of the following factors:

1. Physical, mental or emotional condition existing prior to adoption;
2. Hereditary tendency, congenital problem or birth injury leading to substantial risk of future disability; or
3. Individual circumstances of the child related to age, racial or ethnic background or close relationship with one or more siblings.

A child with special needs will be eligible for adoption assistance if (i) the child cannot or should not be returned to the home of his parents and (ii) reasonable efforts to place the child in an appropriate adoptive home without the provision of adoption assistance have been unsuccessful. An exception may be made to the requirement that efforts be made to place the child in an adoptive home without the provision of adoption assistance when the child has developed significant emotional ties with his foster parents while in their care and that the foster parents wish to adopt the child.

§ 63.2–1301. Types of adoption assistance payments

A. Title IV-E maintenance payments shall be made to the adoptive parents on behalf of an adopted child placed if it is determined that the child is a child with special needs and the child meets the requirements set forth in § 473 of Title IV-E of the Social Security Act (42 U.S.C. § 673).

B. State-funded maintenance payments shall be made to the adoptive parents on behalf of an adopted child if it is determined that the child does not meet the requirements set forth in § 473 of Title IV-E of the Social Security Act (42 U.S.C. § 673) but the child is a child with special needs. For this purpose of state-funded maintenance payments only, a child with special needs may include:

1. A child for whom the factors set forth in subdivision 1 or 2 of § 63. 2–1300 are present at the time of adoption but are not diagnosed until after the final order of adoption, when no more than one year has elapsed from the date of diagnosis; or

2. A child who has lived with his foster parents for at least 12 months and has developed significant emotional ties with his foster parents while in their care, when the foster parents wish to adopt the child and state-funded maintenance payments are necessary to enable the adoption.

C. State special services payments shall be made to the adoptive parents and other persons on behalf of a child in the custody of the local board or in the custody of a licensed child-placing agency and placed for adoption, pursuant to this chapter, if it is determined that:

1. The child is a child with special needs; and

2. The adoptive parents are capable of providing the permanent family relationships needed by the child in all respects except financial.

D. Nonrecurring expense payments shall be made to the adoptive parents for expenses related to the adoption including reasonable and necessary adoption fees, court costs, attorney fees and other legal service fees, as well as any other expenses that are directly related to the legal adoption of a child with special needs including costs related to the adoption study, any health and psychological examinations, supervision of the placement prior to adoption and any transportation costs and reasonable costs of lodging and food for the child and the adoptive parents when necessary to complete the placement or adoption process for which the adoptive parents carry ultimate liability for payment and that have not been reimbursed from any other source, as set forth in 45 C.F.R. § 1356.41. However, the total amount of nonrecurring expense payments made to adoptive parents for the adoption of a child shall not exceed $2,000 or an amount established by federal law.

§ 63.2–1302. Adoption assistance payments; maintenance; special needs; payment agreements; continuation of payments when adoptive parents move to another jurisdiction; procedural requirements

A. Adoption assistance payments may include:

1. Title IV-E or state-funded maintenance payments that shall be payable monthly to provide for the support and care of the child; however, Title IV-E or state-funded

maintenance payments shall not exceed the foster care payment that would otherwise be made for the child; and

2. State special services payments to provide special services to the child that the adoptive parents cannot afford and that are not covered by insurance or otherwise, including, but not limited to:

   a. Medical, surgical and dental care;

   b. Hospitalization;

   c. Individual remedial educational services;

   d. Psychological and psychiatric treatment;

   e. Speech and physical therapy; and

   f. Special services, equipment, treatment and training for physical and mental handicaps.

   State special services payments may be paid to the vendor of the goods or services directly or to the adoptive parents.

B. Adoption assistance payments shall cease when the child with special needs reaches the age of 18 years. If it is determined that the child has a mental or physical handicap, or an educational delay resulting from such handicap, warranting the continuation of assistance, adoption assistance payments may be made until the child reaches the age of 21 years.

C. Adoption assistance payments shall be made on the basis of an adoption assistance agreement entered into by the local board and the adoptive parents or, in cases in which the child is in the custody of a licensed child-placing agency, an agreement between the local board, the licensed child-placing agency and the adoptive parents.

Prior to entering into an adoption assistance agreement, the local board or licensed child-placing agency shall ensure that adoptive parents have received information about their child's eligibility for adoption assistance; about their child's special needs and, to the extent possible, the current and potential impact of those special needs. The local board or licensed child-placing agency shall also ensure that adoptive parents receive information about the process for appeal in the event of a disagreement between the adoptive parent and the local board or the adoptive parent and the child-placing agency and information about the procedures for revising the adoption assistance agreement.

Adoptive parents shall submit annually to the local board within thirty days of the anniversary date of the approved agreement an affidavit which certifies that (i) the child on whose behalf they are receiving adoption assistance payments remains in their care, (ii) the child's condition requiring adoption assistance continues to exist, and (iii) whether or not changes to the adoption assistance agreement are requested.

Title IV-E and state-funded maintenance payments made pursuant to this section shall be changed only in accordance with the provisions of § 473 of Title IV–E of the Social Security Act (42 U.S.C. § 673).

D. Responsibility for adoption assistance payments for a child placed for adoption shall be continued by the local board that initiated the agreement in the event that the adoptive parents live in or move to another jurisdiction.

E. Payments may be made under this chapter from appropriations for foster care services for the maintenance and medical or other services for children who have special needs in accordance with § 63.2–1301. Within the limitations of the appropriations to the Department, the Commissioner shall reimburse any agency making payments under this chapter. Any such agency may seek and accept funds from other sources, including federal, state, local, and private sources, to carry out the purposes of this chapter.

§ 63.2–1303. Qualification for adoption assistance payments

Qualification for adoption assistance payments shall be determined by the local board in response to an application for adoption assistance submitted in accordance with regulations adopted by the Board.

§ 63.2–1304. Appeal to Commissioner regarding adoption assistance

Any applicant for or recipient of adoption assistance aggrieved by any decision of a local board or licensed child-placing agency in granting, denying, changing or discontinuing adoption assistance, may, within 30 days after receiving written notice of such decision, appeal therefrom to the Commissioner. Any applicant or recipient aggrieved by the failure of the local board or licensed child-placing agency to make a decision within a reasonable time may ask for review by the Commissioner. The Commissioner may delegate the duty and authority to duly qualified hearing officers to consider and make determinations on any appeal or review. The Commissioner shall provide an opportunity for a hearing, reasonable notice of which shall be given in writing to the applicant or recipient and to the proper local board in such manner and form as the Commissioner may prescribe. The Commissioner may make or cause to be made an investigation of the facts. The Commissioner shall give fair and impartial consideration to the testimony of witnesses, or other evidence produced at the hearing, reports of investigation of the local board and local director or licensed child-placing agency or of investigations made or caused to be made by the Commissioner, or any facts that the Commissioner may deem proper to enable him to decide fairly the appeal or review. The decision of the Commissioner shall be binding and considered a final agency action for purposes of judicial review of such action pursuant to the provisions of the Administrative Process Act (§ 2.2–4000 et seq.).

NOTES

To address the significant number of children living in foster care placements, state and federal governments enacted incentive programs to promote the possibility of permanent homes for these children. The Virginia assistance program illustrates a state program. But the Adoption and Safe Families Act of 1997, a federal statute, provides under Title II, Section 201, that a state may receive incentive grants if it has successfully promoted adoptions. Overall, the federal statute seeks to promote state initiatives that result in more children finding permanent homes. In addition, under the federal Income Tax Credit for Adoption Assistance, 26 U.S.C.A. §§ 36C, 137 (2016), Congress provides an individual with an income tax credit for all qualified, non-employer related adoption expenses. And there is a special credit if the individual adopts a special needs child. To be covered, the adoption expenses must be reasonable and necessary.

For commentary on financial assistance to parents for adopting special needs children, *see, e.g.*, Hannah Roman, *Foster Parenting As Work*, 27 YALE J. L. & FEMINISM 179 (2016); Sharon McCarthy, Vicki Blohm, Daniel Pollack, *If You Move, You Lose: The Interstate Medicaid Obligation to Special Needs Adopted Children,* 35 N. ILL. U. L. REV. 347 (2015); DeLeith D. Gossett, *If Charity Begins at Home, Why Do We Go Searching Abroad? Why the Federal Adoption Tax Credit Should Not Subsidize International Adoptions,* 17 LEWIS & CLARK L. REV. 839 (2013).

7. STEPPARENT ADOPTION

In re Adoption of GLV

Supreme Court of Kansas, 2008
190 P.3d 245

■ DAVIS, JUSTICE.

G.L.V. and M.J.V. are twin brothers, born on October 17, 1994. Their parents were never married and lived together only briefly prior to the time that the boys were born. In 1995, the mother filed a paternity action, resulting in a determination that the father was the natural father of the twins, and an order was issued requiring the father to pay child support. Three weeks after their birth, the father left the area and did not return until 1997. Upon his return, the father filed an action to secure visitation rights to the twins and was awarded weekend visitation; however, he exercised his visitation rights only two or three times. During the instant adoption proceedings, the father testified he sought aid to enforce visitation from the sheriff but was advised his only remedy would be through court proceedings. Because he did not have funds to hire a lawyer, he did not pursue enforcement of his visitation rights. Absent his two weekend visits, the father has had no direct contact with his twin sons since 1997. Nevertheless, the paternal grandparents and other members of the father's family have maintained a relationship with the twins.

Although the father was ordered by the district court to pay child support in 1994, his payments for the first several years were infrequent, leading to a significant arrearage. Since April 2003, however, the father has been regularly employed and has consistently made monthly child support payments of $366 through an income withholding order. From April 2003 until June 2006, he paid $21,003.86 in child support on an obligation of $14,274, with the overage applied toward the arrearage. The natural father is currently married and has three children by that marriage and one stepchild.

The natural mother of the twins married the petitioner stepfather in 2004. On June 13, 2006, the stepfather filed a petition to adopt the twins without obtaining the consent of the natural father. The stepfather requested the district court grant the adoption in light of the fact that father had not had any contact with the children for 9 years and had never voluntarily paid child support. The district court held an evidentiary hearing on August 29, 2006, during which the father and mother testified. The father acknowledged in his testimony that he had not stayed in touch with the children but insisted that this was due to their mother's attempts to keep the children from him. The father also testified that he covers G.L.V. and M.J.V. under his health insurance policy but could not recall whether he had ever told their mother about the health insurance or provided her with an insurance card. The mother testified that she had never prevented the father from visiting the children. She further explained that her husband, the twins' stepfather, was the only "father figure" that her children had ever known. She testified that the stepfather regularly helps G.L.V. and M.J.V. with their homework and is actively involved in their sports events and scouting program.

After hearing argument from both sides, the district court took the matter under advisement in order to consider its decision in light of the amendment recently made to K.S.A. 59–2136(d), the statute controlling contested stepparent adoptions. The amendment, which became effective in 2006 upon publication, added the following statement to the end of K.S.A. 59–2136(d): "The court may consider the best interests of the child and the fitness of the nonconsenting parent in determining whether a stepparent adoption should be granted." K.S.A.2007 Supp. 59–2136(d). Prior to the amendment, the statute contained no explicit reference to either the best interests of the child or the fitness of the nonconsenting parent in a stepparent adoption. See L. 2006, ch. 22, sec. 1. The district court found that "[i]n this case, the father fails miserably the 'love and affection' test." However, the court also found that the father paid a substantial amount of child support during the prior 2 years. Thus, the court found that "[a]dherence to the precedents of the Kansas Supreme Court would require the Court to deny the adoption."

Considering the question of the best interests of the boys, the court found that "[c]onsideration of the best interest of the children does not clearly favor one parent over the other," in that both parents have the children's best interests at heart, differing only as to what they believe those interests to be. In addition, the court noted that "the father is African American and the mother and the petitioner [stepfather] are Caucasian. Severing ties with the father not only severs ties with his family but also may sever cultural ties." Based on these findings, the court concluded that "the precedents of *K.J.B.* and *B.M.W.* dictate that the petition for adoption should be denied and that the 2006 amendment to K.S.A. 59–2136(d) does not change this outcome."

The stepfather appealed the denial of the adoption petition, claiming that the district court misinterpreted the 2006 amendment to the stepparent adoption statute. A divided panel of the Court of Appeals affirmed, concluding that the 2006 amendment to K.S.A. 59–2136(d) did not abrogate the parental duties test (based on the two-sided ledger) previously adopted by the Kansas Supreme Court in *B.M.W.* and *K.J.B.* even though it granted a district court discretionary authority to consider the best interests of the child and the fitness of the nonconsenting parent. *G.L.V.*, 38 Kan.App.2d at 154–55, 163 P.3d 334.

The most recent version of the stepparent adoption statute, K.S.A.2007 Supp. 59–2136(d), states:

> "[T]he consent of [the natural] father must be given to the adoption unless such father has failed or refused to assume the duties of a parent for two consecutive years next preceding the filing of the petition for adoption or is incapable of giving such consent. In determining whether a father's consent is required under this subsection, the court may disregard incidental visitations, contacts, communications or contributions. In determining whether the father has failed or refused to assume the duties of a parent for two consecutive years next preceding the filing of the petition for adoption, there shall be a rebuttable presumption that if the father, after having knowledge of the child's birth, has knowingly failed to provide a substantial portion of the child support as required by judicial decree, when financially able to do so, for a period of two years next preceding the filing of the petition for adoption, then such father has failed or refused to assume the duties of a parent. *The court may consider the best interests of the child and the fitness of the nonconsenting parent in determining whether a stepparent adoption should be granted.*" (Emphasis added.)

The final sentence in the stepparent adoption statute—that relating to the best interests of the child and the fitness of the nonconsenting parent—was added when the statute was amended in 2006. See L. 2006, ch. 22, sec. 1. The Court of Appeals decision in this case is the only opinion of a Kansas appellate court interpreting the amended statute; the matter therefore comes before this court on petition for review as a case of first impression.

In 1990, the legislature amended the adoption laws by enacting a new section specifically dealing with stepparent adoptions. See K.S.A.1990 Supp. 59–2136(d); L. 1990, ch. 145, sec. 26. This new section required a known father's consent in stepparent adoptions "unless such father has failed or refused to assume the duties of a parent for two consecutive years." The amended statute also included language from the pre-1990 adoption law that "the court may disregard incidental visitations, contacts, communications or contributions" when making its determination of whether the natural father's consent is required. K.S.A.1990 Supp. 59–2136(d).

In 1991, the stepparent adoption statute was again amended to clarify that the 2 consecutive years described in the statute were to be "next preceding the filing of the petition for adoption" and to include the language as to the rebuttable presumption of relinquishing duties when a father has failed to pay a substantial portion of court-ordered child support. K.S.A.1991 Supp. 59–2136(d); L. 1991, ch. 167, sec. 1.

As this discussion of the development of Kansas stepparent adoption law demonstrates, we have consistently repeated that all surrounding circumstances are to be considered when determining whether a natural parent must consent to a stepparent adoption—that is, whether the natural parent has "assume[d] the duties of a parent for two consecutive years next preceding the filing of the petition for adoption or is incapable of giving such consent." See K.S.A.2007 Supp. 59–2136(d); *B.M.W.,* 268 Kan. at 882, 2 P.3d 159. This statement recognizes that there are numerous duties associated with being a parent to a child, and all such duties—even though not explicitly enumerated—may be considered. We have focused primarily on two very basic and important duties of parents—love and affection on one hand and financial support on the other—in the context of stepparent adoptions because these duties are contemplated by the statute. In addition, these two important duties—which have formed the basis for the two-sided ledger approach—are capable of being measured and documented, whereas other parental duties may be less tangible.

We emphasize that the two-sided ledger approach is not under attack in this appeal. The legislature has been aware of this court's interpretation of K.S.A. 59–2136(d) and has not amended the statute to provide an alternative framework for addressing stepparent adoptions. See *B.M.W.,* 268 Kan. at 880–84, 2 P.3d 159. Although the legislature amended the statute in 2006, it did not alter the language regarding the assumption of parental duties. The stepfather's petition for review in this case raises only issues relating to the 2006 amendment:

"Whether the best interests of the children involved in a contested stepparent adoption matter is an overriding factor, or alternatively:

"Whether the two sided ledger standard of *K.J.B.* and *B.M.W.* should now be a three column ledger."

In the case before this court, the stepfather does not dispute the district court's findings that the natural father has assumed his parental duties by paying all of the court-ordered child support due during the 2 years preceding the adoption petition. The question before us, put simply, is whether the 2006 amendment in K.S.A.2007 Supp. 59–2136(d) permits a district court to override the statute's explicit requirement that a natural father who has assumed the duties of a parent give his consent to the stepparent adoption if it determines that the adoption is in the child's best interests. We hold that it does not. Our decision is guided by two important considerations with reference to K.S.A.2007 Supp. 59–2136(d). First, a natural parent who has assumed his or her parental responsibilities has a fundamental right, protected by the United States and Kansas Constitutions, to raise his or her child, and the consent requirement in the stepparent adoption statute codifies these constitutional protections. Second, K.S.A.2007 Supp. 59–2136(d) expresses the public policy of Kansas by implicitly incorporating the determination that the best interests of the child is served by fostering the child's relationship with the natural parent in cases where the parent has assumed the duties of a parent toward the child. These two aspects of the statute have existed both before and after the 2006 amendment; the following discussion addresses each consideration in detail.

The stepfather argues on appeal that when the legislature amended K.S.A. 59–2136(d) in 2006 to include the best interests of the child as a consideration in stepparent adoptions, it intended the best interests to be either an overarching concern or, at a minimum, a concern on equal footing with the court's consideration of whether the nonconsenting parent assumed the parental duties of love and affection and financial support. Placed in the context of our previous discussion, the stepfather is essentially arguing that a court's determination of the best interests of the child may override a nonconsenting parent's fundamental rights *even where that parent has assumed his or her parental responsibilities.* We disagree with the stepfather's interpretation for two important reasons: First, this interpretation is inconsistent with the plain language of the statute, and second, this interpretation is inconsistent with the legislature's implicit recognition that the best interests of the child are protected in the usual case by protecting the natural parent-child relationship.

This is not to say that the 2006 amendment has no effect on stepparent adoptions. The additional language expressly authorizing a court to consider the best interests of the child in determining whether to grant a stepparent adoption provides the court with additional discretionary powers to consider the best interests of the child in denying the adoption—even where a natural parent has not assumed the duties of a parent as articulated by this court—for unique reasons. For example, a court may determine, based upon testimony of the child or other evidence, that the child desires to remain the son or daughter of the natural parent based upon the parent's promise of commitment to the child, based upon friction in the stepparent family, or a pattern of instability in the stepparent history. The provision does not, however, permit a court to override the requirement in K.S.A.2007 Supp. 59–2136(d) of mandatory consent when a natural parent has assumed his or her parental responsibilities.

The decisions of the district court and Court of Appeals are affirmed.

NOTES

Stepparent adoption presumes a valid marriage between a biological parent and his or her spouse, who then becomes a stepparent. The Kansas Supreme Court's decision in *In re* Adoption of G.L.V. illustrates the necessity of obtaining the consent of the natural parent prior to permitting adoption by a stepparent. The decision also reaffirms the fundamental right of a parent to the care, custody and control of a child, even when it would appear that the child's individual best interest would be better served by severing the parent's relationship. Although adoption can sever all intestate inheritance from a biological parent when a child is adopted by third party, this is not the case under, for example, the Uniform Probate Code. Under the Code, if a child is adopted by a stepparent, the child can still inherit *from either genetic parent* under state intestate statutes. *See* UNIF. PROB. CODE § 2–119(c) (2008).

Stepparent adoption will prove advantageous to same-sex couples unable to marry prior to 2015, but now entitled to that right. *See* Obergefell v. Hodges, 135 S.Ct. 2584 (2015). Because marriage permits stepparent adoption, it will be easier for a third party spouse to adopt a child genetically connected to his or her spouse. For commentary *see* Josh Blackman and Howard M. Wasserman, *The Process of Marriage Equality*, 43 HASTINGS CONST. L. Q. 243 (2016); Aaron M. House, *Obergefell's Impact on Wrongful Death in Missouri and Kansas,* 84 UMKC L. REV. 733 (2016); Douglas NeJaime, *Marriage Equality and the New Parenthood*, 129 HARV. L. REV. 1185 (2016).

8. EQUITABLE ADOPTION

Lankford v. Wright

Supreme Court of North Carolina, 1997
489 S.E.2d 604

■ FRYE, JUSTICE.

. . .

The sole issue in this case is whether North Carolina recognizes the doctrine of equitable adoption. We hold that the doctrine should be recognized in this state, and therefore, we reverse the decision of the Court of Appeals.

Plaintiff, Barbara Ann Newton Lankford, was born to Mary M. Winebarger on 15 January 1944. When plaintiff was a child, her natural mother entered into an agreement with her neighbors, Clarence and Lula Newton, whereby the Newtons agreed to adopt and raise plaintiff as their child. Shortly thereafter, plaintiff moved into the Newton residence and became known as Barbara Ann Newton, the only child of Clarence and Lula Newton.

The Newtons held plaintiff out to the public as their own child, and plaintiff was at all times known as Barbara Ann Newton. Plaintiff's school records referred to plaintiff as Barbara Ann Newton and indicated that Clarence and Lula Newton were her parents. Plaintiff's high-school diploma also referred to plaintiff as Barbara Ann Newton. After Clarence Newton died in 1960, the newspaper obituary listed Barbara Ann Newton as his surviving daughter. Later, with Lula Newton's assistance, plaintiff obtained a Social Security card issued to her under the name of Barbara Ann Newton.

After plaintiff joined the Navy, plaintiff and Lula Newton frequently wrote letters to each other. In most of the letters, plaintiff referred to Lula Newton as her mother and Lula Newton referred to plaintiff as her daughter. Lula Newton also established several bank accounts with plaintiff, where Lula Newton deposited money plaintiff sent to her while plaintiff was in the Navy. On several occasions, plaintiff took leaves of absence from work to care for Lula Newton during her illness.

In 1975, Lula Newton prepared a will. When she died in 1994, the will was not accepted for probate because some unknown person had defaced a portion of the will. The will named plaintiff as co-executrix of the estate and made specific bequests to plaintiff. Since the will could not be probated, Lula Newton died intestate.

After Lula Newton's death, plaintiff filed for declaratory judgment seeking a declaration of her rights and status as an heir of the estate of Lula Newton. Defendants, the administrators and named heirs of Lula Newton, filed a motion for summary judgment. The trial court granted defendants' motion. The North Carolina Court of Appeals affirmed the order granting summary judgment, reasoning that plaintiff was not adopted according to N.C.G.S. §§ 48–1 to –38 and that North Carolina does not recognize the doctrine of equitable adoption. This Court granted plaintiff's petition for discretionary review, and we now conclude that the doctrine of equitable adoption should be recognized in North Carolina.

"It is a fundamental premise of equitable relief that equity regards as done that which in fairness and good conscience ought to be done." Thompson v. Soles, 299 N.C. 484, 489, 263 S.E.2d 599, 603 (1980). "Equity regards substance, not form," In re Will of Pendergrass, 251 N.C. 737, 743, 112 S.E.2d 562, 566 (1960), and "will not allow technicalities of procedure to defeat that which is eminently right and just," *id.* at 746, 112 S.E.2d at 568. These principles form the essence of the doctrine of equitable adoption, and it is the duty of this Court to protect and promote them.

Equitable adoption is a remedy to "protect the interest of a person who was supposed to have been adopted as a child but whose adoptive parents failed to undertake the legal steps necessary to formally accomplish the adoption." Gardner v. Hancock, 924 S.W.2d 857, 858 (Mo.Ct.App.1996). The doctrine is applied in an intestate estate to "give effect to the intent of the decedent to adopt and provide for the child." *Id.* It is predicated upon

> principles of contract law and equitable enforcement of the agreement to adopt for the purpose of securing the benefits of adoption that would otherwise flow from the adoptive parent under the laws of intestacy had the agreement to adopt been carried out; as such it is essentially a matter of equitable relief. Being only an equitable remedy to enforce a contract right, it is not intended or applied to create the legal relationship of parent and child, with all the legal consequences of such a relationship, nor is it meant to create a legal adoption.

2 Am.Jur.2d *Adoption* § 53 (1994) (footnotes omitted).

Adoption did not exist at common law and is of purely statutory origin. Wilson v. Anderson, 232 N.C. 212, 215, 59 S.E.2d 836, 839 (1950). Equitable adoption, however, does not confer the incidents of formal statutory adoption; rather, it merely confers rights of inheritance upon the foster child in the event of intestacy of the foster parents.[1] In essence, the doctrine invokes the principle that equity regards that as done which ought to be done. The doctrine is not intended to replace statutory requirements or to create the parent-child relationship; it simply recognizes the foster child's right to inherit from the person or persons who contracted to adopt the child and who honored that contract in all respects except through formal statutory procedures. As an equitable matter, where the child in question has faithfully performed the duties of a natural child to the foster parents, that child is entitled to be placed in the position in which he would have been had he been adopted. Likewise, based on principles of estoppel, those claiming under and through the deceased are estopped to assert that the child was not legally adopted or did not occupy the status of an adopted child.

Further, the scope of the doctrine is limited to facts comparable to those presented here. Thirty-eight jurisdictions have considered equitable adoption; at least twenty-seven have recognized and applied the doctrine. *See, e.g., First Nat'l Bank in* Fairmont v. Phillips, 176 W.Va. 395, 344 S.E.2d 201 (1985). A majority of the jurisdictions recognizing the doctrine have successfully limited its application to claims made by an equitably adopted child against the estate of the foster parent. Geramifar v. Geramifar, 113 Md.App. 495, 688 A.2d 475 (1997). By its own terms, equitable adoption applies only in limited circumstances. The elements necessary to establish the existence of an equitable adoption are:

(1) an express or implied agreement to adopt the child,

(2) reliance on that agreement,

(3) performance by the natural parents of the child in giving up custody,

(4) performance by the child in living in the home of the foster parents and acting as their child,

(5) partial performance by the foster parents in taking the child into their home and treating the child as their own, and

(6) the intestacy of the foster parents.

See 2 Am.Jur.2d *Adoption* § 54 (1994). These elements, particularly the requirement of intestacy, limit the circumstances under which the doctrine may be applied. Specifically, the doctrine acts only to recognize the inheritance rights of a child whose foster parents died intestate and failed to perform the formalities of a legal adoption, yet treated the child as their own for all intents and purposes. The doctrine is invoked for the sole benefit of the foster child in determining heirship upon the intestate death of the person or persons contracting to adopt. Whether the doctrine applies is a factual question, and each element must be proven by clear, cogent, and convincing evidence. *See, e.g., First Nat'l Bank in* Fairmont v. Phillips, 176 W.Va. 395, 344 S.E.2d 201.

In this case, the evidence in the record tends to show that the above elements can be satisfied by clear, cogent, and convincing evidence. The record demonstrates that the Newtons agreed to adopt plaintiff; that the Newtons and plaintiff relied on that agreement; that plaintiff's natural mother gave up custody of plaintiff to the Newtons; that plaintiff lived in the Newtons' home, cared for them in their old age, and otherwise acted as their child; that the Newtons treated plaintiff as their child by taking her into their home, giving her their last name, and raising her as their child; and that Mrs. Newton died intestate several years after Mr. Newton died. These facts fit squarely within the parameters of the doctrine of equitable adoption and are indicative of the dilemma the doctrine is intended to remedy.

We note that our decision to recognize the doctrine of equitable adoption is not precluded by prior decisions of this Court as asserted by defendants and decided by the Court of Appeals. In Ladd v. Estate of Kellenberger, 314 N.C. 477, 334 S.E.2d 751 (1985), we specifically stated that "[w]e find no occasion to address the question of whether North Carolina recognizes the doctrine of equitable adoption." *Id.* at 479, 334 S.E.2d at 753. Likewise, in Chambers v. Byers, 214 N.C. 373, 199 S.E. 398 (1938), our holding was limited to whether the agreement at issue was an enforceable contract to make a will. Thus, neither *Ladd* nor *Chambers* foreclosed the possibility of future recognition of equitable adoption by this Court.

The dissent points out that a minority of jurisdictions have declined to recognize the doctrine of equitable adoption. However, we again note that an overwhelming majority of states that have addressed the question have recognized and applied the doctrine. More importantly, it is the unique role of the courts to fashion equitable remedies to protect and promote the principles of equity such as those at issue in this case. We are convinced that acting in an equitable manner in this case does not interfere with the legislative scheme for adoption, contrary to the assertions of the dissent. Recognition of the doctrine of equitable adoption does not create a legal adoption, and therefore does not impair the statutory procedures for adoption.

In conclusion, a decree of equitable adoption should be granted where justice, equity, and good faith require it. The fairness of applying the doctrine once the prerequisite facts have been established is apparent. Accordingly, we reverse the Court of Appeals' decision which affirmed the trial court's entry of summary judgment for defendants and remand to the trial court for further proceedings not inconsistent with this opinion.

REVERSED AND REMANDED.

■ MITCHELL, CHIEF JUSTICE, dissenting.

In its opinion, the majority for the first time accepts the doctrine of equitable adoption for North Carolina. As applied by the majority in this case, the doctrine results in neither an adoption nor equity. Therefore, although I am convinced the majority is engaged in an honest but unfortunate attempt to do good in the present case, I must dissent.

"Equity" is that established set of principles under which substantial justice may be attained in particular cases where the prescribed or customary forms of ordinary law seem to be inadequate. 27A Am.Jur.2d *Equity* § 1 (1994). Equity "is a complex system of established law and is not merely a reflection of the judge's sense of what is appropriate." *Id.* § 2. It arose in response to the restrictive and inflexible rules of the common law, and not as a means of avoiding legislation that courts deemed unwise or inadequate.

For purposes of governing and regulating judicial action, equity courts over the centuries "have formulated certain rules or principles which are described by the term 'maxims.' " *Id.* § 108. It is these maxims which must control the equity jurisdiction of the courts if their judgments are to reflect anything other than the peculiar preferences of the individual judges involved.

> A court of equity has no more right than has a court of law to act on its own notion of what is right in a particular case; it must be guided by the established rules and precedents. Where rights are defined and established by existing legal principles, they may not be changed or unsettled in equity. A court of equity is thus bound by any explicit statute or directly applicable rule of law, regardless of its views of the equities.

Id. § 109 (footnotes omitted).

One maxim of equity, as the majority explains, is that equity regards as done that which in fairness and good conscience ought to be done. A court's notion of what is good or desirable does not determine what "ought to be done" in applying equity. The maxim of equity upon which the majority relies must yield to other controlling and established rules or maxims. One such maxim is that a court of equity, however benevolent its motives, is "bound by any explicit statute or directly applicable rule of law, regardless of its view of the equities." *Id.* Thus, no equitable remedy may properly be applied to disturb statutorily defined and established rights, such as those rights created by North Carolina statutes controlling intestate succession or those controlling legal adoption.

The North Carolina Intestate Succession Act provides a comprehensive and extensive legislative scheme controlling intestate succession by, through, and from adopted children. N.C.G.S. § 29–17(a) provides:

> A child, *adopted in accordance with Chapter 48 of the General Statutes* or in accordance with the applicable law of any other jurisdiction, and the heirs of such child, are entitled by succession to any property by, through and from his adoptive parents and their heirs the same as if he were the natural legitimate child of the adoptive parents.

N.C.G.S. § 29–17(a) (1995) (emphasis added). The extensive scheme created by the legislature is clear and unambiguous. It provides, in pertinent part, that only those children who are adopted *in compliance with chapter 48* or adopted according to the requirements of another jurisdiction are eligible to take by intestate succession. Therefore, the maxim relied upon by the majority may not properly be applied here.

> Equity will not interfere where a statute applies and dictates requirements for relief. Use of equitable principles to trump an

> apposite statute thus is legally indefensible. The disregard of an unambiguous law based on sympathy is unjustifiable under the rubric of equity.

27A Am.Jur.2d *Equity* § 246 (footnotes omitted).

It is well established that "[w]here an extensive legislative scheme governs, it is incumbent upon chancellors to restrain their equity powers." *Id.* The application of the doctrine of equitable adoption by the majority in this case violates this principle of equity requiring greater restraint when dealing with statutory law than when addressing the common law. The majority's application of the doctrine of equitable adoption here negates the rights of other heirs such as defendants which are expressly provided for in the extensive legislative scheme established by the North Carolina Intestate Succession Act. In the instant case, the application of the doctrine of equitable adoption denies other rightful heirs their statutory intestate shares, in effect voiding the intestate succession hierarchy enacted by our legislature. This result is contrary to established maxims of equity.

Further, contrary to established maxims of equity, the decision of the majority also "trumps" another applicable extensive legislative scheme. Adoption did not exist at common law in North Carolina. Therefore, we have expressly and correctly held that adoption "can be accomplished only in accordance with provisions of statutes enacted by the legislative branch of the State government." Wilson v. Anderson, 232 N.C. 212, 215, 59 S.E.2d 836, 839 (1950). The North Carolina General Assembly has enacted a comprehensive and extensive legislative scheme governing adoptions contained in chapter 48 of the General Statutes. Plaintiff does not fall within the requirements of these statutes. Therefore, I believe that the majority errs in failing to apply restraint in the exercise of its equity powers and in applying its own notion of what "ought to be done" in order to improperly "trump" an apposite statute. 27A Am.Jur.2d *Equity* § 246.

Presently, all states recognize a parent-child relationship through adoption if the certain and unambiguous statutory procedures of each specific state are followed. A strong minority of courts that have reviewed the issue have declined to recognize the doctrine of equitable adoption. *See* Wilks v. Langley, 248 Ark. 227, 235, 451 S.W.2d 209, 213 (1970) (holding inheritance under theory of "virtual adoption" unknown in Arkansas); Maui Land & Pineapple Co. v. Naiapaakai Heirs of Makeelani, 69 Haw. 565, 568, 751 P.2d 1020, 1022 (1988) ("to depart from the statutes by creating a doctrine of equitable adoption would import mischief and uncertainty into the law"); In re Estate of Edwards, 106 Ill.App.3d 635, 637, 62 Ill.Dec. 407, 435 N.E.2d 1379, 1381 (1982) ("Illinois has not expressly recognized the theory of equitable adoption"); Lindsey v. Wilcox, 479 N.E.2d 1330, 1333 (Ind.Ct.App.1985) ("the doctrine of equitable adoption has never been approved in Indiana and it continues to be denied judicial approval"); In re Estate of Robbins, 241

Kan. 620, 621, 738 P.2d 458, 460 (1987) ("Kansas courts do not recognize the doctrine of equitable adoption"); Pierce v. Pierce, 198 Mont. 255, 259, 645 P.2d 1353, 1356 (1982) (the adoptive parent or parents must follow the required procedures set forth in the Uniform Adoption Act in order for an adoption to occur); Alley v. Bennett, 298 S.C. 218, 221, 379 S.E.2d 294, 295 (1989) (the method of adoption provided by statute is exclusive); Couch v. Couch, 35 Tenn.App. 464, 476, 248 S.W.2d 327, 333 (1951) ("The right of adoption was unknown to the common law. It is of statutory origin, and to create the contemplated relation the procedure fixed by the statute must be substantially followed.").

Asserting their belief that adoption is singularly defined by statute, these courts have properly deferred to the judgment of their legislators and the procedures established in their state adoption statutes. These courts have also deferred to their legislative bodies to enact laws governing the many complex issues that will arise if the doctrine of equitable adoption is recognized. Such issues would include whether the equitably "adopted" child would inherit from his or her natural parents or from a natural sibling who had not been equitably adopted. Moreover, a court deciding to recognize "equitable adoption" would have to determine for inheritance purposes the relationship between the equitably adopted child's issue and the equitably adoptive parents, versus the child's biological parents. The complexities abound.

The North Carolina General Assembly clearly enacted chapter 48 of the General Statutes of North Carolina with the intent to establish the exclusive procedure by which a minor child may be adopted. The preface to chapter 48 states the legislative intent in adopting this chapter.

> The General Assembly finds that it is in the public interest to establish a *clear judicial process* for adoptions, to promote the integrity and finality of adoptions, to encourage prompt, conclusive disposition of adoption proceedings, and to structure services to adopted children, biological parents, and adoptive parents that will provide for the needs and protect the interests of all parties to an adoption, particularly adopted minors.

N.C.G.S. § 48–1–100(a) (1995) (emphasis added). The legislature intended that adoption in North Carolina be accomplished only through the formal judicial proceedings provided for in the extensive legislative scheme created in chapter 48. Therefore, equity may not properly interfere by creating a new form of partial or total adoption.

In effect, this Court preempts statutes enacted by our legislature in order to recognize the doctrine of equitable adoption. However, because our legislature has extensively, comprehensively, and unambiguously acted, both with regard to adoption and with regard to intestate succession, I am persuaded that the majority improperly "trumps" clear legislative intent in the name of equity.

Despite plaintiff's foster parents' verbal acknowledgments and holding plaintiff out as their natural child, they never legally adopted her by complying with the statutory process. "A mere contract to adopt a child, however, is not a contract to devise or bequeath property to that child." Ladd v. Estate of Kellenberger, 314 N.C. 477, 486, 334 S.E.2d 751, 758 (1985). Thus, it is my opinion that this Court should not declare plaintiff to have been "equitably adopted," thereby subrogating the rights of the statutorily determined heirs for purposes of intestate succession.

Finally, another principle of equity prevents the proper application here of the maxim that equity regards as done that which ought to be done. Defendants in this case include the heirs of Lula Newton under the North Carolina Intestate Succession Act. There is no allegation, contention, or evidence that they are anything other than innocent third parties to the transactions between plaintiff and her natural parents on the one hand and the Newtons on the other concerning any promise to adopt. This Court, like most courts, has expressly recognized and held that the maxim that equity regards as done that which ought to be done *ought not* to be and "will not be enforced to the injury of innocent third parties." . . .

The record in the present case does not indicate that either plaintiff or defendants are anything other than innocents. Therefore, general principles of equity do not arise concerning what "ought to be done" as between them; "where equities are equal, 'the law must prevail.' " 27A Am.Jur.2d *Equity* § 139 (footnotes omitted).

In the present case, the controlling maxims of equity clearly require that this Court restrain its equity powers so as not to overrule comprehensive statutory schemes and, thereby, do harm to innocents. For these reasons, I respectfully dissent from the decision of the majority and would affirm the holding of the Court of Appeals which affirmed the order of the trial court.

■ PARKER, J., joins in this dissenting opinion.

NOTES

Equitable adoption is a misnomer, it is not adoption, but only an equitable device by which a "child" who met the conditions required by the *Lankford* decision may inherit under the state's intestate statute from a "parent" who meant to adopt him or her but never did. For application and commentary, *see, e.g.*, Lee-Ford Tritt, *Sperms and Estates: An Unadulterated Functionally Based Approach to Parent-Child Property Succession*, 62 SMU L. REV. 367 (2009); Michael J. Higdon, *When Informal Adoption Meets Intestate Succession: The Cultural Myopia of the Equitable Adoption Doctrine*, 43 WAKE FOREST L. REV. 223 (2008).

9. INTERCOUNTRY ADOPTION

HAGUE CONVENTION ON THE PROTECTION OF CHILDREN AND COOPERATION IN RESPECT OF INTERCOUNTRY ADOPTION

May 29, 1993, 32 I.L.M. 1134 (1993)

CHAPTER II-REQUIREMENTS FOR INTERCOUNTRY ADOPTIONS

Article 4

An adoption within the scope of the Convention shall take place only if the competent authorities of the State of origin-

a) have established that the child is adoptable;

b) have determined, after possibilities for placement of the child within the State of origin have been given due consideration, that an Intercountry adoption is in the child's best interests;

c) have ensured that

(1) the persons, institutions and authorities whose consent is necessary for adoption, have been counseled as may be necessary and duly informed of the effects of their consent, in particular whether or not an adoption will result in the termination of the legal relationship between the child and his or her family of origin.

(2) such persons, institutions and authorities have given their consent freely, in the required legal form, and expressed or evidenced in writing,

(3) the consents have not been induced by payment or compensation of any kind and have not been withdrawn, and

(4) the consent of the mother, where required, has been given only after the birth of the child, and

d) have ensured, having regard to the age and degree of maturity of the child, that

(1) he or she has been counseled and duly informed of the effects of the adoption and of his or her consent to the adoption, where such consent is required,

(2) consideration has been given to the child's wishes and opinions,

(3) the child's consent to the adoption, where such consent is required, has been given freely, in the required legal form, and expressed or evidenced in writing, and

(4) such consent has not been induced by payment or compensation of any kind.

NOTES

This brief portion of the Hague Convention in reference to intercountry adoption identifies simply the consent requirements, but the Convention also includes provisions related to central authorities and accredited bodies, to procedural requirements, and to recognition by other states. The United States ratified the Convention in 2007 seeking to, among other goals, provide safeguards for parents of children, adopters, and for the children being adopted. Approximately seventy-five countries have implemented the Convention. For additional commentary on the Convention, *see, e.g.*, Richard R. Carlson, *A Child's Right to a Family versus a State's Discretion to Institutionalize the Child,* 47 GEO. J. INT'L L. 937 (2016); David M. Smolin, *Surrogacy as the Sale of Children: Applying Lessons Learned from Adoption to the Regulation of the Surrogacy Industry's Global Marketing of Children,* 43 PEPP. L. REV. 265 (2016); William Giacofci, Note and Comment, *Curbing Intercountry Adoption Abuses Through the Alien Tort Statute,* 18 ROGER WILLIAMS U. L. REV. 110 (2013); Shani M. King, *Owning Laura Silsby's Shame: How the Haitian Child Trafficking Scheme Embodies Western Disregard for the Integrity of Poor Families*, 25 HARV. HUM. RTS. J. 1 (2012); Barbara Yngvesson, *Transnational Adoption and European Immigration Politics: Producing the National Body in Sweden*, 19 IND. J. GLOBAL LEGAL STUD. 327 (2012); Rachael M. Schupp-Star, Note and Comment, *The Hague Convention on the Protection of Children and Cooperation in Respect of Intercountry Adoption: The Need for a Uniform Standard for Intercountry Adoption by Homosexuals,* 16 ROGER WILLIAMS U. L. REV. 139 (2011); Ann Laquer Estin, *Families Across Borders: The Hague Children's Convention and the Case for International Family Law in the United States*, 62 FLA. L. REV. 47 (2010); David M. Smolin, *Child Laundering and the Hague Convention on Intercountry Adoption: The Future and Past of Intercountry Adoption*, 48 U. LOUISVILLE L. REV. 441 (2010); Elizabeth Burleson, *International Human Rights Law, Coparent Adoption and the Recognition of Gay and Lesbian Families*, 55 LOY. L. REV. 791 (2009).

C. ADOPTION OF ADULTS

Adoption of Swanson

Supreme Court of Delaware, 1993
623 A.2d 1095

■ MOORE, JUSTICE.

Richard Sorrels appeals the denial of his petition in the Family Court to adopt James A. Swanson,[1] a consenting adult.[2] We confront an

[1] Pseudonyms have been used for both parties to this adoption proceeding.

[2] Although not required by Delaware law, Mr. Swanson's natural father also consented to the adoption.

issue of first impression: Is a pre-existing parent-child relationship required under our adult adoption statutes, 13 Del.C. § 951–56, in order for one adult to adopt another? . . .

When Richard Sorrels sought to adopt James Swanson, his companion of 17 years, they were, respectively, 66 and 51 years of age. The adoption had two purposes—to formalize the close emotional relationship that had existed between them for many years and to facilitate their estate planning. Apparently, they sought to prevent collateral claims on their respective estates from remote family members, and to obtain the reduced inheritance tax rate which natural and adopted children enjoy under Delaware law. Admittedly, there was no pre-existing parent-child relationship between them, and on that basis the Family Court denied the petition.

Adult adoptions in Delaware are governed by our Domestic Relations Law, 13 Del.C. § 951 through 956. Section 953 provides that "[i]f the petition complies with the requirements of §§ 951 and 952 of this title, and if the person or persons to be adopted appear in court and consent to the adoption, the Family Court may render a decree ordering the issuance of a certificate of adoption to the petitioner."[3] Although the statute mentions no other requirements beyond those listed in Sections 951–952, the Family Court sua sponte concluded that approval of an adult adoption was contingent upon a pre-existing family relationship.

Indisputably, the legislature, by providing for adoption of minors, intended to allow for the creation and formalization of parent-child relationships between nonrelated adults and children. It is reasonable to infer that the legislature, by providing for adult adoptions, sought to extend this principle to those situations where no adoption occurred before the age of majority or where the parent-child relationship developed during adulthood. It is reasonable to infer that the legislature, by providing for adult adoptions, intended to allow for the formalization of the parent-child relationship where there is an existing parent-child relationship between nonrelated individuals. . . . It is simply illogical that the legislature enacted the adult adoption statute to make familial inheritance rights available to all. Furthermore, it is unlikely that the legislature intended to extend adoption to all other kinds of relationships, including friendships and sexual relationships. Petitioner's interpretation of the statute would lead to these results. Thus, the Family Court implied a new requirement into the adult adoption process. As a result, we are faced with a simple question of statutory construction—did the Family Court err as a matter of law in formulating

[3] 13 Del.C. § 951 provides that: Any person, or any husband and wife jointly, desiring to adopt any person or persons upwards of 18 years of age, shall file a petition in the Family Court of the county in which the petitioner or the person to be adopted resides. 13 Del.C. § 952 describes the contents of the petition: The petition shall state the name, sex and date of birth of the person or persons whose adoption is sought and that the petitioner or petitioners desire to adopt such person or persons. The petition shall be signed by the petitioner or petitioners.

or applying legal principles when it interpreted Section 953 to require a preexisting parent-child relationship?

We begin with the basic rule of statutory construction that requires a court to ascertain and give effect to the intent of the legislature. If the statute as a whole is unambiguous and there is no reasonable doubt as to the meaning of the words used, the court's role is limited to an application of the literal meaning of those words. However, where, as here, the Court is faced with a novel question of statutory construction, it must seek to ascertain and give effect to the intention of the General Assembly as expressed by the statute itself.

There is no reference in Section 953 to any condition of a pre-existing parent-child relationship. Instead, the statute only compels a person seeking an adult adoption to sign and file a petition containing certain basic personal data. If, after having done so, the adoptee appears in court and consents to the adoption, the Family Court may grant the petition for adoption. 13 Del.C. § 953.[4] When statutory language is clear, unambiguous, and consistent with other provisions of the same legislation, the court must give effect to its intent. Moreover, 13 Del.C. § 953, the relevant adult adoption statute, has existed in equivalent form since 1915, without any material change by the General Assembly. That is indicative of legislative satisfaction with the provisions of the statute.

Regardless of one's views as to the wisdom of the statute, our role as judges is limited to applying the statute objectively and not revising it. A court may not engraft upon a statute language which has been clearly excluded therefrom. Thus, where, as here, provisions are expressly included in one part of a statute, but omitted from another, it is reasonable to conclude that the legislature was aware of the omission and intended it. As a result, the omission from the adult adoption procedure for investigation and supervision of prospective placements, found in the requirements for adopting minors, persuades us that it was not the result of an accident. If anything, it is the best evidence of a legislative policy against imposing unnecessary conditions upon the adult adoption process.

Many jurisdictions limit inquiry into the motives or purposes of an adult adoption. However, most recognize that adult adoptions for the purpose of creating inheritance rights are valid. In one of the earliest cases, the Supreme Judicial Court of Massachusetts upheld an adoption of three adults, aged 43, 39 and 25 respectively, by a 70 year old person who intended the adoption to operate in lieu of a will. Collamore v. Learned, Mass.Supr., 171 Mass. 99, 50 N.E. 518 (1898). The court ruled

---

[4] Although the use of the verb "shall" in legislation generally connotes a mandatory requirement, while the verb "may" is deemed permissive, we have cautioned that use of this test is contextual, and thus, mere use of the term "may" does not control legislative intent where, as here, the full setting of the statute suggests a different construction. Miller v. Spicer, Del.Supr., 602 A.2d 65, 67 (1991).

that motive, although proper in that case, had no effect on the validity of the adoption.

A similar result obtained in Sheffield v. Franklin, 151 Ala. 492, 44 So. 373 (1907). The court concluded that the law placed no limit on the age of the person to be adopted even if it altered inheritance rights. Likewise, in Ex Parte Libertini, 244 Md. 542, 224 A.2d 443 (1966), the Maryland Court of Appeals permitted the adoption of an unmarried thirty-five year old woman by an unmarried fifty-six year old woman, initiated for reasons of inheritance and maternal feelings. The court rejected outright the lower court's conclusion that granting the adoption would pervert the entire adoptive process. The court noted that an adoption for the purpose of inheritance does not change the social or domestic relationship of the parties. Rather, its purpose and effect bestows on the adoptee the right of a natural heir to inherit property. This motive was not improper, the court concluded, and therefore had no bearing on a determination of the adoption's propriety.

Cases upholding adoptions for the purpose of improving the adoptee's inheritance rights continue to grow. In Berston v. Minnesota Dept. of Public Welfare, 206 N.W.2d 28 (Minn.1973), the trial court denied the adoption of an adult woman by her natural son on the public policy ground that the purpose of the adoption—to make the petitioner's mother his heir in order to bring her into the terms of a trust established by the petitioner's father after he divorced the mother—would thwart the intent of the settlor of the trust. The Minnesota Supreme Court ruled that the broad language of the adult adoption statute unequivocally foreclosed any limiting construction.[6] Thus, considerations of public policy were matters for reappraisal by legislative amendment. See also Harper v. Martin, Ky.App., 552 S.W.2d 690 (1977) (approving of the adoption of a forty-seven year old male by a terminally ill petitioner for the express purpose of making him the heir at law of a third person); Matter of Fortney's Estate, 5 Kan.App.2d 14, 611 P.2d 599, 604–05 (1980) (upholding an adult adoption originally effectuated for purposes of inheritance); but see Matter of Griswold's Estate, 140 N.J.Super. 35, 354 A.2d 717 (1976) (ruling that an adoption to make an adoptee a beneficiary of a trust was an abuse of the adoption process). If anything, Griswold's Estate is contrary to well established Delaware law. See Haskell v. Wilmington Trust Co., Del.Supr., 304 A.2d 53, 54–5 (1973); Riggs Nat. Bank v. Zimmer, Del.Ch., 304 A.2d 69, 74, aff'd sub nom. Jackson v. Riggs Nat. Bank, Del.Supr., 314 A.2d 178, 182 (1973).

The general disinclination to examine the motives of the petitioner has been extended beyond the area of inheritance rights. In 333 East

[6] Minn.St. 259.21 to 259.32 governed adoption in Minnesota at that time. There were only two references to adult adoptions in these sections. Section 259.22 stated in part that any person who resided in the state for one year or more may petition to adopt a child or an adult. Section 259.24, which dealt with consent, provided that in the adoption of an adult, written consent only shall be required. As in Delaware, the other sections of the statute dealing with notice, investigation and a hearing on the petition, referred only to the adoption of a minor.

53rd Street Associates v. Mann, 1st Dept., 121 A.D.2d 289, 503 N.Y.S.2d 752 (1986), a petitioner adopted an adult woman in order to ensure that she would succeed to the tenancy of a rent controlled apartment. The building's owner sought a declaratory judgment that the adoptee had no rights in the apartment. The appellate court found nothing inherently wrong with an adoption intended to confer an economic benefit on the adopted person.

On the other hand, the New York Court of Appeals ruled that a fifty-seven year old man could not adopt a fifty year old male with whom he shared a homosexual relationship. Matter of Adoption of Robert Paul P., 63 N.Y.2d 233, 481 N.Y.S.2d 652, 471 N.E.2d 424 (1984). The court reasoned that adoption is not a quasi-matrimonial device to provide unmarried partners with a legal imprimatur for their sexual relationship.[7] Id. 481 N.Y.S.2d at 653, 471 N.E.2d at 425. The court also determined that New York's adult adoption process requires the adoption to be in the best interests of the adoptee, and thus, the financial and emotional condition of the petitioner must still be investigated. Delaware's adult adoption process clearly abandons the requirement for such an investigation. It suggests no corresponding need to determine that an adult adoption be in the best interests of the adoptee. We also note the compelling dissent in Matter of Adoption of Robert Paul P., 481 N.Y.S.2d at 656, 471 N.E.2d at 428 (Meyer, J., dissenting), taking the majority to task for imposing limitations on the process that are not found in New York's adult adoption statute.

There are, of course, common sense limitations on any adult adoption. That is why our statute appears to confer reasonable discretion upon the Family Court's approval of an adult adoption. Solely by way of example, no court should countenance an adoption to effect a fraudulent, illegal or patently frivolous purpose. See, e.g., In re Jones, 122 R.I. 716, 411 A.2d 910 (1980), where an older married man sought to adopt his 20 year old paramour to the economic detriment of his wife and family. Delaware law is not necessarily inconsistent with the results in Adoption of Robert Paul P. and In re Jones, supra. Adult adoptions intended to foster a sexual relationship would be against public policy as violative of the incest statute. See 11 Del.C. § 766(b), which defines the crime of incest to include sexual intercourse between a parent and child "without regard to . . . relationships by adoption."

A statute cannot be construed to produce an absurd, meaningless or patently inane result. However, where, as here, the petition contemplates an adoption that is not only within the scope of the statute, but which is

---

[7] There remains, however, an active debate, Bowers v. Hardwick, 478 U.S. 186, 106 S.Ct. 2841, 92 L.Ed.2d 140 (1986), notwithstanding, whether such relationships enjoy constitutionally protected status under the Equal Protection Clause. See Symposium, Life After Hardwick, 27 Harv.C.R.BC.L.L.Rev. 531 (1992); Tracey Rich, Note, Sexual Orientation in the Wake of Bowers v. Hardwick, 22 Ga.L.Rev. 773 (1988).

also widely recognized as a proper exercise of the authority granted by the statute, we can divine no reason why this petition should be denied.

Since the primary object of statutory construction is to reach a result in conformity with legislative policy, once that policy is determined we need only test the construction by the rules of reasonableness and conformity with that policy. In this case, our construction of the statute—permitting the adoption of one adult by another for economic reasons—is consistent with a policy promoting limited judicial inquiry into the purposes or motives behind such a relationship. . . .

It is beyond the province of courts to question the policy or wisdom of an otherwise valid law. Instead, each judge must take and apply the law as they find it, leaving any changes to the duly elected representatives of the people. . . . Accordingly, the order of the Family Court dismissing the petition is REVERSED. The Family Court is directed to issue an appropriate decree of adoption.

NOTES

Often, prior to the legalization of same-sex marriage throughout the country, *see* Obergefell v. Hodges, 135 S.Ct. 2584 (2015), same-sex adults adopted one another in order to achieve the economic benefits associated with "form family" structure, such as with inheritance, taxation, and family trust benefits. Because adoption confers upon another the status of "issue" this practice may still continue, but if the goal is to achieve "family" by adoption, then same-sex marriage seems preferable. For commentary, *see, e.g.*, Jackie Messler, Comment, *The Inconsistent Inheritance Rights of Adult Adoptees and a Proposal for Uniformity*, 5 MARQ. L. REV. 1043 (2012); Sarah Ratliff, Comment, *Adult Adoption: Intestate Succession and Class Gifts Under the Uniform Probate Code,* 105 NW. U. L. REV. 1777 (2011); Russell E. Utter, Jr., Note, *The Benefits and Pitfalls of Adult Adoption in Estate Planning and Its Likely Future in Missouri*, 80 UMKC L. REV. 255 (2011).

Although a key purpose of the "modern" adoption statutes introduced in the United States during the 19th century was to provide families for minor children, a review of the literal language of many of our statutes could be read to include adoption of adults. In the English language the word "children" can refer to relationship as well as age, and this was the word used in many of the statutes. Although adoption of adults has never been widespread in this country, it has been used both to avoid embarrassment or even prosecution for same-sex cohabitation, and for inheritance purposes including circumvention of testamentary limitations. It has significant usage today and varying statutes now deal specifically with adult adoption. It is important to consult these to determine any special limitations or procedures. Some states limit adult adoption to situations in which there was at least some informal relationship between the parties before the adopter reached the age for adoption as an adult. Only consent of the adopter and adoptee ordinarily is needed. In some situations, parents of a person in long term or permanent foster care have maintained their parental rights, but upon reaching adulthood (or in some jurisdictions an earlier specified age) the child's consent will suffice and a foster parent may adopt without consent from the natural parents. States differ in their provisions for inheritance by or through adoption. For historical reference, *see* Walter Wadlington, *Adoption of Adults: A Family Law Anomaly,* 54 CORNELL L. REV. 566 (1969).

INDEX

References are to Pages